ISBN-10:0991104838
ISBN-13: 978-0-9911048-3-3

Library of Congress Control Number 2014949186

Published in the USA
First printing in paperback in August 2014.

The text type set in Arial Unicode.

Indus Script

Meluhha metalwork hieroglyphs

S. Kalyanaraman

Sarasvati Research Center

Indus Script

--Meluhha metalwork hieroglyphs

Table of contents

Executive summary and significance of Meluhha cipher for Bronze Age Technology narratives and history of Ancient India	4
Legacy of *meluhha* language & Asur, Assur metal workers and traders	19
Section A. Meluhha hieroglyphs on m1893 Mohenjo-daro seal; rebus readings of native-metal-smith guild	67
Section B: Āraṭṭa आरट्ट	72
Section C. Meluhha metalwork hieroglyphs	157
Section D: Copper, brass	599
Section E: Bronze, tin	651
Section F: *Cire perdue* (lost wax) castings, forge	753
Index	795

Indus Script

-- Meluhha metalwork hieroglyphs

Executive summary and significance of Meluhha cipher for Bronze Age Technology narratives and history of Ancient India

This is a Sarasvati civilization narrative of technology in Ancient India. It narrates how *cīmarakāra* 'coppersmiths' evolved into *dhokra kamar* '*cire perdue* – los wax casting – technique' specialist artisans. Both categories of metallurgists are attested in Meluhha metalwork hieroglyphs called the Indus Script. A note on *cīmara* 'copper' and *dhokra* '*cire perdue*' introduces Section F: *Cire perdue* (lost wax) castings, forge. As a Bronze Age technology narrative, this evolution of *cīmara kāra* can also be called Neolithic - bronze age transition.

Indus Script inscriptions are Meluhha metalwork trade and process catalogs in Meluhha language. Meluhha lapidaries who worked with shells, carnelian or agate or lapis lazuli to create drilled beads could do metalwok smelting other metallic stones which were mineral ores and metallic compounds. Bronze Age necessitated a writing system to document the quantum leap in technological complexity of casting techniques using metallic stones, in smelters, to produce new resources of metalware, ingots, and hard alloys, called करडा [*karaḍā*] in Meluhha -- hard alloys of copper, tin, zinc, arsenical bronze, tin bronze, brass, pewter, iron, lead, gold or silver. One such alloy was documented in a hieroglyph composition and Meluhha cipher using the backbone-spine metaphor:

baraḍo = spine; backbone (Tulu) Rebus: *baran, bharat* 'mixed alloys' (5 copper, 4 zinc and 1 tin) (Punjabi) PLUS *gaṇḍa* 'four' Rebus: *kaṇḍa* 'furnace, fire-altar' (Santali)

Zinc had its own hieroglyph. It was shown on two Mohenjo-daro seals now in British Museum.
Svastika hieroglyph was also shown on a Mohenjo-daro seal m1225 with inscriptions on two sides:

m1225a Side b: '*svastika*' hieroglyph: Rebus: *jasta, sattva* , *satthiya, zasath* 'zinc'
PLUS 'four' strokes:
|||| Numeral 4: *gaṇḍa* 'four' Rebus: *kaṇḍa* 'furnace, fire-altar' (Santali) PLUS | *koḍa* 'one' Rebus: *koḍ* 'workshop' Thus, zinc fire-altar, workshop

Side a: *balad* m. 'ox ', gng. *bald*, (Ku.) *barad*, id. (Nepali. Tarai) Rebus: *bharat* (5 copper, 4 zinc and 1 tin)(Punjabi) *pattar* 'trough' Rebus*: pattar* 'guild, goldsmith'. Thus, copper-zinc-tin alloy (worker) guild.

kanac 'corner' Rebus: *kañcu* 'bronze' (Telugu) *dula* 'two' Rebus: *dul* 'cast metal' kolom 'three' Rebus: *kolami* 'smithy, forge' Numeral || *dula* 'two' Rebus: *dul* 'cast metal'Numeral III *kolom* 'three' Rebus: *kolami* 'smithy, forge'

kuṭila 'bent' CDIAL 3230 kuṭi— in cmpd. 'curve', *kuṭika—* 'bent' MBh. Rebus: *kuṭila, katthīl* = bronze (8 parts copper and 2 parts tin) kastīra n. ' tin ' lex.H. *kathīr* m. 'tin, pewter'; G. *kathīr* n. ' pewter '.2. H. (Bhoj.?) *kathīl, °lā* m. ' tin, pewter '; M. *kathīl* n. ' tin ', *kathlẽ* n. ' large tin vessel '(CDIAL 2984) kanka 'rim of jar' Rebus: karṇīka 'account

(scribe)' karṇī 'supercargo'

Meluhha hieroglyphs are used to compose and transcribe Indus Script Inscriptions. The readings of Meluhha hieroglyphs are presented as a decipherment of Indus script.

Meluhha hieroglyphs document Bronze Age trade on Tin Road from Malhar, India to Haifa, Israel.

The script transcribes Proto-Indian speech -- Meluhha (mleccha) language glosses.

Cryptic cipher, with an average deployment of 5 hieroglyph signs, often with a hieroglyphic pictorial motif, like an interlocking rebus reading puzzle, details technical specifications of early Bronze Age catalogs of Meluhha metalwork. Including the pictorial motif hieroglyphs, and dotted circles, over 550 hieroglhyphs are used in Meluhha hieroglyph cipher.

Meluhha cipher is validated by 1. readings of Indus Script inscriptions which transcribe Meluhha language and 2. their English translations.

Rebus cipher deploys homonymous glosses of Meluhha. This work presents plaintext readings of hieroglyphs and ciphertext rebus renderings of traded resources and products of Bronze Age – mostly stone, mineral, metal and alloyed artifacts.

An outstanding feature of a writing system called Indus Script is orthographic integrity and fidelity achieved on tiny writing space -- often as small as a thumbnail -- with stunning precision in pictographs rendered as rebus hieroglyphs or logographs transcribing Meluhha language.

This logographic writing system is distinguished from the then contemporary cuneiform of the Ancient Near East and Fertile Crescent which was a syllabic writing system for languages such as Sumerian, Elamite and Akkadian.

It has been a truly humbling experience, a pilgrim's progress, for the author to unravel an ancient writing system and underlying glosses of the ancestral language dating back to ca. 4th millennium BCE.

This work is a celebration of an announciement that what is perhaps one of the earliest writing systems of the world was originated by miners, smelters and smiths of ancient India. In all humility, the work is dedicated in awe and admiration to the guilds of workers of the Bronze Age who created the Sarasvati–Sindhu or Hindu civilization.

The inventive genius of an early writing system is matched by the metallurgical knowledge and inventions by Meluhha artisans of new alloys using a combination of metallic mineral ores and stones.

A herald of a literary event has become a tribute to the Bronze Age toiling masses of the world who have made the world an information society, a harmonious environ to live in for subsequent generations.

Reading through the set of over 2,000 Indus script inscriptions – most of which are unique though there are some sets of duplicate inscriptions -- is a pilgrim's progress unraveling and reliving the work processes evolved in Bronze Age metal work of Meluhhans, ancestors of present-day *Bhāratam janam* (a term used in Rigveda to refer to Bhārata people). Marathi language retains a remarkable cultural continuum of the term used to denote a special alloy metal: भरत [bharata] *n* A factitious metal compounded of copper, pewter, tin &c. भरती [bharatī] Composed of the metal भरत. भरताचें भांडें [bharatācēm bhāṇḍēṃ] *n* A vessel made of the metal भरत. The Indus writing system provides a frequently deployed hieroglyph to denote this alloy. Thus, Indus Script is a technology legacy from the Sarasvati civilization ancestors of present-day people of the sub-continent.

A remarkable semantic unity among present-day Indian languages is established traceable to the days of Sarasvati Hindu civilization ca 4th millennium BCE. Many glosses identified by the deciphered Melhha Indus Script hieroglyphs are demonstrated in ciphertexts of the lexical repertoire of all Indian languages validating a hypothesis that Meluhha-Mleccha was the fountain-spring of *Indian sprachbund* and a veritable *lingua franca* of the nation founded by the organized brilliance of the Bronze Age experts like smelters, artisans – metal- and stone-workers, stone-cutters, inventors of new metal alloys, *cire perdue* casting experts, in particular and traders. This semantic unity of Indian *sprachbund* from Bronze Age days, explains why anyone of the present-day glosses from any one of the Indian languages adequately explains and validates Meluhha rebus cipher.

Metallurgical repertoire of Meluhhans in Bronze Age is well articulated in Meluhha language, for example, in the following Lothal seal m1151, Harappa seals h465, h530, Mohenjodaro seals m993, m1225, m1226, m7; incribed rod m2090 and tablet m389.

Distance between Harappa and Lothal is 1562 kms. (970 miles). It is remarkable that in both these settlements and in 40 others of Sarasvati Sindhu river basins, the Meluhha cipher was deployed over an extended area – with over 2,000 settlements --, for an extended period of time involving 5 or 6 generations.

There is textual vidence that during historical times, what was referred to as *mlecchita vikalpa* (lit. Meluhha cipher) was identified as one of the 64 arts (including two allied communication arts called *akṣára muṣṭika kathanam* and *deśabhāṣā jñānam* – lit. fist-finger gesture narrations and knowledge of spoken language) to be learned by the youth (cf. Vātsyāyana's *Kāmasūtra* वात्स्यायन कामसूत्र in a section titled: *vidyā samuddeśa* lit. objective of schooling or eduation.

It is reasonable to infer that Bronze Age artisans of ancient India had an organized system for learning the use of a writing system which used Meluhha cipher.

Meluhha cipher keys

The keys are:

- Plain text is a list of Meluhha spoken language glosses. This language or *parole* is a precursor to all present-day Indian languages and can be referred to as Proto-Indian. (Two abbreviations are used evidencing the glosses: CDIAL: Comparative Dictionary of Indo-Aryan Languages by R. Turner; DEDR: Dravidian Etymological Dictionary of Dravidian Languages by Burrow and Emeneau and Munda Etyma of Hawaii University)
- Plain text is converted into cipher text by use of hieroglyphs which are either direct pictographs or combinations of pictographs (using ligaturing principle). The ligaturing principle is best evidenced by the 'composite animal' hieroglyph which combines pictographs of : human face, trunk of elephant, tail as serpent-hood, horns of zebu, forelegs of bovine, hindlegs of tiger, scarves on shoulder.
- Homonyms of Meluhha glosses which match the pictographs yield the communicated message.

The method used for Indus writing system (and identification of hieroglyph components in complex ciphers) is best explained by citing some specific examples of application of the cipher to create cipher texts.

m0302 Mohenjo-daro seal

Explaining the application of Meluhha cipher to create cipher texts which are epigraphs on seals, tablets and other artifacts with writing or inscriptions

Meluhha cipher rebus readings start with the pictorial motif hieroglyphs and reading text of inscription starting from the face of the animal reading each hieroglyph sign (including ligatures of orthographic strokes as pictographs or logographs) in sequence:

m1151A,a *ibha* 'elephant' Rebus: *ib* 'iron' *ibbo* 'merchant' (Gujarati) Circumscript: gaṇḍa 'four' Rebus: kaṇḍa 'furnace, fire-altar' (Santali)
aya kammaṭa.'coiner, mint alloy' Together, *aya kāṇḍa* 'alloy metalware'

kanka 'rim of jar' Rebus: karṇīka 'account (scribe)' karṇī 'supercargo' INFIXED sal 'splinter' Rebus: sal 'workshop'.

h465A खोंड [khōṇḍa] m A young bull, a bullcalf. (Marathi) Rebus: kõdār 'turner' (Bengali); कोंद kōnda 'engraver, lapidary setting or infixing gems' (Marathi) G. sãghāṛɔ m. 'lathe' ; संघाट joinery; M. sãgaḍ 'double-canoe' Rebus: sangataras 'stone-cutter, mason' Circumscript: dula 'two' Rebus: dul 'cast metal' PLUS | *koḍa* 'one' Rebus: *koḍ* 'workshop' PLUS मेढा [*mēḍhā*] A twist or tangle arising in thread or cord, a curl or snarl.(Marathi)(CDIAL 10312).L. *meṛh* f. 'rope tying oxen to each other and to post on threshing floor'(CDIAL 10317) Rebus: *meḍ* 'iron'. *mẽṛhet* 'iron' (Mu.Ho.)

 *kanka* 'rim of jar' Rebus: *karṇīka* 'account (scribe)' *karṇī* 'supercargo'

h530A खोंड [khōṇḍa] m A young bull, a bullcalf. (Marathi) Rebus: kõdār 'turner' (Bengali); कोंद kōnda 'engraver, lapidary setting or infixing gems' (Marathi) G. sãghāṛɔ m. 'lathe' ; संघाट joinery; M. sãgaḍ 'double-canoe' Rebus: sangataras 'stone-cutter, mason'

|||| Numeral 4: gaṇḍa 'four' Rebus: kaṇḍa 'furnace, fire-altar' (Santali) dula 'pair' Rebus: dul 'cast metal'
PLUS | *koḍa* 'one' Rebus: *koḍ* 'workshop'

kharedo = a currycomb (Gujarati) खरारा [*kharārā*] *m* (H) A currycomb. 2 Currying a horse. (Marathi) Rebus: करडा [*karaḍā*] Hard from alloy--iron, silver &c. (Marathi) *kharādī* ' turner' (Gujarati)

कांड *kāṇḍa* 'arrow' Rebus: *kāṇḍa* 'pots and pans, metalware, tools'. Rebus 2: kaṇḍ 'fire-altar' (Santali)

m993A खोंड [khōṇḍa] m A young bull, a bullcalf. (Marathi) Rebus: kõdār 'turner' (Bengali); कोंद kōnda 'engraver, lapidary setting or infixing gems' (Marathi) G. sãghāṛɔ m. 'lathe' ; संघाट joinery; M. sãgaḍ 'double-canoe' Rebus: sangataras 'stone-cutter, mason' खांडा [*khāṇḍā*] *m* A jag, notch, or indentation (as upon the edge of a tool or weapon). Rebus: *kāṇḍa* 'tools, pots and pans and metal-ware'

PLUS | *koḍa* 'one' Rebus: *koḍ* 'workshop' *aḍaren* 'cover of pot or lid' Rebus: *aduru* 'native, unsmelted metal'

dhāḷ 'a slope'; 'inclination of a plane' (G.); *ḍhāḷiyum* = adj. sloping, inclining (G.) Rebus: *ḍhālako* = a large metal ingot (G.) *ḍhālakī* = a metal heated and poured into a mould; a solid piece of metal; an ingot (Gujarati) PLUS *dula* 'pair' Rebus: *dul* 'cast metal' *sal* 'splinter' Rebus: *sal* 'workshop'. Thus, *ḍhālako dul sal* 'ingot, cast metal workshop'.

m1226a *balad* m. ' ox ', gng. *bald*, (Ku.) *barad*, id. (N. Tarai) Rebus: *bharat* (5 copper, 4 zinc and 1 tin)(Punjabi) *pattar* 'trough' Rebus: *pattar* 'guild'. Thus, copper-zinc-tin alloy (worker) guild.

Bronze alloy  workshop kañcu sal starting with bronze which is a tin + copper alloy or tin bronze (as distinguished from arsenical bronze, i.e. naturally occurring copper + arsenic).

ayo ḍhālako 'alloy metal ingot'

aya aḍaren (homonym: aduru)'alloy native metal'

muka 'ladle' (Tamil)(DEDR 4887) Rebus: *mũh* 'ingot' (Santali) *baṭa* = a kind of iron (Gujarati) *baṭa* = rimless pot (Kannada) Thus, iron ingot.

kolmo 'three' Rebus: *kolami* 'smithy, forge'.

kānḍa 'arrow' (Sanskrit) Rebus:*khānḍa* 'tools, pots and pans, metal-ware'. Rebus 2: kanḍ 'fire-altar' (Santali)

m7a *खोंड [khōṇḍa] m A young bull, a bullcalf. (Marathi) Rebus: kōdār 'turner' (Bengali); कोंद kōnda 'engraver, lapidary setting or infixing gems' (Marathi) G. sãghāṛɔ m. 'lathe' ; संघाट joinery; M. sāgaḍ 'double-canoe' Rebus: sangataras. संगतराश lit. 'to collect stones, stone-cutter, mason.'*

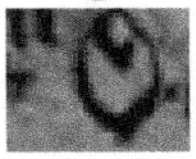

Bronze alloy workshop kañcu sal starting with bronze which is a tin + copper alloy or tin bronze (as distinguished from arsenical bronze, i.e. naturally occurring copper + arsenic).

aya kammaṭa.'coiner, mint alloy'

kuṭila 'bent' CDIAL 3230 kuṭi— in cmpd. 'curve', *kuṭika—* 'bent' MBh. Rebus: kuṭila, katthīl = bronze (8 parts copper and 2 parts tin) dula 'pair' Rebus: dul 'cast metal'. Thus cast bronze.

bhaṭa 'warrior' (Sanskrit) Rebus: *baṭa* a kind of iron (Gujarati). Rebus: *bhaṭa* 'furnace' (Santali)

meḍ 'body' Rebus: meḍ 'iron' (Ho.)

Variant: *meḍ 'body' Rebus: meḍ 'iron' (Ho.) काठी [kāṭhī] f (काष्ट S) 'frame or structure of the body' (Marathi) Rebus: खंडी [khanḍī] measure of weight (Marathi) கண்டி; kanṭi, n. < Mhr. khanḍil. [T. Tu. khanḍi, M. kanḍi.] Candy, a weight, about 500 lbs.*PLUS | *koḍa* 'one' Rebus: *koḍ* 'workshop' dula 'pair' Rebus: dul 'cast metal'. Thus, the 'body' flanked by two linear strokes denote: iron cast workshop.

kanka 'rim of jar' Rebus: karṇīka 'account (scribe)' karṇī 'supercargo'

loa 'ficus religiosa' Rebus: *lo* 'iron' (Sanskrit) PLUS unique ligatures: लोखंड [lōkhaṇḍa] *n* (लोह S) Iron. लोखंडाचे चणे खावविणें or चारणें To oppress grievously.लोखंडकाम [lōkhaṇḍakāma] *n* Iron work; that portion (of a building, machine &c.) which consists of iron. 2 The business of an ironsmith.लोखंडी [lōkhaṇḍī] *a* (लोखंड) Composed of iron; relating to iron. (Marathi) *bhaṭa* 'warrior' (Sanskrit) Rebus: *baṭa* a kind of iron (Gujarati). Rebus: *bhaṭa* 'furnace' (Santali) Thus, together, the ligatured hieroglyph reads rebus: *loa bhaṭa* 'iron furnace'

kanac 'corner' Rebus: *kañcu* 'bronze' dula 'pair' Rebus: dul 'cast metal' Thus cast bronze.

mogge 'sprout, bud' Rebus*: mũh* 'ingot'

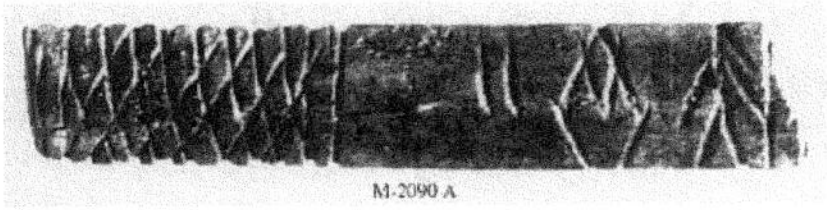

m2090A Pictorial motif hieroglyph: Pali. *akkhika* 'mesh of a net'; S. *akho* m. 'mesh of a net' Rebus: L. P. *akkhā* m. ' one end of a bag or sack thrown over a beast of burden '; Or. *akhā* ' gunny bag '; Bi. *ākhā, ãkhā* ' grain bag carried by pack animal '; H. *ākhā* m. ' one of a pair of grain bags used as panniers '; M. *ãkhā* m. ' netting in which coco -- nuts, &c., are carried ', *ãkhẽ* n. ' half a

bullock -- load ' (CDIAL 17) అంకెము [aṅkemu] *ankemu.* [Telugu] n. One pack or pannier, being half a bullock load. అండెము [aṇḍemu id. (Telugu)
Ka. aṇḍige one pannier or pack, half a bullock load. *Te.* aṇḍemu,aṇḍiyamu id.; aḍigamu a sort of pannier.(DEDR 127) sal 'splinter' Rebus: sal 'workshop'

kanac 'corner' Rebus: *kañcu* 'bronze' *meḍ* 'body' Rebus: *meḍ* 'iron' (Ho.) काठी [kāṭhī] *f* (काष्ट S) 'frame or structure of the body' (Marathi) Rebus: खंडी [khaṇḍī] measure of weight (Marathi) *கண்டி; kaṇṭi, n. < Mhr. khaṇḍil. [T. Tu. khaṇḍi, M. kaṇḍi.]* Candy, a weight, stated to be roughly equivalent to 500 lbs.

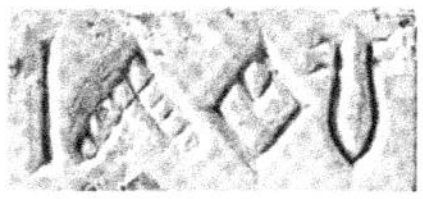
m389A

| *koḍa* 'one' Rebus: *koḍ* 'workshop'
aḍaren 'cover of pot or lid' Rebus: *aduru* 'native, unsmelted metal' Duplicated: dula 'pair' Rebus: dul 'cast metal'

kanac 'corner' Rebus: *kañcu* 'bronze'

rim-of-jar' hieroglyph *kanka* (Santali) *karṇika* 'scribe'(Sanskrit) Rebus: *karṇī,* supercargo for a boat shipment. *karṇīka* 'account (scribe)'.कारणी *kāraṇī* 'the supercargo of a ship' (Marathi)

m447A *खोंड [khōṇḍa] m A young bull, a bullcalf. (Marathi) Rebus: kõdār 'turner' (Bengali); कोंद kōnda 'engraver, lapidary setting or infixing gems' (Marathi) G. sãghārɔ m. 'lathe' ; संघाट joinery; M. sãgaḍ 'double-canoe' Rebus: sangataras 'stone-cutter, mason' Circumscript: dula 'two' Rebus: dul 'cast metal' dhāḷ* 'a slope'; 'inclination of a plane' (G.); *ḍhāḷiyum* = adj. sloping, inclining (G.) Rebus: *ḍhālako* = a large metal ingot (G.) *ḍhālakī* = a metal heated and poured into a mould; a solid piece of metal; an ingot (Gujarati) INFIXED *khuṭo* ' leg, foot ', °ṭī ' goat's leg ' Rebus: *khōṭā* 'alloy' (Marathi)

Seal published by Omananda Saraswati. In Pl. 275: Omananda Saraswati 1975. Ancient Seals of Haryana (in Hindi). Rohtak.

This pictorial motif gets normalized in Indus writing system as a hieroglyph sign:

baraḍo = spine; backbone (Tulu) Rebus: *baran, bharat* 'mixed alloys' (5 copper, 4 zinc and 1 tin) (Punjabi) Tir. mar -- kaṇḍḗ ' back (of the body) '; S. kaṇḍo m. ' back ', L. kaṇḍ f., kaṇḍā m. ' backbone ', awāṇ. kaṇḍ, °ḍī ' back 'H. kāṭā m. ' spine ', G. kāṭɔ m., M. kāṭā m.; Pk. kaṁḍa -- m. ' backbone '.(CDIAL 2670) Rebus: kaṇḍ 'fire-altar' (Santali) The hieroglyph ligature to convey the semantics of 'bone' and rebus reading is: 'four short numeral strokes ligature' |||| Numeral 4: gaṇḍa 'four' Rebus: kaṇḍa 'furnace, fire-altar' (Santali)

This is one possible explanation for the ancient name of the Hindu nation: Bhāratam, mentioned in Ṛgveda – the Bhāratam janam were metalworkers producing *bharat* mixed alloy of copper, zinc and tin.

Water-carrier PLUS rim-of-jar' ligatured sign glyph read rebus: *kuṭhi karṇī* 'furnace supercargo'.

kuṭi; Rebus: *kuṭhi* 'furnace'.

h3a *खोंड [khōṇḍa] m A young bull, a bullcalf. (Marathi) Rebus: kõdār 'turner' (Bengali); कोंद kōnda 'engraver, lapidary setting or infixing gems' (Marathi) kuṭhi karṇī* 'furnace supercargo'. *aya kāṇḍa* 'alloy metalware'

Water-carrier PLUS rim-of-jar' ligatured sign glyph read rebus: *kuṭhi karṇī* 'furnace supercargo'. PLUS | *koḍa* 'one' Rebus: *koḍ* 'workshop'

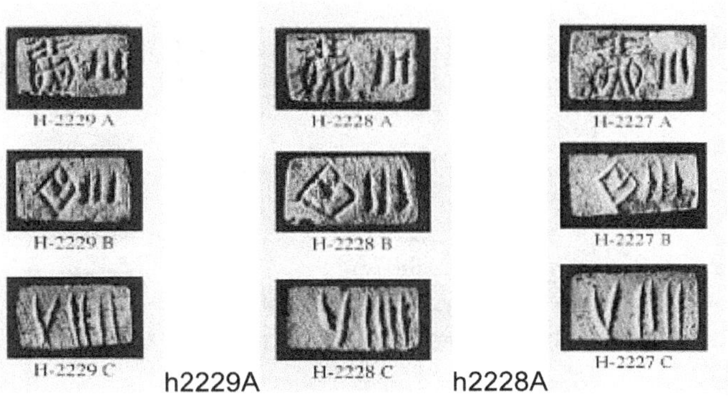

h2229A h2228A h2227A

 h2225A  h2223A  h2222A  h2221A  h2220A  h2219A

 h2218A

Water-carrier PLUS rim-of-jar' ligatured sign glyph read rebus: *kuṭhi karṇī* 'furnace supercargo'.PLUS ||| *kolom* 'three' Rebus: *kolami* 'smithy, forge'. Thus together: furnace, smithy, forge

kanac 'corner' Rebus: *kañcu* 'bronze' PLUS III *kolom* 'three' Rebus: *kolami* 'smithy, forge' Thus together: bronze smithy, forge

baṭa 'rimless, broad-mouthed pot' Rebus: *bhaṭa* 'furnace' (Gujarati.); *baṭa* 'a kind of iron' (Gujarati)

|||| Numeral 4: gaṇḍa 'four' Rebus: kaṇḍa 'furnace, fire-altar' (Santali)

 h838A  h429A  m215a  Lothal 42a

 h838A  m429A  m215a  Lothal 42a

 h499a  m1779a  h81A 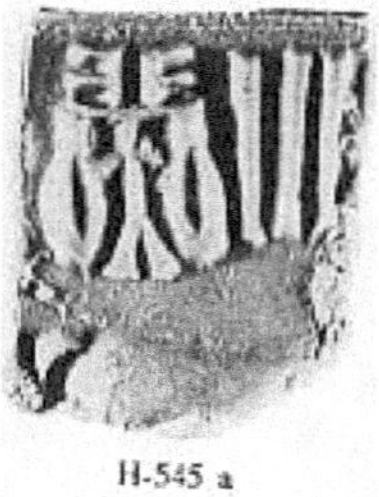 h545a

Water-carrier PLUS rim-of-jar' ligatured sign glyph read rebus: *kuṭhi karṇī* 'furnace supercargo'.PLUS ||| *kolom* 'three' Rebus: *kolami* 'smithy, forge'. Thus together: furnace, smithy, forge

III *kolom* 'three' Rebus: *kolami* 'smithy, forge'

Pictorial hieroglyphs on these seals:

खोंड [khōṇḍa] m A young bull, a bullcalf. (Marathi) Rebus: kõdār 'turner' (Bengali); कोंद kōnda 'engraver, lapidary setting or infixing gems' (Marathi) G. sãghāṛɔ m. 'lathe' ; संघाट joinery; M. sãgaḍ 'double-canoe' Rebus: sangataras 'stone-cutter, mason'

balad m. ' ox ', gng. *bald*, (Ku.) *barad*, id. (N. Tarai) Rebus: *bharat* (5 copper, 4 zinc and 1 tin)(Punjabi) *pattar* 'trough' Rebus*: pattar* 'guild'. Thus, copper-zinc-tin alloy (worker) guild.

 m193A  m187a  Lothal 102a

|||| Numeral 4: gaṇḍa 'four' Rebus: kaṇḍa 'furnace, fire-altar' (Santali)

Water-carrier PLUS rim-of-jar' ligatured sign glyph read rebus: *kuṭhi karṇī* 'furnace supercargo'.

खोंड *[khōṇḍa] m A young bull, a bullcalf. (Marathi) Rebus: kōdār 'turner' (Bengali);* कोंद *kōnda 'engraver, lapidary setting or infixing gems' (Marathi) G. sãghāṛɔ m. 'lathe' ;* संघाट *joinery; M. sāgaḍ 'double-canoe' Rebus: sangataras 'stone-cutter, mason'* Numeral 2: dula 'two' Rebus: dul 'cast metal' PLUS III *kolom* 'three' Rebus: *kolami* 'smithy, forge'

Kalibangan 22a खोंड *[khōṇḍa] m A young bull, a bullcalf. (Marathi) Rebus: kōdār 'turner' (Bengali);* कोंद *kōnda 'engraver, lapidary setting or infixing gems' (Marathi) G. sãghāṛɔ m. 'lathe' ;* संघाट *joinery; M. sāgaḍ 'double-canoe' Rebus: sangataras 'stone-cutter, mason'* dula 'pair' Rebus: dul 'cast metal' PLUS kolom 'three' Rebus: kolami 'smithy, forge'
kuṭhi karṇī 'furnace supercargo'.(of cast metal from smithy)

 *kanac* 'corner' Rebus: *kañcu* 'bronze' PLUS Ligature: | *koḍa* 'one' Rebus: *koḍ* 'workshop' PLUS infixed: kolom 'three' Rebus: 'smithy, forge'.

Variant:
kanac 'corner' Rebus: *kañcu* 'bronze' PLUS Ligature: | *koḍa* 'one' Rebus: *koḍ* 'workshop' PLUS infixed: kolom 'three' Rebus: 'smithy, forge'. Thus, together, bronze smithy, forge.

Two types of bronze metalwork are named in Meluhha hieroglyphs:

 *kanac* 'corner' Rebus: *kañcu* 'bronze'

 *kuṭila* 'bent' CDIAL 3230 kuṭi— in cmpd. 'curve', *kuṭika—* 'bent' MBh. Rebus: *kuṭila, katthīl* = bronze (8 parts copper and 2 parts tin)

Reduplication of hieroglyphs is intended to convey 'metal castings': *dula* 'pair' Rebus: *dul* 'cast metal' (This is consistent with the evidence of *dhokra kamar* work of *cire perdue* (lost-wax) casting).

Copper plate  showing 'hare' fronting a thorny 'bush'. *ranga ronga, ranga conga* = thorny, spikey, armed with thorns; *edel dare ranga conga dareka* = this cotton tree grows with spikes on it (Santali) [Note the thorns on the round object in front of the bull onthe Ur cylinder seal impression – U 16220]

Rebus 'alloy of tin, lead and antimony': *ranga, rang* pewter is an alloy of tin, lead, and antimony (an~jana) (Santali).

kulai 'a hare' (Santali) Allograph: *kul* 'tiger' (Santali) Rebus: *kolhe*'smelter'. (Hieroglyph attached) Together, the 'hare' PLUS 'bush' read: Smelter of alloy of tin, lead and antimony, kolhe ranga. *Vikalpa: kāṭī, kāṭī* 'thorn bush' (Marathi) S. *kaṇḍī* f. ' thorn bush '*(CDIAL 2679) Rebus:* खंडी [khaṇḍī] *f* A measure of weight and capacity, a candy. It consists (in Bombay) of twenty Bombay maunds, or, for particular substances, of eight maunds: (at Poona) of twenty Poona maunds, and generally of twenty maunds; varying there- fore as the maund varies. 2 Applied to a great quantity (Marathi) This gloss खंडी [khaṇḍī] constitutes the estimated measure by weight of the supercargo. An allograph is 'body, stature' following the 'supercargo' hieroglyph: 'rim of jar'.

Foot with anklet; copper alloy (*cire perdue*). Mohenjodaro (After Fig. 5.11 in Agrawal. D.P. 2000. *Ancient Metal Technology & Archaeology of South Asia*. Delhi: Aryan Books International. *khuṭo* ' leg, foot ', °ṭī ' goat's leg ' Rebus: *khōṭā* 'alloy' (Marathi)

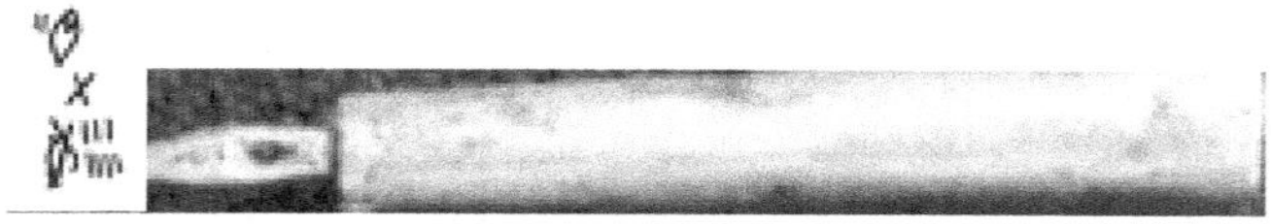

Gold pendant with Indus script inscription. The pendant is needle-like with cylindrical body. It is made from a hollow cylinder with soldered ends and perforated oint. Museum No. MM 1374.50.271; Marshall 1931: 521, pl. CLI, B3 (After Fig. 4.17 a,b in: JM Kenoyer, 1998, p. 196)

The inscription scripted in free-hand writing, is a professional calling card of the artisan who wore the gold pendant:

 Bronze alloy workshop kañcu sal starting with bronze which is a tin + copper alloy or tin bronze (as distinguished from arsenical bronze, i.e. naturally occurring copper + arsenic).

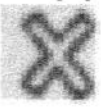 *dāṭu* 'cross'(Telugu) Rebus: *dhatu* 'mineral' (Santali).

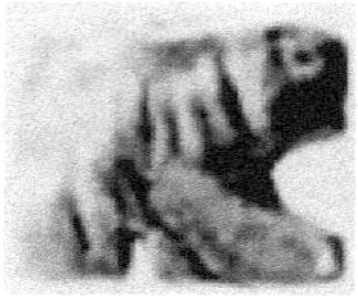

h336A

h336B

4424

ayo 'fish' Rebus: *aya* 'iron' *ayas* 'metal'

||| Numeral: kolom 'three' Rebus: kolami 'smithy, forge'

|||| Numeral: *gaṇḍa* 'four' Rebus: *kaṇḍa* 'furnace, fire-altar' (Santali) Rebus: *kāṇḍa* 'tools, pots and pans and metal-ware'

Bhirrana bronze age artifacts. (Bhirrana settlement is evidenced from 7th millennium BCE) on the banks of Vedic River Sarasvati

Chert blades and Core, Harappan Period (c. 2500 – 1900 BC), Bhirrana

A cache of beads in a small vase, beads of carnelian, lapis lazuli, shell, Harappan Period (c. 2500 – 1900 BC), Bhirrana

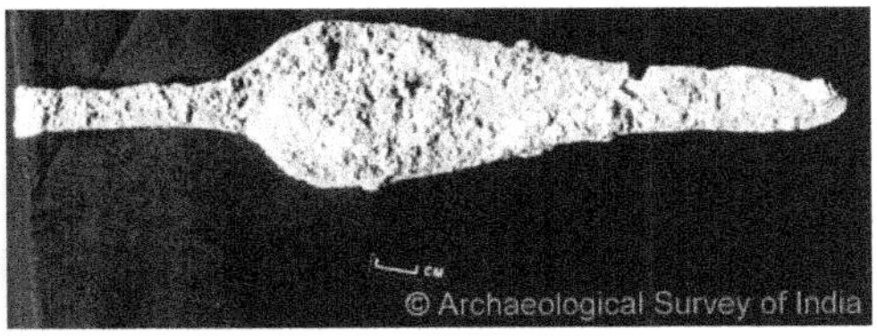

Copper spearhead, (c. 2500 – 1900 BC)

A 'Sheffield of Ancient India: Chanhu-Daro's metal working industry 10 X photos of copper knives, spears, razors, axes and dishes. Many of these items of metalware were made using *cire perdue* metalcasting technique, the way the Nahal Mishmar artifacts were produced. Illustrated London News 1936 - November 21st http://www.iln.org.uk/iln_years/year/1936a.htm

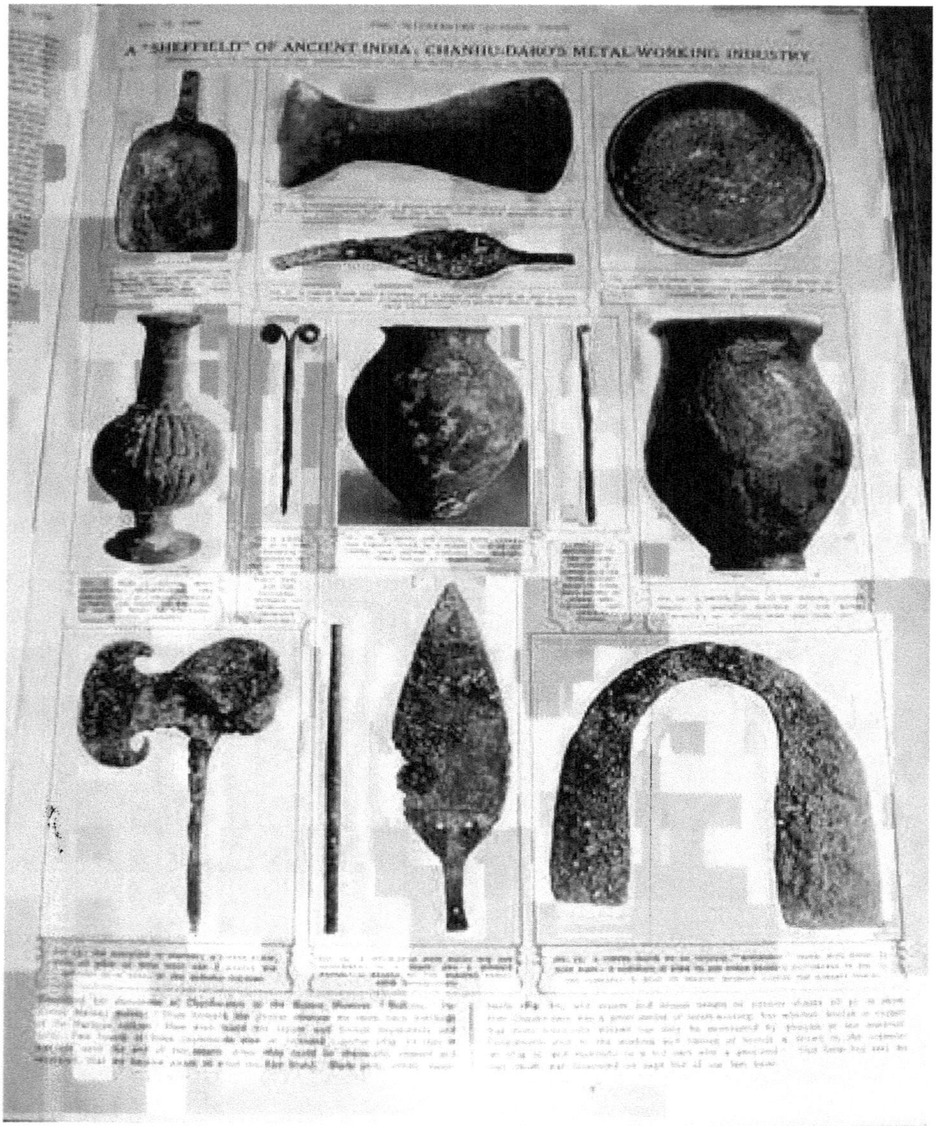
A "SHEFFIELD" OF ANCIENT INDIA: CHANHU-DARO'S METAL WORKING INDUSTRY

Bronze statue (*cire perdue*) of a woman holding a small bowl, Mohenjodaro; copper alloy made using *cire perdue* casting method (DK 12728; Mackay 1938: 274, Pl. LXXIII, 9-11). The cire perdue casting method was done by Meluhhan artisans called *dhokra kamar.* There are inscriptions from Mohenjo-daro and Dholavira attesting to this professional title which continues to be used to the present-day in India. (The inscription hieroglyphs and archaeological contexts are detailed in Section F)

Two contentious academic debates on identity of Meluhha speakers and language spoken by ancient artisans and traders providing the foundation of indian *sprachbund* are resolved:

1.Meluhha speakers were ancient Hindus of *Bhārat* and Bronze Age artisans/traders of Ancient Near East and Fertile crescent – exemplified by later-day legatees called Asur of Chattisgarh and Assur of Ancient Near East.

2. Meluhha language was the *lingua franca* of ancient India. Vedic was a version of poetic diction called *chandas* of Indian *sprachbund.* Thus, the roots for hundreds of glosses of present-day languages of India of over one billion people are traced back in millennial time to rebus ciphertexts of Meluhha hieroglyphs as trade documents of Bronze Age.

Meluhha Indus Script epigraphs thus constitute the oldest written documents of the roots of Hindu civilization, of activities of artisans and traders, whose donkey caravans frequented the Tin Road from India through Ancient Near East to Fertile Crescent, including stretches of maritime sojourns along Rivers Sarasvati and Sindhu and the Persian Gulf channel of Indian Ocean. The Meluhha documents attest the contribution made by Meluhhans to the evolution of Bronze Age. The Meluhha guilds and their trade caravans form the nucleus corporate forms to transform Araṭṭa into a राष्ट्रम् rāṣṭram, a multi-national formation for peoples' progress.

Malhar, India produced the evidence of iron smelter ca. 1800 BCE. Haifa, Israel produced evidence of two tin pure ingots inscribed with Meluhha hieroglyphs. The distance between Malhar and Haifa is 2,818 miles virtually defining the Tin Road which Meluhha speakers traversed over 2 millennia of Bronze Age, documenting their activities on tablets, seals and even on metal artifacts.

The enquiry starts with 1. zebu, humped bull, on ancient writing systems of Meluhha hieroglyphs in Fertile Crescent, Ancient Near East and Ancient India, and 2. Araṭṭa. Meluhha hieroglyphs on inscriptions are technical specifications of trade cargo. Zebu, *bos indicus,* Meluhha gloss *khũṭ,* is read rebus 'native-metal-smith-guild', of seafaring traders on Persian Gulf Maritime route supercargo boats and Tin Road donkey caravans. A synonym for zebu is *aḍar ḍangra* read rebus: *aduru ḍhangar* 'native-unsmelted-metal blacksmith' (Santali); *aduru* denotes 'unsmelted, native metal'. Meluhha zebu and other hieroglyphs presented in this work elaborate on and complement efforts at decipherment of Indus script. The efforts are seen in *Philosophy of Symbolic forms in Meluhha cipher, Meluhha -- a visible language* and *Indus Script cipher* include Corpora of Meluhha Epigraphs.

The most frequently occurring pictorial motif hieroglyph is a young bull. Meluhha cipher reading of the plainpictorial motif is: *कोंद kōnda 'engraver, lapidary setting or infixing gems' (Marathi) kōḍu 'horn' Rebus: 'workshop'sãghārɔ m. 'lathe' (Gujarati) Rebus: sangataras. संगतराश lit. 'to collect stones, stone-cutter, mason.* Thus, an artisan -- lapidary, metalworker, turner is the author of the exquisite Meluhha Indus script, Meluhha writing system. He or she is an Asur, Assur, a worshipper of the sun and fire. He or she is also a worshipper of *śiva शिव* 'auspicious, propitious, lucky'*';* शिवक: is a linga, an image of the auspicious – as evidenced by 1. five stone lingas found in Harappa; and 2. the practice of women wearing sindhur, red vermilion at the parting of the hair shown on two terracotta toys of Nausharo – two indicators of abiding Hindu tradition from the days of Meluhha artisans and their writing system.

The most frequently occurring sign hieroglyph is 'rim-of'-jar'. Meluhha cipher reading of the plaintext gloss is: *karṇī,* supercargo for a boat shipment. *karṇīka* 'account (scribe)'.

'rim-of-jar' hieroglyph *kanka* (Santali) *karṇika* 'scribe'(Sanskrit) Rebus: *karṇī,* supercargo for a boat shipment. *karṇīka* 'account (scribe)'. कारणी *kāraṇī* 'the supercargo of a ship' (Marathi)

The gloss *bharat* had two ancient semantic connotations: 1. An alloy of copper, zinc and tin; the plaintext representation of the gloss *bharat* is the hieroglyph: spine, backbone: *barado* = spine; backbone (Tulu) Rebus: *baran, bharat* 'mixed alloys' (5 copper, 4 zinc and 1 tin) (Punjabi)
2. Name of a Hindu nation mentioned by Viśvāmitra in R̥gveda as *Bhāratam janam.*

The hieroglyph as part of plaintext is found in neolithic times ca. 7000-4300 BCE.

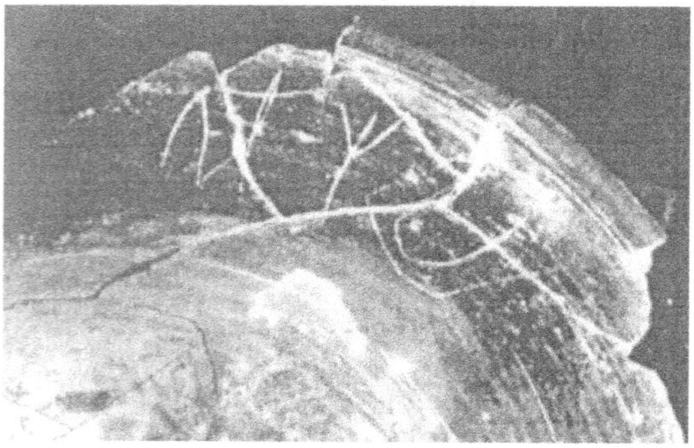

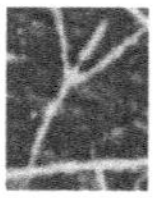

Inscribed pottery from Sanur. Neolithic. Photograph: Archaeological Survey of India. Rebus ciphertext readings of plaintext hieroglyphs: From l.: : *baraḍo* = spine; backbone Rebus: *bharat* 'mixed alloy (copper, zinc, tin) *kolmo* 'paddy plant' Rebus: *kolami* 'smithy, forge' *baṭa* 'rimless, broad-mouthed pot' Rebus: *bhaṭa* 'furnace' (Gujarati.); *baṭa* 'a kind of iron' (Gujarati)
(B.B. Lal, 1960. From Megalithic to the Harappa: Tracing back the graffiti on pottery. Ancient India, No.16, pp.4-24.
http://www.indologica.com/volumes/vol23-24/vol23-24_art04_LAL.pdf)

Chronological sequencing of Meluhha Indus script with referece to Vedic language is rendered easy based on the following facts: Most of Meluhha Indus Script epigraphs belong to the Bronze Age from ca. 3000 BCE. Nicholas Kazanas has demonstrated in a philological excursus that Vedic predates Avestan: "...Avestan moved away from the Indo-Iraian unity, and it did this when the use of *as-* as auxiliary in the periphrastic perfect was well-established in the Brāhmaṇa texts ...the RV was complete by c3300BCE except for the interpolations...the Iranians had been with the Indoaryans and at some unknown date moved out of larger Saptasindhu west and north into Iran." (Kazanas,N., 2011, Vedic and Avestan) http://www.omilosmeleton.gr/pdf/en/indology/Vedic_and_Avestan.pdf Kazanas has also shown based on a study of evolution of cultural motifs that material manifestation of the archaeological finds post-dates early Vedic tradition expressed in Ṛgveda (RV): "RV by general consent was composed around the Sarasvati, then it follows that the Indiaryans were were ensconced in Saptasidhu by c.3200 and that the Indus-Sarasvati Civilization was a material manifestation of the early oral Vedic tradition expressed in the RV." (Item 19. In: Kazanas, N., 2009, Indo-European Lingistics ad Indo-Aryan Indigenism) http://www.omilosmeleton.gr/pdf/en/indology/IEL&IAI.pdf

Legacy of *meluhha* language & Asur, Assur metal workers and traders

Vedic glosses *asūrta-, sūrta-, asūryá-, asūrá-* are explained as related to the sun. Marcos Albino notes: "*asūrta-* is an extended exocentric compound based on svàr/sūr 'sun', thati t is not a negative formation with the "possessive *suffix –ta*, and that *sūrta-* isa decompositional formation..Ved. asūryá-, too, is an extended exocentric compound. Ved. *asūré* is an "absence" formation of the type *arajjáu* 'without rope.'" http://www.ejvs.laurasianacademy.com/ejvs20/asurta.pdf That Asur, Assur lineage smelters and metal workers *par excellence* [evidenced by the Delhi non-rusting iron pillar and dhokra kamar *cire perdue* (lost-wax casting] artifacts and Nahal Mishmar exquisite lost-wax castings of ca. 5th millennium BCE], were sun-worshippers is evidenced by a breathtaking bronze hieroglyphic presentation in Sit-Shamshi bronze of the Louvre Museum. Asur, Assur reached out to the Sun with the ziggurat as *dhatu garbha* (cognate: *dagoba*). शतपथ ब्राह्मण *Śatapatha Brāhmaṇa* (of Yajurveda) III.2.1.23-24 states that the Devas (i.e. Vedic speakers) robbed the language from Asuras. This is a way of saying that languages of Asura and others in Saptasindhu evolved into the Indian *sprachbund*. One explanation for this provided in the statement itself is that it is *upajijñāsya,* 'to be excogitated or found out; enigmatical'. The language referred to in the statement is *mleccha* (cognate *meluhha*). The Hindu tradition refers to both Asura and Deva as the children of Kaśyapa. The same *Brāhmaṇa* notes that the language (*vāc*) is sent by Devas to Gandharvas in exchange fo Soma in their possession. One way of explaining this enigmatic statement is that Vedic diction elaborated the *mleccha* language of Gandharva (people of Gandhāra) using glosses like *ayas* (alloy metal) and *amśu* (from Tocharian *ancu*, iron).

Upajijñāsya commended by the ancient text is the *raison d'etre* for this work, *Deciphered Meluhha Indus Script hieroglyphs.*

Bronze model of temple, also named Sit-shamshi (ceremony of the rising sun) , 12th century BCE. Susa. Louvre Museum. Sb 2743. Sully Rez-de-chaussée Iran, la Susiane à l'époque médio-élamite. Found by J. de Morgan between 1904 and 1905

Elamite inscription: "*I, Shilhak-Inshushinak, son of Shutruk-Nahhunte, beloved servant of Inshushinak, king of Anzan and Susa, who made the kingdom grow, protector of Elam, I built a bronze sit-shamshi*"

The Sit-Shamshi bronze may be an evocation of *sandhyāvandanam*, an ancient daily practice which abides into the present day, of water ablutions and offerings of prayer to Sun divinity, *svàr/sūr* glosses which yield *asur*, and also *assur* -- Aššur (Akkadian) (English| Ashur/Assyria, Assyrian/ *Aššur*, Assyrian Neo-Aramaic/ Ātûr ; Hebrew אַשּׁוּר

/ *Aššûr*, Arabic: آشور / ALA-LC: *Āshūr*). The city was occupied from the Sumerian period ca. 2600-2500 BCE through to the 14th century CE. Akkadian gloss *dullu* 'work' may be a cognate of Meluhha *dul* 'cast metal' (Santali) and religious leader *šangū* cognate of Meluhha *sanghvi,* 'guide of pilgrims' caravan' (Gujarati)

Carved stone sunflowers. Ar of Elam in the Louvre Museum.

Relief spinner Louvre Museum Sb2834. Young woman spinning and servant holding a fan. Fragment of a relief. Bitumen mastic. Neo-Elamite period (8th – 6th century BCE). Found in Susa. The bas-relief was first cited in J, de Morgan's Memoires de la Delegation en Perse, 1900, vol. i. plate xi Ernest Leroux. Paris.

Seven Meluhha hieroglyphs are read on these Susa art pieces: From Sit-Shamshi bronze: 1. rimmed storage jar; 2. three stalks; 3. Ziggurat; From Carved Stone sunflowers: 4. Safflower;

From Relief spinner: 5. Spinner; 6. Stools with bovine legs; 7. Fish with six round ligatures. Meluhha readings of these seven hieroglyphs are:

1. kanka 'rim of jar' Rebus: karṇīka 'account (scribe)' karṇī 'supercargo'

2. ढांक [ḍhāṅka] *n* ढांकळ *f* C An old and decaying tree: also the stump or naked stalks and stem remaining (of a little plant).(Marathi) WPah.kṭg. *ḍāṅg* f. (obl. -- *a*) ' stick ', *ḍaṅgrɔ* m. ' stalk (of a plant) ' Rebus: *ḍhangar* blacksmith' kolom 'three' Rebus: kolami 'smithy, forge' Vikalpa: *khōṇḍa* A tree of which the head and branches are broken off, a stock or stump: also the lower portion of the trunk—that below the branches. (Marathi) Rebus 1: *kōdā* 'to turn in a lathe' (Bengali) Rebus 2: *koḍ* 'workshop' (Gujarati)

3. *dagoba* 'ziggurat' *dhatu garbha* lit. earth as womb containing minerals(ores)(Sanskrit)

4. *karaḍa* -- m. 'safflower', *°ḍā* -- f. ' a tree like the karañja ' (Prakrit); M. *karḍī*, *°ḍaī* f. ' safflower, *carthamus tinctorius* and its seed '. (CDIAL 2788). Rebus: करडा [*karaḍā*] Hard from alloy--iron, silver &c. (Marathi) *kharādī*' turner, a person who fashions or shapes objects on a lathe' (Gujarati)

5. *kāti* 'spinner' rebus: 'wheelwright.' *kola* 'woman' (Nahali). Rebus: *kolhe*' smelter'. *meḍhi, miḍhī, meṇḍhī* = a plait in a woman's hair; a plaited or twisted strand of hair (Punjabi) Rebus: *meḍ* 'iron' (Ho.) *dhaṭu* m. (also dhaṭhu) m. 'scarf' (Western Pahari) (CDIAL 6707) Rebus: *dhatu* 'minerals' (Santali) Assamese. *xaï* 'friend', xaiyā 'partner in a game'; Sinhala. saha 'friend' (< nom. sákhā or < sahāya -- ?). sákhi (nom. sg. sákhā) m. 'friend' RigVeda. (CDIAL 13074) Rebus: Oriya. *sāhi, sāi* ' part of town inhabited by people of one caste or tribe '(CDIAL 13323)

6. *khuṭo* 'leg, foot'. *khũṭ* 'community, guild' (Santali) Kur. *kaṇḍō* a stool. Malt. *kanḍo* stool, seat. (DEDR 1179) Rebus: *kaṇḍ* 'fire-altar, furnace' (Santali) kāṇḍa 'stone ore'. kol 'tiger' Rebus: k*olhe* 'smelter' iger's paws. kola 'tiger' (Telugu); kola 'tiger, jackal' (Kon.). Rebus: kol 'working in iron' (Tamil) The ligatured legs of seat indicae: smelter guild: *kolhe khũṭ*

7. *ayo* 'fish' (Munda). Rebus: *ayas* 'metal' (Sanskrit) aya 'metal' (Gujarati) Numeral 6: *āra* 'six', Rebus: *āra* 'brass,

Harosheth hagoyim 'smithy of nations'. Cognate with Meluhha *kharoṣṭī goy*, 'blacksmith's lip clan' खरोष्टी kharōṣṭī , 'A kind of alphabet; Lv.1.29'. compound as composed of khar + ōṣṭī 'blacksmith + lip'. Often, there is an alternative (perhaps, erroneous) transliteration as kharōṣṭī. The compound is composed of: *khar + ōṣṭī* (or, उष्ट mfn. 'burnt' (CDIAL 2386); uṣṭa -- 'settled' (Sanskrit) (CDIAL 2385) ṓṣṭha m. ' lip ' RigVeda. Pali. oṭṭha -

Repertoire of Meluhha smithy, forge metalwork

Mohenjodaro. Terracotta tablet, Pl. CXVIII,9 (Marshall, 1931).

Pictorial motif hieroglyphs carried in procession:

(Note: The illegible pictorial motif – first from r. -- is inferred to be spoked-wheel comparable to the standard held aloft on Tukulti Ninurta fire-altar). Spokes-of-wheel, nave-of-wheel *āra* 'spokes' Rebus: *āra 'brass'*. cf. erka = ekke (Tbh. of arka) aka (Tbh. of arka) copper (metal); crystal (Kannada) Glyph: *eraka*'nave of wheel' Rebus: eraka 'copper'; cf. erka = ekke (Tbh. of arka) aka (Tbh. of arka) copper (metal); crystal (Kannada)

Scarf *dhatu* 'scarf' (Western Pahari) Rebus: *dhatu* 'mineral ore'

Young bull *kõda* 'young bull-calf' Rebus: *kõdār* 'turner' (Bengali);

Standard device (lathe + portable furnace) *śagaḍī* = lathe (Gujarati) *san:gaḍa*, 'lathe, portable furnace'; rebus: battle; *jangaḍiyo* 'military guard who accompanies treasure into the treasury' (Gujarati) Rebus: *sanghāḍo* (Gujarati) cutting stone, gilding (Gujarati); *sangatarāśū* = stone cutter (Telugu)

- Humped zebu, *bos indicus*, or related species *bos taurus indicus* (also called indicine) is a signature hieroglyph of Hindu civilization. The species of humped bulls held in veneration, also gets the gloss brahmani or brahman bull. It is notable that the early name for a writing system in ancient India was Brahmi a synonym of Sarasvati, name of a river and also a feminine divinity of arts, crafts, writing and learning. The word zebu derives from Tibetan word Zen or Zeba, 'hump of the camel',
- Meluhha hieroglyphs evolved as Indus Writing ca. 3500 BCE -----perhaps the earliest writing system of the world --, spread into the Ancient Near East and the Fertile Crescent.
- The gloss 'meluhha' has variant pronunciations in *milakkha, mleccha* in Indian *sprachbund* (language union). The gloss is attested on an Akkadian cylinder of Shu-ilishu, Meluhha interpreter.
- Meluhha Cipher is defined as hieroglyphs read rebus using Meluhha glosses.
- Meluhha hieroglyphs in epigraphs (also called Indus Script) are deciphered as technical specifications of trade cargo of material resources such as minerals, metals and stone products, metalware, tools, pots and pans.
- Dictionary of Meluhha hieroglyphs detailed in this monograph 1. validates the Meluhha cipher and 2. provides proof that deployment of Zebu (*bos indicus*) hieroglyph is intended to denote the professional repertoire of native-metal-smith-guild.
- Facets and roots of Hindu civilization are evidenced in about 2,600 archaeological sites of Sarasvati and Sindhu river basins (Ancient India). Artisans were engaged in

minerals, metals, stone-turner work. Trader boats, caravans traversed along the Persian Gulf maritime route as well as Tin Road from Aratta to Assur and beyond to Kanesh and Fertile Crescent. The trade is documented on about 7000 epigraphs of Ancient Near East and Ancient India. Meluhha settlements are attested in cuneiform texts.

The material resources used and Bronze Age products produced by lapidary and metalwork artisans with expertise in *cire perdue* metal casting technique, were traded along the Tin Road from Meluhha (Araṭṭa) to Assur onwards to Kanesh and the Fertile Crescent.

- The Meluhha (also called Indus) writing system was founded in Meluhha languages and consisted of hieroglyphs read rebus.
- Meluhha settlements along Persian Gulf and in Ancient Near East served as intermediaries for trade in Meluhhan resources. This is exemplified by Shu Ilishu cylinder seal showing an Akkadian Meluhha interpreter.

A personal cylinder seal of Shu-ilishu, a translator of the Meluhhan language (*Expedition* 48 (1): 42-43) with cuneiform writing exists. The rollout of Shu-ilishu's cylinder seal. Courtesy of the Département des Antiquités Orientales, Musée du Louvre, Paris. "The presence in Akkad of a translator of the Meluhhan language suggests that he may have been literate and could read the undeciphered Indus script. This in turn suggests that there may be bilingual Akkadian/Meluhhan tablets somewhere in Mesopotamia. Although such documents may not exist, Shu-ilishu's cylinder seal offers a glimmer of hope for the future in unraveling the mystery of the Indus script." (Gregory L. Possehl,Shu-ilishu's cylinder seal, Expedition, Vol. 48, Number 1, pp. 42-43).

- Decipherment and rebus readings are detailed in:

  Section A. Meluhha hieroglyphs on m1893 Mohenjo-daro seal; rebus readings of native-metal-smith guild

  Section B: Āraṭṭa आरट्ट

  Section C. Meluhha metalwork hieroglyphs

Section D: Copper, brass
Section E: Bronze, tin
Section F: *Cire perdue* (lost wax) castings, forge

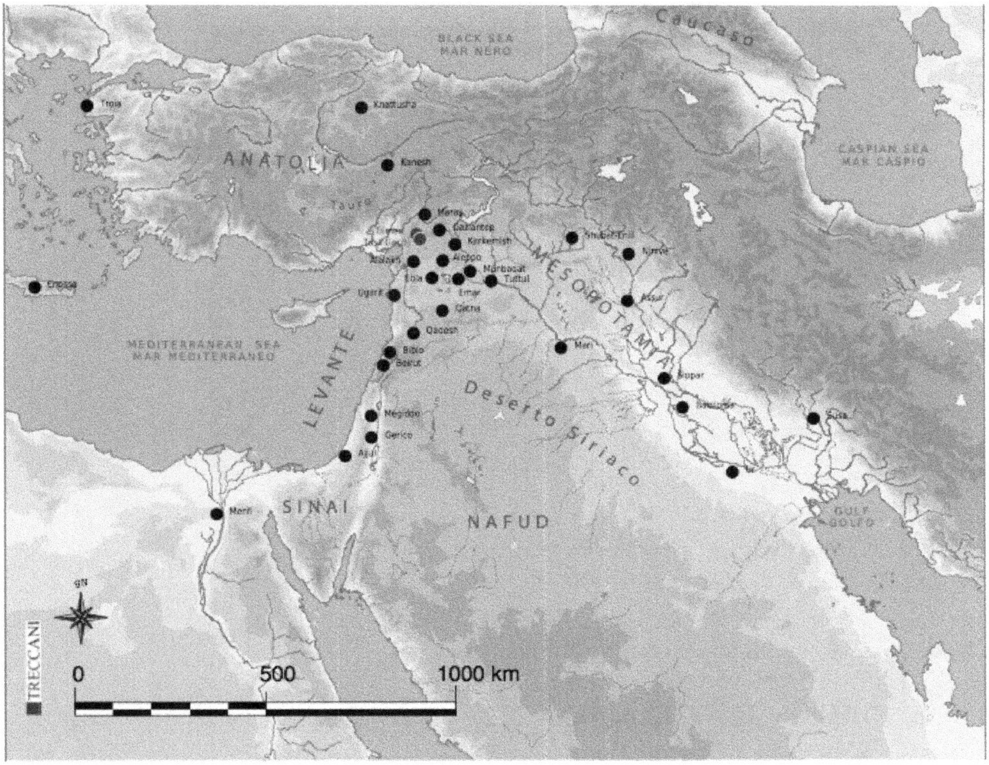

Source: N. Marchetti (ed.), Kinku. Sigilli dell'età del Bronzo dalla regione di Gaziantep in Turchia. Bologna, Museo Civico Medievale, 29 aprile -4 settembre 2011 (OrientLab 1), Dipartimento di Archeologia – Ante Quem, Bologna 2011. http://www.orientlab.net/pubs/

Thanks to Nicolo Marchetti of Bologna University and Refik Duru's introduction on documentation of excavations of U. Bahadir Alkim of Istanbul University. Marchetti's work published in 2011 provides examples of bronze seal impressions of glyptics base on excavations at Tilmen Hoyuk and Tash Gecit Hoyuk, located in south-eastern Anatolia near the Turkey-Syria border. Some seals also have added engravings of name of the seal owner in the period after cuneiform writing had begun to be used.

Some of the glyptics can be hypothesized to be retained memories of Meluhha hieroglyphs deployed on the Tin Road my Meluhha traders and artisans. It is unclear if the choice of the glyptics was influenced by hieroglyphs discussed herein, starting with the zebu hieroglyph. The glyptics of Tilmen Hoyuk and Tash Gecit Hoyuk could also be retained memories of associating with the trade in metals exemplified by the cipher of Meluhha hieroglyphs.

Testa di sovrano paleobabilonese in diorite da Susa, probabilmente XIX secolo a.C. (altezza 15 cm; Parigi, Musée du Louvre, Sb 95; da Matthiae 2000: 88).

Testa cosiddetta di Yarimlim in steatite, da Alalakh, palazzo reale del livello VII, XVII secolo a.C. (altezza 19 cm; Antakya Arkeoloji Müzesi, 10022; da Matthiae 2000: 171).

Impronta di sigillo cilindrico in serpentinite da Zincirli Höyük, Bronzo Antico IIIA (altezza 5,8 cm; Berlino, Staatliche Museen, S1053; da Moortgat 1940: n° 776).

Meluhha hieroglyphs? -- *kol* 'tiger' *kola* 'woman' Rebus: *kolhe* 'smelters' *balad* m. ' ox ', gng. *bald*, (Ku.) *barad*, id. (N. Tarai) Rebus: *bharat* (5 copper, 4 zinc and 1 tin)(Punjabi)

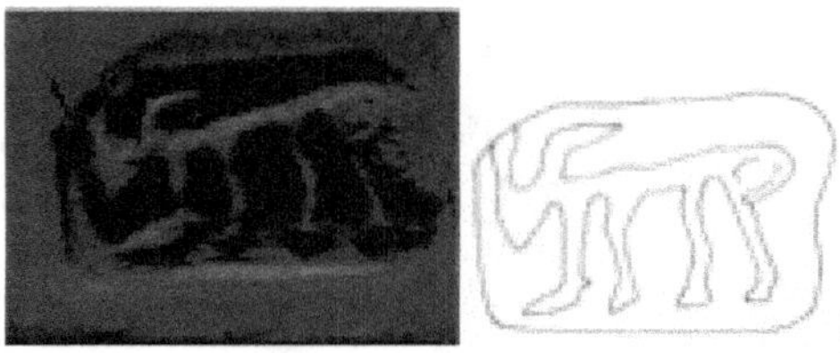

Meluhha hieroglyph? -- mlekh 'goat' Rebus: milakkhu 'copper'.

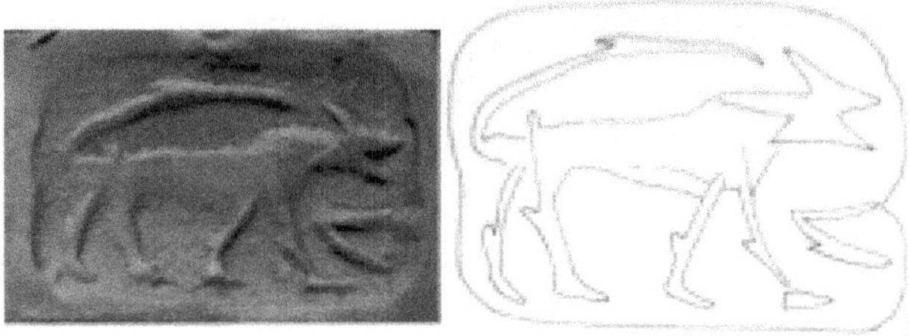

Meluhha hieroglyph? -- *kol* 'tiger' *kola* 'woman' Rebus: *kolhe* 'smelters'

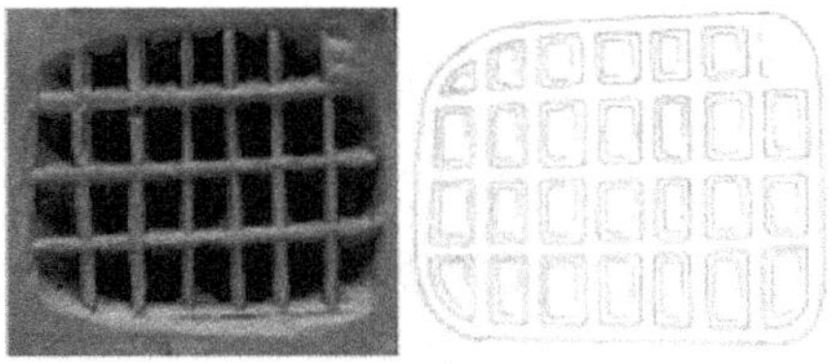

Meluhha hieroglyph? *khaṇḍ* 'field, division' (Sanskrit) Rebus: *khāṇḍa* 'tools, pots and pans, metal-ware'. Rebus 2: kaṇḍ 'fire-altar' (Santali)

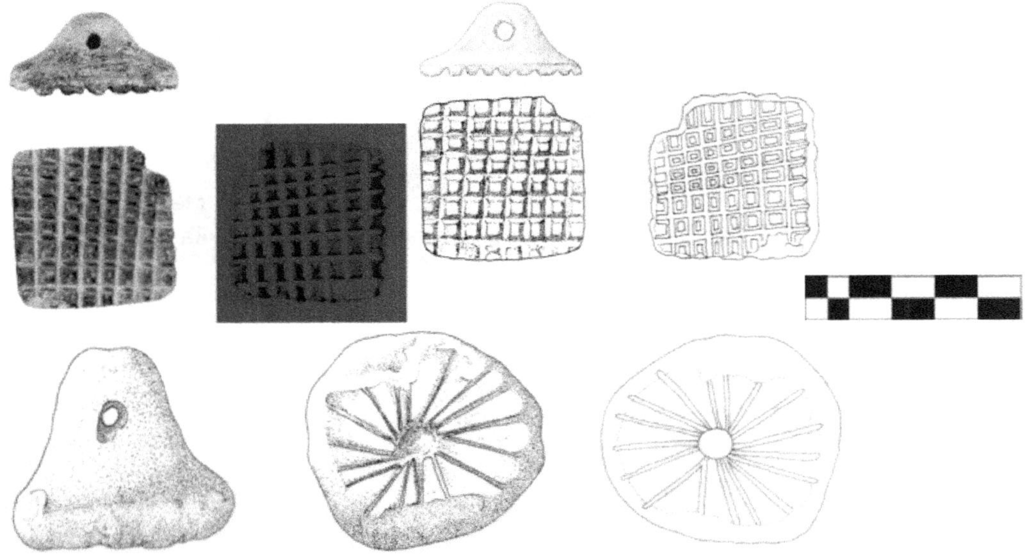

Meluhha hieroglyph? -- *āra* 'spokes' Rebus: *āra 'brass'*. cf. erka = ekke (Tbh. of arka) aka (Tbh. of arka) copper (metal); crystal (Kannada) Glyph: eraka'nave of wheel' Rebus: eraka 'copper'; cf. erka = ekke (Tbh. of arka) aka (Tbh. of arka) copper (metal); crystal (Kannada)

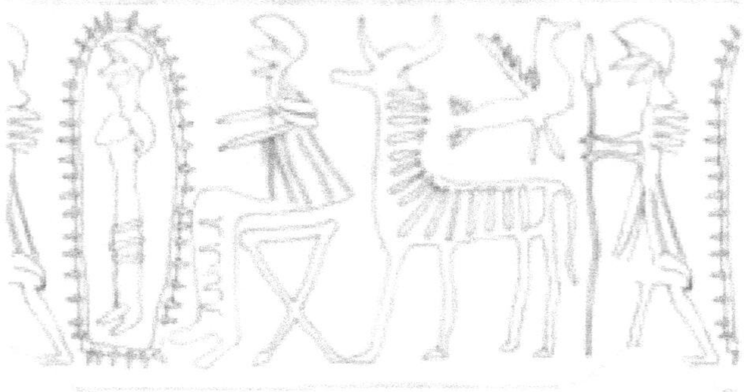

Meluhha speakers? *baṭa* 'quail' Rebus: *baṭha* 'smelter, furnace'

Meluhha speakers? -- *tagara* 'ram' Rebus: *tagara* 'tin'? Rebus: *damgar* 'merchant' (Akkadian)

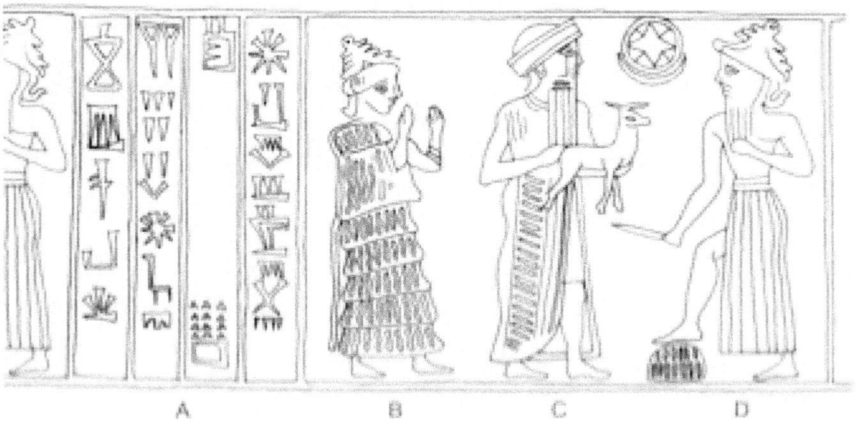

Meluhhan? mlekh ‘goat’ Rebus: milakkhu ‘copper’.

Tracing the migrations of zebu

While a number of zebu hieroglyphs occur on artifacts from Ancient India, humped bull hieroglyphs are also seen on Ancient Near East and Fertile Crescent artifacts. A few examples are presented framed by a hypothesis that Meluhha speakers used the ‘humped bull’ hieroglyph to document artisanal processes or trade transactions:

Seal from Ur showing *tabernae montana* hieroglyph + zebu hieroglyph

Ur cylinder seal impression (cut down into Ur III mausolea from Larsalevel; U. 16220), Iraq. BM 122947; enstatite; Legrain, 1951, No. 632; Collon, 1987, Fig. 611. Source: Editors of Time-Life Books, 1994, Ancient India: Land of Mystery, p. 12. The legend reads: "The seal was discovered in a pre-2000 BCE tomb in Ur, but the bull image is stylistically like those found in the Indus Valley. The seal and similar ones unearthed elsewhere in Mesopotamia offer compelling evidence of trade contacts between Harappans and Mesopotamians." Trader who? Trading, what?

Pictorial motif hieroglyphs:
ḍhanga'tall, long-shanked; *maran: ḍhangi aimai kanae* '= she is a big tall woman' (Santali)
ḍhãgo ' lean ', m. ' skeleton ' (Ku.) (CDIAL 5524) Rebus: *ḍhangar* 'blacksmith' (Maithili)

bicha 'scorpion' (Santali) Rebus: *bica*, bica-diri 'stone ore' (Munda etyma) *kuṭire bica duljad.ko talkena*, they were feeding the furnace with ore (Santali)
ranga ronga, ranga conga = thorny, spikey, armed with thorns; *edel dare ranga conga dareka* = this cotton tree grows with spikes on it (Santali) [Note the thorns on the round object in front of the bull onthe Ur cylinder seal impression – U 16220]

Rebus 'alloy of tin, lead and antimony': *ranga, rang* pewter is an alloy of tin, lead, and antimony (*añjana*) (Santali).
http://www.hindunet.org/saraswati/munda/mundanine.htm

tagaraka '*tabernae montana* fragrant flower' (Sanskrit) *tagara* 'tin' (Tamil)

nāga 'serpent' Rebus: *nāga* 'lead' (Sanskrit) *anakku* 'tin' (Akkadian)

ayo 'fish' Rebus: *aya* 'iron' (Gujarati) *ayas* 'metal' (Sanskrit)

khũṭ, 'zebu' Rebus read rebus 'guild', A synonym is *aḍar ḍangra* Rebus: *aduru ḍhangar* 'native-metal- or black-smith' (Kannada.Santali). dangra 'bull' (Punjabi) Rebus: *ḍhangar* 'blacksmith' (Maithili) *adar dangra* 'zebu' *bos indicus* (Santali) Rebus: ಗಣಿಯಿಂದ ತೆಗದು ಕರಗದೆ ಇರುವ ಅದುರು (Kannada) aduru *gan.iyinda tegadu karagade iruva aduru* = ore taken from the mine and not subjected to melting in a furnace (Ka. Siddhānti Subrahmaṇya' Śastri's new interpretation of the AmarakoŚa, Bangalore, Vicaradarpana Press, 1872, p.330). *adar* = fine sand (Tamil) *aduru* native metal (Kannada); *ayil* iron (Tamil) *ayir, ayiram* any ore (Malayalam); *ajirda karba* very hard iron (Tulu)(DEDR 192).

ಕೂಟ kûṭa. 1. (= ಕೂಟು, ಕೂಡು 2). A verbal noun of ಕೂಡು 1: A joining; a coming in contact with; a junction; connection, union (ಸನ್ಧಿ, ಶ್ಲೇಷ Nr.; ಸೇರಿ Čt. I, 48; ಯೋಗ, ಸೇವೆ Nn. 105; ಮಿಲನ 107; ಯೋಗ, ಸಂಗ 113; ಅಭಿಸಂಗ 122; ಪ್ರಸಂಗ, ಮಿಲನ 139; ಅಭಿಸಂಗ Mr. 492; ಯೋಗ 514; ಸನ್ಧಿ 487; ಸಾಕಂ, etc. 585); an assembly, a crowd (My.); a heap, a quantity (My.); company, fellowship (ಸಾಂಗ್ಯ, ಮಿಲನ Nn. 116; ಸಮಿತಿ, ಸಾಂಗತ್ಯ 141; ವಿಧಾನ, ತನ್ತ್ರ Nn. 75; ವಿಧಿ Mr. 483; ಶಾಸ್ತ್ರ Mr. 502; My.; T. ಕೂಟ್ಟು, ಕೂಟ್ಟಮ್; Tē. ಕೂಟಮಿ; Sk. ಕೂಟ). 2, sexual intercourse (ಮೈಥುನ, ರತ Nn. 73; ರತ, ಸುರತ 155; ಸಂಭೋಗ, ರತಿ 168; ಮೈಥುನ, etc. Mr. 529; Bp. 40, 30; 42, 15. 23; My.; at the present time the *only* meaning in S. Mhr.; Tē. ಕೂಟಮಿ; Sk. ಕುಟೀರ, ಕುಟೀರ). ಆಟಂ ಪಾಟಂ ಕೂಟಂ (Śmd. 246). ಆಟಪಾಟಕೂಟಂಗಳ ಕೇಳಿಗೆ ಅಯ್ದುಸದು ತೊಡಿತ್ತು (198). ನದಿಗಳ ಕೂಟ (ನದ್ಯುಸಂಗಮ Nr.). ಧರ್ಮ ಕಾಮ ಅರ್ಥ ಈ 3 ಪುರುಷಾರ್ಥಗಳ ಕೂಟ (ತ್ರಿವರ್ಗ Si. 255). ಸೊಣ್ಠಿ ಹಿಪ್ಪಲಿ ಮೆಣಸು ಈ ಮೂರರ ಕೂಟ (ತ್ರಿಕಟು 385). ಮೂರು ಅಗ್ನಿಗಳ ಕೂಟ (ತ್ರೇತೆ 424). ಕಿರಿದು ಕೂಟಂ (ಕೊಂಟೆ Čt. I, 18). ತೆರೆದ ಕಣ್ಣಿನ ಮುಟ್ಟಿ ಮುದಿಗುವ ತೆಲಸಸ್ತ್ರ ಅರಿಯದರ ಕೂಟ (company); ಬಡ ಕೂಟ ತಪ್ಪಿಸಿ ಇರೋದು ಕೊಣ್ಣಸ್ತಿ! (Sp.). See Prv. s. ಸೋಲು; Grj. 2, after 106; Rāv. 11, 83; Śāv. 1, 50; J. 6, 34. 35; 15, 6. 47; 24, 48. — ಕೂಟ ಕೂಡು. To assemble (My.).

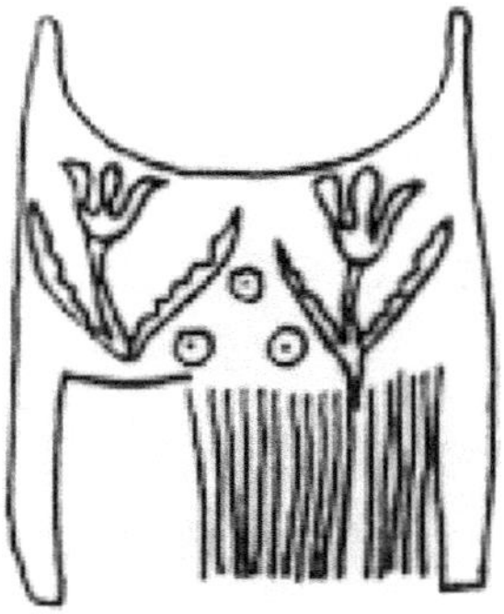

Note: The tagaraka motif appears on a Tell Abraq comb (TA 1649; 11x8.2x0.4cm); decorated bone comb in a context datable to ca. 2100-2000 BCE at Tell Abraq, emirate of Umm al-Qaiwain, United Arab Emirates, on the southern coast of the Arabian Gulf (Fig. 2 a and b in: D.T. Potts, 1993, A new Bactrian find from southeastern Arabia, Antiquity 67 (1993): 591-6) How is tagaraka linked to comb? Tagaraka is a hair fragrance, that is why. [The homonym, takarai, or tagaraka is a five-petalled tabernaemontana flower used as a hair-fragrance]. tagar = a flowering shrub; a plant in bloom (Gujarati) tagara = the shrub tabernaemontana coronaria, and a fragrant hair powder or perfume obtained from it, incense (Vin 1.203); tagara-mallika_ two kinds of gandha_ (Punjabi) t.agara (tagara) a spec. plant; fragrant wood (Pkt.) tagara = a kind of flowering tree (Telugu)

See at www.harappa.com Slide 124 Inscribed Ravi sherd (1998 find at Harappa: Kenoyer and Meadow); the sherd contains the same sign (ca. 3300 BCE). This is perhaps the oldest writing system in the world.
Tell Abraq axe with epigraph ('tulip' glyph + a person raising his arm above his shoulder and wielding a tool +

dotted circles on body) [After Fig. 7 Holly Pittman, 1984, *Art of the Bronze Age: Southeastern Iran, Western Central Asia, and the Indus Valley*, New York, The Metropolitan Museum of Art, pp. 29-30].

tabar = a broad axe (Punjabi). Rebus: *tam(b)ra* 'copper' *tagara* '*tabernae montana*', 'tulip'. Rebus: *tagara* 'tin'. Glyph: *eṛaka* 'upraised arm' (Tamil); rebus: *eraka* = copper (Kannada)

http://bharatkalyan97.blogspot.com/2014/01/a-perfumed-flower-as-meluhha-hieroglyph.html

British Museum. http://www.britishmuseum.org/images/ps332856_m.jpg

c. 2900 BCE. Khafajah chlorite vessel hieroglyphs including the zebu hieroglyph

kol 'tiger' *kola* 'woman' Rebus: *kolhe* 'smelters' *dula* 'pair' Rebus: *dul* 'cast metal'

arye 'lion' Rebus *āra* 'brass'.

khũṭ, 'zebu' Rebus read rebus 'guild', A synonym is *aḍar ḍangra* Rebus: *aduru ḍhangar* 'native-metal-smith, black-smith working on native metal' (Kannada.Santali).

A zebu on a plaque from the Elamite Diyala Valley (Lamberg-Karlovsky and Potts 2001: 225).

Zebu and leaves. In front of the standard

device and the stylized tree of 9 leaves, are the black buck antelopes. Black paint on red ware of Kulli style. Mehi. Second-half of 3rd millennium BCE. [After G.L. Possehl, 1986, *Kulli: an exploration of an ancient civilization in South Asia*, Centers of Civilization, I, Durham, NC: 46, fig. 18 (Mehi II.4.5), based on Stein 1931: pl. 30.

Rebus reading: Zebu is Pictorial motif hieroglyphL adar dangra 'zebu' *bos indicus* Rebus: native-metal-smith; *khũṭ* zebu' *bos indicus* Rebus: guild or community

lo 'iron' (Assamese, Bengali); loa 'iron' (Gypsy) Glyph: *lo* = nine (Santali); *no* = nine (Bengali) *on-patu* = nine (Tamil)

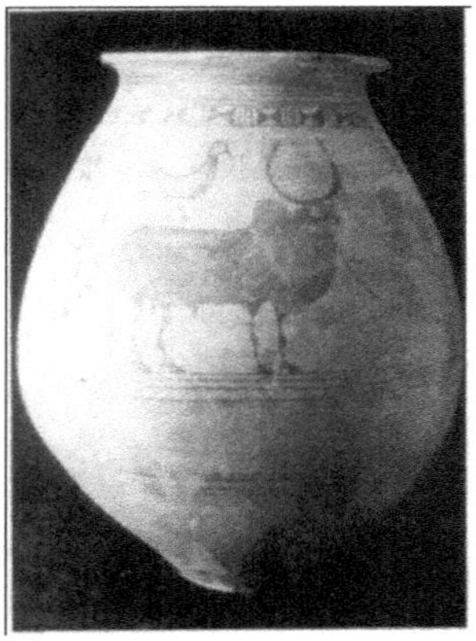

Hieroglyph: standard device: śagaḍī = lathe (Gujarati) san:gaḍa, 'lathe, portable furnace'; rebus: battle; jangaḍiyo 'military guard who accompanies treasure into the treasury' (Gujarati) Rebus: sanghāḍo (Gujarati) cutting stone, gilding (Gujarati); sangatarāśū = stone cutter (Telugu)సంగడము [saṅgaḍamu] sangaḍamu. [from Skt. సంగతమ్.] Help, assistance, aid, సహాయము. Friendship, స్నేహము. Meeting, చేరిక. Nearness, సమీపము. A retinue, పరిచారము. Service, సేవ. An army, సేన. సంగాతము [saṅgātamu] san-gātamu. [from Skt. సంగతమ్.] n. Friendship (Telugu)This rebus reading connoting 'friendship' together with the 'guild or community' suggested by the gloss khũṭ is indicative of an early corporate enterprise or common cause activities in metalwork or stonework.

A zebu bull tied to a post; a bird above. Large painted storage jar discovered in burned rooms at Nausharo, ca. 2600 to 2500 BCE. Cf. Fig. 2.18, J.M. Kenoyer, 1998, Cat. No. 8.

khũṭ 'zebu' Rebus: '(native metal) guild'

baṭa 'quail'; *bhaṭa* 'furnace' (Gujarati); *baṭa* 'a kind of iron' (Gujarati)

Thus, the epigraph on the storage jar reads: iron native-metal stone-worker guild (with) iron furnace).

Zebu together with other hieroglyphs (ficus religiosa leaf, leafless tree, tiger, ram) occur as cryptographs on pottery items of Kulli, Baluchistan. These non-random selections of hieroglyph combinations by artisans of Kulli may connote early use ca. 3000 BCE of a writing system to denote rebus Meluhha language descriptive artisanal or trade transactions in minerals and metals in Ancient Near East – in Sarasvati civilization area, in particular.

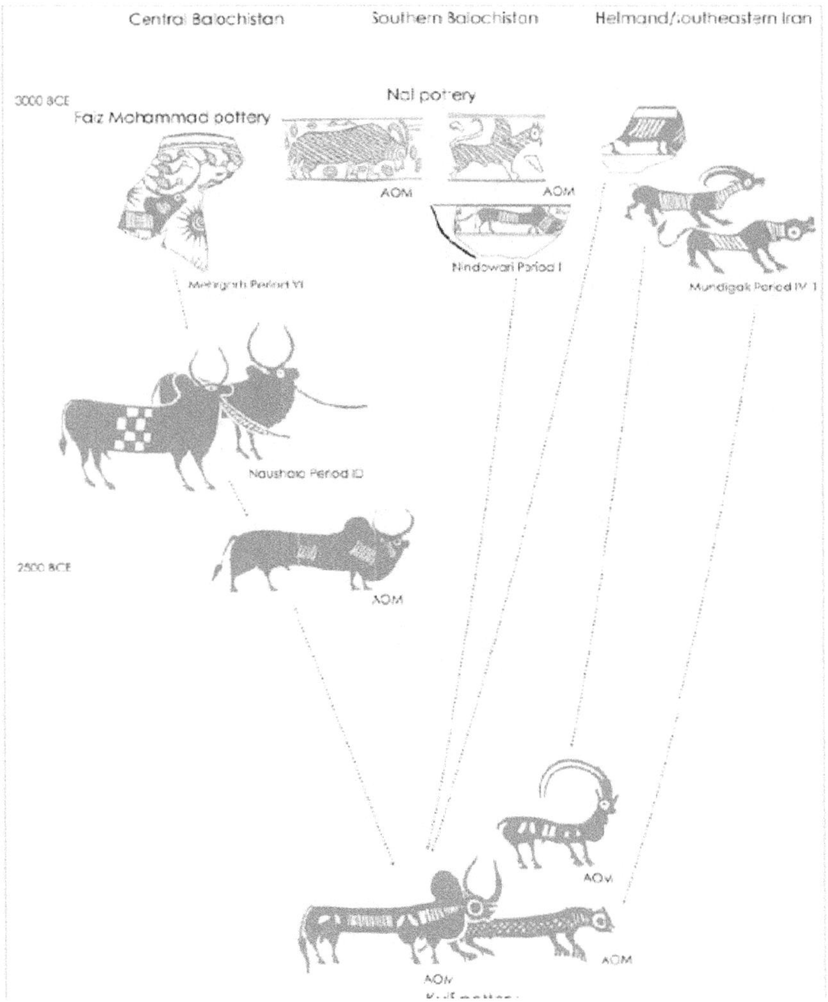

AOM: Ancient Orient Museum, Tokyo.
After Fig. 17: Chronological relationships of animal motifs (zebu, feline, caprid) between Kulli pottery and other ceramic styles. Bulletin of Ancient Orient Museum Vol. XXXIII. 2013/ Pottery from Balochistan in Ancient Orient Museum, Tokyo, Part 2: the late third millennium BCE

by Akinori Uesugi

Kulli bowl. Ancient Orient Museum, Tokyo.

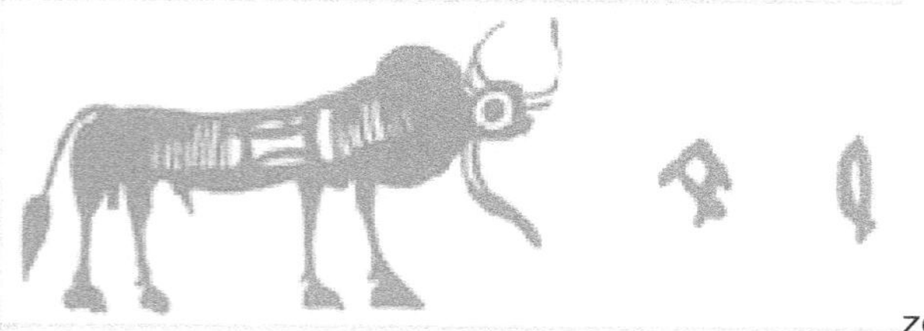

zebu + fish. ayo 'fish' Rebus: aya 'iron' (Gujarati) ayas 'metal' (Sanskrit)

After item 9 in Fig. 13 ibid.

tiger + tree. kol 'tiger' Rebus: kolhe 'smelter'. *khōṇḍa* A stock or stump (Marathi); 'leafless tree' (Marathi)Rebus: *kõdār* 'turner' (Bengali); *kõdā* 'to turn in a lathe' (Bengali).

After item 13 Fig. 17 ibid.

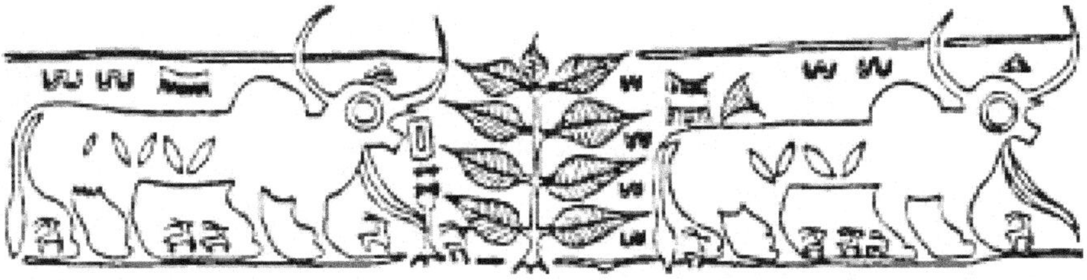

A numeral count of nine leaves: ficus religiosa

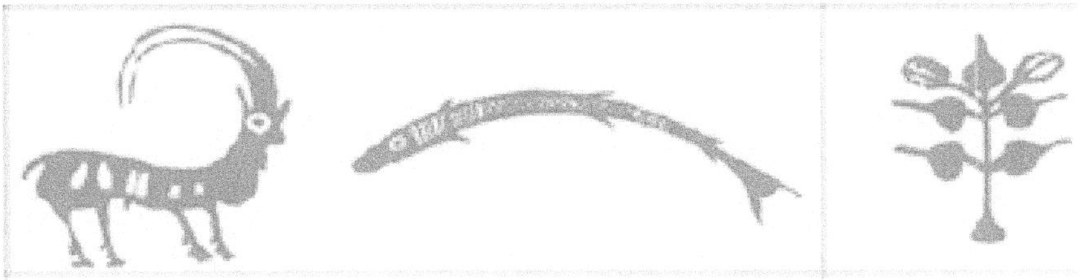

ṭagara'ram' Rebus: *tagara* 'tin' Vikalpa: *miṇḍāl* 'markhor' (Tōrwālī) *meḍho* a ram, a sheep (Gujarati)(CDIAL 10120) Rebus: *mẽṛhẽt, meḍ* 'iron' (Mu.Ho.)

ayo 'fish' Rebus: aya 'iron' (Gujarati) ayas 'metal' (Sanskrit) Hieroglyph: numeral nine: *lo,no* 'nine'; *lo* 'ficus religiosa' Rebus *lo* 'copper'.

Examples of Meluhha Indus Script cipher yielding deciphered Meluhha hieroglyphs-- Style of ligaturing of Meluhha hieroglyphs for distinctive technical specifications of mineral/metal/stone resources

Decipherment of most of the Indus Script corpora inscriptions are detailed in other sections of this work, applying the same cipher yielding rebus readings of ciphertexts

C-23 a

Chanhudaro 23a *miṇḍāl* 'markhor' (Tōrwālī)*meḍho* a ram, a sheep (Gujarati)(CDIAL 10120) Rebus: *mẽṛhẽt, meḍ* 'iron' (Mu.Ho.)

loa 'ficus religiosa' Rebus: *lo* 'iron' (Sanskrit) PLUS unique ligatures: लोखंड [lōkhaṇḍa] *n* (लोह S) Iron. लोखंडाचे चणे खावविणें or चारणें To oppress grievously.लोखंडकाम [lōkhaṇḍakāma] *n* Iron work; that portion (of a building, machine &c.) which consists of iron. 2 The business of an ironsmith.लोखंडी [lōkhaṇḍī] *a* (लोखंड) Composed of iron; relating to iron. (Marathi)
sal 'splinter' Rebus: sal 'workshop'
kolom 'three' Rebus: kolami 'smithy, forge' INFIXED kolom, 'three' Rebus: kolami 'smithy, forge' PLUS

 *kanac* 'corner' Rebus: *kañcu* 'bronze'. Thus bronze smithy. *kamaḍha* 'archer, bow' Rebus: *kammaṭa* 'mint, coiner'.

|||| Numeral 4: gaṇḍa 'four' Rebus: kaṇḍa 'furnace, fire-altar' (Santali) dula 'pair' Rebus: dul 'cast metal'
ḍaṅgrɔ m. ' axe ', poet. *ḍaṅgru* m., °*re* f.; J. *ḍāgrā* m. ' small weapon like axe ', P. *ḍaṅgorī* f. ' small staff or club ' (CDIAL 5520) Rebus: damgar 'merchant' (Akkadian)

Rebus: *ḍhangar* blacksmith'.

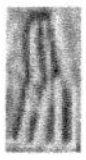  Strands of yarn/rope' hieroglyph: Hieroglyph: 'strands of yarn' Rebus reading: *dhā'tu* 'strand of rope' Rebus: *dhatu* 'mineral ore' (Santali)

Duplicated: dula 'pair' Rebus: dul 'cast metal' PLUS *kamaḍha* 'archer, bow' Rebus: *kammaṭa* 'mint, coiner'. Thus, cast metal mint.

 *kanac* 'corner' Rebus: *kañcu* 'bronze'.

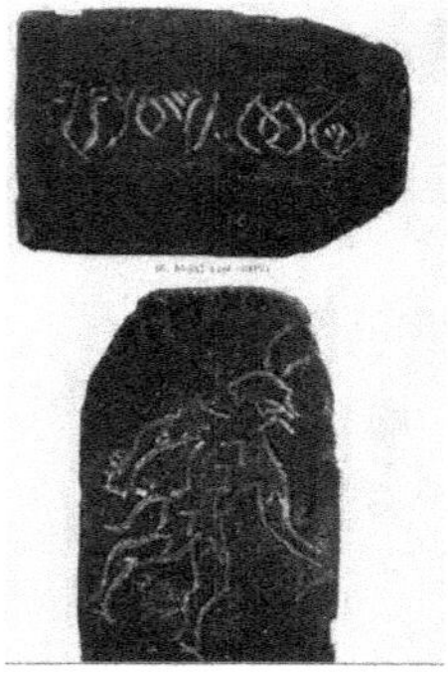

H582A Copper plate. Read rebus as at h2050A

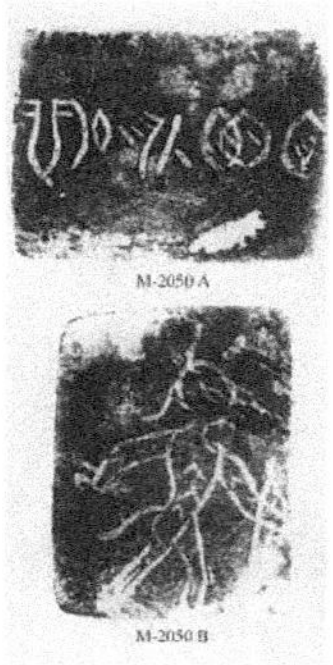

h2050A Two inscribed sides of copper plate.

 *dula* 'pair' Rebus: *dul* 'cast (metal)' PLUS *kana, kanac* = corner (Santali); Rebus: *kañcu* = bronze (Telugu) PLUS infixed kolmo 'paddy plant' Rebus: kolami 'smithy, forge'. Thus, cast bronze smithy, forge. Or, *mogge* 'sprout, bud' Rebus: *mũh* 'ingot' (Santali)Thus, cast bronze ingot. Read as: *kañcu dul mũh 'bronze cast ingot'*

 *dul* 'cast (metal)' PLUS *kana, kanac* = corner *kañcu* = bronze (Telugu) Thus, cast bronze. notch, or indentation (as upon the edge of a tool pots and pans and metal-ware' Thus, cast

dula 'pair' Rebus: (Santali); Rebus: PLUS खांडा [*khāṇḍā*] *m* A jag, or weapon). Rebus: *kāṇḍa* 'tools, bronze metalware.

 *dhāḷ* 'a slope'; 'inclination of a plane' (G.); *ḍhāḷiyum* = adj. sloping, inclining (G.) Rebus: *ḍhālako* = a large metal ingot (G.) *ḍhālakī* = a metal heated and poured into a mould; a solid piece of metal; an ingot (Gujarati) PLUS खांडा [*khāṇḍā*] *m* A jag, notch, or indentation (as upon the edge of a tool or weapon). Rebus: *kāṇḍa* 'tools, pots and pans and metal-ware' Thus, the pair of sign hieroglyphs from r. read rebus: copper, bronze ingots, metalware

 *kolmo* 'paddy plant' Rebus: *kolami* 'smithy, forge' Vikalpa: *mogge* 'sprout, bud' Rebus: *mũh* 'ingot' (Santali) dolu 'plant of shoot height' Rebus: dul 'cast metal'

dulo 'hole' Rebus: dul 'cast metal'

 *kuṭila* 'bent' CDIAL 3230 kuṭi— in cmpd. 'curve', *kuṭika—* 'bent' MBh. Rebus: *kuṭila, katthīl* = bronze (8 parts copper and 2 parts tin)

 *kanka* 'rim of jar' Rebus: *karṇīka* 'account (scribe)' *karṇī* 'supercargo'

Side B: Pictorial hieroglyph: *kamaḍha* 'archer' Rebus: *kammaṭa* 'mint, coiner'.

h2054A Copper plate. Side A: Read rebus as at h2050A Side A. Side B: Allograph: With infixed 'crab' hieroglyph and pot superscripted with 'ficus' hieroglyph: kamaḍha = *ficus religiosa* (Sanskrit); kamar.kom 'ficus' (Santali) rebus: kamaṭa = portable furnace for melting precious metals Telugu; kampaṭṭam = mint (Tamil) Vikalpa: Fig leaf 'loa'; rebus: loh '(copper) metal'. loha-kāra 'metalsmith' (Sanskrit). Vikalpa:

 'Arrow' sign hieroglyph (variant) This is a ligature of 'lid of pot' hieroglyph superscript on 'a linear stroke' numeral hieroglyph.*aḍaren* 'cover of pot or lid' Rebus: *aduru* 'native, unsmelted metal' PLUS koḍ = one (Santali); koḍ 'workshop' (G.)

Duplicated: dula 'pair' Rebus: dul 'cast metal' Thus, native metal castings PLUS mint furnace.

h204A

h1114A

m472A

h754A

h753A

h750A

h751A

h752A

h1799A

dula 'pair' Rebus: *dul* 'cast (metal)' PLUS*kana, kanac* = corner (Santali); Rebus: *kañcu* = bronze (Telugu) PLUS infixed kolmo 'paddy plant' Rebus: kolami 'smithy, forge'. Thus, cast bronze smithy, forge. Or, *mogge* 'sprout, bud' Rebus: *mũh* 'ingot' (Santali)Thus, cast bronze ingot. Read as: *kañcu dul mũh 'bronze cast ingot' aya aḍaren (homonym: aduru)*'alloy native metal' ranku 'liquid measure' Rebus: ranku 'tin'

kolmo 'paddy plant' Rebus: *kolami* 'smithy, forge' Vikalpa: *mogge* 'sprout, bud' Rebus: *mũh* 'ingot' (Santali) dolu 'plant of shoot height' Rebus: dul 'cast metal'

kanka 'rim of jar' Rebus: *karṇīka* 'account (scribe)' *karṇī* 'supercargo' *kharedo* = a currycomb (Gujarati) खरारा [*kharārā*] *m* (H) A currycomb. 2 Currying a horse. (Marathi) Rebus: करडा [*karaḍā*] Hard from alloy--iron, silver &c. (Marathi) *kharādī* ' turner' (Gujarati)

112: M-314 A col (400%)

m314A Inscription with 18 hieroglyphs is a veritable catalogue of Bronze Age Meluhha metal resources and metallurgical processes.

āra 'spokes' Rebus: *āra 'brass'*. cf. erka = ekke (Tbh. of arka) aka (Tbh. of arka) copper (metal); crystal (Kannada) Glyph: *eraka*'nave of wheel' Rebus: eraka 'copper'; cf. erka = ekke (Tbh. of arka) aka (Tbh. of arka) copper (metal); crystal (Kannada) *erako* 'moltencast copper' PLUS
sal 'splinter' Rebus: sal 'workshop' Thus, moltencast copper, brass workshop.
aya aḍaren (homonym: aduru)'alloy native metal'
aya kammaṭa.'coiner, mint alloy'
ayo ḍhālako 'alloy metal ingot'
kāṇḍa 'arrow' (Sanskrit) Rebus:*khāṇḍa* 'tools, pots and pans, metal-ware'. Rebus 2: kaṇḍ 'fire-altar' (Santali)
sal 'splinter' Rebus: sal 'workshop' circumscript four times: kaṇḍ 'fire-altar' (Santali) *ḍhanga* = a crook used for pulling down the branches of trees, for goats, sheep and camels (P.) Rebus:*ḍhangar* blacksmith'.

muka 'ladle' (Tamil)(DEDR 4887) Rebus: *mũh* 'ingot' (Santali) *baṭa* = a kind of iron (G.) *baṭa* = rimless pot (Kannada) Thus, iron ingot.

kolmo 'paddy plant' Rebus: *kolami* 'smithy, forge' Vikalpa: *mogge* 'sprout, bud' Rebus: *mũh* 'ingot' (Santali) dolu 'plant of shoot height' Rebus: dul 'cast metal' DUPLICATED: dula 'pair' Rebus: dul 'cast metal'. Thus, smithy for casting.

kanka 'rim of jar' Rebus: karṇīka 'account (scribe)' karṇī 'supercargo'
kolom 'three' Rebus: kolami 'smithy, forge'
kanac 'corner' Rebus: *kañcu* 'bronze' PLUS dola'hole' Rebus: dul 'cast metal' Thus cast bronze.

  Strands of yarn/rope' hieroglyph: Hieroglyph: 'strands of yarn' Rebus reading: *dhā'tu* 'strand of rope' Rebus: *dhatu* 'mineral ore' (Santali)

kamaḍha 'archer' Rebus: *kampaṭṭam* = mint (Ta.) ; *kammaṭa* 'coiner, mint' (Telugu)

 *kolmo* 'paddy plant' Rebus: *kolami* 'smithy, forge' Vikalpa: *mogge* 'sprout, bud' Rebus: *mũh* 'ingot' (Santali) dolu 'plant of shoot height' Rebus: dul 'cast metal'

PLUS*kana, kanac* = corner (Santali); Rebus: *kañcu* = bronze (Telugu)

 *kuṭila* 'bent' CDIAL 3230 kuṭi— in cmpd. 'curve', *kuṭika—* 'bent' MBh. Rebus: *kuṭila, katthīl* = bronze (8 parts copper and 2 parts tin)

m1881a *balad* m. ' ox ', gng. *bald*, (Ku.) *barad*, id. (N. Tarai) Rebus: *bharat* (5 copper, 4 zinc and 1 tin)(Punjabi) *pattar* 'trough' Rebus*: pattar* 'guild'. Thus, copper-zinc-tin alloy (worker) guild.

 *khaṇḍ* 'field, division' (Sanskrit) Rebus: *khāṇḍa* 'tools, pots and pans, metal-ware'. Rebus 2: kaṇḍ 'fire-altar' (Santali) dula 'pair' Rebus: dul 'cast metal' Thus, duplicated 'division' hieroglyph sign reads: cast metal metal-ware.

 *kanka* 'rim of jar' Rebus: *karṇīka* 'account (scribe)' *karṇī* 'supercargo' INFIXED खांडा [*khāṇḍā*] *m* A jag, notch, or indentation (as upon the edge of a tool or weapon). Rebus: *kāṇḍa* 'tools, pots and pans and metal-ware'

 *baraḍo* = spine; backbone (Tulu) Rebus: *baran, bharat* 'mixed alloys' (5 copper, 4 zinc and 1 tin) (Punjabi) *bhaṭa* 'warrior' (Sanskrit) Rebus: *baṭa* a kind of iron (Gujarati). Rebus: *bhaṭa* 'furnace' (Santali)

 *kanka* 'rim of jar' Rebus: *karṇīka* 'account (scribe)' *karṇī* 'supercargo'

h270A *खोंड [khōṇḍa] m A young bull, a bullcalf. (Marathi) Rebus: kōdār 'turner' (Bengali); कोंद kōnda 'engraver, lapidary setting or infixing gems' (Marathi) G. sãghārɔ m. 'lathe' ; संघाट joinery; M. sāgaḍ 'double-canoe' Rebus: sangataras. संगतराश lit. 'to collect stones, stone-cutter, mason.'*

 *khaṇḍ* 'field, division' (Sanskrit) Rebus: *khāṇḍa* 'tools, pots and pans, metal-ware'. Rebus 2: kaṇḍ 'fire-altar' (Santali) dula 'pair' Rebus: dul 'cast metal' Thus, duplicated 'division' hieroglyph sign reads: cast metal metal-ware.

 *kanka* 'rim of jar' Rebus: *karṇīka* 'account (scribe)' *karṇī* 'supercargo'PLUS infixed: sal 'splinter' Rebus: sal 'workshop'*dula* 'pair' Rebus: *dul* 'cast (metal)' PLUS*kana, kanac* = corner (Santali); Rebus: *kañcu* = bronze (Telugu) PLUS infixed kolmo 'paddy plant' Rebus: kolami 'smithy, forge'. Thus, cast bronze smithy, forge. Or, *mogge* 'sprout, bud' Rebus: *mũh* 'ingot' (Santali)Thus, cast bronze ingot. Read as: *kañcu dul mũh 'bronze cast ingot'*
kamaḍha = crab; *kampaṭṭam* = mint (Ta.) ; *kammaṭa* 'coiner, mint' (Telugu)

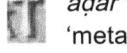

 *aḍar* 'harrow'; rebus: *aduru* 'native unsmelted metal' *ayo* 'fish' Rebus: *aya* 'iron' *ayas* 'metal'

  *baroṭi* 'twelve' *bhārata* 'a factitious alloy of copper, pewter, tin' (Marathi) *aḍaren* 'cover of pot or lid' Rebus: *aduru* 'native, unsmelted metal'
kanka 'rim of jar' Rebus: *karṇīka* 'account (scribe)' *karṇī* 'supercargo'

H-1966 A

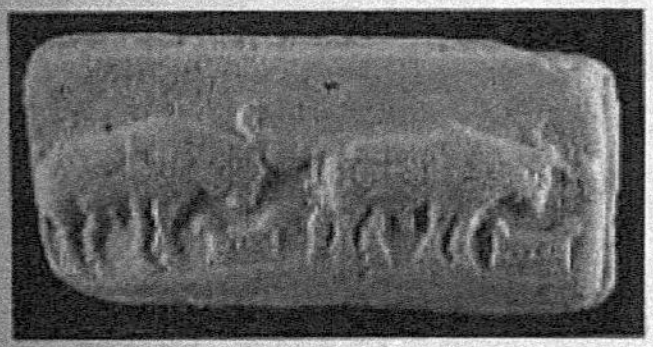

H-1966 B

h1966A

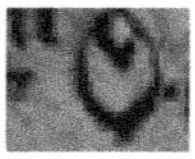 Bronze alloy workshop kañcu sal starting with bronze which is a tin + copper alloy or tin bronze (as distinguished from arsenical bronze, i.e. naturally occurring copper + arsenic).

|||| Numeral 4: gaṇḍa 'four' Rebus: kaṇḍa 'furnace, fire-altar' (Santali)

kolom 'three' Rebus: kolami 'smithy, forge'

 *kuṭila* 'bent' CDIAL 3230 kuṭi— in cmpd. 'curve', *kuṭika*— 'bent' MBh. Rebus: *kuṭila, katthīl* = bronze (8 parts copper and 2 parts tin)

ayo ḍhālako 'alloy metal ingot' (Santali); koḍ 'workshop' (G.)

kānḍa 'arrow' (Sanskrit) Rebus:*khānḍa* 'tools, pots and pans, metal-ware'. Rebus 2: kaṇḍ 'fire-altar' (Santali)

balad m. ' ox ', gng. *bald*, (Ku.) *barad*, id. (N. Tarai) Rebus: *bharat* (5 copper, 4 zinc and 1 tin)(Punjabi) *pattar* 'trough' Rebus*: pattar* 'guild'. Thus, copper-zinc-tin alloy (worker) guild. DUPLICATED: dula 'pair' Rebus: dul 'cast metal'. Thus, cast alloy of copper-zinc-tin.

A Chanhudaro seal impression vividly emphasizes that both 1. pictorial motifs and 2. hieroglyph signs of text have to be treated as signifiers of equal value and as integral to the message conveyed by an epigraph. The sign hieroglyphs occupy the field with sizes comparable to the 'tiger' pictorial motif subject only to space provided by dimensions of the seal. Attempts to read only the text of signs igoring the value of the pictorial motif is likely to be an incomplete decipherment, particularly when pictorial motif hieroglyphs dominate the occupied space of a seal or tablet as 'field symbols'.

 Chanhudaro Excavations, Pl. LI, 18 Text

 6118. Pictorial motif hieroglyphs :

 Worshipper: *bhaṭā* G. *bhuvɔ* m. ' worshipper in a temple ' rather < bhr̥ta -- (CDIAL 9554) Yājñ.com., Rebus: *bhaṭā* 'kiln, furnace'

 A variant of 'adorant' hieroglyph sign is shown with a 'rimless, broad-mouthed pot' which is *baṭa* read rebus: *bhaṭa* 'furnace'. If the 'pot' ligature is a phonetic determinant, the gloss for the 'adorant' is *bhaṭa* 'worshipper'. If the 'kneeling' posture is the key hieroglyphic representation, the gloss is *eragu* 'bow' Rebus: *erako* 'moltencast copper'. Thus, the pair of hieroglyphs on Chanhudaro seal: 'adorant' PLUS 'tiger' connote: *erako kolhe* 'copper smelter'.

bhṛtaka -- m. ' hired servant ' Mn. *bhaṭa* -- m. ' hired soldier, servant ' MBh S. *bhaṛu* ' clever, proficient ', m. ' an adept '; Ku. *bhaṛ* m. ' hero, brave man ', gng. adj. ' mighty '; B. *bhaṛ* ' soldier, servant, nom. prop. ', *bhaṛil* ' servant, hero '(CDIAL 9588) Rebus: M. *bhaḍ* f. 'crackling fuel'(CDIAL 9365) S. *baṭhu* m. ' large pot in which grain is parched, large cooking fire ', *baṭhī* f. ' distilling furnace '; L. *bhaṭṭh* m. ' grain -- parcher's oven ', *bhaṭṭhī* f. ' kiln, distillery ', awāṇ. *bhaṭh*; P. *bhaṭṭh* m., *°ṭhī* f. ' furnace ', *bhaṭṭhā* m. ' kiln '; N. *bhāṭi* ' oven or vessel in which clothes are steamed for washing '; A. *bhaṭā* ' brick -- or lime -- kiln '; B. *bhāṭi* ' kiln '; Or. *bhāṭi* ' brick -- kiln, distilling pot '; Mth. *bhaṭhī, bhaṭṭī* ' brick -- kiln, furnace, still '; Aw.lakh. *bhāṭhā* ' kiln '; H. *bhaṭṭhā* m. ' kiln ', *bhaṭ* f. ' kiln, oven, fireplace '; M. *bhaṭṭā* m. ' pot of fire ', *bhaṭṭī* f. ' forge (CDIAL 9656) Vikalpa: erugu = to bow, to salute or make obeisance (Telugu)er-agu = obeisance (Kannada), ir_ai (Tamil) [Note image of an offering adorant] eraka, erka = copper (Kannada) erako 'moltencast copper'(Gujarati)

మండి [*maṇḍi]* or మండి *maṇḍi*. [Telugu] n. Kneeling down with one leg, an attitude in archery, ఒక కాలితో నేలమీద మోకరించుట, ఆలీఢపాదము. Rebus: *maṇḍi* 'market'.
Note: the style of kneeling person is indicative of worship. That a smelter/forge *kole.l* is a temple is emphatic from the etyma; the gloss *kole.l* means: smithy, temple: *Ta.* kol working in iron,blacksmith; kollaṉ blacksmith. *Ma.* kollan blacksmith, artificer. *Ko.* kole·l smithy, temple in Kota village. *To.* kwala·l Kota smithy. *Ka.*kolime, kolume, kulame, kulime, kulume, kulme fire-pit, furnace; (Bell.; U.P.U.) konimi
blacksmith;(Gowda) kolla id. *Koḍ.* kollë blacksmith. *Te.* kolimi furnace.*Go.* (SR.) kollusānā to mend implements; (Ph.) kolstānā, kulsānā to forge; (Tr.) kōlstānā to repair (of ploughshares); (SR.) kolmi smithy (*Voc.* 948). *Kuwi* (F.)kolhali to forge.(DEDR 2133)

tiger (without the head turned back): *kul* 'tiger' (Santali); *kōlu* id. (Telugu) kōlupuli = Bengal tiger (Telugu)कोल्हा [kōlhā] कोल्हें [kōlhēṃ] A jackal (Marathi) Rebus: *kole.l* 'temple, smithy' (Kota.) *kol* = pañcalōha, a metallic alloy containing five metals (Tamil): copper, brass, tin, lead and iron (Sanskrit); an alternative list of five metals: gold, silver, copper, tin (lead), and iron (dhātu; Nānārtharatnākara. 82; Mangarāja's Nighaṇṭu. 498)(Kannada) *kol, kolhe*, 'the *koles*, iron smelters speaking a language akin to that of Santals' (Santali) krammara 'look back' (Telugu) Rebus: kamar 'metalsmith' (Santali)

khōṇḍa A stock or stump (Marathi); 'leafless tree' (Marathi) Rebus: *kōdār* 'turner' (Bengali); Allograph: young bull.

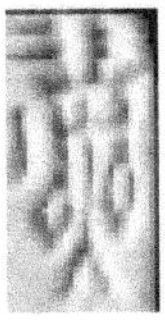

water-carrier hieroglyph *kuṭi*; Rebus: *kuṭhi* 'smelter furnace'. PLUS 'rim of jar':

kanka 'rim of jar' Rebus: karṇīka 'account (scribe)' karṇī 'supercargo' water-carrier hieroglyph kuṭi; Rebus: kuṭhi 'furnace'. Together, the pair of sign hieroglyphs read rebus: *kuṭhi kanka* 'smelter/furnace supercargo'.

dhāḷ 'a slope'; 'inclination of a plane' (Gujarati); *ḍhāḷiyum* = adj. sloping, inclining (Gujarati) Rebus: *ḍhālako* = a large metal ingot (Gujarati) *ḍhālakī* = a metal heated and poured into a mould; a solid piece of metal; an ingot (Gujarati)PLUS dula 'two' Rebus: dul 'cast metal'. Thus, cast metal ingot.

 Variant: *dāṭu* 'cross'(Telugu) Rebus: *dhatu* 'mineral' (Santali).

The epigraph as a whole reads: *dul dhatu* 'cast minerals' *kuṭhi kanka* 'smelter/furnace supercargo'.

m1429

Mohenjo-daro three-sided moulded tablet. Side 1: flat bottomed boat with a central hut with leafy fronds at the top of two poles flanking two ingots; two birds sit on the deck and a large double rudder extends from the rear of the boat. Side 2: snout nosed gharial with a fish in its mouth. Side 3: Eight Meluhha hieroglyphs of Indus Script. MD 602, Islamabad Museum, NMP 1384 4.6X1.2X1.5 cm

Picorial hieroglyphs:

Side 1: *baṭa* 'quail' Rebus: *baṭa* 'iron' (Gujarati) *dula* 'pair' Rebus d*ul* 'cast metal' Together, cast iron: *dul baṭa* PLUS *tamar* 'palm' (Hebrew) Rebus: *tamba* 'copper' (Santali) *tamra* id. (Sanskrit) *dula* 'pair' Rebus d*ul* 'cast metal' Together, cast copper. Shows supercargo of furnae cast copper, furnace cccast bronze, iron castings. Boat: bagalo = an Arabian merchant vessel (Gujarati) bagala = an Arab boat of a particular description (Kannada) Rebus:1. bhāgala 'gate in the wall of a town' (Gujarati)2. bangala = kumpaṭi = an:ga_ra śakaṭī = a chafing dish a portable stove a goldsmith's portable furnace (Telugu)

Side 2: *ayo 'fish' Rebus: aya* 'iron' (Gujarati) *ayas* 'metal' (Sanskrit) PLUS *kāru* 'crocodile' Rebus: *khar* 'blacksmith' (Kashmiri) *ayakara* 'metalsmith'

Side 3: Text of epigraph 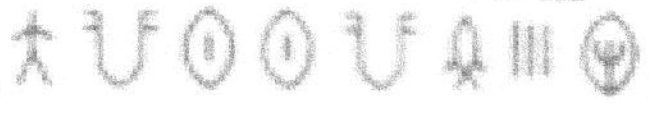 : Supercargo of cast bronze, alloy metal supercargo; cast bronze metalware supercargo; iron ore.

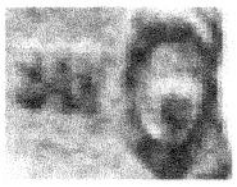

kolom 'three' Rebus: *kolami* 'smithy, forge'.

kolmo 'paddyplat' Rebus: kolami 'smithy, forge' infixed in: *dol* 'two' *dula* दुल । युग्मम् m. a pair, a couple, esp. of two similar things (Rām. 966). Rebus: *dul* meṛeḍ cast iron (Mundari. Santali) *dul* 'to cast metal in a mould' (Santali) Rebus: *dul* 'cast (metal)' *kana, kanac* = corner (Santali); Rebus: *kañcu* = bronze (Telugu) PLUS *kuṭila* 'bent'; Rebus: *kuṭila, katthīl* = bronze (8 parts copper and 2 parts tin) Thus, the oval composition PLUS 'numeral three' reads: smithy for cast bronze, bronze alloy: *dul kañcu kuṭila kolami*

ayo 'fish' Rebus: aya 'iron' (Gujarati) *ayas* 'metal' (Sanskrit)

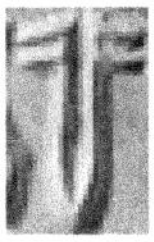

kanka 'rim of jar' Rebus: karṇīka 'account (scribe)' karṇī 'supercargo'

dol 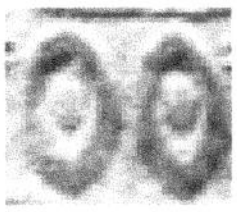 'two' *dula* दुल । युग्मम् m. a pair, a couple, esp. of two similar things (Rām. 966). Rebus: *dul* meṛeḍ cast iron (Mundari. Santali) *dul* 'to cast metal in a mould' (Santali) Rebus: *dul* 'cast (metal)' *kana, kanac* = corner (Santali); Rebus: *kañcu* = bronze (Telugu) PLUS *kuṭila* 'bent'; Rebus: *kuṭila, katthīl* = bronze (8 parts copper and 2 parts tin) PLUS infixed 'notch': खांडा [khāṇḍā] *m* A jag, notch, or indentation (as upon the edge of a tool or weapon). (Marathi) Rebus: *khāṇḍā* 'tools, pots and pans, metal-ware. The pair of ligatured hieroglyphs reads: metalware of cast bronze, bronze alloy', *dul kañcu kuṭila khāṇḍā*

kanka 'rim of jar' Rebus: karṇīka 'account (scribe)' karṇī 'supercargo'

h1027a *खोंड [khōṇḍa] m A young bull, a bullcalf. (Marathi) Rebus: kōdār 'turner' (Bengali); कोंद kōnda 'engraver, lapidary setting or infixing gems' (Marathi) G. sãghārɔ m. 'lathe' ; संघाट joinery; M. sāgaḍ 'double-canoe' Rebus: sangataras. संगतराश lit. 'to collect stones, stone-cutter, mason.'*

dula 'pair' Rebus: *dul* 'cast (metal)' PLUS*kana, kanac* = corner (Santali); Rebus: *kañcu* = bronze (Telugu) PLUS infixed kolmo 'paddy plant' Rebus: kolami 'smithy, forge'. Thus, cast bronze smithy, forge. Or, *mogge* 'sprout, bud' Rebus: *mũh* 'ingot' (Santali)Thus, cast bronze ingot. Read as: *kañcu dul mũh 'bronze cast ingot'*

aḍar 'harrow'; rebus: *aduru* 'native unsmelted metal' *ayo* 'fish' Rebus: *aya* 'iron' *ayas*

'metal'

Three sign sequence:

muka 'ladle' (Tamil)(DEDR 4887) Rebus: *mũh* 'ingot' (Santali) *baṭa* = rimless pot (Kannada) Rebus:) *baṭa* = a kind of iron (G.)) *bhaṭa* furnace (Gujarati) Thus, iron ingot.

kolom 'three' Rebus: kolami 'smithy, forge' *kāṇḍa* 'arrow' (Sanskrit) Rebus:*khāṇḍa* 'tools, pots and pans, metal-ware'. Rebus 2: kaṇḍ 'fire-altar' (Santali) Thus, the three sign sequence reads: iron ingot, furnace smithy, fire-altar metalware.

A seal impression from Ur provides an example of ligatured Meluhha hieroglyphs:

Seal impression, Ur (Upenn; U.16747); dia. 2.6, ht. 0.9 cm.; Gadd, PBA 18 (1932), pp. 11-12, pl. II, no. 12; Porada 1971: pl.9, fig.5; Parpola, 1994, p. 183; water carrier with a skin (or pot?) hung on each end of the yoke across his shoulders and another one below the crook of his left arm; the vessel on the right end of his yoke is over a receptacle for the water; a star on either side of the head (denoting supernatural?). The whole object is enclosed by 'parenthesis' marks. The parenthesis is perhaps a way of splitting of the ellipse (Hunter, G.R., *JRAS*, 1932, 476). An unmistakable example of an 'hieroglyphic' seal.

meḍha 'polar star' (Marathi). Rebus: meḍ (Ho.); mẽṛhet 'iron' (Munda.Ho.) dula 'pair' Rebus: dul 'cast metal'. Thus, the two 'star' sign hieroglyphs flanking the composition denote iron castings.

Ligatured sign hieroglyph: 'rim-of-jar' PLUS 'water-carrier'

kanka 'rim of jar' Rebus: karṇīka 'account (scribe)' karṇī 'supercargo' कर्णधार [*karṇadhāra*] *m* S (A holder of the ear.) A helmsman or steersman. Thus, together, the ligatured hieroglyph reads: supercargo for a boat.

Functions served by tablet inscriptions for deposits into Guild storeroom

Example from Harappa:

H-1930 A H-1930 B

h1930A

Bronze alloy workshop kañcu sal starting with bronze which is a tin + copper alloy or tin bronze (as distinguished from arsenical bronze, i.e. naturally occurring copper + arsenic).

kuṭila 'bent' CDIAL 3230 kuṭi— in cmpd. 'curve', *kuṭika—* 'bent' MBh. Rebus: *kuṭila, katthīl* = bronze (8 parts copper and 2 parts tin)

kanac 'corner' Rebus: *kañcu* 'bronze' kolmo 'paddy plant' Rebus: kolami 'smithy, forge'.

Text on Obverse of tablet: dula 'pair' Rebus: dul 'cast metal' Thus, together *dul kolami kuṭhār* 'metal smithy castings storeroom'

dula 'pair' Rebus; dul 'cast metal' *baṭa* = a kind of iron (Gujarati) *baṭa* = rimless pot (Kannada) Thus, iron ingot.

Variant:

kəṭhā'r, kc. *kuṭhār* m. ' granary, storeroom '(Western Pahari)(CDIAL 3550). *koṭhārī m.* ' storekeeper' (Gujarati)(CDIAL 3551) Thus, storeroom (of) *kolom* 'three' Rebus: *kolami* 'smithy, forge'.

The tablets in Harapa were used to document the metalwork products, metalware from 'workers' platforms' deposited into the storeroom of the citadel.

A seal-cutter would then assemble the superboat cargo using inscriptions on seals as documents with specifications to support bills of lading for trade on the Tin Road caravans and boatloads on Persian Gulf PLUS Rivers Sarasvati and Sindhu maritime routes.

h20a *खोंड [khōṇḍa] m A young bull, a bullcalf. (Marathi) Rebus: kõdār 'turner' (Bengali); कोंद kōnda 'engraver, lapidary setting or infixing gems' (Marathi) G. sãghāṛɔ m. 'lathe' ; संघाट joinery; M. sãgaḍ 'double-canoe' Rebus: sangataras. संगतराश lit. 'to collect stones, stone-cutter, mason.'* *kamaḍha* = crab; *kampaṭṭam* = mint (Ta.) ; *kammaṭa* 'coiner, mint' (Telugu) Vikalpa: *ḍato* = claws of crab (Santali); *dhātu* = mineral (Sanskrit)

dhāḷ 'a slope'; 'inclination of a plane' (G.); *ḍhāḷiyum* = adj. sloping, inclining (G.) Rebus: *ḍhālako* = a large metal ingot (G.) *ḍhālakī* = a metal heated and poured into a mould; a solid piece of metal; an ingot (Gujarati) PLUS खांडा [*khāṇḍā*] *m* A jag, notch, or indentation (as upon the edge of a tool or weapon). Rebus: *kāṇḍa* 'tools, pots and pans and metal-ware' Thus, the pair of sign hieroglyphs from r. read rebus: copper, bronze ingots, metalware castings (of mint, minerals).

dula 'pair' Rebus: *dul* 'cast (metal)' PLUS*kana, kanac* = corner (Santali); Rebus: *kañcu* = bronze (Telugu) PLUS infixed kolmo 'paddy plant' Rebus: kolami 'smithy, forge'. Thus, cast bronze smithy, forge. Or, *mogge* 'sprout, bud' Rebus: *mũh* 'ingot' (Santali)Thus, cast bronze ingot. Read as: *kañcu dul mũh 'bronze cast ingot'*

dula 'two' Rebus: dul 'cast metal' *ayo* 'fish' Rebus: *aya* 'iron' *ayas* 'metal'

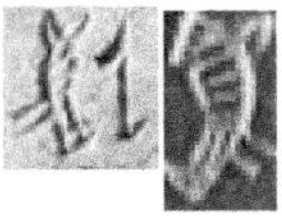

The pair of hieroglyph signs are compositions: bicha 'scorpion' (Assamese) Rebus: *bica* 'stone ore' (Santali) The pairing sign is a composition of: sloping stroke PLUS two short strokes of a 'splinter':*dhāḷ* 'a slope'; 'inclination of a plane' (Gujarati); *ḍhāḷiyum* = adj. sloping, inclining (Gujarati) Rebus: *ḍhālako* = a large metal ingot (Gujarati) *ḍhālakī* = a metal heated and poured into a mould; a solid piece of metal; an ingot (Gujarati)PLUS*sal* 'splinter' Rebus: *sal* 'workshop'. Thus the composition reads: *ḍhālako sal* 'ingot workshop'.

dāṭu 'cross'(Telugu) Rebus: *dhatu* 'mineral' (Santali).

kanka 'rim of jar' Rebus: *karṇīka* 'account (scribe)' *karṇī* 'supercargo'

 *baraḍo* = spine; backbone (Tulu) Rebus: *baran, bharat* 'mixed alloys' (5 copper, 4 zinc and 1 tin) (Punjabi)

m753A *खोंड [khōṇḍa] m A young bull, a bullcalf. (Marathi) Rebus: kōdār 'turner' (Bengali); कोंद kōnda 'engraver, lapidary setting or infixing gems' (Marathi) G. sãghāṛɔ m. 'lathe' ; संघाट joinery; M. sãgaḍ 'double-canoe' Rebus: sangataras. संगतराश lit. 'to collect stones, stone-cutter, mason.'* G. *sãghāṛɔ* m. 'lathe' ; *sãgāḍā* m. ' frame of a building ', *°ḍī* f ' lathe '(CDIAL 12859) Rebus*: sangataras.* संगतराश lit. 'to collect stones, stone-cutter, mason.'

dula 'pair' Rebus: *dul* 'cast (metal)' PLUS*kana, kanac* = corner (Santali); Rebus: *kañcu* = bronze (Telugu) PLUS infixed kolmo 'paddy plant' Rebus: kolami 'smithy, forge'. Thus, cast bronze smithy, forge. Or, *mogge* 'sprout, bud' Rebus: *mũh* 'ingot' (Santali)Thus, cast bronze ingot. Read as: *kañcu dul mũh 'bronze cast ingot'*

 Three sign sequence:

 *muka* 'ladle' (Tamil)(DEDR 4887) Rebus: *mũh* 'ingot' (Santali) *baṭa* = rimless pot (Kannada) Rebus:) *baṭa* = a kind of iron (G.)) *bhaṭa* furnace (Gujarati) Thus, iron ingot.

kolom 'three' Rebus: kolami 'smithy, forge' *kānḍa* 'arrow' (Sanskrit) Rebus:*khānḍa* 'tools, pots and pans, metal-ware'. Rebus 2: kanḍ 'fire-altar' (Santali) Thus, the three sign sequence reads: iron ingot, furnace smithy, fire-altar metalware.

Styles of composing texts of inscriptions

A string of Meluhha hieroglyphs constitute text of an inscription in the Indus script corpora. An example of a long text on a tiny Mohenjo-daro tablet is m355, as a veritable Meluhha metalwork hieroglyphs catalog read rebus as a trade consignment (boat supercargo) message communicated by Meluhha artisans and traders:

m355a, b with a string of 26 hieroglyphs

 *loa* 'ficus religiosa' Rebus: *lo* 'iron' (Sanskrit) PLUS unique ligatures:  लोखंड [lōkhaṇḍa] *n* (लोह S) Iron. लोखंडाचे चणे खावविणें or चारणें To oppress grievously.लोखंडकाम [lōkhaṇḍakāma] *n* Iron work; that portion (of a building, machine &c.) which consists of iron. 2 The business of an ironsmith.लोखंडी [lōkhaṇḍī] *a* (लोखंड) Composed of iron; relating to iron. (Marathi) *bhaṭa* 'warrior' (Sanskrit) Rebus: *baṭa* a kind of iron (Gujarati). Rebus: *bhaṭa* 'furnace' (Santali) Thus, together, the ligatured hieroglyph reads rebus: *loa bhaṭa* 'iron furnace'

kuṭila 'bent' CDIAL 3230 kuṭi— in cmpd. 'curve', *kuṭika—* 'bent' MBh. Rebus: *kuṭila, katthīl* = bronze (8 parts copper and 2 parts tin) dula 'pair' Rebus: dul 'cast metal' Thus, bronze castings. (Santali); koḍ 'workshop' (Gujarati)

 कांड *kāṇḍa* 'arrow' Rebus: *kāṇḍa* 'pots and pans, metalware, tools'. Rebus 2: kaṇḍ 'fire-altar' (Santali)

 dula 'pair' Rebus: dul 'cast metal' PLUS | *koḍa* 'one' Rebus: *koḍ* 'workshop' PLUS INFIXED खांडा [*khāṇḍā*] *m* A jag, notch, or indentation (as upon the edge of a tool or weapon). Rebus: *kāṇḍa* 'tools, pots and pans and metal-ware' Thus metware castings workshop.

 *kanac* 'corner' Rebus: *kañcu* 'bronze' sal 'splinter' Rebus: sal 'workshop' *aya aḍaren* (homonym: aduru) 'alloy native metal' *aya kāṇḍa* 'alloy metalware'

 *muka* 'ladle' (Tamil)(DEDR 4887) Rebus: *mũh* 'ingot' (Santali) *baṭa* = rimless pot (Kannada) Rebus:) *baṭa* = a kind of iron (G.)) *bhaṭa* furnace (Gujarati) Thus, iron ingot.kolom 'three' Rebus: kolami 'smithy, forge'

dula 'two' Rebus: dul 'cast metal'

 *kanac* 'corner' Rebus: *kañcu* 'bronze' PLUS gaṇḍa 'four' Rebus: kaṇḍa 'furnace, fire-altar' (Santali)

 kanka 'rim of jar' Rebus: karṇīka 'account (scribe)' karṇī 'supercargo'

  *khuṭo* ' leg, foot ', °ṭī ' goat's leg ' Rebus: *khōṭā* 'alloy' (Marathi) *aḍaren* 'cover of pot or lid' Rebus: *aduru* 'native, unsmelted metal' Duplicated: dula 'pair' Rebus: dul 'cast metal' PLUS

 mēḍu height, rising ground, hillock (Kannada) Rebus: *mẽṛhẽt, meḍ* 'iron' (Munda.Ho.)

 *kanac* 'corner' Rebus: *kañcu* 'bronze' sal 'splinter' Rebus: sal 'workshop'

 *dula* 'pair' Rebus: *dul* 'cast (metal)' PLUS*kana, kanac* = corner (Santali); Rebus: *kañcu* = bronze (Telugu) PLUS infixed kolmo 'paddy plant' Rebus: kolami 'smithy, forge'. Thus, cast bronze smithy, forge. Or, *mogge* 'sprout, bud' Rebus: *mũh* 'ingot' (Santali)Thus, cast bronze ingot. Read as: *kañcu dul mũh 'bronze cast ingot'*
ayo ḍhālako 'alloy metal ingot' kolom 'three' Rebus: kolami 'smithy, forge'
Circumscript: *kuṭila* 'bent' CDIAL 3230 kuṭi— in cmpd. 'curve', *kuṭika*— 'bent' MBh. Rebus: *kuṭila, katthīl* = bronze (8 parts copper and 2 parts tin) dula 'pair' Rebus: dul 'cast metal' Thus, bronze castings. INFIXED dulo 'hole' Rebus: dul 'cast metal'

 kanka 'rim of jar' Rebus: karṇīka 'account (scribe)' karṇī 'supercargo'

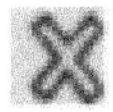 *dāṭu* 'cross'(Telugu) Rebus: *dhatu* 'mineral' (Santali).PLUS sal 'splinter' Rebus: sal 'workshop' PLUS

 *kharedo* = a currycomb (Gujarati) खरारा [*kharārā*] *m* (H) A currycomb. 2 Currying a horse. (Marathi) Rebus: करडा [*karaḍā*] Hard from alloy--iron, silver &c. (Marathi) *kharādī* ' turner' (Gujarati)

 *dula* 'pair' Rebus: *dul* 'cast (metal)' PLUS*kana, kanac* = corner (Santali); Rebus: *kañcu* = bronze (Telugu) Thus, cast bronze. PLUS खांडा [*khāṇḍā*] *m* A jag, notch, or

indentation (as upon the edge of a tool or weapon). Rebus: *kāṇḍa* 'tools, pots and pans and metal-ware' Thus, cast bronze metalware.

PLUS

mogge 'sprout, bud' Rebus: *mũh* 'ingot' (Santali)

Styles of ligaturing to write down Meluhha hieroglyphs

A distinguishing feature of the Meluhha hieroglyph writing system is the fact that within a very small document space of say, a steatite square seal, extraordinary orthographic precision is displayed in configuring the hieroglyphs as may be seen from the following examples:

Characteristic ligatures on 'body or structure/stature of body' hieoglyph

h477A *खोंड [khōṇḍa] m A young bull, a bullcalf. (Marathi) Rebus: kõdār 'turner' (Bengali); कोंद kōnda 'engraver, lapidary setting or infixing gems' (Marathi) G. sãghārɔ m. 'lathe' ; संघाट joinery; M. sãgaḍ 'double-canoe' Rebus: sangataras 'stone-cutter, mason'*

'Fetters on heel' hieroglyph: dula 'pair' Rebus: dul 'cast metal' PLUS खोडा [khōḍā] *m* Stocks (for criminals). Pr. चालला तर गाडा नाहीं तर खोडा. 2 A frame to encumber an animal whilst grazing; a pasture-clog. 3 fig. An encumbering or embarrassing (appendage, business &c.) 4 Paralytic or cramped state (of the body or a limb). खोडा चढविणें (झोंबीमध्यें) In wrestling. To twine one's feet in a certain entangling manner around the feet of the antagonist athlete. Hence to embarrass, hamper, fetter gen. खोंट khōṭa *f* The heel. Rebus: खोट [khōṭa] *f* A mass of metal (unwrought or of old metal melted down); an ingot or wedge. खोटसाळ [khōṭasāḷa] *a* (खोट & साळ from शाला) Alloyed--a metal. L.*khoṭ* f. ' alloy, impurity ', *°ṭā* ' alloyed ', awāṇ. *khoṭā* ' forged '; P. *khoṭ* m. ' base, alloy '(CDIAL 3931) PLUS

meḍ 'body' Rebus: *meḍ* 'iron' (Ho.) काठी [kāṭhī] *f* (काष्ट S) 'frame or structure of the body' (Marathi) Rebus: खंडी [khaṇḍī] measure of weight (Marathi) கண்டி; *kaṇṭi, n. < Mhr. khaṇḍil. [T. Tu. khaṇḍi, M. kaṇḍi.]* Candy, a weight, stated to be roughly equivalent to 500 lbs. PLUS खांडा [*khāṇḍā*] *m* A jag, notch, or indentation (as upon the edge of a tool or weapon). Rebus: *kāṇḍa* 'tools, pots and pans and metal-ware'

Thus, alloy metalware.

ranku 'liquid measure' Rebus: ranku 'tin'

dula 'pair' Rebus: dul 'cast (metal)' kolmo 'rice plant' Rebus: kolami 'smithy/forge'

mēḍu height, rising ground, hillock (Kannada) Rebus: *mẽṛhẽt, meḍ* 'iron' (Munda.Ho.) Duplicated: dula 'pair' Rebus: dul 'cast metal'

Note: The reference is to the casting of pewter (an alloy of tin, copper and antimony)

An artifact, said to be part of a vase, made of antimony dating to about 3000 BC was found at Telloh, Chaldea (part of present-day Iraq) indicating the ability to render metallic silvery-white mineral antimony malleable. The sulfideof antimony is known as *kohl,* an ancient gloss of Proto-Indian used for cosmetics. A lustrous gray metalloid such as sulfide mineral stibnite was referred to by the category term: *meḍ* 'iron' (Ho.)

Most of the ligatured hieroglyphs with ligatures to the 'body or structure/stature of body' hieroglyph are related to the early metallurgical innovations of creating hard alloys by castings of combined mineral ores rendered malleable.

Seafaring maritime merchants, artisans of Meluhha on *bagala* boat

m6a *खोंड [khōṇḍa] m A young bull, a bullcalf. (Marathi) Rebus: kõdār 'turner' (Bengali); कोंद kōnda 'engraver, lapidary setting or infixing gems' (Marathi) G. sãghāṛɔ m. 'lathe' ; संघाट joinery; M. sãgaḍ 'double-canoe' Rebus: sangataras 'stone-cutter, mason'*

āra 'spokes' Rebus: *āra 'brass'*. cf. erka = ekke (Tbh. of arka) aka (Tbh. of arka) copper (metal); crystal (Kannada) Glyph: *eraka*'nave of wheel' Rebus: eraka 'copper'; cf. erka = ekke (Tbh. of arka) aka (Tbh. of arka) copper (metal); crystal (Kannada) *erako* 'moltencast copper'

 *kanac* 'corner' Rebus: *kañcu* 'bronze'

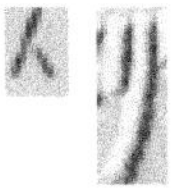

notch+slanted stroke reads rebus: *ḍhālako kāṇḍa* 'ingot, tools, pots and pans and metal-ware'.*dhāḷ* 'a slope'; 'inclination of a plane' (G.); *ḍhāḷiyum* = adj. sloping, inclining (G.) Rebus: *ḍhālako* = a large metal ingot (G.) *ḍhālakī* = a metal heated and poured into a mould; a solid piece of metal; an ingot (Gujarati) PLUS खांडा [*khāṇḍā*] *m* A jag, notch, or indentation (as upon the edge of a tool or weapon). Rebus: *kāṇḍa* 'tools, pots and pans and metal-ware'

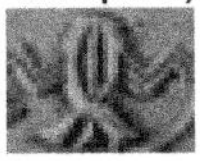

Pa. *vagguli* -- m.f., *°lī* -- f. ' bat ', Pk. *vagguli* -- m.; G. *vāgoḷ* f. ' flying fox ', M. *vāgūḷ, °gaḷ, vāghūḷ, °ghaḷ* (CDIAL 11584) Rebus: bagalo = an Arabian merchant vessel (G.) bagala = an Arab boat of a particular description (Ka.); bagalā (M.); bagarige, bagarage = a kind of vessel (Ka.)

m661a *खोंड [khōṇḍa] m A young bull, a bullcalf. (Marathi) Rebus: kõdār 'turner' (Bengali); कोंद kōnda 'engraver, lapidary setting or infixing gems' (Marathi) G. sãghāṛɔ m. 'lathe' ; संघाट joinery; M. sãgaḍ 'double-canoe' Rebus: sangataras. संगतराश lit. 'to collect stones, stone-cutter, mason.'*

'Arrow' sign hieroglyph (variant) This is a ligature of 'lid of pot' hieroglyph superscript on 'a linear stroke' numeral hieroglyph.*aḍaren* 'cover of pot or lid' Rebus: *aduru* 'native, unsmelted metal' PLUS koḍ = one (Santali); koḍ 'workshop' (Gujarati)

kanka 'rim of jar' Rebus: *karṇika* 'account (scribe)' *karṇī* 'supercargo' PLUS INFIXED: खांडा [*khāṇḍā*] *m* A jag, notch, or indentation (as upon the edge of a tool or weapon). Rebus: *kāṇḍa* 'tools, pots and pans and metal-ware'

aḍar 'harrow'; rebus: *aduru* 'native unsmelted metal'
ayo 'fish' Rebus: *aya* 'iron' *ayas* 'metal'

 *kamaḍha* 'crab' Rebus: *kammaṭa* 'mint, coiner'.*ḍato* = claws of crab (Santali) Rebus: *dhātu* 'mineral ore' PLUS खांडा [*khāṇḍā*] *m* A jag, notch, or indentation (as upon the edge of a tool or weapon). Rebus: *kāṇḍa* 'tools, pots and pans and metal-ware' Thus, mint metalware, ore.

 *kanka* 'rim of jar' Rebus: *karṇīka* 'account (scribe)' *karṇī* 'supercargo'

There are two distinct 'arrow' hieroglyphs with unique ligaturing, thus providing distinct rebus Meluhha semantics:

 'Arrow' sign hieroglyph (variant) This is a ligature of 'lid of pot' hieroglyph superscript on 'a linear stroke' numeral hieroglyph.*aḍaren* 'cover of pot or lid' Rebus: *aduru* 'native, unsmelted metal' PLUS koḍ = one (Santali); koḍ 'workshop' (Gujarati)

 कांड *kāṇḍa* 'arrow' Rebus: *kāṇḍa* 'pots and pans, metalware, tools'. Rebus 2: kaṇḍ 'fire-altar' (Santali)

 A triplet of fishes with unique ligatures are distinctive technical specifications of  *ayo* 'fish' Rebus: *aya* 'iron' (Gujarati) *ayas* 'metal' (Sanskrit)

In this sequence, the three fishes read rebus from r.:

aya aduru 'unsmelted native alloy metal'
ayo ḍhālako 'native metal ingot'

Styles of ligatured 'fish' hieroglyph signs

 ayo 'fish'(Munda); ayas 'iron' (Sanskrit) Rebus: *ayas* 'metal' (Vedic)
PLUS
aḍaren 'lid' Rebus: aduru 'unsmelted native metal'.

 ayo 'fish' Rebus: ayas 'iron' (Gujarati) ayas 'metal' (Vedic) PLUS infixed hieroglyph of slanted stroke: *dhāḷ* 'a slope'; 'inclination of a plane' (Gujarati); *ḍhāḷiyum* = adj. sloping, inclining (Gujarati) Rebus: *ḍhālako* = a large metal ingot (Gujarati) *ḍhālakī* = a metal heated and poured into a mould; a solid piece of metal; an ingot (Gujarati) Thus, the ligatured hieroglyph reads: *ayo ḍhālako* 'native metal ingot'.

 ayo 'fish' Rebus: aya 'iron' (Gujarati) ayas 'metal' (Vedic) notch (infixed ligature) Rebus: *kāṇḍa* 'pots and pans, metalware', Thus, the composite hieroglyph reads rebus: metalware of alloyed metal.

ayo 'fish' Rebus: aya 'iron' (Gujarati) ayas 'metal' (Vedic) PLUS ligatured fins: *khambhaṛā* m. 'fin' (Lahnda); khambh 'wing' (Punjabi) Allograph: Garh. *khambu* ' pillar '.(CDIAL 13640) Rebus: kammaṭa 'coiner, mint'. Thus 'fish' hieroglyph gets ligatured with fins to denote alloyed metal (of) mint to read: *aya kammaṭa.*'coiner, mint alloy'.

ayo 'fish' Rebus: ayas 'iron' (Gujarati) ayas 'metal' (Vedic) aḍaren 'lid' Rebus: aduru 'native unsmelted metal'

ayo 'fish' Rebus: aya 'iron' (Gujarati) ayas 'metal' (Vedic) PLUS gaṇḍā 'four' Rebus: kaṇḍā 'fire-altar'

Other examples of formation of ligatured hieroglyph signs

m1160a *ibha* 'elephant' Rebus: *ib* 'iron' *ibbo* 'merchant' (Gujarati) | *koḍa* 'one' Rebus: *koḍ* 'workshop'

aḍar 'harrow'; rebus: *aduru* 'native unsmelted metal' Ligatured to: *meḍ 'body' Rebus: meḍ 'iron' (Ho.) Rebus: खंडी [khaṇḍī] measure of weight (Marathi) கண்டி; kaṇṭi, n. < Mhr. khaṇḍil. [T. Tu. khaṇḍi, M. kaṇḍi.] Candy, a weight, about 500 lbs.*काठी [kāṭhī] *f* (काष्ट S) 'frame or structure of the body' (Marathi) Rebus: खंडी [khaṇḍī] measure of weight (Marathi) *கண்டி; kaṇṭi, n. < Mhr. khaṇḍil. [T. Tu. khaṇḍi, M. kaṇḍi.]* Candy, a weight, stated to be roughly equivalent to 500 lbs. *bhaṭa* 'warrior' (Sanskrit) Rebus: *baṭa* a kind of iron (Gujarati). Rebus: *bhaṭa* 'furnace' (Santali)
m370A

kana, kanac = corner (Santali); Rebus: *kañcu* = bronze (Telugu) PLUS खांडा [*khāṇḍā*] *m* A jag, notch, or indentation (as upon the edge of a tool or weapon). Rebus: *kāṇḍa* 'tools, pots and pans and metal-ware' Thus, bronze metalware.

kuṭila 'bent' CDIAL 3230 kuṭi— in cmpd. 'curve', *kuṭika—* 'bent' MBh. Rebus: *kuṭila, katthīl* = bronze (8 parts copper and 2 parts tin) Duplicated: dula 'pair' Rebus: dul 'cast metal' Thus, cast bronze.

kanka 'rim of jar' Rebus: *karṇīka* 'account (scribe)' *karṇī* 'supercargo'

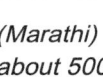

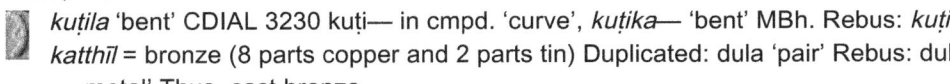

kaṇḍo 'stool, seat' Rebus: *kāṇḍa* 'metalware' *kaṇḍa* 'fire-altar' PLUS 'notch': PLUS खांडा [*khāṇḍā*] *m* A jag, notch, or indentation (as upon the edge of a tool or weapon). Rebus: *kāṇḍa* 'tools, pots and pans and metal-ware' *loa* 'ficus religiosa' Rebus: *lo* 'iron' (Sanskrit) PLUS unique ligatures: लोखंड [lōkhaṇḍa] *n* (लोह S) Iron. लोखंडाचे चणे खावविणें or चारणें To oppress grievously.लोखंडकाम [lōkhaṇḍakāma] *n* Iron work; that portion (of a building, machine &c.) which consists of iron. 2 The business of an ironsmith.लोखंडी [lōkhaṇḍī] *a* (लोखंड) Composed of iron; relating to iron. (Marathi)
ayo ḍhālako 'alloy metal ingot'
kamaḍha 'crab' Rebus: *kammaṭa* 'mint, coiner'.
ḍato = claws of crab (Santali) Rebus: *dhātu* 'mineral ore'

dula 'pair' Rebus: *dul* 'cast (metal)' PLUS *kana, kanac* = corner (Santali); Rebus: *kañcu* = bronze (Telugu) PLUS infixed kolmo 'paddy plant' Rebus: kolami 'smithy, forge'. Thus, cast bronze smithy, forge. Or, *mogge* 'sprout, bud' Rebus: *mũh* 'ingot' (Santali)Thus, cast bronze ingot. Read as: *kañcu dul mũh 'bronze cast ingot' aya aḍaren (homonym: aduru)*'alloy native metal'

m976a *खोंड [khōṇḍa] m A young bull, a bullcalf. (Marathi) Rebus: kõdār 'turner' (Bengali); कोंद kōnda 'engraver, lapidary setting or infixing gems' (Marathi) G. sãghāṛɔ m. 'lathe' ; संघाट joinery; M. sãgaḍ 'double-canoe' Rebus: sangataras 'stone-cutter, mason'*

kanac 'corner' Rebus: *kañcu* 'bronze'

koḍi 'flag' (Ta.)(DEDR 2049). Rebus 1: *koḍ* 'workshop' (Kuwi) Rebus 2: *khõḍ* m. 'pit', *khõḍü* f. 'small pit' (Kashmiri. CDIAL 3947).

PLUS खांडा [*khāṇḍā*] *m* A jag, notch, or indentation (as upon the edge of a tool or weapon). Rebus: *kāṇḍa* 'tools, pots and pans and metal-ware'

cīmara 'black ant' Rebus: *cīmara* 'copper'. *cīmara kāra* -- ' coppersmith 'PLUS *Kur.* xolā tail. *Malt.* qoli id. (DEDR 2135). Rebus: kolhe 'smelter' Thus, copper smelter.

m101a *खोंड [khōṇḍa] m A young bull, a bullcalf. (Marathi) Rebus: kõdār 'turner' (Bengali); कोंद kōnda 'engraver, lapidary setting or infixing gems' (Marathi) G. sãghāṛɔ m. 'lathe' ; संघाट joinery; M. sãgaḍ 'double-canoe' Rebus: sangataras 'stone-cutter, mason'*

Bronze alloy workshop kañcu sal starting with bronze which is a tin + copper alloy or tin bronze (as distinguished from arsenical bronze, i.e. naturally occurring copper + arsenic).

water-carrier hieroglyph *kuṭi*; Rebus: *kuṭhi* 'smelter furnace' PLUS *kāṇḍa* 'arrow' (Sanskrit) Rebus:*khāṇḍa* 'tools, pots and pans, metal-ware'. Rebus 2: kaṇḍ 'fire-altar' (Santali)

kanka 'rim of jar' Rebus: karṇīka 'account (scribe)' karṇī 'supercargo'

mēḍu height, rising ground, hillock (Kannada)(DEDR 5058) Rebus: *mẽṛhẽt, meḍ* 'iron' (Mu.Ho.)

kolmo 'paddy plant' Rebus: kolami 'smithy, forge'.

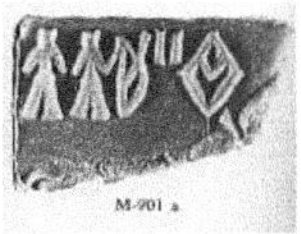

m901a खोंड *[khōṇḍa] m A young bull, a bullcalf. (Marathi) Rebus: kōdār 'turner' (Bengali);* कोंद *kōnda 'engraver, lapidary setting or infixing gems' (Marathi) G. sãghārɔ m. 'lathe' ;* संघाट *joinery; M. sãgaḍ 'double-canoe' Rebus: sangataras 'stone-cutter, mason'*

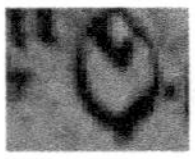

Bronze alloy workshop kañcu sal starting with bronze which is a tin + copper alloy or tin bronze (as distinguished from arsenical bronze, i.e. naturally occurring copper + arsenic).

'Bow and arrow' sign hieroglyph 'Archer + bow + arrow' ligatured hieroglyph upraised arm: eraka 'upraised arm' Rebus: erako 'moltencast copper' *kamaḍha* 'archer, bow' Rebus: *kammaṭa* 'mint, coiner'.

meḍ 'body' Rebus: meḍ 'iron' (Ho.) काठी *[kāṭhī] f (*काष्ट *S) 'frame or structure of the body' (Marathi)* Rebus: खंडी [khaṇḍī] measure of weight (Marathi) கண்டி; *kaṇṭi, n. < Mhr. khaṇḍil. [T. Tu. khaṇḍi, M. kaṇḍi.]* Candy, a weight, stated to be roughly equivalent to 500 lbs.

m1311a

Bronze alloy workshop kañcu sal starting with bronze which is a tin + copper alloy or tin bronze (as distinguished from arsenical bronze, i.e. naturally occurring copper + arsenic).

|||| Numeral 4: gaṇḍa 'four' Rebus: kaṇḍa 'furnace, fire-altar' (Santali) dula 'pair' Rebus: dul 'cast metal'

khareḍo = a currycomb (Gujarati) खरारा [*kharārā*] *m* (H) A currycomb. 2 Currying a horse. (Marathi) Rebus: करडा [*karaḍā*] Hard from alloy--iron, silver &c. (Marathi) *kharādī*' turner' (Gujarati)

kāṇḍa 'arrow' (Sanskrit) Rebus:*khāṇḍa* 'tools, pots and pans, metal-ware'. Rebus 2: kaṇḍ 'fire-altar' (Santali)

h1030a*खोंड [khōṇḍa] m A young bull, a bullcalf. (Marathi) Rebus: kōdār 'turner' (Bengali);* कोंद *kōnda 'engraver, lapidary setting or infixing gems' (Marathi) G. sãghārɔ m. 'lathe' ;* संघाट *joinery; M. sãgaḍ 'double-canoe' Rebus: sangataras.* संगतराश *lit. 'to collect stones, stone-cutter, mason.'*

Bronze alloy workshop kañcu sal starting with bronze which is a tin + copper alloy or tin bronze (as distinguished from arsenical bronze, i.e. naturally occurring copper + arsenic).

kuṭila 'bent' CDIAL 3230 kuṭi— in cmpd. 'curve', *kuṭika*— 'bent' MBh. Rebus: kuṭila, katthīl = bronze (8 parts copper and 2 parts tin) dula 'pair' Rebus: dul 'cast metal' Thus the circumscript: cast bronze, *dul kuṭila* The cirumscript is ligatured to: *bhaṭa* 'warrior' (Sanskrit) Rebus: *baṭa* a kind of iron (Gujarati). Rebus: *bhaṭa* 'furnace' (Santali) Thus, together, th ligatured hieroglyph reads rebus: *loa bhaṭa* 'iron furnace'. Thus, iron furnace for cast metal.

kanka 'rim of jar' Rebus: karṇīka 'account (scribe)' karṇī 'supercargo'

Rebus reading of the pair of hieroglyph signs: *meḍ 'body' Rebus: meḍ 'iron' (Ho.).*Vikalpa: 'frame or structure of the body': काठी [kāṭhī] *f* (काष्ट S) The stalk, stem, or trunk of a plant. A staff, rod, pole, wand, stick gen.; a flagstaff, a walking stick, the mast or the yard of a ship or boat etc. The frame or structure of the body: also (viewed by some as arising from the preceding sense, Measuring rod) stature.(Marathi) Rebus: काटी or कांटी [kāṭī or kāṇṭī] *a* (In नंदभाषा) Twenty.(Marathi) Thus, the supercargo may be twenty maunds or approx. 500 lbs., खंडी [khaṇḍī] *f* A measure of weight and capacity, a candy. It consists (in Bombay) of twenty Bombay maunds, or, for particular substances, of eight maunds: (at Poona) of twenty Poona maunds, and generally of twenty maunds; varying there- fore as the maund varies. Thus, together the 'rim of jar' PLUS 'body' hieroglyphs may be a weight measure of the boatload of supercargo.

கண்டி; kaṇṭi, n. < Mhr. khaṇḍil. [T. Tu. khaṇḍi, M. kaṇḍi.] 1. Candy, a weight, stated to be roughly equivalent to 500 lbs.; பாரமென் னும் நிறையளவு. खंडीगणती or खंडोगणती [khaṇḍīgaṇatī or khaṇḍōgaṇatī] *ad* By candies; counting or reckoning by candies. खंडीवारी [khaṇḍīvārī] *ad* By scores, heaps, candies. खंडी [khaṇḍī] Applied to a great quantity; as खंडीभर पोरें, खंडीभर मेंढ्या, खंडीभर काम, खंडीभर बोलतो-लिहितो&c. 3 A land measure, 120 bighás. Synonym in (Telugu)is: బారువ [bāruva] *bāruva*. [from Skt. భారము.] n. A certain weight equal to twenty maunds. ఇరువై మణుగులగల పరిమాణము.

The pairing of hieroglyph signs explains why the supercargo of a ship is called कारणी *kāraṇī* and denoted by the most frequently occurring hieroglyph in the corpora: 'rim of jar' : *karṇika, kanka* (Sanskrit. Santali)

The importance of the 'Candy' as a great quantity by weight may explain another hieroglyph sign: dotted circle: *Ma.* kaṇti gap in a hedge or fence, breach in a wall, mountain pass. ? *Ko.* kaṇḍy small elevation of land. *Ka.* kaṇḍi, kiṇḍi, gaṇḍi chink, hole, opening. *Koḍ.* kaṇḍi narrow passage (e.g. doorway, mountain pass, hole in a fence). *Tu.* kaṇḍi, khaṇḍi, gaṇḍi hole, opening, window; kaṇḍeriyuni to make a cut. *Te.* gaṇḍi, gaṇḍika hole, orifice, breach, gap, lane; gaṇṭu to cut, wound; *n.* cut, wound, notch; gaṇṭi wound; gaṇḍrincu to cut, divide; gaṇḍrikalu pieces, fragments. *Kuwi* (F.) gundṛa piece; (S.) ganḍra trunk of a tree;gandranga rath'nai to cut in pieces; (Isr.) ganḍra piece.(DEDR 1176).

h1050am47a *खोंड [khōṇḍa] m A young bull, a bullcalf. (Marathi) Rebus: kōdār 'turner' (Bengali);* कोंद *kōnda 'engraver, lapidary setting or infixing gems' (Marathi) G. sãghāṛɔ m. 'lathe' ;* संघाट *joinery; M. sāgaḍ 'double-canoe' Rebus: sangataras 'stone-cutter, mason'*

Bronze alloy workshop kañcu sal starting with bronze which is a tin + copper alloy or tin bronze (as distinguished from arsenical bronze, i.e. naturally occurring copper + arsenic).

aya aḍaren (homonym: aduru)'alloy native metal'

Circumscript 1: Four cirumscript short strokes: *gaṇḍa* 'four' Rebus: *kaṇḍa* 'furnace, fire-altar' (Santali) खांडा [*khāṇḍā*] *m* A jag, notch, or indentation (as upon the edge of a tool or weapon). Rebus: *kāṇḍa* 'tools, pots and pans and metal-ware' PLUS Circumscript 2: *kuṭila* 'bent' CDIAL 3230 kuṭi— in cmpd. 'curve', *kuṭika—* 'bent' MBh. Rebus: *kuṭila, katthīl* = bronze (8 parts copper and 2 parts tin) *dula* 'pair' Rebus: *dul* 'cast metal'. Thus two bent lines () together read as circumscript: cast bronze, *dul kuṭila. kolmo* 'paddy plant' Rebus: *kolami* 'smithy,forge'. Thus the composite hieroglyph with two circumscript ligatures, reads: metalware (from) cast bronze smithy-forge furnace'.

M-1693 a

m1693a

खोंड [khōṇḍa] m A young bull, a bullcalf. (Marathi) Rebus: kõdār 'turner' (Bengali); कोंद kōnda 'engraver, lapidary setting or infixing gems' (Marathi) G. sãghāṛɔ m. 'lathe' ; संघाट joinery; M. sāgaḍ 'double-canoe' Rebus: sangataras 'stone-cutter, mason'

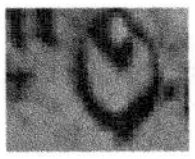

Bronze alloy workshop kañcu sal starting with bronze which is a tin + copper alloy or tin bronze (as distinguished from arsenical bronze, i.e. naturally occurring copper + arsenic).

aya aḍaren (homonym: aduru)'alloy native metal'

muka 'ladle' (Tamil)(DEDR 4887) Rebus: *mũh* 'ingot' (Santali) *baṭa* = a kind of iron (Gujarati) *baṭa* = rimless pot (Kannada) Thus, iron ingot.

kolom 'three' Rebus: kolami 'smithy, forge'

kamaḍha 'crab' Rebus: *kammaṭa* 'mint, coiner'.

ḍato = claws of crab (Santali) Rebus: *dhātu* 'mineral ore' PLUS 'notch' hieroglyph sign ligature: खांडा [*khāṇḍā*] *m* A jag, notch, or indentation (as upon the edge of a tool or weapon). Rebus: *kāṇḍa* 'tools, pots and pans and metal-ware'

Two slanted strokes ligatured (joined) with 'splinter' hieroglyph: *ḍhāḷ* 'a slope'; 'inclination of a plane' (Gujarati); *ḍhāḷiyum* = adj. sloping, inclining (Gujarati) Rebus: *ḍhālako* = a large metal ingot (Gujarati) *ḍhālakī* = a metal heated and poured into a mould; a solid piece of metal; an ingot (Gujarati) Two strokes: dula 'pair' Rebus: dul 'cast metal'. Thus *dul ḍhālako* 'cast metal ingot'. *sal* 'splinter' Rebus: *sal* 'workshop'. Thus the ligatured hieroglyph sign reads: cast metal ingot workshop, *dul ḍhālako sal*

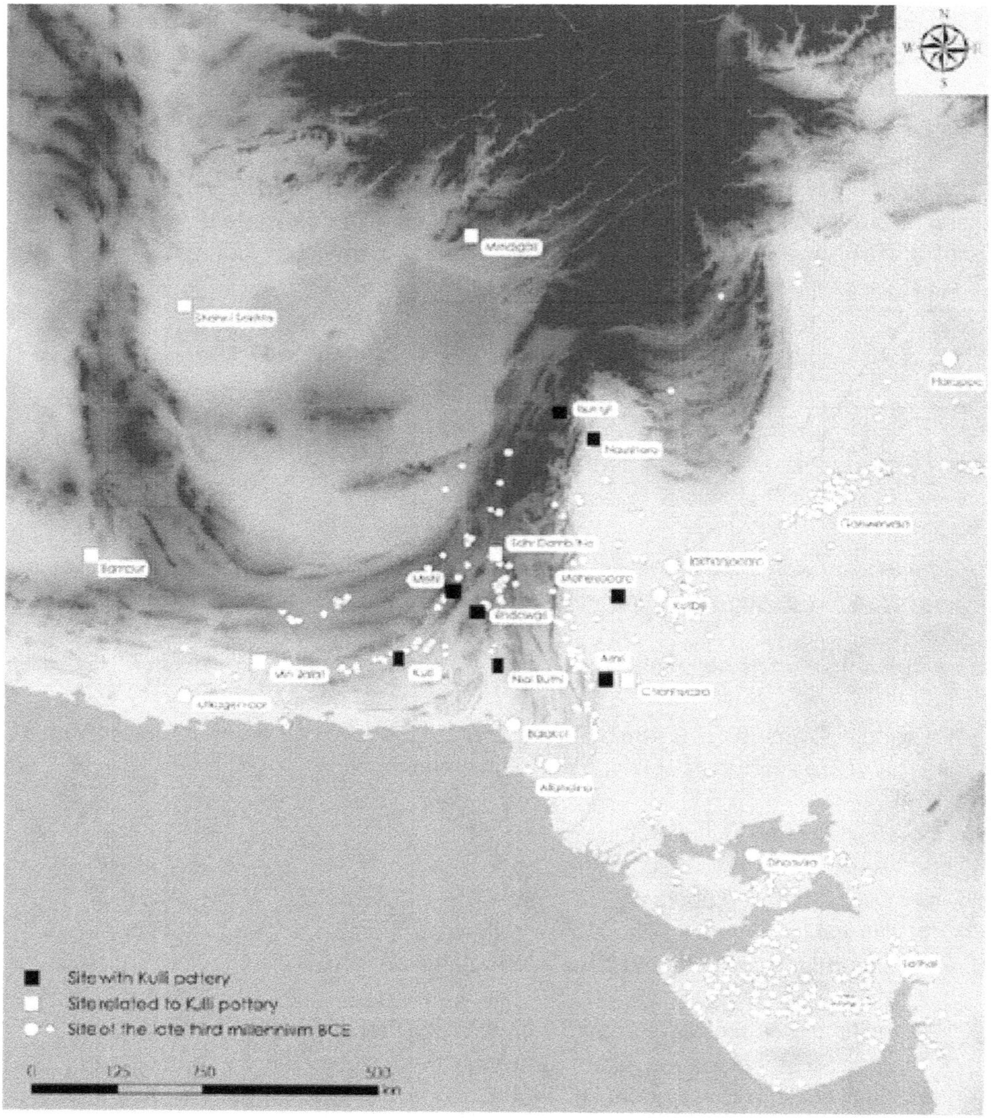

After Fig. 6. Distribution map of representative sites with the Kulli pottey and relevant sites, ibid.
https://www.academia.edu/7823764/Pottery_from_Balochistan_in_Ancient_Orient_Museum_Tokyo_Part_2_the_late_third_millennium_BCE

https://www.academia.edu/4727024/Pottery_from_Balochistan_in_Ancient_Orient_Museum_Tokyo_Part_1_From_the_late_fourth_to_the_early_third_millennia_BCE

Zebu horns are ligatured to a person with upraised arm ligatured to the hindpart of a bovine (with tail); obverse of the tablet shows a one-horned young bull with text hieroglyphs:

81: M-1224 B col (300%)

82: M-1224 E col 2 (300%)

Mohenjo-daro tablet: m1224A,B. *खोंड [khōṇḍa] m A young bull, a bullcalf. (Marathi) Rebus: kõdār 'turner' (Bengali); कोंद kōnda 'engraver, lapidary setting or infixing gems' (Marathi) G. sãghāṛɔ m. 'lathe' ; संघाट joinery; M. sãgaḍ 'double-canoe' Rebus: sangataras. संगतराश lit. 'to collect stones, stone-cutter, mason.'*

eraka 'upraised arm' Rebus: eraka 'copper'
zebu horns: *khũṭ*, 'zebu' Rebus read rebus 'guild', A synonym is *aḍar ḍangra* Rebus: *aduru ḍhangar* 'native-metal-smith, black-smith working on native metal' (Kannada.Santali).

Kalibangan cylinder seal impression

'Leafless tree' hieroglyph occurs on Kalibangan 65a cylinder seal:

Hieroglyphs:

Two persons fencing flanking a woman

Composite animal: tiger, bangled person with headgear of scarf and 'markhor' horns, sprout

Text: sprout (tabernae Montana?), leafless tree, numeral three

Bangled person ligatured to tiger: May denote a jeweler: *maniār, °rā, maneārā* m. ' seller or maker of glass bangles ' (Punjabi)(CDIAL 9733).

maṇikārá m. ' jeweller ' VS. [maṇí -- 1, kāra -- 1]
Pa. *maṇikāra* -- m. ' jeweller ', Pk. *maṇiāra* -- m., K. *manar, manürü* m.;
P. *maniār, °rā, maneārā* m. ' seller or maker of glass bangles '; Or. *maṇihārī* ' jeweller ';
Bi. *manihār* ' glass bangle maker '; H. *maniyār, °rā, manihār, manhiyār* m. ' bracelet maker and seller '; G. *maṇīyār, °īhār* m. ' seller of bangles '; M. *maṇyar, °ṇer, °ṇerī* m. ' jeweller ', Si. *miṇiyara, miṇīr* (CDIAL 9733) maṇí1 m. ' jewel, ornament ' RV.Pa. *maṇi* -- m. ' jewel ', NiDoc. *mani, maṁni*, Pk. *maṇi*<-> m.f.; Gy. pal. *máni* ' button '; K. *man* m. ' precious stone ', *muñu* m., *müñü* f. ' pupil of eye '; S. *maṇi* f. ' jewel ', *maṇyo* m. ' jewels '; P. *maṇī* f. ' jewel ', N. *mani*, Or. *maṇī*, Mth. *manī*, H. *man* m., *manī* f., *maniyā* m.; M. *maṇī* m. ' pearl, jewel ';
Si. *miṇa*, pl. *miṇi* ' jewel '; -- ext. -- *kk* -- : Gy. gr. *minrikló* m. ' ornament ', rum. *mərənkló*, hung. *miriklo* ' pearl, coral ', boh. *miliklo*, germ. *merikle* ' agate ', eng. *mérikli* ' bead ';
Kal.rumb.*mŕãdotdot;ŕik* ' bead necklace '; K. *manka* m. ' snake -- stone '; L. *maṇkā* m. ' bead ', awāṇ. *miṇkā*; P. *maṇkā* m. ' bead, jewel '; G. *maṇkɔ* m. ' gem, bead '; M.*maṇkā* m. ' large gem or bead '. (CDIAL 9731).

Ta. karaṭi, karuṭi, keruṭi fencing, school or gymnasium where wrestling and fencing are taught. *Ka.* garaḍi, garuḍi fencing school. *Tu.* garaḍi, garoḍi id. *Te.*gariḍi, gariḍī id., fencing.

(DEDR 1262). Allographs: garuḍa 'eagle'. करडी [*karaḍī*] *f* (See करडई) Safflower: also its seed. Rebus: karaḍa 'hard alloy' of arka 'copper'. Rebus: fire-god: @B27990. #16671. Remo <karandi>E155 {N} ``^fire-^god".(Munda).

kola 'woman' Rebus: *kolhe* 'smelter'

kol 'tiger' Rebus: *kol* 'working in iron'; *kolhe* 'smelter'.

dhatu 'scarf' (Western Pahari) Rebus: dhatu 'mineral ore' (Santali)

Horns of markhor: *miṇḍāl* 'markhor' (Tōrwālī)*meḍho* a ram, a sheep (Gujarati)(CDIAL 10120) Rebus: *mẽṛhẽt, meḍ* 'iron' (Mu.Ho.)

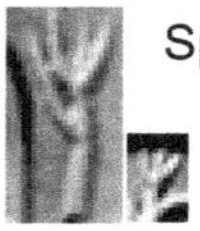

Sprout above horns and in front of the composite pictorial motif hieroglyph: mogge 'sprout, bud' Rebus: mũh 'ingot'

Vikalpa: Two hieroglyphs: numeral three and paddy plant: *kolmo 'three' kolom* 'paddy plant' Rebus: *kolami* 'smithy, forge'

khōṇḍa A stock or stump (Marathi); 'leafless tree' (Marathi). Rebus: *kõdār* 'turner' (Bengali); *kõdā* 'to turn in a lathe' (Bengali).

tagaraka '*tabernae montana*' Rebus; *tagara* 'tin'

Comparable composition of a tiger ligatured to a scarfed woman occurs in a Nausharo seal 9:

Ns-9 A

The pictorial motif hieroglyph has the same readings as on the Kalibangan 65 cylinder seal – indicating a mineral ore smelter: *dhatu kolhe.* The ligatures of: ram's horn and sprout as head-dress read rebus: tagara 'ram' Rebus: tagara 'tin' PLUS *kolmo* 'paddy plant' Rebus: *kolami* 'smithy, forge'.

Text reading: *sal* 'splinter' Rebus: *sal* 'workshop'

mogge 'flower-bud, sprout' Rebus: *mũh* 'ingot' (Santali)

dhatu 'strands of yar' Rebus: dhatu 'mineral ore'

baṭa 'pot' Rebus: *baṭa* 'a kind of iron' (Gujarati) *bhaṭa* 'furnace'.
kolom 'three' Rebus: kolami 'smithy, forge' Dhanga 'peak' Rebus: Dhangar 'blacksmith'

dol 'two' *dula* दुल । युग्मम् m. a pair, a couple, esp. of two similar things (Rām. 966). Rebus: *dul* meṛeḍ cast iron (Mundari. Santali) *dul* 'to cast metal in a mould' (Santali) Rebus: *dul* 'cast (metal)' *kana, kanac* = corner (Santali); Rebus: *kañcu* = bronze (Telugu) PLUS *kuṭila* 'bent'; Rebus: *kuṭila, katthīl* = bronze (8 parts copper and 2 parts tin) PLUS infixed 'notch': खांडा [khāṇḍā] *m* A jag, notch, or indentation (as upon the edge of a tool or weapon). (Marathi) Rebus: *khāṇḍā* 'tools, pots and pans, metal- The pair of ligatured hieroglyphs reads: metalware of cast bronze, bronze alloy', *dul kañcu kuṭila khāṇḍā*

meḍ 'body' Rebus: *meḍ* 'iron' (Ho.)
koḍa 'one' Rebus*: koḍ* 'workshop'

kanka 'rim of jar' Rebus: *karṇīka* 'account (scribe)' *karṇī* 'supercargo'

Comparable hieroglyphs of humped bull, tree, bird, occur on a Failaka seal:

Failaka seal. The Yale tablet is dated to ca. the second half of the twentieth century B.C.... Trade3 on the Persian gulf was in existence well before that time-- about 2350 B.C.-- when Sargon, the first Akkadian king referred to ships from or destined for Melukhkha, Magan and Tilmun (Dilmun) at his wharves. in the Third Dynasty of Ur (around 2000), when trade apparently was centred at Magan. It is even better documented on other tablets from Ur (from about 1900 and from about 1800), belonging to various kings of Larsa. At this time the trade was centered at Tilmun... Cuneiform inscriptions naming Inzak, the god of Tilmun, were found on Failaka and, a long time ago, one on Bahrein... Failaka can be equated with Tilmun, or at least was an important part of it. (Briggs Buchanan, A dated seal impression connecting Babylonia and ancient India, Archaeology, Vol. 20, No.2, 1967, pp. 104-107).

khōṇḍa A stock or stump (Marathi); 'leafless tree' (Marathi). Rebus: *kõdār* 'turner' (Bengali); *kõdā* 'to turn in a lathe' (Bengali).

Hieroglyhph: *karaṛa* 'a very large aquatic bird' (Sindhi) Rebus: करडा [*karaḍā*] Hard from alloy--iron, silver &c. (Marathi) Vikalpa: *baṭa* 'quail' Rebus: *bhaṭa* 'furnace'. *baṭa* 'a kind of iron' (Gujarati) Pair of birds: dula 'pair' Rebus: dul 'cast metal' *khōṇḍa* A stock or stump (Marathi); 'leafless tree' (Marathi). Rebus: *kõdār* 'turner' (Bengali); *kõdā* 'to turn in a lathe' (Bengali).

Ku. *balad* m. ' ox ', gng. *bald*, N. (Tarai) *barad*, id. Rebus: L. bhāraṇ ' to spread or bring out from a kiln '; M. bhārṇẽ, bhāḷṇẽ ' to make strong by charms (weapons, rice, water), enchant, fascinate (CDIAL 9463) Ash. barī ' blacksmith, artisan (CDIAL 9464). Baran, bharat 'mixed alloys' (5 copper, 4 zinc and 1 tin) (Punjabi) bharana id. (Bengali) bharan or toul was created by adding some brass or zinc into pure bronze. bharata = casting metals in moulds (Bengali) *bharata* 'a factitious metal compounded of copper, pewter, tin' (Marathi)

குடி[1]-த்தல் kuṭi-, *11 v. tr.* cf. *kuḍ*. [K. *kuḍi*, M. *kuṭi*.] 1. [T. *kuḍucu*.] To drink, as from a cup, from the breast; பருகுதல். கடலைவற்றக் குடித்திடுகின்ற செவ்வேற் கூற்றம் (கந்தபு. தாரக. 183).*kuṭi.* 'to drink' (Malayalam) Rebus: *kuṭhi.* 'smelter, furnace' (Santali). The pair of 'drinking' persons are thus seen as: *kolhe* 'smelters' working with *baṭa* 'a kind of iron'.

P.Kjærum, *Failaka/Dilmun, The Second Millennium Settlements,vol 1:1*: "The Stamp and Cylinder Seals", 1983. 43, 143.

'Long-shanked person' hieroglyph: *ḍhanga*'tall, long-shanked; *maran: ḍhangi aimai kanae* '= she is a big tall woman' (Santali.) *ḍhāgo* ' lean ', m. ' skeleton ' (Ku.) (CDIAL 5524) Rebus: *ḍhangar* 'blacksmith' (Maithili)

करडी [*karaḍī*] *f* (See करडई) Safflower: also its seed. Rebus: *karaḍa* 'hard alloy' of arka 'copper'. Rebus: fire-god: @B27990. #16671.
Remo <karandi>E155 {N} ``^fire-^god".(Munda) Rebus:. *kharāḍī* ' turner' (Gujarati)

Ku. *balad* m. ' ox ', gng. *bald*, N. (Tarai) *barad*, id. Rebus: L. bhāraṇ ' to spread or bring out from a kiln '; M. bhārṇẽ, bhāḷṇẽ ' to make strong by charms (weapons, rice, water), enchant, fascinate (CDIAL 9463) Ash. barī ' blacksmith, artisan (CDIAL 9464). Baran, bharat 'mixed alloys' (5 copper, 4 zinc and 1 tin) (Punjabi) bharana id. (Bengali) bharan or toul was created by adding some brass or zinc into pure bronze. bharata = casting metals in moulds (Bengali) *bharata* 'a factitious metal compounded of copper, pewter, tin' (Marathi)

Some hieroglyphs which recur on Ancient Near seals such as British Museum cylinder seal No. 89308 and their Meluhha rebus readings are:

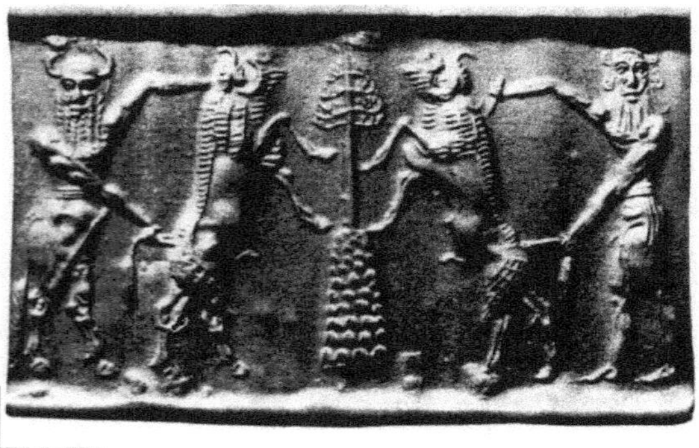

Cylinder seal impression, Mesopotamia [Scene said to epresent Gilgamesh and Ea-bani in conflict with bulls in a wooded and mountainous country; British Museum No. 89308]

Bull-man with zebu horn and a person with six hair-curls in conflict flanking ficus religiosa hieroglyph
Sign 232 *loa* 'ficus religiosa' Rebus: *lo* 'copper'. *āra* 'six' Rebus: *āra-kūṭa*, 'brass'

Bull-man, bull hieroglyphs: ḍangar 'bull' read rebus *ḍhangar* 'blacksmith'; *ṭagara* 'ram' Rebus: *damgar* 'merchant' (Akkadian) ṭhakkura, 'idol', *ṭhākur* ' blacksmith ', ṭhākur m. 'master'.

mountain डोंगर [ḍōṅgara] m A hill. डोंगरकणगर or डोंगरकंगर [ḍōṅgarakaṇagara or ḍōṅgarakaṅgara] m (डोंगर & कणगर form of redup.) Hill and mountain; hills comprehensively or indefinitely.
डोंगरकोळी [ḍōṅgarakōḷī] m A caste of hill people or an individual of it. (Marathi) ḍāngā = hill, dry upland (Bengali); ḍāg mountain-ridge (Hindi)(CDIAL 5476). Rebus: dhangar 'blacksmith' (Maithili) dhokra 'cire perdue metallurgist'.
http://bharatkalyan97.blogspot.com/2014/04/continuity-in-hieroglyph-motifs-from.html

Winged Hero Contesting with a Lion for a Bull
Cylinder seal and impression Mesopotamia, Neo-Babylonian period (ca.1000–539B.C.)
Carnelian 38.5 x 18 mm Seal no. 747 A winged person, humped bull and lion.
http://www.themorgan.org/collections/collections.asp?id=198

eraka 'wing' Rebus: eraka 'copper'

arye 'lion' Rebus: *āra* 'brass'.

khũṭ, 'zebu' Rebus read rebus 'guild', A synonym is *aḍar ḍangra* Rebus: *aduru ḍhangar* 'native-metal- or black-smith' (Kannada.Santali). dangra 'bull' (Punjabi) Rebus: *ḍhangar* 'blacksmith' (Maithili) *adar dangra* 'zebu' *bos indicus* (Santali) Rebus: ಗಣಿಯಿಂದ ತೆಗದು ಕರಗದೆ ಇರುವ ಅದುರು (Kannada) aduru *gan.iyinda tegadu karagade iruva aduru* = ore taken from the mine and not subjected to melting in a furnace (Ka. Siddhānti Subrahmaṇya' Śastri's new interpretation of the AmarakoŚa, Bangalore, Vicaradarpana Press, 1872, p.330).

Griffin Demon Grasping Bull Cylinder seal and impression Mesopotamia, Middle Assyrian period (ca. fourteenth century B.C.) Chalcedony 20 x 10 mm Seal no. 595

eruvai 'eagle' Rebus: eruvai 'copper' eraka 'wing' Rebus: eraka 'copper'
khũṭ, 'zebu' Rebus read rebus 'guild', A synonym is *aḍar ḍangra* Rebus: *aduru ḍhangar* 'native-metal- or black-smith' (Kannada.Santali). dangra 'bull' (Punjabi) Rebus: *ḍhangar* 'blacksmith' (Maithili)

http://www.themorgan.org/collections/collections.asp?id=644

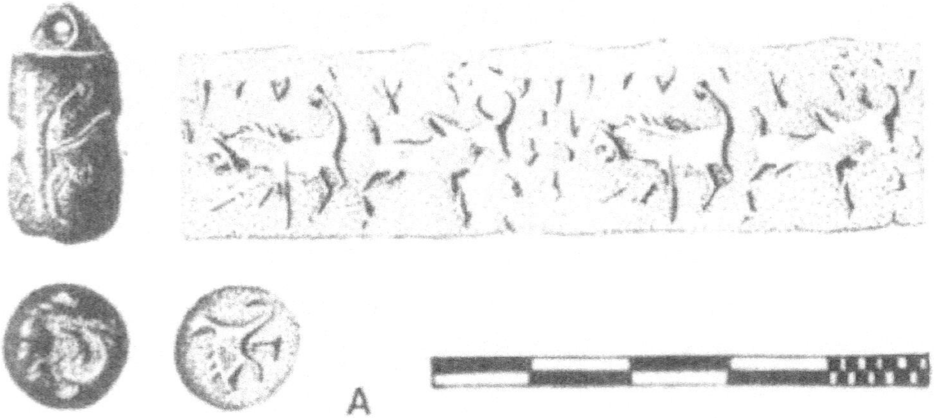

Sibri cylinder seal with Indus writing hieroglyphs: notches, zebu, tiger, scorpion?. Source: Jarrige, Catherine, Jean-François Jarrige, Richard H. Meadow, and Gonzague Quivron, editors (1995/1996) Mehrgarh: Field Reports 1974-1985 - From Neolithic Times to the Indus Civilization. The Reports of Eleven Seasons of Excavations in Kachi District, Balochistan, by the French Archaeological Mission to Pakistan. Sindh, Pakistan: The Department of Culture and Tourism, Government of Sindh, Pakistan, in Collaboration with the French Ministry of Foreign Affairs. http://bharatkalyan97.blogspot.com/2013/07/ancient-near-east-transition-fro-bullae.html

Each dot on the corner of the + glyph and the short numeral strokes on a cylinder seal of Sibri, may denote a notch: खांडा [khāṇḍā] *m* A jag, notch, or indentation (as upon the edge of a tool or weapon). (Marathi) Rebus:*khāṇḍā* 'tools, pots and pans, metal-ware',

kol 'tiger' Rebus: *kol* 'working in iron'; *kolhe* 'smelter'.

adar dangra 'zebu' *bos indicus* (Santali) Rebus: *aduru* native metal (Kannada); *ḍhangar* 'blacksmith' (Maithili)
http://bharatkalyan97.blogspot.com/2014/04/continuity-in-hieroglyph-motifs-from.html

Shahdad standard with zebu hieroglyph.

kanḍo 'stool, seat' Rebus: *kāṇḍā* 'metalware, tools, pots and pans'(Marathi).

kuṭi 'tree' Rebus: kuṭhi 'smelter'

kol 'tiger' Rebus: *kol* 'working in iron'; *kolhe* 'smelter'.

adar dangra 'zebu' *bos indicus* (Santali) Rebus: *aduru* native metal (Kannada); *ḍhangar* 'blacksmith' (Maithili)

Twisted rope: मेढा [*mēḍhā*] A twist or tangle arising in thread or cord, a curl or snarl.(Marathi)(CDIAL 10312).L. *meṛh* f. 'rope tying oxen to each other and to post on threshing floor'(CDIAL 10317) Rebus: *meḍ* 'iron'. *mẽṛhet* 'iron' (Mu.Ho.)

Genetic studies tracing migrations of domesticated 'humped bull'

In a monograph titled "Worldwide Patterns of Ancestry, Divergence, and Admixture in Domesticated Cattle", Jared E. Decker et al present a conclusion: "In Asia, Africa, North and South America, humpless (*Bos taurus taurus* or taurine) and humped (*Bos taurus indicus* or indicine) cattle were crossbred to produce hybrids adapted to the environment and local production systems."
http://www.plosgenetics.org/article/info:doi/10.1371/journal.pgen.1004254

From the perspective of analyzing the deployment of zebu (humped bull) as a hieroglyph in archaeological (trade) contexts, the detailed genetic tree of single domestication or two separate domestications involving aurochs and zebu is more significant than the search for a "recent common ancestor of *Bos taurus* (the western cow) and *Bos indicus* (the zebu) may have lived as much as 1m years ago—well before *Homo sapiens*existed."

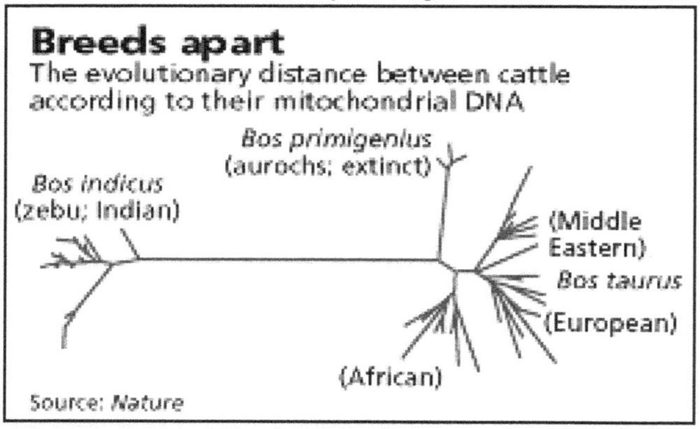

http://www.economist.com/node/587270

The general consensus of genetic studies is that domestication event of *bos indicus* or *bos taurus indicus* occurred in the Sarasvati civilization (also called Indus Civilization of the Indian subcontinent). "Recent mtDNA evidence for domesticated zebu (humped cattle, *B. indicus*) suggests that two major lineages of *B. indicus* are currently present in modern animals. One (called I1) predominates in southeast Asia and southern China and is likely to have been domesticated in the Indus Valley region of what is today Pakistan. Evidence of the transition of wild to domestic *B. indicus* is in evidence in Harappan sites such as Mehrgarh about 7,000 years ago. The second strain, I2, may have been captured in East Asia, but apparently was also domesticated in the Indian subcontinent, based on the presence of a broad range of

diverse genetic elements. The evidence is not entirely clear as of yet."
http://archaeology.about.com/od/domestications/qt/cattle.htm

Section A. Meluhha hieroglyphs on m1893 Mohenjo-daro seal; rebus readings of native-metal-smith guild

The deployment of zebu hieroglyph on Shahdad standard provides a framework for starting the enquiry into and validating Meluhha cipher with the decipherment of a zebu Meluhh inscription on a Mohenjo-daro seal. Section B is an enquiry into the region termed Araṭṭa to identify Meluhha people who participated defining the roots of Hindu civilization, followed by Section C, D and E presenting deciphered Meluhha hieroglyphs related to Meluhha metallurgy, copper/brass and bronze. Section F names the artisans who had the skills in using cire perdue method of casting, they are referred to as dhokra kamar in two Meluhha inscriptions of Dholavira and Mohenjo-daro.

m1893

There are two segments on this seal: 1. 'zebu' pictorial motif hieroglyph; 2. Text of five 'signs' as hiereoglyphs. Reading the hieroglyphs starts from the face of the animal in sequence.

Segment 1: Pictorial motif hieroglyph: *adar dangra* 'zebu' *bos indicus* Rebus: *aduru ḍhangar* native-metal-smith; *khũṭ* 'zebu' *bos indicus* Rebus: 'guild or community'.

'Zebu' Pictorial motif hieroglyph: (Kathiawar) *khũṭ* m. ' Brahmani bull '.(CDIAL 3899) (Kathiawar) *khũṭro* m. ' entire bull used for agriculture, not for breeding'(Gujarati). Rebus 1: *khũṭ* 'community' (Guild). Cf. *khũṭ* a community, sect, society, division, clique, schism, stock (Santali) kūṭa a house, dwelling (Sanskrit)
Rebus2 *kuṭ hi, kut.i* (Or.; Sad. *koṭhi*) the smelting furnace of the blacksmith; kuṭire bica duljad.ko talkena, they were feeding the furnace with ore.

adar dangra 'zebu' *bos indicus* (Santali) Rebus: ಗಣಿಯಿಂದ ತೆಗದು ಕರಗದೆ ಇರುವ ಅದುರು (Kannada) aduru *gan.iyinda tegadu karagade iruva aduru* = ore taken from the mine and not subjected to melting in a furnace (Ka. Siddhānti Subrahmaṇya' Śastri's new interpretation of the AmarakoŚa, Bangalore, Vicaradarpana Press, 1872, p.330). *adar* = fine sand (Tamil) *aduru* native metal (Kannada); *ayil* iron (Tamil) *ayir, ayiram* any ore (Malayalam); *ajirda karba* very hard iron (Tulu)(DEDR 192). Rebus: *ḍhangar* 'blacksmith' (Maithili)

Segment 2: Text of five 'signs' as hieroglyphs read from l. to r.

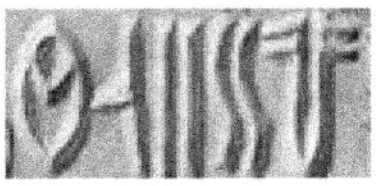

Text of inscription on m1893

Meluhha rebus readings of the full text of the inscription:

1. *kana, kanac* = corner (Santali); Rebus: *kañcu* = bronze (Telugu)
2. *koḍi* 'flag' (Tamil)(DEDR 2049). Rebus 1: *koḍ* 'workshop' (Kuwi)
3. dol 'two' dula दुल । युग्मम् m. a pair, a couple, esp. of two similar things (Rām. 966). Rebus: dul meṛeḍ cast iron (Mundari. Santali) *dul* 'to cast metal in a mould' (Santali) Rebus: dul 'cast (metal)'
4. *kuṭila* 'bent'; Rebus: *kuṭila, katthīl* = bronze (8 parts copper and 2 parts tin)
5. *kanka* (Santali) karṇika 'scribe'(Sanskrit) Rebus: *karṇī,* supercargo for a boat shipment. *karṇīka* account scribe.

Zebu is ligatured as distinctive high horns to create a composite hieroglyph 'composite animal motif' as in m0301: human face, body or forepart of a ram, body and forelegs of a unicorn, horns of a zebu, trunk of an elephant, hindlegs of a tiger and an upraised serpent-like tail:

m1927a

1927b

Mohenjo-daro Seal 1927 with epigraphs on two-side is a confirmation that the horns ligatured to the composite animal on m1927b are horns of zebu.

The pictorial motif hieroglyphs message on the seal:

khũṭ 'zebu' Rebus: '(native metal) guild' This refrain is detailed by the zebu horns affixed to the compositive animal hieroglyph. A synonym is *aḍar ḍangra* read rebus: *aduru ḍhangar* 'blacksmith' (Santali)

The composite animal hieroglyph can thus be seen as an expansion of the message conveyed by the zebu hieroglyph expanding the blacksmith guild activities to other minerals and metals beyond *aduru* 'native, unsmelted metal'. The text message seems to be identical on both sides of the seal m1927: bronze workshop; metal smithy castings; forge. The zebu side a of the seal seems to denote the work of a native-metal-smith; the composite animal side b of the seal seems to denote the expanded work of a blacksmith working with stones, minerals and metals. The composite hieroglyph on m1927b was perhaps called: व्याळ [vyāḷa] *m* (व्याल S) A serpent. Ex. जैसें पायास दंशिलें महा व्याळें ॥ तों मस्तकासीं वृश्चिकें दंशिलें ॥. 2 Applied popularly to the नाग or भुजंग.व्याल [vyāla] *m* S A serpent. (Marathi) யாளவரி yāḷa-vari n. < vyāḷayāḷi யாளி yāḷi, n. < vyāḷa. [K. yāḷi.] A mythological lion-faced animal with elephantine proboscis and tusks; யானையின் தந்தமும் துதிக்கையுஞ் சிங்கத்தின் முகமுமுடையதாகக் கருதப் படும் மிருகம். உழுவையும் யாளியு முளியமும் (குறிஞ் சிப். 252). 1 A vicious elephant; व्यालं बाल-मृणालतन्तुभिरसौ रोद्धुं समुज्जृम्भते Bh.2.6. -2 A beast of prey; वसन्त्यस्मिन् महारण्ये व्यालाश्च रुधिराशनाः Rām.2.119. 19; वनं व्यालनिषेवितम् Rām. -3 A snake; H.3.29. -4 A tiger; Māl.3. -5 A leopard. व्यालकः A vicious or wicked elephant.

The text message on the seal:

kanac 'corner' Rebus: kañcu 'bronze'
sal 'splinter' Rebus: sal 'workshop'

|| dula 'pair or two' Rebus: dul 'cast metal'
||| kolom 'three' Rebus: kolami 'smithy, forge'
kolmo 'paddy plant' Rebus: kolami 'smithy, forge'

Bronze alloy workshop kañcu sal starting with bronze which is a tin + copper alloy or tin bronze (as distinguished from arsenical bronze, i.e. naturally occurring copper + arsenic).

dula 'two' Rebus: dul 'cast metal'
dolom 'three' Rebus: kolami 'smithy, forge'
kolmo 'paddy plant' Rebus: kolami 'smithy, forge'. Vikalpa: *mogge* 'sprout, bud' Rebus: *mũh* 'ingot'

Lothal 220A Zebu horns. Native metal smith guild

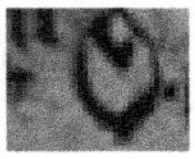

Bronze alloy workshop kañcu sal starting with bronze which is a tin + copper alloy or tin bronze (as distinguished from arsenical bronze, i.e. naturally occurring copper + arsenic).

meḍ 'body' Rebus: *meḍ* 'iron' (Ho.) काठी [kāṭhī] *f* (काष्ट S) 'frame or structure of the body' (Marathi) Rebus: खंडी [khaṇḍī] measure of weight (Marathi) கண்டி; *kaṇṭi, n. < Mhr. khaṇḍil. [T. Tu. khaṇḍi, M. kaṇḍi.]* Candy, a weight, stated to be roughly equivalent to 500 lbs.

'Flag' hieroglyph together with splinter hieroglyph occurs twice on Kalibangan seal 10A, reinforcing the rebus semantics of *koḍ* 'workshop':
The pictorial motif hieroglyph connotes 'turner':
खोंड [khōṇḍa] m A young bull, a bullcalf. (Marathi) Rebus: kõdār 'turner' (Bengali); कोंद kõnda 'engraver, lapidary setting or infixing gems' (Marathi) G. sãghārɔ m. 'lathe' ; संघाट joinery; M. sãgaḍ 'double-canoe' Rebus: sangataras. संगतराश lit. 'to collect stones, stone-cutter, mason.'

First segment of text on K-10A reads: *kanac* 'corner' Rebus: *kañcu* 'bronze' *ranku* 'liquid

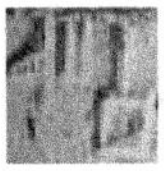

measure' Rebus *ranku* 'tin' sal 'splinter' Rebus: *sal* 'workshop' *koḍ* 'workshop'. It is possible *sal* 'workshop' is a smelter-smithy while *koḍ* is a forge.

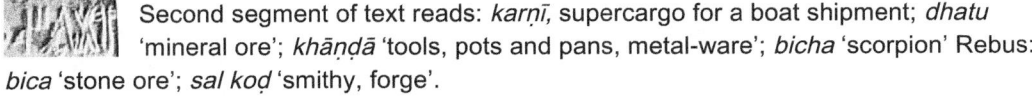

Second segment of text reads: *karṇī,* supercargo for a boat shipment; *dhatu* 'mineral ore'; *khāṇḍā* 'tools, pots and pans, metal-ware'; *bicha* 'scorpion' Rebus: *bica* 'stone ore'; *sal koḍ* 'smithy, forge'.

Read together with the 'zebu' hieroglyph Segments 1 and 2 on Seal m1893 read rebus: supoercargo account of bronze, metal casting with tin, (of) native-metal-smith guild or community. Thus, the text m1893 describes: bronze workshop, cast metal bronze, supercargo (account scribe) *kanka* (Santali) karṇika 'scribe'(Sanskrit) Rebus: *karṇī,* supercargo for a boat shipment.

Each sign in the text is a hieroglyph read rebus:

kana, kanac = corner (Santali); Rebus: kañcu = bronze (Telugu) kā´ṁsya ' made of bell -- metal ' KātyŚr., n. ' bell -- metal ' Yājñ., ' cup of bell -- metal ' MBh., *°aka* -- n. ' bell -- metal '. 2. *kāṁsiya -- . [kaṁsá -- 1]1. Pa. *kaṁsa* -- m. (?) ' bronze ', Pk. *kaṁsa* -- , *kāsa* -- n. ' bell -- metal, drinking vessel, cymbal '; L. (Jukes) *kājā* adj. ' of metal ', awāṇ. *kāsā* ' jar ' (← E with -- *s* -- , not*ñj*); N. *kāso* ' bronze, pewter, white metal ', *kas -- kuṭ* ' metal alloy '; A. *kāh* ' bell -- metal ', B. *kāsā*, Or. *kāsā*, Bi. *kāsā*; Bhoj. *kās* ' bell -- metal ', *kāsā* ' base metal '; H.*kās*, *kāsā* m. ' bell -- metal ', G. *kāsũ* n., M. *kāsẽ* n.; Ko. *kāśẽ* n. ' bronze '; Si. *kasa* ' bell -- metal '.2. L. *kāihā* m. ' bell -- metal ', P. *kāssī*, *kāsī* f., H. *kāsī* f.(CDIAL 2987) కంచము [kañcamu] *kanṭsamu*. [Telugu] n. A metal plate or dish. కంచుకంచము a dish made of bell metal. కంచరవాడు [kañcaravāḍu] or కంచరి *kanṭsara-vaḍu*. [Telugu] n. A brazier, a coppersmith. కంచుపని చేయువాడు. కంచరది a woman of that caste. కంచరిపురుగు *kanṭsari-purugu*. n. A kind of beetle called the death watch. కంచు *kanṭsu*. n. Bell metal. కంచుకుండ a bowl or vessel or bell metal. కంచువాద్యము a cymbal made of bell metal. కంచుతీసినట్లు as bright or dazzling as the glitter of polished metal. Sunbright. ఆమె కంచుగీచినట్లు పలికె she spoke shrilly or with a voice as clear as a bell.

koḍi 'flag' (Tamil)(DEDR 2049). Rebus 1: *koḍ* 'workshop' (Kuwi) Rebus 2: *khŏḍ* m. 'pit', *khŏḍü* f. 'small pit' (Kashmiri. CDIAL 3947).

'Number 2 hieroglyph: dol 'two' Rebus: dul 'cast (metal)'

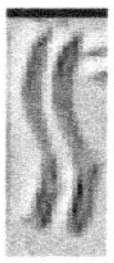

'Bent' pair of lines hieroglyph: kuṭila 'bent'; Rebus: kuṭila, katthīl = bronze (8 parts copper and 2 parts tin) [cf. āra-kūṭa, 'brass' (Sanskrit) CDIAL 3230 kuṭi— in cmpd. 'curve', *kuṭika*— 'bent' MBh. [√kuṭ 1] Ext. in H. *kuṛuk* f. 'coil of string or rope'; M. *kuḍċā* m. 'palm contracted and hollowed', *kuḍapṇẽ* 'to curl over, crisp, contract'. CDIAL 3231 kuṭilá— 'bent, crooked' KātyŚr., *°aka*— Pañcat., n. 'a partic. plant' [√kuṭ 1] Pa. *kuṭila*— 'bent', n. 'bend'; Pk. *kuḍila*— 'crooked', *°illa*— 'humpbacked', *°illaya*— 'bent'DEDR 2054 *(a) Ta.* koṭu curved, bent, crooked; koṭumai crookedness, obliquity; koṭukki hooked bar for fastening doors, clasp of an ornament. A pair of curved lines: *dol* 'likeness, picture, form' [e.g., two tigers, two bulls, sign-pair.] Kashmiri. dula दुल । युग्मम् m. a pair, a couple, esp. of two similar things (Rām. 966). Rebus: dul meṛeḍ cast iron (Mundari. Santali) *dul* 'to cast metal in a mould' (Santali) pasra meṛed, pasāra meṛed = syn. of koṭe meṛed = forged iron, in contrast to dul meṛed, cast iron (Mundari.) Thus, dul kut.ila 'cast bronze'.

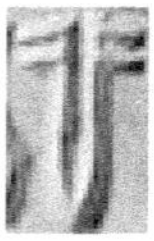

'rim-of-jar' hieroglyph *kanka* (Santali) karṇika 'scribe'(Sanskrit)
Rebus: *karṇī*, supercargo for a boat shipment. *karṇīka* 'account (scribe)'.कारणी kāraṇī ' the supercargo of a ship' (Marathi) कर्णधार [karṇadhāra] *m* S (A holder of the ear.) A helmsman or steersman देशकुळकरणी [dēśakuḷakaraṇī] *m* An hereditary officer of a Mahál. He frames the general account from the accounts of the several Khots and Kulkarṇ̈ís of the villages within the Mahál; the district-accountant.

76: H-180 A col (300%)

h180A Pictorial motifs hieroglyphs: kola 'tiger' Rebus: kolhe 'smelters' dula 'pair' Rebus: dul 'cast metal'. Rebus: *kuṭhi* 'a furnace for smelting iron ore, to smelt iron';*koṭe* 'forged (metal)(Santali)

r-anku, ranku = fornication, adultery (Telugu); rebus: *ranku* 'tin' (Santali) Alternative: *kamḍa, khamḍa* 'copulation' (Santali) Rebus: *kammaṭi* a coiner (Kanada) *kuṭi* 'pudendum muliebre'. *kuṭhi* 'smelter'.

kola 'woman'; rebus: kol 'iron'. kola 'blacksmith' (Kannada); kollë 'blacksmith' (Koḍ)
The glyphic elements shown on the tablet are: copulation, vagina, crocodile. h180 tablet.
Glyph: 'crocodile': karā 'crocodile'. Rebus: khar 'blacksmith'. kāru a wild crocodile or alligator (Telugu)Rebus: kāruvu 'artisan'
kuṭhi = pubes. kola 'foetus' [Glyph of a foetus emerging from *pudendum muliebre* on a Harappa tablet.] kuṭhi = the pubes (lower down than paṇḍe) (Santali)

Rebus: kuṭhi 'a furnace for smelting iron ore to smelt iron'; *kolheko kuṭhieda* koles smelt iron (Santali) kuṭhi, kuṭi (Or.; Sad. koṭhi) (1) the smelting furnace of the blacksmith; kuṭire bica duljad.ko talkena, they were feeding the furnace with ore; (2) the name of ēkuṭi has been given to the fire which, in lac factories, warms the water bath for softening the lac so that it can be spread into sheets; to make a smelting furnace; kuṭhi-o of a smelting furnace, to be made; the smelting furnace of the blacksmith is made of mud, cone-shaped, 2' 6" dia. At the base and 1' 6" at the top. The hole in the centre, into which the mixture of charcoal and iron ore is poured, is about 6" to 7" in dia. At the base it has two holes, a smaller one into which the nozzle of the bellow is inserted, as seen in fig. 1, and a larger one on the opposite side through which the molten iron flows out into a cavity (Mundari) kuṭhi = a factory; lil kuṭhi = an indigo factory (koṭhi - Hindi) (Santali.Bodding)

kuṭhi = an earthen furnace for smelting iron; make do., smelt iron; *kolheko do kuṭhi benaokate baliko dhukana*, the Kolhes build an earthen furnace and smelt iron-ore, blowing the bellows; tehen:ko kuṭhi yet kana, they are working (or building) the furnace to-day (H. koṭhī) (Santali. Bodding)

Text of epigraph from r.:

koḍi 'flag' (Tamil)(DEDR 2049). Rebus 1: *koḍ* 'workshop' (Kuwi) Rebus 2: *khōḍ* m. 'pit', *khōḍü* f. 'small pit' (Kashmiri. CDIAL 3947).

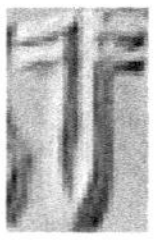

ranku 'antelope' Rebus: *ranku* 'tin.
'rim-of-jar' hieroglyph *kanka* (Santali) karṇika 'scribe'(Sanskrit)
Rebus: *karṇī,* supercargo for a boat shipment. *karṇīka* 'account (scribe)'.कारणी kāraṇī ' the supercargo of a ship' (Marathi) कर्णधार [karṇadhāra] *m* S (A holder of the ear.) A helmsman or steersman देशकुळकरणी [dēśakuḷakaraṇī] *m* An hereditary officer of a Mahál. He frames the general account from the accounts of the several Khots and Kulkarṇís of the villages within the Mahál; the district-accountant.

ranku 'liquid measure' Rebus: *ranku* 'tin'
kolmo 'paddy plant' Rebus: *kolami* 'smithy, forge'

Ligatured sign hieroglyph: 'rim-of-jar' PLUS 'water-carrier'

kanka 'rim of jar' Rebus: karṇīka 'account (scribe)' karṇī 'supercargo' कर्णधार [*karṇadhāra*] *m* S (A holder of the ear.) A helmsman or steersman. Thus, together, the ligatured hieroglyph reads: supercargo for a boat

Section B: Āraṭṭa आरट्ट

See:

http://bharatkalyan97.blogspot.in/2014/01/locating-aratta-with-archaeological.html

http://bharatkalyan97.blogspot.in/2014/01/aratta-as-lata.html

http://bharatkalyan97.blogspot.in/2014/01/the-most-vexed-problem-of-indian.html

Araṭṭa as Lāṭa

http://en.wikipedia.org/wiki/Talk%3AAratta A challenge to scholars and researchers to create a falsifiable hypothesis on the location of Araṭṭa

A breath-taking discovery in Khasi Hills reported on March 26, 2013 takes the Tin Road of Bronze Age from Khasi hills to Āraṭṭa आरट्ट and beyond into trade routes of the Ancient Near East and the Fertile Crescent.

Iron used in Pawel Orokop in Khasi hills 2000 years ago - Evidence of ancient smelting 'technology' found in Meghalaya

http://www.telegraphindia.com/1130326/jsp/frontpage/story_16715810.jsp#.U94kn4BdVB8

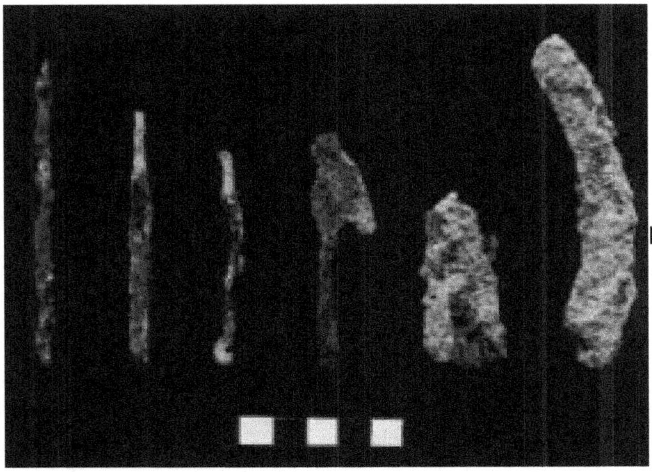

Iron artefacts, Malhar, Dist. Chandauli.

Iron smelter. Damaged circular clay furnace, comprising iron slag and tuyeres and other waste materials stuck with its body, exposed at lohsanwa mound, Period II, Malhar, Dist. Chandauli.Source: Tiwari, Rakesh, The origins of iron-working in India, ca. 1800 BCE.

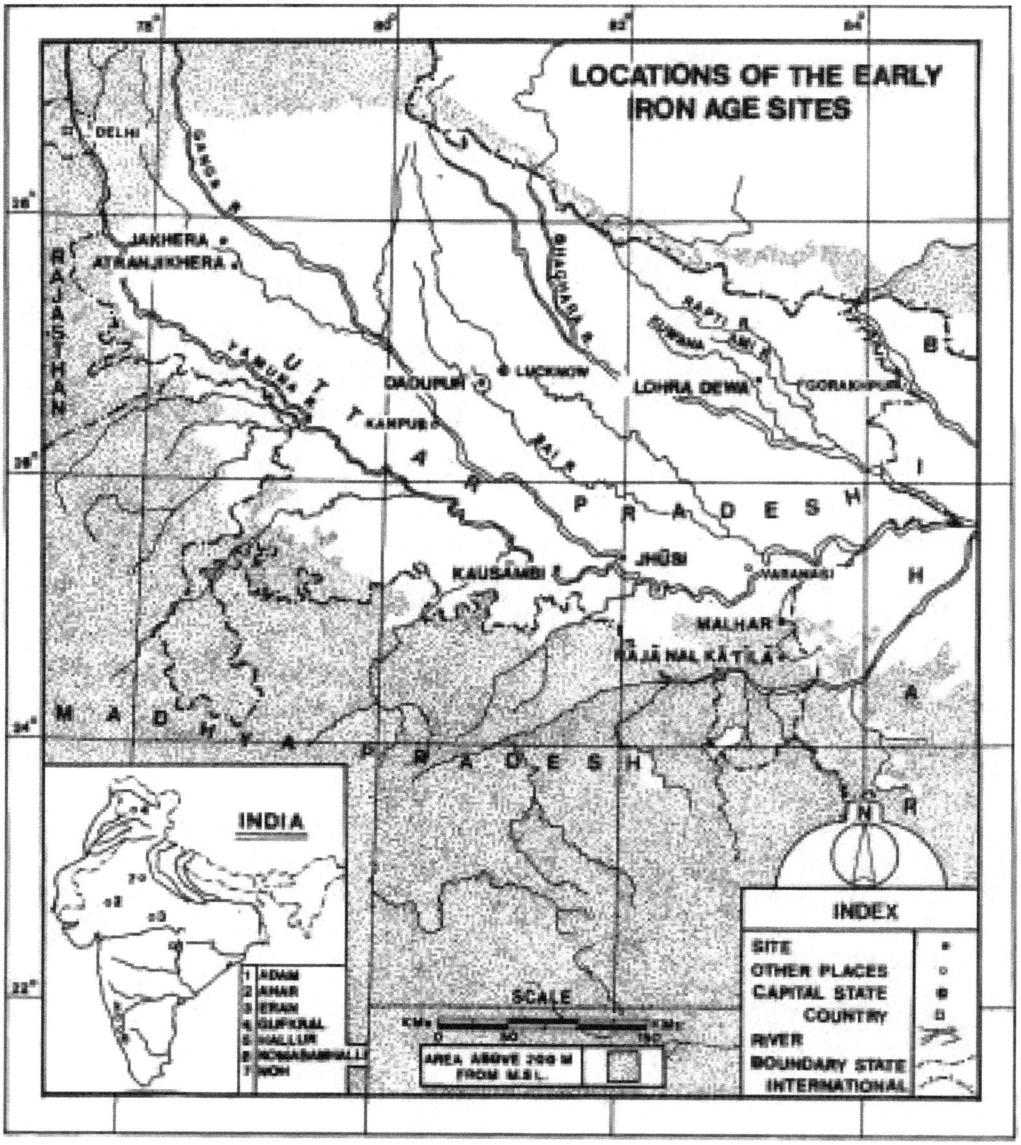

Map showing locations of the Early Iron Age sites in the Central Ganga Plain, the Eastern Vindhyas, and different regions of India.

http://archaeologyonline.net/artifacts/iron-ore

See Tiwari, Rakesh, RK Srivastava, KS Saraswat and KK Singh, 'Outcome of Malhar excavation: summary and discussion', *Pragdhara* 14, Directorate of Archaeology, Uttar Pradesh, pp. 185-200.

A possibility, in the context of Dholavira find of a two-sided bronze age seal, which uses Meluhha hieroglyphs to denote *dhokra kamar* lost-wax metal casters, is that Araṭṭa mentioned in cuneiform texts (Sumer) may refer to Lāṭa (cognate with Rāṭa following the phonetic changes of r~~l).

A region in the Rann of Kutch, bordering Baluchistan, with a number of archaeological sites such a Surkotada, Kanmer may constitute Araṭṭa as Lāṭa. Such an identification is consistent with cuneiform texts mentioning the mountains to cross before Enmerkar could reach Lugalbanda.

In Monier Williams Sanskrit dictionary आरट्ट *m. is defined in plural as* name of a people and country in पञ्च-नद or the Panjab (Mahabharata). In Sumerian texts it is described as full of gold, silver, lapis lazuli and other precious stones and materials, as well as artisans to work them. It was home to female diinity Inanna. Great Khorasan Road was renowned for gem trade from the Himalayas to Mesopotamia.

Hence, this is an addendum to the discussions on http://bharatkalyan97.blogspot.in/2014/01/aratta-as-meluhha-speech-area-re.html Araṭṭa as Meluhha speech area -- re-visiting Baudhāyana śrautasūtra evidence

The consecration (coronation) of Prince Vijaya, 543 BC – 505 BCE, or Sihor of Kathiawar, Gujarat (Detail from the Ajanta Mural of Cave No 17).

Āraṭṭa or *Arāṭṭa* may also link phonetically with Lāṭa mentioned in ancient Indian texts.

Rock Edicts of Ashoka found in Girnar, near Junagad in Saurashtra refer to: *Yona-Kamboja-*

Gandharam Ristika Petenikanam ye va pi amne Aparata... Could the reference to Ristika here a recollection of Marhashi, Marhaši (*Mar-ḫaši*[KI], *Marhashi*, *Marhasi*, *Parhasi*, *Barhasi*; in earlier sources Waraḫše) a 3rd millennium BCE polity situated east of Elam? An inscription attributed to Lugal-Anne-Mundu of Adab (albeit in much later copies) mentions it among the seven provinces of his empire, between the names of Elam and Gutium. This inscription also recorded that he confronted their governor (ensi), Migir-Enlil of Marhashi, who had led a coalition of 13 rebel chiefs against him.

Some Meluhha glosses:

.

खालट [khālaṭa] a Lowish or low--a country or tract: low, depressed, dumpy--a thing. खालाट [khālāṭa] n खालाटी or ठी f (खालीं & ठाय) The low country; the country as it descends from the foot of the Sayhádri-range towards the coast. Opp. to वलाठी. Applied also, in the Konkaṉ, to the land lying immediately along the coast, as वलाटी is to the land lying inwards and ascending towards the Gháṭs. 2 The name of the vowelmarks ु and ू; these occurring under the line of writing; as वेलाटी (from वलाटी or वर & ठाय) is the name of those occurring over it.

खालाटकर [khālāṭakara] c An inhabitant of खालाटी.
वलाट [valāṭa] n वलाटी or ठी f (वर & ठाय Upper-country.) The land as it rises from the coast towards the foot of the Sayhádri range. Opp. to खालाटी The descending country. 2 Applied in the Konkaṉ to the inward or eastern portion of this land, as खालाटी is to that bordering upon the sea.

वलाटकर [valāṭakara] c An inhabitant of वलाटी.
लाट [lāṭa] f A wave. 2 The cross piece of a बगाड (hook-swing); also of a machine for pounding lime, pohe &c. 3 The roller of an oilmill; also of a certain kind of sugarmill. 4 A beam or rail laid across and before the idol in an idol-house. 5 A roller for leveling ground. 6 The beam of a lime and pebble mill. 7 A large beam or piece of timber in general. लाट्या [lāṭyā] m C (लाटणें) A cylindrical roller or muller of a mortar. 2 Any mass (as of dough, earth &c.) so shaped. लाठ [lāṭha] f A contrivance (with three poles &c.) to draw water out of deep wells. लाठा [lāṭhā] m unc A rolling-pin.

लाड [lāḍa] m A caste or an individual of it. They sell betel-leaf, areca-nut, tobacco, bháng &c.

लाड [lāḍa] f (Commonly राड) The muck-pit in the festival of Shimgá.
राट [rāṭa] m R (Usually रहाट) A waterwheel &c. राड [rāḍa] a Foul, turbid, muddy--water &c.
रहाट [rahāṭa] m (H) A machine (composed of two wheels connected by a beam) for drawing water. 2 The wheel of a machine or an engine in general; as of the above contrivance for drawing water, of a spinning machine, a rope-machine &c.: also, by synecdoche, such machine.

रहाटगाडगें [rahāṭagāḍagēṃ] n A wheel with wreaths or a wreath of pots around it, erected over the mouth of a well to draw up water; the Persian waterwheel. 2 fig. The wheel of fortune; constant alternations or vicissitudes; succession of ups and downs, of good and evil; an alternation or reciprocal succession in general. 3 fig. Dealing or business with; a rotation or course of giving and receiving, receiving and giving.

रहाटणें [rahāṭaṇēṃ] v i (रहाट) To be much practised or exercised in; to be conversant with. 2 (Poetry.) To behave.

रहाटपाळणा [rahāṭapāḷaṇā] m The fabric of swinging boxes erected at fairs &c.; a revolving swing or cradle in general.

रहाटवड [rahāṭavaḍa] f C The materials required for, or the articles and items composing, a रहाट or waterwheel.

रहाटवणी [rahāṭavaṇī] n C (रहाट & पाणी) Water drawn up by a waterwheel; as disting. from that of a stream &c.

रहाटागर [rahāṭāgara] m n (रहाट & आगर) A plantation irrigated by means of a waterwheel.

रहाटी [rahāṭī] f (Dim. of रहाट) A waterwheel worked with the feet. 2 fig. Course, custom, established usage respecting. 3 (Poetry.) Behaviour, demeanour. 4 unc (राई) A dense wood or grove.

रहाट्या [rahāṭyā] a (रहाट) Employed or fit to be employed in working a waterwheel--a man or beast. 2 In games of play. A person that plays on both sides. 3 Applied to a vacillating person who espouses sometimes the one side and sometimes the other, a trimmer, turncoat, timeserver. 4 fig. A conductor or manager. 5 One serving (at weddings &c.) without remuneration. 6 A person pressed as a guide, carrier of burdens &c. from village to village; a carrier on of the रहाट (wheel or course of business).

araghaṭṭa m. ' wheel for raising water ' Pañcat., °aka- m. Pa. araghaṭṭa -- m., Pk. arahaṭṭa -- , rah° m.; K. arahaṭh, dat. °ṭas m. ' Persian wheel '; S. arṭu m. ' Persian wheel, spinning wheel '; L. aruṭṭ, araṭ m. ' Persian wheel ', mult. raṭṭ m. ' wheel of a well on which rope ladder and pots are hung '; P. cuharhṭā m. ' a well with four Persian wheels '; Ku. rahaṭ ' spindle '; N. rohoṭe piṅ ' a wheel on which seats are slung and used at fairs '; Or. araṭa ' spinning wheel ', Bi. rahṭā; Mth. rahaṭ, rā° ' wheel at the top of a well '; Aw. lakh. rãhaṭā ' spindle '; H. arhaṭ, rahaṭ, rẽṭ m. ' Persian wheel ', °ṭī f. ' small do. ', rahṭā m. ' Persian wheel, spinning wheel '; OG. arahaṭa m., G. rahẽṭ, re_ṭ, m. ' waterwheel ', re_ṭiyɔ, °ṭurɔ m. ' spinning wheel '; M. rahāṭ, rāṭ ' Persian wheel '. -- Poss. X halá -- : S. halaṭru m. ' Persian wheel with bullocks and apparatus included ', P. halhaṭ m. ' Persian wheel '.S.kcch. araṭ m. ' spinning wheel '. (CDIAL 596).

मराठा [marāṭhā] a (महाराष्ट्र S The great territory.) Relating to the Maráṭhá country. 2 Relating to the Maráṭhá people; but with some distinctiveness or speciality. Applied to the Kuṇbí it contradistinguishes him from the Bráhman and the high castes on the one hand, and from the Parwárí and all outcastes on the other. मराठा, as likewise the term राजा or राव, is arrogated to themselves by many who claim descent from the (extinct) Kshatriya or Military tribe, and who wear accordingly the जानवें or characteristic thread. Such, although they eat with the common Kuṇbi, esteem themselves higher and scruple at intermarriage.

gurjararāṣṭra ' kingdom of the Gurjaras '. [gur- jará -- , rāṣṭrá --] B. gujrāṭ. 4211 *gurjaratrā ' country of the Gurjaras '. [gurjará --]Pk. gujjarattā -- f., H. gujarāt m., G. gujrāt f. 4210 gurjará m. ' name of a people ' Pañcat.Pk. gujjara -- m.; K. gujoru, °juru m. ' pastoral wandering tribe ' (lw. with j); P. gujjar m. ' a caste of milkmen '; H. gūjar m. ' inferior caste of Rajputs '; OMarw. gujarī f. ' a Gūjar woman '; OG. gūjaraḍī f. ' a woman of Gujarat ', G. gujrī f.; M. gūjar m. ' an inhabitant of Gujarat ', °rḍā m. (contemptuous), Ko. gujaru. (CDIAL 4213)

mahārāṣṭra n. ' kingdom ' MW., m. ' name of a people ' MārkP., °ṭraka -- , °ṭrīya -- adj., °ṭrī -- f. ' their language '. [mahā -- , rāṣṭrá --]
Pk. marahaṭṭha -- m., inscr. mahāraṭhi; N. marāṭhi ' of or belonging to the Marāṭhās, the Marāṭhī language '; H. marhaṭṭā m. ' a Marāṭhā '; G. marāṭhɔ m., marāṭhī ' the language '; M. marāṭhā m., marāṭhī adj., f. ' the language '; Si. maharaṭa ' the land of the Marāṭhās '. (CDIAL 9952)

rāḍhā f. ' district in West Bengal ' Kathās., °ḍha -- m. ' belonging to this district ' [MIA. < rāṣṭrá -- ??] Pk. rāḍhā -- f. ' name of a district ', B. rāṛ(h), Or. rāṛha, H. rāṛh m.
rāḍhīya -- .rāḍhīya ' belonging to Rāḍhā ' Prab.com. [rāḍhā --] (CDIAL 10698, 10699)

Raṭṭha (nt.) [Vedic rāṣṭra] reign, kingdom, empire; country, realm Sn 46 (expld at Nd2 536 as "raṭṭhañ ca janapadañ ca koṭṭhāgārañ ca . . . nagarañ ca"), 287, 444, 619; J iv 389 (°ŋ araṭṭhaŋ karoti); PvA 19 (°ŋ kāreti to reign, govern). Pabbata° mountain -- kingdom SnA 26; Magadha° the kingdom of Magadha PvA 67. -- vāsin inhabitant of the realm, subject DhA iii.481 Raṭṭhaka (adj.) [Sk. rāṣṭraka] belonging to the kingdom, royal, sovereign J iv.91 (senāvāhana). Raṭṭhika [fr. raṭṭha, cp. Sk. rāṣṭrika] 1. one belonging to a kingdom, subject in general, inhabitant J ii.241 (brāhmaṇa gahapati -- r. -- do ārik' ādayo). -- 2. an official of the kingdom [op Sk. rāṣṭriya a pretender; also king's brother in -- law] A iii.76=300 (r. pettanika senāya senāpatika).(Pali)

súrāṣṭra ' having good dominion ' TS., m. ' a country in the west of India ' MBh. [su -- 2, rāṣṭrá --] (CDIAL 13504) Pk. suraṭṭha -- n. ' name of a country '. saurāṣṭra ' coming from Surāṣṭra ', m. pl. ' its people ' VarBr̥S., n. ' a partic. metre ' Col. [súrāṣṭra --] (CDIAL 13621)
G. M. soraṭh m. ' a district in Kathiawar '; -- Pk. sōraṭṭha -- n. ' a partic. metre '; S. soraṭhi f. ' a partic. musical mode ', P. soraṭh f.; N. soraṭh ' a Gurung song and dance"; H. soraṭh f. ' a partic. musical mode ', G. M. soraṭh m. (M. also f.); -- P. H. sorṭhā m. ' a partic. metre ', OMarw. soraṭho m. rāṣṭrá n. ' kingdom, country ' RV., ' people ' Mn. [√rāj2]Pa. Pk. raṭṭha -- n. ' kingdom, country '; Ku. rāṭh ' faction, clan, separate division of a joint -- family group '; Si. raṭa ' country, district ', Md. ra ' (abl. rañuṅ). - rāṣṭrín ' possessing a kingdom ' ŚBr., rāṣṭrika -- m. ' governor ' Hariv. [rāṣṭrá --] Pa. raṭṭhika -- m. ' governor ', Pk. raṭṭhiya -- m., OSi. raṭiya. -- L. P. rāṭh
N. rāṛi ' blanket '; B. rāṛi ' belonging to Rāṛh '; Or. rāṛhi ' native of West Bengal, a class of fisherman '; H. rāṛhī ' coming from Rāṛh '.(CDIAL 10724, 10721)

From: Fleet, John F. Corpus Inscriptionum Indicarum: Inscriptions of the Early Guptas. Vol. III. Calcutta: Government of India, Central Publications Branch, 1888, 84-88, we have a discussion on Mandasor Inscription of Kumaragupta and Bandhuvarman. This refers to the district of lāṭa http://www.sdstate.edu/projectsouthasia/upload/Mandasor-of-Kumara.pdf A Sun-temple was built at the city of Das'apura (Mandasor) under the rule of Bandhuvarman (436 CE) by a guild of silk-weavers who were immigrants from lāṭa vishaya which is described as adorned with shrines of gods (devakula), halls of temples (devasabha), viharas, prasada-mala and vimana-mala.

Lāṭa is the ancient name of Southern or Central Gujarāt and ancient Konkan-- perhaps the region between the rivers Mahi and lower Tapti. or between rivers Mahi and Kim (Broach). Dipavamsa (p.54) refers to Simhapura (Sihapura) as the capital of Lāṭa. Ptolemy refers to Lārike [Rāṣṭrika, Lāṭika (Prakrit)]along the sea-coast, east of Indo-Sythia. Baroda copper plate inscription refers to the capital of Lāṭes'vara as Elapur. the legend of Vijaya and his followers may be in Singhapur (Simhapura or Singur), in the Lala Rattha (Lāṭa Rāṣṭra) (Mahavamsa VI.34). The Sanskrit phrase, Apara-Malava-Pashcimena Lata-desa is a reference to this region. Al Biruni refers (Al Biruni's India, p. 205) to it as Lardesh to the extreme hilly west of Bengal where Hooghly district and modern Singur is located. There is however an epic reference to one Sinhapura kingdom with little historical proof, located on the upper Indus which shared borders with Ursa, Abhisara, Bahlika, Darada and Kamboja. (Mahabharata: 2.27.18-22).

It was thought by some early historians that the Republican Gramaneyas of Sabhaparva of Mahabharata[18] may have been the ancestors of the Sinhalese.[19] The original home of the Gramaneyas seems to have been the Sinhapura of Gandhara/Kamboja, but the people shifted to lower Indus and then, after defeat by Pandava Nakula, to Saurashtra Peninsula, centuries prior to common era. There they seem to have founded a principality in Saurashtra Peninsula, centuries prior to common era which they named Sinhapura probably to commemorate their past connections with Sinhapura of Gandhara/Kamboja (According to Dr Hema Chandra Ray, K. M. De Silva et al. also, there is an evidence that the Kambojas who inhabited a region bordering upper Indus, had at one time established themselves in a country near Sindh. The authors have also furnished references to this Southward migration of the Kambojas to a country near Sind (See: History of Ceylon, 1959, p. 93, Hem Chandra Ray, K. M. De Silva, Simon Gregory Perera. Cunningham mentions 'Hingur' as an ancient place name located 40 miles East from the apex of Indus Delta (Ancient Geography of India, map facing p. 248, A Cunningham). The Delta of Indus is still known as Lar and the Sinhapura of Sinhalese traditions was also located somewhere in this region. Scholars say that 'Hingur' could well be a corrupted version of Sinhapura (Ancient Kamboja, People and the Country, 1981, p. 351, Dr J. L. Kamboj).]
http://en.wikipedia.org/wiki/Prince_Vijaya

Prof. TP Verma's paper on Āraṭṭa आरट्ट (this also refers to Prof. BB Lal's identification as Ararat mountain):

http://www.scribd.com/doc/202260732/Aratta-in-Literature-TP-Verma-Hindi

Locating Araṭṭa with archaeological evidence and philological argument http://bharatkalyan97.blogspot.in/2014/01/aratta-as-lata.html Araṭṭa as Lāṭa The following notes provide further evidence and arguments to support the identification of Araṭṭa as Lāṭa (ancient Gujarat). The location of Araṭṭa has baffled many researchers who have located the region in a wide area ranging from Armenia (Ararat or Urartu mountain) to Afghanistan (as the source of lapis lazuli stone).

To make some progress in resolving the problem of locating Araṭṭa, some archaeological evidences are presented.

Chanhu-daro, Dholavira, Tin road

Evidence for Chanhu-daro as the Sheffield of ancient India and Dholavira as the port-town with trade links which could have extended through the Persian Gulf and through Mari to the Fertile Crescent (evidenced by the finds of cire perdue arsenic-bronze artifacts at Nahal Mishmar) and the Tin road through Assur and Kanish (Anatolia) (evidenced by over 20,000 merchants' letters found on cuneiform tablets), it is becoming clear that -- together with tin ore and the technique of lost-wax metal casting -- gold and precious stones came from Afghanistan and Gujarat (evidenced by the Queen Pu-abi tomb finds.

If Gandhara was Afghanistan, Araṭṭa also mentioned in *Baudhāyana śrautasūtra* was Gujarat (Rann of Kutch or northern part of Lāṭa).

Pu-abi had the title "nin" or "eresh", a Sumerian word which can denote a queen or a priestess.)

Puabi's 25 pieces of jewellery constituting the diadem and other ornaments from the Royal Cemetery of Ur in Mesopotamia discovered by Leonard Woolley.

Puabi or Shab'ad "The Sumerian princess": Jewelry and headdress of gold and imported precious stones such as carnelian and lapis lazuli from India and Afghanistan. From the Royal Cemetery of Ur. Early Dynastic, ca. 2400 BC. The National Museum of Iraq - Baghdad.

The headdress of gold, lapis lazuli, and carnelian includes a frontlet with beads and pendant gold rings, two wreaths of poplar leaves, a wreath of willow leaves and inlaid rosettes, and a string of lapis lazuli beads, discovered on Queen Puabi's body in her tomb at the Royal Cemetery of Ur, ca 2550 BCE. The rosette is safflower hieroglyph read rebus in Meluhha: करडी [karaḍī] f (See करडई) 'safflower' (Prakrit) Rebus: करडा [karaḍā] ' Hard from alloy--iron, silver &c.' (Marathi) [Note: अकीक [akīka] m (A) A cornelian (Marathi). वैडूर्य [vaiḍūrya] n (Properly वैदूर्य S) A turquois or lapis lazuli.] The hieroglyph safflower was chosen because it also denoted the fire-god करडी [karaḍī] (Remo)

Polished beads found in the tomb of Queen Puabi

Carnelian beads of Puabi could not have come from Afghanistan.

Middle Assyrian, Ashur, wall painting fragments of Palace of Tukulti Ninurta

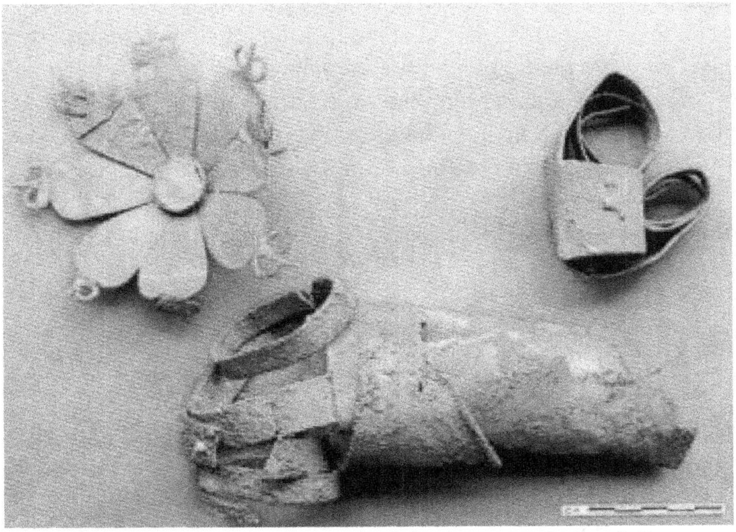

Kunal, silver ornaments. Safflower-shaped hieroglyph is shown on the top left.

Enmerkar's campaign to Aratta

Enmerkar was the ruler and builder of Uruk in Sumer, according to Sumerian king list. A legend is called *Enmerkar and the Lord of Aratta* composed ca. 21st century BCE. The king of Aratta is unnamed.

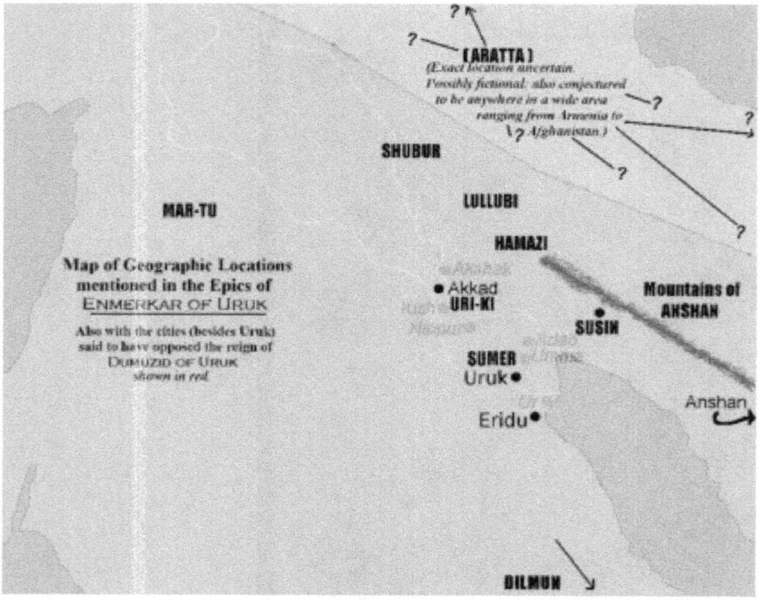

Places mentioned in the Enmerkar Epics

Enmerkar sends an envoy along with his specific threats to destroy Aratta if Aratta does not pay him the tributes, highlighting that Enmerkar was reared on the soil of Aratta. The king of Aratta replies that submission to Uruk is out of the question, because Inanna herself had chosen him to his office. The envoy responds that Inanna has been installed as queen at *E-ana* and has even promised Enmerkar to make Aratta bow to Uruk. Enmerkar actually sends the barley to Aratta as demanded by the king of Aratta, along with the herald and makes another demand to send even more precious stones.

What more information is needed to locate Aratta? Aratta was a region which could supply precious stones.

Gujarat was well known as the repository of the carnelian precious stones. It was also a trade entrepot handling lapis lazuli acquired from Gandhara (Afghanistan).

"The lord of Aratta, in a fit of pride, refuses and instead asks Enmerkar to deliver to him these precious stones himself. Upon hearing this, Enmerkar spends ten years preparing an ornate sceptre, then sends it to Aratta with his messenger. This frightens the lord of Aratta, who now sees that Inanna has indeed forsaken him, but he instead proposes to arrange a one-on-one combat between two champions of the two cities, to determine the outcome of the still-diplomatic conflict with Enmerkar. The king of Uruk responds by accepting this challenge, while increasing his demands for the people of Aratta to make a significant offering for the *E-*

ana and the *abzu*, or face destruction and dispersal. To relieve the herald who, beleaguered, can no longer remember all the messages with which he is charged, Enmerkar then resorts to an invention: writing on tablets. The herald again traverses the "seven mountains" to Aratta, with the tablets, and when the king of Aratta tries to read the message, Ishkur, the storm-god, causes a great rain to produce wild wheat and chickpeas that are then brought to the king. Seeing this, the king declares that Inanna has not forsaken the primacy of Aratta after all, and summons his champion." http://en.wikipedia.org/wiki/Enmerkar_and_the_Lord_of_Aratta

Arguing for locating Aratta in Iran, Samuel Noah Kramer notes:"A problem arises, however, in trying to locate Aratta in relation to Anshan. Is it to be sought north of Anshan in the direction of Lake Urmia and the Caspian Sea, or to the east in the direction of Bauchistan and India, or to the south in the direction of Laristan and the Persian Gulf? Once again, it is a Sumerian epic tale which may give us the answer. This poem, which may be entitled 'Lugalbanda and Mount Hurum', remained largely unintelligible until 1955, when a large six-column tablet from the Hilprecht Collection of the Friedrich-Schiller University in Jena became availale; it tells the following story. Enmerkar, the lord of Erech, has decided to journey to Aratta in order to make it a vassal state. Accompanied by a vast host of Erechites under the command of seven unnamed heroes and Lugalbanda, who, to quote the words of the poem, 'was their eight', he arrives at Mount Hurum. Then and there Lugalbanda falls ill. His brothers and friends do all they can to revive him, but to no avail. Taking for dead, they decide that they will leave his corpse on Mount Hurum, proceed on their journey to Aratta, and on their return from the campaign, pick up his body and carry it back to Erech. But Lugalbanda is not dead. Abandoned and forsaken, he prays to the gods of the sun, moon, ad the Venus star, and they restore his health. He wanders all over the highland steppe, ad there we must leave him for the present, since our available texts break off at this point. It is clear from this poem that Mount Hurum was situated between Erech and Aratta, and since it is not unreasonable to assume that Mount Hurum was the original home of the Hurrian people from the neighborhood of Lake Van, we may conclude that Aratta lay in the vicinity of Lake Urmia or perhaps even farther east."(Kramer, Samual N., *The Sumerians*, p.275) http://people.ucls.uchicago.edu/~cjuriss/ModernWorld/Documents/Jurisson-UNIT-2-Kramer-The-Sumerians-Legacy.pdf

Ancient names of the region of Gujarat (which supplied carnelian stones)

Lāṭa or Lāḍa (cf. Biddhasālabhanjikā) was the ancient name of Gujarat and the northern Konkan (Marco Polo, Vol. II, p. 302n.). The name is also mentioned in Vātsyāyana's *Kāmasūtra*. Dhauli inscription calls it Lāthikā. Girnar inscription of Asoka calls it Rāsthikā (Risthika).

Lāḍa is cognate with Rāḍha of Bengal. (Mahavamsa). The link of Rāḍha with Lāḍa may also be seen in the narrative that Prince Sihabahu had left his maternal grand father's kingdom in *Vanga* and founded Sihapura in Lata Rashtra. (Mahavamsa 6.34).

Lāṭa was also called Ollā.(Rajasekhara's Viddhasalābhanjikā, Acts II and IV). Ollā is a phonetic variant of Ballabhi or Balabhi (now called Wallay or Walā).

The region south of Mahi or Narmada upto river Purva (or as far as Daman) was called Lāṭa and 'it corresponded roughly with southern Gujarat'. (cf.Gauuda P., ch. 55; Dowson's Classical Dictionary of Hindu mythology; Dr. Bhandarkar's Hist. of the Dekkan, see XI, p 42).

According to Prof. Buhler, Lāṭa is central Gujarat, the district between Mahi and Kim rivers and its chief city was Broach. (cf. Additional notes. It-sing's Records of the Buddhist religion by Takakusu, p. 217; Alberuni's India, I, p. 205).

Copper plate inscription found at Baroda names Lāṭeyvara to be Elapur (v. II) also with the genealogy of the kings of Lāṭesvara (JASB, vol. VIII, 1839, p. 292).

Lāṭa has been identified with Central and Southern Gujarat in the Rewah stone inscription of Karna.

Lāṭarāṣṭra or Lāṭaviṣaya had the capital city of Sihapura according to Dipavamsa. Upon the death of Sihabahu of Sinhapura (*Lala Rattha = Lata Rashtra = Latadesa = Gujarat*), his son Summita became king of Lata. He married a Madra princess by whom he had three sons. (Mahavamsa, Trans Geiger, p 62.)

Śaktisangam Tantra locates Lāṭa to the west of Avanti and to the northwest of Vidarbha.

The appearance of the terms *Rathika*, *Ristika* (*Rashtrika*) or *Lathika* in conjunction with the terms *Kambhoja* and *Gandhara* in some Ashokan inscriptions of 2nd century BCE from Mansera and Shahbazgarhi in North Western Frontier Province (present day Pakistan), Girnar (Saurashtra) and Dhavali (Kalinga) and the use of the epithet "Ratta" in many later inscriptions has prompted a claim that the earliest Rashtrakutas (ca. 6$^{tth\text{-}7th}$ centuries) were descendants of the *Arattas*, natives of the Punjab region from the time of Mahabharata, who later migrated south and set up kingdoms there. (Hultzsch in Reu 1933, p2). The term "Ratta" is implied in *Maharatta* ruling families from modern Maharashtra region.(Altekar, 1934, pp. 20-21).

"Uttarakāṇḍa of the Rāmāyaṇa Ch. 100,verse10) refers to Vāhīka who were also known as Jarttikā (Jāt?) and Araṭṭa (Araṭṭa were the Arattai of the *Periplus of the Erythrean Sea*, p. 41) and that their capital was Śākala (Sialkot). Another portion of the same passage suggests that in the Araṭṭa countries religion was in disrepute; it was thus an impure region, and the Aryans of mid-India were forbidden to go there. This is also reflected in the Vārttikā of Pāṇini by Kātyāyana who derives the word Vāhīka from 'vahi' or 'bahi' meaning 'outside', -- suggesting those who were outside the pale of Aryandom. According to Pāṇiniand his scholiast Patañjali, Vāhīka was another name for the Punjab (IV, 2, 117; V, 3,114; Ind. Ant., I, 122)."(Law, Bimala Churn, 1943, *Tribes in Ancient India*, Poona, Meharchand Munshiram). This points to the possibility that Araṭṭa people of *Baudhāyana śrautasūtra* migrated further southwards from the Punjab, just as Uttaramādra migrated beyond the Himalayas.

Jean Przylusky notes that Bahlika (Balkh) was an Iranian settlement of the Madras who were known as Bahlika-Uttaramadras. (An Ancient People of Panjab, The Udumbras, *Journal Asiatique*, 1926, p 11).

Note: Jarttikā (Jāt?) and Araṭṭa as Vāhīka could relate to the eastern and south-western location of the people in present-day as Jāt in Rajasthan and as Araṭṭa (Gurjara) in Gujarat.

Indian *sprachbund* or linguistic argument for Araṭṭa as Lāṭa

In the course of a search for the cipher for Meluhha hieroglyphs (aka Indus script), it has been noted that Meluhha (Mleccha) was the *lingua franca*, the proto-Prakrit vernacular, as distinct from Sanskrit which was a literary version of speech.

There is a philological rule in Indian sprachbund: "ralayorabhedaH"

(This means that there is abheda meaning there is maitri 'friendship' between

"ra" and "la") in pronunciation of words.

Mleccha (Meluhha) would frequently interchange *r-* and *l-* sounds as evidenced in the name of Lāṭa which could also be pronounced as Rāṭa, a derivation from rāṣṭra (Sanskrit).

The following are variants of the Sanskrit gloss: rāṣṭrá n. ' kingdom, country ' RV., ' people ' Mn. Pa. Pk. *raṭṭha* -- n. ' kingdom, country '; Ku. *rāṭh* ' faction, clan, separate division of a joint -- family group '; Si. *raṭa* ' country, district ', Md. *ra* ' (abl. *rařuṅ*). -- See rāḍhā (CDIAL 10721). rāṣṭrakūṭa m. ' name of a people ' inscr. (orig. or by pop. etym. 'head of the kingdom'). S. *rāṭhoṛu* m. ' a caste of Rajputs, bold hardy man '; H. *rāṭhaur* m. ' a tribe of Rajputs (a caste name) ', G. *rāṭhɔṛ* m. -- Poss. hypochoristic in L. *rāṭh* m. ' title of Jats, Gujjars, and Ḍogras, cruel hardhearted man '; P. *rāṭh* m. ' gentleman, noble -- hearted fellow ' rather than < rāṣṭrín (CDIAL 10722). 10724 rāṣṭrín ' possessing a kingdom ' ŚBr., *rāṣṭrika* -- m. ' governor ' Hariv. Pa. *raṭṭhika* -- m. ' governor ', Pk. *raṭṭhiya* -- m., OSi. *raṭiya.* -- L. P. *rāṭh* see rāṣṭrakūṭa (CDIAL 10724).

The Pali, Prakrit form *raṭṭha* is instructive and means a region ruled by a ruler. A region without such a ruler, say, a janapada could have been called *a-raṭṭha* or *Araṭṭa.*

It is not mere coincidence that the following etyma occur and could perhaps be related to the products produced in (like the bead necklace of Puabi in Ur): K. *lar* f. ' string of necklace '; L. *laṛī* f. ' strand of cord ', mult. *laṛ* m., P. *laṛī* f.; Ku. *laṛ* ' garland, string ', *laṛo* ' cord ', *laṛi* ' garland, string of beads '; N. *lari, lariyā* ' skein of cotton removed after spinning '; Mth. *lar* ' strand of rope '; OAw. *laṛī* f. ' string of pearls ', H. *laṛ, laṛī* f., OMarw. *laṛa* f., M. *laḍ, laḍī* f.(CDIAL 10921). *lāḍ* m. ' act of caressing ', *lāḍo* m. ' bride- groom ', *lāḍī* f. ' bride ', *lāḍak* m. ' best man '.(CDIAL 11012).

Considering that Lāṭa consistently refers to Gujarat region in many early epigraphs, it is reasonable to assume that some areas of the region which did not have a ruler and was a *janapada* (trans. republic) -- at some point of time as we traverse the mists of the past -- could have been called *Araṭṭa.*

The horse argument for locating Araṭṭa

Smt. Jayasree Saranathan has provided me the following guidance:

I think Aratta lies to west of river Indus and is known for horse breeding. Please refer Mahabharata sources where Aratta horses were mentioned to have been used in wars. Aratta was also known for irreligious and matriarchal culture. A place with a combination of all these - breeding of war-horses, matriarchy and unchaste women - to be the location of Aratta which was ruled by Sindhu kings in Mahabharata times. I am even tempted to connect it to Susa. I am giving below the Mahabharata sources.

Mbh.6.86.4544	Disregarding those arrows, the impetuous Vrikodara, with heart filled with rage, slew in that battle all the steeds, born in Aratta, of the king of the Sindhus.
Mbh.6.91.4754	And smiling the while, several warriors on thy side, with a large number of steeds consisting of the best of the Kamvoja breed as also of those born in the country of the Rivers, and of those belonging to Aratta and Mahi and Sindhu, and of those of Vanayu also that were white in hue, and lastly those of hilly countries, surrounded the Pandava army
Mbh.7.23.1157	Mighty steeds of gigantic size, of the Aratta breed, bore the mighty-armed Vrihanta of red eyes mounted on his golden car, that prince, viz, who, rejecting the opinions of all the Bharatas, hath singly, from his reverence for Yudhishthira.
Mbh.7.191.10590	Kritavarman, O king, also fled away, borne by his swift steeds, and surrounded by the remnant of his Bhoja, Kalinga, Aratta, and Valhika troops.
Mbh.8.45.2428	In former days a chaste woman was abducted by robbers hailing from Aratta.

In ancient texts, there are references to both Araṭṭa horses and Saindhava horses. It should be noted that Rann of Kutch is on the mouth of Sindhu and Sarasvati rivers.

Not far from Dholavira is a site called Surkotada. Surkotada site contains horse remains dated to ca. 2000 BCE, which is considered a significant observation with respect to Indus Valley Civilisation. Sándor Bökönyi (1997), on examining the bone samples found at Surkotada, opined that at least six samples probably belonged to true horse.During 1974, Archeological Survey of India undertook excavation in this site and J.P.Joshi and A.K.Sharma reported findings of horse bones at all levels (cira 2100-1700 BCE).

Sources:
Bökönyi, Sándor (1997), "Horse remains from the prehistoric site of Surkotada, Kutch, late 3rd millennium B.C.", *South Asian Studies* 13 (1): 297

Singh, Upinder (2008). A history of ancient and early medieval India: from the stone age to the 12th century: New Delhi: Pearson Education. p. 158. Jump up
Cf. Meadow, R. H. and Patel, 1997.
Jump upArcheological Survey of India. Indian Archeology 1974-75.
Jump upEdwin Bryant, Edwin Fransic Bryant. The Quest for Origins of Vedic Culture:The Indo Aryan Migration Debate. Oxford University Press. 2001 Page 171.http://en.wikipedia.org/wiki/Surkotada#Horse_remains

MBh also locates Araṭṭas in the region where 5 rivers + Sindhu flow: There where forests of Pilus stand, and those five rivers flow, viz, the Satadru, the Vipasa, the Iravati, the Candrabhaga, and the Vitasa and which have the Sindhu for their sixth, there in those regions removed from the Himavat, are the countries called by the name of the Arattas. (Mbh.8.44.2385)

[quote] Written byThe Editors of Encyclopædia Britannica
Last Updated April 11, 2014

Enmerkar, ancient Sumerian hero and king of Uruk (Erech), a city-state in southern Mesopotamia, who is thought to have lived at the end of the 4th or beginning of the 3rd millennium BC. Along withLugalbanda and Gilgamesh, Enmerkar is one of the three most significant figures in the surviving Sumerian epics.

Although scholars once assumed that there was only one epic relating Enmerkar's subjugation of a rival city, Aratta, it is now believed that two separate epics tell this tale. One is called *Enmerkar and the Lord of Aratta*. The longest Sumerian epic yet discovered, it is the source of important information about the history and culture of the Sumero-Iranian border area. According to this legend, Enmerkar, son of the sun god Utu, was envious of Aratta's wealth of metal and stone, which he needed in order to build various shrines, especially a temple for the god Enki in Eridu. Enmerkar therefore requested his sister, the goddess Inanna, to aid him in acquiring material and manpower from Aratta; she agreed and advised him to send a threatening message to the lord of Aratta. The lord of Aratta, however, demanded that Enmerkar first deliver large amounts of grain to him. Though Enmerkar complied, the lord of Aratta refused to complete his part of the agreement; threatening messages were again sent out by both men, each claiming the aid and sanction of the goddess Inanna. The text becomes fragmented at that point in the narrative, but in the end Enmerkar was apparently victorious.

The other epic relating the defeat of Aratta is known as *Enmerkar and Ensuhkeshdanna* In this tale the ruler of Aratta, Ensuhkeshdanna (or Ensukushsiranna), demanded that Enmerkar become his vassal. Enmerkar refused and, declaring himself the favourite of the gods, commanded Ensuhkeshdanna to submit to him. Although the members of Ensuhkeshdanna's council advised him to comply with Enmerkar, he listened instead to a local priest, who promised to make Uruk subject to Aratta. When the priest arrived in Uruk, however, he was outwitted and killed by a wise old woman, Sagburru, and the two sons of the goddess Nidaba. After he learned the fate of his priest, Ensuhkeshdanna's will was broken and he yielded to Enmerkar's demands.

A third epic, *Lugalbanda and Enmerkar*, tells of the heroic journey to Aratta made by Lugalbanda in the service of Enmerkar. According to the epic, Uruk was under attack by Semitic nomads. In order to save his domain, Enmerkar required the aid of Inanna, who was in Aratta. Enmerkar requested volunteers to go to Inanna, but only Lugalbanda would agree to undertake the dangerous mission. The epic concerns the events of Lugalbanda's journey and the message given him from Inanna for Enmerkar. Although obscure, Inanna's reply seems to indicate that Enmerkar was to make special water vessels and was also to catch strange fish from a certain river. [unquote]
http://www.britannica.com/EBchecked/topic/188536/Enmerkar#ref66187

Written byThe Editors of Encyclopædia Britannica

Ensuhkeshdanna, also spelled Ensukushsiranna, legendary ruler of the ancient Sumerian city-state of Araṭṭa and rival of the king of Uruk (Erech), Enmerkar.

http://www.britannica.com/EBchecked/topic/188757/Ensuhkeshdanna#ref152568

Enmerkar and the Lord of Āraṭṭa आरट्ट

Source (for translation): Black, J.A., Cunningham, G., Robson, E., and Zólyomi, G., The Electronic Text Corpus of Sumerian Literature, Oxford 1998-.

Standard of Ur. British Museum.

Peace panel

War panel

"This object was found in one of the largest graves in the Royal Cemetery at Ur, lying in the corner of a chamber above the right shoulder of a man. Its original function is not yet understood." Leonard Woolley, the excavator at Ur, imagined that it was carried on a pole as a standard, hence its common name. Another theory suggests that it formed the soundbox of a musical instrument.

When found, the original wooden frame for the mosaic of shell, red limestone and lapis lazuli had decayed, and the two main panels had been crushed together by the weight of the soil. The bitumen acting as glue had disintegrated and the end panels were broken. As a result, the present restoration is only a best guess as to how it originally appeared.

The main panels are known as 'War' and 'Peace'. 'War' shows one of the earliest representations of a Sumerian army. Chariots, each pulled by four donkeys, trample enemies; infantry with cloaks carry spears; enemy soldiers are killed with axes, others are paraded naked and presented to the king who holds a spear.

The 'Peace' panel depicts animals, fish and other goods brought in procession to a banquet. Seated figures, wearing woollen fleeces or fringed skirts, drink to the accompaniment of a musician playing a lyre. Banquet scenes such as this are common on cylinder seals of the period, such as on the seal of the 'Queen' Pu-abi, also in the British Museum."

References

C.L. Woolley and P.R.S. Moorey, *Ur of the Chaldees*, revised edition (Ithaca, New York, Cornell University Press, 1982)

D. Collon, *Ancient Near Eastern art* (London, The British Museum Press, 1995)

M. Roaf, *Cultural atlas of Mesopotamia* (New York, 1990)

See this object in our Collection database online

Further reading

J. Aruz, *Art of the First Cities: The Third Millennium B.C. from the Mediterranean to the Indus* (New York, 2003)
D. Collon, *Ancient Near Eastern Art* (London, 1995)
H. Crawford, *Sumer and Sumerians* (Cambridge, 2004)
N. Postgate, *Early Mesopotamia: Society and Economy at the Dawn of History.* (London, 1994)
N. Yoffee, *Myths of the Archaic State: Evolution of the Earliest Cities, States, and Civilization* (Cambridge, 2005)
R. Zettler, and L. Horne, (eds.) *Treasures from the Royal Tomb at Ur* (Philadelphia, 1998)

http://www.britishmuseum.org/explore/highlights/highlight_image.aspx?image=12_standardur.jpg&retpage=19094

See: http://www.gatewaystobabylon.com/myths/texts/classic/enmerkaratta.htm

Go vernacular to resolved the vexed problem of locating and identifying people involved with the roots of Hindu civilization

Let us focus on one segment of the Ur standard Peace panel top row rightmost hieroglyph showing a lyre or harp played on by a person accompanied by a woman: The hieroglyph denotes read Meluhha rebus, *tam(b)ra* 'copper'.

The harp or lyre compares with a Uruk frieze:

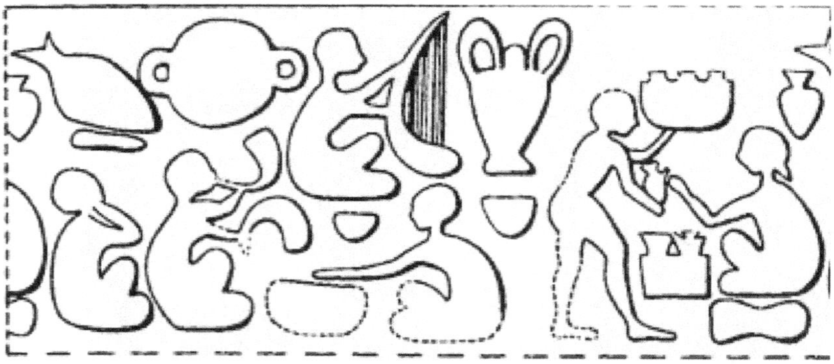

Protoliterate orchestra seal impression from Chogha Mish http://oi.uchicago.edu/pdf/oip101_text.pdf

Hieroglyph: *tambura* 'harp'; rebus: *tambra* 'copper'.
http://bharatkalyan97.blogspot.com/2014/04/meluhha-metallurgy-to-bronze-age.html

Lyre-player, from one of the steles of king Gudea Hieroglyph: *tambura* 'harp'; Rebus: tam(b)ra 'copper' (Santali)

m73a *खोंड [khōṇḍa] m A young bull, a bullcalf. (Marathi) Rebus: kõdār 'turner' (Bengali); कोंद kōnda 'engraver, lapidary setting or infixing gems' (Marathi) G. sãghāṛɔ m. 'lathe' ; संघाट joinery; M. sãgaḍ 'double-canoe' Rebus: sangataras 'stone-cutter, mason'*

tambur 'lyre' Rebus: *tāmra* 'copper' (Sanskrit) *tamba* id. (Santali)
kāṇḍa 'arrow' (Sanskrit) Rebus:*khāṇḍa* 'tools, pots and pans, metal-ware'. Rebus 2: kaṇḍ 'fire-altar' (Santali)

 khareḍo = a currycomb (Gujarati) Rebus: kharādī ' turner'

"The Tambur (spelled in keeping with TDK conventions) is a fretted string instrument of Turkey and the former lands of the Ottoman Empire. Like the ney, the armudi (lit. pear-shaped) kemence and the kudum, it constitutes one of the four instruments of the basic quartet of Turkish classical musicTurkish classical aka *Türk Sanat Müziği* (lit. Turkish Artistic Music). Of the two variants, one is played with a plectrum (*mızraplı tambur*) and the other with a bow (*yaylı tambur*). The player is called a *tamburî*.... There are several hypotheses as to the origin of the instrument. One suggests that it descended from the kopuz, a string instrument still in use among the Turkic peoples of Central Asia and the Caspian region... The name itself derives from the *tanbur*(tunbur). Tanbur in turn might have descended from the Sumerian *pantur*. The name (and its variants such as *tamboura*, *dombura*) also denotes a wide spectrum of pear-shaped string instruments in Persia and Central Asia yet these share only their names with the Ottoman court instrument and in fact are more akin to bağlamas or sazes. In ancient Hittite texts, we come across a string instrument called *tibula*,[2] which is most likely to have been the ancestor of the Ottoman court instrument via Byzantine*tambouras*. This latter hypothesis could also account for the favor the instrument received in the Ottoman court vis-à-vis its rival, the oud. As of the 17th century, the tanbur had already taken its present form and structure and assumed the preponderant role it still holds in Classical Turkish Music performance."

Turkish tambur on the left.

Bulgarian tambura.

http://en.wikipedia.org/wiki/Turkish_tambur

"Theterm *Tanbur*, *Tanbūr*, *Tanbura*, *Tambur*, *Tambura* or *Tanboor* (Persian: تنبور) can refer to various long-necked, string instrument originating in Southern or Central Asia .[1]According to the *New Grove Dictionary of Music and Musicians*, "terminology presents a complicated situation. Nowadays the term tanbur (or tambur) is applied to a variety of distinct and related long-necked string instruments used in art and folk traditions in Afghanistan, Pakistan, Turkey, Tajikestan, Kazakhstan, Uzbekistan... Tanburs have been present in Mesopotamia since the Akkadian era, or the third millenniumBCE." http://en.wikipedia.org/wiki/Tanbur Sources: Scheherezade Qassim Hassan, R. Conway Morris, John Baily, Jean During. "Tanbūr", *The New Grov Dictionary of Music and Musicians*, ed. S. Sadie and J. Tyrrell (London: Macmillan, 2001), xxv, pp. 61-62.

"Three figurines have been found in Susa that belong to 1500 BCE, and in hands of one of them is a tanbur-like instrument." "تنبور (ای تمبور/ طنبور)". Encyclopaedia Islamica. Retrieved March 3, 2013. Tanbur is cognate with Arabic *tunbur*(طنبور), long-necked lute.

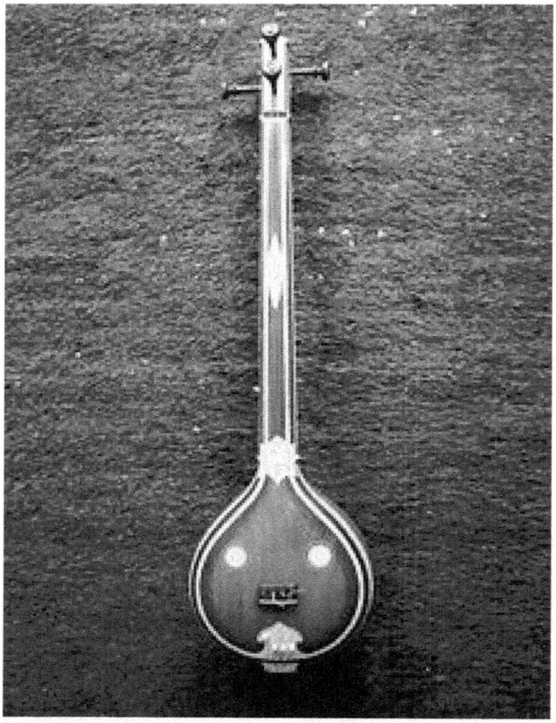

Carnatic style Tanjore tambura.

See:

http://bharatkalyan97.blogspot.in/2014/01/the-most-vexed-problem-of-indian.html The most vexed problem of civilization studies: identifying people. Archaeologists, go vernacular.

After referring to the contributions made by many scholars to Harappan civilization (1921-2013), RS Bisht makes a passing mention that it as also known as Indus-Sarasvati civilization.

This is in Dr. YD Sharma Memorial Lectue delivered at Kokata on 31 August 2013 (Published in Puratattva 2013) which concludes after 18 pages: "Finally, comes up the most vexed problem of the identification of the people who built the Harappan civilization. In this case also diametrically opposite views are held by the scholars. Efforts have been made to identify with the Dravidians, the Proto-Elamites, the Mundas, the Aryans or even to a lost tribe. In this connection it is most pertinent to refer to the detailed anthropological studies carried out by a group of experts led by Hemphill, who hold that there are only two breaks in the anthropological records in the northwestern Indian subcontinent -- one occurs around 4500

BCE, in the beginning of the Chalcolithic era and the second around c. 800 BCE that falls in the Iron Age. The controversy will remain alive until and until the Harappan script is deciphered." (p.25)

The anthropological argument mentioned by Bisht is in the following citation:

Brian E. Hemphill, Alexander F. Christensen & S. I. Mustafakulov, “Trade or Travel: An Assessment of Interpopulational Dynamics among Bronze Age Indo-Iranian Populations,” *South Asian Archaeology*, 1995, ed. Raymond Allchin & Bridget Allchin (New Delhi: Oxford & IBH Publishing, 1997), vol. 2, pp. 855-871.

Hemphill's observation was that there was no trace of “demographic disruption” in the North-West of the subcontinent between 4500 and 800 BCE.

When this 'demographic' observation negated the possibility of any massive intrusion, of non-Harappans into India, why should there be a 'vexed' problem identifying Indians while evaluating the archaeological efforts of 92 years between 1992 to 2013?

I wish Bisht had paused and deliberated on this identity problem a bit more to indicate pointers which could resolve the 'vexed' problem instead of merely using the non-decipherment of Indus writing as the crutch?

Michel Danino hopes that genetics will help resolve the problem of identity. Genetics may not help if one starts with the problematic assumption that the language and culture somehow follow the same set of evolutionary rules.

Semantics of language are cultural indicators. Replacing anthropological construct of 'demographic disruption', one can postulate continuity of cultural practices and using cultural indicators to affirm that there was no 'cultural' disruption between 4500 BCE and 800 BCE.

This may be one approach to resolve the 'vexed' Indian identity problem in Indian civilization studies.

Indeed, it is commonsense to study culture for effective civilization studies not to have any vexatious theories prejudging identity of people in the civilization continuum.

One tool for studying culture is language but more important is the discipline of semantics -- as distinct from study of phonetics or syntax. Mere glossary won't help but the glosses have to be explained with 'meaning' as the meaning evolved over time in socio-cultural interactions.

Semantics as the study of meaning postulates relation between *signifiers*, like words, phrases, signs, and symbols, and what they stand for, their denotation (translation of a sign to its literal meaning). Denotation should be contrasted with connotation, which translates a sign to meanings associated with it.

Let us take some examples signifiers.

Signifier 1

The cultural practice of wearing characteristic marking *sindhur* (red vermilion mark) on the forehead or parting of the hair is a signifier of an Indian woman.

We have to terracotta figurines of Nausharo which show such signifiers.

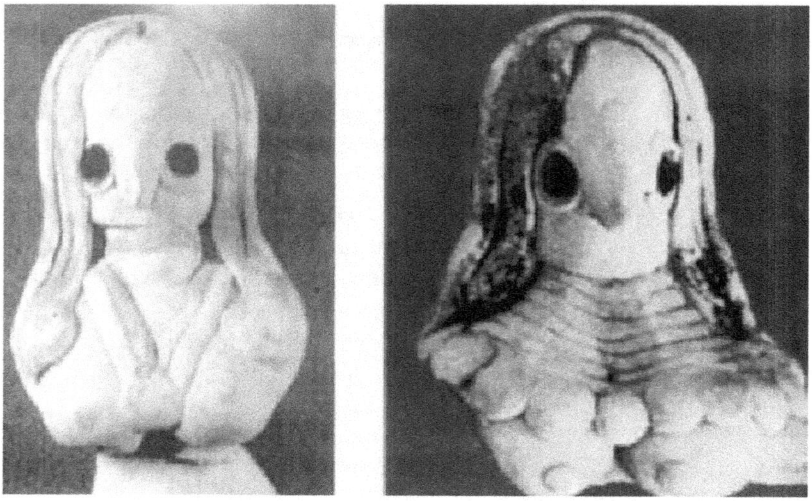

Nausharo: female figurines. Wearing sindhur at the parting of the hair. Hair painted black, ornaments golden and sindhur red. Period 1B, 2800 – 2600 BCE. 11.6 x 30.9 cm.[After Fig. 2.19, Kenoyer, 1998].

Don't these two figurines provide a signifier which identifies Indians, say between 4500 BCE to 800 BCE on the assumption that this practice of wearing sindhur (red vermilion) continues even into the present times?

Signifier 2

The cultural practice of venerating linga, a polished pillar-like stone is a signifier of Indians from 4500 BCE to the present day.

Two decorated bases and a lingam, Mohenjodaro.
Lingam, grey sandstone in situ, Harappa, Trench Ai, Mound F, Pl. X (c) (After Vats). "In an earthenware jar, No. 12414, recovered from Mound F, Trench IV, Square I
Terracotta sivalinga, Kalibangan.

Trefoil or three dotted circles on the pedestal of the linga stone and also decorated on the shawl of the priest statue of Mohenjodaro can be explained as a Meluhha hieroglyph composition:

toluvè hole (Tulu); toḷ (toṭp-, toṭṭ-) to perforate, bore with an instrument (Tamil)(DEDR 3528) Rebus: toṟu (-v-, -t-) to worship, adore, pay homage to; toṟukai worshipping, adoration, prayer (Tamil)tuṟil salutation, obeisance, bow (Kannada)(DEDR 3525). S. *dūlahu* m. ' a fine person ' ← P. *dūlā* m. ' brave man ' (CDIAL 6446) Three: kolom 'three' Rebus: kolami 'smithy, forge'. Smithy is a temple: kole.l 'smithy' Rebus: kole.l 'temple.

Thus, the deployment of the 'three perforated hole' hieroglyphs as a trefoil is to pay homage, to worship in adoration. This Meluhha linguistic explanation is consistent with the obeisance to linga as a representation of divinity in the Hindu civilization area.

The 'hole' hiereoglyph is exemplified in the narratives of 'dotted circles' decorating Persian Gulf seals such as the following: Dilmun seal from Barbar; six heads of antelope radiating from a circle; similar to animal protomes in Failaka, Anatolia and Indus. Obverse of the seal shows four dotted circles. [Poul Kjaerum, The Dilmun Seals as evidence of long distance relations in the early second millennium BC, pp. 269-277.] A tree is shown on this Dilmun seal. The ligatured six heads of 'antelopes' are shown around the center-piece: leafless tree.

meḍho a ram, a sheep (Gujarati)(CDIAL 10120) Rebus: *mẽṛhẽt, meḍ* 'iron' (Mu.Ho.)
āra 'six' Rebus: *āra* 'brass'

khōṇḍa A stock or stump (Marathi); 'leafless tree' (Marathi). Rebus: *kõdār* 'turner' (Bengali); *kõdā* 'to turn in a lathe' (Bengali).

See also: Glyph: 'tree': *kuṭi* 'tree'. Rebus: *kuṭhi* 'smelter furnace' (Santali). Thus, the message denotes: smelter furnace turner iron and brass: *kuṭhi kõdār āra meḍ* The seal thus connotes: smithy-forge with turned metal artifacts (from) PLUS smelter iron, brass of heavy weight: *kaṇḍi* 'hole' Rebus: 20 maunds or 500 lbs.

Back of proto-Dilmun style seal from Saar (2622:05; dia. 1.9 cm.) Three lines across the back of the seal:

kolom 'three' Rebus: *kolami* 'smithy, forge'. Dotted circles shown on a 'standard device' in the round, in an ivory piece from Mohenjo-daro pointing to the beads with drilled holes drilled (as 'dotted circles' on the bottom crucible or portable furnace) using a gimlet of a lathe: *sãghāṛɔ* m. 'lathe' (Gujarati). *kaṇḍi, kiṇḍi, gaṇḍi* chink, hole (Kannada); a Meluhha homonym denotes a bead: Pa. kandi (pl.-l) necklace, beads. Ga. (Punjabi) kandi (pl.-l) bead, (pl.) necklace; (S.2) kandiṭ bead. (DEDR 1215)

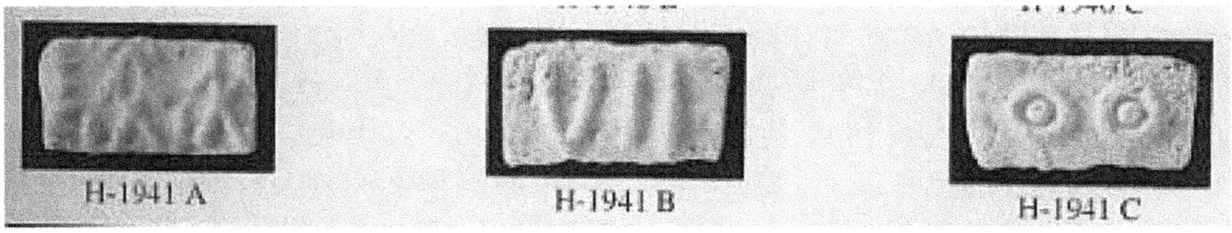

h1941A

Side A:

meḍ 'body' Rebus: *meḍ* 'iron' (Ho.) काठी [kāṭhī] *f* (काष्ट S) 'frame or structure of the body' (Marathi) Rebus: खंडी [khaṇḍī] measure of weight (Marathi) *கண்டி; kaṇṭi, n. < Mhr. khaṇḍil. [T. Tu. khaṇḍi, M. kaṇḍi.]* Candy, a weight, stated to be roughly equivalent to 500 lbs.

aya aḍaren (homonym: aduru)'alloy native metal'

khareḍo = a currycomb (Gujarati) खरारा [*kharārā*] *m* (H) A currycomb. 2 Currying a horse. (Marathi) Rebus: करडा [*karaḍā*] Hard from alloy--iron, silver &c. (Marathi) *kharādī* ' turner' (Gujarati)

Side B: *baṭa* = rimless pot (Kannada) Rebus:) *baṭa* = a kind of iron (G.)) *bhaṭa* furnace (Gujarati) dula 'two' Rebus: dul 'cast metal' dulo 'hole' Rebus: dul 'cast metal'

Side C: dula 'two' Rebus: dul 'cast metal' dulo 'hole' Rebus: dul 'cast metal' Thus metal castings.

h1936A

Side A: *khaṇḍ* 'field, division' (Sanskrit) Rebus: *khāṇḍa* 'tools, pots and pans, metal-ware'. Rebus 2: kaṇḍ 'fire-altar' (Santali) dula 'two' Rebus: dul 'cast metal.

meḍ 'body' Rebus: *meḍ* 'iron' (Ho.) काठी [kāṭhī] *f* (काष्ट S) 'frame or structure of the body' (Marathi) Rebus: खंडी [khaṇḍī] measure of weight (Marathi) *கண்டி; kaṇṭi, n. < Mhr. khaṇḍil. [T. Tu. khaṇḍi, M. kaṇḍi.]* Candy, a weight, stated to be roughly equivalent to 500 lbs. *baṭa* = rimless pot (Kannada) Rebus:) *baṭa* = a kind of iron (G.)) *bhaṭa* furnace (Gujarati) dula 'two' Rebus: dul 'cast metal' dulo 'hole' Rebus: dul 'cast metal'

Side C: three: kolom 'three' Rebus: kolami 'smithy, forge'PLUS dulo 'hole' Rebus: dul 'cast metal' Thus metal smithy castings.

h1721A :

dula 'hole'(Ku.N.); M. *ḍuḷū* n. ' little hole ', *ḍolā* m. (CDIAL 6452) *Ta.* toḷ (toṭp-, toṭṭ-) to perforate, bore with an instrument; toḷkal perforating; toḷku excavation, pit; toḷḷal hole; toḷḷai hole, perforation, pit, anything tubular, fault, defect; toḷai (-pp-, -tt-) to perforate, bore; *n.* hole; tuḷai (-pp-, -tt-) to make a hole, bore, drill, punch, pierce as with an arrow; *n.* hole, orifice, aperture, perforation, hollow as of a tube, bamboo, gateway, passage, flaw in a diamond; tuḷavai hole; tōḷ (tōṭp-, tōṭṭ-) to perforate, bore through, dig out, scoop; *n.* hole; toṇṭi hole. *Ma.* toḷḷa hole, cavity; tuḷa hole, bored hole; tuḷayuka to be perforated; tuḷekka to perforate, pierce, bore. *Ko.* toyḷ- (toḷc-) to

pierce; toyḷ hole in pen-post; toḷ hole, vagina; teḷi·(g)hole in wall between two houses (for handing through fire, etc.). *To.* tüḷy gate-post of pen with holes for bars; tüḷy- (tüḷc-) to make hole in stone or tree. *Ka.* toḷe hole, bored hole; toḷḷe hollow, hole, cavity, deficit, debt; ṭoḷḷe hollow, cavity; ṭoḷḷu, toḷḷu state of being hollow, void, or empty within; toli hole, socket. *Tu.* toluvè hole;tolpuni, doḷpuni to prick; toḷu hole; empty; ḍoḷḷu, ṭoḷḷu, toḷḷè void, hollow. *Te.* toli, tolika hole; tol(u)cu to bore, perforate, hollow, dig, scoop, carve; doṇḍi hole; (K.)dol(u)cu to make a hole; ḍolla hollow, concave. *Go.* (Tr.) tullānā to be bored, pierced; *caus.* tulhuttānā; (Mu.) tullih- to scrape out or bore out the pulp of a gourd (*Voc.* 1762)(DEDR 3528)
Rebus: *dul* 'cast metal'. This rebus reading explains the uniquely inscribed 'dotted circle' on the 'standard device', that is, a lathe/gimlet and on Indus script artifacts with Indus script, treating the 'dotted circle as a hieroglyph to denote: tuḷa hole, bored hole (Malayalam) Rebus: *dul* 'cast metal'.
ayo ḍhālako 'alloy metal ingot'
kanac 'corner' Rebus: *kañcu* 'bronze'

Signifier 3

A tre-foil is a signifier of some 'importance', something or someone venerated (say, an ancestor)

The trefoil signifiers appears in the civilization in the following examples:

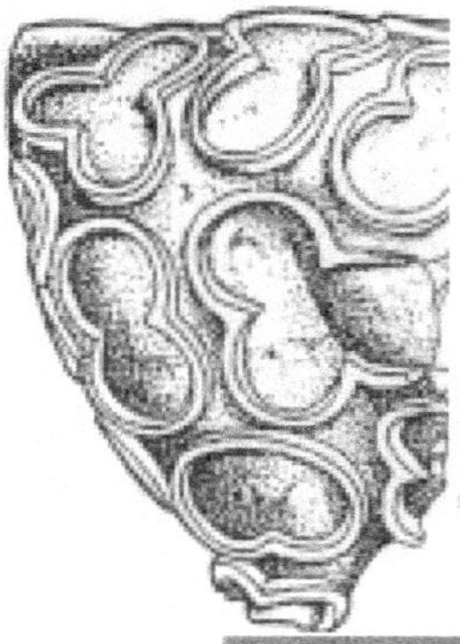

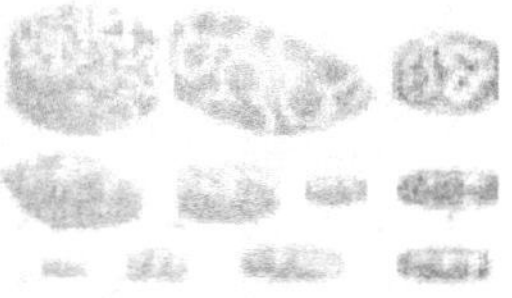

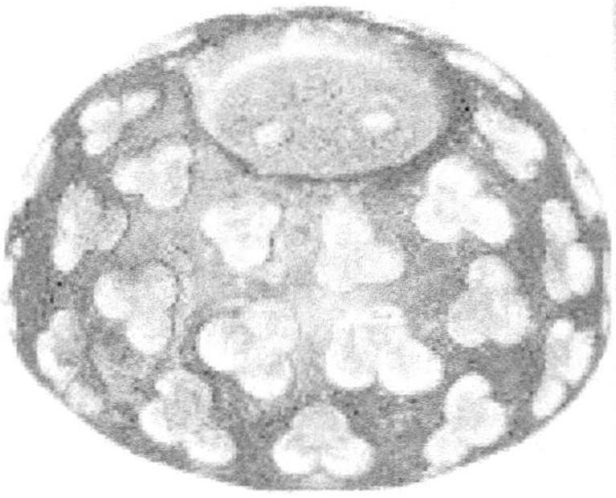

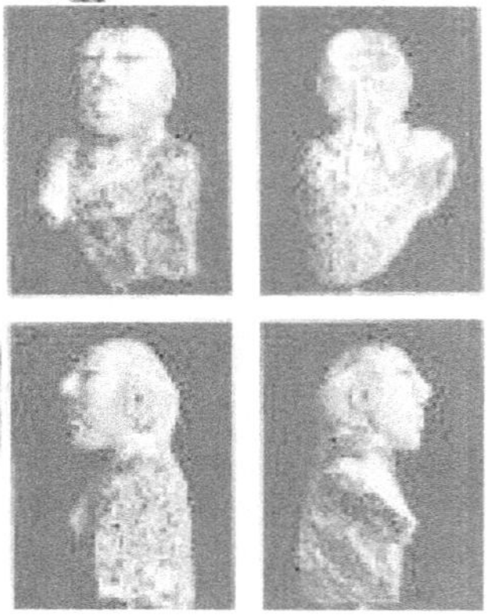

Statue, Uruk (W.16017), c. 3000 B.C.; bull with trefoil inlays; shell mass with inlays of lapis lazuli; 5.3 cm. long; Vorderasiatisches Museum, Berlin; Parpola, 1994, p. 213.

Steatite statue fragment; Mohenjodaro (Sd 767); trefoil-decorated bull; traces of red pigment remain inside the trefoils. After Ardeleanu-Jansen 1989: 196, fig. 1; Parpola, 1994, p. 213.

Trefoils painted on steatite beads, Harappa (After Vats, Pl. CXXXIII, Fig.2)

Trefoil inlay decorated base (for linga icon?); smoothed, polished pedestal of dark red stone; National Museum of Pakistan, Karachi; After Mackay 1938: I, 411; II, pl. 107:35; Parpola, 1994, p. 218.

Statue (DK 1909), Mohenjodaro; four views; white steatite, with remnants of red paint inside the trefoils of the robe; height 17 cm.; National Museum of Pakistan, Karachi; After Marshall 1931a:pl.98; Parpola, 1994, p. 212.

What word in spoken language, was used to denote this signifier? Would it be not be a reasonable and useful exercise to trace such signifiers in the Indian *sprachbund*, on the assumption that the present-day words (from one or more languages of the Indians) contain such signifiers with the same denotation which was in vogue in the early days of the civilization?

History is all around us. Civilization continuum is a living reality. Why should we still treat it as a 'vexed' problem when we can look for signifiers in the archaeological record or even in the anthropological record, to identify Indians in the Indian civilization?

One wonders why the identity problem is looked upon as an intractable problem. The problem can be resolved, if only we look for signifiers -- like the three examples cited above -- which are already available instead of hoping for some new or high-tech genetic markers which may create more problems than they can really resolve.

What gloss connoted a trefoil in Indian *sprachbund*?

I find a word in Malayalam and Vedic which may provide the word as a signifier which matches with trefoil as a 'symbol'.

These examples may provide signifiers of cloth, of someone of importance, or young animal as may be seen from these artifacts displaying the trefoil.

These artifacts evoke the following glosses from Indian *sprachbund* with literal meanings of 'trefoil' signifiers:

Glosses (words and semantics):

पोतृ pōtṛ " Purifier " , Name of one of the 16 officiating priests at a sacrifice (the assistant of the

Brahman (Rigveda)

போற்றி pōṟṟi , < id. *n.* 1. Praise, applause, commendation; புகழ்மொழி. (W.) 2.Brahman temple-priest of Malabar; கோயிற் பூசைசெய்யும் மலையாளநாட்டுப் பிராமணன். (W.) 3. See போத்தி, 1.--*int.* Exclamation of praise; துதிச்சொல்வகை. பொய்தீர் காட்சிப் புரையோய் போற்றி (சிலப். 13, 92).

potṛ. pōtrá ' *cleaning instrument ' (' the Potṛ's soma vessel ' RV.). [√pū]
Bi. *pot* ' jeweller's polishing stone '

பொத்தல் pottal , *n.* < id. [K. *poṭṭare*, M. *pottu*, Tu. *potre.*] 1. Hole, orifice.

pṓta, *pōtalaka, pōtalikā* young animal, heifer; *pōāla* -- m. ' child, bull
potṛā m. ' baby clothes '*potrẽ* n. ' rag for smearing cowdung '. pōta ' covering (?) ' RV., ' rough hempen cloth ' AV *pusta* --2 n. ' working in clay ' (prob. ← Drav., Tam. *pūcu* &c. Pkt. *potta* -- , *°taga* -- , *°tia* -- n. ' cotton cloth ' செம்பொத்தி cem-potti, n. prob. id. +. A kind of cloth.

Te. poṭṭi, poṭṭiya scorpion;
Tu. poṭṭè tender ear of corn; *Pa.* poṭ grain in embryonic stage.
Ta. poṭṭu chaff
Ta. poṭṭu drop, spot, round mark worn on forehead. *Ma.* poṭṭu, poṟṟu a circular mark on the forehead, mostly red. *Ka.* boṭṭu, baṭṭu drop, mark on the forehead. *Koḍ.* boṭṭï round mark worn on the forehead. *Tu.* boṭṭa a spot, mark, a drop; (B-K.) buṭṭe a dot. *Te.* boṭṭu a drop, the sectarian mark worn on the forehead. *Kol.* (SR.) boṭla drop. *Pa.* boṭ id. *Ga.* (Punjabi)boṭu drop, spot. *Konḍa* boṭu drop of water, mark on forehead. *Kuwi* (F.) būttū, (Isr.) buṭu tattoo.

Rebus readings:

pōta ' boat '

H. *pot* m. ' glass bead ', G. M. *pot* f.; -- Bi. *pot* ' jeweller's polishing stone '; Pk. *pottī* -- f. ' glass '; S. *pūti* f. ' glass bead ', P. *pot* f.; N. *pote* ' long straight bar of jewelry '; B. *pot* ' glass bead ', *puti, pũti* ' small bead '; Or. *puti* ' necklace of small glass beads '

Discussion

While it may be debated if a 'temple priest' of the civilization was called *pōṟṟi* as the gloss is used today in Malayalam, or *pōtṛ* as the gloss is used today in the performance of a vedic *yajña*, there seems to be a substantial semantic evidence to relate to the other characteristics of the artifacts deploying the trefoil symbol: cloth, young animal.

Both symbols -- cloth and young animal -- have *pottu* as word signifiers. If *pōṟṟi* or *pottu* is the word signifier, there is a rebus reading possible: *pot* 'boat' or pot 'bead' or *pote* 'long straight bar of jewelry'.

We seem to be looking at trefoil as a hieroglyph read rebus.

1. Shown *pota* 'cloth' worn as a shawl by the important person, the trefoil hieroglyph can be read rebus as the homonymous word: *pōtṛ* 'temple priest'.

2. Shown on *pota* 'young animal or heifer', or on beads, the trefoil hieroglyph can be read either as *pot*'boat' or *pote* 'long straight bar of jewelry or bead'.

These three examples of signifiers have thus provided a framework for resolving the 'vexed' problem of identity.

A conclusion is drawn by rebus readings of hieroglyphs deployed on about 7000 inscribed objects, over an extensive area along the Persian Gulf and along the Tin Road into the Fertile Crescent.

The conclusion is that Meluhha was the spoken idiom the people who denotated these Meluhha hieroglyphs and their rebus readings, almost all in the context of lapidary or smithy or forge. A corollary conclusion is that the Meluhhans were from the Indian *sprachbund.*

The substantive road traveled is the cultural continuum of Indian civilization. Hence, we do not have to find alternative excuses of substitutes such as Harappan or Indus civilization. If locus has to be a signifier the civilization can be called Sindhu-Sarasvati civilization without any hesitation because the civilization lives on not only on these river basins but has left traces which can be found even today in many parts of Eurasia --signifiers such as Tocharian *ancu* 'iron' or Vedic *amśu* 'soma'; Kota language *kole.l* as signifier word for 'smithy' as well as 'temple'.

Would it be ok to venture a suggestion that the problem of identity calls for special efforts on the part of archaeologists to attempt to use the vernacular words to signify artifacts such as pots and pans discovered in the digs, instead of using ONLY English words as signifiers?

Go vernacular, is the lesson to resolve the 'vexed' problem.

“At the present time, the archaeological evidence is not sufficient to identify with certainty the residential city of the Lord of Aratta...In place of a legendary land of Aratta, we can visualize a specific area and begin to see the interaction of Sumerian and early Iranian civilizations in the finds from excavated sites. Aratta is emerging from the shadows.” Yousef Majidzadeh *Journal of Near Eastern Studies* Vol. 35, No. 2 (Apr., 1976), pp. 105-113

Evidence from ancient Tamil texts

Thanks to Jayasree Saranathan for the following excerpts from http://jayasreesaranathan.blogspot.com/2014_01_01_archive.html Identifying Harappan people - inputs from Mahabharata and Silappadhikaram [quote] Given below is a note by Dr S.Kalyanaraman on the need to take into account the cultural symbols and Indian sprachbund in the analysis of Harappan sites that can be aptly called as Indus- Saraswathi civilization. He points out the Nausharo images with sindhur on the forehead, stones resembling linga and trefoil in the Indus images as some of the items to prove the cultural identity of the Harappan people as Vedic.

On my part I wish to point out in brief that Harappan culture was indeed the post-Mahabharata culture that saw the growth of trade after Pandavas wrested control from Kauravas over Gandhara, - the main route to central Asia - which was the maternal country of the Kauravas. This connection of Kauravas to Gandhara justifies the overt interest that their maternal uncle, Shakuni had in wiping out Pandavas from the political scene of that time. This also justifies why the entire Bharat including southerner Pandyas chose to fight on the side of Pandavas and Krishna though Sarangadwaja (the Pandyan king who fought on the side of Pandavas) had a personal grouse against Krishna.

The Indus - saraswathi settlements were a necessity of time as Arabian sea engulfed Dwaraka forcing the people to look for newer places to settle, after their protector Krisha exited from the world. Their previous abode in the Gangetic plain from where they left (18 clans according to Mahabharata) along with Krishna to escape trouble from Jarasandha was the last one in their mind for a place to live. Mahabharata tells that Arjuna guided them out of Dwaraka and settled them. Where were they settled is the question. Going towards Ganges was ruled out and the only option was to go north or north west of Dwaraka / Kutch. The route explained in Mahabharata precisely puts them in the now known Indus - Saraswathi region that includes Dwaraka bound Gujarat too. The details can be read at http://jayasreesaranathan.blogspot.in/2010/07/ivc-was-post-mahabharata-culture-world.html

Now coming to the issue of the so-called scripts on the Indus seals, any analysis without taking into account the local or indigenous inputs can't give correct results. I wish to point out that there is reference at two places in Silappadhikaram on the bundles or trade goods that are stamped with seals that bear "KaNNEzhutthu"(கண்ணெழுத்து) - meaning, " letters by the eyes" which are signs or symbols that indicate the nature of goods, the trader etc which can be easily understood just by looking at it.

In one place this is being told in the context of goods that had reached Pumpukar. Another reference is to the goods sent by Satakarni (Gauthami putra Satakarni of the 1st century AD) to the Cheran king. These goods contained the wealth and goods of North India and bore Kannezhutthu - the letters by the eye... The verses clearly indicate what the seals convey. They being sent by Satakarni containing the wealth of North India do imply that they had been sent from Indus regions. The detailed article on this is written in Tamil in my Tamil blog. Read it here: http://thamizhan-thiravidana.blogspot.in/2012/10/109-ogham_4138.html
When we have cross-referential inputs like this from within India, it is matter of waste of time to look elsewhere or differently to decipher the Indus seals. [unquote]

Comments of Come Carpentier (Private communication, July 2014):

"The ancient battlefield and the modern town are named after the clan of the Kurus to which the leaders of the two camps in the war belonged. It was a fratricidal struggle within the most prominent royal clan in Northern India. According to the oldest annals, the Kurus came from the mountains in the North (*kuru* means mountain and has become *gora*in slav languages and *oros* in greek) and married by tradition women from the kingdoms of Madra and Gandhara, both now in Pakistan. They had apparently mingled their blood with the ancient Puru and Pancala tribes, indigenous to the Saraswati region while retaining the memory of their origins in the northern land of the blessed in Uttarakuru, beyond the Hindu Kush in Central Asia. They may have been "Indo-Aryan" Tokharians from the area which is now populated by various Turkic tribes, between the Pamir range, Kazakhstan and the Tien Shan range that Roman geographers including Pliny call Ottorokorai. The Rig Veda sings the victorious campaign of King Mandhata who conquered the "four great islands" in the North and returned with a large following of Uttarakurus long before the era of the two great epics. It seems that those were the ancestors of the Kauravas who struck an alliance with their victors and eventually succeeded them. The part of Jambudvipa or India where they settled became known as Kururastra and it may not be a coincidence that the Sumerians said they came from Kura Aratta, a highland lying behind seven mountain ranges to the North East. The Mahabharata is not the only text which indicates that in that area of Bactria and Transoxiana also lived a tribe made up or at least ruled by warrior women.

The *Strirajya* (women's kingdom) appears to be the cradle of the Amazons who rode into Asia Minor centuries later and were, according to the Greeks an Indo-Iranian speaking people. According to those diverse but generally convergent stories, the Kurus were a vedic matrilineal polygamous and polyandric clan related to the neighbouring Bahlikas, Kambojas, Daradas and Rishikas and descended from Prajapati Karddama and his son Ila. The Ili river in the region of the Uighur still bears the trace of that name and the peaks of the Pamir may have been the Meru of Vedic mythology. However even before some moved to India, the Tocharian Kurus, probably related to the so-called Andronovo culture, appear to have been kinsmen of the Puru-Bharatas and other *panca janas* of India and were therefore not invading Aryans. Indeed had they not created in their Central Asian home a colony of the original Ilavarta as many Indian traditional scholars affirm? In modern archaeology that "Outer Indo-Aryan land" is called the Bactria-Margiana Archeological Complex or BMAC. Another branch of that federation went south west and gave their name to Khurasan (kurasthana) and Iran (Aryana) where one of their descendents Kurush or Cyrus founded the first Persian empire."

Meluhha language and Meluhha tin

Bronze Age Trade and Writing System of Meluhha (Mleccha) Evidenced by Tin Ingots from the Near vicinity of Haifa

[For Bronze Age Trade Workshop in 5ICAANE, April 5, 2006]

Abstract

The discovery of two pure tin ingots in a ship-wreck near Haifa has produced two "Rosetta" stones to decode the "Indus script". The epigraphs on the tin ingots have been deciphered as related to ranku "antelope", "liquid measure"; read rebus: ranku 'tin'. As J.D. Muhly noted, the emergence of Bronze Age trade and writing system may be two related initiatives which started approximately in the Third Millennium B.C. It is surmised that the maritime-trade links between Ugarit and Meluhha might have extended from Crete to Haifa. Linking archaeology and philology is a challenging task. What language could the writings on Haifa tin ingots be? The breakthrough invention of alloying may have orthographic parallels of ligatured signs and ligatured pictorial motifs (such as a bovine body with multiple animal heads, combination of animal heads, combination of lathe and furnace on a standard device, ligaturing on a heifer, damr.a -- unicorn -- with one curved horn, pannier, kammarsala). A ligature of a tiger's face to the upper body of a woman is also presented in the round. The hieroglyphic code has been deciphered as words of Mleccha. Mleccha (Meluhha) was the language in which Yudhishthira and Vidura converse in the Mahabharata about the non-metallic killer devices of a fortification that was made of shellac. There is a depiction of a Meluhha trader accompanied by a woman carrying a kamandalu. There are, however, substratum words in Sumerian such as tibira "merchant" and sanga "priest" which are cognate with tam(b)ra "copper" (Santali) and sanghvi "priest" (Gujarati).

Lipshur litanies state: 'Melukkha...is the land of carnelian' (Sumerian NA4.GUG, Akkadian sa_mtu). In the 17th century BC, the Neo-Assyrian king Esarhaddon called himself, 'king of the kings of Dilmun, Magan, and Melukkha'. The Sumerian myth Enki and the World Order has Enki exclaiming: 'Let the magilum-boats of Melukkha transport gold and silver for exchange!' Enki and Ninkhursag (lines 1-9, Tr. by B. Alster) has references to the products of Melukkha: 'The land Tukrish shall transport gold from Kharali, lapis lazuli, and bright...to you. The land Melukkha shall bring carnelian, desirable and precious, sissoo-wood from Magan, excellent mangroves, on big-ships! The land Markhashi will (bring) precious stones, dus'ia-stones, (to hand) on the breast, mighty, diorite-stones, u-stones, s'umin-stones to you!'

This monograph presents four 'rosetta stones' to decipher the Indus script. 1. First and second are pure tin ingots with Sarasvati hieroglyphs discovered in the Haifa shipwreck; 2. Third is an Akkadian cylinder seal attesting to Meluhha as a language of bronze-age traders (sea-faring merchants); 3. Fourth is a cylinder seal from Ur showing tabaernamonta flower (used as hair-fragrance) which is read in Meluhha as tagaraka, rebus: tagara 'tin'. The cryptography of the writing system is mlecchita vikalpa (which is recognized by Vatsyayana as one of 64 arts).

Two tin ingots found in Haifa inscribed with Meluhha hieroglyphs:

- *ranku* = tin (Santali)
- *ranku* = liquid measure (Santali)
- *ranku* a species *of deer; ran:kuka (Sanskrit)(CDIAL 10559).*
- *dāṭu = cross Telugu; dhatu* = mineral (Santali)
- Hindi. *dhāṭnā* 'to send out, pour out, cast (metal)' (CDIAL 6771).

Akkadian cylinder seal of Shu-Ilishu, Meluhha interpreter, shows Meluhha trader carrying an antelope: *mlekh* 'goat' Rebs: *milakkkhu* 'copper' (Pali), Meluhha! [*mleccha mukha* 'copper' (Sanskrit)]

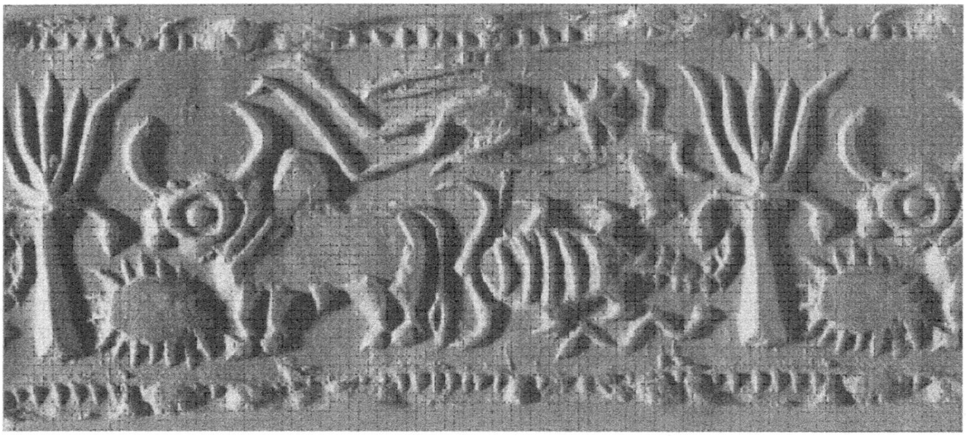

Seal from Ur showing *tabernae montana* hieroglyph + zebu hieroglyph

Bronze age trade and cryptography: *mlecchita vikalpa*

The picture of the two Haifa tin ingots incised with epigraphs was published by J.D. Muhly [New evidence for sources of and trade in bronze age tin, in: Alan D. Franklin, Jacqueline S. Olin, and Theodore A. Wertime, The Search for Ancient Tin, 1977, Seminar organized by Theodore A. Wertime and held at the Smithsonian Institution and the National Bureau of Standards, Washington, D.C., March 14-15, 1977]. Muhly notes:"... copper is likely to be a local product; the tin was almost always an import... There is certainly no tin on Cyprus, so at best the ingots could have been transhipped from that island. How did they then find their way to Haifa? Are we dealing with a ship en route from Cyprus, perhaps to Egypt, which ran into trouble and sank off the coast of Haifa? If so, that certainly rules out Egypt as a source of tin. Ingots of tin are rare before Roman times and, in the eastern Mediterranean, unknown from any period. What the ingots do demonstrate is that metallic tin was in use during the Late Bronze Age...rather extensive use of metallic tin in the ancient eastern Mediterranean, which will probably come as a surprise to many people." (Muhly, J.D., 1976, Copper and Tin, Hamden, Archon Books, p.47). We do not know where the tin ingots were moulded, and where the epigraphs were incised, but it is possible to read the epigraphs using references to cryptography in Mahabharata and mlecchita vikalpa 'cryptography' mentioned by Vatsyayana in vidya samuddes'ah (objective of education in 64 arts).

In the old Akkadian period, the ingots of tin are called s'uqlu and weigh about 25 kg. The two ingots found at Haifa weigh about 5 kg. each.(details of the find and archaeological, archaeo-metallurgical contexts are elaborated at http://www.hindunet.org/saraswati/roots.htm)

Two remarkable insights provided by Muhy and Potts have made this possible. Muhly noted, the emergence of bronze age trade and writing system may be two related initiatives which started circa 3rd millennium Before Common Era (BCE). Potts identified a glyph in what is clearly an Indus script epigraph as tabernaemontana flower which in Indic family of languages and in many ancient ayurveda texts is called tagaraka, read rebus tagara ‘tin’, also tagara ‘hair fragrance’.

This work reads the epigraphs inscised on the tin ingots as Sarasvati hieroglyphs of mleccha (meluhha) language which is part of the Indic language family. (These are called ‘Sarasvati hieroglyphs’ because, about 80% of the archaeological sites of the so-called Indus Valley civilization are on the banks of this Vedic river). The epigraphs ‘certify’ the metal as ranku, ‘tin’ (moulded out of) bat.a, a furnace; ranku is represented by two homonys: antelope, liquid-measure both phonetically read as ranku. bat.a is represented by X glyph, bat.a is a homonym meaning ‘road’. Thus, bot the epigraphs connote ‘tin (out of) furnace’. The two tin ingots become the two ‘rosetta stones’ validating the decipherment of sarasvati hieroglyphs (so-called Indus script) as the repertoire of a smithy/metalsmith-merchant engaged in the bronze-age trade of minerals, metals and alloys and using types of furnaces/smelters.

It will be an erroneous assumption to make that a writing system emerged only to write long texts. The system could have emerged to convey messages about valued artifacts in bronze age trade.. “Obviously no script could have survived indefinitely as a simple mixture of pictures and puns; its scope would have been far too restricted and it would have had in course of time to evolve into a syllabic script,” notes Chadwick in: Gerard Clauson and John Chadwick, 1969, Indus script deciphered?, Antiquity XLIII.

Yes, indeed. The Sarasvati hieroglyphs continued to be used on products manufactured in mints, such as early punch-marked coins of Asia Minor and India. The writing system of Sarasvati hieroglyphs continued on three media and not for writing long texts: 1. Line 1 of Sohgaura copper plate followed by text in Brahmi script to represent the facilities provided to itinerant smiths/merchants for metalwork; 2. About 5 devices on punch-marked coins to represent the repertoire of a mint; and 3. On sculptures of Barhut stupa and many representations in Angkor Wat, representing extraordinary ligatured glyptics such as those of makara. Two Sarasvati hieroglyphs became abiding metaphors: 1. narrow-necked jar which is shown on a Yajurveda manuscript discovered in Gujarat; 2. svastika which adorns many temple walls in India. It is possible that the glyphs and the underlying rebus or pun words, provided the basis for the choice of graphs used in the syllabic-phonetic scripts of Brahmi or Kharoshthi. "A lengthy prehistoric sequence has been established at the important site of Mehrgarh in Pakistani Baluchistan, where an aceramic occupation beginning around 7000 BCE that formed the foundation for the later ceramic Neolithis and Chalcolithic cultures in the region has recently been documented. Despite innovations and changes in the prehistoric sequence of the greater Indus Valley, there is an essential thread of unity and a strong stamp of cultural identity throughout that underscores the essentially indigenous, deeply rooted nature of Indian civilization. While points of contact with other regions are attested, they can hardly have accounted for the strength and individuality of civilization in the subcontinent." (Potts, 1995, p. 1457).

It is also possible that the glyph, for example, of a scorpion – and the underlying metaphor, meaning as kacc 'iron' -- could also have survived in the kudurru of Nebuchadnezzar, to depict him as a hero, an iron-man (illustrated).

Kudurru (boundary stone) marking of Nebuchadnezzar I (1126-1050 BCE), marking the king's land grant to Ritti-Marduk for military service in the inscription (not shown). The symbols appear in six registers. The first register is the eight-pointed star of Ishtar, the crescent of Sin and the sun-disk of Shamash. The second register represents the shrines of Anu, Enlil, and Ea. The third register consists of serpent daises upon which are the hoe of Marduk, the wedge of Nabu, and an unidentified symbol. The fourth register includes an eagle-headed scepter, a double-lion-headed mace, a horse's head on a double base with an arch, and a bird on a rod. The firth register shows the goddes Gula seated on a throne, with a dog (her symbol) lying beside her, and a scorpion-man, with the legs and feet of a bird, holding a bow and arrow. The last register includes double lightning forks supported by a bull (Adad), a tortoise, a scorpion, and a lamp on a pedestal (the symbol of Nusku, the god of light). A snake twists along the side of the kudurru. Ht. 56 cm. London, British Museum (After the notes in: Karen Rhea Nemet-Nejat, 1998, Daily life in Ancient Mesopotamia, London, Greenwood Press, p. 262). The 'star' sign denoted AN, sky god and also was the cuneiform sign to represent the word and syllable: AN. Many of these logographs are found among the Harappan glyphs. It is notable that the pictorial motifs are associated with weapons.

Mlecchita vikalpa

The term, mlecchita vikalpa, is used by Vatsyayana in Kamasutra in the verse related to vidyasamuddes'ah (objectives of education). Together with art of talking with letters and fingers (hand-sign language), and knowledge of dialects, Vatsyayana lists mlecchita-vikalpa as cryptography (cipher-writing) – as three of the 64 arts (education) to be learnt by a youth.

• Va_tsya_yana lists 64 arts to be studied (1.3.15).
• (47) aksara-mustika-kathana--art of talking with letters and fingers
• (48) mlecchita-vikalpa—cypher writing
• (49) desa-bhasa-jnana--art of knowing provincial dialects

The term, mlecchita, means 'made by mleccha', that is, mlecchita vikalpa refers to cryptography of copper-smiths. (It has been noted elsewhere that milakkhu in Pali and mleccha-mukha in Sanskrit, both mean 'copper'. It is no mere coincidence that many epigraphs of the historical periods were inscribed on copper-plates recording economic transactions and edicts by rulers. It is also no mere coincidence that there are about 250 epigraphs with Sarasvati hieroglyphs inscribed on copper plates and metal objects.

Linking archaeology and philology is an exploration in cryptography. What language could the writings on Haifa tin ingots be based on? The breakthrough invention of alloying may have orthographic parallels of ligatured signs and ligatured pictorial motifs (such as a bovine body with multiple animal heads, combination of animal heads, combination of lathe and furnace on a standard device, ligaturing on a heifer, damr.a -- unicorn -- with one curved horn, pannier, kammarsala). A ligature of a tiger's face to the upper body of a woman is also presented in the round. The hieroglyphic code has been cracked as words of Mleccha. Mleccha (Meluhha) was the language in which Yudhishthira and Vidura converse in the Mahabharata about the non-metallic killer devices of a fortification made of shellac. There is a depiction of a Meluhha trader (accompanied by a woman carrying a kamandalu). There are, however, substratum words in Sumerian such as tibira 'merchant' and sanga 'priest' which are cognate with tam(b)ra 'copper' (Santali) and sanghvi 'priest' (Gujarati). (Kalyanaraman, S., 2003, Sarasvati, 7 vols. 1. Civilization, 2. Rigveda, 3. River; 4. Bharati, 5. Technology, 6. Language, 7. Epigraphs, Bangalore, Babasaheb Apte Smarak Samiti http://www.hindunet.org/saraswatihttp://spaces.msn.com/members/sarasvati97) Such a collation of disparate evidences point to the indic family of languages as a possible part of the crypt.

Find-spot of the first two 'rosetta stones'

At the port of Dor, south of Haifa, fisherfolk had raised about 7 tonnes of copper and tin ingots in the 1970's. In 1976 two ingots were found in a shipwreck in the sea near this Phoenician port. Ingot 1 and Ingot 2; Museum of Ancient Art, Municipal Corporation of Haifa.
These two tin ingots contain epigraphs in 'Indus script' which will be elaborated in this monograph as Sarasvati hieroglyphs using underlying Indic language family (mleccha, meluhha!)

To what period the two ingots belonged is uncertain. The conjectures are that they could have come from Ugarit or Cyprus.

The glyphs incised on the ingots DO NOT resemble Cypro-Minoan symbols used in Cyprus or Hittite hieroglyphs used in Ugarit or Cretan hieroglyphs ca. 1500 to 1100 BC. (Appendix A: A Note on Cypro-Minoan symbols, Hittite hieroglyphs and Cretan hieroglphs on Phaistos Disk
One possibility is that they were weighed at Ugarit and stamped as they travelled through the long overland caravan route right upto the western end. [Sources: Anon., 1980, Ingots from wrecked ship may help to solve ancient mystery, Inst. Archaeo-Metallurgical Studies Newsletter, No. 1, 1-2; Maddin, R., T.S. Wheeler and J. Muhly, 1977, Tin in the ancient Near East: old questions and new finds, Expedition, 19, 35-47] .

Hypothesis: The epigraphs on the ingots could have been incised by tin-smiths/merchants, the underlying language of Indic family being: mleccha (meluhha).

Evidence of Meluhhan presence: a third 'rosetta stone'

One region from which these tin ingots could have originated may be from smithe/merchants who spoke the Meluhha (mleccha) language which is part of the Indic language family. Such Meluhha speakers might have been in colonies of traders in Mari.

An Akkadian cylinder seal provides evidence for the presence of a Meluhhan in Mesopotamia.

Akkadian seal (after Powell, p. 390: The Bronze Age Civilization of Central Asia, New York, 1980). The translator of the Meluhhan (Sindhu Sarasvati) language (EME.BAL.ME.LUH.HA.KI) is received by a person of high rank and sitting by his lap. Another Meluhhan sitting by three jars makes a greeting gesture. Two persons enter: one carries an animal, the other a kamandalu (alchemical water-vessel?). British Museum tablet #79987 enumerates a 'man of Meluhha' named (...)-ibra in a list of foes of Naram-Sin, King of Akkad, ca. 2250 BC. Cylinder seal impression; Legend: Shu-ilishu, Meluhha interpreter. Louvre AO 22310 (De Clercq Coll.); greenstone; De Clercq and Menant, 1888, No. 83. Collon, 1987, Fig. 637. Note: British Museum tablet #79987 enumerates a 'man of Meluhha' named (...)-ibra in a list of foes of Naram-Sin, King of Akkad, ca. 2250 BCE. "During the second half of the 3rd millennium BC, textual sources frequently refer to trade with Dilmun, Magan and Meluhha. Dilmun is known to be the island of Bahrain, Magan is probably present-day Makran and the territory opposite it in Oman, while at this period it seems that Meluhha referred to the Indus Valley where the flourishing cities of Mohenjo Daro and Harappa have been excavated. The Indus Valley civilisation used square stamp seals but under the impetus of trade some cylinder seals appear and a Meluhhan interpreter used a typical Akkadian seal." (Collon, 1987)

The Meluhhan being introduced carries an antelope on his arm.The Meluhhan is accompanied by a lady carrying a kaman.d.alu. Since he needed an interpreter, it is clear that the Meluhhan did not speak Akkadian. Antelope carried by the Meluhhan is a hieroglyph: mlekh 'goat' (Br.); mr..eka Telugu; me_t.am (Tamil); mes.am (Sanskrit) Read rebus: me-la-hha.Thus, the antelope conveys the message that the carrier is a Meluhha (speaker). The hieroglyph is thus a phonetic determinant.

If the two tin ingots with epigraphs containing Sarasvati hieroglyphs constitute the first two 'rosetta stones', this cylinder seal constitutes the third 'rosetta stone' attesting to Meluhha as a non-Akkadian language.

There is evidence for the presence of meluhhan (Indus valley people) along the Persian Gulf region, along the sea/river route to Mari, on the right bank of Euphrates river, Mesopotamia.

"...More recent arcaheological researches in East Arabia have brought to light many finds which are related to the presence of Indus valley people. In the settlements of Hili 8 and Maysar-1, both of which have been investigated, Indus valley pottery is frequently found. Seals with Indus valley script and typical iconography indicate influences in Makkan down to the level of business organization. Marks identifying pottery in Makkan were taken from those used in the Indus valley, including the use of the signs on pottery used in the Indus valley. The discovery of a sea-port-- which may be ascribed to the Harappans-- at Ra's al-Junayz on Oman's east coast by an Italian expedition would seem to indicate that trade routes should be viewed in a more differentiated fashion than has been done upto now." [Sege Cleuziou, Preliminary report on the second and third excavation campaigns at Hili 8, Archaeology in the United Arab Emirates, vol. 2/3, 1978/79, 30ff.; Gerd Weisgerber, '...und Kupfer in Oman', Der Anschnitt, vol. 32, 1980, 62-110; Gerd Weisgerber, Makkan and Meluhha- 3rd millennium copper production in Oman and evidence of contact with the Indus valley, Paper read in Cambridge 1981 and to appear in South Asia Archaeology 1981; Tosi, M. 1982. A possible Harappan Seaport in Eastern Arabia: Ra's Al Junayz in the Sultanate of Oman, paper read at the 1st International Conference on Pakistan Archaeology, Peshawar]." Gerd Weisgerber, Dilmun--a trading entrepot; evidence from historical and archaeological sources, 135-142 in: Shaikha Haya Ali Al Khalifa and Michael Rice (eds.) Bahrain through the ages: the archaeology, London, KPI, 1986. [Simo Parpola/Asko Parpola/Robert H. Brunswig, The Meluhha village. evidence of acculturation of Harappan traders in the later third millennium Mesopotamia?, Journal of the Economic and Political History of the Orient, vol. 20, 1977, 129-165. 'If the tablets and their sealed envelopes had not been found, in fact, we might never have suspected the existence of a merchant colony.' (T. Ozguc, An Assyrian trading outpost, Scientific American, 1962, 97 ff.).

The city-state of Lagash (ca. 2060: king Shulgi) records a toponym about the presence of a 'Melukkhan village'. (A. Parpola and S. Parpola, 1975, On the relationship of the Sumerian Toponym Meluhha and Sanskrit Mleccha, Studia Orientalia 46). The word 'Melukkha' also appears, occasionally, as a personal name in cuneiform texts of the Old Akkadian and Ur III periods. Seals of the Indian civilization have been found in Mesopotamia and Iran at Kish (modern Tell Ingharra), Ur, Tell Asmar, Nippur (modern Nuffar), and Susa; a shard with an inscription has been found at Ras al-Junayz, the southeastern extremity of the Oman Peninsula; seal impressions of the civilization have been found at Umma (Tell Jokha) and Tepe Yahya; pottery of the civilization has been found at Ras al-Junayz, Asimah, Maysar, Hili 8, Tell Abraq -- in Oman and United Arab Emirates. Susa, Qalat al-Bahrain, Shimal (Ras al-Khaimah) and Tell Abraq (Umm al-Qaiwain) -- sites around the Arabian Gulf -- have yielded cubical weights of banded chert (unit weight: 13.63 grams) which are the hall-mark of the civilization.

In Ras al-Janyz, in the southeast coast of Oman, a large quantity of bitumen was found in a mud-brick storeroom; the surmise is that the bitumen was used to caulk reed or wooden boats. This find also points to a significant presence of traders from the Indian civilization, during the late third and early second millennium, in Magan (Oman). A copper seal with a Sarasvati hieroglyph was discovered at Ras-al-Junayz. (The port has a green-back turtle reserve). Turtle or tortoise shells were an item of trade from Meluhha, according to Mesopotamian records. “Mats, sarcophagi, coffins and jars, used for funeral practices, were often covered and sealed with bitumen. Reed and wood boats were also caulked with bitumen. Abundant lumps of bituminous mixtures used for that particular purpose have been found in storage rooms of houses at Ra's al-Junayz in Oman. Bitumen was also a widespread adhesive in antiquity and served to repair broken ceramics, fix eyes and horns on statues (e.g. at Tell al-Ubaid around 2500 BC). Beautiful decorations with stones, shells, mother of pearl, on palm trees, cups, ostrich eggs, musical instruments (e.g. the Queen's lyre) and other items, such as rings, jewellery and games, have been excavated from the Royal tombs in Ur.” [Connan, J., 1999, 'Use and Trade of Bitumen in Antiquity and Prehistory: Molecular Archaeology Reveals Secrets of Past Civilizations', Philosophical Transactions of the Royal Society London B 353: 33-50.]
http://www.journals.royalsoc.ac.uk/(qoptgors11gb1p45iz5i3wup)/app/home/contribution.asp?r

eferrer=parent&backto=issue,4,14;journal,86,116;linkingpublicationresults,1:102022,1See also: http://www.sabi-abyad.nl/tellsabiabyad/projecten/index/0/19/?sub=32&language=enwhich has a map pointing to origin of bitumen somewhere between Iraq and Israel.

Sea-faring merchants of Melukkha (Meluhha) and trade route of tin ingots

Mleccha trade was first mentioned by Sargon of Akkad (Mesopotamia 2370 B.C.) who stated that boats from Dilmun, Magan and Meluhha came to the quay of Akkad (Hirsch, H., 1963, Die Inschriften der Konige Von Agade, Afo, 20, pp. 37-38; Leemans, W.F., 1960, Foreign Trade in the Old Babylonian Period, p. 164; Oppenheim, A.L., 1954, The seafaring merchants of Ur, JAOS, 74, pp. 6-17). The Mesopotamian imports from Meluhha were: woods, copper (ayas), gold, silver, carnelina, cotton. Gudea sent expeditions in 2200 B.C. to Makkan and Meluhha in search of hard wood. Seal impression with the cotton cloth from Umma (Scheil, V., 1925, Un Nouvea Sceau Hindou Pseudo-Sumerian, RA, 22/3, pp. 55-56) and cotton cloth piece stuck to the base of a silver vase from Mohenjodaro (Wheeler, R.E.M., 1965, Indus Civilization) are indicative evidence. Babylonian and Greek names for cotton were: sind, sindon. This is an apparent reference to the cotton produced in the black cotton soils of Sind and Gujarat. Ca. 2150-2000 BC, ivory from Meluhha is mentioned in connection with ivory bird figurines (Oppenheim 1954: II, 15 n.24). About 2000 BCEat Ur, ivory is attributed to Dilmun (Bahrein), perhaps shipped up the Gulf from the Indus where tusks and ivory objects were plentiful. Isin-Larsa period (ca. 2000-1800 BCE)texts refer to rods, combs, inlays, boxes, spoons, and 'breastplates' of ivory donated to temples by merchants returning from Dilmun (Oppenheim 1954: 6-12).

'Melukkha' is cognate with Pali 'milakkha' or Sanskrit 'mleccha'. In Pali, 'milakkha' also means, 'copper'. In Sanskrit, 'mleccha-mukha' means 'copper'.

The trading route through Mari on the Euphrates to Ugarit (Mediterranean Sea) and on to Minoan Crete. This routing may explain the presence of Harappan script inscription on tin ingots found at Haifa, Israel!

[After Potts, 1995] The body of water called the Red Sea, Gulf of Aden, Arabian Gulf, Gulf of

Oman and the Arabian Sea were referred to by Herodotus as the Erythraean Sea. Dilmun is identified with Bahrain, Magan with Oman and Melukkha with the Indian Civilization. Sargon of Akkad boasts that ships from Dilmun, Magan and Melukkha docked at the quay of his capital Akkad. This inscription affirms that Melukkha was accessible by the sea-route, through the Arabian gulf.There is significant evidence for the presence of people and goods from and frequent interaction with the Indian Civilization in the Mesopotamian and Gulf areas. There is, however, little evidence of a Sumerian, Akkadian or Babylonian presence in India.

"Tin procurement at Mari was highly organized (Dossin 1970; Villard 1984: nos. 555-6). It travelled in the form of ingots weighing about 5 kg. each. It reached Mari by donkey caravan from Susa (Susiana) and Anshan (Elam) through Eshnunna (Tell Asmar). The relevant records contain the names of Elamite rulers and Elamite agents (Heltzer 1989). Tin was transmitted westwards, both as an item of royal gift-exchange and as a trade commodity...it may well often have travelled by sea up the Gulf from distribution centres in the Indus Valley. In the Old Babylonian period tin was shipped through Dilmun (Leemans 1960: 35), as it had been a millennium earlier to judge by references in the Ebla texts...Strabo (xv.ii.10) referred specifically to Drangiana, the modern region of Seistan in south-west Iran (into Afghanistan) as a source of tin. Muhly (1973: 260) associated this directly with Gudea's report of receiving tin from Meluhha...A number of scholars have pointed out the possibility that tin arrived with gold and lapis lazuli in Sumer through the same trade network, linking Afghanistan with the head of the Gulf, both by land and sea (Stech and Piggott 1986: 41-4)." (P.R.S. Moorey, 1994, Ancient Mesopotamian Materials and Industries, Oxford, Clarendon Press pp. 298-299).
Map showing locations of Mari and Ugarit. The trading route through Mari on the Euphrates to Ugarit (Mediterranean Sea) and on to Haifa. This may explain the presence of Harappan script inscription on tin ingots found at Haifa, Israel ! [Map after Markus Wafler, 'Zu Status und Lage von Taba_l', Orientalia]. Meluhha and interaction areas (After Fig. 2 in P.R.S. Moorey, 1994, Ancient Mesopotamian Materials and Industries, Oxford, Clarendon Press).

Tin from Meluhha; Mleccha as a language

Tin used in Indus Valley civilization is well attested. (Hegde 1978; Chakrabarti 1979; Muhly 1985: 283; Stech and Pigott 1986: 43-4). Gudea c. 2100 BC, identified Meluhha as the source of his tin (Falkenstein 1966: i.48: Cylinder B: XIV). "...tin may well often have travelled by sea up the Gulf from distribution centres in the Indus Valley. In the Old Babylonian period tin was shipped through Dilmun (Leemans 1960: 35)... It is now known that Afghanistan has two zones of tin mineralization. One embraces much of eastern Afghanistan from south of Kandahar to Badakshan in the north-east corner of the country (Shareq et al. 1977); the other lies to the west and extends from Seistan north towards Herat (Cleuziou and Berthoud 1982), the valley of the Sarkar river, where the hills are granitic. Here tin appears commonly as cassiterite, frequently associated with copper, gold, and lead, and in quantities sufficient to attract attention in antiquity. Bronzes at Mundigak, and the controversial Snake Cave artefacts, indicate local use of bronze by at least the third millennium BCE(Shaffer 1978: 89, 115, 144). A number of scholars have pointed out the possibility that tin arrived with gold and lapis lazuli in Sumer through the same trade network, linking Afghanistan with the head of the Gulf, both by land and sea (Stech and Pigott 1986: 41-4)." (P.R.S. Moorey, 1994, Ancient Mesopotamian Materials and Industries, Oxford, Clarendon Press p. 298-299).

van:ga is also tin with the possible association of chalcolithic cultures in Bengal (2nd millennium B.C.) with possible links with the culture of Thailand of the same period (Solheim, W.C., Sciene, Vol. 157, p. 896). Hegde suggests the possibility that water-concentrated placer deposits referred to as 'stream tin' (alluvial cassiterite or mineral tin) in the proximity of Aravalli and Chota Nagpur Hills might have also been the sources of tin.

Meluhha (ancient Sindhu (Indus)-Sarasvati valley) could have been the early source of ancient tin. “There is an extensive belt of placer deposits in the Malay peninsula which stretches over a distance of 1000 miles. The location of the early tin mines is lost to history, but the first documented use of tin seems to be in Mesopotamia, followed soon by Egypt. The tin probably came in through the Persian Gulf, or down what would later be the Silk Route. Some tin has been found in central Africa, and could have supplied a small amount to Egypt. However, the earliest needs for the mineral must have been met by Indian sources, the material being carried westward by migrations from southern and eastern Asia toward the Mediterranean area or from nearby sources.”http://www.ancientroute.com/resource/metal/tin.htm

There is evidence from a cylinder seal of Gudea, the king of Lagash (2143 – 2124 BCE) that tin came from Melukkha. (Muhly, J.D., 1976, Copper and Tin, Hamden, Archon Books, pp. 306-7).

Meluhha is the region where bharatiya languages, such as mleccha (cognate, melukkha, meluhha) were spoken; Mahabharata attests, in the context of a cryptographic reference, that Vidura and Yudhishthira spoke in mleccha. (Appendix B Cryptography and reference to mleccha as language in Mahabharata, and to khanaka, the miner contains text from the epic with a translation).

An Akkadian cylinder seal has been cited earlier as the second 'rosetta stone' attesting to meluhha as a language. A cognate term in Indic language family is: mleccha.

The antelope carried by the bearded Me-lah-ha on an Akkadian cylinder seal may be a phonetic determinant: mel.aka or mr..eka (Telugu)(melu-hha; also, melech, 'king'; plural form, 'melechim'). [cf. Melech Hamashiah: King Messiah; Akad: {Akkad} A city in Mesopotamia (now Iraq) which was part of Nimrod's kingdom, founded by Melech Sargon around 2350 BCE Genesis 10:10; KPJayaswal notes that mleccha was the Samskr.tam representation of Hebrew melekh meaning, 'king' and that the utterance: he lavah! he lavah! in the S'atapatha Bra_hman.a was a specimen of mleccha speech; that this spech is cognate with Hebrew e_loa_h (plural e_lo_him) meaning, 'God' (Jayaswal, KP, 1914, 'Kleine Mitteilungen', Zeitschrift der Deutschen Morgenlandischen Gesellschraft,, vol. LXXII, p. 719). For the specimen of mleccha speech, an alternative explanation is provided in Maha_bha_s.ya with a variation, helayo helayo; Sa_yan.a_ca_rya notes that the speimen of Asura/mleccha speech is a variant of he 'rayo, he 'raya meaning, 'O the (spiteful) enemies', explained by the asuras' inability to pronounce the sounds, - r- and –y-. (Maha_bha_s.ya 1.1.1; KC Chatterjee, 1957, Patanjali's Maha_bha_s.ya, Calcutta, pp. 10-11; Sa_yan.a on S'atapatha Bra_hman.a, 3.2.1.23).] The word me-la-hha may also be cognate with: mer.h, med.h, 'copper merchant'. Another example of a substrate term: Sumerian tibira, tabira (Akkadian. LU2 URUDU-NAGAR =. "[person] copper-carpenter"); a word indicating borrowing from a substrate. In Pkt. tambira = copper. According to Gernot Wilhelm, the Hurrian version of tabira is: tab-li 'copper founder'; tab-iri 'the one who has cast (copper)'.

This may explain why two statuettes made of solid gold and solid silver of Elamite kings also shown carrying an antelope in their hands: melech, 'king'.Elamite worshipper, Susa, Iran 12th century BCE (middle Elamite period), excavated by Ronald de Mecquenem in 1904.

Melakkha, island-dwellersAccording to the great epic, Mlecchas lived on islands: "sa sarva_n mleccha nr.patin sa_gara dvi_pa va_sinah, aram a_ha_ryàm àsa ratna_ni vividha_ni ca, andana aguru vastra_n.i man.i muktam anuttamam, ka_ñcanam rajatam vajram vidrumam ca maha_ dhanam: (Bhima) arranged for all the mleccha kings, who dwell on the ocean islands, to bring varieties of gems, sandalwood, aloe, garments, and incomparable jewels and pearls, gold, silver, diamonds, and extremely valuable coral... great wealth." (MBh. 2.27.25-26).

According to Geiger and Kern, Pa_li term, mila_ca meaning 'forest dweller' was the original variant of milakkha and was used in Ja_takas and Di_gha Nika_ya (Ja_taka, XIV, 486; XVII, 524; Geiger, Wilhelm, Pa_li Literature and Language, tr. BK Ghosh, Calcutta, 1956; repr., 2958, New Delhi, 1978; Kern, H., Toevoegselen op't Woordenbock van Childers, 2 pts., NR., XVI, nos. 4 and 5).This term, mleccha, should be differentiated from another term, pa_s.an.d.a, who were opposed to the doctrines of the times. There is no indication, whatsoever, in any text that mleccha were pa_s.an.d.a; the mleccha were in *Bhāratam janam* – the people of the nation of *Bhārata* (RV 3.53.12). Similarly, there is no indication whatsoever that mleccha were a distinct linguistic entity. The only differentiation indicated in the early texts that mleccha is 'unrefined' speech, that is, the lingua franca (as distinct from the dialects used in mantra-s or Samskr.tam). Thus mleccha is a reference to a common dialect, the spoken tongue in the Indic language family.

What distinquished *mleccha* and *ārya*, when used in reference to language-speakers or dialect-speakers, were only places of habitation, norms of behaviour and dialectical variations in parole (ordinary spoken language) juxtaposed to grammatically 'correct' Samskrtam or inscriptional Prakrits or Pali.

Mleccha in Sanskrit is milakkha or milakkhu in Pali, and the term describes those who dwell on the outskirts of a village. (Shendge, Malati, 1977, The civilized demons: the Harappans in Rigveda, Abhinav Publications).

A milakkhu is disconnected from vāc [refined speech, for e.g. as Samskrtam, as distinguished from the natural (spoken dialect or lingua franca) Prakrt] and does not speak Vedic; he spoke Prakrt. "na a_rya_ mlecchanti bha_s.a_bhir ma_yaya_ na caranty uta: aryas do not speak with crude dialects like mlecchas, nor do they behave with duplicity (MBh. 2.53.8). a dear friend of Vidura who was a professional excavator is sent by Vidura to help the Pa_n.d.avas in confinement; this friend of Vidura has a conversation with Yudhisthira, the eldest Pa_n.d.ava: "... vidurenkoto mleccha-vācàsi pāṇḍava...": on the fourteenth evening of the dark fortnight, Purocana will put fire in the door of your house. 'The Pandavas are leaders of the people, and they are to be burned to death with their mother.' This, Pa_rtha (Yudhis.t.ira), is the determined plan of Dhrtarās.t.ra's son, as I have heard it. When you were leaving the city, Vidura spoke a few words to you in the dialect of the mlecchas, and you replied to him, 'So be it'. I say this to gain your trust.

This passage shows that there were two Arya-s distinguished by language group, Yudhis.t.ra and Vidura. Both are aryas, who could speak mleccha language (mleccha vācasi); Dhrtarās.t.ra and his people (who could also speak mleccha) are NOT arya (respected persons) only because of their behaviour. Mleccha was the *lingua franca*.

"Tin from 'Meluhha'...According to the Larsa texts, merchants were there (in Mari and Lrsa) to purchase copper and tin: the copper came from Magan in Oman, via Tilmun (Bahrain), but the origin of the tin is left in question. Tin mines in north-west Iran or the Transcaucasus are highly unlikely. Fortunately, there is evidence for another tin source in texts from Lagash. Lagash, about 50 km east of Larsa, was of minor importance except under the governorship of Gudea (ca. 2143-2124 BC). His inscriptions indicate extensive trade: gold from Cilicia in Anatolia, marble from Amurra in Syria, and cedar wood from the Amanus Mountains between these two countries, while up through the Persian Gulf or 'Southern Sea' came more timber, porphyry (strictly a purplish rock), lapis lazuli and tin. (Burney, 1977, 86; Muhly, 1973, 306-7, 449 note 542; Muhly, J.D., 1973, Tin trade routes of the Bronze Age, Scientific American, 1973, 61, 404-13). One inscription has been translated:

Copper and tin, blocks of lapis lazuli and ku ne (meaning unknown), bright carnelian from Meluhha.

"This is the only reference to tin from Meluhha...either Meluhha was a name vague enough to embrace Badakhshan (the northernmost province of Afghanistan) as well as some portion of the Indian subcontinent including the Indus valley, or 'tin from Meluhha' means that the metal came from some port in Meluhha -- just as 'copper from Tilmun' means copper from elsewhere shipped through the island of Bahrain. Whichever interpretation is correct, the result is the same. Tin must have come from somewhere in India, or from elsewhere along a trade route down the Indus valley. India is not without its tin locations, rare though they are...The largest deposits in India proper are in the Hazaribagh district of Bihar. 'Old workings' are said to exist... (Wheeler, R.E.M., 1953, The Indus Civilization, CUP, 58)...Tin bronzes from Gujarat are at the southernmost limit of Indus influence. The copper could have come from Rajasthan, though copper ingots at the port of Lothal, at the head of the Gulf of Cambay, suggest imports from Oman or some other Near Eastern copper mining district. Tin supplying Harappa and Mohenjo-daro, most famous of the Indus cities, may have been sent overland to Lothal for export, though the scarcity of tin in the Indus cities makes this idea unconvincing.

"At Harappa, three copper alloys were used in the period 2500-2000 BC: copper and up to 2% nickel; copper and up to 5% nickel; copper with ca. 10% tin and a trace of arsenic. Ingots of tin as well as of copper were found at Harappa. (Lamberg-Karlovsky, C.C., 1967, Archaeology and metallurgy in prehistoric Afghanistan, India and Pakistan, American Anthropologist, 1967, 69, 145-62). The rarity of the metal is seen at Mohenjo-daro where, of 64 artifacts examined, only nine were of tin bronze. (Tylecote, R.F., 1976, A History of Metallurgy, The Metals Society, p. 11). Ingots of tin bronze have also been found at Chanhu-daro. Yet in spite of its scarcity, tin bronze was widely used. Its occasional abundance and, in the case of the bronzes from Luristan in southern Iran, the high quality of the tin bronzes produced, equally underline the fact that rich source of tin existed somewhere...

"The archaeological evidence from Afghanistan is not unequivocal...What is surprising is the discovery in 1962 of corroded pieces of sheet metal bearing traces of an embossed design and made of a low tin content bronze (5.15%)...The uncorroded metal is thought to have contained nearer 7% tin. (Caley, E.R., 1972, Results of an examination of fragments of corroded metal from the 1962 excavation at Snake Cave, Afghanistan, Trans. American Phil. Soc., New Ser. , 62, 43-84). These fragments came from the deepest level in the Snake Cave, contemporary with the earliest occupation dated by 14C to around 5487 and 5291 BC. (Shaffer, J.G., in Allchin F.R. and N. Hammond (eds.), 1979, The Archaeology of Afghanistan, Academic Press, 91, 141-4)...If this dating is acceptable, not only is this metal the earliest tin bronze known from anywhere, but it is also an isolated occurrence of far older than its nearest rival and quite unrelated to the main development of bronze age metallurgy...

"Even more exciting is the evidence from Shortugai... In 1975, French archaeologists discovered on the surface at Shortugai, sherds of Indus pottery extending over more than a millennium - the whole span of the Indus civilization. (Lyonnet, B., 1977, Decouverte des sites de l'age du bronze dans le N.E. de l'Afghanistan: leurs rapports avec la civilisation de l'Indus, Annali Instituto Orientali di Napoli, 37, 19-35)... Particularly important is a Harappan seal bearing an engraved rhinoceros and an inscription which reinforces the belief that the site was a trading post. Shortugai is only 800 km from Harappa, as the crow flies, though the journey involves hundreds of kilometres of mountainous terrain through the Hindu Kush...Lyonnet's conclusion was that the most likely explanation for their existence was an interest in 'the mineral resources of the Iranian Plateau and of Central Asia', to which can now be added those of Afghanistan itself. Indus contacts extended well into Turkmenia where the principal bronze age settlements, such as Altin-depe and Namasga-depe, lie close to the Iranian border...

"A fine copper axe-adze from Harappa, and similar bronze examples from Chanhu-daro and, in Baluchistan, at Shahi-tump, are rare imports of the superior shaft-hole implements developed initially in Mesopotamia before 3000 BC. In northern Iran examples have been found at Shah Tepe, Tureng Tepe, and Tepe Hissar in level IIIc (2000-1500 BC)...Tin was more commonly used in eastern Iran, an area only now emerging from obscurity through the excavation of key sites such as Tepe Yahya and Shahdad. In level IVb (ca. 3000 BCE)at Tepe yahya was found a dagger of 3% tin bronze. (Lamberg-Karlovsky, C.C. and M., 1971, An early city in Iran, Scientific American, 1971, 224, No. 6, 102-11; Muhly, 1973, Appendix 11, 347);

perhaps the result of using a tin-rich copper ore. However, in later levels tin bronze became a 'significant element in its material culture' comparatble with other evidence from south-east Iran where at Shadad bronze shaft-hole axes and bronze vessels were found in graves dated to ca. 2500 BC. (Burney, C., 1975, From village to empire: an introduction to Near Eastern Archaeology, 1977, Phaidon). The richness of Tepe Yahha, Shahr-i-Sokhta, and Shadad, are all indicative of trade and 'an accumulation of wealth unsuspected from the area'. (Lamberg-Karlovsky, 1973, reviewing Masson and Sarianidi (1972) in Antiquity, 43-6)....Namazga-depe and neighbouring sites are a long way from the important tin reserves of Fergana...The origin of Near Eastern tin remains unproven; the geological evidence would favour the deposits of Fergana and the Tien Shan range..." (Penhallurick, R.D., 1986, Tin in Antiquity, London, Institute of Metals, pp. 18-32). See Appendix D Some excerpts from Muhly, Forbes, Serge Cleuziou and Thierry Berthoud on sources of tin; tin of Melukkha !

[The cuneiform characters meluh-ha should be read with an alternative phonetic value: me-lah-ha. (Parpola, Asko, S. Koskenniemi, S. Parpola and P. Aalto, 1970, Decipherment of the Proto Dravidian Inscriptions of the Indus Valley, no. 3, Copenhagen, p. 37; me-la_h-ha are a clan from a Sindhi tribe known as Moha_na.)]

D.K. Chakrabari (1979, The problem of tin in early India--a preliminary survey, in: Man and Environment, Vol. 3, pp. 61-74) opines that during the pre-Harappan and Harappan periods, the main supply of tin was from the western regions: Khorasan and the area between Bukhara and Samarkand. The ancient tin mines in the Kara Dagh District in NW Iran and in the modern Afghan-Iranian Seistan could have been possible sources. Harappan metal-smiths used to conserve tin by storing and re-using scrap pieces of bronze, making low-tin alloys and substituting tin by arsenic. It is possible that some of the imported tin (like lapis lazuli) was exported to Mesopotamia.

Source: http://sarasvatihieroglyphs.blogspot.com/2006/04/bronze-age-trade-and-mleccha-writing.html

Abstract

Aṣṣur is an ancient city on the western bank of river Tigris, occupied from ca. 2600 BCE through 14th century CE. Aṣṣur is also the name of chief deity of the city.

Asur are the name of a people who live in Jharkhand and West Bengal, India who are traditionally engaged in metalworks of iron. Asura are deities in India from the days of Vedic traditions; in Rigveda, *asura* means 'powerful, mighty'. Sarasvatī is described with attribute *āsurī* and *Varuṇa* is an asura. The gloss is also linked to Ahura Mazda and *Deva Asura*, "*Asura* [who] rules over the Divinities." (*AV* 1.10.1, cf. *RV* II.27.10)

The language the ancestors of Ashur traders spoke was Meluhha, enshrined in hieroglyphs of Meluhha recorded on unique designs of sculptural artifacts and on cylinder seals related to Tukulti-Ninurta (an Ashur) and earlier rulers.[i]Tukulti-Ninurta prays before an altar with a staff -- clump of wood, and decorated with safflower hieroglyphs. These hieroglyphs are read rebus in Meluhha of Indian *sprachbund*.

The Tukulti-Ninurta altar is is a temple model for fire-god. This is evidenced by a gloss from Remo (Austro-asiatic) language, spoken by Bonda people in Malkangiri district of southern Odisha, India. Fire-god is called *karandi*.

This is rebus for the safflower adorning volutes on either side of the altar hieroglyph. Safflower as a hieroglyph: करडी [*karaḍī*] Safflower: Rebus: *karandi* 'fire-god'.

This is rebus for the safflower adorning volutes on either side of the altar hieroglyph. Safflower as a hieroglyph: करडी [*karaḍī*] Safflower: Rebus: *karandi* 'fire-god'.

Ashur Tin Road for bronze-armed armies

The traders from Mesopotamia had established merchant settlements in Anatolia. See: (Barjamovic, Gojko, 2011, A journey through Anatolia in 1865 BCE. Barjamovic_2011_A_Journey_Through_Anatolia.pdfhttp://www.academia.edu/attachments/31847751/download_file)

Evidence on early Assyria comes surprisingly from karum kanesh linking Ashur and Kanesh/Nesha in Kultepe, near Kayseri on the ancient Tin road. The merchants who mediated the tin trade were Assur or Ashur.

Cuneiform tablet case, 1920–1840 B.C.; Old Assyrian Trading Colony period.Central Anatolia, Kültepe (Karum Kanesh).Clay; L. 6 5/8 in. (16.8 cm).Gift of Mr. and Mrs. J.J. Klejman, 1966 (66.245.5b) [quote] When the merchants from Ashur in Assyria came to Anatolia early in the second millennium B.C., they brought with them the writing techniques invented in Mesopotamia: the script known as cuneiform ("wedge-shaped") and the medium of clay tablets encased in clay envelopes. The merchants also brought their art in the form of cylinder seals, which marked the traded goods, storerooms, and written records. The Assyrian merchants wrote in the Assyrian language, but tablets and cuneiform were later adopted in Anatolia by the Hittites, who wrote their own language with the imported techniques.

The records of the Assyrian trading colonies, of which Kültepe (ancient Karum Kanesh) was one, provide detailed information about one part of a lively international tradein the early second millennium B.C. that extended from Egypt to the Caucasus to Central Asia and the Indus Valley. The Assyrian tablets describe the exchange of tin and textiles from Ashur for silver from Anatolia as well as detail the specifics of contracts and lawsuits, and about bandits and other misfortunes.

The tablet contained in this case (66.245.5a) is the record of court testimony describing an ownership dispute of a business firm. The case is sealed with two different cylinder seals rolled across the front and back of the envelope in five parallel rows separated by plain clay. Both seals illustrate presentation scenes in which worshippers approach a larger seated figure holding a cup. The obverse, shown here, is also inscribed in cuneiform. [unquote]

(http://www.metmuseum.org/toah/works-of-art/66.245.5b

See: Kraus, Nick, 2011, From Ashur to Anatolia: the merchant middlemen of Mesopotamia

http://cnersundergraduatejournal.files.wordpress.com/2011/06/from-ashur-to-anatolia-the-merchant-middlemen-of-mesopotamia.pdf)

20,000 tablets were discovered at Karum-Kanesh, an Assyrian trading center in Anatolia. (van de Mieroop 2004, *A history of the acient Near East ca. 3000-323 BCE*, Oxford, Blackwell: 95). Estimates of volumes of trade: 100,000 textiles, 100 tons of tin across just 40 years. (van de Mieroop 2004: 97).

"The Assyrian merchants traded tin (ultimately transshipped from Afghanistan) and Assyrian and Babylonian textiles for the gold and silver of Anatolia. The trade was undertaken by donkey caravans, taking three months for the journey from Nesha to Ashur. Over the fifty years described by the archive, 80 tons of tin was exported to Anatolia, enough to make 800 tons of bronze (KH 27); certainly not all of this was devoted to bronze weapon making, but the large quantity of tin imports permitted the development of true bronze-armed armies."(Hamblin, William J., 2006, *Warfare in the ancient Near East to 1600 BCE: holy warriors at the dawn of history*, Routledge, p.291).

"A building inscription of Ilu-Shumma from the Ishtar Temple at Ashur links the copper trade with the inhabitants of southern Mesopotamian cities, who mediated in the exchange of copper coming from the region of Oman. At this same time, textiles from Mesopotamia and tin from Iran or beyond were traded for silver in Anatolia, where Ashur's traders had established permanent trading colonies in a number of princedoms with the consent of the local rulers and carried on trade with Anatolian merchants. Thousands of cuneiform texts discovered in these settlements known as *karums*, especially in Kultepe (Kanesh), not far from Kayseri, provide a glimpse into the business practices of merchants from Ashur and their relations with Anatolian princes as well as with their home city. At the time when Assyrian merchants were trading in

Anatolia, a certain Erishum 1, son of Ilu-shumma, ruled in Ashur. Several of his building inscriptions are preserved. One example also turned up in Kanesh, which may indicate that it was probably during his reign that trading colonies were established in Anatolia. The year-officials (eponyms) listed in Old Assyrian clay tablets in Anatolia seem to confirm this date. Other rulers of Ashur who governed the city-state during the period when trading centers were established in Anatolia were Ikunum, Sargon I, Puzur-Ashur II, Naram-Sin, and Erishum II. Since these were followed by the 'interrugnum' of Shamshi-Adad, they must date from the nineteenth century BCE. Ikunum and Sargon I are not only attested in the Assyrian king list but also in inscriptions they left behind in Ashur. The latter is also known from impressions of his seal found at Kanesh...Shalmanser I (1273-1244 BCE) incorporated the region of Hanigalbat into his realm, establishing an Assyrian administration there. Assyria and the Hittites now confronted one another on the Euphrates, and Tukulti-Ninurta I (1243-1207 BCE) even claimed to have fought successfully against Babylonia, which suffered a heavy defeat... The copper hoard from the Ashur temple...Some of the bronzes have a low tin content, such as the two beaker fragments while in others, notably the dagger blades, the percentage of tin is much higher. The alloy used for the bronze mace head is unlike any of the others, with over 3 percent arsenic, 9 percent lead, and 4 percent antimony. Although the exact compositions have not yet been determined, it appears that the alloy of the statuette in catalogue number 12 is an arsenic-rich lead bronze, while that of the statuette in catalogue number 13 is bronze with a high proportion of tin...Assyria emerges into recorded history in the twentieth century BCE at a time when the state had become a redistribution center for tin and had subsequently established markets in Anatolia. For two centuries the state prospered, as may readily be judged from the contents of thousands of texts preserved and under Shamshi-Adad I (1815-1782 BCE), a major geographical expansion of the state ensued. Soon after the latter king's reign, however, Assyria was conquered, first by Hammurabi of Babylon (ca. 1759 BCE), then a half-century later by the Mitanni, in both cases suffering vassalage..." (Harper, Prudence Oliver, ed., 1995, *Assyrian origins: discoveries at Ashur on the Tigris: antiquities in the Vorderasiatisches Museum, Berlin*, Metropolitan Museum of Art, New York, p.23, 24, 37, 125).

(After Fig. 17. Cult relief found in a well located in the Ashur temple at Ashur. Old Assyrian period, early 2nd millennium BCE, limestone, h. 52 ½ in. (1.36in) *Vorderasiatisches Museum.*)

Meluhha hieroglyphs: *lo* 'pot to overflow' *kāṇḍa* 'water'.

Rebus: *lokhaṇḍ* (overflowing pot) 'metal tools, pots and pans, metalware' (Marathi).

<kanda> {N} ``large earthen water ^pot kept and filled at the house''. @1507. #14261. (Munda) Rebus: khanda 'a trench used as a fireplace when cooking has to be done for a large number of people' (Santali) kand 'fire-altar' (Santali)

దళము [daḷamu] *daḷamu.* [Skt.] n. A leaf. ఆకు. A petal. A

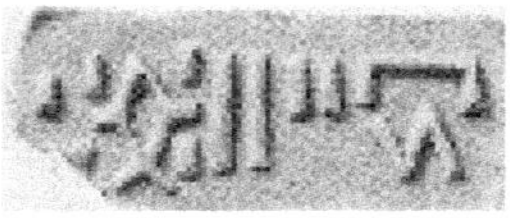

part, భాగము. dala n. ' leaf, petal ' MBh. Pa. Pk. *dala* -- n. ' leaf, petal ', G. M. *daḷ* n.(CDIAL 6214). <DaLO>(MP) {N} ``^branch, ^twig''. *Kh.<DaoRa>(D) `dry leaves when fallen', ~<daura>, ~<dauRa> `twig', Sa.<DAr>, Mu.<Dar>, ~<Dara> `big branch of a tree', ~<DauRa> `a twig or small branch with fresh leaves on it', So.<kOn-da:ra:-n> `branch', H.<DalA>, B.<DalO>, O.<DaLO>, Pk.<DAlA>. %7811. #7741.(Munda etyma)
Rebus: *ḍhālako* = a large metal ingot (Gujarati) *ḍhālakī* = a metal heated and poured into a mould; a solid piece of metal; an ingot (Gujarati)

'Overflowng pot' sign hieroglyph on Mohenjodaro pectoral

m1656A

खोंड [khōṇḍa] m A young bull, a bullcalf. (Marathi) Rebus: kõdār 'turner' (Bengali); कोंद kōnda 'engraver, lapidary setting or infixing gems' (Marathi) G. sãghāṛɔ m. 'lathe' ; संघाट joinery; M. sãgaḍ 'double-canoe' Rebus: sangataras. संगतराश lit. 'to collect stones, stone-cutter, mason.'

m367a *karaḍakum* 'a streamlet' (Gujarati); [*karaḍamu* 'a wave' (Telugu) Rebus: करडा [*karaḍā*] Hard from alloy--iron, silver &c. (Marathi) *kharādī* ' turner'

खोंड [khōṇḍa] m A young bull, a bullcalf. (Marathi) Rebus: kõdār 'turner' (Bengali); कोंद kōnda 'engraver, lapidary setting or infixing gems' (Marathi) G. sãghāṛɔ m. 'lathe' ; संघाट joinery; M. sãgaḍ 'double-canoe' Rebus: sangataras. संगतराश lit. 'to collect stones, stone-cutter, mason.' (Gujarati) *sãgāḍā* m. ' frame of a building ', *sãgāḍī* f. ' lathe ' *kanḍo* stool, seat
Rebus: *kāṇḍā* 'metalware, tools, pots and pans'(Marathi).
Thus, the ligatured sign denotes: hard alloy metalware.

m751A
dāṭu 'cross'(Telugu) Rebus: *dhatu* 'mineral' (Santali). *karaḍamu* 'a wave' (Telugu) Rebus: करडा [*karaḍā*] Hard from alloy--iron, silver &c. (Marathi) dula 'pair' Rebus: dul 'cast metal'

खोंड [khōṇḍa] m A young bull, a bullcalf. (Marathi) Rebus: kõdār 'turner' (Bengali); कोंद kōnda 'engraver, lapidary setting or infixing gems' (Marathi) G. sãghāṛɔ m. 'lathe' ; संघाट joinery; M. sãgaḍ 'double-canoe' Rebus: sangataras. संगतराश lit. 'to collect stones, stone-cutter, mason.'

Thus, the epigraph reads: mineral, cast hard alloy mineral of turner-stone-worker.

Stone pedestal of the god Nuska; Ashur, Temple of Ishtar; Middle Assyrian, reign of Tukulti-Ninurta I, ca. 1243–1207 BCE Provenience: Aṣṣur. Alabaster; H. 23 5/8 in. (60 cm); W. 22 1/2 in. (57 cm); Staatliche Museen zu Berlin, Vorderasiatische Museum

Hieroglyphs:1. करंडा [*karaṇḍā*] A clump, chump, or block of wood. 4 The stock or fixed portion of the staff of the large leaf-covered summerhead or umbrella. करांडा [karāṇḍā] *m* C A cylindrical piece as sawn or chopped off the trunk or a bough of a tree; a clump, chump, or block.

Allograph: 2. करडी [*karaḍī*] *f* (See करडई) Safflower: also its seed.

Rebus: *karaḍa* 'hard alloy' (Marathi)

Hieroglyph: *kaṇḍ* 'furnace, fire-altar' (Santali) Rebus: *kāṇḍā* 'metalware, tools, pots and pans' (Marathi).

A view of the fire-altar pedestal of Tukulti-Ninurta I, Ishtar temple, Assur. Shows the king standing flanked by two standard-bearers; the standard has a spoked-wheel hieroglyph on the top of the staffs and also on the volutes of the altar frieze.The mediation with deities by king is adopted by Assurnasirpal II.

The two standards (staffs) are topped by a spoked wheel. *āra* 'spokes' Rebus: *āra 'brass'*. eraka 'nave of wheel' Rebus: eraka 'copper'. This rebus reading is consistent with the prayer offered to the *karaṇḍa* 'hard alloy'.

Rebus: karaḍa 'hard alloy' of arka 'copper'. <karandi>E155 {N} ``^fire-^god". @B27990. #16671. Re<karandi>E155 {N} ``^fire-^god".(Munda)

http://bharatkalyan97.blogspot.in/2013/11/meluhha-tree-of-life-update-nov-8-2013.html

[i] cf.1. Kalyanaraman, S., 2013, *Meluhha – Tree of life*, Herndon, Sarasvati Research Center and 2. Kalyanaraman, S., 2013, *Meluhha – A visible language*, Herndon, Sarasvati Research Center.

Tin road to Kultepe

"So far, the excavations at Kultepe have brought to light ca. 23,500 tablets, of which 23,000 tablets are from level II and only 500 from level Ib. A very large portion of these finds were from the excavations in the kārum area...The written documents inform us that the kārum was a fortified city protected by city walls. The kārum II city is composed of quarters, separated by squares and streets...Metal was of primary importance in this international trade center; the metal workshops lay in various parts of the settlement...Copper, bronze, silver, gold, electrum, and lead vessels, weapons, belt-buckles and spools, cymbals, pins, zoomorphic and anthropomorphic figurines, and rings with various functions constitute an important collection...The vessels were formed by using forging and casting techniques, while riveting and soldering were used for joining the handles and the other details. "(Kulakoglu, Fikri, Kultepe Kanesh-Karum: the earliest international trade center in Anatolia, pp. 46-47 in: Kulakoglu, Fikri & Selmin Kangal, eds., *Anatolia's prologue, Kultepe Kanesh, Assyrians in Istanbul*, Kayseri Metropolitan Municipality Cultural Publication No. 78, Istanbul ISBN 978-975-8046-79-9.)

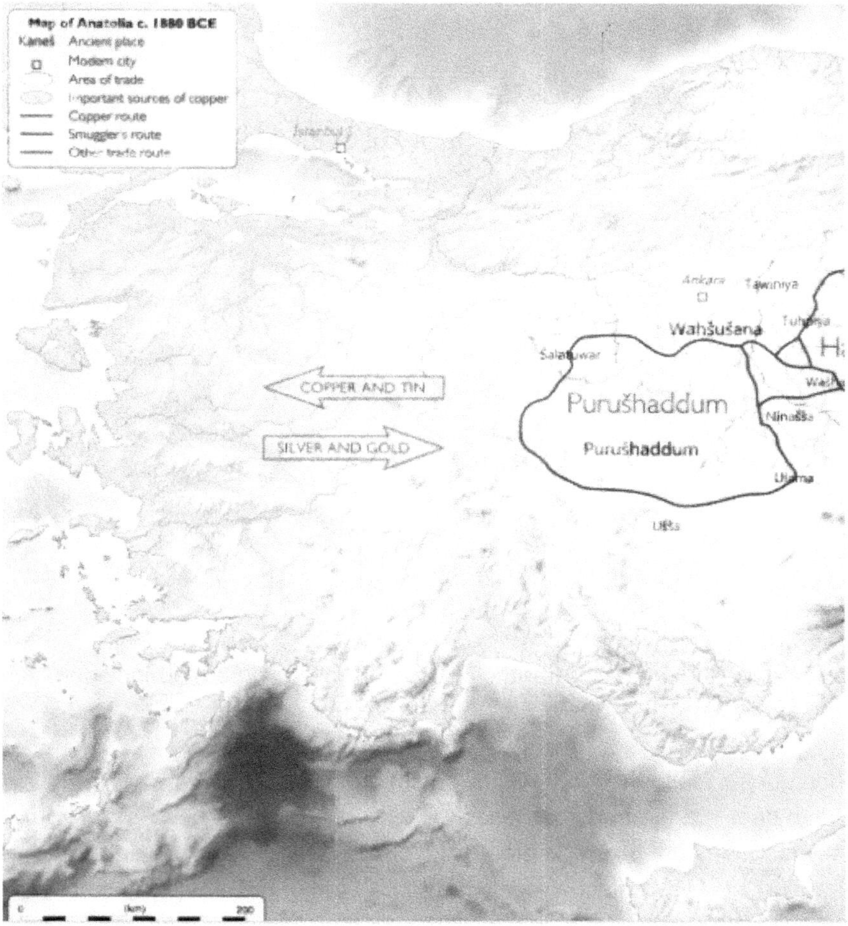

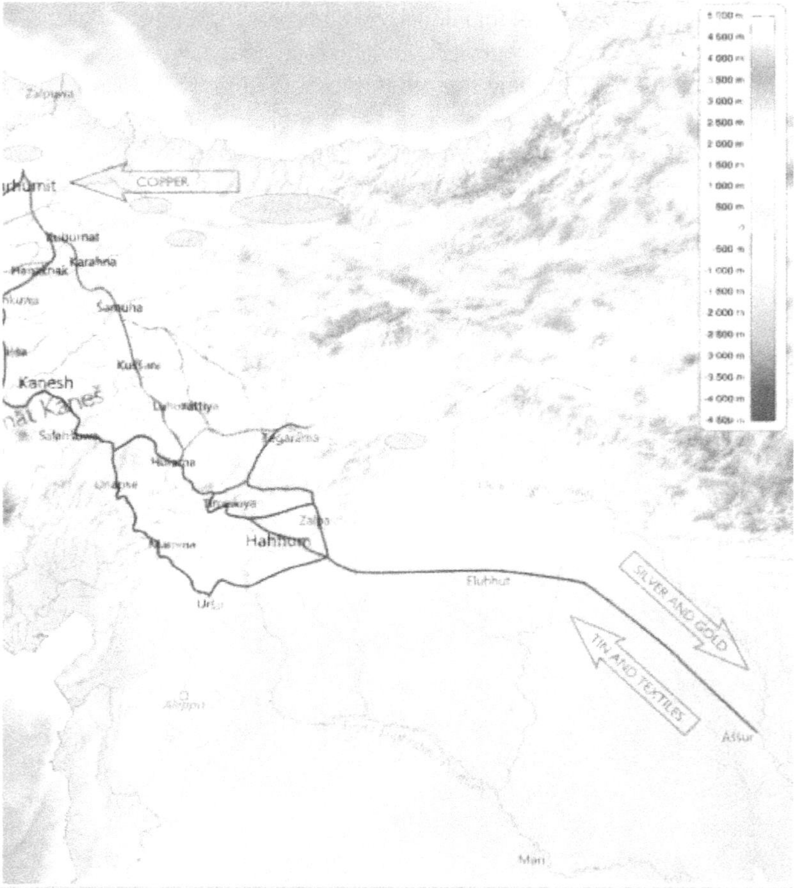

A segment of the Tin Road: Aśśur - Kaneś. After the Map of Anatolia c 1880 BCE included in Anatolia's Prologue...(Catalogue)

"Direct textual evidence goes back to the 1930s BCE, but the network of trading colonies in the region may well have been established generations earlier. The texts we have come from the archives of an Assyrian merchant colony settled at the site of Kultepe (ancient Kanesh) near Kayseri in Central Turkey. They reflect a widely developed system of financial institutions and judicial establishments with a trde based on specialised agents, complex partnerships and an extensive physical infrastructure geared to accommdate it...Assur was located on a rocky spur at a river ford where a caravan route from north to south crossed a track leading from east to west...To be an Assyrian was to be a merchant...Some forty Assyrian colonies (*karum*) and stations (*wabartum*) existed during the heyday of the trade, more than thirty of them in what is today Turkey...The constituent element of the Assyrian trade was the import of tin and woollen textiles from Assur to Anatolia. The merchandise was mostly bought on the market in and taken to Anatolia to be sold mainly in one of three major market cities -- Kanesh, Durhumit or Purushaddum." (Barjamovic, Gojko, A journey through Anatolia in 1865 BCE, p.160 in: Kulakoglu, Fikri & Selmin Kangal, eds., *Anatolia's prologue, Kultepe Kanesh,*

Assyrians in Istanbul, Kayseri Metropolitan Municipality Cultural Publication No. 78, Istanbul ISBN 978-975-8046-79-9.)).

"The essence of the trade was to ship tin, woolen textiles and lapis lazuli to Anatolia to sell it there in order to acquire, directly or indirectly, silver and gold, which was shipped back to Assur. Tin, essential for the Anatoian production of bronze (an alloy of ca. 90 percent copper and 1- percent tin) was imported in Assur from Susa, perhaps by Elamite caravans, and ultimately originated from Central Asia. It was bought in Assur for silver and had the form of slabs that weighed 10 pounds. Its price was fairly standardized, usually ranging between 16 and 14 shekels of tin for 1 shekel of silver, with occasional fluctuations presumably due to changes in the supply...every year several tons of this metal were shipped to Anatolia. The amounts of lapis lazuli, which came from the same area as the tin, were modest (usually one or two pounds) and were obtained in Assur's 'city hall'. Nearly all textiles traded were woolen products, textiles made of linen were rare...The textile product frequently exported and in the biggest numbers was called kutānum. It was the name for a sheet of woolen cloth...The average price of kutānu bought in Assur ranged between 3.5 and 6 shekels of silver...'caravan accounts'...The following specimen is a short one and deals with one single donkey-load (CCT 3,5a): 'Thus Assur-idi, say to Assur-nada: 'you sent me 10 pounds of silver. Thereof 130 pounds of tin under seals, at a rate of 16 1/2 shekels (of tin) per (shekels of silver), its silver 7 pounds 52 2/3 shekels. 4 dark textiles and 5 kutānu-textiles cost 1/2 pound of silver. 7 shekels were lost in the refining (of the silver). 17 shekels the price of 1 donkey, 5 shekels its harness, 20 shekels the price of 2 dark textile that Asssu-taklaku left for you...I took it from this silver. 12 pounds 5 shekels of 'hand-tin', its price at 15:1 is 48 1/3 shekels of silver. All this Assur-taklaku is leading to you. It (the silver sent) has been spent for you.' "(Veenhof, Klaas R., The structure of old Assyrian overland trade, pp.57-58 in: Kulakoglu, Fikri & Selmin Kangal, eds., *Anatolia's prologue, Kultepe Kanesh, Assyrians in Istanbul*, Kayseri Metropolitan Municipality Cultural Publication No. 78, Istanbul ISBN 978-975-8046-79-9.)

After Fig. 241. Mould for lead figurine. 1830-1700 BCE. Steatite. Ankara museum of Anatolian civilisations. Kt. k/k, 063, inv. no. 1938 1/a. Meluhha hieroglyphs: donkey, caravan trader, eye (of woman). *sang* 'priest' (Sumerian) Rebus: *sangi* 'pilgrim, association' (Gujarati) S. *saṅgu* m. ' body of pilgrims '*sãgo* m. 'caravan'. *kola* 'woman' Rebus: *kol* 'working in iron' *kaṇ 'eye'* Rebus:*kaṇṇahāra* 'helmsman, sailor' (Prākṛt) khara1 m. ' donkey ' KātyŚr., *°rī* -- f. Pāṇ.NiDoc. Pk. *khara* -- m., Gy. pal. *ķăr* m., *kắri* f., arm. *xari*, eur. gr. *kher*, *kfer*, rum. *xerú*, Kt. *kur*, Pr. *korū´*, Dm. *khar* m., *°ri* f., Tir. *kh**l*r*, Paš. lauṛ. *khar* m., *khăr* f., Kal. urt. *khār*, Phal.*khār* m., *khári* f., K. *khar* m., *khürü* f., pog. kash. ḍoḍ. *khar*, S. *kharu* m., P. G. M. *khar* m., OM. *khari* f.; -- ext. Ash. *kərəṭék*, Shum. *xareṭá*; <-> L. *kharkā* m., *°kī* f. -- Kho. *khairánu* ' donkey's foal ' (+?). Bshk. Kt. *kur* ' donkey ' (for loss of aspiration Morgenstierne ID 334)(CDIAL 3818). Rebus: khār 'blacksmith'

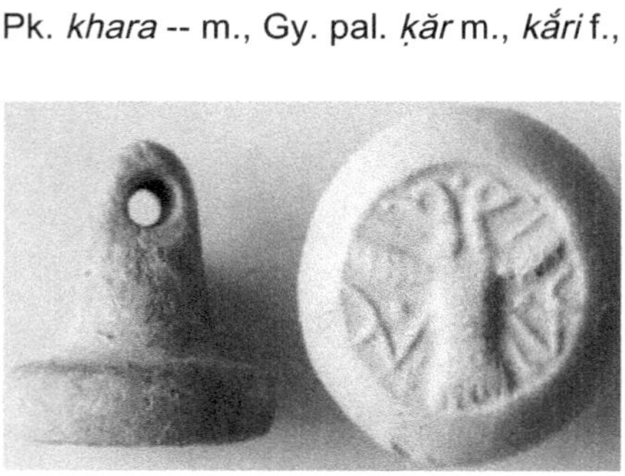

(Kashmiri) Rebus: *khũṭ* 'community, guild' (Santali)

After Fig. 485. Seal. 1830-1700 BCE. Green-gray stone. Ankara museum of Anatolian civilizations. Kt 98/k 067, inv. no. 1-66-98. Meluhha hieroglyphs: dula 'pair' eruvai 'eagle' Rebus: dul 'cast metal' eruvai 'copper'.

After Fig.477. Seal 1950-1835 BCE. Serpentine. Ankara museum of Anatolian civilisations. Kt. 99/k. 085, inv. no. 1-23-99. Meluhha hieroglyphs: *nāga 'serpent' Rebus: nāga 'lead' ḍangar* 'bull'

Rebus: *ḍhangar*'blacksmith'.

After Fig. 469. Seal. 1950-1835 BCE. Hematite. Ankara museum of Anatolian civilisations. Kt. 02/k. 079, inv. no. 1-93-02. Meluhha hieroglyphs: gr̥ālu 'calf'; ḍālu, dālu calf. khāḍū m. 'hill goat'; *rāngo* 'water buffalo bull' (Ku.N.)(CDIAL 10559) Rebus: ranku 'tin' raṅga3 n. ' tin ' lex. [Cf. nāga -- 2, vaṅga -- 1]Pk. *raṁga* -- n. ' tin '; P. *rāg* f., *rāgā* m. ' pewter, tin ' (← H.) karaṇḍa 'duck' (Sanskrit) karaṛa 'a very large aquatic bird' (Sindhi) Rebus: करडा [karaḍā] Hard from alloy--iron, silver &c. (Marathi) kārṇī m. 'super cargo of a ship '(Marathi) *meḍha* 'polar star' (Marathi). Rebus: meḍ (Ho.); mẽṛhet 'iron' (Munda.Ho.)

After Fig. 450 Bulla. 1950-1835 BCE. Clay. Ankara museum of Anatolian civilisations. Kt. 91/k. 113, inv. no. 1-422-91. Meluhha hieroglyphs: star, calf (See Rebus readings cited earlier: iron, maritime)

After Fig. 410. Tablet: A notary document. 1830-1700 BCE. Clay. Ankara Museum of Anatolian civilisations. Kt. n/k.032, inv. no. 165-32-64. Top register seal impression.Hieroglyphs: lion, goat looking back, two tigers. *kol* 'tiger' Rebus: *kol* 'working in iron'. *dula* 'pair' Rebus: *dul* 'cast metal'. *arye* 'lion' Rebus: *arā* 'brass' mlekh 'goat' Rebus: *milakkhu* 'copper'. *krammara* 'look back' Rebus: *kamar* 'smith, artisan'. Thus, *milakkhu kamar* 'copper smith'.

After Fig. 410. Tablet: A notary document. 1830-1700 BCE. Clay. Ankara Museum of Anatolian civilisations. Kt. n/k.032, inv. no. 165-32-64. Top register seal impression.Hieroglyphs: lion, goat looking back, two tigers. *kol* 'tiger' Rebus: *kol* 'working in iron'. *dula* 'pair' Rebus: *dul* 'cast metal'. *arye* 'lion' Rebus: *arā* 'brass' mlekh 'goat'

Rebus: *milakkhu* 'copper'. *krammara* 'look back' Rebus: *kamar* 'smith, artisan'. Thus, *milakkhu kamar* 'copper smith'.

"The development of metallurgy in Anatolia is argued to be the result of complex long-term engagements and interactions among diversified highland and lowland communities.Patterns in the various ways people acquired, produced, traded and consumed metals are givenfocus in this review of recent advancements in the study of Anatolian metalwork. In this paper,we draw attention to research conducted primarily in the Taurus Mountains and Central Anatoliaduring the last decade to examine the changing relationship between society and technologyduring the Chalcolithic and Bronze Age. Specifically, we examine institutions of metalproduction and trade using archaeological evidence to highlight the existence of a complex sociopolitical environment rich in regional technological traditions before major political andeconomic interaction with Syro-Mesopotamia. We stress two conclusions: first, the developmentof indigenous metal production institutions correlates to localized social arrangements inAnatolia. Second, the development of a hierarchy of production sites occurred to mitigate uncertainty in access to necessary metal resources...When past scholars assumed that the development of social complexity and the demand for metal raw materials was a lowland Mesootamian causation, they did not take into account the potential for autonomous social institutions and cultural development in the periphery of powerful states and empires. In addition, the discovery of debris in the Balkans dating to before 5000 ca. BE suggests that the development of metallurgy is likely unrelated to the emergence of complex political economy in Syro-Mesopotamia. The emergence of early complex technologies must take into account the potential for indigenous developments and the structure of the interregional interaction."(Yener, Aslihan K., Joseph W. Lehner, 2014, Organization and specialization of early mining and metal technologies in Anatolia, in: Roberts, BW & CP Thornton, eds., *Reader in early metallurgy: old and new world perspectives*, New York: Springer, pp.529-557; p.530.)

In the context of the finds of Nahal Mishmar hoard (with many artifacts made of *cire perdue* technique), Thornton et al argue that there is as yet no actual evidence that native copper was melted and cast prior to the invention of furnace smelting. (Thornton CP, JM Golden, DJ Killick, VC Piggott, TH Rehren, & BW Roberts, 2010, A chalcolithic error: rebuttal to Amzallag 2009 in: *American Journal of Archaeology* 114 (2010) 305-15.)

A resolution for this debate about indigenous metallurgical developments and transmission of technologies from a particular location is possible. This can start with a review of the possibility that many hieroglyphs deployed on thousands of artifacts (on cylinder seals, in particular) can be explained as related to Meluhha-speaking technologists who were itinerant artisans/traders moving from Meluhha (ancient India) and prospecting for metal sources in the ancient Near East and the in the Fertile Crescent. As yet unresolved is the source of tin; I suggest, agreeing with Muhly, that the source of tin was Meluhha, prospecting for cassiterite and sediment-held lead-zinc-copper carbonates in a process comparable to the panning for gold nuggets in ancient India along the river-bed of *hiraṇyavartanī Sarasvatī*

Tin road trade transactions and meanings of Meluhha hieroglyphs in *kārum*, 'quay, merchant quarter'

kārum, lit. "quay, merchant quarter" is explained in context as a trading colony.

Semantics of Indian *sprachbund* can explain the gloss as a 'place for business' as in Punjabi *kārā* m. 'business'.

कारस्थान [kārasthāna] *n* (कार्य & स्थान) Economy, frugality, thrift. 2 A plot or counsel; a deeply concerted scheme. 3 Economy, arrangement, order (as of a kingdom or family).(Marathi) WPah.kṭg. *kammuɔ* ' busy ';Kho. *kórum* (obl.pl. *kormān* BKhoT 69) ' work 'kárman1 n. ' act, work ' RV.Shum. *lām*, Gaw. *lam*, Woṭ. *kam*, Kal. *krum*, Kho. *korum* (obl. *kormo*), Bshk. *lām*, Mai.Tor. *kām*, Sv. *kəram*, Phal. *kram*, Sh. gil. *krom̥* m. (→ Ḍ. *krom* m.), koh. *kom*, . *kōm*, K. *kam* m., *kömü* f., S. *kamu* m., L. P. *kamm* m., G. *kām* n. ' work ', *kāmũ* n. ' an office administration '; M. *kām* n., Ko. *kāma* n., Si. *kama*.(CDIAL 2892). kāra1 ' making, doing ' Prāt., m. (in cmpds.) ' action '. [√kr̥1] Pa. Pk. *kāra* -- m. ' doing, way of doing '; P. *kārā* m. ' action, business, evildoing '; Or. *kār* ' work, act; G. *kār* m. ' action, trouble '. -- X *kr̥tríma* -- : Pk. *kārima*<-> ' artificial ', G. *kārmũ* ' wonderful, strange '.(CDIAL 3053).

Cuneiform Tablet and Envelope: Old Assyrian Letter 2000.197.A-C (Object Number) Kultepe (Cappadocia), Asia c. 1927-1836 BCE tablet: 4.93 x 4.72 x 1.62 cm (1 15/16 x 1 7/8 x 5/8

More than 23,000 cuneiform tablets of ca. 4,500 years Before Present and many examples of Meluhha hieroglyphs on envelopes have been found at Kanesh, evidence of a trading colony called*karum* dealing in textiles, tin, gold and silver. A large majority date to the period ca. 1910-1830 BCE. Many tablets attest to trade between Assur and Kanesh.

The distance between Assur and Kanesh is about 1200 kms. The Tin road traversed by donkey-caravans also extended beyond Assur on Tigris-Euphrates doab to Meluhha (Sarasvati civilization); the road also covered transactions of seafaring traders transacting in Meluhha-Magan-Dilmun-Elam network. As Amanda H. Podany notes: "Kanesh had access to silver; Assur had access to tin and fine textiles. From around 1950 to 1740 BCE, Assyrian merchants traveled regularly to Kanesh, bringing goods to sell. Some of the assyrians settled there in order to manage their businesses. They brought with them the cuneiform script, in which they recorded their transactions and they also brought their expertise in creating treaties and contracts to consolidate and confirm their activities. Theirs were the houses in which the tens of thousands of cuneiform tablets were found...a copy of a treaty drawn uip between the king of Kanesh and the Assyrian merchants...one can see that the treaty begins with a listing of gods: 'O Adad...gods of the land of Kanesh...Sin, Shamash.' " (Podany, Amanda H., 2013, The Ancient Near East: A very short introduction, OUP, p.64).

The envelope and tablet in British Museum shows the sender's seal with figures approaching a seated king with a bull-man at the end of the scene. I suggest that the bullman with overflowing water from his shoulders is a Meluhha blacksmith.
ḍangar 'bull' Rebus: *ḍhangar* 'blacksmith'. *lo* 'pot to overflow'A person with a vase with overflowing water; sun sign. C. 18th cent. BCE. E. Porada,1971, Remarks on seals found in the Gulf states, Artibus Asiae, 33, 31-7.] *kāṇḍa* 'water'. Rebus: लोखंड *lokhaṇḍ* Iron tools, vessels, or articles in general.

A comparable hieroglyph of overflowing water from the shoulders of a person appears on another tablet case (bottom register seal impression):

Met Museum Accession Number: 66.245.18b
Cuneiform tablet case impressed with three cylinder seals, for cuneiform tablet 66.246.18a: quittance for a loan in copper. ca. 20th–19th century B.C.E. Anatolia, probably from Kültepe (Karum Kanesh) Old Assyrian Trading Colony

Source: http://bharatkalyan97.blogspot.com/2014/04/tin-road-assur-kanesh-trade.html

Meluhha hieroglyphs are a rebus writing system of Bronze Age Ancient Near East

As Sigmund Freud noted, the dream is a rebus.

A *rebus* is an allusional device that uses pictures to represent words or parts of words.

So, too a Meluhha hieroglyph is a rebus, a writing system on Tin Road of Bronze Age extending from Ashur on Tigris river to Kanesh (Kultepe, Anatolia).

It is a travesty of scholarship to call such a rebus writing system as 'illiterate' or 'proto-literate' because the rebus method is made up at least two vocables: one vocable denoting the picture and the other similar sounding vocable denoting the solution to the puzzle that is, the cipher.

Works of art with picture-puzzles make Meluhha, a Visible language. Rebus, a code of literacy, yields meanings of Meluhha hieroglyphs. Such a cipher is attested by Vātsyāyana (ca. 6th century BCE work) as *mlecchita vikalpa*(that is, alternative rendering of Meluhha/Mleccha speech or vocables -- and listed as one of the 64 arts to be learnt by youth as *vidyāsamuddeśa*, 'chief branches of knowledge').

Vocable is a sememe or a word that is capable of being spoken and recognized meaningfully.

A vivid representation of the rebus principle of literacy is provided by Narmer Palette. (Egyptian hieroglyphs: N'r 'cuttle-fish' + m'r 'awl' Rebus: Nar-mer, name of king.) A dream is a rebus. History of Civilizations of ancient times has a record of two remarkable dreams: the first is the dream in the Epic of Tukulti-Ninurta and the second is the dream of Māyā, mother of Gautama Buddha. There are thousands of picture-puzzles which occur on cylinder seals of Ancient Near East which are explained on many Museum catalogs as banquet scenes or animal hunts or war scenes. Many of these picture-puzzles are indeed rebus or comparable to the interpretation of dreams and attempts have not been made to identify the possible language groups who might have deployed such picture-puzzles, principally during the Bronze Age. Rebus signifiers and the signified relate to innovations of the Bronze Age such as: bronze/brass alloys to substitute for arsenical copper, casting methods (such as *cire perdue* casting), alloying ores such as tin, zinc, lead and exchanges along the Tin Road set up by Meluhha artisans/traders also called Assur as metal smelters par excellence. It will be a leap of faith to assume that the picture-puzzles are nonsensical or belong to pro-literate cultures because a contemporary observer is unable to decipher the cipher. While early tokens and bullae (token envelopes) were recognized as ancient accounting methods and categorisation of products, the Proto-Elamite script yet remains undeciphered.

Robert K. Englund provides a succinct state of the art report on Proto-Elamite: "(Tokens) These clay objects consist on the one hand of simple geometrical forms, for instance cones, spheres, etc. and on the other, of complex shapes or of simpler, but incised, forms. Simple, geometrically formed tokens were found encased within clay balls (usually called 'bullae') dating to the period immediately preceding that characterized by the development of the earliest proto-cuneiform texts; these tokens most certainly assumed numerical functions in emerging urban centers of the late fourth millennium BCE...a strong argument from silence can be made that Sumerian is not present in the earliest literate communities, particularly given the large numbers of sign sequences which, with high likelihood, represent personal names and thus should be amenable to grammatical and lexical analyses comparable to those made of later Sumerian onomastics...large numbers of inscribed tablets...which for purposes of graphotactical analysis and context-related semantic categorization of signs and sign combinations represents a text massof high promise...we can utilize language decipherments from texts of later periods in working hypotheses dealing with the linguistic affiliation of archaic scribes...There may, however, have been much more population movement in the area than we imagine, including early Hurrian elements and, if Whittaker, Ivanov, and others are correct, even Indo-Europeans. Fn 44. Rubio (1999: 1-16 has reviewed recent publications, and the pioneering initial work by Landsberger on possible substrate lexemes in Sumerian, and concludes that the fairly extensive list of non-Sumerian words attested in Sumerian texts did not represent a single early Mesopotamian language, but rather reflected a long history of Wanderworter from a myriad of languages, possibly including some loans from Indo-European, and many from early Semitic."

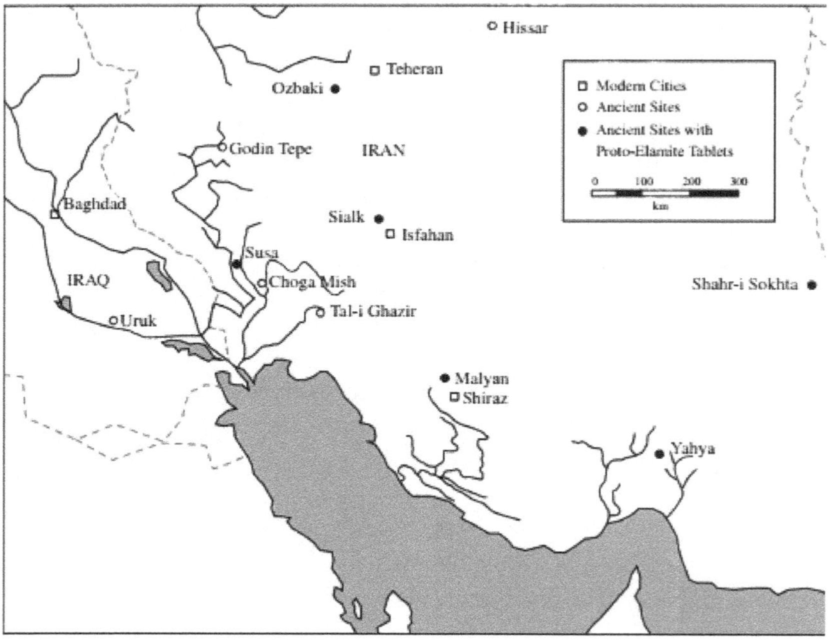

Major sites of Late Uruk and proto-Elamite inscriptions in Persia

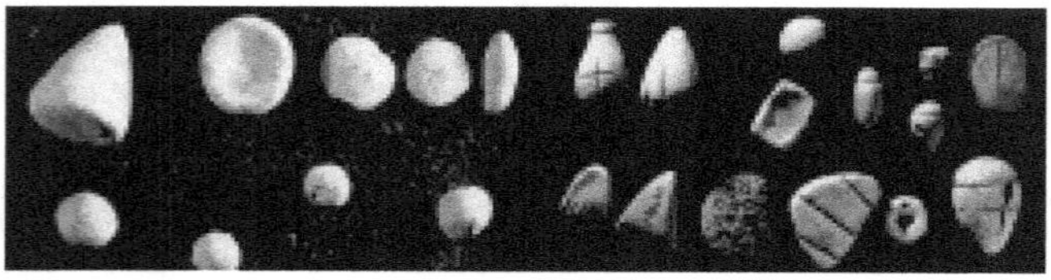

Examples of simple (left) and complex (right) 'tokens' from Uruk (digital images courtesy of CDLI).

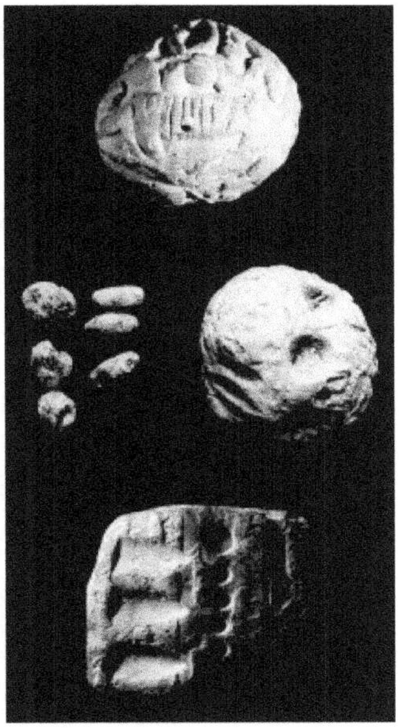

Examples of sealed (top), sealed and impressed (middle) bullae, and a 'numerical' tablet (all from Susa--top: Sb 1932; middle: Sb 1940; bottom: Sb 2313; digital images courtesy of CDLI).

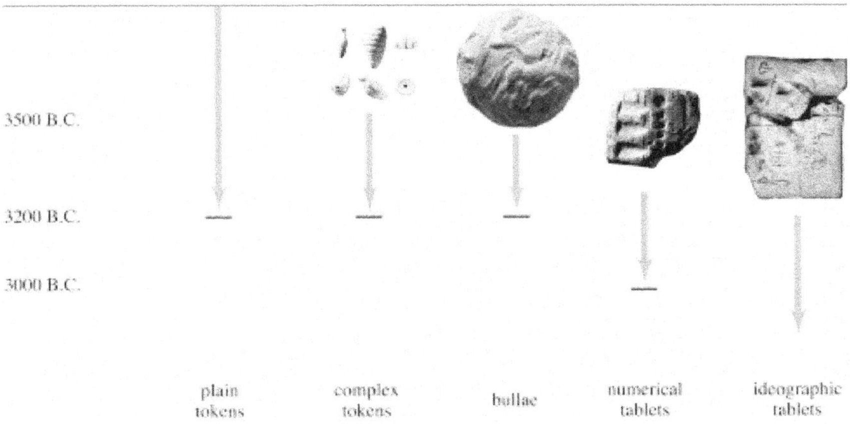

Development of cuneiform, after Schmandt-Besserat (1992).

At the same site of Susa a pot was discovered unambiguously defining the meaning of the hieroglyph which adorned the mouth of the pot since the pot contained metal artifacts (reported by Maurizio Tosi):

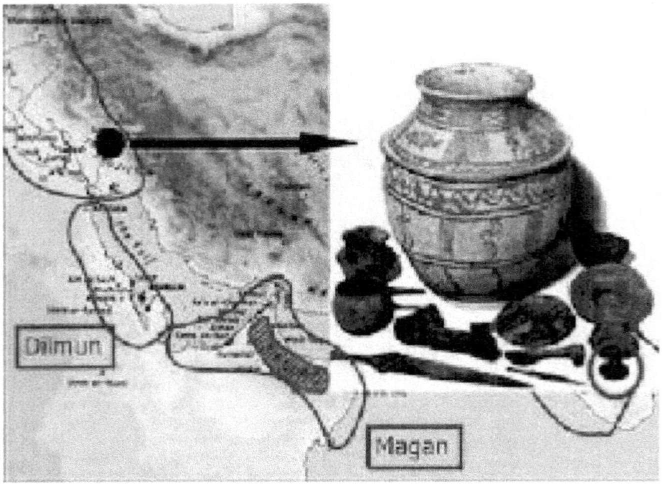

The 'fish' hieroglyph shown on this pot is a Meluhha hieroglyph *ayo* 'fish' (Munda) Rebus *ayo* 'alloy metal' (Gujarati; *ayas*, Sanskrit).

In this evolutionary scheme of 'writing systems' shown on the chart after Schmandt-Besserat-- call them proto-literate or illiterate -- depending upon the definitions assumed for the term 'literate' -- a parallel development ca 3500 BCE is left out: the formation and evolution of Meluhha hieroglyphs (aka Indus writing). The date of ca 3500 BCE is related to the first evidence of writing identified in Harappa excavations by HARP with the following potsherd with a dominant hieroglyph, signifying tabernae montana fragrant wild tulip read rebus:*tagaraka* (hieroglyph) rebus: *tagara* 'tin (ore)' in Meluhha (Indian sprachbund or proto-Indian).

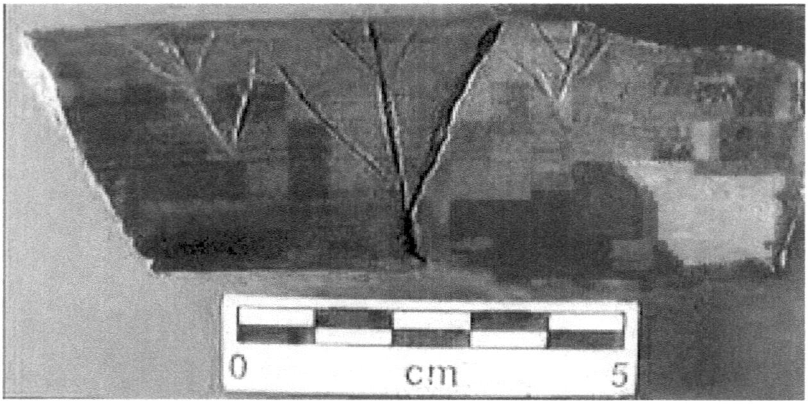

Bronze Age innovations created by Wanderworter --seafaring and land caravans of Meluhha artisans and merchants speaking a version of Proto-Indian --result in the messaging system using hieroglyphs of Meluhha read rebus.

Forcefully refuting claims (characterised as a hoax) of 'illiteracy', Massimo Vidale argues that it is a cop-out to avoid researches into meanings of picture-puzzles by assuming that 'signs' as distinct from 'pictorial motifs' have to be either alphabets or syllables resulting in inscriptions longer than 5 signs and assuming that such glyphs cannot be read as logographs. This is shoot-and-scoot scholarship because the claimants have not so far responded to the refutation by Massimo Vidale indicating the use of the writing system in the context of trade in an extensive contact area from the Fertile Crescent to the Ganga-Yamuna river basin.

Allegedly scholarly, but disdainful,claims of 'illiteracy' do NOT cnnstitute an advance in knowledge to promote the study of now nearly 7000 artifacts with what I have called Meluhha hieroglyphs (aka Indus script) in Ancient Near East (not counting the Tin Road related documents). Witzel et al have erred on a simple assumption that the 'signs' of the script have to be syllabic or alphabetic. They ignored the possibility that they could be logographs including the crocodile, tiger, buffalo etc.which could have been read rebus as Meluhha hieroglyphs. I have shown that almost all the so-called 'signs' and 'pictorial motis' of Indus writing are Meluhha hieroglyphs.

The average number of hieroglyphs, about 5 or 6 are adequate to represent the vocables as pictures (hieroglyphs) to support a trading system complementing the innovations of the Bronze Age stone and metalcrafts. Most of the Meluhha hieroglyphs signify metalware and stoneware together with brief accounts of methods used to smelt or forge or cast artifacts. One most frequently deployed hieroglyph is a 'standard device' shown mostly in front of a one-horned young bull. This *sangaḍa* hieroglyph had rebus readings:*sā̃gāḍā* m. ' frame of a building '; *sangara* 'fortification'; *jangaḍ* accounting for mercatile transactions 'goods entrusted on approval basis'.

Take for example this cylinder seal picture-puzzle which can be resolved by Meluhha hieroglyphs and Meluhha cipher:

Cylinder seal. Provenience: Khafaje Kh. VII 256 Jemdet Nasr (ca. 3000 - 2800 BCE) Frankfort, Henri: *Stratified Cylinder Seals from the Diyala Region.* Oriental Institute Publications 72. Chicago: University of Chicago Press, no. 34.

karaṇḍa 'duck' (Sanskrit) karaṛa 'a very large aquatic bird' (Sindhi) Rebus: करडा [*karaḍā*] Hard from alloy--iron, silver &c. (Marathi)

karaḍa 'panther' Rebus: *karaḍā* 'hard alloy'.
khōṇḍa A stock or stump (Marathi); 'leafless tree' (Marathi). Rebus: *kõdār* 'turner' (Bengali); *kõdā* 'to turn in a lathe' (Bengali).

kāṇḍa 'flowing water' Rebus: *kāṇḍā* 'metalware, tools, pots and pans'.
kul 'tiger' (Santali); *kōlu* id. (Telugu) kōlupuli = Bengal tiger (Telugu)कोल्हा [kōlhā] कोल्हें [kōlhēṃ] A jackal (Marathi) Rebus: *kole.l* 'temple, smithy' (Kota.) *kol* = pañcalōha, a metallic alloy containing five metals (Tamil): copper, brass, tin, lead and iron (Sanskrit); an alternative list of five metals: gold, silver, copper, tin (lead), and iron (dhātu; Nānārtharatnākara. 82; Mangarāja's Nighaṇṭu. 498)(Kannada) *kol, kolhe*, 'the *koles*, iron smelters speaking a language akin to that of Santals' (Santali)

sãgāḍā m. ' frame of a building ', *°ḍī* f. ' lathe '(CDIAL 12859) Rebus*: sangataras.* संगतराश lit. 'to collect stones, stone-cutter, mason.'

Such rebus readings are consistent with Robert K. Englund's summing up pointing to the possibility of non-Sumerian participants in the Bronze Age stoneware, metalware repertoire which constituted a veritable multi-national, industrial revolution of Bronze Age.
Tukulti Ninurta's altar with hieroglyphs happened in a domain where cuneiform was used -- say between Assur and Kanesh on Tin Road. Do the hieroglyphs on the altar mean Tukulti was illiterate? Tukulti altar displays on one side: safflower, rod on altar and on another side 2. spoked wheel. These are hieroglyphs related to bronze age alloys and fire-god *karandi* in Remo language (Munda family). The identification of Meluhha hieroglyphs proceeded from DT Potts' brilliant ingisht identifying *tabernae montana* wild tulip glyph on Tell Abraq axe, also on a vase and on a comb. TA 1649 Tell Abraq.(D.T. Potts, South and Central Asian elements at Tell Abraq (Emirate of Umm al-Qaiwain, United Arab Emirates), c. 2200 BC—CE 400. Potts' insight is complemented by the view of an archaeometallurgist who sees a link between the evolution of Bronze Age from a chalcolithic phase and the emergence of writing systems: "The Early Bronze Age of the 3rd millennium BCE saw the first development of a truly international age of metallurgy... The question is, of course, why all this took place in the 3rd millennium BCE... It seems to me that any attempt to explain why things suddenly took off about 3000 BCE has to explain the most important development, the birth of the art of writing... As for the concept of a Bronze Age one of the most significant events in the 3rd millennium was the development of true tin-bronze alongside an arsenical alloy of copper..." (J.D. Muhly, 1973, *Copper and Tin*, Conn.: Archon., Hamden; Transactions of Connecticut Academy of Arts and Sciences, vol. 43, p. 221f.) In this context, it is apposite to underscore the use of Meluhha hieroglyphs on two pure tin ingots which were discovered in a shipwreck at Haifa. (S. Kalyanaraman, 2010, The Bronze Age Writing System of Sarasvati Hieroglyphics as Evidenced by Two "Rosetta Stones" –

Decoding Indus script as repertoire of the mints/smithy/mine-workers of Meluhha, *Journal of Indo-Judaic Studies, Number 11, pp. 47-74).*

Potts has explained further that nomadism was a remarkable phenomenon in ancient Iran. "Although evidence of 'proto-Median' agriculture and settled life may be difficult to find outside of Iran -- particularly as their 'homeland' remains vague and ill-defined -- linguistic studies suggest that some of the earliest Iranian speakers to reach the Iranian plateau did have an agricultural background and were familiar with both ploughing ad irrigation." Potts cites J. Puhvel, 'The Indo-European and Indo-Aryan plough: A linguistic study of technological diffusion,' *Technology and Culture* 5/2. 1964: 184-186, the posited Indo-Iraia verb stem **karś*- meaning 'to plough', may have been a loanword.' (Potts 2014 - *Nomadism in Iran: From Antiquity to the Modern Era*. New York: Oxford University Press, p. 75)

This hieroglyph is central to the entire corpora; it is the rosetta stone; it is a signifier *tagaraka*, wild fragrant tulip and the signified word is: *tagara*, TIN (cassiterite ore).

Massimo's arguments are convincing in the context of Wanderworter evidence from an extensive area deploying Meluhha hieroglyphs.

Massimo Vidale provided an effective rebuttal of the claim made by Steve Farmer, Richard Sproat & Michael Witzel that Harappan civilization was illiterate. (Massimo Vidale, 2007, 'The collapse melts down: a reply to Farmer, Sproat and Witzel', *East and West,* vol. 57, no. 1-4, pp. 333 to 366). Excerpts: "My purpose is to reply to 'The collapse of the Indus script thesis: the myth of a literate Harappan civilization', by Steve Farmer, Richard Sproat & Michael Witzel, in Electronic Journal of Vedic Studies (EJVS), 11, 2, 2004, pp. 19-57. I actually think that the Indus script was probably a protohistoric script, somehow conveying the sounds and words of one or more still unidentified languages. Although proofs are obviously lacking (the only demonstration would be a successful translation), this is the most reasonable assumption: and I must confess that I have lived so far rather content with such uncertainty...In order to decipher a lost writing system, you have to guess the language, guess the content, and you need relevant contexts on which independently and reasonably test your ideas...Farmer, Sproat & Witzel loudly stated that they have solved the mystery, that the Indus script is not writing, and that they can read or interpret part of the signs, I disagree with their arguments and, perhaps more, with the tone and language adopted by the authors...The authors would like to throw the ball to their opponents, asking them to refute their views by providing a sound decipherment in linguistic terms. But they have raised the problem, proposing a different interpretation and the first readings, and they have to provide a demonstration of their thesis by interpreting and explaining to us the symbolic sequences following the equivalent of their condition 4 (as stated at p. 48)...(but for the moment even Farmer & others will admit that their deities on vessels and seals and the solar cult advertised at Dholavira did not cost them such an impressive outburst of imagination)."

The epigraphs or artifacts so rendered as signifiers, as hieroglyphs are read rebus as Bronze Act metalware, stoneware repertoire. *Cire perdue* casting gets a name: *dhokra* (Meluhha) and the specialist artisans are called*dhokra kamar* (Meluhha).

Zinc is *sattiya, jasta* and the signifier is the svastika (sattiya). Pewter is *tuthnag*, the signifier includes a snake. Sharpness of alloyed metal derived from alloying is *padm*, the signifier is the snake-hood, *paṭam.*

Meluhha artisans and traders operating along the Tin Road had carried with them the signifiers and signifieds and deployed them as epigraphs or artifacts to convey what they were specialists in. They had also produced 1. the flagposts found in Nahar Mishmar arsenical copper artifacts and 2. the leopard weights of Shahi Tump (Baluchistan).

Both the dreams are narrated in ancient texts and also on sculptures and epigraphs. The ancient texts describe the life-activities which the dreams signified. The hieroglyphs used on sculptures ad epigraphs provide for rebus representations of the dreams.

Rebus readings of the images (signifiers) yield the glosses related to life-activities (signifieds).

Both the dreams are presented in visible language of Meluhha using hieroglyphs, read rebus.

Dream of Tukulti-Ninurta and Māyā's dream are signified by visible language

"The dream is a rebus." (Freud, Sigmund, 1959, *Interpretation of Dreams*, p. 1).

One method of derivings meanings of the symbolism in dreams (or unconscious thought) is rebus.

Defining rebus as a picture-puzzle, Sigmund Frued elaborates the concept of displacement of emphasis and affect:

"A correct judgment of the picture-puzzle results only if I make no such objections to the whole and its parts, but if, on the contrary, I take pains to replace each picture by the syllable or word which it is capable of representing by means of any sort of reference, the words which are thus brought together are no longer meaningless, but may constitute a most beautiful and sensible expression. Now the dream is a picture-puzzle of this sort, and our predecessors in the field of dream interpretation have made the mistake of judging the rebus as an artistic composition. As such it appears nonsensical and worthless." (Freud, Sigmund, 1913, Trans. by AA Brill, Interpretation of Dreams, Chapter VI, The dream-work, New York, The Macmillan Company http://www.bartleby.com/285/6.html)

The meanings of the visible images are signified by rebus readings of Meluhha language of Assur (Ancient Near East) and Asur (Ancient India).
The signifier of Māyā's dream is an elephant. The word which signifies an elephant is *ibha*(Meluhha~Sanskrit). Rebus reading provides the signified: *ib* 'iron'. This is a condensation of the life activities of Māyā's clan, *koliya, Koliya* are *koles*, who are iron workers of yore from several generations. Her unconscious thought conditioned by the life of iron workers and smelters who were associated with her lineage identifies them by the product of their labour, *ib* 'iron'. The signifier for this life-activity of working in iron is*ibha*, 'elephant'.

The inscription on the Tukulti Ninurta altar says: god Nusku.
The image is that of an ancestor of Tukulti Ninurta -- ancestor remembered in his dream?-- kneeling before the empty throne of the fire-god Nusku, occupied by what appears to be a flame.

Interpretation of the dream as rebus yields the meaning, the prayer is to fire-god *Karandi.* So, what is depicted is a flame while signifying the fire-god Karandi. In Meluhha language, the rebus reading of a clump of wood is करंडा [*karaṇḍā*].

Tukulti Ninurta's ancestor is an Assur, yes, the Assur whose lineage continues to be called Assur in some parts of India: Chattisgarh, Bastar, Santal paraganas, speaking an Asuri language (Meluhha dialect in the Munda language traditions of Indian *sprachbund*). This is good evidence that Assur of India had travelled far and wide into on the banks of Tigris river establishing the Tin Road between Assur and Kanesh (Kultepe, Anatolia). So, unconscious thought relates to the life-activities of the Assur people on this Tin Road trading in bronze-age artifacts. Hence, the presence of the following hieroglyphs on the Tukulti Ninurta altar: 1. करडी [*karaḍī*] *f* करडई) 'Safflower':, 2. nave of spoked wheel *eraka, arā* (nave, spokes) carried aloft on flagposts as trade announcements. Two flagposts are shown signifying *dula* 'pair' rebus: *dul* 'cast (metal)'.

The trade announcements are comparable to the flagposts shown on Mohenjo-daro tablets (which show hieroglyphs of spoked wheel, scarf, one-horned young bull, lathe-portable furnace --*eraka* 'copper', *dul* 'cast (metal), *arā* 'brass', *dhatu* 'ore', *konda* 'turner's lathe', *sangada* 'citadel, guild'.)

Signifier is hieroglyph: safflower करडी [*karaḍī*].

Signified is rebus: करडा [*karaḍā*] Hard from alloy--iron, silver &c. A color of horses, iron grey.

The signifier of Tukulti-Ninurta's dream is a fire-altar. The narrative of the dream is associated with the messages of the dream signifiers of the signifieds, signifiers of spoked wheels, safflowers signified as hard metal alloys of copper of the Bronze age. The word which signifies a fire-altar is *kaṇḍa* (Meluhha~Santali) The narrative is a prayer to fire-god. How to represent this prayer in a visible language detailing the life-activities which have imbued the images and related meanings into the unconscious mind? *kāṇḍa* is a stem or stick of the sugarcane; such a stem or stick is shown in visible language as the center-piece of the nuska-Ninurta fire altar image before which he kneels down and prays in adoration. He prays to karandi, the fire-god, the signified for which the visible language uses the signified: the stick. *karandi* 'fire-god' (Munda, Remo). Signifier: करंडा [*karaṇḍā*] A clump, chump, or block of wood. 4 The stock or fixed portion of the staff of the large leaf-covered summerhead or umbrella. करांडा [karāṇḍā] *m* C A cylindrical piece as sawn or chopped off the trunk or a bough of a tree; a clump, chump, or block. (Marathi)

The apparent, underlying assumption in the two rebus readings is that the language which provides the glosses is Meluhha and that Tukulti-Ninurta's fire-altar and sculptors who narrated Māyā's elephant are rebus representations of the life activities of Tukulti-Ninurta's clan of Assur and Māyā's clan of Koliyas.

Visible images in works of art are signifiers. Associated words of the spoken language become the signifieds. This is the rebus code.

"In the Assyro-Babylonian tradition, visual representation was considered to be part of an extreme semantic constellation. Like the ideogram in the script, the visual sign had the potential of referring to a chain of referents, linked to it and to one another by a logic that may escape the contemporary viewer but that could be deciphered in antiquity through hermeneutic readings. Such readings were obviously not accessible to a general public, most of whom were most likely nonliterate; however, the potential of signs referring to other signs in a continuous chain of meanings was a knowledge not limited to the literate. The ominous nature of things was a subject of concern fo all in Babylonian and Assyrian society. It seems clear from numerous texts that signs in the environment could be read and deciphered by people other than the scholarly elite or the priesthood. For omens related to the destiny of king or country, court diviners and the priesthood studied the signs, using their scholarly knowledge of astronomy and hermeneutics. But the reading of omina in the environment was also a part of the daily lives of people in general, as we know from textual references to egirru (omens of chance utterances) or to dreams and dream interpretation. Like other signs in the world, visual images could never be seen as the relationship between one signified and one signifier. An image was a pluridimensional sign that carried latent meanings beyond the one manifest on the surface. Since many works of art were made without any intent of presentation to mortal viewers, the polyvalence inherent in their imagery was not always a code intended for a particular audience, whether literate or nonliterate, although one can imagine that the system was at times deliberately manipulated for the purposes of generating a required meaing...polyvalence was considered to be in the very nature of the image-sign. The audience or intended viewer was not of the greatest import in many cases because the work of art was put a position where it was only to be viewed by the king, his courtiers, or temple officials. In these cases whatever meanings were generated through the imagery had much less to do with the good opinion of the chance viewer than they did with the power of the image as a eans of creating an incessant presence. In attempting to catalog ancient Near Eastern images by means of an iconography of one-to-one relationships of signifiers and signifieds, of symbols and gods, for example, we have perhaps limited our readings unnecessarily in a way that the Babylonians and Assyrians would not have done." (Zainab Bahrani, 2011, *The graven image: representation in Babylonia and Assyria*, Univ. of Pennsylvania Press, p. 185-186).

Sigmund Freud refers to a syntax of dreams noting that the pictorial language of the dream uses what Freud explains as 'condensation and displacement' (Freud 1959).

Dream depicted on Tukulti-Ninurta altar
'I have revealed to Atrahasis a dream, and it is thus that he has learned the secret of the gods.' (Epic of Gilgamesh, Ninevite version, XI, 187.)
The Pedestal of Tukulti-Ninurta I

Artifact: Stone monument
Provenience: Assur

Period: Middle Assyrian period (ca. 1400-1000 BC)

Current location: Vorderasiatisches Museum, Berlin

Text genre, language: Royal inscription; Akkadian

CDLI page
Description: Although the cult pedestal of the Middle Assyrian king Tukulti-Ninurta mentions in its short inscription that it is dedicated to the god Nuska, the relief on the front that depicts the king in a rare kind of narrative, standing and kneeling in front of the very same pedestal was frequently discussed by art-historians. More strikingly on top of the depicted pedestal there is not the lamp, the usual divine symbol for the god Nuska, but most likely the representation of a tablet and a stylus, symbols for the god Nabû. (Klaus Wagensonner, University of Oxford) *Editions*: Grayson, A.K. 1987. *The Royal Inscriptions of Mesopotamia. Assyrian Period, I: Assyrian Rulers of the Third and Second Millennia B.C. (to 1115 B.C.)*, Toronto, p. 279ff.

An inscription of Gudea of Lagash (2143-2124 BCE) narrates that he had a dream. He describes the dream to goddess Nina: "In the dream a man, whose stature reached up to heaven (and) reached down to earth, who according to the tiara around his head was a god...at whose feet was a storm, to whose right and left a lion ws at rest, commanded me to built his house (i.e., temple)...a second (man), like a warrior...held in his hand a tablet of lapus-lazuli, (and) outlined the pattern of a temple." (Thureau-Dangin, Die Sumerischen und Akkadischen Konigsinschriften, 94-95 Cylinder A, 4, 14--5,4).

A similar dream is explained on the Tukulti-Ninurta altar. The kneeling adorant prays in front of the altar. The visible image of this prayer is presented on one of the altar. The image on the altar is a rebus.

Tukulti-Ninurta I (1244-1208 BCE) of Assur, narrates the dreams which led to his conquests of Babylon in his epic, a lengthy poem of about 750 to 800 lines. (Lambert, WG, 1957, Three unpublished fragments of the Tukulti-Ninurta Epic, *Archiv fur Orientforschung* 18, Bd, 1957-1958, pp. 38-51).

Narratives from the dream are visible on the hieroglyphs presented on the altar.

Dream of Māyā, mother of Gautama Buddha details ancient texts and sculptural representations providing signifiers of the dream: in particular, the descent of an elephant which is a hieroglyph read rebus, consistent with the dream as a rebus. The narrative is accompanied by Meluhha hieroglyphs which include a scribe of the guild of metal-/stone-work artisans who might have been involved in the construction of the monuments in Bharhut and Nagarjunakonda -- commemorative pilgrimages of Bauddham. Māyā's dream is a sacred, hallowed tradition in Bauddham and the narrative is revered in ancient sculptures and ancient texts. This tradition is further elaborated by the use of Meluhha hieroglyphs which are read rebus, validating the Meluhha hieroglyph cipher for the ancient, unambiguous vernacular of Indian *sprachbund.*

Detail of the top of the sandstone Vedica pillar, half-roundel at top of vedika pillar with composite creatures in relief:

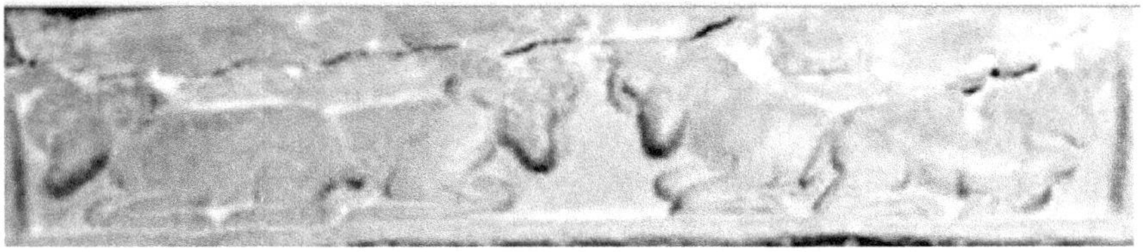

The top register o this relief shows ligatured antelopes back-to-back; the next register from the top shows a bull ligatured to a makara (crocodile with curved fish tail).

Detail of the roundel:

Segments of the sculpture showing: 1. scribe; 2. stacks of straw asociated with epigraphs (incribed ovals -- cartouches -- atop the stacks) and the row of seated artisans. There are two hieroglyphs on these segments: 1. scribe; 2. straw-stacks. Both can be read as Meluhha hieroglyphs.

The scribe shown on Nagarjunakonda sculpture is *kaṇḍa kanka* 'stone scribe'.

The gloss is reinforced by the hieroglyph: stack of straw: *kaṇḍa*

Māyā is a Koliya, i.e. she is a kole, a community working in iron. *kol* 'working in iron' (Tamil).

Koles are the outstanding smelters of iron.

There is an article by Suniti Kumar Chatterjee explaining that the word 'kol' meant 'man' in general.

An old Munda word, kol means 'man'. S. K. Chatterjee called the Munda family of languages as Kol, as the word, according to him, is (in the Sanskrit-Prākṛt form Kolia) an early Aryan modification of an old Munda word meaning 'man'.[i] Przyluski accepts this explanation.[ii]

---

[i] Chatterjee, SK, The study of kol, Calcutta Review, 1923, p. 455
[ii] Przyluski, Non-aryan loans in Indo-Aryan, in: Bagchi, PC, *Pre-aryan and pre-dravidian,* pp.28-29

The crocodile ligatured to the bull is: *kāru* 'crocodile' Rebus: *khar* 'blacksmith' (Kashmiri) *ayakara*'fish+crocodile' rebus: 'metal-smith'. *adar* 'zebu' rebus: *aduru* 'unsmelted metal or ore' (Kannada) aduru native metal (Kannada); ayil iron (Tamil) ayir, ayiram any ore (Malayalam); ajirda karba very hard iron (Tulu)(DEDR 192). aduru =*gaṇiyinda tegadu karagade iruva aduru* = ore taken from the mine and not subjected to melting in a furnace.[i]

[i] Kannada. Siddhānti Subrahmaṇya śāstri's new interpretation of the Amarakośa, Bangalore,Vicaradarpana Press, 1872, p. 330.

Note: In this remarkable ligature, the crocodile+fish hieroglyphs are NOT ligatured to the trunk of an elephant because the scribe wants to precisely communicate the nature of the profession of the artisan guild involved with the prayer to the Buddha narrating his birth. If the elephant was intended, the rebus readings would have included: *ibha* 'elephant' (Samskrtam) *ibbo* 'merchant' (Hemacandra Desināmamāla -Gujarati) *ib* 'iron' (Santali).

Vikalpa 1: the bull is: *ḍangar* 'bull'
Rebus: *dhangar* 'blacksmith' (Maithili) *ḍangar* 'blacksmith' (Hindi).

Vikalpa2: Ku. *balad* m. ' ox ', gng. *bald*, N. (Tarai) *barad*, id. Rebus: L. bhāraṇ ' to spread or bring out from a kiln '; M. bhārṇẽ, bhāḷṇẽ ' to make strong by charms (weapons, rice, water), enchant, fascinate (CDIAL 9463) Ash. barī ' blacksmith, artisan (CDIAL 9464). Baran, bharat ' mixed alloys' (5 copper, 4 zinc and 1 tin) (Punjabi) bharana id. (Bengali) bharan or toul was created by adding some brass or zinc into pure bronze. bharata = casting metals in moulds (Bengali) *bharata* 'a factitious metal compounded of copper, pewter, tin' (Marathi)

The two antelopes joined back-to-back: pusht 'back'; rebus: pusht 'ancestor'. pus̲h̲t bah pus̲h̲t 'generation to generation.' The ram could also be denoted by *ṭagara* 'antelope'; takar, *n.* [தகர் T. *tagaru*, K. *tagar.*] 1. Sheep; ஆட்டின்பொது. (திவா.) 2. Ram; செம் மறியாட்டுக்கடா. (திவா.) பொருநகர் தாக்கற்குப் பேருந் தகைத்து (குறள், 486). Rebus: *ṭagara* 'tin'. dula 'pair' (Kashmiri); rebus: dul 'cast metal' (Munda). Thus the pair of antelopes on the top register denotes: tin smith artisan, dul *ṭagara* 'cast tin'.

The associated hieroglyphs, in the context of depicting the narratives of Māyā's dream, in particular (and their rebus readings) pointing to a continuum of writing systems from the days of Meluhha hieroglyphs (aka Indus writing) – document the expertise of koliya, metal smelters:

- stack of straw: *kaṇḍa* Rebus: *khāṇḍā* 'metal tools, pots and pans' (Marathi) Rebus: *kāṇḍa* 'tools, pots and pans and metal-ware' (Gujarati)
- scribe: *karṇīka* 'account (scribe)' *karṇī* 'supercargo'
- bull ligatured to makara (crocodile + fish tail) : *balad + ayakara* Rebus: *bharata* 'casting metal in moulds' *baran, bharat* 'mixed alloys' (5 copper, 4 zinc and 1 tin) (Punjabi) + *ayakara* metalsmith
- back-to-back ligatured antelopes: *dul ṭagara* 'cast tin'; pus̲h̲t bah pus̲h̲t 'generation to generation.'

Māyā had a dream in which she saw an elephant (*ibha* 'elephant' rebus: *ib* 'iron'). The 'elephant' hieroglyph evokes the rebus rendering of iron smelting competence of her group of Koliya. King Śuddhodana and his soothsayers interpreted the dream that she would bear a son who with detached passion would satisfy the world with sweetness of his ambrosia.

Source: http://bharatkalyan97.blogspot.in/2014/03/meluhha-hieroglyph-is-rebus-writing.html

Section C. Meluhha metalwork hieroglyphs

An exquisite Harappa tablet with inscriptions on both sides is an example of the veritable standard of Meluhha metallurgy described using Meluhha hieroglyphs.

63: H-1997 A col (250%)

64: H-1997 B col (250%)

h1997A,B Side B:

balad m. ' ox ', gng. *bald*, (Ku.) *barad*, id. (N. Tarai) Rebus: *bharat* (5 copper, 4 zinc and 1 tin)(Punjabi) *pattar* 'trough' Rebus*: pattar* 'guild'. Thus, copper-zinc-tin alloy (worker) guild.

Duplicated: dula 'pair' Rebus; dul 'cast metal' Thus *bharat* alloy castings.

khōṇḍa A stock or stump (Marathi); 'leafless tree' (Marathi) Rebus: *kõdār* 'turner' (Bengali); *kõdā* 'to turn in a lathe' (Bengali).

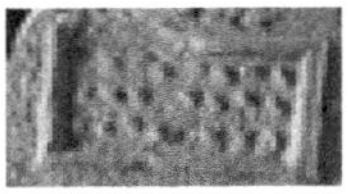

Side A: Text box enclosing 24 incisions or a pair of 12 incisions: dula 'pair' Rebus: dul 'cast metal'

baroṭi 'twelve' *bhārata* 'a factitious alloy of copper, pewter, tin' (Marathi) dulo 'hole' Rebus: dul 'cast metal'. Thus *bharat* alloy castings.
Text of inscription:

aḍaren 'cover of pot or lid' Rebus: *aduru* 'native, unsmelted metal' LIGATURED to ayo 'fish' Rebus: ayas 'metal' (Vedi) Thus, *aya aḍaren (homonym: aduru)*'alloy native metal'

baraḍo = spine; backbone (Tulu) Rebus: *baran, bharat* 'mixed alloys' (5 copper, 4 zinc and 1 tin) (Punjabi)

kanka 'rim of jar' Rebus: *karṇīka* 'account (scribe)' *karṇī* 'supercargo'

khareḍo = a currycomb (Gujarati) खरारा [*kharārā*] *m* (H) A currycomb. 2 Currying a horse. (Marathi) Rebus: करडा [*karaḍā*] Hard from alloy--iron, silver &c. (Marathi) *kharādī* ' turner' (Gujarati)

Limitations of the suggested rebus readings and need for revisions

Some rebus readings may need revisions as explained in the reading of the unique hieroglyph on Lothal 51 seal. Some metal artifacts found during archaeological excavations of Sarasvati civilization may have to be metallurgically analysed for determining the mineral contents.

Lothal 51A

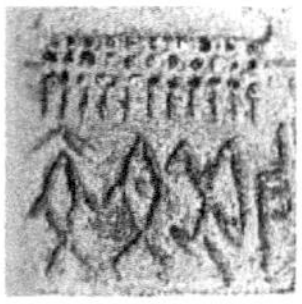

What was the *bica* 'stone ore' depicted by a 'scorpion' ligatured Meluhha hieroglyph?

Text of inscription: *aya aḍaren (homonym: aduru)*'alloy native metal' *aya kāṇḍa* 'alloy metalware'

kamaḍha 'crab' Rebus: *kammaṭa* 'mint, coiner'.*ḍato* = claws of crab (Santali) Rebus: *dhātu* 'mineral ore'

PLUS खांडा [*khāṇḍā*] *m* A jag, notch, or indentation (as upon the edge of a tool or weapon). Rebus: *kāṇḍa* 'tools, pots and pans and metal-ware' Thus, mint metalware, ore.

kolom 'three' Rebus: kolami 'smithy, forge' with circumscript: | *koḍa* 'one' Rebus: *koḍ* 'workshop' dula 'pair' Rebus: dul 'cast metal'. Thus metal smithy castings workshop.

An answer is provided by glosses for three mineral ores in Asuri parole to distinguish among three types of ferrite (iron) ores: *pola* (magnetite), *gota* (laterite), *bichi* (hematite) -- all three Meluhha glosses -- are three varieties of minerals with sources for alloying metals.

bichi, hematite

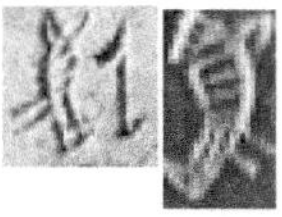 The pair of hieroglyph signs are compositions: bicha 'scorpion' (Assamese) Rebus: *bica* 'stone ore' (Santali) The pairing sign is a composition of: sloping stroke PLUS two short strokes of a 'splinter':*dhāḷ* 'a slope'; 'inclination of a plane' (Gujarati); *ḍhāḷiyum* = adj. sloping, inclining (Gujarati) Rebus: *ḍhālako* = a large metal ingot (Gujarati) *ḍhālakī* = a metal heated and poured into a mould; a solid piece of metal; an ingot (Gujarati)PLUS*sal* 'splinter' Rebus: *sal* 'workshop'. Thus the composition reads: *ḍhālako sal* 'ingot workshop'.

 *bicha* 'scorpion' (Assamese) Rebus: *bica* 'stone ore' (Santali)

Note: In addition to bica 'stone ore', a mineral/metal denoted with the use of comparable unique ligatures is the following hieroglyph:

 *loa* 'ficus religiosa' Rebus: *lo* 'iron' (Sanskrit), *lōha* 'copper' (Prakrit) PLUS unique ligatures: लोखंड [lōkhaṇḍa] *n* (लोह S) Iron. लोखंडाचे चणे खावविणें or चारणें To oppress grievously.लोखंडकाम [lōkhaṇḍakāma] *n* Iron work; that portion (of a building, machine &c.) which consists of iron. 2 The business of an ironsmith.लोखंडी [lōkhaṇḍī] *a* (लोखंड) Composed of iron; relating to iron. (Marathi) The gloss *loh* refers to 'copper' later applied to 'iron'. lōhá ' red, copper -- coloured ' ŚrS., ' made of copper ' ŚBr., m.n. ' copper ' VS., ' iron ' MBh. [*rudh --]Pa. *lōha* -- m. ' metal, esp. copper or bronze '; Pk. *lōha* -- m. ' iron' B. *lo*, *no*, Or. *lohā*, *luhā*, Mth. *loh*, Bhoj. *lohā*, Aw.lakh. *lōh*, H. *loh*, *lohā* m., G. M. *loh* n.; Si. *loho*, *lō* ' metal, ore, iron 'WPah.kṭg. (kc.) *lóɔ* ' iron ', J. *lohā* m., Garh. *loho*; Md. *lō* ' metal '.Pk. *lōhāra* -- m. ' blacksmith ', S. *luhāru* m., L. *lohār* m., *°rī* f., awāṇ. *luhār* (CDIAL 11158, 11159).

pola, magnetite

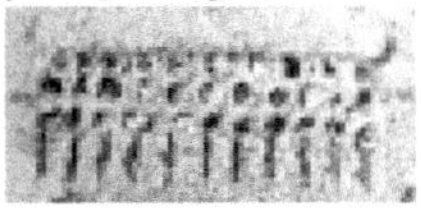 The hieroglyph is stylized beehive or honeycomb ligatured with horns and 'currycomb' hieroglyph.
This has two rows of 12 PLUS 12 holes connoting cast two rows of:

 *baroṭi* 'twelve' *bhārata* 'a factitious alloy of copper, pewter, tin' (Marathi) dula 'pair' Rebus: dul 'cast metal'. The cast metal is pewter called in Meluhha *baraḍo* = spine; backbone (Tulu) Rebus: *baran, bharat* 'mixed alloys' (5 copper, 4 zinc and 1 tin) (Punjabi).

kōḍu horn (Kannada. Tulu. Tamil) Rebus: *kōḍu horn Rebus: 'workshop'.* Also ligatured is a hieroglyph ligature which denotes a hard alloy (perhaps derived from adding magnetite ore):

 *khareḍo* = a currycomb (Gujarati) खरारा [*kharārā*] *m* (H) A currycomb. 2 Currying a horse. (Marathi) Rebus: करडा [*karaḍā*] Hard from alloy--iron, silver &c. (Marathi) *kharādī* ' turner' (Gujarati)

Rebus reading of the hieroglyph: *polā* 'hollow, (honecomb)' Rebus: *pola*, 'magnetite' ore PLUS *kōḍu* horn Rebus: *kōḍu* 'workshop' PLUS *khareḍo* 'currycomb' Rebus: *karaḍā* 'hard alloy'

పొల [pola] or పొలసు *pola*. పొలుసు [polusu][Telugu] A scale of a fish. చేపమీది పొలుసు. *Tu.* poḍasů scales of fish. *Te.* pola, polasu, polusu id. *Kui* plōkosi id. (DEDR 4480). పొలుపు [polupu] or పోల్పు *polupu.* [Telugu] Firmness,స్థైర్యము. "పొలుపుమీరిన నెలవంకబొమలు జూచి, రమణదళుకొత్తు బింబాధరంబుజూచి." Rukmang. i. 158

Russian gloss, *bulat* is cognate *pola* 'magnetite' iron in Asuri (Meluhha) language?

Magnetite is the most magnetic of all the naturally occurring igneous and metamorphic rocks with black or brownish-black with a metallic luster. These magnetite ore stones could have been identified as *pola* iron by Meluhha speakers. Kannada gloss *pola* meaning 'point of the compass' may link with the characteristic of magnetite iron used to create a compass.

1. Ku. *nak -- poṛ* ' nostril '; N. *poro* ' small hole ' (or < 2); G. *poṛũ* n. ' thin scaly crust ' (semant. cf. *pōppa --); M. *poḷ, °ḷẽ* n. ' honeycomb ' (or < 3: semant. cf. *pōka--) L. *polā* ' hollow, porous, loose (of soil) '; M. see 1.4. Pk. *polla -- , °aḍa --* , *pulla --* ' hollow '; P. *pollā* ' hollow ', *pol* m., *pulāī* f. ' hollowness '; Or. *pola* ' hollow ', sb. ' puffed -- up pastry ', *polā* ' empty '; G. *poli* f. ' cavity ', *polũ, polrũ* ' hollow ', *polāṇ* n. ' hollowness '; M. *pol* n. ' empty tube or grain ', *polā* ' hollow '; WPah.kṭg. *pollɔ* ' hollow ', J. *polā*.(CDIAL 8398) *Br.* pōlō hollow, empty; Ta. poḷḷal boring a hole, chiselling, hole, rent, fissure, hollow in a tree; poḷ, poḷḷai hole; Kuwi. porongo hollow; (Isr.) poloṅgā hollow in a tree. (DEDR 4560)

gota, laterite

The gloss used by Meluhha speakers for laterite iron ores is *gota.*

In rebus readings of some hieroglyphs, the decipherment has been suggested as:
dulo 'hole' Rebus: dul 'cast metal'.

An alternative reading could be that the hieroglyph denoted goda, laterite, deploying small globular shapes to denote *goṭ* ' a fruit, whole piece'. In Munda etyma, the gloss *goṭ* is used as a numeral intensive suffix. Rebus reading of the hieroglyph can thus refer to metal castings achieved using *gota*, 'laterite' mineral ore. This is a possible alternative technical specification reading as alloys with laterite ores -- for hieroglyphs deciphered as dul 'cast metal'.

Thus, when three linear strokes are deployed the rebus reading could be: *kolmo goṭa* 'count of three' Rebus: *kolami got* 'furnace for laterite stone ore'. Almost all hieroglyphs with use of numeral counts can be read with this suffix: *goṭa* 'numerative particle'.

Laterites are rusty soil types with iron oxides rich in iron and aluminium. They are formed in hot and wet tropical areas. Laterites can be easily cut with a spade into regular-sized blocks.

P. *goṭṭā* ' gold or silver lace ', H. *goṭā* m. ' edging of such ' (→ K. *goṭa* m. ' edging of gold braid ', S. *goṭo* m. ' gold or silver lace '); M. *goṭ* ' hem of a garment, metal wristlet '(CDIAL 4271)

Kur. goṭā any seed which forms inside a fruit or shell. *Malt.* goṭa a seed or berry(DEDR 069) N. *goṭo* ' piece ', *goṭi* ' chess piece '; A. *goṭ* ' a fruit, whole piece ', *°ṭā* ' globular, solid ', *guṭi* ' small ball, seed, kernel '; B. *goṭā* ' seed, bean, whole '; Or. *goṭā* ' whole, undivided ', M. *goṭā* m. ' roundish stone ' (CDIAL 4271) <gOTa>(P) {ADJ} ``^whole''. {SX} ``^numeral ^intensive suffix''. *Kh., Sa., Mu., Ho<goTA>,B.<goTa> `undivided'; Kh.<goThaG>(P), Sa.<goTAG>,~<gOTe'j>, Mu.<goTo>; Sad.<goT>, O., Bh.<goTa>; cf.Ju.<goTo> `piece', O.<goTa> `one'. %11811. #11721. <goTa>(BD) {NI} ``the ^whole''. *@. #10971. (Munda etyma)

Rebus: <gota> {N} ``^stone''. @3014. #10171. Note: The stone may be gota, laterite mineral ore stone. *khoṭ* m. 'base, alloy' (Punjabi) Rebus: koṭe 'forging (metal)(Mu.) Rebus: goṭī f. 'lump of silver' (G.) goṭi = silver (G.) koḍ 'workshop' (Gujarati).

A lapis lazuli square stamp seal deploys 'zebu' pictorial motif hieroglyph. This is read rebus in http://bharatkalyan97.blogspot.com/2011/10/decoding-lapis-lazuli-indus-seal.html
Link: http://www.docstoc.com/docs/100340942/Decoding-a-lapis-lazuli-Indus-seal-(context)-Silk-road-and-Indus-valley-contacts---Kalyanaraman-(2011)

Face of the lapis lazuli seal.
http://www.britishmuseum.org/explore/highlights/highlight_image.aspx?image=ps267035.jpg&retpage=18837 Modern impression of the seal.

Rebus readings

kandhi 'a lump, a piece' (Santali) Rebus: *kandi* 'beads' (Pa.)(DEDR 1215)
Twelve notches: *baroṭi* 'twelve' *bhārata* 'a factitious alloy of copper, pewter, tin' (Marathi) *dula* 'pair' Rebus: *dul* 'cast metal'. *dul meḍ* 'cast iron' (Mundari)
24 peaks or four sets of six dots: bhaṭa 'six' (Gujarati) Rebus: baṭa 'a kind of iron' (Gujarati) bhaṭṭā 'kiln' (Punjabi)

 ḍāg mountain-ridge (H.)(CDIAL 5476). Rebus: dhangar 'blacksmith' (Maithili) Rebus: damgar 'merchant' (Akkadian)
ṭagara 'ram' Rebus: *tagara* 'tin'
meḍ 'body' Rebus: *meḍ* 'iron' (Ho.)

ḍhol 'a drum beaten on one end by a stick and on the other by the hand' (Santali) *dhollu* 'drummer' (Western Pahari) *dul* 'cast metal'
Zebu: *aḍar ḍangra* 'zebu' (Santali) Rebus: *aduru* 'unsmelted, native metal'; *ḍhangar* 'blacksmith'. *khũṭ* 'zebu' Rebus: *khũṭ* 'guild'

Mohenjo-daro seal. Pictorial motif hieroglyph on this seal: zebu; followed by text of inscription on two lines: Line 1:

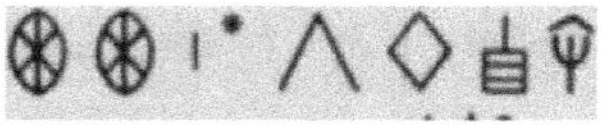

from l. to r. This text of line 1 on the Zebu seal is identical to top line of the two texts of inscriptions (2925 and 2923) on two bronze implements of Mohenjo-daro (m2118A,B and m2121A,B),

That epigaph segments on bronze implements are identical to the epigraph segment on a zebu hieroglyph seal is instructive: zebu is read rebus in Meluhha as native-metal-smith-guild pointing to the possibility that the inscriptions on the seal and also the two bronze implements relate to metalwork.

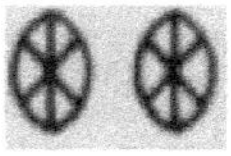

Reading the hieroglyphs from l. to r., the reduplicated wheel-nave-sign hieroglyph is comparable to the wheel-nave-sign hieroglyph which occurs on Tukulti-ninurta's altar carried aloft as a standard. Rebus reading of this hieroglyph has been discussed in http://bharatkalyan97.blogspot.com/2014/07/tin-road-meluhha-aratta-assur-kanesh.html

Excerpt:

A view of the fire-altar pedestal of Tukulti-Ninurta I, Ishtar temple, Assur. Shows the king standing flanked by two standard-bearers; the standards have spoked-wheel hieroglyph on the top of the staffs and also on the volutes of the altar frieze.The mediation with deities by king is adopted by Assurnasirpal II.

The two standards (staffs) are topped by a spoked wheel. *āra* 'spokes' Rebus: *āra 'brass'.* cf. erka = ekke (Tbh. of arka) aka (Tbh. of arka) copper (metal); crystal (Kannada) Glyph: eraka'nave of wheel' Rebus: eraka 'copper'; cf. erka = ekke (Tbh. of arka) aka (Tbh. of arka) copper (metal); crystal (Kannada)

The spoked-wheel hieroglyph by itself reads rebus: *eraka āra.* 'copper, brass'.

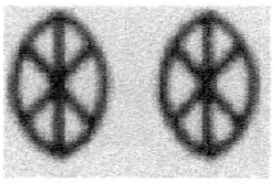

Duplication of a hieroglyph on the Tukulti-Ninurta I altar is denoted by Meluhha gloss: *dol* 'pair' Rebus: *dul* 'cast (metal)'. Thus, the reduplicated wheel-nave-hieroglyphs are read rebus as: cast copper (metal), bronze: *dul eraka āra.*

It is notable that the reduplicated wheel-nave-hieroglyph which occurs on the bronze implements of Mohenjo-daro and other hieroglyphs shown on epigraphs 2923 and 2925 also occur on the monolithic Dholavira signboard, clearly announcing on the gateway as an advertisement hoarding indicating metalwork competence offered at the site location:

Dholavira sign board Text of 10 Meluhha hieroglyphs.

Dholavira (Kotda) on Kadir island, Kutch, Gujarat; 10 signs inscription found near the westernchamber of the northern gate of the citadel high mound (Bisht, 1991: 81, Pl. IX)

Dholavira Sign board mounted on gate to announce to seafarers:
molten cast furnace, mint, moltencast copperwork, native-metalwork, silver; metal-caster-mineral-smith

Rebus reading of Dholavira signboard hieroglyphs in three segments from l.:

1. Copper,brass, iron smelter, furnace;
2. Copper, brass, bronze, native metal workshop;
3. Cast copper (metal), bronze, coiner's mint

Segment 1: *eraka āra.*'copper, brass',; *lo kuṭhi* iron 'smelting furnace'; *koṭe* 'forged (metal) (Santali)
Segment 2: *eraka āra kañcu aḍaren koḍ* = 'copper, brass, bronze, native metal workshop
Segment 3: cast copper (metal), bronze: *dul eraka āra kammaṭa* 'cast copper (Metal), bronze', coiner's mint

era = knave of wheel; rebus: era = copper; *erako* = molten cast (Gujarati) *khuṇṭī or khuṭī* a peg or wooden pin (Marathi) *kuṭhi* 'smelting furnace'; *koṭe* 'forged (metal) (Santali)
loa = a species of fig tree, ficus glomerata, the fruit of ficus glomerata (Santali) Rebus: *lo* 'iron' (Assamese, Bengali)
kana, kanac = corner (Santali); *kañcu* = bronze (Telugu)*kan-* copper work (Tamil)
aḍaren, ḍaren lid, cover (Santali) Rebus: *aduru* 'native metal' (Kannada)
koḍ = one (Santali); koḍ 'workshop' (Gujarati)
dol 'pair'; dul 'cast' Vikalpa: kund opening in the nave or hub of a wheel to admit the axle (Santali) kundam, kund a sacrificial fire-pit (Sanskrit)
kamaḍha = crab; *kampaṭṭam* = mint (Tamil) ; *kammaṭa* 'coiner, mint' (Telugu) Vikalpa: *ḍato* = claws of crab (Santali); *dhātu* = mineral (Sanskrit)

With these rebus readings from Dholavira Signboard, it is possible to decipher the line 1 of the inscription on the two Mohenjo-daro bronze implements:

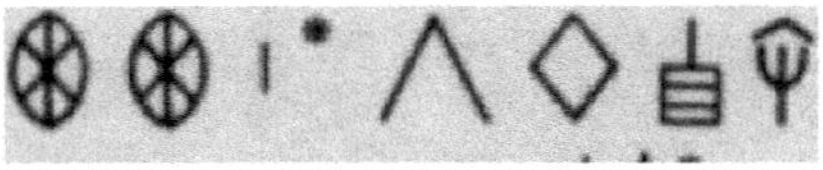
from l. to r.

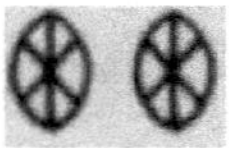
Reduplicated spokes-wheel-nave hieroglyph: *dul eraka āra*

'Notch' hieroglyph: खांडा [khāṇḍā] *m* A jag, notch Rebus: *khāṇḍā* 'tools, pots and pans, metal-ware'. Vikalpa: *koḍa* = one (Santali); *koḍ* 'workshop' (Gujarati)

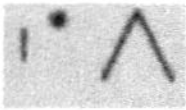
aḍaren, ḍaren lid, cover (Santali) Rebus: aduru 'native metal' (Kannada)

kana, kanac = corner (Santali); *kañcu* = bronze (Telugu)*kaṉ* copper work (Tamil)

ranku 'liquid measure' (Santali) Rebus: ranku 'tin' (Santali)

kolmo 'paddy plant' Rebus: kolami 'smithy, forge'; ligatured with aḍaren, ḍaren lid, cover (Santali) Rebus: aduru 'native metal' (Kannada) Vikalpa: मोख [mōkha] sprout or shoot. (Marathi) *Kuwi* (Su.) mṛogla shoot of bamboo; (Punjabi) moko sprout (DEDR 4997) *Tu.* mugiyuni to close, contract, shut up; muguru sprout, shoot, bud; tender, delicate; muguruni, mukuruni to bud, sprout; muggè, moggè flower-bud, germ; (BRR; Bhattacharya, non-brahmin informant) mukkè bud. *Kor.* (O.) mūke flower-bud. (DEDR 4893) Rebus: mũh '(copper) ingot' (Santali) mũhã = the quantity of iron produced at one time in a native smelting furnace of the Kolhes; iron produced by the Kolhes and formed like a four-cornered piece a little pointed at each end (Santali) PLUS
aḍaren, ḍaren lid, cover (Santali) Rebus: aduru 'native metal' (Kannada) Thus, native metal smithy or native metal ingot.

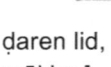

Line 1 of epigraph reads: cast copper brass; tools, pots and pans, metalware workshop; bronze, tin; native metal smithy-forge (Alternative: ingot) Note: It is possible that the hieroglyph ligature superscript ^ denoted *mũh* 'ingot'.

m2121A,B

Text 2925 Mohenjo-daro inscribed bronze implement (MIC Plate CXXVI-5)

Line 2: āra 'six',

Rebus: āra 'brass,

Hieroglyph of 7 inverted U-shaped glyphs: kuṭila 'bent'; Rebus: kuṭila, katthīl = bronze (8 parts copper and 2 parts tin) [cf. āra-kūṭa, 'brass' (Sanskrit) (CDIAL 3230) Thus, the two hieroglyphs together on line 2 read: bronze, brass.

m2118A,B

2923 Mohenjo-daro inscribed bronze implement (MIC Plate CXXVI-2)
Line 2: l. to r.

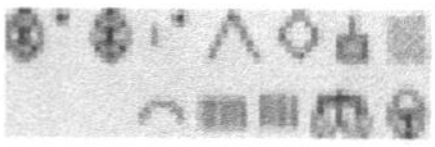

Hieroglyph 'sprout': kolmo 'paddy plant' Rebus: kolami 'smithy, forge' Vikalpa: मोख [mōkha] . Add:--3 Sprout or shoot. (Marathi) *Kuwi* (Su.) mṛogla shoot of bamboo; (Punjabi) moko sprout (DEDR 4997) *Tu.* mugiyuni to close, contract, shut up; muguru sprout, shoot, bud; tender, delicate; muguruni, mukuruni to bud, sprout; muggè, moggè flower-bud, germ; (BRR; Bhattacharya, non-brahmin informant) mukkè bud. *Kor.* (O.) mūke flower-bud. (DEDR 4893) Rebus: mũh '(copper) ingot' (Santali) mũhã = the quantity of iron produced at one time in a native smelting furnace of the Kolhes; iron produced by the Kolhes and formed like a four-cornered piece a little pointed at each end (Santali)

 kuṭi'water carrier'(Telugu) kuṭi= smelter, furnace (Santali)

|||| Numeral 4: gaṇḍa 'four' Rebus: kaṇḍa 'furnace, fire-altar' (Santali)

|||||| Numeral 6: āra 'six', Rebus: āra 'brass,

 kuṭila 'bent'; Rebus: kuṭila, katthīl = bronze (8 parts copper and 2 parts tin) [cf. āra-kūṭa, 'brass' (Sanskrit) (CDIAL 3230)

Thus, Line 2 with five hieroglyphs together reads rebus in sequence: smithy-forge; smelter, furnace; fire-altar (pit); brass, bronze.

 Text 2924 Inscribed bronze implement (MIC Plate CXXVI-3)

|||||| Numeral 6: āra 'six', Rebus: āra 'brass,

 Hieroglyph 'rim of jar' Rebus: .कारणी kāraṇī 'the supercargo of a ship'. meḍ'body' Rebus: meḍ 'iron'

 hieroglyph:'notch, jag' Rebus: 'tools, pots and pans, metalware' खांडा [khāṇḍā] *m* A jag, notch

Rebus: *khāṇḍā* 'tools, pots and pans, metal-ware' (of) *kañcu* 'bronze'.

The oval is a variant of 'rhombus' sign hieroglyph: *kana, kanac* 'corner' Rebus: *kañcu* 'bronze'.
meḍ 'body' Rebus: *meḍ* 'iron'

m2124 Text 2926  Inscribed bronze implement (MIC Plate CXXVII-1)

|||| Numeral 4: ganda 'four' Rebus: kaṇḍa 'furnace, fire-altar' (Santali)

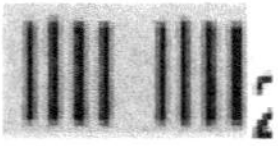 m2123 Text 2928 Inscribed bronze implement (MIC Plate CXXXII-1)

|||| Numeral 4: ganda 'four' Rebus: kaṇḍa 'furnace, fire-altar' (Santali)
dula 'pair' Rebus: dul 'cast (metal)'. Thus, the reduplicated hieroglyphs read rebus: dul kaṇḍa 'cast metal furnace, fire-altar'.

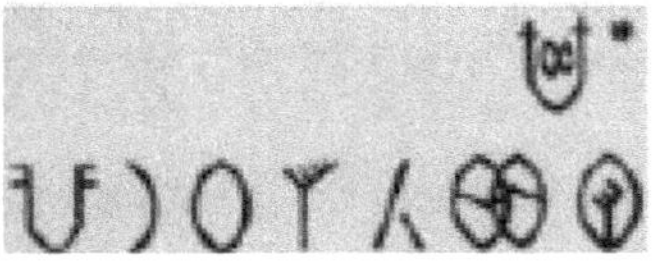
Text 2903 Incised copper tablet

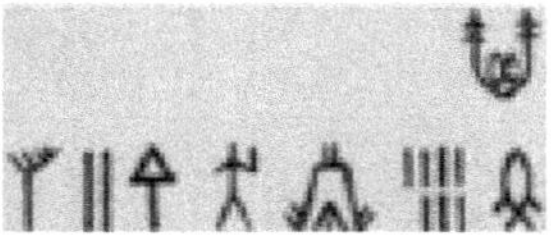
Text 2901 Incised copper tablet

Line 1 hieroglyph  read rebus: kamaḍha 'crab' Rebus: kammaṭa 'coiner, mint'. loa 'ficus religiosa'; Rebs: lo 'iron'. Thus, the ligatured hieroglyph reads: lo kammaṭa 'iron mint'.

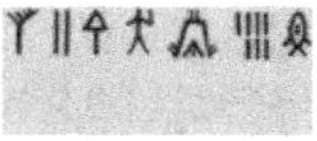
Text 2911 Incised copper tablets Markhor

1.

Two other examples of epigraphs on two sides of a bronze rod from Kalibangan point to the possibility that the writing system was used by metal workers:

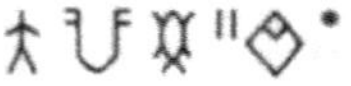 Hieroglyphs on Line 1 read rebus l. to r.:

 *meḍ* 'body' Rebus: *meḍ* 'iron'

4. *kan-ka* (Santali) karṇika 'scribe'(Sanskrit)
Rebus: *karṇī,* supercargo for a boat shipment. *karṇīka* 'account (scribe)'.कारणी kāraṇī 'the supercargo of a ship' (Marathi) कर्णधार [karṇadhāra] *m* S (A holder of the ear.) A helmsman or steersman देशकुळकरणी [dēśakuḷakaraṇī] *m* An hereditary officer of a Mahál. He frames the general account from the accounts of the several Khots and Kulkarṇís of the villages within the Mahál; the district-accountant.

5. ayo 'fish'(Munda); ayas 'iron' (Sanskrit) Rebus: *ayas* 'metal'

6. Hieroglyph 'double-quote' hieroglyph: sal 'splinter'; rebus: sal 'workshop' (Santali) Vikalpa: aṭar 'splinter' (Malayalam); aḍaruni 'to crack' (Tulu) aduru 'native metal (Kannada)

7. *kana, kanac* 'corner' Rebus: *kañcu* 'bronze'.

Thus, together, Line 1 reads rebus in sequence from r. to l. bronze workshop; metal supercargo; iron. Line reads rebus: kuṭila 'bent'; Rebus: kuṭila, katthīl = bronze (8 parts copper and 2 parts tin) [cf. āra-kūṭa, 'brass' (Sanskrit) (CDIAL 3230)

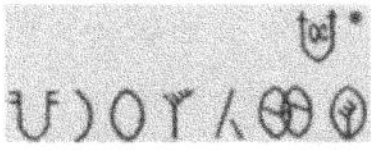

2903 Mohenjo-daro incised copper tablet

Line 1 of this epigraph has the ligatured hieroglyph:

loa 'ficus religiosa' Rebus: *lo* 'copper, iron' (Sanskrit) Duplicated: dula 'pair' Rebus: dul 'cast metal' Thus copper casting. Infixed with *kamaḍha* 'crab' Rebus: *kammaṭa* 'mint, coiner'. *ḍato* = claws of crab (Santali) Rebus: *dhātu* 'mineral ore'

A comparable ligatured hieroglyph occurs on a Mohenjo-daro copper plate which has been interpreted as related to a coiner's mint: http://bharatkalyan97.blogspot.com/2014/07/tin-road-meluhha-aratta-assur-kanesh.html

Excerpt:

The following are examples of Meluhha writing on copper plates (obverse and reverse):

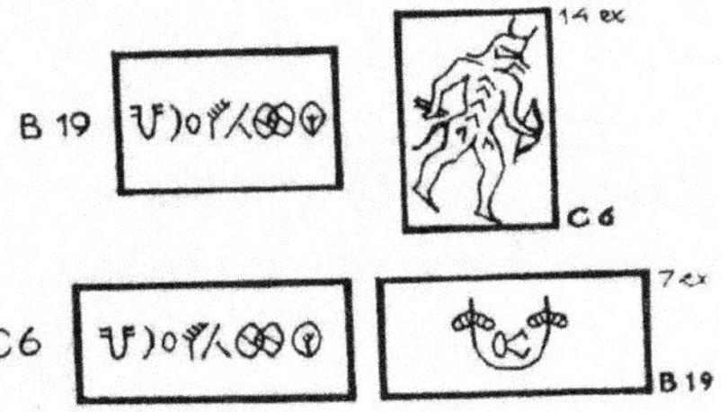

Text of inscription on B19 copper plate with that on C6 copper plate.

Obverse has two allographs: 1. Archer; 2. Ligatured 'crab' 'leaf' hieroglyph.

Meluhha provides the glosses for the rebus readings of these allograph hieroglyphs:

Obverse 1:

kamāṭhiyo = archer; kāmaṭhum = a bow; kāmaḍ, kāmaḍum = a chip of bamboo (Gujarati) kāmaṭhiyo a bowman; an archer (Sanskrit) Rebus: kammaṭi a coiner (Kannada); kampaṭṭam coinage, coin, mint (Tamil) kammaṭa = mint, gold furnace (Telugu)

Obverse 2:

kamaḍha 'crab'; Rebus: kammaṭa = mint, gold furnace (Telugu)
ḍato = claws of crab (Santali) Rebus: dhātu 'mineral ore'.
kamaḍha = *ficus religiosa* (Sanskrit); kamar.kom 'ficus' (Santali) rebus: kamaṭa = portable furnace for melting precious metals Telugu; kampaṭṭam = mint (Tamil) Vikalpa: Fig leaf 'loa'; rebus: loh '(copper) metal'. loha-kāra 'metalsmith' (Sanskrit).

Thus, the message conveyed by the pictorial hieroglyphs and ligatured 'sign' hieroglyphs is IDENTICAL: coiner's mint.

Susa storage jar was found with 'fish' Meluhha hieroglyph on the rim of the storage jar. Susa had contacts with Meluhha.

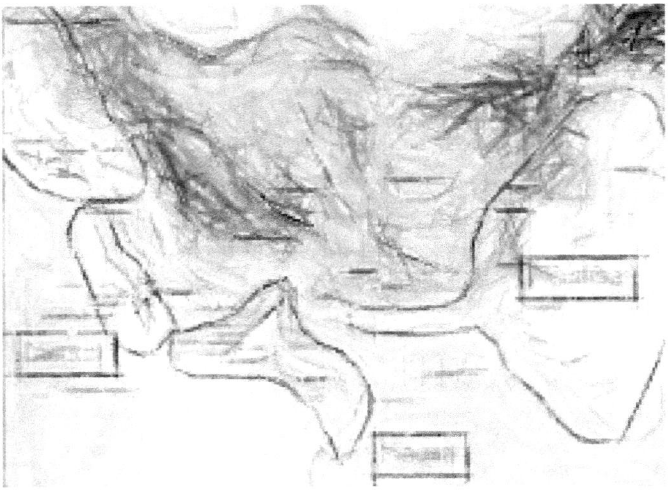

The jar contained 'metal' artifacts, demonstrating conclusively that the contents of the storage jar were denoted in writing by the Meluhha hieroglyph: 'fish' which read ayo 'fish' Rebus: aya 'iron' (Gujarati); ayas 'metal' (Sanskrit).

A'fish' glyph with variants has 1241 occurrences in Indus script epigraphs, apart from 14 objects (inscribed with epigraphs) shaped like fish. See: Bos indicus and fish glyphs of Indus script: metal-smith-guild The decoding of fish as 'ayo' is validated by reviewing the fish glyphs in the context of Indus script and Hindu civilization continuum and other fish glyph variants are explained in the context of pasra, 'smithy guild'.

See:
http://www.scribd.com/doc/235304379/Indus-Script-Cipher-Jul-2014 Indus script cipher ppt
http://www.scribd.com/doc/235304477/Indus-Writing-System-in-Susa-July-2014 Indus writing system in Susa pdf

Zebu as Meluhha hieroglyph: corpora of inscriptions in Ancient Near East

Harappa h083 Text 4236  *khũṭ* 'zebu' Rebus: '(native metal) guild'

Rebus reading of Text 4236:

dāṭu 'cross'(Telugu) Rebus: *dhatu* 'mineral' (Santali). This is a likely reading if the message is intended to convey a mineral-artisan-guild: *dhatu khũṭ*

Vikalpa 1: *ḍag2 ' step, pace '. 2. *ḍig -- 2. 3. *dag -- 2. 1. N. *ḍag* ' step, stride ', H. *ḍag* f., OMarw. *ḍaga* f., G. *ḍag*, *ḍaglũ* n.; M. *ḍag* f. ' pace ', *ḍagṇẽ* ' to step over '; -- Or. *ḍagara* ' footstep, road '; Mth. *ḍagar* ' road ', H. *ḍagar* f., *ḍagrā* m., G. *ḍagar* f. 2. P. *ḍĩgh* f. ' foot, step '; N. *ḍeg*, *ḍek* ' pace '; Mth. *ḍeg* ' footstep '; H. *ḍig*, *ḍeg* f. ' pace '. 3. L. *dagg* m. ' road ', *daggaṛ rāh* m. ' wide road ' (mult. *ḍaggar rāh* < *daggaṛ*?); P. *dagaṛ* m. ' road ', H. *dagṛā* m.(CDIAL

5523).Rebus: *ḍhangar* 'blacksmith' (Maithili) *ḍagar* 'road' (Hindi) Rebus: *damgar* 'merchant'; *tamkāru* id. (Akkadian)

The message of the h083 seal may denote: 'blacksmith guild': *ḍhangar khũṭ*

Vikalpa 2: *bāṭa* 'road' (Telugu). Rebus: *bhaṭa* 'furnace' (Santali)
h084 *khũṭ* 'zebu' Rebus: '(native metal) guild'

h586 Text 4237 *khũṭ* 'zebu' 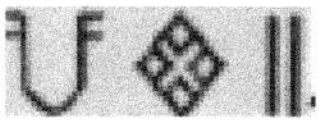 Rebus: '(native metal) guild': Epigraph message: Supercargo of cast bronze.

dula 'pair or two' Rebus: dul 'cast metal'
kana 'corner' Rebus: kañcu 'bronze'

 kanka 'rim of jar' Rebus: *karṇīka* 'account (scribe)' *karṇī* 'supercargo'

'native metal guild'.

h1767B h1767A *khũṭ* 'zebu' Rebus: '(native metal) guild'

Numeral three: kolom 'three' Rebus: kolami 'smithy, forge'
kamaḍha 'crab' Rebus: *kammaṭa* 'mint, coiner'.
ḍato = claws of crab (Santali) Rebus: dhātu 'mineral ore'

khaṇḍ 'field, division' (Sanskrit) Rebus: *khāṇḍa* 'tools, pots and pans, metal-ware'. Rebus 2: kaṇḍ 'fire-altar' (Santali)

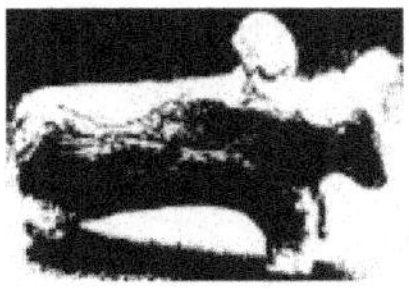

baṭa = rimless pot (Kannada) Rebus: *baṭa* = a kind of iron (G .) *bhaṭa* 'furnace' (Santali)
Meheergarh Zebu *khũṭ* 'zebu' Rebus: '(native metal) guild'

Nausharo 01 *khũṭ* 'zebu' Rebus: ' (native metal) guild'

m0258a Text 1340 *khũṭ* 'zebu' Rebus: '(native metal) guild'
kanac 'corner' Rebus: *kañcu* 'bronze'
sal 'splinter' Rebus: *sal* 'workshop'
khuṭo ' leg, foot ', °ṭī ' goat's leg ' Rebus: *khōṭā* 'alloy' (Marathi)
muka 'ladle' (Tamil)(DEDR 4887) Rebus: *mũh* 'ingot' (Santali) *baṭa* = rimless pot (Kannada) Rebus: *baṭa* = a kind of iron (Gujarati)
kamaḍha 'bow' Rebus: kammaṭa 'coiner, mint'

Line 2: copper furnace pincer instrument to draw things out of the fire

 सांड [sāṇḍa] *f* (षद S) An outlet for superfluous water (as through a dam or mound); a sluice, a floodvent. Rebus: सांडणी [sāṇḍaṇī] *f* (H) An instrument of goldsmiths. It is hooked or curved at the extremity; and is used to draw things out of the fire.

 loa 'ficus religiosa' (Santal) Rebus: loh 'copper' (Sanskrit)

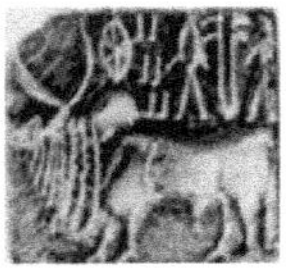  m0260 Text 2567 *khũṭ* 'zebu' Rebus: '(native metal) guild'
eraka 'nave of wheel' Rebus: erako 'moltencast copper'; *āra* 'spokes' Rebus: *āra 'brass'.*

sal 'splinter' Rebus: sal 'workshop'
gaṇḍa 'four' Rebus: kaṇḍ 'fire-altar'
ayo 'fish' Rebus: aya 'iron' (Gujarati) ayas 'metal' (Sanskrit.Vedic)

 kanka 'rim of jar' Rebus: *karṇīka* 'account (scribe)' *karṇī* 'supercargo'
meḍ 'body' Rebus: meḍ 'iron'

 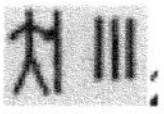 m0262 Text 2249 *khũṭ* 'zebu' Rebus: '(native metal) guild'
kolom 'three' Rebus: kolami 'smithy, forge'
meḍ 'body' Rebus: meḍ 'iron' ligatured with: | *koḍa* = one (Santali); *koḍ* 'workshop' (Gujarati)

  m0265 Text 2155 *khũṭ* 'zebu' Rebus: '(native metal) guild'Rebus reading: metalware, metal tools, miscellaneous articles, casting smithy/forge, supercargo (scribe), iron.

 Read in context, it is assumed to be a combination of a slanted stroke ligatured to a notch,which provide possible rebus readings of a smithy/forge: notch+slanted stroke reads rebus: *ḍhālako kāṇḍa* 'ingots, pots and pans, metalware, tools'

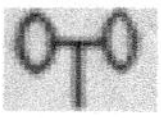 If frame of a cart is depicted, possible rebus reading: अगडा [agaḍā] *m* The tie connecting the जूं & दांडी of a गाडा or load-cart; the shaft and thill-yoke-tie. Rebus: 'lumber, miscellaneous articles': अगडतगड [*agaḍatagaḍa*] *n* अगडबगड *n* (Fanciful formations, or from H) Trash, trumpery, rubbish, lumber, miscellaneous articles.

|| ||| dula 'pair' Rebus: dul 'cast metal'; kolom 'three' Rebus: kolami 'smithy, forge'

 kanka 'rim of jar' Rebus: *karṇīka* 'account (scribe)' *karṇī* 'supercargo'
meḍ 'body' Rebus: meḍ 'iron' (Ho.)

 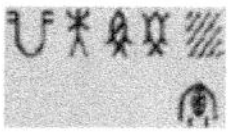 m1005 Text 1001 *khũṭ* 'zebu'
Rebus: '(native metal) guild'

The  composite, ligature hieroglyph: 'arched wheel-spokes-nave' Rebus reading: *eraka āra* 'copper, bronze' *maṇḍa* 'market'

sal ‘splinter’ Rebus: sal ‘workshop’
eraka 'nave of wheel’ Rebus: *eraka* ‘copper’; . *āra* 'spokes' Rebus: *āra ‘brass’.*
मंडप [maṇḍapa] *m* (S) An open shed or hall adorned with flowers and erected on festive occasions, as at marriages &c.: also an arched way of light sticks for the vine &c. to climb and overspread. 2 An open building consecrated to a god. 3 fig. A canopy of clouds. Ex. पावसानें मं0 घातला. मंडन [maṇḍana] *n* (S) corruptly मंडण *n* Ornament or decoration: also the adorning material; jewels, trinkets &c. 2 Adorning, dressing out, bedecking. 3 In disputation; as opp. to खंडन. Establishing, proving, maintaining (of a position). 4 A festive occasion in general. 5 (For मेघमंडन) Overspreading (of clouds); canopy. *v*घाल.

Rebus: मंडली [maṇḍalī] *f* (S) An assembly, a company, a congregated or a corporate body. मंडई [maṇḍī] *f* (H) A green market, the place in a city whither vegetables and fruits are brought to be disposed of by wholesale.

From r.: ayo ‘fish’ Rebus: aya ‘iron’ ayas ‘metal’ (Sanskrit) Technical specificationsof two types of iron/metal: *ayo ḍhālako* ‘alloy metal ingot’ *aya kammaṭa.*’coiner, mint alloy’
meḍ ‘body’ meḍ ‘iron’ PLUS கோடு kōṭu ‘horn’ (Tamil.Kannada) Rebus: koḍ = the place where artisans work (Gujarati)

kanka ‘rim of jar’ Rebus: *karṇīka* ‘account (scribe)’ *karṇī* ‘supercargo’

m1102 *khũṭ* ‘zebu’ Rebus: ‘(native metal) guild’

m1105 Text *khũṭ* ‘zebu’ Rebus: ‘(native metal) guild’ The composite, ligature hieroglyph: ‘arched wheel-spokes-nave’ Rebus reading: *eraka āra* ‘copper, bronze’ *maṇḍa* ‘market’

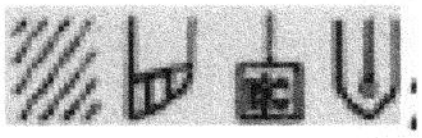

m1106 Text 2331 *khũṭ* ‘zebu’ Rebus: ‘(native metal) guild’
muka ‘ladle’ (Tamil)(DEDR 4887) Rebus: mũh ‘ingot’ (Santali) baṭa = a kind of iron (G .) baṭa = rimless pot (Kannada)
ranku ‘liquid measure’ Rebus: ranku ‘tin’ (Santali): ‘(native metal) guild’ *ḍato* 'claws or pincers of crab' (Santali) Rebus: *dhatu* ‘mineral ore’ (Santali) Thus the ligatured hieroglyph sign reads: ranku dhatu ‘tin mineral’ or perhaps, cassiterite.

khuṭo ‘ leg, foot ’, °ṭī ‘ goat's leg ’ Rebus: khōṭā ‘alloy’ (Marathi)
m1109 Text 1327 *khũṭ* ‘zebu’ Rebus: ‘(native metal) guild’

āra 'spokes' Rebus: *āra 'brass'*. cf. erka = ekke (Tbh. of arka) aka (Tbh. of arka) copper (metal); crystal (Kannada) Glyph: eraka'nave of wheel' Rebus: eraka 'copper'; cf. erka = ekke (Tbh. of arka) aka (Tbh. of arka) copper (metal); crystal (Kannada)
sal 'splinter' Rebus: sal 'workshop'
ayo 'fish' Rebus: aya 'iron' (Gujarati) ayas 'metal' (Vedic) PLUS infixed ligature 'notch' hieroglyph: *kāṇḍa* 'notch' Rebus: *khāṇḍa* 'tools, pots and pans, metal-ware'. Rebus 2: kaṇḍ 'fire-altar' (Santali) Thus, together, the composite hieroglyph of fish-infixed-notch is read rebus: *ayaskāṇḍa* 'excellent quantity of iron tools, pots and pans, metalware'.
kaṇḍa 'arrow' Rebus: fire-altar.

m1116 Text 1329 *khūṭ* 'zebu' Rebus: '(native metal) guild'

 Line 2. Message: ingot forge, cast mineral, bronze.

 Ligature of 'paddy plant' hieroglyph and 'ingot' hieroglyph. *kolmo* 'paddy plant' Rebus: *kolami* 'smithy, forge' *ḍhālako* 'ingot'. Thus, 'ingot forge'.This may be a stylized variant of the hieroglyph providing a variant rebus cipher reading the hieroglyph as cast metal furnace.

 |||| Numeral 4: gaṇḍa 'four' Rebus: kaṇḍa 'furnace, fire-altar' (Santali) dula 'pair' Rebus: dul 'cast metal'

  Variant of compositive hieroglyph: Ligature of two pincers back-to-back. PLUS anvil:खरवई [kharavī] *f* An instrument of braziers,--the anvil on which vessels are hung to be hammered. Rebus: khara 'blacksmith'. *ḍato* 'claws or pincers of crab' (Santali) Rebus: *dhatu* 'mineral ore' (Santali) dula 'pair' Rebus: dul 'cast metal'. Thus, the composite hieroglyph reads rebus: dul dhatu 'cast mineral '.
kanac 'corner' Rebus: kañcu 'bronze' (Telugu)

 Line 1. Message: tin ingot, large ingot, supercargo of metalware, tools, pots and pans.

ranku 'deer' Rebus: ranku 'tin'
ḍhālako 'ingot'.

  Ligatured hieroglyph: rim of jar + notch:
kanka 'rim of jar' Rebus: *karṇīka* 'account (scribe)' *karṇī* 'supercargo' PLUS infixed hieroglyph 'notch' Rebus: *kāṇḍa* 'pots and pans, metalware, tools'. Thus, the composite hieroglyph denotes supercargo of metalware.

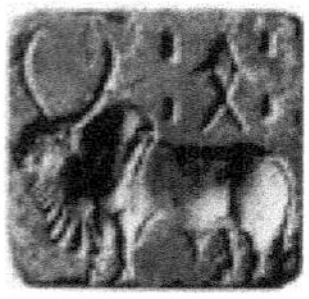
kāṇḍa 'arrow' (Sanskrit) Rebus:*khāṇḍa* 'tools, pots and pans, metal-ware'. Rebus 2: kaṇḍ 'fire-altar' (Santali)

m1118 Text 3157  *khūṭ* 'zebu' Rebus: '(native metal) guild'
gaṇḍa 'four' Rebus: kaṇḍ 'fire-altar'. ayo 'fish' Rebus aya 'iron' (Gujarati); ayas 'metal' (Sanskrit) The particular metal type: *aya*

kāṇḍa 'alloy metalware'

m1120 Text 2362 *khũṭ* 'zebu' Rebus: '(native metal) guild' 'Arrow' sign hieroglyph (variant) This is a ligature of 'lid of pot' hieroglyph superscript on 'a linear

stroke' numeral hieroglyph. aḍaren 'lid of pot' Rebus: aduru 'unsmelted, native metal' *koḍa* 'one' Rebus: *koḍ* 'workshop' dula 'pair' Rebus: dul 'cast metal'; *kamaḍha* 'crab' Rebus: *kammaṭa* 'mint, coiner'. Thus, cast metal mint.

kanka 'rim of jar' Rebus: *karṇīka* 'account (scribe)' *karṇī* 'supercargo'

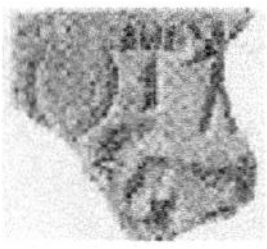
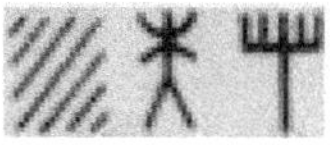

m1122 Text 2610 *khũṭ* 'zebu' Rebus: '(native metal) guild'
aḍar 'harrow'; rebus: *aduru* 'native unsmelted metal'
meḍ 'body' Rebus: meḍ 'iron' koḍ 'horn' koḍ 'workshop'.

Zebu horns in ligatured composite hieroglyphs

A. Zebu is ligatured to a tiger (horns of a zebu attached to a tiger):
m1168 Text 2360
khũṭ 'zebu' Rebus: '(native metal) guild'

Pictorial motif hieroglyph: tiger + zebu (horns): kol 'tiger'+ *khũṭ* 'zebu'
Thus, the hieroglyph composition reads rebus: *kolhe khũṭ* 'smelter guild'
Text 2360 signs as hieroglyphs: supercargo (of) native metal guild
aḍaren, ḍaren lid, cover (Santali) Rebus: *aduru* 'native metal' (Kannada)

kanka 'rim of jar' Rebus: *karṇīka* 'account (scribe)' *karṇī* 'supercargo'

m1516 Copper tablet (Tiger ligatured to zebu horns and with bovine hindlegs?)
m1517 Copper tablet (Ditto) Text 1709/2910

Pictorial motif hieroglyphs: *kolhe khũṭ* 'smelter (native metal) guild'

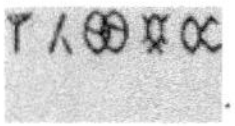

Read rebus From r.:
kamaḍha 'crab' Rebus: *kammaṭa* 'mint, coiner'.
ayo 'fish' (Munda) Rebus: *aya* ?iron' (Gujarati) *ayas* 'metal' (Sanskrit)

Ta. kaṇai cylindrical or globular shape. *Ma. kaṇa roller* of mills, the cylindrical wood of an oilpress. *Ka.* kaṇe, kaṇi heavy wooden roller which stands upright in the mortar of an oil-mill, pair of such rollers used for a sugar-mill. (DEDR 1168). Rebus: kan- 'copper'
kolmo 'paddy plant' Rebus: kolami 'smithy, forge'.

 Read in context, the composite hieroglyph is assumed to be a combination of a slanted stroke ligatured to a notch,which provide possible rebus readings of a smithy/forge: notch+slanted stroke reads rebus: *ḍhālako kāṇḍa* 'ingots, pots and pans, metalware, tools'

dhāḷ 'a slope'; 'inclination of a plane' (Gujarati); *ḍhāḷiyum* = adj. sloping, inclining (Gujarati) Rebus: *ḍhālako* = a large metal ingot (Gujarati) *ḍhālakī* = a metal heated and poured into a mould; a solid piece of metal; an ingot (Gujarati) PLUS खांडा [*khāṇḍā*] *m* A jag, notch, or indentation (as upon the edge of a tool or weapon). Rebus: *kāṇḍa* 'tools, pots and pans and metal-ware'

Vikalpa: *ḍag2 ' step, pace '. 2. *ḍig -- 2. 3. *dag -- 2. 1. N. *ḍag* ' step, stride ', H. *ḍag* f., OMarw. *ḍaga* f., G. *ḍag*, *ḍaglũ* n.; M. *ḍag* f. ' pace ', *ḍagṇẽ* ' to step over '; -- Or. *ḍagara* ' footstep, road '; Mth. *ḍagar* ' road ', H. *ḍagar* f., *ḍagrā* m., G. *ḍagar* f. 2. P. *ḍīgh* f. ' foot, step '; N. *ḍeg*, *ḍek* ' pace '; Mth. *ḍeg* ' footstep '; H. *ḍig*, *ḍeg* f. ' pace '. 3. L. *dagg* m. ' road ', *daggaṛ rāh* m. ' wide road ' (mult. *ḍaggar rāh* < *daggaṛ*?); P. *dagaṛ* m. ' road ', H. *dagṛā* m.(CDIAL 5523).Rebus: *ḍhangar* 'blacksmith' (Maithili)

Thus, the ligatured hieroglyph of notch+slanted stroke reads rebus: *ḍhālako kāṇḍa* 'ingots, pots and pans, metalware, tools'

The text 1709/2910 inscriptions denote: copper, metal mint, smithy/forge (producing) ingots, metalware tools, pots and pans.

Zebu horns ligatured to an elephant with body of a ram, trunk of an elephant, hindlegs of a tiger, upraised serpent-like tail

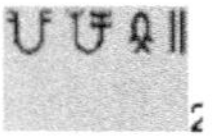 m0571 Text 2913 Copperplate

Hieroglyph composition: elephant + zebu + tail
khũṭ 'zebu' (denoted by the ligatured horns of zebu) Rebus: '(native metal) guild'

ibha 'elephant' Rebus: *ib* 'iron'; *ibbo* 'merchant' (Gujarati. Des'i)

Kur. xolā tail. *Malt.* qoli id. (DEDR 2135). Rebus: kolhe 'smelter'

Message: iron smelter merchant guild.

Text 2913 message:
dula 'pair or two' Rebus: dul 'cast metal' *aḍar* 'harrow'; rebus: *aduru* 'native unsmelted metal' Rebus: *dul aduru* 'cast native unsmelted metal'
ayo 'fish' Rebus: aya 'iron' (Gujarati) ayas 'metal' (Vedic)

Ligatured hieroglyph sign: Pair of harrows + paddy plant:

Rebus: *dul aduru* 'cast native unsmelted metal' PLUS kolmo 'paddy plant' Rebus: kolami 'smithy, forge'. Thus the composite hieroglyph denotes unsmelted, native metal smithy castings.

 kanka 'rim of jar' Rebus: *karṇīka* 'account (scribe)' *karṇī* 'supercargo'

In the following epigraphs, elephant's face is replaced by a human face, while retaining 1. Zebu horns; and 2. elephant's trunk in the composition of ligatured hieroglyphs:

The composition of the hieroglyph of composite animal is read rebus:

khũṭ 'zebu' (denoted by the ligatured horns of zebu) Rebus: '(native metal) guild'

ibha 'elephant' Rebus: *ib* 'iron'; *ibbo* 'merchant' (Gujarati. Des'i)

Kur. xolā tail. *Malt.* qoli id. (DEDR 2135). Rebus: kolhe 'smelter'

Message: iron smelter merchant guild.

Other ligaturing elements are: body of a ram and hindlegs of tiger read rebus:

ṭagara'ram' Rebus; tagara 'tin'
kol 'tiger' Rebus; kolhe 'smelter'
mũh 'human face' Rebus: mũh 'ingot'

Thus, the message conveyed by the composite animal hieroglyph is: ingot (from) iron smelter, tin smelter merchant guild.

Distinct alloys identified in Meluhha inscriptions using distinct hieroglyphs: significance of the 'rhombus' hieroglyph with four corners marked

Included in this inscription is the uniquely ligatured hieroglyph sign: Ligatured sign hieroglyph: 'Pair of harrows': *dul aduru* 'cast native unsmelted metal' PLUS kolmo 'paddy plant' Rebus: kolami 'smithy, forge'. Thus the composite hieroglyph denotes native metal smithy castings. Or, *mogge* 'sprout, bud' Rebus: *mũh* 'ingot': native cast metal ingot.

m478a

खोंड [khōṇḍa] m A young bull, a bullcalf. (Marathi) Rebus: kõdār 'turner' (Bengali); कोंद kōnda 'engraver, lapidary setting or infixing gems' (Marathi) G. sãghāṛɔ m. 'lathe' ; संघाट joinery; M. sãgaḍ 'double-canoe' Rebus: sangataras 'stone-cutter, mason'

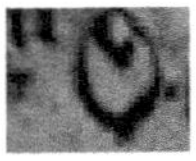

Bronze alloy workshop kañcu sal starting with bronze which is a tin + copper alloy or tin bronze (as distinguished from arsenical bronze, i.e. naturally occurring copper + arsenic).*aya aḍaren (homonym: aduru)*'alloy native metal'

Ligatured sign hieroglyph: 'Pair of harrows': *dul aduru* 'cast native unsmelted metal' PLUS kolmo 'paddy plant' Rebus: kolami 'smithy, forge'. Thus the composite hieroglyph denotes native metal smithy castings. Or, *mogge* 'sprout, bud' Rebus*: mũh* 'ingot': native cast metal ingot.

'rim-of-jar' hieroglyph *kanka* (Santali) *karṇika* 'scribe'(Sanskrit)

Rebus: *karṇī,* supercargo for a boat shipment. *karṇīka* 'account (scribe)'.कारणी *kāraṇī*' the supercargo of a ship' (Marathi)

m705A Read rebus as at m706A

m706A

खोंड [khōṇḍa] m A young bull, a bullcalf. (Marathi) Rebus: kõdār 'turner' (Marathi) Rebus: (Bengali); कोंद kōnda 'engraver, lapidary setting or infixing gems' G. sãghāṛɔ m. 'lathe' ; संघाट joinery; M. sãgaḍ 'double-canoe' sangataras 'stone-cutter, mason'

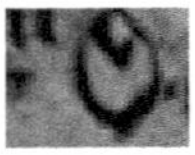

kana,kanac 'corner' Rebus: Bronze alloy workshop kañcu sal starting with bronze which is a tin + copper alloy or tin bronze (as distinguished from arsenical bronze, i.e. naturally occurring copper + arsenic).

aya kammaṭa.'coiner, mint alloy'

Ligatured sign hieroglyph: 'Pair of harrows': *dul aduru* 'cast native unsmelted metal' PLUS kolmo 'paddy plant' Rebus: kolami 'smithy, forge'. Thus the composite hieroglyph denotes native metal smithy castings. Or, *mogge* 'sprout, bud' Rebus*: mũh* 'ingot': native cast metal ingot.

kanka 'rim of jar' Rebus: karṇīka 'account (scribe)' karṇī 'supercargo'

h135A First three signs: Bronze-workshop, bronze smithy.

Bronze alloy workshop kañcu sal starting with bronze which is a tin + copper alloy or tin bronze (as distinguished from arsenical bronze, i.e. naturally occurring copper + arsenic).

dula 'pair' Rebus: *dul* 'cast (metal)' PLUS*kana, kanac* = corner (Santali); Rebus: *kañcu* = bronze (Telugu) PLUS infixed kolmo 'paddy plant' Rebus: kolami 'smithy, forge'. Thus, cast bronze smithy, forge. Or, *mogge* 'sprout, bud' Rebus: *mũh* 'ingot' (Santali)Thus, cast bronze ingot. Read as: *kañcu dul mũh 'bronze cast ingot'*

aya kāṇḍa 'alloy metalware'

Ligatured sign hieroglyph: 'Pair of harrows': *dul aduru* 'cast native unsmelted metal' PLUS kolmo 'paddy plant' Rebus: kolami 'smithy, forge'. Thus the composite hieroglyph denotes native metal smithy castings.

kanka 'rim of jar' Rebus: karṇīka 'account (scribe)' karṇī 'supercargo'

h14a

खोंड [khōṇḍa] m A young bull, a bullcalf. (Marathi) Rebus: kõdār 'turner' (Bengali); कोंद kōnda 'engraver, lapidary setting or infixing gems' (Marathi) G. sãghāṛɔ m. 'lathe' ; संघाट joinery; M. sãgaḍ 'double-canoe' Rebus: sangataras 'stone-cutter, mason'

baroṭi 'twelve' *bhārata* 'a factitious alloy of copper, pewter, tin' (Marathi)
dula 'doubled' Rebus: *dul* 'cast metal'. Thus cast copper-pewter-tin alloy.

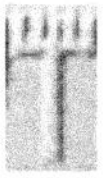

aḍar 'harrow'; rebus: *aduru* 'native unsmelted metal'

Read in context, the composite hieroglyph is assumed to be a combination of a slanted stroke ligatured to a notch,which provide possible rebus readings of a smithy/forge: notch+slanted stroke reads rebus: *ḍhālako kāṇḍa* 'ingot, tools, pots and pans and metal-ware'

ḍhāḷ 'a slope'; 'inclination of a plane' (Gujarati); *ḍhāḷiyum* = adj. sloping, inclining (Gujarati) Rebus: *ḍhālako* = a large metal ingot (Gujarati) *ḍhālakī* = a metal heated and poured into a mould; a solid piece of metal; an ingot (Gujarati) PLUS खांडा [*khāṇḍā*] *m* A jag, notch, or indentation (as upon the edge of a tool or weapon). Rebus: *kāṇḍa* 'tools, pots and pans and metal-ware'

aya kammaṭa.'coiner, mint alloy'

Ligatured sign hieroglyph: 'Pair of harrows': *dul aduru* 'cast native unsmelted metal' PLUS kolmo 'paddy plant' Rebus: kolami 'smithy, forge'. Thus the composite hieroglyph denotes native metal smithy castings.

kanka 'rim of jar' Rebus: karṇīka 'account (scribe)' karṇī 'supercargo'

m750a21A *खोंड [khōṇḍa] m A young bull, a bullcalf. (Marathi) Rebus: kõdār 'turner' (Bengali); कोंद kōnda 'engraver, lapidary setting or infixing gems' (Marathi) G. sãghāṛɔ m. 'lathe' ; संघाट joinery; M. sãgaḍ 'double-canoe' Rebus: sangataras. संगतराश lit. 'to collect stones, stone-cutter, mason.'*

āra 'spokes' Rebus: *āra 'brass'.* cf. erka = ekke (Tbh. of arka) aka (Tbh. of arka) copper (metal); crystal (Kannada) Glyph: *eraka*'nave of wheel' Rebus: eraka 'copper'; cf. erka = ekke (Tbh. of arka) aka (Tbh. of arka) copper (metal); crystal (Kannada) *erako* 'moltencast copper' PLUS

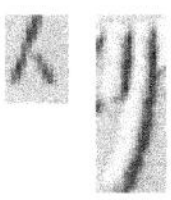

notch+slanted stroke reads rebus: *ḍhālako kāṇḍa* 'ingot, tools, pots and pans and metal-ware'.*ḍhāḷ* 'a slope'; 'inclination of a plane' (G.); *ḍhāḷiyum* = adj. sloping, inclining (G.) Rebus: *ḍhālako* = a large metal ingot (G.) *ḍhālakī* = a metal heated and poured into a mould; a solid piece of metal; an ingot (Gujarati) PLUS खांडा [*khāṇḍā*

] *m* A jag, notch, or indentation (as upon the edge of a tool or weapon). Rebus: *kāṇḍa* 'tools, pots and pans and metal-ware' *Thus, together, the pair reads: āra erako khāṇḍā* 'brass, moltencast copper metalware'.

Ligatured sign hieroglyph: 'Pair of harrows': *dul aduru* 'cast native unsmelted metal' PLUS kolmo 'paddy plant' Rebus: kolami 'smithy, forge'. Thus the composite hieroglyph denotes native metal smithy castings. Or, *mogge* 'sprout, bud' Rebus*: mũh* ingot': native cast metal ingot.

kanka 'rim of jar' Rebus: karṇīka 'account (scribe)' karṇī 'supercargo'

Sign hieroglyphs distinctly specify copper-brass or bronze' products.

Seal m1701a Pictorial hieroglyph:

खोंड [khōṇḍa] m A young bull, a bullcalf. (Marathi) Rebus: kõdār 'turner' (Bengali); कोंद kōnda 'engraver, lapidary setting or infixing gems' (Marathi) G. sãghāṛɔ m. 'lathe' ; संघाट joinery; M. sāgaḍ 'double-canoe' Rebus: sangataras 'stone-cutter, mason'

Text message is composed of two sign hieroglyphs flanking a 'strands-of-rope' hieroglyph. The rebus readings note how the two sign hieroglyphs are technical specifications of two metals, brass and bronze: *dhā́tu* 'strand of rope' Rebus: dhatu 'mineral ore' (Santali)

The text message is: l. to r.: copper, brass, mineral ores, bronze of the lathe-turner's workshop.

The 'rhombus, corner' (or oval variant) hieroglyph is read uniquely and distinguished from 'spokes-of-wheel,nave-of-wheel' hieroglyph; this may be seen from the following tablet which deploys both hieroglyphs on two sides of a Harappa tablet h1882A and B.

H-1882 A

H-1882 B

One connotes *eraka, erako* 'copper, moltencast copper;, *āra* 'brass' + sal 'workshop'; the other connotes *kañcu* 'bronze' + *kolami* 'smithy, forge'.

Another example is tablet m1318 which is a combination of both the hieroglyphs: 'spokes-of-wheel-knave-of-wheel' hieroglyph is infixed in 'rhombus, corner' hieroglyph.

m924A m152a m903a

 Bronze alloy workshop kañcu sal starting with bronze which is a tin + copper alloy or tin bronze (as distinguished from arsenical bronze, i.e. naturally occurring copper + arsenic).

Ligatured sign hieroglyph: 'Pair of harrows': *dul aduru* 'cast native unsmelted metal' PLUS kolmo 'paddy plant' Rebus: kolami 'smithy, forge'. Thus the composite hieroglyph denotes native metal smithy and castings. Or, *mogge* 'sprout, bud' Rebus*: mũh* ingot': native cast metal ingot.

 *kanka* 'rim of jar' Rebus: *karṇīka* 'account (scribe)' *karṇī* 'supercargo'

These four examples of a uniquely ligatured hieroglyph sign point to the significance of the 'rhombus' variant of 'corner' hieroglyph sign detailing four corners of the rhombus. This 'rhombus' is an indication that the artisan smith works with four types of alloys:

Native metal alloy (arsenical bronze -- *kañcu*)
Copper-tin bronze (*kuṭila, katthīl* = bronze), i.e. *erako + ranku*
Copper-tin-zinc pewter (*bhārata* 'a factitious alloy of copper, pewter, tin')
Copper-zinc brass (*āra*)

m1318a

 Ligature of copper, brass -- *eraka, āra*; the PLUS bronze -- *kañcu.*

 *ḍāg* mountain-ridge (Hindi)(CDIAL 5476). Rebus: *dhangar* 'blacksmith'

 kanka 'rim of jar' Rebus: karṇīka 'account (scribe)' karṇī 'supercargo'

 m145A*खोंड [khōṇḍa] m A young bull, a bullcalf. (Marathi) Rebus: kōdār 'turner' (Bengali); कोंद kōnda 'engraver, lapidary setting or infixing gems' (Marathi) G. sãghāṛɔ m. 'lathe' ; संघाट joinery; M. sãgaḍ 'double-canoe' Rebus: sangataras. संगतराश lit. 'to collect stones, stone-cutter, mason.'*

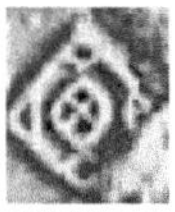 Ligature of copper, brass -- *eraka, āra*; the PLUS bronze -- *kañcu.*

 *meḍ 'body' Rebus: meḍ 'iron' (Ho.) काठी [kāṭhī] f (काष्ट S) 'frame or structure of the body' (Marathi) Rebus: खंडी [khaṇḍī] measure of weight (Marathi) கண்டி; kaṇṭi, n. < Mhr. khaṇḍil. [T. Tu. khaṇḍi, M. kaṇḍi.] Candy, a weight, about 500 lbs.*PLUS | *koḍa* 'one' Rebus: *koḍ* 'workshop'. Thus, iron workshop.

 *kharedo* = a currycomb (Gujarati) खरारा [*kharārā*] *m* (H) A currycomb. 2 Currying a horse. (Marathi) Rebus: करडा [*karaḍā*] Hard from alloy--iron, silver &c. (Marathi) *kharādī* ' turner' (Gujarati)

kanka 'rim of jar' Rebus: karṇīka 'account (scribe)' karṇī 'supercargo'

In the following examples epigraphs which include the composite animal hieroglyph, the related text messages are read rebus (without repeating the reading of the composite animal hieroglyph):

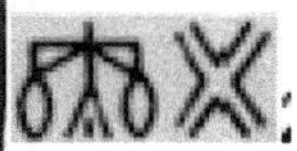

h168
ingot (from) iron smelter, tin smelter merchant guild
M1175a Text 2493
ingot (from) iron smelter, tin smelter merchant guild

dāṭu 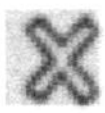 'cross'(Telugu) Rebus: *dhatu* 'mineral' (Santali). This is a likely reading if the message is intended to convey a mineral-artisan-guild: *dhatu khũṭ* Vikalpa*: bāṭa* 'road' (Telugu) Rebus: *baṭa* a kind of iron (Gujarati). Rebus: *bhaṭa* 'furnace' (Santali)

 kuṭi'water carrier'(Telugu) kuṭi= smelter, furnace (Santali)

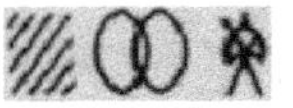 m0299 Text 138
ingot (from) iron smelter, tin smelter merchant guild

bhaṭa 'warrior' (Sanskrit) Rebus: *bhaṭa* 'furnace' (Santali)Rebus: *baṭa* a kind of iron (Gujarati). Rebus: *bhaṭa* 'furnace' (Santali)

 *Ta.* kaṇai cylindrical or globular shape. *Ma.* kaṇa roller of mills, the cylindrical wood of an oilpress. *Ka.* kaṇe, kaṇi heavy wooden roller which stands upright in the mortar of an oil-mill, pair of such rollers used for a sugar-mill. (DEDR 1168). Rebus: kan- 'copper'

 m0301 Text 2258
ingot (from) iron smelter, tin smelter merchant guild

Text 2258 message: supercargo (of) *bharata, bharan* 'pewter alloy (alloy of copper, zinc and tin or copper, pewter and tin)'

 *baraḍo* = spine; backbone (Tulu) Rebus: *baran, bharat* 'mixed alloys' (5 copper, 4 zinc and 1 tin) (Punjabi)

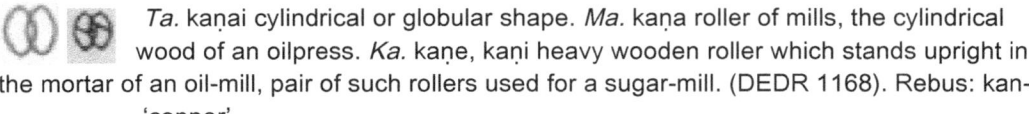

'Backbone, spine' hieroglyph: *baraḍo* = spine; backbone; the back; baraḍo thābaḍavo = lit. to strike on the backbone or back; hence, to encourage; baraḍo bhāre thato = lit. to have a painful backbone, i.e. to do something which will call for a severe beating (Gujarati)bārṇe, bāraṇe = an offering of food to a demon; a meal after fasting, a breakfast (Tulu) barada, barda, birada = a vow (Gujarati)bharaḍo a devotee of S'iva; a man of the bharaḍā caste in the bra_hman.as (Gujarati) baraṛ = name of a caste of jat- around Bhaṭiṇḍa; bararaṇḍā melā = a special fair held in spring (Punjabi) bharāḍ = a religious service or entertainment performed by a bharāḍi_; consisting of singing the praises of some idol or god with playing on the d.aur (drum) and dancing; an order of aṭharā akhād.e = 18 gosāyi_ group; bharād. and bhāratī are two of the 18 orders of gosāyi_ (Marathi)

Allograph: ox, bull: : Ku. *balad* m. ' ox ', gng. *bald*, N. (Tarai) *barad*, id.

Rebus: bāraṇiyo = one whose profession it is to sift ashes or dust in a goldsmith's workshop (Gujarati) In the Punjab, the mixed alloys were generally called, bharat (5 copper, 4 zinc and 1 tin). In Bengal, an alloy called bharan or toul was created by adding some brass or zinc into pure bronze. bharata = casting metals in moulds; bharavum = to fill in; to put in; to pour into (Gujarati) Bengali. ভরন [bharana] n an inferior metal obtained from an alloy of coper, zinc and tin.L. bhāraṇ ' to spread or bring out from a kiln '; M. bhārṇē, bhāḷṇē ' to make strong by charms (weapons, rice, water), enchant, fascinate (CDIAL 9463) Ash. barī ' blacksmith, artisan (CDIAL 9464). Baran, bharat 'mixed alloys' (5 copper, 4 zinc and 1 tin) (Punjabi) bharana id. (Bengali) bharan or toul was created by adding some brass or zinc into pure bronze. bharata = casting metals in moulds (Bengali) *bharata* 'a factitious metal compounded of copper, pewter, tin' (Marathi)

 *kanka* 'rim of jar' Rebus: *karṇīka* 'account (scribe)' *karṇī* 'supercargo'

m1172
ingot (from) iron smelter, tin

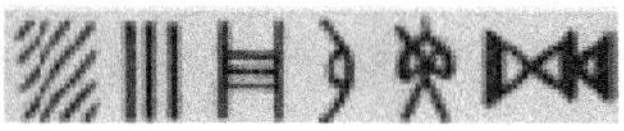

smelter merchant guild
m1173 Text 1191
ingot (from) iron smelter, tin smelter merchant guild

 Ligature of two pincers back-to-back. PLUS anvil:
खरवई [kharavī] *f* An instrument of braziers,--the anvil on which vessels are hung to be hammered. Rebus: khara 'blacksmith'. *ḍato* 'claws or pincers of crab' (Santali) Rebus: *dhatu* 'mineral ore' (Santali) dula 'pair' Rebus: dul 'cast metal'. Thus, the composite hieroglyph reads rebus: *dul dhatu khara* 'cast metal mineral blacksmith'.

bhaṭa 'warrior' (Sanskrit)Rebus: *baṭa* a kind of iron (Gujarati). Rebus: *bhaṭa* 'furnace' (Santali)

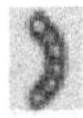 Variant कुटिल *kuṭila* 'bent' Rebus: 'bronze'. The scribe of Meluhha hieroglyphs may perhaps have intended to technically specify two types of bronze: arsenic bronze and tin bronze. The bent hieroglyph sign gets duplicated back-to-back to constitute a circumflex with hieroglyph signs such as 'paddy plant' or 'flower bud or sprout'.

panǰār 'ladder, stairs'(Bshk.)(CDIAL 7760) Rebus: pasra 'smithy' (Santali) Vikalpa: H. sainī, senī f. ' ladder ' Rebus: Pa. sēṇi -- f. ' guild, division of army '; Pk. sēṇi -- f. ' row, collection '; śrḗṇi (metr. often śrayaṇi --) f. ' line, row, troop ' RV. *śrēṇikā* f. 'house ~ ladder' Rebus:*śreṇi* in meaning "guild" (Sanskrit) Pa. *sēṇi* -- f. ' guild, division of army '(Pali)(CDIAL 10718) *seniya* 'soldier'.

kolom 'three' Rebus: kolami 'smithy, forge'.

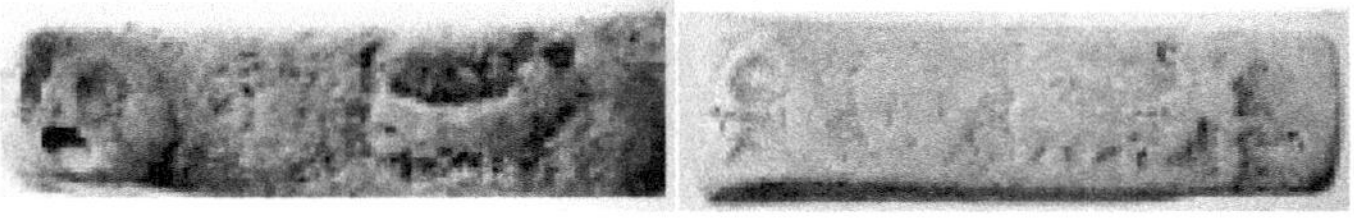

m449A, B Tablet Text 2836
ingot (from) iron smelter, tin

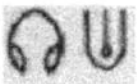 smelter merchant guild

muka 'ladle' (Tamil)(DEDR 4887) Rebus: mũh 'ingot' (Santali) baṭa = rimless pot (Kannada) baṭa = a kind of iron (Gujarati)

m1402 A,B
ingot (from) iron smelter, tin smelter merchant guild

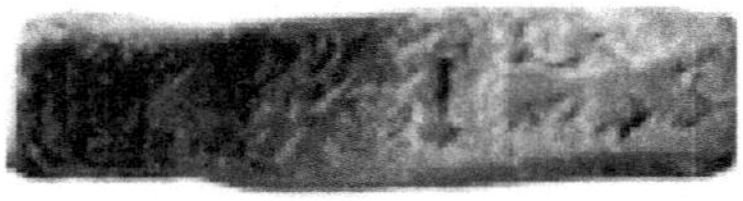

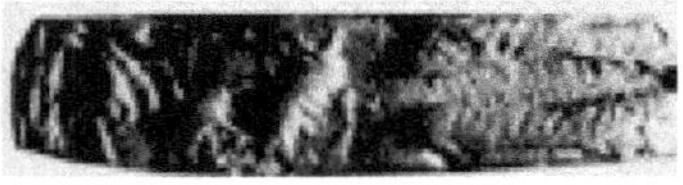

m1430 A,B,C:The composite  animal appears together with other hieroglyph compositions: m1430A: Pict 101: Person throwing a spear at a buffalo and placing one foot on its head; three persons standing near a tree at the center. m1430B: composite animal. m1402C:body of an ox and three heads (bull, antelope, bison) at right; a goat standing on its hindlegs and browsing from a tree at the center. Focus on 'serpent' tail: *nāga* 'snake' Rebus: *nāga* 'lead' (Sanskrit) anakku 'tin' (Akkadian) *Kur.* xolā tail. *Malt.* qoli id. (DEDR 2135). Focus on human face: mukha, *mũh* 'face' Rebus: *mũh* 'ingot'. Zebu horns: *khũṭ* 'zebu' (Gujarati) Rebus: *khũṭ* '(native metal) community, guild' (Santali) kola 'tiger' Rebus: kolhe 'smelters' kol 'working in iron' ibha 'elephant' Rebus: ib 'iron' body of an ox: balad 'bull' Rebus: *baran, bharat* 'mixed alloys' (5 copper, 4 zinc and 1 tin) (Punjabi) dhatu 'scarf' Rebus: dhatu 'mineral ore'.

rāngo 'water buffalo bull' (Ku.N.)(CDIAL 10559) Rebus: ranku 'tin' raṅga3 n. ' tin ' lex. [Cf. nāga -- 2, vaṅga -- 1]Pk. *raṁga* -- n. ' tin '; P. *rāg* f., *rāgā* m. ' pewter, tin ' (← H.)
Text 2819 Rebus readings: mlekh 'goat' (Br.) Rebus: milakkhu 'copper' (Pali)
ingot (from) iron smelter, tin smelter merchant guild

loa 'ficus religiosa' Rebus: *lo* 'copper'

 *kanka* 'rim of jar' Rebus: *karṇīka* 'account (scribe)' *karṇī* 'supercargo'

Text rebus readings of 'strands of rope' hieroglyph sign: See reading of Nausharo seal 9.

 *dhatu* 'strands of rope' Rebus: *dhatu* 'mineral ore' (Santali)

h162A

Metalware from furnace (smelter): Sign hieroglyphs: 'water-carrier' ligatured with 'rim of jar':
m1123A kuṭi 'water-carrier' +

'rim-of-jar' hieroglyph *kanka* (Santali) karṇika 'scribe'(Sanskrit) Rebus: *karṇī,* supercargo for a boat shipment. *karṇīka* 'account (scribe)'.कारणी kāraṇī 'the supercargo of a ship' (Marathi) कर्णधार [karṇadhāra] *m* S (A holder of the ear.) A helmsman or steersman देशकुळकरणी [dēśakuḷakaraṇī] *m* An hereditary officer of a Mahál. He frames the general account from the accounts of the several Khots and Kulkarṇís of the villages within the Mahál; the district-accountant.

L-43 a

Lothal 43a

खोंड [khōṇḍa] m A young bull, a bullcalf. (Marathi) Rebus: kõdār 'turner' (Bengali); कोंद kōnda 'engraver, lapidary setting or infixing gems' (Marathi) G. sãghāṛɔ m. 'lathe' ; संघाट joinery; M. sãgaḍ 'double-canoe' Rebus: sangataras. संगतराश lit. 'to collect stones, stone-cutter, mason.'

kolmo 'paddy plant' Rebus; *kolami* 'smithy, forge' *ranku* 'liquid measure' Rebus: *ranku* 'tin'.

'rim-of-jar' hieroglyph *kanka* (Santali) karṇika 'scribe'(Sanskrit) PLUS *kuṭi* 'water-carrier' Rebus*: kuṭhi* 'smelter/furnace'. The text of inscription reads: smithy, forge, tin, furnace supercargo.

m795a

खोंड [khōṇḍa] m A young bull, a bullcalf. (Marathi) Rebus: kõdār 'turner' (Bengali); कोंद kōnda 'engraver, lapidary setting or infixing gems' (Marathi) G. sãghāṛɔ m. 'lathe' ; संघाट joinery; M. sãgaḍ 'double-canoe' Rebus: sangataras. संगतराश lit. 'to collect stones, stone-cutter, mason.'

खांडा [*khāṇḍā*] *m* A jag, notch, or indentation (as upon the edge of a tool or weapon). Rebus: *kāṇḍa* 'tools, pots and pans and metal-ware' *karaṛa* 'a very large aquatic bird' (Sindhi) Rebus: करडा [*karaḍā*] Hard from alloy--iron, silver &c. (Marathi) Vikalpa: *baṭa* 'quail' Rebus: *baṭha* 'smelter, furnace' *baṭa* 'iron' (Gujarati)

'rim-of-jar' hieroglyph *kanka* (Santali) karṇika 'scribe'(Sanskrit) PLUS *kuṭi* 'water-carrier' Rebus*: kuṭhi* 'smelter/furnace'.

H-1853 A H-1853 B

h1853A

khareḍo = a currycomb (Gujarati) खरारा [*kharārā*] *m* (H) A currycomb. 2 Currying a horse. (Marathi)

Rebus: करडा [*karaḍā*] Hard from alloy--iron, silver &c. (Marathi) *kharādī* ' turner' (Gujarati) *khaṇḍ* 'field, division' (Sanskrit) Rebus: *khāṇḍa* 'tools, pots and pans, metal-ware'. Rebus 2: kaṇḍ 'fire-altar' (Santali) dula 'pair' Rebus: dul 'cast metal' Thus, duplicated 'division' hieroglyph sign reads: cast metal metal-ware.

dul kuṭila 'cast bronze'.PLUS infixed 'splinter': sal 'splinter' Rebus: sal 'workshop' Thus, cast bronze workshop

M-321 a

m321A

खोंड [khōṇḍa] m A young bull, a bullcalf. (Marathi) Rebus: kõdār 'turner'

(Bengali); कोंद kōnda 'engraver, lapidary setting or infixing gems' (Marathi) G. sãghāṛɔ m. 'lathe' ; संघाट joinery; M. sāgaḍ 'double-canoe' Rebus: sangataras. संगतराश lit. 'to collect stones, stone-cutter, mason.'
khaṇḍ 'field, division' (Sanskrit) Rebus: *khāṇḍa* 'tools, pots and pans, metal-ware'. Rebus 2: kaṇḍ 'fire-altar' (Santali) dula 'pair' Rebus: dul 'cast metal' Thus, duplicated 'division' hieroglyph sign reads: cast metal metal-ware.
dul kuṭila 'cast bronze'.PLUS infixed 'three': kolom 'three' Rebus: kolami 'smithy, forge' Thus, cast bronze smithy

Alamgirpr 3A *gaṇḍa* 'four' Rebus: *kaṇḍ* 'fire-altar'

kolom 'three' Rebus: *kolami* 'smithy, forge'
kuṭila 'bronze'

m1918a Pictorial motif hieroglyphs: *rāngo* 'water buffalo bull' (Ku.N.)(CDIAL 10559) Rebus: ranku 'tin' raṅga3 n. ' tin ' lex. [Cf. nāga -- 2, vaṅga -- 1]Pk. *raṁga* -- n. ' tin '; P. *rāg* f., *rāgā* m. ' pewter, tin ' (← H.)
kol 'spearing' kolsa = to kick the foot forward, the foot to come into contact with anything when walking or running; kolsa pasirkedan = I kicked it over (Santali.lex.)mēṛsa = v.a. toss, kick with the foot, hit with the tail (Santali.lex.) me~ṛhe~t iron; ispat m. = steel; dul m. = cast iron; kolhe m. iron manufactured by the Kolhes(Santali)
Rebus: kol 'working in iron' kolhe 'smelters'

Hieroglyph signs:
kana, kanac = corner (Santali); Rebus: *kañcu* = bronze (Telugu) PLUS slanted stroke: *ḍhālako* Rebus: ingot. Together, the ligatured hieroglyph sign reads: *kañcu ḍhālako* 'bronze ingot'
kolmo 'paddy plant' Rebus: *kolami* 'smithy, forge' *meḍ* 'body' (Santali) Rebus: *meḍ* 'iron' (Ho.)

m82A *खोंड [khōṇḍa] m A young bull, a bullcalf. (Marathi) Rebus: kōdār 'turner' (Bengali); कोंद kōnda 'engraver, lapidary setting or infixing gems' (Marathi) G. sãghāṛɔ m. 'lathe' ; संघाट joinery; M. sāgaḍ 'double-canoe' Rebus: sangataras. संगतराश lit. 'to collect stones, stone-cutter, mason.'*
ieroglyph iṟumpu 'ant' (Kannada)(DEDR 864) Rebus: *Ta.* irumpu iron, instrument, weapon. *Ma.* irumpu, irimpu iron. *Ko.* ib id. *To.* ib needle. *Koḍ.* irïmbï iron. *Te.* inumu id. *Kol.* (Kin.) inum (*pl.* inmul) iron, sword. *Kui* (Friend-Pereira) rumba (DEDR 486). Allograph: ibha 'elephant' Rebus: ib 'iron' (Santali); id. (Kota)

kolmo 'paddy plant' Rebus: kolami 'smithy, forge'
kamaḍha = crab; *kampaṭṭam* = mint (Tamil) ; *kammaṭa* 'coiner, mint' (Telugu) Vikalpa: *ḍato* = claws of crab (Santali); *dhātu* = mineral (Sanskrit)

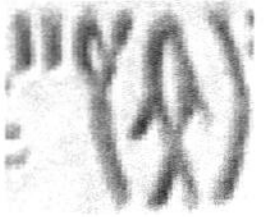

dul kuṭila 'cast bronze'. (Paired bent lines) PLUS ayo 'fish' Rebus: aya 'iron' ayas 'metal' PLUS sal 'splinter' Rebus: sal 'workshop'. Thus cast bronze alloy workshop.

kanka 'rim of jar' Rebus: *karṇīka* 'account (scribe)' *karṇī* 'supercargo'

Lothal 48a

Pictorial moti hieroglyphs: *miṇḍāl* 'markhor' (Tōrwālī)*meḍho* a ram, a sheep (Gujarati)(CDIAL 10120) Rebus: *mẽṛhẽt, meḍ* 'iron' (Mu.Ho.)
sangada 'lathe', 'portable furnace' G. *sãghāṛɔ* m. 'lathe' ; *sãgāḍā* m. ' frame of a building ', *°ḍī* f. ' lathe '(CDIAL 12859) Rebus:sangataras. संगतराश lit. 'to collect stones, stone-cutter, mason.'
Hieroglyph signs: kolmo 'paddy plant' Rebus: kolami 'smithy, forge'

 Hieroglyph 'rim of jar' Rebus: .कारणी kāraṇī 'the supercargo of a ship'.

aya kāṇḍa 'alloy metalware'
dula 'pair' Rebus: dul 'cast metal'
kanac 'corner' Rebus: kañcu 'bronze'

dāṭu 'cross'(Telugu) Rebus: *dhatu* 'mineral' (Santali).

m1770a
खोंड [khōṇḍa] m A young bull, a bullcalf. (Marathi) Rebus: kõdār 'turner' (Bengali); कोंद kōnda 'engraver, lapidary setting or infixing gems' (Marathi) G. sãghāṛɔ m. 'lathe' ; संघाट joinery; M. sãgaḍ 'double-canoe' Rebus: sangataras. संगतराश lit. 'to collect stones, stone-cutter, mason.'
Text inscription: Hieroglyph signs: kolmo 'paddy plant' Rebus: kolami 'smithy, forge' dula 'pair' Rebus: dul 'cast metal'
meḍ 'body' Rebus: *meḍ* 'iron' (Mu.Ho.) Thus, cast metal iron smithy: *meḍ kolami* 'cast iron smithy, forge'

baraḍo = spine; backbone (Tulu) Rebus: *baran, bharat* 'mixed alloys' (5 copper, 4 zinc and 1 tin) (Punjabi)

 Hieroglyph 'rim of jar' Rebus: .कारणी kāraṇī 'the supercargo of a ship'.

Kalibangan 45A: native metal smithy supercargo; blacksmith guild; alloy metal

K-45 A

खोंड [khōṇḍa] m A young bull, a bullcalf. (Marathi) Rebus: kõdār 'turner' (Bengali); कोंद kōnda 'engraver, lapidary setting or infixing gems' (Marathi) G. sãghāṛɔ m. 'lathe' ; संघाट joinery; M. sãgaḍ 'double-canoe' Rebus: sangataras. संगतराश lit. 'to collect stones, stone-cutter, mason.'
aḍaren 'cover of pot or lid' Rebus: *aduru* 'native, unsmelted metal'PLUS kolmo 'paddy plant' Rebus: kolami 'smithy, forge'

 kanka 'rim of jar' Rebus: *karṇīka* 'account (scribe)' *karṇī* 'supercargo'

ḍhanga = a crook used for pulling down the branches of trees, for goats, sheep and camels (Punjabi) Rebus:*ḍhangar* blacksmith'.

Thus, together, the ligatured hieroglyph denotes: native metal workshop.
khuṭo ' leg, foot ', °ṭī ' goat's leg ' Rebus: *khōṭā* 'alloy' (Marathi)

m1730a *खोंड [khōṇḍa] m A young bull, a bullcalf. (Marathi) Rebus: kõdār 'turner' (Bengali); कोंद kōnda 'engraver, lapidary setting or infixing gems' (Marathi) G.*

sãghāṛɔ m. 'lathe' ; संघाट joinery; M. sãgaḍ 'double-canoe' Rebus: sangataras. संगतराश lit. 'to collect stones, stone-cutter, mason.'

Circumscribe by four splinters:

gaṇḍa 'four' (Santali) Rebus: *kaṇḍ* 'fire-altar' (Santali) *sal* 'splinter' Rebus: *sal* 'workshop' Thus fire-altar + workshop.

kolmo 'paddy plant' Rebus: *kolami* 'smithy, forge'. The ligatured hieroglyph sign reads: fire-altar, workshop, smithy, forge.

Read in context, the composite hieroglyph is assumed to be a combination of a slanted stroke ligatured to a notch,which provide possible rebus readings of a smithy/forge: notch+slanted stroke reads rebus: *ḍhālako kāṇḍa* 'ingot, tools, pots and pans and metal-ware'

dhāḷ 'a slope'; 'inclination of a plane' (Gujarati); *ḍhāḷiyum* = adj. sloping, inclining (Gujarati) Rebus: *ḍhālako* = a large metal ingot (Gujarati) *ḍhālakī* = a metal heated and poured into a mould; a solid piece of metal; an ingot (Gujarati) PLUS खांडा [*khāṇḍā*] *m* A jag, notch, or indentation (as upon the edge of a tool or weapon). Rebus: *kāṇḍa* 'tools, pots and pans and metal-ware'

ayo 'fish' Rebus*:* aya 'iron' *ayas* 'metal' (Vedic)

ranku 'liquid measure' Rebus: ranku 'tin'

kanac 'corner' Rebus: *kañcu* 'bronze'

Hieroglyph 'rim of jar' Rebus: .कारणी kāraṇī 'the supercargo of a ship'.

m1669a

खोंड [khōṇḍa] m A young bull, a bullcalf. (Marathi) Rebus: kõdār 'turner' (Bengali); कोंद kōnda 'engraver, lapidary setting or infixing gems' (Marathi) G. sãghāṛɔ m. 'lathe' ; संघाट joinery; M. sãgaḍ 'double-canoe' Rebus: sangataras. संगतराश lit. 'to collect stones, stone-cutter, mason.'

kolmo 'paddy plant' Rebus: *kolami* 'smithy, forge'.

Hieroglyph 'rim of jar' Rebus: .कारणी kāraṇī 'the supercargo of a ship'.

m898a *खोंड [khōṇḍa] m A young bull, a bullcalf. (Marathi) Rebus: kõdār 'turner' (Bengali); कोंद kōnda 'engraver, lapidary setting or infixing gems' (Marathi) G. sãghāṛɔ m. 'lathe' ; संघाट joinery; M. sãgaḍ 'double-canoe' Rebus: sangataras.*

संगतराश lit. 'to collect stones, stone-cutter, mason.'

kolom 'three' Rebus: kolami 'smithy, forge' Phonetic determinant: kolmo 'paddy plant' Rebus: kolami 'smithy, forge'

kole.l 'temple' Rebus: kole.l 'smithy'

m210a

खोंड [khōṇḍa] m A young bull, a bullcalf. (Marathi) Rebus: kōdār 'turner' (Bengali); कोंद kōnda 'engraver, lapidary setting or infixing gems' (Marathi) G. sãghāṛɔ m. 'lathe' ; संघाट joinery; M. sãgaḍ 'double-canoe' Rebus: sangataras. संगतराश lit. 'to collect stones, stone-cutter, mason.'

mogge 'sprout, bud' Rebus*: mũh* 'ingot'

 *kanac* 'corner' Rebus: *kañcu* 'bronze'

 *koḍi* 'flag' (Ta.)(DEDR 2049). Rebus 1: *koḍ* 'workshop' (Kuwi) Rebus 2: *khŏḍ* m. 'pit', *khŏḍü* f. 'small pit' (Kashmiri. CDIAL 3947).

Sign hieroglyph: Numeral counts of four and three organized in two rows:

h9a *खोंड [khōṇḍa] m A young bull, a bullcalf. (Marathi) Rebus: kōdār 'turner' (Bengali); कोंद kōnda 'engraver, lapidary setting or infixing gems' (Marathi) G. sãghāṛɔ m. 'lathe' ; संघाट joinery; M. sãgaḍ 'double-canoe' Rebus: sangataras. संगतराश lit. 'to collect stones, stone-cutter, mason.'*

|||| Numeral 4: gaṇḍa 'four' Rebus: kaṇḍa 'furnace, fire-altar' (Santali)

||| Numeral three: kolom 'three' Rebus: kolami 'smithy, forge'

ayo 'fish' Rebus: *aya* 'iron' *ayas* 'metal'

Kis-2 a

Khirasara 2a

|||| Numeral 4: gaṇḍa 'four' Rebus: kaṇḍa 'furnace, fire-altar' (Santali)

||| Numeral three: kolom 'three' Rebus: kolami 'smithy, forge'

PLUS

 सांड [sāṇḍa] *f* (षद S) An outlet for superfluous water (as through a dam or mound); a sluice, a floodvent. Rebus: सांडणी [sāṇḍaṇī] *f* (H) An instrument of goldsmiths. It is hooked or curved at the extremity; and is used to draw things out of the fire.
सांठा [*sāṇṭhā*] *m* (संचय S) A collection, heap, hoard, store, stock.साटें [*sāṭēṃ*] *n* (संचय S) A whole investment; the total quantity of merchandise (brought to market by one merchant).

 *kanka* 'rim of jar' Rebus: *karṇīka* 'account (scribe)' *karṇī* 'supercargo'

M 578a

M578b

m578a, b A combination of bull + ranku 'antelope' Rebus: ranku 'tin'+ badhia 'boa' Rebus: barea 'merchant' + ibha 'elephant' Rebus: ib 'iron': *balad* m. ' ox ', gng. *bald*, (Ku.) *barad*, id. (N. Tarai) Rebus: *bharat* (5 copper, 4 zinc and 1 tin)(Punjabi) *pattar* 'trough'
Duplicated: dula 'pair' Rebus: dul 'cast metal'. Thus, cast bharat alloy merchant.

|||| Numeral 4: gaṇḍa 'four' Rebus: kaṇḍa 'furnace, fire-altar' (Santali)

||| Numeral three: kolom 'three' Rebus: kolami 'smithy, forge'

PLUS

सांड [sāṇḍa] *f* (षद S) An outlet for superfluous water (as through a dam or mound); a sluice, a floodvent. Rebus: सांडणी [sāṇḍaṇī] *f* (H) An instrument of goldsmiths. It is hooked or curved at the extremity; and is used to draw things out of the fire.
सांठा [*sāṇṭhā*] *m* (संचय S) A collection, heap, hoard, store, stock.साटें [*sāṭēṃ*] *n* (संचय S) A whole investment; the total quantity of merchandise (brought to market by one merchant).

loa 'ficus religiosa' Rebus: *lo* 'iron' (Sanskrit)

kanka 'rim of jar' Rebus: *karṇīka* 'account (scribe)' *karṇī* 'supercargo'

m1534AB Read rebus as at m578 a,b

m1777a

खोंड [khōṇḍa] m A young bull, a bullcalf. (Marathi) Rebus: kõdār 'turner' (Bengali); कोंद kōnda 'engraver, lapidary setting or infixing gems' (Marathi) G. sãghārɔ m. 'lathe' ; संघाट joinery; M. sāgaḍ 'double-canoe' Rebus: sangataras. संगतराश lit. 'to collect stones, stone-cutter, mason.'

|||| Numeral 4: gaṇḍa 'four' Rebus: kaṇḍa 'furnace, fire-altar' (Santali)

||| Numeral three: kolom 'three' Rebus: kolami 'smithy, forge'

सांड [sāṇḍa] *f* (षद S) An outlet for superfluous water (as through a dam or mound); a sluice, a floodvent. Rebus: सांडणी [sāṇḍaṇī] *f* (H) An instrument of goldsmiths. It is hooked or curved at the extremity; and is used to draw things out of the fire.
सांठा [*sāṇṭhā*] *m* (संचय S) A collection, heap, hoard, store, stock.साटें [*sāṭēṃ*] *n* (संचय S) A whole investment; the total quantity of merchandise (brought to market by one merchant).

kanka 'rim of jar' Rebus: *karṇīka* 'account (scribe)' *karṇī* 'supercargo'

m1342a|||| Numeral 4: gaṇḍa 'four' Rebus: kaṇḍa 'furnace, fire-altar' (Santali)

||| Numeral three: kolom 'three' Rebus: kolami 'smithy, forge'

सांड [sāṇḍa] *f* (षद S) An outlet for superfluous water (as through a dam or mound); a sluice, a floodvent. Rebus: सांडणी [sāṇḍaṇī] *f* (H) An instrument of goldsmiths. It is hooked or curved at the extremity; and is used to draw things out of the fire.
सांठा [*sāṇṭhā*] *m* (संचय S) A collection, heap, hoard, store, stock.साटें [*sāṭēṃ*] *n* (संचय S) A whole investment; the total quantity of merchandise (brought to market by one merchant).

meḍ 'body' Rebus: *meḍ* 'iron' (Ho.) काठी [kāṭhī] *f* (काष्ट S) 'frame or structure of the body' (Marathi) Rebus: खंडी [khaṇḍī] measure of weight (Marathi) கண்டி; *kaṇṭi, n. < Mhr. khaṇḍil. [T. Tu. khaṇḍi, M. kaṇḍi.]* Candy, a weight, stated to be roughly equivalent to 500 lbs.

 *dāṭu* 'cross'(Telugu) Rebus: *dhatu* 'mineral' (Santali). sal 'splinter' Rebus: sal 'workshop' PLUS gaṇḍa 'four' Rebus: kaṇḍa 'furnace, fire-altar' (Santali)

 *kanka* 'rim of jar' Rebus: *karṇīka* 'account (scribe)' *karṇī* 'supercargo'

 h156A

 m1775a *खोंड [khōṇḍa] m A young bull, a bullcalf. (Marathi) Rebus: kõdār 'turner' (Bengali); कोंद kōnda 'engraver, lapidary setting or infixing gems' (Marathi) G. sãghāṛɔ m. 'lathe' ; संघाट joinery; M. sãgaḍ 'double-canoe' Rebus: sangataras. संगतराश lit. 'to collect stones, stone-cutter, mason.'*

|||| Numeral 4: gaṇḍa 'four' Rebus: kaṇḍa 'furnace, fire-altar' (Santali)

||| Numeral three: kolom 'three' Rebus: kolami 'smithy, forge'

 PLUS circumscript: dula 'pair' Rebus: dul 'cast metal' *kuṭila* 'bent' CDIAL 3230 kuṭi— in cmpd. 'curve', *kuṭika—* 'bent' MBh. Rebus: *kuṭila, katthīl* = bronze (8 parts copper and 2 parts tin) Thus, cast bronze.

 *kanka* 'rim of jar' Rebus: *karṇīka* 'account (scribe)' *karṇī* 'supercargo'

  h817A Read rebus as at text of m1775a PLUS Ligature: two peaks: mēḍu height, rising ground, hillock (Kannada) Rebus: *meḍ* 'iron' (Ho.) dula 'pair' Rebus: dul 'cast metal' PLUS |||| Numeral 4: gaṇḍa 'four' Rebus: kaṇḍa 'furnace, fire-altar' (Santali)

 *khareḍo* = a currycomb (Gujarati) खरारा [*kharārā*] *m* (H) A currycomb. 2 Currying a horse. (Marathi) Rebus: करडा [*karaḍā*] Hard from alloy--iron, silver &c. (Marathi) *kharādī* ' turner' (Gujarati)

Sign hieroglyph variants of lid or cover of pot:
The sign glyph on m1168A has been read rebus as tiger ligatured with zebu horns. Thus, native metal smith guild.
kol 'tiger' Rebus: kolhe 'smelter'
aḍaren 'cover of pot or lid' Rebus: *aduru* 'native, unsmelted metal'

 *kanka* 'rim of jar' Rebus: *karṇīka* 'account (scribe)' *karṇī* 'supercargo'

 h474a *खोंड [khōṇḍa] m A young bull, a bullcalf. (Marathi) Rebus: kõdār 'turner' (Bengali); कोंद kōnda 'engraver, lapidary setting or infixing gems' (Marathi) G.*

sãghāṛɔ m. 'lathe' ; संघाट joinery; M. sãgaḍ 'double-canoe' Rebus: sangataras. संगतराश lit. 'to collect stones, stone-cutter, mason.'
aḍaren 'cover of pot or lid' Rebus: *aduru* 'native, unsmelted metal' Duplicated: dula 'pair' Rebus: dul 'cast metal' Thus native metal casting. (Last sign illegible.)

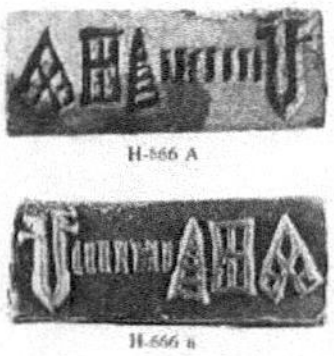

h666A *aḍaren* 'cover of pot or lid' Rebus: *aduru* 'native, unsmelted metal' *khaṇḍ* 'field, division' (Sanskrit) Rebus: *khāṇḍa* 'tools, pots and pans, metal-ware'. Rebus 2: kaṇḍ 'fire-altar' (Santali) dula 'pair' Rebus: dul 'cast metal' Thus cast metalware.

mēḍu height, (Munda.Ho.)  rising ground, hillock (Kannada) Rebus: *mẽṛhẽt, meḍ* 'iron'

|||| Numeral 4: gaṇḍa 'four' Rebus: kaṇḍa 'furnace, fire-altar' (Santali)

||| Numeral three: kolom 'three' Rebus: kolami 'smithy, forge'

 *kanka* 'rim of jar' Rebus: *karṇīka* 'account (scribe)' *karṇī* 'supercargo'

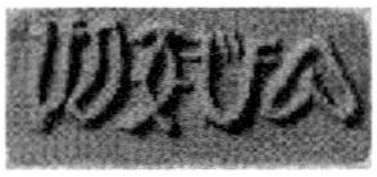

m407a *aḍaren* 'cover of pot or lid' Rebus: *aduru* 'native, unsmelted metal'
 *kanka* 'rim of jar' Rebus: *karṇīka* 'account (scribe)' *karṇī* 'supercargo' sal 'splinter' Rebus: sal 'workshop'
aya aḍaren (homonym: aduru)'alloy native metal'
 *kuṭila* 'bent' CDIAL 3230 kuṭi— in cmpd. 'curve', *kuṭika*— 'bent' MBh. Rebus: *kuṭila, katthīl* = bronze (8 parts copper and 2 parts tin) Duplicated: dula 'pair' Rebus: dul 'cast metal'
 *kanka* 'rim of jar' Rebus: *karṇīka* 'account (scribe)' *karṇī* 'supercargo'

h47a *खोंड [khōṇḍa] m A young bull, a bullcalf. (Marathi) Rebus: kõdār 'turner' (Bengali); कोंद kōnda 'engraver, lapidary setting or infixing gems' (Marathi) G. sãghāṛɔ m. 'lathe' ; संघाट joinery; M. sãgaḍ 'double-canoe' Rebus: sangataras. संगतराश lit. 'to collect stones, stone-cutter, mason.'*
aḍaren 'cover of pot or lid' Rebus: *aduru* 'native, unsmelted metal'
Variant:

 *dula* 'pair' Rebus: dul 'cast metal' *mogge* 'sprout, bud' Rebus: *mũh* 'ingot' (Santali) Thus, cast metal ingot.

 *kanka* 'rim of jar' Rebus: *karṇīka* 'account (scribe)' *karṇī* 'supercargo'

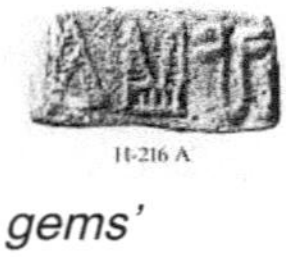

h216A

h441a *खोंड [khōṇḍa] m A young bull, a bullcalf. (Marathi) Rebus: kõdār 'turner' (Bengali); कोंद kōnda 'engraver, lapidary setting or infixing gems' (Marathi) G. sãghāṛɔ m. 'lathe' ; संघाट joinery; M. sãgaḍ 'double-canoe'*

Rebus: sangataras. संगतराश lit. 'to collect stones, stone-cutter, mason.'
aḍaren 'cover of pot or lid' Rebus: *aduru* 'native, unsmelted metal'

 Ligature: two peaks: mēḍu height, rising ground, hillock (Kannada) Rebus: *meḍ* 'iron' (Ho.) dula 'pair' Rebus: dul 'cast metal' PLUS |||| Numeral 4: gaṇḍa 'four' Rebus: kaṇḍa 'furnace, fire-altar' (Santali)

 *kanka* 'rim of jar' Rebus: *karṇīka* 'account (scribe)' *karṇī* 'supercargo'

Signs hieroglyph composition: rimless, wide pot + ladle:

 m1736a *खोंड [khōṇḍa] m A young bull, a bullcalf. (Marathi) Rebus: kõdār 'turner' (Bengali); कोंद kōnda 'engraver, lapidary setting or infixing gems' (Marathi) G. sãghārɔ m. 'lathe' ; संघाट joinery; M. sãgaḍ 'double-canoe' Rebus: sangataras. संगतराश lit. 'to collect stones, stone-cutter, mason.'*

 *kuṭila* 'bent' CDIAL 3230 kuṭi— in cmpd. 'curve', *kuṭika—* 'bent' MBh. Rebus: *kuṭila, katthīl* = bronze (8 parts copper and 2 parts tin) Duplicated: dula 'pair' Rebus: dul 'cast metal'

 *kanka* 'rim of jar' Rebus: *karṇīka* 'account (scribe)' *karṇī* 'supercargo'

aya kammaṭa.'coiner, mint alloy'
aya kāṇḍa 'alloy metalware'

 *muka* 'ladle' (Tamil)(DEDR 4887) Rebus: *mũh* 'ingot' (Santali) *baṭa* = rimless pot (Kannada) Rebus:) *baṭa* = a kind of iron (G.)) *bhaṭa* furnace (Gujarati) Thus, iron ingot.
kolom 'three' Rebus: kolami 'smithy, forge'
kāṇḍa 'arrow' (Sanskrit) Rebus:*khāṇḍa* 'tools, pots and pans, metal-ware'. Rebus 2: kaṇḍ 'fire-altar' (Santali)

Ligatured sign hieroglyph X PLUS 'sprout':

 m57a *खोंड [khōṇḍa] m A young bull, a bullcalf. (Marathi) Rebus: kõdār 'turner' (Bengali); कोंद kōnda 'engraver, lapidary setting or infixing gems' (Marathi) G. sãghārɔ m. 'lathe' ; संघाट joinery; M. sãgaḍ 'double-canoe' Rebus: sangataras. संगतराश lit. 'to collect stones, stone-cutter, mason.'*

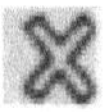 *dāṭu* 'cross'(Telugu) Rebus: *dhatu* 'mineral' (Santali). *kolmo* 'paddy plant' Rebus: *kolami* 'smithy, forge' Vikalpa: *mogge* 'sprout, bud' Rebus: *mũh* 'ingot' (Santali) dolu 'plant  of shoot height' Rebus: dul 'cast metal' PLUS sal 'splinter' Rebus: sal 'workshop'Thus, cast metal, mineral smithy workshop. *kamaḍha* = crab; *kampaṭṭam* = mint (Ta.) ; *kammaṭa* 'coiner, mint' (Telugu) Vikalpa: *ḍato* = claws of crab (Santali); *dhātu* = mineral (Sanskrit)
ayo ḍhālako 'alloy metal ingot'
dula 'two' Rebus: dul 'cast metal' *aya kāṇḍa* 'alloy metalware'

 Sign hieroglyph: hoof/thigh/leg:

 m290a kol 'tiger' Rebus: kolhe 'smelter'
khuṭo ' leg, foot ', °ṭī ' goat's leg ' Rebus: *khōṭā* 'alloy' (Marathi) khar 'donkey' Rebus: khar 'blacksmith' PLUS xoli 'tail' Rebus: kol 'iron'

 m1864a *खोंड [khōṇḍa] m A young bull, a bullcalf. (Marathi) Rebus: kõdār 'turner' (Bengali); कोंद kōnda 'engraver, lapidary setting or infixing gems' (Marathi) G. sãghāṛɔ m. 'lathe' ; संघाट joinery; M. sãgaḍ 'double-canoe' Rebus: sangataras. संगतराश lit. 'to collect stones, stone-cutter, mason.'*

khuṭo ' leg, foot ', °ṭī ' goat's leg ' Rebus: *khōṭā* 'alloy' (Marathi)
 *kanka* 'rim of jar' Rebus: *karṇīka* 'account (scribe)' *karṇī* 'supercargo'

  mēḍu height, rising ground, hillock (Kannada) Rebus: *mẽṛhẽt, meḍ* 'iron' (Munda.Ho.)
 ḍāg mountain-ridge (H.)(CDIAL 5476). Rebus: dhangar 'blacksmith' (Maithili)
(Last sign illegible)

m1690a *खोंड [khōṇḍa] m A young bull, a bullcalf. (Marathi) Rebus: kõdār 'turner' (Bengali); कोंद kōnda 'engraver, lapidary setting or infixing gems' (Marathi) G. sãghāṛɔ m. 'lathe' ; संघाट joinery; M. sãgaḍ 'double-canoe' Rebus: sangataras. संगतराश lit. 'to collect stones, stone-cutter, mason.'*
khuṭo ' leg, foot ', °ṭī ' goat's leg ' Rebus: *khōṭā* 'alloy' (Marathi)
ayo 'fish' Rebus: *aya* 'iron' *ayas* 'metal'
mogge 'sprout, bud' Rebus: *mũh* 'ingot' (Santali) ligatured to: *sangada* 'lathe', 'portable furnace'

 *kanka* 'rim of jar' Rebus: *karṇīka* 'account (scribe)' *karṇī* 'supercargo'

 *dula* 'pair' Rebus: *dul* 'cast (metal)' PLUS*kana, kanac* = corner (Santali); Rebus: *kañcu* = bronze (Telugu) PLUS infixed kolmo 'paddy plant' Rebus: kolami 'smithy, forge'. Thus, cast bronze smithy, forge. Or, *mogge* 'sprout, bud' Rebus: *mũh* 'ingot' (Santali)Thus, cast bronze ingot. Read as: *kañcu dul mũh 'bronze cast ingot' aya kammaṭa.*'coiner, mint alloy'
dula 'two' Rebus: dul 'cast metal' *ayo* 'fish' Rebus: *aya* 'iron' *ayas* 'metal'
 'Arrow' sign hieroglyph (variant) This is a ligature of 'lid of pot' hieroglyph superscript on 'a linear stroke' numeral hieroglyph.*aḍaren* 'cover of pot or lid' Rebus: *aduru* 'native, unsmelted metal' PLUS koḍ = one (Santali); koḍ 'workshop' (G.)

h476a *खोंड [khōṇḍa] m A young bull, a bullcalf. (Marathi) Rebus: kõdār 'turner' (Bengali); कोंद kōnda 'engraver, lapidary setting or infixing gems' (Marathi) G. sãghārɔ m. 'lathe' ; संघाट joinery; M. sãgaḍ 'double-canoe' Rebus: sangataras. संगतराश lit. 'to collect stones, stone-cutter, mason.'*

khuṭo ' leg, foot ', °ṭī ' goat's leg ' Rebus: *khōṭā* 'alloy' (Marathi)
bhaṭa 'warrior' (Sanskrit) Rebus: *baṭa* a kind of iron (Gujarati). Rebus: *bhaṭa* 'furnace' (Santali)

kanka 'rim of jar' Rebus: *karṇīka* 'account (scribe)' *karṇī* 'supercargo'

)(Sign pairs creating a hieroglyph:
m1691a

खोंड [khōṇḍa] m A young bull, a bullcalf. (Marathi) Rebus: kõdār 'turner' (Bengali); कोंद kōnda 'engraver, lapidary setting or infixing gems' (Marathi) G. sãghārɔ m. 'lathe' ; संघाट joinery; M. sãgaḍ 'double-canoe' Rebus: sangataras. संगतराश lit. 'to collect stones, stone-cutter, mason.'

kuṭila 'bent'  CDIAL 3230 kuṭi— in cmpd. 'curve', *kuṭika*— 'bent' MBh. Rebus: *kuṭila, katthīl* = bronze (8 parts copper and 2 parts tin) Duplicated: dula 'pair' Rebus; dul 'cast metal'

kanka 'rim of jar' Rebus: *karṇīka* 'account (scribe)' *karṇī* 'supercargo'
aya kammaṭa.'coiner, mint alloy'

The pair of hieroglyph signs are compositions: bicha 'scorpion' (Assamese) Rebus: *bica* 'stone ore' (Santali) The pairing sign is a composition of: sloping stroke PLUS two short strokes of a 'splinter':*dhāḷ* 'a slope'; 'inclination of a plane' (Gujarati); *ḍhāḷiyum* = adj. sloping, inclining (Gujarati) Rebus: *ḍhālako* = a large metal ingot (Gujarati) *ḍhālakī* = a metal heated and poured into a mould; a solid piece of metal; an ingot (Gujarati)PLUS*sal* 'splinter' Rebus: *sal* 'workshop'. Thus the composition reads: *ḍhālako sal* 'ingot workshop'.

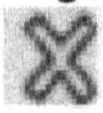
dāṭu 'cross'(Telugu) Rebus: *dhatu* 'mineral' (Santali).

kanka 'rim of jar' Rebus: *karṇīka* 'account (scribe)' *karṇī* 'supercargo'

m809A *खोंड [khōṇḍa] m A young bull, a bullcalf. (Marathi) Rebus: kõdār 'turner' (Bengali); कोंद kōnda 'engraver, lapidary setting or infixing gems' (Marathi) G. sãghārɔ m. 'lathe' ; संघाट joinery; M. sãgaḍ 'double-canoe' Rebus: sangataras. संगतराश lit. 'to collect stones, stone-cutter, mason.'*

kuṭila 'bent' CDIAL 3230 kuṭi— in cmpd. 'curve', *kuṭika*— 'bent' MBh. Rebus: *kuṭila, katthīl* = bronze (8 parts copper and 2 parts tin) Duplicated: dula 'pair' Rebus; dul 'cast metal'
ranku 'liquid measure' Rebus: ranku 'tin' sal 'splinter' Rebus: sal 'workshop'

mēḍu height, rising ground, hillock (Kannada) Rebus: *mẽṛhẽt, meḍ* 'iron' (Munda.Ho.) ḍãg mountain-ridge (H.)(CDIAL 5476). Rebus: dhangar

'blacksmith' (Maithili) *kāṇḍa* 'arrow' (Sanskrit) Rebus:*khāṇḍa* 'tools, pots and pans, metal-ware'. Rebus 2: kaṇḍ 'fire-altar' (Santali)

M-1272 A

m1972A

kuṭila 'bent' CDIAL 3230 kuṭi— in cmpd. 'curve', *kuṭika*— 'bent' MBh. Rebus: *kuṭila, katthīl* = bronze (8 parts copper and 2 parts tin)
Duplicated: dula 'pair' Rebus; dul 'cast metal'
PLUS *khaṇḍ* 'field, division' (Sanskrit) Rebus: *khāṇḍa* 'tools, pots and pans, metal-ware'. Rebus 2: kaṇḍ 'fire-altar' (Santali) dula 'pair' Rebus: dul 'cast metal' Thus cast metalware.

kanka 'rim of jar' Rebus: *karṇīka* 'account (scribe)' *karṇī* 'supercargo' sal 'splinter' Rebus: sal 'workshop'. Thus, cast metal is from workshop and cargo includes metalware. 'Arrow' sign hieroglyph (variant) This is a ligature of 'lid of pot' hieroglyph

superscript on 'a linear stroke' numeral hieroglyph.*aḍaren* 'cover of pot or lid' Rebus: *aduru* 'native, unsmelted metal' PLUS koḍ = one (Santali); koḍ 'workshop' (G.)
kāṇḍa 'arrow' (Sanskrit) Rebus:*khāṇḍa* 'tools, pots and pans, metal-ware'. Rebus 2: kaṇḍ 'fire-altar' (Santali)

Infixed 'sprout' hieroglyph ligatured with: 'rimless broad-mouthed pot'; ''two bent or curved lines circumscribed around the 'sprout' hieroglyph

smithy/forge (with) fire-altar: *kolami* PLUS *dul kuṭila* 'cast bronze'. Thus, *dul kuṭila* *kolami* 'cast bronze smithy/forge.
VIkalpa:

dula 'pair' Rebus: *dul* 'cast (metal)' PLUS*kana, kanac* = corner (Santali); Rebus: *kañcu* = bronze (Telugu) PLUS infixed kolmo 'paddy plant' Rebus: kolami 'smithy, forge'. Thus, cast bronze smithy, forge. Or, *mogge* 'sprout, bud' Rebus: *mũh* 'ingot' (Santali)Thus, cast bronze ingot. Read as: *kañcu dul mũh 'bronze cast ingot'*

L-88 a

Lothal 88a: *mogge* 'sprout, bud' Rebus: *mũh* 'ingot' (Santali) dula 'pair' Rebus: dul 'cast metal' kolom 'three' Rebus: kolami 'smithy, forge' PLUS 'notch' खांडा [*khāṇḍā*] *m* A jag, notch, or indentation (as upon the edge of a tool or weapon). Rebus: *kāṇḍa* 'tools, pots and pans and metal-ware' PLUS *aḍaren* 'cover of pot or lid' Rebus: *aduru* 'native, unsmelted metal' ligatured to: *koḍa* 'one' Rebus: | *koḍ* 'workshop'. Thus, native metal workshop metalware.
khaṇḍ 'field, division' (Sanskrit) Rebus: *khāṇḍa* 'tools, pots and pans, metal-ware'. Rebus 2: kaṇḍ 'fire-altar' (Santali)

karaṇḍa 'duck' (Sanskrit) karaṛa 'a very large aquatic bird' (Sindhi) Rebus: करडा [*karaḍā*] Hard from alloy--iron, silver &c. (Marathi) *kharādī* ' turner' (Gujarati) Duck looks back: krammara 'look back' Rebus: kamar 'smith, artisan' Thus, hard alloy smith.

H-207 A

h207A

dhāḷ 'a slope'; 'inclination of a plane' (G.); *ḍhāḷiyum* = adj. sloping, inclining (G.) Rebus: *ḍhālako* = a large metal ingot (G.) *ḍhālakī* = a metal heated and poured into a mould; a solid piece of metal; an ingot (Gujarati)

dula 'pair' Rebus: dul 'cast metal'. sal splinter' Rebus: sal 'workshop Thu cast metal ingot workshop.

kolmo 'paddy plant' Rebus: *kolami* 'smithy, forge' Vikalpa: *mogge* 'sprout, bud' Rebus: *mũh* 'ingot' (Santali) dolu 'plant of shoot height' Rebus: dul 'cast metal'

kanka 'rim of jar' Rebus: *karṇīka* 'account (scribe)' *karṇī* 'supercargo'

a  *kharedo* = a currycomb (Gujarati) खरारा [*kharārā*] *m* (H) A currycomb. 2 Currying horse. (Marathi) Rebus: करडा [*karaḍā*] Hard from alloy--iron, silver &c. (Marathi) *kharādī* ' turner' (Gujarati)

m263a *balad* m. ' ox ', gng. *bald*, (Ku.) *barad*, id. (N. Tarai) Rebus: *bharat* (5 copper, 4 zinc and 1 tin)(Punjabi) *pattar* 'trough' Rebus*: pattar* 'guild'. Thus, copper-zinc-tin alloy (worker) guild.

beads: Pa. kandi (pl. -l) necklace, beads. Ga. (Punjabi) kandi (pl. -l) bead, (pl.) necklace; (S.2) kandiṭ bead. (DEDR 1215) Rebus: *கண்டி; kaṇṭi, n. < Mhr. khaṇḍil. [T. Tu. khaṇḍi, M. kaṇḍi.] 1. Candy, a weight, stated to be roughly equivalent to 500 lbs.; பாரமென் னும் நிறையளவு.* खंडीगणती or खंडोगणती [khaṇḍīgaṇatī or khaṇḍōgaṇatī] *ad* By candies; counting or reckoning by candies. खंडीवारी [khaṇḍīvārī] *ad* By scores, heaps, candies. खंडी [khaṇḍī] Applied to a great quantity; as खंडीभर पोरें, खंडीभर मेंढ्या, खंडीभर काम, खंडीभर बोलतो-लिहितो&c

koḍi 'flag' (Ta.)(DEDR 2049). Rebus 1: *koḍ* 'workshop' (Kuwi) Rebus 2: *khōḍ* m. 'pit', *khōḍü* f. 'small pit' (Kashmiri. CDIAL 3947).

dula 'pair' Rebus: *dul* 'cast (metal)' PLUS*kana, kanac* = corner (Santali); Rebus: *kañcu* = bronze (Telugu) PLUS *i*nfixed kolmo 'paddy plant' Rebus: kolami 'smithy, forge'. Thus, cast bronze smithy, forge. Or, *mogge* 'sprout, bud' Rebus: *mũh* 'ingot' (Santali)Thus, cast bronze ingot. Read as: *kañcu dul mũh 'bronze cast ingot'*
. *kamaḍha* = crab; *kampaṭṭam* = mint (Ta.) ; *kammaṭa* 'coiner, mint' (Telugu) Vikalpa: *ḍato* = claws of crab (Santali); *dhātu* = mineral (Sanskrit)

dhāḷ 'a slope'; 'inclination of a plane' (G.); *ḍhāḷiyum* = adj. sloping, inclining (G.) Rebus: *ḍhālako* = a large metal ingot (G.) *ḍhālakī* = a metal heated and poured into a mould; a solid piece of metal; an ingot (Gujarati) dula 'pair' Rebus: dul 'cast metal'. sal splinter' Rebus: sal 'workshop Thu cast metal ingot workshop.

m1457A,B: Side B: मेढा [mēḍhā] 'a curl or snarl; twist in thread' (Marathi) Rebus: mẽṛhẽt, meḍ 'iron' (Mu.Ho.)

Top line:Side A

dulo 'hole' Rebus: dul 'cast metal'
kanka 'rim of jar' Rebus: *karṇīka* 'account (scribe)' *karṇī* 'supercargo'
bhaṭa 'warrior' (Sanskrit) Rebus: *baṭa* a kind of iron (Gujarati). Rebus: *bhaṭa* 'furnace' (Santali)

kolmo 'paddy plant' Rebus: *kolami* 'smithy, forge' Vikalpa: *mogge* 'sprout, bud' Rebus: *mūh* 'ingot' (Santali) dolu 'plant of shoot height' Rebus: dul 'cast metal'

Bottom line Side A:

kolmo 'paddy plant' Rebus: *kolami* 'smithy, forge' Vikalpa: *mogge* 'sprout, bud' Rebus: *mūh* 'ingot' (Santali) dolu 'plant of shoot height' Rebus: dul 'cast metal'

dula 'pair' Rebus: *dul* 'cast (metal)' PLUS*kana, kanac* = corner (Santali); Rebus: *kañcu* = bronze (Telugu)
ayo 'fish' Rebus: *aya* 'iron' *ayas* 'metal'

aḍar 'harrow'; rebus: *aduru* 'native unsmelted metal'

h1049a *खोंड [khōṇḍa] m A young bull, a bullcalf. (Marathi) Rebus: kõdār 'turner' (Bengali); कोंद kōnda 'engraver, lapidary setting or infixing gems' (Marathi) G. sãghāṛɔ m. 'lathe' ; संघाट joinery; M. sãgaḍ 'double-canoe' Rebus: sangataras. संगतराश lit. 'to collect stones, stone-cutter, mason.'* .

kolmo 'paddy plant' Rebus: *kolami* 'smithy, forge' dolu 'plant of shoot height' Rebus: dul 'cast metal' ligatured to: *mūdh* ' ridge of roof ' (Assamese)(CDIAL 10247) Rebus: *mund* 'Toda *mund* hut, house, temple' (Toda) Thus, temple of smithy: kole.l The rebus hieroglyph to denote this is: xoli 'tail' Rebus: kole.l
sal 'splinter' Rebus: sal 'workshop'
PLUS |||| Numeral 4: gaṇḍa 'four' Rebus: kaṇḍa 'furnace, fire-altar' (Santali)
mogge 'sprout, bud' Rebus: *mūh* 'ingot' (Santali)

h1953A, B Nativemetal smith guild.

Side A: from r. read rebus:

Composite hieroglyph with ligature.

kolmo 'paddy plant' Rebus: kolami 'smithy/forge'

dula 'pair' Rebus: dul 'cast metal'. The circumscribing ligature may be seen as made up of two curved lines back-to-back: ()kuṭila 'bent' CDIAL 3230 kuṭi— in cmpd. 'curve', *kuṭika—* 'bent' MBh. Rebus: *kuṭila, katthīl* = bronze (8 parts copper and 2 parts tin) [cf. *āra-kūṭa*, 'brass' (Sanskrit)

Thus, the composite hieroglyph is read rebus as: smithy/forge (with) fire-altar: *kolami* PLUS *dul kuṭila* 'cast bronze'. Thus, *dul kuṭila kolami* 'cast bronze smithy/forge'.

ayo 'fish' Rebus: aya 'iron' (Gujarati) ayas 'metal' (Vedic) PLUS ligatured fins: *khambhaṛā* m. 'fin' (Lahnda); khambh 'wing' (Punjabi) Allograph: Garh. *khambu* ' pillar '.(CDIAL 13640) Rebus: kammaṭa 'coiner, mint'. Thus 'fish' hieroglyph gets ligatured with fins to denote alloyed metal (of) mint. [An allograph for *khambh* is: *khambha* 'pillar' (Bhoj)(CDIAL 13639)]

aḍar 'harrow'; rebus: *aduru* 'native unsmelted metal'

ayo 'fish' Rebus: aya 'iron' (Gujarati) ayas 'metal' (Vedic)
कांड *kāṇḍa* 'arrow' Rebus: *kāṇḍa* 'pots and pans, metalware, tools'.
cf. *ayaskāṇḍa* 'excellent quantity of iron' (Panini)

Side B:
khũṭ 'zebu' Rebus: '(native metal) guild'
ayo 'fish' Rebus: aya 'iron' (Gujarati) ayas 'metal' (Vedic)
dula 'pair or two' Rebus: *dul* 'cast metal'
baṭa = rimless pot (Kannada) Rebus: *baṭa* = a kind of iron (G .) *bhaṭa* 'furnace' (Santali)

h103A First 3 signs as at h592a PLUS

dula 'pair'  Rebus: dul 'cast metal' *mogge* 'sprout, bud' Rebus: *mũh* 'ingot' (Santali) Thus, cast metal ingot.

 *kanka* 'rim of jar' Rebus: *karṇīka* 'account (scribe)' *karṇī* 'supercargo'

 *muka* 'ladle' (Tamil)(DEDR 4887) Rebus: *mũh* 'ingot' (Santali) *baṭa* = rimless pot (Kannada) Rebus:) *baṭa* = a kind of iron (G.)) *bhaṭa* furnace (Gujarati) Thus, iron ingot.
kolom 'three' Rebus: kolami 'smithy, forge'
kāṇḍa 'arrow' (Sanskrit) Rebus:*khāṇḍa* 'tools, pots and pans, metal-ware'. Rebus 2: kaṇḍ 'fire-altar' (Santali)
PLUS | *koḍa* 'one' Rebus: *koḍ* 'workshop' dula 'two' Rebus: dul 'cast metal' Thus, casting workshop INFIXED *koḍa* 'one' Rebus: *koḍ* 'workshop' PLUS *aḍaren* 'cover of pot or lid' Rebus: *aduru* 'native, unsmelted metal' Thus, native metal workshop. PLUS
 water-carrier hieroglyph *kuṭi*; Rebus: *kuṭhi* 'smelter furnace'. Thus, smelter workshop.

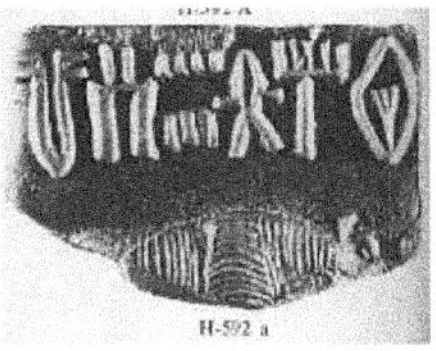

h592a *balad* m. ' ox ', gng. *bald*, (Ku.) *barad*, id. (N. Tarai) Rebus: *bharat* (5 copper, 4 zinc and 1 tin)(Punjabi) *pattar* 'trough' Rebus: *pattar* 'guild'. Thus, copper-zinc-tin alloy (worker) guild.

 *dula* 'pair' Rebus: *dul* 'cast (metal)' PLUS*kana, kanac* = corner (Santali); Rebus: *kañcu* = bronze (Telugu) PLUS *i*nfixed kolmo 'paddy plant' Rebus: kolami 'smithy, forge'. Thus, cast bronze smithy, forge. Or, *mogge* 'sprout, bud' Rebus: *mũh* 'ingot' (Santali)Thus, cast bronze ingot. Read as: *kañcu dul mũh*

'bronze cast ingot'

 *aḍar* 'harrow'; rebus: *aduru* 'native unsmelted metal'

ayo 'fish' Rebus: *aya* 'iron' *ayas* 'metal'
|||| Numeral 4: gaṇḍa 'four' Rebus: kaṇḍa 'furnace, fire-altar' (Santali)
||| Numeral three: kolom 'three' Rebus: kolami 'smithy, forge'

 सांड [sāṇḍa] *f* (षद S) An outlet for superfluous water (as through a dam or mound); a sluice, a floodvent. Rebus: सांडणी [sāṇḍaṇī] *f* (H) An instrument of goldsmiths. It is hooked or curved at the extremity; and is used to draw things out of the fire.
सांठा [*sāṇṭhā*] *m* (संचय S) A collection, heap, hoard, store, stock.साटें [*sāṭēṃ*] *n* (संचय S) A whole investment; the total quantity of merchandise (brought to market by one merchant).

 *kanka* 'rim of jar' Rebus: *karṇīka* 'account (scribe)' *karṇī* 'supercargo'

H-282 A

h282A
dula 'pair' Rebus: *dul* 'cast (metal)' PLUS*kana, kanac* = corner (Santali); Rebus: *kañcu* = bronze (Telugu) PLUS infixed kolmo 'paddy plant' Rebus: kolami 'smithy, forge'. Thus, cast bronze smithy, forge. Or, *mogge* 'sprout, bud' Rebus: *mũh* 'ingot' (Santali)Thus, cast bronze ingot. Read as: *kañcu dul mũh 'bronze cast ingot'*

 *aḍar* 'harrow'; rebus: *aduru* 'native unsmelted metal'

ayo 'fish' Rebus: *aya* 'iron' *ayas* 'metal'
kəṭhā´r, kc. *kuṭhār* m. ' granary, storeroom '(WPah.)(CDIAL 3550). *koṭhārī m.* ' storekeeper'

 (Gujarati)(CDIAL 3551) Thus, storeroom (of) *kolom* 'three' Rebus: *kolami* 'smithy, forge'. dula 'pair' Rebus: dul 'cast metal' Thus, together *dul kolami kuṭhār* 'metal smithy castings storeroom'

 *kuṭila* 'bent' CDIAL 3230 kuṭi— in cmpd. 'curve', *kuṭika*— 'bent' MBh. Rebus: *kuṭila, katthīl* = bronze (8 parts copper and 2 parts tin)

 The pair of hieroglyph signs are compositions: bicha 'scorpion' (Assamese) Rebus: *bica* 'stone ore' (Santali) The pairing sign is a composition of: sloping stroke PLUS two short strokes of a 'splinter':*ḍhāḷ* 'a slope'; 'inclination of a plane' (Gujarati); *ḍhāḷiyum* = adj. sloping, inclining (Gujarati) Rebus: *ḍhālako* = a large metal ingot (Gujarati) *ḍhālakī* = a metal heated and poured into a mould; a solid piece of metal; an ingot (Gujarati)PLUS*sal* 'splinter' Rebus: *sal* 'workshop'. Thus the composition reads: *ḍhālako sal* 'ingot workshop'.

 *dāṭu* 'cross'(Telugu) Rebus: *dhatu* 'mineral' (Santali).

ranku 'liquid measure' Rebus: ranku 'tin'

kolmo 'paddy plant' Rebus: *kolami* 'smithy, forge' Vikalpa: *mogge* 'sprout, bud' Rebus: *mũh* 'ingot' (Santali) dolu 'plant of shoot height' Rebus: dul 'cast metal'

kanka 'rim of jar' Rebus: *karṇīka* 'account (scribe)' *karṇī* 'supercargo'

M-1324 A

m1324A*dula* 'pair' Rebus: *dul* 'cast (metal)' PLUS*kana, kanac* = corner (Santali); Rebus: *kañcu* = bronze (Telugu) PLUS infixed kolmo 'paddy plant' Rebus: kolami 'smithy, forge'. Thus, cast bronze smithy, forge. Or, *mogge* 'sprout, bud' Rebus: *mũh* 'ingot' (Santali)Thus, cast bronze ingot. Read as: *kañcu dul mũh 'bronze cast ingot'*

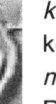

water-carrier hieroglyph *kuṭi*; Rebus: *kuṭhi* 'smelter furnace'. PLUS 'rim of jar':

kanka 'rim of jar' Rebus: karṇīka 'account (scribe)' karṇī 'supercargo'

m1699A Rebus reading as at m1324A

h1999A Rebus reading as at m1324A PLUS kuṭi 'tree' Rebus: kuṭhi 'smelter'

M-1699 A

H-1999 A

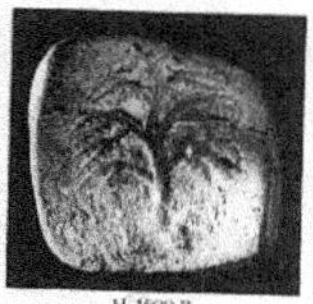

H-1999 B

h38a Rebus reading as at m1324A PLUS खोंड *[khōṇḍa] m A young bull, a bullcalf. (Marathi) Rebus: kõdār 'turner' (Bengali);* कोंद *kõnda 'engraver, lapidary setting or infixing gems' (Marathi) G. sãghāṛɔ m. 'lathe' ;* संघाट *joinery; M. sãgaḍ 'double-canoe' Rebus: sangataras.* संगतराश *lit. 'to collect stones, stone-cutter, mason.'*

m1661A खोंड *[khōṇḍa] m A young bull, a bullcalf. (Marathi) Rebus: kõdār 'turner' (Bengali);* कोंद *kõnda 'engraver, lapidary setting or infixing gems' (Marathi) G. sãghāṛɔ m. 'lathe' ;* संघाट *joinery; M. sãgaḍ 'double-canoe' Rebus: sangataras.* संगतराश *lit. 'to collect stones, stone-cutter, mason.'*

kuṭila 'bent'  CDIAL 3230 kuṭi— in cmpd. 'curve', *kuṭika*— 'bent' MBh. Rebus: *kuṭila*, *katthīl* = bronze (8 parts copper and 2 parts tin)

kəṭhā´r, kc. *kuṭhār* m. ' granary, storeroom '(WPah.)(CDIAL 3550). *koṭhārī m.* ' storekeeper'

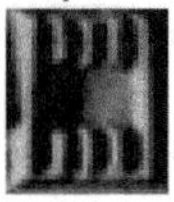

(Gujarati)(CDIAL 3551) Thus, storeroom (of) *kolom* 'three' Rebus: *kolami* 'smithy, forge'. Dula 'pair' Rebus: dul 'cast metal' Thus, together *dul kolami kuṭhār* 'metal smithy castings storeroom'

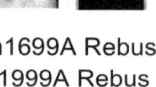

kolmo 'paddy plant' Rebus: *kolami* 'smithy, forge' Vikalpa: *mogge* 'sprout, bud' Rebus: *mũh* 'ingot' (Santali) dolu 'plant of shoot height' Rebus: dul 'cast metal'

Sign composite hieroglyph: Ligature of two bent lines + paddy plant

M-1892 a bis

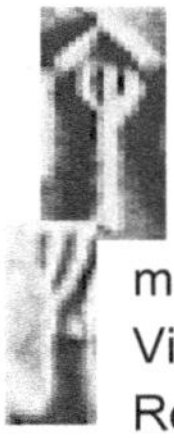

Native metal smith guild. Sign composite hieroglyph on m1892 has been read rebus. *aḍaren* 'cover of pot or lid' Rebus: *aduru* 'native, unsmelted metal' PLUS *kolmo* 'paddy plant' Rebus: *kolami* 'smithy, forge' Vikalpa: *mogge* 'sprout, bud' Rebus: *mũh* 'ingot' (Santali) dolu 'plant of shoot height' Rebus: dul 'cast metal'
Thus, native metal casting and smithy.
ranku 'liquid measure' Rebus: ranku 'tin'

kanac 'corner' Rebus: *kañcu* 'bronze'
aḍaren 'cover of pot or lid' Rebus: *aduru* 'native, unsmelted metal' PLUS 'notch': खांडा [*khāṇḍā*] *m* A jag, notch, or indentation

āra 'spokes' Rebus: *āra 'brass'*. cf. erka = ekke (Tbh. of arka) aka (Tbh. of arka) copper (metal); crystal (Kannada) Glyph: *eraka*'nave of wheel' Rebus: eraka 'copper'; cf. erka = ekke (Tbh. of arka) aka (Tbh. of arka) copper (metal); crystal (Kannada) *erako* 'moltencast copper' Duplicated: dula 'pair' Rebus: dul 'cast metal' Thus cast copper, brass casting.

koḍi 'flag' (Ta.)(DEDR 2049). Rebus 1: *koḍ* 'workshop' (Kuwi) Rebus 2: *khõḍ* m. 'pit', *khõḍü* f. 'small pit' (Kashmiri. CDIAL 3947).

mēḍu height, rising ground, hillock (Kannada) Rebus: *mẽṛhẽt, meḍ* 'iron' (Munda.Ho.)

muka 'ladle' (Tamil)(DEDR 4887) Rebus: *mũh* 'ingot' (Santali) *baṭa* = rimless pot (Kannada) Rebus:) *baṭa* = a kind of iron (G.)) *bhaṭa* furnace (Gujarati) Thus, iron ingot.

m2024a

dula 'pair' Rebus: *dul* 'cast (metal)' PLUS*kana, kanac* = corner (Santali); Rebus: *kañcu* = bronze (Telugu) PLUS infixed kolmo 'paddy plant' Rebus: kolami 'smithy, forge'. Thus, cast bronze smithy, forge. Or, *mogge* 'sprout, bud' Rebus: *mũh* 'ingot' (Santali)Thus, cast bronze ingot. Read as: *kañcu dul mũh 'bronze cast ingot'*

Ligature: two peaks: mēḍu height, rising ground, hillock (Kannada) Rebus: *meḍ* 'iron' (Ho.) dula 'pair' Rebus: dul 'cast metal' PLUS |||| Numeral 4: gaṇḍa 'four' Rebus: kaṇḍa 'furnace, fire-altar' (Santali)

dula 'pair' Rebus: dul 'cast metal' *mogge* 'sprout, bud' Rebus: *mũh* 'ingot' (Santali) Thus, cast metal ingot.

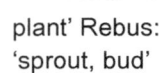

kanka 'rim of jar' Rebus: *karṇīka* 'account (scribe)' *karṇī* 'supercargo'

 Banawali 19A  m711A  m977a 

m1797A खोंड *[khōṇḍa] m A young bull, a bullcalf. (Marathi) Rebus: kõdār 'turner' (Bengali);* कोंद *kōnda 'engraver, lapidary setting or infixing gems' (Marathi) G. sãghāṛɔ m. 'lathe' ;* संघाट *joinery; M. sãgaḍ 'double-canoe' Rebus: sangataras.* संगतराश *lit. 'to collect stones, stone-cutter, mason.'*

dula 'pair' Rebus: *dul* 'cast (metal)' PLUS *kana, kanac* = corner (Santali); Rebus: *kañcu* = bronze (Telugu) PLUS infixed kolmo 'paddy plant' Rebus: kolami 'smithy, forge'. Thus, cast bronze smithy, forge. Or, *mogge* 'sprout, bud' Rebus: *mũh* 'ingot' (Santali)Thus, cast bronze ingot. Read as: *kañcu dul mũh 'bronze cast ingot'*

 *kanka* 'rim of jar' Rebus: *karṇīka* 'account (scribe)' *karṇī* 'supercargo'. Thus, smithy ingots supercargo.

h412A

खोंड *[khōṇḍa] m A young bull, a bullcalf. (Marathi) Rebus: kõdār 'turner' (Bengali);* कोंद *kōnda 'engraver, lapidary setting or infixing gems' (Marathi) G. sãghāṛɔ m. 'lathe' ;* संघाट *joinery; M. sãgaḍ 'double-canoe' Rebus: sangataras.* संगतराश *lit. 'to collect stones, stone-cutter, mason.'*

 *kana, kanac* = corner (Santali); Rebus: *kañcu* = bronze (Telugu) PLUS खांडा [*khāṇḍā*] *m* A jag, notch, or indentation (as upon the edge of a tool or weapon). Rebus: *kāṇḍa* 'tools, pots and pans and metal-ware' Thus, bronze metalware.

 *kanka* 'rim of jar' Rebus: *karṇīka* 'account (scribe)' *karṇī* 'supercargo'

ayo 'fish' Rebus: *aya* 'iron' *ayas* 'metal'

ayo ḍhālako 'alloy metal ingot'

 water-carrier hieroglyph *kuṭi*; Rebus: *kuṭhi* 'smelter furnace'.

 h654a *mogge* 'sprout, bud' Rebus: *mũh* 'ingot' PLUS | *koḍa* 'one' Rebus: *koḍ* 'workshop'

 *kanka* 'rim of jar' Rebus: *karṇīka* 'account (scribe)' *karṇī* 'supercargo'

 *dula* 'pair' Rebus: *dul* 'cast (metal)' PLUS *kana, kanac* = corner (Santali); Rebus: *kañcu* = bronze (Telugu) PLUS infixed kolmo 'paddy plant' Rebus: kolami 'smithy, forge'. Thus,

cast bronze smithy, forge. Or, *mogge* 'sprout, bud' Rebus: *mũh* 'ingot' (Santali)Thus, cast bronze ingot. Read as: *kañcu dul mũh 'bronze cast ingot'*

h482A, B Side B: *ayo* 'fish' Rebus: *aya* 'iron' *ayas* 'metal' PLUS *karāvu* 'crocodile' (Telugu) *khara* 'blacksmith' (Kashmiri) ayakara 'metalsmith' (Pali)

Side A: svastika hieroglyph: Rebus: jasta, satva, 'zinc' (Hindi.Kannada) zasath ज़स्ज़्थ् or zasuth ज़सुथ् । त्रपु m. (sg. dat. zastas ज़स्तस्), zinc, spelter, pewter (cf. Hindī *jast*)(Kashmiri) *kuṭi* 'tree' Rebus: *kuṭhi* 'smelter'

kanka 'rim of jar' Rebus: *karṇīka* 'account (scribe)' *karṇī* 'supercargo'

dula  'pair' Rebus: *dul* 'cast (metal)' PLUS *kana, kanac* = corner (Santali); Rebus: *kañcu* = bronze (Telugu) PLUS infixed kolmo 'paddy plant' Rebus: kolami 'smithy, forge'. Thus, cast bronze smithy, forge. Or, *mogge* 'sprout, bud' Rebus: *mũh* 'ingot' (Santali)Thus, cast bronze ingot. Read as: *kañcu dul mũh 'bronze cast ingot'*

m1452A

dula 'pair' Rebus: *dul* 'cast (metal)' PLUS *kana, kanac* = corner (Santali); Rebus: *kañcu* = bronze (Telugu) PLUS infixed kolmo 'paddy plant' Rebus: kolami 'smithy, forge'. Thus, cast bronze smithy, forge. Or, *mogge* 'sprout, bud' Rebus: *mũh* 'ingot' (Santali)Thus, cast bronze ingot. Read as: *kañcu dul mũh 'bronze cast ingot'*

ayo ḍhālako 'alloy metal ingot'

baraḍo = spine; backbone (Tulu) Rebus: *baran, bharat* 'mixed alloys' (5 copper, 4 zinc and 1 tin) (Punjabi) Obverse:

खोंड [khōṇḍa] m A young bull, a bullcalf. (Marathi) Rebus: kōdār 'turner' (Bengali); कोंद kōnda 'engraver, lapidary setting or infixing gems' (Marathi PLUS krammara 'turn back' Rebus: kamar 'smith' PLUS Kur. xolā tail. *Malt.* qoli id. (DEDR 2135). Rebus: kolhe 'smelter' Thus, copper smelter. Thus, smelter, turner, engraver. ranku 'liquid measue' Rebus: ranku 'tin'

mogge 'sprout, bud' Rebus: *mũh* 'ingot'

kanka 'rim of jar' Rebus: *karṇīka* 'account (scribe)' *karṇī* 'supercargo'

Kalibangan62a*dula* 'pair' Rebus: *dul* 'cast (metal)' PLUS *kana, kanac* = corner (Santali); Rebus: *kañcu* = bronze (Telugu) PLUS infixed kolmo 'paddy plant' Rebus: kolami 'smithy, forge'. Thus, cast bronze smithy, forge. Or, *mogge*

'sprout, bud' Rebus: *mũh* 'ingot' (Santali)Thus, cast bronze ingot. Read as: *kañcu dul mũh 'bronze cast ingot' ayo ḍhālako* 'alloy metal ingot'

baraḍo = spine; backbone (Tulu) Rebus: *baran, bharat* 'mixed alloys' (5 copper, 4 zinc and 1 tin) (Punjabi)

kanka 'rim of jar' Rebus: *karṇīka* 'account (scribe)' *karṇī* 'supercargo'

m249A *balad* m. ' ox ', gng. *bald*, (Ku.) *barad*, id. (N. Tarai) Rebus: *bharat* (5 copper, 4 zinc and 1 tin)(Punjabi) *pattar* 'trough' Rebus*: pattar* 'guild'. Thus, copper-zinc-tin alloy (worker) guild.

dula 'pair' Rebus: *dul* 'cast (metal)' PLUS *kana, kanac* = corner (Santali); Rebus: *kañcu* = bronze (Telugu) PLUS infixed kolmo 'paddy plant' Rebus: kolami 'smithy, forge'. Thus, cast bronze smithy, forge. Or, *mogge* 'sprout, bud' Rebus: *mũh* 'ingot'

(Santali)Thus, cast bronze ingot. Read as: *kañcu dul mũh 'bronze cast ingot' ayo ḍhālako* 'alloy metal ingot'

baraḍo = spine; backbone (Tulu) Rebus: *baran, bharat* 'mixed alloys' (5 copper, 4 zinc and 1 tin) (Punjabi)

kanka 'rim of jar' Rebus: *karṇīka* 'account (scribe)' *karṇī* 'supercargo'

araṇe 'lizard' Rebus: *airaṇ* 'anvil'. The stylized hieroglyph sig connotes such a snarling iron. The hieroglyph may be a variant of:  *kana, kanac* = corner (Santali); Rebus: *kañcu* = bronze (Telugu) PLUS खांडा [*khāṇḍā*] *m* A jag, notch, or indentation (as upon the edge of a tool or weapon). Rebus: *kāṇḍa* 'tools, pots and pans and metal-ware' Thus, bronze metalware.

The stylized curved line may denote a lizard's tail. – as seen on many epigraphs such as Lothal 26 and Harappa 688.

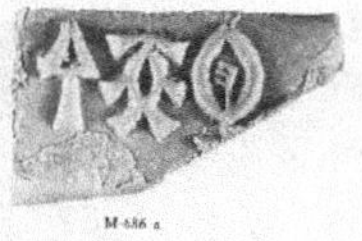

loa 'ficus religiosa' Rebus: *lo* 'iron' (Sanskrit) PLUS unique ligatures: लोखंड [lōkhaṇḍa] *n* (लोह S) Iron. लोखंडाचे चणे खावविणें or चारणें To oppress grievously.लोखंडकाम [lōkhaṇḍakāma] *n* Iron work; that portion (of a building, machine &c.) which consists of iron. 2 The business of an ironsmith.लोखंडी [lōkhaṇḍī] *a* (लोखंड) Composed of iron; relating to iron. (Marathi) *bhaṭa* 'warrior' (Sanskrit) Rebus: *baṭa* a kind of iron (Gujarati). Rebus: *bhaṭa* 'furnace' (Santali) Thus, together, th ligatured hieroglyph reads rebus: *loa bhaṭa* 'iron furnace'

m686a

dula 'pair' Rebus: *dul* 'cast (metal)' PLUS*kana, kanac* = corner (Santali); Rebus: *kañcu* = bronze (Telugu) PLUS infixed kolmo 'paddy plant' Rebus: kolami 'smithy, forge'. Thus, cast bronze smithy, forge. Or, *mogge* 'sprout, bud' Rebus: *mũh* 'ingot' (Santali)Thus, cast bronze ingot. Read as: *kañcu dul mũh 'bronze cast ingot' aya aḍaren (homonym: aduru)*'alloy native metal'

kāṇḍa 'arrow' (Sanskrit) Rebus:*khāṇḍa* 'tools, pots and pans, metal-ware'. Rebus 2: kaṇḍ 'fire-altar' (Santali)

m1784a Read rebus as at m917a

m917a Read rebus as at GharaBiro 1a PLUS *खोंड [khōṇḍa] m A young bull, a bullcalf. (Marathi) Rebus: kōdār 'turner' (Bengali); कोंद kōnda 'engraver, lapidary setting or infixing gems' (Marathi) G. sãghāṛɔ m. 'lathe' ; संघाट joinery; M. sãgaḍ 'double-canoe' Rebus: sangataras. संगतराश lit. 'to collect stones, stone-cutter, mason.'*

GharoBiro 1a

dula 'pair' Rebus: *dul* 'cast (metal)' PLUS*kana, kanac* = corner (Santali); Rebus: *kañcu* = bronze (Telugu) PLUS infixed kolmo 'paddy plant' Rebus: kolami 'smithy, forge'. Thus, cast bronze smithy, forge. Or, *mogge* 'sprout, bud' Rebus: *mũh* 'ingot' (Santali)Thus, cast bronze ingot. Read as: *kañcu dul mũh 'bronze cast ingot' aya aḍaren (homonym: aduru)*'alloy native metal'

 *kuṭila* 'bent' CDIAL 3230 kuṭi— in cmpd. 'curve', *kuṭika*— 'bent' MBh. Rebus: *kuṭila, katthīl* = bronze (8 parts copper and 2 parts tin) Duplicated: dula 'pair' Rebus: dul 'cast metal' Thus, cast bronze.

 *kanka* 'rim of jar' Rebus: *karṇīka* 'account (scribe)' *karṇī* 'supercargo'

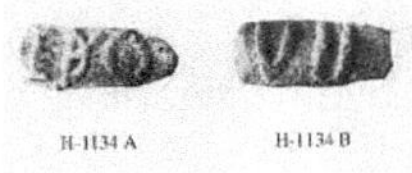

h1134A *dula* 'pair' Rebus: *dul* 'cast (metal)' PLUS *kana, kanac* = corner (Santali); Rebus: *kañcu* = bronze (Telugu) PLUS infixed kolmo 'paddy plant' Rebus: kolami 'smithy, forge'. Thus, cast bronze smithy, forge. Or,

 *mogge* 'sprout, bud' Rebus: *mũh* 'ingot' (Santali)Thus, cast bronze ingot. Read as: *kañcu dul mũh 'bronze cast ingot' aya aḍaren (homonym: aduru)*'alloy native metal'

kamaḍha 'bow and arrow' Rebus: *kammaṭa* 'mint, coiner'.

 *kana, kanac* = corner (Santali); Rebus: *kañcu* = bronze (Telugu) PLUS खांडा [*khāṇḍā*] *m* A jag, notch, or indentation (as upon the edge of a tool or weapon). Rebus: *kāṇḍa* 'tools, pots and pans and metal-ware' Thus, bronze metalware.

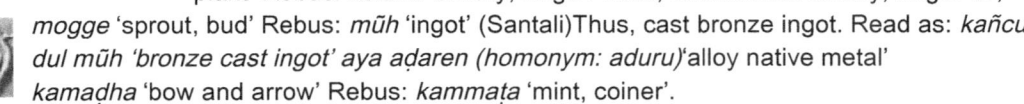

Side B: *baṭa* = rimless pot (Kannada) Rebus:) *baṭa* = a kind of iron (G.)) *bhaṭa* furnace (Gujarati) Thus, iron ingot. PLUS dula 'two' Rebus: dul 'cast metal'. Thus, furnace for metal castings.

h207A

खोंड [khōṇḍa] m A young bull, a bullcalf. (Marathi) Rebus: kõdār 'turner' (Bengali); कोंद kōnda 'engraver, lapidary setting or infixing gems' (Marathi) G. sãghāṛɔ m. 'lathe' ; संघाट joinery; M. sãgaḍ 'double-canoe' Rebus: sangataras. संगतराश lit. 'to collect stones, stone-cutter, mason.'

kamaḍha 'bow and arrow' Rebus: *kammaṭa* 'mint, coiner'. *kana, kanac* = corner (Santali); Rebus: *kañcu* = bronze (Telugu) PLUS kolom 'three' Rebus: kolami 'smithy, forge'. Thus bronze smithy.

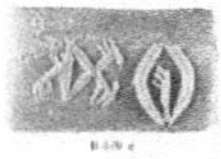

h679a

dula 'pair' Rebus: *dul* 'cast (metal)' PLUS *kana, kanac* = corner (Santali); Rebus: *kañcu* = bronze (Telugu) PLUS infixed kolmo 'paddy plant' Rebus: kolami 'smithy,

 forge'. Thus, cast bronze smithy, forge. Or, *mogge* 'sprout, bud' Rebus: *mũh* 'ingot' (Santali)Thus, cast bronze ingot. Read as: *kañcu dul mũh 'bronze cast ingot' aya aḍaren (homonym: aduru)*'alloy native metal'

kamaḍha 'crab' Rebus: *kammaṭa* 'mint, coiner'.

ḍato = claws of crab (Santali) Rebus: *dhātu* 'mineral ore'

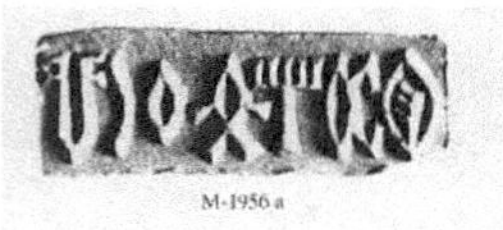

h1956a *dula* 'pair' Rebus: *dul* 'cast (metal)' PLUS *kana, kanac* = corner (Santali); Rebus: *kañcu* = bronze (Telugu) PLUS infixed kolmo 'paddy plant' Rebus: kolami 'smithy, forge'. Thus, cast bronze smithy, forge. Or, *mogge* 'sprout, bud' Rebus: *mũh* 'ingot' (Santali)Thus, cast bronze ingot. Read as: *kañcu dul mũh 'bronze cast ingot'*

kamaḍha 'crab' Rebus: *kammaṭa* 'mint, coiner'.

aḍar 'harrow'; rebus: *aduru* 'native unsmelted metal'
ayo 'fish' Rebus: *aya* 'iron' *ayas* 'metal'
dulo 'hole' Rebus: dul 'cast metal'

kuṭila 'bent' CDIAL 3230 kuṭi— in cmpd. 'curve', *kuṭika*— 'bent' MBh. Rebus: *kuṭila, katthīl* = bronze (8 parts copper and 2 parts tin) Duplicated: dula 'pair' Rebus: dul 'cast metal' Thus, cast bronze.

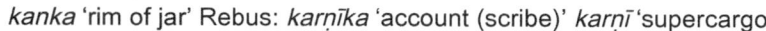

kanka 'rim of jar' Rebus: *karṇīka* 'account (scribe)' *karṇī* 'supercargo'

m707a *खोंड [khōṇḍa] m A young bull, a bullcalf. (Marathi) Rebus: kōdār 'turner' (Bengali); कोंद kōnda 'engraver, lapidary setting or infixing gems' (Marathi) G. sãghāṛɔ m. 'lathe' ; संघाट joinery; M. sāgaḍ 'double-canoe' Rebus: sangataras. संगतराश lit. 'to collect stones, stone-cutter, mason.'*
First four signs read rebus as at h1956a.
'notch': खांडा [*khāṇḍā*] *m* A jag, notch, or indentation (as upon the edge of a tool or weapon). Rebus: *kāṇḍa* 'tools, pots and pans and metal-ware'

dula 'pair' Rebus: dul 'cast metal' *mogge* 'sprout, bud' Rebus: *mũh* 'ingot' (Santali) Thus, cast metal ingot.

kanka 'rim of jar' Rebus: *karṇīka* 'account (scribe)' *karṇī* 'supercargo'

m494A*kana, kanac* = corner (Santali); Rebus: *kañcu* = bronze (Telugu) PLUS खांडा [*khāṇḍā*] *m* A jag, notch, or indentation (as upon the edge of a tool or weapon). Rebus: *kāṇḍa* 'tools, pots and pans and metal-ware' Thus, bronze metalware.

kamaḍha 'crab' Rebus: *kammaṭa* 'mint, coiner'.
baraḍo = spine; backbone (Tulu) Rebus: *baran, bharat* 'mixed alloys' (5 copper, 4 zinc and 1 tin) (Punjabi)

 *kanka*  'rim of jar' Rebus: *karṇīka* 'account (scribe)' *karṇī* 'supercargo'

'rim   water-carrier hieroglyph *kuṭi*; Rebus: *kuṭhi* 'smelter furnace'. PLUS of jar':

kanka 'rim of jar' Rebus: karṇīka 'account (scribe)' karṇī 'supercargo'

baṭa = rimless pot (Kannada) Rebus:) *baṭa* = a kind of iron (G.)) *bhaṭa* furnace (Gujarati) PLUS duplicated: dula 'pair' Rebus: dul 'cast metal' Thus furnace for castings.

PLUS | *koḍa* 'one' Rebus: *koḍ* 'workshop'

kolmo 'paddy plant' Rebus: *kolami* 'smithy, forge' Vikalpa: *mogge* 'sprout, bud' Rebus: *mũh* 'ingot' (Santali) dolu 'plant of shoot height' Rebus: dul 'cast metal'

m495A

kana, kanac = corner (Santali); Rebus: *kañcu* = bronze (Telugu) PLUS खांडा [*khāṇḍā*] *m* A jag, notch, or indentation (as upon the edge of a tool or weapon). Rebus: *kāṇḍa* 'tools, pots and pans and metal-ware' Thus, bronze metalware.

kamaḍha 'crab' Rebus: *kammaṭa* 'mint, coiner'.

baraḍo = spine; backbone (Tulu) Rebus: *baran, bharat* 'mixed alloys' (5 copper, 4 zinc and 1 tin) (Punjabi)

kanka 'rim of jar' Rebus: *karṇīka* 'account (scribe)' *karṇī* 'supercargo'

water-carrier hieroglyph *kuṭi*; Rebus: *kuṭhi* 'smelter furnace'. *baṭa* = rimless pot (Kannada) Rebus:) *baṭa* = a kind of iron (G.)) *bhaṭa* furnace (Gujarati) PLUS triplicated: kolom 'three' Rebus: kolami 'smithy, forge'. Ths iron furnace, smithy.

kolmo 'paddy plant' Rebus: *kolami* 'smithy, forge' Vikalpa: *mogge* 'sprout, bud' Rebus: *mũh* 'ingot' (Santali) dolu 'plant of shoot height' Rebus: dul 'cast metal'

m1781a

खोंड [khōṇḍa] m A young bull, a bullcalf. (Marathi) Rebus: kõdār 'turner' (Bengali); कोंद kōnda 'engraver, lapidary setting or infixing gems' (Marathi) G. sãghāṛɔ m. 'lathe' ; संघाट joinery; M. sãgaḍ 'double-canoe' Rebus: sangataras. संगतराश lit. 'to collect stones, stone-cutter, mason.'

dula 'pair' Rebus: *dul* 'cast (metal)' PLUS*kana, kanac* = corner (Santali); Rebus: *kañcu* = bronze (Telugu) PLUS infixed kolmo 'paddy plant' Rebus: kolami 'smithy, forge'. Thus, cast bronze smithy, forge. Or, *mogge* 'sprout, bud' Rebus: *mũh* 'ingot' (Santali)Thus, cast bronze ingot. Read as: *kañcu dul mũh 'bronze cast ingot'*

ayo ḍhālako 'alloy metal ingot' *kāṇḍa* 'arrow' (Sanskrit) Rebus:*khāṇḍa* 'tools, pots and pans, metal-ware'. Rebus 2: kaṇḍ 'fire-altar' (Santali)

m1079A

dula 'pair' Rebus: *dul* 'cast (metal)' PLUS*kana, kanac* = corner (Santali); Rebus: *kañcu* = bronze (Telugu) PLUS infixed kolmo 'paddy plant' Rebus: kolami 'smithy, forge'. Thus, cast bronze smithy, forge. Or, *mogge* 'sprout, bud' Rebus: *mũh* 'ingot' (Santali)Thus, cast bronze ingot. Read as: *kañcu dul mũh 'bronze cast ingot'*

ayo ḍhālako 'alloy metal ingot'*muka* 'ladle' (Tamil)(DEDR 4887) Rebus: *mũh* 'ingot' (Santali) *baṭa* = rimless pot (Kannada) Rebus:) *baṭa* = a kind of iron (G.)) *bhaṭa* furnace (Gujarati) Thus, iron ingot.

kolom 'three' Rebus: kolami 'smithy, forge'

dula 'pair' Rebus: dul 'cast metal' *mogge* 'sprout, bud' Rebus: *mũh* 'ingot' (Santali) Thus, cast metal ingot.

kanka 'rim of jar' Rebus: *karṇīka* 'account (scribe)' *karṇī* 'supercargo'

m236A *balad* m. ' ox ', gng. *bald*, (Ku.) *barad*, id. (N. Tarai) Rebus: *bharat* (5 copper, 4 zinc and 1 tin)(Punjabi) *pattar* 'trough' Rebus*: pattar* 'guild'. Thus, copper-zinc-tin alloy (worker) guild.

dula 'pair' Rebus: *dul* 'cast (metal)' PLUS*kana, kanac* = corner (Santali); Rebus: *kañcu* = bronze (Telugu) PLUS infixed kolmo 'paddy plant' Rebus: kolami 'smithy, forge'. Thus, cast bronze smithy, forge. Or, *mogge* 'sprout, bud' Rebus: *mũh* 'ingot' (Santali)Thus, cast bronze ingot. Read as: *kañcu dul mũh 'bronze cast ingot' ayo ḍhālako* 'alloy metal ingot' *aya kammaṭa.*'coiner, mint alloy'

muka 'ladle' (Tamil)(DEDR 4887) Rebus: *mũh* 'ingot' (Santali) *baṭa* = rimless pot (Kannada) Rebus:) *baṭa* = a kind of iron (G.)) *bhaṭa* furnace (Gujarati) Thus, iron ingot. kolom 'three' Rebus: kolami 'smithy, forge' *kāṇḍa* 'arrow' (Sanskrit) Rebus:*khāṇḍa* 'tools, pots and pans, metal-ware'. Rebus 2: kaṇḍ 'fire-altar' (Santali)

H-445 A bis

h445A

खोंड [khōṇḍa] m A young bull, a bullcalf. (Marathi) Rebus: kōdār 'turner' (Bengali); कोंद kōnda 'engraver, lapidary setting or infixing gems' (Marathi) G. sãghāṛɔ m. 'lathe' ; संघाट joinery; M. sãgaḍ 'double-canoe' Rebus: sangataras. संगतराश lit. 'to collect stones, stone-cutter, mason.'

'notch': खांडा [*khāṇḍā*] *m* A jag, notch, or indentation (as upon the edge of a tool or weapon). Rebus: *kāṇḍa* 'tools, pots and pans and metal-ware'

kana, kanac = corner (Santali); Rebus: *kañcu* = bronze (Telugu) PLUS खांडा [*khāṇḍā*] *m* A jag, notch, or indentation (as upon the edge of a tool or weapon). Rebus: *kāṇḍa* 'tools, pots and pans and metal-ware' Thus, bronze metalware. *aya kāṇḍa* 'alloy metalware'

M-405 a

m405a First 3 signs read rebus as m30a. PLUS

kuṭila 'bent' CDIAL 3230 kuṭi— in cmpd. 'curve', *kuṭika—* 'bent' MBh. Rebus: *kuṭila, katthīl* = bronze (8 parts copper and 2 parts tin)

Duplicated: dula 'pair' Rebus: dul 'cast metal' Thus, cast bronze.

kanka 'rim of jar' Rebus: *karṇīka* 'account (scribe)' *karṇī* 'supercargo'

m30a *खोंड [khōṇḍa] m A young bull, a bullcalf. (Marathi) Rebus: kōdār 'turner' (Bengali); कोंद kōnda 'engraver, lapidary setting or infixing gems' (Marathi) G. sãghāṛɔ m. 'lathe' ; संघाट joinery; M. sãgaḍ 'double-canoe' Rebus: sangataras. संगतराश lit. 'to collect stones, stone-cutter, mason.'*

dula 'pair' Rebus: *dul* 'cast (metal)' PLUS*kana, kanac* = corner (Santali); Rebus: *kañcu* = bronze (Telugu) PLUS infixed kolmo 'paddy plant' Rebus: kolami 'smithy, f orge'. Thus, cast bronze smithy, forge. Or, *mogge* 'sprout, bud' Rebus: *mũh* 'ingot' (Santali)Thus, cast bronze ingot. Read as: *kañcu dul mũh 'bronze cast* *ingot' aya aḍaren (homonym: aduru)*'alloy native metal' *aya kammaṭa.*'coiner, mint alloy'

mēḍu height, rising ground, hillock (Kannada) Rebus: *mẽṛhẽt, meḍ* 'iron' (Munda.Ho.) |||| Numeral 4: gaṇḍa 'four' Rebus: kaṇḍa 'furnace, fire-altar' (Santali)

||| Numeral three: kolom 'three' Rebus: kolami 'smithy, forge'

dula 'pair' Rebus: dul 'cast metal' *mogge* 'sprout, bud' Rebus: *mũh* 'ingot' (Santali) Thus, cast metal ingot.

kanka 'rim of jar' Rebus: *karṇīka* 'account (scribe)' *karṇī* 'supercargo'

m814a First 3 signs read rebus as m30a PLUS

muka 'ladle' (Tamil)(DEDR 4887) Rebus: *mũh* 'ingot' (Santali) *baṭa* = rimless pot (Kannada) Rebus:) *baṭa* = a kind of iron (G.)) *bhaṭa* furnace (Gujarati) Thus, iron ingot.

kolom 'three' Rebus: kolami 'smithy, forge'

baraḍo = spine; backbone (Tulu) Rebus: *baran, bharat* 'mixed alloys' (5 copper, 4 zinc and 1 tin) (Punjabi) *kanka* 'rim of jar' Rebus: *karṇīka* 'account (scribe)' *karṇī* 'supercargo'

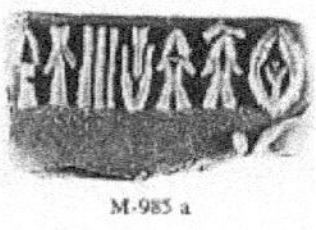

m985a First five signs read rebus as at m814a PLUS

'Arrow' sign hieroglyph (variant) This is a ligature of 'lid of pot' hieroglyph superscript on 'a linear stroke' numeral hieroglyph.*aḍaren* 'cover of pot or lid' Rebus: *aduru* 'native, unsmelted metal' PLUS koḍ = one (Santali); koḍ 'workshop' (G.)

kāṇḍa 'arrow' (Sanskrit) Rebus:*khāṇḍa* 'tools, pots and pans, metal-ware'. Rebus 2: kaṇḍ 'fire-altar' (Santali)

h759A 'young bull' :*खोंड [khōṇḍa] m A young bull, a bullcalf. (Marathi) Rebus: kõdār 'turner' (Bengali); कोंद kōnda 'engraver, lapidary setting or infixing gems' (Marathi) G. sãghāṛɔ m. 'lathe' ; संघाट joinery; M. sãgaḍ 'double-canoe' Rebus: sangataras. संगतराश lit. 'to collect stones, stone-cutter, mason.'*

dula 'pair' Rebus: *dul* 'cast (metal)' PLUS*kana, kanac* = corner (Santali); Rebus: *kañcu* =

bronze (Telugu) PLUS infixed kolmo 'paddy plant' Rebus: kolami 'smithy, forge'. Thus, cast bronze smithy, forge. Or, *mogge* 'sprout, bud' Rebus: *mũh* 'ingot' (Santali)Thus, cast bronze ingot. Read as: *kañcu dul mũh 'bronze cast ingot' aya kammaṭa.*'coiner, mint alloy' *kāṇḍa* 'arrow' (Sanskrit) Rebus:*khāṇḍa* 'tools, pots and pans, metal-ware'. Rebus 2: kaṇḍ 'fire-altar' (Santali)

m1953a

dula 'pair' Rebus: *dul* 'cast (metal)' PLUS*kana, kanac* = corner (Santali); Rebus: *kañcu* =

bronze (Telugu) PLUS infixed kolmo 'paddy plant' Rebus: kolami 'smithy, forge'. Thus, cast bronze smithy, forge. Or, *mogge* 'sprout, bud' Rebus: *mũh* 'ingot' (Santali)Thus, cast bronze ingot. Read as: *kañcu dul mũh 'bronze cast ingot' ayo ḍhālako* 'alloy metal ingot'*dula* 'pair' Rebus: *dul* 'cast (metal)' PLUS

kana, kanac = corner (Santali); Rebus: *kañcu* = bronze (Telugu) Thus, cast bronze. PLUS खांडा [*khāṇḍā*] *m* A jag, notch, or indentation (as upon the edge of a tool or weapon). Rebus: *kāṇḍa* 'tools, pots and pans and metal-ware' Thus, cast bronze metalware.

kolmo 'paddy plant' Rebus: *kolami* 'smithy, forge' Vikalpa: *mogge* 'sprout, bud' Rebus: *mũh* 'ingot' (Santali) dolu 'plant of shoot height' Rebus: dul 'cast metal'

Lothal 82a

dula 'pair' Rebus: *dul* 'cast (metal)' PLUS*kana, kanac* = corner (Santali); Rebus: *kañcu* = bronze (Telugu) PLUS infixed kolmo 'paddy plant' Rebus: kolami 'smithy, forge'. Thus, cast bronze smithy, forge. Or, *mogge* 'sprout, bud' Rebus: *mũh* 'ingot' (Santali)Thus, cast bronze ingot. Read as: *kañcu dul mũh 'bronze cast ingot' aya kāṇḍa* 'alloy metalware' sal 'splinter' Rebus: sal 'workshop' Thus alloy metalware workshop.

kuṭila 'bent' CDIAL 3230 kuṭi— in cmpd. 'curve', *kuṭika—* 'bent' MBh. Rebus: *kuṭila, katthīl* = bronze (8 parts copper and 2 parts tin) *ayo* 'fish' Rebus: *aya* 'iron' *ayas* 'metal'

h240A First two signs read as at Lothal 82a PLUS dula 'two' Rebus: dul 'cast metal'

kuṭila 'bent' CDIAL 3230 kuṭi— in cmpd. 'curve', *kuṭika—* 'bent' MBh. Rebus: *kuṭila, katthīl* = bronze (8 parts copper and 2 parts tin) Duplicated: dula 'pair' Rebus: dul 'cast metal' Thus, cast bronze.

kanka 'rim of jar' Rebus: *karṇīka* 'account (scribe)' *karṇī* 'supercargo'

m504A Copper plate.
kana, kanac = corner (Santali); Rebus: *kañcu* = bronze (Telugu) with infixed three numeral strokes' sign hieroglyph *kolom* 'three' Rebus: *kolami* 'smithy, forge' *ayo ḍhālako* 'alloy metal ingot'

loa 'ficus
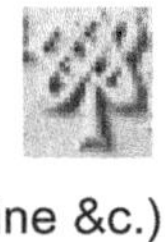
religiosa' Rebus: *lo* 'iron' (Sanskrit) PLUS unique ligatures: लोखंड [lōkhaṇḍa] *n* (लोह S) Iron. लोखंडाचे चणे खावविणें or चारणें To oppress grievously.लोखंडकाम [lōkhaṇḍakāma] *n* Iron work; that portion (of a building, machine &c.) which consists of iron. 2 The business of an ironsmith.लोखंडी [lōkhaṇḍī] *a* (लोखंड) Composed of iron; relating to iron. (Marathi)

kanka 'rim of jar' Rebus: *karṇīka* 'account (scribe)' *karṇī* 'supercargo'

m392a

dula 'pair' Rebus: *dul* 'cast (metal)' PLUS*kana, kanac* = corner (Santali); Rebus: *kañcu* = bronze (Telugu) PLUS infixed kolmo 'paddy plant' Rebus: kolami 'smithy, forge'. Thus, cast bronze smithy, forge. Or, *mogge* 'sprout, bud' Rebus: *mũh* 'ingot' (Santali)Thus, cast bronze ingot. Read as: *kañcu dul mũh 'bronze cast ingot'* dula 'two' Rebus: dul 'cast metal' *ayo* 'fish' Rebus: *aya* 'iron' *ayas* 'metal' ranku 'liquid measure' Rebus: ranku 'tin'

kolmo 'paddy plant' Rebus: *kolami* 'smithy, forge' Vikalpa: *mogge* 'sprout, bud' Rebus: *mũh* 'ingot' (Santali) dolu 'plant of shoot height' Rebus: dul 'cast metal'

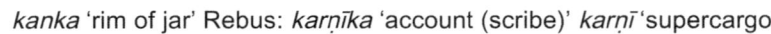

 *kanka* 'rim of jar' Rebus: *karṇīka* 'account (scribe)' *karṇī* 'supercargo'

M-1265 a

m1265a

dula 'pair' Rebus: *dul* 'cast (metal)' PLUS*kana, kanac* = corner (Santali); Rebus: *kañcu* = bronze (Telugu) PLUS infixed kolmo 'paddy plant' Rebus: kolami 'smithy, forge'. Thus, cast bronze smithy, forge. Or, *mogge* 'sprout, bud' Rebus: *mũh* 'ingot' (Santali)Thus, cast bronze ingot. Read as: *kañcu dul mũh 'bronze cast ingot'* dula 'two' Rebus: dul 'cast metal' *aya kammaṭa.*'coiner, mint alloy'

baroṭi 'twelve' *bhārata* 'a factitious alloy of copper, pewter, tin' (Marathi)

 *kanka* 'rim of jar' Rebus: *karṇīka* 'account (scribe)' *karṇī* 'supercargo'

M-811 A

m811A *खोंड [khōṇḍa] m A young bull, a bullcalf. (Marathi) Rebus: kõdār 'turner' (Bengali); कोंद kōnda 'engraver, lapidary setting or infixing gems' (Marathi) G. sãghāṛɔ m. 'lathe' ; संघाट joinery; M. sãgaḍ 'double-canoe' Rebus: sangataras. संगतराश lit. 'to collect stones, stone-cutter, mason.'*

dula 'pair' Rebus: *dul* 'cast (metal)' PLUS*kana, kanac* = corner (Santali); Rebus: *kañcu* = bronze (Telugu) PLUS infixed kolmo 'paddy plant' Rebus: kolami 'smithy, forge'. Thus, cast bronze smithy, forge. Or, *mogge* 'sprout, bud' Rebus: *mũh* 'ingot' (Santali)Thus, cast bronze ingot. Read as: *kañcu dul mũh 'bronze cast ingot'* dula 'two' Rebus: dul 'cast metal' *aya kāṇḍa* 'alloy metalware'

H-661 A

h661A*dula* 'pair' Rebus: *dul* 'cast (metal)' PLUS*kana, kanac* = corner (Santali); Rebus: *kañcu* = bronze (Telugu) PLUS infixed kolmo 'paddy plant' Rebus: kolami 'smithy, forge'. Thus, cast bronze smithy, forge. Or, *mogge* 'sprout, bud' Rebus: *mũh* 'ingot' (Santali)Thus, cast bronze ingot. Read as: *kañcu dul mũh 'bronze cast ingot'* dula 'two' Rebus: dul 'cast metal'

baroṭi 'twelve' *bhārata* 'a factitious alloy of copper, pewter, tin' (Marathi)

 *kanka* 'rim of jar' Rebus: *karṇīka* 'account (scribe)' *karṇī* 'supercargo'

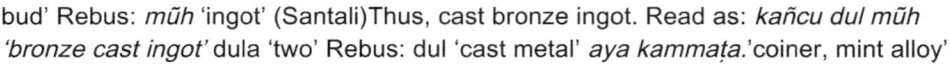

m1676a खोंड [khōṇḍa] m A young bull, a bullcalf. (Marathi) Rebus: kõdār 'turner' (Bengali); कोंद kōnda 'engraver, lapidary setting or infixing gems' (Marathi) G. sãghāṛɔ m. 'lathe' ; संघाट joinery; M. sãgaḍ 'double-canoe' Rebus: sangataras. संगतराश lit. 'to collect stones, stone-cutter, mason.'

dula 'pair' Rebus: *dul* 'cast (metal)' PLUS *kana, kanac* = corner (Santali); Rebus: *kañcu* = bronze (Telugu) PLUS infixed kolmo 'paddy plant' Rebus: kolami 'smithy, forge'. Thus, cast bronze smithy, forge. Or, *mogge* 'sprout, bud' Rebus: *mũh* 'ingot' (Santali)Thus, cast bronze ingot. Read as: *kañcu dul mũh 'bronze cast ingot'* dula 'two' Rebus: dul 'cast metal' *aya kāṇḍa* 'alloy metalware' *kaṇḍo* 'stool, seat' Rebus: *kāṇḍa* 'metalware' *kaṇḍa* 'fire-altar' PLUS

mēḍu height, rising ground, hillock (Kannada) Rebus: *mẽṛhẽt, meḍ* 'iron' (Munda.Ho.) Thus, iron alloy metalware

ranku 'liquid measure' Rebus: ranku 'tin. sal 'splinter' Rebus: sal 'workshop' *aya kammaṭa.*'coiner, mint alloy'

kana, kanac = corner (Santali); Rebus: *kañcu* = bronze (Telugu) PLUS खांडा [*khāṇḍā*] *m* A jag, notch, or indentation (as upon the edge of a tool or weapon). Rebus: *kāṇḍa* 'tools, pots and pans and metal-ware' Thus, bronze metalware.

The pair of hieroglyph signs are compositions: bicha 'scorpion' (Assamese) Rebus: *bica* 'stone ore' (Santali) The pairing sign is a composition of: sloping stroke PLUS two short strokes of a 'splinter':*dhāḷ* 'a slope'; 'inclination of a plane' (Gujarati); *ḍhāḷiyum* = adj. sloping, inclining (Gujarati) Rebus: *ḍhālako* = a large metal ingot (Gujarati) *ḍhālakī* = a metal heated and poured into a mould; a solid piece of metal; an ingot (Gujarati)PLUS *sal* 'splinter' Rebus: *sal* 'workshop'. Thus the composition reads: *ḍhālako sal* 'ingot workshop'.

'Arrow' sign hieroglyph (variant) This is a ligature of 'lid of pot' hieroglyph superscript on 'a linear stroke' numeral hieroglyph.*aḍaren* 'cover of pot or lid' Rebus: *aduru* 'native, unsmelted metal' PLUS koḍ = one (Santali); koḍ 'workshop' (G.)

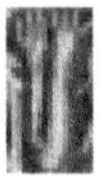

dula 'pair' Rebus: dul 'cast metal' *mogge* 'sprout, bud' Rebus: *mũh* 'ingot' (Santali) Thus, cast metal ingot.

kanka 'rim of jar' Rebus: *karṇīka* 'account (scribe)' *karṇī* 'supercargo'

m1698a खोंड [khōṇḍa] m A young bull, a bullcalf. (Marathi) Rebus: kõdār 'turner' (Bengali); कोंद kōnda 'engraver, lapidary setting or infixing gems' (Marathi) G. sãghāṛɔ m. 'lathe' ; संघाट joinery; M. sãgaḍ 'double-canoe' Rebus: sangataras. संगतराश lit. 'to collect stones, stone-cutter, mason.'

dula 'pair' Rebus: *dul* 'cast (metal)' PLUS *kana, kanac* = corner (Santali); Rebus: *kañcu* = bronze (Telugu) PLUS infixed kolmo 'paddy plant' Rebus: kolami 'smithy, forge'. Thus, cast bronze smithy, forge. Or, *mogge* 'sprout, bud' Rebus: *mũh* 'ingot' (Santali)Thus, cast bronze ingot. Read as: *kañcu dul mũh 'bronze cast ingot'*

kanac 'corner' Rebus: *kañcu* 'bronze' sal 'splinter' Rebus: sal 'workshop'.

muka 'ladle' (Tamil)(DEDR 4887) Rebus: *mũh* 'ingot' (Santali) *baṭa* = rimless pot (Kannada)

Rebus:) *baṭa* = a kind of iron (G.)) *bhaṭa* furnace (Gujarati) Thus, iron ingot.
kolom 'three' Rebus: kolami 'smithy, forge' *aḍaren* 'cover of pot or lid' Rebus: *aduru* 'native, unsmelted metal'

kanka 'rim of jar' Rebus: *karṇīka* 'account (scribe)' *karṇī* 'supercargo'

m173A *खोंड [khōṇḍa] m A young bull, a bullcalf. (Marathi) Rebus: kōdār 'turner' (Bengali); कोंद kōnda 'engraver, lapidary setting or infixing gems' (Marathi) G. sãghārɔ m. 'lathe' ; संघाट joinery; M. sãgaḍ 'double-canoe' Rebus: sangataras. संगतराश lit. 'to collect stones, stone-cutter, mason.'*

dula 'pair' Rebus: *dul* 'cast (metal)' PLUS *kana, kanac* = corner (Santali); Rebus: *kañcu* = bronze (Telugu) PLUS infixed kolmo 'paddy plant' Rebus: kolami 'smithy, forge'. Thus, cast bronze smithy, forge. Or, *mogge* 'sprout, bud' Rebus: *mũh* 'ingot' (Santali)Thus, cast bronze ingot. Read as: *kañcu dul mũh 'bronze cast ingot'*

ranku 'antelope' Rebus: ranku 'tin'

kuṭila 'bent' CDIAL 3230 kuṭi— in cmpd. 'curve', *kuṭika—* 'bent' MBh. Rebus: *kuṭila, katthīl* = bronze (8 parts copper and 2 parts tin)

loa 'ficus religiosa' Rebus: *lo* 'iron' (Sanskrit) PLUS unique ligatures: लोखंड [lōkhaṇḍa] *n* (लोह S) Iron. लोखंडाचे चणे खाववणें or चारणें To oppress grievously.लोखंडकाम [lōkhaṇḍakāma] *n* Iron work; that portion (of a building, machine &c.) which consists of iron. 2 The business of an ironsmith.लोखंडी [lōkhaṇḍī] *a* (लोखंड) Composed of iron; relating to iron. (Marathi)

kanka 'rim of jar' Rebus: *karṇīka* 'account (scribe)' *karṇī* 'supercargo'

M-1355 a

m1355a Thus, cast bronze. PLUS खांडा [*khāṇḍā*] *m* A jag, notch, or indentation (as upon the edge of a tool or weapon). Rebus: *kāṇḍa* 'tools, pots and pans and metal-ware' Thus, cast bronze metalware.

kana, kanac = corner (Santali); Rebus: *kañcu* = bronze (Telugu) PLUS खांडा [*khāṇḍā*] *m* A jag, notch, or indentation (as upon the edge of a tool or weapon). Rebus: *kāṇḍa* 'tools, pots and pans and metal-ware' Thus, bronze metalware.

muka 'ladle' (Tamil)(DEDR 4887) Rebus: *mũh* 'ingot' (Santali) *baṭa* = rimless pot (Kannada) Rebus:) *baṭa* = a kind of iron (G.)) *bhaṭa* furnace (Gujarati) Thus, iron ingot.

kolom 'three' Rebus: kolami 'smithy, forge'

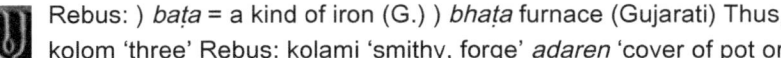

dhāḷ 'a slope'; 'inclination of a plane' (G.); *ḍhāḷiyum* = adj. sloping, inclining (G.) Rebus: *ḍhālako* = a large metal ingot (G.) *ḍhālakī* = a metal heated and poured into a mould; a solid piece of metal; an ingot (Gujarati) dula 'pair' Rebus: dul 'cast metal'. sal splinter' Rebus: sal 'workshop Thu cast metal ingot workshop. (Last sign illegible)

m1323A

dula 'pair' Rebus: *dul* 'cast (metal)' PLUS*kana, kanac* = corner (Santali); Rebus: *kañcu* = bronze (Telugu) PLUS infixed kolmo 'paddy plant' Rebus: kolami 'smithy, forge'. Thus, cast bronze smithy, forge. Or, *mogge* 'sprout, bud' Rebus: *mũh* 'ingot' (Santali)Thus, cast bronze ingot. Read as: *kañcu dul mũh 'bronze cast ingot'*

muka 'ladle' (Tamil)(DEDR 4887) Rebus: *mũh* 'ingot' (Santali) *baṭa* = rimless pot (Kannada) Rebus:) *baṭa* = a kind of iron (G.)) *bhaṭa* furnace (Gujarati) Thus, iron ingot.

kolom 'three' Rebus: kolami 'smithy, forge' ranku 'liquid measure' Rebus: ranku 'tin'.

kolmo 'paddy plant' Rebus: *kolami* 'smithy, forge' Vikalpa: *mogge* 'sprout, bud' Rebus: *mũh* 'ingot' (Santali) dolu 'plant of shoot height' Rebus: dul 'cast metal'
kamaḍha = crab; *kampaṭṭam* = mint (Ta.) ; *kammaṭa* 'coiner, mint' (Telugu)

kanka 'rim of jar' Rebus: *karṇīka* 'account (scribe)' *karṇī* 'supercargo'

m959a *खोंड [khōṇḍa] m A young bull, a bullcalf. (Marathi) Rebus: kõdār 'turner' (Bengali); कोंद kōnda 'engraver, lapidary setting or infixing gems' (Marathi) G. sãghāṛɔ m. 'lathe' ; संघाट joinery; M. sãgaḍ 'double-canoe' Rebus: sangataras. संगतराश lit. 'to collect stones, stone-cutter, mason.'*

dula 'pair' Rebus: *dul* 'cast (metal)' PLUS*kana, kanac* = corner (Santali); Rebus: *kañcu* = bronze (Telugu) PLUS infixed kolmo 'paddy plant' Rebus: kolami 'smithy, forge'. Thus, cast bronze smithy, forge. Or, *mogge* 'sprout, bud' Rebus: *mũh* 'ingot' (Santali)Thus, cast bronze ingot. Read as: *kañcu dul mũh 'bronze cast ingot' aya aḍaren (homonym: aduru)*'alloy native metal' PLUS *aya kāṇḍa* 'alloy metalware'

muka 'ladle' (Tamil)(DEDR 4887) Rebus: *mũh* 'ingot' (Santali) *baṭa* = rimless pot (Kannada) Rebus:) *baṭa* = a kind of iron (G.)) *bhaṭa* furnace (Gujarati) Thus, iron ingot.

kolom 'three' Rebus: kolami 'smithy, forge'
kāṇḍa 'arrow' (Sanskrit) Rebus:*khāṇḍa* 'tools, pots and pans, metal-ware'. Rebus 2: kaṇḍ 'fire-altar' (Santali)

m1200c
|||| Numeral 4: gaṇḍa 'four' Rebus: kaṇḍa 'furnace, fire-altar' (Santali)

||| Numeral three: kolom 'three' Rebus: kolami 'smithy, forge'
kolmo 'paddy plant' Rebus: *kolami* 'smithy, forge' Vikalpa: *mogge* 'sprout, bud' Rebus: *mũh* 'ingot' (Santali) dolu 'plant of shoot height' Rebus: dul 'cast metal'

m673a *खोंड [khōṇḍa] m A young bull, a bullcalf. (Marathi) Rebus: kõdār 'turner' (Bengali); कोंद kōnda 'engraver, lapidary setting or infixing gems' (Marathi) G.*

sãghāṛɔ m. 'lathe' ; संघाट joinery; M. sãgaḍ 'double-canoe' Rebus: sangataras. संगतराश lit. 'to collect stones, stone-cutter, mason.'

Text of inscription: reead rebus as at m1200c.

B-10 a

Banawali 10a *miṇḍāl* 'markhor' (Tōrwālī) *meḍho* a ram, a sheep (G.)(CDIAL 10120) Rebus: *mẽṛhẽt, meḍ* 'iron' (Mu.Ho.) Text of inscription: reead rebus as at m1200c.

Banawali 12a *miṇḍāl* 'markhor' (Tōrwālī) *meḍho* a ram, a sheep (G.)(CDIAL 10120) Rebus: *mẽṛhẽt, meḍ* 'iron' (Mu.Ho.) Text of inscription: reead rebus as at m1200c.

m784a *खोंड [khōṇḍa] m A young bull, a bullcalf. (Marathi) Rebus: kõdār 'turner' (Bengali); कोंद kōnda 'engraver, lapidary setting or infixing gems' (Marathi) G. sãghāṛɔ m. 'lathe' ; संघाट joinery; M. sãgaḍ 'double-canoe' Rebus: sangataras. संगतराश lit. 'to collect stones, stone-cutter, mason.'*

baṭa = rimless pot (Kannada) Rebus:) *baṭa* = a kind of iron (G.)) *bhaṭa* furnace (Gujarati) PLUS infixed:

kolmo 'paddy plant' Rebus: *kolami* 'smithy, forge' Vikalpa: *mogge* 'sprout, bud' Rebus: *mũh* 'ingot' (Santali) dolu 'plant of shoot height' Rebus: dul 'cast metal' Thus, iron castings, furnace.

kolmo 'paddy plant' Rebus: *kolami* 'smithy, forge' Vikalpa: *mogge* 'sprout, bud' Rebus: *mũh* 'ingot' (Santali) dolu 'plant of shoot height' Rebus: dul 'cast metal' Thus, metal castings.

koḍi 'flag' (Ta.)(DEDR 2049). Rebus 1: *koḍ* 'workshop' (Kuwi) Rebus 2: *khõḍ* m. 'pit', *khõḍü* f. 'small pit' (Kashmiri. CDIAL 3947)

m760a *खोंड [khōṇḍa] m A young bull, a bullcalf. (Marathi) Rebus: kõdār 'turner' (Bengali); कोंद kōnda 'engraver, lapidary setting or infixing gems' (Marathi) G. sãghāṛɔ m. 'lathe' ; संघाट joinery; M. sãgaḍ 'double-canoe' Rebus: sangataras. संगतराश lit. 'to collect stones, stone-cutter, mason.'* *baṭa* = rimless pot (Kannada) Rebus:) *baṭa* = a kind of iron (G.)) *bhaṭa* furnace (Gujarati) PLUS infixed:

kolmo 'paddy plant' Rebus: *kolami* 'smithy, forge' Vikalpa: *mogge* 'sprout, bud' Rebus: *mũh* 'ingot' (Santali) dolu 'plant of shoot height' Rebus: dul 'cast metal' Thus, iron castings, furnace.

kanka 'rim of jar' Rebus: *karṇīka* 'account (scribe)' *karṇī* 'supercargo'

dula 'pair' Rebus: *dul* 'cast (metal)' PLUS*kana, kanac* = corner (Santali); Rebus: *kañcu* = bronze (Telugu) PLUS infixed kolmo 'paddy plant' Rebus: kolami 'smithy, forge'.

Thus, cast bronze smithy, forge. Or, *mogge* 'sprout, bud'
aḍar 'harrow'; rebus: *aduru* 'native unsmelted metal'

ayo ‘fish’ Rebus: *aya* ‘iron’ *ayas* ‘metal’

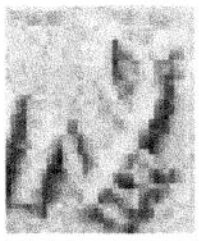

Spine, backbone’ hieroglyph:
m339A

M-330 A

baraḍo = spine; backbone (Tulu) Rebus: *baran, bharat* ‘mixed alloys’ (5 copper, 4 zinc and 1 tin) (Punjabi) water-carrier hieroglyph *kuṭi*; Rebus: *kuṭhi* ‘smelter furnace’. PLUS ‘rim of jar’:

kanka ‘rim of jar’ Rebus: karṇīka ‘account (scribe)’ karṇī ‘supercargo’

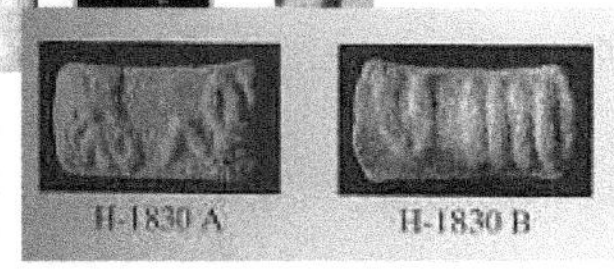

h1830 Side A: Read rebus as at m339A. Side B: |||| Numeral 4: *gaṇḍa* 'four' Rebus: *kaṇḍa* 'furnace, fire-altar' (Santali) PLUS *baṭa* = rimless pot (Kannada) Rebus:) *baṭa* = a kind of iron (G.)) *bhaṭa* furnace (Gujarati) Thus, iron furnace, fire-altar.

h1791
Side A:

khareḍo =  a currycomb (Gujarati) खरारा [*kharārā*] *m* (H) A currycomb. 2 Currying a horse. (Marathi) Rebus: करडा [*karaḍā*] Hard from alloy--iron, silver &c. (Marathi) *kharādī* ‘ turner’ (Gujarati)

kanka ‘rim of jar’ Rebus: *karṇīka* ‘account (scribe)’ *karṇī* ‘supercargo’ *bhaṭa* ‘warrior’ (Sanskrit) Rebus: *baṭa* a kind *aya kammaṭa.*’coiner, mint alloy’of iron (Gujarati). Rebus: *bhaṭa* ‘furnace’ (Santali) Side B:

baraḍo = spine; backbone (Tulu) Rebus: *baran, bharat* ‘mixed alloys’ (5 copper, 4 zinc and 1 tin) (Punjabi)

h742A
baraḍo = spine; backbone (Tulu) Rebus: *baran, bharat* ‘mixed alloys’ (5 copper, 4 zinc and 1 tin) (Punjabi) Duplicated: dula ‘pair’ Rebus: dul ‘cast metal’ Note: The four affixes of ‘bones of the spine’ on the second variant of the epigraph text, indicate a furnace: |||| Numeral 4: gaṇḍa 'four' Rebus: kaṇḍa 'furnace, fire-altar' (Santali) Thus the pair of hieroglyphs read: bharat PLUS bharat *kāṇḍa* ‘bharat alloy furnace & tools, pots and pans and metal-ware’.

bhaṭa ‘warrior’ (Sanskrit) Rebus: *baṭa* a kind of iron (Gujarati). Rebus: *bhaṭa* ‘furnace’ (Santali)

khareḍo = a currycomb (Gujarati) खरारा [*kharārā*] *m* (H) A currycomb. 2 Currying a horse. (Marathi) Rebus: करडा [*karaḍā*] Hard from alloy--iron, silver &c. (Marathi) *kharādī* ‘ turner’ (Gujarati) Cast Bharata alloy, iron furnace, supercargo, turned hard alloys.

kanka ‘rim of jar’ Rebus: *karṇīka* ‘account (scribe)’ *karṇī* ‘supercargo’

M-1829 a

m1829a खोंड [khōṇḍa] m A young bull, a bullcalf. (Marathi) Rebus: kõdār 'turner' (Bengali); कोंद kōnda 'engraver, lapidary setting or infixing gems' (Marathi) G. sãghāṛɔ m. 'lathe' ; संघाट joinery; M. sāgaḍ 'double-canoe' Rebus: sangataras. संगतराश lit. 'to collect stones, stone-cutter, mason.'

baraḍo = spine; backbone (Tulu) Rebus: *baran, bharat* 'mixed alloys' (5 copper, 4 zinc and 1 tin) (Punjabi) *kāṇḍa* 'arrow' (Sanskrit) Rebus:*khāṇḍa* 'tools, pots and pans, metal-ware'. Rebus 2: kaṇḍ 'fire-altar' (Santali)

H-503 A

h503A खोंड [khōṇḍa] m A young bull, a bullcalf. (Marathi) Rebus: kõdār 'turner' (Bengali); कोंद kōnda 'engraver, lapidary setting or infixing gems' (Marathi) G. sãghāṛɔ m. 'lathe' ; संघाट joinery; M. sāgaḍ 'double-canoe' Rebus: sangataras. संगतराश lit. 'to collect stones, stone-cutter, mason.' Rebus readings of text as at m829a.

M-1200 a

m1200a खोंड [khōṇḍa] m A young bull, a bullcalf. (Marathi) Rebus: kõdār 'turner' (Bengali); कोंद kōnda 'engraver, lapidary setting or infixing gems' (Marathi) G. sãghāṛɔ m. 'lathe' ; संघाट joinery; M. sāgaḍ 'double-canoe' Rebus: sangataras. संगतराश lit. 'to collect stones, stone-cutter, mason.'

baraḍo = spine; backbone (Tulu) Rebus: *baran, bharat* 'mixed alloys' (5 copper, 4 zinc and 1 tin) (Punjabi) *kāṇḍa* 'arrow' (Sanskrit) Rebus:*khāṇḍa* 'tools, pots and pans, metal-ware'. Rebus 2: kaṇḍ 'fire-altar' (Santali)

muka 'ladle' (Tamil)(DEDR 4887) Rebus: *mũh* 'ingot' (Santali) *baṭa* = rimless pot (Kannada) Rebus:) *baṭa* = a kind of iron (G.)) *bhaṭa* furnace (Gujarati) Thus, iron ingot.

Variant:

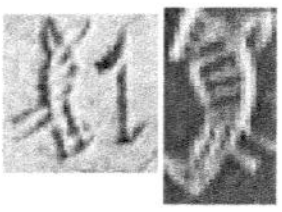

The pair of hieroglyph signs are compositions: bicha 'scorpion' (Assamese) Rebus: *bica* 'stone ore' (Santali) The pairing sign is a composition of: sloping stroke PLUS two short strokes of a 'splinter':*ḍhāḷ* 'a slope'; 'inclination of a plane' (Gujarati); *ḍhāḷiyum* = adj. sloping, inclining (Gujarati) Rebus: *ḍhālako* = a large metal ingot (Gujarati) *ḍhālakī* = a metal heated and poured into a mould; a solid piece of metal; an ingot (Gujarati)PLUS*sal* 'splinter' Rebus: *sal* 'workshop'. Thus the composition reads: *ḍhālako sal* 'ingot workshop'.

kanka 'rim of jar' Rebus: *karṇīka* 'account (scribe)' *karṇī* 'supercargo'

m276a Rhinoceros/boar: baḍhia = a castrated boar, a hog (Santali) baḍhi 'a caste who work both in iron and wood' (Santali) *baṟea* 'merchant' PLUS pattar 'trough' Rebus: pattar 'guild' Thus iron-wood artisan-merchant guild.

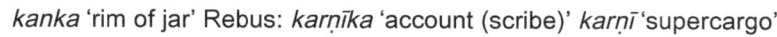

baraḍo = spine; backbone (Tulu) Rebus: *baran, bharat* 'mixed alloys' (5 copper, 4 zinc and 1 tin) (Punjabi) *kāṇḍa* 'arrow' (Sanskrit) Rebus:*khāṇḍa* 'tools, pots and pans, metal-ware'. Rebus 2: kaṇḍ 'fire-altar' (Santali)

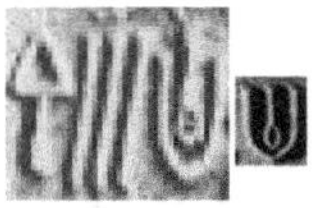

Three sign sequence:
muka 'ladle' (Tamil)(DEDR 4887) Rebus: *mũh* 'ingot' (Santali) *baṭa* = rimless pot (Kannada) Rebus:) *baṭa* = a kind of iron (G.)) *bhaṭa* furnace (Gujarati) Thus, iron ingot.
kolom 'three' Rebus: kolami 'smithy, forge' *kāṇḍa* 'arrow' (Sanskrit) Rebus:*khāṇḍa* 'tools, pots and pans, metal-ware'. Rebus 2: kaṇḍ 'fire-altar' (Santali) Thus, the three sign sequence reads: iron ingot, furnace smithy, fire-altar metalware.

m848a *खोंड [khōṇḍa] m A young bull, a bullcalf. (Marathi) Rebus: kõdār 'turner' (Bengali); कोंद kōnda 'engraver, lapidary setting or infixing gems' (Marathi) G. sãghāṛɔ m. 'lathe' ; संघाट joinery; M. sãgaḍ 'double-canoe' Rebus: sangataras. संगतराश lit. 'to collect stones, stone-cutter, mason.'*

baraḍo = spine; backbone (Tulu) Rebus: *baran, bharat* 'mixed alloys' (5 copper, 4 zinc and 1 tin) (Punjabi) *kāṇḍa* 'arrow' (Sanskrit) Rebus:*khāṇḍa* 'tools, pots and pans, metal-ware'. Rebus 2: kaṇḍ 'fire-altar' (Santali)

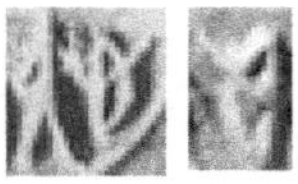

'Bow and arrow' sign hieroglyph 'Archer + bow + arrow' ligatured hieroglyph upraised arm: eraka 'upraised arm' Rebus: erako 'moltencast copper' *kamaḍha* 'archer, bow' Rebus: *kammaṭa* 'mint, coiner'.

kolmo 'paddy plant' Rebus: *kolami* 'smithy, forge' Vikalpa: *mogge* 'sprout, bud' Rebus: *mũh* 'ingot' (Santali) dolu 'plant of shoot height' Rebus: dul 'cast metal'

h1827 Side A:

baraḍo = spine; backbone (Tulu) Rebus: *baran, bharat* ' mixed alloys' (5 copper, 4 zinc and 1 tin) (Punjabi) *kāṇḍa* 'arrow' (Sanskrit) Rebus:*khāṇḍa* 'tools, pots and pans, metal-ware'. Rebus 2: kaṇḍ 'fire-altar' (Santali)

kanka 'rim of jar' Rebus: *karṇīka* 'account (scribe)' *karṇī* 'supercargo'

khareḍo = a currycomb (Gujarati) खरारा [*kharārā*] *m* (H) A currycomb. 2 Currying a horse. (Marathi) Rebus: करडा [*karaḍā*] Hard from alloy--iron, silver &c. (Marathi) *kharādī* ' turner' (Gujarati)
Side B: *baṭa* = rimless pot (Kannada) Rebus:) *baṭa* = a kind of iron (G.)) *bhaṭa* furnace (Gujarati) PLUS dula 'two' Rebus: dul 'cast metal' Thus furnace iron hard alloy castings.

dāṭu 'cross'(Telugu) Rebus: *dhatu* 'mineral' (Santali).

koḍi 'flag' (Ta.)(DEDR 2049). Rebus 1: *koḍ* 'workshop' (Kuwi) Rebus 2: *khõḍ* m. 'pit', *khõḍü* f. 'small pit' (Kashmiri. CDIAL 3947).

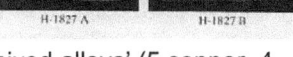

kanac 'corner' Rebus: *kañcu* 'bronze'

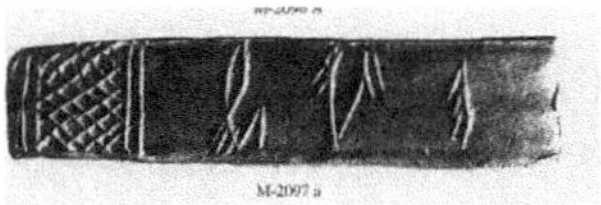

m2097A Read rebus as at Side A h1827

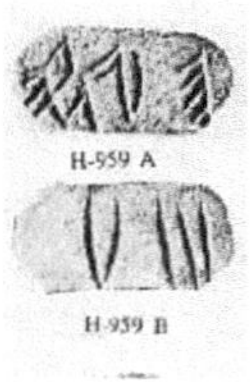

h959A Side A read rebus as at Side A h1827 PLUS Side B: *baṭa* = rimless pot (Kannada) Rebus:) *baṭa* = a kind of iron (G.)) *bhaṭa* furnace (Gujarati) PLUS ||| Numeral three: kolom 'three' Rebus: kolami 'smithy, forge' Thus iron furnace, smithy.

The following 10 identical inscriptions with 3 hieroglyph signs read rebus as at Side A h1827

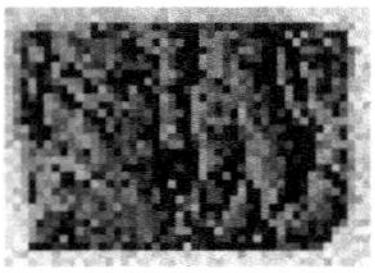

h934A

h354A

h352A

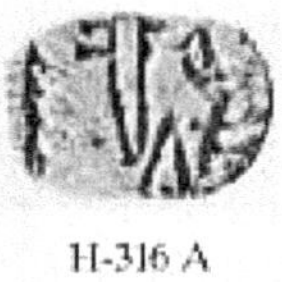

h316A

h314A

h313A

h312A

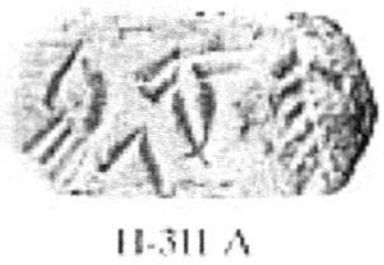

h311A

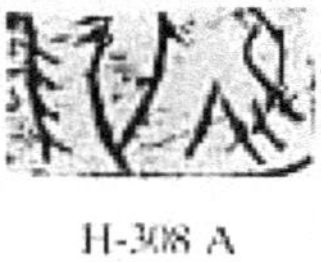

h308A

h233A Tablet shaped like a sickle.

m1732a *खोंड [khōṇḍa] m A young bull, a bullcalf. (Marathi) Rebus: kõdār 'turner' (Bengali); कोंद kōnda 'engraver, lapidary setting or infixing gems' (Marathi) G. sãghāṛɔ m. 'lathe' ; संघाट joinery; M. sãgaḍ 'double-canoe' Rebus: sangataras. संगतराश lit. 'to collect stones, stone-cutter, mason.'*

baraḍo = spine; backbone (Tulu) Rebus: *baran, bharat* 'mixed alloys' (5 copper, 4 zinc and 1 tin) (Punjabi)

kanka 'rim of jar' Rebus: *karṇīka* 'account (scribe)' *karṇī* 'supercargo'

kana, kanac = corner (Santali); Rebus: *kañcu* = bronze (Telugu) PLUS खांडा [*khāṇḍā*] *m* A jag, notch, or indentation (as upon the edge of a tool or weapon). Rebus: *kāṇḍa* 'tools, pots and pans and metal-ware' Thus, bronze metalware.

aya kāṇḍa 'alloy metalware'

m1743A *खोंड [khōṇḍa] m A young bull, a bullcalf. (Marathi) Rebus: kõdār 'turner' (Bengali); कोंद kōnda 'engraver, lapidary setting or infixing gems' (Marathi) G. sãghāṛɔ m. 'lathe' ; संघाट joinery; M. sãgaḍ 'double-canoe' Rebus: sangataras.*

संगतराश lit. 'to collect stones, stone-cutter, mason.'

kolmo 'paddy plant' Rebus: *kolami* 'smithy, forge' Vikalpa: *mogge* 'sprout, bud' Rebus: *mũh* 'ingot' (Santali) dolu 'plant of shoot height' Rebus: dul 'cast metal'

dula 'pair' Rebus: *dul* 'cast (metal)' PLUS*kana, kanac* = corner (Santali); Rebus: *kañcu* = bronze (Telugu) Thus, cast bronze.

kanka 'rim of jar' Rebus: *karṇīka* 'account (scribe)' *karṇī* 'supercargo'

baraḍo = spine; backbone (Tulu) Rebus: *baran, bharat* 'mixed alloys' (5 copper, 4 zinc and 1 tin) (Punjabi)

m189a खोंड [khōṇḍa] m A young bull, a bullcalf. (Marathi) Rebus: kõdār 'turner' (Bengali); कोंद kōnda 'engraver, lapidary setting or infixing gems' (Marathi) G. sãghāṛɔ m. 'lathe' ; संघाट joinery; M. sãgaḍ 'double-canoe' Rebus: sangataras. संगतराश lit. 'to collect stones, stone-cutter, mason.'

baraḍo = spine; backbone (Tulu) Rebus: *baran, bharat* 'mixed alloys' (5 copper, 4 zinc and 1 tin) (Punjabi)

kanka 'rim of jar' Rebus: *karṇīka* 'account (scribe)' *karṇī* 'supercargo'

dhāḷ 'a slope'; 'inclination of a plane' (G.); *ḍhāḷiyum* = adj. sloping, inclining (G.) Rebus: *ḍhālako* = a large metal ingot (G.) *ḍhālakī* = a metal heated and poured into a mould; a solid piece of metal; an ingot (Gujarati) PLUS *dula* 'pair' Rebus: *dul* 'cast *metal' sal* 'splinter' Rebus: *sal* 'workshop'. Thus, *ḍhālako dul sal* 'ingot, cast metal workshop'.

m786a खोंड [khōṇḍa] m A young bull, a bullcalf. (Marathi) Rebus: kõdār 'turner' (Bengali); कोंद kōnda 'engraver, lapidary setting or infixing gems' (Marathi) G. sãghāṛɔ m. 'lathe' ; संघाट joinery; M. sãgaḍ 'double-canoe' Rebus: sangataras.

संगतराश lit. 'to collect stones, stone-cutter, mason.'

baraḍo = spine; backbone (Tulu) Rebus: *baran, bharat* 'mixed alloys' (5 copper, 4 zinc and 1 tin) (Punjabi)

kanka 'rim of jar' Rebus: *karṇīka* 'account (scribe)' *karṇī* 'supercargo'

ayo ḍhālako 'alloy metal ingot'

kamaḍha 'crab' Rebus: *kammaṭa* 'mint, coiner'.

ḍato = claws of crab (Santali) Rebus: *dhātu* 'mineral ore'

kanka 'rim of jar' Rebus: *karṇīka* 'account (scribe)' *karṇī* 'supercargo'

m127a खोंड [khōṇḍa] m A young bull, a bullcalf. (Marathi) Rebus: kõdār 'turner' (Bengali); कोंद kōnda 'engraver, lapidary setting or infixing gems' (Marathi) G. sãghāṛɔ m. 'lathe' ; संघाट joinery; M. sãgaḍ 'double-canoe' Rebus: sangataras.

संगतराश lit. 'to collect stones, stone-cutter, mason.'

baraḍo = spine; backbone (Tulu) Rebus: *baran, bharat* 'mixed alloys' (5 copper, 4 zinc and 1 tin) (Punjabi)

kanka 'rim of jar' Rebus: *karṇīka* 'account (scribe)' *karṇī* 'supercargo'
aya aḍaren (homonym: aduru)'alloy native metal'

kanka 'rim of jar' Rebus: *karṇīka* 'account (scribe)' *karṇī* 'supercargo'
kamaḍha 'crab' Rebus: *kammaṭa* 'mint, coiner'.

ḍato = claws of crab (Santali) Rebus: *dhātu* 'mineral ore'. The ligatures: sal 'splinter' Rebus: sal 'workshop' Thus mineral ore, mint workshop.

m1819A *खोंड [khōṇḍa] m A young bull, a bullcalf. (Marathi) Rebus: kōdār 'turner' (Bengali); कोंद kōnda 'engraver, lapidary setting or infixing gems' (Marathi) G. sãghāṛɔ m. 'lathe' ; संघाट joinery; M. sãgaḍ 'double-canoe' Rebus: sangataras.*

संगतराश lit. 'to collect stones, stone-cutter, mason.'
baraḍo = spine; backbone (Tulu) Rebus: *baran, bharat* 'mixed alloys' (5 copper, 4 zinc and 1 tin) (Punjabi)

kanka 'rim of jar' Rebus: *karṇīka* 'account (scribe)' *karṇī* 'supercargo'

m301A Zebu horns on compolsite animal. Native metal smith guild. Text of inscription read rebus as at m1819A

m1195a  Read rebus as at m1819A

h892 Side B:
baraḍo = spine; backbone (Tulu) Rebus: *baran, bharat* ' mixed alloys' (5 copper, 4 zinc and 1 tin) (Punjabi)

Ligature: two peaks: mēḍu height, rising ground, hillock (Kannada) Rebus: *meḍ* 'iron' (Ho.) dula 'pair' Rebus: dul 'cast metal' PLUS |||| Numeral 4: gaṇḍa 'four' Rebus: kaṇḍa 'furnace, fire-altar' (Santali)

kanka 'rim of jar' Rebus: *karṇīka* 'account (scribe)' *karṇī* 'supercargo'

khareḍo = a currycomb (Gujarati) खरारा [*khararā*] *m* (H) A currycomb. 2 Currying a horse. (Marathi) Rebus: करडा [*karaḍā*] Hard from alloy--iron, silver &c. (Marathi) *kharādī* ' turner' (Gujarati)

Side A: |||| Numeral 4: gaṇḍa 'four' Rebus: kaṇḍa 'furnace, fire-altar' (Santali) *baṭa* = rimless pot (Kannada) Rebus:) *baṭa* = a kind of iron (G.)) *bhaṭa* furnace (Gujarati) Thus, iron furnace, fire-altar.

m832a
खोंड [khōṇḍa] m A young bull, a bullcalf. (Marathi) Rebus: kōdār 'turner' (Bengali); कोंद kōnda 'engraver, lapidary setting or infixing gems' (Marathi) G. sãghāṛɔ m. 'lathe' ; संघाट joinery; M. sãgaḍ 'double-canoe' Rebus: sangataras. संगतराश lit. 'to collect stones, stone-cutter, mason.'

Text of inscription subset read rebus as at h892 Side B

h218A Read rebus as subset at h892 Side B

h740A

meḍ 'body' Rebus: *meḍ* 'iron' (Ho.) काठी [kāṭhī] *f* (काष्ट S) 'frame or structure of the body' (Marathi) Rebus: खंडी [khaṇḍī] measure of weight (Marathi) *கண்டி; kaṇṭi, n. < Mhr. khaṇḍil. [T. Tu. khaṇḍi, M. kaṇḍi.]* Candy, a weight, stated to be roughly equivalent to 500 lbs.

baraḍo = spine; backbone (Tulu) Rebus: *baran, bharat* 'mixed alloys' (5 copper, 4 zinc and 1 tin) (Punjabi)

bhaṭa 'warrior' (Sanskrit) Rebus: *baṭa* a kind of iron (Gujarati). Rebus: *bhaṭa* 'furnace' (Santali)

kanka 'rim of jar' Rebus: *karṇīka* 'account (scribe)' *karṇī* 'supercargo'

khareḍo = a currycomb (Gujarati) खरारा [*kharārā*] *m* (H) A currycomb. 2 Currying a horse. (Marathi) Rebus: करडा [*karaḍā*] Hard from alloy--iron, silver &c. (Marathi) *kharādī* ' turner' (Gujarati)

h1080a

baraḍo = spine; backbone (Tulu) Rebus: *baran, bharat* 'mixed alloys' (5 copper, 4 zinc and 1 tin) (Punjabi)

bhaṭa 'warrior' (Sanskrit) Rebus: *baṭa* a kind of iron (Gujarati). Rebus: *bhaṭa* 'furnace' (Santali)

kanka 'rim of jar' Rebus: *karṇīka* 'account (scribe)' *karṇī* 'supercargo'

Ligatured hieroglyph: 'double pincer back-to-back'
'Duplicated pincers back-to-back or linked' sign hieroglyph

h37a *खोंड [khōṇḍa] m A young bull, a bullcalf. (Marathi) Rebus: kõdār 'turner' (Bengali); कोंद kōnda 'engraver, lapidary setting or infixing gems' (Marathi) G. sãghāṛɔ m. 'lathe' ; संघाट joinery; M. sāgaḍ 'double-canoe' Rebus: sangataras. संगतराश lit. 'to collect stones, stone-cutter, mason.'*

kamaḍha 'crab' Rebus: *kammaṭa* 'mint, coiner'.
ḍato = claws of crab (Santali) Rebus: *dhātu* 'mineral ore' Duplicated: dula 'pair' Rebus: dul 'cast metal' Thus, minerals castings and mint.

kanka 'rim of jar' Rebus: *karṇīka* 'account (scribe)' *karṇī* 'supercargo'

 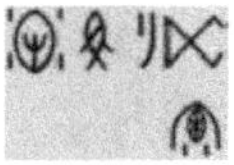 Mohenjo-daro m0256 Text 1332 *khũṭ* ‘zebu’ Rebus: ‘(native metal) guild’

 The composite, ligature hieroglyph: ‘arched wheel-spokes-nave’ Rebus reading: *eraka āra* ‘copper, bronze' *maṇḍa* ‘market’ (See related glosses in m1005 decipherment)

Line 2: *dhatu sal* mineral ore workshop, *ayas ḍhālako* = a large alloyed metal ingot + *kolami kaṇḍ* smithy fire-altar PLUS *dul kuṭila* ‘cast bronze’.
kamaḍha ‘crab’ Rebus: *kammaṭa* ‘mint, coiner’.
ḍato 'claws or pincers of crab' (Santali) Rebus: *dhatu* ‘mineral ore’ (Santali)

 Variant: Read in context, the composite hieroglyph is assumed to be a combination of a slanted stroke ligatured to a notch,which provide possible rebus readings of a smithy/forge: notch+slanted stroke reads rebus: *ḍhālako kāṇḍa* ‘ingot, tools, pots and pans and metal-ware’

dhāḷ ‘a slope’; ‘inclination of a plane’ (Gujarati); *ḍhāḷiyum* = adj. sloping, inclining (Gujarati) Rebus: *ḍhālako* = a large metal ingot (Gujarati) *ḍhālakī* = a metal heated and poured into a mould; a solid piece of metal; an ingot (Gujarati) PLUS खांडा [*khāṇḍā*] *m* A jag, notch, or indentation (as upon the edge of a tool or weapon). Rebus: *kāṇḍa* ‘tools, pots and pans and metal-ware’

ayo ‘fish’ Rebus: aya ‘iron’ (Gujarati) ayas ‘metal’ (Vedic) PLUS infixed ligature of slanted stroke: *dhāḷ* ‘a slope’; ‘inclination of a plane’ (Gujarati); *ḍhāḷiyum* = adj. sloping, inclining (Gujarati) Rebus: *ḍhālako* = a large metal ingot (Gujarati) *ḍhālakī* = a metal heated and poured into a mould; a solid piece of metal; an ingot (Gujarati)

 Composite hieroglyph with ligatures.

gaṇḍa ‘four’ Rebus: *kaṇḍ* ‘fire-altar’
kolmo ‘paddy plant’ Rebus: kolami ‘smithy/forge’

dula ‘pair’ Rebus: dul ‘cast metal’. The circumscribing ligature may be seen as made up of two curved lines back-to-back: ()kuṭila ‘bent’ CDIAL 3230 kuṭi— in cmpd. ‘curve’, *kuṭika*— ‘bent’ MBh. Rebus: kuṭila, katthīl = bronze (8 parts copper and 2 parts tin) [cf. āra-kūṭa, ‘brass’ (Sanskrit)

 Or, *dula* ‘pair’ Rebus: *dul* ‘cast (metal)’ PLUS *kana, kanac* = corner (Santali); Rebus: *kañcu* = bronze (Telugu) PLUS infixed kolmo ‘paddy plant’ Rebus: kolami ‘smithy, forge’. Thus, cast bronze smithy, forge. Or, *mogge* ‘sprout, bud’ Rebus: *mũh* ‘ingot’ (Santali)Thus, cast bronze ingot. Read as: *kañcu dul mũh ‘bronze cast ingot’*

Thus, the composite hieroglyph is read rebus as: smithy/forge (with) fire-altar: kolami kaṇḍ PLUS dul kuṭila ‘cast bronze’.

m365a *kamaḍha* = crab; *kampaṭṭam* = mint (Ta.) ; *kammaṭa* 'coiner, mint' (Telugu) Vikalpa: *ḍato* = claws of crab (Santali); *dhātu* = mineral (Sanskrit)

 *dhāḷ* 'a slope'; 'inclination of a plane' (G.); *ḍhāḷiyum* = adj. sloping, inclining (G.) Rebus: *ḍhālako* = a large metal ingot (G.) *ḍhālakī* = a metal heated and poured into a mould; a solid piece of metal; an ingot (Gujarati) PLUS खांडा [*khāṇḍā*] *m* A jag, notch, or indentation (as upon the edge of a tool or weapon). Rebus: *kāṇḍa* 'tools, pots and pans and metal-ware' Thus, the pair of sign hieroglyphs from r. read rebus: copper, bronze ingots, metalware castings (of mint, minerals).

 *aḍar* 'harrow'; rebus: *aduru* 'native unsmelted metal'
aya kāṇḍa 'alloy metalware '*muka* 'ladle' (Tamil)(DEDR 4887) Rebus: *mũh* 'ingot' (Santali) *baṭa* = rimless pot (Kannada) Rebus:) *baṭa* = a kind of iron (G.)) *bhaṭa* furnace (Gujarati) Thus, iron ingot.

kolom 'three' Rebus: kolami 'smithy, forge'
kamaḍha = crab; *kampaṭṭam* = mint (Ta.) ; *kammaṭa* 'coiner, mint' (Telugu) Vikalpa: *ḍato* = claws of crab (Santali); *dhātu* = mineral (Sanskrit) *dhāḷ* 'a slope'; 'inclination of a plane' (G.); *ḍhāḷiyum* = adj. sloping, inclining (G.) Rebus: *ḍhālako* = a large metal ingot (G.) *ḍhālakī* = a metal heated and poured into a mould; a solid piece of metal; an ingot (Gujarati) dula 'pair' Rebus: dul 'cast metal'. sal splinter' Rebus: sal 'workshop Thu cast metal ingot workshop.

m307a First two signs read rebus as at m365a PLUS dula 'two' Rebus: dul 'cast metal'

kuṭila 'bent'  CDIAL 3230 kuṭi— in cmpd. 'curve', *kuṭika*— 'bent' MBh. Rebus: *kuṭila, katthīl* = bronze (8 parts copper and 2 parts tin) Duplicated: dula 'pair' Rebus: dul 'cast metal' Thus, cast bronze.

 *kanka* 'rim of jar' Rebus: *karṇīka* 'account (scribe)' *karṇī* 'supercargo'

Pictorial motif hieroglyphs: kol 'tiger' Rebus: kolhe 'smelters' kol 'working in iron' Duplicated: dula 'pair' Rebus: dul 'cast metal' Thus, iron castings. PLUS kola 'woman' Rebus: kol 'working in iron' See m0308: *kaṇṇahāra* -- m. 'helmsman, sailor'. (काण*kāṇa* 'one-eyed', *āra* 'six', 'rings of hair' symbolic forms).
kannār 'coppersmiths'; *kan* 'copper'.

Kalibangan 6a Catalog of alloy turner, engraver, (lapidary) mint workshop. *खोंड [khōṇḍa] m A young bull, a bullcalf. (Marathi) Rebus: kōdār 'turner' (Bengali); कोंद kōnda 'engraver, lapidary setting or infixing gems' (Marathi) G. sãghāṛɔ m. 'lathe' ; संघाट joinery; M. sãgaḍ 'double-canoe' Rebus: sangataras. संगतराश lit. 'to collect stones, stone-cutter, mason.'* G. *sãghāṛɔ* m. 'lathe' ; *sãgāḍā* m. ' frame of a building ', °*ḍī* f. ' lathe '(CDIAL 12859) Rebus*: sangataras.*

संगतराश lit. 'to collect stones, stone-cutter, mason.'

koḍi 'flag' (Ta.)(DEDR 2049). Rebus 1: *koḍ* 'workshop' (Kuwi) Rebus 2: *khŏḍ* m. 'pit', *khŏḍū* f. 'small pit' (Kashmiri. CDIAL 3947).

kana, kanac 'corner' Rebus: *kañcu* 'bronze'

āra 'spokes' Rebus: *āra 'brass'.* cf. erka = ekke (Tbh. of arka) aka (Tbh. of arka) copper (metal); crystal (Kannada) Glyph: *eraka*'nave of wheel' Rebus: eraka 'copper'; cf. erka = ekke (Tbh. of arka) aka (Tbh. of arka) copper (metal); crystal (Kannada) *erako* 'moltencast copper'

kamaḍha = crab; *kampaṭṭam* = mint (Ta.) ; *kammaṭa* 'coiner, mint' (Telugu) Vikalpa: *ḍato* = claws of crab (Santali); *dhātu* = mineral (Sanskrit)

khuṭo ' leg, foot ', °ṭī ' goat's leg ' Rebus: *khōṭā* 'alloy' (Marathi)

kanka 'rim of jar' Rebus: *karṇīka* 'account (scribe)' *karṇī* 'supercargo'

kole.l 'temple' Rebus: kole.l 'smithy'

m64a

खोंड [khōṇḍa] m A young bull, a bullcalf. (Marathi) Rebus: kōdār 'turner' (Bengali); कोंद kōnda 'engraver, lapidary setting or infixing gems' (Marathi) G. sãghāṛɔ m. 'lathe' ; संघाट joinery; M. sāgaḍ 'double-canoe' Rebus: sangataras. संगतराश lit. 'to collect stones, stone-cutter, mason.'

kamaḍha 'crab' Rebus: *kammaṭa* 'mint, coiner'.
ḍato = claws of crab (Santali) Rebus: *dhātu* 'mineral ore' PLUS ligature: *aḍaren* 'cover of pot or lid' Rebus: *aduru* 'native, unsmelted metal' thus, native metal , mineral mint.

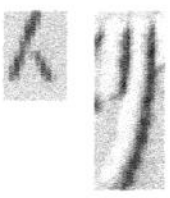
notch+slanted stroke reads rebus: *ḍhālako kāṇḍa* 'ingot, tools, pots and pans and metal-ware'.*ḍhāḷ* 'a slope'; 'inclination of a plane' (G.); *ḍhāḷiyum* = adj. sloping, inclining (G.) Rebus: *ḍhālako* = a large metal ingot (G.) *ḍhālakī* = a metal heated and poured into a mould; a solid piece of metal; an ingot (Gujarati) PLUS खांडा [*khāṇḍā*] *m* A jag, notch, or indentation (as upon the edge of a tool or weapon). Rebus: *kāṇḍa* 'tools, pots and pans and metal-ware'
kamaḍha 'crab' Rebus: *kammaṭa* 'mint, coiner'.
ḍato = claws of crab (Santali) Rebus: *dhātu* 'mineral ore' PLUS ligature: 'notch': खांडा [*khāṇḍā*] *m* A jag, notch, or indentation (as upon the edge of a tool or weapon). Rebus: *kāṇḍa* 'tools, pots and pans and metal-ware'

ḍhanga = a crook used for pulling down the branches of trees, for goats, sheep and camels (P.) Rebus:*ḍhangar* blacksmith' PLUS 'notch': खांडा [*khāṇḍā*] *m* A jag, notch, or indentation (as upon the edge of a tool or weapon). Rebus: *kāṇḍa* 'tools, pots and pans and metal-ware'. Thus, blacksmith metwalre.

h2040A *kamaḍha* 'crab' Rebus: *kammaṭa* 'mint, coiner'. *ḍato* = claws of crab (Santali) Rebus: *dhātu* 'mineral ore' PLUS

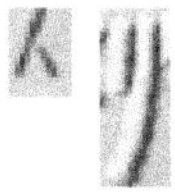

notch+slanted stroke reads rebus: *ḍhālako kāṇḍa* 'ingot, tools, pots and pans and metal-ware'.*dhāḷ* 'a slope'; 'inclination of a plane' (G.); *ḍhāḷiyuṁ* = adj. sloping, inclining (G.) Rebus: *ḍhālako* = a large metal ingot (G.) *ḍhālakī* = a metal heated and poured into a mould; a solid piece of metal; an ingot (Gujarati) PLUS खांडा [*khāṇḍā*] *m* A jag, notch, or indentation (as upon the edge of a tool or weapon). Rebus: *kāṇḍa* 'tools, pots and pans and metal-ware'

dula 'pair' Rebus: *dul* 'cast (metal)' PLUS*kana, kanac* = corner (Santali); Rebus: *kañcu* = bronze (Telugu) PLUS infixed kolmo 'paddy plant' Rebus: kolami 'smithy, forge'. Thus, cast bronze smithy, forge. Or, *mogge* 'sprout, bud' Rebus: *mũh* 'ingot' (Santali)Thus, cast bronze ingot. Read as: *kañcu dul mũh 'bronze cast ingot'*

kanka 'rim of jar' Rebus: *karṇīka* 'account (scribe)' *karṇī* 'supercargo'

m149A

खोंड [khōṇḍa] m A young bull, a bullcalf. (Marathi) Rebus: kōdār 'turner' (Bengali); कोंद kōnda 'engraver, lapidary setting or infixing gems' (Marathi) G. sãghāṛɔ m. 'lathe' ; संघाट joinery; M. sāgaḍ 'double-canoe' Rebus: sangataras. संगतराश lit. 'to collect stones, stone-cutter, mason.'

The first two signs of text of inscription is read rebus as at h2040A

ḍhanga = a crook used for pulling down the branches of trees, for goats, sheep and camels (P.) Rebus:*ḍhangar* blacksmith'.

dula 'pair' Rebus: dul 'cast metal' *mogge* 'sprout, bud' Rebus: *mũh* 'ingot' (Santali) Thus, cast metal ingot.

kanka 'rim of jar' Rebus: *karṇīka* 'account (scribe)' *karṇī* 'supercargo'

h421a

खोंड [khōṇḍa] m A young bull, a bullcalf. (Marathi) Rebus: kōdār 'turner' (Bengali); कोंद kōnda 'engraver, lapidary setting or infixing gems' (Marathi) G. sãghāṛɔ m. 'lathe' ; संघाट joinery; M. sāgaḍ 'double-canoe' Rebus: sangataras. संगतराश lit. 'to collect stones, stone-cutter, mason.'

The first two signs of text of inscription is read rebus as at h2040A

aya kammaṭa.'coiner, mint alloy'

kanka 'rim of jar' Rebus: *karṇīka* 'account (scribe)' *karṇī* 'supercargo'

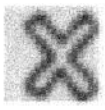 *dāṭu* 'cross'(Telugu) Rebus: *dhatu* 'mineral' (Santali).
PLUS *kaṇḍo* 'stool, seat' Rebus: *kāṇḍa* 'metalware' *kaṇḍa* 'fire-altar'

M-873 a

m873a
खोंड [khōṇḍa] m A young bull, a bullcalf. (Marathi) Rebus: kõdār 'turner' (Bengali); कोंद kōnda 'engraver, lapidary setting or infixing gems' (Marathi) G. sãghāṛɔ m. 'lathe' ; संघाट joinery; M. sãgaḍ 'double-canoe' Rebus: sangataras. संगतराश lit. 'to collect stones, stone-cutter, mason.'

The first two signs of text of inscription is read rebus as at h2040A
aya kāṇḍa 'alloy metalware'

Three sign sequence:

muka 'ladle' (Tamil)(DEDR 4887) Rebus: *mũh* 'ingot' (Santali) *baṭa* = rimless pot (Kannada) Rebus:) *baṭa* = a kind of iron (G.)) *bhaṭa* furnace (Gujarati) Thus, iron ingot.
kolom 'three' Rebus: kolami 'smithy, forge' *kāṇḍa* 'arrow' (Sanskrit) Rebus:*khāṇḍa* 'tools, pots and pans, metal-ware'. Rebus 2: kaṇḍ 'fire-altar' (Santali) Thus, the three sign sequence reads: iron ingot, furnace smithy, fire-altar metalware.

H-483 A

h483A
खोंड [khōṇḍa] m A young bull, a bullcalf. (Marathi) Rebus: kõdār 'turner' (Bengali); कोंद kōnda 'engraver, lapidary setting or infixing gems' (Marathi) G. sãghāṛɔ m. 'lathe' ; संघाट joinery; M. sãgaḍ 'double-canoe' Rebus: sangataras. संगतराश lit. 'to collect stones, stone-cutter, mason.'

The first two signs of text of inscription is read rebus as at h2040A
ayo ḍhālako 'alloy metal ingot'

 *dula* 'pair' Rebus: *dul* 'cast (metal)' PLUS*kana, kanac* = corner (Santali); Rebus: *kañcu* = bronze (Telugu) Thus, cast bronze.
dula 'two' Rebus: dul 'cast metal'

 *kanka* 'rim of jar' Rebus: *karṇīka* 'account (scribe)' *karṇī* 'supercargo'

M-501 A

m501A The first two signs of text of inscription is read rebus as at h2040A

dāṭu 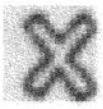 'cross'(Telugu) Rebus: *dhatu* 'mineral' (Santali).

 *kanka* 'rim of jar' Rebus: *karṇīka* 'account (scribe)' *karṇī* 'supercargo'

M-1444 A

M-1444 a

M-2040 a

M-2040 b

m1444A The first two signs of text of inscription is read rebus as at h2040A As at m501A
m2040a The first two signs of text of inscription is read rebus as at h2040A As at m501A PLUS Side B: ranku 'antelope' Rebus: ranku

'tin' PLUS

 *dāṭu* 'cross'(Telugu) Rebus: *dhatu* 'mineral' (Santali) PLUS

 *kuṭila* 'bent' CDIAL 3230 kuṭi— in cmpd. 'curve', *kuṭika—* 'bent' MBh. Rebus: *kuṭila, katthīl* = bronze (8 parts copper and 2 parts tin) Duplicated: dula 'pair' Rebus: dul 'cast metal' Thus, cast bronze.

m1764a

खोंड [khōṇḍa] m A young bull, a bullcalf. (Marathi) Rebus: kõdār 'turner' (Bengali); कोंद kōnda 'engraver, lapidary setting or infixing gems' (Marathi) G. sãghāṛɔ m. 'lathe' ; संघाट joinery; M. sãgaḍ 'double-canoe' Rebus: sangataras. संगतराश lit. 'to collect stones, stone-cutter, mason.'

The first two signs of text of inscription is read rebus as at h2040A

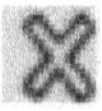 *dāṭu* 'cross'(Telugu) Rebus: *dhatu* 'mineral' (Santali).
PLUS *kaṇḍo* 'stool, seat' Rebus: *kāṇḍa* 'metalware' *kaṇḍa* 'fire-altar'

h1893 Side A: The first two signs of text of inscription is read rebus as at h2040A kolom 'three' Rebus; kolami 'smithy, forge' *kolmo* 'paddy plant' Rebus: *mũh* 'ingot' (Santali) dolu

 *kolami* 'smithy, forge' Vikalpa: *mogge* 'sprout, bud' Rebus: 'plant of shoot height' Rebus: dul 'cast metal'

 Side B: *āra* 'spokes' Rebus: *āra 'brass'.* cf. erka = ekke (Tbh. of arka) aka (Tbh. of arka) copper (metal); crystal (Kannada) Glyph: *eraka* 'nave of wheel' Rebus: eraka 'copper'; cf. erka = ekke (Tbh. of arka) aka (Tbh. of arka) copper (metal); crystal (Kannada) *erako* 'moltencast copper' Duplicated: dula 'pair' Rebus: dul 'cast metal' Thus cast copper, brass casting. PLUS 'notch': metalware.

 *meḍ* 'body' Rebus: *meḍ* 'iron' (Ho.) PLUS | *koḍa* 'one' Rebus: *koḍ* 'workshop' dula 'pair' Rebus: dul 'cast metal'. Thus, the 'body' flanked by two linear strokes denote: iron cast workshop.

water-  carrier hieroglyph *kuṭi*; Rebus: *kuṭhi* 'smelter furnace'.

 *kanac* 'corner' Rebus: *kañcu* 'bronze'

m396a The first two signs of text of inscription is read rebus as at h2040A

aya kāṇḍa 'alloy metalware'

kəṭhā'r, kc. *kuṭhār* m. ' granary, storeroom '(WPah.)(CDIAL 3550). *koṭhārī m.* ' storekeeper'

 (Gujarati)(CDIAL 3551) Thus, storeroom (of) *kolom* 'three' Rebus: *kolami* 'smithy, forge'. Dula 'pair' Rebus: dul 'cast metal' Thus, together *dul kolami kuṭhār* 'metal smithy castings storeroom'

iingot.

 *kuṭila* 'bent' CDIAL 3230 kuṭi— in cmpd. 'curve', *kuṭika—* 'bent' MBh. Rebus: *kuṭila, katthīl* = bronze (8 parts copper and 2 parts tin) Duplicated: dula 'pair' Rebus: dul 'cast

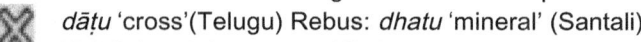

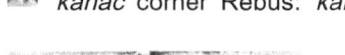

metal' Thus, cast bronze.

 *kana, kanac* = corner (Santali); Rebus: *kañcu* = bronze (Telugu) PLUS खांडा [*khāṇḍā*] *m* A jag, notch, or indentation (as upon the edge of a tool or weapon). Rebus: *kāṇḍa* 'tools, pots and pans and metal-ware' Thus, bronze metalware.

ayo ḍhālako 'alloy metal ingot'

kəṭhā´r, kc. *kuṭhār* m. ' granary, storeroom '(WPah.)(CDIAL 3550). *koṭhārī m.* ' storekeeper'

 (Gujarati)(CDIAL 3551) Thus, storeroom (of) *kolom* 'three' Rebus: *kolami* 'smithy, forge'. Dula 'pair' Rebus: dul 'cast metal' Thus, together *dul kolami kuṭhār* 'metal smithy castings storeroom'

 *cīmara* 'black ant' Rebus: *cīmara* 'copper'. *cīmara kāra* -- ' coppersmith '

m777A *खोंड [khōṇḍa] m A young bull, a bullcalf. (Marathi) Rebus: kõdār 'turner' (Bengali); कोंद kōnda 'engraver, lapidary setting or infixing gems' (Marathi) G. sãghāṛɔ m. 'lathe' ; संघाट joinery; M. sãgaḍ 'double-canoe' Rebus: sangataras. संगतराश lit. 'to collect stones, stone-cutter, mason.'*

The first two signs of text of inscription is read rebus as at h2040A

aya aḍaren (homonym: aduru)'alloy native metal'

kāṇḍa 'arrow' (Sanskrit) Rebus:*khāṇḍa* 'tools, pots and pans, metal-ware'. Rebus 2: kaṇḍ 'fire-altar' (Santali)

dulo 'hole' Rebus: dul 'cast metal' flanking: *ḍhanga* = a crook used for pulling down the branches of trees, for goats, sheep and camels (P.) Rebus:*ḍhangar* blacksmith'.Thus, specialist smith in metal castings.

m1723a *खोंड [khōṇḍa] m A young bull, a bullcalf. (Marathi) Rebus: kõdār 'turner' (Bengali); कोंद kōnda 'engraver, lapidary setting or infixing gems' (Marathi) G. sãghāṛɔ m. 'lathe' ; संघाट joinery; M. sãgaḍ 'double-canoe' Rebus: sangataras. संगतराश lit. 'to collect stones, stone-cutter, mason.'*

kamaḍha 'crab' Rebus: *kammaṭa* 'mint, coiner'.

 *muka* 'ladle' (Tamil) Rebus: *mũh* 'ingot' (Santali) *baṭa* = rimless pot (Kannada) Rebus:) *baṭa* = a kind of iron (G.)) *bhaṭa* furnace (Gujarati) Thus, iron ingot.

kolom 'three' Rebus: kolami 'smithy, forge'

 *dula* 'pair' Rebus: *dul* 'cast (metal)' PLUS*kana, kanac* = corner (Santali); Rebus: *kañcu* = bronze (Telugu) Thus, cast bronze.

dula 'two' Rebus: dul 'cast metal'

 *kanka* 'rim of jar' Rebus: *karṇīka* 'account (scribe)' *karṇī* 'supercargo'

m121A

खोंड [khōṇḍa] m A young bull, a bullcalf. (Marathi) Rebus: kõdār 'turner' (Bengali); कोंद kōnda 'engraver, lapidary setting or infixing gems' (Marathi) G. sãghāṛɔ m. 'lathe' ; संघाट joinery; M. sãgaḍ 'double-canoe' Rebus: sangataras. संगतराश lit. 'to collect stones, stone-cutter, mason.'

kamaḍha 'crab' Rebus: *kammaṭa* 'mint, coiner'.
ayo ḍhālako 'alloy metal ingot'
dulo 'hole' Rebus: dul 'cast metal'

 *kuṭila* 'bent' CDIAL 3230 kuṭi— in cmpd. 'curve', *kuṭika—* 'bent' MBh. Rebus: *kuṭila,*

 *katthīl* = bronze (8 parts copper and 2 parts tin)
kanka 'rim of jar' Rebus: *karṇīka* 'account (scribe)' *karṇī* 'supercargo'

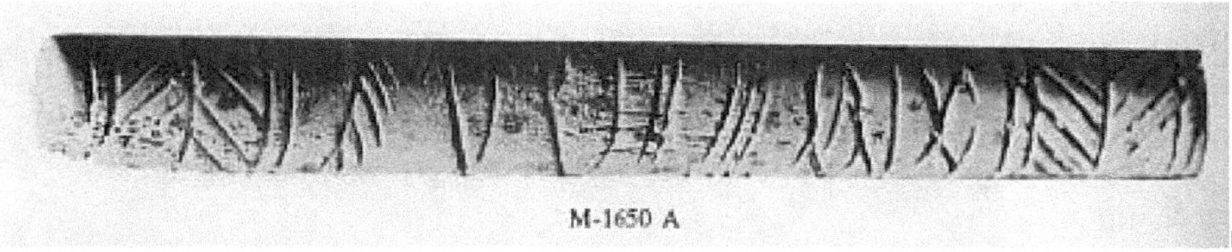
m1650A

kamaḍha 'crab' Rebus: *kammaṭa* 'mint, coiner'. *ayo* 'fish' Rebus: *aya* 'iron' *ayas* 'metal' kolom 'three' Rebus: kolami 'smithy, forge' *baṭa* = rimless pot (Kannada) Rebus:) *baṭa* = a kind of iron (G.)) *bhaṭa* furnace (Gujarati)

m568A Copper plate. *kamaḍha* 'crab' Rebus: *kammaṭa* 'mint, coiner'. *aya kammaṭa.*'coiner, mint alloy'

 *dula* 'pair' Rebus: *dul* 'cast (metal)' PLUS*kana, kanac* = corner (Santali); Rebus: *kañcu* = bronze (Telugu) Thus, cast bronze.

 *dhāḷ* 'a slope'; 'inclination of a plane' (G.); *ḍhāḷiyum* = adj. sloping, inclining (G.) Rebus: *ḍhālako* = a large metal ingot (G.) *ḍhālakī* = a metal heated and poured into a mould; a solid piece of metal; an ingot (Gujarati) PLUS खांडा [*khāṇḍā*] *m* A jag, notch, or indentation (as upon the edge of a tool or weapon). Rebus: *kāṇḍa* 'tools, pots and pans and metal-ware'

 *kolmo* 'paddy plant' Rebus: *kolami* 'smithy, forge' Vikalpa: *mogge* 'sprout, bud' Rebus: *mũh* 'ingot' (Santali) dolu 'plant of shoot height' Rebus: dul 'cast metal'

m1516A Copper plate. Side B: zebu horns. Tiger ligatured to zebu body. Hence, native metal smith guild. kola 'tiger' Rebus: kolhe 'smelter' kol 'working in iron. Side A: *kamaḍha* = crab; *kampaṭṭam* = mint (Ta.) ; *kammaṭa* 'coiner, mint' (Telugu) Vikalpa: *ḍato* = claws of crab (Santali); *dhātu* = mineral (Sanskrit) *aya kammaṭa.*'coiner, mint alloy'

 *kuṭila* 'bent' CDIAL 3230 kuṭi— in cmpd. 'curve', *kuṭika—* 'bent' MBh. Rebus: *kuṭila,* *katthīl* = bronze (8 parts copper and 2 parts tin)

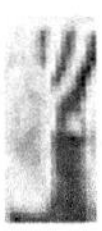 *kolmo* 'paddy plant' Rebus: *kolami* 'smithy, forge' Vikalpa: *mogge* 'sprout, bud' Rebus: *mũh* 'ingot' (Santali) dolu 'plant of shoot height' Rebus: dul 'cast metal'

m1186A
Text of inscription read rebus:

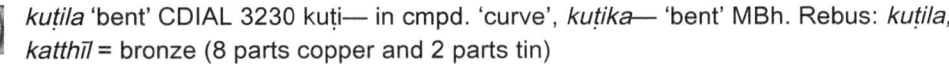

kamaḍha 'crab' Rebus: *kammaṭa* 'mint, coiner'.

ḍato = claws of crab (Santali) Rebus: *dhātu* 'mineral ore'
aya kāṇḍa 'alloy metalware'

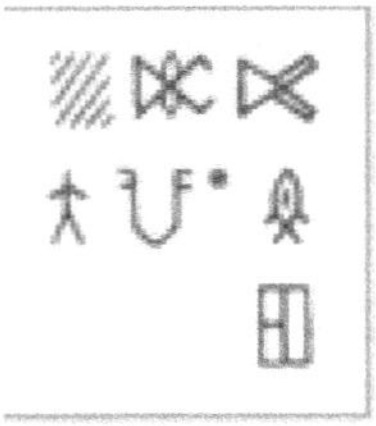

kanka 'rim of jar' Rebus: *karṇīka* 'account (scribe)' *karṇī* 'supercargo'
Pictorial motif hieroglyphs:
Kur. kaṇḍō a stool. Malt. Kanḍo stool, seat. (DEDR 1179) Rebus:

kāṇḍa 'metalware' *kaṇḍa* 'fire-altar'

meḍ 'body' Rebus: *meḍ* 'iron' (Ho.) काठी [kāṭhī] *f* (काष्ट S) 'frame or structure of the body' (Marathi) Rebus: खंडी [khaṇḍī] measure of weight (Marathi) கண்டி; *kaṇṭi, n. < Mhr. khaṇḍil. [T. Tu. khaṇḍi, M. kaṇḍi.]* Candy, a weight, stated to be roughly equivalent to 500 lbs.
kole.l 'temple. Rebus: kole.l 'smithy'

bagalo 'Pleiades' Rebus: *bagala* 'Arab boat' Headdress: *kūdī* 'bunch of twigs' (Sanskrit) Rebus: *kuṭhi* 'smelter furnace' (Santali)
||| Numeral three: kolom 'three' Rebus: kolami 'smithy, forge' PLUS |||| Numeral 4: gaṇḍa 'four' Rebus: kaṇḍa 'furnace, fire-altar' (Santali)

dhaṭu m. (also dhaṭhu) m. 'scarf' (WPah.) (CDIAL 6707) Allograph: ḍato = claws of crab (Santali) Rebus: dhātu = mineral (Sanskrit), dhatu id. (Santali) [Scarf as head dress of the horned person standing beween ficus leaves emanating from the sides of a jar.]
See the human face ligatured to a ram's body (an indication of the hieroglyphic nature of the orthographic composition):

loa 'ficus religiosa' Rebus: *lo* 'iron' (Sanskrit) PLUS unique ligatures: लोखंड [lōkhaṇḍa] *n* (लोह S) Iron. लोखंडाचे चणे खावविणें or चारणें To oppress grievously.लोखंडकाम [lōkhaṇḍakāma] *n* Iron work; that portion (of a building, machine &c.) which consists of iron. 2 The business of an ironsmith.लोखंडी [lōkhaṇḍī] *a* (लोखंड) Composed of iron; relating to iron. (Marathi)

Kneeling adorant. *bhaṭa* 'worshipper' *bhaṭa* 'furnace' *baṭa* 'iron' (Gujarati)

Offering bowl with ladle. *muka* 'ladle' (Tamil)(DEDR 4887) Rebus: *mũh* 'ingot' (Santali) *baṭa* = rimless pot (Kannada) Rebus:) *baṭa* = a kind of iron (G.)) *bhaṭa* furnace (Gujarati) Thus, iron ingot.

mũh 'face' (Santali). Rebus: mũh metal ingot (Santali) mũhã = the quantity of iron produced at one time in a native smelting furnace of the Kolhes; iron produced by the Kolhes and formed like a four-cornered piece a little pointed at each end; mūhā mẽṛhẽt = iron smelted by the Kolhes and formed into an equilateral lump a little pointed at each end; kolhe tehen mẽṛhẽtko mūhā akata = the Kolhes have to-day produced pig iron (Santali.lex.)

miṇḍāl 'markhor' (Tor.wali) meḍho 'a ram, a sheep' (G.)(CDIAL 10120)mēṇḍha'ram'(CDIAL

9606).मेंढा [mēṇḍhā] m (मेष S through H) A male sheep, a ram or tup. मेंढका or क्या [mēṇḍhakā or kyā] a (मेंढा) A shepherd (Marathi) Rebus: meḍ 'iron' (Ho.) mēṇḍh 'gold' as in: मेंढसर [mēṇḍhasara] m A bracelet of gold thread. (Marathi)

m725a *खोंड [khōṇḍa] m A young bull, a bullcalf. (Marathi) Rebus: kõdār 'turner' (Bengali); कोंद kōnda 'engraver, lapidary setting or infixing gems' (Marathi) G. sãghārɔ m. 'lathe' ; संघाट joinery; M. sãgaḍ 'double-canoe' Rebus: sangataras. संगतराश lit. 'to collect stones, stone-cutter, mason.'*

kamaḍha 'crab' Rebus: *kammaṭa* 'mint, coiner'.
ḍato = claws of crab (Santali) Rebus: *dhātu* 'mineral ore'

dāṭu 'cross'(Telugu) Rebus: *dhatu* 'mineral' (Santali).

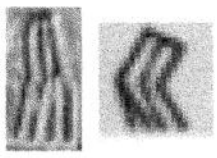

Strands of yarn/rope' hieroglyph: Hieroglyph: 'strands of yarn' Rebus reading: *dhā'tu* 'strand of rope' Rebus: *dhatu* 'mineral ore' (Santali)
sal 'splinter' Rebus: sal 'workshop'
kamaḍha 'crab' Rebus: *kammaṭa* 'mint, coiner' PLUS dulo 'hole' Rebus: dul 'cast metal'

kanka 'rim of jar' Rebus: *karṇīka* 'account (scribe)' *karṇī* 'supercargo'

m628a *खोंड [khōṇḍa] m A young bull, a bullcalf. (Marathi) Rebus: kõdār 'turner' (Bengali); कोंद kōnda 'engraver, lapidary setting or infixing gems' (Marathi) G. sãghārɔ m. 'lathe' ; संघाट joinery; M. sãgaḍ 'double-canoe' Rebus: sangataras. संगतराश lit. 'to collect stones, stone-cutter, mason.'*
kamaḍha 'crab' Rebus: *kammaṭa* 'mint, coiner'

kuṭila 'bent' CDIAL 3230 kuṭi— in cmpd. 'curve', *kuṭika—* 'bent' MBh. Rebus: *kuṭila, katthīl* = bronze (8 parts copper and 2 parts tin) PLUS 'notch': Thus, bronze metalware.

kanka 'rim of jar' Rebus: *karṇīka* 'account (scribe)' *karṇī* 'supercargo' PLUS 'notch' Thus metalware supercargo.
kolom 'three' Rebus: kolami 'smithy, forge'
ayo 'fish' Rebus: *aya* 'iron' *ayas* 'metal'

kanka 'rim of jar' Rebus: *karṇīka* 'account (scribe)' *karṇī* 'supercargo'

meḍ 'body' Rebus: *meḍ* 'iron' (Ho.) काठी [kāṭhī] *f* (काष्ट S) 'frame or structure of the body' (Marathi) Rebus: खंडी [khaṇḍī] measure of weight (Marathi) *கண்டி; kaṇṭi, n. < Mhr. khaṇḍil. [T. Tu. khaṇḍi, M. kaṇḍi.]* Candy, a weight, stated to be roughly equivalent to 500 lbs.

m310A kola 'tiger' Rebus: kolhe 'smelter' krammara 'looks back' Rebus: kamar 'smith' heraka 'spy' Rebus: erako 'moltencast copper'

khōṇḍa A stock or stump (Marathi); 'leafless tree' (Marathi) Rebus: *kõdār* 'turner' (Bengali); *kõdā* 'to turn in a lathe' (Bengali).

kamaḍha 'crab' Rebus: *kammaṭa* 'mint, coiner'.
aḍaren 'lid of pot' Rebus: *aduru* native metal (Kannada) kole.l 'temple' Rebus: kole.l 'smithy'

kanka 'rim of jar' Rebus: *karṇīka* 'account (scribe)' *karṇī* 'supercargo'

m62a *खोंड [khōṇḍa] m A young bull, a bullcalf. (Marathi) Rebus: kõdār 'turner' (Bengali); कोंद kōnda 'engraver, lapidary setting or infixing gems' (Marathi) G. sãghārɔ m. 'lathe' ; संघाट joinery; M. sãgaḍ 'double-canoe' Rebus: sangataras. संगतराश lit. 'to collect stones, stone-cutter, mason.'*

kamaḍha 'crab' Rebus: *kammaṭa* 'mint, coiner'.
ḍato = claws of crab (Santali) Rebus: *dhātu* 'mineral ore' Duplicated: dula 'pair' Rebus: dul 'cast metal' The two 'crab' hieroglyphs flank a pot: *baṭa* = rimless pot (Kannada) Rebus:) *baṭa* = a kind of iron (G.)) *bhaṭa* furnace (Gujarati). Thus, the three sign hieroglyphs read rebus: iron ore furnace castings.

kanka 'rim of jar' Rebus: *karṇīka* 'account (scribe)' *karṇī* 'supercargo'
dula 'two' Rebus: dul 'cast metal' Thus, cast metal supercargo.
aya kāṇḍa 'alloy metalware'

Banawali 4a *खोंड [khōṇḍa] m A young bull, a bullcalf. (Marathi) Rebus: kõdār 'turner' (Bengali); कोंद kōnda 'engraver, lapidary setting or infixing gems' (Marathi) G. sãghārɔ m. 'lathe' ; संघाट joinery; M. sãgaḍ 'double-canoe' Rebus: sangataras. संगतराश lit. 'to collect stones, stone-cutter, mason.'*
Ranku 'antelope' Rebus: *ranku* 'tin'
kamaḍha 'crab' Rebus: *kammaṭa* 'mint, coiner'.
ḍato = claws of crab (Santali) Rebus: *dhātu* 'mineral ore'

kanka 'rim of jar' Rebus: *karṇīka* 'account (scribe)' *karṇī* 'supercargo'

Lothal 58a Read rebus as the last 3 signs at Banawali 4a.

Kalibangan 91A Read as at Banawali 4a first sign PLUS

kanka 'rim of jar' Rebus: *karṇīka* 'account (scribe)' *karṇī* 'supercargo'
PLUS sal 'splinter' Rebus: sal 'workshop'. Thus, workshop supercargo.

m17a खोंड [khōṇḍa] m A young bull, a bullcalf. (Marathi) Rebus: kõdār 'turner' (Bengali); कोंद kōnda 'engraver, lapidary setting or infixing gems' (Marathi) G. sãghāṛɔ m. 'lathe' ; संघाट joinery; M. sãgaḍ 'double-canoe' Rebus: sangataras. संगतराश lit. 'to collect stones, stone-cutter, mason.'

kamaḍha 'crab' Rebus: *kammaṭa* 'mint, coiner'.

ḍato = claws of crab (Santali) Rebus: *dhātu* 'mineral ore'

kana, kanac = corner (Santali); Rebus: *kañcu* = bronze (Telugu) PLUS खांडा [*khāṇḍā*] *m* A jag, notch, or indentation (as upon the edge of a tool or weapon). Rebus: *kāṇḍa* 'tools, pots and pans and metal-ware' Thus, bronze metalware. PLUS infixed ligature: dulo 'hole' Rebus: dul 'cast metal'. PLUS sal 'splinter' Rebus: sal 'workshop; Thus workshop metalware castings.

kolom 'three' Rebus: kolami 'smithy, forge' Duplicated: dula 'pair' Rebus: dul 'cast metal'. Thus smithy for castings.

kolmo 'paddy plant' Rebus: *kolami* 'smithy, forge' Vikalpa: *mogge* 'sprout, bud' Rebus: *mũh* 'ingot' (Santali) dolu 'plant of shoot height' Rebus: dul 'cast metal'

m1879a *balad* m. ' ox ', gng. *bald*, (Ku.) *barad*, id. (N. Tarai) Rebus: *bharat* (5 copper, 4 zinc and 1 tin)(Punjabi) *pattar* 'trough' Rebus*: pattar* 'guild'. Thus, copper-zinc-tin alloy (worker) guild.

kamaḍha 'crab' Rebus: *kammaṭa* 'mint, coiner'.

ḍato = claws of crab (Santali) Rebus: *dhātu* 'mineral ore'

ḍhanga = a crook used for pulling down the branches of trees, for goats, sheep and camels (P.) Rebus:*ḍhangar* blacksmith'.

aya kammaṭa.'coiner, mint alloy'

kəṭhā´r, kc. *kuṭhār* m. ' granary, storeroom '(WPah.)(CDIAL 3550). *koṭhārī m.* ' storekeeper'

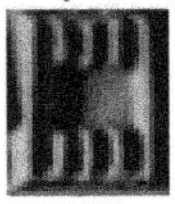

(Gujarati)(CDIAL 3551) Thus, storeroom (of) *kolom* 'three' Rebus: *kolami* 'smithy, forge'. Dula 'pair' Rebus: dul 'cast metal' Thus, together *dul kolami kuṭhār* 'metal smithy castings storeroom'

kanka 'rim of jar' Rebus: *karṇīka* 'account (scribe)' *karṇī* 'supercargo'

m1134A Rhinoceros/boar: baḍhia = a castrated boar, a hog (Santali) baḍhi 'a caste who work both in iron and wood' (Santali) *baṟea* 'merchant'

kamaḍha 'crab' Rebus: *kammaṭa* 'mint, coiner'.

ḍato = claws of crab (Santali) Rebus: *dhātu* 'mineral ore'

kana, kanac = corner (Santali); Rebus: *kañcu* = bronze (Telugu) PLUS खांडा [*khāṇḍā*] *m* A jag, notch, or indentation (as upon the edge of a tool or weapon). Rebus: *kāṇḍa* 'tools, pots and pans and metal-ware' Thus, bronze metalware. PLUS infixed hieroglyph: kole.l 'temple' Rebus; kole.l 'smithy'

kanac 'corner' Rebus: *kañcu* 'bronze'

āra 'spokes' Rebus: *āra 'brass'*. cf. erka = ekke (Tbh. of arka) aka (Tbh. of arka) copper (metal); crystal (Kannada) Glyph: *eraka*'nave of wheel' Rebus: eraka 'copper';

cf. erka = ekke (Tbh. of arka) aka (Tbh. of arka) copper (metal); crystal (Kannada) *erako* ‘moltencast copper’ Duplicated: dula ‘pair’ Rebus: dul ‘cast metal’ Thus cast copper, brass casting.

m148A *खोंड [khōṇḍa] m A young bull, a bullcalf. (Marathi) Rebus: kõdār ‘turner’ (Bengali); कोंद kōnda ‘engraver, lapidary setting or infixing gems’ (Marathi) G. sãghāṛɔ m. ‘lathe’ ; संघाट joinery; M. sãgaḍ ‘double-canoe’ Rebus: sangataras. संगतराश lit. ‘to collect stones, stone-cutter, mason.’*
kamaḍha ‘crab’ Rebus: *kammaṭa* ‘mint, coiner’.

 *ḍato* = claws of crab (Santali) Rebus: *dhātu* ‘mineral ore’

 *kanac* ‘corner’ Rebus: *kañcu* ‘bronze’
kanka ‘rim of jar’ Rebus: *karṇīka* ‘account (scribe)’ *karṇī* ‘supercargo’

m632A खोंड [khōṇḍa] m A young bull, a bullcalf. (Marathi) Rebus: kõdār ‘turner’ (Bengali); कोंद kōnda ‘engraver, lapidary setting or infixing gems’ (Marathi) G. sãghāṛɔ m. ‘lathe’ ; संघाट joinery; M. sãgaḍ ‘double-canoe’ Rebus: sangataras. संगतराश lit. ‘to collect stones, stone-cutter, mason.’
ḍato = claws of crab (Santali) Rebus: *dhātu* ‘mineral ore’ PLUS | *koḍa* ‘one’ Rebus: *koḍ* ‘workshop’ Thus, mineral ore workshop.
ḍhanga = a crook used for pulling down the branches of trees, for goats, sheep and camels (P.) Rebus: *ḍhangar* blacksmith’.

 *kanka* ‘rim of jar’ Rebus: *karṇīka* ‘account (scribe)’ *karṇī* ‘supercargo’PLUS infixed: kolom ‘three’ Rebus: kolami ‘smithy, forge’. Thus, smithy supercargo.
kamaḍha ‘crab’ Rebus: *kammaṭa* ‘mint, coiner’.
ayo ‘fish’ Rebus: *aya* ‘iron’ *ayas* ‘metal’

 *aḍar* 'harrow'; rebus: *aduru* 'native unsmelted metal'

ayo ‘fish’ Rebus: *aya* ‘iron’ *ayas* ‘metal’

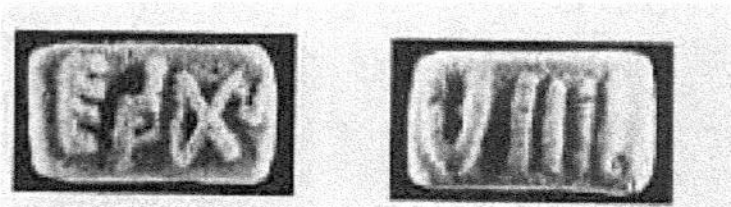

H-1817 A H-1817 B

h1817A Side A: *ḍato* = claws of crab (Santali) Rebus: *dhātu* ‘mineral ore’ PLUS *aḍaren* ‘lid of pot’ Rebus: aduru ‘unsmelted, native metal’ Thus, native metal mineral.

 *ḍhanga* = a crook used for pulling down the branches of trees, for goats, sheep and camels (P.) Rebus: *ḍhangar* blacksmith’ PLUS ‘notch’: खांडा [*khāṇḍā*] *m* A jag, notch, or indentation (as upon the edge of a tool or weapon). Rebus: *kāṇḍa* ‘tools, pots and pans and metal-ware’. Thus, blacksmith metalware.

a  *kharedo* = a currycomb (Gujarati) खरारा [*kharārā*] *m* (H) A currycomb. 2 Currying horse. (Marathi) Rebus: करडा [*karaḍā*] Hard from alloy--iron, silver &c. (Marathi) *kharādī* ‘ turner’ (Gujarati)
Side B: *baṭa* = rimless pot (Kannada) Rebus:) *baṭa* = a kind of iron (G.)) *bhaṭa* furnace (Gujarati) |||| Numeral 4: gaṇḍa 'four' Rebus: kaṇḍa 'furnace, fire-altar' (Santali)

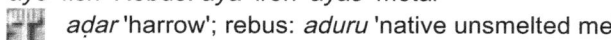

m1390A *ibha* ‘elephant’ Rebus: *ib* ‘iron’ *ibbo* ‘merchant’ (Gujarati)
Text of inscription read rebus as at h1817A

m1053a *ḍato* = claws of crab (Santali) Rebus: *dhātu* 'mineral ore' PLUS : *ḍhālako kāṇḍa* 'ingot, tools, pots and pans and metal-ware'.*dhāḷ* 'a slope'; 'inclination of a plane' (G.); *ḍhāḷiyum* = adj. sloping, inclining (G.) Rebus: *ḍhālako* = a large metal ingot (G.) *ḍhālakī* = a metal heated and poured into a mould; a solid piece of metal; an ingot (Gujarati) thus, mineral ingot.

ḍhanga = a crook used for pulling down the branches of trees, for goats, sheep and camels (P.) Rebus:*ḍhangar* blacksmith' PLUS 'notch': खांडा [*khāṇḍā*] *m* A jag, notch, or indentation (as upon the edge of a tool or weapon). Rebus: *kāṇḍa* 'tools, pots and pans and metal-ware'. Thus, blacksmith metalware.

baroṭi 'twelve' *bhārata* 'a factitious alloy of copper, pewter, tin' (Marathi)

kanka 'rim of jar' Rebus: *karṇīka* 'account (scribe)' *karṇī* 'supercargo'

m1800a *खोंड [khōṇḍa] m A young bull, a bullcalf. (Marathi) Rebus: kõdār 'turner' (Bengali); कोंद kōnda 'engraver, lapidary setting or infixing gems' (Marathi) G. sãghāṛɔ m. 'lathe' ; संघाट joinery; M. sãgaḍ 'double-canoe' Rebus: sangataras. संगतराश lit. 'to collect stones, stone-cutter, mason.'*

ḍato = claws of crab (Santali) Rebus: *dhātu* 'mineral ore' *kamaḍha* 'crab' Rebus: *kammaṭa* 'mint, coiner'.

ḍhanga = a crook used for pulling down the branches of trees, for goats, sheep and camels (P.) Rebus:*ḍhangar* blacksmith' PLUS 'notch': खांडा [*khāṇḍā*] *m* A jag, notch, or indentation (as upon the edge of a tool or weapon). Rebus: *kāṇḍa* 'tools, pots and pans and metal-ware'. Thus, blacksmith metalware.

m939a Read rebus as at m1800a

m1989a

kamaḍha 'crab' Rebus: *kammaṭa* 'mint, coiner'.

ḍato = claws of crab (Santali) Rebus: *dhātu* 'mineral ore'

|||| Numeral 4: gaṇḍa 'four' Rebus: kaṇḍa 'furnace, fire-altar' (Santali)

||| Numeral three: kolom 'three' Rebus: kolami 'smithy, forge'

सांड [sāṇḍa] *f* (षंद S) An outlet for superfluous water (as through a dam or mound); a sluice, a floodvent. Rebus: सांडणी [sāṇḍaṇī] *f* (H) An instrument of goldsmiths. It is hooked or curved at the extremity; and is used to draw things out of the fire.

सांठा [*sāṇṭhā*] *m* (संचय S) A collection, heap, hoard, store, stock.साटें [*sāṭēṃ*] *n* (संचय S) A whole investment; the total quantity of merchandise (brought to market by one merchant).

 *kanka* 'rim of jar' Rebus: *karṇīka* 'account (scribe)' *karṇī* 'supercargo'

 *dāṭu* 'cross'(Telugu) Rebus: *dhatu* 'mineral' (Santali). PLUS *kaṇḍo* 'stool, seat' Rebus: *kāṇḍa* 'metalware' *kaṇḍa* 'fire-altar'

m842a *खोंड [khōṇḍa] m A young bull, a bullcalf. (Marathi) Rebus: kõdār 'turner' (Bengali); कोंद kōnda 'engraver, lapidary setting or infixing gems' (Marathi) G. sãghāṛɔ m. 'lathe' ; संघाट joinery; M. sãgaḍ 'double-canoe' Rebus: sangataras. संगतराश lit. 'to collect stones, stone-cutter, mason.'*

ḍato = claws of crab (Santali) Rebus: *dhātu* 'mineral ore' Ligatured hieroglyph: *Kur.* xolā tail. *Malt.* qoli id. (DEDR 2135). Rebus: kolhe 'smelter' Thus, mineral copper smelter.

h99A *kamaḍha* 'crab' Rebus: *kammaṭa* 'mint, coiner'.
ḍato = claws of crab (Santali) Rebus: *dhātu* 'mineral ore' Ligatured hieroglyph: *Kur.* xolā tail. *Malt.* qoli id. (DEDR 2135). Rebus: kolhe 'smelter' Thus, mineral copper smelter.

 *kharedo* = a currycomb (Gujarati) खरारा [*kharārā*] *m* (H) A currycomb. 2 Currying a horse. (Marathi) Rebus: करडा [*karaḍā*] Hard from alloy--iron, silver &c. (Marathi) *kharādī* ' turner' (Gujarati)

m1662A *खोंड [khōṇḍa] m A young bull, a bullcalf. (Marathi) Rebus: kõdār 'turner' (Bengali); कोंद kōnda 'engraver, lapidary setting or infixing gems' (Marathi) G. sãghāṛɔ m. 'lathe' ; संघाट joinery; M. sãgaḍ 'double-canoe' Rebus: sangataras. संगतराश lit. 'to collect stones, stone-cutter, mason.'*

ḍato = claws of crab (Santali) Rebus: *dhātu* 'mineral ore' Ligatured hieroglyph: *Kur.* xolā tail. *Malt.* qoli id. (DEDR 2135). Rebus: kolhe 'smelter' Thus, mineral copper smelter.

 *kanac* 'corner' Rebus: *kañcu* 'bronze' sal 'splinter' Rebus: sal 'workshop'

 *baroṭi* 'twelve' *bhārata* 'a factitious alloy of copper, pewter, tin' (Marathi)

Three sign sequence:
muka 'ladle' (Tamil)(DEDR 4887) Rebus: *mũh* 'ingot' (Santali) *baṭa* = rimless pot (Kannada) Rebus:) *baṭa* = a kind of iron (G.)) *bhaṭa* furnace (Gujarati) Thus, iron ingot.
kolom 'three' Rebus: kolami 'smithy, forge' *kāṇḍa* 'arrow' (Sanskrit) Rebus:*khāṇḍa* 'tools, pots and pans, metal-ware'. Rebus 2: kaṇḍ 'fire-altar' (Santali) Thus, the three sign sequence reads: iron ingot, furnace smithy, fire-altar metalware.

ayo 'fish' Rebus: *aya* 'iron' *ayas* 'metal'

h1075A *kamaḍha* 'crab' Rebus: *kammaṭa* 'mint, coiner'.
ḍato = claws of crab (Santali) Rebus: *dhātu* 'mineral ore' PLUS | *koḍa* 'one' Rebus: *koḍ* 'workshop' Thus, mint or mineral workshop.
ḍhanga = a crook used for pulling down the branches of trees, for goats, sheep and camels (P.) Rebus: *ḍhangar* blacksmith'.

kanka 'rim of jar' Rebus: *karṇīka* 'account (scribe)' *karṇī* 'supercargo' PLUS sal 'splinter' Rebus: sal 'workshop' Thus workshop supercargo.

m153a *खोंड [khōṇḍa] m A young bull, a bullcalf. (Marathi) Rebus: kõdār 'turner' (Bengali); कोंद kōnda 'engraver, lapidary setting or infixing gems' (Marathi) G. sãghārɔ m. 'lathe' ; संघाट joinery; M. sãgaḍ 'double-canoe' Rebus: sangataras. संगतराश lit. 'to collect stones, stone-cutter, mason.'*

cīmara 'black ant' Rebus: *cīmara* 'copper'. *cīmara kāra* -- ' coppersmith '

meḍ 'body' Rebus: *meḍ* 'iron' (Ho.) काठी [kāṭhī] *f* (काष्ठ S) 'frame or structure of the body' (Marathi) Rebus: खंडी [khanḍī] measure of weight (Marathi) *கண்டி; kaṇṭi, n. < Mhr. khanḍil. [T. Tu. khanḍi, M. kanḍi.]* Candy, a weight, stated to be roughly equivalent to 500 lbs. PLUS

aḍar 'harrow'; rebus: *aduru* 'native unsmelted metal' Thus, unsmelted iron native metal.

kuṭila 'bent' CDIAL 3230 kuṭi— in cmpd. 'curve', *kuṭika*— 'bent' MBh. Rebus: *kuṭila, katthīl* = bronze (8 parts copper and 2 parts tin) Duplicated: dula 'pair' Rebus: dul 'cast metal' Thus, cast bronze. PLUS infixed: Variant:

karaṇḍa 'duck' (Sanskrit) karaṛa 'a very large aquatic bird' (Sindhi) Rebus: करडा [*karaḍā*] Hard from alloy--iron, silver &c. (Marathi) *kharādī* ' turner' (Gujarati) Thus, castings of an alloy of copper, native metal and tin.

M-1275 A

m1275A *kamaḍha* 'crab' Rebus: *kammaṭa* 'mint, coiner'.
ḍato = claws of crab (Santali) Rebus: *dhātu* 'mineral ore'
dula 'two' Rebus: dul 'cast metal'
ayo 'fish' Rebus: *aya* 'iron' *ayas* 'metal'
ḍhanga = a crook used for pulling down the branches of trees, for goats, sheep and camels (P.) Rebus: *ḍhangar* blacksmith'.

dula 'pair' Rebus: dul 'cast metal' *mogge* 'sprout, bud' Rebus: *mũh* 'ingot' (Santali) Thus, cast metal ingot.

kanka 'rim of jar' Rebus: *karṇīka* 'account (scribe)' *karṇī* 'supercargo'

M-943 a

m943a *खोंड [khōṇḍa] m A young bull, a bullcalf. (Marathi) Rebus: kõdār 'turner' (Bengali); कोंद kōnda 'engraver, lapidary setting or infixing gems' (Marathi) G.*

sãghāṛɔ m. 'lathe' ; संघाट joinery; M. sãgaḍ 'double-canoe' Rebus: sangataras. संगतराश lit. 'to collect stones, stone-cutter, mason.'
kamaḍha 'crab' Rebus: *kammaṭa* 'mint, coiner'.
ḍato = claws of crab (Santali) Rebus: *dhātu* 'mineral ore'

 *aḍar* 'harrow'; rebus: *aduru* 'native unsmelted metal'

ayo 'fish' Rebus: *aya* 'iron' *ayas* 'metal'

 *baraḍo* = spine; backbone (Tulu) Rebus: *baran, bharat* 'mixed alloys' (5 copper, 4 zinc and 1 tin) (Punjabi)

 *kanka* 'rim of jar' Rebus: *karṇīka* 'account (scribe)' *karṇī* 'supercargo'

 m469A 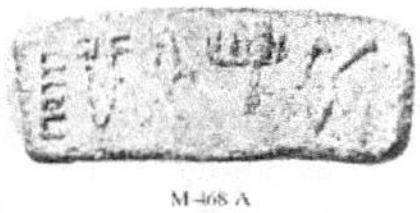 m468A  h767A

 h748A  h203A *kamaḍha* 'crab' Rebus: *kammaṭa* 'mint, coiner'.
ḍato = claws of crab (Santali) Rebus: *dhātu* 'mineral ore'

 *aḍar* 'harrow'; rebus: *aduru* 'native unsmelted metal'

 *ayo* 'fish' Rebus: *aya* 'iron' *ayas* 'metal'
kanka 'rim of jar' Rebus: *karṇīka* 'account (scribe)' *karṇī* 'supercargo'

 *khareḍo* = a currycomb (Gujarati) खरारा [*kharārā*] *m* (H) A currycomb. 2 Currying a horse. (Marathi) Rebus: करडा [*karaḍā*] Hard from alloy--iron, silver &c. (Marathi) *kharādī* ' turner' (Gujarati)

 m395A *kamaḍha* 'crab' Rebus: *kammaṭa* 'mint, coiner'.
ḍato = claws of crab (Santali) Rebus: *dhātu* 'mineral ore'

 *aḍar* 'harrow'; rebus: *aduru* 'native unsmelted metal'
ayo 'fish' Rebus: *aya* 'iron' *ayas* 'metal'
kānḍa 'arrow' (Sanskrit) Rebus:*khānḍa* 'tools, pots and pans, metal-ware'. Rebus 2: kaṇḍ 'fire-altar' (Santali)

m1884A *balad* m. ' ox ', gng. *bald*, (Ku.) *barad*, id. (N. Tarai) Rebus: *bharat* (5 copper, 4 zinc and 1 tin)(Punjabi) *pattar* 'trough' Rebus*: pattar* 'guild'. Thus, copper-zinc-tin alloy (worker) guild.

 *aḍar* 'harrow'; rebus: *aduru* 'native unsmelted metal' Duplicated: dula 'pair' Rebus: dul 'cast metal'. Thus native metal castings. Sal 'splinter' Rebus: sal 'workshop'
āra 'six' Rebus: *āra-kūṭa*, 'brass' *ayo* 'fish' Rebus: *aya* 'iron' *ayas* 'metal' *kāṇḍa* 'arrow' (Sanskrit) Rebus:*khāṇḍa* 'tools, pots and pans, metal-ware'. Rebus 2: kaṇḍ 'fire-altar' (Santali)

m1971A *kamaḍha* 'crab' Rebus: *kammaṭa* 'mint, coiner'.
ḍato = claws of crab (Santali) Rebus: *dhātu* 'mineral ore'

 *aḍar* 'harrow'; rebus: *aduru* 'native unsmelted metal' *ayo* 'fish' Rebus: *aya* 'iron' *ayas* 'metal'

 *muka* 'ladle' (Tamil)(DEDR 4887) Rebus: *mũh* 'ingot' (Santali) *baṭa* = rimless pot (Kannada) Rebus:) *baṭa* = a kind of iron (G.)) *bhaṭa* furnace (Gujarati) Thus, iron ingot.
kolom 'three' Rebus: kolami 'smithy, forge'
ḍato = claws of crab (Santali) Rebus: *dhātu* 'mineral ore'
kāṇḍa 'arrow' (Sanskrit) Rebus:*khāṇḍa* 'tools, pots and pans, metal-ware'. Rebus 2: kaṇḍ 'fire-altar' (Santali)

m1295a *kamaḍha* 'crab' Rebus: *kammaṭa* 'mint, coiner'.
ḍato = claws of crab (Santali) Rebus: *dhātu* 'mineral ore'

 *aḍar* 'harrow'; rebus: *aduru* 'native unsmelted metal'
ayo 'fish' Rebus: *aya* 'iron' *ayas* 'metal'
dula 'pair' Rebus: *dul* 'cast (metal)' PLUS*kana, kanac* = corner (Santali); Rebus: *kañcu* = bronze (Telugu) Thus, cast bronze.PLUS *dhāḷ* 'a slope'; 'inclination of a plane' (G.); *ḍhāḷiyum* = adj. sloping, inclining (G.) Rebus: *ḍhālako* = a large metal ingot (G.) *ḍhālakī* = a metal heated and poured into a mould; a solid piece of metal; an ingot (Gujarati) Thus, bronze ingot.

 *kolmo* 'paddy plant' Rebus: *kolami* 'smithy, forge' Vikalpa: *mogge* 'sprout, bud' Rebus: *mũh* 'ingot' (Santali) dolu 'plant of shoot height' Rebus: dul 'cast metal'

m618A *kamaḍha* = crab; *kampaṭṭam* = mint (Ta.) ; *kammaṭa* 'coiner, mint' (Telugu) Vikalpa: *ḍato* = claws of crab (Santali); *dhātu* = mineral (Sanskrit) Duplicated: dula 'pair' Rebus: dul 'cast metal'. Thus mint castings or mineral castings.

m393a *kamaḍha* = crab; *kampaṭṭam* = mint (Ta.) ; *kammaṭa* 'coiner, mint' (Telugu) Vikalpa: *ḍato* = claws of crab (Santali); *dhātu* = mineral (Sanskrit) Duplicated: dula 'pair' Rebus: dul 'cast metal'. Thus mint castings or mineral castings. sal 'splinter' Rebus: sal 'workshop' Thus, metal castings workshop

dula 'pair' Rebus: *dul* 'cast (metal)' PLUS *kana, kanac* = corner (Santali); Rebus: *kañcu* = bronze (Telugu) PLUS infixed kolmo 'paddy plant' Rebus: kolami 'smithy, forge'. Thus, cast bronze smithy, forge. Or, *mogge* 'sprout, bud' Rebus: *mũh* 'ingot' (Santali)Thus, cast bronze ingot. Read as: *kañcu dul mũh 'bronze cast ingot'*

aya kammaṭa.'coiner, mint alloy'

||| Numeral 4: gaṇḍa 'four' Rebus: kaṇḍa 'furnace, fire-altar' (Santali) PLUS ||| Numeral three: kolom 'three' Rebus: kolami 'smithy, forge'

सांड [sāṇḍa] *f* (षद S) An outlet for superfluous water (as through a dam or mound); a sluice, a floodvent. Rebus: सांडणी [sāṇḍaṇī] *f* (H) An instrument of goldsmiths. It is hooked or curved at the extremity; and is used to draw things out of the fire.

सांठा [*sāṇṭhā*] *m* (संचय S) A collection, heap, hoard, store, stock.साटें [*sāṭēṃ*] *n* (संचय S) A whole investment; the total quantity of merchandise (brought to market by one merchant).

kanka 'rim of jar' Rebus: *karṇīka* 'account (scribe)' *karṇī* 'supercargo'

dāṭu 'cross'(Telugu) Rebus: *dhatu* 'mineral' (Santali).
PLUS *kaṇḍo* 'stool, seat' Rebus: *kāṇḍa* 'metalware' *kaṇḍa* 'fire-altar'

m0263 Text 1336 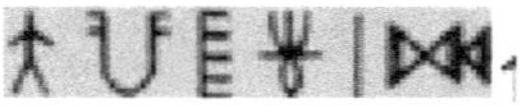 *khũṭ* 'zebu' Rebus: '(native metal) guild'

Ligature of two pincers back-to-back. PLUS anvil: खरवई [kharavī] *f* An instrument of braziers,--the anvil on which vessels are hung to be hammered. Rebus: khara 'blacksmith'. *ḍato* 'claws or pincers of crab' (Santali) Rebus: *dhatu* 'mineral ore' (Santali) dula 'pair' Rebus: dul 'cast metal'. Thus, the composite hieroglyph reads rebus: dul dhatu khara 'cast metal mineral blacksmith'.

| *koḍa* = one (Santali); *koḍ* 'workshop' (Gujarati)

Ligature of 'paddy plant' hieroglyph and 'ingot' hieroglyph. *kolmo* 'paddy plant' Rebus: *kolami* 'smithy, forge' *ḍhālako* 'ingot'. Thus, 'ingot forge'. Or, variant:

|||| Numeral 4: gaṇḍa 'four' Rebus: kaṇḍa 'furnace, fire-altar' (Santali) dula 'pair' Rebus: dul 'cast metal'

kharedo = a currycomb (Gujarati) खरारा [*khararā*] *m* (H) A currycomb. 2 Currying a horse. (Marathi) Rebus: करडा [*karaḍā*] Hard from alloy--iron, silver &c. (Marathi) *kharādī* ' turner' (Gujarati)

h66a *खोंड [khōṇḍa] m A young bull, a bullcalf. (Marathi) Rebus: kōdār 'turner' (Bengali); कोंद kōnda 'engraver, lapidary setting or infixing gems' (Marathi) G.*

sãghāṛɔ m. 'lathe' ; संघाट joinery; M. sãgaḍ 'double-canoe' Rebus: sangataras. संगतराश lit. 'to collect stones, stone-cutter, mason.'

koḍi 'flag' (Ta.)(DEDR 2049). Rebus 1: *koḍ* 'workshop' (Kuwi) Rebus 2: *khŏḍ* m. 'pit', *khŏḍü* f. 'small pit' (Kashmiri. CDIAL 3947).

PLUS *kharedo* = a currycomb (Gujarati) खरारा [*kharārā*] *m* (H) A currycomb. 2 Currying a horse. (Marathi) Rebus: करडा [*karaḍā*] Hard from alloy--iron, silver &c. (Marathi) *kharādī* ' turner' (Gujarati) Thus, hard alloy workshop.

aya aḍaren (homonym: aduru)'alloy native metal'

khaṇḍ 'field, division' (Sanskrit) Rebus: *khāṇḍa* 'tools, pots and pans, metal-ware'. Rebus 2: kaṇḍ 'fire-altar' (Santali) dula 'pair' Rebus: dul 'cast metal' Thus, duplicated 'division' hieroglyph sign reads: cast metal metal-ware.

h160A

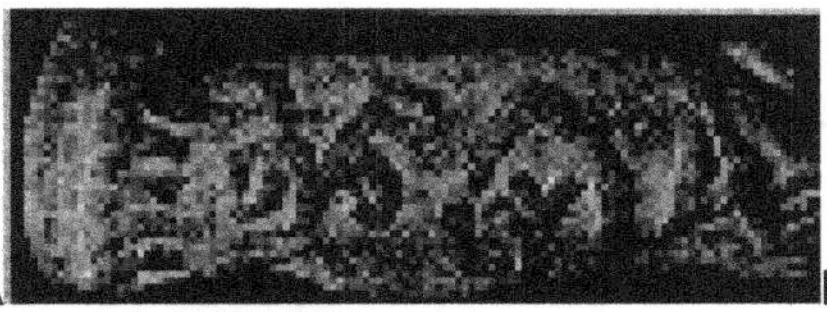
h189A

h775A

h1808A

h470A

m1419A

h670a

h681

m1962a

m1986a

h152a

ḍhanga = a crook used for pulling down the branches of trees, for goats, sheep and camels (P.) Rebus:*ḍhangar* blacksmith'. PLUS

 *kharedo* = a currycomb (Gujarati) खरारा [*kharārā*] *m* (H) A currycomb. 2 Currying a horse. (Marathi) Rebus: करडा [*karaḍā*] Hard from alloy--iron, silver &c. (Marathi) *kharādī* ' turner' (Gujarati) Thus, a blacksmith who is a specialist in hard alloys or hard alloy smith.

 *dula* 'pair' Rebus: *dul* 'cast (metal)' PLUS*kana, kanac* = corner (Santali); Rebus: *kañcu* = bronze (Telugu) PLUS infixed kolmo 'paddy plant' Rebus: kolami 'smithy, forge'. Thus, cast bronze smithy, forge. Or, *mogge* 'sprout, bud' Rebus: *mũh* 'ingot' (Santali)Thus, cast bronze ingot. Read as: *kañcu dul mũh 'bronze cast ingot'*

  water-carrier hieroglyph *kuṭi*; Rebus: *kuṭhi* 'smelter furnace'. PLUS 'rim of jar':

 kanka 'rim of jar' Rebus: karṇīka 'account (scribe)' karṇī 'supercargo'

m371A First three  signs from l. read rebus as at h152a and ten other duplicated inscriptions on tablets. PLUS dula 'two' Rebus: dul 'cast metal'

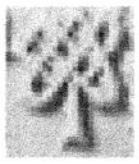 *loa* 'ficus religiosa' Rebus: *lo* 'iron' (Sanskrit) PLUS unique ligatures: लोखंड [lōkhaṇḍa] *n* (लोह S) Iron. लोखंडाचे चणे खावविणें or चारणें To oppress grievously.लोखंडकाम [lōkhaṇḍakāma] *n* Iron work; that portion (of a building, machine &c.) which consists of iron. 2 The business of an ironsmith.लोखंडी [lōkhaṇḍī] *a* (लोखंड) Composed of iron; relating to iron. (Marathi)

 *meḍ* 'body' Rebus: *meḍ* 'iron' (Ho.) काठी [kāṭhī] *f* (काष्ट S) 'frame or structure of the body' (Marathi) Rebus: खंडी [khaṇḍī] measure of weight (Marathi) *கண்டி; kaṇṭi, n. < Mhr. khaṇḍil. [T. Tu. khaṇḍi, M. kaṇḍi.]* Candy, a weight, stated to be roughly equivalent to 500 lbs.

 *khaṇḍ* 'field, division' (Sanskrit) Rebus: *khāṇḍa* 'tools, pots and pans, metal-ware'. Rebus 2: kaṇḍ 'fire-altar' (Santali) dula 'pair' Rebus: dul 'cast metal' Thus, duplicated 'division' hieroglyph sign reads: cast metal metal-ware.

 *ḍato* = claws of crab (Santali) Rebus: *dhātu* 'mineral ore' Duplicated: dula 'pair' Rebus: dul 'cast metal' PLUS ligature:

 mēḍu height, rising ground, hillock (Kannada) Rebus: *mẽṛhẽt, meḍ* 'iron' (Munda.Ho.)

PLUS | *koḍa* 'one' Rebus: *koḍ* 'workshop'. Thus, iron castings workshop.

 |||| Numeral 4: gaṇḍa 'four' Rebus: kaṇḍa 'furnace, fire-altar' (Santali) dula 'pair' Rebus: dul 'cast metal'

 *kharedo* = a currycomb (Gujarati) खरारा [*kharārā*] *m* (H) A currycomb. 2 Currying a horse. (Marathi) Rebus: करडा [*karaḍā*] Hard from alloy--iron, silver &c. (Marathi) *kharādī* ' turner' (Gujarati)

 *kanka* 'rim of jar' Rebus: *karṇīka* 'account (scribe)' *karṇī* 'supercargo'

 *meḍ* 'body' Rebus: *meḍ* 'iron' (Ho.) काठी [kāṭhī] *f* (काष्ट S) 'frame or structure of the body' (Marathi) Rebus: खंडी [khaṇḍī] measure of weight (Marathi) *கண்டி; kaṇṭi, n. < Mhr. khaṇḍil. [T. Tu. khaṇḍi, M. kaṇḍi.]* Candy, a weight, stated to be roughly equivalent to 500 lbs.

NOTE: The occurrence of 'body' or 'stature' hieroglyph as a terminating sequence after the 'rim of jar' hieroglyph is a quantification by the scribe-artisan-trader of the weight of supercargo to be about 50 lbs. or . खंडी [khaṇḍī] = 20 maunds.

h1662A *खोंड [khōṇḍa] m A young bull, a bullcalf. (Marathi) Rebus: kõdār 'turner' (Bengali); कोंद kōnda 'engraver, lapidary setting or infixing gems' (Marathi) G. sãghāṛɔ m. 'lathe' ; संघाट joinery; M. sãgaḍ 'double-canoe' Rebus: sangataras. संगतराश lit. 'to collect stones, stone-cutter, mason.'*

ḍato = claws of crab (Santali) Rebus: *dhātu* 'mineral ore' Duplicated: dula 'pair' Rebus: dul 'cast metal'

 mēḍu height, rising ground, hillock (Kannada) Rebus: *mẽṛhẽt, meḍ* 'iron' (Munda.Ho.) sal 'splinter' Rebus: sal 'workshop'

  *loa* 'ficus religiosa' Rebus: *lo* 'iron' (Sanskrit) PLUS unique ligatures: लोखंड [lōkhaṇḍa] *n* (लोह S) Iron. लोखंडाचे चणे खावविणें or चारणें To oppress grievously.लोखंडकाम [lōkhaṇḍakāma] *n* Iron work; that portion (of a building, machine &c.) which consists of iron. 2 The business of an ironsmith.लोखंडी [lōkhaṇḍī] *a* (लोखंड) Composed of iron; relating to iron. (Marathi) *bhaṭa* 'warrior' (Sanskrit) Rebus: *baṭa* a kind of iron (Gujarati). Rebus: *bhaṭa* 'furnace' (Santali) Thus, together, th ligatured hieroglyph reads rebus: *loa bhaṭa* 'iron furnace'

 *dhāḷ* 'a slope'; 'inclination of a plane' (G.); *ḍhāḷiyum* = adj. sloping, inclining (G.) Rebus: *ḍhālako* = a large metal ingot (G.) *ḍhālakī* = a metal heated and poured into a mould; a solid piece of metal; an ingot (Gujarati) PLUS खांडा [*khāṇḍā*] *m* A jag, notch, or indentation (as upon the edge of a tool or weapon). Rebus: *kāṇḍa* 'tools, pots and pans and metal-ware' Thus, the pair of sign hieroglyphs from r. read rebus: copper, bronze ingots, metalware castings.

 *meḍ* 'body' Rebus: *meḍ* 'iron' (Ho.) काठी [kāṭhī] *f* (काष्ट S) 'frame or structure of the body' (Marathi) Rebus: खंडी [khaṇḍī] measure of weight (Marathi) *கண்டி; kaṇṭi, n. < Mhr. khaṇḍil. [T. Tu. khaṇḍi, M. kaṇḍi.]* Candy, a weight, stated to be roughly equivalent to 500 lbs.

 *kanka* 'rim of jar' Rebus: *karṇīka* 'account (scribe)' *karṇī* 'supercargo'

kolom 'three' Rebus: kolami 'smithy, forge' DUPLICATED. dula 'pair' Rebus: dul 'cast metal' Thus, smithy for castings.

m78a खोंड [khōṇḍa] m A young bull, a bullcalf. (Marathi) Rebus: kõdār 'turner' (Bengali); कोंद kōnda 'engraver, lapidary setting or infixing gems' (Marathi) G. sãghāṛɔ m. 'lathe' ; संघाट joinery; M. sãgaḍ 'double-canoe' Rebus: sangataras. संगतराश lit. 'to collect stones, stone-cutter, mason.'

ḍato = claws of crab (Santali) Rebus: *dhātu* 'mineral ore' Duplicated: dula 'pair' Rebus: dul 'cast metal' PLUS ligature:

mēḍu height, rising ground, hillock (Kannada) Rebus: *mẽṛhẽt, meḍ* 'iron' (Munda.Ho.)

PLUS dula 'two' Rebus: dul 'cast metal' Thus iron castings.

Khara 'donkey' Rebus: khar 'blacksmith' PLUS *Kur.* xolā tail. *Malt.* qoli id. (DEDR 2135). Rebus: kolhe 'smelter' Thus, copper smelter. Thus, blacksmith-copper smelter.

kanka 'rim of jar' Rebus: *karṇīka* 'account (scribe)' *karṇī* 'supercargo'

m243a *balad* m. ' ox ', gng. *bald*, (Ku.) *barad*, id. (N. Tarai) Rebus: *bharat* (5 copper, 4 zinc and 1 tin)(Punjabi) *pattar* 'trough' Rebus*: pattar* 'guild'. Thus, copper-zinc-tin alloy (worker) guild.

ḍato = claws of crab (Santali) Rebus: *dhātu* 'mineral ore' Duplicated: dula 'pair' Rebus: dul 'cast metal' PLUS ligature:

mēḍu height, rising ground, hillock (Kannada) Rebus: *mẽṛhẽt, meḍ* 'iron' (Munda.Ho.)

loa 'ficus religiosa' Rebus: *lo* 'iron' (Sanskrit) PLUS unique ligatures: लोखंड [lōkhaṇḍa] *n* (लोह S) Iron. लोखंडाचे चणे खावविणें or चारणें To oppress grievously.लोखंडकाम [lōkhaṇḍakāma] *n* Iron work; that portion (of a building, machine &c.) which consists of iron. 2 The business of an ironsmith.लोखंडी [lōkhaṇḍī] *a* (लोखंड) Composed of iron; relating to iron. (Marathi) *bhaṭa* 'warrior' (Sanskrit) Rebus: *baṭa* a kind of iron (Gujarati). Rebus: *bhaṭa* 'furnace' (Santali) Thus, together, th ligatured hieroglyph reads rebus: *loa bhaṭa* 'iron furnace'

dhāḷ 'a slope'; 'inclination of a plane' (G.); *ḍhāḷiyum* = adj. sloping, inclining (G.) Rebus: *ḍhālako* = a large metal ingot (G.) *ḍhālakī* = a metal heated and poured into a mould; a solid piece of metal; an ingot (Gujarati).Ligatures: dula 'pair' Rebus: dul 'cast metal' PLUS mēḍu height, rising ground, hillock (Kannada) Rebus: *mẽṛhẽt, meḍ* 'iron' (Munda.Ho.) Thus iron ingot castings.

ranku 'liquid measure' Rebus: ranku 'tin'

kamaḍha 'bow and arrow' Rebus:: *kampaṭṭam* = mint (Ta.) ; *kammaṭa* 'coiner, mint' (Telugu)

m220a

खोंड [khōṇḍa] m A young bull, a bullcalf. (Marathi) Rebus: kõdār 'turner' (Bengali); कोंद kōnda 'engraver, lapidary setting or infixing gems' (Marathi) G. sãghāṛɔ m. 'lathe' ; संघाट joinery; M. sãgaḍ 'double-canoe' Rebus: sangataras. संगतराश lit. 'to collect stones, stone-cutter, mason.'

ḍato = claws of crab (Santali) Rebus: *dhātu* 'mineral ore' Duplicated: dula 'pair' Rebus: dul 'cast metal' PLUS ligature:

 mēḍu height, rising ground, hillock (Kannada) Rebus: *mẽṛhẽt, meḍ* 'iron' (Munda.Ho.)

 *kanka* 'rim of jar' Rebus: *karṇīka* 'account (scribe)' *karṇī* 'supercargo'PLUS | खांडा [*khāṇḍā*] *m* A jag, notch, or indentation (as upon the edge of a tool or weapon). Rebus: *kāṇḍa* 'tools, pots and pans and metal-ware' Thus, metalware supercargo.

 The hieroglyph a variant of:  *kana, kanac* = corner (Santali); Rebus: *kañcu* = bronze (Telugu) PLUS खांडा [*khāṇḍā*] *m* A jag, notch, or indentation (as upon the edge of a tool or weapon). Rebus: *kāṇḍa* 'tools, pots and pans and metal-ware' Thus, bronze metalware.

ranku 'liquid measure' Rebus: ranku 'tin'

 *kanka* 'rim of jar' Rebus: *karṇīka* 'account (scribe)' *karṇī* 'supercargo'

 Lothal 104A *ḍato* = claws of crab (Santali) Rebus: *dhātu* 'mineral ore' Duplicated: dula 'pair' Rebus: dul 'cast metal'
baṭa = rimless pot (Kannada) Rebus:) *baṭa* = a kind of iron (G.)) *bhaṭa* furnace (Gujarati) Duplicated: dula 'pair' Rebus: dul 'cast metal' Thus, iron castings furnace.

 Variant: 'A slanted stroke between two hillocks': *dhāḷ* 'a slope'; 'inclination of a plane' (G.); *ḍhāḷiyum* = adj. sloping, inclining (G.) Rebus: *ḍhālako* = a large metal ingot (G.) *ḍhālakī* = a metal heated and poured into a mould; a solid piece of metal; an ingot (Gujarati).Ligatures: dula 'pair' Rebus: dul 'cast metal' PLUS mēḍu height, rising ground, hillock (Kannada) Rebus: *mẽṛhẽt, meḍ* 'iron' (Munda.Ho.) Thus iron ingot castings.

 m119A *खोंड [khōṇḍa] m A young bull, a bullcalf. (Marathi) Rebus: kõdār 'turner' (Bengali); कोंद kōnda 'engraver, lapidary setting or infixing gems' (Marathi) G. sãghāṛɔ m. 'lathe' ; संघाट joinery; M. sāgaḍ 'double-canoe' Rebus: sangataras. संगतराश lit. 'to collect stones, stone-cutter, mason.'*

ḍato = claws of crab (Santali) Rebus: *dhātu* 'mineral ore' Duplicated: dula 'pair' Rebus: dul 'cast metal' Thus, mineral ore castings.

 *kuṭila* 'bent' CDIAL 3230 kuṭi— in cmpd. 'curve', *kuṭika*— 'bent' MBh. Rebus: *kuṭila, katthīl* = bronze (8 parts copper and 2 parts tin)

dula 'two' Rebus: dul 'cast metal' Thus cast bronze.

kəṭhā´r, kc. *kuṭhār* m. ' granary, storeroom '(WPah.)(CDIAL 3550). *koṭhārī m.* ' storekeeper'

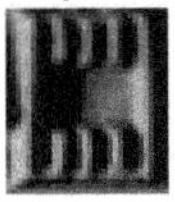 (Gujarati)(CDIAL 3551) Thus, storeroom (of) *kolom* 'three' Rebus: *kolami* 'smithy, forge'. Dula 'pair' Rebus: dul 'cast metal' Thus, together *dul kolami kuṭhār* 'metal smithy castings storeroom'

kamaḍha 'archer' Rebus: *kammaṭa* 'mint, coiner'.

 *kolmo* 'paddy plant' Rebus: *kolami* 'smithy, forge' Vikalpa: *mogge* 'sprout, bud' Rebus: *mũh* 'ingot' (Santali) dolu 'plant of shoot height' Rebus: dul 'cast metal'

 *aḍaren* 'lid of pot' Rebus: aduru 'unsmelted, native metal'

 Ligature: two peaks: mēḍu height, rising ground, hillock (Kannada) Rebus: *meḍ* 'iron' (Ho.) dula 'pair' Rebus: dul 'cast metal' PLUS |||| Numeral 4: gaṇḍa 'four' Rebus: kaṇḍa 'furnace, fire-altar' (Santali)

 water-carrier hieroglyph *kuṭi*; Rebus: *kuṭhi* 'smelter furnace'.

 m102A

खोंड [khōṇḍa] m A young bull, a bullcalf. (Marathi) Rebus: kõdār 'turner' (Bengali); कोंद kōnda 'engraver, lapidary setting or infixing gems' (Marathi) G. sãghāṛɔ m. 'lathe' ; संघाट joinery; M. sāgaḍ 'double-canoe' Rebus: sangataras. संगतराश lit. 'to collect stones, stone-cutter, mason.'

ḍato = claws of crab (Santali) Rebus: *dhātu* 'mineral ore' Duplicated: dula 'pair' Rebus: dul 'cast metal' Thus, mineral ore castings. PLUS ligature:

 mēḍu height, rising ground, hillock (Kannada) Rebus: *mẽṛhẽt, meḍ* 'iron' (Munda.Ho.)

 *kuṭila* 'bent' CDIAL 3230 kuṭi— in cmpd. 'curve', *kuṭika—* 'bent' MBh. Rebus: *kuṭila, katthīl* = bronze (8 parts copper and 2 parts tin)

kolom 'three' Rebus: kolami 'smithy, forge'

  water-carrier hieroglyph *kuṭi*; Rebus: *kuṭhi* 'smelter furnace'. PLUS 'rim of jar':

 kanka 'rim of jar' Rebus: karṇīka 'account (scribe)' karṇī 'supercargo'

m855a *खोंड [khōṇḍa] m A young bull, a bullcalf. (Marathi) Rebus: kõdār 'turner' (Bengali); कोंद kōnda 'engraver, lapidary setting or infixing gems' (Marathi) G. sãghāṛɔ m. 'lathe' ; संघाट joinery; M. sāgaḍ 'double-canoe' Rebus: sangataras. संगतराश lit. 'to collect stones, stone-cutter, mason.'*

ḍato = claws of crab (Santali) Rebus: *dhātu* 'mineral ore' Duplicated: dula 'pair' Rebus: dul 'cast metal' Thus, mineral ore castings.

 *dāṭu* 'cross'(Telugu) Rebus: *dhatu* 'mineral' (Santali).

kanac 'corner' Rebus: *kañcu* 'bronze' sal 'splinter' Rebus: sal 'workshop'

 सांड [sāṇḍa] *f* (षद S) An outlet for superfluous water (as through a dam or mound); a sluice, a floodvent. Rebus: सांडणी [sāṇḍaṇī] *f* (H) An instrument of goldsmiths. It is

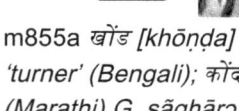

hooked or curved at the extremity; and is used to draw things out of the fire.
सांठा [*sāṇṭhā*] *m* (संचय S) A collection, heap, hoard, store, stock.साटें [*sāṭēṃ*] *n* (संचय S) A whole investment; the total quantity of merchandise (brought to market by one merchant).

kolmo 'paddy plant' Rebus: *kolami* 'smithy, forge' Vikalpa: *mogge* 'sprout, bud' Rebus: *mũh* 'ingot' (Santali) dolu 'plant of shoot height' Rebus: dul 'cast metal'

kana, kanac = corner (Santali); Rebus: *kañcu* = bronze (Telugu) PLUS खांडा [*khāṇḍā*] *m* A jag, notch, or indentation (as upon the edge of a tool or weapon). Rebus: *kāṇḍa* 'tools, pots and pans and metal-ware' Thus, bronze metalware.

Fowl hieroglyphs: கோழி kōḻi, *n.* < கொழு-. [T. *kōḍi*, K. M. *kōḷi*, Tu. *kōri.*] 1. Gallinaceous fowl; குக்குடம். குப்பை கிளைப்போவாக் கோழிபோல் (நாலடி, 341).Rebus 1: *koḍ* 'workshop' (Kuwi) Rebus 2: *khōḍ* m. 'pit', *khōḍü* f. 'small pit' (Kashmiri. CDIAL 3947).

m132A *खोंड [khōṇḍa] m A young bull, a bullcalf. (Marathi) Rebus: kõdār 'turner' (Bengali); कोंद kōnda 'engraver, lapidary setting or infixing gems' (Marathi) G. sãghāṛɔ m. 'lathe' ; संघाट joinery; M. sãgaḍ 'double-canoe' Rebus: sangataras. संगतराश lit. 'to collect stones, stone-cutter, mason.'*

ḍato = claws of crab (Santali) Rebus: *dhātu* 'mineral ore' Duplicated: dula 'pair' Rebus: dul 'cast metal' Thus, mineral ore castings. PLUS ligature:

mēḍu height, rising ground, hillock (Kannada) Rebus: *mẽṛhẽt, meḍ* 'iron' (Munda.Ho.) kolom 'three' Rebus: kolami 'smithy, forge'

water-carrier hieroglyph *kuṭi*; Rebus: *kuṭhi* 'smelter furnace'. PLUS 'rim of jar':

kanka 'rim of jar' Rebus: karṇīka 'account (scribe)' karṇī 'supercargo'

m1685a *खोंड [khōṇḍa] 'turner' (Bengali); कोंद (Marathi) G. sãghāṛɔ Rebus: sangataras.*

m A young bull, a bullcalf. (Marathi) Rebus: kõdār kōnda 'engraver, lapidary setting or infixing gems' m. 'lathe' ; संघाट joinery; M. sãgaḍ 'double-canoe' संगतराश lit. 'to collect stones, stone-cutter, mason.'

ḍato = claws of crab (Santali) Rebus: *dhātu* 'mineral ore' Duplicated: dula 'pair' Rebus: dul 'cast metal' Thus, mineral ore castings. PLUS ligature:

mēḍu height, rising ground, hillock (Kannada) Rebus: *mẽṛhẽt, meḍ* 'iron' (Munda.Ho.) kolom 'three' Rebus: kolami 'smithy, forge'

kuṭila 'bent' CDIAL 3230 kuṭi— in cmpd. 'curve', *kuṭika—* 'bent' MBh. Rebus: *kuṭila, katthīl* = bronze (8 parts copper and 2 parts tin) Duplicated: dula 'pair' Rebus: dul 'cast metal' Thus, cast bronze.

kuṭila 'bent' CDIAL 3230 kuṭi— in cmpd. 'curve', *kuṭika—* 'bent' MBh. Rebus: *kuṭila, katthīl* = bronze (8 parts copper and 2 parts tin) Triplicated: kolom 'three' Rebus: kolami

'smithy, forge'. Thus bronze smithy.

bhaṭa 'warrior' (Sanskrit) Rebus: *baṭa* a kind of iron (Gujarati). Rebus: *bhaṭa* 'furnace' (Santali)

Circumscript: *kuṭila* 'bent' CDIAL 3230 kuṭi— in cmpd. 'curve', *kuṭika*— 'bent' MBh. Rebus: *kuṭila, katthīl* = bronze (8 parts copper and 2 parts tin) Duplicated: dula 'pair' Rebus: dul 'cast metal' Thus, furnace bronze castings.

kanka 'rim of jar' Rebus: *karṇīka* 'account (scribe)' *karṇī* 'supercargo'

meḍ 'body' Rebus: *meḍ* 'iron' (Ho.) काठी [kāṭhī] *f* (काष्ट S) 'frame or structure of the body' (Marathi) Rebus: खंडी [khaṇḍī] measure of weight (Marathi) *கண்டி; kaṇṭi, n. < Mhr. khaṇḍil. [T. Tu. khaṇḍi, M. kaṇḍi.]* Candy, a weight, stated to be roughly equivalent to 500 lbs.

m1685a *खोंड [khōṇḍa] m A young bull, a bullcalf. (Marathi) Rebus: kõdār 'turner' (Bengali); कोंद kōnda 'engraver, lapidary setting or infixing gems' (Marathi) G. sãghārɔ m. 'lathe' ; संघाट joinery; M. sãgaḍ 'double-canoe' Rebus: sangataras. संगतराश lit. 'to collect stones, stone-cutter, mason.'*

ḍato = claws of crab (Santali) Rebus: *dhātu* 'mineral ore' Duplicated: dula 'pair' Rebus: dul 'cast metal' Thus, mineral ore castings. PLUS ligature:

mēḍu height, rising ground, hillock (Kannada) Rebus: *mẽṛhẽt, meḍ* 'iron' (Munda.Ho.)

kuṭila 'bent' CDIAL 3230 kuṭi— in cmpd. 'curve', *kuṭika*— 'bent' MBh. Rebus: *kuṭila, katthīl* = bronze (8 parts copper and 2 parts tin) Duplicated: dula 'pair' Rebus: dul 'cast metal' Thus, cast bronze.

kuṭila 'bent' CDIAL 3230 kuṭi— in cmpd. 'curve', *kuṭika*— 'bent' MBh. Rebus: *kuṭila, katthīl* = bronze (8 parts copper and 2 parts tin) Triplicated: kolom 'three' Rebus: kolami 'smithy, forge'. Thus bronze smithy.

| *koḍa* 'one' Rebus: *koḍ* 'workshop'

kolom 'three' Rebus: kolami 'smithy, forge' Duplicated: dula 'pair' Rebus: dul 'cast metal' Thus smithy for castings.

ayo 'fish' Rebus: *aya* 'iron' *ayas* 'metal'

kanka 'rim of jar' Rebus: *karṇīka* 'account (scribe)' *karṇī* 'supercargo'

meḍ 'body' Rebus: *meḍ* 'iron' (Ho.) काठी [kāṭhī] *f* (काष्ट S) 'frame or structure of the body' (Marathi) Rebus: खंडी [khaṇḍī] measure of weight (Marathi) *கண்டி; kaṇṭi, n. < Mhr. khaṇḍil. [T. Tu. khaṇḍi, M. kaṇḍi.]* Candy, a weight, stated to be roughly equivalent to 500 lbs.

h473a *खोंड [khōṇḍa] m A young bull, a bullcalf. (Marathi) Rebus: kõdār 'turner' (Bengali); कोंद kōnda 'engraver, lapidary setting or infixing gems' (Marathi) G.*

sãghāṛɔ m. 'lathe' ; संघाट joinery; M. sãgaḍ 'double-canoe' Rebus: sangataras. संगतराश lit. 'to collect stones, stone-cutter, mason.'

ḍato = claws of crab (Santali) Rebus: *dhātu* 'mineral ore' Duplicated: dula 'pair' Rebus: dul 'cast metal' Thus, mineral ore castings. PLUS ligature:

mēḍu height, rising ground, hillock (Kannada) Rebus: *mẽṛhẽt, meḍ* 'iron' (Munda.Ho.)

सांड [sāṇḍa] *f* (षद S) An outlet for superfluous water (as through a dam or mound); a sluice, a floodvent. Rebus: सांडणी [sāṇḍaṇī] *f* (H) An instrument of goldsmiths. It is hooked or curved at the extremity; and is used to draw things out of the fire. सांठा [*sāṇṭhā*] *m* (संचय S) A collection, heap, hoard, store, stock.साटें [*sāṭēṃ*] *n* (संचय S) A whole investment; the total quantity of merchandise (brought to market by one merchant).

kanac 'corner' Rebus: *kañcu* 'bronze'

h7a

खोंड [khōṇḍa] m A young bull, a bullcalf. (Marathi) Rebus: kōdār 'turner' (Bengali); कोंद kōnda 'engraver, lapidary setting or infixing gems' (Marathi) G. sãghāṛɔ m. 'lathe' ; संघाट joinery; M. sãgaḍ 'double-canoe' Rebus: sangataras. संगतराश lit. 'to collect stones, stone-cutter, mason.'

kuṭila 'bent' CDIAL 3230 kuṭi— in cmpd. 'curve', *kuṭika—* 'bent' MBh. Rebus: *kuṭila, katthīl* = bronze (8 parts copper and 2 parts tin) Ligatured to: *dhāḷ* 'a slope'; 'inclination of a plane' (G.); *ḍhāḷiyum* = adj. sloping, inclining (G.) Rebus: *ḍhālako* = a large metal ingot (G.) *ḍhālakī* = a metal heated and poured into a mould; a solid piece of metal; an ingot (Gujarati) Thus, bronze ingots. PLUS

ḍato = claws of crab (Santali) Rebus: *dhātu* 'mineral ore' Duplicated: dula 'pair' Rebus: dul 'cast metal' Thus, mineral ore castings.

'notch': खांडा [*khāṇḍā*] *m* A jag, notch, or indentation (as upon the edge of a tool or weapon). Rebus: *kāṇḍa* 'tools, pots and pans and metal-ware' Thus, bronze metalware castings.

dāṭu 'cross'(Telugu) Rebus: *dhatu* 'mineral' (Santali).

ḍhanga = a crook used for pulling down the branches of trees, for goats, sheep and camels (P.) Rebus:*ḍhangar* blacksmith'

kuṭila 'bent' CDIAL 3230 kuṭi— in cmpd. 'curve', *kuṭika—* 'bent' MBh. Rebus: *kuṭila, katthīl* = bronze (8 parts copper and 2 parts tin) Duplicated: dula 'pair' Rebus: dul 'cast metal' Thus, cast bronze.

Sign hieroglyph: 'a crook used for pulling down the branches of trees'

h172A *ḍhanga* = a crook used for pulling down the branches of trees, for goats, sheep and camels (P.) Rebus:*ḍhangar* blacksmith'

kanka 'rim of jar' Rebus: *karṇīka* 'account (scribe)' *karṇī* 'supercargo' Thus, smithy supercargo.

khareḍo = a currycomb (Gujarati) खरारा [*kharārā*] *m* (H) A currycomb. 2 Currying a horse. (Marathi) Rebus: करडा [*karaḍā*] Hard from alloy--iron, silver &c. (Marathi) *kharādī* ' turner' (Gujarati)

dula 'pair' Rebus: *dul* 'cast (metal)' PLUS*kana, kanac* = corner (Santali); Rebus: *kañcu* = bronze (Telugu) Thus, cast bronze.

m888A *खोंड [khōṇḍa] m A young bull, a bullcalf. (Marathi) Rebus: kōdār 'turner' (Bengali); कोंद kōnda 'engraver, lapidary setting or infixing gems' (Marathi) G. sãghāṛɔ m. 'lathe' ; संघाट joinery; M. sãgaḍ 'double-canoe' Rebus: sangataras. संगतराश lit. 'to collect stones, stone-cutter, mason.'*

ḍhanga = a crook used for pulling down the branches of trees, for goats, sheep and camels (P.) Rebus:*ḍhangar* blacksmith'

kanka 'rim of jar' Rebus: *karṇīka* 'account (scribe)' *karṇī* 'supercargo' Thus, smithy supercargo.

aya kammaṭa.'coiner, mint alloy'

ayo 'fish' Rebus: *aya* 'iron' *ayas* 'metal'

kānḍa 'arrow' (Sanskrit) Rebus:*khānḍa* 'tools, pots and pans, metal-ware'. Rebus 2: kaṇḍ 'fire-altar' (Santali)

h101a *ḍhanga* = a crook used for pulling down the branches of trees, for goats, sheep and camels (P.) Rebus:*ḍhangar* blacksmith'

dula 'pair' Rebus: dul 'cast metal' *mogge* 'sprout, bud' Rebus: *mũh* 'ingot' (Santali) Thus, cast metal ingot.

kanka 'rim of jar' Rebus: *karṇīka* 'account (scribe)' *karṇī* 'supercargo'

h758A

h757A *ḍhanga* = a crook used for pulling down the branches of trees, for goats, sheep and camels (P.) Rebus:*ḍhangar* blacksmith'

bhaṭa 'warrior' (Sanskrit) Rebus: *baṭa* a kind of iron (Gujarati). Rebus: *bhaṭa* 'furnace' (Santali)

kanka 'rim of jar' Rebus: *karṇīka* 'account (scribe)' *karṇī* 'supercargo'

  Sign hieroglyph; ‘Antelope with short tail’ stylized as a ‘quadruped’ sign:

m1276A ranku ‘antelope’ Rebus: ranku ‘tin’

  *kanka* ‘rim of jar’ Rebus: *karṇīka* ‘account (scribe)’ *karṇī* ‘supercargo’ ‘notch’: खांडा [*khāṇḍā*] *m* A jag, notch, or indentation (as upon the edge of a tool or weapon). Rebus: *kāṇḍa* ‘tools, pots and pans and metal-ware’

aya aḍaren (homonym: aduru)‘alloy native metal’

 water-carrier hieroglyph *kuṭi*; Rebus: *kuṭhi* ‘smelter furnace’.

PLUS

kāṇḍa ‘arrow’ (Sanskrit) Rebus:*khāṇḍa* ‘tools, pots and pans, metal-ware’. Rebus 2: kaṇḍ 'fire-altar' (Santali)

 m0116 Zebu. Native metal smith guild.

ranku ‘antelope’ Rebus: ranku ‘tin’

dulo ‘hole’ Rebus: dul ‘cast metal’

 *kanka* ‘rim of jar’ Rebus: *karṇīka* ‘account (scribe)’ *karṇī* ‘supercargo’ PLUS infixed ‘notch’: खांडा [*khāṇḍā*] *m* A jag, notch, or indentation (as upon the edge of a tool or weapon). Rebus: *kāṇḍa* ‘tools, pots and pans and metal-ware’

kāṇḍa ‘arrow’ (Sanskrit) Rebus:*khāṇḍa* ‘tools, pots and pans, metal-ware’. Rebus 2: kaṇḍ 'fire-altar' (Santali) PLUS ‘notch’: खांडा [*khāṇḍā*] *m* A jag, notch, or indentation (as upon the edge of a tool or weapon). Rebus: ‘metalware’

 |||| Numeral 4: gaṇḍa 'four' Rebus: kaṇḍa 'furnace, fire-altar' (Santali) dula ‘pair’ Rebus: dul ‘cast metal’

ḍato = claws of crab (Santali) Rebus: *dhātu* ‘mineral ore’ Duplicated: dula ‘pair’ Rebus: dul ‘cast metal’ Thus, mineral ore castings.

 *kanac* ‘corner’ Rebus: *kañcu* ‘bronze’

 m926a *खोंड [khōṇḍa] m A young bull, a bullcalf. (Marathi) Rebus: kõdār ‘turner’ (Bengali); कोंद kōnda ‘engraver, lapidary setting or infixing gems’ (Marathi) G. sãghāṛɔ m. ‘lathe’ ; संघाट joinery; M. sãgaḍ ‘double-canoe’ Rebus: sangataras. संगतराश lit. ‘to collect stones, stone-cutter, mason.’*

khar ‘donkey’ Rebus: khara ‘blacksmith’

 *kanka* 'rim of jar' Rebus: *karṇīka* 'account (scribe)' *karṇī* 'supercargo' PLUS infixed 'notch': खांडा [*khāṇḍā*] *m* A jag, notch, or indentation (as upon the edge of a tool or weapon). Rebus: *kāṇḍa* 'tools, pots and pans and metal-ware' Thus, metalware supercargo.

 *kana, kanac* = corner (Santali); Rebus: *kañcu* = bronze (Telugu) PLUS खांडा [*khāṇḍā*] *m* A jag, notch, or indentation (as upon the edge of a tool or weapon). Rebus: *kāṇḍa* 'tools, pots and pans and metal-ware' Thus, bronze metalware. Duplicated: dula 'pair' Rebus: dul 'cast metal' Thus cast bronze metalware.

Circumscript:

 *kuṭila* 'bent' CDIAL 3230 kuṭi— in cmpd. 'curve', *kuṭika*— 'bent' MBh. Rebus: *kuṭila, katthīl* = bronze (8 parts copper and 2 parts tin) Duplicated: dula 'pair' Rebus: dul 'cast metal' Thus, cast bronze. INFIXED: karaṇḍa 'duck' (Sanskrit) karaṛa 'a very large aquatic bird' (Sindhi) Rebus: करडा [*karaḍā*] Hard from alloy--iron, silver &c. (Marathi) *kharādī* ' turner' (Gujarati) Thus, hard alloy, cast bronze.

 *kanka* 'rim of jar' Rebus: *karṇīka* 'account (scribe)' *karṇī* 'supercargo'

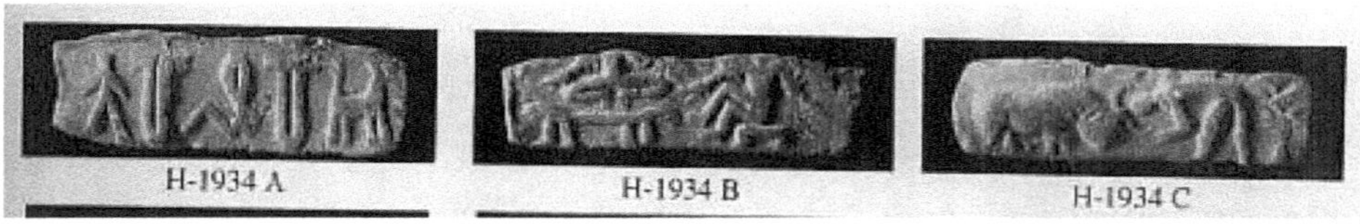

h1934A

Side A: ranku 'antelope' Rebus: ranku 'tin' PLUS *Kur.* xolā tail. *Malt.* qoli id. (DEDR 2135). Rebus: kolhe 'smelter' Thus, tin smelter or castings.

 *kanka* 'rim of jar' Rebus: *karṇīka* 'account (scribe)' *karṇī* 'supercargo'

 *baraḍo* = spine; backbone (Tulu) Rebus: *baran, bharat* 'mixed alloys' (5 copper, 4 zinc and 1 tin) (Punjabi)

 *kanka* 'rim of jar' Rebus: *karṇīka* 'account (scribe)' *karṇī* 'supercargo'

 *meḍ* 'body' Rebus: *meḍ* 'iron' (Ho.) काठी [kāṭhī] *f* (काष्ट S) 'frame or structure of the body' (Marathi) Rebus: खंडी [khaṇḍī] measure of weight (Marathi) *கண்டி; kaṇṭi, n. < Mhr. khaṇḍil. [T. Tu. khaṇḍi, M. kaṇḍi.]* Candy, a weight, stated to be roughly equivalent to 500 lbs.

Side B: *kamaḍha* 'penance' Rebus: *kammaṭa* 'mint, coiner'. *kaṇḍo* 'stool, seat' Rebus: *kāṇḍa* 'metalware' *kaṇḍa* 'fire-altar'

Side C: *balad* m. ' ox ', gng. *bald*, (Ku.) *barad*, id. (N. Tarai) Rebus: *bharat* (5 copper, 4 zinc and 1 tin)(Punjabi) PLUS ṭakkarā f. ' blow on the head ' Rājat. Pk. *ṭakkara* -- m. ' collision ', K. *ṭakara* m.; S. *ṭakaru* m. ' knocking the head against anything, butting ', *ṭakiraṇu* ' to knock against, encounter, be compared with '; L.*ṭakkaraṇ* ' to meet, agree '; P. *ṭakkar* f. ' pushing, knocking ', *ṭakkarṇā* ' to collide, meet '; Ku. *ṭakkar* ' shock, jerk, loss '; N. *ṭakar* ' obstacle, collision '(CDIAL 5424) Rebus: tagaram 'tin' Rebus: *ḍhangar* blacksmith' Rebus: damgar 'merchant' . Thus, alloy of bharat (copper + zinc + tin) PLUS tin (mineral), that is, adding tin to copper+ pewter to create *baroṭi* 'twelve' *bhārata* 'a factitious alloy of copper, pewter, tin' (Marathi)

m213A

खोंड [khōṇḍa] m A young bull, a bullcalf. (Marathi) Rebus: kōdār 'turner' (Bengali); कोंद kōnda 'engraver, lapidary setting or infixing gems' (Marathi) G. sãghāṛɔ m. 'lathe' ; संघाट joinery; M. sãgaḍ 'double-canoe' Rebus: sangataras. संगतराश lit. 'to collect stones, stone-cutter, mason.'

khar 'donkey' Rebus: khara 'blacksmith'

kolmo 'paddy plant' Rebus: *kolami* 'smithy, forge' Vikalpa: *mogge* 'sprout, bud' Rebus: *mũh* 'ingot' (Santali) dolu 'plant of shoot height' Rebus: dul 'cast metal'

sal 'splinter' Rebus: sal 'workshop' Thus workshop for castings.

loa 'ficus religiosa' Rebus: *lo* 'iron' (Sanskrit) PLUS unique ligatures: लोखंड [lōkhaṇḍa] *n* (लोह S) Iron. लोखंडाचे चणे खावविणें or चारणें To oppress grievously.लोखंडकाम [lōkhaṇḍakāma] *n* Iron work; that portion (of a building, machine &c.) which consists of iron. 2 The business of an ironsmith.लोखंडी [lōkhaṇḍī] *a* (लोखंड) Composed of iron; relating to iron. (Marathi)

kanka 'rim of jar' Rebus: *karṇīka* 'account (scribe)' *karṇī* 'supercargo'

Unnumbered khar 'donkey' Rebus: khara 'blacksmith

kolmo 'paddy plant' Rebus: *kolami* 'smithy, forge' Vikalpa: *mogge* 'sprout, bud' Rebus: *mũh* 'ingot' (Santali) dolu 'plant of shoot height' Rebus: dul 'cast metal'

loa 'ficus religiosa' Rebus: *lo* 'iron' (Sanskrit) PLUS unique ligatures: लोखंड [lōkhaṇḍa] *n* (लोह S) Iron. लोखंडाचे चणे खावविणें or चारणें To oppress grievously.लोखंडकाम [lōkhaṇḍakāma] *n* Iron work; that portion (of a building, machine &c.) which consists of iron. 2 The business of an ironsmith.लोखंडी [lōkhaṇḍī] *a* (लोखंड) Composed of iron; relating to iron. (Marathi)

kanka 'rim of jar' Rebus: *karṇīka* 'account (scribe)' *karṇī* 'supercargo'

सांड [sāṇḍa] *f* (षद S) An outlet for superfluous water (as through a dam or mound); a sluice, a floodvent. Rebus: सांडणी [sāṇḍaṇī] *f* (H) An instrument of goldsmiths. It is hooked or curved at the extremity; and is used to draw things out of the fire. सांठा [*sāṇṭhā*] *m* (संचय S) A collection, heap, hoard, store, stock.साटें [*sāṭēṃ*] *n* (संचय S) A whole investment; the total quantity of merchandise (brought to market by one merchant).

muka 'ladle' (Tamil)(DEDR 4887) Rebus: *mũh* 'ingot' (Santali) *baṭa* = rimless pot (Kannada) Rebus:) *baṭa* = a kind of iron (G.)) *bhaṭa* furnace (Gujarati) Thus, iron ingot.

 *kanka* 'rim of jar' Rebus: *karṇīka* 'account (scribe)' *karṇī* 'supercargo'

 mēḍu height, rising ground, hillock (Kannada) Rebus: *mẽṛhẽt, meḍ* 'iron' (Munda.Ho.)
aya kāṇḍa 'alloy metalware'

 *cīmara* 'black ant' Rebus: *cīmara* 'copper'. *cīmara kāra* -- ' coppersmith '

kamaḍha 'archer' Rebus: *kampaṭṭam* = mint (Ta.) ; *kammaṭa* 'coiner, mint' (Telugu)

 h22a *खोंड [khōṇḍa] m A young bull, a bullcalf. (Marathi) Rebus: kõdār 'turner' (Bengali); कोंद kōnda 'engraver, lapidary setting or infixing gems' (Marathi) G. sãghāṛɔ m. 'lathe' ; संघाट joinery; M. sãgaḍ 'double-canoe' Rebus: sangataras. संगतराश lit. 'to collect stones, stone-cutter, mason.'*

ranku 'antelope' Rebus: ranku 'tin'

 *kolmo* 'paddy plant' Rebus: *kolami* 'smithy, forge' Vikalpa: *mogge* 'sprout, bud' Rebus: *mũh* 'ingot' (Santali) dolu 'plant of shoot height' Rebus: dul 'cast metal'
sal 'splinter' Rebus: sal 'workshop'

 *dula* 'pair' Rebus: *dul* 'cast (metal)' PLUS*kana, kanac* = corner (Santali); Rebus: *kañcu* = bronze (Telugu) PLUS infixed kolmo 'paddy plant' Rebus: kolami 'smithy, forge'. Thus, cast bronze smithy, forge. Or, *mogge* 'sprout, bud' Rebus: *mũh* 'ingot' (Santali)Thus, cast bronze ingot. Read as: *kañcu dul mũh 'bronze cast ingot'*
ayo ḍhālako 'alloy metal ingot'

ranku 'antelope' Rebus: ranku 'tin'

 *kuṭila* 'bent' CDIAL 3230 kuṭi— in cmpd. 'curve', *kuṭika*— 'bent' MBh. Rebus: *kuṭila, katthīl* = bronze (8 parts copper and 2 parts tin)

 *kanka* 'rim of jar' Rebus: *karṇīka* 'account (scribe)' *karṇī* 'supercargo'

 m880a *खोंड [khōṇḍa] m A young bull, a bullcalf. (Marathi) Rebus: kõdār 'turner' (Bengali); कोंद kōnda 'engraver, lapidary setting or infixing gems' (Marathi) G. sãghāṛɔ m. 'lathe' ; संघाट joinery; M. sãgaḍ 'double-canoe' Rebus: sangataras. संगतराश lit. 'to collect stones, stone-cutter, mason.'*

ranku 'antelope' Rebus: ranku 'tin'

 *kanac* 'corner' Rebus: *kañcu* 'bronze'

 *kanka* 'rim of jar' Rebus: *karṇīka* 'account (scribe)' *karṇī* 'supercargo'

 *kanac* 'corner' Rebus: *kañcu* 'bronze' Duplicated: dula 'pair' Rebus: dul 'cast metal' Thus cast bronze.

 *kanka* 'rim of jar' Rebus: *karṇīka* 'account (scribe)' *karṇī* 'supercargo'

h2190A Side A: ranku

antelope' Rebus: ranku 'tin'

 *kanka* 'rim of jar' Rebus: *karṇīka* 'account (scribe)' *karṇī* 'supercargo'

 *meḍ* 'body' Rebus: *meḍ* 'iron' (Ho.) काठी [kāṭhī] *f* (काष्ट S) 'frame or structure of the body' (Marathi) Rebus: खंडी [khaṇḍī] measure of weight (Marathi) கண்டி; *kaṇṭi, n. < Mhr. khaṇḍil. [T. Tu. khaṇḍi, M. kaṇḍi.]* Candy, a weight, stated to be roughly equivalent to 500 lbs.

Side B:

 *kanac* 'corner' Rebus: *kañcu* 'bronze'kolom 'three' Rebus: kolami 'smithy, forge' Thus, bronze smithy.

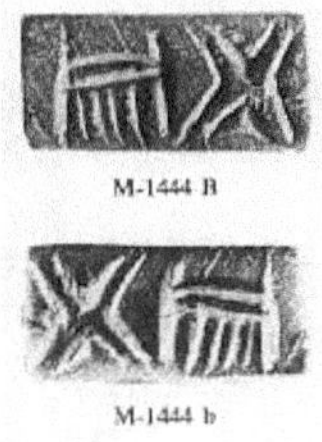

m1444B, b ranku 'antelope' Rebus: ranku 'tin'

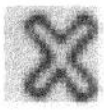 *dāṭu* 'cross'(Telugu) Rebus: *dhatu* 'mineral' (Santali).

m1838a *खोंड [khōṇḍa] m A young bull, a bullcalf. (Marathi) Rebus: kõdār 'turner' (Bengali); कोंद kōnda 'engraver, lapidary setting or infixing gems' (Marathi) G. sãghārɔ m. 'lathe' ; संघाट joinery; M. sãgaḍ 'double-canoe' Rebus: sangataras. संगतराश lit. 'to collect stones, stone-cutter, mason.'*

ranku 'antelope' Rebus: ranku 'tin'

 *kuṭila* 'bent' CDIAL 3230 kuṭi— in cmpd. 'curve', *kuṭika—* 'bent' MBh. Rebus: *kuṭila, katthīl* = bronze (8 parts copper and 2 parts tin)

 *kolmo* 'paddy plant' Rebus: *kolami* 'smithy, forge' Vikalpa: *mogge* 'sprout, bud' Rebus: *mũh* 'ingot' (Santali) dolu 'plant of shoot height' Rebus: dul 'cast metal'

m1350A ranku 'anelope' Rebus: ranku 'tin.

kuṭila 'bent'  CDIAL 3230 kuṭi— in cmpd. 'curve', *kuṭika—* 'bent' MBh. Rebus: *kuṭila, katthīl* = bronze (8 parts copper and 2 parts tin)

 *kanka* 'rim of jar' Rebus: *karṇīka* 'account (scribe)' *karṇī* 'supercargo' PLUS infixed: sal 'splinter' Rebus: sal 'workshop' Thus, workshop supercargo.

 *dula* 'pair' Rebus: *dul* 'cast (metal)' PLUS*kana, kanac* = corner (Santali); Rebus: *kañcu* = bronze (Telugu) PLUS infixed kolmo 'paddy plant' Rebus: kolami 'smithy, forge'. Thus, cast bronze smithy, forge. Or, *mogge* 'sprout, bud' Rebus: *mũh* 'ingot' (Santali)Thus, cast bronze ingot. Read as: *kañcu dul mũh 'bronze cast ingot'*

aḍar 'harrow'; rebus: *aduru* 'native unsmelted metal'

ayo 'fish' Rebus: *aya* 'iron' *ayas* 'metal'

beads: Pa. kandi (pl. -l) necklace, beads. Ga. (Punjabi) kandi (pl. -l) bead, (pl.) necklace; (S.2) kandiṭ bead. (DEDR 1215) Rebus: *கண்டி; kaṇṭi, n. < Mhr. khaṇḍil. [T. Tu. khaṇḍi, M. kaṇḍi.] 1. Candy, a weight, stated to be roughly equivalent to 500 lbs.; பாரமென் னும் நிறையளவு.* खंडीगणती or खंडोगणती [khaṇḍīgaṇatī or khaṇḍōgaṇatī] *ad* By candies; counting or reckoning by candies. खंडीवारी [khaṇḍīvārī] *ad* By scores, heaps, candies. खंडी [khaṇḍī] Applied to a great quantity; as खंडीभर पोरें, खंडीभर मेंढ्या, खंडीभर काम, खंडीभर बोलतो-लिहितो&c

kolmo 'paddy plant' Rebus: *kolami* 'smithy, forge' Vikalpa: *mogge* 'sprout, bud' Rebus: *mũh* 'ingot' (Santali) dolu 'plant of shoot height' Rebus: dul 'cast metal'

M-935 A

m935A *खोंड [khōṇḍa] m A young bull, a bullcalf. (Marathi) Rebus: kõdār 'turner' (Bengali); कोंद kōnda 'engraver, lapidary setting or infixing gems' (Marathi) G. sãghārɔ m. 'lathe' ; संघाट joinery; M. sãgaḍ 'double-canoe' Rebus: sangataras. संगतराश lit. 'to collect stones, stone-cutter, mason.'*

ranku 'antelope' Rebus: ranku 'tin'

kuṭila 'bent' CDIAL 3230 kuṭi— in cmpd. 'curve', *kuṭika—* 'bent' MBh. Rebus: *kuṭila, katthīl* = bronze (8 parts copper and 2 parts tin)

kanka 'rim of jar' Rebus: *karṇīka* 'account (scribe)' *karṇī* 'supercargo'

m120a *खोंड [khōṇḍa] m A young bull, a bullcalf. (Marathi) Rebus: kõdār 'turner' (Bengali); कोंद kōnda 'engraver, lapidary setting or infixing gems' (Marathi) G. sãghārɔ m. 'lathe' ; संघाट joinery; M. sãgaḍ 'double-canoe' Rebus: sangataras 'stone-cutter, mason'*

ranku 'antelope' Rebus: ranku 'tin'

dula 'pair' Rebus: *dul* 'cast (metal)' PLUS*kana, kanac* = corner (Santali); Rebus: *kañcu* = bronze (Telugu) Thus, cast bronze.

kanka 'rim of jar' Rebus: *karṇīka* 'account (scribe)' *karṇī* 'supercargo' PLUS infixed 'notch': खांडा [*khāṇḍā*] *m* A jag, notch, or indentation (as upon the edge of a tool or weapon). Rebus: *kāṇḍa* 'tools, pots and pans and metal-ware'

सांड [sāṇḍa] *f* (षद S) An outlet for superfluous water (as through a dam or mound); a sluice, a floodvent. Rebus: सांडणी [sāṇḍaṇī] *f* (H) An instrument of goldsmiths. It is hooked or curved at the extremity; and is used to draw things out of the fire.

सांठा [*sāṇṭhā*] *m* (संचय S) A collection, heap, hoard, store, stock.साटें [*sāṭēṃ*] *n* (संचय S) A whole investment; the total quantity of merchandise (brought to market by one merchant).

bhaṭa 'warrior' (Sanskrit) Rebus: *baṭa* a kind of iron (Gujarati). Rebus: *bhaṭa* 'furnace' (Santali)

kanka 'rim of jar' Rebus: *karṇīka* 'account (scribe)' *karṇī* 'supercargo'

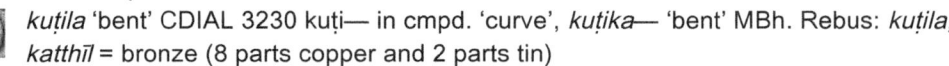

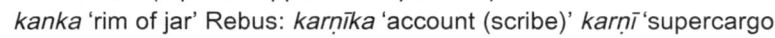

M-1336 a

INFIXED

m1336a ranku 'antelope' Rebus: ranku 'tin' ranku 'liquid measure' Rebus: ranku 'tin'

kanka 'rim of jar' Rebus: *karṇīka* 'account (scribe)' *karṇī* 'supercargo' kolom 'three' Rebus: kolami 'smithy, forge'

m39a

खोंड [khōṇḍa] m A young bull, a bullcalf. (Marathi) Rebus: kõdār 'turner' (Bengali); कोंद kōnda 'engraver, lapidary setting or infixing gems' (Marathi) G. sãghāṛɔ m. 'lathe' ; संघाट joinery; M. sãgaḍ 'double-canoe' Rebus: sangataras. संगतराश lit. 'to collect stones, stone-cutter, mason.'

ranku 'antelope' Rebus: ranku 'tin'

cīmara 'black ant' Rebus: *cīmara* 'copper'. *cīmara kāra* -- ' coppersmith ' sal 'splinter' Rebus: sal 'workshop' खांडा [*khāṇḍā*] *m* A jag, notch, or indentation (as upon the edge of a tool or weapon). Rebus: *kāṇḍa* 'tools, pots and pans and metal-ware'

aya aḍaren (homonym: aduru)'alloy native metal'

aya kammaṭa.'coiner, mint alloy'

muka 'ladle' (Tamil)(DEDR 4887) Rebus: *mũh* 'ingot' (Santali) *baṭa* = rimless pot (Kannada) Rebus:) *baṭa* = a kind of iron (G.)) *bhaṭa* furnace (Gujarati) Thus, iron ingot.

'Sign hieroglyph: 'division of field':

L-86 a

Lothal 86A | *koḍa* 'one' Rebus: *koḍ* 'workshop' *khaṇḍ* 'field, division' (Sanskrit) Rebus: *khānḍa* 'tools, pots and pans, metal-ware'. Rebus 2: kaṇḍ 'fire-altar' (Santali)

dula 'pair' Rebus: *dul* 'cast (metal)' PLUS*kana, kanac* = corner (Santali);

Rebus: *kañcu* = bronze (Telugu) Thus, cast bronze.

kolmo 'paddy plant' Rebus: *kolami* 'smithy, forge' Vikalpa: *mogge* 'sprout, bud' Rebus: *mũh* 'ingot' (Santali) dolu 'plant of shoot height' Rebus: dul 'cast metal'

h2A

खोंड [khōṇḍa] m A young bull, a bullcalf. (Marathi) Rebus: kõdār 'turner' (Bengali); कोंद kōnda 'engraver, lapidary setting or infixing gems' (Marathi) G. sãghāṛɔ m. 'lathe' ; संघाट joinery; M. sãgaḍ 'double-canoe' Rebus: sangataras. संगतराश lit. 'to collect stones, stone-cutter, mason.'

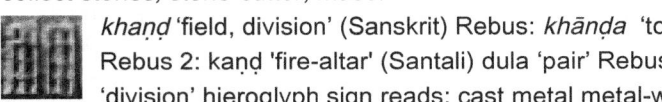

khaṇḍ 'field, division' (Sanskrit) Rebus: *khānḍa* 'tools, pots and pans, metal-ware'. Rebus 2: kaṇḍ 'fire-altar' (Santali) dula 'pair' Rebus: dul 'cast metal' Thus, duplicated 'division' hieroglyph sign reads: cast metal metal-ware. *ḍhanga* = a crook used for pulling down the branches of trees, for goats, sheep and camels (P.)

Rebus:*ḍhangar* blacksmith'.

 *kanka* 'rim of jar' Rebus: *karṇīka* 'account (scribe)' *karṇī* 'supercargo'

 PLUS infixed sal 'splinter' Rebus: sal 'workshop'
baraḍo = spine; backbone (Tulu) Rebus: *baran, bharat* 'mixed alloys' (5 copper, 4 zinc and 1 tin) (Punjabi)

 *kanka* 'rim of jar' Rebus: *karṇīka* 'account (scribe)' *karṇī* 'supercargo' *aya kāṇḍa* 'alloy metalware'

 m1794a
खोंड [khōṇḍa] m A young bull, a bullcalf. (Marathi) Rebus: kōdār 'turner' (Bengali); कोंद kōnda 'engraver, lapidary setting or infixing gems' (Marathi) G. sãghāṛɔ m. 'lathe' ; संघाट joinery; M. sãgaḍ 'double-canoe' Rebus: sangataras. संगतराश lit. 'to collect stones, stone-cutter, mason.'

 *khaṇḍ* 'field, division' (Sanskrit) Rebus: *khāṇḍa* 'tools, pots and pans, metal-ware'. Rebus 2: kaṇḍ 'fire-altar' (Santali) dula 'pair' Rebus: dul 'cast metal' Thus, duplicated 'division' hieroglyph sign reads: cast metal metal-ware.

 *kanka* 'rim of jar' Rebus: *karṇīka* 'account (scribe)' *karṇī* 'supercargo'
PLUS infixed kolom 'three' Rebus: kolami 'smithy, forge'

 *khareḍo* = a currycomb (Gujarati) खरारा [*kharārā*] *m* (H) A currycomb. 2 Currying a horse. (Marathi) Rebus: करडा [*karaḍā*] Hard from alloy--iron, silver &c. (Marathi) *kharādī* ' turner' (Gujarati)

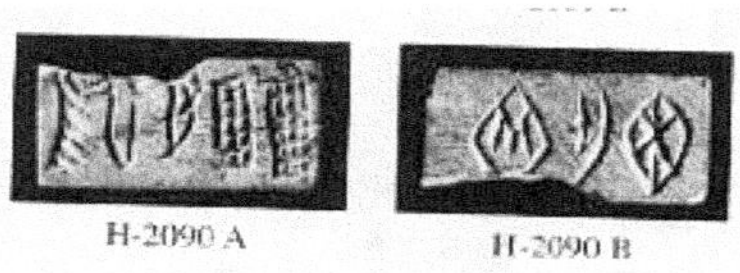

h2090

h2089

 *khaṇḍ* 'field, division' (Sanskrit) Rebus: *khāṇḍa* 'tools, pots and pans, metal-ware'. Rebus 2: kaṇḍ 'fire-altar' (Santali) dula 'pair' Rebus: dul 'cast metal' Thus, duplicated 'division' hieroglyph sign reads: cast metal metal-ware.
kamaḍha 'archer, bow' Rebus: *kammaṭa* 'mint, coiner'.

 *kanka* 'rim of jar' Rebus: *karṇīka* 'account (scribe)' *karṇī* 'supercargo'

 *khareḍo* = a currycomb (Gujarati) खरारा [*kharārā*] *m* (H) A currycomb. 2 Currying a horse. (Marathi) Rebus: करडा [*karaḍā*] Hard from alloy--iron, silver &c. (Marathi) *kharādī* ' turner' (Gujarati)

 *āra* 'spokes' Rebus: *āra 'brass'.* cf. erka = ekke (Tbh. of arka) aka (Tbh. of arka) copper (metal); crystal (Kannada) Glyph: *eraka*'nave of wheel' Rebus: eraka 'copper'; cf. erka = ekke (Tbh. of arka) aka (Tbh. of arka) copper (metal); crystal (Kannada) *erako* 'moltencast copper' Duplicated: dula 'pair'

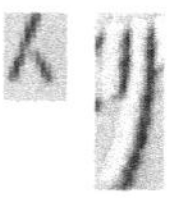 *ḍhālako kāṇḍa* 'ingot, tools, pots and pans and metal-ware'.*ḍhāḷ* 'a slope'; 'inclination of a plane' (G.); *ḍhāḷiyum* = adj. sloping, inclining (G.) Rebus: *ḍhālako* = a large metal ingot (G.) *ḍhālakī* = a metal heated and poured into a mould; a solid piece of metal; an ingot (Gujarati) PLUS खांडा [*khāṇḍā*] *m* A jag, notch, or indentation (as upon the edge of a

tool or weapon). Rebus: *kāṇḍa* 'tools, pots and pans and metal-ware' *Thus, together, the pair reads: āra erako khāṇḍā* 'brass, moltencast copper metalware'.

 alloy workshop *kañcu sal* starting with bronze which is a tin + copper alloy or tin bronze (as distinguished from arsenical bronze, i.e. naturally occurring copper + arsenic).

H-229 A

h229A

kuṭila 'bent' CDIAL 3230 kuṭi— in cmpd. 'curve', *kuṭika—* 'bent' MBh. Rebus: *kuṭila, katthīl* = bronze (8 parts copper and 2 parts tin)

khaṇḍ 'field, division' (Sanskrit) Rebus: *khāṇḍa* 'tools, pots and pans, metal-ware'. Rebus 2: kaṇḍ 'fire-altar' (Santali) *kamaḍha* 'archer, bow' Rebus: *kammaṭa* 'mint, coiner'.

 *kanka* 'rim of jar' Rebus: *karṇīka* 'account (scribe)' *karṇī* 'supercargo'

 *kharedo* = a currycomb (Gujarati) खरारा [*kharārā*] *m* (H) A currycomb. 2 Currying a horse. (Marathi) Rebus: करडा [*karaḍā*] Hard from alloy--iron, silver &c. (Marathi) *kharādī* ' turner' (Gujarati)

H-211 A

h211A

 *khaṇḍ* 'field, division' (Sanskrit) Rebus: *khāṇḍa* 'tools, pots and pans, metal-ware'. Rebus 2: kaṇḍ 'fire-altar' (Santali) dula 'pair' Rebus: dul 'cast metal' Thus, duplicated 'division' hieroglyph sign reads: cast metal metal-ware.

kamaḍha 'archer, bow' Rebus: *kammaṭa* 'mint, coiner'.

 *kanka* 'rim of jar' Rebus: *karṇīka* 'account (scribe)' *karṇī* 'supercargo'

 *kharedo* = a currycomb (Gujarati) खरारा [*kharārā*] *m* (H) A currycomb. 2 Currying a horse. (Marathi) Rebus: करडा [*karaḍā*] Hard from alloy--iron, silver &c. (Marathi) *kharādī* ' turner' (Gujarati)

m633a *खोंड [khōṇḍa] m A young bull, a bullcalf. (Marathi) Rebus: kõdār 'turner' (Bengali); कोंद kōnda 'engraver, lapidary setting or infixing gems' (Marathi) G. sãghāṛɔ m. 'lathe' ; संघाट joinery; M. sãgaḍ 'double-canoe' Rebus: sangataras. संगतराश lit. 'to collect stones, stone-cutter, mason.'*

 *khaṇḍ* 'field, division' (Sanskrit) Rebus: *khāṇḍa* 'tools, pots and pans, metal-ware'. Rebus 2: kaṇḍ 'fire-altar' (Santali) dula 'pair' Rebus: dul 'cast metal' Thus, duplicated 'division' hieroglyph sign reads: cast metal metal-ware.

 *kanka* 'rim of jar' Rebus: *karṇīka* 'account (scribe)' *karṇī* 'supercargo' PLUS INFIXED: खांडा [*khāṇḍā*] *m* A jag, notch, or indentation (as upon the edge of a tool or weapon). Rebus: *kāṇḍa* 'tools, pots and pans and metal-ware'

aya kāṇḍa 'alloy metalware'

 'Arrow' sign hieroglyph (variant) This is a ligature of 'lid of pot' hieroglyph superscript on 'a linear stroke' numeral hieroglyph.*aḍaren* 'cover of pot or lid' Rebus: *aduru* 'native, unsmelted metal'

 *kolmo* 'paddy plant' Rebus: *kolami* 'smithy, forge' Vikalpa: *mogge* 'sprout, bud' Rebus: *mũh* 'ingot' (Santali) dolu 'plant of shoot height' Rebus: dul 'cast metal'

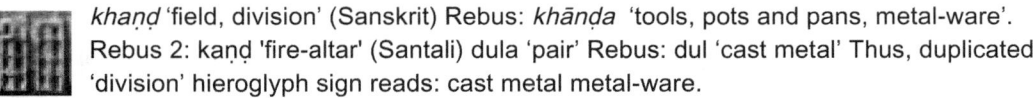

m1731a *खोंड [khōṇḍa] m A young bull, a bullcalf. (Marathi) Rebus: kõdār 'turner' (Bengali); कोंद kōnda 'engraver, lapidary setting or infixing gems' (Marathi) kōḍu 'horn' Rebus: 'workshop'sãghāṛɔ m. 'lathe' (Gujarati) Rebus: sangataras. संगतराश lit. 'to collect stones, stone-cutter, mason.'*

khaṇḍ 'field, division' (Sanskrit) Rebus: *khāṇḍa* 'tools, pots and pans, metal-ware'. Rebus 2: kaṇḍ 'fire-altar' (Santali) dula 'pair' Rebus: dul 'cast metal' Thus, duplicated 'division' hieroglyph sign reads: cast metal metal-ware.

kanka 'rim of jar' Rebus: *karṇīka* 'account (scribe)' *karṇī* 'supercargo' PLUS INFIXED: खांडा [*khāṇḍā*] *m* A jag, notch, or indentation (as upon the edge of a tool or weapon). Rebus: *kāṇḍa* 'tools, pots and pans and metal-ware'

|||| Numeral 4: gaṇḍa 'four' Rebus: kaṇḍa 'furnace, fire-altar' (Santali)

kolmo 'paddy plant' Rebus: *kolami* 'smithy, forge' Vikalpa: *mogge* 'sprout, bud' Rebus: *mūh* 'ingot' (Santali) dolu 'plant of shoot height' Rebus: dul 'cast metal'

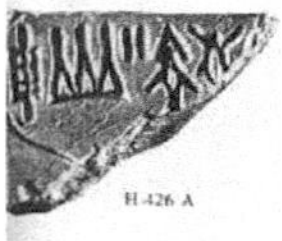

h426A *खोंड [khōṇḍa] m A young bull, a bullcalf. (Marathi) Rebus: kõdār 'turner' (Bengali); कोंद kōnda 'engraver, lapidary setting or infixing gems' (Marathi) G. sãghāṛɔ m. 'lathe' ; संघाट joinery; M. sãgaḍ 'double-canoe' Rebus: sangataras. संगतराश lit. 'to collect stones, stone-cutter, mason.'*

khaṇḍ 'field, division' (Sanskrit) Rebus: *khāṇḍa* 'tools, pots and pans, metal-ware'. Rebus 2: kaṇḍ 'fire-altar' (Santali) PLUS | *koḍa* 'one' Rebus: *koḍ* 'workshop'

ḍãg mountain-ridge (H.)(CDIAL 5476). Rebus: dhangar 'blacksmith' (Maithili) sal 'splinter' Rebus: sal 'workshop' *aya kāṇḍa* 'alloy metalware' *aya kammaṭa.*'coiner, mint alloy'

m1907a Rhinoceros/boar: baḍhia = a castrated boar, a hog (Santali) baḍhi 'a caste who work both in iron and wood' (Santali) *baṟea* 'merchant' pattar 'trough' Rebus: pattar 'guild'

khaṇḍ 'field, division' (Sanskrit) Rebus: *khāṇḍa* 'tools, pots and pans, metal-ware'. Rebus 2: kaṇḍ 'fire-altar' (Santali) PLUS | *koḍa* 'one' Rebus: *koḍ* 'workshop'

ḍãg mountain-ridge (H.)(CDIAL 5476). Rebus: dhangar 'blacksmith' (Maithili) sal 'splinter' Rebus: sal 'workshop'

dula 'two' Rebus: dul 'cast metal' PLUS kolom 'three' Rebus: kolami 'smithy, forge'

kolmo 'paddy plant' Rebus: *kolami* 'smithy, forge' Vikalpa: *mogge* 'sprout, bud' Rebus: *mūh* 'ingot' (Santali) dolu 'plant of shoot height' Rebus: dul 'cast metal'

m937A *खोंड [khōṇḍa] m A young bull, a bullcalf. (Marathi) Rebus: kõdār 'turner' (Bengali); कोंद kōnda 'engraver, lapidary setting or infixing gems' (Marathi) G. sãghāṛɔ m. 'lathe' ; संघाट joinery; M. sãgaḍ 'double-canoe' Rebus: sangataras. संगतराश lit. 'to collect stones, stone-cutter, mason.'* *khaṇḍ* 'field, division' (Sanskrit) Rebus:

khāṇḍa 'tools, pots and pans, metal-ware'. Rebus 2: kaṇḍ 'fire-altar' (Santali)

 *kuṭila* 'bent' CDIAL 3230 kuṭi— in cmpd. 'curve', *kuṭika*— 'bent' MBh. Rebus: *kuṭila, katthīl* = bronze (8 parts copper and 2 parts tin) sal 'splinter' Rebus: sal 'workshop' PLUS | *koḍa* 'one' Rebus: *koḍ* 'workshop'

  mēḍu height, rising ground, hillock (Kannada) Rebus: *mẽṛhẽt, meḍ* 'iron' (Munda.Ho.)

 ḍāg mountain-ridge (H.)(CDIAL 5476). Rebus: dhangar 'blacksmith' (Maithili) *kanka* 'rim of jar' Rebus: *karṇīka* 'account (scribe)' *karṇī* 'supercargo'

M-849 a

m849a *खोंड [khōṇḍa] m A young bull, a bullcalf. (Marathi) Rebus: kõdār 'turner' (Bengali); कोंद kōnda 'engraver, lapidary setting or infixing gems' (Marathi) G. sãghāṛɔ m. 'lathe' ; संघाट joinery; M. sãgaḍ 'double-canoe' Rebus: sangataras. संगतराश lit. 'to collect stones, stone-cutter, mason.' khaṇḍ* 'field, division' (Sanskrit) Rebus: *khāṇḍa* 'tools, pots and pans, metal-ware'. Rebus 2: kaṇḍ 'fire-altar' (Santali) *kamaḍha* 'crab' Rebus: *kammaṭa* 'mint, coiner'. *ḍato* = claws of crab (Santali) Rebus: *dhātu* 'mineral ore' sal 'splinter' Rebus: sal 'workshop'

 |||| Numeral 4: gaṇḍa 'four' Rebus: kaṇḍa 'furnace, fire-altar' (Santali) dula 'pair' Rebus: dul 'cast metal'

water-  carrier hieroglyph *kuṭi*; Rebus: *kuṭhi* 'smelter furnace'.

 Unnumbered Zebu. Native metal smith guild. *khaṇḍ* 'field, division' (Sanskrit) Rebus: *khāṇḍa* 'tools, pots and pans, metal-ware'. Rebus 2: kaṇḍ 'fire-altar' (Santali) Duplicated circumscript: dula 'pair' Rebus: dul 'cast metal' Thus, duplicated 'division' hieroglyph sign reads: cast metal metal-ware.

 *meḍ* 'body' Rebus: *meḍ* 'iron' (Ho.) काठी [kāṭhī] *f* (काष्ट S) 'frame or structure of the body' (Marathi) Rebus: खंडी [khaṇḍī] measure of weight (Marathi) *கண்டி; kaṇṭi, n. < Mhr. khaṇḍil. [T. Tu. khaṇḍi, M. kaṇḍi.]* Candy, a weight, stated to be roughly equivalent to 500 lbs. karaṇḍa 'duck' (Sanskrit) karaṛa 'a very large aquatic bird' (Sindhi) Rebus: करडा [*karaḍā*] Hard from alloy--iron, silver &c. (Marathi) *kharādī* ' turner' (Gujarati) Circumscript:

 *kuṭila* 'bent' CDIAL 3230 kuṭi— in cmpd. 'curve', *kuṭika*— 'bent' MBh. Rebus: *kuṭila, katthīl* = bronze (8 parts copper and 2 parts tin) Duplicated: dula 'pair' Rebus: dul 'cast metal' Thus, cast bronze.

 *khareḍo* = a currycomb (Gujarati) खरारा [*kharārā*] *m* (H) A currycomb. 2 Currying a horse. (Marathi) Rebus: करडा [*karaḍā*] Hard from alloy--iron, silver &c. (Marathi) *kharādī* ' turner' (Gujarati)

M-1329 A

m1329A *khaṇḍ* 'field, division' (Sanskrit) Rebus: *khāṇḍa* 'tools, pots and pans, metal-ware'. Rebus 2: kaṇḍ 'fire-altar' (Santali)

meḍ 'body' Rebus: *meḍ* 'iron' (Ho.) काठी [kāṭhī] *f* (काष्ट S) 'frame or structure of the body' (Marathi) Rebus: खंडी [khaṇḍī] measure of weight (Marathi) *கண்டி; kaṇṭi, n. < Mhr. khaṇḍil. [T. Tu. khaṇḍi, M. kaṇḍi.]* Candy, a weight, stated to be roughly equivalent to 500 lbs. karaṇḍa 'duck' (Sanskrit) खांडा [*khāṇḍā*] *m* A jag, notch, or indentation (as upon the edge of a tool or weapon). Rebus: *kāṇḍa* 'tools, pots and pans and metal-ware'

PLUS | *koḍa* 'one' Rebus: *koḍ* 'workshop' *ayo* 'fish' Rebus: *aya* 'iron' *ayas* 'metal' mēḍu height, rising ground, hillock (Kannada) Rebus: *meḍ* 'iron' (Ho.) kolom 'three' Rebus: kolami 'smithy, forge' Thus, *meḍ kolami* 'iron smithy-forge'

āra 'spokes' Rebus: *āra 'brass'*. cf. erka = ekke (Tbh. of arka) aka (Tbh. of arka) copper (metal); crystal (Kannada) Glyph: *eraka*'nave of wheel' Rebus: eraka 'copper'; cf. erka = ekke (Tbh. of arka) aka (Tbh. of arka) copper (metal); crystal (Kannada) *erako* 'moltencast copper'

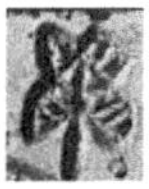

Uniquely ligatured 'ficus religiosa' hieroglyph:

m1748A

खोंड [khōṇḍa] m A young bull, a bullcalf. (Marathi) Rebus: kõdār 'turner' (Bengali); कोंद kōnda 'engraver, lapidary setting or infixing gems' (Marathi) G. sãghārɔ m. 'lathe' ; संघाट joinery; M. sãgaḍ 'double-canoe' Rebus: sangataras. संगतराश lit. 'to collect stones, stone-cutter, mason.'

loa 'ficus religiosa' Rebus: *lo* 'iron' (Sanskrit) PLUS unique ligatures: लोखंड [lōkhaṇḍa] *n* (लोह S) Iron. लोखंडाचे चणे खावविणें or चारणें To oppress grievously.लोखंडकाम [lōkhaṇḍakāma] *n* Iron work; that portion (of a building, machine &c.) which consists of iron. 2 The business of an ironsmith.लोखंडी [lōkhaṇḍī] *a* (लोखंड) Composed of iron; relating to iron. (Marathi) *kolom 'three' Rebus:* kolami 'smithy, forge' with circumcript: | *koḍa* 'one' Rebus: *koḍ* 'workshop' dula 'pair' Rebus: dul 'cast metal'. Thus metal smithy castings workshop.

m133A *खोंड [khōṇḍa] m A young bull, a bullcalf. (Marathi) Rebus: kõdār 'turner' (Bengali); कोंद kōnda 'engraver, lapidary setting or infixing gems' (Marathi) G. sãghārɔ m. 'lathe' ; संघाट joinery; M. sãgaḍ 'double-canoe' Rebus: sangataras. संगतराश lit. 'to collect stones, stone-cutter, mason.'*

loa 'ficus religiosa' Rebus: *lo* 'iron' (Sanskrit) PLUS unique ligatures: लोखंड [lōkhaṇḍa] *n* (लोह S) Iron. लोखंडाचे चणे खावविणें or चारणें To oppress grievously.लोखंडकाम [lōkhaṇḍakāma] *n* Iron work; that portion (of a building, machine &c.) which consists of iron. 2 The business of an ironsmith.लोखंडी [lōkhaṇḍī] *a* (लोखंड) Composed of iron; relating to iron. (Marathi)

kuṭila 'bent' CDIAL 3230 kuṭi— in cmpd. 'curve', *kuṭika—* 'bent' MBh. Rebus: *kuṭila, katthīl* = bronze (8 parts copper and 2 parts tin) Duplicated: dula 'pair' Rebus: dul 'cast metal' Thus, cast bronze.

kana, kanac = corner (Santali); Rebus: *kañcu* = bronze (Telugu) PLUS खांडा [*khāṇḍā*] *m* A jag, notch, or indentation (as upon the edge of a tool or weapon). Rebus: *kāṇḍa* 'tools, pots and pans and metal-ware' Thus, bronze metalware. INFIXED: kolom 'three' Rebus: kolami 'smithy, forge'.

bicha 'scorpion' (Assamese) Rebus: *bica* 'stone ore' (Santali) *ayo* 'fish' Rebus: *aya* 'iron' *ayas* 'metal' *aya kammaṭa.*'coiner, mint alloy' *kamaḍha* 'crab' Rebus: *kammaṭa* 'mint, coiner'.
ḍato = claws of crab (Santali) Rebus: *dhātu* 'mineral ore'

kolom 'three' Rebus: kolami 'smithy, forge' with circumcript: | *koḍa* 'one' Rebus: *koḍ* 'workshop' dula 'pair' Rebus: dul 'cast metal'. Thus metal smithy castings workshop.

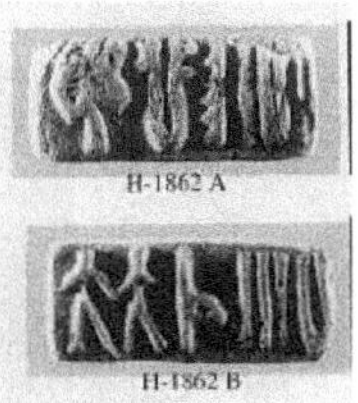
h1862 Side A:

loa 'ficus religiosa' Rebus: *lo* 'iron' (Sanskrit) PLUS unique ligatures: लोखंड [lōkhaṇḍa] *n* (लोह S) Iron. लोखंडाचे चणे खावविणें or चारणें To oppress grievously.लोखंडकाम [lōkhaṇḍakāma] *n* Iron work; that portion (of a building, machine &c.) which consists of iron. 2 The business of an ironsmith.लोखंडी [lōkhaṇḍī] *a* (लोखंड) Composed of iron; relating to iron. (Marathi)

kanka 'rim of jar' Rebus: *karṇīka* 'account (scribe)' *karṇī* 'supercargo'

kharedo = a currycomb (Gujarati) खरारा [*kharārā*] *m* (H) A currycomb. 2 Currying a horse. (Marathi) Rebus: करडा [*karaḍā*] Hard from alloy--iron, silver &c. (Marathi) *kharādī* ' turner' (Gujarati)

kolom 'three' Rebus: kolami 'smithy, forge' *baṭa* = rimless pot (Kannada) Rebus:) *baṭa* = a kind of iron (G.)) *bhaṭa* furnace (Gujarati) Side B: Duplicated 'body': dula 'pair' Rebus: dul 'cast metal' PLUS *meḍ* 'body' Rebus: *meḍ* 'iron' (Ho.) काठी [kāṭhī] *f* (काष्ट S) 'frame or structure of the body' (Marathi) Rebus: खंडी [khaṇḍī] measure of weight (Marathi) *கண்டி; kaṇṭi, n. < Mhr. khaṇḍil. [T. Tu. khaṇḍi, M. kaṇḍi.]* Candy, a weight, stated to be roughly equivalent to 500 lbs. Thus, iron castings.

koḍi 'flag' (Ta.)(DEDR 2049). Rebus 1: *koḍ* 'workshop' (Kuwi) Rebus 2: *khōḍ* m. 'pit', *khōḍü* f. 'small pit' (Kashmiri. CDIAL 3947). *kolom* 'three' Rebus: kolami 'smithy, forge' *baṭa* = rimless pot (Kannada) Rebus:) *baṭa* = a kind of iron (G.)) *bhaṭa* furnace (Gujarati)

m212A

खोंड [khōṇḍa] m A young bull, a bullcalf. (Marathi) Rebus: kõdār 'turner' (Bengali); कोंद kōnda 'engraver, lapidary setting or infixing gems' (Marathi) G. sãghāṛɔ m. 'lathe' ; संघाट joinery; M. sãgaḍ 'double-canoe' Rebus: sangataras. संगतराश lit. 'to collect stones, stone-cutter, mason.'

loa 'ficus religiosa' Rebus: *lo* 'iron' (Sanskrit) PLUS unique ligatures: लोखंड [lōkhaṇḍa] *n* (लोह S) Iron. लोखंडाचे चणे खावविणें or चारणें To oppress grievously.लोखंडकाम [lōkhaṇḍakāma] *n* Iron work; that portion (of a building, machine &c.) which consists of

iron. 2 The business of an ironsmith.लोखंडी [lōkhaṇḍī] *a* (लोखंड) Composed of iron; relating to iron. (Marathi)

kolom ‘three’ Rebus: kolami ‘smithy, forge’

| *koḍa* ‘one’ Rebus: *koḍ* ‘workshop’ PLUS |||| Numeral 4: gaṇḍa 'four' Rebus: kaṇḍa 'furnace, fire-altar' (Santali)

m1128A *rāngo* ‘water buffalo bull’ (Ku.N.)(CDIAL 10559) Rebus: rango ‘pewter’ *pattar* ‘trough’ Rebus: *pattar* ‘guild’.Thus, pewter guild.

loa ‘ficus religiosa’ Rebus: *lo* ‘iron’ (Sanskrit) PLUS unique ligatures: लोखंड [lōkhaṇḍa] *n* (लोह S) Iron. लोखंडाचे चणे खावविणें or चारणें To oppress grievously.लोखंडकाम [lōkhaṇḍakāma] *n* Iron work; that portion (of a building, machine &c.) which consists of iron. 2 The business of an ironsmith.लोखंडी [lōkhaṇḍī] *a* (लोखंड) Composed of iron; relating to iron. (Marathi)

kuṭila ‘bent’ CDIAL 3230 kuṭi— in cmpd. ‘curve’, *kuṭika—* ‘bent’ MBh. Rebus: *kuṭila, katthīl* = bronze (8 parts copper and 2 parts tin)

m1317a

loa ‘ficus religiosa’ Rebus: *lo* ‘iron’ (Sanskrit) PLUS unique ligatures: लोखंड [lōkhaṇḍa] *n* (लोह S) Iron. लोखंडाचे चणे खावविणें or चारणें To oppress grievously.लोखंडकाम [lōkhaṇḍakāma] *n* Iron work; that portion (of a building, machine &c.) which consists of iron. 2 The business of an ironsmith.लोखंडी [lōkhaṇḍī] *a* (लोखंड) Composed of iron; relating to iron. (Marathi)

water-carrier hieroglyph *kuṭi*; Rebus: *kuṭhi* ‘smelter furnace’. PLUS ‘rim of jar’:

kanka ‘rim of jar’ Rebus: karṇīka ‘account (scribe)’ karṇī ‘supercargo’

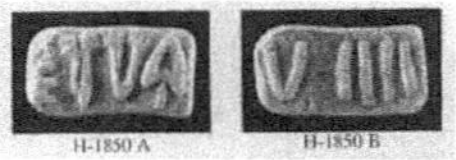

h1850A,B

loa ‘ficus religiosa’ Rebus: *lo* ‘iron’ (Sanskrit) PLUS unique ligatures: लोखंड [lōkhaṇḍa] *n* (लोह S) Iron. लोखंडाचे चणे खावविणें or चारणें To oppress grievously.लोखंडकाम [lōkhaṇḍakāma] *n* Iron work; that portion (of a building, machine &c.) which consists of iron. 2 The business of an ironsmith.लोखंडी [lōkhaṇḍī] *a* (लोखंड) Composed of iron; relating to iron. (Marathi)

dula ‘pair’ Rebus: dul ‘cast metal’ *mogge* ‘sprout, bud’ Rebus: *mūh* ‘ingot’ (Santali) Thus, cast metal ingot.

kanka ‘rim of jar’ Rebus: *karṇīka* ‘account (scribe)’ *karṇī* ‘supercargo’

kharedo = a currycomb (Gujarati) खरारा [*kharārā*] *m* (H) A currycomb. 2 Currying a horse. (Marathi) Rebus: करडा [*karaḍā*] Hard from alloy--iron, silver &c. (Marathi) *kharādī* ‘ turner’ (Gujarati) Side B: *baṭa* = rimless pot (Kannada) Rebus:) *baṭa* = a kind of iron (G.)) *bhaṭa* furnace (Gujarati) |||| Numeral 4: gaṇḍa 'four' Rebus: kaṇḍa 'furnace, fire-altar' (Santali)

Kalibangan 53A

 *loa* ‘ficus religiosa’ Rebus: *lo* ‘iron’ (Sanskrit) PLUS unique ligatures: लोखंड [lōkhaṇḍa] *n* (लोह S) Iron. लोखंडाचे चणे खावविणें or चारणें To oppress grievously.लोखंडकाम [lōkhaṇḍakāma] *n* Iron work; that portion (of a building, machine &c.) which consists of iron. 2 The business of an ironsmith.लोखंडी [lōkhaṇḍī] *a* (लोखंड) Composed of iron; relating to iron. (Marathi)

 ḍāg mountain-ridge (H.)(CDIAL 5476). Rebus: dhangar ‘blacksmith’ (Maithili)

m990a *खोंड [khōṇḍa] m A young bull, a bullcalf. (Marathi) Rebus: kõdār ‘turner’ (Bengali); कोंद kōnda ‘engraver, lapidary setting or infixing gems’ (Marathi) G. sãghāṛɔ m. ‘lathe’ ; संघाट joinery; M. sāgaḍ ‘double-canoe’ Rebus: sangataras. संगतराश lit. ‘to collect stones, stone-cutter, mason.’*

loa ‘ficus  religiosa’ Rebus: *lo* ‘iron’ (Sanskrit) PLUS unique ligatures: लोखंड [lōkhaṇḍa] *n* (लोह S) Iron. लोखंडाचे चणे खावविणें or चारणें To oppress grievously.लोखंडकाम [lōkhaṇḍakāma] *n* Iron work; that portion (of a building, machine &c.) which consists of iron. 2 The business of an ironsmith.लोखंडी [lōkhaṇḍī] *a* (लोखंड) Composed of iron; relating to iron. (Marathi)

 *kanka* ‘rim of jar’ Rebus: *karṇīka* ‘account (scribe)’ *karṇī* ‘supercargo’

 water-carrier hieroglyph *kuṭi*; Rebus: *kuṭhi* ‘smelter furnace’. PLUS *kāṇḍa* ‘arrow’ (Sanskrit) Rebus:*khāṇḍa* ‘tools, pots and pans, metal-ware’. Rebus 2: kaṇḍ 'fire-altar' (Santali)

h1102A

 *loa* ‘ficus religiosa’ Rebus: *lo* ‘iron’ (Sanskrit) PLUS unique ligatures: लोखंड [lōkhaṇḍa] *n* (लोह S) Iron. लोखंडाचे चणे खावविणें or चारणें To oppress grievously.लोखंडकाम [lōkhaṇḍakāma] *n* Iron work; that portion (of a building, machine &c.) which consists of iron. 2 The business of an ironsmith.लोखंडी [lōkhaṇḍī] *a* (लोखंड) Composed of iron; relating to iron. (Marathi)

 *kanka* ‘rim of jar’ Rebus: *karṇīka* ‘account (scribe)’ *karṇī* ‘supercargo’

 *khareḍo* = a currycomb (Gujarati) खरारा [*kharārā*] *m* (H) A currycomb. 2 Currying a horse. (Marathi) Rebus: करडा [*karaḍā*] Hard from alloy--iron, silver &c. (Marathi) *kharādī* ‘ turner’ (Gujarati)

dula ‘two’ Rebus: dul ‘cast metal’ *baṭa* ‘rimless, broad-mouthed pot’ Rebus: *bhaṭa* ‘furnace’ (Gujarati.); *baṭa* ‘a kind of iron’ (Gujarati)

h290B

h289B

 *loa* ‘ficus religiosa’ Rebus: *lo* ‘iron’ (Sanskrit) PLUS unique ligatures: लोखंड [lōkhaṇḍa] *n* (लोह S) Iron. लोखंडाचे चणे खावविणें or चारणें To

oppress grievously.लोखंडकाम [lōkhaṇḍakāma] *n* Iron work; that portion (of a building, machine &c.) which consists of iron. 2 The business of an ironsmith.लोखंडी [lōkhaṇḍī] *a* (लोखंड) Composed of iron; relating to iron. (Marathi)

m273A *miṇḍāl* 'markhor' (Tōrwālī)*meḍho* a ram, a sheep (Gujarati)(CDIAL 10120) Rebus: *mẽṛhẽt, meḍ* 'iron' (Mu.Ho.)

loa 'ficus religiosa' Rebus: *lo* 'iron' (Sanskrit) PLUS unique ligatures: लोखंड [lōkhaṇḍa] *n* (लोह S) Iron. लोखंडाचे चणे खावविणें or चारणें To oppress grievously.लोखंडकाम [lōkhaṇḍakāma] *n* Iron work; that portion (of a building, machine &c.) which consists of iron. 2 The business of an ironsmith.लोखंडी [lōkhaṇḍī] *a* (लोखंड) Composed of iron; relating to iron. (Marathi)

m1666a *खोंड [khōṇḍa] m A young bull, a bullcalf. (Marathi) Rebus: kōdār 'turner' (Bengali); कोंद kōnda 'engraver, lapidary setting or infixing gems' (Marathi) G. sãghāṛɔ m. 'lathe' ; संघाट joinery; M. sāgaḍ 'double-canoe' Rebus: sangataras. संगतराश lit. 'to collect stones, stone-cutter, mason.'*

loa 'ficus religiosa' Rebus: *lo* 'iron' (Sanskrit) PLUS unique ligatures: लोखंड [lōkhaṇḍa] *n* (लोह S) Iron. लोखंडाचे चणे खावविणें or चारणें To oppress grievously.लोखंडकाम [lōkhaṇḍakāma] *n* Iron work; that portion (of a building, machine &c.) which consists of iron. 2 The business of an ironsmith.लोखंडी [lōkhaṇḍī] *a* (लोखंड) Composed of iron; relating to iron. (Marathi) *khaṇḍ* 'field, division' (Sanskrit) Rebus: *khāṇḍa* 'tools, pots and pans, metal-ware'. Rebus 2: kaṇḍ 'fire-altar' (Santali)

kanka 'rim of jar' Rebus: *karṇīka* 'account (scribe)' *karṇī* 'supercargo'
INFIXED kolom 'three' Rebus: kolami 'smithy, forge'

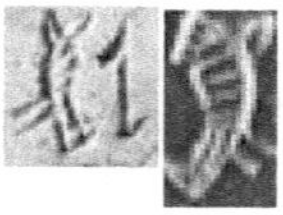

The pair of hieroglyph signs are compositions: bicha 'scorpion' (Assamese) Rebus: *bica* 'stone ore' (Santali) The pairing sign is a composition of: sloping stroke PLUS two short strokes of a 'splinter':*dhāḷ* 'a slope'; 'inclination of a plane' (Gujarati); *ḍhāḷiyum* = adj. sloping, inclining (Gujarati) Rebus: *ḍhālako* = a large metal ingot (Gujarati) *ḍhālakī* = a metal heated and poured into a mould; a solid piece of metal; an ingot (Gujarati)PLUS*sal* 'splinter' Rebus: *sal* 'workshop'. Thus the composition reads: *ḍhālako sal* 'ingot workshop'.

dāṭu 'cross'(Telugu) Rebus: *dhatu* 'mineral' (Santali).

kanka 'rim of jar' Rebus: *karṇīka* 'account (scribe)' *karṇī* 'supercargo'

h10a *खोंड [khōṇḍa] m A young bull, a bullcalf. (Marathi) Rebus: kōdār 'turner' (Bengali); कोंद kōnda 'engraver, lapidary setting or infixing gems' (Marathi) G. sãghāṛɔ m. 'lathe' ; संघाट joinery; M. sāgaḍ 'double-canoe' Rebus: sangataras. संगतराश lit. 'to collect stones, stone-cutter, mason.'*
dula 'pair' Rebus: dul 'cast metal'

loa 'ficus religiosa' Rebus: *lo* 'iron' (Sanskrit) PLUS unique ligatures: लोखंड [lōkhaṇḍa] *n* (लोह S) Iron. लोखंडाचे चणे खावविणें or चारणें To oppress grievously.लोखंडकाम [lōkhaṇḍakāma] *n* Iron work; that portion (of a building, machine &c.) which consists of iron. 2 The business of an ironsmith.लोखंडी [lōkhaṇḍī] *a* (लोखंड) Composed of iron; relating to iron. (Marathi) Thus, iron castings. *kamaḍha* 'archer, bow' Rebus: *kammaṭa* 'mint, coiner'. |||| Numeral 4: gaṇḍa 'four' Rebus: kaṇḍa 'furnace, fire-altar' (Santali) Duplicated: dula 'pair' Rebus: dul 'cast metal' ranku 'liquid measure' Rebus: ranku 'tin' Duplicated: dula 'pair' Rebus: dul 'cast metal' Thus, tin castings.

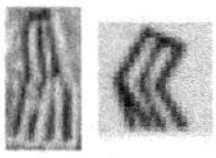

Strands of yarn/rope' hieroglyph: Hieroglyph: 'strands of yarn' Rebus reading: *dhā'tu* 'strand of rope' Rebus: *dhatu* 'mineral ore' (Santali)

āra 'spokes' Rebus: *āra 'brass'*. cf. erka = ekke (Tbh. of arka) aka (Tbh. of arka) copper (metal); crystal (Kannada) Glyph: *eraka*'nave of wheel' Rebus: eraka 'copper'; cf. erka = ekke (Tbh. of arka) aka (Tbh. of arka) copper (metal); crystal (Kannada) *erako* 'moltencast copper'

M-1814 A

m1814A *खोंड [khōṇḍa] m A young bull, a bullcalf. (Marathi) Rebus: kõdār 'turner' (Bengali);* *कोंद kōnda 'engraver, lapidary setting or infixing gems' (Marathi) G. sãghārɔ m. 'lathe' ; संघाट joinery; M. sãgaḍ 'double-canoe' Rebus: sangataras. संगतराश lit. 'to collect stones, stone-cutter, mason.'*
aya kammaṭa.'coiner, mint alloy'

aḍar 'harrow'; rebus: *aduru* 'native unsmelted metal' *ayo* 'fish' Rebus: *aya* 'iron' *ayas* 'metal' *kānḍa* 'arrow' (Sanskrit) Rebus:*khānḍa* 'tools, pots and pans, metal-ware'. Rebus 2: kaṇḍ 'fire-altar' (Santali)

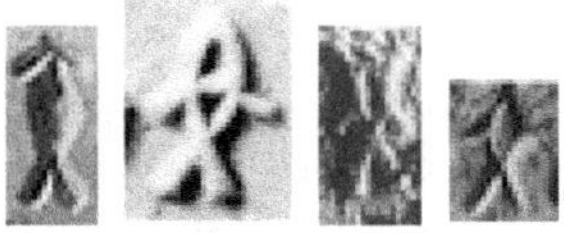

'Fish' hieroglyph with infixes and ligatures

<aḍara>(L) {N} ``^scales of a fish, sharp bark of a tree" Rebus: aduru 'unsmelted, native metal'

m1898a *khũṭ* 'zebu' Rebus: '(native metal) guild'

ayo 'fish' Rebus: aya 'iron' (Gujarati) ayas 'metal' (Vedic) PLUS *khambhaṛā* m. 'fin' (Lahnda); khambh 'wing' (Punjabi) Allograph: Garh. *khambu* ' pillar '.(CDIAL 13640) Rebus: *kammaṭa* 'coiner, mint'. Thus, the ligatured hieroglyph sign reads rebus: *aya kammaṭa* 'iron, alloyed metal mint'.

m445A *aya kammaṭa* 'iron, alloyed metal mint'.

baraḍo = spine; backbone (Tulu) Rebus: *baran, bharat* 'mixed alloys' (5 copper, 4 zinc and 1 tin) (Punjabi)

kanka 'rim of jar' Rebus: *karṇīka* 'account (scribe)' *karṇī* 'supercargo'

m360A *aya aḍaren (homonym: aduru)*'alloy native metal'

 Ligatured sign hieroglyph: 'Pair of harrows': *dul aduru* 'cast native unsmelted metal' PLUS kolmo 'paddy plant' Rebus: kolami 'smithy, forge'. Thus the composite hieroglyph denotes native metal smithy castings. Or, *mogge* 'sprout, bud' Rebus*: mũh* 'ingot': native cast metal ingot.

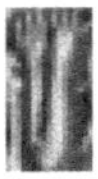 *dula* 'pair' Rebus: dul 'cast metal' *mogge* 'sprout, bud' Rebus: *mũh* 'ingot' (Santali) Thus, cast metal ingot.

 *kanka* 'rim of jar' Rebus: *karṇīka* 'account (scribe)' *karṇī* 'supercargo'

 *meḍ* 'body' Rebus: *meḍ* 'iron' (Ho.) काठी [kāṭhī] *f* (काष्ट S) 'frame or structure of the body' (Marathi) Rebus: खंडी [khaṇḍī] measure of weight (Marathi) *கண்டி; kaṇṭi, n. < Mhr. khaṇḍil. [T. Tu. khaṇḍi, M. kaṇḍi.]* Candy, a weight, stated to be roughly equivalent to 500 lbs.

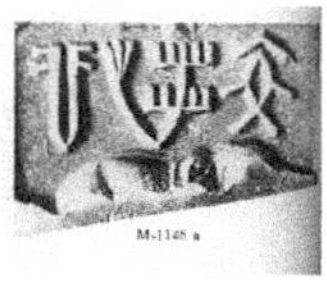 m1146a *balad* m. ' ox ', gng. *bald*, (Ku.) *barad*, id. (N. Tarai) Rebus: *bharat* (5 copper, 4 zinc and 1 tin)(Punjabi) *pattar* 'trough' Rebus*: pattar* 'guild'. Thus, copper-zinc-tin alloy (worker) guild.
aya aḍaren (homonym: aduru)'alloy native metal'

 Ligatured sign hieroglyph: 'Pair of harrows': *dul aduru* 'cast native unsmelted metal' PLUS kolmo 'paddy plant' Rebus: kolami 'smithy, forge'. Thus the composite hieroglyph denotes native metal smithy castings. Or, *mogge* 'sprout, bud' Rebus*: mũh* 'ingot': native cast metal ingot.

 *kanka* 'rim of jar' Rebus: *karṇīka* 'account (scribe)' *karṇī* 'supercargo'

 m252a *balad* m. ' ox ', gng. *bald*, (Ku.) *barad*, id. (N. Tarai) Rebus: *bharat* (5 copper, 4 zinc and 1 tin)(Punjabi) *pattar* 'trough' Rebus*: pattar* 'guild'. Thus, copper-zinc-tin alloy (worker) guild.
aya aḍaren (homonym: aduru)'alloy native metal'

 dula 'two' Rebus: dul 'cast metal' PLUS *baṭa* = rimless pot (Kannada) Rebus:) *baṭa* = a kind of iron (G.)) *bhaṭa* furnace (Gujarati) Thus, furnace for castings.

baroṭi 'twelve' *bhārata* 'a factitious alloy of copper, pewter, tin' (Marathi)

 *khaṇḍ* 'field, division' (Sanskrit) Rebus: *khānḍa* 'tools, pots and pans, metal-ware'. Rebus 2: kaṇḍ 'fire-altar' (Santali) dula 'pair' Rebus: dul 'cast metal' Thus, duplicated 'division' hieroglyph sign reads: cast metal metal-ware.

water-carrier hieroglyph *kuṭi*; Rebus: *kuṭhi* 'smelter furnace'. PLUS 'rim of jar':

   kanka 'rim of jar' Rebus: karṇīka 'account (scribe)' karṇī 'supercargo'

 *kharedo* = a currycomb (Gujarati) खरारा [*kharārā*] *m* (H) A currycomb. 2 Currying a horse. (Marathi) Rebus: करडा [*karaḍā*] Hard from alloy--iron, silver &c. (Marathi) *kharādī* ' turner' (Gujarati)

m784a *खोंड [khōṇḍa] m A young bull, a bullcalf. (Marathi) Rebus: kõdār 'turner' (Bengali); कोंद kōnda 'engraver, lapidary setting or infixing gems' (Marathi) G. sãghāṛɔ m. 'lathe' ; संघाट joinery; M. sãgaḍ 'double-canoe' Rebus: sangataras. संगतराश lit. 'to collect stones, stone-cutter, mason.'*

aya aḍaren (homonym: aduru)'alloy native metal'*kamaḍha* 'crab' Rebus: *kammaṭa* 'mint, coiner'.

ḍato = claws of crab (Santali) Rebus: *dhātu* 'mineral ore'

 *kharedo* = a currycomb (Gujarati) खरारा [*kharārā*] *m* (H) A currycomb. 2 Currying a horse. (Marathi) Rebus: करडा [*karaḍā*] Hard from alloy--iron, silver &c. (Marathi) *kharādī* ' turner' (Gujarati) dulo 'hole' Rebus: dul 'cast metal'

m1847a *खोंड [khōṇḍa] m A young bull, a bullcalf. (Marathi) Rebus: kõdār 'turner' (Bengali); कोंद kōnda 'engraver, lapidary setting or infixing gems' (Marathi) G. sãghāṛɔ m. 'lathe' ; संघाट joinery; M. sãgaḍ 'double-canoe' Rebus: sangataras. संगतराश lit. 'to collect stones, stone-cutter, mason.'*

aya aḍaren (homonym: aduru)'alloy native metal'

kamaḍha 'crab' Rebus: *kammaṭa* 'mint, coiner'.

ḍato = claws of crab (Santali) Rebus: *dhātu* 'mineral ore'

 *kolom 'three' Rebus:* kolami 'smithy, forge' with circumcript: | *koḍa* 'one' Rebus: *koḍ* 'workshop' dula 'pair' Rebus: dul 'cast metal'. Thus metal smithy castings workshop.

Lothal 9a *खोंड [khōṇḍa] m A young bull, a bullcalf. (Marathi) Rebus: kõdār 'turner' (Bengali); कोंद kōnda 'engraver, lapidary setting or infixing gems' (Marathi) G. sãghāṛɔ m. 'lathe' ; संघाट joinery; M. sãgaḍ 'double-canoe' Rebus: sangataras. संगतराश lit. 'to collect stones, stone-cutter, mason.'*

aya aḍaren (homonym: aduru)'alloy native metal'

kamaḍha 'crab' Rebus: *kammaṭa* 'mint, coiner'.

ḍato = claws of crab (Santali) Rebus: *dhātu* 'mineral ore'

PLUS खांडा [*khāṇḍā*] *m* A jag, notch, or indentation (as upon the edge of a tool or weapon). Rebus: *kāṇḍa* 'tools, pots and pans and metal-ware'

 *kolom 'three' Rebus:* kolami 'smithy, forge' with circumcript: | *koḍa* 'one' Rebus: *koḍ* 'workshop' dula 'pair' Rebus: dul 'cast metal'. Thus metal smithy castings workshop.

m1351a Read rebus as at Lothal 9a.

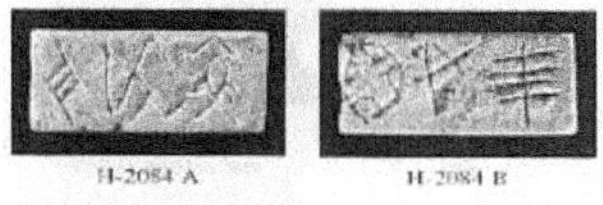

h2084A Side A read rebus as at Lothal 9a. Side B: | *koḍa* 'one' Rebus: *koḍ* 'workshop' PLUS |||| Numeral 4: gaṇḍa 'four' Rebus: kaṇḍa 'furnace, fire-altar' (Santali) *kamaḍha* 'archer, bow' Rebus: *kammaṭa* 'mint, coiner'.

kanac 'corner' Rebus: *kañcu* 'bronze'

m1705a Read rebus as at m1809a

m1809a खोंड *[khōṇḍa] m A young bull, a bullcalf. (Marathi) Rebus: kōdār 'turner' (Bengali);* कोंद *kōnda 'engraver, lapidary setting or infixing gems' (Marathi) G. sãghāṛɔ m. 'lathe' ;* संघाट *joinery; M. sãgaḍ 'double-canoe' Rebus: sangataras.* संगतराश *lit. 'to collect stones, stone-cutter, mason.' aya aḍaren (homonym: aduru)*'alloy native metal'

kamaḍha 'crab' Rebus: *kammaṭa* 'mint, coiner'.

ḍato = claws of crab (Santali) Rebus: *dhātu* 'mineral ore'

kanka 'rim of jar' Rebus: *karṇīka* 'account (scribe)' *karṇī* 'supercargo'

m1751a खोंड *[khōṇḍa] m A young bull, a bullcalf. (Marathi) Rebus: kõdār 'turner' (Bengali);* कोंद *kōnda 'engraver, lapidary setting or infixing gems' (Marathi) G. sãghāṛɔ m. 'lathe' ;* संघाट *joinery; M. sãgaḍ 'double-canoe' Rebus: sangataras.* संगतराश *lit. 'to collect stones, stone-cutter, mason.' aya aḍaren (homonym: aduru)*'alloy native metal'

kanka 'rim of jar' Rebus: *karṇīka* 'account (scribe)' *karṇī* 'supercargo'

kamaḍha 'crab' Rebus: *kammaṭa* 'mint, coiner'.

ḍato = claws of crab (Santali) Rebus: *dhātu* 'mineral ore'

PLUS *kolmo* 'paddy plant' Rebus: *kolami* 'smithy, forge' Vikalpa: *mogge* 'sprout, bud' Rebus: *mũh* 'ingot' (Santali) dolu 'plant of shoot height' Rebus: dul 'cast metal' Thus, mineral ore, metal smithy castings and mint.

H-251 A bis

H-251 C bis

h251 Side A: *aya aḍaren (homonym: aduru)*'alloy native metal'

meḍ 'body' Rebus: *meḍ* 'iron' (Ho.) काठी [kāṭhī] *f* (काष्ट S) 'frame or structure of the body' (Marathi) Rebus: खंडी [khaṇḍī] measure of weight (Marathi) கண்டி; *kaṇṭi, n. < Mhr. khaṇḍil. [T. Tu. khaṇḍi, M. kaṇḍi.]* Candy, a weight, stated to be roughly equivalent to 500 lbs.

kanka 'rim of jar' Rebus: *karṇīka* 'account (scribe)' *karṇī* 'supercargo'

khareḍo = a currycomb (Gujarati) खरारा [*kharārā*] *m* (H) A currycomb. 2 Currying a horse. (Marathi) Rebus: करडा [*karaḍā*] Hard from alloy--iron, silver &c. (Marathi) *kharādī* ' turner' (Gujarati) Side B: *balad* m. ' ox ', gng. *bald*, (Ku.) *barad*, id. (N. Tarai) Rebus: *bharat* (5 copper, 4 zinc and 1 tin)(Punjabi) *pattar* 'trough' Rebus*: pattar* 'guild'. Thus, copper-zinc-tin alloy (worker) guild.

m672A खोंड *[khōṇḍa] m A young bull, a bullcalf. (Marathi) Rebus: kõdār 'turner' (Bengali);* कोंद *kōnda 'engraver, lapidary setting or infixing gems' (Marathi) G. sãghāṛɔ m. 'lathe' ;* संघाट *joinery; M. sãgaḍ 'double-canoe' Rebus: sangataras.* संगतराश *lit. 'to collect stones, stone-cutter, mason.'*

aya aḍaren (homonym: aduru)'alloy native metal'

ranku 'liquid measure' Rebus: ranku 'tin'

 *kolmo* 'paddy plant' Rebus: *kolami* 'smithy, forge' Vikalpa: *mogge* 'sprout, bud' Rebus: *mūh* 'ingot' (Santali) dolu 'plant of shoot height' Rebus: dul 'cast metal'

 *kanka* 'rim of jar' Rebus: *karṇīka* 'account (scribe)' *karṇī* 'supercargo'

 m1310A First 5 signs read rebus as at m672A PLUS |||| Numeral 4: gaṇḍa 'four' Rebus: kaṇḍa 'furnace, fire-altar' (Santali)

 *kolmo* 'paddy plant' Rebus: *kolami* 'smithy, forge' Vikalpa: *mogge* 'sprout, bud' Rebus: *mūh* 'ingot' (Santali) dolu 'plant of shoot height' Rebus: dul 'cast metal'

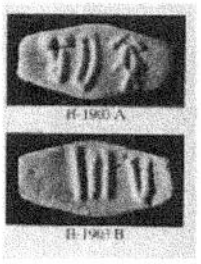 h1903A,B *aya aḍaren (homonym: aduru)*'alloy native metal'

 *kuṭila* 'bent' CDIAL 3230 kuṭi— in cmpd. 'curve', *kuṭika—* 'bent' MBh. Rebus: *kuṭila, katthīl* = bronze (8 parts copper and 2 parts tin) Duplicated: dula 'pair' Rebus: dul 'cast metal' Thus, cast bronze.

 *kanka* 'rim of jar' Rebus: *karṇīka* 'account (scribe)' *karṇī* 'supercargo'

Side B: *baṭa* = rimless pot (Kannada) Rebus:) *baṭa* = a kind of iron (G.)) *bhaṭa* furnace (Gujarati)

||| Numeral three: kolom 'three' Rebus: kolami 'smithy, forge'

 h291A *aya aḍaren (homonym: aduru)*'alloy native metal' *ḍhālako kāṇḍa* 'ingot, tools, pots and pans and metal-ware'.*dhāḷ* 'a slope'; 'inclination of a plane' (G.); *ḍhāḷiyum* = adj. sloping, inclining (G.) Rebus: *ḍhālako* = a large metal ingot (G.) *ḍhālakī* = a metal heated and poured into a mould; a solid piece of metal; an ingot (Gujarati)

 *kuṭila* 'bent' CDIAL 3230 kuṭi— in cmpd. 'curve', *kuṭika—* 'bent' MBh. Rebus: *kuṭila, katthīl* = bronze (8 parts copper and 2 parts tin) Duplicated: dula 'pair' Rebus: dul 'cast metal' Thus, cast bronze.

 *kanka* 'rim of jar' Rebus: *karṇīka* 'account (scribe)' *karṇī* 'supercargo'

 *khareḍo* = a currycomb (Gujarati) खरारा [*kharārā*] *m* (H) A currycomb. 2 Currying a horse. (Marathi) Rebus: करडा [*karaḍā*] Hard from alloy--iron, silver &c. (Marathi) *kharādī* ' turner' (Gujarati)

 m1086a *balad* m. ' ox ', gng. *bald,* (Ku.) *barad,* id. (N. Tarai) Rebus: *bharat* (5 copper, 4 zinc and 1 tin)(Punjabi) *pattar* 'trough' Rebus*: pattar* 'guild'. Thus, copper-zinc-tin alloy (worker) guild. *aya aḍaren (homonym: aduru)*'alloy native metal' *aya kammaṭa.*'coiner, mint alloy' PLUS *kāṇḍa* 'alloy metalware'

 m399A *aya aḍaren (homonym: aduru)*'alloy native metal'

muka 'ladle' (Kannada) 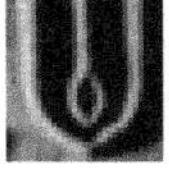 (Tamil)(DEDR 4887) Rebus: *mūh* 'ingot' (Santali) *baṭa* = rimless pot Rebus:) *baṭa* = a kind of iron (G.)) *bhaṭa* furnace (Gujarati) Thus, iron ingot.

kolom 'three' Rebus: kolami 'smithy, forge'

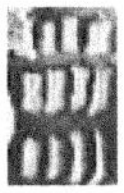 *baroṭi* 'twelve' *bhārata* 'a factitious alloy of copper, pewter, tin' (Marathi)

 *kanka* 'rim of jar' Rebus: *karṇīka* 'account (scribe)' *karṇī* 'supercargo'

 Allahdino 3A *खोंड [khōṇḍa] m A young bull, a bullcalf. (Marathi) Rebus: kōdār 'turner' (Bengali); कोंद kōnda 'engraver, lapidary setting or infixing gems' (Marathi) G. sãghāṛɔ m. 'lathe' ; संघाट joinery; M. sāgaḍ 'double-canoe' Rebus: sangataras. संगतराश lit. 'to collect stones, stone-cutter, mason.' aya aḍaren (homonym: aduru)*'alloy native metal'

 *muka* 'ladle' (Tamil)(DEDR 4887) Rebus: *mũh* 'ingot' (Santali) *baṭa* = rimless pot (Kannada) Rebus:) *baṭa* = a kind of iron (G.)) *bhaṭa* furnace (Gujarati) Thus, iron ingot.

 kolom 'three' Rebus: kolami 'smithy, forge' *kuṭila* 'bent' CDIAL 3230 kuṭi— in cmpd. 'curve', *kuṭika*— 'bent' MBh. Rebus: *kuṭila, katthīl* = bronze (8 parts copper and 2 parts tin) Duplicated: dula 'pair' Rebus: dul 'cast metal' Thus, cast bronze.

 *kanka* 'rim of jar' Rebus: *karṇīka* 'account (scribe)' *karṇī* 'supercargo'

 m1958A *aya aḍaren (homonym: aduru)*'alloy native metal'

 *muka* 'ladle' (Tamil)(DEDR 4887) Rebus: *mũh* 'ingot' (Santali) *baṭa* = rimless pot (Kannada) Rebus:) *baṭa* = a kind of iron (G.)) *bhaṭa* furnace (Gujarati) Thus, iron ingot.

kolom 'three' Rebus: kolami 'smithy, forge' dulo 'hole' Rebus: dul 'cast metal'.

 *kuṭila* 'bent' CDIAL 3230 kuṭi— in cmpd. 'curve', *kuṭika*— 'bent' MBh. Rebus: *kuṭila, katthīl* = bronze (8 parts copper and 2 parts tin)

 *kanka* 'rim of jar' Rebus: *karṇīka* 'account (scribe)' *karṇī* 'supercargo'

 m534A Copper plate inscription. *aya aḍaren (homonym: aduru)*'alloy native metal'

 *muka* 'ladle' (Tamil)(DEDR 4887) Rebus: *mũh* 'ingot' (Santali) *baṭa* = rimless pot (Kannada) Rebus:) *baṭa* = a kind of iron (G.)) *bhaṭa* furnace (Gujarati) Thus, iron ingot.

kolom 'three' Rebus: kolami 'smithy, forge' dulo 'hole' Rebus: dul 'cast metal'.

 *dula* 'pair' Rebus: *dul* 'cast (metal)' PLUS*kana, kanac* = corner (Santali); Rebus: *kañcu* = bronze (Telugu) Thus, cast bronze. PLUS खांडा [*khāṇḍā*] *m* A jag, notch, or indentation (as upon the edge of a tool or weapon). Rebus: *kāṇḍa* 'tools, pots and pans and metal-ware' Thus, cast bronze metalware.

 *kolmo* 'paddy plant' Rebus: *kolami* 'smithy, forge' Vikalpa: *mogge* 'sprout, bud' Rebus: *mũh* 'ingot' (Santali) dolu 'plant of shoot height' Rebus: dul 'cast metal'

ranku'antelope; Rebus: ranku 'tin' PLUS | *koḍa* 'one' Rebus: *koḍ* 'workshop'

 *kolmo* 'paddy plant' Rebus: *kolami* 'smithy, forge' Vikalpa: *mogge* 'sprout, bud' Rebus: *mũh* 'ingot' (Santali) dolu 'plant of shoot height' Rebus: dul 'cast metal'

 h141a *aya aḍaren (homonym: aduru)*'alloy native metal' *ayo ḍhālako* 'alloy metal ingot' sal 'splinter' Rebus: sal 'workshop'

'Arrow' sign hieroglyph (variant) This is a ligature of 'lid of pot' hieroglyph superscript on 'a linear stroke' numeral hieroglyph.*aḍaren* 'cover of pot or lid' Rebus: *aduru* 'native, unsmelted metal' PLUS koḍ = one (Santali); koḍ 'workshop' (Gujarati) kolom 'three' Rebus: kolami 'smithy, forge'

kuṭila 'bent' CDIAL 3230 kuṭi— in cmpd. 'curve', *kuṭika—* 'bent' MBh. Rebus: *kuṭila, katthīl* = bronze (8 parts copper and 2 parts tin) dula 'two' Rebus: dul 'cast metal'

kolmo 'paddy plant' Rebus: *kolami* 'smithy, forge' Vikalpa: *mogge* 'sprout, bud' Rebus: *mūh* 'ingot' (Santali) dolu 'plant of shoot height' Rebus: dul 'cast metal'

h657A

kuṭila 'bent' CDIAL 3230 kuṭi— in cmpd. 'curve', *kuṭika—* 'bent' MBh. Rebus: *kuṭila, katthīl* = bronze (8 parts copper and 2 parts tin) dula 'two' Rebus: dul 'cast metal'

aya aḍaren (homonym: aduru)'alloy native metal' *aya kāṇḍa* 'alloy metalware'

notch+slanted stroke reads rebus: *ḍhālako kāṇḍa* 'ingot, tools, pots and pans and metal-ware'.*dhāḷ* 'a slope'; 'inclination of a plane' (G.); *ḍhāḷiyum* = adj. sloping, inclining (G.) Rebus: *ḍhālako* = a large metal ingot (G.) *ḍhālakī* = a metal heated and poured into a mould; a solid piece of metal; an ingot (Gujarati) PLUS खांडा [*khāṇḍā*] *m* A jag, notch, or indentation (as upon the edge of a tool or weapon). Rebus: *kāṇḍa* 'tools, pots and pans and metal-ware' *Thus, together, the pair reads: āra erako khāṇḍā* 'brass, moltencast copper metalware'.

kolmo 'paddy plant' Rebus: *kolami* 'smithy, forge' Vikalpa: *mogge* 'sprout, bud' Rebus: *mūh* 'ingot' (Santali) dolu 'plant of shoot height' Rebus: dul 'cast metal'

m1885a *aya aḍaren (homonym: aduru)*'alloy native metal' *aya kammaṭa.*'coiner, mint alloy'

baroṭi 'twelve' *bhārata* 'a factitious alloy of copper, pewter, tin' (Marathi)

water-carrier hieroglyph *kuṭi*; Rebus: *kuṭhi* 'smelter furnace'.

m1917A *kola* 'tiger' Rebus: kolhe 'smelter' kol 'working in iron' pattar 'trough' Rebus: pattar 'guild, goldsmith'.

aya aḍaren (homonym: aduru)'alloy native metal' *ayo ḍhālako* 'alloy metal ingot'

kamaḍha dhātu  'crab' Rebus: *kammaṭa* 'mint, coiner'.*ḍato* = claws of crab (Santali) Rebus: 'mineral ore'

PLUS खांडा [*khāṇḍā*] *m* A jag, notch, or indentation (as upon the edge of a tool or weapon). Rebus: *kāṇḍa* 'tools, pots and pans and metal-ware' Thus, mint metalware, ore.

kolom 'three' Rebus: kolami 'smithy, forge' with circumscript: | *koḍa* 'one' Rebus: *koḍ* 'workshop' dula 'pair' Rebus: dul 'cast metal'. Thus metal smithy castings workshop.

| *koḍa* 'one' Rebus: *koḍ* 'workshop' PLUS ||| kolom 'three' Rebus: kolami 'smithy, forge' PLUS || sal 'splinter' Rebus sal 'workshop'

m1966A *aya aḍaren (homonym: aduru)*'alloy native metal' *ayo ḍhālako* 'alloy metal ingot'

kamaḍha 'crab' Rebus: *kammaṭa* 'mint, coiner'.*ḍato* = claws of crab (Santali) Rebus: *dhātu* 'mineral ore'

PLUS खांडा [*khāṇḍā*] *m* A jag, notch, or indentation (as upon the edge of a tool or weapon). Rebus: *kāṇḍa* 'tools, pots and pans and metal-ware' Thus, mint metalware, ore.

kolom 'three' Rebus: kolami 'smithy, forge' with circumscript: | *koḍa* 'one' Rebus: *koḍ* 'workshop' dula 'pair' Rebus: dul 'cast metal'. Thus metal smithy castings workshop.

m1113 m1113a '(native metal)

Pictorial motif hieroglyph: *khũṭ* 'zebu' Rebus: guild'

Text 1331 on m1113:

ayo 'fish' Rebus: aya 'iron' (Gujarati) ayas 'metal' (Vedic) PLUS aḍaren 'lid' Rebus: aduru 'native unsmelted metal'

sal 'splinter' Rebus: sal 'workshop'

ayo 'fish' Rebus: ayas 'iron' (Gujarati) ayas 'metal' (Vedic) PLUS infixed hieroglyph of slanted stroke: *dhāḷ* 'a slope'; 'inclination of a plane' (Gujarati); *ḍhāḷiyum* = adj. sloping, inclining (Gujarati) Rebus: *ḍhālako* = a large metal ingot (Gujarati) *ḍhālakī* = a metal heated and poured into a mould; a solid piece of metal; an ingot (Gujarati) Thus, the ligatured hieroglyph reads: *ayo ḍhālako* 'native metal ingot'.

ḍato 'claws or pincers of crab' (Santali) Rebus: *dhatu* 'mineral ore' (Santali) PLUS xola 'tail' Rebus: kolhe 'smelter'.

Vikalpa: *kamaḍha* 'crab' Rebus: *kammaṭa* 'mint, coiner'.*ḍato* = claws of crab (Santali) Rebus: *dhātu* 'mineral ore'

PLUS खांडा [*khāṇḍā*] *m* A jag, notch, or indentation (as upon the edge of a tool or weapon). Rebus: *kāṇḍa* 'tools, pots and pans and metal-ware' Thus, mint metalware, ore.

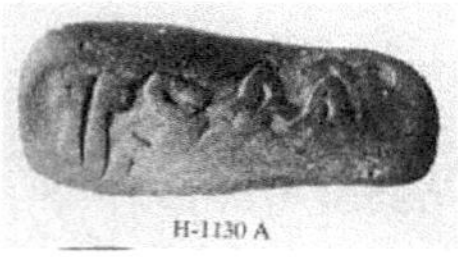

h1130A *aya aḍaren (homonym: aduru)*'alloy native metal' *ayo* 'fish' Rebus: *aya* 'iron' *ayas* 'metal'

baraḍo = spine; backbone (Tulu) Rebus: *baran, bharat* 'mixed alloys' (5 copper, 4 zinc and 1 tin) (Punjabi)

kanka 'rim of jar' Rebus: *karṇīka* 'account (scribe)' *karṇī* 'supercargo'

m0302A Composite animal with zebu horns. Native metal smith guild. Text 1380 ingot (from) iron smelter, tin smelter merchant guild. Focus on 'serpent' tail: *nāga* 'snake' Rebus: *nāga* 'lead' (Sanskrit) anakku 'tin' (Akkadian) *Kur.* xolā tail. *Malt.* qoli id. (DEDR 2135). Focus on human face: mukha, *mũh* 'face' Rebus*: mũh* 'ingot'. Zebu horns: *khũṭ* 'zebu' (Gujarati) Rebus: *khũṭ* '(native metal) community, guild' (Santali) kola 'tiger' Rebus: kolhe 'smelters' kol 'working in iron' ibha 'elephant' Rebus: ib 'iron' body of an ox: balad 'bull' Rebus: *baran, bharat* 'mixed alloys' (5 copper, 4 zinc and 1 tin) (Punjabi) dhatu 'scarf' Rebus: dhatu 'mineral ore'.

ayo 'fish'(Munda); ayas 'iron' (Sanskrit) Rebus: *ayas* 'metal' (Vedic)PLUS aḍaren 'lid' Rebus: aduru 'unsmelted native metal'. Thus the epigraph denotes rebus: iron, copper mineral smithy, unsmelted native metal alloy, fire-altar (furnace)

ayo 'fish'(Munda); ayas 'iron' (Sanskrit) Rebus: *ayas* 'metal' (Vedic)PLUS infixed ligature of slanted stroke: *dhāḷ* 'a slope'; 'inclination of a plane' (Gujarati); *ḍhāḷiyum* = adj. sloping, inclining (Gujarati) Rebus: *ḍhālako* = a large metal ingot (Gujarati) *ḍhālakī* = a metal heated and poured into a mould; a solid piece of metal; an ingot (Gujarati)
kāṇḍā 'arrow' Rebus: khāṇḍā 'tools, pots and pans, metalware'.

h148 *aya aḍaren (homonym: aduru)*'alloy native metal' *aya kammaṭa.*'coiner, mint alloy' kāṇḍā 'arrow' Rebus: khāṇḍā 'tools, pots and pans, metalware'.

m1890a *balad* m. ' ox ', gng. *bald,* (Ku.) *barad,* id. (N. Tarai) Rebus: *bharat* (5 copper, 4 zinc and 1 tin)(Punjabi) *pattar* 'trough' Rebus*: pattar* 'guild'. Thus, copper-zinc-tin alloy (worker) guild.
aya aḍaren (homonym: aduru)'alloy native metal' *aya kammaṭa.*'coiner, mint alloy' *muka* 'ladle' (Tamil)(DEDR 4887) Rebus: *mũh* 'ingot' (Santali) *baṭa* = rimless pot (Kannada) Rebus:) *baṭa* = a kind of iron (G.)) *bhaṭa* furnace (Gujarati) Thus, iron ingot.
kāṇḍā 'arrow' Rebus: khāṇḍā 'tools, pots and pans, metalware'

h58a *खोंड [khōṇḍa] m A young bull, a bullcalf. (Marathi) Rebus: kõdār 'turner' (Bengali); कोंद kōnda 'engraver, lapidary setting or infixing gems' (Marathi) G. sãghāṛɔ m. 'lathe' ; संघाट joinery; M. sãgaḍ 'double-canoe' Rebus: sangataras. संगतराश lit. 'to collect stones, stone-cutter, mason.'*
aya aḍaren (homonym: aduru)'alloy native metal' *ayo ḍhālako* 'alloy metal ingot'

dula 'pair' Rebus: dul 'cast metal' *mogge* 'sprout, bud' Rebus: *mũh* 'ingot' (Santali) Thus, cast metal ingot.

 and 
kanka 'rim of jar' Rebus: *karṇīka* 'account (scribe)' *karṇī* 'supercargo' *ḍhanga* = a crook used for pulling down the branches of trees, for goats, sheep camels (P.) Rebus:*ḍhangar* blacksmith'. PLUS

khareḍo = a currycomb (Gujarati) खरारा [*kharārā*] *m* (H) A currycomb. 2 Currying a horse. (Marathi) Rebus: करडा [*karaḍā*] Hard from alloy--iron, silver &c. (Marathi) *kharādī* ' turner' (Gujarati)

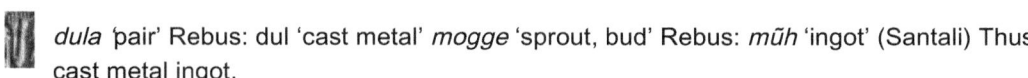

dula 'pair' Rebus: *dul* 'cast (metal)' PLUS*kana, kanac* = corner (Santali); Rebus: *kañcu* = bronze (Telugu) PLUS infixed kolmo 'paddy plant' Rebus: kolami 'smithy, forge'. Thus, cast bronze smithy, forge. Or, *mogge* 'sprout, bud' Rebus: *mũh* 'ingot' (Santali)Thus, cast bronze ingot. Read as: *kañcu dul mũh 'bronze cast ingot'*

water-carrier hieroglyph *kuṭi*; Rebus: *kuṭhi* 'smelter furnace'. PLUS 'rim of jar':

kanka 'rim of jar' Rebus: karṇīka 'account (scribe)' karṇī 'supercargo'

H-2055 A

h2055A *aya aḍaren (homonym: aduru)*'alloy native metal' *aya kammaṭa.*'coiner, mint alloy'
kanka 'rim of jar' Rebus: *karṇīka* 'account (scribe)' *karṇī* 'supercargo'

meḍ 'body' Rebus: *meḍ* 'iron' (Ho.) काठी [kāṭhī] *f* (काष्ट S) 'frame or structure of the body' (Marathi) Rebus: खंडी [khaṇḍī] measure of weight (Marathi) கண்டி; *kanṭi, n. < Mhr. khaṇḍil. [T. Tu. khaṇḍi, M. kaṇḍi.]* Candy, a weight, stated to be roughly equivalent to 500 lbs.

M-486 b

m486b *balad* m. ' ox ', gng. *bald*, (Ku.) *barad*, id. (N. Tarai) Rebus: *bharat* (5 copper, 4 zinc and 1 tin)(Punjabi) *pattar* 'trough' Rebus*: pattar* 'guild'. Thus, copper-zinc-tin alloy (worker) guild. *aya aḍaren (homonym: aduru)*'alloy native metal' *kānḍa* 'arrow' (Sanskrit) Rebus:*khānḍa* 'tools, pots and pans, metal-ware'. Rebus 2: kaṇḍ 'fire-altar' (Santali)

M-1095 a bis

m1095a *balad* m. ' ox ', gng. *bald*, (Ku.) *barad*, id. (N. Tarai) Rebus: *bharat* (5 copper, 4 zinc and 1 tin)(Punjabi) *pattar* 'trough' Rebus*: pattar* 'guild'. Thus, copper-zinc-tin alloy (worker) guild. *aya aḍaren (homonym: aduru)*'alloy native metal' *aya kammaṭa.*'coiner, mint alloy'

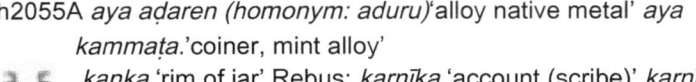

mēḍu height, rising ground, hillock (Kannada) Rebus: *meḍ* 'iron' (Ho.) kolom 'three'

Rebus: kolami 'smithy, forge' Thus, *meḍ kolami* 'iron smithy-forge'
kanka 'rim of jar' Rebus: *karṇīka* 'account (scribe)' *karṇī* 'supercargo'

M-377 a

m377a *aya aḍaren (homonym: aduru)*'alloy native metal' *aya kammaṭa.*'coiner, mint alloy'

The pair of 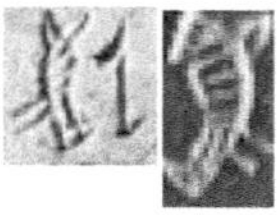 hieroglyph signs are compositions: bicha 'scorpion' (Assamese) Rebus: *bica* 'stone ore' (Santali) The pairing sign is a composition of: sloping stroke PLUS two short strokes of a 'splinter':*dhāḷ* 'a slope'; 'inclination of a plane' (Gujarati); *ḍhāḷiyum* = adj. sloping, inclining (Gujarati) Rebus: *ḍhālako* = a large metal ingot (Gujarati) *ḍhālakī* = a metal heated and poured into a mould; a solid piece of metal; an ingot (Gujarati)PLUS*sal* 'splinter' Rebus: *sal* 'workshop'. Thus the composition reads: *ḍhālako sal* 'ingot workshop'.

dāṭu 'cross'(Telugu) Rebus: *dhatu* 'mineral' (Santali).

kanka 'rim of jar' Rebus: *karṇīka* 'account (scribe)' *karṇī* 'supercargo'

h390a खोंड *[khōṇḍa] m A young bull, a bullcalf. (Marathi) Rebus: kōdār 'turner' (Bengali);* कोंद *kōnda 'engraver, lapidary setting or infixing gems' (Marathi) G. sãghārɔ m. 'lathe' ;* संघाट *joinery; M. sãgaḍ 'double-canoe' Rebus: sangataras.* संगतराश *lit. 'to collect stones, stone-cutter, mason.' aya aḍaren (homonym: aduru)*'alloy native metal'

  'Three' kolom 'three' Rebus: kolami 'smithy, forge' PLUS *ayo* 'fish' Rebus: *aya* 'iron' *ayas* 'metal' PLUS Strands of yarn/rope' hieroglyph: Hieroglyph: 'strands of yarn' Rebus reading: *dhā'tu* 'strand of rope' Rebus: *dhatu* 'mineral ore' (Santali)

 *āra* 'spokes' Rebus: *āra 'brass'*. cf. erka = ekke (Tbh. of arka) aka (Tbh. of arka) copper (metal); crystal (Kannada) Glyph: *eraka*'nave of wheel' Rebus: eraka 'copper'; cf. erka = ekke (Tbh. of arka) aka (Tbh. of arka) copper (metal); crystal (Kannada) *erako* 'moltencast copper' Duplicated: dula 'pair' Rebus: dul 'cast metal' Thus cast copper, brass casting.

m962A *खोंड [khōṇḍa] m A young bull, a bullcalf. (Marathi) Rebus: kōdār 'turner' (Bengali); कोंद kōnda 'engraver, lapidary setting or infixing gems' (Marathi) G. sãghāṛɔ m. 'lathe' ; संघाट joinery; M. sãgaḍ 'double-canoe' Rebus: sangataras. संगतराश lit. 'to collect stones, stone-cutter, mason.'*

aya aḍaren (homonym: aduru)'alloy native metal' *aya kammaṭa.*'coiner, mint alloy' *ayo* 'fish' Rebus: *aya* 'iron' *ayas* 'metal'
kāṇḍa 'arrow' (Sanskrit) Rebus:*khāṇḍa* 'tools, pots and pans, metal-ware'. Rebus 2: kaṇḍ 'fire-altar' (Santali)

m572A *aya aḍaren (homonym: aduru)*'alloy native metal' *ayo ḍhālako* 'alloy metal ingot' *ayo* 'fish' Rebus: *aya* 'iron' *ayas* 'metal' PLUS

 *kuṭila* 'bent' CDIAL 3230 kuṭi— in cmpd. 'curve', *kuṭika*— 'bent' MBh. Rebus: *kuṭila, katthīl* = bronze (8 parts copper and 2 parts tin)
Duplicated: dula 'pair' Rebus: dul 'cast metal' Thus, cast bronze.

 mēḍu height, rising ground, hillock (Kannada) Rebus: *mẽṛhẽt, meḍ* 'iron' (Munda.Ho.)

 *kanka* 'rim of jar' Rebus: *karṇīka* 'account (scribe)' *karṇī* 'supercargo'

m573a Line 2 read as at m572A. Line 1:

 *kanac* 'corner' Rebus: *kañcu* 'bronze'

 *meḍ* 'body' Rebus: *meḍ* 'iron' (Ho.) काठी [kāṭhī] *f* (काष्ट S) 'frame or structure of the body' (Marathi) Rebus: खंडी [khaṇḍī] measure of weight (Marathi) *கண்டி; kaṇṭi, n. < Mhr. khaṇḍil. [T. Tu. khaṇḍi, M. kaṇḍi.]* Candy, a weight, stated to be roughly equivalent to 500 lbs.

m1521 Side A read rebus as at m572A
Side B: Rhinoceros/boar: baḍhia = a castrated boar, a hog (Santali) baḍhi 'a caste who work both in iron and wood' (Santali) *baṟea* 'merchant'

Lothal 111a *aya aḍaren (homonym: aduru)*'alloy native metal' *aya kammaṭa.*'coiner, mint alloy'

kuṭila  'bent' CDIAL 3230 kuṭi— in cmpd. 'curve', *kuṭika*— 'bent' MBh. Rebus: *kuṭila,*

katthīl = bronze (8 parts copper and 2 parts tin) Duplicated: dula 'pair' Rebus: dul 'cast metal' Thus, cast bronze.
kanka 'rim of jar' Rebus: *karṇīka* 'account (scribe)' *karṇī* 'supercargo'

m1817a *खोंड [khōṇḍa] m A young bull, a bullcalf. (Marathi) Rebus: kõdār 'turner' (Bengali); कोंद kōnda 'engraver, lapidary setting or infixing gems' (Marathi) G. sãghāṛɔ m. 'lathe' ; संघाट joinery; M. sãgaḍ 'double-canoe' Rebus: sangataras. संगतराश lit. 'to collect stones, stone-cutter, mason.' aya aḍaren (homonym: aduru)*'alloy native metal'

loa 'ficus religiosa' Rebus: *lo* 'iron' (Sanskrit) PLUS unique ligatures: लोखंड [lōkhaṇḍa] *n* (लोह S) Iron. लोखंडाचे चणे खावविणें or चारणें To oppress grievously.लोखंडकाम [lōkhaṇḍakāma] *n* Iron work; that portion (of a building, machine &c.) which consists of iron. 2 The business of an ironsmith.लोखंडी [lōkhaṇḍī] *a* (लोखंड) Composed of iron; relating to iron. (Marathi)

kanka 'rim of jar' Rebus: *karṇīka* 'account (scribe)' *karṇī* 'supercargo'

h794A *aya aḍaren (homonym: aduru)*'alloy native metal' *ayo* 'fish' Rebus: *aya* 'iron' *ayas* 'metal' PLUS 'four' circumscript strokes: *aya kāṇḍa* 'alloy metalware' Side B: *baṭa* = rimless pot (Kannada) Rebus:) *baṭa* = a kind of iron (G.)) *bhaṭa* furnace (Gujarati) PLUS dula 'two' Rebus: dul 'cast metal'.

h46A

खोंड [khōṇḍa] m A young bull, a bullcalf. (Marathi) Rebus: kõdār 'turner' (Bengali); कोंद kōnda 'engraver, lapidary setting or infixing gems' (Marathi) G. sãghāṛɔ m. 'lathe' ; संघाट joinery; M. sãgaḍ 'double-canoe' Rebus: sangataras. संगतराश lit. 'to collect stones, stone-cutter, mason.' aya aḍaren (homonym: aduru)'alloy native metal'
ranku 'antelope' Rebus: ranku 'tin'.

kuṭila 'bent' CDIAL 3230 kuṭi— in cmpd. 'curve', *kuṭika*— 'bent' MBh. Rebus: *kuṭila,*

katthīl = bronze (8 parts copper and 2 parts tin)
kanka 'rim of jar' Rebus: *karṇīka* 'account (scribe)' *karṇī* 'supercargo'

m1744a *खोंड [khōṇḍa] m A young bull, a bullcalf. (Marathi) Rebus: kõdār 'turner' (Bengali); कोंद kōnda 'engraver, lapidary setting or infixing gems' (Marathi) G. sãghāṛɔ m. 'lathe' ; संघाट joinery; M. sãgaḍ 'double-canoe' Rebus: sangataras. संगतराश lit. 'to collect stones, stone-cutter, mason.' aya aḍaren (homonym: aduru)*'alloy native metal'

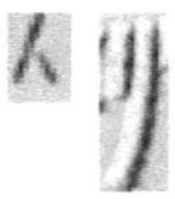

notch+slanted stroke reads rebus: *ḍhālako kāṇḍa* 'ingot, tools, pots and pans and metal-ware'.*ḍhāḷ* 'a slope'; 'inclination of a plane' (G.); *ḍhāḷiyum* = adj. sloping, inclining (G.) Rebus: *ḍhālako* = a large metal ingot (G.) *ḍhālakī* = a metal heated and poured into a mould; a solid piece of metal; an ingot (Gujarati) PLUS खांडा [*khāṇḍā*] *m* A jag, notch, or indentation (as upon the edge of a tool or weapon). Rebus: *kāṇḍa* 'tools, pots and pans and metal-ware' *Thus, together, the pair reads: āra erako khāṇḍā* 'brass, moltencast copper metalware'.

aḍaren 'lid of pot' Rebus: aduru 'unsmelted, native metal' PLUS

Pa. kandi (pl. -l) necklace, beads. Ga. (Punjabi) kandi (pl. -l) bead, (pl.) necklace; (S.2) kandiṭ bead. (DEDR 1215) Rebus: *கண்டி; kaṇṭi, n. < Mhr. khaṇḍil. [T. Tu. khaṇḍi, M. kaṇḍi.] 1. Candy, a weight, stated to be roughly equivalent to 500 lbs.; பாரமென் னும் நிறையளவு.* खंडीगणती or खंडोगणती [khaṇḍīgaṇatī or khaṇḍōgaṇatī] *ad* By candies; counting or reckoning by candies. खंडीवारी [khaṇḍīvārī] *ad* By scores, heaps, candies. खंडी [khaṇḍī] Applied to a great quantity; as खंडीभर पोरें, खंडीभर मेंढ्या, खंडीभर काम, खंडीभर बोलतो-लिहितो&c

'Arrow' sign hieroglyph (variant) This is a ligature of 'lid of pot' hieroglyph superscript on 'a linear stroke' numeral hieroglyph.*aḍaren* 'cover of pot or lid' Rebus: *aduru* 'native, unsmelted metal' PLUS koḍ = one (Santali); koḍ 'workshop' (Gujarati) PLUS Inverted variant:*aḍaren* 'lid of pot' Rebus: aduru 'unsmelted, native metal' PLUS

kolmo 'paddy plant' Rebus: *kolami* 'smithy, forge' Vikalpa: *mogge* 'sprout, bud' Rebus: *mũh* 'ingot' (Santali) dolu 'plant of shoot height' Rebus: dul 'cast metal'
kamaḍha 'archer, bow' Rebus: *kammaṭa* 'mint, coiner'.

khareḍo = a currycomb (Gujarati) खरारा [*kharārā*] *m* (H) A currycomb. 2 Currying a horse. (Marathi) Rebus: करडा [*karaḍā*] Hard from alloy--iron, silver &c. (Marathi) *kharādī* ' turner' (Gujarati)

M-323 a

m323a *खोंड [khōṇḍa] m A young bull, a bullcalf. (Marathi) Rebus: kõdār 'turner' (Bengali); कोंद kōnda 'engraver, lapidary setting or infixing gems' (Marathi) G. sãghāṛɔ m. 'lathe' ; संघाट joinery; M. sāgaḍ 'double-canoe' Rebus: sangataras. संगतराश lit. 'to collect stones, stone-cutter, mason.' aya aḍaren (homonym: aduru)*'alloy native metal'

aḍar 'harrow'; rebus: *aduru* 'native unsmelted metal'
ayo 'fish' Rebus: *aya* 'iron' *ayas* 'metal' *kāṇḍa* 'arrow' (Sanskrit) Rebus:*khāṇḍa* 'tools, pots and pans, metal-ware'. Rebus 2: kaṇḍ 'fire-altar' (Santali)

M-969 A

m969A *खोंड [khōṇḍa] m A young bull, a bullcalf. (Marathi) Rebus: kõdār 'turner' (Bengali); कोंद kōnda 'engraver, lapidary setting or infixing gems' (Marathi) G. sãghāṛɔ m. 'lathe' ; संघाट joinery; M. sāgaḍ 'double-canoe' Rebus: sangataras. संगतराश lit. 'to collect stones, stone-cutter, mason.' aya aḍaren (homonym: aduru)*'alloy native metal'

water-carrier hieroglyph *kuṭi*; Rebus: *kuṭhi* 'smelter furnace'. PLUS 'rim of jar':

kanka 'rim of jar' Rebus: karṇīka 'account (scribe)' karṇī 'supercargo'

M-1916 a

m1916a kola 'tiger' Rebus: kolhe 'smelter' kol 'working in iron' pattar 'trough' Rebus: pattar 'guild, goldsmith'.

Pa. kandi (pl. -l) necklace, beads. Ga. (Punjabi) kandi (pl. -l) bead, (pl.) necklace; (S.2) kandiṭ bead. (DEDR 1215) Rebus: *கண்டி; kaṇṭi, n. < Mhr. khaṇḍil. [T. Tu. khaṇḍi, M. kaṇḍi.] 1. Candy, a weight, stated to be*

roughly equivalent to 500 lbs.; பாரமென் னும் நிறையளவு. खंडीगणती or खंडोगणती [khaṇḍīgaṇatī or khaṇḍōgaṇatī] *ad* By candies; counting or reckoning by candies. खंडीवारी [khaṇḍīvārī] *ad* By scores, heaps, candies. खंडी [khaṇḍī] Applied to a great quantity; as खंडीभर पोरें, खंडीभर मेंढ्या, खंडीभर काम, खंडीभर बोलतो-लिहितो&c

sal 'splingter' Rebus sal' workshop'

meḍ 'body' Rebus: *meḍ* 'iron' (Ho.) काठी [kāṭhī] *f* (काष्ट S) 'frame or structure of the body' (Marathi) Rebus: खंडी [khaṇḍī] measure of weight (Marathi) *கண்டி; kaṇṭi, n. < Mhr. khaṇḍil. [T. Tu. khaṇḍi, M. kaṇḍi.]* Candy, a weight, stated to be roughly equivalent to 500 lbs.

kharedo = a currycomb (Gujarati) खरारा [*kharārā*] *m* (H) A currycomb. 2 Currying a horse. (Marathi) Rebus: करडा [*karaḍā*] Hard from alloy--iron, silver &c. (Marathi) *kharādī* ' turner' (Gujarati)

kanka 'rim of jar' Rebus: *karṇīka* 'account (scribe)' *karṇī* 'supercargo'

M-1845 a

h1845a *खोंड [khōṇḍa] m A young bull, a bullcalf. (Marathi) Rebus: kõdār 'turner' (Bengali); कोंद kōnda 'engraver, lapidary setting or infixing gems' (Marathi) G. sãghāṛɔ m. 'lathe' ; संघाट joinery; M. sãgaḍ 'double-canoe' Rebus: sangataras. संगतराश lit. 'to collect stones, stone-cutter, mason.' aya aḍaren (homonym: aduru)*'alloy native metal'

dula 'pair' Rebus: *dul* 'cast (metal)' PLUS *kana, kanac* = corner (Santali); Rebus: *kañcu* = bronze (Telugu) PLUS infixed kolmo 'paddy plant' Rebus: kolami 'smithy, forge'. Thus, cast bronze smithy, forge. Or, *mogge* 'sprout, bud' Rebus: *mũh* 'ingot' (Santali)Thus, cast bronze ingot. Read as: *kañcu dul mũh 'bronze cast ingot'*

kanka 'rim of jar' Rebus: *karṇīka* 'account (scribe)' *karṇī* 'supercargo'

L-23 a

Lothal 23a *खोंड [khōṇḍa] m A young bull, a bullcalf. (Marathi) Rebus: kõdār 'turner' (Bengali); कोंद kōnda 'engraver, lapidary setting or infixing gems' (Marathi) G. sãghāṛɔ m. 'lathe' ; संघाट joinery; M. sãgaḍ 'double-canoe' Rebus: sangataras. संगतराश lit. 'to collect stones, stone-cutter, mason.' aya aḍaren (homonym: aduru)*'alloy native metal'

aḍaren 'cover of pot or lid' Rebus: *aduru* 'native, unsmelted metal' Duplicated: dula 'pair' Rebus: dul 'cast metal'

kanka 'rim of jar' Rebus: *karṇīka* 'account (scribe)' *karṇī* 'supercargo'

M-1001 a

m1001a *खोंड [khōṇḍa] m A young bull, a bullcalf. (Marathi) Rebus: kõdār 'turner' (Bengali); कोंद kōnda 'engraver, lapidary setting or infixing gems' (Marathi) G. sãghāṛɔ m. 'lathe' ; संघाट joinery; M. sãgaḍ 'double-canoe' Rebus: sangataras. संगतराश lit. 'to collect stones, stone-cutter, mason.' aya aḍaren (homonym: aduru)*'alloy native metal'

 *aḍaren* 'cover of pot or lid' Rebus: *aduru* 'native, unsmelted metal' Duplicated: dula 'pair' Rebus: dul 'cast metal'

 *kanka* 'rim of jar' Rebus: *karṇīka* 'account (scribe)' *karṇī* 'supercargo'

m1081A *balad* m. ' ox ', gng. *bald*, (Ku.) *barad*, id. (N. Tarai) Rebus: *bharat* (5 copper, 4 zinc and 1 tin)(Punjabi) *pattar* 'trough' Rebus*: pattar* 'guild'. Thus, copper-zinc-tin alloy (worker) guild.

 *kamaḍha* 'crab' Rebus: *kammaṭa* 'mint, coiner'.*ḍato* = claws of crab (Santali) Rebus: *dhātu* 'mineral ore' PLUS खांडा [*khāṇḍā*] *m* A jag, notch, or indentation (as upon the edge of a tool or weapon). Rebus: *kāṇḍa* 'tools, pots and pans and metal-ware' Thus, mint metalware, ore.

 *baroṭi* 'twelve' *bhārata* 'a factitious alloy of copper, pewter, tin' (Marathi)
ayo 'fish' Rebus: *aya* 'iron' *ayas* 'metal' *aya aḍaren (homonym: aduru)*'alloy native metal'
aya kāṇḍa 'alloy metalware'

 *kanka* 'rim of jar' Rebus: *karṇīka* 'account (scribe)' *karṇī* 'supercargo'

 *kana, kanac* = corner (Santali); Rebus: *kañcu* = bronze (Telugu) PLUS खांडा [*khāṇḍā*] *m* A jag, notch, or indentation (as upon the edge of a tool or weapon). Rebus: *kāṇḍa* 'tools, pots and pans and metal-ware' Thus, bronze metalware. PLUS three infixes: kolom 'three' Rebus: kolami 'smithy, forge'

 beads: Pa. kandi (pl. -l) necklace, beads. Ga. (Punjabi) kandi (pl. -l) bead, (pl.) necklace; (S.2) kandiṭ bead. (DEDR 1215) Rebus: *கண்டி; kaṇṭi, n. < Mhr. khaṇḍil. [T. Tu. khaṇḍi, M. kaṇḍi.] 1. Candy, a weight, stated to be roughly equivalent to 500 lbs.; பாரமென் னும் நிறையளவு.* खंडीगणती or खंडोगणती [khaṇḍīgaṇatī or khaṇḍōgaṇatī] *ad* By candies; counting or reckoning by candies. खंडीवारी [khaṇḍīvārī] *ad* By scores, heaps, candies. खंडी [khaṇḍī] Applied to a great quantity; as खंडीभर पोरें, खंडीभर मेंढ्या, खंडीभर काम, खंडीभर बोलतो-लिहितो&c PLUS 'guild'.Thus, pewter guild.

aḍaren 'cover of pot or lid' Rebus: *aduru* 'native, unsmelted metal'

 m89A *खोंड [khōṇḍa] m A young bull, a bullcalf. (Marathi) Rebus: kōdār 'turner' (Bengali); कोंद kōnda 'engraver, lapidary setting or infixing gems' (Marathi) G. sãghārɔ m. 'lathe' ; संघाट joinery; M. sãgaḍ 'double-canoe' Rebus: sangataras. संगतराश lit. 'to collect stones, stone-cutter, mason.' aya aḍaren (homonym: aduru)*'alloy native metal' dula 'two' Rebus: dul 'cast metal' *baṭa* = rimless pot (Kannada) Rebus:) *baṭa* = a kind of iron (G.)) *bhaṭa* furnace (Gujarati) PLUS sal 'splinter' Rebus: sal 'workshop' dulo 'hole' Rebus: dul 'cast metal' PLUS ligature: 'lid of pot': *aḍaren* 'cover of pot or lid' Rebus: *aduru* 'native, unsmelted metal' Duplicated: dula 'pair' Rebus: dul 'cast metal' The hieroglyph denotes cast metal ingot.

  *kanka* 'rim of jar' Rebus: *karṇīka* 'account (scribe)' *karṇī* 'supercargo'

h593a The pictorial motif is of a composite animal. Focus on 'serpent' tail: *nāga* 'snake' Rebus: *nāga* 'lead' (Sanskrit) anakku 'tin' (Akkadian) *Kur.* xolā tail. *Malt.* qoli id. (DEDR 2135). Focus on human face: mukha, *mũh* 'face' Rebus*: mũh* 'ingot'. Zebu horns: *khũṭ* 'zebu' (Gujarati) Rebus: *khũṭ* '(native metal) community, guild' (Santali) kola 'tiger' Rebus: kolhe 'smelters' kol 'working in iron' ibha 'elephant' Rebus: ib 'iron' body of an ox: balad 'bull' Rebus: *baran, bharat* 'mixed alloys' (5 copper, 4 zinc and 1 tin) (Punjabi) dhatu 'scarf' Rebus: dhatu 'mineral ore'.
aya kāṇḍa 'alloy metalware' PLUS sal 'splinter' Rebus: sal 'workshop'
aya kammaṭa.'coiner, mint alloy'
aya aḍaren (homonym: aduru)'alloy native metal'

dula 'pair' Rebus: dul 'cast metal' *mogge* 'sprout, bud' Rebus: *mũh* 'ingot' (Santali) Thus, cast metal ingot.

kanka 'rim of jar' Rebus: *karṇīka* 'account (scribe)' *karṇī* 'supercargo'

Lothal 66f *ayo* 'fish' Rebus: *aya* 'iron' *ayas* 'metal'

m298a *खोंड [khōṇḍa] m A young bull, a bullcalf. (Marathi) Rebus: kõdār 'turner' (Bengali); कोंद kōnda 'engraver, lapidary setting or infixing gems' (Marathi) G. sãghāṛɔ m. 'lathe' ; संघाट joinery; M. sãgaḍ 'double-canoe' Rebus: sangataras. संगतराश lit. 'to collect stones, stone-cutter, mason.'* Text read rebus as at Lothal 66f. *ayo* 'fish' Rebus: *aya* 'iron' *ayas* 'metal'
Pictorial motif hieroglyphs: *balad* m. ' ox ', gng. *bald*, (Ku.) *barad*, id. (N. Tarai) Rebus: *bharat* (5 copper, 4 zinc and 1 tin)(Punjabi) *pattar* 'trough' Rebus*: pattar* 'guild'. Thus, copper-zinc-tin alloy (worker) guild. PLUS *खोंड [khōṇḍa] m A young bull, a bullcalf. (Marathi) Rebus: kõdār 'turner' (Bengali); कोंद kōnda 'engraver, lapidary setting or infixing gems' (Marathi) G. sãghāṛɔ m. 'lathe' ; संघाट joinery; M. sãgaḍ 'double-canoe' Rebus: sangataras. संगतराश lit. 'to collect stones, stone-cutter, mason.'*

Kalibangan 34A *miṇḍāl* 'markhor' (Tōrwālī) *meḍho* a ram, a sheep (G.)(CDIAL 10120) Rebus: *mẽṛhẽt, meḍ* 'iron' (Mu.Ho.)
ayo 'fish' Rebus: *aya* 'iron' *ayas* 'metal'

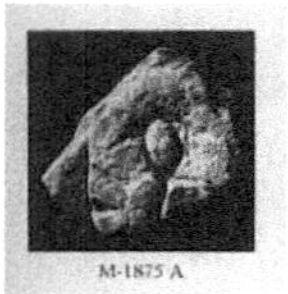
m1875A dulo 'hole' Rebus: dul 'cast metal' PLUS

aḍaren 'cover of pot or lid' Rebus: *aduru* 'native, unsmelted metal'
Duplicated: dula 'pair' Rebus: dul 'cast metal'

Louvre cylinder seal *miṇḍāl* 'markhor' (Tōrwālī) *meḍho* a ram, a sheep (G.)(CDIAL 10120) Rebus: *mẽṛhẽt, meḍ* 'iron' (Mu.Ho.) *ayo* 'fish' Rebus: *aya* 'iron' *ayas* 'metal'

kolmo 'paddy plant' Rebus: *kolami* 'smithy, forge' Vikalpa: *mogge* 'sprout, bud' Rebus: *mũh* 'ingot' (Santali) dolu 'plant of shoot height' Rebus: dul 'cast metal'

kōḍu 'horn' Rebus: *kōḍu* 'workshop' PLUS *kūdī* 'bunch of twigs' (Sanskrit) Rebus: *kuṭhi* 'smelter furnace' (Santali)

meḍ 'body' Rebus: *meḍ* 'iron' (Ho.) काठी [kāṭhī] *f* (काष्ट S) 'frame or structure of the body' (Marathi) Rebus: खंडी [khaṇḍī] measure of weight (Marathi) *கண்டி; kaṇṭi, n. < Mhr. khaṇḍil. [T. Tu. khaṇḍi, M. kaṇḍi.]* Candy, a weight, stated to be roughly equivalent to 500 lbs. PLUS *kaṇḍo* 'stool, seat' Rebus: *kāṇḍa* 'metalware' *kaṇḍa* 'fire-altar'

nāga 'snake' Rebus: *nāga* 'lead' (Sanskrit) anakku 'tin' (Akkadian)
Rhinoceros/boar: baḍhia = a castrated boar, a hog (Santali) baḍhi 'a caste who work both in iron and wood' (Santali) *baṟea* 'merchant'

rāngo 'water buffalo bull' (Ku.N.)(CDIAL 10559) Rebus: rango 'pewter'

dula 'two' Rebus: dul 'cast metal' PLUS kola 'tiger' Rebus: kol 'working in iron' Thus iron castings. Flanking:
meḍ 'body' Rebus: *meḍ* 'iron' (Ho.)PLUS eraka 'upraised hand' Rebus; erako 'moltencast copper' PLUS kolmo 'paddy plant' Rebus: kolami 'smithy, forge'.

dula 'hole' Rebus: dul 'cast metal' PLUS *balad* m. ' ox ', gng. *bald*, (Ku.) *barad*, id. (N. Tarai) Rebus: *bharat* (5 copper, 4 zinc and 1 tin)(Punjabi) Thus, cast *bharat* 'alloy of copper, zinc and tin' PLUS eruvai 'eagle' Rebus: eruvai 'copper'

khōṇḍa A stock or stump (Marathi); 'leafless tree' (Marathi) Rebus: *kõdār* 'turner' (Bengali); *kõdā* 'to turn in a lathe' (Bengali).

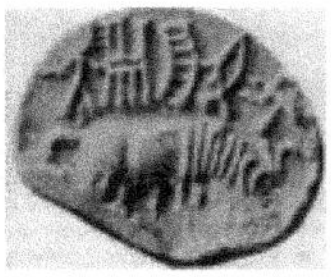

BM 120573 *balad* m. ' ox ', gng. *bald*, (Ku.) *barad*, id. (N. Tarai) Rebus: *bharat* (5 copper, 4 zinc and 1 tin)(Punjabi) *pattar* 'trough' Rebus: *pattar* 'guild'. Thus, copper-zinc-tin alloy (worker) guild.

loa 'ficus religiosa' Rebus: *lo* 'iron' (Sanskrit) PLUS unique ligatures: लोखंड [lōkhaṇḍa] *n* (लोह S) Iron. लोखंडाचे चणे खावविणें or चारणें To oppress grievously.लोखंडकाम [lōkhaṇḍakāma] *n* Iron work; that portion (of a building, machine &c.) which consists of iron. 2 The business of an ironsmith.लोखंडी [lōkhaṇḍī] *a* (लोखंड) Composed of iron; relating to iron. (Marathi)
ayo 'fish' Rebus: *aya* 'iron' *ayas* 'metal'

kuṭila 'bent' CDIAL 3230 kuṭi— in cmpd. 'curve', *kuṭika—* 'bent' MBh. Rebus: *kuṭila, katthīl* = bronze (8 parts copper and 2 parts tin) Duplicated: dula 'pair' Rebus: dul 'cast metal' Thus, cast bronze.
ranku 'antelope' Rebus: ranku 'tin'

meḍ 'body' Rebus: *meḍ* 'iron' (Ho.) काठी [kāṭhī] *f* (काष्ट S) 'frame or structure of the body' (Marathi) Rebus: खंडी [khaṇḍī] measure of weight (Marathi) *கண்டி; kaṇṭi, n. < Mhr. khaṇḍil. [T. Tu. khaṇḍi, M. kaṇḍi.]* Candy, a weight, stated to be roughly equivalent to 500 lbs.

Chanhudaro 9a *खोंड [khōṇḍa] m A young bull, a bullcalf. (Marathi) Rebus: kõdār 'turner' (Bengali); कोंद kōnda 'engraver, lapidary setting or infixing gems' (Marathi) G. sãghāṛɔ m. 'lathe' ; संघाट joinery; M. sãgaḍ 'double-canoe' Rebus: sangataras. संगतराश lit. 'to collect stones, stone-cutter, mason.'*
ayo 'fish' Rebus: *aya* 'iron' *ayas* 'metal'

muka 'ladle' (Tamil)(DEDR 4887) Rebus: *mũh* 'ingot' (Santali) *baṭa* = rimless pot (Kannada) Rebus:) *baṭa* = a kind of iron (G.)) *bhaṭa* furnace (Gujarati) Thus, iron ingot.

kolom 'three' Rebus: kolami 'smithy, forge'*dula* 'pair' Rebus: *dul* 'cast (metal)' PLUS*kana, kanac* = corner (Santali); Rebus: *kañcu* = bronze (Telugu) PLUS infixed kolmo 'paddy plant' Rebus: kolami 'smithy, forge'. Thus, cast bronze smithy, forge. Or, *mogge* 'sprout, bud' Rebus: *mũh* 'ingot' (Santali)Thus, cast bronze ingot. Read as:
kañcu dul mũh 'bronze cast ingot'
ayo ḍhālako 'alloy metal ingot

'water-carrier hieroglyph *kuṭi*; Rebus: *kuṭhi* 'smelter furnace'.

h24a *खोंड [khōṇḍa] m A young bull, a bullcalf. (Marathi) Rebus: kõdār 'turner' (Bengali); कोंद kōnda 'engraver, lapidary setting or infixing gems' (Marathi) G. sãghāṛɔ m. 'lathe' ; संघाट joinery; M. sãgaḍ 'double-canoe' Rebus: sangataras. संगतराश lit. 'to collect stones, stone-cutter, mason.' ayo ḍhālako* 'alloy metal ingot'
muka 'ladle' (Tamil)(DEDR 4887) Rebus: *mũh* 'ingot' (Santali)

baṭa = rimless pot (Kannada) Rebus:) *baṭa* = a kind of iron (G.)) *bhaṭa* furnace (Gujarati) Thus, iron ingot.
kolom 'three' Rebus: kolami 'smithy, forge'

baraḍo = spine; backbone (Tulu) Rebus: *baran, bharat* 'mixed alloys' (5 copper, 4 zinc and 1 tin) (Punjabi)

kəṭhā´r,  kc. *kuṭhār* m. ' granary, storeroom '(WPah.)(CDIAL 3550). *koṭhārī m.* ' storekeeper' (Gujarati)(CDIAL 3551) Thus, storeroom (of) *kolom* 'three' Rebus: *kolami* 'smithy, forge'. Dula 'pair' Rebus: dul 'cast metal' Thus, together *dul kolami*

kuṭhār 'metal smithy castings storeroom'

kanka 'rim of jar' Rebus: *karṇīka* 'account (scribe)' *karṇī* 'supercargo'

h956a *खोंड [khōṇḍa] m A young bull, a bullcalf. (Marathi) Rebus: kõdār 'turner' (Bengali); कोंद kōnda 'engraver, lapidary setting or infixing gems' (Marathi) G. sãghāṛɔ m. 'lathe' ; संघाट joinery; M. sãgaḍ 'double-canoe' Rebus: sangataras. संगतराश lit. 'to collect stones, stone-cutter, mason.' ayo* 'fish' Rebus: *aya* 'iron' *ayas* 'metal'

Three sign sequence:

muka 'ladle' (Tamil)(DEDR 4887) Rebus: *mũh* 'ingot' (Santali) *baṭa* = rimless pot (Kannada) Rebus:) *baṭa* = a kind of iron (G.)) *bhaṭa* furnace (Gujarati) Thus, iron ingot.

kharedo = a currycomb (Gujarati) खरारा [*kharārā*] *m* (H) A currycomb. 2 Currying a horse. (Marathi) Rebus: करडा [*karaḍā*] Hard from alloy--iron, silver &c. (Marathi) *kharādī* ' turner' (Gujarati)

kolom 'three' Rebus: kolami 'smithy, forge' *kāṇḍa* 'arrow' (Sanskrit) Rebus:*khāṇḍa* 'tools, pots and pans, metal-ware'. Rebus 2: kaṇḍ 'fire-altar' (Santali) Thus, the three sign sequence reads: iron ingot, furnace smithy, fire-altar metalware

h860a खोंड *[khōṇḍa] m A young bull, a bullcalf. (Marathi) Rebus: kõdār 'turner' (Bengali);* कोंद *kōnda 'engraver, lapidary setting or infixing gems' (Marathi) G. sãghāṛɔ m. 'lathe' ;* संघाट *joinery; M. sãgaḍ 'double-canoe' Rebus: sangataras.* संगतराश *lit. 'to collect stones, stone-cutter, mason.'*

ayo ḍhālako 'alloy metal ingot'

aya kammaṭa.'coiner, mint alloy'

Three sign sequence:

muka 'ladle' (Tamil)(DEDR 4887) Rebus: *mũh* 'ingot' (Santali) *baṭa* = rimless pot (Kannada) Rebus:) *baṭa* = a kind of iron (G.)) *bhaṭa* furnace (Gujarati) Thus, iron ingot.

kolom 'three' Rebus: kolami 'smithy, forge' *kāṇḍa* 'arrow' (Sanskrit) Rebus:*khāṇḍa* 'tools, pots and pans, metal-ware'. Rebus 2: kaṇḍ 'fire-altar' (Santali) Thus, the three sign sequence reads: iron ingot, furnace smithy, fire-altar metalware

H-1813 A H-1813 B

h1813A Read rebus as at h1811A

H-1811 A H-1811 B

h1811A Side B: | *koḍa* 'one' Rebus: *koḍ* 'workshop' PLUS ||| kolom 'three' Rebus: kolami 'smithy, forge' PLUS || sal 'splinter' Rebus sal 'workshop'

सांड [sāṇḍa] *f* (षद S) An outlet for superfluous water (as through a dam or mound); a sluice, a floodvent. Rebus: सांडणी [sāṇḍaṇī] *f* (H) An instrument of goldsmiths. It is hooked or curved at the extremity; and is used to draw things out of the fire.

सांठा [*sāṇṭhā*] *m* (संचय S) A collection, heap, hoard, store, stock.साटें [*sāṭēṃ*] *n* (संचय S) A whole investment; the total quantity of merchandise (brought to market by one merchant).

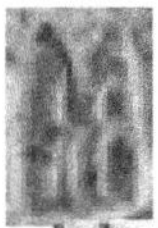

Ligature: two peaks: mēḍu height, rising ground, hillock (Kannada) Rebus: *meḍ* 'iron' (Ho.) dula 'pair' Rebus: dul 'cast metal' PLUS |||| Numeral 4: gaṇḍa 'four' Rebus: kaṇḍa 'furnace, fire-altar' (Santali)

'Arrow' sign hieroglyph (variant) This is a ligature of 'lid of pot' hieroglyph superscript on 'a linear stroke' numeral hieroglyph.*aḍaren* 'cover of pot or lid' Rebus: *aduru* 'native, unsmelted metal' PLUS infixed: *kamaḍha* 'crab' Rebus: *kammaṭa* 'mint, coiner'. *ḍato* = claws of crab (Santali) Rebus: *dhātu* 'mineral ore'

|||| Numeral 4: gaṇḍa 'four' Rebus: kaṇḍa 'furnace, fire-altar' (Santali)

Side A: *ayo* 'fish' Rebus: *aya* 'iron' *ayas* 'metal'

muka 'ladle' (Tamil)(DEDR 4887) Rebus: *mũh* 'ingot' (Santali) *baṭa* = rimless pot (Kannada) Rebus:) *baṭa* = a kind of iron (G.)) *bhaṭa* furnace (Gujarati) Thus, iron ingot.
kolom 'three' Rebus: kolami 'smithy, forge'

kamaḍha 'crab' Rebus: *kammaṭa* 'mint, coiner'.
ḍato = claws of crab (Santali) Rebus: *dhātu* 'mineral ore'
baṭa = rimless pot (Kannada) Rebus:) *baṭa* = a kind of iron (G.)) *bhaṭa* furnace (Gujarati) INFIXED खांडा [*khāṇḍā*] *m* A jag, notch, or indentation (as upon the edge of a tool or weapon). Rebus: *kāṇḍa* 'tools, pots and pans and metal-ware'

khareḍo = a currycomb (Gujarati) खरारा [*kharārā*] *m* (H) A currycomb. 2 Currying a horse. (Marathi) Rebus: करडा [*karaḍā*] Hard from alloy--iron, silver &c. (Marathi) *kharādī* ' turner' (Gujarati)

h136A

kolmo 'paddy plant' Rebus: *kolami* 'smithy, forge' Vikalpa: *mogge* 'sprout, bud' Rebus: *mũh* 'ingot' (Santali) dolu 'plant of shoot height' Rebus: dul 'cast metal'

सांड [sāṇḍa] *f* (षद S) An outlet for superfluous water (as through a dam or mound); a sluice, a floodvent. Rebus: सांडणी [sāṇḍaṇī] *f* (H) An instrument of goldsmiths. It is hooked or curved at the extremity; and is used to draw things out of the fire.
सांठा [*sāṇṭhā*] *m* (संचय S) A collection, heap, hoard, store, stock.साटें [*sāṭēṃ*] *n* (संचय S) A whole investment; the total quantity of merchandise (brought to market by one merchant).

muka 'ladle' (Tamil)(DEDR 4887) Rebus: *mũh* 'ingot' (Santali) *baṭa* = rimless pot (Kannada) Rebus:) *baṭa* = a kind of iron (G.)) *bhaṭa* furnace (Gujarati) Thus, iron ingot.
kolom 'three' Rebus: kolami 'smithy, forge'

aya aḍaren (homonym: aduru)'alloy native metal'

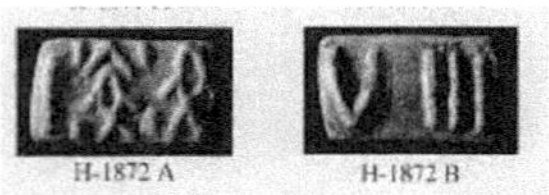
h1872A *aya aḍaren (homonym: aduru)*'alloy native metal' *aya kāṇḍa* 'alloy metalware' *baṭa* = rimless pot (Kannada) Rebus:) *baṭa* = a kind of iron (G.)) *bhaṭa* furnace (Gujarati)
kolom 'three' Rebus: kolami 'smithy, forge'

m1837a *खोंड [khōṇḍa] m A young bull, a bullcalf. (Marathi) Rebus: kõdār 'turner' (Bengali); कोंद kōnda 'engraver, lapidary setting or infixing gems' (Marathi) G. sãghāṛɔ m. 'lathe' ; संघाट joinery; M. sãgaḍ 'double-canoe' Rebus: sangataras. संगतराश lit. 'to collect stones, stone-cutter, mason.' ayo* 'fish' Rebus: *aya* 'iron' *ayas* 'metal' dula 'pair' Rebus: dul 'cast metal' smelter/furnace'.

water-carrier hieroglyph *kuṭi*; Rebus: *kuṭhi* 'smelter furnace'.

h815A *ayo* 'fish' Rebus: *aya* 'iron' *ayas* 'metal' dula 'pair' Rebus: dul 'cast metal'

'Arrow' sign hieroglyph (variant) This is a ligature of 'lid of pot' hieroglyph superscript on 'a linear stroke' numeral hieroglyph.*aḍaren* 'cover of pot or lid' Rebus: *aduru* 'native, unsmelted metal' PLUS koḍ = one (Santali); koḍ 'workshop' (Gujarati) *kāṇḍa* 'arrow' (Sanskrit) Rebus:*khāṇḍa* 'tools, pots and pans, metal-ware'. Rebus 2: kaṇḍ 'fire-altar' (Santali)

h230A Read rebus as at h815A

h248A *ayo* 'fish' Rebus: *aya* 'iron' *ayas* 'metal' dula 'pair' Rebus: dul 'cast metal' ranku 'antelope' Rebus: ranku 'tin'

kuṭila  'bent' CDIAL 3230 kuṭi— in cmpd. 'curve', *kuṭika*— 'bent' MBh. Rebus: *kuṭila, katthīl* = bronze (8 parts copper and 2 parts tin)

 *kanka* 'rim of jar' Rebus: *karṇīka* 'account (scribe)' *karṇī* 'supercargo'

 *khareḍo* = a currycomb (Gujarati) खरारा [*kharārā*] *m* (H) A currycomb. 2 Currying a horse. (Marathi) Rebus: करडा [*karaḍā*] Hard from alloy--iron, silver &c. (Marathi) *kharādī* ' turner' (Gujarati) *kamaḍha* 'crab' Rebus: *kammaṭa* 'mint, coiner'.
ḍato = claws of crab (Santali) Rebus: *dhātu* 'mineral ore'

h245A *ayo* 'fish' Rebus: *aya* 'iron' *ayas* 'metal' dula 'pair' Rebus: dul 'cast metal'

 *kanka* 'rim of jar' Rebus: *karṇīka* 'account (scribe)' *karṇī* 'supercargo' gaṇḍa 'four' Rebus: kaṇḍa 'furnace, fire-altar' (Santali) PLUS

 *dula* 'pair' Rebus: *dul* 'cast (metal)' PLUS*kana, kanac* = corner (Santali); Rebus: *kañcu* = bronze (Telugu) PLUS infixed kolmo 'paddy plant' Rebus: kolami 'smithy, forge'. Thus, cast bronze smithy, forge. Or, *mogge* 'sprout, bud' Rebus: *mūh* 'ingot' (Santali)Thus, cast bronze ingot. Read as: *kañcu dul mūh 'bronze cast ingot'*

m1720A *खोंड [khōṇḍa] m A young bull, a bullcalf. (Marathi) Rebus: kōdār 'turner' (Bengali); कोंद kōnda 'engraver, lapidary setting or infixing gems' (Marathi) G. sãghāṛɔ m. 'lathe' ; संघाट joinery; M. sāgaḍ 'double-canoe' Rebus: sangataras. संगतराश lit. 'to collect stones, stone-cutter, mason.'*

aya kammaṭa.'coiner, mint alloy'
ayo ḍhālako 'alloy metal ingot'

 *kanka* 'rim of jar' Rebus: *karṇīka* 'account (scribe)' *karṇī* 'supercargo' *kaṇḍo* 'stool, seat' Rebus: *kāṇḍa* 'metalware' *kaṇḍa* 'fire-altar'

PLUS

 *dāṭu* 'cross'(Telugu) Rebus: *dhatu* 'mineral' (Santali).

h874A

aya kammaṭa.'coiner, mint alloy'

ayo ḍhālako 'alloy metal ingot'

kānḍa 'arrow' (Sanskrit) Rebus:*khānḍa* 'tools, pots and pans, metal-ware'. Rebus 2: kaṇḍ 'fire-altar' (Santali)

 Side B: mēḍu height, rising ground, hillock (Kannada) Rebus: *meḍ* 'iron' (Ho.) kolom 'three' Rebus: kolami 'smithy, forge' Thus, *meḍ kolami* 'iron smithy-forge'

 *kanka* 'rim of jar' Rebus: *karṇīka* 'account (scribe)' *karṇī* 'supercargo'

 *khareḍo* = a currycomb (Gujarati) खरारा [*khararā*] *m* (H) A currycomb. 2 Currying a horse. (Marathi) Rebus: करडा [*karaḍā*] Hard from alloy--iron, silver &c. (Marathi) *kharādī* ' turner' (Gujarati)

 m250a *balad* m. ' ox ', gng. *bald*, (Ku.) *barad*, id. (N. Tarai) Rebus: *bharat* (5 copper, 4 zinc and 1 tin)(Punjabi) *pattar* 'trough' Rebus*: pattar* 'guild'. Thus, copper-zinc-tin alloy (worker) guild.

aya kāṇḍa 'alloy metalware' *ayo ḍhālako* 'alloy metal ingot' gaṇḍa 'four' Rebus: kaṇḍa 'furnace, fire-altar' (Santali) PLUS

 *dula* 'pair' Rebus: *dul* 'cast (metal)' PLUS*kana, kanac* = corner (Santali); Rebus: *kañcu* = bronze (Telugu) PLUS infixed kolmo 'paddy plant' Rebus: kolami 'smithy, forge'. Thus, cast bronze smithy, forge. Or, *mogge* 'sprout, bud' Rebus: *mũh* 'ingot' (Santali)Thus, cast bronze ingot. Read as: *kañcu dul mũh 'bronze cast ingot'*

h2019A,B *aya aḍaren (homonym: aduru)*'alloy native metal' *aya kammaṭa.*'coiner, mint alloy'

 *kanka* 'rim of jar' Rebus: *karṇīka* 'account (scribe)' *karṇī* 'supercargo'

 *meḍ* 'body' Rebus: *meḍ* 'iron' (Ho.) काठी [kāṭhī] *f* (काष्ट S) 'frame or structure of the body' (Marathi) Rebus: खंडी [khaṇḍī] measure of weight (Marathi) கண்டி; *kaṇṭi, n. < Mhr. khaṇḍil. [T. Tu. khaṇḍi, M. kaṇḍi.]* Candy, a weight, stated to be roughly equivalent to 500 lbs.

Side B: *ayo* 'fish' Rebus: *aya* 'iron' *ayas* 'metal' dula 'two' Rebus: dul 'cast metal' ranku 'liquid measure' Rebus: ranku 'tin'

 *dāṭu* 'cross'(Telugu) Rebus: *dhatu* 'mineral' (Santali).

 *kuṭila* 'bent' CDIAL 3230 kuṭi— in cmpd. 'curve', *kuṭika—* 'bent' MBh. Rebus: *kuṭila, katthīl* = bronze (8 parts copper and 2 parts tin)

h1124A *ayo* 'fish' Rebus: *aya* 'iron' *ayas* 'metal' *aya aḍaren (homonym: aduru)*'alloy native metal' *aya kāṇḍa* 'alloy metalware'

m1827a Read rebus as at m1836a

m1836a *खोंड [khōṇḍa] m A young bull, a bullcalf. (Marathi) Rebus: kõdār 'turner' (Bengali); कोंद kōnda 'engraver, lapidary setting or infixing gems' (Marathi) G. sãghāṛɔ m. 'lathe' ; संघाट joinery; M. sãgaḍ 'double-canoe' Rebus: sangataras. संगतराश lit. 'to collect stones, stone-cutter, mason.'*
ayo ḍhālako 'alloy metal ingot' *kāṇḍa* 'arrow' (Sanskrit) Rebus:*khāṇḍa* 'tools, pots and pans, metal-ware'. Rebus 2: kaṇḍ 'fire-altar' (Santali)

m186a
Read rebus as at m657a

m657a *खोंड [khōṇḍa] m A young bull, a bullcalf. (Marathi) Rebus: kõdār 'turner' (Bengali); कोंद kōnda 'engraver, lapidary setting or infixing gems' (Marathi) G. sãghāṛɔ m. 'lathe' ; संघाट joinery; M. sãgaḍ 'double-canoe' Rebus: sangataras. संगतराश lit. 'to collect stones, stone-cutter, mason.'*
aya kammaṭa.'coiner, mint alloy' *kāṇḍa* 'arrow' (Sanskrit) Rebus:*khāṇḍa* 'tools, pots and pans, metal-ware'. Rebus 2: kaṇḍ 'fire-altar' (Santali)

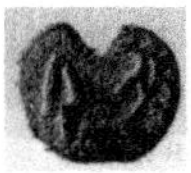

h819a Read rebus as at m657a
m1907A Read rebus as at m657a PLUS Side B: *baṭa* = rimless pot (Kannada) Rebus:) *baṭa* = a kind of iron (G.)) *bhaṭa* furnace (Gujarati PLUS gaṇḍa 'four' Rebus: kaṇḍa 'furnace, fire-altar' (Santali)

m185a Read rebus as at m978A

m978A *खोंड [khōṇḍa] m A young bull, a bullcalf. (Marathi) Rebus: kõdār 'turner' (Bengali); कोंद kōnda 'engraver, lapidary setting or infixing gems' (Marathi) G. sãghāṛɔ m. 'lathe' ; संघाट joinery; M. sãgaḍ 'double-canoe' Rebus: sangataras. संगतराश lit. 'to collect stones, stone-cutter, mason.'* *ayo* 'fish' Rebus: *aya* 'iron' *ayas* 'metal' *kāṇḍa* 'arrow' (Sanskrit) Rebus:*khāṇḍa* 'tools, pots and pans, metal-ware'. Rebus 2: kaṇḍ 'fire-altar' (Santali)

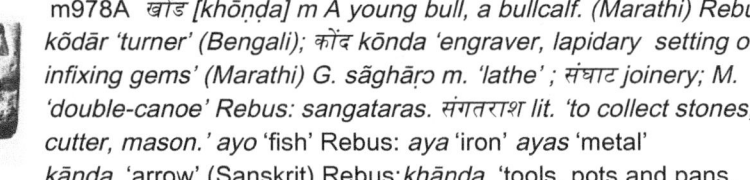

Banawali 3A *खोंड [khōṇḍa] m A young bull, a bullcalf. (Marathi) Rebus: kõdār 'turner' (Bengali); कोंद kōnda 'engraver, lapidary setting or infixing gems' (Marathi) G. sãghāṛɔ m. 'lathe' ; संघाट joinery; M. sãgaḍ 'double-canoe' Rebus: sangataras. संगतराश lit. 'to collect stones, stone-cutter, mason.'* gaṇḍa 'four' Rebus: kaṇḍa 'furnace, fire-altar' (Santali) *PLUS ayo* 'fish' Rebus: *aya* 'iron' *ayas* 'metal'

kāṇḍa 'arrow' (Sanskrit) Rebus:*khāṇḍa* 'tools, pots and pans, metal-ware'. Rebus 2: kaṇḍ 'fire-altar' (Santali)

m208a Read rebus as at h525a

h525a *खोंड [khōṇḍa] m A young bull, a bullcalf. (Marathi) Rebus: kõdār 'turner' (Bengali); कोंद kōnda 'engraver, lapidary setting or infixing gems' (Marathi) G. sãghāṛɔ m. 'lathe' ; संघाट joinery; M.* *sãgaḍ* *'double-canoe' Rebus: sangataras. संगतराश lit. 'to collect stones,* *stone-* *cutter, mason.'*

ayo ḍhālako 'alloy metal ingot'

aya kammaṭa.'coiner, mint alloy' *kāṇḍa* 'arrow' (Sanskrit) Rebus:*khāṇḍa* 'tools, pots and pans, metal-ware'. Rebus 2: kaṇḍ 'fire-altar' (Santali)

h698A Read rebus as at h1770

h243A Read rebus as at h1770A

h1770

ayo 'fish' Rebus: *aya* 'iron' *ayas* 'metal'
kāṇḍa 'arrow' (Sanskrit) Rebus:*khāṇḍa* 'tools, pots and pans, metal-ware'. Rebus 2: kaṇḍ 'fire-altar' (Santali)

kharedo = a currycomb (Gujarati) खरारा [*kharārā*] *m* (H) A currycomb. 2 Currying a horse. (Marathi) Rebus: करडा [*karaḍā*] Hard from alloy--iron, silver &c. (Marathi) *kharādī* ' turner' (Gujarati) Side B: *balad* m. ' ox ', gng. *bald*, (Ku.) *barad*, id. (N. Tarai) Rebus: *bharat* (5 copper, 4 zinc and 1 tin)(Punjabi) *pattar* 'trough' Rebus*: pattar* 'guild'. Thus, copper-zinc-tin alloy (worker) guild.

h2053A,B Side A: *ayo* 'fish' Rebus: *aya* 'iron' *ayas* 'metal' |||| Numeral 4: gaṇḍa 'four' Rebus: kaṇḍa 'furnace, fire-altar' (Santali)

||| Numeral three: kolom 'three' Rebus: kolami 'smithy, forge' सांड [sāṇḍa] *f* (षद S) An outlet for superfluous water (as through a dam or mound); a sluice, a floodvent. Rebus: सांडणी [sāṇḍaṇī] *f* (H) An instrument of goldsmiths. It is hooked or curved at the extremity; and is used to draw things out of the fire. सांठा [*sāṇṭhā*] *m* (संचय S) A collection, heap, hoard, store, stock.साटें [*sāṭēṃ*] *n* (संचय S) A whole investment; the total quantity of merchandise (brought to market by one merchant).

erako 'upraised hand' Rebus: erako 'moltencast copper' PLUS *meḍ* 'body' Rebus: *meḍ* 'iron' (Ho.) काठी [kāṭhī] *f* (काष्ट S) 'frame or structure of the body' (Marathi) Rebus: खंडी [khaṇḍī] measure of weight (Marathi) கண்டி; *kaṇṭi, n. < Mhr. khaṇḍil. [T. Tu. khaṇḍi, M. kaṇḍi.]* Candy, a weight, stated to be roughly equivalent to 500 lbs. *kāṇḍa* 'arrow' (Sanskrit) Rebus:*khāṇḍa* 'tools, pots and pans, metal-ware'. Rebus 2: kaṇḍ 'fire-altar' (Santali)

dula 'two' rebus: dul 'cast metal'*kolmo* 'paddy plant' Rebus: *kolami* 'smithy, forge' Vikalpa: *mogge* 'sprout, bud' Rebus: *mũh* 'ingot' (Santali) dolu 'plant of shoot height' Rebus: dul 'cast metal'

Side B:

 'Arrow' sign hieroglyph (variant) This is a ligature of 'lid of pot' hieroglyph superscript on 'a linear stroke' numeral hieroglyph.*aḍaren* 'cover of pot or lid' Rebus: *aduru* 'native, unsmelted metal' PL US Duplicated: dula 'pair' Rebus: dul 'cast metal' INFIXED *kamaḍha* 'crab' Rebus: *kammaṭa* 'mint, coiner'.*ḍato* = claws of crab (Santali) Rebus: *dhātu* 'mineral ore

M-1544 A

m1544A *ayo ḍhālako* 'alloy metal ingot'

 *kolmo* 'paddy plant' Rebus: *kolami* 'smithy, forge' Vikalpa: *mogge* 'sprout, bud' Rebus: *mūh* 'ingot' (Santali) dolu 'plant of shoot height' Rebus: dul 'cast metal'

 *kanka* 'rim of jar' Rebus: *karṇīka* 'account (scribe)' *karṇī* 'supercargo'

M-2107 a

m2107a *aya kammaṭa.*'coiner, mint alloy' sal 'splinter' Rebus: sal 'workshop' PLUS खांडा [*khāṇḍā*] *m* A jag, notch, or indentation (as upon the edge of a tool or weapon). Rebus: *kāṇḍa* 'tools, pots and pans and metal-ware'
dula 'pair' Rebus: *dul* 'cast (metal)' PLUS*kana, kanac* = corner (Santali); Rebus: *kañcu* = bronze (Telugu) Thus, cast bronze.

 *khareḍo* = a currycomb (Gujarati) खरारा [*kharārā*] *m* (H) A currycomb. 2 Currying a horse. (Marathi) Rebus: करडा [*karaḍā*] Hard from alloy--iron, silver &c. (Marathi) *kharādī* ' turner' (Gujarati)
kolom 'three' Rebus: kolami 'smithy, forge'

m1719a *खोंड [khōṇḍa] m A young bull, a bullcalf. (Marathi) Rebus: kõdār 'turner' (Bengali); कोंद kōnda 'engraver, lapidary setting or infixing gems' (Marathi) G. sãghāṛɔ m. 'lathe' ; संघाट joinery; M. sãgaḍ 'double-canoe' Rebus: sangataras. संगतराश lit. 'to collect stones, stone-cutter, mason.'*
Text of inscription as at m226A PLUS kole.l 'temple' Rebus: kole.l 'smithy

m228A *खोंड [khōṇḍa] m A young bull, a bullcalf. (Marathi) Rebus: kõdār 'turner' (Bengali); कोंद kōnda 'engraver, lapidary setting or infixing gems' (Marathi) G. sãghāṛɔ m. 'lathe' ; संघाट joinery; M. sãgaḍ 'double-canoe' Rebus: sangataras. संगतराश lit. 'to collect stones, stone-cutter, mason.'*
aya kammaṭa.'coiner, mint alloy'
kəṭhā´r, kc. *kuṭhār* m. ' granary, storeroom '(WPah.)(CDIAL 3550). *koṭhārī m.* ' storekeeper' (Gujarati)(CDIAL 3551) Thus, storeroom (of) *kolom* 'three' Rebus: *kolami* 'smithy, forge'. Dula 'pair' Rebus: dul 'cast metal' Thus, together *dul kolami kuṭhār* 'metal smithy castings storeroom'

 *kanka* 'rim of jar' Rebus: *karṇīka* 'account (scribe)' *karṇī* 'supercargo'

H-321 A

h321A

H-298 A

h298A Read rebus as at h350A

H-350 A

h350A *aya kammaṭa.*'coiner, mint alloy'
kəṭhā´r, kc. *kuṭhār* m. ' granary, storeroom '(WPah.)(CDIAL 3550). *koṭhārī m.* ' storekeeper' (Gujarati)(CDIAL 3551) Thus, storeroom (of) *kolom* 'three' Rebus: *kolami* 'smithy, forge'. dula 'pair' Rebus: dul 'cast metal' Thus,  together *dul kolami kuṭhār* 'metal smithy castings storeroom'

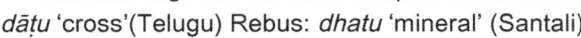

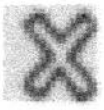 *dāṭu* 'cross'(Telugu) Rebus: *dhatu* 'mineral' (Santali).

 *kanka* 'rim of jar' Rebus: *karṇīka* 'account (scribe)' *karṇī* 'supercargo'

M-967 A

m967A *खोंड [khōṇḍa] m A young bull, a bullcalf. (Marathi) Rebus: kõdār 'turner' (Bengali); कोंद kōnda 'engraver, lapidary setting or infixing gems' (Marathi) G. sãghāṛɔ m. 'lathe' ; संघाट joinery; M. sãgaḍ 'double-canoe' Rebus: sangataras. संगतराश lit. 'to collect stones, stone-cutter, mason.' dula* 'pair' Rebus: dul 'cast metal' PLUS

 *kharedo* = a currycomb (Gujarati) खरारा [*kharārā*] *m* (H) A currycomb. 2 Currying a horse. (Marathi) Rebus: करडा [*karaḍā*] Hard from alloy--iron, silver &c. (Marathi) *kharādī* ' turner' (Gujarati) Thus, cast hard alloys.

 *kanac* 'corner' Rebus: *kañcu* 'bronze' *ḍhanga* = a crook used for pulling down the branches of trees, for goats, sheep and camels (P.) Rebus:*ḍhangar* blacksmith' *ayo* 'fish' Rebus: *aya* 'iron' *ayas* 'metal'

m627A *खोंड [khōṇḍa] m A young bull, a bullcalf. (Marathi) Rebus: kõdār 'turner' (Bengali); कोंद kōnda 'engraver, lapidary setting or infixing gems' (Marathi) G. sãghāṛɔ m. 'lathe' ; संघाट joinery; M. sãgaḍ 'double-canoe' Rebus: sangataras. संगतराश lit. 'to collect stones, stone-cutter, mason.' ayo* 'fish' Rebus: *aya* 'iron' *ayas* 'metal' *kañcu* 'bronze' *ḍhanga* = a crook used for pulling down the branches of trees, for goats, sheep and camels (P.) Rebus:*ḍhangar* blacksmith' *khaṇḍ* 'field, division' (Sanskrit) Rebus: *khānḍa* 'tools, pots and pans, metal-ware'. Rebus 2: kaṇḍ 'fire-altar' (Santali)

 *kanka* 'rim of jar' Rebus: *karṇīka* 'account (scribe)' *karṇī* 'supercargo'
aya aḍaren (homonym: aduru)'alloy native metal'

 *khaṇḍ* 'field, division' (Sanskrit) Rebus: *khānḍa* 'tools, pots and pans, metal-ware'. Rebus 2: kaṇḍ 'fire-altar' (Santali) dula 'pair' Rebus: dul 'cast metal' Thus, duplicated 'division' hieroglyph sign reads: cast metal metal-ware.

h1690A Text of inscription as at m627A PLUS kola 'tiger' Rebus: kolhe 'smelters' kol 'working in iron' pattar 'trough' Rebus: pattar 'guild, goldsmith'
ayo 'fish' Rebus: *aya* 'iron' *ayas* 'metal'
ḍhanga = a crook used for pulling down the branches of trees, for goats, sheep and camels (P.) Rebus:*ḍhangar* blacksmith'

 *khaṇḍ* 'field, division' (Sanskrit) Rebus: *khānḍa* 'tools, pots and pans, metal-ware'. Rebus 2: kaṇḍ 'fire-altar' (Santali) *kanka* 'rim of jar' Rebus: *karṇīka* 'account (scribe)' *karṇī* 'supercargo'

aya aḍaren (homonym: aduru)'alloy native metal'

H-763 A

h763A *ayo ḍhālako* 'alloy metal ingot'

ranku 'antelope' Rebus: ranku 'tin'

 *kuṭila* 'bent' CDIAL 3230 kuṭi— in cmpd. 'curve', *kuṭika*— 'bent' MBh.

 Rebus: *kuṭila, katthīl* = bronze (8 parts copper and 2 parts tin) *kanka* 'rim of jar' Rebus: *karṇīka* 'account (scribe)' *karṇī* 'supercargo'

 *kharedo* = a currycomb (Gujarati) खरारा [*kharārā*] *m* (H) A currycomb. 2 Currying a horse. (Marathi) Rebus: करडा [*karaḍā*] Hard from alloy--iron, silver &c. (Marathi) *kharādī* ' turner' (Gujarati)

m492A *aya kammaṭa.*'coiner, mint alloy'

 *dula* 'pair' Rebus: *dul* 'cast (metal)' PLUS*kana, kanac* = corner (Santali); Rebus: *kañcu* = bronze (Telugu) PLUS infixed kolmo 'paddy plant' Rebus: kolami 'smithy, forge'. Thus, cast bronze smithy, forge. Or, *mogge* 'sprout, bud' Rebus: *mũh* 'ingot' (Santali)Thus, cast bronze ingot. Read as: *kañcu dul mũh 'bronze cast ingot'*

 सांड [sāṇḍa] *f* (षद S) An outlet for superfluous water (as through a dam or mound); a sluice, a floodvent. Rebus: सांडणी [sāṇḍaṇī] *f* (H) An instrument of goldsmiths. It is hooked or curved at the extremity; and is used to draw things out of the fire.
सांठा [*sāṇṭhā*] *m* (संचय S) A collection, heap, hoard, store, stock.साटें [*sāṭēṃ*] *n* (संचय S) A whole investment; the total quantity of merchandise (brought to market by one merchant).

 *kanka* 'rim of jar' Rebus: *karṇīka* 'account (scribe)' *karṇī* 'supercargo'

 'Arrow' sign hieroglyph (variant) This is a ligature of 'lid of pot' hieroglyph superscript on 'a linear stroke' numeral hieroglyph.*aḍaren* 'cover of pot or lid' Rebus: *aduru* 'native, unsmelted metal' PLUS koḍ = one (Santali); koḍ 'workshop' (Gujarati)

m238a *balad* m. ' ox ', gng. *bald*, (Ku.) *barad*, id. (N. Tarai) Rebus: *bharat* (5 copper, 4 zinc and 1 tin)(Punjabi) *pattar* 'trough' Rebus*: pattar* 'guild'. Thus, copper-zinc-tin alloy (worker) guild.
ayo ḍhālako 'alloy metal ingot'

 *dula* 'pair' Rebus: *dul* 'cast (metal)' PLUS*kana, kanac* = corner (Santali); Rebus: *kañcu* = bronze (Telugu) PLUS infixed kolmo 'paddy plant' Rebus: kolami 'smithy, forge'. Thus, cast bronze smithy, forge. Or, *mogge* 'sprout, bud' Rebus: *mũh* 'ingot' (Santali)Thus, cast bronze ingot. Read as: *kañcu dul mũh 'bronze cast ingot'*

 *kanka* 'rim of jar' Rebus: *karṇīka* 'account (scribe)' *karṇī* 'supercargo'

h161a *ayo ḍhālako* 'alloy metal ingot'

 dula 'pair' Rebus: dul 'cast metal' PLUS | *koḍa* 'one' Rebus: *koḍ* 'workshop' PLUS INFIXED खांडा [*khāṇḍā*] *m* A jag, notch, or indentation (as upon the edge of a tool or

weapon). Rebus: *kāṇḍa* 'tools, pots and pans and metal-ware' Thus metalware castings workshop.

 *kuṭila* 'bent' CDIAL 3230 kuṭi— in cmpd. 'curve', *kuṭika—* 'bent' MBh. Rebus: *kuṭila, katthīl* = bronze (8 parts copper and 2 parts tin)

 'Arrow' sign hieroglyph (variant) This is a ligature of 'lid of pot' hieroglyph superscript on 'a linear stroke' numeral hieroglyph.*aḍaren* 'cover of pot or lid' Rebus: *aduru* 'native, unsmelted metal' PLUS koḍ = one (Santali); koḍ 'workshop' (Gujarati)

 *dula* 'pair' Rebus: dul 'cast metal' *mogge* 'sprout, bud' Rebus: *mũh* 'ingot' (Santali) Thus, cast metal ingot.

 *kanka* 'rim of jar' Rebus: *karṇīka* 'account (scribe)' *karṇī* 'supercargo'

H-201 A

h201A Read rebus as at h743A

H-200 A

h200A Read rebus as at h743A

h743A *aya kammaṭa.*'coiner, mint alloy'

 *aḍaren* 'cover of pot or lid' Rebus: *aduru* 'native, unsmelted metal' Duplicated: dula 'pair' Rebus: dul 'cast metal'

 *dula* 'pair' Rebus: dul 'cast metal' *mogge* 'sprout, bud' Rebus: *mũh* 'ingot' (Santali) Thus, cast metal ingot.

 *kanka* 'rim of jar' Rebus: *karṇīka* 'account (scribe)' *karṇī* 'supercargo'

H-2200 A

h2200A *aya kammaṭa.*'coiner, mint alloy'

 *baraḍo* = spine; backbone (Tulu) Rebus: *baran, bharat* 'mixed alloys' (5 copper, 4 zinc and 1 tin) (Punjabi)

 *kanka* 'rim of jar' Rebus: *karṇīka* 'account (scribe)' *karṇī* 'supercargo'

 *khareḍo* = a currycomb (Gujarati) खरारा [*kharārā*] *m* (H) A currycomb. 2 Currying a horse. (Marathi) Rebus: करडा [*karaḍā*] Hard from alloy--iron, silver &c. (Marathi) *kharādī* ' turner' (Gujarati)

H-199 A

h199A *aya kammaṭa.*'coiner, mint alloy'

 *aḍaren* 'cover of pot or lid' Rebus: *aduru* 'native, unsmelted metal' Duplicated: dula 'pair' Rebus: dul 'cast metal'

notch+slanted stroke   reads rebus: *ḍhālako kāṇḍa* 'ingot, tools, pots and pans and metal-ware'.*dhāḷ* 'a slope'; 'inclination of a plane' (G.); *ḍhāḷiyum* = adj. sloping, inclining (G.) Rebus: *ḍhālako* = a large metal ingot (G.) *ḍhālakī* = a metal heated and poured into a mould; a solid piece of metal; an ingot (Gujarati) PLUS खांडा [*khāṇḍā*] *m* A jag, notch, or indentation (as upon the edge of a tool or weapon). Rebus: *kāṇḍa* 'tools, pots and pans and metal-ware' Circumscript: sal 'splinter' Rebus: sal 'workshop'

kanka 'rim of jar' Rebus: *karṇīka* 'account (scribe)' *karṇī* 'supercargo'

m547A Copper plate. *aya kāṇḍa* 'alloy metalware' |||| Numeral 4: gaṇḍa 'four' Rebus: kaṇḍa 'furnace, fire-altar' (Santali) ||| kolom 'three' Rebus: kolami 'smithy, forge' PLUS || sal 'splinter' Rebus sal 'workshop'

सांड [sāṇḍa] *f* (षद S) An outlet for superfluous water (as through a dam or mound); a sluice, a floodvent. Rebus: सांडणी [sāṇḍaṇī] *f* (H) An instrument of goldsmiths. It is hooked or curved at the extremity; and is used to draw things out of the fire.
सांठा [*sāṇṭhā*] *m* (संचय S) A collection, heap, hoard, store, stock.साटें [*sāṭēṃ*] *n* (संचय S) A whole investment; the total quantity of merchandise (brought to market by one merchant).
erako 'upraised hand' Rebus: erako 'moltencast copper' PLUS

meḍ 'body' Rebus: *meḍ* 'iron' (Ho.) काठी [kāṭhī] *f* (काष्ट S) 'frame or structure of the body' (Marathi) Rebus: खंडी [khaṇḍī] measure of weight (Marathi) கண்டி; *kaṇṭi, n. < Mhr. khaṇḍil. [T. Tu. khaṇḍi, M. kaṇḍi.]* Candy, a weight, stated to be roughly equivalent to 500 lbs.
kāṇḍa 'arrow' (Sanskrit) Rebus:*khāṇḍa* 'tools, pots and pans, metal-ware'. Rebus 2: kaṇḍ 'fire-altar' (Santali)
dula 'two' Rebus: dul 'cast metal'

kolmo 'paddy plant' Rebus: *kolami* 'smithy, forge' Vikalpa: *mogge* 'sprout, bud' Rebus: *mũh* 'ingot' (Santali) dolu 'plant of shoot height' Rebus: dul 'cast metal'

m397A *ayo ḍhālako* 'alloy metal ingot'

baroṭi 'twelve' *bhārata* 'a factitious alloy of copper, pewter, tin' (Marathi)

dula 'pair' Rebus: dul 'cast metal' *mogge* 'sprout, bud' Rebus: *mũh* 'ingot' (Santali) Thus, cast metal ingot.

kanka 'rim of jar' Rebus: *karṇīka* 'account (scribe)' *karṇī* 'supercargo'

m1651A (Ivory rod) *aya kammaṭa.*'coiner, mint alloy'

dula 'pair' Rebus: *dul* 'cast (metal)' *kañcu* = bronze (Telugu) PLUS 'smithy, forge'. Thus, cast bronze *mũh* 'ingot' (Santali)Thus, cast *cast ingot'*

PLUS*kana, kanac* = corner (Santali); Rebus: infixed kolmo 'paddy plant' Rebus: kolami smithy, forge. Or, *mogge* 'sprout, bud' Rebus: bronze ingot. Read as: *kañcu dul mũh 'bronze*

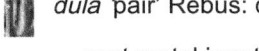

kolmo 'paddy plant' Rebus: *kolami* 'smithy, forge' Vikalpa: *mogge* 'sprout, bud' Rebus: *mūh* 'ingot' (Santali) dolu 'plant of shoot height' Rebus: dul 'cast metal'

ḍhanga = a crook used for pulling down the branches of trees, for goats, sheep and camels (P.) Rebus:*ḍhangar* blacksmith'

kanka 'rim of jar' Rebus: *karṇīka* 'account (scribe)' *karṇī* 'supercargo'

khareḍo = a currycomb (Gujarati) खरारा [*kharārā*] *m* (H) A currycomb. 2 Currying a horse. (Marathi) Rebus: करडा [*karaḍā*] Hard from alloy--iron, silver &c. (Marathi) *kharādī* ' turner' (Gujarati)

Hieroglyphs on the edges: dula 'pair' Rebus: dul 'cast metal'

m2018a

m2017B Rhinoceros/boar: baḍhia = a castrated boar, a hog (Santali) baḍhi 'a caste who work both in iron and wood' (Santali) *baṟea* 'merchant'

Circumscript: *kuṭila* 'bent' CDIAL 3230 kuṭi— in cmpd. 'curve', *kuṭika*— 'bent' MBh. Rebus: *kuṭila, katthīl* = bronze (8 parts copper and 2 parts tin) Duplicated: dula 'pair' Rebus: dul 'cast metal' Thus, cast bronze. PLUS *baṭa* 'quail' Rebus: *baṭha* 'smelter, furnace' *baṭa* 'a kind of iron' (Gujarati) Thus, together bronze furnace castings.

m1199A *खोंड [khōṇḍa] m A young bull, a bullcalf. (Marathi) Rebus: kōdār 'turner' (Bengali); कोंद kōnda 'engraver, lapidary setting or infixing gems' (Marathi) G. sãghāṛɔ m. 'lathe' ; संघाट joinery; M. sãgaḍ 'double-canoe' Rebus: sangataras. संगतराश lit. 'to collect stones, stone-cutter, mason.'*

ayo 'fish' Rebus: *aya* 'iron' *ayas* 'metal'

kamaḍha 'crab' Rebus: *kammaṭa* 'mint, coiner'.

kuṭila 'bent' CDIAL 3230 kuṭi— in cmpd. 'curve', *kuṭika*— 'bent' MBh. Rebus: *kuṭila, katthīl* = bronze (8 parts copper and 2 parts tin)

kanka 'rim of jar' Rebus: *karṇīka* 'account (scribe)' *karṇī* 'supercargo'

m255a *balad* m. ' ox ', gng. *bald*, (Ku.) *barad*, id. (N. Tarai) Rebus: *bharat* (5 copper, 4 zinc and 1 tin)(Punjabi) *pattar* 'trough' Rebus*: pattar* 'guild'. Thus, copper-zinc-tin alloy (worker) guild. *ayo ḍhālako* 'alloy metal ingot'

kanac 'corner' Rebus: *kañcu* 'bronze'

kanka 'rim of jar' Rebus: *karṇīka* 'account (scribe)' *karṇī* 'supercargo'

rāngo 'water buffalo bull' (Ku.N.)(CDIAL 10559) Rebus: rango 'pewter'

aya kāṇḍa 'alloy metalware'

dula 'two' Rebus: dul 'cast metal'

kāṇḍa 'arrow' (Sanskrit) Rebus:*khāṇḍa* 'tools, pots and pans, metal-ware'. Rebus 2: kaṇḍ 'fire-altar' (Santali)

m1361a Read rebus as at m1992a

m1992a *aya kammaṭa.*'coiner, mint alloy' *khuṭo* ' leg, foot ', °ṭī ' goat's leg ' Rebus: *khōṭā* 'alloy' (Marathi)

kanka 'rim of jar' Rebus: *karṇīka* 'account (scribe)' *karṇī* 'supercargo'

m217A,a

First 3 sign hieroglyphs read rebus as at m255a PLUS INFIXED dula 'two' Rebus: dul 'cast metal'. Thus, cast metal alloy ingot of bronze (copper, zinc and tin) *खोंड [khōṇḍa] m A young bull, a bullcalf. (Marathi) Rebus: kõdār 'turner' (Bengali); कोंद kōnda 'engraver, lapidary setting or infixing gems' (Marathi) G. sãghāṛɔ m. 'lathe' ; संघाट joinery; M. sãgaḍ 'double-canoe' Rebus: sangataras. संगतराश lit. 'to collect stones, stone-cutter, mason.'*

m230A *खोंड [khōṇḍa] m A young bull, a bullcalf. (Marathi) Rebus: kõdār 'turner' (Bengali); कोंद kōnda 'engraver, lapidary setting or infixing gems' (Marathi) G. sãghāṛɔ m. 'lathe' ; संघाट joinery; M. sãgaḍ 'double-canoe' Rebus: sangataras. संगतराश lit. 'to collect stones, stone-cutter, mason.' ayo ḍhālako* 'alloy metal ingot'

baraḍo = spine; backbone (Tulu) Rebus: *baran, bharat* 'mixed alloys' (5 copper, 4 zinc and 1 tin) (Punjabi)

kanka 'rim of jar' Rebus: *karṇīka* 'account (scribe)' *karṇī* 'supercargo'

meḍ 'body' Rebus: *meḍ* 'iron' (Ho.) काठी [kāṭhī] *f* (काष्ट S) 'frame or structure of the body' (Marathi) Rebus: खंडी [khaṇḍī] measure of weight (Marathi) *கண்டி; kaṇṭi, n. < Mhr. khaṇḍil. [T. Tu. khaṇḍi, M. kaṇḍi.]* Candy, a weight, stated to be roughly equivalent to 500 lbs.

m502A

Lothal 55a Text of inscription read rebus as at Lothal 35a.

Lothal 35a *खोंड [khōṇḍa] m A young bull, a bullcalf. (Marathi) Rebus: kõdār 'turner' (Bengali); कोंद kōnda 'engraver, lapidary setting or infixing gems' (Marathi) G. sãghāṛɔ m. 'lathe' ; संघाट joinery; M. sãgaḍ 'double-canoe' Rebus: sangataras. संगतराश lit. 'to collect stones, stone-cutter, mason.'*

ayo ḍhālako 'alloy metal ingot'

 *baraḍo* = spine; backbone (Tulu) Rebus: *baran, bharat* 'mixed alloys' (5 copper, 4 zinc and 1 tin) (Punjabi)

 *kanka* 'rim of jar' Rebus: *karṇīka* 'account (scribe)' *karṇī* 'supercargo'

M-1849 A

m1849A *खोंड [khōṇḍa] m A young bull, a bullcalf. (Marathi) Rebus: kõdār 'turner' (Bengali); कोंद kōnda 'engraver, lapidary setting or infixing gems' (Marathi) G. sãghāṛɔ m. 'lathe' ; संघाट joinery; M. sãgaḍ 'double-canoe' Rebus: sangataras. संगतराश lit. 'to collect stones, stone-cutter, mason.' ayo ḍhālako* 'alloy metal ingot' Circumscript: gaṇḍa 'four' Rebus: kaṇḍa 'furnace, fire-altar' (Santali)

PLUS

 *dula* 'pair' Rebus: *dul* 'cast (metal)' PLUS *kana, kanac* = corner (Santali); Rebus: *kañcu* = bronze (Telugu) PLUS infixed kolmo 'paddy plant' Rebus: kolami 'smithy, forge'. Thus, cast bronze smithy, forge. Or, *mogge* 'sprout, bud' Rebus: *mũh* 'ingot' (Santali)Thus, cast bronze ingot. Read as: *kañcu dul mũh 'bronze cast ingot'*

 *khareḍo* = a currycomb (Gujarati) खरारा [*kharārā*] *m* (H) A currycomb. 2 Currying a horse. (Marathi) Rebus: करडा [*karaḍā*] Hard from alloy--iron, silver &c. (Marathi) *kharādī*' turner' (Gujarati)

m847a *खोंड [khōṇḍa] m A young bull, a bullcalf. (Marathi) Rebus: kõdār 'turner' (Bengali); कोंद kōnda 'engraver, lapidary setting or infixing gems' (Marathi) G. sãghāṛɔ m. 'lathe' ; संघाट joinery; M. sãgaḍ 'double-canoe' Rebus: sangataras. संगतराश lit. 'to collect stones, stone-cutter, mason.' ayo ḍhālako* 'alloy metal ingot' *aya kāṇḍa* 'alloy metalware'

 *baroṭi* 'twelve' *bhārata* 'a factitious alloy of copper, pewter, tin' (Marathi)

 *kanka* 'rim of jar' Rebus: *karṇīka* 'account (scribe)' *karṇī* 'supercargo'

H-761 B

h761B *ayo* 'fish' Rebus: *aya* 'iron' *ayas* 'metal' *ḍhanga* = a crook used for pulling down the branches of trees, for goats, sheep and camels (P.) Rebus:*ḍhangar* blacksmith'. *bhaṭa* 'warrior' (Sanskrit) Rebus: *baṭa* a kind of iron (Gujarati). Rebus: *bhaṭa* 'furnace' (Santali)

 *khareḍo* = a currycomb (Gujarati) खरारा [*kharārā*] *m* (H) A currycomb. 2 Currying a horse. (Marathi) Rebus: करडा [*karaḍā*] Hard from alloy--iron, silver &c. (Marathi) *kharādī*' turner' (Gujarati)

m731A *खोंड [khōṇḍa] m A young bull, a bullcalf. (Marathi) Rebus: kõdār 'turner' (Bengali); कोंद kōnda 'engraver, lapidary setting or infixing gems' (Marathi) G. sãghāṛɔ m. 'lathe' ; संघाट joinery; M. sãgaḍ 'double-canoe' Rebus: sangataras. संगतराश lit. 'to collect stones, stone-cutter, mason.' ayo* 'fish' Rebus: *aya* 'iron' *ayas* 'metal'

water-carrier  hieroglyph *kuṭi*; Rebus: *kuṭhi* 'smelter furnace'.

Chanhudaro 21A खोंड *[khōṇḍa] m A young bull, a bullcalf. (Marathi) Rebus: kõdār 'turner' (Bengali);* कोंद *kōnda 'engraver, lapidary setting or infixing gems' (Marathi) G. sãghāṛɔ m. 'lathe' ;* संघाट *joinery; M. sãgaḍ 'double-canoe' Rebus: sangataras.* संगतराश *lit. 'to collect stones, stone-cutter, mason.' aya kammaṭa.*'coiner, mint alloy'

water-carrier hieroglyph *kuṭi*; Rebus: *kuṭhi* 'smelter furnace'. PLUS 'rim of jar':

 kanka 'rim of jar' Rebus: karṇīka 'account (scribe)' karṇī 'supercargo'

 *aḍar* 'harrow';

h2241A *aya kammaṭa.*'coiner, mint alloy'
rebus: *aduru* 'native unsmelted metal'

m1727a खोंड *[khōṇḍa] m A young bull, a bullcalf. (Marathi) Rebus: kõdār 'turner' (Bengali);* कोंद *kōnda 'engraver, lapidary setting or infixing gems' (Marathi) G. sãghāṛɔ m. 'lathe' ;* संघाट *joinery; M. sãgaḍ 'double-canoe' Rebus: sangataras.* संगतराश *lit. 'to collect stones, stone-cutter, mason.'*
aya kammaṭa.'coiner, mint alloy'

 mēḍu height, rising ground, hillock (Kannada) Rebus: *mẽṛhẽt, meḍ* 'iron' (Munda.Ho.)

 'Arrow' sign hieroglyph (variant) This is a ligature of 'lid of pot' hieroglyph superscript on 'a linear stroke' numeral hieroglyph.*aḍaren* 'cover of pot or lid' Rebus: *aduru* 'native, unsmelted metal' PLUS koḍ = one (Santali); koḍ 'workshop' (Gujarati)

kāṇḍa 'arrow' (Sanskrit) Rebus:*khāṇḍa* 'tools, pots and pans, metal-ware'. Rebus 2: kaṇḍ 'fire-altar' (Santali)

m1891a *balad* m. ' ox ', gng. *bald*, (Ku.) *barad*, id. (N. Tarai) Rebus: *bharat* (5 copper, 4 zinc and 1 tin)(Punjabi) *pattar* 'trough' Rebus*: pattar* 'guild'. Thus, copper-zinc-tin alloy (worker) guild.
aya kammaṭa.'coiner, mint alloy'

 mēḍu height, rising ground, hillock (Kannada) Rebus: *mẽṛhẽt, meḍ* 'iron' (Munda.Ho.)

||| Numeral three: kolom 'three' Rebus: kolami 'smithy, forge'
Duplicated: dula 'pair' Rebus: dul 'cast metal' Thus metal smithy castings.

 *kanka* 'rim of jar' Rebus: *karṇīka* 'account (scribe)' *karṇī* 'supercargo'

 *khareḍo* = a currycomb (Gujarati) खरारा [*kharārā*] *m* (H) A currycomb. 2 Currying a horse. (Marathi) Rebus: करडा [*karaḍā*] Hard from alloy--iron, silver &c. (Marathi) *kharādī*' turner' (Gujarati)

m1418A Side B: kolom 'three' Rebus: kolami 'smithy, forge' Circumscript:

 *kuṭila* 'bent' CDIAL 3230 kuṭi— in cmpd. 'curve', *kuṭika*— 'bent' MBh. Rebus: *kuṭila, katthīl* = bronze (8 parts copper and 2 parts tin) Duplicated:

dula 'pair' Rebus: dul 'cast metal' Thus, cast bronze. PLUS *bhaṭa* 'warrior' (Sanskrit) Rebus: *baṭa* a kind of iron (Gujarati). Rebus: *bhaṭa* 'furnace' (Santali)

 *baraḍo* = spine; backbone (Tulu) Rebus: *baran, bharat* 'mixed alloys' (5 copper, 4 zinc and 1 tin) (Punjabi)

dula 'two' Rebus: dul 'cast metal'
Side A: kolom 'three' Rebus: kolami 'smithy, forge'
aya kammaṭa.'coiner, mint alloy'

 *aḍar* 'harrow'; rebus: *aduru* 'native unsmelted metal'
bhaṭa 'warrior' (Sanskrit) Rebus: *baṭa* a kind of iron (Gujarati). Rebus: *bhaṭa* 'furnace' (Santali)

 *kanka* 'rim of jar' Rebus: *karṇīka* 'account (scribe)' *karṇī* 'supercargo'

dula 'two' Rebus: dul 'cast metal'

H-2141 A H-2141 B

h2141A

H-2140 A H-2140 B

h2140A Side A; *aya kāṇḍa* 'alloy metalware'

 *baraḍo* = spine; backbone (Tulu) Rebus: *baran, bharat* 'mixed alloys' (5 copper, 4 zinc and 1 tin) (Punjabi)

 *kanka* 'rim of jar' Rebus: *karṇīka* 'account (scribe)' *karṇī* 'supercargo'

 *kamaḍha* 'crab' Rebus: *kammaṭa* 'mint, coiner'.*ḍato* = claws of crab (Santali) Rebus: *dhātu* 'mineral ore'

PLUS खांडा [*khāṇḍā*] *m* A jag, notch, or indentation (as upon the edge of a tool or weapon). Rebus: *kāṇḍa* 'tools, pots and pans and metal-ware' Thus, mint metalware, ore. Side B: *baṭa* = rimless pot (Kannada) Rebus:) *baṭa* = a kind of iron (G.)) *bhaṭa* furnace (Gujarati) PLUS gaṇḍa 'four' Rebus: kaṇḍa 'furnace, fire-altar' (Santali)

M-88 A

m88a *खोंड [khōṇḍa] m A young bull, a bullcalf. (Marathi) Rebus: kõdār 'turner' (Bengali); कोंद kōnda 'engraver, lapidary setting or infixing gems' (Marathi) G. sãghārɔ m. 'lathe' ; संघाट joinery; M. sãgaḍ 'double-canoe' Rebus: sangataras. संगतराश lit. 'to collect stones, stone-cutter, mason.'*
ayo ḍhālako 'alloy metal ingot'

loa 'ficus  religiosa' Rebus: *lo* 'iron' (Sanskrit) PLUS unique ligatures: लोखंड [lōkhaṇḍa] *n* (लोह S) Iron. लोखंडाचे चणे खावविणें or चारणें To oppress grievously.लोखंडकाम [lōkhaṇḍakāma] *n* Iron work; that portion (of a building, machine &c.) which consists of iron. 2 The business of an ironsmith.लोखंडी [lōkhaṇḍī] *a* (लोखंड) Composed of iron; relating to iron. (Marathi)

| *koḍa* 'one' Rebus: *koḍ* 'workshop' Duplicated: dula 'pair' Rebus: dul 'cast metal' Thus cast metal workshop. INFIXED ||| kolom 'three' Rebus: kolami 'smithy, forge' Thus, metal smithy castings, forge workshop.

h1024a *खोंड [khōṇḍa] m A young bull, a bullcalf. (Marathi) Rebus: kõdār 'turner' (Bengali); कोंद kōnda 'engraver, lapidary setting or infixing gems' (Marathi) G. sãghārɔ m. 'lathe' ; संघाट joinery; M. sãgaḍ 'double-canoe' Rebus: sangataras. संगतराश lit. 'to collect stones, stone-cutter, mason.' aya kāṇḍa* 'alloy metalware'

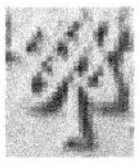

loa 'ficus religiosa' Rebus: *lo* 'iron' (Sanskrit) PLUS unique ligatures: लोखंड [lōkhaṇḍa] *n* (लोह S) Iron. लोखंडाचे चणे खाववणें or चारणें To oppress grievously.लोखंडकाम [lōkhaṇḍakāma] *n* Iron work; that portion (of a building, machine &c.) which consists of iron. 2 The business of an ironsmith.लोखंडी [lōkhaṇḍī] *a* (लोखंड) Composed of iron; relating to iron. (Marathi) *ḍhanga* = a crook used for pulling down the branches of trees, for goats, sheep and camels (P.) Rebus:*ḍhangar* blacksmith'.

kanka 'rim of jar' Rebus: *karṇīka* 'account (scribe)' *karṇī* 'supercargo'

Ligatured 'pot' signs

m1908a Ligature on the nose of the animal khar 'donkey' Rebus: khara 'blacksmith':

mēḍu height, rising ground, hillock (Kannada) Rebus: *mẽṛhẽt, meḍ* 'iron' (Munda.Ho.) Thus, read rebus together: iron smith.

Dotted circles on the body of the animal: dulo 'hole' Rebus: dul 'cast metal' Thus, the pictorial motif is read rebus as iron castings.
ḍhālako kāṇḍa 'ingot, tools, pots and pans and metal-ware'.*ḍhāḷ* 'a slope'; 'inclination of a plane' (G.); *ḍhāḷiyum* = adj. sloping, inclining (G.) Rebus: *ḍhālako* = a large metal ingot (G.) *ḍhālakī* = a metal heated and poured into a mould; a solid piece of metal; an ingot (Gujarati)

dula 'pair' Rebus: dul 'cast metal' *mogge* 'sprout, bud' Rebus: *mũh* 'ingot' (Santali) Thus, cast metal ingot.

kanka 'rim of jar' Rebus: *karṇīka* 'account (scribe)' *karṇī* 'supercargo'

Kalibangan 40A bha 'elephant' Rebus: ib 'iron' ibbo 'merchant' (Gujarati)

dula 'pair' Rebus: dul 'cast metal' *mogge* 'sprout, bud' Rebus: *mũh* 'ingot' (Santali) Thus, cast metal ingot.
ḍhālako kāṇḍa 'ingot, tools, pots and pans and metal-ware'.*ḍhāḷ* 'a slope'; 'inclination of a plane' (G.); *ḍhāḷiyum* = adj. sloping, inclining (G.) Rebus: *ḍhālako* = a large metal ingot (G.) *ḍhālakī* = a metal heated and poured into a mould; a solid piece of metal; an ingot (Gujarati) PLUS खांडा [*khāṇḍā*] *m* A jag, notch, or indentation (as upon the edge of a tool or weapon). Rebus: *kāṇḍa* 'tools, pots and pans and metal-ware'

 *kanac* 'corner' Rebus: *kañcu* 'bronze' PLUS खांडा [*khāṇḍā*] *m* A jag, notch, or indentation (as upon the edge of a tool or weapon). Rebus: *kāṇḍa* 'tools, pots and pans and metal-ware'

 Variant: beads: Pa. kandi (pl. -l) necklace, beads. Ga. (Punjabi) kandi (pl. -l) bead, (pl.) necklace; (S.2) kandiṭ bead. (DEDR 1215) Rebus: *கண்டி; kaṇṭi, n. < Mhr. khaṇḍil. [T. Tu. khaṇḍi, M. kaṇḍi.] 1. Candy, a weight, stated to be roughly equivalent to 500 lbs.; பாரமென் னும் நிறையளவு.* खंडीगणती or खंडोगणती [khaṇḍīgaṇatī or khaṇḍōgaṇatī] *ad* By candies; counting or reckoning by candies. खंडीवारी [khaṇḍīvārī] *ad* By scores, heaps, candies. खंडी [khaṇḍī] Applied to a great quantity; as खंडीभर पोरें, खंडीभर मेंढ्या, खंडीभर काम, खंडीभर बोलतो-लिहितो&c

kaṇḍo 'stool, seat' Rebus: *kāṇḍa* 'metalware' *kaṇḍa* 'fire-altar'

khuṭo ' leg, foot ', °ṭī ' goat's leg ' Rebus: *khōṭā* 'alloy' (Marathi)

m713A *खोंड [khōṇḍa] m A young bull, a bullcalf. (Marathi) Rebus: kōdār 'turner' (Bengali); कोंद kōnda 'engraver, lapidary setting or infixing gems' (Marathi) G. sãghāṛɔ m. 'lathe' ; संघाट joinery; M. sãgaḍ 'double-canoe' Rebus: sangataras. संगतराश lit. 'to collect stones, stone-cutter, mason.'*

 *dula* 'pair' Rebus: dul 'cast metal' *mogge* 'sprout, bud' Rebus: *mūh* 'ingot' (Santali) sal 'splinter' Rebus: sal 'workshop' Thus, workshop ingot castings.

khuṭo ' leg, foot ', °ṭī ' goat's leg ' Rebus: *khōṭā* 'alloy' (Marathi)

 *dula* 'pair' Rebus: *dul* 'cast (metal)' PLUS*kana, kanac* = corner (Santali); Rebus: *kañcu* = bronze (Telugu) PLUS *i*nfixed kolmo 'paddy plant' Rebus: kolami 'smithy, forge'. Thus, cast bronze smithy, forge. Or, *mogge* 'sprout, bud' Rebus: *mūh* 'ingot' (Santali)Thus, cast bronze ingot. Read as: *kañcu dul mūh 'bronze cast ingot'*

aya kāṇḍa 'alloy metalware'

h598A *खोंड [khōṇḍa] m A young bull, a bullcalf. (Marathi) Rebus: kōdār 'turner' (Bengali); कोंद kōnda 'engraver, lapidary setting or infixing gems' (Marathi) G. sãghāṛɔ m. 'lathe' ; संघाट joinery; M. sãgaḍ 'double-canoe' Rebus: sangataras. संगतराश lit. 'to collect stones, stone-cutter, mason.'*

dula 'pair' (Sanskrit) 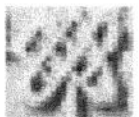 Rebus: dul 'cast metal' PLUS *loa* 'ficus religiosa' Rebus: *lo* 'iron' PLUS unique ligatures: लोखंड [lōkhaṇḍa] *n* (लोह S) Iron. लोखंडाचे चणे खावविणें or चारणें To oppress grievously.लोखंडकाम [lōkhaṇḍakāma] *n* Iron work; that portion (of a building, machine &c.) which consists of iron. 2 The business of an ironsmith.लोखंडी [lōkhaṇḍī] *a* (लोखंड) Composed of iron; relating to iron. (Marathi) Thus, together, iron castings PLUS INFIXED *kamaḍha* 'crab' Rebus: *kammaṭa* 'mint, coiner'.

ḍato = claws of crab (Santali) Rebus: *dhātu* 'mineral ore'. Thus mint, mineral ore iron castings.

 The pair of hieroglyph signs are compositions: bicha 'scorpion' (Assamese) Rebus: *bica* 'stone ore' (Santali) The pairing sign is a composition of: sloping stroke PLUS two short strokes of a 'splinter':*dhāḷ* 'a slope'; 'inclination of a plane' (Gujarati); *ḍhāḷiyum* = adj. sloping, inclining (Gujarati) Rebus: *ḍhālako* = a large metal ingot (Gujarati) *ḍhālakī* = a metal heated and poured into a mould; a solid piece of

metal; an ingot (Gujarati)PLUS*sal* 'splinter' Rebus: *sal* 'workshop'. Thus the composition reads: *ḍhālako sal* 'ingot workshop'.

dhāḷ 'a slope'; 'inclination of a plane' (G.); *ḍhāḷiyum* = adj. sloping, inclining (G.) Rebus: *ḍhālako* = a large metal ingot (G.) *ḍhālakī* = a metal heated and poured into a mould; a solid piece of metal; an ingot (Gujarati) PLUS *dula* 'pair' Rebus: *dul* 'cast *metal' sal* 'splinter' Rebus: *sal* 'workshop'. Thus, *ḍhālako dul sal* 'ingot, cast metal workshop'.
aya kammaṭa.'coiner, mint alloy' PLUS sal 'splinter' Rebus: sal 'workshop'. Thus mint alloy workshop.
kəṭhā´r, kc. *kuṭhār* m. ' granary, storeroom '(WPah.)(CDIAL 3550). *koṭhārī m.* ' storekeeper'

(Gujarati)(CDIAL 3551) Thus, storeroom (of) *kolom* 'three' Rebus: *kolami* 'smithy, forge'. Dula 'pair' Rebus: dul 'cast metal' Thus, together *dul kolami kuṭhār* 'metal smithy castings storeroom'

kanka 'rim of jar' Rebus: *karṇīka* 'account (scribe)' *karṇī* 'supercargo'

m1759a *खोंड [khōṇḍa] m A young bull, a bullcalf. (Marathi) Rebus: kõdār 'turner' (Bengali); कोंद kōnda 'engraver, lapidary setting or infixing gems' (Marathi) G. sãghāṛɔ m. 'lathe' ; संघाट joinery; M. sãgaḍ 'double-canoe' Rebus: sangataras. संगतराश lit. 'to collect stones, stone-cutter, mason.'*

dula 'pair' Rebus: dul 'cast metal' *mogge* 'sprout, bud' Rebus: *mũh* 'ingot' (Santali) Thus, cast metal ingot. PLUS INFIXED | *koḍa* 'one' Rebus: *koḍ* 'workshop'. Thus cast metal ingot workshop.
sal 'splinter' Rebus: sal 'workshop'
dula 'pair' Rebus: *dul* 'cast (metal)' PLUS*kana, kanac* = corner (Santali); Rebus: *kañcu* = bronze (Telugu) Thus, cast bronze.
dula 'two' Rebus: dul 'cast metal' (May indicate cast metal of other alloys, other than bronze castings)

kanka 'rim of jar' Rebus: *karṇīka* 'account (scribe)' *karṇī* 'supercargo'

m758A *खोंड [khōṇḍa] m A young bull, a bullcalf. (Marathi) Rebus: kõdār 'turner' (Bengali); कोंद*

kōnda 'engraver, lapidary setting or infixing gems' (Marathi) G. sãghāṛɔ m. 'lathe' ; संघाट joinery; M. sãgaḍ 'double-canoe' Rebus: sangataras. संगतराश lit. 'to collect stones, stone-cutter, mason.'

dula 'pair' Rebus: dul 'cast metal' *mogge* 'sprout, bud' Rebus: *mũh* 'ingot' (Santali) Thus, cast metal ingot.PLUS infixed:

| *koḍa* 'one' Rebus: *koḍ* 'workshop' PLUS ligatured:

baroṭi 'twelve' *bhārata* 'a factitious alloy of copper, pewter, tin' (Marathi). Thus, bharata alloy casting workshop.

kamaḍha = crab; *kampaṭṭam* = mint (Ta.) ; *kammaṭa* 'coiner, mint' (Telugu) Vikalpa: *ḍato* = claws of crab (Santali); *dhātu* = mineral (Sanskrit)

kanka 'rim of jar' Rebus: *karṇīka* 'account (scribe)' *karṇī* 'supercargo' PLUS INFIXED:sal 'splinter' Rebus: sal 'workshop' Thus workshop supercargo.

aya kammaṭa.'coiner, mint alloy' PLUS खांडा [*khāṇḍā*] *m* A jag, notch, or indentation (as upon the edge of a tool or weapon). Rebus: *kāṇḍa* 'tools, pots and pans and metal-ware'

kanka 'rim of jar' Rebus: *karṇīka* 'account (scribe)' *karṇī* 'supercargo' PLUS INFIXED: खांडा [*khāṇḍā*] *m* A jag, notch, or indentation (as upon the edge of a tool or weapon). Rebus: *kāṇḍa* 'tools, pots and pans and metal-ware'

kanka 'rim of jar' Rebus: *karṇīka* 'account (scribe)' *karṇī* 'supercargo'

M-1801 a

m1801a *खोंड [khōṇḍa] m A young bull, a bullcalf. (Marathi) Rebus: kõdār 'turner' (Bengali); कोंद kōnda 'engraver, lapidary setting or infixing gems' (Marathi) G. sãghāṛɔ m. 'lathe' ; संघाट joinery; M. sãgaḍ 'double-canoe' Rebus: sangataras. संगतराश lit. 'to collect stones, stone-cutter, mason.'*

dula 'pair'  Rebus: dul 'cast metal' *mogge* 'sprout, bud' Rebus: *mũh* 'ingot' (Santali) Thus, cast metal ingot.

INFIXED

āra 'spokes' Rebus: *āra 'brass'*. cf. erka = ekke (Tbh. of arka) aka (Tbh. of arka) copper (metal); crystal (Kannada) Glyph: *eraka*'nave of wheel' Rebus: eraka 'copper'; cf. erka = ekke (Tbh. of arka) aka (Tbh. of arka) copper (metal); crystal (Kannada) *erako* 'moltencast copper'. Thus, read rebus: moltencast copper, brass ingot castings.

kanka 'rim of jar' Rebus: *karṇīka* 'account (scribe)' *karṇī* 'supercargo'

| *koḍa* 'one' Rebus: *koḍ* 'workshop'

|||| Numeral 4: gaṇḍa 'four' Rebus: kaṇḍa 'furnace, fire-altar' (Santali) dula 'pair' Rebus: dul 'cast metal'

kharedo = a currycomb (Gujarati) खरारा [*kharārā*] *m* (H) A currycomb. 2 Currying a horse. (Marathi) Rebus: करडा [*karaḍā*] Hard from alloy--iron, silver &c. (Marathi) *kharādī* ' turner' (Gujarati)

'Arrow' sign hieroglyph (variant) This is a ligature of 'lid of pot' hieroglyph superscript on 'a linear stroke' numeral hieroglyph.

aḍaren 'cover of pot or lid' Rebus: *aduru* 'native, unsmelted metal' PLUS koḍ = one (Santali); koḍ 'workshop' (Gujarati)

Thus, together, the ligatured hieroglyph denotes: native metal workshop.

Pair of such ligatured hieroglyphs: dula 'pair' Rebus: dul 'cast metal'. The pair denotes: native metal casting workshop'.

m388a

metal) 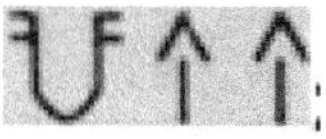 m0264 Text 2607 *khũṭ* 'zebu' Rebus: '(native guild'

dula 'pair' Rebus: dul 'cast metal'; aḍaren 'lid of pot' Rebus: aduru 'unsmelted, native metal' *koḍa* 'one' Rebus: *koḍ* 'workshop'

kanka 'rim of jar' Rebus: *karṇīka* 'account (scribe)' *karṇī* 'supercargo'

Lothal 98A dula 'pair' Rebus: dul 'cast metal'; aḍaren 'lid of pot' Rebus: aduru 'unsmelted, native metal'. Thus as a pair: cast unsmelted metal (from*) koḍa* 'one' Rebus: *koḍ* 'workshop'
aḍar 'harrow'; rebus: *aduru* 'native unsmelted metal'

ayo 'fish' Rebus: aya 'iron' (Gujarati) ayas 'metal' (Sanskrit)
कांड *kāṇḍa* 'arrow' Rebus: *kāṇḍa* 'pots and pans, metalware, tools'.

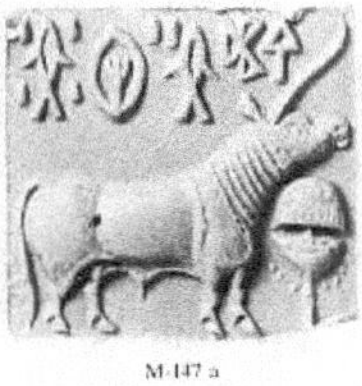

m147a*खोंड [khōṇḍa] m A young bull, a bullcalf. (Marathi) Rebus: kõdār 'turner' (Bengali); कोंद kōnda 'engraver, lapidary setting or infixing gems' (Marathi) G. sãghārɔ m. 'lathe' ; संघाट joinery; M. sãgaḍ 'double-canoe' Rebus: sangataras. संगतराश lit. 'to collect stones, stone-cutter, mason.'*

कांड *kāṇḍa* 'arrow' Rebus: *kāṇḍa* 'pots and pans, metalware, tools'.
kamaḍha 'crab' Rebus: *kammaṭa* 'mint, coiner'.
ḍato = claws of crab (Santali) Rebus: *dhātu* 'mineral ore'

ayo 'fish' Rebus: *aya* 'iron' *ayas* 'metal' sal 'splinter' Rebus: sal 'workshop'*dula* 'pair' Rebus: *dul* 'cast (metal)' PLUS*kana, kanac* = corner (Santali); Rebus: *kañcu* = bronze (Telugu) PLUS infixed kolmo 'paddy plant' Rebus: kolami 'smithy, forge'. Thus, cast bronze smithy, forge. Or, *mogge* 'sprout, bud' Rebus: *mũh* 'ingot' (Santali)Thus, cast bronze ingot. Read as: *kañcu dul mũh 'bronze cast ingot'*
aya kāṇḍa 'alloy metalware'

m3a *खोंड [khōṇḍa] m A young bull, a bullcalf. (Marathi) Rebus: kõdār 'turner' (Bengali); कोंद kōnda 'engraver, lapidary setting or infixing gems' (Marathi) G.*

sãghāṛɔ m. 'lathe' ; संघाट joinery; M. sãgaḍ 'double-canoe' Rebus: sangataras 'stone-cutter, mason' kōḍu 'horn' Rebus: 'workshop'sãghāṛɔ m. 'lathe' (Gujarati) Rebus: sangataras. संगतराश lit. 'to collect stones, stone-cutter, mason. Inverted variant:
kaṇḍo 'stool, seat' Rebus: *kāṇḍa* 'metalware' *kaṇḍa* 'fire-altar' (Phonetic determinant) PLUS

कांड *kāṇḍa* 'arrow' Rebus: *kāṇḍa* 'pots and pans, metalware, tools'. Rebus 2: kaṇḍ 'fire-altar' (Santali)

dula 'two' Rebus: dul 'cast metal' *khuṭo* ' leg, foot ', °ṭī ' goat's leg ' Rebus: *khōṭā* 'alloy' (Marathi)
Thus, alloy metal metalware.

h90A *ibha* 'elephant' Rebus: *ib* 'iron' *ibbo* 'merchant' (Gujarati) Inverted variant:
kaṇḍo 'stool, seat' Rebus: *kāṇḍa* 'metalware' *kaṇḍa* 'fire-altar' (Phonetic determinant) PLUS *kāṇḍa* 'arrow' (Sanskrit) Rebus:*khāṇḍa* 'tools, pots and pans, metal-ware'. Rebus 2: kaṇḍ 'fire-altar' (Santali)

koḍi 'flag'  (Ta.)(DEDR 2049). Rebus 1: *koḍ* 'workshop' (Kuwi) Rebus 2: *khŏḍ* m. 'pit', *khŏḍü* f. 'small pit' (Kashmiri. CDIAL 3947).

khuṭo ' leg, foot ', °ṭī ' goat's leg ' Rebus: *khōṭā* 'alloy' (Marathi)

cīmara 'black ant' Rebus: *cīmara* 'copper'. *cīmara kāra* -- ' coppersmith 'खांडा [*khāṇḍā*] *m* A jag, notch, or indentation (as upon the edge of a tool or weapon). Rebus: *kāṇḍa* 'tools, pots and pans and metal-ware' PLUS | *koḍa* 'one' Rebus: *koḍ* 'workshop'

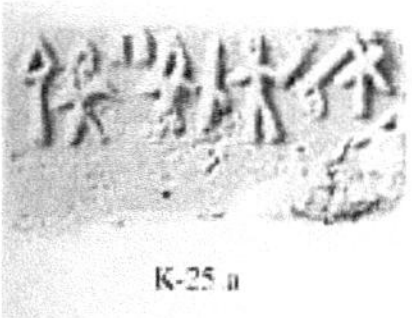

Kalibangan 25a 'Arrow' sign hieroglyph (variant) This is a ligature of 'lid of pot' hieroglyph superscript on 'a linear stroke' numeral hieroglyph.*aḍaren* 'cover of pot or lid' Rebus: *aduru* 'native, unsmelted metal' PLUS koḍ = one (Santali); koḍ 'workshop' (Gujarati) *ḍhanga* = a crook used for pulling down the branches of trees, for goats, sheep and camels (P.) Rebus:*ḍhangar* blacksmith'. eraka 'upraised hand' Rebus: erako 'moltencast copper'
meḍ 'body' Rebus: *meḍ* 'iron' (Ho.) काठी [kāṭhī] *f* (काष्ट S) 'frame or structure of the body'

(Marathi) Rebus: खंडी [khaṇḍī] measure of weight (Marathi) கண்டி; *kaṇṭi, n. < Mhr. khaṇḍil. [T. Tu. khaṇḍi, M. kaṇḍi.]* Candy, a weight, stated to be roughly equivalent to 500 lbs.

notch+slanted stroke reads rebus: *ḍhālako kāṇḍa* 'ingot, tools, pots and pans and metal-ware'.*ḍhāḷ* 'a slope'; 'inclination of a plane' (G.); *ḍhāḷiyum* = adj. sloping, inclining (G.) Rebus: *ḍhālako* = a large metal ingot (G.) *ḍhālakī* = a metal heated and poured into a mould; a solid piece of metal; an ingot (Gujarati) PLUS खांडा [*khāṇḍā*] *m* A jag, notch, or indentation (as upon the edge of a tool or weapon). Rebus: *kāṇḍa* 'tools, pots and pans and metal-ware' *Thus, together, the pair reads: āra erako khāṇḍā* 'brass, moltencast copper metalware'.
ayo 'fish' Rebus: *aya* 'iron' *ayas* 'metal' sal 'splinter' Rebus: sal 'workshop'

aya kāṇḍa 'alloy metalware' *kāṇḍa* 'arrow' (Sanskrit) Rebus:*khāṇḍa* 'tools, pots and pans, metal-ware'. Rebus 2: kaṇḍ 'fire-altar' (Santali)

h232A'

Arrow' sign hieroglyph (variant) This is a ligature of 'lid of pot' hieroglyph superscript on 'a linear stroke' numeral hieroglyph.*aḍaren* 'cover of pot or lid' Rebus: *aduru* 'native, unsmelted metal' PLUS koḍ = one (Santali); koḍ 'workshop' (Gujarati) *baraḍo* = spine; backbone (Tulu) Rebus: *baran, bharat* 'mixed alloys' (5 copper, 4 zinc and 1 tin) (Punjabi)

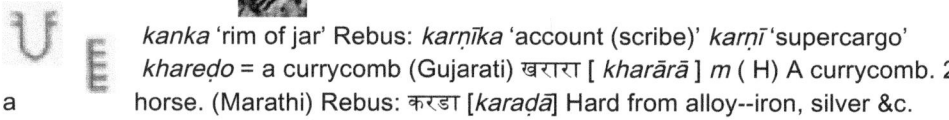

kanka 'rim of jar' Rebus: *karṇīka* 'account (scribe)' *karṇī* 'supercargo' *khareḍo* = a currycomb (Gujarati) खरारा [*kharārā*] *m* (H) A currycomb. 2 Currying a horse. (Marathi) Rebus: करडा [*karaḍā*] Hard from alloy--iron, silver &c. (Marathi) *kharādī* ' turner' (Gujarati)

m81a *खोंड [khōṇḍa] m A young bull, a bullcalf. (Marathi) Rebus: kõdār 'turner' (Bengali); कोंद kōnda 'engraver, lapidary setting or infixing gems' (Marathi) G. sãghāṛɔ m. 'lathe' ; संघाट joinery; M. sãgaḍ 'double-canoe' Rebus: sangataras. संगतराश lit. 'to collect stones, stone-cutter, mason.'*

'Arrow' sign hieroglyph (variant) This is a ligature of 'lid of pot' hieroglyph

superscript on 'a linear stroke' numeral hieroglyph.*aḍaren* 'cover of pot or lid' Rebus: *aduru* 'native, unsmelted metal' PLUS koḍ = one (Santali); koḍ 'workshop' (Gujarati)

khaṇḍ 'field, division' (Sanskrit) Rebus: *khāṇḍa* 'tools, pots and pans, metal-ware'. Rebus 2: kaṇḍ 'fire-altar' (Santali) dula 'pair' Rebus: dul 'cast metal' Thus, duplicated 'division' hieroglyph sign reads: cast metal metal-ware.

sal 'splinter' Rebus: sal 'workshop'

aya kammaṭa.'coiner, mint alloy'

kamaḍha 'crab' Rebus: *kammaṭa* 'mint, coiner'.*ḍato* = claws of crab (Santali) Rebus: *dhātu* 'mineral ore'

PLUS खांडा [*khāṇḍā*] *m* A jag, notch, or indentation (as upon the edge of a tool or weapon). Rebus: *kāṇḍa* 'tools, pots and pans and metal-ware' Thus, mint metalware, ore.

dula two, pair' Rebus: dul 'cast metal' PLUS *dhāḷ* 'a slope'; 'inclination of a plane' (G.); *ḍhāḷiyum* = adj. sloping, inclining (G.) Rebus: *ḍhālako* = a large metal ingot (G.) *ḍhālakī* = a metal heated and poured into a mould; a solid piece of metal; an ingot (Gujarati) PLUS kolom 'three' Rebus: kolami 'smithy, forge'. Thus cast metal ingot smithy.

m123a *खोंड [khōṇḍa] m A young bull, a bullcalf. (Marathi) Rebus: kõdār 'turner' (Bengali); कोंद kōnda 'engraver, lapidary setting or infixing gems' (Marathi) G. sãghāṛɔ m. 'lathe' ; संघाट joinery; M. sãgaḍ 'double-canoe' Rebus: sangataras. संगतराश lit. 'to collect stones, stone-cutter, mason.'* metal'

'Arrow' sign  hieroglyph (variant) This is a ligature of 'lid of pot' hieroglyph superscript on ‘a linear stroke’ numeral hieroglyph.*aḍaren* ‘cover of pot or lid’ Rebus: *aduru* ‘native, unsmelted metal’ PLUS koḍ = one (Santali); koḍ ‘workshop’ (Gujarati) PLUS dulo ‘hole’ Rebus: dul ‘cast metal’

 *koḍi* ‘flag’ (Ta.)(DEDR 2049). Rebus 1: *koḍ* ‘workshop’ (Kuwi) Rebus 2: *khŏḍ* m. ‘pit’, *khŏḍü* f. ‘small pit’ (Kashmiri. CDIAL 3947).
bhaṭa ‘warrior’ (Sanskrit) Rebus: *baṭa* a kind of iron (Gujarati). Rebus: *bhaṭa* ‘furnace’ (Santali) PLUS खांडा [*khāṇḍā*] *m* A jag, notch, or indentation (as upon the edge of a tool or weapon). Rebus: *kāṇḍa* ‘tools, pots and pans and metal-ware’

 *khareḍo* = a currycomb (Gujarati) खरारा [*kharārā*] *m* (H) A currycomb. 2 Currying a horse. (Marathi) Rebus: करडा [*karaḍā*] Hard from alloy--iron, silver &c. (Marathi) *kharādī* ‘ turner’ (Gujarati)

h68A *balad* m. ‘ ox ’, gng. *bald*, (Ku.) *barad*, id. (N. Tarai) Rebus: *bharat* (5 copper, 4 zinc and 1 tin)(Punjabi) *pattar* ‘trough’ Rebus: *pattar* ‘guild’. Thus, copper-zinc-tin alloy (worker) guild.

‘Arrow’ sign  hieroglyph (variant) This is a ligature of ‘lid of pot’ hieroglyph superscript on ‘a linear stroke’ numeral hieroglyph.*aḍaren* ‘cover of pot or lid’ Rebus: *aduru* ‘native, unsmelted metal’ PLUS koḍ = one (Santali); koḍ ‘workshop’ (Gujarati) Duplicated: dula ‘pair’ Rebus: dul ‘cast metal’ Thus, native metal workshop castings. PLUS dula ‘hole’ Rebus: dul ‘cast metal’. (The second ‘arrow’ has a ‘hole’ hieroglyph ligature as a phonetic –senabtic determinant of metal casting work).

sal ‘splinter’ Rebus: sal ‘workshop’
| *koḍa* ‘one’ Rebus: *koḍ* ‘workshop’

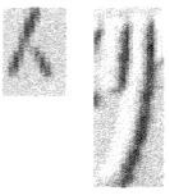 notch+slanted stroke reads rebus: *ḍhālako kāṇḍa* ‘ingot, tools, pots and pans and metal-ware’.*dhāḷ* ‘a slope’; ‘inclination of a plane’ (G.); *ḍhāḷiyum* = adj. sloping, inclining (G.) Rebus: *ḍhālako* = a large metal ingot (G.) *ḍhālakī* = a metal heated and poured into a mould; a solid piece of metal; an ingot (Gujarati) PLUS खांडा [*khāṇḍā*] *m* A jag, notch, or indentation (as upon the edge of a tool or weapon). Rebus: *kāṇḍa* ‘tools, pots and pans and metal-ware’ *Thus, together, the pair reads: āra erako khāṇḍā* ‘brass, moltencast copper metalware’.

 अगडा [agaḍā] *m* The tie connecting the जूं & दांडी of a गाडा or load-cart; the shaft and thill-yoke-tie. Rebus: ‘lumber, miscellaneous articles’: अगडतगड [*agaḍatagaḍa*] *n* अगडबगड *n* (Fanciful formations, or from H) Trash, trumpery, rubbish, lumber, miscellaneous articles. arka) copper (metal); crystal (Kannada) *erako* ‘moltencast copper’ Duplicated: dula ‘pair’ Rebus: dul ‘cast metal’ Thus cast copper, brass casting.
dula ‘two’ Rebus: dul ‘cast metal’ PLUS kolom ‘three’ Rebus: kolami ‘smithy, forge’

 *kanka* ‘rim of jar’ Rebus: *karṇīka* ‘account (scribe)’ *karṇī* ‘supercargo’

खोंड *[khōṇḍa] m A young bull, a bullcalf. (Marathi) Rebus: kõdār 'turner' (Bengali);* कोंद *kōnda 'engraver, lapidary setting or infixing gems' (Marathi) G. sãghāṛɔ m. 'lathe' ;* संघाट *joinery; M. sãgaḍ 'double-canoe' Rebus: sangataras.* संगतराश *lit. 'to collect stones, stone-cutter, mason.'*

'Arrow' sign hieroglyph (variant) This is a ligature of 'lid of pot' hieroglyph superscript on 'a linear stroke' numeral hieroglyph.*aḍaren* 'cover of pot or lid' Rebus: *aduru* 'native, unsmelted metal' PLUS koḍ = one (Santali); koḍ 'workshop' (Gujarati) PLUS dula 'hole' Rebus: dul 'cast metal'

kolmo 'paddy plant' Rebus: *kolami* 'smithy, forge' Vikalpa: *mogge* 'sprout, bud' Rebus: *mũh* 'ingot' (Santali) dolu 'plant of shoot height' Rebus: dul 'cast metal'

dula 'pair' Rebus: *dul* 'cast (metal)'
sal 'splinter' Rebus: sal 'workshop' PLUS kolom 'three' Rebus: kolami 'smithy, forge'

ayo 'fish' Rebus: *aya* 'iron' *ayas* 'metal'

kanka 'rim of jar' Rebus: *karṇīka* 'account (scribe)' *karṇī* 'supercargo'

meḍ 'body' Rebus: *meḍ* 'iron' (Ho.) काठी [kāṭhī] *f* (काष्ट S) 'frame or structure of the body' (Marathi) Rebus: खंडी [khaṇḍī] measure of weight (Marathi) *கண்டி; kaṇṭi, n. < Mhr. khaṇḍil. [T. Tu. khaṇḍi, M. kaṇḍi.]* Candy, a weight, stated to be roughly equivalent to 500 lbs.

'Foot, hoof' sign hieroglyph

h1798a खोंड *[khōṇḍa] m A young bull, a bullcalf. (Marathi) Rebus: kõdār 'turner' (Bengali);* कोंद *kōnda 'engraver, lapidary setting or infixing gems' (Marathi) G. sãghāṛɔ m. 'lathe' ;* संघाट *joinery; M. sãgaḍ 'double-canoe' Rebus: sangataras.* संगतराश *lit. 'to collect stones, stone-cutter, mason.'*

khuṭo ' leg, foot ', °ṭī ' goat's leg ' Rebus: *khōṭā* 'alloy' (Marathi)

kanka 'rim of jar' Rebus: *karṇīka* 'account (scribe)' *karṇī* 'supercargo'

m1858A खोंड *[khōṇḍa] m A young bull, a bullcalf. (Marathi) Rebus: kõdār 'turner' (Bengali);* कोंद *kōnda 'engraver, lapidary setting or infixing gems' (Marathi) G. sãghāṛɔ m. 'lathe' ;* संघाट *joinery; M. sãgaḍ 'double-canoe' Rebus: sangataras.* संगतराश *lit. 'to collect stones, stone-cutter, mason.'*

khuṭo ' leg, foot ', °ṭī ' goat's leg ' Rebus: *khōṭā* 'alloy' (Marathi) erako 'upraised arm' Rebus: erako 'moltencast copper' PLUS

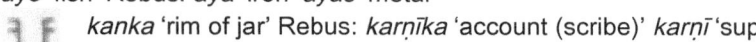

meḍ 'body' Rebus: *meḍ* 'iron' (Ho.) काठी [kāṭhī] *f* (काष्ट S) 'frame or structure of the body' (Marathi) Rebus: खंडी [khaṇḍī] measure of weight (Marathi) *கண்டி; kaṇṭi, n. < Mhr. khaṇḍil. [T. Tu. khaṇḍi, M. kaṇḍi.]* Candy, a weight, stated to be roughly equivalent to 500 lbs.

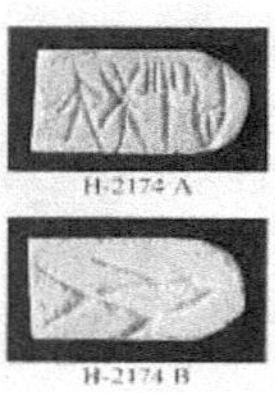

h2174A

meḍ 'body' Rebus: *meḍ* 'iron' (Ho.) काठी [kāṭhī] *f* (काष्ट S) 'frame or structure of the body' (Marathi) Rebus: खंडी [khaṇḍī] measure of weight (Marathi) *கண்டி; kaṇṭi, n. < Mhr. khaṇḍil. [T. Tu. khaṇḍi, M. kaṇḍi.]*

Candy, a weight, stated to be roughly equivalent to 500 lbs.

loa 'ficus religiosa' Rebus: *lo* 'iron' (Sanskrit) PLUS unique ligatures: लोखंड [lōkhaṇḍa] *n* (लोह S) Iron. लोखंडाचे चणे खावविणें or चारणें To oppress grievously.लोखंडकाम [lōkhaṇḍakāma] *n* Iron work; that portion (of a building, machine &c.) which consists of iron. 2 The business of an ironsmith.लोखंडी [lōkhaṇḍī] *a* (लोखंड) Composed of iron; relating to iron. (Marathi) *bhaṭa* 'warrior' (Sanskrit) Rebus: *baṭa* a kind of iron (Gujarati). Rebus: *bhaṭa* 'furnace' (Santali) Thus, together, th ligatured hieroglyph reads rebus: *loa bhaṭa* 'iron furnace'

aḍar 'harrow'; rebus: *aduru* 'native unsmelted metal'

khuṭo ' leg, foot ', °ṭī ' goat's leg ' Rebus: *khōṭā* 'alloy' (Marathi) *ayo* 'fish' Rebus: *aya* 'iron' *ayas* 'metal'

m52a *खोंड [khōṇḍa] m A young bull, a bullcalf. (Marathi) Rebus: kõdār 'turner' (Bengali); कोंद kōnda 'engraver, lapidary setting or infixing gems' (Marathi) G. sãghāṛɔ m. 'lathe' ; संघाट joinery; M. sãgaḍ 'double-canoe' Rebus: sangataras. संगतराश lit. 'to collect stones, stone-cutter, mason.'*

khuṭo ' leg, foot ', °ṭī ' goat's leg ' Rebus: *khōṭā* 'alloy' (Marathi)

mēḍu height, rising ground, hillock (Kannada) Rebus: *mẽṛhẽt, meḍ* 'iron' (Munda.Ho.) PLUS *kaṇḍo* 'stool, seat' Rebus: *kāṇḍa* 'metalware' *kaṇḍa* 'fire-altar'

dula 'pair' Rebus: *dul* 'cast (metal)' PLUS*kana, kanac* = corner (Santali); Rebus: *kañcu* = bronze (Telugu) PLUS infixed kolmo 'paddy plant' Rebus: kolami 'smithy, forge'. Thus, cast bronze smithy, forge. Or, *mogge* 'sprout, bud' Rebus: *mũh* 'ingot' (Santali)Thus, cast bronze ingot. Read as: *kañcu dul mũh 'bronze cast ingot'*

aya aḍaren (homonym: aduru)'alloy native metal'

aḍar 'harrow'; rebus: *aduru* 'native unsmelted metal' *aya kāṇḍa* 'alloy metalware'

dula 'two' Rebus: dul 'cast metal'

kuṭila 'bent' CDIAL 3230 kuṭi— in cmpd. 'curve', *kuṭika*— 'bent' MBh. Rebus: *kuṭila, katthīl* = bronze (8 parts copper and 2 parts tin) Duplicated: dula 'pair' Rebus: dul 'cast metal' Thus, cast bronze.

kanka 'rim of jar' Rebus: *karṇīka* 'account (scribe)' *karṇī* 'supercargo'

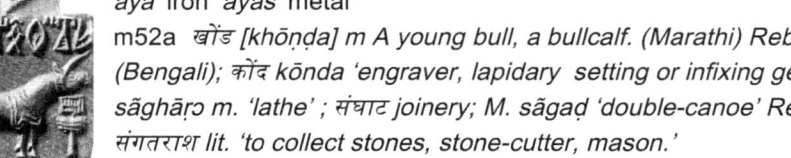

खोंड [khōṇḍa] m A young bull, a bullcalf. (Marathi) Rebus: kõdār 'turner' (Bengali); कोंद kōnda 'engraver, lapidary setting or infixing gems' (Marathi)

G. sãghārɔ m. 'lathe' ; संघाट joinery; M. sãgaḍ 'double-canoe' Rebus: sangataras. संगतराश lit. 'to collect stones, stone-cutter, mason.'

dulo 'hole' Rebus: dul 'cast metal'

khuṭo ' leg, foot ', °ṭī ' goat's leg ' Rebus: *khōṭā* 'alloy' (Marathi) kolom 'three' Rebus: kolami 'smithy, forge'

kanka 'rim of jar' Rebus: *karṇīka* 'account (scribe)' *karṇī* 'supercargo' PLUS INFIXED: खांडा [*khāṇḍā*] *m* A jag, notch, or indentation (as upon the edge of a tool or weapon). Rebus: *kāṇḍa* 'tools, pots and pans and metal-ware'

'Bow and arrow' sign hieroglyph 'Archer + bow + arrow' ligatured hieroglyph upraised arm: eraka 'upraised arm' Rebus: erako 'moltencast copper' *kamaḍha* 'archer, bow' Rebus: *kammaṭa* 'mint, coiner'.

loa 'ficus religiosa' Rebus: *lo* 'iron' (Sanskrit) PLUS unique ligatures: लोखंड [lōkhaṇḍa] *n* (लोह S) Iron. लोखंडाचे चणे खावविणें or चारणें To oppress grievously.लोखंडकाम [lōkhaṇḍakāma] *n* Iron work; that portion (of a building, machine &c.) which consists of iron. 2 The business of an ironsmith.लोखंडी [lōkhaṇḍī] *a* (लोखंड) Composed of iron; relating to iron. (Marathi)

kanka 'rim of jar' Rebus: *karṇīka* 'account (scribe)' *karṇī* 'supercargo'

h130A

H-130 A

khuṭo ' leg, foot ', °ṭī ' goat's leg ' Rebus: *khōṭā* 'alloy' (Marathi) kolom 'three' Rebus: kolami 'smithy, forge'

'Bow and arrow' sign hieroglyph 'Archer + bow + arrow' ligatured hieroglyph upraised arm: eraka 'upraised arm' Rebus: erako 'moltencast copper' *kamaḍha* 'archer, bow' Rebus: *kammaṭa* 'mint, coiner'.

Variant: kana, kanac = corner (Santali); Rebus: *kañcu* = bronze (Telugu) PLUS kolom 'three' Rebus: kolami 'smithy, forge' Thus, bronze forge.

ranku 'liquid measure' Rebus: ranku 'tin' PLUS sal 'splinter' Rebus: sal 'workshop'

dula 'pair' Rebus: *dul* 'cast (metal)' PLUS*kana, kanac* = corner (Santali); Rebus: *kañcu* = bronze (Telugu) PLUS infixed kolmo 'paddy plant' Rebus: kolami 'smithy, forge'. Thus, cast bronze smithy, forge. Or, *mogge* 'sprout, bud' Rebus: *mũh* 'ingot' (Santali)Thus, cast bronze ingot. Read as: *kañcu dul mũh 'bronze cast ingot'*

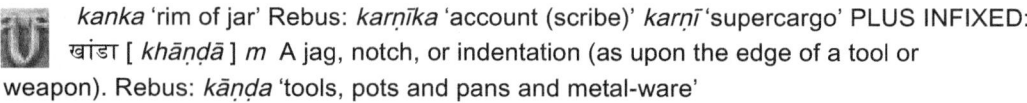

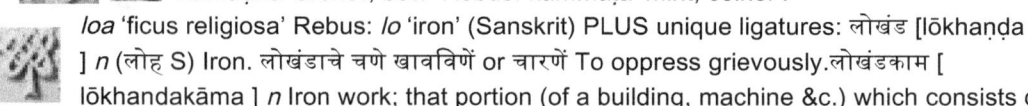

aya kāṇḍa 'alloy metalware' *muka* 'ladle' (Tamil)(DEDR 4887) Rebus: *mũh* 'ingot' (Santali) *baṭa* = rimless pot (Kannada) Rebus:) *baṭa* = a kind of iron (G.)) *bhaṭa* furnace (Gujarati) Thus, iron ingot. PLUS kolom 'three' Rebus: kolami 'smithy, forge' *dula* 'pair' Rebus: *dul* 'cast (metal)' PLUS*kana, kanac* = corner (Santali); Rebus: *kañcu* = bronze (Telugu) Thus, cast bronze.

dula 'two' Rebus: dul 'cast metal'

 *kolmo* 'paddy plant' Rebus: *kolami* 'smithy, forge' Vikalpa: *mogge* 'sprout, bud' Rebus: *mũh* 'ingot' (Santali) dolu 'plant of shoot height' Rebus: dul 'cast metal'

m391A

khuṭo ' leg, foot ', °ṭī ' goat's leg ' Rebus: *khōṭā* 'alloy' (Marathi)
PLUS

 *kolmo* 'paddy plant' Rebus: *kolami* 'smithy, forge' Vikalpa: *mogge* 'sprout, bud' Rebus: *mũh* 'ingot' (Santali) dolu 'plant of shoot height' Rebus: dul 'cast metal'

 *kuṭila* 'bent' CDIAL 3230 kuṭi— in cmpd. 'curve', *kuṭika—* 'bent' MBh. Rebus: *kuṭila, katthīl* = bronze (8 parts copper and 2 parts tin)PLUS

 'Bow and arrow' sign hieroglyph 'Archer + bow + arrow' ligatured hieroglyph upraised arm: eraka 'upraised arm' Rebus: erako 'moltencast copper' *kamaḍha* 'archer, bow' Rebus: *kammaṭa* 'mint, coiner'.

 *kanac* 'corner' Rebus: *kañcu* 'bronze'
sal 'splinter' Rebus: sal 'workshop'

The hieroglyph may be a variant of:  *kana, kanac* = corner (Santali); Rebus: *kañcu* = bronze (Telugu) PLUS kolom 'three' Rebus: kolami 'smithy, forge.

 *kuṭila* 'bent' CDIAL 3230 kuṭi— in cmpd. 'curve', *kuṭika—* 'bent' MBh. Rebus: *kuṭila, katthīl* = bronze (8 parts copper and 2 parts tin) Duplicated: dula 'pair' Rebus: dul 'cast metal' Thus, cast bronze. INFIXED dulo 'hole' Rebus: dul 'cast metal'
ayo ḍhālako 'alloy metal ingot' kolom 'three' Rebus: kolami 'smithy, forge'

 *kanka* 'rim of jar' Rebus: *karṇika* 'account (scribe)' *karṇī* 'supercargo' PLUS INFIXED: खांडा [*khāṇḍā*] *m* A jag, notch, or indentation (as upon the edge of a tool or weapon). Rebus: *kāṇḍa* 'tools, pots and pans and metal-ware'

 *dula* 'pair' Rebus: *dul* 'cast (metal)' PLUS*kana, kanac* = corner (Santali); Rebus: *kañcu* = bronze (Telugu) Thus, cast bronze.

 *dāṭu* 'cross'(Telugu) Rebus: *dhatu* 'mineral' (Santali).

INFIXED sal 'splinter' Rebus: sal 'workshop' PLUS Numeral 4: gaṇḍa 'four' Rebus: kaṇḍa 'furnace, fire-altar' (Santali)

kolmo 'paddy plant' Rebus: *kolami* 'smithy, forge' Vikalpa: *mogge* 'sprout, bud' Rebus: *mũh* 'ingot' (Santali) dolu 'plant of shoot height' Rebus: dul 'cast metal'

m376a

khuṭo ' leg, foot ', °ṭī ' goat's leg ' Rebus: *khōṭā* 'alloy' (Marathi) *bhaṭa* 'warrior' (Sanskrit) Rebus: *baṭa* a kind of iron (Gujarati). Rebus: *bhaṭa* 'furnace' (Santali)

baraḍo = spine; backbone (Tulu) Rebus: *baran, bharat* 'mixed alloys' (5 copper, 4 zinc and 1 tin) (Punjabi) sal 'splinter' Rebus: sal 'workshop

kanac 'corner' Rebus: *kañcu* 'bronze'

kuṭila 'bent' CDIAL 3230 kuṭi— in cmpd. 'curve', *kuṭika—* 'bent' MBh. Rebus: *kuṭila,*

katthīl = bronze (8 parts copper and 2 parts tin) PLUS 'Bow and arrow' sign hieroglyph 'Archer + bow + arrow' ligatured hieroglyph *kamaḍha* 'archer, bow' Rebus: *kammaṭa* 'mint, coiner'.

khuṭo ' leg, foot ', °ṭī ' goat's leg ' Rebus: *khōṭā* 'alloy' (Marathi)

Ingot + metal-ware rebus readings (Sign hieroglyphs composition: slanted stroke + notch or jag stroke)

MS5065 *khũṭ* 'zebu' Rebus: '(native metal) guild'

dhāḷ 'a slope'; 'inclination of a plane' (G.); *ḍhāḷiyum* = adj. sloping, inclining (G.) Rebus: *ḍhālako* = a large metal ingot (G.) *ḍhālakī* = a metal heated and poured into a mould; a solid piece of metal; an ingot (Gujarati) PLUS खांडा [*khāṇḍā*] *m* A jag, notch, or indentation (as upon the edge of a tool or weapon). Rebus: *kāṇḍa* 'tools, pots and pans and metal-ware'

khareḍo = a currycomb (Gujarati) खरारा [*kharārā*] *m* (H) A currycomb. 2 Currying a horse. (Marathi) Rebus: करडा [*karaḍā*] Hard from alloy--iron, silver &c. (Marathi) *kharādī* ' turner' (Gujarati)

aḍaren 'cover of pot or lid' Rebus: *aduru* 'native, unsmelted metal'.

m256a *khũṭ* 'zebu' Rebus: '(native metal) guild'
Sign hieroglyph on m256 as at MS 5065 has been read rebus:

 Read in context, the composite hieroglyph is assumed to be a combination of a slanted stroke ligatured to a notch,which provide possible rebus readings of a smithy/forge: notch+slanted stroke reads rebus: *ḍhālako kāṇḍa* 'ingot, tools, pots and pans and metal-ware'

dhāḷ 'a slope'; 'inclination of a plane' (Gujarati); *ḍhāḷiyum* = adj. sloping, inclining (Gujarati) Rebus: *ḍhālako* = a large metal ingot (Gujarati) *ḍhālakī* = a metal heated and poured into a mould; a solid piece of metal; an ingot (Gujarati) PLUS खांडा [*khāṇḍā*] *m* A jag, notch, or indentation (as upon the edge of a tool or weapon). Rebus: *kāṇḍa* 'tools, pots and pans and metal-ware'

 अगडा [agaḍā] *m* The tie connecting the जूं & दांडी of a गाडा or load-cart; the shaft and thill-yoke-tie. Rebus: 'lumber, miscellaneous articles': अगडतगड [*agaḍatagaḍa*] *n* अगडबगड *n* (Fanciful formations, or from H) Trash, trumpery, rubbish, lumber, miscellaneous articles.

 dula 'two' Rebus: dul 'cast metal' ||| Numeral three: kolom 'three' Rebus: kolami 'smithy, forge'
kanka 'rim of jar' Rebus: *karṇīka* 'account (scribe)' *karṇī* 'supercargo' *meḍ* 'body' Rebus: *meḍ* 'iron' (Ho.) काठी [kāṭhī] *f* (काष्ट S) 'frame or structure of the body' (Marathi) Rebus: खंडी [khaṇḍī] measure of weight (Marathi) *கண்டி; kaṇṭi, n. < Mhr. khaṇḍil. [T. Tu. khaṇḍi, M. kaṇḍi.]* Candy, a weight, stated to be roughly equivalent to 500 lbs.

h1679A m879A h451A Three seals with identical inscriptions.

खोंड [khōṇḍa] m A young bull, a bullcalf. (Marathi) Rebus: kõdār 'turner' (Bengali); कोंद kōnda 'engraver, lapidary setting or infixing gems' (Marathi) 'lathe' ; संघाट joinery; M.
G. sãghārɔ m. sãgaḍ 'double-canoe' Rebus: sangataras. संगतराश lit. 'to collect stones, stone-cutter, mason.'

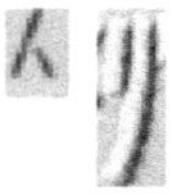 notch+slanted stroke reads rebus: *ḍhālako kāṇḍa* 'ingot, tools, pots and pans and metal-ware'.*dhāḷ* 'a slope'; 'inclination of a plane' (G.); *ḍhāḷiyum* = adj. sloping, inclining (G.) Rebus: *ḍhālako* = a large metal ingot (G.) *ḍhālakī* = a metal heated and poured into a mould; a solid piece of metal; an ingot (Gujarati) PLUS खांडा [*khāṇḍā*] *m* A jag, notch, or indentation (as upon the edge of a tool or weapon). Rebus: *kāṇḍa* 'tools, pots and pans and metal-ware'

 *meḍ* 'body' Rebus: *meḍ* 'iron' (Ho.) काठी [kāṭhī] *f* (काष्ट S) 'frame or structure of the body' (Marathi) Rebus: खंडी [khaṇḍī] measure of weight (Marathi) *கண்டி; kaṇṭi, n. < Mhr. khaṇḍil. [T. Tu. khaṇḍi, M. kaṇḍi.]* Candy, a weight, stated to be roughly equivalent to 500 lbs.

 *kharedo* = a currycomb (Gujarati) खरारा [*kharārā*] *m* (H) A currycomb. 2 Currying a horse. (Marathi) Rebus: करडा [*karaḍā*] Hard from alloy--iron, silver &c. (Marathi) *kharādī* ' turner' (Gujarati)

 *kanka* 'rim of jar' Rebus: *karṇīka* 'account (scribe)' *karṇī* 'supercargo'

H-1684 A

h1684A *खोंड [khōṇḍa] m A young bull, a bullcalf. (Marathi) Rebus: kõdār 'turner' (Bengali); कोंद kōnda 'engraver, lapidary setting or infixing gems' (Marathi) G. sãghāṛɔ m. 'lathe' ; संघाट joinery; M. sãgaḍ 'double-canoe' Rebus: sangataras. संगतराश lit. 'to collect stones, stone-cutter, mason.'*

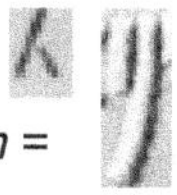 notch+slanted stroke reads rebus: *ḍhālako kāṇḍa* 'ingot, tools, pots and pans and metal-ware'.*dhāḷ* 'a slope'; 'inclination of a plane' (G.); *ḍhāḷiyum* = adj. sloping, inclining (G.) Rebus: *ḍhālako* = a large metal ingot (G.) *ḍhālakī* = a metal heated and poured into a mould; a solid piece of metal; an ingot (Gujarati) PLUS खांडा [*khāṇḍā*] *m* A jag, notch, or indentation (as upon the edge of a tool or weapon). Rebus: *kāṇḍa* 'tools, pots and pans and metal-ware'

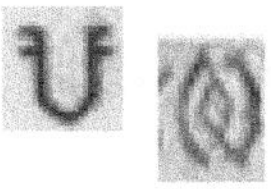 *kanka* 'rim of jar' Rebus: *karṇīka* 'account (scribe)' *karṇī* 'supercargo'
dula 'pair' Rebus: *dul* 'cast (metal)' PLUS*kana, kanac* = corner (Santali); Rebus: *kañcu* = bronze (Telugu) Thus, cast bronze.

| *koḍa* 'one' Rebus: *koḍ* 'workshop' PLUS ||| kolom 'three' Rebus: kolami 'smithy, forge' PLUS || sal 'splinter' Rebus sal 'workshop'

 Superscript ligature:

 'Arrow' sign hieroglyph (variant) This is a ligature of 'lid of pot' hieroglyph superscript on 'a linear stroke' numeral hieroglyph.*aḍaren* 'cover of pot or lid' Rebus: *aduru* 'native, unsmelted metal' PLUS koḍ = one (Santali); koḍ 'workshop' (Gujarati) PLUS superscript: मंडप [manḍapa] *m* (S) An open shed or hall adorned with flowers and erected on festive occasions, as at marriages &c.: also an arched way of light sticks for the vine &c. to climb and overspread. 2 An open building consecrated to a god. 3 fig. A canopy of clouds. Ex. पावसानें मं0 घातला. मंडन [manḍana] *n* (S) corruptly मंडण *n* Ornament or decoration: also the adorning material; jewels, trinkets &c. 2 Adorning, dressing out, bedecking. 3 In disputation; as opp. to खंडन. Establishing, proving, maintaining (of a position). 4 A festive occasion in general. 5 (For मेघमंडन) Overspreading (of clouds); canopy. *V*घाल.

Rebus: मंडली [manḍalī] *f* (S) An assembly, a company, a congregated or a corporate body. मंडई [manḍī] *f* (H) A green market, the place in a city whither vegetables and fruits are brought to be disposed of by wholesale.

h521a Read rebus as at h69A

M-1856 a

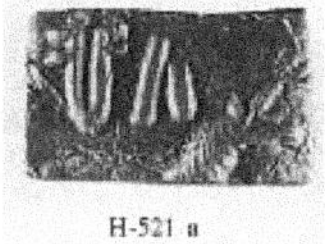
H-521 a

h1856a Read rebus as at h69A

h69A *खोंड [khōṇḍa] m A young bull, a bullcalf. (Marathi) Rebus: kõdār 'turner' (Bengali); कोंद kōnda 'engraver, lapidary setting or infixing gems' (Marathi)*

G. sãghāṛɔ m. 'lathe' ; संघाट joinery; M. sãgaḍ 'double-canoe' Rebus: sangataras. संगतराश lit. 'to collect stones, stone-cutter, mason.'

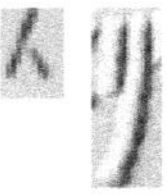

notch+slanted stroke reads rebus: *ḍhālako kāṇḍa* 'ingot, tools, pots and pans and metal-ware'.*dhāḷ* 'a slope'; 'inclination of a plane' (G.); *ḍhāḷiyum* = adj. sloping, inclining (G.) Rebus: *ḍhālako* = a large metal ingot (G.) *ḍhālakī* = a metal heated and poured into a mould; a solid piece of metal; an ingot (Gujarati) PLUS खांडा [*khāṇḍā*] *m* A jag, notch, or indentation (as upon the edge of a tool or weapon). Rebus: *kāṇḍa* 'tools, pots and pans and metal-ware'

kanka 'rim of jar' Rebus: *karṇīka* 'account (scribe)' *karṇī* 'supercargo'

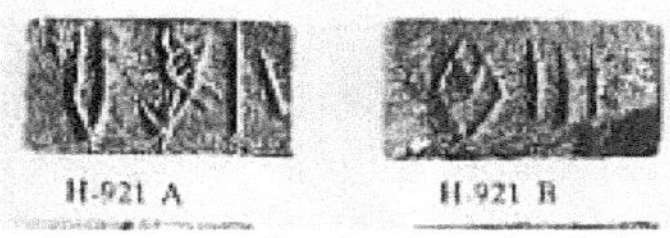

h921A,B

notch+slanted stroke reads rebus: *ḍhālako kāṇḍa* 'ingot, tools, pots and pans and metal-ware'.*dhāḷ* 'a slope'; 'inclination of a plane' (G.); *ḍhāḷiyum* = adj. sloping, inclining (G.) Rebus: *ḍhālako* = a large metal ingot (G.) *ḍhālakī* = a metal heated and poured into a mould; a solid piece of metal; an ingot (Gujarati) PLUS खांडा [*khāṇḍā*] *m* A jag, notch, or indentation (as upon the edge of a tool or weapon). Rebus: *kāṇḍa* 'tools, pots and pans and metal-ware'

baraḍo = spine; backbone (Tulu) Rebus: *baran, bharat* 'mixed alloys' (5 copper, 4 zinc and 1 tin) (Punjabi)

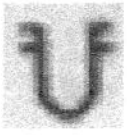

kanka 'rim of jar' Rebus: *karṇīka* 'account (scribe)' *karṇī* 'supercargo'

M-1097 A

m1097A *balad* m. ' ox ', gng. *bald*, (Ku.) *barad*, id. (N. Tarai) Rebus: *bharat* (5 copper, 4 zinc and 1 tin)(Punjabi) *pattar* 'trough' Rebus*: pattar* 'guild'. Thus, copper-zinc-tin alloy (worker) guild.

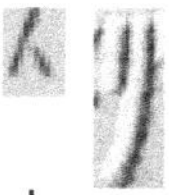

notch+slanted stroke reads rebus: *ḍhālako kāṇḍa* 'ingot, tools, pots and pans and metal-ware'.*dhāḷ* 'a slope'; 'inclination of a plane' (G.); *ḍhāḷiyum* = adj. sloping, inclining (G.) Rebus: *ḍhālako* = a large metal ingot (G.) *ḍhālakī* = a metal heated and poured into a mould; a solid piece of metal; an ingot (Gujarati) PLUS खांडा [*khāṇḍā*] *m* A jag, notch, or indentation (as upon the edge of a tool or weapon). Rebus: *kāṇḍa* 'tools, pots and pans and metal-ware'

khar 'donkey' Rebus: khara 'blacksmith' (Kashmiri) PLUS *Kur.* xolā tail. *Malt.* qoli id. (DEDR 2135). Rebus: kolhe 'smelter' Thus, copper smelter.

kana, kanac = corner (Santali); Rebus: *kañcu* = bronze (Telugu)
INFIXED dulo 'hole' Rebus: dul 'cast metal' Thus bronze castings.

m226A *खोंड [khōṇḍa] m A young bull, a bullcalf. (Marathi) Rebus: kõdār 'turner' (Bengali); कोंद kōnda 'engraver, lapidary setting or infixing gems' (Marathi) G.*

sãghāṛɔ m. 'lathe' ; संघाट joinery; M. sãgaḍ 'double-canoe' Rebus: sangataras. संगतराश lit. 'to collect stones, stone-cutter, mason.'

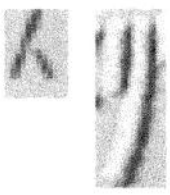

notch+slanted stroke reads rebus: *ḍhālako kāṇḍa* 'ingot, tools, pots and pans and metal-ware'.*dhāḷ* 'a slope'; 'inclination of a plane' (G.); *ḍhāḷiyum* = adj. sloping, inclining (G.) Rebus: *ḍhālako* = a large metal ingot (G.) *ḍhālakī* = a metal heated and poured into a mould; a solid piece of metal; an ingot (Gujarati) PLUS खांडा [*khāṇḍā*] *m* A jag, notch, or indentation (as upon the edge of a tool or weapon). Rebus: *kāṇḍa* 'tools, pots and pans and metal-ware'

khuṭo ' leg, foot ', °ṭī ' goat's leg ' Rebus: *khōṭā* 'alloy' (Marathi)

koḍi 'flag' (Ta.)(DEDR 2049). Rebus 1: *koḍ* 'workshop' (Kuwi) Rebus 2: *khōḍ* m. 'pit', *khōḍū* f. 'small pit' (Kashmiri. CDIAL 3947).

kanka 'rim of jar' Rebus: *karṇīka* 'account (scribe)' *karṇī* 'supercargo'

M-1366 A

m1366

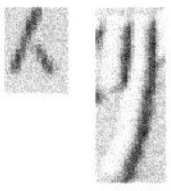

notch+slanted stroke reads rebus: *ḍhālako kāṇḍa* 'ingot, tools, pots and pans and metal-ware'.*dhāḷ* 'a slope'; 'inclination of a plane' (G.); *ḍhāḷiyum* = adj. sloping, inclining (G.) Rebus: *ḍhālako* = a large metal ingot (G.) *ḍhālakī* = a metal heated and poured into a mould; a solid piece of metal; an ingot (Gujarati) PLUS खांडा [*khāṇḍā*] *m* A jag, notch, or indentation (as upon the edge of a tool or weapon). Rebus: *kāṇḍa* 'tools, pots and pans and metal-ware'

kəṭhā´r, kc. *kuṭhār* m. ' granary, storeroom '(WPah.)(CDIAL 3550). *koṭhārī m.* ' storekeeper'

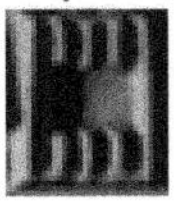

(Gujarati)(CDIAL 3551) Thus, storeroom (of) *kolom* 'three' Rebus: *kolami* 'smithy, forge'. Dula 'pair' Rebus: dul 'cast metal' Thus, together *dul kolami kuṭhār* 'metal smithy castings storeroom'

dula 'pair' Rebus: *dul* 'cast (metal)' PLUS*kana, kanac* = corner (Santali); Rebus: *kañcu* = bronze (Telugu) PLUS infixed kolmo 'paddy plant' Rebus: kolami 'smithy, forge'. Thus, cast bronze smithy, forge. Or, *mogge* 'sprout, bud' Rebus: *mũh* 'ingot' (Santali)Thus, cast bronze ingot. Read as: *kañcu dul mũh 'bronze cast ingot'*

Side B:

Variant: dula 'pair' Rebus: dul 'cast metal' PLUS | *koḍa* 'one' Rebus: *koḍ* 'workshop' PLUS INFIXED kolom three' Rebus: kolami 'smithy, forge' Thus metalware castings forge. PLUS ligature: dula 'two' Rebus: dul 'cast metal'*dhāḷ* 'a slope'; 'inclination of a plane' (G.); *ḍhāḷiyum* = adj. sloping, inclining (G.) Rebus: *ḍhālako* = a large metal ingot (G.) *ḍhālakī* = a metal heated and poured into a mould; a solid piece of metal; an ingot (Gujarati) Thus, cast metal ingot smithy, forge workshop.

kanka 'rim of jar' Rebus: *karṇīka* 'account (scribe)' *karṇī* 'supercargo'

m201A m1740a turner's metalware+ ingots PLUS *kuṭi* 'water-carrier' Rebus*: kuṭhi* 'smelter/furnace'.
खोंड [khōṇḍa] m A young bull, a bullcalf. (Marathi) Rebus: kõdār 'turner' (Bengali); कोंद kōnda 'engraver, lapidary setting or infixing gems' (Marathi) G. sãghāṛɔ m. 'lathe' ; संघाट joinery; M. sãgaḍ 'double-canoe' Rebus: sangataras. संगतराश lit. 'to collect stones, stone-cutter, mason.'

notch+slanted stroke reads rebus: *ḍhālako kāṇḍa* 'ingot, tools, pots and pans and metal-ware'.*dhāḷ* 'a slope'; 'inclination of a plane' (G.); *ḍhāḷiyum* = adj. sloping, inclining (G.) Rebus: *ḍhālako* = a large metal ingot (G.) *ḍhālakī* = a metal heated and poured into a mould; a solid piece of metal; an ingot (Gujarati) PLUS खांडा [*khāṇḍā*] *m* A jag, notch, or indentation (as upon the edge of a tool or weapon). Rebus: *kāṇḍa* 'tools, pots and pans and metal-ware'

m1133a Rhinoceros/boar: baḍhia = a castrated boar, a hog (Santali) baḍhi 'a caste who work both in iron and wood' (Santali) *baṟea* 'merchant'

water-carrier hieroglyph *kuṭi*; Rebus: *kuṭhi* 'smelter furnace'.
PLUS 'rim of jar':
kanka 'rim of jar' Rebus: karṇīka 'account (scribe)' karṇī 'supercargo'

meḍ 'body' Rebus: *meḍ* 'iron' (Ho.) काठी [kāṭhī] *f* (काष्ट S) 'frame or structure of the body' (Marathi) Rebus: खंडी [khaṇḍī] measure of weight (Marathi) *கண்டி; kaṇṭi, n. < Mhr. khaṇḍil. [T. Tu. khaṇḍi, M. kaṇḍi.]* Candy, a weight, stated to be roughly equivalent to 500 lbs.

khareḍo = a currycomb (Gujarati) खरारा [*kharārā*] *m* (H) A currycomb. 2 Currying a horse. (Marathi) Rebus: करडा [*karaḍā*] Hard from alloy--iron, silver &c. (Marathi) *kharādī* ' turner' (Gujarati)

kanka 'rim of jar' Rebus: *karṇīka* 'account (scribe)' *karṇī* 'supercargo'

सांड [sāṇḍa] *f* (षद S) An outlet for superfluous water (as through a dam or mound); a sluice, a floodvent. Rebus: सांडणी [sāṇḍaṇī] *f* (H) An instrument of goldsmiths. It is hooked or curved at the extremity; and is used to draw things out of the fire.
सांठा [*sāṇṭhā*] *m* (संचय S) A collection, heap, hoard, store, stock.साटें [*sāṭēṃ*] *n* (संचय S) A whole investment; the total quantity of merchandise (brought to market by one merchant).

ḍãg mountain-ridge (H.)(CDIAL 5476). Rebus: dhangar 'blacksmith' (Maithili)

Mountain-range or mountain-ridge hieroglyph

m20a *खोंड [khōṇḍa] m A young bull, a bullcalf. (Marathi) Rebus: kõdār 'turner' (Bengali); कोंद kōnda 'engraver, lapidary setting or infixing gems' (Marathi) G. sãghāṛɔ m. 'lathe' ; संघाट joinery; M. sãgaḍ 'double-canoe' Rebus: sangataras. संगतराश lit. 'to collect stones, stone-cutter, mason.'*

Variant: dula 'pair' Rebus: dul 'cast metal' PLUS | *koḍa* 'one' Rebus: *koḍ* 'workshop' PLUS INFIXED kolom three' Rebus: kolami 'smithy, forge' Thus metalware castings forge.PLUS dulo 'hole' Rebus: dul 'cast metal' Thus, cast metal forge PLUS Ligature:

 *kuṭila* 'bent' CDIAL 3230 kuṭi— in cmpd. 'curve', *kuṭika*— 'bent' MBh. Rebus: *kuṭila, katthīl* = bronze (8 parts copper and 2 parts tin) Duplicated: dula 'pair' Rebus: dul 'cast metal' Thus, cast bronze. Thus, cast bronze forge.

 ḍāg mountain-ridge (H.)(CDIAL 5476). Rebus: dhangar 'blacksmith' (Maithili)

āra 'six' Rebus: *āra* 'brass'. Vikalpa: dula 'pair' Rebus: dul 'cast metal' PLUS kolom 'three' Rebus: kolami 'smithy, forge' Thus cast metal forge.

 *kanac* 'corner' Rebus: *kañcu* 'bronze' PLUS sal 'splinter' Rebus: sal 'workshop' dula 'two' Rebus: dul 'cast metal' PLUS kolom 'three' Rebus: kolami 'smithy, forge' Thus, metal smithy castings.

 *kolmo* 'paddy plant' Rebus: *kolami* 'smithy, forge' Vikalpa: *mogge* 'sprout, bud' Rebus: *mũh* 'ingot' (Santali) dolu 'plant of shoot height' Rebus: dul 'cast metal'

m1820a Read rebus as at first 3 signs of m1773

M-1820 a

M-1773 A (100%)

M-1773 a (100%)

m1773A,a *खोंड [khōṇḍa] m A young bull, a bullcalf. (Marathi) Rebus: kõdār 'turner' (Bengali); कोंद kōnda 'engraver, lapidary setting or infixing gems' (Marathi) G. sãghāṛɔ m. 'lathe' ; संघाट joinery; M. sãgaḍ 'double-canoe' Rebus: sangataras. संगतराश lit. 'to collect stones, stone-cutter, mason.'* ranku 'liquid measure' Rebus: ranku 'tin'

 ḍãg mountain-ridge (H.)(CDIAL 5476). Rebus: dhangar 'blacksmith' (Maithili)

 *dula* 'pair' Rebus: dul 'cast metal' *mogge* 'sprout, bud' Rebus: *mũh* 'ingot' (Santali) Thus, cast metal ingot.

 *kanka* 'rim of jar' Rebus: *karṇīka* 'account (scribe)' *karṇī* 'supercargo'

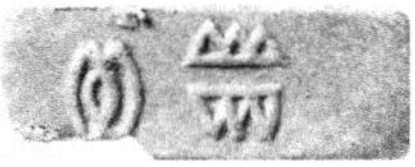

m326c

 ḍãg mountain-ridge (H.)(CDIAL 5476). Rebus: dhangar 'blacksmith' (Maithili) dula 'pair' Rebus: dul 'cast metal' Thus cast metal smith. *āra* 'six' Rebus: *āra* 'brass'

 *dula* 'pair' Rebus: *dul* 'cast (metal)' PLUS*kana, kanac* = corner (Santali); Rebus: *kañcu* = bronze (Telugu) Thus, cast bronze.

 m358A kolom 'three' Rebus: kolami 'smithy, forge' PLUS खांडा [*khāṇḍā*] *m* A jag, notch, or indentation (as upon the edge of a tool or weapon). Rebus: *kāṇḍa* 'tools, pots and pans and metal-ware'

 कांड *kāṇḍa* 'arrow' Rebus: *kāṇḍa* 'pots and pans, metalware, tools'. Rebus 2: kaṇḍ 'fire-altar' (Santali)

aya kammaṭa.'coiner, mint alloy'

 *dula* 'pair' Rebus: *dul* 'cast (metal)' PLUS*kana, kanac* = corner (Santali); Rebus: *kañcu* = bronze (Telugu) PLUS infixed kolmo 'paddy plant' Rebus: kolami 'smithy, forge'. Thus, cast bronze smithy, forge. Or, *mogge* 'sprout, bud' Rebus: *mũh* 'ingot' (Santali)Thus, cast bronze ingot. Read as: *kañcu dul mũh 'bronze cast ingot'* sal 'splinter' Rebus: sal 'workshop'

 mēḍu height, rising ground, hillock (Kannada) Rebus: *mẽṛhẽt, meḍ* 'iron' (Munda.Ho.) PLUS | *koḍa* 'one' Rebus: *koḍ* 'workshop' Thus, iron workshop.

h1909A

 mēḍu height, rising ground, hillock (Kannada) Rebus: *mẽṛhẽt, meḍ* 'iron' (Munda.Ho.)

 *kanac* 'corner' Rebus: *kañcu* 'bronze'

 *kanka* 'rim of jar' Rebus: *karṇīka* 'account (scribe)' *karṇī* 'supercargo'

Side B: *baṭa* = rimless pot (Kannada) Rebus: *baṭa* = a kind of iron (G.)) *bhaṭa* furnace (Gujarati) PLUS dula 'two' Rebus: dul 'cast metal' Thus, furnace metal castings.

 Dholavira *खोंड [khōṇḍa] m A young bull, a bullcalf. (Marathi) Rebus: kōdār 'turner' (Bengali); कोंद kōnda 'engraver, lapidary setting or infixing gems' (Marathi) G. sãghāṛɔ m. 'lathe' ; संघाट joinery; M. sãgaḍ 'double-canoe' Rebus: sangataras. संगतराश lit. 'to collect stones, stone-cutter, mason.'*

mēḍu height,  rising ground, hillock (Kannada) Rebus: *mẽṛhẽt, meḍ* 'iron' (Munda.Ho.)

 ḍãg mountain-ridge (H.)(CDIAL 5476). Rebus: dhangar 'blacksmith' (Maithili) dula 'pair' Rebus: dul 'cast metal' Thus cast metal smith. *āra* 'six' Rebus: *āra* 'brass'

कांड *kāṇḍa* 'arrow' Rebus: *kāṇḍa* 'pots and pans, metalware, tools'. Rebus 2: kaṇḍ 'fire-altar' (Santali)

K-28 A

Kalibangan 28A *balad* m. ' ox ', gng. *bald*, (Ku.) *barad*, id. (N. Tarai) Rebus: *bharat* (5 copper, 4 zinc and 1 tin)(Punjabi) *pattar* 'trough' Rebus*: pattar* 'guild'. Thus, copper-zinc-tin alloy (worker) guild.

mēḍu height, rising ground, hillock (Kannada) Rebus: *mẽṛhẽt, meḍ* 'iron' (Munda.Ho.)

cīmara 'black ant' Rebus: *cīmara* 'copper'. *cīmara kāra* -- ' coppersmith ' sal 'splinter' Rebus: sal 'workshop'

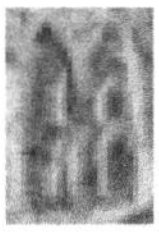
Ligature: two peaks: mēḍu height, rising ground, hillock (Kannada) Rebus: *meḍ* 'iron' (Ho.) dula 'pair' Rebus: dul 'cast metal' PLUS |||| Numeral 4: gaṇḍa 'four' Rebus: kaṇḍa 'furnace, fire-altar' (Santali)

kanka 'rim of jar' Rebus: *karṇīka* 'account (scribe)' *karṇī* 'supercargo'

khōṇḍa A stock or stump (Marathi); 'leafless tree' (Marathi) Rebus: *kõdār* 'turner' (Bengali); *kõdā* 'to turn in a lathe' (Bengali).

ḍhanga = a crook used for pulling down the branches of trees, for goats, sheep and camels (P.) Rebus:*ḍhangar* blacksmith'.

m325A *खोंड [khōṇḍa] m A young bull, a bullcalf. (Marathi) Rebus: kõdār 'turner' (Bengali); कोंद kōnda 'engraver, lapidary setting or infixing gems' (Marathi) G. sãghāṛɔ m. 'lathe' ; संघाट joinery; M. sãgaḍ 'double-canoe' Rebus: sangataras. संगतराश lit. 'to collect stones, stone-cutter, mason.'*

mēḍu height, rising ground, hillock (Kannada) Rebus: *mẽṛhẽt, meḍ* 'iron' (Munda.Ho.)

kanac 'corner' Rebus: *kañcu* 'bronze' sal 'splinter' Rebus; sal 'workshop'

dula 'pair' Rebus: *dul* 'cast (metal)' PLUS*kana, kanac* = corner (Santali); Rebus: *kañcu* = bronze (Telugu) PLUS infixed kolmo 'paddy plant' Rebus: kolami 'smithy, forge'. Thus, cast bronze smithy, forge. Or, *mogge* 'sprout, bud' Rebus: *mūh* 'ingot' (Santali)Thus, cast bronze ingot. Read as: *kañcu dul mūh 'bronze cast ingot'*

aya kammaṭa.'coiner, mint alloy' *aya kāṇḍa* 'alloy metalware' Thus, alloy mint metalware.

h70a *खोंड [khōṇḍa] m A young bull, a bullcalf. (Marathi) Rebus: kõdār 'turner' (Bengali); कोंद kōnda 'engraver, lapidary setting or infixing gems' (Marathi) G.*

sãghāṛɔ m. 'lathe' ; संघाट joinery; M. sãgaḍ 'double-canoe' Rebus: sangataras. संगतराश lit. 'to collect stones, stone-cutter, mason.'

 mēḍu height, rising ground, hillock (Kannada) Rebus: *mẽṛhẽt, meḍ* 'iron' (Munda.Ho.) kolom 'three' Rebus: kolami 'smithy, forge'

 *kolmo* 'paddy plant' Rebus: *kolami* 'smithy, forge' Vikalpa: *mogge* 'sprout, bud' Rebus: *mũh* 'ingot' (Santali) dolu 'plant of shoot height' Rebus: dul 'cast metal'

Lothal 20a *खोंड [khōṇḍa] m A young bull, a bullcalf. (Marathi) Rebus: kõdār 'turner' (Bengali); कोंद kōnda 'engraver, lapidary setting or infixing gems' (Marathi) G. sãghāṛɔ m. 'lathe' ; संघाट joinery; M. sãgaḍ 'double-canoe' Rebus: sangataras. संगतराश lit. 'to collect stones, stone-cutter, mason.'*

 mēḍu height, rising ground, hillock (Kannada) Rebus: *mẽṛhẽt, meḍ* 'iron' (Munda.Ho.) PLUS |||| Numeral 4: gaṇḍa 'four' Rebus: kaṇḍa 'furnace, fire-altar' (Santali) Thus, iron furnace.

 *kolmo* 'paddy plant' Rebus: *kolami* 'smithy, forge' Vikalpa: *mogge* 'sprout, bud' Rebus: *mũh* 'ingot' (Santali) dolu 'plant of shoot height' Rebus: dul 'cast metal'

m1095A *balad* m. ' ox ', gng. *bald*, (Ku.) *barad*, id. (N. Tarai) Rebus: *bharat* (5 copper, 4 zinc and 1 tin)(Punjabi) *pattar* 'trough' Rebus*: pattar* 'guild'. Thus, copper-zinc-tin alloy (worker) guild.

 mēḍu height, rising ground, hillock (Kannada) Rebus: *mẽṛhẽt, meḍ* 'iron' (Munda.Ho.) PLUS |||| Numeral 4: gaṇḍa 'four' Rebus: kaṇḍa 'furnace, fire-altar' (Santali) Thus, iron furnace.

 dula 'pair' Rebus: dul 'cast metal'
'Arrow' sign hieroglyph (variant) This is a ligature of 'lid of pot' hieroglyph superscript on 'a linear stroke' numeral hieroglyph.*aḍaren* 'cover of pot or lid' Rebus: *aduru* 'native, unsmelted metal' PLUS koḍ = one (Santali); koḍ 'workshop' (Gujarati) PLUS dulo 'hole' Rebus: dul 'cast metal' ranku 'liquid measure' Rebus: ranku 'tin'

  Strands of yarn/rope' hieroglyph: Hieroglyph: 'strands of yarn' Rebus reading: *dhā´tu* 'strand of rope' Rebus: *dhatu* 'mineral ore' (Santali)

 *kanac* 'corner' Rebus: *kañcu* 'bronze'

Nausharo 8a *खोंड [khōṇḍa] m A young bull, a bullcalf. (Marathi) Rebus: kõdār 'turner' (Bengali); कोंद kōnda 'engraver, lapidary setting or infixing gems' (Marathi) G. sãghāṛɔ m. 'lathe' ; संघाट joinery; M. sãgaḍ 'double-canoe' Rebus: sangataras. संगतराश lit. 'to collect stones, stone-cutter, mason.'*

mēḍu height,  rising ground, hillock (Kannada) Rebus: *mẽṛhẽt, meḍ* 'iron' (Munda.Ho.)

PLUS |||| Numeral 4: gaṇḍa 'four' Rebus: kaṇḍa 'furnace, fire-altar' (Santali) Thus, iron furnace.
kolom 'three' Rebus: kolami 'smithy, forge'

 *kanka* 'rim of jar' Rebus: *karṇīka* 'account (scribe)' *karṇī* 'supercargo'

m859a खोंड *[khōṇḍa] m A young bull, a bullcalf. (Marathi) Rebus: kõdār 'turner' (Bengali); कोंद kōnda 'engraver, lapidary setting or infixing gems' (Marathi) G. sãghāṛɔ m. 'lathe' ; संघाट joinery; M. sãgaḍ 'double-canoe' Rebus: sangataras. संगतराश lit. 'to collect stones, stone-cutter, mason.'*

 mēḍu height, risi |||| Numeral 4: gaṇḍa 'four' Rebus: kaṇḍa 'furnace, fire-altar' (Santali) Thus, iron furnace. ng ground, hillock (Kannada) Rebus: *mẽṛhẽt, meḍ* 'iron' (Munda.Ho.) PLUS |||| Numeral 4: gaṇḍa 'four' Rebus: kaṇḍa 'furnace, fire-altar' (Santali) Thus, iron furnace. PLUS ||| Numeral 3: kolom 'three' Rebus: kolami 'smithy, forge'

 *dula* 'pair' Rebus: dul 'cast metal' *mogge* 'sprout, bud' Rebus: *mũh* 'ingot' (Santali) Thus, cast metal ingot.

 *kanka* 'rim of jar' Rebus: *karṇīka* 'account (scribe)' *karṇī* 'supercargo'

h174A

 mēḍu height, rising ground, hillock (Kannada) Rebus: *mẽṛhẽt, meḍ* 'iron' (Munda.Ho.) PLUS |||| Numeral 4: gaṇḍa 'four' Rebus: kaṇḍa 'furnace, fire-altar' (Santali) Thus, iron furnace. PLUS ||| Numeral 3: kolom 'three' Rebus: kolami 'smithy, forge'

 *kanka* 'rim of jar' Rebus: *karṇīka* 'account (scribe)' *karṇī* 'supercargo'

 *khareḍo* = a currycomb (Gujarati) खरारा [*kharārā*] *m* (H) A currycomb. 2 Currying a horse. (Marathi) Rebus: करडा [*karaḍā*] Hard from alloy--iron, silver &c. (Marathi) *kharādī* ' turner' (Gujarati)

m1813a Read rebus as at First 3 signs on h453A

m861a Read rebus as at First 3 signs on h453A

h453A खोंड *[khōṇḍa] m A young bull, a bullcalf. (Marathi) Rebus: kõdār 'turner' (Bengali); कोंद kōnda 'engraver, lapidary setting or infixing gems' (Marathi) G. sãghāṛɔ m. 'lathe' ; संघाट joinery; M. sãgaḍ 'double-canoe' Rebus: sangataras. संगतराश lit. 'to collect stones, stone-cutter, mason.'*

 mēḍu height, rising ground, hillock (Kannada) Rebus: *mẽṛhẽt, meḍ* 'iron' (Munda.Ho.) PLUSPLUS ||| Numeral 3: kolom 'three' Rebus: kolami 'smithy, forge'

aya  *kanka* 'rim of jar' Rebus: *karṇīka* 'account (scribe)' *karṇī* 'supercargo' *kammaṭa.*'coiner, mint alloy'

h139A

 mēḍu height, rising ground, hillock (Kannada) Rebus: *mẽṛhẽt, meḍ* 'iron' (Munda.Ho.)

 *kanac* 'corner' Rebus: *kañcu* 'bronze'

 *koḍi* 'flag' (Ta.)(DEDR 2049). Rebus 1: *koḍ* 'workshop' (Kuwi) Rebus 2: *khŏḍ* m. 'pit', *khŏḍü* f. 'small pit' (Kashmiri. CDIAL 3947).

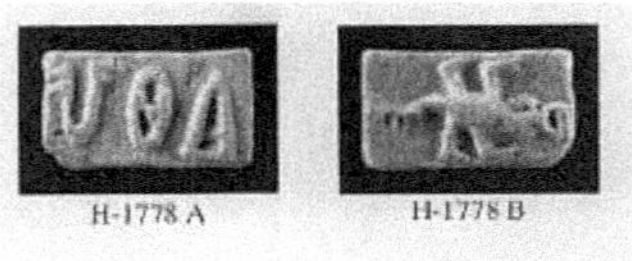

h1778A

 mēḍu height, rising ground, hillock (Kannada) Rebus: *mẽṛhẽt, meḍ* 'iron' (Munda.Ho.)

 *kanac* 'corner' Rebus: *kañcu* 'bronze'

 *kanka* 'rim of jar' Rebus: *karṇīka* 'account (scribe)' *karṇī* 'supercargo' SideB: 'fish + crocodile': ayo 'fish' + kharavu 'crocodile' Rebus: ayakara 'metalsmith' (Pali) PLUS ligature on the tail: PLUS |||| Numeral 4: gaṇḍa 'four' Rebus: kaṇḍa 'furnace, fire-altar' (Santali) Thus, iron furnace metalsmith.

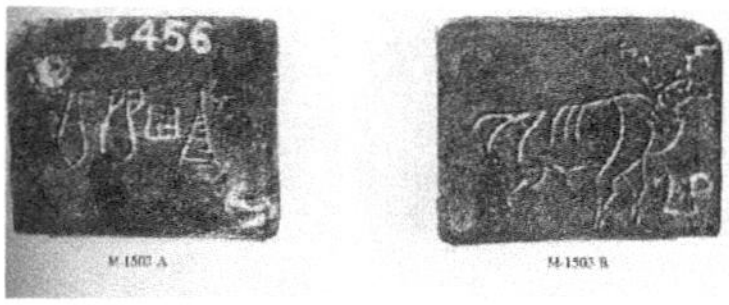

m1503A Side B: *miṇḍāl* 'markhor' (Tōrwālī) *meḍho* a ram, a sheep (G.)(CDIAL 10120) Rebus: *mẽṛhẽt, meḍ* 'iron' (Mu.Ho.)

h157A Read rebus as at  m1363a

m1363a

 mēḍu height, rising ground, hillock (Kannada) Rebus: *mẽṛhẽt, meḍ* 'iron' (Munda.Ho.)

khaṇḍ 'field, division' (Sanskrit) Rebus: *khāṇḍa* 'tools, pots and pans, metal-ware'. Rebus 2: kaṇḍ 'fire-altar' (Santali)

 water-carrier hieroglyph *kuṭi*; Rebus: *kuṭhi* 'smelter furnace'.

m1803a *खोंड [khōṇḍa] m A young bull, a bullcalf. (Marathi) Rebus: kõdār 'turner' (Bengali); कोंद kōnda 'engraver, lapidary setting or infixing gems' (Marathi) G. sãghāṛɔ m. 'lathe' ; संघाट joinery; M. sãgaḍ 'double-canoe' Rebus: sangataras. संगतराश lit. 'to collect stones, stone-cutter, mason.'*
Text of inscription read rebus as at m2045

m1512A Read rebus as at m2045

m2045 Copper plate.

mēḍu height, rising ground, hillock (Kannada) Rebus: *mẽṛhẽt, meḍ* 'iron' (Munda.Ho.) *khaṇḍ* 'field, division' (Sanskrit) Rebus: *khānḍa* 'tools, pots and pans, metal-ware'. Rebus 2: kaṇḍ 'fire-altar' (Santali)

dula 'pair' Rebus: dul 'cast metal' *mogge* 'sprout, bud' Rebus: *mūh* 'ingot' (Santali) Thus, cast metal ingot.

kanka 'rim of jar' Rebus: *karṇīka* 'account (scribe)' *karṇī* 'supercargo' Side B: *balad* m. ' ox ', gng. *bald*, (Ku.) *barad*, id. (N. Tarai) Rebus: *bharat* (5 copper, 4 zinc and 1 tin)(Punjabi) *pattar* 'trough' Rebus: *pattar* 'guild'. Thus, copper-zinc-tin alloy (worker) guild.

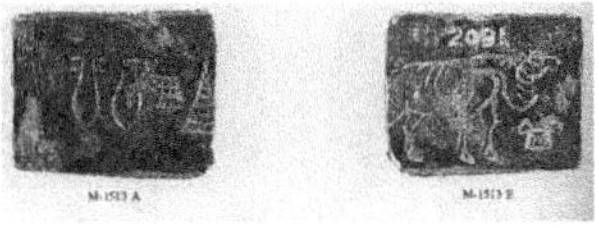

m1513 Copper plate. Side B: *rāngo* 'water buffalo bull' (Ku.N.)(CDIAL 10559) Rebus: rango 'pewter' *pattar* 'trough' Rebus: *pattar* 'guild'.Thus, pewter guild. Side A: Read rebus at m2045

m269A Read rebus as at m1513 for Side B: and Side A Text of inscription as at m516A

m516A

Santali) Thus, cast metal ingot.

kanka 'rim of jar' Rebus: *karṇīka* 'account (scribe)' *karṇī* 'supercargo'

mēḍu height, rising ground, hillock (Kannada) Rebus: *mẽṛhẽt, meḍ* 'iron' (Munda.Ho.) *khaṇḍ* 'field, division' (Sanskrit) Rebus: *khānḍa* 'tools, pots and pans, metal-ware'. Rebus 2: kaṇḍ 'fire-altar' (Santali)

m556A

m552A m559A m557A m551A

All 5 copper plate inscriptions (m556, m552, m559, m551) read rebus as at Side B of m2045

m374A

mēḍu height, rising ground, hillock (Kannada) Rebus: *mẽṛhẽt, meḍ* 'iron' (Munda.Ho.)
khaṇḍ 'field, division' (Sanskrit) Rebus: *khānḍa* 'tools, pots and pans, metal-ware'. Rebus 2: kaṇḍ 'fire-altar' (Santali)
khaṇḍ 'field, division' (Sanskrit) Rebus: *khānḍa* 'tools, pots and pans, metal-ware'. Rebus 2: kaṇḍ 'fire-altar' (Santali) PLUS kolom 'three' Rebus: kolami 'smithy, forge'

 *kuṭila* 'bent' CDIAL 3230 kuṭi— in cmpd. 'curve', *kuṭika*— 'bent' MBh. Rebus: *kuṭila, katthīl* = bronze (8 parts copper and 2 parts tin)

 *kanka* 'rim of jar' Rebus: *karṇīka* 'account (scribe)' *karṇī* 'supercargo'

Kalibangan 63A

mēḍu height, rising ground, hillock (Kannada) Rebus: *mẽṛhẽt, meḍ* 'iron' (Munda.Ho.)

 *dula* 'pair' Rebus: dul 'cast metal' *mogge* 'sprout, bud' Rebus: *mũh* 'ingot' (Santali) Thus, cast metal ingot. PLUS INFIXED | *koḍa* 'one' Rebus: *koḍ* 'workshop' Thus, cast metal ingot workshop.

 *kanka* 'rim of jar' Rebus: *karṇīka* 'account (scribe)' *karṇī* 'supercargo'

 *khareḍo* = a currycomb (Gujarati) खरारा [*kharārā*] *m* (H) A currycomb. 2 Currying a horse. (Marathi) Rebus: करडा [*karaḍā*] Hard from alloy--iron, silver &c. (Marathi) *kharādī* ' turner' (Gujarati)

h096 Text 4249

ingot (from) iron smelter, tin smelter merchant guild

Focus on 'serpent' tail: *nāga* 'snake' Rebus: *nāga* 'lead' (Sanskrit) anakku 'tin' (Akkadian) *Kur.* xolā tail. *Malt.* qoli id. (DEDR 2135). Focus on human face: mukha, *mũh* 'face' Rebus*: mũh* 'ingot'. Zebu horns: *khũṭ* 'zebu' (Gujarati) Rebus: *khũṭ* '(native metal) community, guild' (Santali) kola 'tiger' Rebus: kolhe 'smelters' kol 'working in iron' ibha 'elephant' Rebus: ib 'iron' body of an ox: balad 'bull' Rebus:

baran, bharat 'mixed alloys' (5 copper, 4 zinc and 1 tin) (Punjabi) dhatu 'scarf' Rebus: dhatu 'mineral ore'.

Seal h096 message: bronze supercargo workshop: ingot (from) iron smelter, tin smelter merchant guild.

gaṇḍa 'four' Rebus: kaṇḍ 'fire-altar' PLUS kanac 'corner' Rebus: kañcu 'bronze' PLUS ligature:

'Arrow' sign hieroglyph (variant) This is a ligature of 'lid of pot' hieroglyph superscript on 'a linear stroke' numeral hieroglyph.*aḍaren* 'cover of pot or lid' Rebus: *aduru* 'native, unsmelted metal' This ligatured hieroglyph thus denotes: use of native metal to achieve the bronze alloy metal.

kanka 'rim of jar' Rebus: karṇīka 'account (scribe)' karṇī 'supercargo'

koḍi 'flag' (Ta.)(DEDR 2049). Rebus 1: *koḍ* 'workshop' (Kuwi) Rebus 2: *khŏḍ* m. 'pit', *khōḍü* f. 'small pit' (Kashmiri. CDIAL 3947).

M-1313 A

m1313A gaṇḍa 'four' Rebus: kaṇḍ 'fire-altar' PLUS

kana, kanac = corner (Santali); Rebus: *kañcu* = bronze (Telugu) PLUS खांडा [*khāṇḍā*] *m* A jag, notch, or indentation (as upon the edge of a tool or weapon). Rebus: *kāṇḍa* 'tools, pots and pans and metal-ware' Thus, bronze metalware.

| *koḍa* 'one' Rebus: *koḍ* 'workshop' Duplicated: dula 'pair' Rebus: dul 'cast metal' Thus cast metal workshop. INFIXED ||| kolom 'three' Rebus: kolami 'smithy, forge' Thus, metal smithy castings, forge workshop.

balad m. ' ox ', gng. *bald,* (Ku.) *barad,* id. (N. Tarai) Rebus: *bharat* (5 copper, 4 zinc and 1 tin)(Punjabi) *pattar* 'trough' Rebus*: pattar* 'guild'. Thus, copper-zinc-tin alloy (worker) guild.

ढांक [ḍhāṅka] *n* ढांकळ *f* C An old and decaying tree: also the stump or naked stalks and stem remaining (of a little plant).(Marathi) WPah.ktg. *ḍāṅg* f. (obl. -- *a*) ' stick ', *ḍaṅgrɔ* m. ' stalk (of a plant) ' Rebus: *ḍhangar* blacksmith'

ṭagara'ram' Rebus: *tagara* 'tin' Vikalpa: *miṇḍāl* 'markhor' (Tōrwālī) *meḍho* a ram, a sheep (G.)(CDIAL 10120) Rebus: *mẽṛhẽt, meḍ* 'iron' (Mu.Ho.)

beads: Pa. kandi (pl. -l) necklace, beads. Ga. (Punjabi) kandi (pl. -l) bead, (pl.) necklace; (S.2) kandiṭ bead. (DEDR 1215) Rebus: கண்டி; *kaṇṭi, n. < Mhr. khaṇḍil. [T. Tu. khaṇḍi, M. kaṇḍi.] 1. Candy, a weight, stated to be roughly equivalent to 500 lbs.;* பாரமென்னும்

நிறையளவு. खंडीगणती or खंडोगणती [khaṇḍīgaṇatī or khaṇḍōgaṇatī] *ad* By candies; counting or reckoning by candies. खंडीवारी [khaṇḍīvārī] *ad* By scores, heaps, candies. खंडी [khaṇḍī] Applied to a great quantity; as खंडीभर पोरें, खंडीभर मेंढ्या, खंडीभर काम, खंडीभर बोलतो-लिहितो&c

m1923a *kul* 'tiger' (Santali); *kōlu* id. (Telugu) kōlupuli = Bengal tiger (Te.) कोल्हा [kōlhā] कोल्हें [kōlhēṃ] A jackal (Marathi) Rebus: *kol, kolhe*, 'the *koles*, iron smelters speaking a language akin to that of Santals' (Santali) kol 'working in iron' (Tamil) pattar 'trough' Rebus: pattar 'trough'

muka 'ladle' (Tamil)(DEDR 4887) Rebus: *mũh* 'ingot' (Santali) *baṭa* = rimless pot (Kannada) Rebus:) *baṭa* = a kind of iron (G.)) *bhaṭa* furnace (Gujarati) Thus, iron ingot.

 *kanac* 'corner' Rebus: *kañcu* 'bronze' PLUS sal 'splinter' Rebus: sal 'workshop' Count of four: |||| Numeral 4: gaṇḍa 'four' Rebus: kaṇḍa 'furnace, fire-altar' (Santali)
ḍhanga = a crook used for pulling down the branches of trees, for goats, sheep and camels (P.) Rebus:*ḍhangar*

 *dula* 'pair' Rebus: dul 'cast metal' *mogge* 'sprout, bud' Rebus: *mũh* 'ingot' (Santali) Thus, cast metal ingot.
kanka 'rim of jar' Rebus: *karṇīka* 'account (scribe)' *karṇī* 'supercargo'

m130A *खोंड [khōṇḍa] m A young bull, a bullcalf. (Marathi) Rebus: kõdār 'turner' (Bengali); कोंद kōnda 'engraver, lapidary setting or infixing gems' (Marathi) G. sãghārɔ m. 'lathe' ; संघाट joinery; M. sãgaḍ 'double-canoe' Rebus: sangataras. संगतराश lit. 'to collect stones, stone-cutter, mason.'*
Count of four: |||| Numeral 4: gaṇḍa 'four' Rebus: kaṇḍa 'furnace, fire-altar' (Santali)

meḍ 'body' Rebus: *meḍ* 'iron' (Ho.) काठी [kāṭhī] *f* (काष्ठ S) 'frame or structure of the body' (Marathi) Rebus: खंडी [khaṇḍī] measure of weight (Marathi) *கண்டி; kaṇṭi, n. < Mhr. khaṇḍil. [T. Tu. khaṇḍi, M. kaṇḍi.]* Candy, a weight, stated to be roughly equivalent to 500 lbs.
dula 'two' Rebus: dul 'cast metal' PLUS sal 'splinter' Rebus: sal 'workshop. *ayo* 'fish' Rebus: *aya* 'iron' *ayas* 'metal'
Ligature: *kaṇḍo* 'stool, seat' Rebus: *kāṇḍa* 'metalware' *kaṇḍa* 'fire-altar'
PLUS

meḍ 'body' Rebus: *meḍ* 'iron' (Ho.) काठी [kāṭhī] *f* (काष्ठ S) 'frame or structure of the body' (Marathi) Rebus: खंडी [khaṇḍī] measure of weight (Marathi) *கண்டி; kaṇṭi, n. < Mhr. khaṇḍil. [T. Tu. khaṇḍi, M. kaṇḍi.]* Candy, a weight, stated to be roughly equivalent to 500 lbs.

kanka 'rim of jar' Rebus: karṇīka 'account (scribe)' karṇī 'supercargo'

m925A *खोंड [khōṇḍa] m A young bull, a bullcalf. (Marathi) Rebus: kõdār 'turner' (Bengali); कोंद kōnda 'engraver, lapidary setting or infixing gems'*

(Marathi) G. sãghāṛɔ m. 'lathe' ; संघाट joinery; M. sãgaḍ 'double-canoe' Rebus: sangataras. संगतराश lit. 'to collect stones, stone-cutter, mason.' Count of four: |||| Numeral 4: gaṇḍa 'four' Rebus: kaṇḍa 'furnace, fire-altar' (Santali) PLUS
ranku 'liquid measure' Rebus: ranku 'tin'

Cirumscribing hieroglyph of four short strokes with infix ligature of another hieroglyph

Seals: m1118 Kalibangan032 *khũṭ* 'zebu' Rebus: '(native metal) guild'

Kalibangan 032 m1118A

ayo 'fish'; ayas 'metal' (Sanskrit) aya = iron (Gujarati)

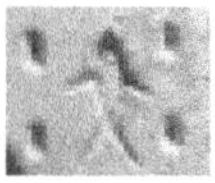

Ayo 'fish' (Munda) + gaṇḍa 'set of four' (Santali)

Harappa tablet (inscribed object in the shape of a fish): h329A, h329B

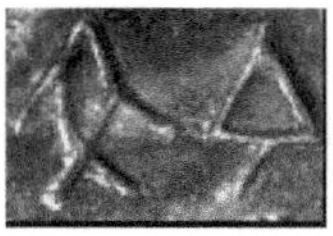

ayo 'fish' (Munda) + *kaṇḍa* 'arrow' (Sanskrit)

Rebus: *ayaskāṇḍa* 'a quantity of iron, excellent iron' (Pāṇ.gaṇ) Side A of h329: *baṭa* = rimless pot (Kannada) Rebus:) *baṭa* = a kind of iron (G.)) *bhaṭa* furnace (Gujarati) PLUS gaṇḍa 'four' Rebus: kaṇḍa 'furnace, fire-altar' (Santali) Vedic gloss ayas 'metal' and Panini's phrase *ayaskāṇḍa* are significant Meluhha glosses in Indian *sprachbund.*

m277A *खोंड [khōṇḍa] m A young bull, a bullcalf. (Marathi) Rebus: kõdār 'turner' (Bengali); कोंद kōnda 'engraver, lapidary setting or infixing gems' (Marathi) G. sãghāṛɔ m. 'lathe' ; संघाट joinery; M. sãgaḍ 'double-canoe' Rebus: sangataras. संगतराश lit. 'to collect stones, stone-cutter, mason.'* Count of four: |||| Numeral 4: gaṇḍa 'four' Rebus: kaṇḍa 'furnace, fire-altar' (Santali) PLUS *aya kammaṭa.*'coiner, mint alloy'

kanka 'rim of jar' Rebus: karṇīka 'account (scribe)' karṇī 'supercargo'

m973a *खोंड [khōṇḍa] m A young bull, a bullcalf. (Marathi) Rebus: kõdār 'turner' (Bengali); कोंद kōnda 'engraver, lapidary setting or infixing gems' (Marathi) G. sãghāṛɔ m. 'lathe' ; संघाट joinery; M. sãgaḍ 'double-canoe' Rebus: sangataras. संगतराश lit. 'to collect stones, stone-cutter, mason.'*

ayo 'fish' Rebus: aya 'iron' (Gujarati) ayas 'metal' (Vedic) PLUS gaṇḍā 'four' Rebus: kaṇḍā 'fire-altar' Thus, iron furnace (in) kolom 'three' Rebus: kolami 'smithy, forge'.

m305A Count of four: |||| Numeral 4: gaṇḍa 'four' Rebus: kaṇḍa 'furnace, fire-altar' (Santali) Circumscript: *aya kammaṭa.*'coiner, mint alloy'

 *kanac* 'corner' Rebus: *kañcu* 'bronze'

ayo 'fish' Rebus: *aya* 'iron' *ayas* 'metal'
meḍha 'polar star' (Marathi). Rebus: meḍ (Ho.); mẽṛhet 'iron' (Munda.Ho.) dula 'pair' Rebus: dul 'cast metal'. Thus, the two 'star' sign hieroglyphs flanking the composition denote iron castings.

kōḍu 'horn' kōḍu 'workshop' *kūdī* 'bunch of twigs' (Sanskrit) Rebus: *kuṭhi* 'smelter furnace' (Santali)
dhatu 'scarf' Rebus: dhatu 'mineral ore'
kamaḍha 'penance' Rebus: *kammaṭa* 'mint, coiner'. Focus on human face: mukha, *mũh* 'face' Rebus: *mũh* 'ingot'.

m1084 *balad* m. ' ox ', gng. *bald*, (Ku.) *barad*, id. (N. Tarai) Rebus: *bharat* (5 copper, 4 zinc and 1 tin)(Punjabi) *pattar* 'trough' Rebus: *pattar* 'guild'. Thus, copper-zinc-tin alloy (worker) guild.

Count of four: |||| Numeral 4: gaṇḍa 'four' Rebus: kaṇḍa 'furnace, fire-altar' (Santali) Circumscript: *aya aḍaren (homonym: aduru)* 'alloy native metal'

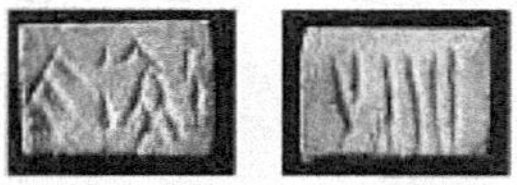

H-2155 A H-2155 B

h2155A,B Count of four: |||| Numeral 4: gaṇḍa 'four' Rebus: kaṇḍa 'furnace, fire-altar' (Santali) Circumscript: *aya kāṇḍa* 'alloy metalware'

khareḍo =  a currycomb (Gujarati) खरारा [*kharārā*] *m* (H) A currycomb. 2 Currying a horse. (Marathi) Rebus: करडा [*karaḍā*] Hard from alloy--iron, silver &c. (Marathi) *kharādī* ' turner' (Gujarati)
SideB: Count of four: |||| Numeral 4: gaṇḍa 'four' Rebus: kaṇḍa 'furnace, fire-altar' (Santali)
baṭa = rimless pot (Kannada) Rebus:) *baṭa* = a kind of iron (G.)) *bhaṭa* furnace (Gujarati) Thus, iron furnace, fire-altar.

M-1978 a bis

m1978a Count of four: |||| Numeral 4: gaṇḍa 'four' Rebus: kaṇḍa 'furnace, fire-altar' (Santali) Circumscript: *aya kāṇḍa* 'alloy metalware'

muka 'ladle' (Tamil)(DEDR 4887) Rebus: *mũh* 'ingot' (Santali) *baṭa* = rimless pot (Kannada) Rebus:) *baṭa* = a kind of iron (G.)) *bhaṭa* furnace (Gujarati) Thus, iron ingot.
kolom 'three' Rebus: kolami 'smithy, forge'

 *dhāḷ* 'a slope'; 'inclination of a plane' (G.); *ḍhāḷiyum* = adj. sloping, inclining (G.) Rebus: *ḍhālako* = a large metal ingot (G.) *ḍhālakī* = a metal heated and poured into a mould; a solid piece of metal; an ingot (Gujarati) PLUS खांडा [*khāṇḍā*] *m* A jag, notch, or indentation (as upon the edge of a tool or weapon). Rebus: *kāṇḍa* 'tools, pots and pans and metal-ware' Thus, the pair of sign hieroglyphs from r. read rebus: copper, bronze ingots, metalware castings

 *kolmo* 'paddy plant' Rebus: *kolami* 'smithy, forge' Vikalpa: *mogge* 'sprout, bud' Rebus: *mũh* 'ingot' (Santali) dolu 'plant of shoot height' Rebus: dul 'cast metal'

B-17 a

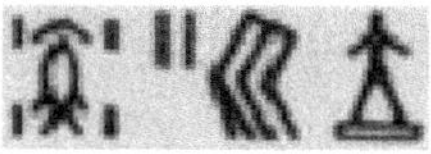

Banawali 17a Text 9201
Pictorial motif hieroglyphs: kol 'tiger' Rebus: kolhe 'smelter'

Ligatured to horns of a zebu: *khũṭ* 'zebu' (Gujarati) Rebus: *khũṭ* '(native metal) community, guild' (Santali)

dhaṭu 'scarf' (Western Pahari). Rebus: *dhatu* 'mineral' (Santali).

sangada 'lathe', 'portable furnace' G. *sãghāṛɔ* m. 'lathe' ; *sãgāḍā* m. ' frame of a building ', *°ḍī* f. ' lathe '(CDIAL 12859) Rebus:
sangataras. संगतराश lit. 'to collect stones, stone-cutter, mason.' संगतराश संज्ञा पुं० [फ़ा०] पत्थर काटने या गढ़नेवाला मजदूर । पत्थरकट । २. एक औजार जो पत्थर काटने के काम में आता है । (Dasa, Syamasundara. Hindi sabdasagara. Navina samskarana. 2nd ed. Kasi : Nagari Pracarini Sabha, 1965-1975.) पत्थर या लकडी पर नकाशी करनेवाला, संगतराश, 'mason'.
Together, the pictorial motif hieroglyphs read rebus: *sangada kolhe dhatu khũṭ* 'stone-cutter-turner-mineral metal smelter guild'.

Text signs as hieroglyphs from r.: Text 9201

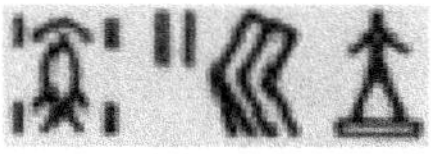

meḍ 'body' Rebus: *meḍ* 'iron'
dhatu 'strands of yarn' rebus: '(Copper) mineral, ore'
sal 'splinter' Rebus: *sal* 'workshop'
ayo 'fish' Rebus: *aya* 'iron' ayas 'metal'; gaṇḍa 'four' Rebus: kaṇḍ 'fire-altar'. aḍaren 'lid' Rebus: aduru 'unsmelted native metal'. Thus the epigraph denotes rebus: iron, copper mineral smithy, unsmelted native metal alloy, fire-altar (furnace)

M-1438 A

m1438a Count of four: |||| Numeral 4: gaṇḍa 'four' Rebus: kaṇḍa 'furnace, fire-altar' (Santali) PLUS
ayo 'fish' Rebus: aya 'iron' (Gujarati) ayas 'metal (Vedic) PLUS

kuṭila 'bent'  CDIAL 3230 kuṭi— in cmpd. 'curve', *kuṭika—* 'bent' MBh. Rebus: *kuṭila, katthīl* = bronze (8 parts copper and 2 parts tin) Duplicated: dula 'pair' Rebus: dul 'cast metal' Thus, cast bronze.

 *kanka* 'rim of jar' Rebus: *karṇīka* 'account (scribe)' *karṇī* 'supercargo'

H-2154 A

H-2154 B

h2154A 'Count of four: |||| Numeral 4: gaṇḍa 'four' Rebus: kaṇḍa 'furnace, fire-altar' (Santali) PLUS
ayo 'fish' Rebus: aya 'iron' (Gujarati) ayas 'metal (Vedic) PLUS

 *kanac* 'corner' Rebus: *kañcu* 'bronze' Side B: *baṭa* = a kind of iron (G.)) *bhaṭa* furnace (Gujarati) PLUS kaṇḍa 'furnace, fire-altar' (Santali)

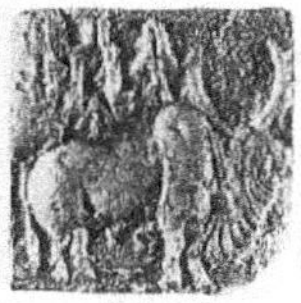

M-1121 a

m1121a *khũṭ* 'zebu' Rebus: '(native metal) guild' ayo 'fish' Rebus: aya 'iron' (Gujarati) ayas 'metal' (Vedic)

 सांड [sāṇḍa] *f* (षद S) An outlet for superfluous water (as through a dam or mound); a sluice, a floodvent. Rebus: सांडणी [sāṇḍaṇī] *f* (H) An instrument of goldsmiths. It is hooked or curved at the extremity; and is used to draw things out of the fire. सांठा [*sāṇṭhā*] *m* (संचय S) A collection, heap, hoard, store, stock.साटें [*sāṭēṃ*] *n* (संचय S) A whole investment; the total quantity of merchandise (brought to market by one merchant).

H-1867 A

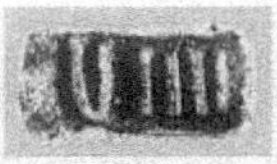

H-1867 B

h1867A Circumscript:

 *kuṭila* 'bent' CDIAL 3230 kuṭi— in cmpd. 'curve', *kuṭika—* 'bent' MBh. Rebus: *kuṭila, katthīl* = bronze (8 parts copper and 2 parts tin) Duplicated: dula 'pair' Rebus: dul 'cast metal' Thus, cast bronze. PLUS ayo 'fish' Rebus: aya 'iron' (Gujarati) ayas 'metal' (Vedic) Thus, bronze metal.

 *kanka* 'rim of jar' Rebus: *karṇīka* 'account (scribe)' *karṇī* 'supercargo'

  water-carrier hieroglyph *kuṭi*; Rebus: *kuṭhi* 'smelter furnace'. PLUS 'rim of jar':

 kanka 'rim of jar' Rebus: karṇīka 'account (scribe)' karṇī 'supercargo'

Side B: Count of four: |||| Numeral 4: gaṇḍa 'four' Rebus: kaṇḍa 'furnace, fire-altar' (Santali) PLUS *baṭa* = rimless pot (Kannada) Rebus: *baṭa* = a kind of iron (G.)) *bhaṭa* furnace (Gujarati)

M-209 a

m209A *खोंड [khōṇḍa] m A young bull, a bullcalf. (Marathi) Rebus: kōdār 'turner' (Bengali); कोंद kōnda 'engraver, lapidary setting or infixing gems' (Marathi) G. sãghāṛɔ m. 'lathe' ; संघाट joinery; M. sãgaḍ 'double-canoe' Rebus: sangataras. संगतराश lit. 'to collect stones, stone-cutter, mason.'*

meḍ  'body' Rebus: *meḍ* 'iron' (Ho.) काठी [kāṭhī] *f* (काष्ट S) 'frame or structure of the body' (Marathi) Rebus: खंडी [khaṇḍī] measure of weight (Marathi) கண்டி; *kaṇṭi, n.* < *Mhr. khaṇḍil. [T. Tu. khaṇḍi, M. kaṇḍi.]* Candy, a weight, stated to be roughly equivalent to 500 lbs.

 *kanka* 'rim of jar' Rebus: *karṇīka* 'account (scribe)' *karṇī* 'supercargo'

 water-carrier hieroglyph *kuṭi*; Rebus: *kuṭhi* 'smelter furnace'. PLUS 'rim of jar':

  kanka 'rim of jar' Rebus: karṇīka 'account (scribe)' karṇī 'supercargo'

M-1312 A

m1312

kanac 'corner' Rebus: *kañcu* 'bronze'

dulo 'hole' Rebus: dul 'cast metal' LIGATURED to

 *kanac* 'corner' Rebus: *kañcu* 'bronze' Thus, cast bronze

ayo 'fish' Rebus: *aya* 'iron' *ayas* 'metal'

m203A *खोंड [khōṇḍa] m A young bull, a bullcalf. (Marathi) Rebus: kõdār 'turner' (Bengali); कोंद kōnda 'engraver, lapidary setting or infixing gems' (Marathi) G. sãghāṛɔ m. 'lathe' ; संघाट joinery; M. sāgaḍ 'double-canoe' Rebus: sangataras. संगतराश lit. 'to collect stones, stone-cutter, mason.'* *ayo* 'fish' Rebus: *aya* 'iron' *ayas* 'metal'

 *kolmo* 'paddy plant' Rebus: *kolami* 'smithy, forge' Vikalpa: *mogge* 'sprout, bud' Rebus: *mũh* 'ingot' (Santali) dolu 'plant of shoot height' Rebus: dul 'cast metal'
Ligatured to:
G. *sãghāṛɔ* m. 'lathe' ; *sãgāḍā* m. ' frame of a building ', °*ḍī* f. ' lathe '(CDIAL 12859) Rebus: *sangataras.* संगतराश lit. 'to collect stones, stone-cutter, mason.'Thus, stone-cutter, cast metal ingot.

 *kanka* 'rim of jar' Rebus: *karṇīka* 'account (scribe)' *karṇī* 'supercargo'
ranku 'liquid measure' Rebus: ranku 'tin'

 *kolmo* 'paddy plant' Rebus: *kolami* 'smithy, forge' Vikalpa: *mogge* 'sprout, bud' Rebus: *mũh* 'ingot' (Santali) dolu 'plant of shoot height' Rebus: dul 'cast metal'

kanka 'rim of jar' Rebus: karṇīka 'account (scribe)' karṇī 'supercargo'

m2014A *ayo* 'fish' Rebus: *aya* 'iron' *ayas* 'metal'
dula 'pair' Rebus: *dul* 'cast (metal)' PLUS*kana, kanac* = corner (Santali); Rebus: *kañcu* = bronze (Telugu) Thus, cast bronze.
dula 'two' Rebus: dul 'cast metal'

kanka 'rim of jar' Rebus: *karṇīka* 'account (scribe)' *karṇī* 'supercargo'

h431A *खोंड [khōṇḍa] m A young bull, a bullcalf. (Marathi) Rebus: kõdār 'turner' (Bengali); कोंद kōnda 'engraver, lapidary setting or infixing gems' (Marathi) G. sãghāṛɔ m. 'lathe' ; संघाट joinery; M. sāgaḍ 'double-canoe' Rebus: sangataras. संगतराश lit. 'to collect stones, stone-cutter, mason.' aya kammaṭa.*'coiner, mint alloy'

kanka 'rim of jar' Rebus: karṇīka 'account (scribe)' karṇī 'supercargo'

m1802A *खोंड [khōṇḍa] m A young bull, a bullcalf. (Marathi) Rebus: kõdār*

'turner' (Bengali); कोंद kōnda 'engraver, lapidary setting or infixing gems' (Marathi) G. sãghāṛɔ m. 'lathe' ; संघाट joinery; M. sãgaḍ 'double-canoe' Rebus: sangataras. संगतराश lit. 'to collect stones, stone-cutter, mason.' aya kammaṭa.'coiner, mint alloy' *kamaḍha* 'crab' Rebus: *kammaṭa* 'mint, coiner'.
ḍato = claws of crab (Santali) Rebus: *dhātu* 'mineral ore'
kanka 'rim of jar' Rebus: karṇīka 'account (scribe)' karṇī 'supercargo'

m1015A *खोंड [khōṇḍa] m A young bull, a bullcalf. (Marathi) Rebus: kõdār 'turner' (Bengali); कोंद kōnda 'engraver, lapidary setting or infixing gems' (Marathi) G. sãghāṛɔ m. 'lathe' ; संघाट joinery; M. sãgaḍ 'double-canoe' Rebus: sangataras. संगतराश lit. 'to collect stones, stone-cutter, mason.' ayo ḍhālako* 'alloy metal ingot'
kamaḍha 'crab' Rebus: *kammaṭa* 'mint, coiner'.
ḍato = claws of crab (Santali) Rebus: *dhātu* 'mineral ore'
kanka 'rim of jar' Rebus: karṇīka 'account (scribe)' karṇī 'supercargo'

m1548A *aya kāṇḍa* 'alloy metalware'T

he pair of hieroglyph signs are compositions: *bicha* 'scorpion' (Assamese) Rebus: *bica* 'stone ore' (Santali) The pairing sign is a composition of: sloping stroke PLUS two short strokes of a 'splinter':*dhāḷ* 'a slope'; 'inclination of a plane' (Gujarati); *ḍhāḷiyum* = adj. sloping, inclining (Gujarati) Rebus: *ḍhālako* = a large metal ingot (Gujarati) *ḍhālakī* = a metal heated and poured into a mould; a solid piece of metal; an ingot (Gujarati)PLUS*sal* 'splinter' Rebus: *sal* 'workshop'. Thus the composition reads: *ḍhālako sal* 'ingot workshop'.

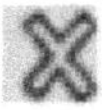

dāṭu 'cross'(Telugu) Rebus: *dhatu* 'mineral' (Santali).

kanka 'rim of jar' Rebus: *karṇīka* 'account (scribe)' *karṇī* 'supercargo'

m1156a Read rebus as at m1548A PLUS *ibha* 'elephant' Rebus: *ib* 'iron' *ibbo* 'merchant' (Gujarati)

h171A Read rebus as at h699A

h699A *aya kāṇḍa* 'alloy metalware' *kamaḍha* 'crab' Rebus: *kammaṭa* 'mint, coiner'.

ḍato = claws of crab (Santali) Rebus: *dhātu* 'mineral ore'*baraḍo* = spine; backbone (Tulu) Rebus: *baran, bharat* 'mixed alloys' (5 copper, 4 zinc and 1 tin) (Punjabi)

kanka 'rim of jar' Rebus: *karṇīka* 'account (scribe)' *karṇī* 'supercargo'

h1123A *aya kāṇḍa* 'alloy metalware' *kamaḍha* 'crab' Rebus: *kammaṭa* 'mint, coiner'. *ḍato* = claws of crab (Santali) Rebus: *dhātu* 'mineral

| *koḍa* 'one' Rebus: *koḍ* 'workshop' Duplicated: dula 'pair' Rebus: dul 'cast metal' Thus cast metal workshop. INFIXED ||| kolom 'three' Rebus: kolami 'smithy, forge' Thus, metal smithy castings, forge workshop.

m2014B *balad* m. ' ox ', gng. *bald*, (Ku.) *barad*, id. (N. Tarai) Rebus: *bharat* (5 copper, 4 zinc and 1 tin)(Punjabi) *pattar* 'trough' Rebus*: pattar* 'guild'. Thus, copper-zinc-tin alloy (worker) guild.

ayo 'fish' Rebus: *aya* 'iron' *ayas* 'metal'
kamaḍha 'crab' Rebus: *kammaṭa* 'mint, coiner'.
ḍato = claws of crab (Santali) Rebus: *dhātu* 'mineral ore'
dula 'pair' Rebus: dul 'cast metal' Thus mineral ore castings and mint

Lothal 38a
खोंड [khōṇḍa] m A young bull, a bullcalf. (Marathi) Rebus: kōdār 'turner' (Bengali); कोंद kōnda 'engraver, lapidary setting or infixing gems' (Marathi) G. sãghāṛɔ m. 'lathe' ; संघाट joinery; M. sāgaḍ 'double-canoe' Rebus: sangataras. संगतराश lit. 'to collect stones, stone-cutter, mason.'

kanka 'rim of jar' Rebus: karṇīka 'account (scribe)' karṇī 'supercargo'

h734A *ayo ḍhālako* 'alloy metal ingot'
aya kammaṭa.'coiner, mint alloy'
ranku 'liquid measure' Rebus: ranku 'tin'

kolmo 'paddy plant' Rebus: *kolami* 'smithy, forge' Vikalpa: *mogge* 'sprout, bud' Rebus: *mũh* 'ingot' (Santali) dolu 'plant of shoot height' Rebus: dul 'cast metal'

kanka 'rim of jar' Rebus: *karṇīka* 'account (scribe)' *karṇī* 'supercargo'

m1988a *aya kammaṭa.*'coiner, mint alloy'
|||| Numeral 4: gaṇḍa 'four' Rebus: kaṇḍa 'furnace, fire-altar' (Santali)
||| kolom 'three' Rebus: kolami 'smithy, forge' PLUS || sal 'splinter' Rebus sal 'workshop'

kolmo 'paddy plant' Rebus: *kolami* 'smithy, forge' Vikalpa: *mogge* 'sprout, bud' Rebus: *mũh* 'ingot' (Santali) dolu 'plant of shoot height' Rebus: dul 'cast metal'

kanka 'rim of jar' Rebus: *karṇīka* 'account (scribe)' *karṇī* 'supercargo'

H-64 a

h64A *खोंड [khōṇḍa] m A young bull, a bullcalf. (Marathi) Rebus: kõdār 'turner' (Bengali); कोंद kōnda 'engraver, lapidary setting or infixing gems' (Marathi) G. sãghāɽɔ m. 'lathe' ; संघाट joinery; M. sãgaḍ 'double-canoe' Rebus: sangataras. संगतराश lit. 'to collect stones, stone-cutter, mason.'*
aya kammaṭa.'coiner, mint alloy'

 *kuṭila* 'bent' CDIAL 3230 kuṭi— in cmpd. 'curve', *kuṭika—* 'bent' MBh. Rebus: *kuṭila, katthīl* = bronze (8 parts copper and 2 parts tin) metal'

 'Arrow' sign hieroglyph (variant) This is a ligature of 'lid of pot' hieroglyph superscript on 'a linear stroke' numeral hieroglyph.*aḍaren* 'cover of pot or lid' Rebus: *aduru* 'native, unsmelted metal' PLUS koḍ = one (Santali); koḍ 'workshop' (Gujarati)

 कांड *kāṇḍa* 'arrow' Rebus: *kāṇḍa* 'pots and pans, metalware, tools'. Rebus 2: kaṇḍ 'fire-altar' (Santali)

H-323 A

h323A *aya kammaṭa.*'coiner, mint alloy' *bhaṭa* 'warrior' (Sanskrit) Rebus: *baṭa* a kind of iron (Gujarati). Rebus: *bhaṭa* 'furnace' (Santali)

 *kanka* 'rim of jar' Rebus: *karṇīka* 'account (scribe)' *karṇī* 'supercargo'

H-954 A

h954A *aya kammaṭa.*'coiner, mint alloy' *aya aḍaren (homonym: aduru)*'alloy native metal'

 *kanka* 'rim of jar' Rebus: *karṇīka* 'account (scribe)' *karṇī* 'supercargo'

 *meḍ* 'body' Rebus: *meḍ* 'iron' (Ho.) काठी [kāṭhī] *f* (काष्ट S) 'frame or structure of the body' (Marathi) Rebus: खंडी [khaṇḍī] measure of weight (Marathi) *கண்டி; kaṇṭi, n. < Mhr. khaṇḍil. [T. Tu. khaṇḍi, M. kaṇḍi.]* Candy, a weight, stated to be roughly equivalent to 500 lbs.

H-1895 A

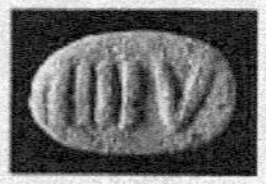

H-1895 B

h1895A *aya kammaṭa.*'coiner, mint alloy' *bhaṭa* 'warrior' (Sanskrit) *bhaṭa* 'warrior' Rebus: *baṭa* a kind of iron (Gujarati). Rebus: *bhaṭa* 'furnace' (Santali)

 *kanka* 'rim of jar' Rebus: *karṇīka* 'account (scribe)' *karṇī* 'supercargo' *baṭa* = rimless pot (Kannada) Rebus: *baṭa* = a kind of iron (G.)) *bhaṭa* furnace (Gujarati) |||| Numeral 4: gaṇḍa 'four' Rebus: kaṇḍa 'furnace, fire-altar' (Santali)

M-1315 A

m1315A *aya kammaṭa.*'coiner, mint alloy'

 *meḍ* 'body' Rebus: *meḍ* 'iron' (Ho.) काठी [kāṭhī] *f* (काष्ट S) 'frame or structure of the body' (Marathi) Rebus: खंडी [khaṇḍī] measure of

weight (Marathi) கண்டி; *kaṇṭi, n. < Mhr. khaṇḍil. [T. Tu. khaṇḍi, M. kaṇḍi.]* Candy, a weight, stated to be roughly equivalent to 500 lbs.

khaṇḍ 'field, division' (Sanskrit) Rebus: *khāṇḍa* 'tools, pots and pans, metal-ware'. Rebus 2: kaṇḍ 'fire-altar' (Santali) dula 'pair' Rebus: dul 'cast metal' Thus, duplicated 'division' hieroglyph sign reads: cast metal metal-ware.

m1887a *balad* m. ' ox ', gng. *bald*, (Ku.) *barad*, id. (N. Tarai) Rebus: *bharat* (5 copper, 4 zinc and 1 tin)(Punjabi) *pattar* 'trough' Rebus*: pattar* 'guild'. Thus, copper-zinc-tin alloy (worker) guild.
aya kammaṭa.'coiner, mint alloy' *aya aḍaren (homonym: aduru)*'alloy native metal'

aḍaren 'cover of pot or lid' Rebus: *aduru* 'native, unsmelted metal' Duplicated: dula 'pair' Rebus: dul 'cast metal'

'Arrow' sign hieroglyph (variant) This is a ligature of 'lid of pot' hieroglyph superscript on 'a linear stroke' numeral hieroglyph.*aḍaren* 'cover of pot or lid' Rebus: *aduru* 'native, unsmelted metal' PLUS koḍ = one (Santali); koḍ 'workshop' (Gujarati)

kanka 'rim of jar' Rebus: *karṇīka* 'account (scribe)' *karṇī* 'supercargo'

h1897A Read rebus as at h781A

h781A *aya kammaṭa.*'coiner, mint alloy'

kuṭila 'bent' CDIAL 3230 kuṭi— in cmpd. 'curve', *kuṭika—* 'bent' MBh. Rebus: *kuṭila, katthīl* = bronze (8 parts copper and 2 parts tin) Duplicated: dula 'pair' Rebus: dul 'cast metal' Thus, cast bronze.

kanka 'rim of jar' Rebus: *karṇīka* 'account (scribe)' *karṇī* 'supercargo'

Side B: *baṭa* = rimless pot (Kannada) Rebus: *baṭa* = a kind of iron (G.)) *bhaṭa* furnace (Gujarati) PLUS kolom 'three' Rebus; kolami 'smithy, forge'

m1965a sal 'splinter' Rebus: sal 'workshop'

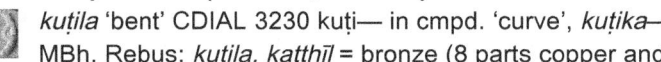

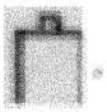

सांड [sāṇḍa] *f* (षद S) An outlet for superfluous water (as through a dam or mound); a sluice, a floodvent. Rebus: सांडणी [sāṇḍaṇī] *f* (H) An instrument of goldsmiths. It is hooked or curved at the extremity; and is used to draw things out of the fire. सांठा [*sāṇṭhā*] *m* (संचय S) A collection, heap, hoard, store, stock.साटें [*sāṭēṃ*] *n* (संचय S) A whole investment; the total quantity of merchandise (brought to market by one merchant).

 *kanka* 'rim of jar' Rebus: *karṇīka* 'account (scribe)' *karṇī* 'supercargo'

  notch+slanted stroke reads rebus: *ḍhālako kāṇḍa* 'ingot, tools, pots and pans and metal-ware'.*dhāḷ* 'a slope'; 'inclination of a plane' (G.); *ḍhāḷiyum* = adj. sloping, inclining (G.) Rebus: *ḍhālako* = a large metal ingot (G.) *ḍhālakī* = a metal heated and poured into a mould; a solid piece of metal; an ingot (Gujarati) PLUS खांडा [*khāṇḍā*] *m* A jag, notch, or indentation (as upon the edge of a tool or weapon). Rebus: *kāṇḍa* 'tools, pots and pans and metal-ware'

 *kolmo* 'paddy plant' Rebus: *kolami* 'smithy, forge' Vikalpa: *mogge* 'sprout, bud' Rebus: *mũh* 'ingot' (Santali) dolu 'plant of shoot height' Rebus: dul 'cast metal'

 m1734  m945a Read rebus as at m975A

m975A *खोंड [khōṇḍa] m A young bull, a bullcalf. (Marathi) Rebus: kõdār 'turner' (Bengali); कोंद kōnda 'engraver, lapidary setting or infixing gems' (Marathi) G. sãghāṛɔ m. 'lathe' ; संघाट joinery; M. sãgaḍ 'double-canoe' Rebus: sangataras. संगतराश lit. 'to collect stones, stone-cutter, mason.'*

Circumscript: Numeral 4: gaṇḍa 'four' Rebus: kaṇḍa 'furnace, fire-altar' (Santali) dula 'pair' Rebus: dul 'cast metal' PLUS

 *kuṭila* 'bent' CDIAL 3230 kuṭi— in cmpd. 'curve', *kuṭika—* 'bent' MBh. Rebus: *kuṭila, katthīl* = bronze (8 parts copper and 2 parts tin)PLUS ligature: sal 'splinter' Rebus: sal 'workshop'

 kanka 'rim of jar' Rebus: karṇīka 'account (scribe)' karṇī 'supercargo' PLUS infixed notch: खांडा [*khāṇḍā*] *m* A jag, notch, or indentation (as upon the edge of a tool or

  Strands of yarn/rope' hieroglyph: Rebus reading: *dhā́tu* 'strand of rope' (Santali)

 Hieroglyph: 'strands of yarn' Rebus: *dhatu* 'mineral ore'

 *dāṭu* 'cross'(Telugu) Rebus: *dhatu* 'mineral' (Santali). PLUS ligature: sal 'splinter' Rebus: sal 'workshop'

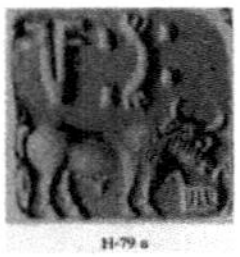

h79a *balad* m. ' ox ', gng. *bald*, (Ku.) *barad*, id. (N. Tarai) Rebus: *bharat* (5 copper, 4 zinc and 1 tin)(Punjabi) *pattar* 'trough' Rebus*: pattar* 'guild'. Thus, copper-zinc-tin alloy (worker) guild.

Circumscript: Numeral 4: gaṇḍa 'four' Rebus: kaṇḍa 'furnace, fire-altar' (Santali) dula 'pair' Rebus: dul 'cast metal' PLUS

 *kuṭila* 'bent' CDIAL 3230 kuṭi— in cmpd. 'curve', *kuṭika—* 'bent' MBh. Rebus: *kuṭila, katthīl* = bronze (8 parts copper and 2 parts tin)PLUS ligature: sal 'splinter' Rebus: sal 'workshop'

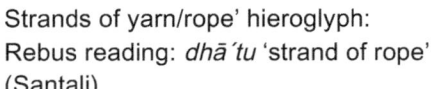

 *kanka* 'rim of jar' Rebus: *karṇīka* 'account (scribe)' *karṇī* 'supercargo'

m137a *खोंड [khōṇḍa] m A young bull, a bullcalf. (Marathi) Rebus: kõdār 'turner' (Bengali); कोंद kōnda 'engraver, lapidary setting or infixing gems' (Marathi) G. sãghāṛɔ m. 'lathe' ; संघाट joinery; M. sãgaḍ 'double-canoe' Rebus: sangataras. संगतराश lit. 'to collect stones, stone-cutter, mason.'* Circumscript: Numeral 4: gaṇḍa 'four' Rebus: kaṇḍa 'furnace, fire-altar' (Santali) dula 'pair' Rebus: dul 'cast metal' PLUS

dula 'two' Rebus: dul 'cast metal' PLUS

āra 'spokes' Rebus: *āra 'brass'*. cf. erka = ekke (Tbh. of arka) aka (Tbh. of arka) copper (metal); crystal (Kannada) Glyph: *eraka*'nave of wheel' Rebus: eraka 'copper'; cf. erka = ekke (Tbh. of arka) aka (Tbh. of arka) copper (metal); crystal (Kannada) *erako* 'moltencast copper' Thus, moltencast copper and brass furnace.castings.

m817A *खोंड [khōṇḍa] m A young bull, a bullcalf. (Marathi) Rebus: kõdār 'turner' (Bengali); कोंद kōnda 'engraver, lapidary setting or infixing gems' (Marathi) G. sãghāṛɔ m. 'lathe' ; संघाट joinery; M. sãgaḍ 'double-canoe' Rebus: sangataras. संगतराश lit. 'to collect stones, stone-cutter, mason.'*

Circumscript: Numeral 4: gaṇḍa 'four' Rebus: kaṇḍa 'furnace, fire-altar' (Santali) dula 'pair' Rebus: dul 'cast metal' PLUS

 *kanac* 'corner' Rebus: *kañcu* 'bronze' Thus, cast bronze.

loa 'ficus religiosa' Rebus: *lo* 'iron' (Sanskrit) PLUS unique ligatures: लोखंड [lōkhaṇḍa] *n* (लोह S) Iron. लोखंडाचे चणे खावविणें or चारणें To oppress grievously.लोखंडकाम [lōkhaṇḍakāma] *n* Iron work; that portion (of a building, machine &c.) which consists of iron. 2 The business of an ironsmith.लोखंडी [lōkhaṇḍī] *a* (लोखंड) Composed of iron; relating to iron. (Marathi)

कांड *kāṇḍa* 'arrow' Rebus: *kāṇḍa* 'pots and pans, metalware, tools'. Rebus 2: kaṇḍ 'fire-altar' (Santali)

m1677a *खोंड [khōṇḍa] m A young bull, a bullcalf. (Marathi) Rebus: kõdār 'turner' (Bengali); कोंद kōnda 'engraver, lapidary setting or infixing gems' (Marathi) G. sãghāṛɔ m. 'lathe' ; संघाट joinery; M. sãgaḍ 'double-canoe' Rebus: sangataras. संगतराश lit. 'to collect stones, stone-cutter, mason.' dula 'two' Rebus: dul 'cast metal' sal 'splinter' Rebus: sal 'workshop'*

āra 'spokes' Rebus: *āra 'brass'*. cf. erka = ekke (Tbh. of arka) aka (Tbh. of arka) copper (metal); crystal (Kannada) Glyph: *eraka*'nave of wheel' Rebus: eraka 'copper'; cf. erka = ekke (Tbh. of arka) aka (Tbh. of arka) copper (metal); crystal (Kannada) *erako* 'moltencast copper' PLUS sal 'splinter' Rebus: sal 'workshop'

dula 'two' Rebus: dul 'cast metal' PLUS *loa* 'ficus religiosa' Rebus: *lo* 'iron' (Sanskrit) PLUS unique ligatures: लोखंड [lōkhaṇḍa] *n* (लोह S) Iron. लोखंडाचे चणे खावविणें or चारणें To oppress grievously.लोखंडकाम [lōkhaṇḍakāma] *n* Iron work; that portion (of a building, machine &c.) which consists of iron. 2 The business of an ironsmith.लोखंडी [lōkhaṇḍī] *a* (लोखंड) Composed of iron; relating to iron. (Marathi)
Thus, copper castings.

कांड *kāṇḍa* 'arrow' Rebus: *kāṇḍa* 'pots and pans, metalware, tools'. Rebus 2: kaṇḍ 'fire-altar' (Santali)

'Notched slant or hook-shaped' sign hieroglyph

Al-4 A

Allahdino 4A *खोंड [khōṇḍa] m A young bull, a bullcalf. (Marathi) Rebus: kōdār 'turner' (Bengali); कोंद kōnda 'engraver, lapidary setting or infixing gems' (Marathi) G. sãghāṛɔ m. 'lathe' ; संघाट joinery; M. sāgaḍ 'double-canoe' Rebus: sangataras. संगतराश lit. 'to collect stones, stone-cutter, mason.'* loungers, newsmongers, gossips, scamps. 2 An order of men. Ex. गोसाव्यांचे अठरा अखाडे आहेत.(M.)

ḍhanga = a crook used for pulling down the branches of trees, for goats, sheep and camels

(P.) Rebus:*ḍhangar* blacksmith'.
kanka 'rim of jar' Rebus: *karṇīka* 'account (scribe)' *karṇī* 'supercargo'

kanka 'rim of jar' Rebus: karṇīka 'account (scribe)' karṇī 'supercargo'

aya kāṇḍa 'alloy metalware'

mēḍu height, rising ground, hillock (Kannada) Rebus: *mẽṛhẽt, meḍ* 'iron' (Munda.Ho.)
|||| Numeral 4: *gaṇḍa* 'four' Rebus: *kaṇḍa* 'furnace, fire-altar' (Santali).
kolom 'three' Rebus*: kolami* 'smithy, forge'

kanka 'rim of jar' Rebus: *karṇīka* 'account (scribe)' *karṇī* 'supercargo'

m881a *खोंड [khōṇḍa] m A young bull, a bullcalf. (Marathi) Rebus: kōdār 'turner' (Bengali); कोंद kōnda 'engraver, lapidary setting or infixing gems' (Marathi) G. sãghāṛɔ m. 'lathe' ; संघाट joinery; M. sāgaḍ 'double-canoe' Rebus: sangataras. संगतराश lit. 'to collect stones, stone-cutter, mason.' ḍhanga* = a crook used for pulling down the branches of trees, for goats, sheep and camels (P.) Rebus:*ḍhangar* blacksmith'. *kolom* 'three' Rebus*: kolami* 'smithy, forge'

notch+slanted stroke reads rebus: *ḍhālako kāṇḍa* 'ingot, tools, pots and pans and metal-ware'.*ḍhāḷ* 'a slope'; 'inclination of a plane' (G.); *ḍhāḷiyum* = adj. sloping, inclining (G.) Rebus: *ḍhālako* = a large metal ingot (G.) *ḍhālakī* = a metal heated and poured into a mould; a solid piece of metal; an ingot (Gujarati) PLUS खांडा [*khāṇḍā*

] *m* A jag, notch, or indentation (as upon the edge of a tool or weapon). Rebus: *kāṇḍa* 'tools, pots and pans and metal-ware'
ayo 'fish' Rebus: *aya* 'iron' *ayas* 'metal'

m972a *खोंड [khōṇḍa] m A young bull, a bullcalf. (Marathi) Rebus: kõdār 'turner' (Bengali); कोंद*

kōnda 'engraver, lapidary setting or infixing gems' (Marathi) G. sãghāṛɔ m. 'lathe' ; संघाट joinery; M. sãgaḍ 'double-canoe' Rebus: sangataras. संगतराश lit. 'to collect stones, stone-cutter, mason.' ḍhanga = a crook used for pulling down the branches of trees, for goats, sheep and camels (P.) Rebus:*ḍhangar* blacksmith'.

meḍ 'body' Rebus: *meḍ* 'iron' (Ho.) काठी [kāṭhī] *f* (काष्ट S) 'frame or structure of the body' (Marathi) Rebus: खंडी [khaṇḍī] measure of weight (Marathi) *கண்டி; kaṇṭi, n. < Mhr. khaṇḍil. [T. Tu. khaṇḍi, M. kaṇḍi.]* Candy, a weight, stated to be roughly equivalent to 500 lbs.

kanka 'rim of jar' Rebus: *karṇīka* 'account (scribe)' *karṇī* 'supercargo'

h1924A *ḍhanga* = a crook used for pulling down the branches of trees, for goats, sheep and camels (P.) Rebus:*ḍhangar* blacksmith'. kolom 'three' Rebus: kolami 'smithy, forge' *kamaḍha* 'crab' Rebus: *kammaṭa* 'mint, coiner'.
ḍato = claws of crab (Santali) Rebus: *dhātu* 'mineral ore'
Side B: kolom 'three' Rebus: kolami 'smithy, forge' PLUS
baṭa = rimless pot (Kannada) Rebus: *baṭa* = a kind of iron (G.)) *bhaṭa* furnace (Gujarati)

m36a *खोंड [khōṇḍa] m A young bull, a bullcalf. (Marathi) Rebus: kõdār 'turner' (Bengali); कोंद kōnda 'engraver, lapidary setting or infixing gems' (Marathi) G. sãghāṛɔ m. 'lathe' ; संघाट joinery; M. sãgaḍ 'double-canoe' Rebus: sangataras. संगतराश lit. 'to collect stones, stone-cutter, mason.'*

ḍhanga = a crook used for pulling down the branches of trees, for goats, sheep and camels (P.) Rebus:*ḍhangar* blacksmith'. PLUS kolom 'three' Rebus: kolami 'smithy, forge' PLUS | *koḍa* 'one' Rebus: *koḍ* 'workshop' *khuṭo* ' leg, foot ', °ṭī ' goat's leg ' Rebus: *khōṭā* 'alloy' (Marathi)

kuṭila 'bent' CDIAL 3230 kuṭi— in cmpd. 'curve', *kuṭika*— 'bent' MBh. Rebus: *kuṭila, katthīl* = bronze (8 parts copper and 2 parts tin) Duplicated: dula 'pair' Rebus: dul 'cast metal' Thus, cast bronze.

koḍi 'flag' (Ta.)(DEDR 2049). Rebus 1: *koḍ* 'workshop' (Kuwi) Rebus 2: *khŏḍ* m. 'pit', *khŏḍü* f. 'small pit' (Kashmiri. CDIAL 3947).
dula 'two' Rebus: dul 'cast metal' sal 'splinter' Rebus: sal 'workshop' *ayo* 'fish' Rebus: *aya* 'iron' *ayas* 'metal'
kəṭhā'r, kc. *kuṭhār* m. ' granary, storeroom '(WPah.)(CDIAL 3550). *koṭhārī m.* ' storekeeper'

(Gujarati)(CDIAL 3551) Thus, storeroom (of) *kolom* 'three' Rebus: *kolami* 'smithy, forge'. Dula 'pair' Rebus: dul 'cast metal' Thus, together *dul kolami kuṭhār* 'metal smithy castings storeroom'

dulo 'hole' Rebus: dul 'cast metal' PLUS *aya kammaṭa.*'coiner, mint alloy'
Thus alloy metal castings.

 *kanka* 'rim of jar' Rebus: *karṇīka* 'account (scribe)' *karṇī* 'supercargo'

M-1749 a bis

m1749a *खोंड [khōṇḍa] m A young bull, a bullcalf. (Marathi) Rebus: kõdār 'turner' (Bengali); कोंद kōnda 'engraver, lapidary setting or infixing gems' (Marathi) G. sãghārɔ m. 'lathe' ; संघाट joinery; M. sãgaḍ 'double-canoe' Rebus: sangataras. संगतराश lit. 'to collect stones, stone-cutter, mason.'*

  'Bow and arrow' sign hieroglyph 'Archer + bow + arrow' ligatured hieroglyph upraised arm: eraka 'upraised arm' Rebus: erako 'moltencast copper'

 *kamaḍha* 'archer, bow' Rebus: *kammaṭa* 'mint,
mēḍu height, rising ground, hillock (Kannada) Rebus: *meḍ* 'iron' (Ho.) kolom 'three' Rebus: kolami 'smithy, forge' Thus, *meḍ kolami* 'iron smithy-forge'
aya kammaṭa.'coiner, mint alloy'

 'Sluice' sign hieroglyph

 m1900a *khũṭ* 'zebu' Rebus: '(native metal) guild' Text message: instrument to draw things out of the fire; tin, supercargo of metalware; alloyed metal of mint; tools, pots and pans, metalware.

 सांड [sāṇḍa] *f* (षद S) An outlet for superfluous water (as through a dam or mound); a sluice, a floodvent. Rebus: सांडणी [sāṇḍaṇī] *f* (H) An instrument of goldsmiths. It is hooked or curved at the extremity; and is used to draw things out of the fire. सांठा [*sāṇṭhā*] *m* (संचय S) A collection, heap, hoard, store, stock.साटें [*sāṭēṃ*] *n* (संचय S) A whole investment; the total quantity of merchandise (brought to market by one merchant). Ranku 'liquid measure' Rebus: ranku 'tin'

ranku 'liquid measure' Rebus: ranku 'tin'

 Ligatured hieroglyph: rim of jar + notch:
kanka 'rim of jar' Rebus: *karṇīka* 'account (scribe)' *karṇī* 'supercargo' PLUS infixed hieroglyph 'notch' Rebus: *kāṇḍa* 'pots and pans, metalware, tools'. Thus, the composite hieroglyph denotes supercargo of metalware.

ayo 'fish' Rebus: aya 'iron' (Gujarati) ayas 'metal' (Vedic) PLUS ligatured fins: *khambhaṛā* m. 'fin' (Lahnda); khambh 'wing' (Punjabi) Allograph: Garh. *khambu* ' pillar '.(CDIAL 13640) Rebus: kammaṭa 'coiner, mint'. Thus 'fish' hieroglyph gets ligatured with fins to denote alloyed metal (of) mint. [An allograph for *khambh* is: *khambha* 'pillar' (Bhoj)(CDIAL 13639)]

kāṇḍa 'arrow' (Sanskrit) Rebus:*khāṇḍa* 'tools, pots and pans, metal-ware'. Rebus 2: kaṇḍ 'fire-altar' (Santali)

m0318a

सांड [sāṇḍa] *f* (षद S) An outlet for superfluous water (as through a dam or mound); a sluice, a floodvent. Rebus: सांडणी [sāṇḍaṇī] *f* (H) An instrument of goldsmiths. It is hooked or curved at the extremity; and is used to draw things out of the fire. सांठा [*sāṇṭhā*] *m* (संचय S) A collection, heap, hoard, store, stock.साटें [*sāṭēṃ*] *n* (संचय S) A whole investment; the total quantity of merchandise (brought to market by one merchant). | *koḍa* 'one' Rebus: *koḍ* 'workshop' sal 'splinter' Rebus: sal 'workshop' dula 'pair' Rebus: dul 'cast metal' Thus, workshop for metal castings.

 *kolmo* 'paddy plant' Rebus: *kolami* 'smithy, forge' Vikalpa: *mogge* 'sprout, bud' Rebus: *mũh* 'ingot' (Santali) dolu 'plant of shoot height' Rebus: dul 'cast metal'

m1233a

सांड [sāṇḍa] *f* (षद S) An outlet for superfluous water (as through a dam or mound); a sluice, a floodvent. Rebus: सांडणी [sāṇḍaṇī] *f* (H) An instrument of goldsmiths. It is hooked or curved at the extremity; and is used to draw things out of the fire. सांठा [*sāṇṭhā*] *m* (संचय S) A collection, heap, hoard, store, stock.साटें [*sāṭēṃ*] *n* (संचय S) A whole investment; the total quantity of merchandise (brought to market by one merchant).

 *kanka* 'rim of jar' Rebus: *karṇīka* 'account (scribe)' *karṇī* 'supercargo'

m1989b

सांड [sāṇḍa] *f* (षद S) An outlet for superfluous water (as through a dam or mound); a sluice, a floodvent. Rebus: सांडणी [sāṇḍaṇī] *f* (H) An instrument of goldsmiths. It is hooked or curved at the extremity; and is used to draw things out of the fire. सांठा [*sāṇṭhā*] *m* (संचय S) A collection, heap, hoard, store, stock.साटें [*sāṭēṃ*] *n* (संचय S) A whole investment; the total quantity of merchandise (brought to market by one merchant).

 *kanka* 'rim of jar' Rebus: *karṇīka* 'account (scribe)' *karṇī* 'supercargo'

kaṇḍo 'stool, seat' Rebus: *kāṇḍa* 'metalware' *kaṇḍa* 'fire-altar'
PLUS

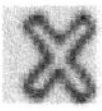 *dāṭu* 'cross'(Telugu) Rebus: *dhatu* 'mineral' (Santali).

M-1424 A

M-1424 A bis

M-1424 B

M-1424 B bis

M-1424 C

m1424A,B

Text of inscription: Side 1

 सांड [sāṇḍa] *f* (षद S) An outlet for superfluous water (as through a dam or mound); a sluice, a floodvent. Rebus: सांडणी [sāṇḍaṇī] *f* (H) An instrument of goldsmiths. It is hooked or curved at the extremity; and is used to draw things out of the fire. सांठा [*sāṇṭhā*] *m* (संचय S) A collection, heap, hoard, store, stock.साटें [*sāṭēṃ*] *n* (संचय S) A whole investment; the total quantity of merchandise (brought to market by one merchant). Three: kolom 'three' Rebus: kolami 'smithy, forge' PLUS *baṭa* = rimless pot (Kannada) Rebus:) *baṭa* = a kind of iron (G.)) *bhaṭa* furnace (Gujarati) Thus, furnace smithy for iron.

 *kanka* 'rim of jar' Rebus: *karṇīka* 'account (scribe)' *karṇī* 'supercargo'
INFIXED sal 'splinte' Rebus: sal 'workshop' Thus, workshop cargo.

 *dula* 'pair' Rebus: *dul* 'cast (metal)' PLUS*kana, kanac* = corner (Santali); Rebus: *kañcu* = bronze (Telugu) PLUS infixed kolmo 'paddy plant' Rebus: kolami 'smithy, forge'. Thus, cast bronze smithy, forge. Or, *mogge* 'sprout, bud' Rebus: *mũh* 'ingot' (Santali)Thus, cast bronze ingot. Read as: *kañcu dul mũh 'bronze cast ingot'*

 *aḍaren* 'cover of pot or lid' Rebus: *aduru* 'native, unsmelted metal' Duplicated: dula 'pair' Rebus: dul 'cast metal'

 *kanka* 'rim of jar' Rebus: *karṇīka* 'account (scribe)' *karṇī* 'supercargo'

Text of inscription Side 2:

kamaḍha 'archer, bow' Rebus: *kammaṭa* 'mint, coiner'.

 *loa* 'ficus religiosa' Rebus: *lo* 'iron' (Sanskrit) PLUS unique ligatures: लोखंड [lōkhaṇḍa] *n* (लोह् S) Iron. लोखंडाचे चणे खावविणें or चारणें To oppress grievously.लोखंडकाम [lōkhaṇḍakāma] *n* Iron work; that portion (of a building, machine &c.) which consists of iron. 2 The business of an ironsmith.लोखंडी [lōkhaṇḍī] *a* (लोखंड) Composed of iron; relating to iron. (Marathi)

 *kanka* 'rim of jar' Rebus: *karṇīka* 'account (scribe)' *karṇī* 'supercargo'
Accompanying pictorial motif:

balad m. ' ox ', gng. *bald*, (Ku.) *barad*, id. (N. Tarai) Rebus: *bharat* (5 copper, 4 zinc and 1 tin)(Punjabi) *pattar* 'trough' Rebus*: pattar* 'guild'. Thus, copper-zinc-tin alloy (worker) guild

m920A *खोंड [khōṇḍa] m A young bull, a bullcalf. (Marathi) Rebus: kõdār 'turner' (Bengali); कोंद kōnda 'engraver, lapidary setting or infixing gems' (Marathi) G. sãghāṛɔ m. 'lathe' ; संघाट joinery; M. sãgaḍ 'double-canoe' Rebus: sangataras. संगतराश lit. 'to collect stones, stone-cutter, mason.'*

सांड [sāṇḍa] *f* (षद S) An outlet for superfluous water (as through a dam or mound); a sluice, a floodvent. Rebus: सांडणी [sāṇḍaṇī] *f* (H) An instrument of goldsmiths. It is hooked or curved at the extremity; and is used to draw things out of the fire.
सांठा [*sāṇṭhā*] *m* (संचय S) A collection, heap, hoard, store, stock.साटें [*sāṭēṃ*] *n* (संचय S) A whole investment; the total quantity of merchandise (brought to market by one merchant).

dula 'two' Rebus: dul 'cast metal' PLUS kolom 'three' Rebus: kolami 'smithy, forge' LIGATURED horizontally to:
| *koḍa* 'one' Rebus: *koḍ* 'workshop' Thus, cast metal, forge workshop.
Circumscript:

kuṭila 'bent' CDIAL 3230 kuṭi— in cmpd. 'curve', *kuṭika—* 'bent' MBh. Rebus: *kuṭila, katthīl* = bronze (8 parts copper and 2 parts tin) Duplicated: dula 'pair' Rebus: dul 'cast metal' Thus, cast bronze.
PLUS *baṭa* 'quail' Rebus: *baṭha* 'smelter, furnace' Vikalpa variant:

karaṇḍa 'duck' (Sanskrit) karaṛa 'a very large aquatic bird' (Sindhi) Rebus: करडा [*karaḍā*] Hard from alloy--iron, silver &c. (Marathi) *kharādī* ' turner' (Gujarati) Duck looks back: krammara 'look back' Rebus: kamar 'smith, artisan' Thus, bronze castings hard alloy smith. Or, smelter bronze castings.

h458A *खोंड [khōṇḍa] m A young bull, a bullcalf. (Marathi) Rebus: kõdār 'turner' (Bengali); कोंद kōnda 'engraver, lapidary setting or infixing gems' (Marathi) G. sãghāṛɔ m. 'lathe' ; संघाट joinery; M. sãgaḍ 'double-canoe' Rebus: sangataras. संगतराश lit. 'to collect stones, stone-cutter, mason.'*

सांड [sāṇḍa] *f* (षद S) An outlet for superfluous water (as through a dam or mound); a sluice, a floodvent. Rebus: सांडणी [sāṇḍaṇī] *f* (H) An instrument of goldsmiths. It is hooked or curved at the extremity; and is used to draw things out of the fire.
सांठा [*sāṇṭhā*] *m* (संचय S) A collection, heap, hoard, store, stock.साटें [*sāṭēṃ*] *n* (संचय S) A whole investment; the total quantity of merchandise (brought to market by one merchant).

kanac 'corner' Rebus: *kañcu* 'bronze'

koḍi 'flag' (Ta.)(DEDR 2049). Rebus 1: *koḍ* 'workshop' (Kuwi) Rebus 2: *khōḍ* m. 'pit', *khōḍü* f. 'small pit' (Kashmiri. CDIAL 3947)

m649A *खोंड [khōṇḍa] m A young bull, a bullcalf. (Marathi) Rebus: kõdār 'turner' (Bengali); कोंद kōnda 'engraver, lapidary setting or infixing gems' (Marathi) G. sãghāṛɔ m. 'lathe' ; संघाट joinery; M. sãgaḍ 'double-canoe' Rebus: sangataras. संगतराश lit. 'to collect stones, stone-cutter, mason.'*

kaṇḍo 'stool, seat' Rebus: *kāṇḍa* 'metalware' *kaṇḍa* 'fire-altar'
PLUS *Kur.* xolā tail. *Malt.* qoli id. (DEDR 2135). Rebus: kolhe 'smelter'

āra 'spokes' Rebus: *āra 'brass'*. cf. erka = ekke (Tbh. of arka) aka (Tbh. of arka) copper (metal); crystal (Kannada) Glyph: *eraka* 'nave of wheel' Rebus: eraka 'copper'; cf. erka = ekke (Tbh. of arka) aka (Tbh. of arka) copper (metal); crystal (Kannada) *erako* 'moltencast copper' Thus, copper, brass smelter.

H-2240 B

h2240B

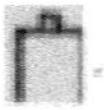

सांड [sāṇḍa] *f* (षद S) An outlet for superfluous water (as through a dam or mound); a sluice, a floodvent. Rebus: सांडणी [sāṇḍaṇī] *f* (H) An instrument of goldsmiths. It is hooked or curved at the extremity; and is used to draw things out of the fire.
सांठा [*sāṇṭhā*] *m* (संचय S) A collection, heap, hoard, store, stock.साटें [*sāṭēṃ*] *n* (संचय S) A whole investment; the total quantity of merchandise (brought to market by one merchant).

kanac 'corner' Rebus: *kañcu* 'bronze'

m67a *खोंड [khōṇḍa] m A young bull, a bullcalf. (Marathi) Rebus: kōdār 'turner' (Bengali); कोंद kōnda 'engraver, lapidary setting or infixing gems' (Marathi) G. sãghārɔ m. 'lathe' ; संघाट joinery; M. sãgaḍ 'double-canoe' Rebus: sangataras. संगतराश lit. 'to collect stones, stone-cutter, mason.'*

सांड [sāṇḍa] *f* (षद S) An outlet for superfluous water (as through a dam or mound); a sluice, a floodvent. Rebus: सांडणी [sāṇḍaṇī] *f* (H) An instrument of goldsmiths. It is hooked or curved at the extremity; and is used to draw things out of the fire.
सांठा [*sāṇṭhā*] *m* (संचय S) A collection, heap, hoard, store, stock.साटें [*sāṭēṃ*] *n* (संचय S) A whole investment; the total quantity of merchandise (brought to market by one merchant).

eraka 'upraised hand' Rebus: erako 'moltencast copper' PLUS *baṭa* = rimless pot (Kannada) Rebus: *baṭa* = a kind of iron (G.)) *bhaṭa* furnace (Gujarati) PLUS

meḍ 'body' Rebus: *meḍ* 'iron' (Ho.) काठी [kāṭhī] *f* (काष्ट S) 'frame or structure of the body' (Marathi) Rebus: खंडी [khaṇḍī] measure of weight (Marathi) *கண்டி; kaṇṭi, n. < Mhr. khaṇḍil. [T. Tu. khaṇḍi, M. kaṇḍi.]* Candy, a weight, stated to be roughly equivalent to 500 lbs. (Kannada) Glyph: *eraka* 'nave of wheel' Rebus: eraka 'copper'; cf. erka = ekke (Tbh. of arka) aka (Tbh. of arka) copper (metal); crystal (Kannada)

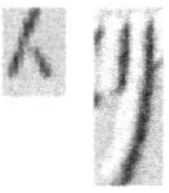

notch+slanted stroke reads rebus: *ḍhālako kāṇḍa* 'ingot, tools, pots and pans and metal-ware'.*ḍhāḷ* 'a slope'; 'inclination of a plane' (G.); *ḍhāḷiyum* = adj. sloping, inclining (G.) Rebus: *ḍhālako* = a large metal ingot (G.) *ḍhālakī* = a metal heated and poured into a mould; a solid piece of metal; an ingot (Gujarati) PLUS खांडा [*khāṇḍā*

] *m* A jag, notch, or indentation (as upon the edge of a tool or weapon). Rebus: *kāṇḍa* 'tools, pots and pans and metal-ware'

 *kuṭila* 'bent' CDIAL 3230 kuṭi— in cmpd. 'curve', *kuṭika*— 'bent' MBh. Rebus: *kuṭila, katthīl* = bronze (8 parts copper and 2 parts tin)

The hieroglyph may be a variant of:  *kana, kanac* = corner (Santali); Rebus: *kañcu* = bronze (Telugu) PLUS kolom 'three' Rebus: kolami 'smithy, forge.

 *kanka* 'rim of jar' Rebus: *karṇīka* 'account (scribe)' *karṇī* 'supercargo'

m740A *खोंड [khōṇḍa] m A young bull, a bullcalf. (Marathi) Rebus: kōdār 'turner' (Bengali); कोंद kōnda 'engraver, lapidary setting or infixing gems' (Marathi) G. sãghārɔ m. 'lathe' ; संघाट joinery; M. sãgaḍ 'double-canoe' Rebus: sangataras. संगतराश lit. 'to collect stones, stone-cutter, mason.'*

 सांड [sāṇḍa] *f* (षद S) An outlet for superfluous water (as through a dam or mound); a sluice, a floodvent. Rebus: सांडणी [sāṇḍaṇī] *f* (H) An instrument of goldsmiths. It is hooked or curved at the extremity; and is used to draw things out of the fire.
सांठा [*sāṇṭhā*] *m* (संचय S) A collection, heap, hoard, store, stock.साटें [*sāṭēṃ*] *n* (संचय S) A whole investment; the total quantity of merchandise (brought to market by one merchant).

 *muka* 'ladle' (Tamil)(DEDR 4887) Rebus: *mũh* 'ingot' (Santali) *baṭa* = rimless pot (Kannada) Rebus: *baṭa*

 *kanka* (Santali) *karṇika* 'scribe'(Sanskrit) Rebus: *karṇī,* supercargo for a boat shipment. INFIXED खांडा [*khāṇḍā*] *m* A jag, notch, or indentation (as upon the edge of a tool or weapon). Rebus: *kāṇḍa* 'tools, pots and pans and metal-ware'

 mēḍu height, rising ground, hillock (Kannada) Rebus: *mẽṛhẽt, meḍ* 'iron' (Munda.Ho.) *aya kāṇḍa* 'alloy metalware'

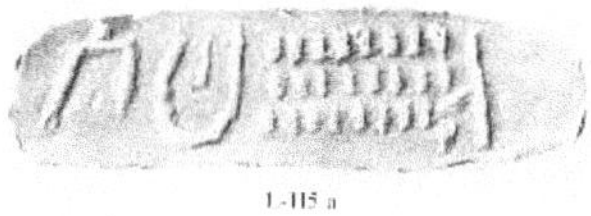

Lothal 115a

 सांड [sāṇḍa] *f* (षद S) An outlet for superfluous water (as through a dam or mound); a sluice, a floodvent. Rebus: सांडणी [sāṇḍaṇī] *f* (H) An instrument of goldsmiths. It is hooked or curved at the extremity; and is used to draw things out of the fire.
सांठा [*sāṇṭhā*] *m* (संचय S) A collection, heap, hoard, store, stock.साटें [*sāṭēṃ*] *n* (संचय S) A whole investment; the total quantity of merchandise (brought to market by one merchant).

 *muka* 'ladle' (Tamil)(DEDR 4887) Rebus: *mũh* 'ingot' (Santali) *baṭa* = rimless pot (Kannada) Rebus: *baṭa* = a kind of iron (G.)) *bhaṭa* furnace (Gujarati) dula 'pair' Rebus: dul 'cast metal' PLUS

 *baroṭi* 'twelve' *bhārata* 'a factitious alloy of copper, pewter, tin' (Marathi)

Thus, factitious alloy castings.

notch+slanted stroke reads rebus: *ḍhālako kāṇḍa* 'ingot, tools, pots and pans and metal-ware'.*dhāḷ* 'a slope'; 'inclination of a plane' (G.); *ḍhāḷiyum* = adj. sloping, inclining (G.) Rebus: *ḍhālako* = a large metal ingot (G.) *ḍhālakī* = a metal heated and poured into a mould; a solid piece of metal; an ingot (Gujarati) PLUS खांडा [*khāṇḍā*] *m* A jag, notch, or indentation (as upon the edge of a tool or weapon). Rebus: *kāṇḍa* 'tools, pots and pans and metal-ware'

m65a *खोंड [khōṇḍa] m A young bull, a bullcalf. (Marathi) Rebus: kõdār 'turner' (Bengali); कोंद kōnda 'engraver, lapidary setting or infixing gems' (Marathi) G. sãghāṛɔ m. 'lathe' ; संघाट joinery; M. sãgaḍ 'double-canoe' Rebus: sangataras. संगतराश lit. 'to collect stones, stone-cutter, mason.'*

सांड [sāṇḍa] *f* (षद S) An outlet for superfluous water (as through a dam or mound); a sluice, a floodvent. Rebus: सांडणी [sāṇḍaṇī] *f* (H) An instrument of goldsmiths. It is hooked or curved at the extremity; and is used to draw things out of the fire. सांठा [*sāṇṭhā*] *m* (संचय S) A collection, heap, hoard, store, stock.साटें [*sāṭēṃ*] *n* (संचय S) A whole investment; the total quantity of merchandise (brought to market by one merchant).

muka 'ladle' (Tamil)(DEDR 4887) Rebus: *mũh* 'ingot' (Santali) *baṭa* = rimless pot (Kannada) Rebus:) *baṭa* = a kind of iron (G.)) *bhaṭa* furnace (Gujarati) Thus, iron ingot furnace.

Variant:

dhāḷ 'a slope'; 'inclination of a plane' (G.); *ḍhāḷiyum* = adj. sloping, inclining (G.) Rebus: *ḍhālako* = a large metal ingot (G.) *ḍhālakī* = a metal heated and poured into a mould; a solid piece of metal; an ingot (Gujarati) PLUS खांडा [*khāṇḍā*] *m* A jag, notch, or indentation (as upon the edge of a tool or weapon). Rebus: *kāṇḍa* 'tools, pots and pans and metal-ware'
Thus, the pair of sign hieroglyphs from r. read rebus: copper, bronze ingots, metalware castings, pots and pans and metal-ware'
ayo 'fish' Rebus: *aya* 'iron' *ayas* 'metal'

कांड *kāṇḍa* 'arrow' Rebus: *kāṇḍa* 'pots and pans, metalware, tools'. Rebus 2: kaṇḍ 'fire-altar' (Santali)

m159A *खोंड [khōṇḍa] m A young bull, a bullcalf. (Marathi) Rebus: kõdār 'turner' (Bengali); कोंद kōnda 'engraver, lapidary setting or infixing gems' (Marathi) G. sãghāṛɔ m. 'lathe' ; संघाट joinery; M. sãgaḍ 'double-canoe' Rebus: sangataras. संगतराश lit. 'to collect stones, stone-cutter, mason.'*

सांड [sāṇḍa] *f* (षद S) An outlet for superfluous water (as through a dam or mound); a sluice, a floodvent. Rebus: सांडणी [sāṇḍaṇī] *f* (H) An instrument of goldsmiths. It is hooked or curved at the extremity; and is used to draw things out of the fire. सांठा [*sāṇṭhā*] *m* (संचय S) A collection, heap, hoard, store, stock.साटें [*sāṭēṃ*] *n* (संचय S) A whole investment; the total quantity of merchandise (brought to market by one merchant).

 *kuṭila* 'bent' CDIAL 3230 kuṭi— in cmpd. 'curve', *kuṭika*— 'bent' MBh. Rebus: *kuṭila, katthīl* = bronze (8 parts copper and 2 parts tin)

 *kanka* (Santali) *karṇika* 'scribe'(Sanskrit) Rebus: *karṇī,* supercargo for a boat shipment. INFIXED खांडा [*khāṇḍā*] *m* A jag, notch, or indentation (as upon the edge of a tool or weapon). Rebus: *kāṇḍa* 'tools, pots and pans and metal-ware'

kuṭila  'bent' CDIAL 3230 kuṭi— in cmpd. 'curve', *kuṭika*— 'bent' MBh. Rebus: *kuṭila, katthīl* = bronze (8 parts copper and 2 parts tin) Duplicated: dula 'pair' Rebus: dul 'cast metal' Thus, cast bronze.

PLUS

|||| Numeral 4: *gaṇḍa* 'four' Rebus: *kaṇḍa* 'furnace, fire-altar' (Santali).

kolom 'three' Rebus*: kolami* 'smithy, forge'

kanka 'rim of jar' Rebus: karṇīka 'account (scribe)' karṇī 'supercargo'

Chanhudaro 8A *खोंड [khōṇḍa] m A young bull, a bullcalf. (Marathi) Rebus: kōdār 'turner' (Bengali); कोंद kōnda 'engraver, lapidary setting or infixing gems' (Marathi) G. sãghāṛɔ m. 'lathe' ; संघाट joinery; M. sāgaḍ 'double-canoe' Rebus: sangataras. संगतराश lit. 'to collect stones, stone-cutter, mason.'*

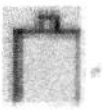 सांड [sāṇḍa] *f* (षद S) An outlet for superfluous water (as through a dam or mound); a sluice, a floodvent. Rebus: सांडणी [sāṇḍaṇī] *f* (H) An instrument of goldsmiths. It is hooked or curved at the extremity; and is used to draw things out of the fire.

सांठा [*sāṇṭhā*] *m* (संचय S) A collection, heap, hoard, store, stock.साटें [*sāṭēṃ*] *n* (संचय S) A whole investment; the total quantity of merchandise (brought to market by one merchant).

 *kanka* (Santali) *karṇika* 'scribe'(Sanskrit) Rebus: *karṇī,* supercargo for a boat shipment. INFIXED खांडा [*khāṇḍā*] *m* A jag, notch, or indentation (as upon the edge of a tool or weapon). Rebus: *kāṇḍa* 'tools, pots and pans and metal-ware' *aya kammaṭa.*'coiner, mint alloy'

 *dula* 'pair' Rebus: *dul* 'cast (metal)' PLUS*kana, kanac* = corner (Santali); Rebus: *kañcu* = bronze (Telugu) PLUS infixed kolmo 'paddy plant' Rebus: kolami 'smithy, forge'. Thus, cast bronze smithy, forge. Or, *mogge* 'sprout, bud' Rebus: *mũh* 'ingot' (Santali)Thus, cast bronze ingot. Read as: *kañcu dul mũh 'bronze cast ingot'*

 *kanka* 'rim of jar' Rebus: *karṇīka* 'account (scribe)' *karṇī* 'supercargo'

m665A *खोंड [khōṇḍa] m A young bull, a bullcalf. (Marathi) Rebus: kōdār 'turner' (Bengali); कोंद kōnda 'engraver, lapidary setting or infixing gems' (Marathi) G. sãghāṛɔ m. 'lathe' ; संघाट joinery; M. sāgaḍ 'double-canoe' Rebus: sangataras. संगतराश lit. 'to collect stones, stone-cutter, mason.'*

सांड [sāṇḍa ] *f* (षद S) An outlet for superfluous water (as through a dam or mound); a sluice, a floodvent. Rebus: सांडणी [sāṇḍaṇī] *f* (H) An instrument of goldsmiths. It is hooked or curved at the extremity; and is used to draw things out of the fire. सांठा [*sāṇṭhā*] *m* (संचय S) A collection, heap, hoard, store, stock.साटें [*sāṭēṃ*] *n* (संचय S) A whole investment; the total quantity of merchandise (brought to market by one merchant). *mogge* 'sprout, bud' Rebus*: mũh* ingot' sal 'splinter' Rebus: sal 'workshop'

|||| Numeral 4: gaṇḍa 'four' Rebus: kaṇḍa 'furnace, fire-altar' (Santali) dula 'pair' Rebus: dul 'cast metal'

ḍāg mountain-ridge (H.)(CDIAL 5476). Rebus: dhangar 'blacksmith' (Maithili) *kamaḍha* 'crab' Rebus: *kammaṭa* 'mint, coiner'.
ḍato = claws of crab (Santali) Rebus: *dhātu* 'mineral ore'

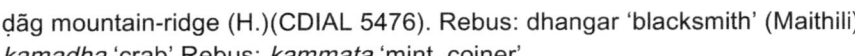

kanka 'rim of jar' Rebus: *karṇīka* 'account (scribe)' *karṇī* 'supercargo'
kəṭhā'r, kc. *kuṭhār* m. ' granary, storeroom '(WPah.)(CDIAL 3550). *koṭhārī m.* '

storekeeper' (Gujarati)(CDIAL 3551) Thus, storeroom (of) *kolom* 'three' Rebus: *kolami* 'smithy, forge'. Dula 'pair' Rebus: dul 'cast metal' Thus, together *dul kolami kuṭhār* 'metal smithy castings storeroom'

kanka 'rim of jar' Rebus: karṇīka 'account (scribe)' karṇī 'supercargo'

  *kanac* 'corner' Rebus: *kañcu* 'bronze'

K-24 a

Kalibangan 24a *खोंड [khōṇḍa] m A young bull, a bullcalf. (Marathi) Rebus: kōdār 'turner' (Bengali); कोंद kōnda 'engraver, lapidary setting or infixing gems' (Marathi) G. sãghāṛɔ m. 'lathe' ; संघाट joinery; M. sãgaḍ 'double-canoe' Rebus: sangataras. संगतराश lit. 'to collect stones, stone-cutter, mason.'*

सांड [sāṇḍa ] *f* (षद S) An outlet for superfluous water (as through a dam or mound); a sluice, a floodvent. Rebus: सांडणी [sāṇḍaṇī] *f* (H) An instrument of goldsmiths. It is hooked or curved at the extremity; and is used to draw things out of the fire. सांठा [*sāṇṭhā*] *m* (संचय S) A collection, heap, hoard, store, stock.साटें [*sāṭēṃ*] *n* (संचय S) A whole investment; the total quantity of merchandise (brought to market by one merchant).

kuṭila 'bent' CDIAL 3230 kuṭi— in cmpd. 'curve', *kuṭika—* 'bent' MBh. Rebus: *kuṭila, katthīl* = bronze (8 parts copper and 2 parts tin) PLUS ligature:
ḍhanga = a crook used for pulling down the branches of trees, for goats, sheep and camels (P.) Rebus:*ḍhangar* blacksmith'. sal 'splinter' Rebus: sal 'workshop'

meḍ 'body' Rebus: *meḍ* 'iron' (Ho.) काठी [kāṭhī] *f* (काष्ट S) 'frame or structure of the body' (Marathi) Rebus: खंडी [khaṇḍī] measure of weight (Marathi) *கண்டி; kaṇṭi, n. < Mhr. khaṇḍil. [T. Tu. khaṇḍi, M. kaṇḍi.]* Candy, a weight, stated to be roughly equivalent to 500 lbs.
PLUS खांडा [*khāṇḍā*] *m* A jag, notch, or indentation (as upon the edge of a tool or weapon). Rebus: *kāṇḍa* 'tools, pots and pans and metal-ware'

dula 'pair' Rebus: dul 'cast metal' *mogge* 'sprout, bud' Rebus: *mūh* 'ingot' (Santali) Thus, cast metal ingot.
kanka 'rim of jar' Rebus: karṇīka 'account (scribe)' karṇī 'supercargo'

m624A *खोंड [khōṇḍa] m A young bull, a bullcalf. (Marathi) Rebus: kõdār 'turner' (Bengali); कोंद kōnda 'engraver, lapidary setting or infixing gems' (Marathi) G. sãghāṛɔ m. 'lathe' ; संघाट joinery; M. sãgaḍ 'double-canoe' Rebus: sangataras. संगतराश lit. 'to collect stones, stone-cutter, mason.'*

सांड [sāṇḍa ] *f* (षद S) An outlet for superfluous water (as through a dam or mound); a sluice, a floodvent. Rebus: सांडणी [sāṇḍaṇī] *f* (H) An instrument of goldsmiths. It is hooked or curved at the extremity; and is used to draw things out of the fire.
सांठा [*sāṇṭhā*] *m* (संचय S) A collection, heap, hoard, store, stock.साटें [*sāṭēṃ*] *n* (संचय S) A whole investment; the total quantity of merchandise (brought to market by one merchant).

'Bow and arrow' sign hieroglyph 'Archer + bow + arrow' ligatured hieroglyph upraised arm: eraka 'upraised arm' Rebus: erako 'moltencast copper' *kamaḍha* 'archer, bow' Rebus: *kammaṭa* 'mint, coiner'.

cīmara 'black ant' Rebus: *cīmara* 'copper'. *cīmara kāra* -- ' coppersmith '

m837a *खोंड [khōṇḍa] m A young bull, a bullcalf. (Marathi) Rebus: kõdār 'turner' (Bengali); कोंद kōnda 'engraver, lapidary setting or infixing gems' (Marathi) G. sãghāṛɔ m. 'lathe' ; संघाट joinery; M. sãgaḍ 'double-canoe' Rebus: sangataras. संगतराश lit. 'to collect stones, stone-cutter, mason.'*

सांड [sāṇḍa] *f* (षद S) An outlet for superfluous water (as through a dam or mound); a sluice, a floodvent. Rebus: सांडणी [sāṇḍaṇī] *f* (H) An instrument of goldsmiths. It is hooked or curved at the extremity; and is used to draw things out of the fire.
सांठा [*sāṇṭhā*] *m* (संचय S) A collection, heap, hoard, store, stock.साटें [*sāṭēṃ*] *n* (संचय S) A whole investment; the total quantity of merchandise (brought to market by one merchant).

'Bow and arrow' sign hieroglyph 'Archer + bow + arrow' ligatured hieroglyph upraised arm: eraka 'upraised arm' Rebus: erako 'moltencast copper' *kamaḍha* 'archer, bow' Rebus: *kammaṭa* 'mint, coiner'.

kanka (Santali) *karṇika* 'scribe'(Sanskrit) Rebus: *karṇī,* supercargo for a boat shipment. INFIXED खांडा [*khāṇḍā*] *m* A jag, notch, or indentation (as upon the edge of a tool or weapon). Rebus: *kāṇḍa* 'tools, pots and pans and metal-ware'

notch+slanted stroke reads rebus: *ḍhālako kāṇḍa* 'ingot, tools, pots and pans and metal-ware'.*ḍhāḷ* 'a slope'; 'inclination of a plane' (G.); *ḍhāḷiyum* = adj. sloping, inclining (G.) Rebus: *ḍhālako* = a large metal ingot (G.) *ḍhālakī* = a metal heated and poured into a mould; a solid piece of metal; an ingot (Gujarati) PLUS खांडा [*khāṇḍā*] *m* A jag, notch, or indentation (as upon the edge of a tool or weapon). Rebus: *kāṇḍa* 'tools, pots and pans and metal-ware'

meḍ 'body' Rebus: *meḍ* 'iron' (Ho.) काठी [kāṭhī] *f* (काष्ट S) 'frame or structure of the body' (Marathi) Rebus: खंडी [khaṇḍī] measure of weight (Marathi) *கண்டி; kaṇṭi, n. < Mhr. khaṇḍil. [T. Tu. khaṇḍi, M. kaṇḍi.]* Candy, a weight, stated to be roughly equivalent to 500 lbs.

kanka 'rim of jar' Rebus: karṇīka 'account (scribe)' karṇī 'supercargo'

M-960 a

m960a *खोंड [khōṇḍa] m A young bull, a bullcalf. (Marathi) Rebus: kõdār 'turner' (Bengali); कोंद kōnda 'engraver, lapidary setting or infixing gems' (Marathi) G. sãghāṛɔ m. 'lathe' ; संघाट joinery; M. sãgaḍ 'double-canoe' Rebus: sangataras. संगतराश lit. 'to collect stones, stone-cutter, mason.'*

सांड [sāṇḍa] *f* (षद S) An outlet for superfluous water (as through a dam or mound); a sluice, a floodvent. Rebus: सांडणी [sāṇḍaṇī] *f* (H) An instrument of goldsmiths. It is hooked or curved at the extremity; and is used to draw things out of the fire.
सांठा [*sāṇṭhā*] *m* (संचय S) A collection, heap, hoard, store, stock.साटें [*sāṭēṃ*] *n* (संचय S) A whole investment; the total quantity of merchandise (brought to market by one merchant).
ranku 'liquid measure' Rebus: ranku 'tin'.

kanka 'rim of jar' Rebus: *karṇīka* 'account (scribe)' *karṇī* 'supercargo'

aya kammaṭa.'coiner, mint alloy'

कांड *kāṇḍa* 'arrow' Rebus: *kāṇḍa* 'pots and pans, metalware, tools'. Rebus 2: kaṇḍ 'fire-altar' (Santali)

M-1707 a

m1707a *खोंड [khōṇḍa] m A young bull, a bullcalf. (Marathi) Rebus: kõdār 'turner' (Bengali); कोंद kōnda 'engraver, lapidary setting or infixing gems' (Marathi) G. sãghāṛɔ m. 'lathe' ; संघाट joinery; M. sãgaḍ 'double-canoe' Rebus: sangataras. संगतराश lit. 'to collect stones, stone-cutter, mason.'*

सांड [sāṇḍa ] *f* (षद S) An outlet for superfluous water (as through a dam or mound); a sluice, a floodvent. Rebus: सांडणी [sāṇḍaṇī] *f* (H) An instrument of goldsmiths. It is hooked or curved at the extremity; and is used to draw things out of the fire.
सांठा [*sāṇṭhā*] *m* (संचय S) A collection, heap, hoard, store, stock.साटें [*sāṭēṃ*] *n* (संचय S) A whole investment; the total quantity of merchandise (brought to market by one merchant).

notch+slanted stroke reads rebus: *ḍhālako kāṇḍa* 'ingot, tools, pots and pans and metal-ware'.*dhāḷ* 'a slope'; 'inclination of a plane' (G.); *ḍhāḷiyum* = adj. sloping, inclining (G.) Rebus: *ḍhālako* = a large metal ingot (G.) *ḍhālakī* = a metal heated and poured into a mould; a solid piece of metal; an ingot (Gujarati) PLUS खांडा [*khāṇḍā*] *m* A jag, notch, or indentation (as upon the edge of a tool or weapon). Rebus: *kāṇḍa* 'tools, pots and pans and metal-ware'
dula 'two' Rebus: dul 'cast metal'

dula 'pair' Rebus: dul 'cast metal' *mogge* 'sprout, bud' Rebus: *mũh* 'ingot' (Santali) Thus, cast metal ingot.

|||| Numeral 4: gaṇḍa 'four' Rebus: kaṇḍa 'furnace, fire-altar' (Santali) dula 'pair' Rebus: dul 'cast metal'

Strands of yarn/rope' hieroglyph: Hieroglyph: 'strands of yarn' Rebus reading: *dhā'tu* 'strand of rope' Rebus: *dhatu* 'mineral ore' (Santali)

m742A *खोंड [khōṇḍa] m A young bull, a bullcalf. (Marathi) Rebus: kōdār 'turner' (Bengali); कोंद kōnda 'engraver, lapidary setting or infixing gems' (Marathi) G. sãghāṛɔ m. 'lathe' ; संघाट joinery; M. sāgaḍ 'double-canoe' Rebus: sangataras. संगतराश lit. 'to collect stones, stone-cutter, mason.'*

सांड [sāṇḍa] *f* (षद S) An outlet for superfluous water (as through a dam or mound); a sluice, a floodvent. Rebus: सांडणी [sāṇḍaṇī] *f* (H) An instrument of goldsmiths. It is hooked or curved at the extremity; and is used to draw things out of the fire.
सांठा [*sāṇṭhā*] *m* (संचय S) A collection, heap, hoard, store, stock.साटें [*sāṭēṃ*] *n* (संचय S) A whole investment; the total quantity of merchandise (brought to market by one merchant).

dhāḷ 'a slope'; 'inclination of a plane' (G.); *ḍhāḷiyum* = adj. sloping, inclining (G.) Rebus: *ḍhālako* = a large metal ingot (G.) *ḍhālakī* = a metal heated and poured into a mould; a solid piece of metal; an ingot (Gujarati) PLUS खांडा [*khāṇḍā*] *m* A jag, notch, or indentation (as upon the edge of a tool or weapon). Rebus: *kāṇḍa* 'tools, pots and pans and metal-ware' Thus, the pair of sign hieroglyphs from r. read rebus: copper, bronze ingots, metalware castings.
dula 'two' Rebus: dul 'cast metal'

kanac 'corner' Rebus: *kañcu* 'bronze'

meḍ 'body' Rebus: *meḍ* 'iron' (Ho.) काठी [kāṭhī] *f* (काष्ट S) 'frame or structure of the body' (Marathi) Rebus: खंडी [khaṇḍī] measure of weight (Marathi) *கண்டி; kaṇṭi, n. < Mhr. khaṇḍil. [T. Tu. khaṇḍi, M. kaṇḍi.]* Candy, a weight, stated to be roughly equivalent to 500 lbs.

m1262a

सांड [sāṇḍa] *f* (षद S) An outlet for superfluous water (as through a dam or mound); a sluice, a floodvent. Rebus: सांडणी [sāṇḍaṇī] *f* (H) An instrument of goldsmiths. It is hooked or curved at the extremity; and is used to draw things out of the fire. सांठा [*sāṇṭhā*] *m* (संचय S) A collection, heap, hoard, store, stock.साटें [*sāṭēṃ*] *n* (संचय S) A whole investment; the total quantity of merchandise (brought to market by one merchant). DUPLICATED: dula 'pair' Rebus: dul 'cast metal' Thus cast metal collection.
dulo 'hole' Rebus: dul 'cast metal' PLUS *kamaḍha* 'crab' Rebus: *kammaṭa* 'mint, coiner'. *ḍato* = claws of crab (Santali) Rebus: *dhātu* 'mineral ore' Thus, mint mineral castings.

 *kanka* 'rim of jar' Rebus: *karṇīka* 'account (scribe)' *karṇī* 'supercargo' PLUS infixed: kolom 'three' Rebus: kolami 'smithy, forge'. PLUS खांडा [*khāṇḍā*] *m* A jag, notch, or indentation (as upon the edge of a tool or weapon). Rebus: *kāṇḍa* 'tools, pots and pans and metal-ware.

|||| Numeral 4: gaṇḍa 'four' Rebus: kaṇḍa 'furnace, fire-altar' (Santali)

 *kolmo* 'paddy plant' Rebus: *kolami* 'smithy, forge' Vikalpa: *mogge* 'sprout, bud' Rebus: *mũh* 'ingot' (Santali) dolu 'plant of shoot height' Rebus: dul 'cast metal'

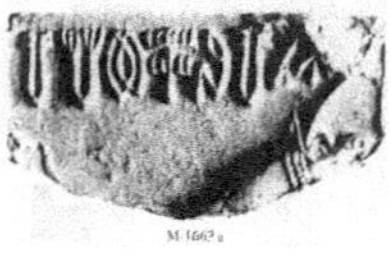

m1663a खोंड [khōṇḍa] m A young bull, a bullcalf. (Marathi) Rebus: kõdār 'turner' (Bengali); कोंद kōnda 'engraver, lapidary setting or infixing gems' (Marathi) G. sãghāṛɔ m. 'lathe' ; संघाट joinery; M. sāgaḍ 'double-canoe' Rebus: sangataras. संगतराश lit. 'to collect stones, stone-cutter, mason.'

 water-carrier hieroglyph *kuṭi*; Rebus: *kuṭhi* 'smelter furnace'.

 'Arrow' sign hieroglyph (variant) This is a ligature of 'lid of pot' hieroglyph superscript on 'a linear stroke' numeral hieroglyph.*aḍaren* 'cover of pot or lid' Rebus: *aduru* 'native, unsmelted metal' PLUS koḍ = one (Santali); koḍ 'workshop' (Gujarati)

 *kanka* 'rim of jar' Rebus: *karṇīka* 'account (scribe)' *karṇī* 'supercargo'

 *baraḍo* = spine; backbone (Tulu) Rebus: *baran, bharat* 'mixed alloys' (5 copper, 4 zinc and 1 tin) (Punjabi)

 *aḍar* 'harrow'; rebus: *aduru* 'native unsmelted metal'

 dula 'pair' Rebus: dul 'cast metal'. Thus native metal castings.
dula 'pair' Rebus: *dul* 'cast (metal)' PLUS*kana, kanac* = corner (Santali); Rebus: *kañcu* = bronze (Telugu) Thus, cast bronze.

 *dula* 'pair' Rebus: dul 'cast metal' *mogge* 'sprout, bud' Rebus: *mũh* 'ingot' (Santali) Thus, cast metal ingot.

kanka 'rim of jar' Rebus: karṇīka 'account (scribe)' karṇī 'supercargo'

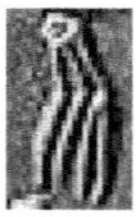 'Strands' sign hieroglyph

m183A *खोंड [khōṇḍa] m A young bull, a bullcalf. (Marathi) Rebus: kõdār 'turner' (Bengali); कोंद kōnda 'engraver, lapidary setting or infixing gems' (Marathi) G. sãghāṛɔ m. 'lathe' ; संघाट joinery; M. sāgaḍ 'double-canoe' Rebus: sangataras. संगतराश lit. 'to collect stones, stone-cutter, mason.'*

  Strands of yarn/rope' hieroglyph: Hieroglyph: 'strands of yarn' Rebus reading: *dhā́tu* 'strand of rope' Rebus: *dhatu* 'mineral ore' (Santali)

 *dhāḷ* ‘a slope’; ‘inclination of a plane’ (G.); *ḍhāḷiyum* = adj. sloping, inclining (G.) Rebus: *ḍhālako* = a large metal ingot (G.) *ḍhālakī* = a metal heated and poured into a mould; a solid piece of metal; an ingot (Gujarati) PLUS खांडा [*khāṇḍā*] *m* A jag, notch, or indentation (as upon the edge of a tool or weapon). Rebus: *kāṇḍa* ‘tools, pots and pans and metal-ware’ Thus, the pair of sign hieroglyphs from r. read rebus: copper, bronze ingots, metalware castings.
ayo ḍhālako ‘alloy metal ingot’

 कांड *kāṇḍa* ‘arrow’ Rebus: *kāṇḍa* ‘pots and pans, metalware, tools’. Rebus 2: kaṇḍ 'fire-altar' (Santali)

K-18 a

Kalibangan 18a *खोंड [khōṇḍa] m A young bull, a bullcalf. (Marathi) Rebus: kõdār ‘turner’ (Bengali); कोंद kōnda ‘engraver, lapidary setting or infixing gems’ (Marathi) G. sãghāṛɔ m. ‘lathe’ ; संघाट joinery; M. sãgaḍ ‘double-canoe’ Rebus: sangataras ‘stone-cutter, mason’*

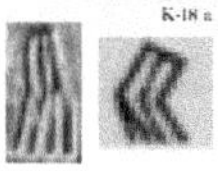 Strands of yarn/rope’ hieroglyph: Hieroglyph: ‘strands of yarn’ Rebus reading: *dhā´tu* ‘strand of rope’ Rebus: *dhatu* ‘mineral ore’ (Santali)

 *dula* ‘pair’ Rebus: dul ‘cast metal’ *mogge* ‘sprout, bud’ Rebus: *mũh* ‘ingot’ (Santali) Thus, cast metal ingot. INFIXED dulo ‘hole’ Rebus: dul ‘cast metal’ sal ‘splinter’ Rebus: sal ‘workshop’

 ḍãg mountain-ridge (H.)(CDIAL 5476). Rebus: dhangar ‘blacksmith’ (Maithili)

  *loa* ‘ficus religiosa’ Rebus: *lo* ‘iron’ (Sanskrit) PLUS unique ligatures: लोखंड [lōkhaṇḍa] *n* (लोह S) Iron. लोखंडाचे चणे खावविणें or चारणें To oppress grievously.लोखंडकाम [lōkhaṇḍakāma] *n* Iron work; that portion (of a building, machine &c.) which consists of iron. 2 The business of an ironsmith.लोखंडी [lōkhaṇḍī] *a* (लोखंड) Composed of iron; relating to iron. (Marathi) *bhaṭa* ‘warrior’ (Sanskrit) Rebus: *baṭa* a kind of iron (Gujarati). Rebus: *bhaṭa* ‘furnace’ (Santali) Thus, together, th ligatured hieroglyph reads rebus: *loa bhaṭa* ‘iron furnace’

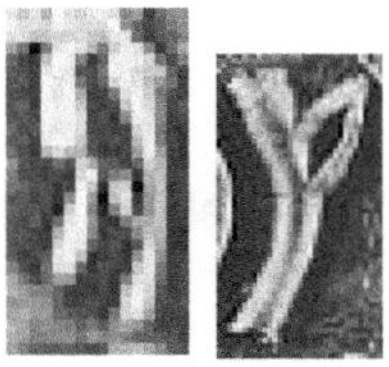 ‘Curved or bent line’ PLUS slanted stroke PLUS slanted notch ligatured sign hieroglyph Variant: ‘bent line’ ligatured with bud?

M-1902 a

 m1902a *khũṭ* ‘zebu’ Rebus: ‘(native metal) guild’
This triplet of sign hieroglyphs combine to read rebus: ‘bent line’ Rebus: *kuṭila* ‘bronze’ PLUS *ḍhālako* = large metal ingots AS WELL AS *kāṇḍa* ‘tools, pots and pans and metal-ware’ supercargo:*kanka* ‘rim of jar’

Rebus: *karṇīka* 'account (scribe)' *karṇī* 'supercargo' (consisting of):
kuṭila 'bent' CDIAL 3230 *kuṭi—* in cmpd. 'curve', *kuṭika—* 'bent' MBh. Rebus: *kuṭila, katthīl* = bronze (8 parts copper and 2 parts tin) cf. āra-kūṭa, 'brass' (Sanskrit)

Hieroglyphs: slanted stroke + notch: Read in context, the composite hieroglyph is assumed to be a combination of a slanted stroke ligatured to a notch,which provide possible rebus readings of a smithy/forge: notch+slanted stroke reads rebus: *ḍhālako kāṇḍa* 'ingots, pots and pans, metalware, tools'

dhāḷ 'a slope'; 'inclination of a plane' (Gujarati); *ḍhāḷiyum* = adj. sloping, inclining (Gujarati) Rebus: *ḍhālako* = a large metal ingot (Gujarati) *ḍhālakī* = a metal heated and poured into a mould; a solid piece of metal; an ingot (Gujarati)PLUS खांडा [*khāṇḍā*] *m* A jag, notch, or indentation (as upon the edge of a tool or weapon). Rebus: *kāṇḍa* 'tools, pots and pans and metal-ware'

ranku 'liquid measure' Rebus: ranku 'tin'
| *koḍa* = one (Santali); *koḍ* 'workshop' (Gujarati)
kuṭi 'water-carrier' Rebus: kuṭhi 'smelter/furnace'.

C-12a

Chanhudaro 12a खोंड [khōṇḍa] m A young bull, a bullcalf. (Marathi) Rebus: kõdār 'turner' (Bengali); कोंद kōnda 'engraver, lapidary setting or infixing gems' (Marathi) G. sãghāṛɔ m. 'lathe' ; संघाट joinery; M. sãgaḍ 'double-canoe' Rebus: sangataras. संगतराश lit. 'to collect stones, stone-cutter, mason.'

kuṭila 'bent'  CDIAL 3230 kuṭi— in cmpd. 'curve', *kuṭika—* 'bent' MBh. Rebus: *kuṭila, katthīl* = bronze (8 parts copper and 2 parts tin)

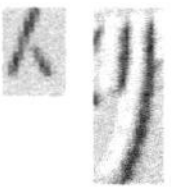

notch+slanted stroke reads rebus: *ḍhālako kāṇḍa* 'ingot, tools, pots and pans and metal-ware'.*dhāḷ* 'a slope'; 'inclination of a plane' (G.); *ḍhāḷiyum* = adj. sloping, inclining (G.) Rebus: *ḍhālako* = a large metal ingot (G.) *ḍhālakī* = a metal heated and poured into a mould; a solid piece of metal; an ingot (Gujarati) PLUS खांडा [*khāṇḍā*] *m* A jag, notch, or indentation (as upon the edge of a tool or weapon). Rebus: *kāṇḍa* 'tools, pots and pans and metal-ware'
kanka 'rim of jar' Rebus: karṇīka 'account (scribe)' karṇī 'supercargo'

| *koḍa* 'one' Rebus: *koḍ* 'workshop'
ranku 'liquid measure' Rebus: ranku 'tin'

kolmo 'paddy plant' Rebus: *kolami* 'smithy, forge' Vikalpa: *mogge* 'sprout, bud' Rebus: *mūh* 'ingot' (Santali) dolu 'plant of shoot height' Rebus: dul 'cast metal'

water-carrier hieroglyph *kuṭi*; Rebus: *kuṭhi* 'smelter furnace'.

m71A Read rebus for first two signs as at m1078A PLUS

kanka 'rim of jar' Rebus: karṇīka 'account (scribe)' karṇī 'supercargo' INFIXED kolom 'three' Rebus: kolamii 'smithy, forge' PLUS *ayo* 'fish' Rebus: *aya* 'iron' *ayas* 'metal' *aya kammaṭa*.'coiner, mint alloy'

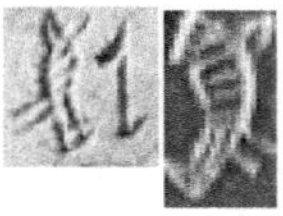

The pair of hieroglyph signs are compositions: bicha 'scorpion' (Assamese) Rebus: *bica* 'stone ore' (Santali) The pairing sign is a composition of: sloping stroke PLUS two short strokes of a 'splinter':*dhāḷ* 'a slope'; 'inclination of a plane' (Gujarati); *ḍhāḷiyum* = adj. sloping, inclining (Gujarati) Rebus: *ḍhālako* = a large metal ingot (Gujarati) *ḍhālakī* = a metal heated and poured into a mould; a solid piece of metal; an ingot (Gujarati)PLUS*sal* 'splinter' Rebus: *sal* 'workshop'. Thus the composition reads: *ḍhālako sal* 'ingot workshop'.

dāṭu 'cross'(Telugu) Rebus: *dhatu* 'mineral' (Santali).

kanka 'rim of jar' Rebus: *karṇīka* 'account (scribe)' *karṇī* 'supercargo'

M-1078 A bis

m1078A Zebu horns ligatured to a young bull. Thus a native metal smith guild PLUS turner, engraver. *खोंड [khōṇḍa] m A young bull, a bullcalf. (Marathi) Rebus: kõdār 'turner' (Bengali); कोंद kōnda 'engraver, lapidary setting or infixing gems' (Marathi) G. sãghāṛɔ m. 'lathe' ; संघाट joinery; M. sãgaḍ 'double-canoe' Rebus: sangataras. संगतराश lit. 'to collect stones, stone-cutter, mason.'*

kuṭila 'bent' CDIAL 3230 kuṭi— in cmpd. 'curve', *kuṭika*— 'bent' MBh. Rebus: *kuṭila, katthīl* = bronze (8 parts copper and 2 parts tin)

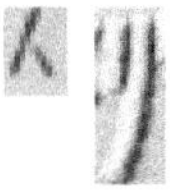

notch+slanted stroke reads rebus: *ḍhālako kāṇḍa* 'ingot, tools, pots and pans and metal-ware'.*dhāḷ* 'a slope'; 'inclination of a plane' (G.); *ḍhāḷiyum* = adj. sloping, inclining (G.) Rebus: *ḍhālako* = a large metal ingot (G.) *ḍhālakī* = a metal heated and poured into a mould; a solid piece of metal; an ingot (Gujarati) PLUS खांडा [*khāṇḍā*] *m* A jag, notch, or indentation (as upon the edge of a tool or weapon). Rebus: *kāṇḍa* 'tools, pots and pans and metal-ware'

kanka (Santali) *karṇika* 'scribe'(Sanskrit) Rebus: *karṇī,* supercargo for a boat shipment. INFIXED खांडा [*khāṇḍā*] *m* A jag, notch, or indentation (as upon the edge of a tool or weapon). Rebus: *kāṇḍa* 'tools, pots and pans and metal-ware' *āra* 'six' Rebus: *āra* 'brass' PLUS sal 'splinter' Rebus: sal 'workshop'

loa 'ficus religiosa' Rebus: *lo* 'iron' (Sanskrit) PLUS unique ligatures: लोखंड [lōkhaṇḍa] *n* (लोह S) Iron. लोखंडाचे चणे खावविणें or चारणें To oppress grievously.लोखंडकाम [lōkhaṇḍakāma] *n* Iron work; that portion (of a building, machine &c.) which consists of iron. 2 The business of an ironsmith.लोखंडी [lōkhaṇḍī] *a* (लोखंड) Composed of iron; relating to iron. (Marathi)

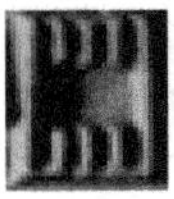

kəṭhā´r, kc. *kuṭhār* m. ' granary, storeroom '(WPah.)(CDIAL 3550). *koṭhārī m.* ' storekeeper' (Gujarati)(CDIAL 3551) Thus, storeroom (of) *kolom* 'three' Rebus: *kolami* 'smithy, forge'. Dula 'pair' Rebus: dul 'cast metal' Thus, together *dul kolami kuṭhār* 'metal smithy castings storeroom'

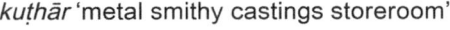

m0257A Text 2314 *khũṭ* 'zebu' Rebus: '(native metal) guild'

Super cargo of cast metal, bronze worksho
kuṭila 'bent' CDIAL 3230 kuṭi— in cmpd. 'curve', *kuṭika*— 'bent' MBh.
Rebus: *kuṭila, katthīl* = bronze (8 parts copper and 2 parts tin) [cf. āra-kūṭa, 'brass'

(Sanskrit)
Read in context, the composite hieroglyph is assumed to be a combination of a slanted stroke ligatured to a notch,which provide possible rebus readings of a smithy/forge: notch+slanted stroke reads rebus: *ḍhālako kāṇḍa* 'ingot, tools, pots and pans and metal-ware'

dhāḷ 'a slope'; 'inclination of a plane' (Gujarati); *ḍhāḷiyum* = adj. sloping, inclining (Gujarati) Rebus: *ḍhālako* = a large metal ingot (Gujarati) *ḍhālakī* = a metal heated and poured into a mould; a solid piece of metal; an ingot (Gujarati) PLUS खांडा [*khāṇḍā*] *m* A jag, notch, or indentation (as upon the edge of a tool or weapon). Rebus: *kāṇḍa* 'tools, pots and pans and metal-ware'

kanka 'rim of jar' Rebus: *karṇīka* 'account (scribe)' *karṇī* 'supercargo'
dula 'pair' Rebus: dul 'cast metal'

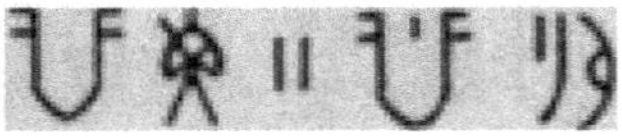

m1114 m1114a Text 2441*khũṭ* 'zebu' Rebus: '(native metal) guild': Text message: Brass workshop; metalware workshop supercargo; iron furnace supercargo.

kuṭila 'bent' CDIAL 3230 kuṭi— in cmpd. 'curve', *kuṭika*— 'bent' MBh. Rebus: *kuṭila, katthīl* = bronze (8 parts copper and 2 parts tin) [cf. *āra-kūṭa*, 'brass' (Sanskrit)]

Read in context, the composite hieroglyph is assumed to be a combination of a slanted stroke ligatured to a notch,which provide possible rebus readings of a smithy/forge: notch+slanted stroke reads rebus: *ḍhālako kāṇḍa* 'ingot, tools, pots and pans and metal-ware'

dhāḷ 'a slope'; 'inclination of a plane' (Gujarati); *ḍhāḷiyum* = adj. sloping, inclining (Gujarati) Rebus: *ḍhālako* = a large metal ingot (Gujarati) *ḍhālakī* = a metal heated and poured into a mould; a solid piece of metal; an ingot (Gujarati) PLUS खांडा [*khāṇḍā*] *m* A jag, notch, or indentation (as upon the edge of a tool or weapon). Rebus: *kāṇḍa* 'tools, pots and pans and metal-ware'

Ligatured hieroglyph: rim of jar + notch:

kanka 'rim of jar' Rebus: *karṇīka* 'account (scribe)' *karṇī* 'supercargo' PLUS infixed hieroglyph 'notch' Rebus: *kāṇḍa* 'pots and pans, metalware, tools'. Thus, the composite hieroglyph denotes supercargo of metalware.
sal 'splinter' Rebus: *sal* 'workshop'

loa 'ficus religiosa' Rebus: *lo* 'iron' (Sanskrit) PLUS unique ligatures: लोखंड [lōkhaṇḍa] *n* (लोह S) Iron. लोखंडाचे चणे खावविणें or चारणें To oppress grievously.लोखंडकाम [lōkhaṇḍakāma] *n* Iron work; that portion (of a building, machine &c.) which consists of iron. 2 The business of an ironsmith.लोखंडी [lōkhaṇḍī

] *a* (लोखंड) Composed of iron; relating to iron. (Marathi) *bhaṭa* 'warrior' (Sanskrit) Rebus: *baṭa* a kind of iron (Gujarati). Rebus: *bhaṭa* 'furnace' (Santali) Thus, together, th ligatured hieroglyph reads rebus: *loa bhaṭa* 'iron furnace'

kanka 'rim of jar' Rebus: *karṇīka* 'account (scribe)' *karṇī* 'supercargo' PLUS infixed hieroglyph 'notch' Rebus: *kāṇḍa* 'pots and pans, metalware, tools'.

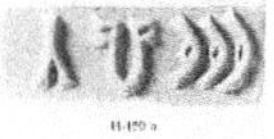

h150a

kuṭila 'bent' CDIAL 3230 kuṭi— in cmpd. 'curve', *kuṭika*— 'bent' MBh. Rebus: *kuṭila, katthīl* = bronze (8 parts copper and 2 parts tin) TRIPLICATED: kolom 'three' Rebus: kolami 'smithy, forge'

kanka 'rim of jar' Rebus: *karṇīka* 'account (scribe)' *karṇī* 'supercargo'

Variant:

notch+slanted stroke reads rebus: *ḍhālako kāṇḍa* 'ingot, tools, pots and pans and metal-ware'.*dhāḷ* 'a slope'; 'inclination of a plane' (G.); *ḍhāḷiyum* = adj. sloping, inclining (G.) Rebus: *ḍhālako* = a large metal ingot (G.) *ḍhālakī* = a metal heated and poured into a mould; a solid piece of metal; an ingot (Gujarati) PLUS खांडा [*khāṇḍā*] *m* A jag, notch, or indentation (as upon the edge of a tool or weapon). Rebus: *kāṇḍa* 'tools, pots and pans and metal-ware'

m1975a

kuṭila 'bent' CDIAL 3230 kuṭi— in cmpd. 'curve', *kuṭika*— 'bent' MBh. Rebus: *kuṭila, katthīl* = bronze (8 parts copper and 2 parts tin)

cīmara 'black ant' Rebus: *cīmara* 'copper'. *cīmara kāra* -- ' coppersmith '

ranku 'liquid measure' Rebus: ranku 'tin' PLUS sal 'splinter' Rebus: sal 'workshop'

dula 'pair' Rebus: dul 'cast metal' *mogge* 'sprout, bud' Rebus: *mũh* 'ingot' (Santali) Thus, cast metal ingot.

kanka 'rim of jar' Rebus: *karṇīka* 'account (scribe)' *karṇī* 'supercargo'

m165a *खोंड [khōṇḍa] m A young bull, a bullcalf. (Marathi) Rebus: kõdār 'turner' (Bengali); कोंद kōnda 'engraver, lapidary setting or infixing gems' (Marathi) G. sãghāṛɔ m. 'lathe' ; संघाट joinery; M. sãgaḍ 'double-canoe' Rebus: sangataras. संगतराश lit. 'to collect stones, stone-cutter, mason.'*

kuṭila 'bent' CDIAL 3230 kuṭi— in cmpd. 'curve', *kuṭika*— 'bent' MBh. Rebus: *kuṭila, katthīl* = bronze (8 parts copper and 2 parts tin)

m966a *खोंड [khōṇḍa] m A young bull, a bullcalf. (Marathi) Rebus: kõdār 'turner' (Bengali); कोंद kōnda 'engraver, lapidary setting or infixing gems' (Marathi) G. sãghāṛɔ m. 'lathe' ; संघाट joinery; M. sãgaḍ 'double-canoe' Rebus: sangataras. संगतराश lit. 'to collect stones, stone-cutter, mason.'*

 *kuṭila* 'bent' CDIAL 3230 kuṭi— in cmpd. 'curve', *kuṭika—* 'bent' MBh. Rebus: *kuṭila, katthīl* = bronze (8 parts copper and 2 parts tin)

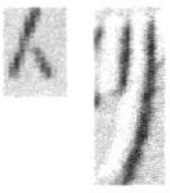 notch+slanted stroke reads rebus: *ḍhālako kāṇḍa* 'ingot, tools, pots and pans and metal-ware'.*dhāḷ* 'a slope'; 'inclination of a plane' (G.); *ḍhāḷiyum* = adj. sloping, inclining (G.) Rebus: *ḍhālako* = a large metal ingot (G.) *ḍhālakī* = a metal heated and poured into a mould; a solid piece of metal; an ingot (Gujarati) PLUS खांडा [*khāṇḍā*] *m* A jag, notch, or indentation (as upon the edge of a tool or weapon). Rebus: *kāṇḍa* 'tools, pots and pans and metal-ware'

kanka 'rim of jar' Rebus: karṇīka 'account (scribe)' karṇī 'supercargo'

 Circumscript: sal 'splinter' Rebus: sal 'workshop' PLUS count of four: |||| Numeral 4: *gaṇḍa* 'four' Rebus: *kaṇḍa* 'furnace, fire-altar' (Santali).INFIXED | *koḍa* 'one' Rebus: *koḍ* 'workshop'

 *kanka* 'rim of jar' Rebus: *karṇīka* 'account (scribe)' *karṇī* 'supercargo'

M-369 a

m369A

kuṭila 'bent' CDIAL  3230 kuṭi— in cmpd. 'curve', *kuṭika—* 'bent' MBh. Rebus: *kuṭila, katthīl* = bronze (8 parts copper and 2 parts tin)

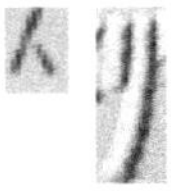 notch+slanted stroke reads rebus: *ḍhālako kāṇḍa* 'ingot, tools, pots and pans and metal-ware'.*dhāḷ* 'a slope'; 'inclination of a plane' (G.); *ḍhāḷiyum* = adj. sloping, inclining (G.) Rebus: *ḍhālako* = a large metal ingot (G.) *ḍhālakī* = a metal heated and poured into a mould; a solid piece of metal; an ingot (Gujarati) PLUS खांडा [*khāṇḍā*] *m* A jag, notch, or indentation (as upon the edge of a tool or weapon). Rebus: *kāṇḍa* 'tools, pots and pans and metal-ware'

 *kanka* 'rim of jar' Rebus: *karṇīka* 'account (scribe)' *karṇī* 'supercargo'
INFIXED sal 'splinter' Rebus: sal 'workshop'

 *dula* 'pair' Rebus: *dul* 'cast (metal)' PLUS*kana, kanac* = corner (Santali); Rebus: *kañcu* = bronze (Telugu) PLUS infixed kolmo 'paddy plant' Rebus: kolami 'smithy, forge'. Thus, cast bronze smithy, forge. Or, *mogge* 'sprout, bud' Rebus: *mũh* 'ingot' (Santali)Thus, cast bronze ingot. Read as: *kañcu dul mũh 'bronze cast ingot'*

 *aḍar* 'harrow'; rebus: *aduru* 'native unsmelted metal'
ayo 'fish' Rebus: *aya* 'iron' *ayas* 'metal'

aya kammaṭa.'coiner, mint alloy'

 The pair of hieroglyph signs are compositions: bicha 'scorpion' (Assamese) Rebus: *bica* 'stone ore' (Santali) The pairing sign is a composition of: sloping stroke PLUS two short strokes of a 'splinter':*dhāḷ* 'a slope'; 'inclination of a plane' (Gujarati); *ḍhāḷiyum* = adj. sloping, inclining (Gujarati) Rebus: *ḍhālako* = a large metal ingot (Gujarati) *ḍhālakī* = a metal heated and poured into a mould; a solid piece of metal; an ingot (Gujarati)PLUS*sal* 'splinter' Rebus: *sal* 'workshop'. Thus the composition reads: *ḍhālako sal* 'ingot workshop'.

 *dāṭu* 'cross'(Telugu) Rebus: *dhatu* 'mineral' (Santali).

 *kanka* 'rim of jar' Rebus: *karṇīka* 'account (scribe)' *karṇī* 'supercargo'

m247a *balad* m. ' ox ', gng. *bald*, (Ku.) *barad*, id. (N. Tarai) Rebus: *bharat* (5 copper, 4 zinc and 1 tin)(Punjabi) *pattar* 'trough' Rebus*: pattar* 'guild'. Thus, copper-zinc-tin alloy (worker) guild.

 *kuṭila* 'bent' CDIAL 3230 kuṭi— in cmpd. 'curve', *kuṭika*— 'bent' MBh. Rebus: *kuṭila, katthīl* = bronze (8 parts copper and 2 parts tin)

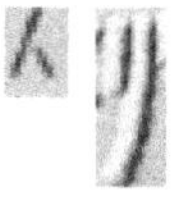 notch+slanted stroke reads rebus: *ḍhālako kāṇḍa* 'ingot, tools, pots and pans and metal-ware'.*dhāḷ* 'a slope'; 'inclination of a plane' (G.); *ḍhāḷiyum* = adj. sloping, inclining (G.) Rebus: *ḍhālako* = a large metal ingot (G.) *ḍhālakī* = a metal heated and poured into a mould; a solid piece of metal; an ingot (Gujarati) PLUS खांडा [*khāṇḍā*] *m* A jag, notch, or indentation (as upon the edge of a tool or weapon). Rebus: *kāṇḍa* 'tools, pots and pans and metal-ware'

 *kanka* 'rim of jar' Rebus: *karṇīka* 'account (scribe)' *karṇī* 'supercargo'
|||| Numeral 4: gaṇḍa 'four' Rebus: kaṇḍa 'furnace, fire-altar' (Santali)
||| Numeral three: kolom 'three' Rebus: kolami 'smithy, forge'

 *kolmo* 'paddy plant' Rebus: *kolami* 'smithy, forge' Vikalpa: *mogge* 'sprout, bud' Rebus: *mũh* 'ingot' (Santali) dolu 'plant of shoot height' Rebus: dul 'cast metal'

m1360a

 *kuṭila* 'bent' CDIAL 3230 kuṭi— in cmpd. 'curve', *kuṭika*— 'bent' MBh. Rebus: *kuṭila, katthīl* = bronze (8 parts copper and 2 parts tin)

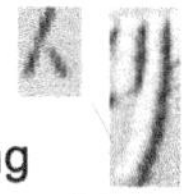 notch+slanted stroke reads rebus: *ḍhālako kāṇḍa* 'ingot, tools, pots and pans and metal-ware'.*dhāḷ* 'a slope'; 'inclination of a plane' (G.); *ḍhāḷiyum* = adj. sloping, inclining (G.) Rebus: *ḍhālako* = a large metal ingot (G.) *ḍhālakī* = a metal heated and poured into a mould; a solid piece of metal; an ingot (Gujarati) PLUS खांडा [*khāṇḍā*] *m* A jag, notch, or indentation (as upon the edge of a tool or weapon). Rebus: *kāṇḍa* 'tools, pots and pans and metal-ware'

 *kanka* 'rim of jar' Rebus: *karṇīka* 'account (scribe)' *karṇī* 'supercargo' INFIXED खांडा [*khāṇḍā*] *m* A jag, notch, or indentation (as upon the edge of a tool or weapon). Rebus: *kāṇḍa* 'tools, pots and pans and metal-ware'
|||| Numeral 4: gaṇḍa 'four' Rebus: kaṇḍa 'furnace, fire-altar' (Santali)
||| Numeral three: kolom 'three' Rebus: kolami 'smithy, forge'

ranku 'liquid measure' Rebus: ranku 'tin'

Lothal 217A

 *kuṭila* 'bent' CDIAL 3230 kuṭi— in cmpd. 'curve', *kuṭika—* 'bent' MBh. Rebus: *kuṭila, katthīl* = bronze (8 parts copper and 2 parts tin)

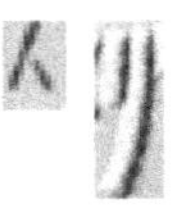 notch+slanted stroke reads rebus: *ḍhālako kāṇḍa* 'ingot, tools, pots and pans and metal-ware'.*dhāḷ* 'a slope'; 'inclination of a plane' (G.); *ḍhāḷiyum* = adj. sloping, inclining (G.) Rebus: *ḍhālako* = a large metal ingot (G.) *ḍhālakī* = a metal heated and poured into a mould; a solid piece of metal; an ingot (Gujarati) PLUS खांडा [*khāṇḍā*] *m* A jag, notch, or indentation (as upon the edge of a tool or weapon). Rebus: *kāṇḍa* 'tools, pots and pans and metal-ware'

 *āra* 'spokes' Rebus: *āra 'brass'.* cf. erka = ekke (Tbh. of arka) aka (Tbh. of arka) copper (metal); crystal (Kannada) Glyph: *eraka*'nave of wheel' Rebus: eraka 'copper'; cf. erka = ekke (Tbh. of arka) aka (Tbh. of arka) copper (metal); crystal (Kannada) *erako* 'moltencast copper' Duplicated: dula 'pair' Rebus: dul 'cast metal' Thus cast copper, brass casting.

 *kanka* 'rim of jar' Rebus: *karṇīka* 'account (scribe)' *karṇī* 'supercargo'

 m68a *खोंड [khōṇḍa] m A young bull, a bullcalf. (Marathi) Rebus: kõdār 'turner' (Bengali); कोंद kōnda 'engraver, lapidary setting or infixing gems' (Marathi) G. sãghārɔ m. 'lathe' ; संघाट joinery; M. sãgaḍ 'double-canoe' Rebus: sangataras. संगतराश lit. 'to collect stones, stone-cutter, mason.'*

 *kuṭila* 'bent' CDIAL 3230 kuṭi— in cmpd. 'curve', *kuṭika—* 'bent' MBh. Rebus: *kuṭila, katthīl* = bronze (8 parts copper and 2 parts tin)

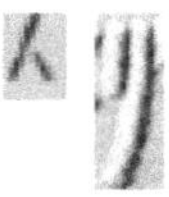 notch+slanted stroke reads rebus: *ḍhālako kāṇḍa* 'ingot, tools, pots and pans and metal-ware'.*dhāḷ* 'a slope'; 'inclination of a plane' (G.); *ḍhāḷiyum* = adj. sloping, inclining (G.) Rebus: *ḍhālako* = a large metal ingot (G.) *ḍhālakī* = a metal heated and poured into a mould; a solid piece of metal; an ingot (Gujarati) PLUS खांडा [*khāṇḍā*] *m* A jag, notch, or indentation (as upon the edge

 *kanka* 'rim of jar' Rebus: *karṇīka* 'account (scribe)' *karṇī* 'supercargo'

 *baraḍo* = spine; backbone (Tulu) Rebus: *baran, bharat* 'mixed alloys' (5 copper, 4 zinc and 1 tin) (Punjabi)

 *kanka* 'rim of jar' Rebus: *karṇīka* 'account (scribe)' *karṇī* 'supercargo'

 *meḍ* 'body' Rebus: *meḍ* 'iron' (Ho.) काठी [kāṭhī] *f* (काष्ट S) 'frame or structure of the body' (Marathi) Rebus: खंडी [khaṇḍī] measure of weight (Marathi) *கண்டி; kaṇṭi, n. < Mhr. khaṇḍil. [T. Tu. khaṇḍi, M. kaṇḍi.]* Candy, a weight, stated to be roughly equivalent to 500 lbs.

 beads: Pa. kandi (pl. -l) necklace, beads. Ga. (Punjabi) kandi (pl. -l) bead, (pl.) necklace; (S.2) kandiṭ bead. (DEDR 1215) Rebus: *கண்டி; kaṇṭi, n. < Mhr. khaṇḍil. [T. Tu. khaṇḍi, M. kaṇḍi.] 1. Candy, a weight, stated to be roughly equivalent to 500 lbs.; பாரமென்னும் நிறையளவு.* खंडीगणती or खंडोगणती [khaṇḍīgaṇatī or khaṇḍōgaṇatī] *ad* By candies; counting or

reckoning by candies. खंडीवारी [khaṇḍīvārī] *ad* By scores, heaps, candies. खंडी [khaṇḍī] Applied to a great quantity; as खंडीभर पोरें, खंडीभर मेंढ्या, खंडीभर काम, खंडीभर बोलतो-लिहितो&c PLUS superscript:

'Arrow' sign hieroglyph (variant) This is a ligature of 'lid of pot' hieroglyph superscript on 'a linear stroke' numeral hieroglyph.*aḍaren* 'cover of pot or lid' Rebus: *aduru* 'native, unsmelted metal' PLUS koḍ = one (Santali); koḍ 'workshop' (Gujarati)

Stylized representation of fire-altar: *gaṇḍa* 'four' sal 'splinter' Rebus: sal 'workshop''Rebus: *kaṇḍa* 'furnace, fire-altar' (Santali) Thus, fire-altar as the workplace of smiths and smelters or 'workshop' producing great quantities of castings.

M-1805 a

m1805a *खोंड [khōṇḍa] m A young bull, a bullcalf. (Marathi) Rebus: kõdār 'turner' (Bengali); कोंद kōnda 'engraver, lapidary setting or infixing gems' (Marathi) G. sãghāṛɔ m. 'lathe' ; संघाट joinery; M. sãgaḍ 'double-canoe' Rebus: sangataras. संगतराश lit. 'to collect stones, stone-cutter, mason.'*

kuṭila 'bent'  CDIAL 3230 kuṭi— in cmpd. 'curve', *kuṭika—* 'bent' MBh. Rebus: *kuṭila, katthīl* = bronze (8 parts copper and 2 parts tin)

notch+slanted stroke reads rebus: *ḍhālako kāṇḍa* 'ingot, tools, pots and pans and metal-ware'.*dhāḷ* 'a slope'; 'inclination of a plane' (G.); *ḍhāḷiyum* = adj. sloping, inclining (G.) Rebus: *ḍhālako* = a large metal ingot (G.) *ḍhālakī* = a metal heated and poured into a mould; a solid piece of metal; an ingot (Gujarati) PLUS खांडा [*khāṇḍā*] *m* A jag, notch, or indentation (as upon the edge of a tool or weapon). Rebus: *kāṇḍa* 'tools, pots and pans and metal-ware'

kanka 'rim of jar' Rebus: *karṇīka* 'account (scribe)' *karṇī* 'supercargo' INFIXED खांडा [*khāṇḍā*] *m* A jag, notch, or indentation (as upon the edge of a tool or weapon). Rebus: *kāṇḍa* 'tools, pots and pans and metal-ware'

ḍhanga = a crook used for pulling down the branches of trees, for goats, sheep and camels (P.) Rebus:*ḍhangar* blacksmith'.

kanka 'rim of jar' Rebus: karṇīka 'account (scribe)' karṇī 'supercargo'

m877a *खोंड [khōṇḍa] m A young bull, a bullcalf. (Marathi) Rebus: kõdār 'turner'*

M-877 a

(Bengali); कोंद kōnda 'engraver, lapidary setting or infixing gems' (Marathi) G. sãghāṛɔ m. 'lathe' ; संघाट joinery; M. sãgaḍ 'double-canoe' Rebus: sangataras. संगतराश lit. 'to collect stones, stone-cutter, mason.'

kuṭila 'bent' CDIAL 3230 kuṭi— in cmpd. 'curve', *kuṭika—* 'bent' MBh. Rebus: *kuṭila, katthīl* = bronze (8 parts copper and 2 parts tin)

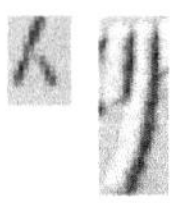

notch+slanted stroke reads rebus: *ḍhālako kāṇḍa* 'ingot, tools, pots and pans and metal-ware'.*dhāḷ* 'a slope'; 'inclination of a plane' (G.); *ḍhāḷiyum* = adj. sloping, inclining (G.) Rebus: *ḍhālako* = a large metal ingot (G.) *ḍhālakī* = a metal heated and poured into a mould; a solid piece of metal; an ingot (Gujarati) PLUS खांडा [*khāṇḍā*] *m* A jag, notch, or indentation (as upon the edge of a tool or weapon). Rebus: *kāṇḍa* 'tools, pots and pans and metal-ware'

 *kanka* 'rim of jar' Rebus: *karṇīka* 'account (scribe)' *karṇī* 'supercargo' INFIXED खांडा [*khāṇḍā*] *m* A jag, notch, or indentation (as upon the edge of a tool or weapon). Rebus: *kāṇḍa* 'tools, pots and pans and metal-ware'

ḍhanga = a crook used for pulling down the branches of trees, for goats, sheep and camels (P.) Rebus:*ḍhangar* blacksmith'.

| *koḍa* 'one' Rebus: *koḍ* 'workshop' Duplicated: dula 'pair' Rebus: dul 'cast metal' Thus cast metal workshop. INFIXED *ayo* 'fish' Rebus: *aya* 'iron' *ayas* 'metal' Thus, workshop for ayas metal castings.

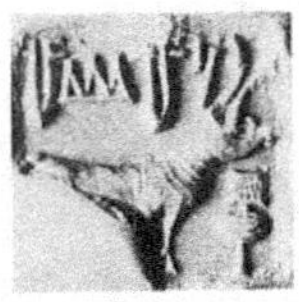

M-870 a

m870a *खोंड [khōṇḍa] m A young bull, a bullcalf. (Marathi) Rebus: kõdār 'turner' (Bengali); कोंद kōnda 'engraver, lapidary setting or infixing gems' (Marathi) G. sãghāṛɔ m. 'lathe' ; संघाट joinery; M. sãgaḍ 'double-canoe' Rebus: sangataras. संगतराश lit. 'to collect stones, stone-cutter, mason.'*

 *kuṭila* 'bent' CDIAL 3230 kuṭi— in cmpd. 'curve', *kuṭika*— 'bent' MBh. Rebus: *kuṭila, katthīl* = bronze (8 parts copper and 2 parts tin)

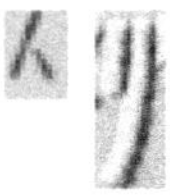 notch+slanted stroke reads rebus: *ḍhālako kāṇḍa* 'ingot, tools, pots and pans and metal-ware'.*dhāḷ* 'a slope'; 'inclination of a plane' (G.); *ḍhāḷiyum* = adj. sloping, inclining (G.) Rebus: *ḍhālako* = a large metal ingot (G.) *ḍhālakī* = a metal heated and poured into a mould; a solid piece of metal; an ingot (Gujarati)

 *kanka* 'rim of jar' Rebus: *karṇīka* 'account (scribe)' *karṇī* 'supercargo'

 ḍãg mountain-ridge (H.)(CDIAL 5476). Rebus: dhangar 'blacksmith' (Maithili)

kanka 'rim of jar' Rebus: karṇīka 'account (scribe)' karṇī 'supercargo'

M-105 a

m105a *खोंड [khōṇḍa] m A young bull, a bullcalf. (Marathi) Rebus: kõdār 'turner' (Bengali); कोंद kōnda 'engraver, lapidary setting or infixing gems' (Marathi) G. sãghāṛɔ m. 'lathe' ; संघाट joinery; M. sãgaḍ 'double-canoe' Rebus: sangataras. संगतराश lit. 'to collect stones, stone-cutter, mason.'*

 *kuṭila* 'bent' CDIAL 3230 kuṭi— in cmpd. 'curve', *kuṭika*— 'bent' MBh. Rebus: *kuṭila, katthīl* = bronze (8 parts copper and 2 parts tin)

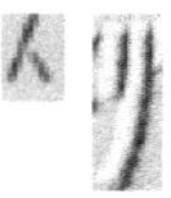 notch+slanted stroke reads rebus: *ḍhālako kāṇḍa* 'ingot, tools, pots and pans and metal-ware'.*dhāḷ* 'a slope'; 'inclination of a plane' (G.); *ḍhāḷiyum* = adj. sloping, inclining (G.) Rebus: *ḍhālako* = a large metal ingot (G.) *ḍhālakī* = a metal heated and poured into a mould; a solid piece of metal; an ingot (Gujarati)

kanka 'rim of jar' Rebus: *karṇīka* 'account (scribe)' *karṇī* 'supercargo' PLUS INFIXED sal 'splinter' Rebus: sal 'workshop'.

aya kāṇḍa 'alloy metalware'

dula 'pair' Rebus: *dul* 'cast (metal)' PLUS *kana, kanac* = corner (Santali); Rebus: *kañcu* = bronze (Telugu) PLUS infixed kolmo 'paddy plant' Rebus: kolami 'smithy, forge'. Thus, cast bronze smithy, forge. Or, *mogge* 'sprout, bud' Rebus: *mũh* 'ingot' (Santali)Thus, cast bronze ingot. Read as: *kañcu dul mũh 'bronze cast ingot'*

kanka 'rim of jar' Rebus: *karṇīka* 'account (scribe)' *karṇī* 'supercargo'

Ligature: two peaks: mēḍu height, rising ground, hillock (Kannada) Rebus: *meḍ* 'iron' (Ho.) dula 'pair' Rebus: dul 'cast metal' PLUS खांडा [*khāṇḍā*] *m* A jag, notch, or indentation (as upon the edge of a tool or weapon). Rebus: *kāṇḍa* 'tools, pots and pans and metal-ware'

M-709 A

m709A *खोंड [khōṇḍa] m A young bull, a bullcalf. (Marathi) Rebus: kõdār 'turner' (Bengali); कोंद kōnda 'engraver, lapidary setting or infixing gems' (Marathi) G. sãghāṛɔ m. 'lathe' ; संघाट joinery; M. sãgaḍ 'double-canoe' Rebus: sangataras. संगतराश lit. 'to collect stones, stone-cutter, mason.'*

kuṭila 'bent' CDIAL 3230 kuṭi— in cmpd. 'curve', *kuṭika—* 'bent' MBh. Rebus: *kuṭila, katthīl* = bronze (8 parts copper and 2 parts tin)

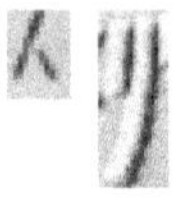

notch+slanted stroke reads rebus: *ḍhālako kāṇḍa* 'ingot, tools, pots and pans and metal-ware'.*dhāl* 'a slope'; 'inclination of a plane' (G.); *ḍhāḷiyum* = adj. sloping, inclining (G.) Rebus: *ḍhālako* = a large metal ingot (G.) *ḍhālakī* = a metal heated and poured into a mould; a solid piece of metal; an ingot (Gujarati) PLUS खांडा [*khāṇḍā*] *m* A jag, notch, or indentation (as upon the edge of a tool or weapon). Rebus: *kāṇḍa* 'tools, pots and pans and metal-ware'

kanka 'rim of jar' Rebus: *karṇīka* 'account (scribe)' *karṇī* 'supercargo' INFIXED खांडा [*khāṇḍā*] *m* A jag, notch, or indentation (as upon the edge of a tool or weapon). Rebus: *kāṇḍa* 'tools, pots and pans and metal-ware'

ḍhanga = a crook used for pulling down the branches of trees, for goats, sheep and camels (P.) Rebus:*ḍhangar* blacksmith'.

खांडा [*khāṇḍā*] *m* A jag, notch, or indentation (as upon the edge of a tool or weapon). Rebus: *kāṇḍa* 'tools, pots and pans and metal-ware' PLUS *bhaṭa* 'warrior' (Sanskrit) Rebus: *baṭa* a kind of iron (Gujarati). Rebus: *bhaṭa* 'furnace' (Santal

kanka 'rim of jar' Rebus: karṇīka 'account (scribe)' karṇī 'supercargo'

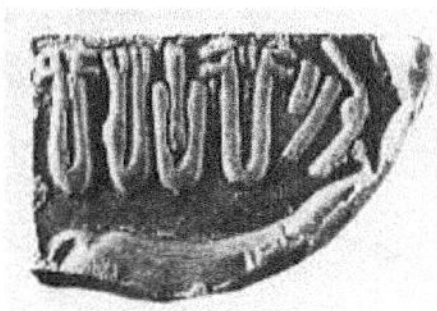

M-754 a

m754a *खोंड [khōṇḍa] m A young bull, a bullcalf. (Marathi) Rebus: kõdār 'turner' (Bengali); कोंद kōnda 'engraver, lapidary setting or infixing gems' (Marathi) G. sãghāṛɔ m. 'lathe' ; संघाट joinery; M. sãgaḍ 'double-canoe' Rebus: sangataras 'stone-cutter, mason'*

kuṭila 'bent' CDIAL 3230 kuṭi— in cmpd. 'curve', *kuṭika—* 'bent' MBh. Rebus: *kuṭila, katthīl* = bronze (8 parts copper and 2 parts tin)

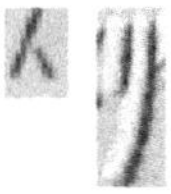

notch+slanted stroke reads rebus: *ḍhālako kāṇḍa* 'ingot, tools, pots and pans and metal-ware'.*dhāḷ* 'a slope'; 'inclination of a plane' (G.); *ḍhāḷiyum* = adj. sloping, inclining (G.) Rebus: *ḍhālako* = a large metal ingot (G.) *ḍhālakī* = a metal heated and poured into a mould; a solid piece of metal; an ingot (Gujarati)

kanka 'rim of jar' Rebus: *karṇīka* 'account (scribe)' *karṇī* 'supercargo' PLUS INFIXED sal 'splinter' Rebus: sal 'workshop'.

muka 'ladle' (Tamil)(DEDR 4887) Rebus: *mũh* 'ingot' (Santali) *baṭa* = rimless pot (Kannada) Rebus:) *baṭa* = a kind of iron (G.)) *bhaṭa* furnace (Gujarati) Thus, iron ingot.

dula 'pair' Rebus: dul 'cast metal' *mogge* 'sprout, bud' Rebus: *mũh* 'ingot' (Santali) Thus, cast metal ingot.

kanka 'rim of jar' Rebus: karṇīka 'account (scribe)' karṇī 'supercargo'

m854A *खोंड [khōṇḍa] m A young bull, a bullcalf. (Marathi) Rebus: kõdār 'turner' (Bengali); कोंद kōnda 'engraver, lapidary setting or infixing gems' (Marathi) G. sãghāṛɔ m. 'lathe' ; संघाट joinery; M. sãgaḍ 'double-canoe' Rebus: sangataras. संगतराश lit. 'to collect stones, stone-cutter, mason.'*

kuṭila 'bent' CDIAL 3230 kuṭi— in cmpd. 'curve', *kuṭika—* 'bent' MBh. Rebus: *kuṭila, katthīl* = bronze (8 parts copper and 2 parts tin)

notch+slanted stroke reads rebus: *ḍhālako kāṇḍa* 'ingot, tools, pots and pans and metal-ware'.*dhāḷ* 'a slope'; 'inclination of a plane' (G.); *ḍhāḷiyum* = adj. sloping, inclining (G.) Rebus: *ḍhālako* = a large metal ingot (G.) *ḍhālakī* = a metal heated and poured into a mould; a solid piece of metal; an ingot (Gujarati) PLUS खांडा [*khāṇḍā*] *m* A jag, notch, or indentation (as upon the edge of a tool or weapon). Rebus: *kāṇḍa* 'tools, pots and pans and metal-ware'

kanka 'rim of jar' Rebus: *karṇīka* 'account (scribe)' *karṇī* 'supercargo' INFIXED खांडा [*khāṇḍā*] *m* A jag, notch, or indentation (as upon the edge of a tool or weapon). Rebus: *kāṇḍa* 'tools, pots and pans and metal-ware'
Circumscript: Numeral 4: gaṇḍa 'four' Rebus: kaṇḍa 'furnace, fire-altar' (Santali) PLUS ranku 'liquid measure' Rebus: ranku 'tin'

h39a *खोंड [khōṇḍa] m A young bull, a bullcalf. (Marathi) Rebus: kõdār 'turner' (Bengali); कोंद kōnda 'engraver, lapidary setting or infixing gems' (Marathi) G. sãghāṛɔ m. 'lathe' ; संघाट joinery; M. sãgaḍ 'double-canoe' Rebus: sangataras. संगतराश lit. 'to collect stones, stone-cutter, mason.'*

 *kuṭila* 'bent' CDIAL 3230 kuṭi— in cmpd. 'curve', *kuṭika—* 'bent' MBh. Rebus: *kuṭila, katthīl* = bronze (8 parts copper and 2 parts tin)

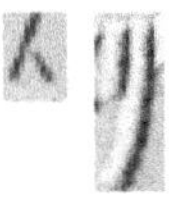 notch+slanted stroke reads rebus: *ḍhālako kāṇḍa* 'ingot, tools, pots and pans and metal-ware'.*dhāḷ* 'a slope'; 'inclination of a plane' (G.); *ḍhāḷiyum* = adj. sloping, inclining (G.) Rebus: *ḍhālako* = a large metal ingot (G.) *ḍhālakī* = a metal heated and poured into a mould; a solid piece of metal; an ingot (Gujarati) PLUS खांडा [*khāṇḍā*] *m* A jag, notch, or indentation (as upon the edge of a tool or weapon). Rebus: *kāṇḍa* 'tools, pots and pans and metal-ware'

 *kanka* 'rim of jar' Rebus: *karṇīka* 'account (scribe)' *karṇī* 'supercargo' INFIXED खांडा [*khāṇḍā*] *m* A jag, notch, or indentation (as upon the edge of a tool or weapon). Rebus: *kāṇḍa* 'tools, pots and pans and metal-ware'

aya aḍaren (homonym: aduru)'alloy native metal'

aya kammaṭa.'coiner, mint alloy'

ayo ḍhālako 'alloy metal ingot'

ranku 'liquid measure' Rebus: ranku 'tin'

 *kolmo* 'paddy plant' Rebus: *kolami* 'smithy, forge' Vikalpa: *mogge* 'sprout, bud' Rebus: *mũh* 'ingot' (Santali) dolu 'plant of shoot height' Rebus: dul 'cast metal'

kanka 'rim of jar' Rebus: karṇīka 'account (scribe)' karṇī 'supercargo'

M-1790 a

m1790a *खोंड [khōṇḍa] m A young bull, a bullcalf. (Marathi) Rebus: kõdār 'turner' (Bengali); कोंद kōnda 'engraver, lapidary setting or infixing gems' (Marathi) G. sãghāṛɔ m. 'lathe' ; संघाट joinery; M. sãgaḍ 'double-canoe' Rebus: sangataras. संगतराश lit. 'to collect stones, stone-cutter, mason.'*

 *kuṭila* 'bent' CDIAL 3230 kuṭi— in cmpd. 'curve', *kuṭika—* 'bent' MBh. Rebus: *kuṭila, katthīl* = bronze (8 parts copper and 2 parts tin)

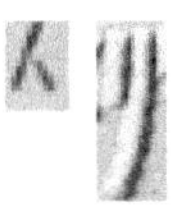 notch+slanted stroke reads rebus: *ḍhālako kāṇḍa* 'ingot, tools, pots and pans and metal-ware'.*dhāḷ* 'a slope'; 'inclination of a plane' (G.); *ḍhāḷiyum* = adj. sloping, inclining (G.) Rebus: *ḍhālako* = a large metal ingot (G.) *ḍhālakī* = a metal heated and poured into a mould; a solid piece of metal; an ingot (Gujarati) PLUS खांडा [*khāṇḍā*] *m* A jag, notch, or indentation (as upon the edge of a tool or weapon). Rebus: *kāṇḍa* 'tools, pots and pans and metal-ware'

 *kanka* 'rim of jar' Rebus: *karṇīka* 'account (scribe)' *karṇī* 'supercargo' INFIXED खांडा [*khāṇḍā*] *m* A jag, notch, or indentation (as upon the edge of a tool or weapon). Rebus: *kāṇḍa* 'tools, pots and pans and metal-ware'

Circumscript: Numeral 4: gaṇḍa 'four' Rebus: kaṇḍa 'furnace, fire-altar' (Santali) PLUS ranku 'liquid measure' Rebus: ranku 'tin'

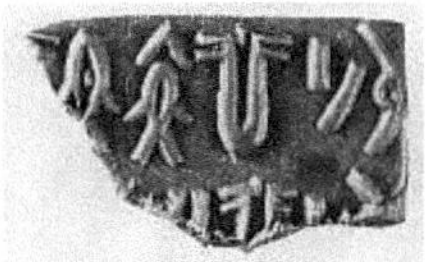

M-1190 a

m1190a

 *kuṭila* 'bent' CDIAL 3230 kuṭi— in cmpd. 'curve', *kuṭika—* 'bent' MBh. Rebus: *kuṭila, katthīl* = bronze (8 parts copper and 2 parts tin)

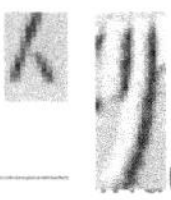 notch+slanted stroke reads rebus: *ḍhālako kāṇḍa* 'ingot, tools,

pots and pans and metal-ware'.*dhāḷ* 'a slope'; 'inclination of a plane' (G.); *ḍhāḷiyum* = adj. sloping, inclining (G.) Rebus: *ḍhālako* = a large metal ingot (G.) *ḍhālakī* = a metal heated and poured into a mould; a solid piece of metal; an ingot (Gujarati) PLUS खांडा [*khāṇḍā*] *m* A jag, notch, or indentation (as upon the edge of a tool or weapon). Rebus: *kāṇḍa* 'tools, pots and pans and metal-ware'

kanka 'rim of jar' Rebus: *karṇīka* 'account (scribe)' *karṇī* 'supercargo' INFIXED खांडा [*khāṇḍā*] *m* A jag, notch, or indentation (as upon the edge of a tool or weapon). Rebus: *kāṇḍa* 'tools, pots and pans and metal-ware'

aya kāṇḍa 'alloy metalware'
aya aḍaren (homonym: aduru)'alloy native metal'

Line 2 illegible. Excepting for 'rim-of-jar' INFIXED 'notch' as read rebus on Line 1.

m326A *खोंड [khōṇḍa] m A young bull, a bullcalf. (Marathi) Rebus: kōdār 'turner' (Bengali); कोंद kōnda 'engraver, lapidary setting or infixing gems' (Marathi) G. sãghāṛɔ m. 'lathe' ; संघाट joinery; M. sãgaḍ 'double-canoe' Rebus: sangataras. संगतराश lit. 'to collect stones, stone-cutter, mason.'*

kuṭila 'bent' CDIAL 3230 kuṭi— in cmpd. 'curve', *kuṭika*— 'bent' MBh. Rebus: *kuṭila, katthīl* = bronze (8 parts copper and 2 parts tin)

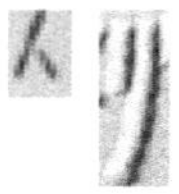

notch+slanted stroke reads rebus: *ḍhālako kāṇḍa* 'ingot, tools, pots and pans and metal-ware'.*dhāḷ* 'a slope'; 'inclination of a plane' (G.); *ḍhāḷiyum* = adj. sloping, inclining (G.) Rebus: *ḍhālako* = a large metal ingot (G.) *ḍhālakī* = a metal heated and poured into a mould; a solid piece of metal; an ingot (Gujarati) PLUS खांडा [*khāṇḍā*] *m* A jag, notch, or indentation (as upon the edge of a tool or weapon). Rebus: *kāṇḍa* 'tools, pots and pans and metal-ware'

kanka 'rim of jar' Rebus: *karṇīka* 'account (scribe)' *karṇī* 'supercargo' INFIXED खांडा [*khāṇḍā*] *m* A jag, notch, or indentation (as upon the edge of a tool or weapon). Rebus: *kāṇḍa* 'tools, pots and pans and metal-ware'
ayo 'fish' Rebus: *aya* 'iron' *ayas* 'metal'

kuṭila 'bent' CDIAL 3230 kuṭi— in cmpd. 'curve', *kuṭika*— 'bent' MBh. Rebus: *kuṭila, katthīl* = bronze (8 parts copper and 2 parts tin) Duplicated: dula 'pair' Rebus: dul 'cast metal' Thus, cast bronze.
kanka 'rim of jar' Rebus: karṇīka 'account (scribe)' karṇī 'supercargo'

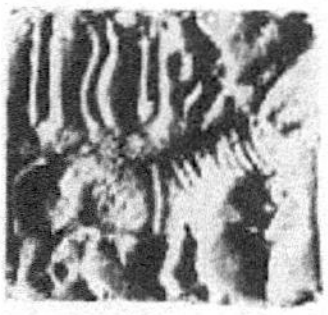

M-974 a

m974a *खोंड [khōṇḍa] m A young bull, a bullcalf. (Marathi) Rebus: kōdār 'turner' (Bengali); कोंद kōnda 'engraver, lapidary setting or infixing gems' (Marathi) G. sãghāṛɔ m. 'lathe' ; संघाट joinery; M. sãgaḍ 'double-canoe' Rebus: sangataras. संगतराश lit. 'to collect stones, stone-cutter, mason.'*

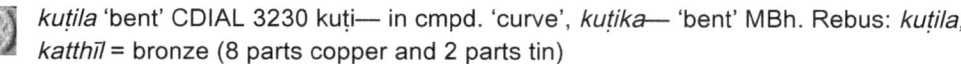

kuṭila 'bent' CDIAL 3230 kuṭi— in cmpd. 'curve', *kuṭika*— 'bent' MBh. Rebus: *kuṭila, katthīl* = bronze (8 parts copper and 2 parts tin)

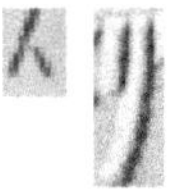 notch+slanted stroke reads rebus: *ḍhālako kāṇḍa* 'ingot, tools, pots and pans and metal-ware'.*dhāḷ* 'a slope'; 'inclination of a plane' (G.); *ḍhāḷiyum* = adj. sloping, inclining (G.) Rebus: *ḍhālako* = a large metal ingot (G.) *ḍhālakī* = a metal heated and poured into a mould; a solid piece of metal; an ingot (Gujarati) PLUS खांडा [*khāṇḍā*] *m* A jag, notch, or indentation (as upon the edge of a tool or weapon). Rebus: *kāṇḍa* 'tools, pots and pans and metal-ware'

 *kanka* 'rim of jar' Rebus: *karṇīka* 'account (scribe)' *karṇī* 'supercargo' INFIXED खांडा [*khāṇḍā*] *m* A jag, notch, or indentation (as upon the edge of a tool or weapon). Rebus: *kāṇḍa* 'tools, pots and pans and metal-ware'

 *kuṭila* 'bent' CDIAL 3230 kuṭi— in cmpd. 'curve', *kuṭika*— 'bent' MBh. Rebus: *kuṭila, katthīl* = bronze (8 parts copper and 2 parts tin) Duplicated: dula 'pair' Rebus: dul 'cast metal' Thus, cast bronze.

kanka 'rim of jar' Rebus: karṇīka 'account (scribe)' karṇī 'supercargo'

M-971 a

m971a *खोंड [khōṇḍa] m A young bull, a bullcalf. (Marathi) Rebus: kõdār 'turner' (Bengali); कोंद kōnda 'engraver, lapidary setting or infixing gems' (Marathi) G. sãghāṛɔ m. 'lathe' ; संघाट joinery; M. sāgaḍ 'double-canoe' Rebus: sangataras. संगतराश lit. 'to collect stones, stone-cutter, mason.'*

 *kuṭila* 'bent' CDIAL 3230 kuṭi— in cmpd. 'curve', *kuṭika*— 'bent' MBh. Rebus: *kuṭila, katthīl* = bronze (8 parts copper and 2 parts tin)

 notch+slanted stroke reads rebus: *ḍhālako kāṇḍa* 'ingot, tools, pots and pans and metal-ware'.*dhāḷ* 'a slope'; 'inclination of a plane' (G.); *ḍhāḷiyum* = adj. sloping, inclining (G.) Rebus: *ḍhālako* = a large metal ingot (G.) *ḍhālakī* = a metal heated and poured into a mould; a solid piece of metal; an ingot (Gujarati) PLUS खांडा [*khāṇḍā*] *m* A jag, notch, or indentation (as upon the edge of a tool or weapon). Rebus: *kāṇḍa* 'tools, pots and pans and metal-ware'

 *kanka* 'rim of jar' Rebus: *karṇīka* 'account (scribe)' *karṇī* 'supercargo' INFIXED खांडा [*khāṇḍā*] *m* A jag, notch, or indentation (as upon the edge of a tool or weapon). Rebus: *kāṇḍa* 'tools, pots and pans and metal-ware'

 *aḍar* 'harrow'; rebus: *aduru* 'native unsmelted metal'
Duplicated: dula 'pair' Rebus: dul 'cast metal' Thus native metal castings.

kanka 'rim of jar' Rebus: karṇīka 'account (scribe)' karṇī 'supercargo'

m113a *खोंड [khōṇḍa] m A young bull, a bullcalf. (Marathi) Rebus: kõdār 'turner' (Bengali); कोंद kōnda 'engraver, lapidary setting or infixing gems' (Marathi) G. sãghāṛɔ m. 'lathe' ; संघाट joinery; M. sāgaḍ 'double-canoe' Rebus: sangataras. संगतराश lit. 'to collect stones, stone-cutter, mason.'*

 *kuṭila* 'bent' CDIAL 3230 kuṭi— in cmpd. 'curve', *kuṭika*— 'bent' MBh. Rebus: *kuṭila, katthīl* = bronze (8 parts copper and 2 parts tin)

 notch+slanted stroke reads rebus: *ḍhālako kāṇḍa* 'ingot, tools, pots and pans and metal-ware'.*dhāḷ* 'a slope'; 'inclination of a plane' (G.); *ḍhāḷiyum* = adj. sloping, inclining (G.) Rebus: *ḍhālako* = a large metal ingot (G.) *ḍhālakī* = a metal heated and

poured into a mould; a solid piece of metal; an ingot (Gujarati) PLUS खांडा [*khāṇḍā*] *m* A jag, notch, or indentation (as upon the edge of a tool or weapon). Rebus: *kāṇḍa* 'tools, pots and pans and metal-ware'

kanka 'rim of jar' Rebus: *karṇīka* 'account (scribe)' *karṇī* 'supercargo' INFIXED खांडा [*khāṇḍā*] *m* A jag, notch, or indentation (as upon the edge of a tool or weapon). Rebus: *kāṇḍa* 'tools, pots and pans and metal-ware'

dula 'pair' Rebus: *dul* 'cast (metal)' PLUS*kana, kanac* = corner (Santali); Rebus: *kañcu* = bronze (Telugu) Thus, cast bronze.

dula 'two' Rebus: dul 'cast metal'

kanka 'rim of jar' Rebus: karṇīka 'account (scribe)' karṇī 'supercargo'

Lothal 28a *खोंड [khōṇḍa] m A young bull, a bullcalf. (Marathi) Rebus: kõdār 'turner' (Bengali); कोंद kōnda 'engraver, lapidary setting or infixing gems' (Marathi) G. sãghāṛɔ m. 'lathe' ; संघाट joinery; M. sãgaḍ 'double-canoe' Rebus: sangataras. संगतराश lit. 'to collect stones, stone-cutter, mason.'*

kuṭila 'bent' CDIAL 3230 kuṭi— in cmpd. 'curve', *kuṭika*— 'bent' MBh. Rebus: *kuṭila, katthīl* = bronze (8 parts copper and 2 parts tin)

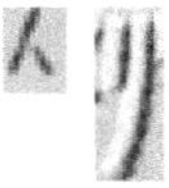
notch+slanted stroke reads rebus: *ḍhālako kāṇḍa* 'ingot, tools, pots and pans and metal-ware'.*dhāḷ* 'a slope'; 'inclination of a plane' (G.); *ḍhāḷiyum* = adj. sloping, inclining (G.) Rebus: *ḍhālako* = a large metal ingot (G.) *ḍhālakī* = a metal heated and poured into a mould; a solid piece of metal; an ingot (Gujarati) PLUS खांडा [*khāṇḍā*] *m* A jag, notch, or indentation (as upon the edge of a tool or weapon). Rebus: *kāṇḍa* 'tools, pots and pans and metal-ware'

kanka 'rim of jar' Rebus: *karṇīka* 'account (scribe)' *karṇī* 'supercargo' INFIXED खांडा [*khāṇḍā*] *m* A jag, notch, or indentation (as upon the edge of a tool or weapon). Rebus: *kāṇḍa* 'tools, pots and pans and metal-ware'

ranku 'liquid measure' Rebus: ranku 'tin'

kolmo 'paddy plant' Rebus: *kolami* 'smithy, forge' Vikalpa: *mogge* 'sprout, bud' Rebus: *mũh* 'ingot' (Santali) dolu 'plant of shoot height' Rebus: dul 'cast metal'

kanka 'rim of jar' Rebus: karṇīka 'account (scribe)' karṇī 'supercargo'

h2128A

H-2128 A

H-2128 B

kuṭila 'bent' CDIAL 3230 kuṭi— in cmpd. 'curve', *kuṭika*— 'bent' MBh. Rebus: *kuṭila, katthīl* = bronze (8 parts copper and 2 parts tin)

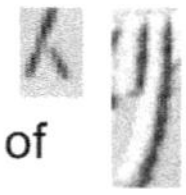
notch+slanted stroke reads rebus: *ḍhālako kāṇḍa* 'ingot, tools, pots and pans and metal-ware'.*dhāḷ* 'a slope'; 'inclination of a plane' (G.); *ḍhāḷiyum* = adj.

sloping, inclining (G.) Rebus: *ḍhālako* = a large metal ingot (G.) *ḍhālakī* = a metal heated and poured into a mould; a solid piece of metal; an ingot (Gujarati) PLUS खांडा [*khāṇḍā*] *m* A jag, notch, or indentation (as upon the edge of a tool or weapon). Rebus: *kāṇḍa* 'tools, pots and pans and metal-ware'

kanka 'rim of jar' Rebus: *karṇīka* 'account (scribe)' *karṇī* 'supercargo' INFIXED खांडा [*khāṇḍā*] *m* A jag, notch, or indentation (as upon the edge of a tool or weapon). Rebus: *kāṇḍa* 'tools, pots and pans and metal-ware'

muka 'ladle' (Tamil)(DEDR 4887) Rebus: *mũh* 'ingot' (Santali) *baṭa* = rimless pot (Kannada) Rebus:) *baṭa* = a kind of iron (G.)) *bhaṭa* furnace (Gujarati)

water-carrier hieroglyph *kuṭi*; Rebus: *kuṭhi* 'smelter furnace'.

mēḍu height, rising ground, hillock (Kannada) Rebus: *meḍ* 'iron' (Ho.) kolom 'three' Rebus: kolami 'smithy, forge' Thus, *meḍ kolami* 'iron smithy-forge'

ranku 'liquid measure' Rebus: ranku 'tin'

meḍ 'body' Rebus: *meḍ* 'iron' (Ho.) काठी [kāṭhī] *f* (काष्ट S) 'frame or structure of the body' (Marathi) Rebus: खंडी [khaṇḍī] measure of weight (Marathi) கண்டி; *kaṇṭi, n. < Mhr. khaṇḍil. [T. Tu. khaṇḍi, M. kaṇḍi.]* Candy, a weight, stated to be roughly equivalent to 500 lbs.

meḍ 'body' Rebus: *meḍ* 'iron' (Ho.) PLUS | *koḍa* 'one' Rebus: *koḍ* 'workshop'

ayo 'fish' Rebus: *aya* 'iron' *ayas* 'metal'

h89A *ibha* 'elephant' Rebus: *ib* 'iron' *ibbo* 'merchant' (Gujarati) First 3 signs read rebus as m755a PLUS *aya kammaṭa.*'coiner, mint alloy' *aya kāṇḍa* 'alloy metalware'

m647a First 3 signs read rebus as m755a PLUS *ayo* 'fish' Rebus: *aya* 'iron' *ayas* 'metal' *aya aḍaren (homonym: aduru)*'alloy native metal'
bhaṭa 'warrior' (Sanskrit) Rebus: *baṭa* a kind of iron (Gujarati). Rebus: *bhaṭa* 'furnace' (Santali)

kanka 'rim of jar' Rebus: karṇīka 'account (scribe)' karṇī 'supercargo'

M-1757 a

m1757a First 3 signs read rebus as m755a PLUS *aya kammaṭa.*'coiner, mint alloy'

|||| Numeral 4: gaṇḍa 'four' Rebus: kaṇḍa 'furnace, fire-altar' (Santali)
dula 'pair' Rebus: dul 'cast metal'

mēḍu height, rising ground, hillock (Kannada) Rebus: *mẽṛhẽt, meḍ* 'iron' (Munda.Ho.)

kaṇḍo 'stool, seat' Rebus: *kāṇḍa* 'metalware' *kaṇḍa* 'fire-altar'

m59a First 3 signs read rebus as m755a PLUS kolom 'three' Rebus: kolami 'smithy, forge'

koḍi 'flag' (Ta.)(DEDR 2049). Rebus 1: *koḍ* 'workshop' (Kuwi) Rebus 2: *khōḍ* m. 'pit', *khōḍü* f. 'small pit' (Kashmiri. CDIAL 3947).

m1672a First 3 signs read rebus as m755a PLUS kolom 'three' Rebus: kolami 'smithy, forge'

ayo 'fish' Rebus: *aya* 'iron' *ayas* 'metal'

कांड *kāṇḍa* 'arrow' Rebus: *kāṇḍa* 'pots and pans, metalware, tools'. Rebus 2: kaṇḍ 'fire-altar' (Santali)

m755a *खोंड [khōṇḍa] m A young bull, a bullcalf. (Marathi) Rebus: kōdār 'turner' (Bengali); कोंद kōnda 'engraver, lapidary setting or infixing gems' (Marathi) G. sãghāṛɔ m. 'lathe' ; संघाट joinery; M. sãgaḍ 'double-canoe' Rebus: sangataras. संगतराश lit. 'to collect stones, stone-cutter, mason.'*

kuṭila 'bent' CDIAL 3230 kuṭi— in cmpd. 'curve', *kuṭika—* 'bent' MBh. Rebus: *kuṭila, katthīl* = bronze (8 parts copper and 2 parts tin)

notch+slanted stroke reads rebus: *ḍhālako kāṇḍa* 'ingot, tools, pots and pans and metal-ware'.*dhāḷ* 'a slope'; 'inclination of a plane' (G.); *ḍhāḷiyum* = adj. sloping, inclining (G.) Rebus: *ḍhālako* = a large metal ingot (G.) *ḍhālakī* = a metal heated and poured into a mould; a solid piece of metal; an ingot (Gujarati) PLUS खांडा [*khāṇḍā*] *m* A jag, notch, or indentation (as upon the edge of a tool or weapon). Rebus: *kāṇḍa* 'tools, pots and pans and metal-ware'

kanka 'rim of jar' Rebus: *karṇīka* 'account (scribe)' *karṇī* 'supercargo' INFIXED खांडा [*khāṇḍā*] *m* A jag, notch, or indentation (as upon the edge of a tool or weapon). Rebus: *kāṇḍa* 'tools, pots and pans and metal-ware'

loa 'ficus religiosa' Rebus: *lo* 'iron' (Sanskrit) PLUS unique ligatures: लोखंड [lōkhaṇḍa] *n* (लोह S) Iron. लोखंडाचे चणे खावविणें or चारणें To oppress grievously.लोखंडकाम [lōkhaṇḍakāma] *n* Iron work; that portion (of a building, machine &c.) which consists of iron. 2 The business of an ironsmith.लोखंडी [lōkhaṇḍī] *a* (लोखंड) Composed of iron; relating to iron. (Marathi)

Ligature: two peaks: mēḍu height, rising ground, hillock (Kannada) Rebus: *meḍ* 'iron' (Ho.) dula 'pair' Rebus: dul 'cast metal' PLUS |||| Numeral 4: gaṇḍa 'four' Rebus: kaṇḍa 'furnace, fire-altar' (Santali)

kanka 'rim of jar' Rebus: karṇīka 'account (scribe)' karṇī 'supercargo'

m387a

 *kuṭila* 'bent' CDIAL 3230 kuṭi— in cmpd. 'curve', *kuṭika*— 'bent' MBh. Rebus: *kuṭila, katthīl* = bronze (8 parts copper and 2 parts tin)

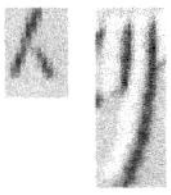 notch+slanted stroke reads rebus: *ḍhālako kāṇḍa* 'ingot, tools, pots and pans and metal-ware'.*dhāḷ* 'a slope'; 'inclination of a plane' (G.); *ḍhāḷiyum* = adj. sloping, inclining (G.) Rebus: *ḍhālako* = a large metal ingot (G.) *ḍhālakī* = a metal heated and poured into a mould; a solid piece of metal; an ingot (Gujarati) PLUS खांडा [*khāṇḍā*] *m* A jag, notch, or indentation (as upon the edge of a tool or weapon). Rebus: *kāṇḍa* 'tools, pots and pans and metal-ware'

 *kanka* 'rim of jar' Rebus: *karṇīka* 'account (scribe)' *karṇī* 'supercargo' INFIXED sal 'splinter' Rebus: sal 'workshop'

kamaḍha 'crab' Rebus: *kammaṭa* 'mint, coiner'.
ḍato = claws of crab (Santali) Rebus: *dhātu* 'mineral ore'
dula 'two' Rebus: dul 'cast metal'

Circumscript: Four strokes: gaṇḍa 'four' Rebus: kaṇḍa 'furnace, fire-altar' (Santali)PLUS *ayo* 'fish' Rebus: *aya* 'iron' *ayas* 'metal'

m820a Read rebus as at First three signs of m964A

m964A *खोंड [khōṇḍa] m A young bull, a bullcalf. (Marathi) Rebus: kõdār 'turner' (Bengali); कोंद kōnda 'engraver, lapidary setting or infixing gems' (Marathi) G. sãghāṛɔ m. 'lathe'; संघाट joinery; M. sãgaḍ 'double-canoe' Rebus: sangataras. संगतराश lit. 'to collect stones, stone-cutter, mason.'*

 *kuṭila* 'bent' CDIAL 3230 kuṭi— in cmpd. 'curve', *kuṭika*— 'bent' MBh. Rebus: *kuṭila, katthīl* = bronze (8 parts copper and 2 parts tin)

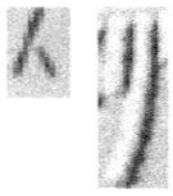 notch+slanted stroke reads rebus: *ḍhālako kāṇḍa* 'ingot, tools, pots and pans and metal-ware'.*dhāḷ* 'a slope'; 'inclination of a plane' (G.); *ḍhāḷiyum* = adj. sloping, inclining (G.) Rebus: *ḍhālako* = a large metal ingot (G.) *ḍhālakī* = a metal heated and poured into a mould; a solid piece of metal; an ingot (Gujarati) PLUS खांडा [*khāṇḍā*] *m* A jag, notch, or indentation (as upon the edge of a tool or weapon). Rebus: *kāṇḍa* 'tools, pots and pans and metal-ware'

 *kanka* 'rim of jar' Rebus: *karṇīka* 'account (scribe)' *karṇī* 'supercargo' INFIXED खांडा [*khāṇḍā*] *m* A jag, notch, or indentation (as upon the edge of a tool or weapon). Rebus: *kāṇḍa* 'tools, pots and pans and metal-ware'
kamaḍha 'crab' Rebus: *kammaṭa* 'mint, coiner'.
ḍato = claws of crab (Santali) Rebus: *dhātu* 'mineral ore'

 *dula* 'two, pair' Rebus: dul 'cast metal' PLUS *dhāḷ* 'a slope'; 'inclination of a plane' (G.); *ḍhāḷiyum* = adj. sloping, inclining (G.) Rebus: *ḍhālako* = a large metal ingot (G.) *ḍhālakī* = a metal heated and poured into a mould; a solid piece of metal; an ingot (Gujarati) PLUS kolom 'three' Rebus: kolami 'smithy, forge'. Thus cast metal ingot smithy.

Rakhigarhi 1A Read rebus for first 3 signs as at m964A PLUS

Ligature: two peaks: mēḍu height, rising ground, hillock (Kannada) Rebus: *meḍ* 'iron' (Ho.) dula 'pair' Rebus: dul 'cast metal' PLUS |||| Numeral 4: gaṇḍa 'four' Rebus: kaṇḍa 'furnace, fire-altar' (Santali)

dula 'pair' Rebus: dul 'cast metal' *mogge* 'sprout, bud' Rebus: *mũh* 'ingot' (Santali) Thus, cast metal ingot.
kanka 'rim of jar' Rebus: karṇīka 'account (scribe)' karṇī 'supercargo'

m292A,a
karāvu 'crocodile' (Telugu) Rebus: khara 'blacksmith' (Kashmiri)

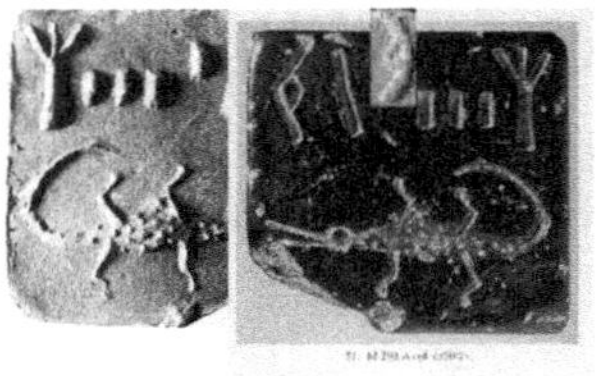

kuṭila 'bent' CDIAL 3230 kuṭi— in cmpd. 'curve', *kuṭika—* 'bent' MBh. Rebus: *kuṭila, katthīl* = bronze (8 parts copper and 2 parts tin)

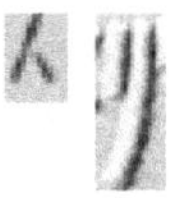

notch+slanted stroke reads rebus: *ḍhālako kāṇḍa* 'ingot, tools, pots and pans and metal-ware'.*ḍhāḷ* 'a slope'; 'inclination of a plane' (G.); *ḍhāḷiyum* = adj. sloping, inclining (G.) Rebus: *ḍhālako* = a large metal ingot (G.) *ḍhālakī* = a metal heated and poured into a mould; a solid piece of metal; an ingot (Gujarati) PLUS खांडा [*khāṇḍā*] *m* A jag, notch, or indentation (as upon the edge of a tool or weapon). Rebus: *kāṇḍa* 'tools, pots and pans and metal-ware'

kolom 'three' Rebus: kolami 'smithy, forge'

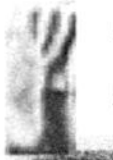

kolmo 'paddy plant' Rebus: *kolami* 'smithy, forge' Vikalpa: *mogge* 'sprout, bud' Rebus: *mũh* 'ingot' (Santali) dolu 'plant of shoot height' Rebus: dul 'cast metal'

h391a *खोंड [khōṇḍa] m A young bull, a bullcalf. (Marathi) Rebus: kõdār 'turner' (Bengali); कोंद kōnda 'engraver, lapidary setting or infixing gems' (Marathi) G. sãghāṛɔ m. 'lathe' ; संघाट joinery; M. sãgaḍ 'double-canoe' Rebus: sangataras. संगतराश lit. 'to collect stones, stone-cutter, mason.'*

kuṭila 'bent' CDIAL 3230 kuṭi— in cmpd. 'curve', *kuṭika—* 'bent' MBh. Rebus: *kuṭila, katthīl* = bronze (8 parts copper and 2 parts tin)

notch+slanted stroke reads rebus: *ḍhālako kāṇḍa* 'ingot, tools, pots and pans and metal-ware'.*ḍhāḷ* 'a slope'; 'inclination of a plane' (G.); *ḍhāḷiyum* = adj. sloping, inclining (G.) Rebus: *ḍhālako* = a large metal ingot (G.) *ḍhālakī* = a metal heated and poured into a mould; a solid piece of metal; an ingot (Gujarati) PLUS खांडा [*khāṇḍā*] *m* A jag, notch, or indentation (as upon the edge of a tool or weapon). Rebus: *kāṇḍa* 'tools, pots and pans and metal-ware'
aya aḍaren (homonym: aduru)'alloy native metal'
kaṇḍo 'stool, seat' Rebus: *kāṇḍa* 'metalware' *kaṇḍa* 'fire-altar'

mēḍu height, rising ground, hillock (Kannada) Rebus: *mẽṛhẽt, meḍ* 'iron' (Munda.Ho.) PLUS | *koḍa* 'one' Rebus: *koḍ* 'workshop'

kanka 'rim of jar' Rebus: karṇīka 'account (scribe)' karṇī 'supercargo'

Chanhudaro 11a *खोंड [khōṇḍa] m A young bull, a bullcalf. (Marathi) Rebus: kõdār 'turner' (Bengali); कोंद kōnda 'engraver, lapidary setting or infixing gems' (Marathi) G. sãghāṛɔ m. 'lathe' ; संघाट joinery; M. sãgaḍ 'double-canoe' Rebus: sangataras. संगतराश lit. 'to collect stones, stone-cutter, mason.'*

kuṭila  'bent' CDIAL 3230 kuṭi— in cmpd. 'curve', *kuṭika—* 'bent' MBh. Rebus: *kuṭila, katthīl* = bronze (8 parts copper and 2 parts tin)

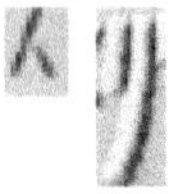 notch+slanted stroke reads rebus: *ḍhālako kāṇḍa* 'ingot, tools, pots and pans and metal-ware'.*dhāḷ* 'a slope'; 'inclination of a plane' (G.); *ḍhāḷiyum* = adj. sloping, inclining (G.) Rebus: *ḍhālako* = a large metal ingot (G.) *ḍhālakī* = a metal heated and poured into a mould; a solid piece of metal; an ingot (Gujarati) PLUS खांडा [*khāṇḍā*] *m* A jag, notch, or indentation (as upon the edge of a tool or weapon). Rebus: *kāṇḍa* 'tools, pots and pans and metal-ware'

Circumscript: Four strokes: gaṇḍa 'four' Rebus: kaṇḍa 'furnace, fire-altar' (Santali)PLUS *ayo* 'fish' Rebus: *aya* 'iron' *ayas* 'metal'

  *loa* 'ficus religiosa' Rebus: *lo* 'iron' (Sanskrit) PLUS unique ligatures: लोखंड [lōkhaṇḍa] *n* (लोह S) Iron. लोखंडाचे चणे खावविणें or चारणें To oppress grievously.लोखंडकाम [lōkhaṇḍakāma] *n* Iron work; that portion (of a building, machine &c.) which consists of iron. 2 The business of an ironsmith.लोखंडी [lōkhaṇḍī] *a* (लोखंड) Composed of iron; relating to iron. (Marathi) *bhaṭa* 'warrior' (Sanskrit) Rebus: *baṭa* a kind of iron (Gujarati). Rebus: *bhaṭa* 'furnace' (Santali) Thus, together, th ligatured hieroglyph reads rebus: *loa bhaṭa* 'iron furnace'

khaṇḍ 'field, division' (Sanskrit) Rebus: *khāṇḍa* 'tools, pots and pans, metal-ware'. Rebus 2: kaṇḍ 'fire-altar' (Santali) ranku 'liquid measure' Rebus: ranku 'tin'

m48a *खोंड [khōṇḍa] m A young bull, a bullcalf. (Marathi) Rebus: kõdār 'turner' (Bengali); कोंद kōnda 'engraver, lapidary setting or infixing gems' (Marathi) G. sãghāṛɔ m. 'lathe' ; संघाट joinery; M. sãgaḍ 'double-canoe' Rebus: sangataras. संगतराश lit. 'to collect stones, stone-cutter, mason.'*

kuṭila 'bent'  CDIAL 3230 kuṭi— in cmpd. 'curve', *kuṭika—* 'bent' MBh. Rebus: *kuṭila, katthīl* = bronze (8 parts copper and 2 parts tin)

 *koḍi* 'flag' (Ta.)(DEDR 2049). Rebus 1: *koḍ* 'workshop' (Kuwi) Rebus 2: *khŏḍ* m. 'pit', *khŏḍü* f. 'small pit' (Kashmiri. CDIAL 3947).

 . notch+slanted stroke reads rebus: *ḍhālako kāṇḍa* 'ingot, tools, pots and pans and metal-ware'.*dhāḷ* 'a slope'; 'inclination of a plane' (G.); *ḍhāḷiyum* = adj. sloping, inclining (G.) Rebus: *ḍhālako* = a large metal ingot (G.) *ḍhālakī* = a metal heated and poured into a mould; a solid piece of metal; an ingot (Gujarati) PLUS खांडा [*khāṇḍā*] *m* A jag, notch, or indentation (as upon the edge of a tool or weapon). Rebus: *kāṇḍa* 'tools, pots and pans and metal-ware'

 ḍãg mountain-ridge (H.)(CDIAL 5476). Rebus: dhangar 'blacksmith' (Maithili)

 *āra* 'spokes' Rebus: *āra 'brass'*. cf. erka = ekke (Tbh. of arka) aka (Tbh. of arka) copper (metal); crystal (Kannada) Glyph: *eraka*'nave of wheel' Rebus: eraka 'copper'; cf. erka = ekke (Tbh. of arka) aka (Tbh. of arka) copper (metal); crystal (Kannada)

erako 'moltencast copper'

kolmo 'paddy plant' Rebus: *kolami* 'smithy, forge' Vikalpa: *mogge* 'sprout, bud' Rebus: *mũh* 'ingot' (Santali) dolu 'plant of shoot height' Rebus: dul 'cast metal'

m84A *खोंड [khōṇḍa] m A young bull, a bullcalf. (Marathi) Rebus: kõdār 'turner' (Bengali); कोंद kōnda 'engraver, lapidary setting or infixing gems' (Marathi) G. sãghāṛɔ m. 'lathe' ; संघाट joinery; M. sãgaḍ 'double-canoe' Rebus: sangataras. संगतराश lit. 'to collect stones, stone-cutter, mason.'*

kuṭila 'bent' CDIAL 3230 kuṭi— in cmpd. 'curve', *kuṭika—* 'bent' MBh. Rebus: *kuṭila, katthīl* = bronze (8 parts copper and 2 parts tin)

koḍi 'flag' (Ta.)(DEDR 2049). Rebus 1: *koḍ* 'workshop' (Kuwi) Rebus 2: *khõḍ* m. 'pit', *khõḍü* f. 'small pit' (Kashmiri. CDIAL 3947).
खांडा [*khāṇḍā*] *m* A jag, notch, or indentation (as upon the edge of a tool or weapon). Rebus: *kāṇḍa* 'tools, pots and pans and metal-ware' *aya kammaṭa.*'coiner, mint alloy'

dula 'pair' Rebus: dul 'cast metal' *mogge* 'sprout, bud' Rebus: *mũh* 'ingot' (Santali) Thus, cast metal ingot. PLUS | *koḍa* 'one' Rebus: *koḍ* 'workshop'

'rim-of-jar' hieroglyph *kanka* (Santali) *karṇika*'scribe'(Sanskrit) Rebus: *karṇī,* supercargo for a

boat shipment. *karṇīka* 'account (scribe)'.कारणी *kāraṇī* 'the supercargo of a ship' (Marathi)

h183A

kuṭila 'bent' CDIAL 3230 kuṭi— in cmpd. 'curve', *kuṭika—* 'bent' MBh. Rebus: *kuṭila, katthīl* = bronze (8 parts copper and 2 parts tin)

ayo 'fish' Rebus: *aya* 'iron' *ayas* 'metal'
kamaḍha 'archer, bow' Rebus: *kammaṭa* 'mint, coiner'. Variant:
dula 'pair' Rebus: *dul* 'cast (metal)' PLUS*kana, kanac* = corner (Santali); Rebus: *kañcu* = bronze (Telugu) Thus, cast bronze.

kharedo = a currycomb (Gujarati) खरारा [*kharārā*] *m* (H) A currycomb. 2 Currying a horse. (Marathi) Rebus: करडा [*karaḍā*] Hard from alloy--iron, silver &c. (Marathi) *kharādī* ' turner' (Gujarati)

m2033A,B,C Side C: *खोंड [khōṇḍa] m A young bull, a bullcalf. (Marathi) Rebus: kõdār 'turner' (Bengali); कोंद kōnda 'engraver, lapidary setting or infixing gems' (Marathi) G. sãghāṛɔ m. 'lathe' ; संघाट joinery; M. sãgaḍ 'double-canoe' Rebus: sangataras 'stone-cutter, mason'*

SideA: *kuṭila* 'bent' CDIAL 3230 kuṭi— in cmpd. 'curve', *kuṭika—* 'bent' MBh. Rebus: *kuṭila, katthīl* = bronze (8 parts copper and 2 parts tin)

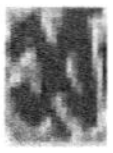
kamaḍha 'crab' Rebus: *kammaṭa* 'mint, coiner'.*ḍato* = claws of crab (Santali) Rebus: *dhātu* 'mineral ore' PLUS खांडा [

khāṇḍā] *m* A jag, notch, or indentation (as upon the edge of a tool or weapon). Rebus: *kāṇḍa* 'tools, pots and pans and metal-ware' Thus, mint metalware, ore.

loa 'ficus religiosa' Rebus: *lo* 'iron' (Sanskrit) PLUS unique ligatures: लोखंड [lōkhaṇḍa] *n* (लोह S) Iron. लोखंडाचे चणे खावविणें or चारणें To oppress grievously.लोखंडकाम [lōkhaṇḍakāma] *n* Iron work; that portion (of a building, machine &c.) which consists of iron. 2 The business of an ironsmith.लोखंडी [lōkhaṇḍī] *a* (लोखंड) Composed of iron; relating to iron. (Marathi) *bhaṭa* 'warrior' (Sanskrit) Rebus: *baṭa* a kind of iron (Gujarati). Rebus: *bhaṭa* 'furnace' (Santali) Thus, together, th ligatured hieroglyph reads rebus: *loa bhaṭa* 'iron furnace'

meḍ 'body' Rebus: *meḍ* 'iron' (Ho.) काठी [kāṭhī] *f* (काष्ट S) 'frame or structure of the body' (Marathi) Rebus: खंडी [khaṇḍī] measure of weight (Marathi) *கண்டி; kaṇṭi, n. < Mhr. khaṇḍil. [T. Tu. khaṇḍi, M. kaṇḍi.]* Candy, a weight, stated to be roughly equivalent to 500 lbs.

kanac 'corner' Rebus: *kañcu* 'bronze' Side B: *kuṭila* 'bent' CDIAL 3230 kuṭi— in cmpd. 'curve', *kuṭika*— 'bent' MBh. Rebus: *kuṭila, katthīl* = bronze (8 parts copper and 2 parts tin) Duplicated: dula 'pair' Rebus: dul 'cast metal' Thus, cast bronze. Karavu 'crocodile' Rebus; khara 'blacksmith' ayo 'fish' Rebus: aya 'iron' (Gujarati) Duplicated: dula 'pair' Rebus: dul 'cast metal' Thus, iron castings. *kamaḍha* 'penance' Rebus: *kammaṭa* 'mint, coiner'. *kaṇḍo* 'stool, seat' Rebus: *kāṇḍa* 'metalware' *kaṇḍa* 'fire-altar'

Side C: *koḍa* 'one' Rebus: *koḍ* 'workshop' kola 'tiger' Rebus: kolhe 'smelter' kol 'working in iron'

h268a *खोंड [khōṇḍa] m A young bull, a bullcalf. (Marathi) Rebus: kõdār 'turner' (Bengali); कोंद kōnda 'engraver, lapidary setting or infixing gems' (Marathi) G. sãghārɔ m. 'lathe' ; संघाट joinery; M. sãgaḍ 'double-canoe' Rebus: sangataras. संगतराश lit. 'to collect stones, stone-cutter, mason.'*

kuṭila 'bent' CDIAL 3230 kuṭi— in cmpd. 'curve', *kuṭika*— 'bent' MBh. Rebus: *kuṭila,*

katthīl = bronze (8 parts copper and 2 parts tin)
mēḍu height, rising ground, hillock (Kannada) Rebus: *meḍ* 'iron' (Ho.) kolom 'three' Rebus: kolami 'smithy, forge' Thus, *meḍ kolami* 'iron smithy-forge'
ayo 'fish' Rebus: *aya* 'iron' *ayas* 'metal' sal 'splinter' Rebus: sal 'workshop'

dula 'pair' Rebus: *dul* 'cast (metal)' PLUS*kana, kanac* = corner (Santali); Rebus: *kañcu* = bronze (Telugu) PLUS infixed kolmo 'paddy plant' Rebus: kolami 'smithy, forge'. Thus, cast bronze smithy, forge. Or, *mogge* 'sprout, bud' Rebus: *mũh* 'ingot' (Santali)Thus, cast bronze ingot. Read as: *kañcu dul mũh 'bronze cast ingot'*

muka 'ladle' (Tamil)(DEDR 4887) Rebus: *mũh* 'ingot' (Santali) *baṭa* = rimless pot (Kannada) Rebus:) *baṭa* = a kind of iron (G.)) *bhaṭa* furnace (Gujarati) Thus, iron ingot.
kolom 'three' Rebus: kolami 'smithy, forge'

|||| Numeral 4: gaṇḍa 'four' Rebus: kaṇḍa 'furnace, fire-altar' (Santali) ||| kolom 'three' Rebus: kolami 'smithy, forge'

 सांड [sāṇḍa] *f* (षद S) An outlet for superfluous water (as through a dam or mound); a sluice, a floodvent. Rebus: सांडणी [sāṇḍaṇī] *f* (H) An instrument of goldsmiths. It is hooked or curved at the extremity; and is used to draw things out of the fire.
सांठा [*sāṇṭhā*] *m* (संचय S) A collection, heap, hoard, store, stock.साटें [*sāṭēṃ*] *n* (संचय S) A whole investment; the total quantity of merchandise (brought to market by one merchant).

kanka 'rim of jar' Rebus: karṇīka 'account (scribe)' karṇī 'supercargo'

M-1930 A

m1930A,B
mēḍu height, rising ground, hillock (Kannada) Rebus: *meḍ* 'iron' (Ho.) kolom 'three' Rebus: kolami 'smithy, forge' Thus, *meḍ kolami* 'iron smithy-forge'

M-1930 B
 *kuṭila* 'bent' CDIAL 3230 kuṭi— in cmpd. 'curve', *kuṭika—* 'bent' MBh. Rebus: *kuṭila, katthīl* = bronze (8 parts copper and 2 parts tin)

 *dula* 'pair' Rebus: *dul* 'cast (metal)' PLUS*kana, kanac* = corner (Santali); Rebus: *kañcu* = bronze (Telugu) PLUS infixed kolmo 'paddy plant' Rebus: kolami 'smithy, forge'. Thus, cast bronze smithy, forge. Or, *mogge* 'sprout, bud' Rebus: *mūh* 'ingot' (Santali)Thus, cast bronze ingot. Read as: *kañcu dul mūh 'bronze cast ingot' PLUS*
gaṇḍa 'four' Rebus: kaṇḍa 'furnace, fire-altar' (Santali) | *koḍa* 'one' Rebus: *koḍ* 'workshop'

 h1657A *खोंड [khōṇḍa] m A young bull, a bullcalf. (Marathi) Rebus: kõdār 'turner' (Bengali); कोंद kōnda 'engraver, lapidary setting or infixing gems' (Marathi) G. sãghāṛɔ m. 'lathe' ; संघाट joinery; M. sãgaḍ 'double-canoe' Rebus: sangataras. संगतराश lit. 'to collect stones, stone-cutter, mason.'*

 *kuṭila* 'bent' CDIAL 3230 kuṭi— in cmpd. 'curve', *kuṭika—* 'bent' MBh. Rebus: *kuṭila, katthīl* = bronze (8 parts copper and 2 parts tin)

 *dāṭu* 'cross'(Telugu) Rebus: *dhatu* 'mineral' (Santali).
dula 'two' Rebus: dul 'cast metal' sal 'splinter' Rebus: sal 'workshop'
ayo 'fish' Rebus: *aya* 'iron' *ayas* 'metal' *aya aḍaren (homonym: aduru)*'alloy native metal'

 *dula* 'pair' Rebus: *dul* 'cast (metal)' PLUS*kana, kanac* = corner (Santali); Rebus: *kañcu* = bronze (Telugu) PLUS infixed kolmo 'paddy plant' Rebus: kolami 'smithy, forge'. Thus, cast bronze smithy, forge. Or, *mogge* 'sprout, bud' Rebus: *mūh* 'ingot' (Santali)Thus, cast bronze ingot. Read as: *kañcu dul mūh 'bronze cast ingot'*
kolom 'three' Rebus: kolami 'smithy, forge'

 *kuṭila* 'bent' CDIAL 3230 kuṭi— in cmpd. 'curve', *kuṭika—* 'bent' MBh. Rebus: *kuṭila, katthīl* = bronze (8 parts copper and 2 parts tin) dula 'two' Rebus: dul 'cast metal' Thus, bronze castings. ranku 'liquid measure' Rebus: ranku 'tin'. *kolmo* 'paddy plant' Rebus:
 *kolami* 'smithy, forge' Vikalpa: *mogge* 'sprout, bud' Rebus: *mūh* 'ingot' (Santali) dolu 'plant of shoot height' Rebus: dul 'cast metal'

kanka 'rim of jar' Rebus: *karṇīka* 'account (scribe)' *karṇī* 'supercargo'

h8a *खोंड [khōṇḍa] m A young bull, a bullcalf. (Marathi) Rebus: kõdār 'turner' (Bengali); कोंद kōnda 'engraver, lapidary setting or infixing gems' (Marathi) G. sãghāṛɔ m. 'lathe' ; संघाट joinery; M. sãgaḍ 'double-canoe' Rebus: sangataras. संगतराश lit. 'to collect stones, stone-cutter, mason.'*

kuṭila 'bent' CDIAL 3230 kuṭi— in cmpd. 'curve', *kuṭika*— 'bent' MBh. Rebus: *kuṭila, katthīl* = bronze (8 parts copper and 2 parts tin)

dāṭu 'cross'(Telugu) Rebus: *dhatu* 'mineral' (Santali). sal 'splinter' Rebus: sal 'workshop'

muka 'ladle' (Tamil)(DEDR 4887) Rebus: *mũh* 'ingot' (Santali) *baṭa* = rimless pot (Kannada) Rebus:) *baṭa* = a kind of iron (G.)) *bhaṭa* furnace (Gujarati) Thus, iron ingot.

kolom 'three' Rebus: kolami 'smithy, forge' *kāṇḍa* ranku 'liquid measure' Rebus: ranku 'tin' *kolmo* 'paddy plant' Rebus: *kolami* 'smithy, forge' Vikalpa: *mogge* 'sprout, bud' Rebus: *mũh* 'ingot' (Santali) dolu 'plant of shoot height' Rebus: dul 'cast metal'

kanka 'rim of jar' Rebus: *karṇīka* 'account (scribe)' *karṇī* 'supercargo'
खांडा [*khāṇḍā*] *m* A jag, notch, or indentation (as upon the edge of a tool or weapon). Rebus: *kāṇḍa* 'tools, pots and pans and metal-ware'

|||| Numeral 4: gaṇḍa 'four' Rebus: kaṇḍa 'furnace, fire-altar' (Santali) dula 'pair' Rebus: dul 'cast metal'

m23A *खोंड [khōṇḍa] m A young bull, a bullcalf. (Marathi) Rebus: kõdār 'turner' (Bengali); कोंद kōnda 'engraver, lapidary setting or infixing gems' (Marathi) G. sãghāṛɔ m. 'lathe' ; संघाट joinery; M. sãgaḍ 'double-canoe' Rebus: sangataras. संगतराश lit. 'to collect stones, stone-cutter, mason.'*

खांडा [*khāṇḍā*] *m* A jag, notch, or indentation (as upon the edge of a tool or weapon). Rebus: *kāṇḍa* 'tools, pots and pans and metal-ware' *kuṭila* 'bent' CDIAL 3230 kuṭi—

in cmpd. 'curve', *kuṭika*— 'bent' MBh. Rebus: *kuṭila, katthīl* = bronze (8 parts copper and 2 parts tin) *aya aḍaren (homonym: aduru)* 'alloy native metal' *ayo* 'fish' Rebus: *aya* 'iron' *ayas* 'metal'

कांड *kāṇḍa* 'arrow' Rebus: *kāṇḍa* 'pots and pans, metalware, tools'. Rebus 2: kaṇḍ 'fire-altar' (Santali)

dāṭu 'cross'(Telugu) Rebus: *dhatu* 'mineral' (Santali). PLUS

dhāḷ 'a slope'; 'inclination of a plane' (G.); *ḍhāḷiyum* = adj. sloping, inclining (G.) Rebus: *ḍhālako* = a large metal ingot (G.) *ḍhālakī* = a metal heated and poured into a mould; a solid piece of metal; an ingot (Gujarati) PLUS खांडा [*khāṇḍā*] *m* A jag, notch, or indentation (as upon the edge of a tool or weapon). Rebus: *kāṇḍa* 'tools, pots and pans and metal-ware' Thus, the pair of sign hieroglyphs from r. read rebus: copper, bronze ingots, metalware castings.

 *aḍaren* 'cover of pot or lid' Rebus: *aduru* 'native, unsmelted metal' Duplicated: dula 'pair' Rebus: dul 'cast metal'

 *koḍi* 'flag' (Ta.)(DEDR 2049). Rebus 1: *koḍ* 'workshop' (Kuwi) Rebus 2: *khōḍ* m. 'pit', *khōḍü* f. 'small pit' (Kashmiri. CDIAL 3947).

 *cīmara* 'black ant' Rebus: *cīmara* 'copper'. *cīmara kāra* -- ' coppersmith '

 *kanac* 'corner' Rebus: *kañcu* 'bronze'

Circumscript: gaṇḍa 'four' Rebus: kaṇḍa 'furnace, fire-altar' (Santali)

 *dula* 'pair' Rebus: *dul* 'cast (metal)' PLUS *kana, kanac* = corner (Santali); Rebus: *kañcu* = bronze (Telugu) Thus, cast bronze. Furnace bronze castings.

 *kanka* 'rim of jar' Rebus: *karṇīka* 'account (scribe)' *karṇī* 'supercargo'

 m234a *balad* m. ' ox ', gng. *bald*, (Ku.) *barad*, id. (N. Tarai) Rebus: *bharat* (5 copper, 4 zinc and 1 tin)(Punjabi) *pattar* 'trough' Rebus: *pattar* 'guild'. Thus, copper-zinc-tin alloy (worker) guild.

 *kuṭila* 'bent' CDIAL 3230 kuṭi— in cmpd. 'curve', *kuṭika*— 'bent' MBh. Rebus: *kuṭila, katthīl* = bronze (8 parts copper and 2 parts tin)

 *aya aḍaren (homonym: aduru)* 'alloy native metal' *ayo* 'fish' Rebus: *aya* 'iron' *ayas* 'metal'

कांड *kāṇḍa* 'arrow' Rebus: *kāṇḍa* 'pots and pans, metalware, tools'. Rebus 2: kaṇḍ 'fire-altar' (Santali)

 *dāṭu* 'cross'(Telugu) Rebus: *dhatu* 'mineral' (Santali).

 *dhāḷ* 'a slope'; 'inclination of a plane' (G.); *ḍhāḷiyum* = adj. sloping, inclining (G.) Rebus: *ḍhālako* = a large metal ingot (G.) *ḍhālakī* = a metal heated and poured into a mould; a solid piece of metal; an ingot (Gujarati) PLUS खांडा [*khāṇḍā*] *m* A jag, notch, or indentation (as upon the edge of a tool or weapon). Rebus: *kāṇḍa* 'tools, pots and pans and metal-ware' Thus, the pair of sign hieroglyphs from r. read rebus: copper, bronze ingots, metalware castings.

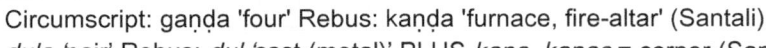

 *aḍaren* 'cover of pot or lid' Rebus: *aduru* 'native, unsmelted metal' Duplicated: dula 'pair' Rebus: dul 'cast metal' PLUS dulo 'hole' Rebus: dul 'cast metal'

 *kanka* 'rim of jar' Rebus: *karṇīka* 'account (scribe)' *karṇī* 'supercargo'

  gaṇḍa 'four' Rebus: kaṇḍa 'furnace, fire-altar' (Santali)

loa 'ficus religiosa' Rebus: *lo* 'iron' (Sanskrit) PLUS unique ligatures: लोखंड [lōkhaṇḍa] *n* (लोह S) Iron. लोखंडाचे चणे खावविणें or चारणें To oppress grievously.लोखंडकाम [lōkhaṇḍakāma] *n* Iron work; that portion (of a building, machine &c.) which consists of iron. 2 The business of an ironsmith.लोखंडी [lōkhaṇḍī] *a* (लोखंड) Composed of iron; relating to iron. (Marathi) *bhaṭa* 'warrior' (Sanskrit) Rebus: *baṭa* a

kind of iron (Gujarati). Rebus: *bhaṭa* 'furnace' (Santali) Thus, together, th ligatured hieroglyph reads rebus: *loa bhaṭa* 'iron furnace'
kamaḍha 'crab' Rebus: *kammaṭa* 'mint, coiner'.
ḍato = claws of crab (Santali) Rebus: *dhātu* 'mineral ore'

Circumscript: gaṇḍa 'four' Rebus: kaṇḍa 'furnace, fire-altar' (Santali) INFIXED *dula* 'pair' Rebus: *dul* 'cast (metal)' PLUS*kana, kanac* = corner (Santali); Rebus: *kañcu* = bronze (Telugu) Thus, cast bronze.

m1664a *खोंड [khōṇḍa] m A young bull, a bullcalf. (Marathi) Rebus: kōdār 'turner' (Bengali); कोंद kōnda 'engraver, lapidary setting or infixing gems' (Marathi) G. sãghāṛɔ m. 'lathe' ; संघाट joinery; M. sãgaḍ 'double-canoe' Rebus: sangataras. संगतराश lit. 'to collect stones, stone-cutter, mason.'*

kuṭila 'bent' CDIAL 3230 kuṭi— in cmpd. 'curve', *kuṭika*— 'bent' MBh. Rebus: *kuṭila, katthīl* = bronze (8 parts copper and 2 parts tin)

notch+slanted stroke reads rebus: *ḍhālako kāṇḍa* 'ingot, tools, pots and pans and metal-ware'.*dhāḷ* 'a slope'; 'inclination of a plane' (G.); *ḍhāḷiyum* = adj. sloping, inclining (G.) Rebus: *ḍhālako* = a large metal ingot (G.) *ḍhālakī* = a metal heated and poured into a mould; a solid piece of metal; an ingot (Gujarati) PLUS खांडा [*khāṇḍā*] *m* A jag, notch, or indentation (as upon the edge of a tool or weapon). Rebus: *kāṇḍa* 'tools, pots and pans and metal-ware'

mēḍu height, rising ground, hillock (Kannada) Rebus: *mẽṛhẽt, meḍ* 'iron' (Munda.Ho.)

kana, kanac = corner (Santali); Rebus: *kañcu* = bronze (Telugu) PLUS kolom 'three' Rebus: kolami 'smithy, forge'.

m373a

kuṭila 'bent' CDIAL 3230 kuṭi— in cmpd. 'curve', *kuṭika*— 'bent' MBh. Rebus: *kuṭila, katthīl* = bronze (8 parts copper and 2 parts tin)

loa 'ficus religiosa' Rebus: *lo* 'iron' (Sanskrit) PLUS unique ligatures: लोखंड [lōkhaṇḍa] *n* (लोह S) Iron. लोखंडाचे चणे खावविणें or चारणें To oppress grievously.लोखंडकाम [lōkhaṇḍakāma] *n* Iron work; that portion (of a building, machine &c.) which consists of iron. 2 The business of an ironsmith.लोखंडी [lōkhaṇḍī] *a* (लोखंड) Composed of iron; relating to iron. (Marathi) Duplicated: dula 'pair' Rebus: dul 'cast metal'

kana, kanac = corner (Santali); Rebus: *kañcu* = bronze (Telugu) PLUS dulo 'hole' Rebus: dul 'cast metal' PLUS sal 'splinter' Rebus: sal 'workshop'

dula 'pair' Rebus: dul 'cast metal'

kharedo = a currycomb (Gujarati) खरारा [*kharārā*] *m* (H) A currycomb. 2 Currying a horse. (Marathi) Rebus: करडा [*karaḍā*] Hard from alloy--iron, silver &c. (Marathi) *kharādī* ' turner' (Gujarati) Thus, hard alloy castings.

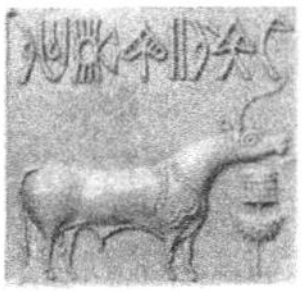

h5a खोंड [khōṇḍa] m A young bull, a bullcalf. (Marathi) Rebus: kõdār 'turner' (Bengali); कोंद kōnda 'engraver, lapidary setting or infixing gems' (Marathi) G. sãghāṛɔ m. 'lathe' ; संघाट joinery; M. sãgaḍ 'double-canoe' Rebus: sangataras. संगतराश lit. 'to collect stones, stone-cutter, mason.'

kuṭila 'bent' CDIAL 3230 kuṭi— in cmpd. 'curve', *kuṭika*— 'bent' MBh. Rebus: *kuṭila, katthīl* = bronze (8 parts copper and 2 parts tin)

loa 'ficus religiosa' Rebus: *lo* 'iron' (Sanskrit) PLUS unique ligatures: लोखंड [lōkhaṇḍa] *n* (लोह S) Iron. लोखंडाचे चणे खावविणें or चारणें To oppress grievously.लोखंडकाम [lōkhaṇḍakāma] *n* Iron work; that portion (of a building, machine &c.) which consists of iron. 2 The business of an ironsmith.लोखंडी [lōkhaṇḍī] *a* (लोखंड) Composed of iron; relating to iron. (Marathi) *bhaṭa* 'warrior' (Sanskrit) Rebus: *baṭa* a kind of iron (Gujarati). Rebus: *bhaṭa* 'furnace' (Santali) Thus, together, th ligatured hieroglyph reads rebus: *loa bhaṭa* 'iron furnace'

kuṭila 'bent' CDIAL 3230 kuṭi— in cmpd. 'curve', *kuṭika*— 'bent' MBh. Rebus: *kuṭila, katthīl* = bronze (8 parts copper and 2 parts tin) dula 'two' Rebus: dul 'cast metal'

loa 'ficus religiosa' Rebus: *lo* 'iron' (Sanskrit) PLUS unique ligatures: लोखंड [lōkhaṇḍa] *n* (लोह S) Iron. लोखंडाचे चणे खावविणें or चारणें To oppress grievously.लोखंडकाम [lōkhaṇḍakāma] *n* Iron work; that portion (of a building, machine &c.) which consists of iron. 2 The business of an ironsmith.लोखंडी [lōkhaṇḍī] *a* (लोखंड) Composed of iron; relating to iron. (Marathi)

cīmara 'black ant' Rebus: *cīmara* 'copper'. *cīmara kāra* -- ' coppersmith '

muka 'ladle' (Tamil)(DEDR 4887) Rebus: *mũh* 'ingot' (Santali) *baṭa* = rimless pot

(Kannada) Rebus:) *baṭa* = a kind of iron (G.)) *bhaṭa* furnace (Gujarati) Thus, iron ingot.

kuṭila 'bent' CDIAL 3230 kuṭi— in cmpd. 'curve', *kuṭika*— 'bent' MBh. Rebus: *kuṭila, katthīl* = bronze (8 parts copper and 2 parts tin)

M-1274 a

h1274a dula 'pair' Rebus: dul 'cast metal' *kuṭila* 'bent' CDIAL 3230 kuṭi— in cmpd. 'curve', *kuṭika*— 'bent' MBh. Rebus: *kuṭila, katthīl* = bronze (8 parts copper and 2 parts tin) Ligature of 'bud' is a semantic reinforcement of castings of ingots: mogge 'bud' Rebus: *mũh* 'ingot'. Thus bronze ingot and castings. dula 'two' Rebus: dul 'cast metal'

aḍar 'harrow'; rebus: *aduru* 'native unsmelted metal' PLUS eraka 'upraised arm' Rebus: erako 'moltencast copper' Ligatured to:

meḍ 'body' Rebus: *meḍ* 'iron' (Ho.) काठी [kāṭhī] *f* (काष्ट S) 'frame or structure of the body' (Marathi) Rebus: खंडी [khaṇḍī] measure of weight (Marathi) கண்டி; *kaṇṭi, n.* < *Mhr. khaṇḍil. [T. Tu. khaṇḍi, M. kaṇḍi.]* Candy, a weight, stated to be roughly equivalent to 500 lbs.

m1810a *खोंड [khōṇḍa] m A young bull, a bullcalf. (Marathi) Rebus: kõdār 'turner' (Bengali); कोंद kōnda 'engraver, lapidary setting or infixing gems'*

(Marathi) G. sãghāṛɔ m. 'lathe' ; संघाट joinery; M. sãgaḍ 'double-canoe' Rebus: sangataras. संगतराश lit. 'to collect stones, stone-cutter, mason.'

 *kuṭila* 'bent' CDIAL 3230 kuṭi— in cmpd. 'curve', *kuṭika—* 'bent' MBh. Rebus: *kuṭila, katthīl* = bronze (8 parts copper and 2 parts tin)

  water-carrier hieroglyph *kuṭi*; Rebus: *kuṭhi* 'smelter furnace'. PLUS 'rim of jar':

 kanka 'rim of jar' Rebus: karṇīka 'account (scribe)' karṇī 'supercargo'

 सांड [sāṇḍa] *f* (षद S) An outlet for superfluous water (as through a dam or mound); a sluice, a floodvent. Rebus: सांडणी [sāṇḍaṇī] *f* (H) An instrument of goldsmiths. It is hooked or curved at the extremity; and is used to draw things out of the fire. सांठा [*sāṇṭhā*] *m* (संचय S) A collection, heap, hoard, store, stock.साटें [*sāṭēṃ*] *n* (संचय S) A whole investment; the total quantity of merchandise (brought to market by one merchant).

  *loa* 'ficus religiosa' Rebus: *lo* 'iron' (Sanskrit) PLUS unique ligatures: लोखंड [lōkhaṇḍa] *n* (लोह S) Iron. लोखंडाचे चणे खावविणें or चारणें To oppress grievously.लोखंडकाम [lōkhaṇḍakāma] *n* Iron work; that portion (of a building, machine &c.) which consists of iron. 2 The business of an ironsmith.लोखंडी [lōkhaṇḍī] *a* (लोखंड) Composed of iron; relating to iron. (Marathi)

bhaṭa 'warrior' (Sanskrit) Rebus: *baṭa* a kind of iron (Gujarati). Rebus: *bhaṭa* 'furnace' (Santali)

 kanka 'rim of jar' Rebus: karṇīka 'account (scribe)' karṇī 'supercargo'

M-1826 a

m1826a *खोंड [khōṇḍa] m A young bull, a bullcalf. (Marathi) Rebus: kõdār 'turner' (Bengali); कोंद kōnda 'engraver, lapidary setting or infixing gems' (Marathi) G. sãghāṛɔ m. 'lathe' ; संघाट joinery; M. sãgaḍ 'double-canoe' Rebus: sangataras. संगतराश lit. 'to collect stones, stone-cutter, mason.'*

kuṭila 'bent'  CDIAL 3230 kuṭi— in cmpd. 'curve', *kuṭika—* 'bent' MBh. Rebus: *kuṭila, katthīl* = bronze (8 parts copper and 2 parts tin)

 'Arrow' sign hieroglyph (variant) This is a ligature of 'lid of pot' hieroglyph superscript on 'a linear stroke' numeral hieroglyph.*aḍaren* 'cover of pot or lid' Rebus: *aduru* 'native, unsmelted metal' PLUS koḍ = one (Santali); koḍ 'workshop' (Gujarati) PLUS dulo 'hole' Rebus: dul 'cast metal'

 कांड *kāṇḍa* 'arrow' Rebus: *kāṇḍa* 'pots and pans, metalware, tools'. Rebus 2: kaṇḍ 'fire-altar' (Santali)

m779A खोंड *[khōṇḍa] m A young bull, a bullcalf. (Marathi) Rebus: kõdār 'turner' (Bengali);* कोंद *kōnda 'engraver, lapidary setting or infixing gems' (Marathi) G. sãghāṛɔ m. 'lathe' ;* संघाट *joinery; M. sãgaḍ 'double-canoe' Rebus: sangataras.* संगतराश *lit. 'to collect stones, stone-cutter, mason.'*

kuṭila 'bent' CDIAL 3230 kuṭi— in cmpd. 'curve', *kuṭika—* 'bent' MBh. Rebus: *kuṭila, katthīl* = bronze (8 parts copper and 2 parts tin)

'Arrow' sign hieroglyph (variant) This is a ligature of 'lid of pot' hieroglyph superscript on 'a linear stroke' numeral hieroglyph.*aḍaren* 'cover of pot or lid' Rebus: *aduru* 'native, unsmelted metal' PLUS koḍ = one (Santali); koḍ 'workshop' (Gujarati) PLUS dulo 'hole' Rebus: dul 'cast metal'

dhāḷ 'a slope'; 'inclination of a plane' (G.); *ḍhāḷiyum* = adj. sloping, inclining (G.) Rebus: *ḍhālako* = a large metal ingot (G.) *ḍhālakī* = a metal heated and poured into a mould; a solid piece of metal; an ingot (Gujarati) PLUS *dula* 'pair' Rebus: *dul* 'cast metal' PLUS | *koḍa* 'one' Rebus: *koḍ* 'workshop'.

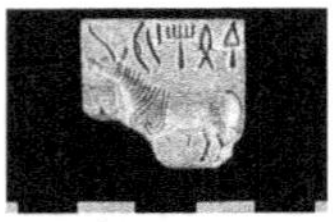

h1669A खोंड *[khōṇḍa] m A young bull, a bullcalf. (Marathi) Rebus: kõdār 'turner' (Bengali);* कोंद *kōnda 'engraver, lapidary setting or infixing gems' (Marathi) G. sãghāṛɔ m. 'lathe' ;* संघाट *joinery; M. sãgaḍ 'double-canoe' Rebus: sangataras.* संगतराश *lit. 'to collect stones, stone-cutter, mason.'*

kuṭila 'bent' CDIAL 3230 kuṭi— in cmpd. 'curve', *kuṭika—* 'bent' MBh. Rebus: *kuṭila, katthīl* = bronze (8 parts copper and 2 parts tin)

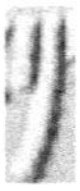

notch+slanted stroke reads rebus: *ḍhālako kāṇḍa* 'ingot, tools, pots and pans and metal-ware'.*dhāḷ* 'a slope'; 'inclination of a plane' (G.); *ḍhāḷiyum* = adj. sloping, inclining (G.) Rebus: *ḍhālako* = a large metal ingot (G.) *ḍhālakī* = a metal heated and poured into a mould; a solid piece of metal; an ingot (Gujarati) PLUS खांडा [*khāṇḍā*] *m* A jag, notch, or indentation (as upon the edge of a tool or weapon). Rebus: *kāṇḍa* 'tools, pots and pans and metal-ware'

aḍar 'harrow'; rebus: *aduru* 'native unsmelted metal'

ayo 'fish' Rebus: *aya* 'iron' *ayas* 'metal'

कांड *kāṇḍa* 'arrow' Rebus: *kāṇḍa* 'pots and pans, metalware, tools'. Rebus 2: kaṇḍ 'fire-altar' (Santali)

Lothal 114a First 2 signs read rebus as at h1669A PLUS

āra 'spokes' Rebus: *āra 'brass'*. cf. erka = ekke (Tbh. of arka) aka (Tbh. of arka) copper (metal); crystal (Kannada) Glyph: *eraka*'nave of wheel' Rebus: eraka 'copper'; cf. erka = ekke (Tbh. of arka) aka (Tbh. of arka) copper (metal); crystal (Kannada) *erako* 'moltencast copper' Duplicated: dula 'pair' Rebus: dul 'cast metal' Thus cast copper, brass casting.

dula 'two' Rebus: dul 'cast metal' *ayo* 'fish' Rebus: *aya* 'iron' *ayas* 'metal'

kuṭila 'bent' CDIAL 3230 kuṭi— in cmpd. 'curve', *kuṭika—* 'bent' MBh. Rebus: *kuṭila, katthīl* = bronze (8 parts copper and 2 parts tin) Duplicated: dula 'pair' Rebus: dul 'cast metal' Thus, cast bronze.

ranku 'liquid measure' Rebus: ranku 'tin'

| *koḍa* 'one' Rebus: *koḍ* 'workshop'

 *kanka* 'rim of jar' Rebus: *karṇīka* 'account (scribe)' *karṇī* 'supercargo'

m1671a *खोंड [khōṇḍa] m A young bull, a bullcalf. (Marathi) Rebus: kōdār 'turner' (Bengali); कोंद kōnda 'engraver, lapidary setting or infixing gems' (Marathi) G. sãghāṛɔ m. 'lathe' ; संघाट joinery; M. sãgaḍ 'double-canoe' Rebus: sangataras. संगतराश lit. 'to collect stones, stone-cutter, mason.'* First 2 signs read rebus as at h1669A PLUS

 *baraḍo* = spine; backbone (Tulu) Rebus: *baran, bharat* 'mixed alloys' (5 copper, 4 zinc and 1 tin) (Punjabi) Circumscript:

 *kuṭila* 'bent' CDIAL 3230 kuṭi— in cmpd. 'curve', *kuṭika*— 'bent' MBh. Rebus: *kuṭila, katthīl* = bronze (8 parts copper and 2 parts tin) Duplicated: dula 'pair' Rebus: dul 'cast metal' Thus, cast bronze. INFIXED *ayo* 'fish' Rebus: *aya* 'iron' *ayas* 'metal'

 *kanka* 'rim of jar' Rebus: *karṇīka* 'account (scribe)' *karṇī* 'supercargo'

Kalibangan 4A First 2 signs read rebus as at h1669A PLUS

Sal 'splinter' Rebus: sal 'workshop'

loa 'ficus religiosa' Rebus: *lo* 'iron' (Sanskrit) PLUS unique ligatures: लोखंड [lōkhaṇḍa] *n* (लोह S) Iron. लोखंडाचे चणे खावविणें or चारणें To oppress grievously.लोखंडकाम [lōkhaṇḍakāma] *n* Iron work; that portion (of a building, machine &c.) which consists of iron. 2 The business of an ironsmith.लोखंडी [lōkhaṇḍī] *a* (लोखंड) Composed of iron; relating to iron. (Marathi) *bhaṭa* 'warrior' (Sanskrit) Rebus: *baṭa* a kind of iron (Gujarati). Rebus: *bhaṭa* 'furnace' (Santali) Thus, together, the ligatured hieroglyph reads rebus: *loa bhaṭa* 'iron furnace' Circumscript:

 *kuṭila* 'bent' CDIAL 3230 kuṭi— in cmpd. 'curve', *kuṭika*— 'bent' MBh. Rebus: *kuṭila, katthīl* = bronze (8 parts copper and 2 parts tin) Duplicated: dula 'pair' Rebus: dul 'cast metal' Thus, cast bronze. INFIXED karaṇḍa 'duck' (Sanskrit) karaṛa 'a very large aquatic bird' (Sindhi) Rebus: करडा [*karaḍā*] Hard from alloy--iron, silver &c. (Marathi) *kharādī* ' turner' (Gujarati) *āra* 'six' Rebus: *āra* 'brass'

m363A First two signs read rebus as at h1669A PLUS
kanka 'rim of jar' Rebus: *karṇīka* 'account (scribe)' *karṇī* 'supercargo'
INFIXED kolom 'three' Rebus: kolami 'smithy, forge'

 *aḍar* 'harrow'; rebus: *aduru* 'native unsmelted metal' *bhaṭa* 'warrior' (Sanskrit) Rebus:

 *baṭa* a kind of iron (Gujarati). Rebus: *bhaṭa* 'furnace' (Santali)
kanka 'rim of jar' Rebus: *karṇīka* 'account (scribe)' *karṇī* 'supercargo'

h145A Ligatured first sign read as two signs read at h1669A PLUS

dula 'pair' Rebus: *dul* 'cast (metal)' PLUS*kana, kanac* = corner (Santali); Rebus: *kañcu* = bronze (Telugu) PLUS infixed kolmo 'paddy plant' Rebus: kolami 'smithy, forge'. Thus, cast bronze smithy, forge. Or, *mogge* 'sprout, bud' Rebus: *mũh* 'ingot' (Santali)Thus, cast bronze ingot. Read as: *kañcu dul mũh 'bronze cast ingot' kamaḍha* = crab; *kampaṭṭam* = mint (Ta.) ; *kammaṭa* 'coiner, mint' (Telugu) Vikalpa: *ḍato* = claws of crab (Santali); *dhātu* = mineral (Sanskrit) *ayo* 'fish' Rebus: *aya* 'iron' *ayas* 'metal'

Chanhudaro 6A *खोंड [khōṇḍa] m A young bull, a bullcalf. (Marathi) Rebus: kõdār 'turner' (Bengali); कोंद kōnda 'engraver, lapidary setting or infixing gems' (Marathi) G. sãghāṛɔ m. 'lathe' ; संघाट joinery; M. sãgaḍ 'double-canoe' Rebus: sangataras. संगतराश lit. 'to collect stones, stone-cutter, mason.'* Ligatured first sign read as two signs read at h1669A PLUS *aya kammaṭa.*'coiner, mint alloy'

कांड *kāṇḍa* 'arrow' Rebus: *kāṇḍa* 'pots and pans, metalware, tools'. Rebus 2: kaṇḍ 'fire-altar' (Santali)

m677a *खोंड [khōṇḍa] m A young bull, a bullcalf. (Marathi) Rebus: kõdār 'turner' (Bengali); कोंद kōnda 'engraver, lapidary setting or infixing gems' (Marathi) G. sãghāṛɔ m. 'lathe' ; संघाट joinery; M. sãgaḍ 'double-canoe' Rebus: sangataras. संगतराश lit. 'to collect stones, stone-cutter, mason.'* Ligatured first sign read as two signs read at h1669A PLUS *aya kammaṭa.*'coiner, mint alloy' *aya kāṇḍa* 'alloy metalware'

muka 'ladle' (Tamil)(DEDR 4887) Rebus: *mũh* 'ingot' (Santali) *baṭa* = rimless pot (Kannada) Rebus:) *baṭa* = a kind of iron (G.)) *bhaṭa* furnace (Gujarati) Thus, iron ingot.

kolom 'three' Rebus: kolami 'smithy, forge'

Ligature: two peaks: mēḍu height, rising ground, hillock (Kannada) Rebus: *meḍ* 'iron' (Ho.) dula 'pair' Rebus: dul 'cast metal' PLUS |||| Numeral 4: gaṇḍa 'four' Rebus: kaṇḍa 'furnace, fire-altar' (Santali)

'Arrow' sign hieroglyph (variant) This is a ligature of 'lid of pot' hieroglyph superscript on 'a linear stroke' numeral hieroglyph.*aḍaren* 'cover of pot or lid' Rebus: *aduru* 'native, unsmelted metal' PLUS koḍ = one (Santali); koḍ 'workshop' (Gujarati)

kuṭila 'bent' CDIAL 3230 kuṭi— in cmpd. 'curve', *kuṭika*— 'bent' MBh. Rebus: *kuṭila, katthīl* = bronze (8 parts copper and 2 parts tin) Duplicated: dula 'pair' Rebus: dul 'cast metal' Thus, cast bronze.

kanka 'rim of jar' Rebus: *karṇīka* 'account (scribe)' *karṇī* 'supercargo'

h59a *खोंड [khōṇḍa] m A young bull, a bullcalf. (Marathi) Rebus: kõdār 'turner' (Bengali); कोंद kōnda 'engraver, lapidary setting or infixing gems' (Marathi) G. sãghāṛɔ m. 'lathe' ; संघाट joinery; M. sãgaḍ 'double-canoe' Rebus: sangataras. संगतराश lit. 'to collect stones, stone-cutter, mason.'*

kuṭila 'bent' CDIAL 3230 kuṭi— in cmpd. 'curve', *kuṭika*— 'bent' MBh. Rebus: *kuṭila, katthīl* = bronze (8 parts copper and 2 parts tin) PLUS sal 'splinter' Rebus: sal 'workshop'

 *kanka* 'rim of jar' Rebus: *karṇīka* 'account (scribe)' *karṇī* 'supercargo'

h589A buffalo hieroglyph: *rāngo* 'water buffalo bull' (Ku.N.)(CDIAL 10559) Rebus: ranku 'tin' raṅga3 n. ' tin ' lex. [Cf. nāga -- 2, vaṅga -- 1]Pk. *raṁga* -- n. ' tin '; P. *rāg* f., *rāgā* m. ' pewter, tin ' (← H.) kolom 'three' Rebus: kolami 'smithy, forge'
sal 'splinter' Rebus: sal 'workshop' kolom 'three' Rebus: kolami 'smithy, forge' Thus, bronze forge.

 *kuṭila* 'bent' CDIAL 3230 kuṭi— in cmpd. 'curve', *kuṭika*— 'bent' MBh. Rebus: *kuṭila,*

 *katthīl* = bronze (8 parts copper and 2 parts tin)
kanka 'rim of jar' Rebus: *karṇīka* 'account (scribe)' *karṇī* 'supercargo'

h36a *खोंड [khōṇḍa] m A young bull, a bullcalf. (Marathi) Rebus: kõdār 'turner' (Bengali); कोंद kōnda 'engraver, lapidary setting or infixing gems' (Marathi) G. sãghāṛɔ m. 'lathe' ; संघाट joinery; M. sãgaḍ 'double-canoe' Rebus: sangataras. संगतराश lit. 'to collect stones, stone-cutter, mason.' erako* 'upraised arm' Rebus: erako 'moltencast copper' PLUS

 *kuṭila* 'bent' CDIAL 3230 kuṭi— in cmpd. 'curve', *kuṭika*— 'bent' MBh. Rebus: *kuṭila, katthīl*

 *meḍ* 'body' Rebus: *meḍ* 'iron' (Ho.) काठी [kāṭhī] *f* (काष्ट S) 'frame or structure of the body' (Marathi) Rebus: खंडी [khaṇḍī] measure of weight (Marathi) *கண்டி; kaṇṭi, n. < Mhr. khaṇḍil. [T. Tu. khaṇḍi, M. kaṇḍi.]* Candy, a weight, stated to be roughly equivalent to 500 lbs.
= bronze (8 parts copper and 2 parts tin)

 *kanka* 'rim of jar' Rebus: *karṇīka* 'account (scribe)' *karṇī* 'supercargo' *ayo ḍhālako* 'alloy metal ingot' *kamaḍha* 'crab' Rebus: *kammaṭa* 'mint, coiner'.=
 *kanka* 'rim of jar' Rebus: *karṇīka* 'account (scribe)' *karṇī* 'supercargo'

m1682a *खोंड [khōṇḍa] m A young bull, a bullcalf. (Marathi) Rebus: kõdār 'turner' (Bengali); कोंद kōnda 'engraver, lapidary setting or infixing gems' (Marathi) G. sãghāṛɔ m. 'lathe' ; संघाट joinery; M. sãgaḍ 'double-canoe' Rebus: sangataras. संगतराश lit. 'to collect stones, stone-cutter, mason.'* First sign read rebus as at h36a.
 *kuṭila* 'bent' CDIAL 3230 kuṭi— in cmpd. 'curve', *kuṭika*— 'bent' MBh. Rebus: *kuṭila, katthīl* = bronze (8 parts copper and 2 parts tin) Duplicated: dula 'pair' Rebus: dul 'cast metal' Thus, cast bronze.
 water-carrier hieroglyph *kuṭi*; Rebus: *kuṭhi* 'smelter furnace'.

Kalibangan 9a *खोंड [khōṇḍa] m A young bull, a bullcalf. (Marathi) Rebus: kõdār 'turner' (Bengali); कोंद kōnda 'engraver, lapidary setting or infixing gems'*

(Marathi) G. sãghāṛɔ m. 'lathe' ; संघाट joinery; M. sãgaḍ 'double-canoe' Rebus: sangataras. संगतराश lit. 'to collect stones, stone-cutter, mason.'

 *kuṭila* 'bent' CDIAL 3230 kuṭi— in cmpd. 'curve', *kuṭika—* 'bent' MBh. Rebus: *kuṭila, katthīl* = bronze (8 parts copper and 2 parts tin) kolom 'three' Rebus: kolami 'smithy, forge'

ayo 'fish' Rebus: *aya* 'iron' *ayas* 'metal'

 *kanka* 'rim of jar' Rebus: *karṇīka* 'account (scribe)' *karṇī* 'supercargo'

 'Arrow' sign hieroglyph (variant) This is a ligature of 'lid of pot' hieroglyph superscript on 'a linear stroke' numeral hieroglyph.*aḍaren* 'cover of pot or lid' Rebus: *aduru* 'native, unsmelted metal' PLUS koḍ = one (Santali); koḍ 'workshop' (Gujarati)

 Kalibangan 11a *खोंड [khōṇḍa] m A young bull, a bullcalf. (Marathi) Rebus: kõdār 'turner' (Bengali); कोंद kōnda 'engraver, lapidary setting or infixing gems' (Marathi) G. sãghāṛɔ m. 'lathe' ; संघाट joinery; M. sãgaḍ 'double-canoe' Rebus: sangataras. संगतराश lit. 'to collect stones, stone-cutter, mason.'*

First sign read rebus as at Kalibangan 9a. dulo 'hole' Rebus; dul 'cast metal'

 *aḍar* 'harrow'; rebus: *aduru* 'native unsmelted metal'

 *khuṭo* ' leg, foot ', °ṭī ' goat's leg ' Rebus: *khōṭā* 'alloy' (Marathi)

 *kanka* 'rim of jar' Rebus: *karṇīka* 'account (scribe)' *karṇī* 'supercargo'

 m1658B

kuṭila 'bent' *katthīl* =  CDIAL 3230 kuṭi— in cmpd. 'curve', *kuṭika—* 'bent' MBh. Rebus: *kuṭila,* bronze (8 parts copper and 2 parts tin)

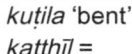

The hieroglyph may be a variant of:  *kana, kanac* = corner (Santali); Rebus: *kañcu* = bronze (Telugu) PLUS kolom 'three' Rebus: kolami 'smithy, forge.

 h927A

 *kuṭila* 'bent' CDIAL 3230 kuṭi— in cmpd. 'curve', *kuṭika—* 'bent' MBh. Rebus: *kuṭila, katthīl* = bronze (8 parts copper and 2 parts tin)

 *koḍi* 'flag' (Ta.)(DEDR 2049). Rebus 1: *koḍ* 'workshop' (Kuwi) Rebus 2: *khōḍ* m. 'pit', *khōḍü* f. 'small pit' (Kashmiri. CDIAL 3947).

 m1910a Rhinoceros/boar: baḍhia = a castrated boar, a hog (Santali) baḍhi 'a caste who work both in iron and wood' (Santali) *baṟea* 'merchant' pattar 'trough' Rebus: pattar 'guild, goldsmith'

mēḍu height, rising ground, hillock (Kannada) Rebus: *mẽṛhẽt, meḍ* 'iron' (Munda.Ho.) PLUS
erako 'upraised hand' Rebus: erako 'moltencast copper' PLUS

meḍ 'body' Rebus: *meḍ* 'iron' (Ho.) काठी [kāṭhī] *f* (काष्ट S) 'frame or structure of the body' (Marathi) Rebus: खंडी [khaṇḍī] measure of weight (Marathi) கண்டி; *kaṇṭi, n. < Mhr. khaṇḍil. [T. Tu. khaṇḍi, M. kaṇḍi.]* Candy, a weight, stated to be roughly equivalent to 500 lbs.

kanka 'rim of jar' Rebus: *karṇīka* 'account (scribe)' *karṇī* 'supercargo' *ḍhanga* = a crook used for pulling down the branches of trees, for goats, sheep and camels (P.) Rebus:*ḍhangar* blacksmith' *aya kammaṭa.*'coiner, mint alloy'

कांड *kāṇḍa* 'arrow' Rebus: *kāṇḍa* 'pots and pans, metalware, tools'. Rebus 2: kaṇḍ 'fire-altar' (Santali)

m98a *खोंड [khōṇḍa] m A young bull, a bullcalf. (Marathi) Rebus: kõdār 'turner' (Bengali); कोंद kōnda 'engraver, lapidary setting or infixing gems' (Marathi) G. sãghārɔ m. 'lathe' ; संघाट joinery; M. sãgaḍ 'double-canoe' Rebus: sangataras. संगतराश lit. 'to collect stones, stone-cutter, mason.'*

kuṭila 'bent' CDIAL 3230 kuṭi— in cmpd. 'curve', *kuṭika—* 'bent' MBh. Rebus: *kuṭila, katthīl* = bronze (8 parts copper and 2 parts tin)
|||| Numeral 4: gaṇḍa 'four' Rebus: kaṇḍa 'furnace, fire-altar' (Santali)

||| Numeral 3: *kolom* 'three' Rebus*: kolami* 'smithy, forge'
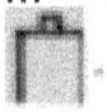
सांड [sāṇḍa] *f* (षद S) An outlet for superfluous water (as through a dam or mound); a sluice, a floodvent. Rebus: सांडणी [sāṇḍaṇī] *f* (H) An instrument of goldsmiths. It is hooked or curved at the extremity; and is used to draw things out of the fire.
सांठा [*sāṇṭhā*] *m* (संचय S) A collection, heap, hoard, store, stock.साटें [*sāṭēṃ*] *n* (संचय S) A whole investment; the total quantity of merchandise (brought to market by one merchant).

kanka 'rim of jar' Rebus: *karṇīka* 'account (scribe)' *karṇī* 'supercargo'

m331f

kuṭila 'bent' CDIAL 3230 kuṭi— in cmpd. 'curve', *kuṭika—* 'bent' MBh. Rebus: *kuṭila, katthīl* = bronze (8 parts copper and 2 parts tin)

loa 'ficus religiosa' Rebus: *lo* 'iron' (Sanskrit) PLUS unique ligatures: लोखंड [lōkhaṇḍa] *n* (लोह S) Iron. लोखंडाचे चणे खावविणें or चारणें To oppress grievously.लोखंडकाम [lōkhaṇḍakāma] *n* Iron work; that portion (of a building, machine &c.) which consists of iron. 2 The business of an ironsmith.लोखंडी [lōkhaṇḍī] *a* (लोखंड) Composed of iron; relating to iron. (Marathi)

aḍaren 'cover of pot or lid' Rebus: *aduru* 'native, unsmelted metal' Duplicated: dula 'pair' Rebus: dul 'cast metal'

 *kuṭila* 'bent' CDIAL 3230 kuṭi— in cmpd. 'curve', *kuṭika—* 'bent' MBh. Rebus: *kuṭila, katthīl* = bronze (8 parts copper and 2 parts tin)

 m1277A

 *kuṭila* 'bent' CDIAL 3230 kuṭi— in cmpd. 'curve', *kuṭika—* 'bent' MBh. Rebus: *kuṭila, katthīl* = bronze (8 parts copper and 2 parts tin) Duplicated: dula 'pair' Rebus: dul 'cast metal' Thus, cast bronze. PLUS mogge 'bud' Rebus*: mũh* 'ingot'. dula 'two' Rebus: dul 'cast metal'

h272A *खोंड [khōṇḍa] m A young bull, a bullcalf. (Marathi) Rebus: kõdār 'turner' (Bengali); कोंद kōnda 'engraver, lapidary setting or infixing gems' (Marathi) G. sãghāṛɔ m. 'lathe' ; संघाट joinery; M. sãgaḍ 'double-canoe' Rebus: sangataras. संगतराश lit. 'to collect stones, stone-cutter, mason.'* First 2 signs read rebus as at m1277A.

  Strands of yarn/rope' hieroglyph: Hieroglyph: 'strands of yarn' Rebus reading: *dhā'tu* 'strand of rope' Rebus: *dhatu* 'mineral ore' (Santali) sal 'splinter' Rebus: sal 'workshop' *aya kammaṭa.*'coiner, mint alloy'

|||| Numeral 4: gaṇḍa 'four' Rebus: kaṇḍa 'furnace, fire-altar' (Santali)

||| Numeral 3: *kolom* 'three' Rebus*: kolami* 'smithy, forge'

 सांड [sāṇḍa] *f* (षद S) An outlet for superfluous water (as through a dam or mound); a sluice, a floodvent. Rebus: सांडणी [sāṇḍaṇī] *f* (H) An instrument of goldsmiths. It is hooked or curved at the extremity; and is used to draw things out of the fire.

सांठा [*sāṇṭhā*] *m* (संचय S) A collection, heap, hoard, store, stock.साटें [*sāṭēṃ*] *n* (संचय S) A whole investment; the total quantity of merchandise (brought to market by one merchant).

 mēḍu height, rising ground, hillock (Kannada) Rebus: *mẽṛhẽt, meḍ* 'iron' (Munda.Ho.)

  m1529A Copper plate.

 *kuṭila* 'bent' CDIAL 3230 kuṭi— in cmpd. 'curve', *kuṭika—* 'bent' MBh. Rebus: *kuṭila, katthīl* = bronze (8 parts copper and 2 parts tin) Duplicated: dula 'pair' Rebus: dul 'cast metal' Thus, cast bronze. dula 'two' Rebus: dul 'cast metal' ranku 'liquid measure' Rebus: ranku 'tin' INFIXED in: dula 'pair' Rebus; dul 'cast metal' खांडा [*khāṇḍā*] *m* A jag, notch, or indentation (as upon the edge of a tool or weapon). Rebus: *kāṇḍa* 'tools, pots and pans and metal-ware' Thus, mint metalware, ore.

 *meḍ* 'body' Rebus: *meḍ* 'iron' (Ho.) काठी [kāṭhī] *f* (काष्ट S) 'frame or structure of the body' (Marathi) Rebus: खंडी [khaṇḍī] measure of weight (Marathi) *கண்டி; kaṇṭi, n. < Mhr. khaṇḍil. [T. Tu. khaṇḍi, M. kaṇḍi.]* Candy, a weight, stated to be roughly equivalent to 500 lbs. dulo 'hole' Rebus: dul 'cast metal'

Side B: Composite animal: bull + rhinoceros + elephant *balad* m. ' ox ', gng. *bald*, (Ku.) *barad*, id. (N. Tarai) Rebus: *bharat* (5 copper, 4 zinc and 1 tin)(Punjabi) *pattar* 'trough' Rebus: *pattar* 'guild'. Thus, copper-zinc-tin alloy (worker) guild. Ibha 'elephant' Rebus: ib 'iron' Rhinoceros/boar: baḍhia = a castrated boar, a hog (Santali) baḍhi 'a caste who work both in iron and wood' (Santali) *baṟea* 'merchant' INSCRIBED on body: kolom 'three' Rebus: kolami 'smith, forge'

h57a *खोंड [khōṇḍa] m A young bull, a bullcalf. (Marathi) Rebus: kõdār 'turner' (Bengali); कोंद kōnda 'engraver, lapidary setting or infixing gems' (Marathi) G. sãghāṛɔ m. 'lathe' ; संघाट joinery; M. sāgaḍ 'double-canoe' Rebus: sangataras. संगतराश lit. 'to collect stones, stone-cutter, mason.'*

kuṭila 'bent' CDIAL 3230 kuṭi— in cmpd. 'curve', *kuṭika*— 'bent' MBh. Rebus: *kuṭila, katthīl* = bronze (8 parts copper and 2 parts tin) Duplicated: dula 'pair' Rebus: dul 'cast metal' Thus, cast bronze. INFIXED

baroṭi 'twelve' *bhārata* 'a factitious alloy of copper, pewter, tin' (Marathi)

water-carrier hieroglyph *kuṭi*; Rebus: *kuṭhi* 'smelter furnace'. *aḍaren* 'cover of pot or lid' Rebus: *aduru* 'native, unsmelted metal'

खोंड [khōṇḍa] m A young bull, a bullcalf. (Marathi) Rebus: kõdār 'turner' (Bengali); कोंद kōnda 'engraver, lapidary setting or infixing gems' (Marathi) G. sãghāṛɔ m. 'lathe' ; संघाट joinery; M. sāgaḍ 'double-canoe' Rebus: sangataras 'stone-cutter, mason'

khareḍo =  a currycomb (Gujarati) खरारा [*kharārā*] *m* (H) A currycomb. 2 Currying a horse. (Marathi) Rebus: करडा [*karaḍā*] Hard from alloy--iron, silver &c. (Marathi) *kharādī* ' turner' (Gujarati)

meḍ 'body' Rebus: *meḍ* 'iron' (Ho.) काठी [kāṭhī] *f* (काष्ट S) 'frame or structure of the body' (Marathi) Rebus: खंडी [khaṇḍī] measure of weight (Marathi) கண்டி; *kaṇṭi, n. < Mhr. khaṇḍil. [T. Tu. khaṇḍi, M. kaṇḍi.]* Candy, a weight, stated to be roughly equivalent to 500 lbs.

loa 'ficus religiosa' Rebus: *lo* 'iron' (Sanskrit) PLUS unique ligatures: लोखंड [lōkhaṇḍa] *n* (लोह S) Iron. लोखंडाचे चणे खावविणें or चारणें To oppress grievously.लोखंडकाम [lōkhaṇḍakāma] *n* Iron work; that portion (of a building, machine &c.) which consists of iron. 2 The business of an ironsmith.लोखंडी [lōkhaṇḍī] *a* (लोखंड) Composed of iron; relating to iron. (Marathi) *bhaṭa* 'warrior' (Sanskrit) Rebus: *baṭa* a kind of iron (Gujarati). Rebus: *bhaṭa* 'furnace' (Santali) Thus, together, the ligatured hieroglyph reads rebus: *loa bhaṭa* 'iron furnace' *sal 'splinter' Rebus: sal 'workshop'*

kuṭila 'bent' CDIAL 3230 kuṭi— in cmpd. 'curve', *kuṭika*— 'bent' MBh. Rebus: *kuṭila, katthīl* = bronze (8 parts copper and 2 parts tin) Duplicated: dula 'pair' Rebus: dul 'cast metal' Thus, cast bronze. INFIXED

bicha 'scorpion' (Assamese) Rebus: *bica* 'stone ore' (Santali)

m1314A *mogge* 'sprout, bud' Rebus: *mūh* 'ingot' (Santali) *āra* 'six' Rebus: *āra* 'brass'खांडा [*khāṇḍā*] *m* A jag, notch, or indentation (as upon the edge of a tool or weapon). Rebus: *kāṇḍa* 'tools, pots and pans and metal-ware'

kanka 'rim of jar' Rebus: *karṇīka* 'account (scribe)' *karṇī* 'supercargo'

kuṭila 'bent' CDIAL 3230 kuṭi— in cmpd. 'curve', *kuṭika—* 'bent' MBh. Rebus: *kuṭila, katthīl* = bronze (8 parts copper and 2 parts tin) Duplicated: dula 'pair' Rebus: dul 'cast metal' Thus, cast bronze.

m846a

h32a *खोंड [khōṇḍa] m A young bull, a bullcalf. (Marathi) Rebus: kõdār 'turner' (Bengali); कोंद kōnda 'engraver, lapidary setting or infixing gems' (Marathi) G. sãghārɔ m. 'lathe' ; संघाट joinery; M. sãgaḍ 'double-canoe' Rebus: sangataras 'stone-cutter, mason'*

kuṭila 'bent' CDIAL 3230 kuṭi— in cmpd. 'curve', *kuṭika—* 'bent' MBh. Rebus: *kuṭila, katthīl* = bronze (8 parts copper and 2 parts tin) Duplicated: dula 'pair' Rebus: dul 'cast metal' Thus, cast bronze.

kanka 'rim of jar' Rebus: *karṇīka* 'account (scribe)' *karṇī* 'supercargo'

h461A *खोंड [khōṇḍa] m A young bull, a bullcalf. (Marathi) Rebus: kõdār 'turner' (Bengali); कोंद kōnda 'engraver, lapidary setting or infixing gems' (Marathi) G. sãghārɔ m. 'lathe' ; संघाट joinery; M. sãgaḍ 'double-canoe' Rebus: sangataras 'stone-cutter, mason'*

bicha 'scorpion' (Assamese) Rebus: *bica* 'stone ore' (Santali) *baṭa* = rimless pot (Kannada) Rebus:) *baṭa* = a kind of iron (G.)) *bhaṭa* furnace (Gujarati) dula 'pair' Rebus: dul 'cast metal' sal 'splinter' Rebus: sal 'workshop'

loa 'ficus religiosa' Rebus: *lo* 'iron' (Sanskrit) PLUS unique ligatures: लोखंड [lōkhaṇḍa] *n* (लोह S) Iron. लोखंडाचे चणे खावविणें or चारणें To oppress grievously.लोखंडकाम [lōkhaṇḍakāma] *n* Iron work; that portion (of a building, machine &c.) which consists of iron. 2 The business of an ironsmith.लोखंडी [lōkhaṇḍī] *a* (लोखंड) Composed of iron; relating to iron. (Marathi)

kanka 'rim of jar' Rebus: *karṇīka* 'account (scribe)' *karṇī* 'supercargo'

meḍ 'body' Rebus: *meḍ* 'iron' (Ho.) काठी [kāṭhī] *f* (काष्ट S) 'frame or structure of the body' (Marathi) Rebus: खंडी [khaṇḍī] measure of weight (Marathi) *கண்டி; kaṇṭi, n. < Mhr. khaṇḍil. [T. Tu. khaṇḍi, M. kaṇḍi.]* Candy, a weight, stated to be roughly equivalent to 500 lbs.

h1372A

kuṭila 'bent' CDIAL 3230 kuṭi— in cmpd. 'curve', *kuṭika—* 'bent' MBh. Rebus: *kuṭila, katthīl* = bronze (8 parts copper and 2 parts tin) Duplicated: dula 'pair'

Rebus: dul 'cast metal' Thus, cast bronze. INFIXED *bhaṭa* 'warrior' (Sanskrit) Rebus: *baṭa* a kind of iron (Gujarati). Rebus: *bhaṭa* 'furnace' (Santali

water-carrier hieroglyph *kuṭi*; Rebus: *kuṭhi* 'smelter furnace'. PLUS 'rim of jar':

kanka 'rim of jar' Rebus: karṇīka 'account (scribe)' karṇī 'supercargo'

MS5059 खोंड *kōdār 'turner' infixing gems' sãgaḍ 'double-*

[khōṇḍa] m A young bull, a bullcalf. (Marathi) Rebus: (Bengali); कोंद *kōnda 'engraver, lapidary setting or (Marathi) G. sãghāṛɔ m. 'lathe' ;* संघाट *joinery; M. canoe' Rebus: sangataras 'stone-cutter, mason'*

kuṭila 'bent' CDIAL 3230 kuṭi— in cmpd. 'curve', *kuṭika*— 'bent' MBh. Rebus: *kuṭila, katthīl* = bronze (8 parts copper and 2 parts tin) Duplicated: dula 'pair' Rebus: dul 'cast metal' Thus, cast bronze. INFIXED dulo 'hole' Rebus: dul 'cast metal'

khaṇḍ 'field, division' (Skt.) Rebus: *khānḍa* 'tools, pots and pans, metal-ware'. Rebus 2: kaṇḍ 'fire-altar' (Santali) dula 'pair' Rebus: dul 'cast metal' Thus, duplicated 'division' hieroglyph sign reads: cast metal metal-ware. *kamaḍha* 'archer, bow' Rebus: *kammaṭa* 'mint, coiner'.

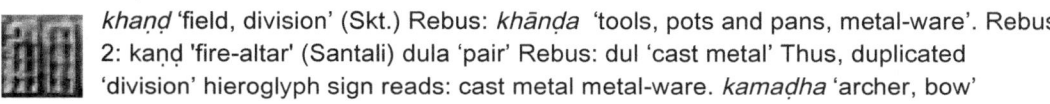

khareḍo = a currycomb (Gujarati) खरारा [*kharārā*] *m* (H) A currycomb. 2 Currying a horse. (Marathi) Rebus: करडा [*karaḍā*] Hard from alloy--iron, silver &c. (Marathi) *kharādī* ' turner' (Gujarati)

araṇe 'lizard' Rebus: *airaṇ* 'anvil'. Vikalpa: *karāvu* 'crocodile' Rebus: khara 'blacksmith'

cīmara 'black ant' Rebus: *cīmara* 'copper'. *cīmara kāra* -- ' coppersmith '

baroṭi 'twelve' *bhārata* 'a factitious alloy of copper, pewter, tin' (Marathi)

'Scorpion sting' sign hieroglyph with unique ligatures and pairing hieroglyph bica 'stone ore' PLUS *ḍhālako* 'a large metal ingot '

bicha 'scorpion' (Assamese) Rebus: *bica* 'stone ore' (Santali)

The pair of hieroglyph signs are compositions: bicha 'scorpion' (Assamese) Rebus: *bica* 'stone ore' (Santali) The pairing sign is a composition of: sloping stroke PLUS two short strokes of a 'splinter':*dhāḷ* 'a slope'; 'inclination of a plane' (Gujarati); *ḍhāḷiyum* = adj. sloping, inclining (Gujarati) Rebus: *ḍhālako* = a large metal ingot (Gujarati) *ḍhālakī* = a metal heated and poured into a mould; a solid piece of metal; an ingot (Gujarati)PLUS*sal* 'splinter' Rebus: *sal* 'workshop'. Thus the composition reads: *ḍhālako sal* 'ingot workshop'.

Nindowari 2a खोंड [khōṇḍa] m A young bull, a bullcalf. (Marathi) Rebus: kõdār 'turner' (Bengali); कोंद kōnda 'engraver, lapidary setting or infixing gems' (Marathi) G. sãghāṛɔ m. 'lathe' ; संघाट joinery; M. sãgaḍ 'double-canoe' Rebus: sangataras 'stone-cutter, mason' bica 'stone ore' PLUS *kamaḍha* 'crab' Rebus: *kammaṭa* 'mint, coiner'.
ḍato = claws of crab (Santali) Rebus: *dhātu* 'mineral ore'

kharedo = a currycomb (Gujarati) खरारा [*kharārā*] *m* (H) A currycomb. 2 Currying a horse. (Marathi) Rebus: करडा [*karaḍā*] Hard from alloy--iron, silver &c. (Marathi) *kharādī* ' turner' (Gujarati)

M-222 a

m222a *खोंड [khōṇḍa] m A young bull, a bullcalf. (Marathi) Rebus: kõdār 'turner' (Bengali); कोंद kōnda 'engraver, lapidary setting or infixing gems' (Marathi) G. sãghāṛɔ m. 'lathe' ; संघाट joinery; M. sãgaḍ 'double-canoe' Rebus: sangataras 'stone-cutter, mason' bica* 'stone ore' *khuṭo* ' leg, foot ', °ṭī ' goat's leg ' Rebus: *khōṭā* 'alloy' (Marathi) *vāgoḷ* f. ' flying fox ' Rebus: bagala 'Arab boat'

m414a *bica* 'stone ore'

kanka 'rim of jar' Rebus: *karṇīka* 'account (scribe)' *karṇī* 'supercargo'

'Arrow' sign hieroglyph (variant) This is a ligature of 'lid of pot' hieroglyph superscript on 'a linear stroke' numeral hieroglyph.*aḍaren* 'cover of pot or lid' Rebus: *aduru* 'native, unsmelted metal' PLUS koḍ = one (Santali); koḍ 'workshop' (Gujarati) *ayo* 'fish' Rebus: *aya* 'iron' *ayas* 'metal'

M-455 A

m455A Read rebus as at m950a

m857a Read rebus as at m950a

M-857 a

M-950 a

m950a *खोंड [khōṇḍa] m A young bull, a bullcalf. (Marathi) Rebus: kõdār 'turner' (Bengali); कोंद kōnda 'engraver, lapidary setting or infixing gems' (Marathi) G. sãghāṛɔ m. 'lathe' ; संघाट joinery; M. sãgaḍ 'double-canoe' Rebus: sangataras 'stone-cutter, mason'* bica 'stone ore' PLUS *ḍhālako* 'a large metal ingot '

dāṭu 'cross'(Telugu) Rebus: *dhatu* 'mineral' (Santali).

kanka 'rim of jar' Rebus: *karṇīka* 'accou

  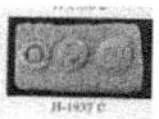

h1937A,B,C Read rebus as at h1939

h1938A,B,C SideA: read rebus as at m950a Side B: *baṭa* = rimless pot (Kannada) Rebus: *baṭa* = a kind of iron (G.)) *bhaṭa* furnace (Gujarati) kolom 'three' Rebus: kolami 'smithy, forge' Side C: dulo 'hole' Rebus: dul 'cast metal' kolom 'three' Rebus: kolami 'smithy, forge'

M-1780 A

m1780A *खोंड [khōṇḍa] m A young bull, a bullcalf. (Marathi) Rebus: kõdār 'turner' (Bengali); कोंद kōnda 'engraver, lapidary setting or infixing gems' (Marathi) G. sãghāṛɔ m. 'lathe' ; संघाट joinery; M. sãgaḍ 'double-canoe' Rebus: sangataras 'stone-cutter, mason'* bica 'stone ore'

'Arrow' sign hieroglyph (variant) This is a ligature of 'lid of pot' hieroglyph superscript on 'a linear stroke' numeral hieroglyph.*aḍaren* 'cover of pot or lid' Rebus: *aduru* 'native, unsmelted metal' PLUS koḍ = one (Santali); koḍ 'workshop' (Gujarati)
dulo 'hole' Rebus: dul 'cast animal' *kanka* (Santali) *karṇika* 'scribe'(Sanskrit)
Rebus: *karṇī,* supercargo for a boat shipment. INFIXED खांडा [*khāṇḍā*] *m* A jag, notch, or indentation (as upon the edge of a tool or weapon). Rebus: *kāṇḍa* 'tools, pots and pans and metal-ware'
kolom 'three' Rebus: kolami 'smithy, forge'

 *dāṭu* 'cross'(Telugu) Rebus: *dhatu* 'mineral' (Santali).

 *kanka* 'rim of jar' Rebus: *karṇīka* 'account (scribe)' *karṇī* 'supercargo'

H-1181 A

H-1181 B

kanka 'rim of jar' Rebus: karṇīka 'account (scribe)' karṇī 'supercargo'

Together, the pair of hieroglyph signs read: *bica ḍhālako sal* 'stone ore ingot workshop'.

H-2066 A

H-2066 B

h2066

h1181 PLUS water-carrier hieroglyph *kuṭi*; Rebus: *kuṭhi* 'smelter furnace'.

PLUS 'rim of jar': *kanka* (Santali) *karṇika* 'scribe'(Sanskrit) Rebus: *karṇī,* supercargo
PLUS

kharedo = a currycomb (Gujarati) खरारा [*kharārā*] *m* (H) A currycomb. 2 Currying a horse. (Marathi) Rebus: करडा [*karaḍā*] Hard from alloy--iron, silver &c. (Marathi) *kharādī* ' turner' (Gujarati)

kanac 'corner' Rebus: *kañcu* 'bronze'

muka 'ladle' (Tamil)(DEDR 4887) Rebus: *mũh* 'ingot' (Santali) *baṭa* = rimless pot (Kannada) Rebus: *baṭa* = a kind of iron (G.)) *bhaṭa* furnace (Gujarati) Thus, iron ingot. PLUS ranku 'liquid measure' Rebus: ranku 'tin'

h761a Read rebus as at Side A h2066, h1181

h299A Read rebus as at Side A h2066 h1181

m97A Read rebus as at Side A h2066 h1181 PLUS खोंड *[khōṇḍa] m A young bull, a bullcalf. (Marathi) Rebus: kõdār 'turner'* *(Bengali);* कोंद *kōnda 'engraver, lapidary setting or infixing gems'* *(Marathi) G. sãghāṛɔ m. 'lathe' ;* संघाट *joinery; M. sãgaḍ 'double-canoe'* *Rebus: sangataras 'stone- cutter, mason')* G. *sãghāṛɔ* m. 'lathe' ; *sãgāḍā* m. ' frame of a building ', *°ḍī* f. ' lathe '(CDIAL 12859) Rebus*: sangataras.* संगतराश lit. 'to collect stones, stone-cutter, mason.'

'Divided room' sign hieroglyph kole.l 'temple' Rebus: kole.l 'smithy' (Kota)

m1911a Rhinoceros/boar: baḍhia = a castrated boar, a hog (Santali) baḍhi 'a caste who work both in iron and wood' (Santali) *baṟea* 'merchant'

kolmo 'paddy plant' Rebus: *kolami* 'smithy, forge' Vikalpa: *mogge* 'sprout, bud' Rebus: *mũh* 'ingot' (Santali) dolu 'plant of shoot height' Rebus: dul 'cast metal' *kamaḍha* 'crab' Rebus: *kammaṭa* 'mint, coiner'.*ḍato* = claws of crab (Santali) Rebus: *dhātu* 'mineral ore' PLUS | *koḍa* 'one' Rebus: *koḍ* 'workshop' sal 'splinter' Rebus: sal 'workshop'

āra 'spokes' Rebus: *āra 'brass'*. cf. erka = ekke (Tbh. of arka) aka (Tbh. of arka) copper (metal); crystal (Kannada) Glyph: *eraka*'nave of wheel' Rebus: eraka 'copper'; cf. erka = ekke (Tbh. of arka) aka (Tbh. of arka) copper (metal); crystal (Kannada) *erako* 'moltencast copper' Duplicated: dula 'pair' Rebus: dul 'cast metal' Thus cast copper, brass casting.

h206A kole.l 'temple' Rebus: kole.l 'smithy' (Kota)

muka 'ladle' (Kannada)

(Tamil)(DEDR 4887) Rebus: *mũh* 'ingot' (Santali) *baṭa* = rimless pot Rebus: *baṭa* = a kind of iron (G.)) *bhaṭa* furnace (Gujarati) Thus, iron

ingot.

cīmara 'black ant' Rebus: *cīmara* 'copper'. *cīmara kāra* -- ' coppersmith ' *ayo* 'fish' Rebus: *aya* 'iron' *ayas* 'metal'

kəṭhā´r, kc. *kuṭhār* m. ' granary, storeroom '(WPah.)(CDIAL 3550). *koṭhārī m.* ' storekeeper' (Gujarati)(CDIAL 3551) Thus, storeroom (of) *kolom* 'three' Rebus: *kolami* 'smithy, forge'. Dula 'pair' Rebus: dul 'cast metal' Thus, together *dul kolami kuṭhār* 'metal smithy castings storeroom'

kanka 'rim of jar' Rebus: *karṇīka* 'account (scribe)' *karṇī* 'supercargo'

m180A *खोंड [khōṇḍa] m A young bull, a bullcalf. (Marathi) Rebus: kõdār 'turner' (Bengali); कोंद kōnda 'engraver, lapidary setting or infixing gems' (Marathi) G. sãghāṛɔ m. 'lathe' ; संघाट joinery; M. sãgaḍ 'double-canoe' Rebus: sangataras 'stone-cutter, mason'* kole.l 'temple' Rebus: kole.l 'smithy' (Kota)

kanka 'rim of jar' Rebus: karṇīka 'account (scribe)' karṇī 'supercargo'

h60a *खोंड [khōṇḍa] m A young bull, a bullcalf. (Marathi) Rebus: kõdār 'turner' (Bengali); कोंद kōnda 'engraver, lapidary setting or infixing gems' (Marathi) G. sãghāṛɔ m. 'lathe' ; संघाट joinery; M. sãgaḍ 'double-canoe' Rebus: sangataras 'stone-cutter, mason'* G. *sãghāṛɔ* m. 'lathe' ; *sãgāḍā* m. ' frame of a building ', *°ḍī* f. ' lathe '(CDIAL 12859) Rebus*: sangataras.* संगतराश lit. 'to collect stones, stone-cutter, mason.
kole.l 'temple' Rebus: kole.l 'smithy' (Kota)

kanka 'rim of jar' Rebus: *karṇīka* 'account (scribe)' *karṇī* 'supercargo' *aḍaren* 'cover of pot or lid' Rebus: *aduru* 'native, unsmelted metal' sal 'splinter' Rebus: sal 'workshop'

āra 'spokes' Rebus: *āra 'brass'.* cf. erka = ekke (Tbh. of arka) aka (Tbh. of arka) copper (metal); crystal (Kannada) Glyph: *eraka*'nave of wheel' Rebus: eraka 'copper'; cf. erka = ekke (Tbh. of arka) aka (Tbh. of arka) copper (metal); crystal (Kannada) *erako* 'moltencast copper' Duplicated: dula 'pair' Rebus: dul 'cast metal' Thus cast copper, brass casting. sal 'splinter' Rebus; sal 'workshop'

m782a *खोंड [khōṇḍa] m A young bull, a bullcalf. (Marathi) Rebus: kõdār 'turner' (Bengali); कोंद kōnda 'engraver, lapidary setting or infixing gems' (Marathi) G. sãghāṛɔ m. 'lathe' ; संघाट joinery; M. sãgaḍ 'double-canoe' Rebus: sangataras 'stone-cutter, mason'* G. *sãghāṛɔ* m. 'lathe' ; *sãgāḍā* m. ' frame of a building ', *°ḍī* f. ' lathe '(CDIAL 12859) Rebus*: sangataras.* संगतराश lit. 'to collect stones, stone-cutter, mason.' kole.l 'temple' Rebus: kole.l 'smithy' (Kota)

kanka 'rim of jar' Rebus: *karṇīka* 'account (scribe)' *karṇī* 'supercargo' खांडा [*khāṇḍā*] *m* A jag, notch, or indentation (as upon the edge of a tool or weapon). Rebus: *kāṇḍa* 'tools, pots and pans and metal-ware' gaṇḍa 'four' Rebus: kaṇḍa 'furnace, fire-altar' (Santali) INFIXED

 *kuṭila* 'bent' CDIAL 3230 kuṭi— in cmpd. 'curve', *kuṭika—* 'bent' MBh. Rebus: *kuṭila, katthīl* = bronze (8 parts copper and 2 parts tin) sal 'splinter' Rebus: sal 'workshop'

 *kanka* 'rim of jar' Rebus: *karṇīka* 'account (scribe)' *karṇī* 'supercargo'

m952A *खोंड [khōṇḍa] m A young bull, a bullcalf. (Marathi) Rebus: kõdār 'turner' (Bengali); कोंद kōnda 'engraver, lapidary setting or infixing gems' (Marathi) G. sãghāṛɔ m. 'lathe' ; संघाट joinery; M. sãgaḍ 'double-canoe' Rebus: sangataras 'stone-cutter, mason'* G. *sãghāṛɔ* m. 'lathe' ; *sãgāḍā* m. ' frame of a building ', *°ḍī* f. ' lathe '(CDIAL 12859) Rebus*: sangataras.* संगतराश lit. 'to collect stones, stone-cutter, mason.' kole.l 'temple' Rebus: kole.l 'smithy' (Kota) INFIXED *baṭa* = rimless pot (Kannada) Rebus: *baṭa* = a kind of iron (G.)) *bhaṭa* furnace (Gujarati) Thus, the temple furnace.

 *kanac* 'corner' Rebus: *kañcu* 'bronze'

m714a *खोंड [khōṇḍa] m A young bull, a bullcalf. (Marathi) Rebus: kõdār 'turner' (Bengali); कोंद kōnda 'engraver, lapidary setting or infixing gems' (Marathi) G. sãghāṛɔ m. 'lathe' ; संघाट joinery; M. sãgaḍ 'double-canoe' Rebus: sangataras 'stone-cutter, mason'* G. *sãghāṛɔ* m. 'lathe' ; *sãgāḍā* m. ' frame of a building ', *°ḍī* f. ' lathe '(CDIAL 12859) Rebus*: sangataras.* संगतराश lit. 'to collect stones, stone-cutter, mason.' kole.l 'temple' Rebus: kole.l 'smithy' (Kota)

 *kanac* 'corner' Rebus: *kañcu* 'bronze' sal 'splinter' Rebus: sal 'workshop' *dula* 'pair' Rebus: *dul* 'cast (metal)' PLUS *kana, kanac* = corner (Santali); Rebus: *kañcu* = bronze (Telugu) PLUS infixed kolmo 'paddy plant' Rebus: kolami 'smithy, forge'. Thus, cast bronze smithy, forge. Or, *mogge* 'sprout, bud' Rebus: *mũh* 'ingot' (Santali)Thus, cast bronze ingot. Read as: *kañcu dul mũh 'bronze cast ingot' kamaḍha* 'crab' Rebus: *kammaṭa* 'mint, coiner'.*ḍato* = claws of crab (Santali) Rebus: *dhātu* 'mineral ore'

 *ayo* 'fish' Rebus: *aya* 'iron' *ayas* 'metal' *muka* 'ladle' (Tamil)(DEDR 4887) Rebus: *mũh* 'ingot' (Santali) *baṭa* = rimless pot (Kannada) Rebus:) *baṭa* = a kind of iron (G.)) *bhaṭa* furnace (Gujarati) Thus, iron ingot.

kolom 'three' Rebus: kolami 'smithy, forge'|||| Numeral 4: gaṇḍa 'four' Rebus: kaṇḍa 'furnace, fire-altar' (Santali)||| Numeral 3: *kolom* 'three' Rebus*: kolami* 'smithy, forge'

 सांड [sāṇḍa] *f* (षद S) An outlet for superfluous water (as through a dam or mound); a sluice, a floodvent. Rebus: सांडणी [sāṇḍaṇī] *f* (H) An instrument of goldsmiths. It is hooked or curved at the extremity; and is used to draw things out of the fire.

सांठा [*sāṇthā*] *m* (संचय S) A collection, heap, hoard, store, stock.साटें [*sāṭēṃ*] *n* (संचय S) A whole investment; the total quantity of merchandise (brought to market by one merchant).

 *kanka* 'rim of jar' Rebus: *karṇīka* 'account (scribe)' *karṇī* 'supercargo'

Lothal 56A kole.l 'temple' Rebus: kole.l 'smithy' (Kota)

 *kanka* 'rim of jar' Rebus: *karṇīka* 'account (scribe)' *karṇī* 'supercargo'

m1292A kole.l 'temple' Rebus: kole.l 'smithy' (Kota) खांडा [*khāṇḍā*] *m* A jag, notch, or indentation (as upon the edge of a tool or

weapon). Rebus: *kāṇḍa* 'tools, pots and pans and metal-ware' *kanka* 'rim of jar' Rebus: *karṇīka* 'account (scribe)' *karṇī* 'supercargo' INFIXED kolom 'three' Rebus: kolami 'smithy, forge'

kuṭila 'bent' CDIAL 3230 kuṭi— in cmpd. 'curve', *kuṭika*— 'bent' MBh. Rebus: *kuṭila, katthīl* = bronze (8 parts copper and 2 parts tin) Duplicated: dula 'pair' Rebus: dul 'cast metal' Thus, cast bronze or bronze castings

m240a *balad* m. ' ox ', gng. *bald*, (Ku.) *barad*, id. (N. Tarai) Rebus: *bharat* (5 copper, 4 zinc and 1 tin)(Punjabi) *pattar* 'trough' Rebus: *pattar* 'guild'. Thus, copper-zinc-tin alloy (worker) guild.
kole.l 'temple' Rebus: kole.l 'smithy' (Kota)

kanac 'corner' Rebus: *kañcu* 'bronze' sal 'splinter' Rebus: sal 'workshop' dula 'two' Rebus: dul 'workshop' *ayo* 'fish' Rebus: *aya* 'iron' *ayas* 'metal' *aya kammaṭa.*'coiner, mint alloy'

कांड *kāṇḍa* 'arrow' Rebus: *kāṇḍa* 'pots and pans, metalware, tools'. Rebus 2: kaṇḍ 'fire-altar' (Santali)

m1273A kole.l 'temple' Rebus: kole.l 'smithy' (Kota)

kanac  'corner' Rebus: *kañcu* 'bronze' sal 'splinter' Rebus: sal 'workshop'

baroṭi 'twelve' *bhārata* 'a factitious alloy of copper, pewter, tin' (Marathi) *kanka* 'rim of jar' Rebus: *karṇīka* 'account (scribe)' *karṇī* 'supercargo'

खोंड [khōṇḍa] m A young bull, a bullcalf. (Marathi) Rebus: kōdār 'turner' (Bengali); कोंद kōnda 'engraver, lapidary setting or infixing gems' (Marathi) G. sãghāṛɔ m. 'lathe' ; संघाट joinery; M. sāgaḍ 'double-canoe' Rebus: sangataras 'stone-cutter, mason' G. *sãghāṛɔ* m. 'lathe' ; *sãgāḍā* m. ' frame of a building ', *°ḍī* f. ' lathe '(CDIAL 12859) Rebus: *sangataras.* संगतरा) *kamaḍha* 'archer, bow' Rebus: *kammaṭa* 'mint, coiner'.

muka 'ladle' (Tamil)(DEDR 4887) Rebus: *mũh* 'ingot' (Santali) *baṭa* = rimless pot (Kannada) Rebus: *baṭa* = a kind of iron (G.)) *bhaṭa* furnace (Gujarati) Thus, iron ingot. *mogge* 'sprout, bud' Rebus: *mũh* 'ingot'

kanka 'rim of jar' Rebus: *karṇīka* 'account (scribe)' *karṇī* 'supercargo'

'Curved lines' sign hieroglyph Variant:

kuṭila 'bent' CDIAL 3230 kuṭi— in cmpd. 'curve', *kuṭika*— 'bent' MBh. Rebus: *kuṭila, katthīl* = bronze (8 parts copper and 2 parts tin) Duplicated: dula 'pair' Rebus: dul 'cast metal' Thus, cast bronze or bronze castings. PLUS *mogge* 'sprout, bud' Rebus*: mũh* ingot'. Thus, bronze ingot castings.

 m1179  M-1179 a bis m1179a Text 2606 

Rebus reading of markhor hieroglyph on m1180a and m1179 seal:

miṇḍāl 'markhor' (Tōrwālī)*meḍho* a ram, a sheep (Gujarati)(CDIAL 10120) Rebus: *mẽṛhẽt, meḍ* 'iron' (Mu.Ho.)
dhatu 'scarf; (Western Pahari) Rebus: dhatu 'mineral ore' (Santali)

Rebus reading of Text 2606:

Variant hieroglyph Sign:  कुटिल kuṭila 'bent' Rebus: 'bronze' Duplicated bent glyph: dula 'pair' Rebus; dul 'cast metal'. Thus the hieroglyph denotes caste bronze.

 *kanka* 'rim of jar' Rebus: *karṇīka* 'account (scribe)' *karṇī* 'supercargo'

The seal impression m417A is a variant ligaturing creating a composition of six heads of animals: of one-horned young bull, of short-horned bull (Bison or ox), of zebu, of tiger, of antelope and another uncertain animal – radiating outward from a hatched ring: m417A

The hieroglyphic pictorial motif composition can be treated as a variant of the 'composite animal' hieroglyph and read rebus accordingly as: ingot (from) iron smelter, tin smelter merchant guild (with the addition of one-horned young bull, the reading includes: metal turner PLUS 'short-horned bull' which reads rebus as follows:
Allograph of *baraḍo* = spine; backbone: ox, bull: : Ku. *balad* m. ' ox ', gng. *bald*, N. (Tarai) *barad*, id.

Rebus: bāraṇiyo = one whose profession it is to sift ashes or dust in a goldsmith's workshop (Gujarati) In the Punjab, the mixed alloys were generally called, bharat (5 copper, 4 zinc and 1 tin). In Bengal, an alloy called bharan or toul was created by adding some brass or zinc into pure bronze. bharata = casting metals in moulds; bharavum = to fill in; to put in; to pour into (Gujarati) Bengali. ভরন [bharana] n an inferior metal obtained from an alloy of coper, zinc and tin.L. bhāraṇ ' to spread or bring out from a kiln '; M. bhārṇẽ, bhāḷṇẽ ' to make strong by charms (weapons, rice, water), enchant, fascinate (CDIAL 9463) Ash. barī ' blacksmith, artisan (CDIAL 9464). Baran, bharat 'mixed alloys' (5 copper, 4 zinc and 1 tin) (Punjabi) bharana id. (Bengali) bharan or toul was created by adding some brass or zinc into pure bronze. bharata = casting metals in moulds (Bengali) *bharata* 'a factitious metal compounded of copper, pewter, tin' (Marathi)

m747a *खोंड [khōṇḍa] m A young bull, a bullcalf. (Marathi) Rebus: kõdār 'turner' (Bengali); कोंद kōnda 'engraver, lapidary setting or infixing gems' (Marathi) G. sãghāṛɔ m. 'lathe' ; संघाट joinery; M. sãgaḍ 'double-canoe' Rebus: sangataras 'stone-cutter, mason'* G. *sãghāṛɔ* m. 'lathe' ; *sãgāḍā* m. ' frame of a building ', *°ḍī* f. ' lathe '(CDIAL 12859) Rebus*: sangataras.* संगतराश lit. 'to collect stones, stone-cutter, mason.'

Bronze ingot castings.

muka 'ladle' (Tamil)(DEDR 4887) Rebus: *mũh* 'ingot' (Santali) *baṭa* = rimless pot (Kannada) Rebus:) *baṭa* = a kind of iron (G.)) *bhaṭa* furnace (Gujarati) Thus, iron ingot.

kamaḍha 'crab' Rebus: *kammaṭa* 'mint, coiner'.

ḍato = claws of crab (Santali) Rebus: *dhātu* 'mineral ore'

kole.l 'temple' Rebus: kole.l 'smithy' (Kota)

m843a *खोंड [khōṇḍa] m A young bull, a bullcalf. (Marathi) Rebus: kõdār 'turner' (Bengali); कोंद kōnda 'engraver, lapidary setting or infixing gems' (Marathi) G. sãghāṛɔ m. 'lathe' ; संघाट joinery; M. sãgaḍ 'double-canoe' Rebus: sangataras 'stone-cutter, mason'* G. *sãghāṛɔ* m. 'lathe' ; *sãgāḍā* m. ' frame of a building ', *°ḍī* f. ' lathe '(CDIAL 12859) Rebus*: sangataras.* संगतराश lit. 'to collect stones, stone-cutter, mason.' Bronze ingot castings *kanka* (Santali) *karṇika* 'scribe'(Sanskrit) Rebus: *karṇī,* supercargo for a boat shipment. INFIXED खांडा [*khāṇḍā*] *m* A jag, notch, or indentation (as upon the edge of a tool or weapon). Rebus: *kāṇḍa* 'tools, pots and pans and metal-ware' karaṇḍa 'duck' (Sanskrit) karaṛa 'a very large aquatic bird' (Sindhi) Rebus: करडा [*karaḍā*] Hard from alloy--iron, silver &c. (Marathi) *kharādī* ' turner' (Gujarati)

dula 'pair' Rebus: dul 'cast metal' *mogge* 'sprout, bud' Rebus: *mũh* 'ingot' (Santali) Thus, cast metal ingot.

water-carrier hieroglyph *kuṭi*; Rebus: *kuṭhi* 'smelter furnace'.

h97A bagala 'pleiades' Rebus: bagalo = an Arabian merchant vessel (G.) bagala = an Arab boat of a particular description (Ka.); bagalā (M.); bagarige, bagarage = a kind of vessel (Ka.)

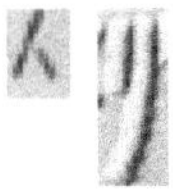

notch+slanted stroke reads rebus: *ḍhālako kāṇḍa* 'ingot, tools, pots and pans and metal-ware'.*dhāḷ* 'a slope'; 'inclination of a plane' (G.); *ḍhāḷiyum* = adj. sloping, inclining (G.) Rebus: *ḍhālako* = a large metal ingot (G.) *ḍhālakī* = a metal heated and poured into a mould; a solid piece of metal; an ingot (Gujarati) PLUS खांडा [*khāṇḍā*] *m* A jag, notch, or indentation (as upon the edge of a tool or weapon). Rebus: *kāṇḍa* 'tools, pots and pans and metal-ware' kole.l 'temple' Rebus: kolami 'smithy' PLUS kolom 'three' Rebus: kolami 'smith, forge' (Hieroglyphic -Phonetic –semantic determinant)

  *bicha* 'scorpion' (Assamese) Rebus: *bica* 'stone ore' (Santali) *muka* 'ladle' (Tamil)(DEDR 4887) Rebus: *mũh* 'ingot' (Santali) *baṭa* = rimless pot (Kannada) Rebus:) *baṭa* = a kind of iron (G.)) *bhaṭa* furnace (Gujarati) Thus, iron ingot. PLUS Bronze ingot castings.

Thus, the boatload supercargo comprised: Bronze ingot castings, iron ingots PLUS metalware from smithy, forge.

MS 5062 *balad* m. ' ox ', gng. *bald*, (Ku.) *barad*, id. (N. Tarai) Rebus: *bharat* (5 copper, 4 zinc and 1 tin)(Punjabi) *pattar* 'trough' Rebus*: pattar* 'guild'. Thus, copper-zinc-tin alloy (worker) guild.
Bronze ingot castings.

water-carrier  hieroglyph *kuṭi*; Rebus: *kuṭhi* 'smelter furnace'.
Ranku 'liquid measure' Rebus: ranku 'tin' PLUS *aḍaren* 'cover of pot or lid' Rebus: *aduru* 'native, unsmelted metal'

 *cīmara* 'black ant' Rebus: *cīmara* 'copper'. *cīmara kāra* -- ' coppersmith '

m1823A खोंड *[khōṇḍa] m A young bull, a bullcalf. (Marathi) Rebus: kōdār 'turner' (Bengali);* कोंद *kōnda 'engraver, lapidary setting or infixing gems' (Marathi) G. sãghāṛɔ m. 'lathe' ;* संघाट *joinery; M. sāgaḍ 'double-canoe' Rebus: sangataras 'stone-cutter, mason'* G. *sãghāṛɔ* m. 'lathe' ; *sãgāḍā* m. ' frame of a building ', *°ḍī* f. ' lathe '(CDIAL 12859) Rebus*: sangataras.* संगतराश lit. 'to collect stones, stone-cutter, mason.' Bronze ingot castings INFIXED 'bud': *mogge* 'sprout, bud' PLUS | *koḍa* 'one' Rebus: *koḍ* 'workshop' Rebus*: mũh* 'ingot' sal 'splinter' Rebus: sal 'workshop' gaṇḍa 'four' Rebus: kaṇḍa 'furnace, fire-altar' (Santali)

 *kolmo* 'paddy plant' Rebus: *kolami* 'smithy, forge' Vikalpa: *mogge* 'sprout, bud' Rebus: *mũh* 'ingot' (Santali) dolu 'plant of shoot height' Rebus: dul 'cast metal'

 Sign hieroglyph X ligatured with four or six rings
gaṇḍa 'four' Rebus: kaṇḍa 'furnace, fire-altar' (Santali) dulo 'hole' Rebus: dul 'cast metal' Thus, metal castings fire-altar

m241aa *balad* m. ' ox ', gng. *bald*, (Ku.) *barad*, id. (N. Tarai) Rebus: *bharat* (5 copper, 4 zinc and 1 tin)(Punjabi) *pattar* 'trough' Rebus*: pattar* 'guild'. Thus, copper-zinc-tin alloy (worker) guild. Metal castings fire-altar. *kaṇḍo* 'stool, seat' Rebus: *kāṇḍa* 'metalware' *kaṇḍa* 'fire-altar' PLUS

 'Arrow' sign hieroglyph (variant) This is a ligature of 'lid of pot' hieroglyph superscript on 'a linear stroke' numeral hieroglyph.*aḍaren* 'cover of pot or lid' Rebus: *aduru* 'native, unsmelted metal' PLUS koḍ = one (Santali); koḍ 'workshop' (Gujarati)

 *kanka* 'rim of jar' Rebus: *karṇīka* 'account (scribe)' *karṇī* 'supercargo'

 *dula* 'pair' Rebus: *dul* 'cast (metal)' PLUS*kana, kanac* = corner (Santali); Rebus: *kañcu* = bronze (Telugu) Thus, cast bronze. dula 'two' Rebus: dul 'cast metal'

 *kanka* 'rim of jar' Rebus: *karṇīka* 'account (scribe)' *karṇī* 'supercargo'

 *meḍ* 'body' Rebus: *meḍ* 'iron' (Ho.) काठी [kāṭhī] *f* (काष्ट S) 'frame or structure of the body' (Marathi) Rebus: खंडी [khaṇḍī] measure of weight (Marathi) கண்டி; *kaṇṭi, n. < Mhr. khaṇḍil. [T. Tu. khaṇḍi, M. kaṇḍi.]* Candy, a weight, stated to be roughly equivalent to 500 lbs.

m1674a *खोंड [khōṇḍa] m A young bull, a bullcalf. (Marathi) Rebus: kõdār 'turner' (Bengali); कोंद kōnda 'engraver, lapidary setting or infixing gems' (Marathi) G. sãghāṛɔ m. 'lathe' ; संघाट joinery; M. sãgaḍ 'double-canoe' Rebus: sangataras 'stone-cutter, mason'* G. *sãghāṛɔ* m. 'lathe' ; *sãgāḍā* m. ' frame of a building ', *°ḍī* f. ' lathe '(CDIAL 12859) Rebus*: sangataras.* संगतराश lit. 'to collect stones, stone-cutter, mason.'

Metal castings fire-altar.

  *kanac* 'corner' Rebus: *kañcu* 'bronze' sal 'splinter' Rebus: sal 'workshop' *ayo ḍhālako* 'alloy metal ingot' Circumscript: *kuṭila* 'bent' CDIAL 3230 kuṭi— in cmpd. 'curve', *kuṭika*— 'bent' MBh. Rebus: *kuṭila, katthīl* = bronze (8 parts copper and 2 parts tin) Duplicated: dula 'pair' Rebus: dul 'cast metal' Thus, cast bronze or bronze castings. PLUS *ayo* 'fish' Rebus: *aya* 'iron' *ayas* 'metal'

 *kanka* 'rim of jar' Rebus: *karṇīka* 'account (scribe)' *karṇī* 'supercargo'

 *meḍ* 'body' Rebus: *meḍ* 'iron' (Ho.) काठी [kāṭhī] *f* (काष्ट S) 'frame or structure of the body' (Marathi) Rebus: खंडी [khaṇḍī] measure of weight (Marathi) கண்டி; *kaṇṭi, n. < Mhr. khaṇḍil. [T. Tu. khaṇḍi, M. kaṇḍi.]* Candy, a weight, stated to be roughly equivalent to 500 lbs.

m112a *खोंड [khōṇḍa] m A young bull, a bullcalf. (Marathi) Rebus: kõdār 'turner' (Bengali); कोंद kōnda 'engraver, lapidary setting or infixing gems' (Marathi) G. sãghāṛɔ m. 'lathe' ; संघाट joinery; M. sãgaḍ 'double-canoe' Rebus: sangataras 'stone-cutter, mason'* G. *sãghāṛɔ* m. 'lathe' ; *sãgāḍā* m. ' frame of a building ', *°ḍī* f. ' lathe '(CDIAL 12859) Rebus*: sangataras.* संगतराश lit. 'to collect stones, stone-cutter, mason.'

Metal castings fire-altar. *kaṇḍo* 'stool, seat' Rebus: *kāṇḍa* 'metalware' *kaṇḍa* 'fire-altar' PLUS

 'Arrow' sign hieroglyph (variant) This is a ligature of 'lid of pot' hieroglyph superscript on 'a linear stroke' numeral hieroglyph.*aḍaren* 'cover of pot or lid' Rebus: *aduru* 'native, unsmelted metal' PLUS koḍ = one (Santali); koḍ 'workshop' (Gujarati)

 *kanka* 'rim of jar' Rebus: *karṇīka* 'account (scribe)' *karṇī* 'supercargo'

loa  'ficus religiosa' Rebus: *lo* 'iron' (Sanskrit) PLUS unique ligatures: लोखंड [lōkhaṇḍa] *n* (लोह S) Iron. लोखंडाचे चणे खावविणें or चारणें To oppress grievously.लोखंडकाम [lōkhaṇḍakāma] *n* Iron work; that portion (of a building, machine &c.)

which consists of iron. 2 The business of an ironsmith.लोखंडी [lōkhaṇḍī] *a* (लोखंड) Composed of iron; relating to iron. (Marathi) |||| Numeral 4: gaṇḍa 'four' Rebus: kaṇḍa 'furnace, fire-altar' (Santali)||| Numeral 3: *kolom* 'three' Rebus*: kolami* 'smithy, forge'
ayo 'fish' Rebus: *aya* 'iron' *ayas* 'metal'

 *dula* 'pair' Rebus: dul 'cast metal' *mogge* 'sprout, bud' Rebus: *mũh* 'ingot' (Santali) Thus, cast metal ingot.

 *kanka* 'rim of jar' Rebus: *karṇīka* 'account (scribe)' *karṇī* 'supercargo'

 sign hieroglyph

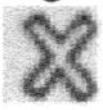 *dāṭu* 'cross'(Telugu) Rebus: *dhatu* 'mineral' (Santali).

 *dāṭu* 'cross'(Telugu) Rebus: *dhatu* 'mineral' (Santali).PLUS gaṇḍa 'four' Rebus: kaṇḍa 'furnace, fire-altar' (Santali) PLUS sal 'splinter' Rebus: sal 'workshop' Thus, mineral fire-altar (furnace) workshop.

 m655A *खोंड [khōṇḍa] m A young bull, a bullcalf. (Marathi) Rebus: kõdār 'turner' (Bengali); कोंद kōnda 'engraver, lapidary setting or infixing gems' (Marathi) G. sãghāṛɔ m. 'lathe' ; संघाट joinery; M. sãgaḍ 'double-canoe' Rebus: sangataras 'stone-cutter, mason'*

Mineral fire-altar workshop

 *kanac* 'corner' Rebus: *kañcu* 'bronze' INFIXED

 *āra* 'spokes' Rebus: *āra 'brass'*. cf. erka = ekke (Tbh. of arka) aka (Tbh. of arka) copper (metal); crystal (Kannada) Glyph: *eraka*'nave of wheel' Rebus: eraka 'copper'; cf. erka = ekke (Tbh. of arka) aka (Tbh. of arka) copper (metal); crystal (Kannada) *erako* 'moltencast copper' Duplicated: dula 'pair' Rebus: dul 'cast metal' Thus cast copper, brass casting.

The hieroglyph composition indicates a spectrum of metalwork on alloys of copper: moltencast copper, brass, bronze castings.
ayo 'fish' Rebus: *aya* 'iron' *ayas* 'metal' sal 'splinter' Rebus: sal 'workshop' *ayo ḍhālako* 'alloy metal ingot'
khuṭo ' leg, foot ', °ṭī ' goat's leg ' Rebus: *khōṭā* 'alloy' (Marathi)

 *kanka* 'rim of jar' Rebus: *karṇīka* 'account (scribe)' *karṇī* 'supercargo'

 m61a *खोंड [khōṇḍa] m A young bull, a bullcalf. (Marathi) Rebus: kõdār 'turner' (Bengali); कोंद kōnda 'engraver, lapidary setting or infixing gems' (Marathi) G. sãghāṛɔ m. 'lathe' ; संघाट joinery; M. sãgaḍ 'double-canoe' Rebus: sangataras 'stone-cutter, mason'*

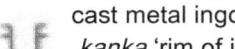

Mineral fire-altar (furnace) workshop

khaṇḍ 'field, division' (Skt.) Rebus: *khāṇḍa* 'tools, pots and pans, metal-ware'. Rebus 2: kaṇḍ 'fire-altar' (Santali) dula 'pair' Rebus: dul 'cast metal' Thus cast metalware or metalware castings.

mēḍu height, rising ground, hillock (Kannada) Rebus: *meḍ* 'iron' (Ho.) kolom 'three' Rebus: kolami 'smithy, forge' Thus, *meḍ kolami* 'iron smithy-forge'

ayo 'fish' Rebus: *aya* 'iron' *ayas* 'metal' sal 'splinter' *ayo ḍhālako* 'alloy metal ingot'

'Arrow' sign hieroglyph (variant) This is a ligature of 'lid of pot' hieroglyph superscript on 'a linear stroke' numeral hieroglyph.*aḍaren* 'cover of pot or lid' Rebus: *aduru* 'native, unsmelted metal' PLUS koḍ = one (Santali); koḍ 'workshop' (Gujarati)

kanka 'rim of jar' Rebus: *karṇīka* 'account (scribe)' *karṇī* 'supercargo'

खोंड [khōṇḍa] m A young bull, a bullcalf. (Marathi) Rebus: kõdār 'turner' (Bengali); कोंद kōnda 'engraver, lapidary setting or infixing gems' (Marathi) G. sãghāṛɔ m. 'lathe' ; संघाट joinery; M. sãgaḍ 'double-canoe' Rebus: sangataras 'stone-cutter, mason'

kaṇḍo 'stool, seat' Rebus: *kāṇḍa* 'metalware' *kaṇḍa* 'fire-altar' PLUS

dāṭu 'cross'(Telugu) Rebus: *dhatu* 'mineral' (Santali). Thus, mineral fire-altar (furnace).

h41A *खोंड [khōṇḍa] m A young bull, a bullcalf. (Marathi) Rebus: kõdār 'turner' (Bengali); कोंद kōnda 'engraver, lapidary setting or infixing gems' (Marathi) G. sãghāṛɔ m. 'lathe' ; संघाट joinery; M. sãgaḍ 'double-canoe' Rebus: sangataras 'stone-cutter, mason'*

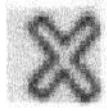

dāṭu 'cross'(Telugu) Rebus: *dhatu* 'mineral' (Santali).

tiger

(without the head turned back): *kul* 'tiger' (Santali); *kōlu* id. (Telugu) kōlupuli = Bengal tiger (Te.) कोल्हा [kōlhā] कोल्हें [kōlhēṃ] A jackal (Marathi) Rebus:
kole.l 'temple, smithy' (Kota.) *kol* = pañcalōha, a metallic alloy containing five metals (Tamil *kol, kolhe*, 'the *koles*, iron smelters

Worshipper: *bhaṭā* G. *bhuvɔ* m. ' worshipper in a temple ' rather < bhṛta --(CDIAL 9554) Yājñ.com., Rebus: *bhaṭā* ' kiln, furnace'

khōṇḍa A stock or stump (Marathi); 'leafless tree' (Marathi) Rebus: *kõdār* 'turner' (Bengali); *kõdā* 'to turn in a lathe' (Bengali). *kuṭi* 'tree' Rebus: *kuṭhi* 'smelter'

water-carrier hieroglyph *kuṭi*; Rebus: *kuṭhi* 'smelter furnace'.

PLUS 'rim of jar': *kanka* (Santali) *karṇika* 'scribe'(Sanskrit)
Rebus: *karṇī*, supercargo

'rim-of-jar'

hieroglyph *kanka* (Santali) *karṇika* 'scribe'(Sanskrit)
Rebus: *karṇī*, supercargo for a boat shipment. *karṇīka* 'account

(scribe)'.कारणी *kāraṇī* 'the supercargo of a ship'
dula 'two' Rebus: dul 'cast metal' PLUS *dhāḷ* 'a slope'; 'inclination of a plane' (G.); *ḍhāḷiyum* = adj. sloping, inclining (G.) Rebus: *ḍhālako* = a large metal ingot (G.) *ḍhālakī* = a metal heated and poured into a mould; a solid piece of metal; an ingot (Gujarati)

 *dāṭu* 'cross'(Telugu) Rebus: *dhatu* 'mineral' (Santali).

m176A

खोंड [khōṇḍa] m A young bull, a bullcalf. (Marathi) Rebus: kõdār 'turner' (Bengali); कोंद kōnda 'engraver, lapidary setting or infixing gems' (Marathi) G. sãghāṛɔ m. 'lathe' ; संघाट joinery; M. sãgaḍ 'double-canoe' Rebus: sangataras 'stone-cutter, mason'

 *dāṭu* 'cross'(Telugu) Rebus: *dhatu* 'mineral' (Santali).

 *kanka* 'rim of jar' Rebus: *karṇīka* 'account (scribe)' *karṇī* 'supercargo'

m291A tiger (without the head turned back): *kul* 'tiger' (Santali); *kōlu* id. (Telugu) kōlupuli = Bengal tiger (Te.) कोल्हा [kōlhā] कोल्हें [kōlhēṃ] A jackal (Marathi) Rebus: *kole.l* 'temple, smithy' (Kota.) *kol* = pañcalōha, a metallic alloy containing five metals (Tamil *kol, kolhe*, 'the *koles*, iron smelters

 *dāṭu* 'cross'(Telugu) Rebus: *dhatu* 'mineral' (Santali).

 *kanka* 'rim of jar' Rebus: *karṇīka* 'account (scribe)' *karṇī* 'supercargo'

baṭa 'rimless, broad-mouthed pot' Rebus: *bhaṭa* 'furnace' (Gujarati.); *baṭa* 'a kind of iron' (Gujarati)

K-61 a

Kalibangan 61a

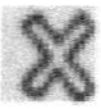 *dāṭu* 'cross'(Telugu) Rebus: *dhatu* 'mineral' (Santali).

 *kanka* 'rim of jar' Rebus: *karṇīka* 'account (scribe)' *karṇī* 'supercargo'

M-1176 a

m1176m1176a Zebu horns. Native metal smith guild. ingot (from) iron smelter, tin smelter merchant guild

 *dāṭu* 'cross'(Telugu) Rebus: *dhatu* 'mineral' (Santali).

water-carrier hieroglyph *kuṭi*; Rebus: *kuṭhi* 'smelter furnace'.

PLUS 'rim of jar': *kanka* (Santali) *karṇika* 'scribe'(Sanskrit) Rebus: *karṇī,* supercargo

m1111 m1111a Text 1333 *khũṭ* 'zebu' Rebus: '(native metal) guild'

 *dāṭu* 'cross'(Telugu) Rebus: *dhatu* 'mineral' (Santali). This is a likely reading if the message is intended to convey a mineral-artisan-guild: *dhatu khūṭ*

 *kuṭila* 'bent' CDIAL 3230 kuṭi— in cmpd. 'curve', *kuṭika—* 'bent' MBh. Rebus: *kuṭila, katthīl* = bronze (8 parts copper and 2 parts tin) Duplicated: dula 'pair' Rebus: dul 'cast metal' Thus, cast bronze or bronze castings.

Thus,

 कुटिल kuṭila 'bent' Rebus: 'bronze'

 'rim of jar' hieroglyph infixed with three short numerical strokes:

 kanka 'rim of jar' Rebus: *karṇīka* 'account (scribe)' *karṇī* 'supercargo' PLUS (infixed) kolom 'three' Rebus: kolami 'smithy/forge'. Thus the ligatured hieroglyph reads rebus: 'supercargo of smithy/forge': *kolami karṇī* 'supercargo'

ḍato 'claws or pincers of crab' (Santali) Rebus: *dhatu* 'mineral ore' (Santali)

 kanka 'rim of jar' Rebus: *karṇīka* 'account (scribe)' *karṇī* 'supercargo'

m1901 *khūṭ* 'zebu' Rebus: '(native metal) guild'

Text of epigraph with hieroglyphs:

The firs sign from r. is hieroglyph composition: rim of jar PLUS water-carrier.

dula 'pair' Rebus: dul 'cast metal'; kuṭila 'bent' CDIAL 3230 *kuṭi—* in cmpd. 'curve', *kuṭika—* 'bent' MBh. Rebus: *kuṭila, katthīl* = bronze (8 parts copper and 2 parts tin) cf. āra-kūṭa, 'brass' (Sanskrit) This composite hieroglyph thus denotes: cast bronze: *dul kuṭila* Ligature: *kaṇḍo* 'stool, seat' Rebus: *kāṇḍa* 'metalware' *kaṇḍa* 'fire-altar'

balad m. ' ox ', gng. *bald*, (Ku.) *barad*, id. (N. Tarai) Rebus: *bharat* (5 copper, 4 zinc and 1 tin)(Punjabi) *pattar* 'trough' Rebus*: pattar* 'guild'. Thus, copper-zinc-tin alloy (worker) guild. eraka 'upraised hand' Rebus: erako 'moltencast copper' (mixed with zinc and tin in furnace to produce bronze castings.)

Rebus readings of the composite hieroglyph on both these seals are:

kuṭi 'water-carrier' Rebus: kuṭhi 'smelter furnace' PLUS

 *kanka* 'rim of jar' Rebus: *karṇīka* 'account (scribe)' *karṇī* 'supercargo' Thus, the composite hieroglyph on m1901 denotes the message: supercargo (from) smelter furnace.

water-carrier hieroglyph kuṭi; Rebus: kuṭhi 'furnace'. Together, the pair of sign hieroglyphs read rebus: *dhatu kuṭhi* 'mineral (ore) smelter/furnace'.

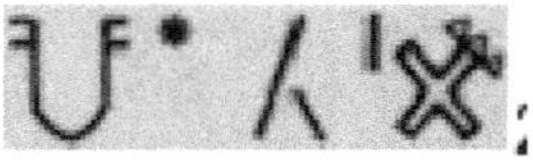

m0261 Text 2535 *khũṭ* 'zebu' Rebus: '(native metal) guild'. The composite hieroglyph sign sequence is read rebus as: ingot, metalware merchant

'Notch' hieroglyph is superscripted to this composite hieroglyph describing the nature of the supercargo: *khāṇḍa* 'notch' Rebus: *khāṇḍa* 'tools, pots and pans, metal-ware'.

The next hieroglyph sign is also a composite with intertwined)(hieroglyphs back to back:

Vikalpa 1: *bāṭa* 'road' (Telugu). Rebus: *bhaṭa* 'furnace' (Santali)
Vikalpa 2: *dāṭu* 'cross'(Telugu) Rebus: *dhatu* 'mineral' (Santali).

Superscript notch read rebus: *kāṇḍa* 'pots and pans, metalware, tools' PLUS Ligatured sign hieroglyph: dhatu 'mineral' + damgar 'merchant'
ṭākuro = hill top (Nepali); *ḍāg* = mountain-ridge (Hindi)(CDIAL 5476). Rebus: Rebus: *damgar* 'merchant'; *tamkāru* id. (Akkadian) Vikalpa: *ḍhangar* 'blacksmith' (Maithili)

Read in context, the composite hieroglyph is assumed to be a combination of a slanted stroke ligatured to a notch,which provide possible rebus readings of a smithy/forge: notch+slanted stroke reads rebus: *ḍhālako kāṇḍa* 'ingot, tools, pots and pans and metal-ware'

dhāḷ 'a slope'; 'inclination of a plane' (Gujarati); *ḍhāḷiyum* = adj. sloping, inclining (Gujarati) Rebus: *ḍhālako* = a large metal ingot (Gujarati) *ḍhālakī* = a metal heated and poured into a mould; a solid piece of metal; an ingot (Gujarati) PLUS खांडा [*khāṇḍā*] *m* A jag, notch, or indentation (as upon the edge of a tool or weapon). Rebus: *kāṇḍa* 'tools, pots and pans and metal-ware'

dāṭu 'cross'(Telugu) Rebus: *dhatu* 'mineral' (Santali). This is a likely reading if the message is intended to convey a mineral-artisan-guild: *dhatu khũṭ*

kanka 'rim of jar' Rebus: *karṇīka* 'account (scribe)' *karṇī* 'supercargo' m896A *खोंड [khōṇḍa] m A young bull, a bullcalf. (Marathi) Rebus: kõdār 'turner' (Bengali); कोंद kōnda 'engraver, lapidary setting or infixing gems' (Marathi) G. sãghāṛɔ m. 'lathe' ; संघाट joinery; M. sãgaḍ 'double-canoe' Rebus: sangataras 'stone-cutter, mason'*

meḍ 'body' Rebus: *meḍ* 'iron' (Ho.) काठी [kāṭhī] *f* (काष्ट S) 'frame or structure of the body' (Marathi) Rebus: खंडी [khaṇḍī] measure of weight (Marathi) *கண்டி; kaṇṭi, n. < Mhr. khaṇḍil. [T. Tu. khaṇḍi, M. kaṇḍi.]* Candy, a weight, stated to be roughly equivalent to 500 lbs.

dula 'two' Rebus: dul 'cast metal' PLUS खांडा [*khāṇḍā*] *m* A jag, notch, or indentation (as upon the edge of a tool or weapon). Rebus: *kāṇḍa* 'tools, pots and pans and metal-ware' Thus, metalware castings.

mēḍu height, rising ground, hillock (Kannada) Rebus: *mẽṛhẽt, meḍ* 'iron' (Munda.Ho.)

kaṇḍo 'stool, seat' Rebus: *kāṇḍa* 'metalware' *kaṇḍa* 'fire-altar' DUPLICATED: dula 'pair' Rebus: dul 'cast metal' Thus, iron metalware castings.

Allahdino 5A *खोंड [khōṇḍa] m A young bull, a bullcalf. (Marathi) Rebus: kõdār 'turner' (Bengali); कोंद kōnda 'engraver, lapidary setting or infixing gems' (Marathi) G. sãghāṛɔ m. 'lathe' ; संघाट joinery; M. sãgaḍ 'double-canoe' Rebus: sangataras 'stone-cutter, mason'*

 water-carrier hieroglyph *kuṭi*; Rebus: *kuṭhi* 'smelter furnace'.

PLUS 'rim of jar': *kanka* (Santali) *karṇika* 'scribe'(Sanskrit) Rebus: *karṇī*, supercargo

 kanka 'rim of jar' Rebus: karṇīka 'account (scribe)' karṇī 'supercargo'

ḍāg  mountain-ridge (H.)(CDIAL 5476). Rebus: dhangar 'blacksmith' (Maithili)

ranku 'liquid measure' Rebus: ranku 'tin' INFIXED: | *koḍa* 'one' Rebus: *koḍ* 'workshop'

m666a *खोंड [khōṇḍa] m A young bull, a bullcalf. (Marathi) Rebus: kõdār 'turner' (Bengali); कोंद kōnda 'engraver, lapidary setting or infixing gems' (Marathi) G. sãghāṛɔ m. 'lathe' ; संघाट joinery; M. sãgaḍ 'double-canoe' Rebus: sangataras 'stone-cutter, mason'*

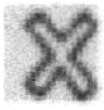 *dāṭu* 'cross'(Telugu) Rebus: *dhatu* 'mineral' (Santali). *ḍhālako kāṇḍa* 'ingot, tools, pots and pans and metal-ware'.*ḍhāḷ* 'a slope'; 'inclination of a plane' (G.); *ḍhāḷiyum* = adj. sloping, inclining (G.) Rebus: *ḍhālako* = a large metal ingot (खांडा [*khāṇḍā*] *m* A jag, notch, or indentation (as upon the edge of a tool or weapon). Rebus: *kāṇḍa* 'tools, pots and pans and metal-ware'

aya kāṇḍa 'alloy metalware' *ḍhanga* = a crook used for pulling down the branches of trees, for goats, sheep and camels (P.) Rebus:*ḍhangar* blacksmith'.dulo 'hole' Rebus: dul 'cast metal'

h1A *खोंड [khōṇḍa] m A young bull, a bullcalf. (Marathi) Rebus: kõdār 'turner' (Bengali); कोंद kōnda 'engraver, lapidary setting or infixing gems' (Marathi) G. sãghāṛɔ m. 'lathe' ; संघाट joinery; M. sãgaḍ 'double-canoe' Rebus: sangataras 'stone-cutter, mason'*

āra 'spokes' Rebus: *āra 'brass'*. cf. erka = ekke (Tbh. of arka) aka (Tbh. of arka)

 copper (metal); crystal (Kannada) Glyph: *eraka*'nave of wheel' Rebus: eraka 'copper'; cf. erka = ekke (Tbh. of arka) aka (Tbh. of arka) copper (metal); crystal (Kannada) *erako* 'moltencast copper' Duplicated: dula 'pair' Rebus: dul 'cast metal' Thus cast copper, brass casting.

ranku 'liquid measure' Rebus: ranku 'tin'

 सांड [sāṇḍa] *f* (षद S) An outlet for superfluous water (as through a dam or mound); a sluice, a floodvent. Rebus: सांडणी [sāṇḍaṇī] *f* (H) An instrument of goldsmiths. It is

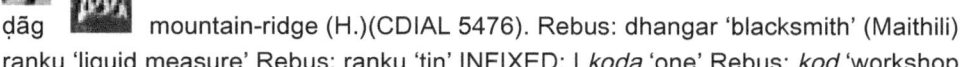

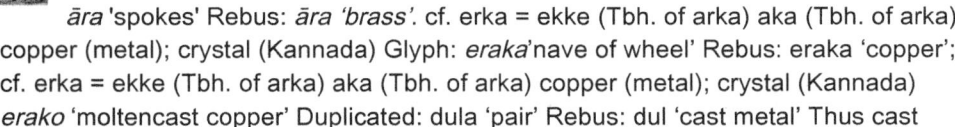

hooked or curved at the extremity; and is used to draw things out of the fire.
सांठा [*sāṇṭhā*] *m* (संचय S) A collection, heap, hoard, store, stock.साटें [*sāṭēṃ*] *n* (संचय S) A whole investment; the total quantity of merchandise (brought to market by one merchant).

 *dāṭu* 'cross'(Telugu) Rebus: *dhatu* 'mineral' (Santali)

 m69a First two signs as at first two signs of h56A PLUS *aya kāṇḍa* 'alloy metalware'

 *dula* 'pair' Rebus: *dul* 'cast (metal)' PLUS*kana, kanac* = corner (Santali); Rebus: *kañcu* = bronze (Telugu) PLUS infixed kolmo 'paddy plant' Rebus: kolami 'smithy, forge'. Thus, cast bronze smithy, forge. Or, *mogge* 'sprout, bud' Rebus: *mũh* 'ingot' (Santali)Thus, cast bronze ingot. Read as: *kañcu dul mũh 'bronze cast ingot'*

kanka 'rim of jar' Rebus: *karṇīka* 'account (scribe)' *karṇī* 'supercargo'

 h56A *खोंड [khōṇḍa] m A young bull, a bullcalf. (Marathi) Rebus: kōdār 'turner' (Bengali); कोंद kōnda 'engraver, lapidary setting or infixing gems' (Marathi) G. sãghāṛɔ m. 'lathe' ; संघाट joinery; M. sãgaḍ 'double-canoe' Rebus: sangataras 'stone-cutter, mason'*

dāṭu 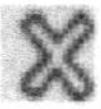 'cross'(Telugu) Rebus: *dhatu* 'mineral' (Santali)

 notch+slanted stroke reads rebus: *ḍhālako kāṇḍa* 'ingot, tools, pots and pans and metal-ware'.*dhāḷ* 'a slope'; 'inclination of a plane' (G.); *ḍhāḷiyum* = adj. sloping, inclining (G.) Rebus: *ḍhālako* = a large metal ingot (G.) *ḍhālakī* = a metal heated and poured into a mould; a solid piece of metal; an ingot (Gujarati) PLUS खांडा [*khāṇḍā*] *m* A jag, notch, or indentation (as upon the edge of a tool or weapon). Rebus: *kāṇḍa* 'tools, pots and pans and metal-ware'

 *baraḍo* = spine; backbone (Tulu) Rebus: *baran, bharat* 'mixed alloys' (5 copper, 4 zinc and 1 tin) (Punjabi) [Note four ligatured bones: gaṇḍa 'four' Rebus: kaṇḍa 'furnace, fire-altar' (Santali)]

kanka 'rim of jar' Rebus: *karṇīka* 'account (scribe)' *karṇī* 'supercargo'

H-237 A

h237A

H-821 A

h821A

h1846A

h1138A

h1845A

h823A

Rebus readings of inscriptions on h823A set of 7 tablets:

 *dāṭu* 'cross'(Telugu) Rebus: *dhatu* 'mineral' (Santali).

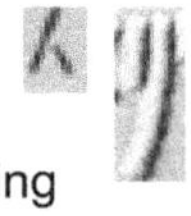 and notch+slanted stroke reads rebus: *ḍhālako kāṇḍa* 'ingot, tools, pots and pans metal-ware'.*dhāḷ* 'a slope'; 'inclination of a plane' (G.); *ḍhāḷiyum* = adj. sloping, inclining (G.) Rebus: *ḍhālako* = a large metal ingot (G.) *ḍhālakī* = a metal heated and poured into a mould; a solid piece of metal; an ingot (Gujarati) PLUS खांडा [*khāṇḍā*] *m* A jag, notch, or indentation (as upon the edge of a tool or weapon). Rebus: *kāṇḍa* 'tools, pots and pans and metal-ware'

aya kammaṭa.'coiner, mint alloy'

kəṭhā´r, kc. *kuṭhār* m. ' granary, storeroom '(WPah.)(CDIAL 3550). *koṭhārī m.* ' storekeeper' (Gujarati)(CDIAL 3551) Thus, storeroom (of) *kolom* 'three' Rebus: *kolami* 'smithy, forge'. Dula 'pair' Rebus: dul 'cast metal' Thus, together *dul kolami kuṭhār* 'metal smithy castings storeroom'

kanka 'rim of jar' Rebus: *karṇīka* 'account (scribe)' *karṇī* 'supercargo'

|||| Numeral 4: gaṇḍa 'four' Rebus: kaṇḍa 'furnace, fire-altar' (Santali) PLUS *baṭa* = rimless pot (Kannada) Rebus: *baṭa* = a kind of iron (G.)) *bhaṭa* furnace (Gujarati)

m1181A *kamaḍha* 'penance' Rebus: *kammaṭa* 'mint, coiner'.
kaṇḍo 'stool, seat' Rebus: *kāṇḍa* 'metalware' *kaṇḍa* 'fire-altar' *kūdī* 'bunch of twigs' (Sanskrit) Rebus: *kuṭhi* 'smelter furnace' (Santali)
kōḍu 'horn' Rebus: *kōḍu* 'workshop'
First 2 signs read rebus as h56A 'mineral metalware, ingots'
aya kāṇḍa 'alloy metalware'

 *kuṭila* 'bent' CDIAL 3230 kuṭi— in cmpd. 'curve', *kuṭika*— 'bent' MBh. Rebus: *kuṭila, katthīl* = bronze (8 parts copper and 2 parts tin) Duplicated: dula 'pair' Rebus: dul 'cast metal' Thus, cast bronze or bronze castings.

 *kanka* 'rim of jar' Rebus: *karṇīka* 'account (scribe)' *karṇī* 'supercargo'

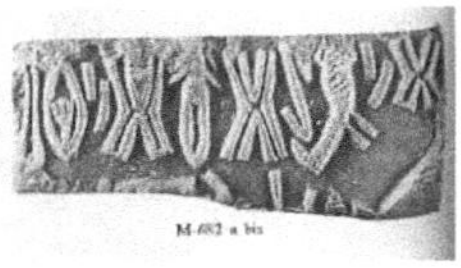

m682a First 2 signs read rebus as at h56A PLUS

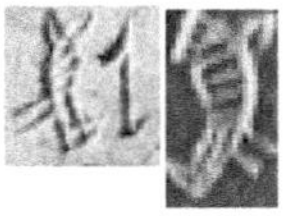

The pair of hieroglyph signs are compositions: bicha 'scorpion' (Assamese) Rebus: *bica* 'stone ore' (Santali) The pairing sign is a composition of: sloping stroke PLUS two short strokes of a 'splinter':*dhāḷ* 'a slope'; 'inclination of a plane' (Gujarati); *ḍhāḷiyum* = adj. sloping, inclining (Gujarati) Rebus: *ḍhālako* = a large metal ingot (Gujarati) *ḍhālakī* = a metal heated and poured into a mould; a solid piece of metal; an ingot (Gujarati)PLUS*sal* 'splinter' Rebus: *sal* 'workshop'. Thus the composition reads: *ḍhālako sal* 'ingot workshop'.

 *dāṭu* 'cross'(Telugu) Rebus: *dhatu* 'mineral' (Santali).

 dulo 'hole' Rebus: dul 'cast metal' PLUS*aḍaren* 'cover of pot or lid' Rebus: *aduru* 'native, unsmelted metal' Duplicated: dula 'pair' Rebus: dul 'cast metal'

Next 2 signs same as first 2 signs and read rebus as at h56A 'mineral metalware, ingots'

 *dula* 'pair' Rebus: *dul* 'cast (metal)' PLUS*kana, kanac* = corner (Santali); Rebus: *kañcu* = bronze (Telugu) PLUS infixed kolmo 'paddy plant' Rebus: kolami 'smithy, forge'. Thus, cast bronze smithy, forge. Or, *mogge* 'sprout, bud' Rebus: *mũh* 'ingot' (Santali)Thus, cast bronze ingot. Read as: *kañcu dul mũh 'bronze cast ingot'*

 *kanka* 'rim of jar' Rebus: *karṇīka* 'account (scribe)' *karṇī* 'supercargo'

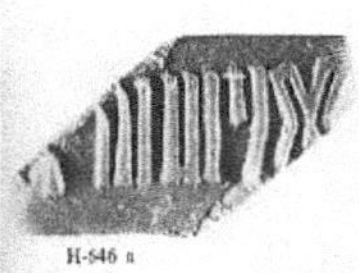

h646a

Banawali 21A First 2 signs read rebus as at h56A 'Mineral metalware ingots'. kolom 'three' Rebus: kolami 'smithy, forge' gaṇḍa 'four' Rebus: kaṇḍa 'furnace, fire-altar' (Santali) dula 'pair'

m1738a *खोंड [khōṇḍa] m A young bull, a bullcalf. (Marathi) Rebus: kõdār 'turner' (Bengali); कोंद kōnda 'engraver, lapidary setting or infixing gems' (Marathi) G. sãghāṛɔ m. 'lathe' ; संघाट joinery; M. sãgaḍ 'double-canoe' Rebus: sangataras 'stone-cutter, mason'* First 2 signs read rebus as at h56A 'Mineral metalware ingots'

m5a *खोंड [khōṇḍa] m A young bull, a bullcalf. (Marathi) Rebus: kõdār 'turner' (Bengali); कोंद kōnda 'engraver, lapidary setting or infixing gems' (Marathi) G. sãghāṛɔ m. 'lathe' ; संघाट joinery; M. sãgaḍ 'double-canoe' Rebus: sangataras 'stone-cutter, mason'* First 2 signs read rebus as at h56A 'Mineral metalware ingots' *aya aḍaren (homonym: aduru)*'alloy native metal' *aya kammaṭa.*'coiner, mint alloy'

Ligatured sign hieroglyph: 'Pair of harrows': *dul aduru* 'cast native unsmelted metal' PLUS kolmo 'paddy plant' Rebus: kolami 'smithy, forge'. Thus the composite hieroglyph denotes native metal smithy castings. Or, *mogge* 'sprout, bud' Rebus*:* *mũh* 'ingot': native cast metal ingot.

H-2135 A

h2135A First 2 signs read rebus as at h56A 'Mineral metalware ingots' ranku 'antelope' Rebus: ranku 'tin'

kuṭila 'bent' CDIAL  3230 kuṭi— in cmpd. 'curve', *kuṭika—* 'bent' MBh. Rebus: *kuṭila, katthīl* = bronze (8 parts copper and 2 parts tin)

 *kanka* 'rim of jar' Rebus: *karṇīka* 'account (scribe)' *karṇī* 'supercargo'

h91A *ibha* 'elephant' Rebus: *ib* 'iron' *ibbo* 'merchant' (Gujarati)First 2 signs read rebus as at h56A 'Mineral metalware ingots' *ayo* 'fish' Rebus: *aya* 'iron' *ayas* 'metal'

 'Arrow' sign hieroglyph (variant) This is a ligature of 'lid of pot' hieroglyph superscript on 'a linear stroke' numeral hieroglyph.*aḍaren* 'cover of pot or lid' Rebus: *aduru* 'native, unsmelted metal' PLUS koḍ = one (Santali); koḍ 'workshop' (Gujarati)

 कांड *kāṇḍa* 'arrow' Rebus: *kāṇḍa* 'pots and pans, metalware, tools'. Rebus 2: kaṇḍ 'fire-altar' (Santali)

m1683a *खोंड [khōṇḍa] m A young bull, a bullcalf. (Marathi) Rebus: kõdār 'turner' (Bengali); कोंद kōnda 'engraver, lapidary setting or infixing gems' (Marathi) G. sãghāṛɔ m. 'lathe' ; संघाट joinery; M. sāgaḍ 'double-canoe' Rebus: sangataras 'stone-cutter, mason'* First 2 signs read rebus as at h56A 'Mineral metalware ingots'

ḍhanga =  a crook used for pulling down the branches of trees, for goats, sheep and camels (P.) Rebus:*ḍhangar* blacksmith'. PLUS

 *kharedo* = a currycomb (Gujarati) खरारा [*kharārā*] *m* (H) A currycomb. 2 Currying a horse. (Marathi) Rebus: करडा [*karaḍā*] Hard from alloy--iron, silver &c. (Marathi) *kharādī* ' turner' (Gujarati)

 *dula* 'pair' Rebus: *dul* 'cast (metal)' PLUS*kana, kanac* = corner (Santali); Rebus: *kañcu* = bronze (Telugu) PLUS infixed kolmo 'paddy plant' Rebus: kolami 'smithy, forge'. Thus, cast bronze smithy, forge. Or, *mogge* 'sprout, bud' Rebus: *mũh* 'ingot' (Santali)Thus, cast bronze ingot. Read as: *kañcu dul mũh 'bronze cast ingot'*

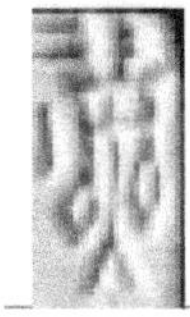  water-carrier hieroglyph *kuṭi*; Rebus: *kuṭhi* 'smelter furnace'.

PLUS 'rim of jar': *kanka* (Santali) *karṇika* 'scribe'(Sanskrit) Rebus: *karṇī,* supercargo 'rim-of-jar' hieroglyph *kanka* (Santali) *karṇika* 'scribe'(Sanskrit) Rebus: *karṇī,* supercargo for a boat shipment. *karṇīka* 'account (scribe)'.कारणी *kāraṇī* 'the supercargo of a ship.

m626a *खोंड [khōṇḍa] m A young bull, a bullcalf. (Marathi) Rebus: kõdār 'turner' (Bengali); कोंद kōnda 'engraver, lapidary setting or infixing gems' (Marathi) G. sãghāṛɔ m. 'lathe' ; संघाट joinery; M. sãgaḍ 'double-canoe' Rebus: sangataras 'stone-cutter, mason'*

The pair of hieroglyph signs are compositions: bicha 'scorpion' (Assamese) Rebus: *bica* 'stone ore' (Santali) The pairing sign is a composition of: sloping stroke PLUS two short strokes of a 'splinter':*dhāḷ* 'a slope'; 'inclination of a plane' (Gujarati); *ḍhāḷiyum* = adj. sloping, inclining (Gujarati) Rebus: *ḍhālako* = a large metal ingot (Gujarati) *ḍhālakī* = a metal heated and poured into a mould; a solid piece of metal; an ingot (Gujarati)PLUS*sal* 'splinter' Rebus: *sal* 'workshop'. Thus the composition reads: *ḍhālako sal* 'ingot workshop'.

dāṭu 'cross'(Telugu) Rebus: *dhatu* 'mineral' (Santali).

kanka 'rim of jar' Rebus: *karṇīka* 'account (scribe)' *karṇī* 'supercargo'

Next 2 signs read rebus as at h56A

dula 'pair' Rebus: *dul* 'cast (metal)' PLUS*kana, kanac* = corner (Santali); Rebus: *kañcu* = bronze (Telugu) PLUS infixed kolmo 'paddy plant' Rebus: kolami 'smithy, forge'. Thus, cast bronze smithy, forge. Or, *mogge* 'sprout, bud' Rebus: *mũh* 'ingot' (Santali)Thus, cast bronze ingot. Read as: *kañcu dul mũh 'bronze cast ingot'*

.

kanka 'rim of jar' Rebus: *karṇīka* 'account (scribe)' *karṇī* 'supercargo'

kamaḍha 'archer, bow' Rebus: *kammaṭa* 'mint, coiner'. *mogge* 'sprout, bud' Rebus: *mũh* 'ingot' (Santali) Cirumscript: gaṇḍa 'four' Rebus: kaṇḍa 'furnace, fire-altar' (Santali)

dula 'pair' Rebus: *dul* 'cast (metal)' PLUS*kana, kanac* = corner (Santali); Rebus: *kañcu* = bronze (Telugu) Thus, cast bronze.

m146a *खोंड [khōṇḍa] m A young bull, a bullcalf. (Marathi) Rebus: kõdār 'turner' (Bengali); कोंद kōnda 'engraver, lapidary setting or infixing gems' (Marathi) G. sãghāṛɔ m. 'lathe' ; संघाट joinery; M. sãgaḍ 'double-canoe' Rebus: sangataras 'stone-cutter, mason'*

First 2 signs read rebus as at h56A 'Mineral metalware ingots'

kuṭila 'bent' CDIAL 3230 kuṭi— in cmpd. 'curve', *kuṭika—* 'bent' MBh. Rebus: *kuṭila, katthīl* = bronze (8 parts copper and 2 parts tin)

bicha 'scorpion' (Assamese) Rebus: *bica* 'stone ore' (Santali)

kanka 'rim of jar' Rebus: *karṇīka* 'account (scribe)' *karṇī* 'supercargo'

m55a *खोंड [khōṇḍa] m A young bull, a bullcalf. (Marathi) Rebus: kõdār 'turner' (Bengali); कोंद kōnda 'engraver, lapidary setting or infixing gems' (Marathi) G. sãghārɔ m. 'lathe' ; संघाट joinery; M. sãgaḍ 'double-canoe' Rebus: sangataras 'stone-cutter, mason'*

First 2 signs read rebus as at h56A 'Mineral metalware ingots'

Ranku 'liquid measure' Rebus: ranku 'tin' (workshop)

 ḍãg mountain-ridge (H.)(CDIAL 5476). Rebus: dhangar 'blacksmith' (Maithili)

 kanka 'rim of jar' Rebus: karṇīka 'account (scribe)' karṇī 'supercargo'

Lothal 14a *खोंड [khōṇḍa] m A young bull, a bullcalf. (Marathi) Rebus: kõdār 'turner' (Bengali); कोंद kōnda 'engraver, lapidary setting or infixing gems' (Marathi) G. sãghārɔ m. 'lathe' ; संघाट joinery; M. sãgaḍ 'double-canoe' Rebus: sangataras 'stone-cutter, mason'*

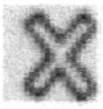 *dāṭu* 'cross'(Telugu) Rebus: *dhatu* 'mineral' (Santali). खांडा [*khāṇḍā*] *m* A jag, notch, or indentation (as upon the edge of a tool or weapon). Rebus: *kāṇḍa* 'tools, pots and pans and metal-ware'

 kanka 'rim of jar' Rebus: karṇīka 'account (scribe)' karṇī 'supercargo'

 *dula* 'pair' Rebus: dul 'cast metal' *mogge* 'sprout, bud' Rebus: *mũh* 'ingot' (Santali) Thus, cast metal ingot.

 dula 'pair' Rebus: dul 'cast metal' PLUS | *koḍa* 'one' Rebus: *koḍ* 'workshop' PLUS INFIXED kolom 'three' Rebus: kolami 'smithy, forge' Thus metalware castings forge.

Lothal 96A

dāṭu 'cross'(Telugu) Rebus: *dhatu* 'mineral' (Santali).

 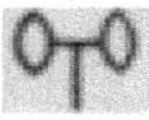 अगडा [agaḍā] *m* The tie connecting the जूं & दांडी of a गाडा or load-cart; the shaft and thill-yoke-tie. Rebus: 'lumber, miscellaneous articles': अगडतगड [*agaḍatagaḍa*] *n* अगडबगड *n* (Fanciful formations, or from H) Trash, trumpery, rubbish, lumber, miscellaneous articles.

 *khareḍo* = a currycomb (Gujarati) खरारा [*kharārā*] *m* (H) A currycomb. 2 Currying a horse. (Marathi) Rebus: करडा [*karaḍā*] Hard from alloy--iron, silver &c. (Marathi) *kharādī* ' turner' (Gujarati)

h665a First 2 signs read rebus as at h56A 'Mineral metalware ingots' gaṇḍa 'four' Rebus: kaṇḍa 'furnace, fire-altar' (Santali)

mogge 'sprout, bud' Rebus: *mũh* 'ingot' (Santali)

m1747a *खोंड [khōṇḍa] m A young bull, a bullcalf. (Marathi) Rebus: kõdār 'turner' (Bengali); कोंद kōnda 'engraver, lapidary setting or infixing gems' (Marathi) G.*

sãghāṛɔ m. 'lathe' ; संघाट joinery; M. sãgaḍ 'double-canoe' Rebus: sangataras 'stone-cutter, mason' First 2 signs read rebus as at h56A 'Mineral metalware ingots'

PLUS | *koḍa* 'one' Rebus: *koḍ* 'workshop'

 *kanka* 'rim of jar' Rebus: *karṇīka* 'account (scribe)' *karṇī* 'supercargo'

The hieroglyph may be a variant of:  *kana, kanac* = corner (Santali); Rebus: *kañcu* = bronze (Telugu) PLUS kolom 'three' Rebus: kolami 'smithy, forge.

m1786a *खोंड [khōṇḍa] m A young bull, a bullcalf. (Marathi) Rebus: kõdār 'turner' (Bengali); कोंद kōnda 'engraver, lapidary setting or infixing gems' (Marathi) G. sãghāṛɔ m. 'lathe' ; संघाट joinery; M. sãgaḍ 'double-canoe' Rebus: sangataras 'stone-cutter, mason'* First 2 signs read rebus as at h56A 'Mineral metalware ingots'

h580A *balad* m. ' ox ', gng. *bald*, (Ku.) *barad*, id. (N. Tarai) Rebus: *bharat* (5 copper, 4 zinc and 1 tin)(Punjabi) *pattar* 'trough' Rebus: *pattar* 'guild'. Thus, copper-zinc-tin alloy (worker) guild.

First 2 signs read rebus as at h56A 'Mineral metalware ingots'

ranku 'liquid measure' Rebus: ranku 'tin' (workshop).

Circumsript:

 *kuṭila* 'bent' CDIAL 3230 kuṭi— in cmpd. 'curve', *kuṭika—* 'bent' MBh. Rebus: *kuṭila, katthīl* = bronze (8 parts copper and 2 parts tin) Duplicated: dula 'pair' Rebus: dul 'cast metal' Thus, cast bronze or bronze castings.

karaṇḍa 'duck' (Sanskrit) karaṛa 'a very large aquatic bird' (Sindhi) Rebus: करडा [*karaḍā*] Hard from alloy--iron, silver &c. (Marathi) *kharādī* ' turner' (Gujarati)

 *kanka* 'rim of jar' Rebus: *karṇīka* 'account (scribe)' *karṇī* 'supercargo'

m1715a *खोंड [khōṇḍa] m A young bull, a bullcalf. (Marathi) Rebus: kõdār 'turner' (Bengali); कोंद kōnda 'engraver, lapidary setting or infixing gems' (Marathi) G. sãghāṛɔ m. 'lathe' ; संघाट joinery; M. sãgaḍ 'double-canoe' Rebus: sangataras 'stone-cutter, mason'* First 2 signs read rebus as at h56A 'Mineral metalware ingots'

 *muka* 'ladle' (Tamil)(DEDR 4887) Rebus: *mũh* 'ingot' (Santali) *baṭa* = rimless pot (Kannada) Rebus:) *baṭa* = a kind of iron (G.)) *bhaṭa* furnace (Gujarati) Thus, iron ingot.

kolom 'three' Rebus: kolami 'smithy, forge'

 *kuṭila* 'bent' CDIAL 3230 kuṭi— in cmpd. 'curve', *kuṭika—* 'bent' MBh. Rebus: *kuṭila,*

 *katthīl* = bronze (8 parts copper and 2 parts tin) Duplicated: dula 'pair' Rebus: dul 'cast metal' Thus, cast bronze or bronze castings.

kanka 'rim of jar' Rebus: karṇīka 'account (scribe)' karṇī 'supercargo'

h1844A

dāṭu 'cross'(Telugu) Rebus: *dhatu* 'mineral' (Santali).
water-carrier hieroglyph *kuṭi*; Rebus: *kuṭhi* 'smelter furnace'.

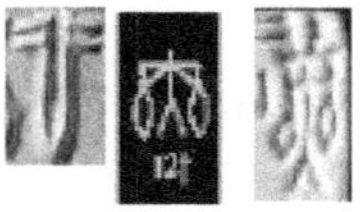

PLUS 'rim of jar': *kanka* (Santali) *karṇika* 'scribe'(Sanskrit) Rebus: *karṇī*, supercargo 'rim-of-jar' hieroglyph *kanka* (Santali) *karṇika* 'scribe'(Sanskrit) Rebus: *karṇī*, supercargo for a boat shipment. *karṇīka* 'account (scribe)'.कारणी *kāraṇī* 'the supercargo of a ship' (Marathi)*gaṇḍa* 'four' Rebus: *kaṇḍa* 'furnace, fire-altar' (Santali). *baṭa* = rimless pot (Kannada) Rebus:) *baṭa* = a kind of iron (G.)) *bhaṭa* furnace (Gujarati)

m134A *खोंड [khōṇḍa] m A young bull, a bullcalf. (Marathi) Rebus: kõdār 'turner' (Bengali); कोंद kōnda 'engraver, lapidary setting or infixing gems' (Marathi) G. sãghāṛɔ m. 'lathe' ; संघाट joinery; M. sãgaḍ 'double-canoe' Rebus: sangataras 'stone-cutter, mason'*

dāṭu 'cross'(Telugu) Rebus: *dhatu* 'mineral' (Santali). dula 'two' Rebus: dul 'cast metal'

kanac 'corner' Rebus: *kañcu* 'bronze'

m70a *खोंड [khōṇḍa] m A young bull, a bullcalf. (Marathi) Rebus: kõdār 'turner' (Bengali); कोंद kōnda 'engraver, lapidary setting or infixing gems' (Marathi) G. sãghāṛɔ m. 'lathe' ; संघाट joinery; M. sãgaḍ 'double-canoe' Rebus: sangataras 'stone-cutter, mason'dāṭu* 'cross'(Telugu) Rebus: *dhatu* 'mineral' (Santali).

dāṭu 'cross'(Telugu) Rebus: *dhatu* 'mineral' (Santali).

kolmo 'paddy plant' Rebus: *kolami* 'smithy, forge' Vikalpa: *mogge* 'sprout, bud' Rebus: *mũh* 'ingot' (Santali) dolu 'plant of shoot height' Rebus: dul 'cast metal'
sal 'splinter' Rebus: sal 'workshop' dula 'two' Rebus: dul 'cast metal' *aya kāṇḍa* 'alloy metalware'

m1165a kola 'tiger' Rebus: kolhe 'smelters' kol 'working in iron' pattar 'trough' Rebus: pattar 'guild, goldsmith' First 2 signs read rebus as at h56A 'Mineral metalware ingots'

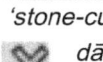

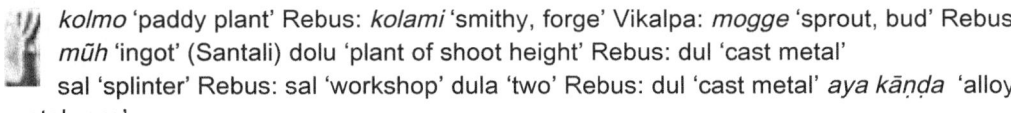

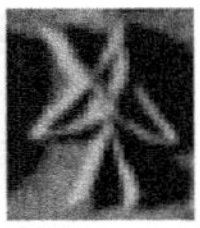 

loa 'ficus religiosa' Rebus: *lo* 'iron' (Sanskrit) PLUS unique ligatures: लोखंड [lōkhaṇḍa] *n* (लोह S) Iron. लोखंडाचे चणे खावविणें or चारणें To oppress grievously.लोखंडकाम [lōkhaṇḍakāma] *n* Iron work; that portion (of a building, machine &c.) which consists of iron. 2 The business of an ironsmith.लोखंडी [lōkhaṇḍī] *a* (लोखंड) Composed of iron; relating to iron. (Marathi) *bhaṭa* 'warrior' (Sanskrit) Rebus: *baṭa* a kind of iron (Gujarati). Rebus: *bhaṭa* 'furnace' (Santali) Thus, together, the ligatured hieroglyph reads rebus: *loa bhaṭa* 'iron furnace'

 *kuṭila* 'bent' CDIAL 3230 kuṭi— in cmpd. 'curve', *kuṭika—* 'bent' MBh. Rebus: *kuṭila,*

 *katthīl* = bronze (8 parts copper and 2 parts tin) Duplicated
kanka 'rim of jar' Rebus: *karṇīka* 'account (scribe)' *karṇī* 'supercargo'

 *meḍ* 'body' Rebus: *meḍ* 'iron' (Ho.) काठी [kāṭhī] *f* (काष्ट S) 'frame or structure of the body' (Marathi) Rebus: खंडी [khaṇḍī] measure of weight (Marathi) கண்டி; *kaṇṭi, n. < Mhr. khaṇḍil. [T. Tu. khaṇḍi, M. kaṇḍi.]* Candy, a weight, stated to be roughly equivalent to 500 lbs.

 h142a First 2 signs read rebus as at h56A 'Mineral metalware ingots'
 *kana, kanac* = corner (Santali); Rebus: *kañcu* = bronze (Telugu) PLUS खांडा [*khāṇḍā*] *m* A jag, notch, or indentation (as upon the edge of a tool or weapon). Rebus: *kāṇḍa* 'tools, pots and pans and metal-ware' Thus, bronze metalware. *kana, kanac* = corner (Santali); Rebus: *kañcu* = bronze (Telugu) PLUS

 'Arrow' sign hieroglyph (variant) This is a ligature of 'lid of pot' hieroglyph superscript on 'a linear stroke' numeral hieroglyph.*aḍaren* 'cover of pot or lid' Rebus: *aduru* 'native, unsmelted metal' PLUS koḍ = one (Santali); koḍ 'workshop' (Gujarati) Circumscript:
 *kuṭila* 'bent' CDIAL 3230 kuṭi— in cmpd. 'curve', *kuṭika—* 'bent' MBh. Rebus: *kuṭila, katthīl* = bronze (8 parts copper and 2 parts tin) Duplicated: dula 'pair' Rebus: dul 'cast metal' Thus, cast bronze or bronze castings.
INFIXED karaṇḍa 'duck' (Sanskrit) karaṛa 'a very large aquatic bird' (Sindhi)
Rebus: करडा [*karaḍā*] Hard from alloy--iron, silver &c. (Marathi) *kharādī* ' turner' (Gujarati)
 *kanka* 'rim of jar' Rebus: *karṇīka* 'account (scribe)' *karṇī* 'supercargo'

 m171A *खोंड [khōṇḍa] m A young bull, a bullcalf. (Marathi) Rebus: kōdār 'turner' (Bengali); कोंद kōnda 'engraver, lapidary setting or infixing gems' (Marathi) G. sãghāṛɔ m. 'lathe' ; संघाट joinery; M. sāgaḍ 'double-canoe' Rebus: sangataras 'stone-cutter, mason'* First 2 signs read rebus as at h56A 'Mineral metalware ingots'

 *dula* 'pair' Rebus: *dul* 'cast (metal)' PLUS*kana, kanac* = corner (Santali); Rebus: *kañcu* = bronze (Telugu) PLUS infixed kolmo 'paddy plant' Rebus: kolami 'smithy, forge'. Thus, cast bronze smithy, forge. Or, *mogge* 'sprout, bud' Rebus: *mũh* 'ingot' (Santali)Thus, cast bronze ingot. Read as: *kañcu dul mũh 'bronze cast ingot'*
ayo ḍhālako 'alloy metal ingot'
 *kuṭila* 'bent' CDIAL 3230 kuṭi— in cmpd. 'curve', *kuṭika—* 'bent' MBh. Rebus: *kuṭila, katthīl* = bronze (8 parts copper and 2 parts tin) Duplicated: dula 'pair' Rebus: dul 'cast metal' Thus, cast bronze or bronze castings.
 *kanka* 'rim of jar' Rebus: *karṇīka* 'account (scribe)' *karṇī* 'supercargo'

  notch+slanted stroke reads rebus: *ḍhālako kāṇḍa* 'ingot, tools, pots and pans and metal-ware'.*ḍhāḷ* 'a slope'; 'inclination of a plane' (G.); *ḍhāḷiyum* = adj. sloping, inclining (G.) Rebus: *ḍhālako* = a large metal ingot (G.) *ḍhālakī* = a metal heated and poured into a mould; a solid piece of metal; an ingot (Gujarati) PLUS खांडा [*khāṇḍā*

] *m* A jag, notch, or indentation (as upon the edge of a tool or weapon). Rebus: *kāṇḍa* 'tools, pots and pans and metal-ware'

kolmo 'paddy plant' Rebus: *kolami* 'smithy, forge' Vikalpa: *mogge* 'sprout, bud' Rebus: *mũh* 'ingot' (Santali) dolu 'plant of shoot height' Rebus: dul 'cast metal'

m267A *rāngo* 'water buffalo bull' (Ku.N.)(CDIAL 10559) Rebus: rango 'pewter' *pattar* 'trough' Rebus: *pattar* 'guild'.Thus, pewter guild.
kaṇḍo 'stool, seat' Rebus: *kāṇḍa* 'metalware' *kaṇḍa* 'fire-altar'

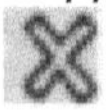
dāṭu 'cross'(Telugu) Rebus: *dhatu* 'mineral' (Santali).
sal 'splinter' Rebus: sal 'workshop'
water-carrier hieroglyph *kuṭi*; Rebus: *kuṭhi* 'smelter furnace'.

PLUS 'rim of jar': *kanka* (Santali) *karṇika* 'scribe'(Sanskrit)
Rebus: *karṇī,* supercargo
'rim-of-jar' hieroglyph *kanka* (Santali) *karṇika* 'scribe'(Sanskrit)
Rebus: *karṇī,* supercargo for a boat shipment. *karṇīka* 'account (scribe)' .कारणी *kāraṇī* 'the supercargo of a ship' (Marathi)

kəṭhā´r, kc. *kuṭhār* m. ' granary, storeroom '(WPah.)(CDIAL 3550). *koṭhārī m.* ' storekeeper' (Gujarati)(CDIAL 3551) Thus, storeroom (of) *kolom* 'three' Rebus: *kolami* 'smithy, forge'. Dula 'pair' Rebus: dul 'cast metal' Thus, together *dul kolami kuṭhār* 'metal smithy castings storeroom'

kanka 'rim of jar' Rebus: *karṇīka* 'account (scribe)' *karṇī* 'supercargo'

m126A *खोंड [khōṇḍa] m A young bull, a bullcalf. (Marathi) Rebus: kõdār 'turner' (Bengali); कोंद kōnda 'engraver, lapidary setting or infixing gems' (Marathi) G. sãghārɔ m. 'lathe' ; संघाट joinery; M. sãgaḍ 'double-canoe' Rebus: sangataras 'stone-cutter, mason'* First 2 signs read rebus as at h56A 'Mineral metalware ingots' *ḍato* = claws of crab (Santali) Rebus: *dhātu* 'mineral ore' dula 'pair' Rebus: dul 'cast metal'

कांड *kāṇḍa* 'arrow' Rebus: *kāṇḍa* 'pots and pans, metalware, tools'. Rebus 2: kaṇḍ 'fire-altar' (Santali)

m26a *खोंड [khōṇḍa] m A young bull, a bullcalf. (Marathi) Rebus: kõdār 'turner' (Bengali); कोंद kōnda 'engraver, lapidary setting or infixing gems' (Marathi) G. sãghārɔ m. 'lathe' ; संघाट joinery; M. sãgaḍ 'double-canoe' Rebus: sangataras 'stone-cutter, mason'* First 2 signs read rebus as at h56A 'Mineral metalware ingots' *ḍato* = claws of crab (Santali) Rebus: *dhātu* 'mineral ore' dula 'pair' Rebus: dul 'cast metal'

kanka 'rim of jar' Rebus: karṇīka 'account (scribe)' karṇī 'supercargo'
meḍ 'body' Rebus: *meḍ* 'iron' (Ho.) काठी [kāṭhī] *f* (काष्ट S) 'frame or structure of the

body' (Marathi) Rebus: खंडी [khaṇḍī] measure of weight (Marathi) *கண்டி; kaṇṭi, n. < Mhr. khaṇḍil. [T. Tu. khaṇḍi, M. kaṇḍi.]* Candy, a weight, stated to be roughly equivalent

to 500 lbs.

m739a खोंड *[khōṇḍa] m A young bull, a bullcalf. (Marathi) Rebus: kõdār 'turner' (Bengali);* कोंद *kōnda 'engraver, lapidary setting or infixing gems' (Marathi) G. sãghārɔ m. 'lathe' ;* संघाट *joinery; M. sãgaḍ 'double-canoe' Rebus: sangataras 'stone-cutter, mason'*

kamaḍha 'crab' Rebus: *kammaṭa* 'mint, coiner'.

ḍato = claws of crab (Santali) Rebus: *dhātu* 'mineral ore'

muka 'ladle' (Tamil)(DEDR 4887) Rebus: *mũh* 'ingot' (Santali) | *koḍa* 'one' Rebus: *koḍ* 'workshop' sal 'splinter' Rebus: sal 'workshop'

aḍar 'harrow'; rebus: *aduru* 'native unsmelted metal' *bhaṭa* 'warrior' (Sanskrit) Rebus: *baṭa* a kind of iron (Gujarati). Rebus: *bhaṭa* 'furnace' (Santali)

kanka 'rim of jar' Rebus: *karṇīka* 'account (scribe)' *karṇī* 'supercargo'

meḍ 'body' Rebus: *meḍ* 'iron' (Ho.) काठी [kāṭhī] *f* (काष्ठ S) 'frame or structure of the body' (Marathi) Rebus: खंडी [khaṇḍī] measure of weight (Marathi) *கண்டி; kaṇṭi, n. < Mhr. khaṇḍil. [T. Tu. khaṇḍi, M. kaṇḍi.]* Candy, a weight, stated to be roughly equivalent to 500 lbs.

h2104A,B

dāṭu 'cross'(Telugu) Rebus: *dhatu* 'mineral' (Santali). *kamaḍha* 'crab' Rebus: *kammaṭa* 'mint, coiner'.

ḍato = claws of crab (Santali) Rebus: *dhātu* 'mineral ore'

kanka 'rim of jar' Rebus: *karṇīka* 'account (scribe)' *karṇī* 'supercargo'

meḍ 'body' Rebus: *meḍ* 'iron' (Ho.) काठी [kāṭhī] *f* (काष्ठ S) 'frame or structure of the body' (Marathi) Rebus: खंडी [khaṇḍī] measure of weight (Marathi) *கண்டி; kaṇṭi, n. < Mhr. khaṇḍil. [T. Tu. khaṇḍi, M. kaṇḍi.]* Candy, a weight, stated to be roughly equivalent to 500 lbs.

kharedo = a currycomb (Gujarati) खरारा [*kharārā*] *m* (H) A currycomb. 2 Currying a horse. (Marathi) Rebus: करडा [*karaḍā*] Hard from alloy--iron, silver &c. (Marathi) *kharādī* ' turner' (Gujarati)

m481A First 2 signs read rebus as at h56A 'Mineral metalware ingots'

dula 'pair' Rebus: *dul* 'cast (metal)' PLUS*kana, kanac* = corner (Santali); Rebus: *kañcu* = bronze (Telugu) PLUS infixed kolmo 'paddy plant' Rebus: kolami 'smithy, forge'. Thus, cast bronze smithy, forge. Or, *mogge* 'sprout, bud' Rebus: *mũh* 'ingot' (Santali)Thus, cast bronze ingot. Read as: *kañcu dul mũh 'bronze cast ingot'*

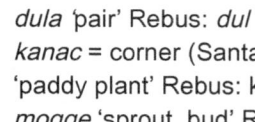

kanka 'rim of jar' Rebus: *karṇīka* 'account (scribe)' *karṇī* 'supercargo'

Circumscript:

kuṭila 'bent' CDIAL 3230 kuṭi— in cmpd. 'curve', *kuṭika—* 'bent' MBh. Rebus: *kuṭila, katthīl* = bronze (8 parts copper and 2 parts tin) Duplicated: dula 'pair' Rebus: dul 'cast metal' Thus, cast bronze or bronze castings. *bhaṭa* 'warrior' (Sanskrit) Rebus: *baṭa* a kind of iron (Gujarati). Rebus: *bhaṭa* 'furnace' (Santali)

Worshipper: *bhaṭā* G. *bhuvɔ* m. ' worshipper in a temple ' rather < bhr̥ta --(CDIAL 9554) Yājñ.com., Rebus: *bhaṭā* ' kiln, furnace' PLUS (Phonetic-semantic determinant): *baṭa* = rimless pot (Kannada) Rebus:) *baṭa* = a kind of iron (G.)) *bhaṭa* furnace (Gujarati)

h133a First 2 signs read rebus as at h56A 'Mineral metalware ingots' *kamaḍha* 'crab' Rebus: *kammaṭa* 'mint, coiner'. *ḍato* = claws of crab (Santali) Rebus: *dhātu* 'mineral ore'

aḍar 'harrow'; rebus: *aduru* 'native unsmelted metal'

ayo 'fish' Rebus: *aya* 'iron' *ayas* 'metal'

kamaḍha 'crab' Rebus: *kammaṭa* 'mint, coiner'.*ḍato* = claws of crab (Santali) Rebus: *dhātu* 'mineral ore' PLUS खांडा [*khāṇḍā*] *m* A jag, notch, or indentation (as upon the edge of a tool or weapon). Rebus: *kāṇḍa* 'tools, pots and pans and metal-ware' Thus, mint metalware, ore.

kanka 'rim of jar' Rebus: *karṇīka* 'account (scribe)' *karṇī* 'supercargo'

h1705A First 2 signs read rebus as at h56A 'Mineral metalware ingots' *kamaḍha* 'crab' Rebus: *kammaṭa* 'mint, coiner'.

ḍato = claws of crab (Santali) Rebus: *dhātu* 'mineral ore' *aya kammaṭa.*'coiner, mint alloy' *aya kāṇḍa* 'alloy metalware'

kuṭila 'bent' CDIAL 3230 kuṭi— in cmpd. 'curve', *kuṭika—* 'bent' MBh. Rebus: *kuṭila, katthīl* = bronze (8 parts copper and 2 parts tin) Duplicated: dula 'pair' Rebus: dul 'cast metal' Thus, cast bronze or bronze castings.

kanka 'rim of jar' Rebus: *karṇīka* 'account (scribe)' *karṇī* 'supercargo'

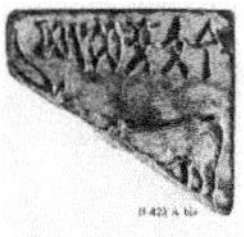

h423A *खोंड [khōṇḍa] m A young bull, a bullcalf. (Marathi) Rebus: kõdār 'turner' (Bengali); कोंद kōnda 'engraver, lapidary setting or infixing gems' (Marathi) G. sãghāṛɔ m. 'lathe' ; संघाट joinery; M. sãgaḍ 'double-canoe' Rebus: sangataras 'stone-cutter, mason'* First 2 signs read rebus as at h56A 'Mineral metalware ingots' *kamaḍha* 'crab' Rebus: *kammaṭa* 'mint, coiner'.*ḍato* = claws of crab (Santali) Rebus: *dhātu* 'mineral ore' *aya kammaṭa.*'coiner, mint alloy' *aya kāṇḍa* 'alloy metalware'

कांड *kāṇḍa* 'arrow' Rebus: *kāṇḍa* 'pots and pans, metalware, tools'. Rebus 2: kaṇḍ 'fire-altar' (Santali)

h1975A First 2 signs read rebus as at h56A 'Mineral metalware ingots'

dula 'pair' Rebus: dul  'cast metal' *mogge* 'sprout, bud' Rebus: *mũh* 'ingot' (Santali)

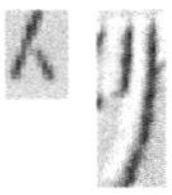

Thus, cast metal ingot.PLUS notch+slanted stroke reads rebus: *ḍhālako kāṇḍa* 'ingot, tools, pots and pans and metal-ware'.*dhāḷ* 'a slope'; 'inclination of a plane' (G.); *ḍhāḷiyum* = adj. sloping, inclining (G.) Rebus: *ḍhālako* = a large metal ingot (G.) *ḍhālakī* = a metal heated and poured into a mould; a solid piece of metal; an ingot (Gujarati) PLUS खांडा [*khāṇḍā*] *m* A jag, notch, or indentation (as upon the edge of a tool or weapon). Rebus: *kāṇḍa* 'tools, pots and pans and metal-ware'

kanka 'rim of jar' Rebus: *karṇīka* 'account (scribe)' *karṇī* 'supercargo'

Side B: *kamaḍha* 'penance' Rebus: *kammaṭa* 'mint, coiner'. *kaṇḍo* 'stool, seat' Rebus: *kāṇḍa* 'metalware' *kaṇḍa* 'fire-altar'Zebu. Native metal smith guild.

h1319A

H-1319 A

dāṭu 'cross'(Telugu) Rebus: *dhatu* 'mineral' (Santali).

PLUS *aḍaren* 'cover of pot or lid' Rebus: *aduru* 'native, unsmelted metal' *khareḍo* = a currycomb (Gujarati) खरारा [*kharārā*] *m* (H) A currycomb. 2 Currying a horse. (Marathi) Rebus: करडा [*karaḍā*] Hard from alloy--iron, silver &c. (Marathi) *kharādī* ' turner' (Gujarati)

| 'One linear stroke' as sign hieroglyph

h086a Text 4233 *khũṭ* 'zebu' Rebus: '(native metal) guild'

koḍa 'one'(Santali) Rebus: *koḍ* 'artisan's workshop'. *ṭākuro* = hill top (Nepali); *ḍãg* = mountain-ridge (Hindi)(CDIAL 5476). Rebus: Rebus: *damgar* 'merchant'; *tamkāru* id. (Akkadian) Vikalpa: *ḍhangar* 'blacksmith' (Maithili)

kaṇḍa 'arrow' Rebus: *kāṇḍa* 'tools, pots and pans and metal-ware.

Thus epigraph h086 reads rebus: *khũṭ* 'zebu' Rebus: '(native metal) guild' (of) *ḍhangar* 'blacksmith' (Maithili) *koḍ* 'artisan's workshop' (for) *kāṇḍa* 'tools, pots and pans and metal-ware.

M-328 a

m0328a *khũṭ* 'zebu' Rebus: '(native metal) guild' kuṭi 'water carrier' Rebus: kuṭhi 'smelter furnace' meḍ 'body' Rebus: meḍ 'iron' (Ho.Mu.) Vikalpa: काठी [kāṭhī] *f* (काष्ठ S) The stalk, stem, or trunk of a plant. A staff, rod, pole, wand, stick gen.; a flagstaff, a walking stick, the mast or the yard of a ship or boat etc. The frame or structure of the body: also (viewed by some as arising from the preceding sense, Measuring rod) stature.(Marathi) Rebus: खंडी [khaṇḍī] A score (of sheep or goats, and of some certain things).

Rebus: काटी or कांटी [kāṭī or kāṇṭī] *a* (In नंदभाषा) Twenty.(Marathi) खंडी [khaṇḍī] *f* A measure of weight and capacity, a candy. It consists (in Bombay) of twenty Bombay maunds, or, for particular substances, of eight maunds: (at Poona) of twenty Poona maunds, and generally of twenty maunds; varying there-fore as the maund varies. 2 Applied to a great quantity; as खंडीभर पोरें, खंडीभर मेंढ्या, खंडीभर काम, खंडीभर बोलतो-लिहितो &c. 3 A land measure, 120 bighás. 4 A score (of sheep or goats, and of some certain things). खंडीगणती or खंडोगणती [khaṇḍīgaṇatī or khaṇḍōgaṇatī] *ad* By candies; counting or reckoning by candies. खंडीवारी [khaṇḍīvārī] By scores, heaps, candies.

h1995A Epigraph: iron workshop; furnace + workshop. *kolom* 'three' Rebus: *kolami* 'smithy, forge' First sign read rebus as at m0328a. *koḍa* 'one'(Santali) Rebus: *koḍ* 'artisan's workshop'.

 water-carrier hieroglyph *kuṭi*; Rebus: *kuṭhi* 'smelter furnace'.

m1828a खोंड *[khōṇḍa] m A young bull, a bullcalf. (Marathi) Rebus: kõdār 'turner' (Bengali); कोंद kōnda 'engraver, lapidary setting or infixing gems' (Marathi) G. sãghāṛɔ m. 'lathe' ; संघाट joinery; M. sãgaḍ 'double-canoe' Rebus: sangataras 'stone-cutter, mason'*

| *koḍa* = one (Santali); *koḍ* 'workshop' (Gujarati)

meḍ 'body' Rebus: meḍ 'iron' (Gujarati) Together, the ligatured hieroglyph reads: *meḍ koḍ* 'iron workshop'. PLUS furnace cargo. water-carrier hieroglyph kuṭi; Rebus: kuṭhi 'furnace'

 *kanka* 'rim of jar' Rebus: *karṇī* 'supercargo'

m1686a खोंड *[khōṇḍa] m A young bull, a bullcalf. (Marathi) Rebus: kõdār 'turner' (Bengali); कोंद kōnda 'engraver, lapidary setting or infixing gems' (Marathi) G. sãghāṛɔ m. 'lathe' ; संघाट joinery; M. sãgaḍ 'double-canoe' Rebus: sangataras 'stone-cutter, mason'*

| *koḍa* = one (Santali); *koḍ* 'workshop' (Gujarati)

meḍ 'body' Rebus: meḍ 'iron' (Gujarati) Together, the ligatured hieroglyph reads: *meḍ koḍ* 'iron workshop'. sal 'splinte' Rebus: sal 'workshop' dula 'two' Rebus: dul 'cast metal' *ayo* 'fish' Rebus: *aya* 'iron' *ayas* 'metal'

 *kuṭila* 'bent' CDIAL 3230 kuṭi— in cmpd. 'curve', *kuṭika—* 'bent' MBh. Rebus: *kuṭila, katthīl* = bronze (8 parts copper and 2 parts tin) Duplicated: dula 'pair' Rebus: dul 'cast metal' Thus, cast bronze or bronze castings.

 *kanka* 'rim of jar' Rebus: *karṇīka* 'account (scribe)' *karṇī* 'supercargo'

h72a खोंड *[khōṇḍa] m A young bull, a bullcalf. (Marathi) Rebus: kõdār 'turner' (Bengali); कोंद kōnda 'engraver, lapidary setting or infixing gems' (Marathi) G. sãghāṛɔ m. 'lathe' ; संघाट joinery; M. sãgaḍ 'double-canoe' Rebus: sangataras 'stone-cutter, mason'* First sign read rebus as at m1686a.

 *khaṇḍ* 'field, division' (Skt.) Rebus: *khāṇḍa* 'tools, pots and pans, metal-ware'. Rebus 2: kaṇḍ 'fire-altar' (Santali) dula 'pair' Rebus: dul 'cast metal' Thus, duplicated 'division' hieroglyph sign reads: cast metal metal-ware.

m2028A  m382A Read rebus as at h72a.

m1202C *First sign read rebus as at h72a.* अगडा [agaḍā] *m* The tie connecting the जूं & दांडी of a गाडा or load-cart; the shaft and thill-yoke-tie. Rebus: 'lumber, miscellaneous articles': अगडतगड [*agaḍatagaḍa*] ; || *dula* 'pair' Rebus: *dul* 'cast metal' ||| *kolom* 'three' Rebus: *kolami* 'smithy, forge'.

M-1839 a

M-1816 a

M-197 a

m1839a m1816a m197a खोंड [khōṇḍa] m A young bull, a bullcalf. (Marathi) Rebus: kõdār 'turner' (Bengali); कोंद kōnda 'engraver, lapidary setting or infixing gems' (Marathi) G. sãghāṛɔ m. 'lathe' ; संघाट joinery; M. sãgaḍ 'double-canoe' Rebus: sangataras 'stone-cutter, mason'

meḍ 'body' Rebus: *meḍ* 'iron' (Ho.) PLUS | *koḍa* 'one' Rebus: *koḍ* 'workshop' dula 'pair' Rebus: dul 'cast metal'. Thus, the 'body' flanked by two linear strokes denote: workshop for iron castings.

water-carrier hieroglyph *kuṭi*; Rebus: *kuṭhi* 'smelter furnace'.

PLUS 'rim of jar': *kanka* (Santali) *karṇika* 'scribe'(Sanskrit)

Rebus: *karṇī,* supercargo

'rim-of-jar' hieroglyph *kanka* (Santali) *karṇika* 'scribe'(Sanskrit)

Rebus: *karṇī,* supercargo for a boat shipment. *karṇīka* 'account (scribe)'.कारणी *kāraṇī* 'the supercargo of a ship' (Marathi)

h1860A,B Side A: First sign read rebus as at m1839a. PLUS *kharedo* = a currycomb (Gujarati) खरारा [*kharārā*] *m* (H) A currycomb. 2 Currying a horse. (Marathi) Rebus: करडा [*karaḍā*] Hard from alloy--iron, silver &c. (Marathi) *kharādī* ' turner' (Gujarati) gaṇḍa 'four' Rebus: kaṇḍa 'furnace, fire-altar' (Santali) PLUS *baṭa* = rimless pot (Kannada) Rebus:) *baṭa* = a kind of iron (G.)) *bhaṭa* furnace (Gujara

m830A खोंड *[khōṇḍa] m A young bull, a bullcalf. (Marathi) Rebus: kõdār 'turner' (Bengali); कोंद kōnda 'engraver, lapidary setting or infixing gems' (Marathi) G. sãghāṛɔ m. 'lathe' ; संघाट joinery; M. sãgaḍ 'double-canoe' Rebus: sangataras 'stone-cutter, mason'* Read rebus as at Side A of h1860

h517A खोंड *[khōṇḍa] m A young bull, a bullcalf. (Marathi) Rebus: kõdār 'turner' (Bengali); कोंद kōnda 'engraver, lapidary setting or infixing gems' (Marathi) G. sãghāṛɔ m. 'lathe' ; संघाट joinery; M. sãgaḍ 'double-canoe' Rebus: sangataras 'stone-cutter, mason'* Read rebus as at m1839a.

h481A खोंड *[khōṇḍa] m A young bull, a bullcalf. (Marathi) Rebus: kõdār 'turner' (Bengali); कोंद kōnda 'engraver, lapidary setting or infixing gems' (Marathi) G. sãghāṛɔ m. 'lathe' ; संघाट joinery; M. sãgaḍ 'double-canoe' Rebus: sangataras*

'stone-cutter, mason'

meḍ 'body' Rebus: *meḍ* 'iron' (Ho.) PLUS | *koḍa* 'one' Rebus: *koḍ* 'workshop' PLUS mēḍu height, rising ground, hillock (Kannada) Rebus: *mẽṛhẽt, meḍ* 'iron' (Munda.Ho.)

m936a खोंड *[khōṇḍa] m A young bull, a bullcalf. (Marathi) Rebus: kõdār 'turner' (Bengali);* कोंद *kōnda 'engraver, lapidary setting or infixing gems' (Marathi) G. sãghāṛɔ m. 'lathe' ;* संघाट *joinery; M. sãgaḍ 'double-canoe' Rebus: sangataras 'stone-cutter, mason'*

ḍãg mountain-ridge (H.)(CDIAL 5476). Rebus: dhangar 'blacksmith' (Maithili)

'*ṭākuro* = hill top (Nepali) *damgar* 'merchant'; *tamkāru* id. (Akkadian) PLUS *kaṇḍa* 'arrow' Rebus: *kāṇḍa* 'tools, pots and pans and metal-ware.

,m1897 *khũṭ* 'zebu' Rebus: '(native metal) guild'

| *koḍa* = one (Santali); *koḍ* 'workshop' (Gujarati) *gaṇḍ* 'four' Rebus: *kaṇḍ* 'fire-altar' *ranku* 'liquid measure' Rebus: *ranku* 'tin'

Epigraph: fire-altar, tin workshop.

m812A खोंड *[khōṇḍa] m A young bull, a bullcalf. (Marathi) Rebus: kõdār 'turner' (Bengali);* कोंद *kōnda 'engraver, lapidary setting or infixing gems' (Marathi) G. sãghāṛɔ m. 'lathe' ;* संघाट *joinery; M. sãgaḍ 'double-canoe' Rebus: sangataras 'stone-cutter, mason'*

| *koḍa* = one (Santali); *koḍ* 'workshop' (Gujarati) dula 'two' Rebus: dul 'cast metal' dulo 'hole' Rebus: dul 'cast metal'

kanka 'rim of jar' Rebus: *karṇīka* 'account (scribe)' *karṇī* 'supercargo'

Lohunjodaro 1A खोंड *[khōṇḍa] m A young bull, a bullcalf. (Marathi) Rebus: kõdār 'turner' (Bengali);* कोंद *kōnda 'engraver, lapidary setting or infixing gems' (Marathi) G. sãghāṛɔ m. 'lathe' ;* संघाट *joinery; M. sãgaḍ 'double-canoe' Rebus: sangataras 'stone-cutter, mason'*

meḍ 'body' Rebus: *meḍ* 'iron' (Ho.) PLUS | *koḍa* 'one' Rebus: *koḍ* 'workshop' ranku 'liquid measure' Rebus: ranku 'tin' *mogge* 'sprout, bud' Rebus*: mũh* 'ingot' *sal* 'splinter' Rebus: sal 'workshop' *aya aḍaren (homonym: aduru)*'alloy native metal'

khuṭo ' leg, foot ', °ṭī ' goat's leg ' Rebus: *khōṭā* 'alloy' (Marathi) *meḍ* 'body' Rebus: *meḍ* 'iron' (Ho.)PLUS *aḍar* en 'lid of pot' Rebus: aduru 'native metal' *khaṇḍ* 'field, division' (Skt.) Rebus: *khāṇḍa* 'tools, pots and pans, metal-ware'. Rebus 2: kaṇḍ 'fire-altar' (Santali)

dula 'pair' Rebus: dul 'cast metal' *mogge* 'sprout, bud' Rebus: *mũh* 'ingot' (Santali) Thus, cast metal ingot.

kanka 'rim of jar' Rebus: karṇīka 'account (scribe)' karṇī 'supercargo'

m831A खोंड *[khōṇḍa] m A young bull, a bullcalf. (Marathi) Rebus: kõdār 'turner' (Bengali);* कोंद *kōnda 'engraver, lapidary setting or infixing gems' (Marathi) G. sãghāṛɔ m. 'lathe' ;* संघाट *joinery; M. sãgaḍ 'double-canoe' Rebus: sangataras 'stone-cutter, mason'* *meḍ* 'body' Rebus: *meḍ* 'iron' (Ho.) PLUS

 *kharedo* = a currycomb (Gujarati) खरारा [*kharārā*] *m* (H) A currycomb. 2 Currying a horse. (Marathi) Rebus: करडा [*karaḍā*] Hard from alloy--iron, silver &c. (Marathi) *kharādī* ' turner' (Gujarati)

 *kana, kanac* = corner (Santali); Rebus: *kañcu* = bronze (Telugu) PLUS खांडा [*khāṇḍā*] *m* A jag, notch, or indentation (as upon the edge of a tool or weapon). Rebus: *kāṇḍa* 'tools, pots and pans and metal-ware' Thus, bronze metalware

H-584 A

h584A खोंड *[khōṇḍa] m A young bull, a bullcalf. (Marathi) Rebus: kõdār 'turner' (Bengali); कोंद kōnda 'engraver, lapidary setting or infixing gems' (Marathi) G. sãghāṛɔ m. 'lathe' ; संघाट joinery; M. sãgaḍ 'double-canoe' Rebus: sangataras 'stone-cutter, mason' balad* m. ' ox ', gng. *bald*, (Ku.) *barad*, id. (N. Tarai) Rebus: *bharat* (5 copper, 4 zinc and 1 tin)(Punjabi) *pattar* 'trough' Rebus: *pattar* 'guild'. Thus, copper-zinc-tin alloy (worker) guild.

meḍ 'body' Rebus: *meḍ* 'iron' (Ho.)PLUS *aḍar* en 'lid of pot' Rebus: aduru 'native metal'
 *kharedo* = a currycomb (Gujarati) खरारा [*kharārā*] *m* (H) A currycomb. 2 Currying a horse. (Marathi) Rebus: करडा [*karaḍā*] Hard from alloy--iron, silver &c. (Marathi) *kharādī* ' turner' (Gujarati)

H-1858 A

H-1858 B

h1858A,B

H-215 A

h215A *meḍ* 'body' Rebus: *meḍ* 'iron' (Ho.)PLUS *aḍar* en 'lid of pot' Rebus: aduru 'native metal' PLUS dulo 'hole' Rebus: dul 'cast metal' Thus, iron castings. PLUS *kharedo* = a currycomb (Gujarati) खरारा [*kharārā*] *m* (H) A currycomb. 2 Currying a horse. (Marathi) Rebus: करडा [*karaḍā*] Hard from alloy--iron, silver &c. (Marathi) *kharādī* ' turner' (Gujarati) Side B of 1858: *baṭa* = rimless pot (Kannada) Rebus:) *baṭa* = a kind of iron (G.)) *bhaṭa* furnace (Gujarati) kolom 'three' Rebus: kolami 'smithy, forge' PLUS

m35a खोंड *[khōṇḍa] m A young bull, a bullcalf. (Marathi) Rebus: kõdār 'turner' (Bengali); कोंद kōnda 'engraver, lapidary setting or infixing gems' (Marathi) G. sãghāṛɔ m. 'lathe' ; संघाट joinery; M. sãgaḍ 'double-canoe' Rebus: sangataras 'stone-cutter, mason' meḍ* 'body' Rebus: *meḍ* 'iron' (Ho.)PLUS

  mēḍu height, rising ground, hillock (Kannada) Rebus: *mẽṛhẽt, meḍ* 'iron' (Munda.Ho.) sal 'splinter' Rebus: sal 'workshop' *aya kāṇḍa* 'alloy metalware' *ayo ḍhālako* 'alloy metal ingot' ranku 'liquid measure' Rebus: ranku 'tin' *kolmo* 'paddy plant' Rebus: *kolami* 'smithy, forge' Vikalpa: *mogge* 'sprout, bud' Rebus: *mũh* 'ingot' (Santali) dolu 'plant of shoot height' Rebus: dul 'cast metal'
 *kanka* 'rim of jar' Rebus: *karṇīka* 'account (scribe)' *karṇī* 'supercargo'

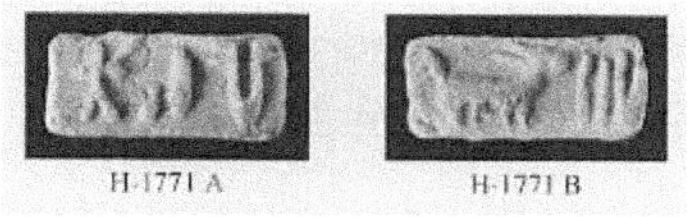

h1771A,B *bhaṭa* 'warrior' (Sanskrit) Rebus: *baṭa* a kind of iron (Gujarati). Rebus: *bhaṭa* 'furnace' (Santali) खांडा [*khāṇḍā*] *m* A jag, notch, or indentation (as upon the edge of a tool or weapon). Rebus: *kāṇḍa* 'tools, pots and pans and metal-ware' | *koḍa* 'one' Rebus: *koḍ* 'workshop' Side B:mlek 'goat' Rebus: milakkhu 'copper' dula 'two' Rebus; dul 'cast metal' *baṭa* 'warrior' 'rimless pot' Rebus: *baṭa* a kind of iron (Gujarati). Rebus: *bhaṭa* 'furnace' (Santali)

Lothal 1a *खोंड [khōṇḍa] m A young bull, a bullcalf. (Marathi) Rebus: kõdār 'turner' (Bengali); कोंद kōnda 'engraver, lapidary setting or infixing gems' (Marathi) G. sãghāṛɔ m. 'lathe' ; संघाट joinery; M. sāgaḍ 'double-canoe' Rebus: sangataras 'stone-cutter, mason' eraka 'upraised hand' Rebus: erako 'moltencast copper' PLUS*

 *kana, kanac* = corner (Santali); Rebus: *kañcu* = bronze (Telugu) PLUS खांडा [*khāṇḍā*] *m* A jag, notch, or indentation (as upon the edge of a tool or weapon). Rebus: *kāṇḍa* 'tools, pots and pans and metal-ware' Thus, bronze metalware. INFIXED kolom 'three' Rebus: kolami 'smithy, forge' sal 'splinter' Rebus: sal 'workshop' *ayo ḍhālako* 'alloy metal ingot' *ḍato* = claws of crab (Santali) Rebus: *dhātu* 'mineral ore'

 *ḍhanga* = a crook used for pulling down the branches of trees, for goats, sheep and camels (P.) Rebus:*ḍhangar* blacksmith' PLUS 'notch': खांडा [*khāṇḍā*] *m* A jag, notch, or indentation (as upon the edge of a tool or weapon). Rebus: *kāṇḍa* 'tools, pots and pans and metal-ware'. Thus, blacksmith metalware.

m71a *खोंड [khōṇḍa] m A young bull, a bullcalf. (Marathi) Rebus: kõdār 'turner' (Bengali); कोंद kōnda 'engraver, lapidary setting or infixing gems' (Marathi) G. sãghāṛɔ m. 'lathe' ; संघाट joinery; M. sāgaḍ 'double-canoe' Rebus: sangataras 'stone-cutter, mason'* eraka 'upraised hand' Rebus: erako 'moltencast copper' PLUS meḍ 'body' Rebus: meḍ 'iron' (Ho.)

kolmo  'paddy plant' Rebus: *kolami* 'smithy, forge' Vikalpa: *mogge* 'sprout, bud' Rebus: *mũh* 'ingot' (Santali) dolu 'plant of shoot height' Rebus: dul 'cast metal' sal 'splinter' Rebus: sal 'workshop' meḍ 'body' Rebus: meḍ 'iron' PLUS | *koḍa* 'one' Rebus: *koḍ* 'workshop' *khuṭo* ' leg, foot ', °ṭī ' goat's leg ' Rebus: *khōṭā* 'alloy' (Marathi)

 water-carrier hieroglyph *kuṭi*; Rebus: *kuṭhi* 'smelter furnace'.

Lothal 2a *खोंड [khōṇḍa] m A young bull, a bullcalf. (Marathi) Rebus: kõdār 'turner' (Bengali); कोंद kōnda 'engraver, lapidary setting or infixing gems' (Marathi) G. sãghāṛɔ m. 'lathe' ; संघाट joinery; M. sāgaḍ 'double-canoe' Rebus: sangataras 'stone-cutter, mason'*

 *kolmo* 'paddy plant' Rebus: *kolami* 'smithy, forge' Vikalpa: *mogge* 'sprout, bud' Rebus: *mũh* 'ingot' (Santali) dolu 'plant of shoot height' Rebus: dul 'cast metal'

 *dhāḷ* 'a slope'; 'inclination of a plane' (G.); *ḍhāḷiyum* = adj. sloping, inclining (G.) Rebus: *ḍhālako* = a large metal ingot (G.) *ḍhālakī* = a metal heated and poured into a mould; a

solid piece of metal; an ingot (Gujarati) PLUS खांडा [*khāṇḍā*] *m* A jag, notch, or indentation (as upon the edge of a tool or weapon). Rebus: *kāṇḍa* 'tools, pots and pans and metal-ware' Thus, the pair of sign hieroglyphs from r. read rebus: copper, bronze ingots, metalware castings.

ayo ḍhālako 'alloy metal ingot' *kamaḍha* 'crab' Rebus: *kammaṭa* 'mint, coiner'.

ḍato = claws of crab (Santali) Rebus: *dhātu* 'mineral ore' *dula* 'two, pair' Rebus: dul 'cast metal' PLUS *ḍhāḷ* 'a slope'; 'inclination of a plane' (G.); *ḍhāḷiyum* = adj. sloping, inclining (G.) Rebus: *ḍhālako* = a large metal ingot (G.) *ḍhālakī* = a metal heated and poured into a mould; a solid piece of metal; an ingot (Gujarati) PLUS kolom 'three' Rebus: kolami 'smithy, forge'. Thus cast metal ingot smithy. खांडा [*khāṇḍā*] *m* A jag, notch, or indentation

(as upon the edge of a tool or weapon). Rebus: *kāṇḍa* 'tools, pots and pans and metal-ware'

|||| Numeral 4: gaṇḍa 'four' Rebus: kaṇḍa 'furnace, fire-altar' (Santali) dula 'pair' Rebus: dul 'cast metal'

h76A *balad* m. ' ox ', gng. *bald*, (Ku.) *barad*, id. (N. Tarai) Rebus: *bharat* (5 copper, 4 zinc and 1 tin)(Punjabi) *pattar* 'trough' Rebus: *pattar* 'guild'. Thus, copper-zinc-tin alloy (worker) guild.

meḍ 'body' Rebus: *meḍ* 'iron' (Ho.) PLUS *Kur.* xolā tail. *Malt.* qoli id. (DEDR 2135). Rebus: kolhe 'smelter' Thus, copper smelter.

baraḍo = spine; backbone (Tulu) Rebus: *baran, bharat* 'mixed alloys' (5 copper, 4 zinc and 1 tin) (Punjabi)

kanka (Santali) *karṇika* 'scribe'(Sanskrit) Rebus: *karṇī,* supercargo for a boat shipment. INFIXED खांडा [*khāṇḍā*] *m* A jag, notch, or indentation (as upon the edge of a tool or weapon). Rebus: *kāṇḍa* 'tools, pots and pans and metal-ware' *aya aḍaren (homonym: aduru)* 'alloy native metal' *aya kammaṭa.* 'coiner, mint alloy' *bhaṭa* 'warrior' (Sanskrit) Rebus: *baṭa* a kind of iron (Gujarati). Rebus: *bhaṭa* 'furnace' (Santali)

kanka 'rim of jar' Rebus: *karṇīka* 'account (scribe)' *karṇī* 'supercargo'

M-1335 A

m1335A

h185A *meḍ* 'body' Rebus: *meḍ* 'iron' (Ho.)

khaṇḍ 'field, division' (Skt.) Rebus: *khāṇḍa* 'tools, pots and pans, metal-ware'. Rebus 2: kaṇḍ 'fire-altar' (Santali) dula 'pair' Rebus: dul 'cast metal'

Thus, duplicated 'division' hieroglyph sign reads: cast metal metal-ware.

M-403 A

m403A eraka 'upraised hand' Rebus: erako 'moltencast copper' *meḍ* 'body' Rebus: *meḍ* 'iron' (Ho.)

कांड *kāṇḍa*

'arrow' Rebus: *kāṇḍa* 'pots and pans, metalware, tools'. Rebus 2: kaṇḍ 'fire-altar' (Santali) | *koḍa* 'one' Rebus: *koḍ* 'workshop' PLUS *aḍaren* 'cover of pot or lid' Rebus: *aduru* 'native, unsmelted metal' *mogge* 'sprout, bud' Rebus: *mūh* 'ingot' (Santali)

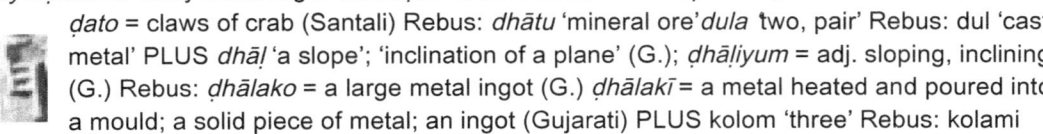

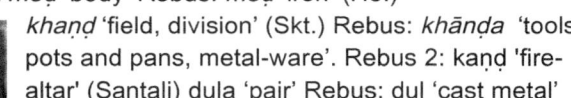

m288a *sāgāḍā* m. ' frame of a building ', °*ḍī* f. ' lathe '(CDIAL 12859) Rebus: *sangataras.* संगतराश lit. 'to collect stones, stone-cutter, mason' PLUS kola 'tiger' Rebus: kolhe 'smelter' kol 'working in iron'

mēḍu height, rising ground, hillock (Kannada) Rebus: *mẽṛhẽt, meḍ* 'iron' (Munda.Ho.) dula 'pair' Rebus: dul 'cast metal'

dhāḷ 'a slope'; 'inclination of a plane' (G.); *ḍhāḷiyum* = adj. sloping, inclining (G.) Rebus: *ḍhālako* = a large metal ingot (G.) *ḍhālakī* = a metal heated and poured into a mould; a solid piece of metal; an ingot (Gujarati) PLUS खांडा [*khāṇḍā*] *m* A jag, notch, or indentation (as upon the edge of a tool or weapon). Rebus: *kāṇḍa* 'tools, pots and pans and metal-ware' Thus, the pair of sign hieroglyphs from r. read rebus: copper, bronze ingots, metalware castings.

kanka 'rim of jar' Rebus: *karṇīka* 'account (scribe)' *karṇī* 'supercargo'

baraḍo = spine; backbone (Tulu) Rebus: *baran, bharat* 'mixed alloys' (5 copper, 4 zinc and 1 tin) (Punjabi)

kanka 'rim of jar' Rebus: *karṇīka* 'account (scribe)' *karṇī* 'supercargo'

meḍ 'body' Rebus: *meḍ* 'iron' (Ho.) काठी [kāṭhī] *f* (काष्ट S) 'frame or structure of the body' (Marathi) Rebus: खंडी [khaṇḍī] measure of weight (Marathi) *கண்டி; kaṇṭi, n. < Mhr. khaṇḍil. [T. Tu. khaṇḍi, M. kaṇḍi.]* Candy, a weight, stated to be roughly equivalent to 500 lbs.

m308A

meḍ 'body' Rebus: *meḍ* 'iron' (Ho.) काठी [kāṭhī] *f* (काष्ट S) 'frame or structure of the body' (Marathi) Rebus: खंडी [khaṇḍī] measure of weight (Marathi) *கண்டி; kaṇṭi, n. < Mhr. khaṇḍil. [T. Tu. khaṇḍi, M. kaṇḍi.]* Candy, a weight, stated to be roughly equivalent to 500 lbs.

kolom 'three' Rebus: kolami 'smithy, forge' PLUS खांडा [*khāṇḍā*] *m* A jag, notch, or indentation (as upon the edge of a tool or weapon). Rebus: *kāṇḍa* 'tools, pots and pans and metal-ware'

kanka 'rim of jar' Rebus: *karṇīka* 'account (scribe)' *karṇī* 'supercargo'

kuṭila 'bent' CDIAL 3230 kuṭi— in cmpd. 'curve', *kuṭika—* 'bent' MBh. Rebus: *kuṭila, katthīl* = bronze (8 parts copper and 2 parts tin)ranku 'antelope' Rebus: ranku 'tin

m304a Blacksmith workshop, ingot smithy

Pictorial motifs hieroglyphs:
kamaḍha 'penance'(Pkt.) Rebus: kammaṭa 'mint, coiner'
tättāru 'buffalo horn'(Munda) Rebus: P. ludh. *ṭhaṭherā* m., Ku. *ṭhaṭhero* m., N. *ṭhaṭero*, Bi. *ṭhaṭherā*, Mth. *ṭhaṭheri*, H. *ṭhaṭherā* m. K. *ṭhōṭhur* m., S. *ṭhāṭhāro* m., P. *ṭhaṭhiār*, *°rā* m. Pk. *ṭhaṭṭhāra* --m.(CDIAL 5493) N. *ṭhaṭṭar* ' an alloy of copper and bell metal '(CDIAL 5491)

kūdī 'bunch of twigs' (Sanskrit) Rebus: *kuṭhi* 'smelter furnace' (Santali)

mukha 'face' Rebus: *mũh* 'ingot' *kolom* 'three' (faces) Rebus: *kolami* 'smithy, forge'
kammarsāla 'waistband' Rebus: *kamar* 'blacksmith' *sal* 'workshop' (Santali)
koḍu 'bracelet' Rebus*: koḍ* 'workshop'
maṇḍā 'raised platform, stool' Rebus: *maṇḍā* 'warehouse' Vikalpa: *kanḍo* stool, seat Rebus: *kāṇḍā* 'metalware, tools, pots and pans'(Marathi).

mēṭu 'rick as of hay' Rebus: meḍ 'iron'
mlekh 'goat' Rebus: milakkkhu 'copper' (Pali) dula 'pair' Rebus: dul 'cast metal'
kol 'tiger' Rebus: kolhe 'smelter' *kaṭavai* 'leap, jump' Rebus: *kaḍavu* 'turning lathe' Leaping: *kũdā* Rebus: *kõdār* 'turner' (Bengali); *kõdā* 'to turn in a lathe' (Bengali) Thus the hieroglyph denotes: *kolhe kõdār* 'smelter, turner'

rāngo 'water buffalo bull' (Ku.N.)(CDIAL 10559) Rebus: ranku 'tin' raṅga3 n. ' tin ' lex. [Cf. nāga -- 2, vaṅga -- 1]Pk. *raṁga* -- n. ' tin '; P. *rāg* f., *rāgā* m. ' pewter, tin ' (← H.); Ku. *rāṅ* ' tin, solder ', gng. *rāk*; N. *rāṅ*, *rāṅo* ' tin, solder ', A. B. *rāṅ*; Or. *rāṅga* ' tin ', *rāṅgā* ' solder, spelter ', Bi. Mth. *rāgā*, OAw. *rāṁga*; H. *rāg* f., *rāgā* m. ' tin, pewter '; Si. *raṅga* ' tin '.(CDIAL 10562). Vikalpa: *kaṭiya* 'buffalo heifer' (Gujarati) Rebus: *kāṭi* 'furnace (Trench)' (Tamil) Kur. *kaṛā* young male buffalo; Rebus*: kāṭhāḷ* 'maritime' (Gujarati) கடலர் kaṭalar, n. < id. Fishermen inhabitants of maritime tracts

ibha 'elephant' Rebus: ib 'iron' (Santali) ibbo 'merchant' (Gujarati)

baḍhia = a castrated boar, a hog (Santali) baḍhi 'a caste who work both in iron and wood' (Santali) *baṟea* 'merchant' Vikalpa: kāṇḍā 'rhinoceros' (Tamil) Rebus: khāṇḍā 'tools, pots and pans, metalware' (Marathi)

Text hieroglyphs: *meḍ* 'body' Rebus: *meḍ* 'iron' (Ho.)
kamaḍha 'crab' Rebus: *kammaṭa* 'mint, coiner'.
ḍato = claws of crab (Santali) Rebus: *dhātu* 'mineral ore'

sal 'splinter' Rebus: *sal* 'workshop' INFIXED in 'rim-of-jar': kanka 'rim of jar' Rebus: *karṇīka* 'account (scribe)' *karṇī* 'supercargo'. Thus, supercargo workshop.

ayo 'fish' Rebus: aya 'iron' (Gujarati) ayas 'metal' (Vedic)

kanka 'rim of jar' Rebus: *karṇīka* 'account (scribe)' *karṇī* 'supercargo'. The pair thus reads: metal supercargo.

M-486 a

h480a kola 'tiger' Rebus: kolhe 'smelter' kol 'working in iron' pattar 'trough' Rebus: pattar 'guild, goldsmith'

meḍ 'body' Rebus: *meḍ* 'iron' (Ho.) काठी [kāṭhī] *f* (काष्ट S) 'frame or structure of the body' (Marathi) Rebus: खंडी [khaṇḍī] measure of weight (Marathi) *கண்டி; kaṇṭi, n. < Mhr. khaṇḍil. [T. Tu. khaṇḍi, M. kaṇḍi.]* Candy, a weight, stated to be roughly equivalent to 500 lbs.

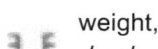

kanka 'rim of jar' Rebus: *karṇīka* 'account (scribe)' *karṇī* 'supercargo'

khaṇḍ 'field, division' (Skt.) Rebus: *khāṇḍa* 'tools, pots and pans, metal-ware'. Rebus 2: kaṇḍ 'fire-altar' (Santali)

Banawali 1a *खोंड [khōṇḍa] m A young bull, a bullcalf. (Marathi) Rebus: kōdār 'turner' (Bengali); कोंद kōnda 'engraver, lapidary setting or infixing gems' (Marathi) G. sãghāṛɔ m. 'lathe' ; संघाट joinery; M. sãgaḍ 'double-canoe' Rebus: sangataras 'stone-cutter, mason'*

meḍ 'body' Rebus: *meḍ* 'iron' (Ho.) काठी [kāṭhī] *f* (काष्ट S) 'frame or structure of the body' (Marathi) Rebus: खंडी [khaṇḍī] measure of weight (Marathi) *கண்டி; kaṇṭi, n. < Mhr. khaṇḍil. [T. Tu. khaṇḍi, M. kaṇḍi.]* Candy, a weight, stated to be roughly equivalent to 500 lbs.

kanka 'rim of jar' Rebus: karṇīka 'account (scribe)' karṇī 'supercargo' *ayo* 'fish' Rebus: *aya* 'iron' *ayas* 'metal' sal 'splinter' Rebus: sal 'workshop'

koḍi 'flag' (Ta.)(DEDR 2049). Rebus 1: *koḍ* 'workshop' (Kuwi) Rebus 2: *khŏḍ* m. 'pit', *khōḍü* f. 'small pit' (Kashmiri. CDIAL 3947). *kamaḍha* 'crab' Rebus: *kammaṭa* 'mint, coiner'.

ḍato = claws of crab (Santali) Rebus: *dhātu* 'mineral ore' dula 'pair' Rebus: dul 'cast metal' PLUS

āra 'spokes' Rebus: *āra 'brass'*. cf. erka = ekke (Tbh. of arka) aka (Tbh. of arka) copper (metal); crystal (Kannada) Glyph: *eraka*'nave of wheel' Rebus: eraka 'copper'; cf. erka = ekke (Tbh. of arka) aka (Tbh. of arka) copper (metal); crystal (Kannada) *erako* 'moltencast copper' Thus, copper and brass castings.

K-16 A

Kalibangan 16A *खोंड [khōṇḍa] m A young bull, a bullcalf. (Marathi) Rebus: kōdār 'turner' (Bengali); कोंद kōnda 'engraver, lapidary setting or infixing gems' (Marathi) G. sãghāṛɔ m. 'lathe' ; संघाट joinery; M. sãgaḍ 'double-canoe' Rebus: sangataras 'stone-cutter, mason'*

meḍ 'body' Rebus: *meḍ* 'iron' (Ho.) काठी [kāṭhī] *f* (काष्ट S) 'frame or structure of the body' (Marathi) Rebus: खंडी [khaṇḍī] measure of weight (Marathi) *கண்டி; kaṇṭi, n. < Mhr. khaṇḍil. [T. Tu. khaṇḍi, M. kaṇḍi.]* Candy, a weight, stated to be roughly equivalent to 500 lbs.

kanka 'rim of jar' Rebus: *karṇīka* 'account (scribe)' *karṇī* 'supercargo'

ayo 'fish' Rebus: *aya* 'iron' *ayas* 'metal'

dhāḷ 'a slope'; 'inclination of a plane' (G.); *ḍhāḷiyum* = adj. sloping, inclining (G.) Rebus: *ḍhālako* = a large metal ingot (G.) *ḍhālakī* = a metal heated and poured into a mould; a solid piece of metal; an ingot (Gujarati) PLUS खांडा [*khāṇḍā*] *m* A jag, notch, or indentation (as upon the edge of a tool or weapon). Rebus: *kāṇḍa* 'tools, pots and pans and metal-ware' Thus, the pair of sign hieroglyphs from r. read rebus: copper, bronze ingots, metalware castings.

āra 'spokes' Rebus: *āra 'brass'*. cf. erka = ekke (Tbh. of arka) aka (Tbh. of arka) copper (metal); crystal (Kannada) Glyph: *eraka*'nave of wheel' Rebus: eraka 'copper';

cf. erka = ekke (Tbh. of arka) aka (Tbh. of arka) copper (metal); crystal (Kannada) *erako* 'moltencast copper'

m1288a

meḍ 'body' Rebus: *meḍ* 'iron' (Ho.) काठी [kāṭhī] *f* (काष्ट S) 'frame or structure of the body' (Marathi) Rebus: खंडी [khaṇḍī] measure of weight (Marathi) *கண்டி; kaṇṭi, n. < Mhr. khaṇḍil. [T. Tu. khaṇḍi, M. kaṇḍi.]* Candy, a weight, stated to be roughly equivalent to 500 lbs.

kanka 'rim of jar' Rebus: *karṇīka* 'account (scribe)' *karṇī* 'supercargo'

kuṭila 'bent' CDIAL 3230 kuṭi— in cmpd. 'curve', *kuṭika—* 'bent' MBh. Rebus: *kuṭila, katthīl* = bronze (8 parts copper and 2 parts tin) *bhaṭa* 'warrior' (Sanskrit) Rebus: *baṭa* a kind of iron (Gujarati). Rebus: *bhaṭa* 'furnace' (Santali)

m87A *खोंड [khōṇḍa] m A young bull, a bullcalf. (Marathi) Rebus: kõdār 'turner' (Bengali); कोंद kōnda 'engraver, lapidary setting or infixing gems' (Marathi) G. sãghāṛɔ m. 'lathe' ; संघाट joinery; M. sãgaḍ 'double-canoe' Rebus: sangataras 'stone-cutter, mason'* *aḍaren* 'cover of pot or lid' Rebus: *aduru* 'native, unsmelted metal' PLUS

meḍ 'body' Rebus: *meḍ* 'iron' (Ho.) काठी [kāṭhī] *f* (काष्ट S) 'frame or structure of the body' (Marathi) Rebus: खंडी [khaṇḍī] measure of weight (Marathi) *கண்டி; kaṇṭi, n. < Mhr. khaṇḍil. [T. Tu. khaṇḍi, M. kaṇḍi.]* Candy, a weight, stated to be roughly equivalent to 500 lbs.

kamaḍha 'archer, bow' Rebus: *kammaṭa* 'mint, coiner'.

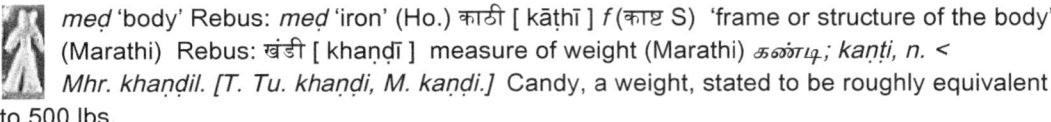

khareḍo = a currycomb (Gujarati) खरारा [*kharārā*] *m* (H) A currycomb. 2 Currying a horse. (Marathi) Rebus: करडा [*karaḍā*] Hard from alloy--iron, silver &c. (Marathi) *kharādī* ' turner' (Gujarati)

h1673A *खोंड [khōṇḍa] m A young bull, a bullcalf. (Marathi) Rebus: kõdār 'turner' (Bengali); कोंद kōnda 'engraver, lapidary setting or infixing gems' (Marathi) G. sãghāṛɔ m. 'lathe' ; संघाट joinery; M. sãgaḍ 'double-canoe' Rebus: sangataras 'stone-cutter, mason'*

mogge 'sprout, bud' Rebus*: mũh* 'ingot' gaṇḍa 'four' Rebus: kaṇḍa 'furnace, fire-altar' (Santali) *meḍ* 'body' Rebus: *meḍ* 'iron' (Ho.) काठी [kāṭhī] *f* (काष्ट S) 'frame or structure of the body' (Marathi) Rebus: खंडी [khaṇḍī] measure of weight (Marathi) *கண்டி; kaṇṭi, n. < Mhr. khaṇḍil. [T. Tu. khaṇḍi, M. kaṇḍi.]* Candy, a weight, stated to be roughly equivalent to 500 lbs.

m386a *sãgāḍā* m. ' frame of a building ', *°ḍī* f. ' lathe '(CDIAL 12859) Rebus*: sangataras.* संगतराश lit. 'to collect stones, stone-cutter, mason. PLUS

ũh 'ingot' gaṇḍa 'four' Rebus: kaṇḍa 'furnace, fire-altar' (Santali) *meḍ* 'body' Rebus: *meḍ* 'iron' (Ho.) काठी [kāṭhī] *f* (काष्ट S) 'frame or structure of the body' (Marathi) Rebus: खंडी [khaṇḍī] measure of weight (Marathi) *கண்டி; kaṇṭi, n. < Mhr. khaṇḍil. [T. Tu. khaṇḍi, M. kaṇḍi.]* Candy, a weight, stated to be roughly equivalent to 500 lbs. खांडा [*khāṇḍā*] *m* A jag, notch, or indentation (as upon the edge of a tool or weapon). Rebus: *kāṇḍa* 'tools, pots and pans and metal-war ganḍa 'four' Rebus: kanḍa 'furnace, fire-altar' (Santali) *mogge* 'sprout, bud' Rebus*: mũh* 'ingot'

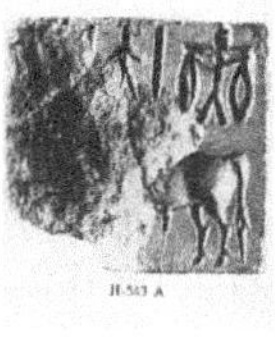 h543A  h544A  m991A

खोंड [khōṇḍa] m A young bull, a bullcalf. (Marathi) Rebus: kōdār 'turner' (Bengali); कोंद kōnda 'engraver, lapidary setting or infixing gems' (Marathi) G. sãghāṛɔ m. 'lathe' ; संघाट joinery; M. sāgaḍ 'double-canoe' Rebus: sangataras 'stone-cutter, mason'

 *khareḍo* = a currycomb (Gujarati) खरारा [*kharārā*] *m* (H) A currycomb. 2 Currying a horse. (Marathi) Rebus: करडा [*karaḍā*] Hard from alloy--iron, silver &c. (Marathi) *kharādī* ' turner' (Gujarati) PLUS

 *ũh* 'ingot' ganḍa 'four' Rebus: kanḍa 'furnace, fire-altar' (Santali) *meḍ* 'body' Rebus: *meḍ* 'iron' (Ho.) काठी [kāṭhī] *f* (काष्ट S) 'frame or structure of the body' (Marathi) Rebus: खंडी [khanḍī] measure of weight (Marathi) *கண்டி; kaṇṭi, n. < Mhr. khanḍil. [T. Tu. khanḍi, M. kanḍi.]* Candy, a weight, stated to be roughly equivalent to 500 lbs.

| *koḍa* 'one' Rebus: *koḍ* 'workshop'

 water-carrier hieroglyph *kuṭi*; Rebus: *kuṭhi* 'smelter furnace'.

खोंड [khōṇḍa] m A young bull, a bullcalf. (Marathi) Rebus: kōdār 'turner' (Bengali); कोंद kōnda 'engraver, lapidary setting or infixing gems' (Marathi) G. sãghāṛɔ m. 'lathe' ; संघाट joinery; M. sāgaḍ 'double-canoe' Rebus: sangataras 'stone-cutter, mason' | *koḍa* 'one' Rebus: *koḍ* 'workshop'

 mēḍu height, rising ground, hillock (Kannada) Rebus: *mẽṛhẽt, meḍ* 'iron' (Munda.Ho.)

 *kanac* 'corner' Rebus: *kañcu* 'bronze'

 *koḍi* 'flag' (Ta.)(DEDR 2049). Rebus 1: *koḍ* 'workshop' (Kuwi) Rebus 2: *khŏḍ* m. 'pit', *khŏḍü* f. 'small pit' (Kashmiri. CDIAL 3947).

 m1741a *खोंड [khōṇḍa] m A young bull, a bullcalf. (Marathi) Rebus: kōdār 'turner' (Bengali); कोंद kōnda 'engraver, lapidary setting or infixing gems' (Marathi) G. sãghāṛɔ m. 'lathe' ; संघाट joinery; M. sāgaḍ 'double-canoe' Rebus: sangataras 'stone-cutter, mason'* खांडा [*khānḍā*] *m* A jag, notch, or indentation (as upon the edge of a tool or weapon). Rebus: *kānḍa* 'tools, pots and pans and metal-ware' *ayo* 'fish' Rebus: *aya* 'iron' *ayas* 'metal'

  *loa* 'ficus religiosa' Rebus: *lo* 'iron' (Sanskrit) PLUS unique ligatures: लोखंड [lōkhanḍa] *n* (लोह S) Iron. लोखंडाचे चणे खावविणें or चारणें To oppress

grievously.लोखंडकाम [lōkhaṇḍakāma] *n* Iron work; that portion (of a building, machine &c.) which consists of iron. 2 The business of an ironsmith.लोखंडी [lōkhaṇḍī] *a* (लोखंड) Composed of iron; relating to iron. (Marathi) *bhaṭa* 'warrior' (Sanskrit) Rebus: *baṭa* a kind of iron (Gujarati). Rebus: *bhaṭa* 'furnace' (Santali) Thus, together, the ligatured hieroglyph reads rebus: *loa bhaṭa* 'iron furnace' dula 'pair' Rebus: dul 'cast metal' PLUS

aḍar 'harrow'; rebus: *aduru* 'native unsmelted metal' *mason'* notch+slanted stroke reads rebus: *ḍhālako kāṇḍa* 'ingot, tools, pots and pans and metal-ware'.*dhāḷ* 'a slope'; 'inclination of a plane' (G.); *ḍhāḷiyum* = adj. sloping, inclining (G.) Rebus: *ḍhālako* = a large metal ingot (G.) *ḍhālakī* = a metal heated and poured into a mould; a solid piece of metal; an ingot (Gujarati) PLUS खांडा [*khāṇḍā*] *m* A jag, notch, or indentation (as upon the edge of a tool or weapon). Rebus: *kāṇḍa* 'tools, pots and pans and metal-ware' *kamaḍha* 'crab' Rebus: *kammaṭa* 'mint, coiner'.*ḍato* = claws of crab (Santali) Rebus: *dhātu* 'mineral ore' PLUS PLUS *Kur.* xolā tail. *Malt.* qoli id. (DEDR 2135). Rebus: kolhe 'smelter' Thus, copper smelter.

H-443 A

h443A *खोंड [khōṇḍa] m A young bull, a bullcalf. (Marathi) Rebus: kõdār 'turner' (Bengali); कोंद kōnda 'engraver, lapidary setting or infixing gems' (Marathi) G. sãghāṛɔ m. 'lathe' ; संघाट joinery; M. sãgaḍ 'double-canoe' Rebus: sangataras 'stone-cutter, mason'* | *koḍa* 'one' Rebus: *koḍ* 'workshop' *ayo* 'fish' Rebus: *aya* 'iron' *ayas* 'metal' *ḍhālako kāṇḍa* 'ingot, tools, pots and pans and metal-ware'.*dhāḷ* 'a slope'; 'inclination of a plane' (G.); *ḍhāḷiyum* = adj. sloping, inclining (G.) Rebus: *ḍhālako* = a large metal ingot (G.) *ḍhālakī* = a metal heated and poured into a mould; a solid piece of metal; an ingot (Gujarati)

H-440 a

h440a *खोंड [khōṇḍa] m A young bull, a bullcalf. (Marathi) Rebus: kõdār 'turner' (Bengali); कोंद kōnda 'engraver, lapidary setting or infixing gems' (Marathi) G. sãghāṛɔ m. 'lathe' ; संघाट joinery; M. sãgaḍ 'double-canoe' Rebus: sangataras 'stone-cutter, mason'*| *koḍa* 'one' Rebus: *koḍ* 'workshop' *aya kammaṭa.*'coiner, mint alloy'

kanka 'rim of jar' Rebus: *karṇīka* 'account (scribe)' *karṇī* 'supercargo'

meḍ

'body' Rebus: *meḍ* 'iron' (Ho.) काठी [kāṭhī] *f* (काष्ट S) 'frame or structure of the body' (Marathi) Rebus: खंडी [khaṇḍī] measure of weight (Marathi) கண்டி; *kaṇṭi, n. < Mhr. khaṇḍil. [T. Tu. khaṇḍi, M. kaṇḍi.]* Candy, a weight, stated to be roughly equivalent to 500 lbs.

M-1982 a

m1982A | *koḍa* 'one' Rebus: *koḍ* 'workshop' *aya kammaṭa.*'coiner, mint alloy' *bhaṭa* 'warrior' (Sanskrit) Rebus: *baṭa* a kind of iron (Gujarati). Rebus: *bhaṭa* 'furnace' (Santali)

kanka 'rim of jar'

Rebus: karṇīka 'account (scribe)' karṇī 'supercargo'

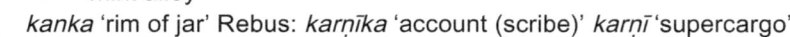

M-951 A

m951A खोंड *[khōṇḍa] m A young bull, a bullcalf. (Marathi) Rebus: kõdār 'turner' (Bengali);* कोंद *kōnda 'engraver, lapidary setting or infixing gems' (Marathi) G. sãghāṛɔ m. 'lathe' ;* संघाट *joinery; M. sãgaḍ 'double-canoe' Rebus: sangataras 'stone-cutter, mason''* | *koḍa* 'one' Rebus: *koḍ* 'workshop' *aya kammaṭa.*'coiner, mint alloy'

kuṭila 'bent' CDIAL 3230 kuṭi— in cmpd. 'curve', *kuṭika*— 'bent' MBh. Rebus: *kuṭila, katthīl* = bronze (8 parts copper and 2 parts tin) Duplicated: dula 'pair' Rebus: dul 'cast metal' Thus, cast bronze or bronze castings.

kanka 'rim of jar' Rebus: karṇīka 'account (scribe)' karṇī 'supercargo'

m1713a खोंड *[khōṇḍa] m A young bull, a bullcalf. (Marathi) Rebus: kõdār 'turner' (Bengali);* कोंद

kōnda 'engraver, lapidary setting or infixing gems' (Marathi) G. sãghāṛɔ m. 'lathe' ; संघाट *joinery; M. sãgaḍ 'double-canoe' Rebus: sangataras 'stone-cutter, mason'* | *koḍa* 'one' Rebus: *koḍ* 'workshop' *aya kammaṭa.*'coiner, mint alloy' *ayo* 'fish' Rebus: *aya* 'iron' *ayas* 'metal' *ḍhanga* = a crook used for pulling down the branches of trees, for goats, sheep and camels (P.)Rebus:*ḍhangar* blacksmith'.

kanac 'corner' Rebus: *kañcu* 'bronze' dula 'two' Rebus: dul 'cast metal' *ayo* 'fish' Rebus: *aya* 'iron' *ayas* 'metal'

Lothal 4a खोंड *[khōṇḍa] m A young bull, a bullcalf. (Marathi) Rebus: kõdār 'turner' (Bengali);* कोंद *kōnda 'engraver, lapidary setting or infixing gems' (Marathi) G. sãghāṛɔ m. 'lathe' ;* संघाट *joinery; M. sãgaḍ 'double-canoe' Rebus: sangataras 'stone-cutter, mason'* | *koḍa* 'one' Rebus: *koḍ* 'workshop' *aya kammaṭa.*'coiner, mint alloy'

सांड [sāṇḍa] *f* (षद S) An outlet for superfluous water (as through a dam or mound); a sluice, a floodvent. Rebus: सांडणी [sāṇḍaṇī] *f* (H) An instrument of goldsmiths. It is hooked or curved at the extremity; and is used to draw things out of the fire.
सांठा [*sāṇṭhā*] *m* (संचय S) A collection, heap, hoard, store, stock.साटें [*sāṭēṃ*] *n* (संचय S) A whole investment; the total quantity of merchandise (brought to market by one merchant). sal 'splinter' Rebus: sal 'workshop'
ayo 'fish' Rebus: *aya* 'iron' *ayas* 'metal' *bhaṭa* 'warrior' (Sanskrit) Rebus: *baṭa* a kind of iron (Gujarati). Rebus: *bhaṭa* 'furnace' (Santali)

kanka 'rim of jar' Rebus: *karṇīka* 'account (scribe)' *karṇī* 'supercargo'
aḍaren 'cover of pot or lid' Rebus: *aduru* 'native, unsmelted metal' PLUS
| *koḍa* 'one' Rebus: *koḍ* 'workshop'

Lothal 79a dulo 'hole' Rebus: dul 'cast metal' PLUS | *koḍa* 'one' Rebus: *koḍ* 'workshop'

kanka 'rim of jar' Rebus: karṇīka 'account (scribe)' karṇī 'supercargo' INFIXED sal 'splinter' Rebus: sal 'workshop'.
kolom 'three' Rebus: kolami 'smithy, forge' PLUS | *koḍa* 'one' Rebus: *koḍ* 'workshop'

Chanhudaro 15a खोंड *[khōṇḍa] m A young bull, a bullcalf. (Marathi) Rebus: kõdār 'turner' (Bengali);* कोंद *kōnda 'engraver, lapidary setting or infixing gems' (Marathi) G. sãghāṛɔ m. 'lathe' ;* संघाट *joinery; M. sãgaḍ 'double-canoe' Rebus: sangataras 'stone-cutter, mason'*

kuṭila 'bent'  CDIAL 3230 kuṭi— in cmpd. 'curve', *kuṭika—* 'bent' MBh. Rebus: *kuṭila, katthīl* = bronze (8 parts copper and 2 parts tin)PLUS | *koḍa* 'one' Rebus: *koḍ* 'workshop'

 *kharedo* = a currycomb (Gujarati) खरारा [*kharārā*] *m* (H) A currycomb. 2 Currying a horse. (Marathi) Rebus: करडा [*karaḍā*] Hard from alloy--iron, silver &c. (Marathi) *kharādī* ' turner' (Gujarati)

 *kanka* 'rim of jar' Rebus: *karṇīka* 'account (scribe)' *karṇī* 'supercargo'

खोंड *[khōṇḍa] m A young bull, a bullcalf. (Marathi) Rebus: kõdār 'turner' (Bengali);* कोंद *kōnda 'engraver, lapidary setting or infixing gems' (Marathi) G. sãghāṛɔ m. 'lathe' ;* संघाट *joinery; M. sãgaḍ 'double-canoe' Rebus: sangataras 'stone-cutter, mason'* PLUS | *koḍa* 'one' Rebus: *koḍ* 'workshop'

 *kuṭila* 'bent' CDIAL 3230 kuṭi— in cmpd. 'curve', *kuṭika—* 'bent' MBh. Rebus: *kuṭila, katthīl* = bronze (8 parts copper and 2 parts tin) PLUS | *koḍa* 'one' Rebus: *koḍ* 'workshop' *kuṭila* 'bent' CDIAL 3230 kuṭi— in cmpd. 'curve', *kuṭika—* 'bent' MBh. Rebus: *kuṭila, katthīl* = bronze (8 parts copper and 2 parts tin) Duplicated: dula 'pair' Rebus: dul 'cast metal' Thus, cast bronze or bronze castings.

 *aḍar* 'harrow'; rebus: *aduru* 'native unsmelted metal' *bhaṭa* 'warrior' (Sanskrit) Rebus: *baṭa* a kind of iron (Gujarati). Rebus: *bhaṭa* 'furnace' (Santali)

 *kanka* 'rim of jar' Rebus: *karṇīka* 'account (scribe)' *karṇī* 'supercargo'

h550A Read rebus as at m135

m135A खोंड *[khōṇḍa] m A young bull, a bullcalf. (Marathi) Rebus: kõdār 'turner' (Bengali);* कोंद *kōnda 'engraver, lapidary setting or infixing gems' (Marathi) G. sãghāṛɔ m. 'lathe' ;* संघाट *joinery; M. sãgaḍ 'double-canoe' Rebus: sangataras 'stone-cutter, mason'*

 *muka* 'ladle' (Tamil)(DEDR 4887) Rebus: *mũh* 'ingot' (Santali) *baṭa* = rimless pot (Kannada) Rebus:) *baṭa* = a kind of iron (G.)) *bhaṭa* furnace (Gujarati) PLUS | *koḍa* 'one' Rebus: *koḍ* 'workshop' kolom 'three' Rebus: kolami 'smithy, forge'

 कांड *kāṇḍa* 'arrow' Rebus: *kāṇḍa* 'pots and pans, metalware, tools'. Rebus 2: kaṇḍ 'fire-altar' (Santali)

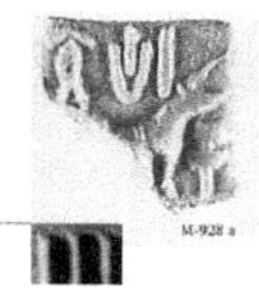

m928a खोंड *[khōṇḍa] m A young bull, a bullcalf. (Marathi) Rebus: kõdār*

'turner' (Bengali); कोंद kōnda 'engraver, lapidary setting or infixing gems' (Marathi) G. sãghāṛɔ m. 'lathe' ; संघाट joinery; M. sãgaḍ 'double-canoe' Rebus: sangataras 'stone-cutter, mason' *muka* 'ladle' (Tamil)(DEDR 4887) Rebus: *mũh* 'ingot' (Santali) *baṭa* = rimless pot (Kannada) Rebus:) *baṭa* = a kind of iron (G.)) *bhaṭa* furnace (Gujarati)
PLUS | *koḍa* 'one' Rebus: *koḍ* 'workshop' kolom 'three' Rebus: kolami 'smithy, forge' *aḍaren* 'cover of pot or lid' Rebus: *aduru* 'native, unsmelted metal' PLUS dula 'pair' Rebus: dul 'cast metal' PLUS *ḍānga* 'peak or summit of hill' (Hindi) Rebus: *ḍhangar* 'blacksmith' (Maithili)

h67a *खोंड [khōṇḍa] m A young bull, a bullcalf. (Marathi) Rebus: kõdār 'turner' (Bengali); कोंद kōnda 'engraver, lapidary setting or infixing gems' (Marathi) G. sãghāṛɔ m. 'lathe' ; संघाट joinery; M. sãgaḍ 'double-canoe' Rebus: sangataras 'stone-cutter, mason'* Circumscript: gaṇḍa 'four' Rebus: kaṇḍa 'furnace, fire-altar' (Santali) INFIXED ranku 'liquid measure' Rebus: ranku 'tin'PLUS | *koḍa* 'one' Rebus: *koḍ* 'workshop'

m141a *खोंड [khōṇḍa] m A young bull, a bullcalf. (Marathi) Rebus: kõdār 'turner' (Bengali); कोंद kōnda 'engraver, lapidary setting or infixing gems' (Marathi) G. sãghāṛɔ m. 'lathe' ; संघाट joinery; M. sãgaḍ 'double-canoe' Rebus: sangataras 'stone-cutter, mason'*

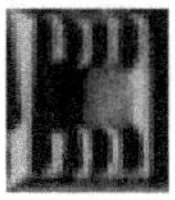

kəṭhā´r, kc. *kuṭhār* m. ' granary, storeroom '(WPah.)(CDIAL 3550). *koṭhārī m.* ' storekeeper' (Gujarati)(CDIAL 3551) Thus, storeroom (of) *kolom* 'three' Rebus: *kolami* 'smithy, forge'. dula 'pair' Rebus: dul 'cast metal' Thus, together *dul kolami kuṭhār* 'metal smithy castings storeroom' | *koḍa* 'one' Rebus: *koḍ* 'workshop' sal 'splinter' Rebus: sal 'workshop' *aya kammaṭa.*'coiner, mint alloy' *ayo ḍhālako* 'alloy metal ingot'

kəṭhā´r, kc. *kuṭhār* m. ' granary, storeroom '(WPah.)(CDIAL 3550). *koṭhārī m.* ' storekeeper' (Gujarati)(CDIAL 3551) Thus, storeroom (of) *kolom* 'three' Rebus: *kolami* 'smithy, forge'.

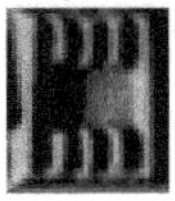

bicha 'scorpion' (Assamese) Rebus: *bica* 'stone ore' (Santali)

kanac 'corner' Rebus: *kañcu* 'bronze'

m1928a *rāngo* 'water buffalo bull' (Ku.N.)(CDIAL 10559) Rebus: rango 'pewter' *pattar* 'trough' Rebus: *pattar* 'guild'.Thus, pewter guild.
| *koḍa* 'one' Rebus: *koḍ* 'workshop' kolom 'three' Rebus: kolami 'smithy, forge'

water-carrier hieroglyph *kuṭi*; Rebus: *kuṭhi* 'smelter furnace'.

h471a *खोंड [khōṇḍa] m A young bull, a bullcalf. (Marathi) Rebus: kõdār 'turner' (Bengali); कोंद kōnda 'engraver, lapidary setting or infixing gems' (Marathi) G.*

sãghāṛɔ m. 'lathe' ; संघाट joinery; M. sãgaḍ 'double-canoe' Rebus: sangataras 'stone-cutter, mason' dula 'two' Rebus: dul 'cast metal' PLUS *dhāḷ* 'a slope'; 'inclination of a plane' (G.); *ḍhāḷiyum* = adj. sloping, inclining (G.) Rebus: *ḍhālako* = a large metal ingot (G.) *ḍhālakī* = a metal heated and poured into a mould; a solid piece of metal; an ingot (Gujarati) INFIXED खांडा [*khāṇḍā*] *m* A jag, notch, or indentation (as upon the edge of a tool or weapon). Rebus: *kāṇḍa* 'tools, pots and pans and metal-ware' Thus, ingots and metalware.

meḍ 'body' Rebus: *meḍ* 'iron' (Ho.) काठी [kāṭhī] *f* (काष्ट S) 'frame or structure of the body' (Marathi) Rebus: खंडी [khaṇḍī] measure of weight (Marathi) கண்டி; *kaṇṭi, n. < Mhr. khanḍil. [T. Tu. khaṇḍi, M. kaṇḍi.]* Candy, a weight, stated to be roughly equivalent to 500 lbs.

kharedo = a currycomb (Gujarati) खरारा [*kharārā*] *m* (H) A currycomb. 2 Currying a horse. (Marathi) Rebus: करडा [*karaḍā*] Hard from alloy--iron, silver &c. (Marathi) *kharādī* ' turner' (Gujarati)

kanka 'rim of jar' Rebus: *karṇīka* 'account (scribe)' *karṇī* 'supercargo'

h448A *खोंड [khōṇḍa] m A young bull, a bullcalf. (Marathi) Rebus: kōdār 'turner' (Bengali); कोंद kōnda 'engraver, lapidary setting or infixing gems' (Marathi) G. sãghāṛɔ m. 'lathe' ; संघाट joinery; M. sãgaḍ 'double-canoe' Rebus: sangataras 'stone-cutter, mason'*

| *koḍa* 'one' Rebus: *koḍ* 'workshop'

notch+slanted stroke reads rebus: *ḍhālako kāṇḍa* 'ingot, tools, pots and pans and metal-ware'.*dhāḷ* 'a slope'; 'inclination of a plane' (G.); *ḍhāḷiyum* = adj. sloping, inclining (G.) Rebus: *ḍhālako* = a large metal ingot (G.) *ḍhālakī* = a metal heated and poured into a mould; a solid piece of metal; an ingot (Gujarati) PLUS खांडा [*khāṇḍā*] *m* A jag, notch, or indentation (as upon the edge of a tool or weapon). Rebus: *kāṇḍa* 'tools, pots and pans and metal-ware'

kanka 'rim of jar' Rebus: *karṇīka* 'account (scribe)' *karṇī* 'supercargo'

h146A

ḍhanga = a crook used for pulling down the branches of trees, for goats, sheep and camels (P.) Rebus:*ḍhangar* blacksmith'. PLUS

kharedo = a currycomb (Gujarati) खरारा [*kharārā*] *m* (H) A currycomb. 2 Currying a horse. (Marathi)
Rebus: करडा [*karaḍā*] Hard from alloy--iron, silver &c. (Marathi) *kharādī* ' turner' (Gujarati)

dula 'pair' Rebus: *dul* 'cast (metal)' PLUS*kana, kanac* = corner (Santali); Rebus: *kañcu* = bronze (Telugu) PLUS infixed kolmo 'paddy plant' Rebus: kolami 'smithy, forge'. Thus, cast bronze smithy, forge. Or, *mogge* 'sprout, bud' Rebus: *mũh* 'ingot' (Santali)Thus, cast bronze ingot. Read as: *kañcu dul mũh 'bronze cast ingot'*

water-carrier hieroglyph *kuṭi*; Rebus: *kuṭhi* 'smelter furnace'.

PLUS 'rim of jar': *kanka* (Santali) *karṇika* 'scribe'(Sanskrit)
Rebus: *karṇī,* supercargo

'rim-of-jar' hieroglyph *kanka* (Santali) *karṇika* 'scribe'(Sanskrit) Rebus: *karṇī,* supercargo for a boat shipment. *karṇīka* 'account (scribe)'.कारणी *kāraṇī* 'the supercargo of a ship' (Marathi)

m756a खोंड [khōṇḍa] m A young bull, a bullcalf. (Marathi) Rebus: kõdār 'turner' (Bengali); कोंद kōnda 'engraver, lapidary setting or infixing gems' (Marathi) G. sãghāṛɔ m. 'lathe' ; संघाट joinery; M. sãgaḍ 'double-canoe' Rebus: sangataras 'stone-cutter, mason' | *koḍa* 'one' Rebus: *koḍ* 'workshop'

kana,  *kanac* = corner (Santali); Rebus: *kañcu* = bronze (Telugu) PLUS खांडा [*khāṇḍā*] *m* A jag, notch, or indentation (as upon the edge of a tool or weapon). Rebus: *kāṇḍa* 'tools, pots and pans and metal-ware' Thus, bronze metalware.

INFIXED kolom 'three' Rebus: kolami 'smithy, forge'

baraḍo = spine; backbone (Tulu) Rebus: *baran, bharat* 'mixed alloys' (5 copper, 4 zinc and 1 tin) (Punjabi) PLUS gaṇḍa 'four' Rebus: kaṇḍa 'furnace, fire-altar' (Santali) *bhaṭa* 'warrior' (Sanskrit) Rebus: *baṭa* a kind of iron (Gujarati). Rebus: *bhaṭa* 'furnace' (Santali)

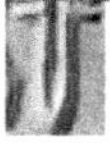

kanka 'rim of jar' Rebus: karṇīka 'account (scribe)' karṇī 'supercargo'

m992a खोंड [khōṇḍa] m A young bull, a bullcalf. (Marathi) Rebus: kõdār 'turner' (Bengali); कोंद kōnda 'engraver, lapidary setting or infixing gems' (Marathi) G. sãghāṛɔ m. 'lathe' ; संघाट joinery; M. sãgaḍ 'double-canoe' Rebus: sangataras 'stone-cutter, mason' | *koḍa* 'one' Rebus: *koḍ* 'workshop'

dula 'pair' Rebus: *dul* 'cast (metal)' PLUS*kana, kanac* = corner (Santali); Rebus: *kañcu* = bronze (Telugu) PLUS infixed kolmo 'paddy plant' Rebus: kolami 'smithy, forge'. Thus, cast bronze smithy, forge. Or, *mogge* 'sprout, bud' Rebus: *mũh* 'ingot' (Santali)Thus, cast bronze ingot. Read as: *kañcu dul mũh 'bronze cast ingot'*

koḍi 'flag' (Ta.)(DEDR 2049). Rebus 1: *koḍ* 'workshop' (Kuwi) Rebus 2: *khŏḍ* m. 'pit', *khŏḍü* f. 'small pit' (Kashmiri. CDIAL 3947).

m863a खोंड [khōṇḍa] m A young bull, a bullcalf. (Marathi) Rebus: kõdār 'turner' (Bengali); कोंद kōnda 'engraver, lapidary setting or infixing gems' (Marathi) G. sãghāṛɔ m. 'lathe' ; संघाट joinery; M. sãgaḍ 'double-canoe' Rebus: sangataras 'stone-cutter, mason'

khōṇḍa A stock or stump (Marathi); 'leafless tree' (Marathi) Rebus: *kõdār* 'turner' (Bengali); *kõdā* 'to turn in a lathe' (Bengali).

| *koḍa* 'one' Rebus: *koḍ* 'workshop'

kanka 'rim of jar' Rebus: *karṇīka* 'account (scribe)' *karṇī* 'supercargo'

INFIXED खांडा [*khāṇḍā*] *m* A jag, notch, or indentation (as upon the edge of a tool or weapon). Rebus: *kāṇḍa* 'tools, pots and pans and metal-ware'

muka 'ladle' (Tamil)(DEDR 4887) Rebus: *mũh* 'ingot' (Santali) *baṭa* = rimless pot (Kannada) Rebus: *baṭa* = a kind of iron (G.)) *bhaṭa* furnace (Gujarati) Thus, iron

ingot. *bicha* 'scorpion' (Assamese) Rebus: *bica* 'stone ore' (Santali)

kanka 'rim of jar' Rebus: karṇīka 'account (scribe)' karṇī 'supercargo'

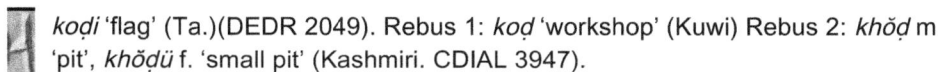

m1684a खोंड [khōṇḍa] m A young bull, a bullcalf. (Marathi) Rebus: kõdār 'turner' (Bengali); कोंद kōnda 'engraver, lapidary setting or infixing gems' (Marathi) G.

sãghāṛɔ m. 'lathe' ; संघाट joinery; M. sãgaḍ 'double-canoe' Rebus: sangataras 'stone-cutter, mason | *koḍa* 'one' Rebus: *koḍ* 'workshop'

beads: Pa. kandi (pl. -l) necklace, beads. Ga. (Punjabi) kandi (pl. -l) bead, (pl.) necklace; (S.2) kandiṭ bead. (DEDR 1215) Rebus: *கண்டி; kaṇṭi, n. < Mhr. khaṇḍil. [T. Tu. khaṇḍi, M. kaṇḍi.] 1. Candy, a weight, stated to be roughly equivalent to 500 lbs.; பாரமென் னும் நிறையளவு.* खंडीगणती or खंडोगणती [khaṇḍīgaṇatī or khaṇḍōgaṇatī] *ad* By candies; counting or reckoning by candies. खंडीवारी [khaṇḍīvārī] *ad* By scores, heaps, candies. खंडी [khaṇḍī] Applied to a great quantity; as खंडीभर पोरें, खंडीभर मेंढ्या, खंडीभर काम, खंडीभर बोलतो-लिहितो&c
mogge 'sprout, bud' Rebus*: mũh* 'ingot'
h305B | *koḍa* 'one' Rebus: *koḍ* 'workshop'

kanac 'corner' Rebus: *kañcu* 'bronze'
kolom 'three' Rebus: kolami 'smithy, forge'

m155A *खोंड [khōṇḍa] m A young bull, a bullcalf. (Marathi) Rebus: kõdār 'turner' (Bengali); कोंद kōnda 'engraver, lapidary setting or infixing gems' (Marathi) G. sãghāṛɔ m. 'lathe' ; संघाट joinery; M. sãgaḍ 'double-canoe' Rebus: sangataras 'stone-cutter, mason'* | *koḍa* 'one' Rebus: *koḍ* 'workshop'

baraḍo = spine; backbone (Tulu) Rebus: *baran, bharat* 'mixed alloys' (5 copper, 4 zinc and 1 tin) (Punjabi) PLUS gaṇḍa 'four' Rebus: kaṇḍa 'furnace, fire-altar' (Santali)

kanka 'rim of jar' Rebus: karṇīka 'account (scribe)' karṇī 'supercargo'

Kalibangan 49a Pictorial motif hieroglyphs:

heraka 'spy' Rebus: erako 'moltencast copper'

khōṇḍa A stock or stump (Marathi); 'leafless tree' (Marathi) Rebus: *kõdār* 'turner' (Bengali); Allograph: young bull.

blacksmith;(Gowda) kolla id. *Koḍ.* kollë blacksmith. *Te.* kolimi furnace.*Go.* (SR.) kollusānā to mend implements; (Ph.) kolstānā, kulsānā to forge; (Tr.) kōlstānā to repair (of ploughshares); (SR.) kolmi smithy (*Voc.* 948). *Kuwi* (F.) kolhali to forge.(DEDR 2133)

tiger (with the head turned back): *kul* 'tiger' (Santali); *kōlu* id. (Telugu) kōlupuli = Bengal tiger (Telugu)कोल्हा [kōlhā] कोल्हें [kōlhēṃ] A jackal (Marathi) Rebus: *kole.l* 'temple, smithy' (Kota.) *kol* = pañcalōha, a metallic alloy containing five metals (Tamil): copper, brass, tin, lead and iron (Sanskrit); an alternative list of five metals: gold, silver, copper, tin (lead), and iron (dhātu; Nānārtharatnākara. 82; Mangarāja's Nighaṇṭu. 498)(Kannada) *kol, kolhe*, 'the *koles*, iron smelters speaking a language akin to that of Santals' (Santali)

H-305 B

krammara 'look back' (Telugu) Rebus: *kamar* 'metalsmith' (Santali)

Text hieroglyph signs:

III *kolom* 'three' Rebus: *kolami* 'smithy, forge'

A pair of 'three' hieroglyphs; *dula* 'pair' Rebus: *dul* 'cast metal'. Thus, casting smithy, forge.

Water-carrier PLUS rim-of-jar' ligatured sign glyph read rebus: *kuṭhi karṇī* 'furnace supercargo'. (paired with)

|||| Numeral 4: *gaṇḍa* 'four' Rebus: *kaṇḍa* 'furnace, fire-altar' (Santali). Thus, the pair of sign hieroglyphs connote: fire-altar, frnace supercargo'

m96A Lothal 16a

Water-carrier PLUS rim-of-jar' ligatured sign glyph read rebus: *kuṭhi karṇī* 'furnace supercargo'. (paired with)

 |||| 

Numeral 4: *gaṇḍa* 'four' Rebus: *kaṇḍa* 'furnace, fire-altar' (Santali). Thus, the pair of sign hieroglyphs connote: fire-altar, furnace supercargo'

'Numerals' as sign hieroglyph strokes

m1308a

kolmo 'paddy plant' Rebus: *kolami* 'smithy, forge' Variant hieroglyph: mogge 'sprout, bud' Rebus: muh 'ingot'

|||| Numeral 4: *gaṇḍa* 'four' Rebus: *kaṇḍa* 'furnace, fire-altar' (Santali).

The following epigraphs have 'young bull PLUS standard' hieroglyphs which denote:

> खोंड *[khōṇḍa] m A young bull, a bullcalf. (Marathi) Rebus: kōdār 'turner' (Bengali);* कोंद *kōnda 'engraver, lapidary setting or infixing gems' (Marathi) G. sãghāṛɔ m. 'lathe' ;* संघाट *joinery; M. sāgaḍ 'double-canoe' Rebus: sangataras 'stone-cutter, mason'*

m710A Furnace for hard alloy ingots

kolmo 'paddy plant' Rebus: *kolami* 'smithy, forge' Variant hieroglyph: mogge 'sprout, bud' Rebus: muh 'ingot'

|||| Numeral 4: *gaṇḍa* 'four' Rebus: *kaṇḍa* 'furnace, fire-altar' (Santali).

kharedo = a currycomb (Gujarati) खरारा [*kharārā*] *m* (H) A currycomb. 2 Currying a horse. (Marathi) Rebus: करडा [*karaḍā*] Hard from alloy--iron, silver &c. (Marathi) *kharādī* ' turner' (Gujarati)

m1742a

kolmo 'paddy plant' Rebus: *kolami* 'smithy, forge' Variant hieroglyph: mogge 'sprout, bud' Rebus: muh 'ingot'
|||| Numeral 4: *gaṇḍa* 'four' Rebus: *kaṇḍa* 'furnace, fire-altar' (Santali).

m749A

kolmo 'paddy plant' Rebus: *kolami* 'smithy, forge' Variant hieroglyph: mogge 'sprout, bud' Rebus: muh 'ingot'
|||| Numeral 4: *gaṇḍa* 'four' Rebus: *kaṇḍa* 'furnace, fire-altar' (Santali).

h518a

kolmo 'paddy plant' Rebus: *kolami* 'smithy, forge' Variant hieroglyph: mogge 'sprout, bud' Rebus: muh 'ingot'
|||| Numeral 4: *gaṇḍa* 'four' Rebus: *kaṇḍa* 'furnace, fire-altar' (Santali).

Banawali 9A
miṇḍāl 'markhor' (Tōrwālī)*meḍho* a ram, a sheep (Gujarati)(CDIAL 10120)
Rebus: *mẽṛhẽt, meḍ* 'iron' (Mu.Ho.)

kolmo 'paddy plant' Rebus: *kolami* 'smithy, forge' Variant hieroglyph: mogge 'sprout, bud' Rebus: muh 'ingot' |||| Numeral 4: *gaṇḍa* 'four' Rebus: *kaṇḍa* 'furnace, fire-altar' (Santali).

Kalibangan 50A Markhor horns: *miṇḍāl* 'markhor' (Tōrwālī)*meḍho* a ram, a sheep (Gujarati)(CDIAL 10120) Rebus: *mẽṛhẽt, meḍ* 'iron' (Mu.Ho.) dhatu 'scarf' Rebus: dhatu 'mineral ore' kola 'woman' Rebus: kolhe 'smelter' kol 'working in iron' kola 'tiger' Rebus: kolhe 'smelter' kol 'working in iron' Twig as headdress: *kūdī* 'bunch of twigs' (Sanskrit) Rebus: *kuṭhi* 'smelter furnace' (Santali)
Pa. *kaṭa* -- m. ' mat ', *°aka* -- m.n. ' ring, bracelet '; Pk. *kaḍaya* -- m.n. ' ring ', *kaḍā* -- f. ' chain '; Gy. wel. *kerō* m. ' bracelet ', gr. *koró*; Dm. *kaṛaī*; Paš. *kāṛa* ' snare (made of horsehair) ' IIFL iii 3, 98 with (?); Phal. *kāṛa* ' bracelet ' (CDIAL 2629) Rebus:) Rebus: खंडी [khaṇḍī] measure of weight (Marathi) கண்டி; *kaṇṭi, n. < Mhr. khaṇḍil. [T. Tu. khaṇḍi, M. kaṇḍi.]* Candy, a weight, stated to be roughly equivalent to 500 lbs.

kolmo 'paddy plant' Rebus: *kolami* 'smithy, forge' Variant hieroglyph: mogge 'sprout, bud' Rebus: muh 'ingot'
|||| Numeral 4: *gaṇḍa* 'four' Rebus: *kaṇḍa* 'furnace, fire-altar' (Santali).

h302B ayo 'fish' Rebs: *aya* 'iron' (Gujarati) *ayas* 'metal' (Vedic)
|||| Numeral 4: *gaṇḍa* 'four' Rebus: *kaṇḍa* 'furnace, fire-altar' (Santali). *baṭa* 'broad-mouthed pot'; *bhaṭa* 'furnace' (Gujarati.); *baṭa* 'a kind of iron' (Gujarati) Thus, metal fire-altar, iron furnace.

h577a

h290A

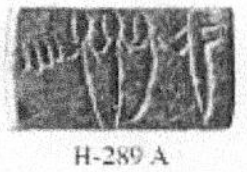
h289A

Pictorial hieroglyph on h577: *balad* m. ' ox ', gng. *bald*, (Ku.) *barad*, id. (N. Tarai) Rebus: *bharat* (5 copper, 4 zinc and 1 tin)(Punjabi) *pattar* 'trough' Rebus*: pattar* 'guild'. Thus, copper-zinc-tin alloy (worker) guild.

|||| Numeral 4: *gaṇḍa* 'four' Rebus: *kaṇḍa* 'furnace, fire-altar' (Santali).

'Three arrows topped by ingots': unsmelted metal ingot, smithy workshop: kolom 'three' Rebus: kolami 'smithy' aḍaren 'lid of pot' Rebus: aduru 'unsmelted, native metal'. *koḍa* 'one' Rebus: *koḍ* 'workshop' dulo 'hole' Rebus: dul 'cast metal'

kanka 'rim of jar' Rebus: *karṇīka* 'account (scribe)' *karṇī* 'supercargo'

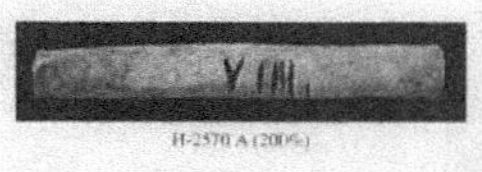
h2570A

h2246C

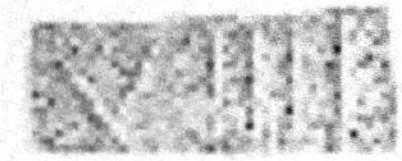
h982B

h910B

h892B

h823B

h771B

h350B

h297B

h215B

baṭa 'rimless, broad-mouthed pot' Rebus: *bhaṭa* 'furnace' (Gujarati.); *baṭa* 'a kind of iron' (Gujarati)

|||| Numeral 4: *gaṇḍa 'four' Rebus: kaṇḍa* 'furnace, fire-altar' (Santali)

m2104a

baṭa 'rimless, broad-mouthed pot' Rebus: *bhaṭa* 'furnace' (Gujarati.); *baṭa* 'a kind of iron' (Gujarati)

|||| Numeral 4: gaṇḍa 'four' Rebus: kaṇḍa 'furnace, fire-altar' (Santali)

*meḍ 'body' Rebus: meḍ 'iron' (Ho.) काठी [kāṭhī] f (काष्ट S) 'frame or structure of the body' (Marathi) Rebus: खंडी [khaṇḍī] measure of weight (Marathi) கண்டி; kaṇṭi, n. < Mhr. khaṇḍil. [T. Tu. khaṇḍi, M. kaṇḍi.] Candy, a weight, about 500 lbs.*PLUS PLUS | *koḍa* 'one' Rebus: *koḍ* 'workshop' dula 'pair' Rebus: dul 'cast metal'. Thus, the 'body' flanked by two linear strokes denote: iron cast workshop.

water-carrier hieroglyph *kuṭi*; Rebus: *kuṭhi* 'smelter furnace'.

m64a खोंड *[khōṇḍa] m A young bull, a bullcalf. (Marathi) Rebus: kõdār 'turner' (Bengali);* कोंद *kōnda 'engraver, lapidary setting or infixing gems' (Marathi) G. sãghāṛɔ m. 'lathe' ;* संघाट *joinery; M. sãgaḍ 'double-canoe' Rebus: sangataras 'stone-cutter, mason'*

|||| Numeral 4: *gaṇḍa* 'four' Rebus: *kaṇḍa* 'furnace, fire-altar' (Santali)
ayo 'fish' Rebus: *aya* 'iron' (Gujarati) *ayas* 'metal'(Vedic)

Read in context, it is assumed to be a combination of a slanted stroke ligatured to a notch,which provide possible rebus readings of a smithy/forge: notch+slanted stroke reads rebus: *ḍhālako kāṇḍa* 'ingots, pots and pans, metalware, tools'.

Thus the segment of text reads rebus:

Three sign sequence:

muka 'ladle' (Tamil)(DEDR 4887) Rebus: *mũh* 'ingot' (Santali) Thus, iron ingot.

kolom 'three' Rebus: kolami 'smithy, forge' *kāṇḍa* 'arrow' (Sanskrit) Rebus:*khāṇḍa* 'tools, pots and pans, metal-ware'. Rebus 2: kaṇḍ 'fire-altar' (Santali) Thus, the three sign sequence reads: iron ingot, furnace smithy, fire-altar metalware.

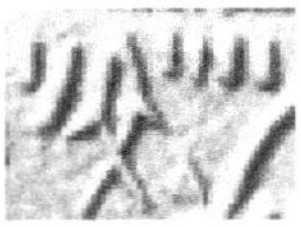

kaṇḍa 'furnace, fire-altar' (Santali) ayo 'fish' Rebus: *aya* 'iron' (Gujarati) *ayas* 'metal'(Vedic)
ḍhālako kāṇḍa 'ingots, pots and pans, metalware, tools' (Read rebus as at m64a).

m1206A *balad* m. ' ox ', gng. *bald*, (Ku.) *barad*, id. (N. Tarai) Rebus: *bharat* (5 copper, 4 zinc and 1 tin)(Punjabi) *pattar* 'trough' Rebus*: pattar* 'guild'. Thus, copper-zinc-tin alloy (worker) guild.
|||| Numeral 4: *gaṇḍa* 'four' Rebus: *kaṇḍa* 'furnace, fire-altar' (Santali)
ayo 'fish' Rebus: *aya* 'iron' (Gujarati) *ayas* 'metal'(Vedic)
kaṇḍa 'arrow' *kāṇḍa* 'tools, pots and pans and metal-ware.

m283A ibha 'elephant' Rebus: ib 'iron' (Santali) ibbo 'merchant' (Gujarati)
|||| Numeral 4: *gaṇḍa* 'four' Rebus: *kaṇḍa* 'furnace, fire-altar' (Santali) dula 'pair' Rebus: dul 'cast metal'. Thus, cast metal fire-altar.
kolmo 'paddy plant' Rebus: *kolami* 'smithy, forge'.

h818A

H-818 A

|||| Numeral 4: *gaṇḍa* 'four' Rebus: *kaṇḍa* 'furnace, fire-altar' (Santali) dula 'pair' Rebus: dul 'cast metal'. Thus, cast metal fire-altar.

Ligature: two peaks: mēḍu height, rising ground, hillock (Kannada) Rebus: *meḍ* 'iron' (Ho.) dula 'pair' Rebus: dul 'cast metal' PLUS |||| Numeral 4: gaṇḍa 'four' Rebus: kaṇḍa 'furnace, fire-altar' (Santali)

kanka 'rim of jar' Rebus: karṇīka 'account (scribe)' karṇī 'supercargo'

m383a|

||| Numeral 4: *gaṇḍa* 'four' Rebus: *kaṇḍa* 'furnace, fire-altar' (Santali) *meḍ* 'body' Rebus: *meḍ* 'iron' (Ho.)

meḍ 'body' Rebus: *meḍ* 'iron' (Ho.) काठी [kāṭhī] *f* (काष्ट S) 'frame or structure of the body' (Marathi) Rebus: खंडी [khaṇḍī] measure of weight (Marathi) *கண்டி; kaṇṭi, n.* < *Mhr. khaṇḍil. [T. Tu. khaṇḍi, M. kaṇḍi.]* Candy, a weight, stated to be roughly equivalent to 500 lbs.

khaṇḍ 'field, division' (Skt.) Rebus: *khāṇḍa* 'tools, pots and pans, metal-ware'. Rebus 2: kaṇḍ 'fire-altar' (Santali) dula 'pair' Rebus: dul 'cast metal' Thus, duplicated 'division' hieroglyph sign reads: cast metal metal-ware.

m262a Zebu. Native metal smith guild.

||| Numeral 4: *gaṇḍa* 'four' Rebus: *kaṇḍa* 'furnace, fire-altar' (Santali) *meḍ* 'body' Rebus: *meḍ* 'iron' (Ho.)

meḍ 'body' Rebus: *meḍ* 'iron' (Ho.) काठी [kāṭhī] *f* (काष्ट S) 'frame or structure of the body' (Marathi) Rebus: खंडी [khaṇḍī] measure of weight (Marathi) *கண்டி; kaṇṭi, n.* < *Mhr. khaṇḍil. [T. Tu. khaṇḍi, M. kaṇḍi.]* Candy, a weight, stated to be roughly equivalent to 500 lbs.

h509A

M-331 d

m331d *kolom* 'three' Rebus: *kolami* 'smithy, forge'.

H-1715 A

h1715A *kolom* 'three' Rebus: *kolami* 'smithy, forge'. *dula* 'pair' Rebus: *dul* 'cast metal'. kuṭila 'bent' CDIAL 3230 kuṭi— in cmpd. 'curve', *kuṭika*— 'bent' MBh. Rebus: kuṭila, katthīl = bronze (8 parts copper and 2 parts tin) cf. āra-kūṭa, 'brass' (Sanskrit)

M-1197 A

m1197A *kolom* 'three' Rebus: *kolami* 'smithy, forge'.

खांडा [khāṇḍā] *m* A jag, notch, or indentation (as upon the edge of a tool or weapon). (Marathi) Rebus: *khāṇḍā* 'tools, pots and pans, metal-ware.

dhāḷ 'a slope'; 'inclination of a plane' (Gujarati); *ḍhāḷiyum* = adj. sloping, inclining (Gujarati) Rebus: *ḍhālako* = a large metal ingot (Gujarati) *ḍhālakī* = a metal heated and poured into a mould; a solid piece of metal; an ingot (Gujarati) PLUS *dula* 'pair' Rebus: *dul* 'cast *metal' sal* 'splinter' Rebus: *sal* 'workshop'. Thus, *ḍhālako dul sal* 'ingot, cast metal workshop'. *kolom* 'three' Rebus: *kolami* 'smithy, forge'.

Rebus representation of an ingot furnace (fire-altar)

h48A *खोंड [khōṇḍa] m A young bull, a bullcalf. (Marathi) Rebus: kõdār 'turner' (Bengali); कोंद kōnda 'engraver, lapidary setting or infixing gems' (Marathi) G. sãghāṛɔ m. 'lathe' ; संघाट joinery; M. sãgaḍ 'double-canoe' Rebus: sangataras 'stone-cutter, mason'*

kolom 'three' Rebus: *kolami* 'smithy, forge'. *mogge* 'sprout, bud' Rebus*: mũh* 'ingot'

|||| Numeral 4: *gaṇḍa* 'four' Rebus: *kaṇḍa* 'furnace, fire-altar' (Santali). Thus, together, read rebus: ingot furnace: *mũh kaṇḍa*

|||| Numeral 4: *gaṇḍa* 'four' Rebus: *kaṇḍa* 'furnace, fire-altar' (Santali) PLUS mogge 'sprout, bud' Rebus: mũh 'ingot'. Thus, fire-altar ingot or ingot furnace.

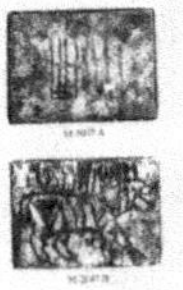

m2047A,B Copper plate. Pictorial motif hieroglyph: *balad* m. ' ox ', gng. *bald*, (Ku.) *barad*, id. (N. Tarai) Rebus: *bharat* (5 copper, 4 zinc and 1 tin)(Punjabi)
||||Numeral 4: *gaṇḍa* 'four' Rebus: *kaṇḍa* 'furnace, fire-altar' (Santali) PLUS mogge 'sprout, bud' Rebus: mũh 'ingot'. Thus, fire-altar ingot or ingot furnace

m546A

Copper plate. |||| Numeral 4: *gaṇḍa* 'four' Rebus: *kaṇḍa* 'furnace, fire-altar' (Santali) PLUS mogge 'sprout, bud' Rebus: mũh 'ingot'. Thus, fire-altar ingot or ingot furnace. kolom 'three' Rebus: kolami 'smithy, forge'

baraḍo = spine; backbone (Tulu) Rebus: *baran, bharat* 'mixed alloys' (5 copper, 4 zinc and 1 tin) (Punjabi) PLUS gaṇḍa 'four' Rebus: kaṇḍa 'furnace, fire-altar' (Santali)

m543A

Copper plate. |||| Numeral 4: *gaṇḍa* 'four' Rebus: *kaṇḍa* 'furnace, fire-altar' (Santali) PLUS mogge 'sprout, bud' Rebus: mũh 'ingot'. Thus, fire-altar ingot or ingot furnace. First 3 signs read rebus as at m546A. *bhaṭa* 'warrior' (Sanskrit) Rebus: *baṭa* a kind of iron (Gujarati). Rebus: *bhaṭa* 'furnace' (Santali)

kanka 'rim of jar' Rebus: karṇīka 'account (scribe)' karṇī 'supercargo' dulo 'hole' Rebus: dul 'cast metal'.

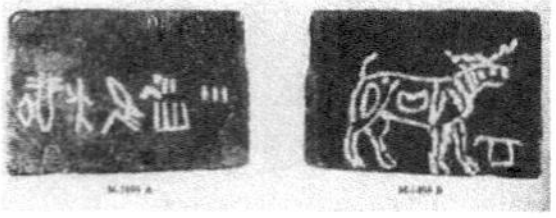

m1498A Pictorial hieroglyph: *miṇḍāl* 'markhor' (Tōrwālī) *meḍho* a ram, a sheep (G.)(CDIAL 10120) Rebus: *mẽṛhẽt, meḍ* 'iron' (Mu.Ho.) pattar 'trough' Rebus: pattar 'guild, goldsmith'.

|||| Numeral 4: *gaṇḍa* 'four' Rebus: *kaṇḍa* 'furnace, fire-altar' (Santali) PLUS mogge 'sprout, bud' Rebus: mũh 'ingot'. Thus, fire-altar ingot.

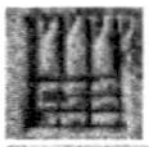

Rebus readings of text as at m543A.

m218A *खोंड [khōṇḍa] m A young bull, a bullcalf. (Marathi) Rebus: kõdār 'turner' (Bengali); कोंद kōnda 'engraver, lapidary setting or infixing gems' (Marathi) G. sãghāṛɔ m. 'lathe' ; संघाट joinery; M. sãgaḍ 'double-canoe' Rebus: sangataras 'stone-cutter, mason'*

|||| Numeral 4: *gaṇḍa* 'four' Rebus: *kaṇḍa* 'furnace, fire-altar' (Santali) PLUS mogge 'sprout, bud' Rebus: mũh 'ingot'. Thus, fire-altar ingot or ingot furnace.

ayo 'fish' Rebus: aya 'iron' (Gujarati) ayas 'metal' (Vedic)

 *kharedo* = a currycomb (Gujarati) खरारा [*kharārā*] *m* (H) A currycomb. 2 Currying a horse. (Marathi) Rebus: करडा [*karaḍā*] Hard from alloy--iron, silver &c. (Marathi) *kharādī* ' turner' (Gujarati)

L-36 a

Lothal 36a *खोंड [khōṇḍa] m A young bull, a bullcalf. (Marathi) Rebus: kõdār 'turner' (Bengali); कोंद kōnda 'engraver, lapidary setting or infixing gems' (Marathi) G. sãghāṛɔ m. 'lathe' ; संघाट joinery; M. sãgaḍ 'double-canoe' Rebus: sangataras 'stone-cutter, mason' kōḍu 'horn' Rebus: 'workshop'sãghāṛɔ m. 'lathe' (Gujarati) Rebus: sangataras. संगतराश lit. 'to collect stones, stone-cutter, mason.*

 *kanac* 'corner' Rebus: *kañcu* 'bronze' PLUS

 *mogge* 'sprout, bud' Rebus*: mũh* 'ingot'

 *koḍi* 'flag' (Ta.)(DEDR 2049). Rebus 1: *koḍ* 'workshop' (Kuwi) Rebus 2: *khŏḍ* m. 'pit', *khōḍü* f. 'small pit' (Kashmiri. CDIAL 3947).

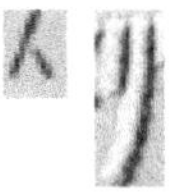 notch+slanted stroke reads rebus: *ḍhālako kāṇḍa* 'ingot, tools, pots and pans and metal-ware'.*dhāḷ* 'a slope'; 'inclination of a plane' (G.); *ḍhāḷiyum* = adj. sloping, inclining (G.) Rebus: *ḍhālako* = a large metal ingot (G.) *ḍhālakī* = a metal heated and poured into a mould; a solid piece of metal; an ingot (Gujarati) PLUS खांडा [*khāṇḍā*] *m* A jag, notch, or indentation (as upon the edge of a tool or weapon). Rebus: *kāṇḍa* 'tools, pots and pans and metal-ware'

gaṇḍa 'four' Rebus: *kaṇḍa* 'furnace, fire-altar' (Santali) PLUS mogge 'sprout' + *gaṇḍa* 'four' Rebus: *mũh kaṇḍa* 'ingot furnace'

M-402 A

h402A *gaṇḍa* 'four' Rebus: *kaṇḍa* 'furnace, fire-altar' (Santali) PLUS mogge 'sprout' + *gaṇḍa* 'four' Rebus: *mũh kaṇḍa* 'ingot furnace' kolom 'three' Rebus: kolami 'smithy, forge' खांडा [*khāṇḍā*] *m* A jag, notch, or indentation (as upon the edge of a tool or weapon). Rebus: *kāṇḍa* 'tools, pots and pans and metal-ware'
bhaṭa 'warrior' (Sanskrit) Rebus: *baṭa* a kind of iron (Gujarati). Rebus: *bhaṭa* 'furnace' (Santali)

 *baraḍo* = spine; backbone (Tulu) Rebus: *baran, bharat* 'mixed alloys' (5 copper, 4 zinc and 1 tin) (Punjabi)

khaṇḍ 'field, division' (Sanskrit) Rebus: *khānḍa* 'tools, pots and pans, metal-ware'. Rebus 2: kaṇḍ 'fire-altar' (Santali)

 mēḍu height, rising ground, hillock (Kannada) Rebus: *mẽṛhẽt, meḍ* 'iron' (Munda.Ho.)

and 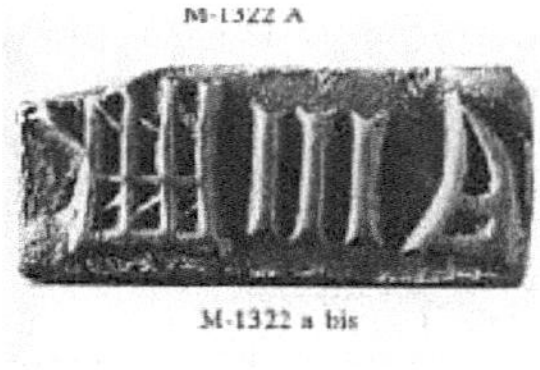 into

m1322a Ligature: *ḍhālako kāṇḍa* 'ingot, tools, pots and pans metal-ware'.*dhāḷ* 'a slope'; 'inclination of a plane' (G.); *ḍhāḷiyum* = adj. sloping, inclining (G.) Rebus: *ḍhālako* = a large metal ingot (G.) *ḍhālakī* = a metal heated and poured a mould; a solid piece of metal; an ingot (Gujarati) PLUS *kolmo* 'paddy plant' Rebus: *kolami* 'smithy, forge' Variant hieroglyph: *mogge* 'sprout, bud' Rebus*: mũh* 'ingot'

|||| Numeral 4: *gaṇḍa* 'four' Rebus: *kaṇḍa* 'furnace, fire-altar' (Santali). Thus, together, read rebus: ingot furnace: *mũh kaṇḍa*

kolom 'three' Rebus: kolami 'smithy, forge'

 mēḍu height, rising ground, hillock (Kannada) Rebus: *mẽṛhẽt, meḍ* 'iron' (Munda.Ho.)

m1724a *खोंड [khōṇḍa] m A young bull, a bullcalf. (Marathi) Rebus: kōdār 'turner' (Bengali); कोंद kōnda 'engraver, lapidary setting or infixing gems' (Marathi) G. sãghāṛɔ m. 'lathe' ; संघाट joinery; M. sāgaḍ 'double-canoe' Rebus: sangataras. संगतराश lit. 'to collect stones, stone-cutter, mason.'*

  Strands of yarn/rope' hieroglyph: Hieroglyph: 'strands of yarn' Rebus reading: *dhā'tu* 'strand of rope' Rebus: *dhatu* 'mineral ore' (Santali)

The hieroglyph may be a variant of:  *kana, kanac* = corner (Santali); Rebus: *kañcu* = bronze (Telugu) PLUS kolom 'three' Rebus: kolami 'smithy, forge. खांडा [*khāṇḍā*] *m* A jag, notch, or indentation (as upon the edge of a tool or weapon). Rebus: *kāṇḍa* 'tools, pots and pans and metal-ware'

kolom 'three' Rebus: kolami 'smithy, forge'

mogge 'sprout, bud' Rebus*: mũh* 'ingot'

|||| Numeral 4: *gaṇḍa* 'four' Rebus: *kaṇḍa* 'furnace, fire-altar' (Santali). Thus, together, read rebus: ingot furnace: *mũh kaṇḍa.*

Chanhudaro 16a *खोंड [khōṇḍa] m A young bull, a bullcalf. (Marathi) Rebus: kōdār 'turner' (Bengali); कोंद kōnda 'engraver, lapidary setting or infixing gems' (Marathi) G. sãghāṛɔ m. 'lathe' ; संघाट joinery; M. sāgaḍ 'double-canoe' Rebus: sangataras. संगतराश lit. 'to collect stones, stone-cutter, mason.'*

kuṭila 'bent'  CDIAL 3230 kuṭi— in cmpd. 'curve', *kuṭika—* 'bent' MBh. Rebus: *kuṭila, katthīl* = bronze (8 parts copper and 2 parts tin) LIGATURE:

  notch+slanted stroke reads rebus: *ḍhālako kāṇḍa* 'ingot, tools, pots and pans and metal-ware'.*dhāḷ* 'a slope'; 'inclination of a plane' (G.); *ḍhāḷiyum* = adj. sloping, inclining (G.) Rebus: *ḍhālako* = a large metal ingot (G.) *ḍhālakī* = a metal heated and

poured into a mould; a solid piece of metal; an ingot (Gujarati) PLUS खांडा [*khāṇḍā*] *m* A jag, notch, or indentation (as upon the edge of a tool or *kanka* (Santali) *karṇika* 'scribe'(Sanskrit) Rebus: *karṇī,* supercargo for a boat shipment. INFIXED खांडा [*khāṇḍā*] *m* A jag, notch, or indentation (as upon the edge of a tool or weapon). Rebus: *kāṇḍa* 'tools, pots and pans and metal-ware'
kolom 'three' Rebus: kolami 'smithy, forge'.
mogge 'sprout, bud' Rebus*: mũh* 'ingot'
|||| Numeral 4: *gaṇḍa* 'four' Rebus: *kaṇḍa* 'furnace, fire-altar' (Santali). Thus, together, read rebus: ingot furnace: *mũh kaṇḍa*

m525A Copper plate. Together, the pair of hieroglyph signs read: *bica ḍhālako sal* 'stone ore ingot workshop'. PLUS

dāṭu 'cross'(Telugu) Rebus: *dhatu* 'mineral' (Santali). *kanka* 'rim of jar' Rebus: *karṇīka* ' account (scribe)' *karṇī* 'supercargo'

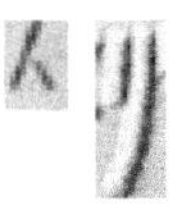

notch+slanted stroke reads rebus: *ḍhālako kāṇḍa* 'ingot, tools, pots and pans and metal-ware'.*dhāḷ* 'a slope'; 'inclination of a plane' (G.); *ḍhāḷiyum* = adj. sloping, inclining (G.) Rebus: *ḍhālako* = a large metal ingot (G.) *ḍhālakī* = a metal heated and poured into a mould; a solid piece of metal; an ingot (Gujarati) PLUS खांडा [*khāṇḍā*] *m* A jag, notch, or indentation (as upon the edge of a tool or weapon). Rebus: *kāṇḍa* 'tools, pots and pans and metal-ware'
Ingot furnace: *mũh kaṇḍa*

m1475 Side A read rebus as at m525A PLUS Side B: *rāngo* 'water buffalo bull' (Ku.N.)(CDIAL 10559) Rebus: rango 'pewter' *pattar* 'trough' Rebus: *pattar* 'guild'.Thus, pewter guild.
Ingot furnace: *mũh kaṇḍa*

h271a *खोंड [khōṇḍa] m A young bull, a bullcalf. (Marathi) Rebus: kõdār 'turner' (Bengali); कोंद kōnda 'engraver, lapidary setting or infixing gems' (Marathi) G. sãghāṛɔ m. 'lathe' ; संघाट joinery; M. sãgaḍ 'double-canoe' Rebus: sangataras 'stone-cutter, mason'* G. *sãghāṛɔ* m. 'lathe' ; *sãgāḍā* m. ' frame of a building ', °*ḍī* f. ' lathe '(CDIAL 12859) Rebus*: sangataras.* संगतराश lit. 'to collect stones, stone-cutter, mason.'
ranku 'liquid measure" Rebus: ranku 'tin' (Santali) Ingot furnace: *mũh kaṇḍa*

khuṭo ' leg, foot ', °ṭī ' goat's leg ' Rebus: *khōṭā* 'alloy' (Marathi)

kanka 'rim of jar' Rebus: *karṇīka* 'account (scribe)' *karṇī* 'supercargo' INFIXED kolom 'three' Rebus: kolami 'smithy, forge'

h28A *खोंड [khōṇḍa] m A young bull, a bullcalf.*  *(Marathi) Rebus: kõdār 'turner' (Bengali); कोंद kōnda 'engraver, lapidary setting or*

infixing gems' (Marathi) G. sãghāṛɔ m. 'lathe' ; संघाट joinery; M. sāgaḍ 'double-canoe' Rebus: sangataras 'stone-cutter, mason' G. *sãghāṛɔ* m. 'lathe' ; *sãgāḍā* m. ' frame of a building ', *°ḍī* f. ' lathe '(CDIAL 12859) Rebus*: sangataras.* संगतराश lit. 'to collect stones, stone-cutter, mason' ranku 'liquid measure" Rebus: ranku 'tin' (Santali) Ingot furnace: *mũh kaṇḍa*
muka 'ladle' (Tamil)(DEDR 4887) Rebus: *mũh* 'ingot' (Santali) *baṭa* = rimless pot (Kannada) Rebus: *baṭa* = a kind of iron (G.)) *bhaṭa* furnace (Gujarati) Thus, iron ingot.
kəṭhā´r, kc. *kuṭhār* m. ' granary, storeroom '(WPah.)(CDIAL 3550). *koṭhārī m.* ' storekeeper'

(Gujarati)(CDIAL 3551) Thus, storeroom (of) *kolom* 'three' Rebus: *kolami* 'smithy, forge'. Dula 'pair' Rebus: dul 'cast metal' Thus, together *dul kolami kuṭhār* 'metal smithy castings storeroom'

m948A *खोंड [khōṇḍa] m A young bull, a bullcalf. (Marathi) Rebus: kõdār 'turner' (Bengali); कोंद kōnda 'engraver, lapidary setting or infixing gems' (Marathi) G. sãghāṛɔ m. 'lathe' ; संघाट joinery; M. sāgaḍ 'double-canoe' Rebus: sangataras 'stone-cutter, mason'*] *koḍa* 'one' Rebus: *koḍ* 'workshop'

loa 'ficus religiosa' Rebus: *lo* 'iron' (Sanskrit) PLUS unique ligatures: लोखंड [lōkhaṇḍa] *n* (लोह S) Iron. लोखंडाचे चणे खावविणें or चारणें To oppress grievously.लोखंडकाम [lōkhaṇḍakāma] *n* Iron work; that portion (of a building, machine &c.) which consists of iron. 2 The business of an ironsmith.लोखंडी [lōkhaṇḍī] *a* (लोखंड) Composed of iron; relating to iron. (Marathi) sal 'splinter' Rebus: sal 'workshop' kolom 'three' Rebus: kolami 'smithy, forge'
mogge 'sprout, bud' Rebus*: mũh* 'ingot'
|||| Numeral 4: *gaṇḍa* 'four' Rebus: *kaṇḍa* 'furnace, fire-altar' (Santali). Thus, together, read rebus: ingot furnace: *mũh kaṇḍa*.

h1671A *खोंड [khōṇḍa] m A young bull, a bullcalf. (Marathi) Rebus: kõdār 'turner' (Bengali); कोंद kōnda 'engraver, lapidary setting or infixing gems' (Marathi) G. sãghāṛɔ m. 'lathe' ; संघाट joinery; M. sāgaḍ 'double-canoe' Rebus: sangataras 'stone-cutter, mason' sal 'splinter' Rebus: sal 'workshop'*
ḍato = claws of crab (Santali); *dhātu* = mineral (Sanskrit)
mogge 'sprout, bud' Rebus*: mũh* 'ingot'
|||| Numeral 4: *gaṇḍa* 'four' Rebus: *kaṇḍa* 'furnace, fire-altar' (Santali). Thus, together, read rebus: ingot furnace: *mũh kaṇḍa*
sal 'splinter' Rebus: sal 'workshop'

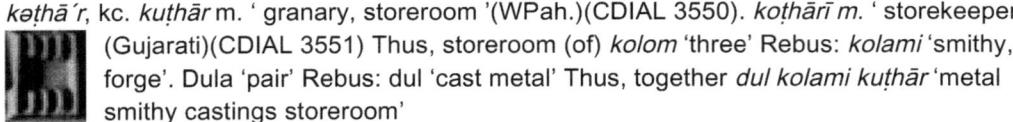

ḍhāḷ 'a slope'; 'inclination of a plane' (G.); *ḍhāḷiyum* = adj. sloping, inclining (G.) Rebus: *ḍhālako* = a large metal ingot (G.) *ḍhālakī* = a metal heated and poured into a mould; a solid piece of metal; an ingot (Gujarati) PLUS खांडा [*khāṇḍā*] *m* A jag, notch, or indentation (as upon the edge of a tool or weapon). Rebus: *kāṇḍa* 'tools, pots and pans and metal-ware' Thus, the pair of sign hieroglyphs from r. read rebus: copper, bronze ingots, metalware castings.
kanka 'rim of jar' Rebus: karṇīka 'account (scribe)' karṇī 'supercargo'

Mohenjo-daro seal M1783a *खोंड [khōṇḍa] m A young bull, a bullcalf. (Marathi) Rebus: kõdār 'turner' (Bengali); कोंद kōnda 'engraver, lapidary setting or infixing gems' (Marathi) G. sãghāṛɔ m. 'lathe' ; संघाट joinery; M.*

 *sãgaḍ 'double-canoe' Rebus: sangataras 'stone-cutter, mason'*मेढा [mēḍhā] A twist or tangle arising in thread or cord, a curl or snarl.(Marathi) Rebus: *meḍ*'iron'. *mẽṛhet* 'iron' (Mu.Ho.)

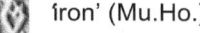

kanac 'corner' Rebus: *kañcu* 'bronze'

sal 'splinter' Rebus: sal 'workshop' kolom 'three' Rebus: kolami 'smithy, forge' mogge 'sprout, bud' Rebus*: mũh* 'ingot'

|||| Numeral 4: *gaṇḍa* 'four' Rebus: *kaṇḍa* 'furnace, fire-altar' (Santali). Thus, together, read rebus: ingot furnace: *mũh kaṇḍa*

kanac 'corner' Rebus: *kañcu* 'bronze'

'Arrow' sign hieroglyph (variant) This is a ligature of 'lid of pot' hieroglyph superscript on 'a linear stroke' numeral hieroglyph.*aḍaren* 'cover of pot or lid' Rebus: *aduru* 'native, unsmelted metal' PLUS koḍ = one (Santali); koḍ 'workshop' (Gujarati)

m356A

 *kharedo* = a currycomb (Gujarati) खरारा [*khararā*] *m* (H) A currycomb. 2 Currying a horse. (Marathi) Rebus: करडा [*karaḍā*] Hard from alloy--iron, silver &c. (Marathi) *kharādī* ' turner' (Gujarati)

ranku 'liquid measure' Rebus: ranku 'tin' ingot furnace: *mũh kaṇḍa*

kamaḍha 'archer, bow' Rebus: *kammaṭa* 'mint, coiner'.

dula 'two' Rebus: dul 'cast metal'

 *āra* 'spokes' Rebus: *āra 'brass'*. cf. erka = ekke (Tbh. of arka) aka (Tbh. of arka) copper (metal); crystal (Kannada) Glyph: *eraka*'nave of wheel' Rebus: eraka 'copper'; cf. erka = ekke (Tbh. of arka) aka (Tbh. of arka) copper (metal); crystal (Kannada) *erako* 'moltencast copper' Duplicated: dula 'pair' Rebus: dul 'cast metal' Thus cast copper, brass casting.

kuṭila 'bent' CDIAL 3230 kuṭi— in cmpd. 'curve', *kuṭika—* 'bent' MBh. Rebus: *kuṭila, katthīl* = bronze (8 parts copper and 2 parts tin)

  *loa* 'ficus religiosa' Rebus: *lo* 'iron' (Sanskrit) PLUS unique ligatures: लोखंड [lōkhaṇḍa] *n* (लोह S) Iron. लोखंडाचे चणे खावविणें or चारणें To oppress grievously.लोखंडकाम [lōkhaṇḍakāma] *n* Iron work; that portion (of a building, machine &c.) which consists of iron. 2 The business of an ironsmith.लोखंडी [lōkhaṇḍī] *a* (लोखंड) Composed of iron; relating to iron. (Marathi) *bhaṭa* 'warrior' (Sanskrit) Rebus: *baṭa* a kind of iron (Gujarati). Rebus: *bhaṭa* 'furnace' (Santali) Thus, together, the ligatured hieroglyph reads rebus: *loa bhaṭa* 'iron furnace'

L-90 a

Lothal 90a

loa 'ficus religiosa' Rebus: *lo* 'iron' (Sanskrit) PLUS unique ligatures: लोखंड [lōkhaṇḍa] *n* (लोह S) Iron. लोखंडाचे चणे खावविणें or चारणें To oppress grievously.लोखंडकाम [lōkhaṇḍakāma] *n* Iron work; that portion (of a building, machine &c.) which consists of iron. 2 The business of an ironsmith.लोखंडी [lōkhaṇḍī] *a* (लोखंड) Composed of iron; relating to iron. (Marathi) *bhaṭa* 'warrior' (Sanskrit) Rebus: *baṭa* a kind of iron (Gujarati). Rebus: *bhaṭa* 'furnace' (Santali) Thus, together, the ligatured hieroglyph reads rebus: *loa bhaṭa* 'iron furnace'

 *mogge* 'sprout, bud' Rebus: *mūh* 'ingot' (Santali)

 *dhāḷ* 'a slope'; 'inclination of a plane' (G.); *ḍhāḷiyum* = adj. sloping, inclining (G.) Rebus: *ḍhālako* = a large metal ingot (G.) *ḍhālakī* = a metal heated and poured into a mould; a solid piece of metal; an ingot (Gujarati) PLUS खांडा [*khāṇḍā*] *m* A jag, notch, or indentation (as upon the edge of a tool or weapon). Rebus: *kāṇḍa* 'tools, pots and pans and metal-ware' Thus, the pair of sign hieroglyphs from r. read rebus: copper, bronze ingots, metalware castings.
kolom 'three' Rebus: kolami 'smithy, forge' ingot furnace: *mūh kaṇḍa*

A variant representation of four 'sprout' hieroglyphs:
 *kolmo* 'paddy plant' Rebus: *kolami* 'smithy, forge' Variant hieroglyph: *mogge* 'sprout, bud' Rebus*: mūh* 'ingot'
|||| Numeral 4: *gaṇḍa* 'four' Rebus: *kaṇḍa* 'furnace, fire-altar' (Santali). Thus, together, read rebus: ingot furnace: *mūh kaṇḍa*

 Zebu. Native metal smith guild. Four 'sprout' hieroglyphs may denote four smithy units: *kolmo* 'paddyplant' Rebus: *kolami* 'smithy,forge'.

 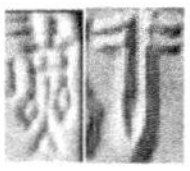 water-carrier hieroglyph *kuṭi*; Rebus: *kuṭhi* 'smelter furnace'. PLUS 'rim of jar':
kanka 'rim of jar' Rebus: karṇīka 'account (scribe)' karṇī 'supercargo'

 h1672A *खोंड [khōṇḍa] m A young bull, a bullcalf. (Marathi) Rebus: kõdār 'turner' (Bengali); कोंद kōnda 'engraver, lapidary setting or infixing gems' (Marathi) G. sãghāṛɔ m. 'lathe' ; संघाट joinery; M. sãgaḍ 'double-canoe' Rebus: sangataras 'stone-cutter, mason'*
kolom 'three' Rebus: *kolami* 'smithy/forge'

 Read in context, the composite hieroglyph is assumed to be a combination of a slanted stroke ligatured to a notch,which provide possible rebus readings of a smithy/forge: notch+slanted stroke reads rebus: *ḍhālako kāṇḍa* 'ingot, tools, pots and pans and metal-ware'

dhāḷ 'a slope'; 'inclination of a plane' (Gujarati); *ḍhāḷiyum* = adj. sloping, inclining (Gujarati) Rebus: *ḍhālako* = a large metal ingot (Gujarati) *ḍhālakī* = a metal heated and poured into a mould; a solid piece of metal; an ingot (Gujarati) PLUS खांडा [*khāṇḍā*] *m* A jag, notch, or indentation (as upon the edge of a tool or weapon). Rebus: *kāṇḍa* 'tools, pots and pans and metal-ware'
 *meḍ* 'body' Rebus: *meḍ* 'iron' (Ho.) काठी [kāṭhī] *f* (काष्ट S) 'frame or structure of the body' (Marathi) Rebus: खंडी [khaṇḍī] measure of weight (Marathi) *கண்டி; kaṇṭi, n. < Mhr. khaṇḍil. [T. Tu. khaṇḍi, M. kaṇḍi.]* Candy, a weight, stated to be roughly equivalent to 500 lbs.

meḍ 'body' Rebus: meḍ 'iron' (Ho.Mu.) Vikalpa: काठी [kāṭhī] *f* (काष्ट S) The stalk, stem, or trunk of a plant. A staff, rod, pole, wand, stick gen.; a flagstaff, a walking stick, the mast or the yard of a ship or boat etc. The frame or structure of the body: also (viewed by some as arising from the preceding sense, Measuring rod) stature.(Marathi) Rebus: काटी or कांटी [kāṭī or kāṇṭī] *a* (In नंदभाषा) Twenty.(Marathi) खंडी [khaṇḍī] *f* A measure of weight and capacity, a candy. It consists (in Bombay) of twenty Bombay maunds, or, for particular substances, of eight maunds: (at Poona) of twenty Poona maunds, and generally of twenty maunds; varying therefore as the maund varies. 2 Applied to a great quantity; as खंडीभर पोरें, खंडीभर मेंढ्या, खंडीभर काम, खंडीभर बोलतो-लिहितो &c. 3 A land measure, 120 bighás. 4 A score (of sheep or goats, and of some certain things). खंडीगणती or खंडोगणती [khaṇḍīgaṇatī or khaṇḍōgaṇatī] *ad* By candies; counting or reckoning by candies. खंडीवारी [khaṇḍīvārī] *ad* By scores, heaps, candies.

 *kharedo* = a currycomb (Gujarati) खरारा [*kharārā*] *m* (H) A currycomb. 2 Currying a horse. (Marathi) Rebus: करडा [*karaḍā*] Hard from alloy--iron, silver &c. (Marathi) *kharādī* ' turner' (Gujarati)

 kanka 'rim of jar' Rebus: karṇīka 'account (scribe)' karṇī 'supercargo'

h585 *khũṭ* 'zebu' Rebus: '(native metal) guild'.

kolom 'three' Rebus: *kolami* 'smithy/forge'

కండె [kaṇḍe] *kaṇḍe*. [Telugu] n. A head or ear of millet or maize. జొన్నకంకి (Telugu) *kāṛ* 'stack of stalks of large millet' (Maithili) kāḍ 2 काँड् m. a section, part in general; a cluster, bundle, multitude (Śiv. 32). kāḍ 1 काँड् । काण्डः m. the stalk or stem of a reed, grass, or the like, straw. In the compound with dan 5 (p. 221*a*, l. 13) the word is spelt kāḍ. Rebus : *khāṇḍa* 'tools, pots and pans, metal-ware'. Rebus 2: kaṇḍ 'fire-altar' (Santali) Vikalpa: kolmo 'paddy plant' Rebus: kolami 'smithy, forge'. Vikalpa: mogge 'bud, sprout' Rebus: mũh 'ingot'

h65A *खोंड [khōṇḍa] m A young bull, a bullcalf. (Marathi) Rebus: kōdār 'turner' (Bengali); कोंद kōnda 'engraver, lapidary setting or infixing gems' (Marathi) G. sãghārɔ m. 'lathe' ; संघाट joinery; M. sāgaḍ 'double-canoe' Rebus: sangataras 'stone-cutter, mason'*

kolom 'three' Rebus: *kolami* 'smithy, forge'. dula 'pair' Rebus: dul 'cast metal' sal 'splinter' Rebus: sal 'workshop' Thus, metal smithy castings workshop.

'Two slanted strokes' hieroglyph: *dhāḷ* 'a slope'; 'inclination of a plane' (Gujarati); *ḍhāḷiyum* = adj. sloping, inclining (Gujarati) Rebus: *ḍhālako* = a large metal ingot (Gujarati) *ḍhālakī* = a metal heated and poured into a mould; a solid piece of metal; an ingot (Gujarati) PLUS dula 'two' Rebus:dul 'cast metal'. Thus, cast metal ingot.

 kanka 'rim of jar' Rebus: karṇīka 'account (scribe)' karṇī 'supercargo'

m416A *balad* m. ' ox ', gng. *bald,* (Ku.) *barad,* id. (N. Tarai) Rebus: *bharat* (5 copper, 4 zinc and 1 tin)(Punjabi) *pattar* 'trough'
kolom 'three' Rebus: *kolami* 'smithy, forge'. dula 'pair' Rebus: dul 'cast metal'

The pair of hieroglyph signs are compositions: *bicha* 'scorpion' (Assamese) ebus: *bica* 'stone ore' (Santali) The pairing sign is a composition of: sloping stroke PLUS two short strokes of a 'splinter':

dhāḷ 'a slope'; 'inclination of a plane' (Gujarati); *ḍhāḷiyum* = adj. sloping, inclining (Gujarati) Rebus: *ḍhālako* = a large metal ingot (Gujarati) *ḍhālakī* = a metal heated and poured into a mould; a solid piece of metal; an ingot (Gujarati)PLUS*sal* 'splinter' Rebus: *sal* 'workshop'. Thus the composition reads: *ḍhālako sal* 'ingot workshop'.Together, the pair of hieroglyph signs read: *bica ḍhālako sal* 'stone ore ingot workshop'.

ranku 'antelope' Rebus: *ranku* 'tin'.

Vikalpa: Ligature: two peaks: mēḍu height, rising ground, hillock (Kannada) Rebus: *meḍ* 'iron' (Ho.) dula 'pair' Rebus: dul 'cast metal' PLUS |||| Numeral 4: gaṇḍa 'four' Rebus: kaṇḍa 'furnace, fire-altar' (Santali)

m1799A

खोंड [khōṇḍa] m A young bull, a bullcalf. (Marathi) Rebus: kõdār 'turner' (Bengali); कोंद kōnda 'engraver, lapidary setting or infixing gems' (Marathi) G. sãghāṛɔ m. 'lathe' ; संघाट joinery; M. sãgaḍ 'double-canoe' Rebus: sangataras 'stone-cutter, mason'

m822a

kolmo 'paddy plant' Rebus: kolami 'smithy, forge'. Vikalpa: mogge 'bud, sprout' Rebus: mũh 'ingot'
kolom 'three' Rebus: kolami 'smithy, forge' dula 'pair' Rebus: dul 'cast metal'. Thus, together, cast metal ingot smithy'

m178a

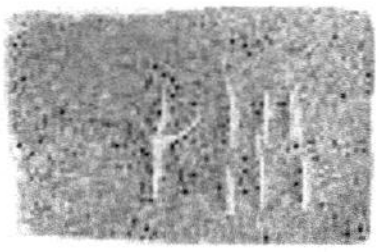

m1365A kolmo 'paddy plant' Rebus: kolami 'smithy, forge'. Vikalpa: mogge 'bud, sprout' Rebus: mũh 'ingot'
kolom 'three' Rebus: kolami 'smithy, forge' dula 'pair' Rebus: dul 'cast metal'. Thus, together, cast metal ingot smithy'

rāngo 'water buffalo bull' (Ku.N.)(CDIAL 10559) Rebus: rango 'pewter'

kolmo ‘paddy plant’ Rebus: kolami ‘smithy, forge’. Vikalpa: mogge ‘bud, sprout’ Rebus: mũh ‘ingot’

kolom ‘three’ Rebus: kolami ‘smithy, forge’ dula ‘pair’ Rebus: dul ‘cast metal’. Thus, together, cast metal ingot smithy’

h884A *खोंड [khōṇḍa] m A young bull, a bullcalf. (Marathi) Rebus: kõdār ‘turner’ (Bengali); कोंद kōnda ‘engraver, lapidary setting or infixing gems’ (Marathi) G. sãghāṛɔ m. ‘lathe’ ; संघाट joinery; M. sãgaḍ ‘double-canoe’ Rebus: sangataras ‘stone-cutter, mason’*

kolom ‘three’ Rebus: kolami ‘smithy, forge’ dula ‘pair’ Rebus: dul ‘cast metal’. Thus, together, cast metal ingot smithy’

khaṇḍ ‘field, division’ (Skt.) Rebus: *khāṇḍa* ‘tools, pots and pans, metal-ware’. Rebus 2: kaṇḍ 'fire-altar' (Santali) dula ‘pair’ Rebus: dul ‘cast metal’ Thus, duplicated ‘division’ hieroglyph sign reads: cast metal metal-ware.

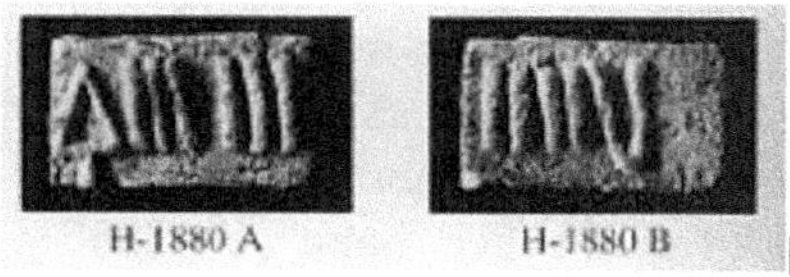

h1880A,B

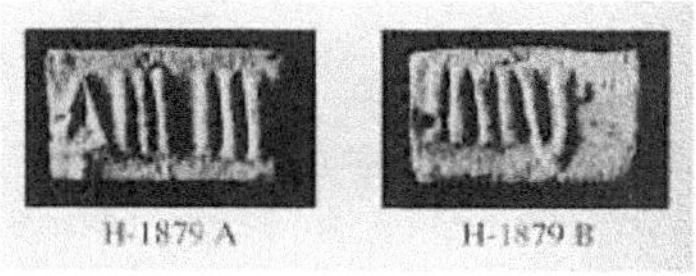

h1879A,B

k*olom* ‘three’ Rebus: *kolami* ‘smithy, forge’ *dula* ‘pair’ Rebus: *dul* ‘cast metal’. Thus, together, cast metal ingot smithy’

kaṇḍa ‘arrow’ Rebus: *khāṇḍa* ‘tools, pots and pans, metal-ware’.

baṭa ‘rimless, broad-mouthed pot’ Rebus: *bhaṭa* ‘furnace’ (Gujarati.); *baṭa* ‘a kind of iron’ (Gujarati)

|||| Numeral 4: gaṇḍa 'four' Rebus: kaṇḍa 'furnace, fire-altar' (Santali)

h1840A *खोंड [khōṇḍa] m A young bull, a bullcalf. (Marathi) Rebus: kõdār ‘turner’ (Bengali); कोंद kōnda ‘engraver, lapidary setting or infixing gems’ (Marathi) G. sãghāṛɔ m. ‘lathe’ ; संघाट joinery; M. sãgaḍ ‘double-canoe’ Rebus: sangataras ‘stone-cutter, mason’*

kanka ‘rim  of jar’ Rebus: karṇīka ‘account (scribe)’ karṇī ‘supercargo’

kolom ‘three’ Rebus: *kolami* ‘smithy, forge’ *dula* ‘pair’ Rebus: *dul* ‘cast metal’. Thus, together, cast metal ingot smithy’

h789A Side A: First 3 signs read as at h1880 PLUS ayo ‘fish’ Rebus: aya ‘iron’ (Gujarati) ayas ‘metal’ (Vedic) PLUS  *khareḍo* = a currycomb (Gujarati) खरारा [*kharārā*] *m* (H) A currycomb. 2 Currying a horse. (Marathi) Rebus: करडा [*karaḍā*] Hard from alloy--iron, silver &c. (Marathi) *kharādī* ‘ turner’ (Gujarati) Side B: kolom ‘three’ Rebus: kolami ‘smithy, forge’ PLUS next sign as at Side B of h1880.

h1028a *खोंड [khōṇḍa] m A young bull, a bullcalf. (Marathi) Rebus: kõdār 'turner' (Bengali); कोंद kōnda 'engraver, lapidary setting or infixing gems' (Marathi) G. sãghāṛɔ m. 'lathe' ; संघाट joinery; M. sãgaḍ 'double-canoe' Rebus: sangataras 'stone-cutter, mason'*

kolom 'three' Rebus: *kolami* 'smithy, forge' *dula* 'pair' Rebus: *dul* 'cast metal'. Thus, together, cast metal ingot smithy'ayo 'fish' Rebus: aya 'iron' (Gujarati) ayas 'metal' (Vedic)

m1758A *खोंड [khōṇḍa] m A young bull, a bullcalf. (Marathi) Rebus: kõdār 'turner' (Bengali); कोंद kōnda 'engraver, lapidary setting or infixing gems' (Marathi) G. sãghāṛɔ m. 'lathe' ; संघाट joinery; M. sãgaḍ 'double-canoe' Rebus: sangataras 'stone-cutter, mason' kolom* 'three' Rebus: *kolami* 'smithy, forge' *dula* 'pair' Rebus: *dul* 'cast metal'. Thus, together, cast metal ingot smithy' *ḍhanga* = a crook used for pulling down the branches of trees, for goats, sheep and camels (P.) Rebus:*ḍhangar* blacksmith'.

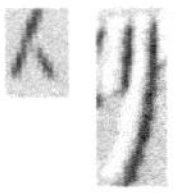

notch+slanted stroke reads rebus: *ḍhālako kāṇḍa* 'ingot, tools, pots and pans and metal-ware'.*dhāḷ* 'a slope'; 'inclination of a plane' (G.); *ḍhāḷiyum* = adj. sloping, inclining (G.) Rebus: *ḍhālako* = a large metal ingot (G.) *ḍhālakī* = a metal heated and poured into a mould; a solid piece of metal; an ingot (Gujarati) PLUS खांडा [*khāṇḍā*] *m* A jag, notch, or indentation (as upon the edge of a tool or weapon). Rebus: *kāṇḍa* 'tools, pots and pans and metal-ware' *aya aḍaren (homonym: aduru)*'alloy native metal' *ayo* 'fish' Rebus: *aya* 'iron' *ayas* 'metal'

कांड *kāṇḍa* 'arrow' Rebus: *kāṇḍa* 'pots and pans, metalware, tools'. Rebus 2: kaṇḍ 'fire-altar' (Santali)

M-1904 a

m1904a mlekh 'goat' Rebus: milakkha 'copper' (Pali)

kolom 'three' Rebus: *kolami* 'smithy, forge' *dula* 'pair' Rebus: *dul* 'cast metal'. Thus, together, cast metal ingot smithy'

kolmo 'paddy plant' Rebus: kolami 'smithy, forge'

h98A .

kolom 'three' Rebus: *kolami* 'smithy, forge' *dula* 'pair' Rebus: *dul* 'cast metal'. Thus, together, cast metal ingot smithy'

ayo 'fish' Rebus: aya 'iron' (Gujarati) ayas 'metal' (Vedic)

kaṇḍa 'arrow' Rebus: *khāṇḍa* 'tools, pots and pans, metal-ware'.

kuṭila 'bent' CDIAL 3230 kuṭi— in cmpd. 'curve', *kuṭika*— 'bent' MBh. Rebus: *kuṭila, katthīl* = bronze (8 parts copper and 2 parts tin)

kanac 'corner' Rebus: *kañcu* 'bronze'. Thus, two types of broze are identified: perhaps, arsenical copper and tin bronze.

Allahdino 2a *खोंड [khōṇḍa] m A young bull, a bullcalf. (Marathi) Rebus: kõdār 'turner' (Bengali); कोंद kōnda 'engraver, lapidary setting or infixing gems' (Marathi) G. sãghāṛɔ m. 'lathe' ; संघाट joinery; M. sãgaḍ 'double-canoe' Rebus: sangataras 'stone-cutter, mason' kolom* 'three' Rebus: kolami 'smithy, forge' *kamaḍha* 'archer, bow' Rebus: *kammaṭa* 'mint, coiner'.
kolmo 'paddy plant' Rebus: *kolami* 'smithy, forge' Vikalpa: *mogge* 'sprout, bud' Rebus: *mũh* 'ingot'  (Santali) dolu 'plant of shoot height' Rebus: dul 'cast metal'

 *koḍi* 'flag' (Ta.)(DEDR 2049). Rebus 1: *koḍ* 'workshop' (Kuwi) Rebus 2: *khŏḍ* m. 'pit', *khŏḍü* f. 'small pit' (Kashmiri. CDIAL 3947).

h1664A *खोंड [khōṇḍa] m A young bull, a bullcalf. (Marathi) Rebus: kõdār 'turner' (Bengali); कोंद kōnda 'engraver, lapidary setting or infixing gems' (Marathi) G. sãghāṛɔ m. 'lathe' ; संघाट joinery; M. sãgaḍ 'double-canoe' Rebus: sangataras 'stone-cutter, mason'*

kolom 'three' Rebus: kolami 'smithy, forge' mogge 'sprout, bud' Rebus: mũh 'ingot'

m1857A, m987a, m179a Read rebus as at h1664.

m1765A *खोंड [khōṇḍa] m A young bull, a bullcalf. (Marathi) Rebus: kõdār 'turner' (Bengali); कोंद kōnda 'engraver, lapidary setting or infixing gems' (Marathi) G. sãghāṛɔ m. 'lathe' ; संघाट joinery; M. sãgaḍ 'double-canoe' Rebus: sangataras 'stone-cutter, mason'* मेढा [*mēḍhā*] A twist or tangle arising in thread or cord, a curl or snarl.(Marathi)(CDIAL 10312).L. *meṛh* f. 'rope tying oxen to each other and to post on threshing floor'(CDIAL 10317) Rebus: *meḍ* 'iron'. *mẽṛhet* 'iron' (Mu.Ho.) | *koḍa* 'one' Rebus: *koḍ* 'workshop'

 *aḍaren* 'cover of pot or lid' Rebus: *aduru* 'native, unsmelted metal' Duplicated: dula 'pair' Rebus: dul 'cast metal'

  *loa* 'ficus religiosa' Rebus: *lo* 'iron' (Sanskrit) PLUS unique ligatures: लोखंड [lōkhaṇḍa] *n* (लोह S) Iron. लोखंडाचे चणे खावविणें or चारणें To oppress grievously.लोखंडकाम [lōkhaṇḍakāma] *n* Iron work; that portion (of a building, machine &c.) which consists of iron. 2 The business of an ironsmith.लोखंडी [lōkhaṇḍī] *a* (लोखंड) Composed of iron; relating to iron. (Marathi) *bhaṭa* 'warrior' (Sanskrit) Rebus: *baṭa* a kind of iron (Gujarati). Rebus: *bhaṭa* 'furnace' (Santali) Thus, together, the ligatured hieroglyph reads rebus: *loa bhaṭa* 'iron furnace'
kəṭhā́r, kc. *kuṭhār* m. ' granary, storeroom '(WPah.)(CDIAL 3550). *koṭhārī m.* ' storekeeper'  (Gujarati)(CDIAL 3551) Thus, storeroom (of) *kolom* 'three' Rebus: *kolami* 'smithy, forge'. Dula 'pair' Rebus: dul 'cast metal' Thus, together *dul kolami kuṭhār* 'metal smithy castings storeroom'

muka 'ladle' (Tamil)(DEDR 4887) Rebus: *mũh* 'ingot' (Santali) *baṭa* = rimless pot (Kannada) Rebus:) *baṭa* = a kind of iron (G.)) *bhaṭa* furnace (Gujarati) Thus, iron ingot. sal 'splinter' Rebus: sal 'workshop'

meḍ 'body' Rebus: *meḍ* 'iron' (Ho.) काठी [kāṭhī] *f* (काष्ट S) 'frame or structure of the body' (Marathi) Rebus: खंडी [khaṇḍī] measure of weight (Marathi) *கண்டி; kaṇṭi, n. < Mhr. khaṇḍil. [T. Tu. khaṇḍi, M. kaṇḍi.]* Candy, a weight, stated to be roughly equivalent to 500 lbs. kolom 'three' Rebus: kolami 'smithy, forge'.

M-1846 a

m1846a *खोंड [khōṇḍa] m A young bull, a bullcalf. (Marathi) Rebus: kõdār 'turner' (Bengali); कोंद kōnda 'engraver, lapidary setting or infixing gems' (Marathi) G. sãghāṛɔ m. 'lathe' ; संघाट joinery; M. sãgaḍ 'double-canoe' Rebus: sangataras 'stone-cutter, mason' kolom 'three' Rebus: kolami 'smithy, forge'*

loa 'ficus   religiosa' Rebus: *lo* 'iron' (Sanskrit) PLUS unique ligatures: लोखंड [lōkhaṇḍa] *n* (लोह S) Iron. लोखंडाचे चणे खावविणें or चारणें To oppress grievously.लोखंडकाम [lōkhaṇḍakāma] *n* Iron work; that portion (of a building, machine &c.) which consists of iron. 2 The business of an ironsmith.लोखंडी [lōkhaṇḍī] *a* (लोखंड) Composed of iron; relating to iron. (Marathi) *bhaṭa* 'warrior' (Sanskrit) Rebus: *baṭa* a kind of iron (Gujarati). Rebus: *bhaṭa* 'furnace' (Santali) Thus, together, the ligatured hieroglyph reads rebus: *loa bhaṭa* 'iron furnace'

khareḍo = a currycomb (Gujarati) खरारा [*kharārā*] *m* (H) A currycomb. 2 Currying a horse. (Marathi) Rebus: करडा [*karaḍā*] Hard from alloy--iron, silver &c. (Marathi) *kharādī* ' turner' (Gujarati)

m1894 *khũṭ* 'zebu' Rebus: '(native metal) guild'. Text message: furnace smithy/forge workshop; iron workshop community; supercargo.
kolom 'three' Rebus: kolami 'smithy, forge'
koḍi 'flag' (Tamil)(DEDR 2049). Rebus 1: *koḍ* 'workshop' (Kuwi) Rebus 2: *khõḍ* m. 'pit', *khõḍü* f. 'small pit' (Kashmiri. CDIAL 3947).

| *koḍa* 'one' Rebus: *koḍ* 'workshop' PLUS gaṇḍa 'four' Rebus: kaṇḍa 'furnace, fire-altar' (Santali) PLUS खांडा [*khāṇḍā*] *m* A jag, notch, or indentation (as upon the edge of a tool or weapon). Rebus: *kāṇḍa* 'tools, pots and pans and metal-ware'
ayo 'fish' Rebus: aya 'iron' (Gujarati) ayas 'metal' (Vedic) PLUS sal 'splinter' Rebus: sal 'workhop' Thus, the pair of hieroglyphs read rebus: iron workshop = *aya sal.*
ḍhanga = a crook used for pulling down the branches of trees, for goats, sheep and camels (Punjabi) Rebus:*ḍhangar* blacksmith'.

kanka 'rim of jar' Rebus: *karṇīka* 'account (scribe)' *karṇī* 'supercargo'

Kalibangan 8a *खोंड [khōṇḍa] m A young bull, a bullcalf. (Marathi) Rebus: kõdār 'turner' (Bengali); कोंद kōnda 'engraver, lapidary setting or infixing gems' (Marathi) G. sãghāṛɔ m. 'lathe' ; संघाट joinery; M. sãgaḍ 'double-canoe' Rebus: sangataras 'stone-cutter, mason'*
kolom 'three' Rebus: kolami 'smithy, forge'
ayo 'fish' Rebus: aya 'iron' (Gujarati) ayas 'metal' (Vedic)
kanka 'rim of jar' Rebus: karṇīka 'account (scribe)' karṇī 'supercargo'

 water-carrier hieroglyph *kuṭi*; Rebus: *kuṭhi* 'smelter furnace'.

m1912a ibha 'elephant' Rebus: ib 'iron' (Santali) ibbo 'merchant' (Gujarati)

kolom 'three' Rebus: kolami 'smithy, forge'
ayo 'fish' Rebus: aya 'iron' (Gujarati) ayas 'metal' (Vedic)
kāṇḍa 'arrow' (Sanskrit) Rebus:*khāṇḍa* 'tools, pots and pans, metal-ware'.
Rebus 2: kaṇḍ 'fire-altar' (Santali)

h1056a *खोंड [khōṇḍa] m A young bull, a bullcalf. (Marathi) Rebus: kõdār 'turner' (Bengali); कोंद kōnda 'engraver, lapidary setting or infixing gems' (Marathi) G. sãghāṛɔ m. 'lathe' ; संघाट joinery; M. sãgaḍ 'double-canoe' Rebus: sangataras 'stone-cutter, mason'* kolom 'three' Rebus: kolami 'smithy, forge'
ayo 'fish' Rebus: aya 'iron' (Gujarati) ayas 'metal' (Vedic)

 *kanka* 'rim of jar' Rebus: *karṇī,* supercargo for a boat shipment. *karṇīka* 'account (scribe) '.कारणी *kāraṇī* 'the supercargo of a ship' (Marathi)

meḍ 'body' Rebus: *meḍ* 'iron' (Ho.) काठी [kāṭhī] *f* (काष्ट S) 'frame or structure of the body' (Marathi) Rebus: खंडी [khaṇḍī] measure of weight (Marathi) *கண்டி; kaṇṭi, n. < Mhr. khaṇḍil. [T. Tu. khaṇḍi, M. kaṇḍi.]* Candy, a weight, stated to be roughly equivalent to 500 lbs.

 *kharedo* = a currycomb (Gujarati) खरारा [*kharārā*] *m* (H) A currycomb. 2 Currying a horse. (Marathi) Rebus: करडा [*karaḍā*] Hard from alloy--iron, silver &c. (Marathi) *kharādī* ' turner' (Gujarati)

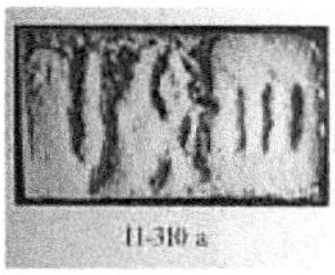

h310a Red rebus as at m1442

m1439A Read rebus as at m1442

m1442A kolom 'three' Rebus: kolami 'smithy, forge'ayo 'fish' Rebus: aya 'iron' (Gujarati) ayas 'metal' (Vedic)

 *kanka* 'rim of jar' Rebus: *karṇī,* supercargo for a boat shipment. *karṇīka* ' account (scribe)'.कारणी *kāraṇī* 'the supercargo of a ship' (Marathi)

m294a ibha 'elephant' Rebus: ib 'iron' (Santali) ibbo 'merchant' (Gujarati) pattar 'trough' Rebus: pattar 'goldsmith guild' (Telugu)

खोंड [khōṇḍa] m A young bull, a bullcalf. (Marathi) Rebus: kõdār 'turner' (Bengali); कोंद kōnda 'engraver, lapidary setting or infixing gems' (Marathi) G. sãghāṛɔ m. 'lathe' ; संघाट joinery; M. sãgaḍ 'double-canoe' Rebus: sangataras 'stone-cutter, mason' Text read rebus as at m1442.

m94a *खोंड [khōṇḍa] m A young bull, a bullcalf. (Marathi) Rebus: kõdār 'turner' (Bengali); कोंद kōnda 'engraver, lapidary setting or infixing gems' (Marathi) G. sãghāṛɔ m. 'lathe' ; संघाट joinery; M. sãgaḍ 'double-canoe' Rebus: sangataras 'stone-cutter, mason'*

kolom ‘three’ Rebus: kolami ‘smithy, forge’
ayo ‘fish’ Rebus: aya ‘iron’ (Gujarati) ayas ‘metal’ (Vedic)
rank ‘liquid measure’ Rebus: ranku ‘tin’ (Santali)
kolmo ‘paddy plant’ Rebus: kolami ‘smithy, forge’ Vikalpa: mogge ‘sprout’ Rebus: mũh ‘ingot’
 kanka ‘rim of jar’ Rebus: karṇīka ‘account (scribe)’ karṇī ‘supercargo’

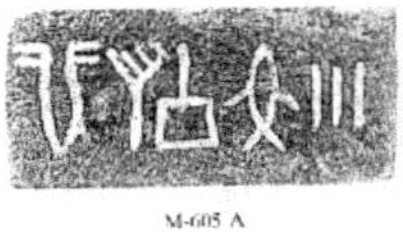

m695A copper plate inscription.
kolom ‘three’ Rebus: kolami ‘smithy, forge’
ayo ‘fish’ Rebus: aya ‘iron’ (Gujarati) ayas ‘metal’ (Vedic)
rank ‘liquid measure’ Rebus: ranku ‘tin’ (Santali)
kolmo ‘paddy plant’ Rebus: kolami ‘smithy, forge’ Vikalpa: mogge ‘sprout’ Rebus: mũh ‘ingot’
kanka ‘rim of jar’ Rebus: karṇīka ‘account (scribe)’ karṇī ‘supercargo’

m916A *खोंड [khōṇḍa] m A young bull, a bullcalf. (Marathi) Rebus: kõdār ‘turner’ (Bengali); कोंद kōnda ‘engraver, lapidary setting or infixing gems’ (Marathi) G. sãghāṛɔ m. ‘lathe’ ; संघाट joinery; M. sãgaḍ ‘double-canoe’ Rebus: sangataras. संगतराश lit. ‘to collect stones, stone-cutter, mason.’*

 *dula* ‘pair’ Rebus: *dul* ‘cast (metal)’ PLUS *kana, kanac* = corner (Santali); Rebus: *kañcu* = bronze (Telugu) PLUS infixed kolmo ‘paddy plant’ Rebus: kolami ‘smithy, forge’. Thus, cast bronze smithy, forge. Or, *mogge* ‘sprout, bud’ Rebus: *mũh* ‘ingot’ (Santali)Thus, cast bronze ingot. Read as: *kañcu dul mũh ‘bronze cast ingot’*
Duplicated: *dula* ‘pair’ Rebus: dul ‘cast metal’ Thus, bronze ingot, casting smithy.
 *kharedo* = a currycomb (Gujarati) खरारा [*kharārā*] *m* (H) A currycomb. 2 Currying a horse. (Marathi) Rebus: करडा [*karaḍā*] Hard from alloy--iron, silver &c. (Marathi) *kharādī* ‘ turner’ (Gujarati)

m27a *खोंड [khōṇḍa] m A young bull, a bullcalf. (Marathi) Rebus: kõdār ‘turner’ (Bengali); कोंद kōnda ‘engraver, lapidary setting or infixing gems’ (Marathi) G. sãghāṛɔ m. ‘lathe’ ; संघाट joinery; M. sãgaḍ ‘double-canoe’ Rebus: sangataras ‘stone-cutter, mason’*
kolom ‘three’ Rebus: kolami ‘smithy, forge’
kuṭila ‘bent’ CDIAL 3230 kuṭi— in cmpd. ‘curve’, *kuṭika—* ‘bent’ MBh. Rebus: kuṭila, katthīl = bronze (8 parts copper and 2 parts tin) cf. āra-kūṭa, ‘brass’ (Sanskrit)
baṭa ‘rimless, broad-mouthed pot’ Rebus: *bhaṭa* ‘furnace’ (Gujarati.); *baṭa* ‘a kind of iron’ (Gujarati) Infixed ‘splinter’: *sal* ‘splinter’ Rebus: *sal* ‘workshop’
 kanka ‘rim of jar’ Rebus: karṇīka ‘account (scribe)’ karṇī ‘supercargo’ Infixed खांडा [*khāṇḍā*] *m* A jag, notch, or indentation (as upon the edge of a tool or weapon). Rebus: *kāṇḍa* ‘tools, pots and pans and metal-ware’ Thus, metalware supercargo.
dul kuṭila ‘cast bronze’. (Paired bent lines) PLUS kolmo ‘paddyplant’ Rebus: kolami ‘smithy, forge’. Thus, cast bronze smithy-forge.
aya aḍaren (homonym: aduru)‘alloy native metal’
kamaḍha ‘crab’ Rebus: *kammaṭa* ‘mint, coiner’. PLUS ligature ‘tail’ hieroglyph:
Kur. xolā tail. *Malt.* qoli id. (DEDR 2135). Rebus: kolhe ‘smelters’. Thus, smelters’ mint.

ḍato = claws of crab (Santali) Rebus: dhātu 'mineral ore'

h450a *खोंड [khōṇḍa] m A young bull, a bullcalf. (Marathi) Rebus: kõdār 'turner' (Bengali); कोंद kōnda 'engraver, lapidary setting or infixing gems' (Marathi) G. sãghāṛɔ m. 'lathe' ; संघाट joinery; M. sãgaḍ 'double-canoe' Rebus: sangataras 'stone-cutter, mason'*

kolom 'three' Rebus: kolami 'smithy, forge'

kuṭila 'bent' CDIAL 3230 kuṭi— in cmpd. 'curve', *kuṭika—* 'bent' MBh. Rebus: kuṭila, katthīl = bronze (8 parts copper and 2 parts tin) cf. āra-kūṭa, 'brass' (Sanskrit)

baṭa 'rimless, broad-mouthed pot' Rebus: *bhaṭa* 'furnace' (Gujarati.); *baṭa* 'a kind of iron' (Gujarati) Infixed 'splinter': *sal* 'splinter' Rebus: *sal* 'workshop'

kanka 'rim of jar' Rebus: karṇīka 'account (scribe)' karṇī 'supercargo' Infixed खांडा [*khāṇḍā*] *m* A jag, notch, or indentation (as upon the edge of a tool or weapon). Rebus: *kāṇḍa* 'tools, pots and pans and metal-ware' Thus, metalware supercargo.

aya kammaṭa.'coiner, mint alloy'

bhaṭa 'warrior' (Sanskrit) Rebus: *baṭa* a kind of iron (Gujarati). Rebus: *bhaṭa* 'furnace' (Santali) kanka 'rim of jar' Rebus: karṇīka 'account (scribe)' karṇī 'supercargo'

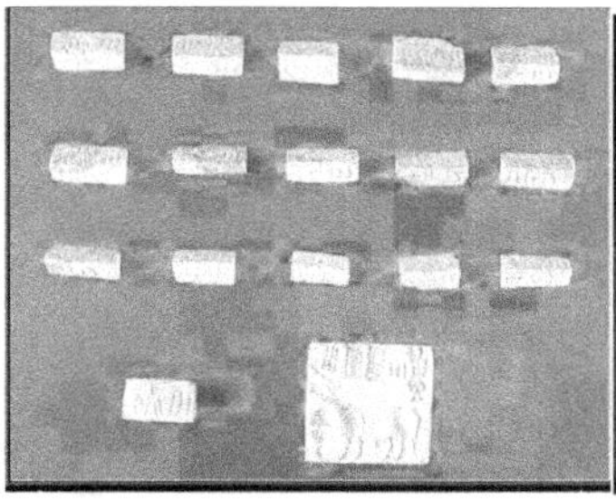

h1682A (Seventeen seals with identical inscriptions were found)

||| Numeral three: kolom 'three' Rebus: kolami 'smithy, forge'

khaṇḍ 'field, division' (Sanskrit) Rebus: *khāṇḍa* 'tools, pots and pans, metal-ware'. Rebus 2: kaṇḍ 'fire-altar' (Santali) dula 'pair' Rebus: dul 'cast metal' Thus, duplicated 'division' hieroglyph sign reads: cast metal metal-ware.

||| Numeral three: kolom 'three' Rebus: kolami 'smithy, forge'

water-carrier hieroglyph *kuṭi*; Rebus: *kuṭhi* 'smelter furnace'. PLUS 'rim of jar': kanka 'rim of jar' Rebus: karṇīka 'account (scribe)' karṇī 'supercargo'

m4a *खोंड [khōṇḍa] m A young bull, a bullcalf. (Marathi) Rebus: kõdār 'turner' (Bengali); कोंद kōnda 'engraver, lapidary setting or infixing gems' (Marathi) G. sãghāṛɔ m. 'lathe' ; संघाट joinery; M. sãgaḍ 'double-canoe' Rebus: sangataras 'stone-cutter, mason'*

||| Numeral three: kolom 'three' Rebus: kolami 'smithy, forge'

khaṇḍ 'field, division' (Sanskrit) Rebus: *khāṇḍa* 'tools, pots and pans, metal-ware'. Rebus 2: kaṇḍ 'fire-altar' (Santali) dula 'pair' Rebus: dul 'cast metal' Thus, duplicated 'division' hieroglyph sign reads: cast metal metal-ware.

kamaḍha 'crab' Rebus: *kammaṭa* 'mint, coiner'. PLUS ligature 'tail' hieroglyph:

Kur. xolā tail. *Malt.* qoli id. (DEDR 2135). Rebus: kolhe 'smelters'. Thus, smelters' mint.
ḍato = claws of crab (Santali) Rebus: dhātu 'mineral ore'
sal 'splinter' Rebus: *sal* 'workshop'
aya kāṇḍa 'alloy metalware'

muka 'ladle' (Tamil)(DEDR 4887) Rebus: *mũh* 'ingot' (Santali) *baṭa* = a kind of iron (Gujarati) *baṭa* = rimless pot (Kannada)

kolom 'three' Rebus: kolami 'smithy, forge'. Thus, iron ingot forge.

கொட்டு[2] koṭṭu [Tu. *koṭṭu*.] hoe with short handle, weeding-hoe (Tamil) Rebus: खोट [khōṭa] *f* A mass of metal (unwrought or of old metal melted down); an ingot or wedge.(Marathi)

Strands of yarn/rope' reading: *dhā'tu* 'strand of

hieroglyph: Hieroglyph: 'strands of yarn' Rebus rope' Rebus: *dhatu* 'mineral ore' (Santali)

h561A *kolom* 'three' Rebus: *kolami* 'smithy, forge' *aya kāṇḍa* 'alloy metalware'

m511B Copper plate. The hieroglyph may be a variant of:  *kana, kanac* = corner (Santali); Rebus: *kañcu* = bronze (Telugu)

kana, kanac = corner (Santali); Rebus: *kañcu* = bronze (Telugu)
kuṭila 'bent' CDIAL 3230 kuṭi— in cmpd. 'curve', *kuṭika*— 'bent' MBh.

Rebus: kuṭila, katthīl = bronze (8 parts copper and 2 parts tin) cf. āra-kūṭa, 'brass' (Sanskrit)

baṭa 'rimless, broad-mouthed pot' Rebus: *bhaṭa* 'furnace' (Gujarati.); *baṭa* 'a kind of iron' (Gujarati) ||| Numeral three: kolom 'three' Rebus: kolami 'smithy, forge'.

h246B *meḍ 'body' Rebus: meḍ 'iron' (Ho.) काठी [kāṭhī] f (काष्ट S) 'frame or structure of the body' (Marathi) Rebus: खंडी [khaṇḍī] measure of weight (Marathi) கண்டி; kaṇṭi, n. < Mhr. khaṇḍil. [T. Tu. khaṇḍi, M. kaṇḍi.] Candy, a weight, about 500 lbs.*eraka 'upraised hand' Rebus: erako 'moltencast copper' PLUS *baṭa* 'rimless, broad-mouthed pot' Rebus: *bhaṭa* 'furnace' (Gujarati.); *baṭa* 'a kind of iron' (Gujarati)

baṭa 'rimless, broad-mouthed pot' Rebus: *bhaṭa* 'furnace' (Gujarati.); *baṭa* 'a kind of iron' (Gujarati) ||| Numeral three: kolom 'three' Rebus: kolami 'smithy, forge'.

 h1796B  h979B 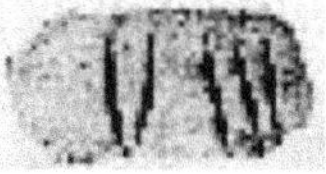 h959B  h949B

 h934B  h927B  h924B  h857B 

h821B  h818B  h793B  h792B 

h790B  h789B 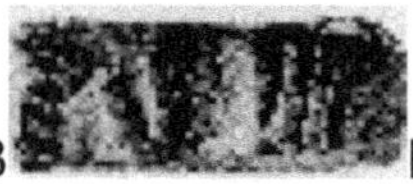 h783B 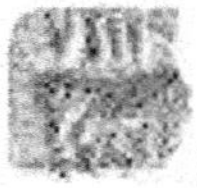 h703B 

h702B  h352B  h319B  h306B 

h303B 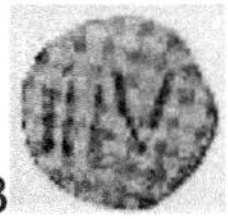 h249B 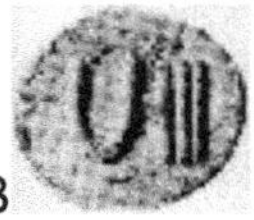 h248B 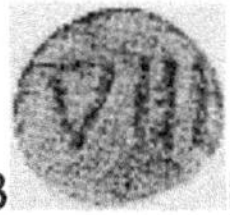 h254B

 h229B  h219B  h216B

 h211B 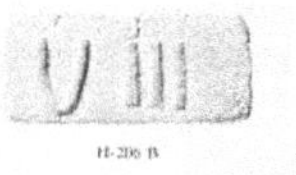 h206B

baṭa 'rimless, broad-mouthed pot' Rebus: *bhaṭa* 'furnace' (Gujarati.); *baṭa* 'a kind of iron' (Gujarati) ||| Numeral three: kolom 'three' Rebus: kolami 'smithy, forge'.

Chanhudaro 1a *खोंड [khōṇḍa] m A young bull, a bullcalf. (Marathi) Rebus: kōdār 'turner' (Bengali); कोंद kōnda 'engraver, lapidary setting or infixing gems' (Marathi) G. sãghāṛɔ m. 'lathe' ; संघाट joinery; M. sāgaḍ 'double-canoe' Rebus: sangataras 'stone-cutter, mason'*

||| Numeral three: kolom 'three' Rebus: kolami 'smithy, forge'.
Kur. xolā tail. *Malt.* qoli id. (DEDR 2135) Rebus: kolhe 'smelters' PLUS ingot: *ḍhālako* = a large metal ingot (Gujarati) Vikalpa: dulo 'hole' Rebus: dul 'cast metal'
koḍi 'flag' (Tamil)(DEDR 2049). Rebus 1: *koḍ* 'workshop' (Kuwi)
Circumscript: kuṭila 'bent' CDIAL 3230 kuṭi— in cmpd. 'curve', *kuṭika*— 'bent' MBh. Rebus: kuṭila, katthīl = bronze (8 parts copper and 2 parts tin) cf. āra-kūṭa, 'brass' (Sanskrit) dula 'pair' Rebus: dul 'cast metal' INFIXED
meḍ 'body' Rebus: *meḍ* 'iron' (Ho.) *bhaṭa* 'warrior' (Sanskrit) Rebus: *baṭa* a kind of iron (Gujarati). Rebus: *bhaṭa* 'furnace' (Santali)

kanka 'rim of jar' Rebus: karṇīka 'account (scribe)' karṇī 'supercargo'
loa 'ficus religiosa' Rebus: *lo* 'iron' (Sanskrit) PLUS unique ligatures: लोखंड [lōkhaṇḍa] *n* (लोह S) Iron. लोखंडाचे चणे खावविणें or चारणें To oppress

grievously.लोखंडकाम [lōkhaṇḍakāma] *n* Iron work; that portion (of a building, machine &c.) which consists of iron. 2 The business of an ironsmith.लोखंडी [lōkhaṇḍī] *a* (लोखंड) Composed of iron; relating to iron. (Marathi) Alternative reading: *bhaṭa* 'warrior' (Sanskrit) Rebus: *baṭa* a kind of iron (Gujarati). Rebus: *bhaṭa* 'furnace' (Santali)
kanac 'corner' Rebus: *kañcu* 'bronze
dula 'pair or two' Rebus: *dul* 'cast metal'
koḍa 'one' Rebus: *koḍ* 'workshop'

K-23 a

Kalibangan 23a *खोंड [khōṇḍa] m A young bull, a bullcalf. (Marathi) Rebus: kōdār 'turner' (Bengali); कोंद kōnda 'engraver, lapidary setting or infixing gems' (Marathi) G. sãghāṛɔ m. 'lathe' ; संघाट joinery; M. sāgaḍ 'double-canoe' Rebus: sangataras 'stone-cutter, mason'*

||| Numeral three: *kolom* 'three' Rebus: *kolami* 'smithy, forge'.
āra 'spokes' Rebus: *āra 'brass'.* eraka 'nave of wheel' Rebus: eraka 'copper'; erako 'moltencast copper'.
sal 'splinter' Rebus: *sal* 'workshop' dula 'two' Rebus: dul 'cast metal' PLUS *ḍhanga* = a crook used for pulling down the branches of trees, for goats, sheep and camels (P.) Rebus:*ḍhangar* blacksmith'. Thus, cast metal smith.

dula 'pair' Rebus: dul 'cast metal' Thus, a guild of metal casters.
kanka 'rim of jar' Rebus: karṇīka 'account (scribe)' karṇī 'supercargo'

m409A supercargo of cast metal bronze ingot from smelters' smithy/forge
||| Numeral three: *kolom* 'three' Rebus: *kolami* 'smithy, forge'. PLUS ligature of 'tail': *Kur. xolā* tail. *Malt.* qoli id. (DEDR 2135) Rebus: kolhe 'smelters'

kanka 'rim of jar' Rebus: karṇīka 'account (scribe)' karṇī 'supercargo'
mogge 'sprout, bud' Rebus*: mũh* 'ingot' circumscript ligature: *dula* 'pair' Rebus: *dul* 'cast metal' PLUS
kuṭila 'bent' CDIAL 3230 kuṭi— in cmpd. 'curve', *kuṭika—* 'bent' MBh. Rebus: kuṭila, katthīl = bronze (8 parts copper and 2 parts tin) cf. āra-kūṭa, 'brass' (Sanskrit) Thus, cast bronze ingot.

Harappan Seal

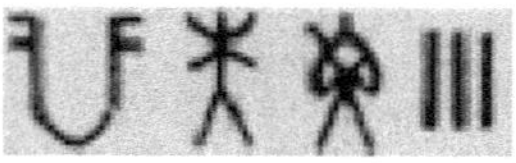

m1108 Text 1339 *khũṭ* 'zebu' Rebus: '(native metal) guild'

||| Numeral three: *kolom* 'three' Rebus: *kolami* 'smithy, forge'.

loa 'ficus religiosa' Rebus: *lo* 'iron' (Sanskrit) PLUS unique ligatures: लोखंड [lōkhaṇḍa] *n* (लोह S) Iron. लोखंडाचे चणे खावविणें or चारणें To oppress grievously.लोखंडकाम [lōkhaṇḍakāma] *n* Iron work; that portion (of a building, machine &c.) which consists of iron. 2 The business of an ironsmith.लोखंडी [lōkhaṇḍī] *a* (लोखंड) Composed of iron; relating to iron. (Marathi)

bhaṭa 'warrior' (Sanskrit) Rebus: *baṭa* a kind of iron (Gujarati). Rebus: *bhaṭa* 'furnace' (Santali) Thus, together, the ligatured hieroglyph reads rebus: *loa bhaṭa* 'iron furnace'

 kanka 'rim of jar' Rebus: karṇīka 'account (scribe)' karṇī 'supercargo'

m401a

||| Numeral three: *kolom* 'three' Rebus: *kolami* 'smithy, forge'.
kamaḍha 'crab' Rebus: *kammaṭa* 'mint, coiner'.
ḍato = claws of crab (Santali) Rebus: dhātu 'mineral ore'

khaṇḍ 'field, division' (Sanskrit) Rebus: *khānḍa* 'tools, pots and pans, metal-ware'. Rebus 2: kaṇḍ 'fire-altar' (Santali) dula 'pair' Rebus: dul 'cast metal' Thus cast metalware.

m1080a, m161a, h49a , m922A खोंड *[khōṇḍa] m A young bull, a bullcalf. (Marathi) Rebus: kōdār 'turner' (Bengali); कोंद kōnda 'engraver, lapidary setting or infixing gems' (Marathi) G. sãghāṛɔ m. 'lathe' ; संघाट joinery; M. sāgaḍ 'double-canoe' Rebus: sangataras 'stone-cutter, mason'*

||| Numeral three: *kolom* 'three' Rebus: *kolami* 'smithy, forge'.
kamaḍha 'crab' Rebus: *kammaṭa* 'mint, coiner'.
ḍato = claws of crab (Santali) Rebus: dhātu 'mineral ore' On m1080a: eraka 'upraised arm' Rebus: erako 'moltencast copper'

khaṇḍ 'field, division' (Sanskrit) Rebus: *khānḍa* 'tools, pots and pans, metal-ware'. Rebus 2: kaṇḍ 'fire-altar' (Santali) dula 'pair' Rebus: dul 'cast metal' Thus cast metalware.

m162a खोंड *[khōṇḍa] m A young bull, a bullcalf. (Marathi) Rebus: kōdār 'turner' (Bengali); कोंद kōnda 'engraver, lapidary setting or infixing gems' (Marathi) G. sãghāṛɔ m. 'lathe' ; संघाट joinery; M. sāgaḍ 'double-canoe' Rebus: sangataras 'stone-cutter, mason'*

||| Numeral three: *kolom* 'three' Rebus: *kolami* 'smithy, forge'.

kamaḍha 'crab' Rebus: *kammaṭa* 'mint, coiner'.
ḍato = claws of crab (Santali) Rebus: dhātu 'mineral ore' *dula* 'pair' Rebus: *dul* 'cast metal'. Thus mineral castings mint

kanac 'corner' Rebus: *kañcu* 'bronze
dula 'pair or two' Rebus: *dul* 'cast metal' Thus, cast bronze.

kolmo 'padd plant' Rebs: *kolami* 'smithy, forge' *dula* 'pair' Rebus: *dul* 'cast metal' Thus, metal smithy castings.
kanka 'rim of jar' Rebus: karṇīka 'account (scribe)' karṇī 'supercargo'

खोंड [khōṇḍa] m A young bull, a bullcalf. (Marathi) Rebus: kõdār 'turner' (Bengali); कोंद kōnda 'engraver, lapidary setting or infixing gems' (Marathi) G. sãghāṛɔ m. 'lathe' ; संघाट joinery; M. sãgaḍ 'double-canoe' Rebus: sangataras 'stone-cutter, mason'

||| Numeral three: *kolom* 'three' Rebus: *kolami* 'smithy, forge'.

Read in context, the composite hieroglyph is assumed to be a combination of a slanted stroke ligatured to a notch,which provide possible rebus readings of a smithy/forge: notch+slanted stroke reads rebus: *ḍhālako kāṇḍa* 'ingot, tools, pots and pans and metal-ware'

ḍhāḷ 'a slope'; 'inclination of a plane' (Gujarati); *ḍhāḷiyum* = adj. sloping, inclining (Gujarati) Rebus: *ḍhālako* = a large metal ingot (Gujarati) *ḍhālakī* = a metal heated and poured into a mould; a solid piece of metal; an ingot (Gujarati) PLUS खांडा [*khāṇḍā*] *m* A jag, notch, or indentation (as upon the edge of a tool or weapon). Rebus: *kāṇḍa* 'tools, pots and pans and metal-ware'
*meḍ 'body' Rebus: meḍ 'iron' (Ho.) काठी [kāṭhī] f (काष्ट S) 'frame or structure of the body' (Marathi) Rebus: खंडी [khaṇḍī] measure of weight (Marathi) கண்டி; kaṇṭi, n. < Mhr. khaṇḍil. [T. Tu. khaṇḍi, M. kaṇḍi.] Candy, a weight, about 500 lbs.*PLUS PLUS | *koḍa* 'one' Rebus: *koḍ* 'workshop'

kharedo = a currycomb (Gujarati) खरारा [*kharārā*] *m* (H) A currycomb. 2 Currying a horse. (Marathi) Rebus: करडा [*karaḍā*] Hard from alloy--iron, silver &c. (Marathi) *kharādī* ' turner' (Gujarati)

kanka 'rim of jar' Rebus: karṇīka 'account (scribe)' karṇī 'supercargo'

h1032a, h62a

खोंड [khōṇḍa] m A young bull, a bullcalf. (Marathi) Rebus: kõdār 'turner' (Bengali); कोंद kōnda 'engraver, lapidary setting or infixing gems' (Marathi) G. sãghāṛɔ m. 'lathe' ; संघाट joinery; M. sãgaḍ 'double-canoe' Rebus: sangataras 'stone-cutter, mason'

||| Numeral three: *kolom* 'three' Rebus: *kolami* 'smithy, forge'.

loa 'ficus religiosa' Rebus: *lo* 'iron' (Sanskrit) PLUS unique ligatures: लोखंड [lōkhaṇḍa] *n* (लोह S) Iron. लोखंडाचे चणे खावविणें or चारणें To oppress grievously.लोखंडकाम [lōkhaṇḍakāma] *n* Iron work; that portion (of a building, machine &c.) which consists of iron. 2 The business of an ironsmith.लोखंडी [lōkhaṇḍī] *a* (लोखंड) Composed of iron; relating to iron. (Marathi)

bhaṭa 'warrior' (Sanskrit) Rebus: *baṭa* a kind of iron (Gujarati). Rebus: *bhaṭa* 'furnace' (Santali)

Thus, together, the ligatured hieroglyph reads rebus: *loa bhaṭa* 'iron furnace'
kanka 'rim of jar' Rebus: karṇīka 'account (scribe)' karṇī 'supercargo'

h642a copper plate. 'Two slanted strokes' hieroglyph: *dhāḷ* 'a slope'; 'inclination of a plane' (Gujarati); *ḍhāḷiyum* = adj. sloping, inclining (Gujarati) Rebus: *ḍhālako* = a large metal ingot (Gujarati) *ḍhālakī* = a metal heated and poured into a mould; a solid piece of metal; an ingot (Gujarati) PLUS dula 'two' Rebus:dul 'cast metal'. Thus, cast metal ingot. | *koḍa* 'one' Rebus: *koḍ* 'workshop'
kolom 'three' Rebus: kolami 'smithy, forge' INFIXED in: kanac 'corner' Rebus: kañcu 'bronze' Thus, bronze smithy-forge
kamaḍha 'archer' Rebus: *kammaṭa* 'mint, coiner'.

|||| Numeral 4: gaṇḍa 'four' Rebus: kaṇḍa 'furnace, fire-altar' (Santali) dula 'pair' Rebus: dul 'cast metal'

Strands of yarn/rope' reading: *dhā´tu* 'strand of

hieroglyph: Hieroglyph: 'strands of yarn' Rebus rope' Rebus: *dhatu* 'mineral ore' (Santali)

खांडा [*khāṇḍā*] *m* A jag, notch, or indentation (as upon the edge of a tool or weapon). Rebus: *kāṇḍa* 'tools, pots and pans and metal-ware'

Chanhudaro 30A *dula* 'pair' Rebus: dul 'cast metal' PLUS *āra* 'spokes' Rebus: *āra 'brass'.* cf. erka = ekke (Tbh. of arka) aka (Tbh. of arka) copper (metal); crystal (Kannada) Glyph: eraka'nave of wheel' Rebus: eraka 'copper'; cf. erka = ekke (Tbh. of arka) aka (Tbh. of arka) copper (metal); crystal (Kannada)

dula 'pair' Rebus: dul 'cast metal'PLUS

loa 'ficus religiosa' Rebus: *lo* 'iron' (Sanskrit) PLUS unique ligatures: लोखंड [lōkhaṇḍa] *n* (लोह S) Iron. लोखंडाचे चणे खावविणें or चारणें To oppress grievously.लोखंडकाम [lōkhaṇḍakāma] *n* Iron work; that portion (of a building, machine &c.) which consists of iron. 2 The business of an ironsmith.लोखंडी [lōkhaṇḍī] *a* (लोखंड) Composed of iron; relating to iron. (Marathi) *bhaṭa* 'warrior' (Sanskrit) Rebus: *baṭa* a kind of iron (Gujarati). Rebus: *bhaṭa* 'furnace' (Santali) Thus, together, the ligatured hieroglyph reads rebus: *loa bhaṭa* 'iron furnace'
sal 'splinter' Rebus: sal 'workshop' dula 'pair' Rebus: dul 'cast metal'. Thus, cast metal workshop.

m1853a *खोंड [khōṇḍa] m A young bull, a bullcalf. (Marathi) Rebus: kõdār 'turner' (Bengali); कोंद kōnda 'engraver, lapidary setting or infixing gems' (Marathi) G. sãghāṛɔ m. 'lathe' ; संघाट joinery; M. sāgaḍ 'double-canoe' Rebus: sangataras 'stone-cutter, mason'*

dula ‘two’ Rebus: dul ‘cast metal’ kolom ‘three’ Rebus: kolami ‘smithy, forge’ Thus, metal smithy castings-forge.

loa ‘ficus religiosa’ Rebus: *lo* ‘iron’ (Sanskrit) PLUS unique ligatures: लोखंड [lōkhaṇḍa] *n* (लोह S) Iron. लोखंडाचे चणे खावविणें or चारणें To oppress grievously.लोखंडकाम [lōkhaṇḍakāma] *n* Iron work; that portion (of a building, machine &c.) which consists of iron. 2 The business of an ironsmith.लोखंडी [lōkhaṇḍī] *a* (लोखंड) Composed of iron; relating to iron. (Marathi) *bhaṭa* ‘warrior’ (Sanskrit) Rebus: *baṭa* a kind of iron (Gujarati). Rebus: *bhaṭa* ‘furnace’ (Santali) Thus, together, the ligatured hieroglyph reads rebus: *loa bhaṭa* ‘iron furnace’

āra 'spokes' Rebus: *āra ‘brass’*. cf. erka = ekke (Tbh. of arka) aka (Tbh. of arka) copper (metal); crystal (Kannada) Glyph: *eraka*’nave of wheel’ Rebus: eraka ‘copper’; cf. erka = ekke (Tbh. of arka) aka (Tbh. of arka) copper (metal); crystal (Kannada) *erako* ‘moltencast copper’ Duplicated: dula ‘pair’ Rebus: dul ‘cast metal’ Thus cast copper, brass casting.

m194A *खोंड [khōṇḍa] m A young bull, a bullcalf. (Marathi) Rebus: kōdār ‘turner’ (Bengali); कोंद kōnda ‘engraver, lapidary setting or infixing gems’ (Marathi) G. sãghārɔ m. ‘lathe’ ; संघाट joinery; M. sãgaḍ ‘double-canoe’ Rebus: sangataras ‘stone-cutter, mason’*

dula ‘two’ Rebus: dul ‘cast metal’ kolom ‘three’ Rebus: kolami ‘smithy, forge’ Thus, metal smithy castings-forge.

kuṭila ‘bent’ CDIAL 3230 kuṭi— in cmpd. ‘curve’, *kuṭika—* ‘bent’ MBh. Rebus: kuṭila, katthīl = bronze (8 parts copper and 2 parts tin) cf. āra-kūṭa, ‘brass’ (Sanskrit)

kanka ‘rim of jar’ Rebus: karṇīka ‘account (scribe)’ karṇī ‘supercargo’

*meḍ ‘body’ Rebus: meḍ ‘iron’ (Ho.) काठी [kāṭhī] f (काष्ट S) ‘frame or structure of the body’ (Marathi) Rebus: खंडी [khaṇḍī] measure of weight (Marathi) கண்டி; kaṇṭi, n. < Mhr. khaṇḍil. [T. Tu. khaṇḍi, M. kaṇḍi.] Candy, a weight, about 500 lbs.*Vikalpa: काठी [kāṭhī] *f* (काष्ट S) frame or structure of the body: also (viewed by some as arising from the preceding sense, Measuring rod) stature.(Marathi) Rebus: काटी or कांटी [kāṭī or kāṇṭī] *a* (In नंदभाषा) Twenty.(Marathi) Measuring twent maunds?

m138A *Read rebus as a tfirst 3 signs of m14A.*

h511a Read rebus as at first 3 signs of m194A

m254a Pictorial motif: *balad* m. ‘ ox ’, gng. *bald*, (Ku.) *barad*, id. (N. Tarai) Rebus: *bharat* (5 copper, 4 zinc and 1 tin)(Punjabi) pattar ‘trough’ Rebus: pattar ‘guild’. Thus, copper-zinc-tin alloy (worker) guild.

dula ‘two’ Rebus: dul ‘cast metal’ kolom ‘three’ Rebus: kolami ‘smithy, forge’ Thus, metal smithy castings-forge.

mogge ‘sprout, bud’ Rebus: *mũh* ‘ingot’

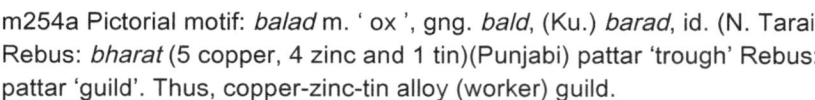

The pair of hieroglyph signs are compositions: *bicha* ‘scorpion’ (Assamese) ebus: *bica* ‘stone ore’ (Santali) The pairing sign is a composition of: sloping stroke PLUS two short strokes of a 'splinter':

dhāḷ 'a slope'; 'inclination of a plane' (Gujarati); *ḍhāḷiyum* = adj. sloping, inclining (Gujarati) Rebus: *ḍhālako* = a large metal ingot (Gujarati) *ḍhālakī* = a metal heated and poured into a mould; a solid piece of metal; an ingot (Gujarati) PLUS *sal* 'splinter' Rebus: *sal* 'workshop'. Thus the composition reads: *ḍhālako sal* 'ingot workshop'.
Togethe, the pair of hieroglyph signs read: *bica ḍhālako sal* 'stone ore ingot workshop'.

m1983a, m404a, h1996A, Kalibangan 19A, m224a read rebus as at first two signs of m254a:

m1983a

m404a

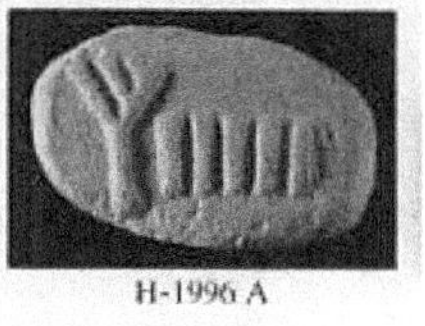

h1996A

Kalibangan 19A

m224a

1368A Read rebus as at m1852A

m1852A खोंड [*khōṇḍa*] *m A young bull, a bullcalf. (Marathi) Rebus: kõdār 'turner' (Bengali);* कोंद *kōnda 'engraver, lapidary setting or infixing gems' (Marathi) G. sãghāṛɔ m. 'lathe' ;* संघाट *joinery; M. sãgaḍ 'double-canoe' Rebus: sangataras 'stone-cutter, mason'*

dula 'two' Rebus: dul 'cast metal' kolom 'three' Rebus: kolami 'smithy, forge' Thus, metal smithy castings-forge.

kuṭila 'bent' CDIAL 3230 *kuṭi—* in cmpd. 'curve', *kuṭika—* 'bent' MBh. Rebus: kuṭila, katthīl = bronze (8 parts copper and 2 parts tin) cf. āra-kūṭa, 'brass' (Sanskrit) kanka 'rim of jar' Rebus: karṇīka 'account (scribe)' karṇī 'supercargo'

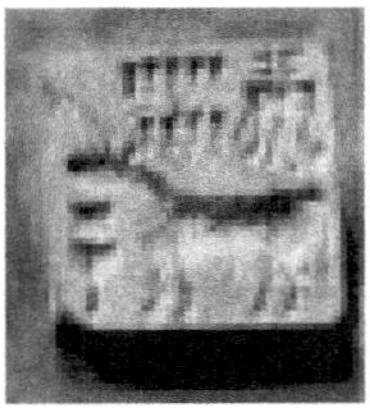

Dholavira *खोंड [khōṇḍa] m A young bull, a bullcalf. (Marathi) Rebus: kõdār 'turner' (Bengali);* कोंद *kōnda 'engraver, lapidary setting or infixing gems' (Marathi) G. sãghāṛɔ m. 'lathe' ;* संघाट *joinery; M. sãgaḍ 'double-canoe' Rebus: sangataras 'stone-cutter, mason'*

dula 'two' Rebus: dul 'cast metal' kolom 'three' Rebus: kolami 'smithy, forge' Thus, metal smithy castings-forge.

gaṇḍa 'four' Rebus: *kaṇḍa* 'furnace, fire-altar' (Santali).

water-carrier hieroglyph *kuṭi*; Rebus: *kuṭhi* 'smelter furnace'. PLUS 'rim of jar':

kanka 'rim of jar' Rebus: karṇīka 'account (scribe)' karṇī 'supercargo'

h4a

खोंड [khōṇḍa] m A young bull, a bullcalf. (Marathi) Rebus: kõdār 'turner' (Bengali); कोंद *kōnda 'engraver, lapidary setting or infixing gems' (Marathi) G. sãghāṛɔ m. 'lathe' ;* संघाट *joinery; M. sãgaḍ 'double-canoe' Rebus: sangataras 'stone-cutter, mason'*

dula 'two' Rebus: dul 'cast metal' kolom 'three' Rebus: kolami 'smithy, forge' Thus, metal smithy castings-forge.

gaṇḍa 'four' Rebus: *kaṇḍa* 'furnace, fire-altar' (Santali).(Note: The significance of two notches flanking the 5+4 numerals is assumed to be a breakup of splinter hieroglyph: sal 'splinter' Rebus: sal 'workshop'. Thus, metal smithy castings-forge workshop.

Read in context, the composite hieroglyph is assumed to be a combination of a slanted stroke ligatured to a notch,which provide possible rebus readings of a smithy/forge: notch+slanted stroke reads rebus: *ḍhālako kāṇḍa* 'ingot, tools, pots and pans and metal-ware'

ḍhāḷ 'a slope'; 'inclination of a plane' (Gujarati); *ḍhāḷiyum* = adj. sloping, inclining (Gujarati) Rebus: *ḍhālako* = a large metal ingot (Gujarati) *ḍhālakī* = a metal heated and poured into a mould; a solid piece of metal; an ingot (Gujarati) PLUS खांडा [*khāṇḍā*] *m* A jag, notch, or indentation (as upon the edge of a tool or weapon). Rebus: *kāṇḍa* 'tools, pots and pans and metal-ware' *ayo* 'fish' Rebus: *aya* 'iron' *ayas* 'metal' (Vedic)

h23a खोंड [khōṇḍa] m A young bull, a bullcalf. (Marathi) Rebus: kõdār 'turner' (Bengali); कोंद kōnda 'engraver, lapidary setting or infixing gems' (Marathi) G. sãghārɔ m. 'lathe' ; संघाट joinery; M. sãgaḍ 'double-canoe' Rebus: sangataras 'stone-cutter, mason'

dula 'two' Rebus: dul 'cast metal' kolom 'three' Rebus: kolami 'smithy, forge' Thus, metal smithy castings-forge.

gaṇḍa 'four' Rebus: *kaṇḍa* 'furnace, fire-altar' (Santali).

mogge 'sprout, bud' Rebus: *mũh* 'ingot'

baraḍo = spine; backbone (Tulu) Rebus: *baran, bharat* 'mixed alloys' (5 copper, 4 zinc and 1 tin) (Punjabi)

*meḍ 'body' Rebus: meḍ 'iron' (Ho.) काठी [kāṭhī] f (काष्ट S) 'frame or structure of the body' (Marathi) Rebus: खंडी [khaṇḍī] measure of weight (Marathi) கண்டி; kaṇṭi, n. < Mhr. khaṇḍil. [T. Tu. khaṇḍi, M. kaṇḍi.] Candy, a weight, about 500 lbs.*eraka 'upraised hand' Rebus: erako

'moltencast copper'

kanka 'rim of jar' Rebus: karṇīka 'account (scribe)' karṇī 'supercargo'

M-955 a

m955a *खोंड [khōṇḍa] m A young bull, a bullcalf. (Marathi) Rebus: kõdār 'turner' (Bengali); कोंद kōnda 'engraver, lapidary setting or infixing gems' (Marathi) G. sãghārɔ m. 'lathe' ; संघाट joinery; M. sãgaḍ 'double-canoe' Rebus: sangataras 'stone-cutter, mason'*

dula 'pair' Rebus: dul 'cast metal'.

koḍa 'one' Rebus: *koḍ* 'workshop'

kamaḍha 'crab' Rebus: *kammaṭa* 'mint, coiner'.

ḍato = claws of crab (Santali) Rebus: dhātu 'mineral ore'

kolom 'three' Rebus: kolami 'smithy, forge'

Lothal 12a *खोंड [khōṇḍa] m A young bull, a bullcalf. (Marathi) Rebus: kõdār 'turner' (Bengali); कोंद kōnda 'engraver, lapidary setting or infixing gems' (Marathi) G. sãghārɔ m. 'lathe' ; संघाट joinery; M. sãgaḍ 'double-canoe' Rebus: sangataras 'stone-cutter, mason'*

dula 'pair' Rebus: dul 'cast metal'.

*meḍ 'body' Rebus: meḍ 'iron' (Ho.) काठी [kāṭhī] f (काष्ट S) 'frame or structure of the body' (Marathi) Rebus: खंडी [khaṇḍī] measure of weight (Marathi) கண்டி; kaṇṭi, n. < Mhr. khaṇḍil. [T. Tu. khaṇḍi, M. kaṇḍi.] Candy, a weight, about 500 lbs.*eraka 'upraised hand' Rebus: erako 'moltencast copper' sal 'splinter Rebus: sal 'workshop'

kolom 'three' Rebus" kolami 'smithy, forge'

dula ‘pair’ Rebus: dul ‘cast metal’

kamaḍha ‘crab’ Rebus: *kammaṭa* ‘mint, coiner’.

ḍato = claws of crab (Santali) Rebus: dhātu ‘mineral ore’

kanka ‘rim of jar’ Rebus: karṇīka ‘account (scribe)’ karṇī ‘supercargo’

M-1725 a

m1725a *खोंड [khōṇḍa] m A young bull, a bullcalf. (Marathi) Rebus: kõdār ‘turner’ (Bengali); कोंद kōnda ‘engraver, lapidary setting or infixing gems’ (Marathi) G. sãghāṛɔ m. ‘lathe’ ; संघाट joinery; M. sāgaḍ ‘double-canoe’ Rebus: sangataras ‘stone-cutter, mason’*

kolom ‘three’ Rebus: kolami ‘smithy, forge’

loa ‘ficus religiosa’ Rebus: *lo* ‘iron’ (Sanskrit) PLUS unique ligatures: लोखंड [lōkhaṇḍa] *n* (लोह S) Iron. लोखंडाचे चणे खावविणें or चारणें To oppress grievously.लोखंडकाम [lōkhaṇḍakāma] *n* Iron work; that portion (of a building, machine &c.) which consists of iron. 2 The business of an ironsmith.लोखंडी [lōkhaṇḍī] *a* (लोखंड) Composed of iron; relating to iron. (Marathi) *bhaṭa* ‘warrior’ (Sanskrit) Rebus: *baṭa* a kind of iron (Gujarati). Rebus: *bhaṭa* ‘furnace’ (Santali) Thus, together, the ligatured hieroglyph reads rebus: *loa bhaṭa* ‘iron furnace’

meḍ ‘body’ Rebus: meḍ ‘iron’

kanka ‘rim of jar’ Rebus: karṇīka ‘account (scribe)’ karṇī ‘supercargo’

khareḍo = a currycomb (Gujarati) खरारा [*kharārā*] *m* (H) A currycomb. 2 Currying a horse. (Marathi) Rebus: करडा [*karaḍā*] Hard from alloy--iron, silver &c. (Marathi) *kharādī* ‘ turner’ (Gujarati)

’Wide-mouthed, rimless pot with infixed three numeral strokes’ sign hieroglyph

kolom ‘three’ Rebus: *kolami* ‘smithy, forge’ infixed in:*baṭa* ‘rimless, broad-mouthed pot’ Rebus: *bhaṭa* ‘furnace’ (Gujarati.); *baṭa* ‘a kind of iron’ (Gujarati)

m297a *खोंड [khōṇḍa] m A young bull, a bullcalf. (Marathi) Rebus: kõdār ‘turner’ (Bengali); कोंद kōnda ‘engraver, lapidary setting or infixing gems’ (Marathi) G. sãghāṛɔ m. ‘lathe’ ; संघाट joinery; M. sāgaḍ ‘double-canoe’ Rebus: sangataras ‘stone-cutter, mason’*

The ‘young bull’ hieroglyph is ligatures to ‘octopus’ hieroglyph: m297a: Seal h1018a: copper plate

veṛhā octopus, said to be found in the Indus (Jaṭki lexicon of A. Jukes, 1900) Rebus: *beṛɔ* m. ‘palace’ (WPah); L. *veṛh*, *vehṛ* m. fencing; Mth. *beṛhī* granary;

L. *veṛhā*, *vehṛā* enclosure containing many houses; *beṛā* building with a courtyard (Western Pahari) (CDIAL 12130)

beṛ ‘fence, enclosure’, *beṛā* ‘fence, hedge’ (Bengali)(CDIAL 12130) Rebus: *beṛhi* ‘granary’ (Maithili)

vēṣṭá— ‘enclosure’ lex., *°aka-* m. ‘fence’, Si. *veṭya* ‘enclosure’; — Pa. *vēṭhaka*— ‘surrounding’; S. *veṛhu* m. ‘encircling’; L. *veṛh*, *vehṛ* m. ‘fencing, enclosure in jungle with a hedge, (Ju.)

blockade', *veṛhā*, *vehṛā* m. 'courtyard, (Ju.) enclosure containing many houses'; P. *veṛhā*, *be°* m. 'enclosure, courtyard'; Ku. *beṛo* 'circle or band (of people)'; A. *beṛ* 'wall of house, circumference of anything'; B. *beṛ* 'fence, enclosure', *beṛā* 'fence, hedge'; Or. *beṛha* 'fence round young trees', *beṛā* 'wall of house'; Mth. *beṛ* 'hedge, wall', *beṛhī* 'granary'; H. *beṛh*, *beṛ*, *beṛhā*, *beṛā* m. 'enclosure, cattle surrounded and carried off by force'; M. *veḍh* m. 'circumference'; WPah.kṭg. *beṛɔ* m. 'palace', J. *beṛā* m. 'id., esp. the female apartments', kul. *beṛā* 'building with a courtyard'; A. also *berā* 'fence, enclosure' (CDIAL 12130) *Konḍa* velgu gōḍa com- pound wall. (DEDR 5538) *Ka.* baḷasu to be surrounded, surround;*n.* act of surrounding or encom- passing, what surrounds, state of being circuitous, one round or turn (as of a rope, etc.); balepuni to enclose, surround, besiege. *Te.* balayu to surround, (K. also) besiege; (K.)(DEDR 5313).

 Read in context, the composite hieroglyph is assumed to be a combination of a slanted stroke ligatured to a notch,which provide possible rebus readings of a smithy/forge: notch+slanted stroke reads rebus: *ḍhālako kāṇḍa* 'ingot, tools, pots and pans and metal-ware'

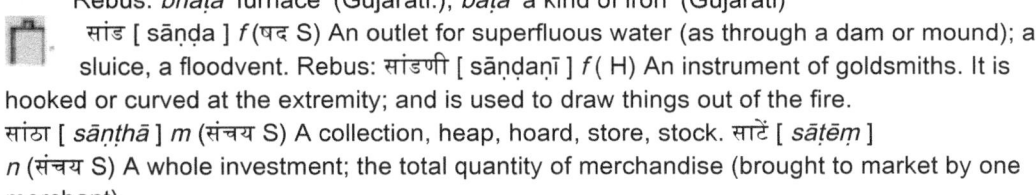

dhāḷ 'a slope'; 'inclination of a plane' (Gujarati); *ḍhāḷiyum* = adj. sloping, inclining (Gujarati) Rebus: *ḍhālako* = a large metal ingot (Gujarati) *ḍhālakī* = a metal heated and poured into a mould; a solid piece of metal; an ingot (Gujarati)PLUS खांडा [*khāṇḍā*] *m* A jag, notch, or indentation (as upon the edge of a tool or weapon). Rebus: *kāṇḍa* 'tools, pots and pans and metal-ware'

 'Wide-mouthed, rimless pot with infixed three numeral strokes' sign hieroglyph *kolom* 'three' Rebus: *kolami* 'smithy, forge' infixed in: *baṭa* 'rimless, broad-mouthed pot' Rebus: *bhaṭa* 'furnace' (Gujarati.); *baṭa* 'a kind of iron' (Gujarati)

 सांड [sāṇḍa] *f* (षंद S) An outlet for superfluous water (as through a dam or mound); a sluice, a floodvent. Rebus: सांडणी [sāṇḍaṇī] *f* (H) An instrument of goldsmiths. It is hooked or curved at the extremity; and is used to draw things out of the fire. सांठा [*sāṇṭhā*] *m* (संचय S) A collection, heap, hoard, store, stock. साटें [*sāṭēṃ*] *n* (संचय S) A whole investment; the total quantity of merchandise (brought to market by one merchant).

aya kammaṭa.'coiner, mint alloy'
kanka 'rim of jar' Rebus: karṇīka 'account (scribe)' karṇī 'supercargo'
meḍ 'body' Rebus: *meḍ* 'iron' (Ho.)

m1135a A composite animal: tusk of a boar, body of young bull, feet of elephant, ears of a donkey. khara 'donkey' Rebus: kara 'blacksmith' (Kashmiri) *खोंडी [khōṇḍī] f An outspread shovelform sack (as formed temporarily out of a कांबळा, to hold or fend off grain, chaff &c.) (Marathi) koḍiyum 'rings on neck' (Gujarati) kondh 'heifer'. kōḍu horn (Kannada. Tulu. Tamil) खोंड [khōṇḍa] m A young bull, a bullcalf. (Marathi) Rebus: kōdār 'turner' (Bengali); kōdā 'to turn in a lathe' (Bengali). कोंद kōnda 'engraver, lapidary setting or infixing gems' (Marathi)* G. *sãghāṛɔ* m. 'lathe' ; *sãgāḍā* m. ' frame of a building ', *°ḍī* f. ' lathe '(CDIAL 12859) Rebus*: sangataras.* संगतराश lit. 'to collect stones, stone-cutter, mason.' Rhinoceros/boar: baḍhia = a castrated boar, a hog (Santali) baḍhi 'a caste who work both in iron and wood' (Santali) *baṟea* 'merchant' *ibha* 'elephant' Rebus: *ib* 'iron' *ibbo* 'merchant' (Gujarati)

'Wide-mouthed, rimless pot with infixed three numeral strokes' sign hieroglyph *kolom* 'three' Rebus: *kolami* 'smithy, forge' infixed in: *baṭa* 'rimless, broad-mouthed pot' Rebus: *bhaṭa* 'furnace' (Gujarati.); *baṭa* 'a kind of iron' (Gujarati)

khareḍo = a currycomb (Gujarati) खरारा [*kharārā*] *m* (H) A currycomb. 2 Currying a horse. (Marathi) Rebus: करडा [*karaḍā*] Hard from alloy--iron, silver &c. (Marathi) *kharādī* ' turner' (Gujarati)
sal 'splinter' Rebus: sal 'workshop'

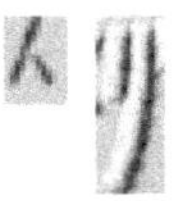
notch+slanted stroke reads rebus: *ḍhālako kāṇḍa* 'ingot, tools, pots and pans and metal-ware'.*dhāḷ* 'a slope'; 'inclination of a plane' (G.); *ḍhāḷiyum* = adj. sloping, inclining (G.) Rebus: *ḍhālako* = a large metal ingot (G.) *ḍhālakī* = a metal heated and poured into a mould; a solid piece of metal; an ingot (Gujarati) PLUS खांडा [*khāṇḍā*] *m* A jag, notch, or indentation (as upon the edge of a tool or weapon). Rebus: *kāṇḍa* 'tools, pots and pans and metal-ware'

kanka 'rim of jar' Rebus: karṇīka 'account (scribe)' karṇī 'supercargo'

Surkotada 2A

kanka 'rim of jar' Rebus: karṇīka 'account (scribe)' karṇī 'supercargo'

dula 'pair' Rebus: *dul* 'cast (metal)' PLUS*kana, kanac* = corner (Santali); Rebus: *kañcu* = bronze (Telugu) PLUS infixed kolmo 'paddy plant' Rebus: kolami 'smithy, forge'. Thus, cast bronze smithy, forge. Or, *mogge* 'sprout, bud' Rebus: *mũh* 'ingot' (Santali)Thus, cast bronze ingot. Read as: *kañcu dul mũh 'bronze cast ingot'*

kolmo 'paddy plant' Rebus: *kolami* 'smithy, forge' Vikalpa: *mogge* 'sprout, bud' Rebus: *mũh* 'ingot' (Santali) dolu 'plant of shoot height' Rebus: dul 'cast metal'

dhāḷ 'a slope'; 'inclination of a plane' (G.); *ḍhāḷiyum* = adj. sloping, inclining (G.) Rebus: *ḍhālako* = a large metal ingot (G.) *ḍhālakī* = a metal heated and poured into a mould; a solid piece of metal; an ingot (Gujarati) PLUS खांडा [*khāṇḍā*] *m* A jag, notch, or indentation (as upon the edge of a tool or weapon). Rebus: *kāṇḍa* 'tools, pots and pans and metal-ware' Thus, the pair of sign hieroglyphs from r. read rebus: copper, bronze ingots, metalware castings.
kanka (Santali) *karṇika* 'scribe'(Sanskrit) Rebus: *karṇī,* supercargo for a boat shipment. INFIXED खांडा [*khāṇḍā*] *m* A jag, notch, or indentation (as upon the edge of a tool or weapon). Rebus: *kāṇḍa* 'tools, pots and pans and metal-ware'

h3a*खोंडी [khōṇḍī] f An outspread shovelform sack (as formed temporarily out of a कांबळा, to hold or fend off grain, chaff &c.) (Marathi) koḍiyum 'rings on neck' (Gujarati) kondh 'heifer'. kōḍu horn (Kannada. Tulu. Tamil) खोंड [khōṇḍa] m A young*

bull, a bullcalf. (Marathi) Rebus: kõdār 'turner' (Bengali); kõdā 'to turn in a lathe' (Bengali). कोंद kōnda 'engraver, lapidary setting or infixing gems' (Marathi) G. *sãghāṛɔ* m. 'lathe' ; *sãgāḍā* m. ' frame of a building ', *°ḍī* f. ' lathe '(CDIAL 12859) Rebus*: sangataras.* संगतराश lit. 'to collect stones, stone-cutter, mason.'

'Wide-mouthed, rimless pot with infixed three numeral strokes' sign hieroglyph *kolom* 'three' Rebus: *kolami* 'smithy, forge' infixed in: *baṭa* 'rimless, broad-mouthed pot' Rebus: *bhaṭa* 'furnace' (Gujarati.); *baṭa* 'a kind of iron' (Gujarati)

khaṇḍ 'field, division' (Skt.) Rebus: *khānḍa* 'tools, pots and pans, metal-ware'. Rebus 2: kaṇḍ 'fire-altar' (Santali) dula 'pair' Rebus: dul 'cast metal' Thus cast metalware or metalware castings.

khuṇṭī or khuṭī a peg or wooden pin (Marathi) *kuṭhi* 'smelting furnace'; *koṭe* 'forged (metal) (Santali)
sal 'splinter' Rebus: sal 'workshop'

|||| Numeral 4: gaṇḍa 'four' Rebus: kaṇḍa 'furnace, fire-altar' (Santali)
||| kolom 'three' Rebus: kolami 'smithy, forge'

सांड [sāṇḍa] *f* (षद S) An outlet for superfluous water (as through a dam or mound); a sluice, a floodvent. Rebus: सांडणी [sāṇḍaṇī] *f* (H) An instrument of goldsmiths. It is hooked or curved at the extremity; and is used to draw things out of the fire.
सांठा [*sāṇṭhā*] *m* (संचय S) A collection, heap, hoard, store, stock.साटें [*sāṭēṃ*] *n* (संचय S) A whole investment; the total quantity of merchandise (brought to market by one merchant).

kanka 'rim of jar' Rebus: *karṇīka* 'account (scribe)' *karṇī* 'supercargo'

M-1785 a

m1785a *खोंडी [khōṇḍī] f An outspread shovelform sack (as formed temporarily out of a कांबळा, to hold or fend off grain, chaff &c.) (Marathi) koḍiyum 'rings on neck' (Gujarati) kondh 'heifer'. kōḍu horn (Kannada. Tulu. Tamil) खोंड [khōṇḍa] m A young bull, a bullcalf. (Marathi) Rebus: kõdār 'turner' (Bengali); kõdā 'to turn in a lathe' (Bengali). कोंद kōnda 'engraver, lapidary setting or infixing gems' (Marathi)* G. *sãghāṛɔ* m. 'lathe' ; *sãgāḍā* m. ' frame of a building ', *°ḍī* f. ' lathe '(CDIAL 12859) Rebus*: sangataras.* संगतराश lit. 'to collect stones, stone-cutter, mason.'
Wide-mouthed, rimless pot with infixed two numeral strokes' sign hieroglyph: isal 'splinter' Rebus: sal 'workshop' nfixed in: *baṭa* 'rimless, broad-mouthed pot' Rebus: *bhaṭa* 'furnace' (Gujarati.); *baṭa* 'a kind of iron' (Gujarati) kolom 'three' Rebus: kolami 'smithy, forge' PLUS *ḍhālako kānḍa* 'ingot, tools, pots and pans and metal-ware'.*dhāḷ* 'a slope'; 'inclination of a plane' (G.); *ḍhāḷiyum* = adj. sloping, inclining (G.) Rebus: *ḍhālako* = a large metal ingot (G.) *ḍhālakī* = a metal heated and poured into a mould; a solid piece of metal; an ingot (Gujarati)

Thus, ingot smithy.
aḍar 'harrow'; rebus: *aduru* 'native unsmelted metal'

kanka ‘rim of jar’ Rebus: karṇīka ‘account (scribe)’ karṇī ‘supercargo’

dulo ‘hole’ Rebus: dul ‘cast metal’ PLUS | *koḍa* ‘one’ Rebus: *koḍ* ‘workshop’

Variant:

kuṭila ‘bent’ CDIAL 3230 kuṭi— in cmpd. ‘curve’, *kuṭika—* ‘bent’ MBh. Rebus: *kuṭila, katthīl* = bronze (8 parts copper and 2 parts tin) Duplicated: dula ‘pair’ Rebus: dul ‘cast metal’ Thus, cast bronze or bronze castings.

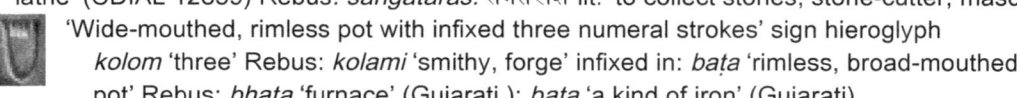

h87A : *rāngo* ‘water buffalo bull’ (Ku.N.)(CDIAL 10559) Rebus: rango ‘pewter’

‘Wide-mouthed, rimless pot with infixed three numeral strokes’ sign hieroglyph

kolom ‘three’ Rebus: *kolami* ‘smithy, forge’ infixed in: *baṭa* ‘rimless, broad-mouthed pot’ Rebus: *bhaṭa* ‘furnace’ (Gujarati.); *baṭa* ‘a kind of iron’ (Gujarati)

khaṇḍ ‘field, division’ (Skt.) Rebus: *khānḍa* ‘tools, pots and pans, metal-ware’. Rebus 2: kaṇḍ 'fire-altar' (Santali) dula ‘pair’ Rebus: dul ‘cast metal’ Thus cast metalware or metalware castings.

kanka ‘rim of jar’ Rebus: *karṇīka* ‘account (scribe)’ *karṇī* ‘supercargo’

M-1815 a

m1815a *खोंडी [khōṇḍī] f An outspread shovelform sack (as formed temporarily out of a कांबळा, to hold or fend off grain, chaff &c.) (Marathi) koḍiyum ‘rings on neck’ (Gujarati) kondh ‘heifer’. kōḍu horn (Kannada. Tulu. Tamil) खोंड [khōṇḍa] m A young bull, a bullcalf. (Marathi) Rebus: kõdār ‘turner’ (Bengali); kõdā ‘to turn in a lathe’ (Bengali). कोंद kōnda ‘engraver, lapidary setting or infixing gems’ (Marathi)* G. *sãghāṛɔ* m. ‘lathe’ ; *sãgāḍā* m. ‘ frame of a building ’, *°ḍī* f. ‘ lathe ’(CDIAL 12859) Rebus*: sangataras.* संगतराश lit. ‘to collect stones, stone-cutter, mason.’

‘Wide-mouthed, rimless pot with infixed three numeral strokes’ sign hieroglyph

kolom ‘three’ Rebus: *kolami* ‘smithy, forge’ infixed in: *baṭa* ‘rimless, broad-mouthed pot’ Rebus: *bhaṭa* ‘furnace’ (Gujarati.); *baṭa* ‘a kind of iron’ (Gujarati)

khaṇḍ ‘field, division’ (Skt.) Rebus: *khānḍa* ‘tools, pots and pans, metal-ware’. Rebus 2: kaṇḍ 'fire-altar' (Santali) dula ‘pair’ Rebus: dul ‘cast metal’ Thus cast metalware or metalware castings.

baṭa ‘rimless, broad-mouthed pot’ Rebus: *bhaṭa* ‘furnace’ (Gujarati.); *baṭa* ‘a kind of iron’ (Gujarati)

m9a *खोंडी [khōṇḍī] f An outspread shovelform sack (as formed temporarily out of a कांबळा, to hold or fend off grain, chaff &c.) (Marathi) koḍiyum ‘rings on neck’ (Gujarati) kondh ‘heifer’. kōḍu horn (Kannada. Tulu. Tamil) खोंड [khōṇḍa] m A young bull, a bullcalf. (Marathi) Rebus: kõdār ‘turner’ (Bengali); kõdā ‘to turn in a lathe’ (Bengali). कोंद kōnda ‘engraver, lapidary setting or infixing gems’ (Marathi)* G. *sãghāṛɔ* m. ‘lathe’ ; *sãgāḍā* m. ‘ frame of a building ’, *°ḍī* f. ‘ lathe ’(CDIAL 12859) Rebus*: sangataras.* संगतराश lit. ‘to collect stones, stone-cutter, mason.’

kolom 'three' Rebus: *kolami* 'smithy, forge' infixed in:

 kanka 'rim of jar' Rebus: karṇīka 'account (scribe)' karṇī 'supercargo'
Thus, supercargo of smithy, forge.

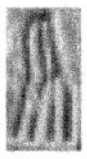  Strands of yarn/rope' hieroglyph: Hieroglyph: 'strands of yarn' Rebus reading: *dhā'tu* 'strand of rope' Rebus: *dhatu* 'mineral ore' (Santali)
PLUS | *koḍa* 'one' Rebus: *koḍ* 'workshop'

m862a खोंडी *[khōṇḍī] f An outspread shovelform sack (as formed temporarily out of a* कांबळा*, to hold or fend off grain, chaff &c.) (Marathi) koḍiyum 'rings on neck' (Gujarati) kondh 'heifer'. kōḍu horn (Kannada. Tulu. Tamil)* खोंड *[khōṇḍa] m A young bull, a bullcalf. (Marathi) Rebus: kōdār 'turner' (Bengali); kōdā 'to turn in a lathe' (Bengali).* कोंद *kōnda 'engraver, lapidary setting or infixing gems' (Marathi)* G. *sãghāṛɔ* m. 'lathe' ; *sãgāḍā* m. ' frame of a building ', *°ḍī* f. ' lathe '(CDIAL 12859) Rebus*: sangataras.* संगतराश lit. 'to collect stones, stone-cutter, mason.'
sal 'splinter' Rebus: sal 'workshop' INFIXED in:

 kanka 'rim of jar' Rebus: karṇīka 'account (scribe)' karṇī 'supercargo' Thus, workshop supercargo.

 *dula* 'pair' Rebus: dul 'cast metal' *mogge* 'sprout, bud' Rebus: *mũh* 'ingot' (Santali) Thus, cast metal ingot.

 kanka 'rim of jar' Rebus: karṇīka 'account (scribe)' karṇī 'supercargo'

m1700a खोंडी *[khōṇḍī] f An outspread shovelform sack (as formed temporarily out of a* कांबळा*, to hold or fend off grain, chaff &c.) (Marathi) koḍiyum 'rings on neck' (Gujarati) kondh 'heifer'. kōḍu horn (Kannada. Tulu. Tamil)* खोंड *[khōṇḍa] m A young bull, a bullcalf. (Marathi) Rebus: kōdār 'turner' (Bengali); kōdā 'to turn in a lathe' (Bengali).* कोंद *kōnda 'engraver, lapidary setting or infixing gems' (Marathi)* G. *sãghāṛɔ* m. 'lathe' ; *sãgāḍā* m. ' frame of a building ', *°ḍī* f. ' lathe '(CDIAL 12859) Rebus*: sangataras.* संगतराश lit. 'to collect stones, stone-cutter, mason.'
kolom 'three' Rebus: *kolami* 'smithy, forge' infixed in:

 kanka 'rim of jar' Rebus: karṇīka 'account (scribe)' karṇī 'supercargo'
Thus, supercargo of smithy, forge.
kamaḍha 'archer, bow' Rebus: *kammaṭa* 'mint, coiner'.

 *kharedo* = a currycomb (Gujarati) खरारा [*kharārā*] *m* (H) A currycomb. 2 Currying a horse. (Marathi) Rebus: करडा [*karaḍā*] Hard from alloy--iron, silver &c. (Marathi) *kharādī* ' turner' (Gujarati)

m1822a खोंडी *[khōṇḍī] f An outspread shovelform sack (as formed temporarily out of a* कांबळा*, to hold or fend off grain, chaff &c.) (Marathi) koḍiyum 'rings on neck' (Gujarati) kondh 'heifer'. kōḍu horn (Kannada. Tulu. Tamil)* खोंड *[khōṇḍa] m A young bull, a bullcalf. (Marathi) Rebus: kõdār 'turner' (Bengali); kõdā 'to turn in a lathe' (Bengali).* कोंद *kōnda 'engraver, lapidary setting or infixing gems' (Marathi)* G. *sãghāṛɔ* m. 'lathe' ; *sãgāḍā* m. ' frame of a building ', *°ḍī* f. ' lathe '(CDIAL 12859) Rebus*: sangataras.* संगतराश lit. 'to collect stones, stone-cutter, mason.'

sal 'splinter' Rebus: sal 'workshop' PLUS *baṭa* = rimless pot (Kannada) Rebus:) *baṭa* = a kind of iron (G.)) *bhaṭa* furnace (Gujarati)

 अगडा [agaḍā] *m* The tie connecting the जूं & दांडी of a गाडा or load-cart; the shaft and thill-yoke-tie. Rebus: 'lumber, miscellaneous articles': अगडतगड [*agaḍatagaḍa*] *n* अगडबगड *n* (Fanciful formations, or from H) Trash, trumpery, rubbish, lumber, miscellaneous articles.
dula 'pair' Rebus: dul 'cast metal' PLUS *ḍhālako kāṇḍa* 'ingot, tools, pots and pans and metal-ware'.*dhāḷ* 'a slope'; 'inclination of a plane' (G.); *ḍhāḷiyum* = adj. sloping, inclining (G.) Rebus: *ḍhālako* = a large metal ingot (G.) *ḍhālakī* = a metal heated and poured into a mould; a solid piece of metal; an ingot (Gujarati) Thus, metal ingot castings. PLUS | *koḍa* 'one' Rebus: *koḍ* 'workshop'

Kalibangan 43a Composite animal. खोंडी *[khōṇḍī] f An outspread shovelform sack (as formed temporarily out of a* कांबळा*, to hold or fend off grain, chaff &c.) (Marathi) koḍiyum 'rings on neck' (Gujarati) kondh 'heifer'. kōḍu horn (Kannada. Tulu. Tamil)* खोंड *[khōṇḍa] m A young bull, a bullcalf. (Marathi) Rebus: kõdār 'turner' (Bengali); kõdā 'to turn in a lathe' (Bengali).* कोंद *kōnda 'engraver, lapidary setting or infixing gems' (Marathi)* G. *sãghāṛɔ* m. 'lathe' ; *sãgāḍā* m. ' frame of a building ', *°ḍī* f. ' lathe '(CDIAL 12859) Rebus*: sangataras.* संगतराश lit. 'to collect stones, stone-cutter, mason.'

balad m. ' ox ', gng. *bald*, (Ku.) *barad*, id. (N. Tarai) Rebus: *bharat* (5 copper, 4 zinc and 1 tin)(Punjabi) *pattar* 'trough' Rebus*: pattar* 'guild'. Thus, copper-zinc-tin alloy (worker) guild.

miṇḍāl 'markhor' (Tōrwālī) *meḍho* a ram, a sheep (G.)(CDIAL 10120) Rebus: *mẽṛhẽt, meḍ* 'iron' (Mu.Ho.)

dulo 'hole' Rebus: dul 'cast metal' PHONETIC reinforcement: dula 'pair' Rebus: dul 'cast metal PLUS
sal 'splinter' Rebus: sal 'workshop' PLUS *baṭa* = rimless pot (Kannada) Rebus:) *baṭa* = a kind of iron (G.)) *bhaṭa* furnace (Gujarati)

dula 'pair' Rebus: dul 'cast metal' *mogge* 'sprout, bud' Rebus: *mūh* 'ingot' (Santali) Thus, cast metal ingot.

 kanka 'rim of jar' Rebus: karṇīka 'account (scribe)' karṇī 'supercargo'
sal 'splinter' Rebus: sal 'workshop' INFIXED in:

 kanka 'rim of jar' Rebus: karṇīka 'account (scribe)' karṇī 'supercargo' Thus, workshop supercargo.
dula 'two' Rebus: dul 'cast metal' (DUPLICATED): *kamaḍha* 'crab' Rebus: *kammaṭa* 'mint, coiner'.
ḍato = claws of crab (Santali) Rebus: *dhātu* 'mineral ore'
Thus, mineral ore, mint castings

h1981A Side A: gaṇḍa 'four' Rebus: kaṇḍa 'furnace, fire-altar' (Santali) *baṭa* = rimless pot (Kannada) Rebus: *baṭa* = a kind of iron (G.)) *bhaṭa* furnace (Gujarati)

dulo 'hole' Rebus: dul 'cast metal'

Side B: gaṇḍa 'four' Rebus: kaṇḍa 'furnace, fire-altar' (Santali)*baṭa* = rimless pot (Kannada) Rebus: *baṭa* = a kind of iron (G.)) *bhaṭa* furnace (Gujarati)
kaṇḍo 'stool, seat' Rebus: *kāṇḍa* 'metalware' *kaṇḍa* 'fire-altar' PLUS dulo 'pair' Rebus; dul 'cast metal' PLUS *kamaḍha* 'crab' Rebus: *kammaṭa* 'mint, coiner'.
ḍato = claws of crab (Santali) Rebus: *dhātu* 'mineral ore' Thus, mineral, mint, metalware furnace

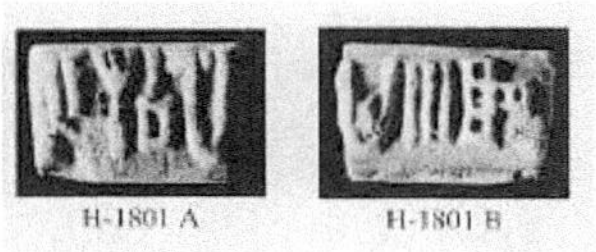

h1801A sal 'splinter' Rebus: sal 'workshop'

 *kolmo* 'paddy plant' Rebus: *kolami* 'smithy, forge' Vikalpa: *mogge* 'sprout, bud' Rebus: *mūh* 'ingot' (Santali) dolu 'plant of shoot height' Rebus: dul 'cast metal'
ranku 'liquid measure' Rebus: ranku 'tin' 'rim-of-jar' hieroglyph *kanka* (Santali)

 *kanka* (Santali) *karṇika* 'scribe'(Sanskrit) Rebus: *karṇī,* supercargo for a boat shipment. INFIXED खांडा [*khāṇḍā*] *m* A jag, notch, or indentation (as upon the edge of a tool or weapon). Rebus: *kāṇḍa* 'tools, pots and pans and metal-ware' *baṭa* = rimless pot (Kannada) Rebus: *baṭa* = a kind of iron (G.)) *bhaṭa* furnace (Gujarati) INFIXED: *ḍato* = claws of crab (Santali) Rebus: *dhātu* 'mineral ore'
kolom 'three' Rebus: kolami 'smithy, forge'

dula 'pair' Rebus: dul 'cast metal' PLUS | *koḍa* 'one' Rebus: *koḍ* 'workshop' PLUS INFIXED kolom
'three' Rebus: kolami 'smithy, forge' Thus metware castings forge. PLUS dula 'pair' Rebus: dul 'cast metal' PLUS | *koḍa* 'one' Rebus: *koḍ* 'workshop' PLUS INFIXED खांडा [*khāṇḍā*] *m* A jag, notch, or indentation (as upon the edge of a tool or weapon). Rebus: *kāṇḍa* 'tools, pots and pans and metal-ware' Thus metware castings workshop.

H-519 A

h519A *baṭa* = rimless pot (Kannada) Rebus: *baṭa* = a kind of iron (G.)) *bhaṭa* furnace (Gujarati)

 kanka 'rim of jar' Rebus: karṇīka 'account (scribe)' karṇī 'supercargo'
| *koḍa* 'one' Rebus: *koḍ* 'workshop'PLUS dula 'two' Rebus: dul 'cast metal' PLUS *ḍhālako kāṇḍa* 'ingot, tools, pots and pans and metal-ware'.*dhāḷ* 'a slope'; 'inclination of a plane' (G.); *ḍhāḷiyum* = adj. sloping, inclining (G.) Rebus: *ḍhālako* = a large metal ingot (G.) *ḍhālakī* = a metal heated and poured into a mould; a solid piece of metal; an ingot (Gujarati) Thus, ingot, metal castings.

 mēḍu height, rising ground, hillock (Kannada) Rebus: *mẽṛhẽt, meḍ* 'iron' (Munda.Ho.) LIGATURE:

 kanka 'rim of jar' Rebus: karṇīka 'account (scribe)' karṇī 'supercargo'

M-519 A

m519A Copper plate.

 *khaṇḍ* 'field, division' (Skt.) Rebus: *khāṇḍa* 'tools, pots and pans, metal-ware'. Rebus 2: kaṇḍ 'fire-altar' (Santali) dula 'pair' Rebus: dul 'cast metal' Thus, duplicated 'division' hieroglyph sign reads: cast metal metal-ware.

 *meḍ* 'body' Rebus: *meḍ* 'iron' (Ho.) काठी [kāṭhī] *f* (काष्ट S) 'frame or structure of the body' (Marathi) Rebus: खंडी [khaṇḍī] measure of weight (Marathi) கண்டி; *kaṇṭi, n. < Mhr. khaṇḍil. [T. Tu. khaṇḍi, M. kaṇḍi.]* Candy, a weight, stated to be roughly equivalent to 500 lbs. PLUS *baṭa* = rimless pot (Kannada) Rebus: *baṭa* = a kind of iron (G.)) *bhaṭa* furnace (Gujarati)

ranku 'liquid measure' Rebus: ranku 'tin'

eraka 'upraised arm' Rebus: erako 'moltencast copper' PLUS

 *meḍ* 'body' Rebus: *meḍ* 'iron' (Ho.) काठी [kāṭhī] *f* (काष्ट S) 'frame or structure of the body' (Marathi) Rebus: खंडी [khaṇḍī] measure of weight (Marathi) கண்டி; *kaṇṭi, n. < Mhr. khaṇḍil. [T. Tu. khaṇḍi, M. kaṇḍi.]* Candy, a weight, stated to be roughly equivalent to 500 lbs.

baṭa = rimless pot (Kannada) Rebus: *baṭa* = a kind of iron (G.)) *bhaṭa* furnace (Gujarati)

 kanka 'rim of jar' Rebus: karṇīka 'account (scribe)' karṇī 'supercargo'

L-217 B

Lothal 217B *खोंडी [khōṇḍī] f An outspread shovelform sack (as formed temporarily out of a कांबळा, to hold or fend off grain, chaff &c.) (Marathi) koḍiyum 'rings on neck' (Gujarati) kondh 'heifer'. kōḍu horn (Kannada. Tulu. Tamil) खोंड [khōṇḍa] m A young bull, a bullcalf. (Marathi) Rebus: kõdār 'turner' (Bengali); kõdā 'to turn in a lathe' (Bengali). कोंद kōnda 'engraver, lapidary setting or infixing gems' (Marathi)* G. *sãghāṛɔ* m. 'lathe' ; *sãgāḍā* m. ' frame of a building ', *°ḍī* f. ' lathe '(CDIAL 12859) Rebus*: sangataras.* संगतराश lit. 'to collect stones, stone-cutter, mason.'

balad m. ' ox ', gng. *bald,* (Ku.) *barad,* id. (N. Tarai) Rebus: *bharat* (5 copper, 4 zinc and 1 tin)(Punjabi) *pattar* 'trough' Rebus*: pattar* 'guild'. Thus, copper-zinc-tin alloy (worker) guild.

'Wide-mouthed, rimless pot with infixed three numeral strokes' sign hieroglyph *kolom* 'three' Rebus: *kolami* 'smithy, forge' infixed in: *baṭa* 'rimless, broad-mouthed pot' Rebus: *bhaṭa* 'furnace' (Gujarati.); *baṭa* 'a kind of iron' (Gujarati)

meḍ 'body' Rebus: *meḍ* 'iron' (Ho.) काठी [kāṭhī] *f* (काष्ट S) 'frame or structure of the body' (Marathi) Rebus: खंडी [khaṇḍī] measure of weight (Marathi) *கண்டி; kaṇṭi, n. < Mhr. khaṇḍil. [T. Tu. khaṇḍi, M. kaṇḍi.]* Candy, a weight, stated to be roughly equivalent to 500 lbs.

kanka 'rim of jar' Rebus: karṇīka 'account (scribe)' karṇī 'supercargo'

baṭa 'rimless, broad-mouthed pot' Rebus: *bhaṭa* 'furnace' (Gujarati.); *baṭa* 'a kind of iron' (Gujarati)

m1103A

Text 1337 *khũṭ* 'zebu' Rebus: '(native metal) guild'

कोठी [kōṭhī] *f* (कोष्ट S) A granary, garner, storehouse, warehouse, treasury, factory, bank. 2 The grain and provisions (as of an army); the commissariatsupplies. Ex.लशकराची कोठी चालली-उतरली- आली-लुटली. 3 The chamber (of a gun, of pipes, of tubes): also the hold or capacity (of a ship, cart, barrow). 4 A chamber, cell, or compartment of the body; of which seventy-two are enumerated. Ex. आतां बाहत्तर कोठ्यांची शुद्धि पिंडामध्यें. 5 A large oblong bamboo basket, to hold rice &c. 6 A common term for the squares in a मिठागर or saltern-enclosure. Rebus: खोटसाळ [khōṭasāḷa] *a* (खोट & साळ from शाला) Alloyed.

muka 'ladle' (Tamil)(DEDR 4887) Rebus: *mũh* 'ingot' (Santali) *baṭa* = rimless pot (Kannada) Rebus: *baṭa* = a kind of iron (G.)) *bhaṭa* furnace (Gujarati) Thus, iron ingot.

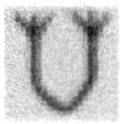

dula 'pair' Rebus: dul 'cast (metal)' kolmo 'rice plant' Rebus: kolami 'smithy/forge' metal.

ranku 'liquid measure' Rebus: ranku 'tin'

āra 'spokes' Rebus: *āra 'brass'.* cf. erka = ekke (Tbh. of arka) aka (Tbh. of arka) copper (metal); crystal (Kannada) Glyph: eraka'nave of wheel' Rebus: eraka 'copper'; cf. erka = ekke (Tbh. of arka) aka (Tbh. of arka) copper (metal); crystal (Kannada)

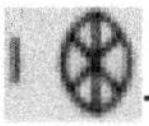

Thus, the pair of sign hieroglyphs are read rebus: *khāṇḍā āra eraka* 'tools, metalware' (of) bronze, coppercast (metal) smithy/forge PLUS खांडा [khāṇḍā] *m* A jag, notch, or indentation (as upon the edge of a tool or weapon). (Marathi) Rebus:*khāṇḍā* 'tools, pots and pans, metal-ware',

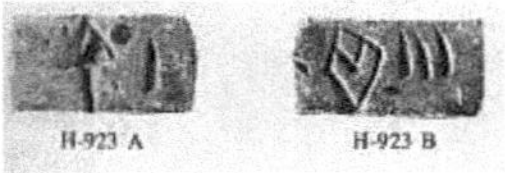

h923A

कांड *kāṇḍa* 'arrow' Rebus: *kāṇḍa* 'pots and pans, metalware, tools'. Rebus 2: kaṇḍ 'fire-altar' (Santali)

{}Phonetic-Semantic reinforcement): खांडा [*khāṇḍā*] *m* A jag, notch, or indentation (as upon the edge of a tool or weapon). Rebus: *kāṇḍa* 'tools, pots and pans and metal-ware'

 *kanac* 'corner' Rebus: *kañcu* 'bronze' kolom 'three' Rebus: kolami 'smithy, forge'

h602A

 *kana, kanac* = corner (Santali); Rebus: *kañcu* = bronze (Telugu) PLUS खांडा [*khāṇḍā*] *m* A jag, notch, or indentation (as upon the edge of a tool or weapon). Rebus: *kāṇḍa* 'tools, pots and pans and metal-ware' Thus, bronze metalware.

 *kuṭila* 'bent' CDIAL 3230 kuṭi— in cmpd. 'curve', *kuṭika*— 'bent' MBh. Rebus: *kuṭila, katthīl* = bronze (8 parts copper and 2 parts tin) Duplicated: dula 'pair' Rebus: dul 'cast metal' Thus, cast bronze or bronze castings.

h1077A Copper plate. खांडा [*khāṇḍā*] *m* A jag, notch, or indentation (as upon the edge of a tool or weapon). Rebus: *kāṇḍa* 'tools, pots and pans and metal-ware'

kuṭila 'bent' CDIAL  3230 kuṭi— in cmpd. 'curve', *kuṭika*— 'bent' MBh. Rebus: *kuṭila, katthīl* = bronze (8 parts copper and 2 parts tin)

The hieroglyph may be a variant of:  *kana, kanac* = corner (Santali); Rebus: *kañcu* = bronze (Telugu) PLUS kolom 'three' Rebus: kolami 'smithy, forge.

 *khareḍo* = a currycomb (Gujarati) खरारा [*kharārā*] *m* (H) A currycomb. 2 Currying a horse. (Marathi) Rebus: करडा [*karaḍā*] Hard from alloy--iron, silver &c. (Marathi) *kharādī* ' turner' (Gujarati)

 *bicha* 'scorpion' (Assamese) Rebus: *bica* 'stone ore' (Santali)

 *khareḍo* = a currycomb (Gujarati) खरारा [*kharārā*] *m* (H) A currycomb. 2 Currying a horse. (Marathi) Rebus: करडा [*karaḍā*] Hard from alloy--iron, silver &c. (Marathi) *kharādī* ' turner' (Gujarati)

H-241 A

h241Aखांडा [*khāṇḍā*] *m* A jag, notch, or indentation (as upon the edge of a tool or weapon). Rebus: *kāṇḍa* 'tools, pots and pans and metal-ware' *meḍ* 'body' Rebus:  *meḍ* 'iron' (Ho.) काठी [kāṭhī] *f* (काष्ट S) 'frame or structure of the body' (Marathi) Rebus: खंडी [khaṇḍī] measure of weight (Marathi) *கண்டி; kaṇṭi, n. Mhr. khaṇḍil. [T. Tu. khaṇḍi, M. kaṇḍi.]* Candy, a weight, stated to be roughly
< equivalent to 500 lbs.

ḍhanga = a crook used for pulling down the branches of trees, for goats, sheep and camels (P.) Rebus:*ḍhangar* blacksmith'. Thus, tools and metalware of iron smith.

M-1397 A
M-1397 B

m1397A,B Side A:

 dula 'pair' Rebus: dul 'cast metal' PLUS | *koḍa* 'one' Rebus: *koḍ* 'workshop' PLUS INFIXED खांडा [*khāṇḍā*] *m* A jag, notch, or indentation (as upon the edge of a tool or weapon). Rebus: *kāṇḍa* 'tools, pots and pans and metal-ware' Thus metware castings workshop.

kuṭila 'bent' CDIAL  3230 kuṭi— in cmpd. 'curve', *kuṭika—* 'bent' MBh. Rebus: *kuṭila, katthīl* = bronze (8 parts copper and 2 parts tin)

 *muka* 'ladle' (Tamil)(DEDR 4887) Rebus: *mūh* 'ingot' (Santali) *baṭa* = rimless pot (Kannada) Rebus: *baṭa* = a kind of iron (G.)) *bhaṭa* furnace (Gujarati) Thus, iron ingot.

 water-carrier hieroglyph *kuṭi*; Rebus: *kuṭhi* 'smelter furnace'.

Side B: Zebu: Native metal smith.

 *muka* 'ladle' (Tamil)(DEDR 4887) Rebus: *mūh* 'ingot' (Santali) *baṭa* = rimless pot (Kannada) Rebus: *baṭa* = a kind of iron (G.)) *bhaṭa* furnace (Gujarati) Thus, iron ingot.

 water-carrier hieroglyph *kuṭi*; Rebus: *kuṭhi* 'smelter furnace'.

H-2051 A

h2051A

 *muka* 'ladle' (Tamil)(DEDR 4887) Rebus: *mūh* 'ingot' (Santali) *baṭa* = rimless pot (Kannada) Rebus: *baṭa* = a kind of iron (G.)) *bhaṭa* furnace (Gujarati) Thus, iron ingot.

 water-carrier hieroglyph *kuṭi*; Rebus: *kuṭhi* 'smelter furnace'.

'Bow and arrow' sign hieroglyph 'Archer + bow + arrow' ligatured hieroglyph upraised arm: eraka 'upraised arm' Rebus: erako 'moltencast copper' *kamaḍha* 'archer, bow' Rebus: *kammaṭa* 'mint, coiner'.

m1695a *खोंड [khōṇḍa] m A young bull, a bullcalf. (Marathi) Rebus: kõdār 'turner' (Bengali); कोंद kōnda 'engraver, lapidary setting or infixing gems' (Marathi) G. sãghāṛɔ m. 'lathe' ; संघाट joinery; M. sãgaḍ 'double-canoe' Rebus: sangataras 'stone-cutter, mason'*

kammaṭa 'mint, coiner'.

notch+slanted stroke reads rebus: *ḍhālako kāṇḍa* 'ingot, tools, pots and pans and metal-ware'.*dhāḷ* 'a slope'; 'inclination of a plane' (G.); *ḍhāḷiyum* = adj. sloping, inclining (G.) Rebus: *ḍhālako* = a large metal ingot (G.) *ḍhālakī* = a metal heated and poured into a mould; a solid piece of metal; an ingot (Gujarati) PLUS खांडा [*khāṇḍā*] *m* A jag, notch, or indentation (as upon the edge of a tool or weapon). Rebus: *kāṇḍa* 'tools, pots and pans and metal-ware'

aḍaren 'cover of pot or lid' Rebus: *aduru* 'native, unsmelted metal' Duplicated: dula 'pair' Rebus: dul 'cast metal'

Ligature: two peaks: mēḍu height, rising ground, hillock (Kannada) Rebus: *meḍ* 'iron' (Ho.) dula 'pair' Rebus: dul 'cast metal' PLUS |||| Numeral 4: gaṇḍa 'four' Rebus: kaṇḍa 'furnace, fire-altar' (Santali)

kanka 'rim of jar' Rebus: karṇīka 'account (scribe)' karṇī 'supercargo'

m1117a Text 2615

Pictorial hieroglyph: *khũṭ* 'zebu' Rebus: '(native metal) guild'.

Text message: coiner-mint, mineral-ore cast, bronze cast

kamaḍha 'bow' Rebus: *kammaṭa* 'coiner, mint' (with resources of): *dhatu* 'mineral ore' PLUS *dul kañcu* 'bronze castings' (*cire perdue*? Perhaps indicated by the duplication of the circumscribing pairs of linear strokes).

Strands of yarn/rope' reading: *dhā´tu* 'strand of *dula* 'pair or two' Rebus: *kanac* 'corner' Rebus: *kañcu* 'bronze dula 'pair or two' Rebus: *dul* 'cast metal'

hieroglyph: Hieroglyph: 'strands of yarn' Rebus rope' Rebus: *dhatu* 'mineral ore' (Santali) *dul* 'cast metal'

m154a खोंड *[khōṇḍa] m A young bull, a bullcalf. (Marathi) Rebus: kõdār 'turner' (Bengali);* कोंद *kōnda 'engraver, lapidary setting or infixing gems' (Marathi) G. sãghāṛɔ m. 'lathe' ;* संघाट *joinery; M. sãgaḍ 'double-canoe' Rebus: sangataras 'stone-cutter, mason'*

kamaḍha 'bow' Rebus: *kammaṭa* 'coiner, mint' (with resources of): *dhatu* 'mineral ore'

koḍi 'flag' (Ta.)(DEDR 2049). Rebus 1: *koḍ* 'workshop' (Kuwi) Rebus 2: *khŏḍ* m. 'pit', *khŏḍü* f. 'small pit' (Kashmiri. CDIAL 3947).sal 'spinter' Rebus: sal 'workshop'

aḍar 'harrow'; rebus: *aduru* 'native unsmelted metal'
ayo 'fish' Rebus: *aya* 'iron' *ayas* 'metal'

कांड *kāṇḍa* 'arrow' Rebus: *kāṇḍa* 'pots and pans, metalware, tools'. Rebus 2: kaṇḍ 'fire-altar' (Santali)
kole.l 'temple' Rebus: kole.l 'smithy' (Kota)

K-17 A

Kalibangan 17A खोंड *[khōṇḍa] m A young bull, a bullcalf. (Marathi) Rebus: kõdār 'turner' (Bengali);* कोंद *kōnda 'engraver, lapidary setting or infixing gems' (Marathi) G. sãghāṛɔ m. 'lathe' ;* संघाट *joinery; M. sãgaḍ 'double-canoe' Rebus: sangataras 'stone-cutter, mason'*

kamaḍha 'archer, bow' Rebus: *kammaṭa* 'mint, coiner'.

kanka 'rim of jar' Rebus: karṇīka 'account (scribe)' karṇī 'supercargo'

M-1745 a

m1745 खोंड *[khōṇḍa] m A young bull, a bullcalf. (Marathi) Rebus: kõdār 'turner' (Bengali);* कोंद *kōnda 'engraver, lapidary setting or infixing gems' (Marathi) G. sãghāṛɔ m. 'lathe' ;* संघाट *joinery; M. sãgaḍ 'double-canoe' Rebus: sangataras 'stone-cutter, mason'*

kamaḍha 'archer, bow' Rebus: *kammaṭa* 'mint, coiner'.
Sal 'splinter' Rebus: sal'workshop'
| *koḍa* 'one' Rebus: *koḍ* 'workshop'

baroṭi 'twelve' *bhārata* 'a factitious alloy of copper, pewter, tin' (Marathi)
dula 'pair' Rebus: dul 'cast metal' PLUS

āra 'spokes' Rebus: *āra 'brass'*. cf. erka = ekke (Tbh. of arka) aka (Tbh. of arka) copper (metal); crystal (Kannada) Glyph: *eraka*'nave of wheel' Rebus: eraka 'copper'; cf. erka = ekke (Tbh. of arka) aka (Tbh. of arka) copper (metal); crystal (Kannada) *erako* 'moltencast copper'

खोंड [khōṇḍa] m A young bull, a bullcalf. (Marathi) Rebus: kõdār 'turner' (Bengali); कोंद kōnda 'engraver, lapidary setting or infixing gems' (Marathi) G. sãghāṛɔ m. 'lathe' ; संघाट joinery; M. sãgaḍ 'double-canoe' Rebus: sangataras 'stone-cutter, mason'

kamaḍha 'archer, bow' Rebus: *kammaṭa* 'mint, coiner'.

| *koḍa* 'one' Rebus: *koḍ* 'workshop'

sal 'splinter' Rebus: sal 'workshop' *dula* 'pair' Rebus: *dul* 'cast (metal)' PLUS*kana, kanac* = corner (Santali); Rebus: *kañcu* = bronze (Telugu) PLUS infixed kolmo 'paddy plant' Rebus: kolami 'smithy, forge'. Thus, cast bronze smithy, forge. Or, *mogge* 'sprout, bud' Rebus: *mũh* 'ingot' (Santali)Thus, cast bronze ingot. Read as: *kañcu dul mũh 'bronze cast ingot'*

kamaḍha 'archer' Rebus: *kammaṭa* 'mint, coiner'.

aya aḍaren (homonym: aduru)'alloy native metal'

Three sign sequence:

muka 'ladle' (Tamil)(DEDR 4887) Rebus: *mũh* 'ingot' (Santali) Thus, iron ingot.

kolom 'three' Rebus: kolami 'smithy, forge' *kāṇḍa* 'arrow' (Sanskrit) Rebus:*khāṇḍa* 'tools, pots and pans, metal-ware'. Rebus 2: kaṇḍ 'fire-altar' (Santali) Thus, the three sign sequence reads: iron ingot, furnace smithy, fire-altar metalware.

K-59 a

Kalibangan 59a

kamaḍha 'archer, bow' Rebus: *kammaṭa* 'mint, coiner'.

| *koḍa* 'one' Rebus: *koḍ* 'workshop'

sal 'splinter' Rebus: sal 'workshop;

खांडा [*khāṇḍā*] *m* A jag, notch, or indentation (as upon the edge of a tool or weapon). Rebus: *kāṇḍa* 'tools, pots and pans and metal-ware' Thus, mint metalware, ore. Kolom 'three' Rebus: kolami 'smithy, forge' sal 'splinter' Rebus: sal 'workshop'

H-467 A

h467A *First 3 signs read rebus as at m878A*

sãgaḍ

kamaḍha

M-878 A

m878A *खोंड [khōṇḍa] m A young bull, a bullcalf. (Marathi) Rebus: kõdār 'turner' (Bengali); कोंद kōnda 'engraver, lapidary setting or infixing gems' (Marathi) G. sãghāṛɔ m. 'lathe' ; संघाट joinery; M. 'double-canoe' Rebus: sangataras 'stone-cutter, mason'* 'archer, bow' Rebus: *kammaṭa* 'mint, coiner'.

kolmo 'paddy plant' Rebus: *kolami* 'smithy, forge' Vikalpa: *mogge* 'sprout, bud' Rebus: *mũh* 'ingot' (Santali) dolu 'plant of shoot height' Rebus: dul 'cast metal' *kanka* (Santali) *karṇika* 'scribe'(Sanskrit) Rebus: *karṇī,* supercargo for a boat shipment. INFIXED खांडा [*khāṇḍā*] *m* A jag, notch, or indentation (as upon the edge of a tool or weapon). Rebus: *kāṇḍa* 'tools, pots and pans and metal-ware' dula 'two' Rebus: dul 'cast metal' PLUS kolom 'three' Rebus: kolami 'smithy, forge'

 *kuṭila* 'bent' CDIAL 3230 kuṭi— in cmpd. 'curve', *kuṭika—* 'bent' MBh. Rebus: *kuṭila,*

 *katthīl* = bronze (8 parts copper and 2 parts tin)

kanka 'rim of jar' Rebus: karṇīka 'account (scribe)' karṇī 'supercargo'

m1903a *rāngo* 'water buffalo bull' (Ku.N.)(CDIAL 10559
kamaḍha 'archer, bow' Rebus: *kammaṭa* 'mint, coiner'.

 *kanac* 'corner' Rebus: *kañcu* 'bronze'

kanka 'rim of  jar' Rebus: karṇīka 'account (scribe)' karṇī 'supercargo'

m1756a *खोंड [khōṇḍa] m A young bull, a bullcalf. (Marathi) Rebus: kõdār 'turner' (Bengali); कोंद kōnda 'engraver, lapidary setting or infixing gems' (Marathi) G. sãghāṛɔ m. 'lathe' ; संघाट joinery; M. sãgaḍ 'double-canoe' Rebus: sangataras 'stone-cutter, mason'*
kamaḍha 'archer, bow' Rebus: *kammaṭa* 'mint, coiner'.

kanka 'rim of  jar' Rebus: karṇīka 'account (scribe)' karṇī 'supercargo'

aya aḍaren (homonym: aduru)'alloy native metal' *aya kammaṭa.*'coiner, mint alloy'

 water-carrier hieroglyph *kuṭi*; Rebus: *kuṭhi* 'smelter furnace'.

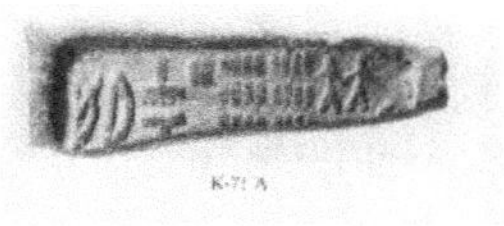

Kalibangan 71A
kamaḍha 'archer, bow' Rebus: *kammaṭa* 'mint, coiner'.
Duplicated: dula 'pair' Rebus: dul 'cast metal' Thus, mint ore castings.

 *aḍar* 'harrow'; rebus: *aduru* 'native unsmelted metal'
Duplicated: dula 'pair' Rebus: dul 'cast metal' Thus, native metal castings.

 *baroṭi* 'twelve' *bhārata* 'a factitious alloy of copper, pewter, tin' (Marathi) Duplicated: dula 'pair' Rebus: dul 'cast metal' Thus pewter alloy castings.

 *meḍ* 'body' Rebus: *meḍ* 'iron' (Ho.) काठी [kāṭhī] *f* (काष्ट S) 'frame or structure of the body' (Marathi) Rebus: खंडी [khaṇḍī] measure of weight (Marathi) *கண்டி; kaṇṭi, n. < Mhr. khaṇḍil. [T. Tu. khaṇḍi, M. kaṇḍi.]* Candy, a weight, stated to be roughly equivalent to 500 lbs.

Duplicated: dula 'pair' Rebus: dul 'cast metal' Thus, iron castings.

m320A खोंड *[khōṇḍa] m A young bull, a bullcalf. (Marathi) Rebus: kōdār 'turner' (Bengali);* कोंद *kōnda 'engraver, lapidary setting or infixing gems' (Marathi) G. sãghārɔ m. 'lathe' ;* संघाट *joinery; M. sãgaḍ 'double-canoe' Rebus: sangataras 'stone-cutter, mason'*
kamaḍha 'archer, bow' Rebus: *kammaṭa* 'mint, coiner'.

kolmo 'paddy plant' Rebus: *kolami* 'smithy, forge' Vikalpa: *mogge* 'sprout, bud' Rebus: *mũh* 'ingot' (Santali) dolu 'plant of shoot height' Rebus: dul 'cast metal'

kanka (Santali) *karṇika* 'scribe'(Sanskrit) Rebus: *karṇī,* supercargo for a boat shipment. INFIXED खांडा [*khāṇḍā*] *m* A jag, notch, or indentation (as upon the edge of a tool or weapon). Rebus: *kāṇḍa* 'tools, pots and pans and metal-ware'

baraḍo = spine; backbone (Tulu) Rebus: *baran, bharat* 'mixed alloys' (5 copper, 4 zinc and 1 tin) (Punjabi) PLUS gaṇḍa 'four' Rebus: kaṇḍa 'furnace, fire-altar' (Santali)

kanka 'rim of jar' Rebus: karṇīka 'account (scribe)' karṇī 'supercargo'

M-354 A

m354A
kamaḍha 'archer, bow' Rebus: *kammaṭa* 'mint, coiner'.

kuṭila 'bent' CDIAL 3230 kuṭi— in cmpd.

'curve', *kuṭika—* 'bent' MBh. Rebus: *kuṭila, katthīl* = bronze (8 parts copper and 2 parts tin) Duplicated: dula 'pair' Rebus: dul 'cast metal' Thus, cast bronze or bronze castings.

sal 'splinter' Rebus: sal 'workshop' Circumscript: gaṇḍa 'four' Rebus: kaṇḍa 'furnace, fire-altar' (Santali) *aya aḍaren (homonym: aduru)*'alloy native metal'

dula 'pair' Rebus: *dul* 'cast (metal)' PLUS*kana, kanac* = corner (Santali); Rebus: *kañcu* = bronze (Telugu) Thus, cast bronze. PLUS खांडा [*khāṇḍā*] *m* A jag, notch, or indentation (as upon the edge of a tool or weapon). Rebus: *kāṇḍa* 'tools, pots and pans and metal-ware' Thus, cast bronze metalware.

mogge 'sprout, bud' Rebus*: mũh* 'ingot'
baṭa = rimless pot (Kannada) Rebus: *baṭa* = a kind of iron (G.)) *bhaṭa* furnace (Gujarati)
Ligatures: gaṇḍa 'four' Rebus: kaṇḍa 'furnace, fire-altar' (Santali) PLUS खांडा [*khāṇḍā*] *m* A jag, notch, or indentation (as upon the edge of a tool or weapon). Rebus: *kāṇḍa* 'tools, pots and pans and metal-ware'

kanka 'rim of jar' Rebus: karṇīka 'account (scribe)' karṇī 'supercargo

h55a खोंड *[khōṇḍa] m A young bull, a bullcalf. (Marathi) Rebus: kõdār 'turner' (Bengali);* कोंद *kōnda 'engraver, lapidary setting or infixing gems' (Marathi) G. sãghāṛɔ m. 'lathe' ;* संघाट *joinery; M. sãgaḍ 'double-canoe' Rebus: sangataras 'stone-cutter, mason'*

kamaḍha 'archer, bow' Rebus: *kammaṭa* 'mint, coiner'.

kanac 'corner' Rebus: *kañcu* 'bronze' sal 'splinter' Rebus: sal 'workshop' gaṇḍa 'four' Rebus: kaṇḍa 'furnace, fire-altar' (Santali)

kolmo 'paddy plant' Rebus: *kolami* 'smithy, forge' Vikalpa: *mogge* 'sprout, bud' Rebus: *mũh* 'ingot' (Santali) dolu 'plant of shoot height' Rebus: dul 'cast metal'

Kalibangan 5A खोंड *[khōṇḍa] m A young bull, a bullcalf. (Marathi) Rebus: kõdār 'turner' (Bengali);* कोंद *kōnda 'engraver, lapidary setting or infixing gems' (Marathi) G. sãghāṛɔ m. 'lathe' ;* संघाट *joinery; M. sãgaḍ 'double-canoe' Rebus: sangataras 'stone-cutter, mason'*

kamaḍha 'archer, bow' Rebus: *kammaṭa* 'mint, coiner'.

kanka (Santali) *karṇika* 'scribe'(Sanskrit) Rebus: *karṇī,* supercargo for a boat shipment. INFIXED खांडा [*khāṇḍā*] *m* A jag, notch, or indentation (as upon the edge of a tool or weapon). Rebus: *kāṇḍa* 'tools, pots and pans and metal-ware'

dula

'pair' Rebus: *dul* 'cast (metal)' PLUS*kana, kanac* = corner (Santali); Rebus: *kañcu* = bronze (Telugu) PLUS infixed kolmo 'paddy plant' Rebus: kolami 'smithy, forge'. Thus, cast bronze smithy, forge. Or, *mogge* 'sprout, bud' Rebus: *mũh* 'ingot' (Santali)Thus, cast bronze ingot. Read as: *kañcu dul mũh 'bronze cast ingot' aya kammaṭa.*'coiner, mint alloy' *ayo ḍhālako* 'alloy metal ingot'

कांड *kāṇḍa* 'arrow' Rebus: *kāṇḍa* 'pots and pans, metalware, tools'. Rebus 2: kaṇḍ 'fire-altar' (Santali)

m1668a खोंड *[khōṇḍa] m A young bull, a bullcalf. (Marathi) Rebus: kõdār 'turner' (Bengali);* कोंद *kōnda 'engraver, lapidary setting or infixing gems' (Marathi) G. sãghāṛɔ m. 'lathe' ;* संघाट *joinery; M. sãgaḍ 'double-canoe' Rebus: sangataras 'stone-cutter, mason'*

kamaḍha 'archer, bow' Rebus: *kammaṭa* 'mint, coiner'.

muka 'ladle' (Kannada)

(Tamil)(DEDR 4887) Rebus: *mũh* 'ingot' (Santali) *baṭa* = rimless pot Rebus: *baṭa* = a kind of iron (G.)) *bhaṭa* furnace (Gujarati) Thus, iron ingot.

ranku 'antelope' Rebus; ranku 'tin' sal 'splinter' Rebus; sal 'workshop'

dula 'pair' Rebus: *dul* 'cast (metal)' PLUS*kana, kanac* = corner (Santali); Rebus: *kañcu* = bronze (Telugu) PLUS infixed kolmo 'paddy plant' Rebus: kolami 'smithy, forge'. Thus,

cast bronze smithy, forge. Or, *mogge* 'sprout, bud' Rebus: *mũh* 'ingot' (Santali)Thus, cast bronze ingot. Read as: *kañcu dul mũh 'bronze cast ingot'*
ayo ḍhālako 'alloy metal ingot'

dula 'pair' Rebus: dul 'cast (metal)' kolmo 'rice plant' Rebus: kolami 'smithy/forge' metal.

kanka 'rim of jar' Rebus: karṇīka 'account (scribe)' karṇī 'supercargo'

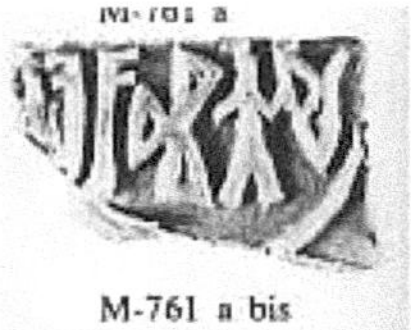
m761A *खोंड [khōṇḍa] m A young bull, a bullcalf. (Marathi) Rebus: kõdār 'turner' (Bengali); कोंद kōnda 'engraver, lapidary setting or infixing gems' (Marathi) G. sãghāṛɔ m. 'lathe' ; संघाट joinery; M. sãgaḍ 'double-canoe' Rebus: sangataras 'stone-cutter, mason'*
kamaḍha 'archer, bow' Rebus: *kammaṭa* 'mint, coiner'.

mēḍu height, rising ground, hillock (Kannada) Rebus: *meḍ* 'iron' (Ho.) kolom 'three' Rebus: kolami 'smithy, forge' Thus, *meḍ kolami* 'iron smithy-forge'

kanka 'rim of jar' Rebus: karṇīka 'account (scribe)' karṇī 'supercargo'

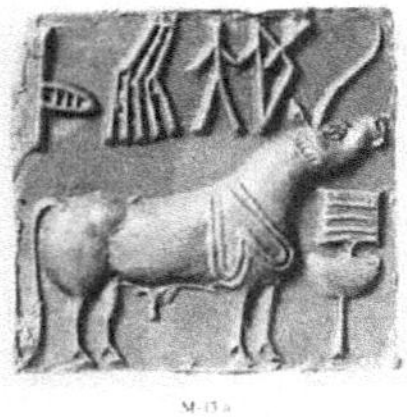
m13a *खोंड [khōṇḍa] m A young bull, a bullcalf. (Marathi) Rebus: kõdār 'turner' (Bengali); कोंद kōnda 'engraver, lapidary setting or infixing gems' (Marathi) G. sãghāṛɔ m. 'lathe' ; संघाट joinery; M. sãgaḍ 'double-canoe' Rebus: sangataras 'stone-cutter, mason'*
kamaḍha 'archer, bow' Rebus: *kammaṭa* 'mint, coiner'.

Strands of yarn/rope' hieroglyph: Hieroglyph: 'strands of yarn' Rebus reading: *dhā́tu* 'strand of rope' Rebus: *dhatu* 'mineral ore' (Santali)

koḍi 'flag' (Ta.)(DEDR 2049). Rebus 1: *koḍ* 'workshop' (Kuwi) Rebus 2: *khõḍ* m. 'pit', *khõḍü* f. 'small pit' (Kashmiri. CDIAL 3947).

m191A *खोंड [khōṇḍa] m A young bull, a bullcalf. (Marathi) Rebus: kõdār 'turner' (Bengali); कोंद kōnda 'engraver, lapidary setting or infixing gems' (Marathi) G. sãghāṛɔ m. 'lathe' ; संघाट joinery; M. sãgaḍ 'double-canoe' Rebus: sangataras 'stone-cutter, mason'*
kamaḍha 'archer, bow' Rebus: *kammaṭa* 'mint, coiner'.

meḍ 'body' Rebus: *meḍ* 'iron' (Ho.) काठी [kāṭhī] *f* (काष्ट S) 'frame or structure of the body' (Marathi) Rebus: खंडी [khaṇḍī] measure of weight (Marathi) *கண்டி; kaṇṭi, n. < Mhr. khaṇḍil. [T. Tu. khaṇḍi, M. kaṇḍi.]* Candy, a weight, stated to be roughly equivalent to 500 lbs.

'Flower-bud or sprout' sign hieroglyph

In the following compositions, a human face (which is commonly ligatured on the composite animal hieroglyph) is ligatured to a bovine with markhor horns: m1180A

m1180a Text 1303

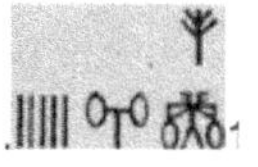

mũh 'face' (Hindi) mogge 'flower-bud, sprout' Rebus: mũh 'ingot' (Santali) dhatu 'scarf' Rebus: dhatu 'mineral ore' (Santali)

Kur. xolā tail. *Malt.* qoli id. (DEDR 2135). dhatu Rebus: *kolhe* 'smelter'. The pictorial  motif hieroglyph composite on m1180 seal denotes: mineral (ore) – tin, lead -- ingot smelter of turner.

Rebus readings of Text 1303: Bronze ingot castings.

muggè, moggè flower-bud, germ; (BRR; Bhattacharya, non-brahmin informant) mukkè bud. *Kor.* (O.) mūke flower-bud. (Tulu)(DEDR 4893). mukula-, () mudgara- bud; Pkt. (*DNM*) moggara id.; Turner, *CDIAL*, no. 10146 Rebus: mũh 'face' (Hindi) mukha id. (Sanskrit) मोख [mōkha] sprout or shoot. (Marathi) *Kuwi* (Su.) mr̥ogla shoot of bamboo; (Punjabi) moko sprout (DEDR 4997) *Tu.* mugiyuni to close, contract, shut up; muguru sprout, shoot, bud; tender, delicate; muguruni, mukuruni to bud, sprout; muggè, moggè flower-bud, germ; (BRR; Bhattacharya, non-brahmin informant) mukkè bud. *Kor.* (O.) mūke flower-bud. (DEDR 4893) Rebus: mũh '(copper) ingot' (Santali) mũhã = the quantity of iron produced at one time in a native smelting furnace of the Kolhes; iron produced by the Kolhes and formed like a four-cornered piece a little pointed at each end (Santali)

kuṭi 'water-carrier' Rebus: kuṭhi 'smelter furnace' PLUS

kanka 'rim of jar' Rebus: *karṇīka* 'account (scribe)' *karṇī* 'supercargo'

Thus, the composite hieroglyph on m1901 denotes the message: supercargo (from) smelter furnace.

If frame of a cart is depicted, possible rebus reading: अगडा [agaḍā] *m* The tie connecting the जूं & दांडी of a गाडा or load-cart; the shaft and thill-yoke-tie. Rebus: 'lumber, miscellaneous articles': अगडतगड [*agaḍatagaḍa*] *n* अगडबगड *n* (Fanciful formations, or from H) Trash, trumpery, rubbish, lumber, miscellaneous articles.

|| dula 'pair' Rebus: dul 'cast metal'

||| kolmo 'three' Rebus: kolami 'smithy, forge'

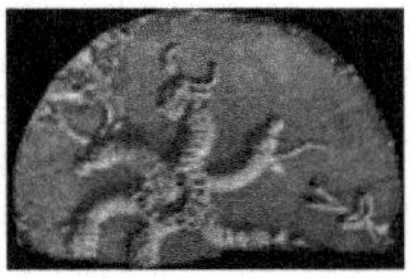

m417A Text 1383 The semi-circular chain which links he faces of animals may be a stylized ladder read rebus: 'guild':

H. sainī, senī f. ' ladder ' Rebus: Pa. sēṇi -- f. ' guild, division of army '; Pk. sēṇi -- f. ' row, collection '; śrḗṇi (metr. often śrayaṇi --) f. ' line, row, troop ' RV. *śrēṇikā* f. 'house ~ ladder' Rebus:*śreṇi* in meaning "guild" (Sanskrit) Pa. *sēṇi* -- f. ' guild, division of army '(Pali)(CDIAL 10718) *seniya* 'soldier'.

Composition of animal faces: *खोंडी [khōṇḍī] f An outspread shovelform sack (as formed temporarily out of a कांबळा, to hold or fend off grain, chaff &c.) (Marathi) koḍiyum 'rings on neck' (Gujarati) kondh 'heifer'. kōḍu horn (Kannada. Tulu. Tamil) खोंड [khōṇḍa] m A young bull, a bullcalf. (Marathi) Rebus: kõdār 'turner' (Bengali); kõdā 'to turn in a lathe' (Bengali). कोंद kōnda 'engraver, lapidary setting or infixing gems' (Marathi)*

balad m. ' ox ', gng. *bald*, (Ku.) *barad*, id. (N. Tarai) Rebus: *bharat* (5 copper, 4 zinc and 1 tin)(Punjabi) *pattar* 'trough' Rebus*: pattar* 'guild'. Thus, copper-zinc-tin alloy (worker) guild.

khũṭ 'zebu' Rebus: '(native metal) guild'

kola 'tiger' Rebus; kolhe 'smelter' kol 'working in iron'

Maybe: *miṇḍāl* 'markhor' (Tōrwālī) *meḍho* a ram, a sheep (G.)(CDIAL 10120) Rebus: *mẽṛhẽt, meḍ* 'iron' (Mu.Ho.)

bhaṭa 'warrior' (Sanskrit) Rebus: *baṭa* a kind of iron (Gujarati). Rebus: *bhaṭa* 'furnace' (Santali) *nāga* 'snake' Rebus: *nāga* 'lead' (Sanskrit) anakku 'tin' (Akkadian)

m840a *खोंड [khōṇḍa] m A young bull, a bullcalf. (Marathi) Rebus: kõdār 'turner' (Bengali);* *कोंद kōnda 'engraver, lapidary setting or infixing gems' (Marathi) G. sãghāṛɔ m. 'lathe' ; संघाट joinery; M. sãgaḍ 'double-canoe' Rebus: sangataras 'stone-cutter, mason'*

mogge 'sprout, bud' Rebus: *mũh* 'ingot' (Santali

kuṭila 'bent' CDIAL 3230 kuṭi— in cmpd. 'curve', *kuṭika*— 'bent' MBh. Rebus: *kuṭila, katthīl* = bronze (8 parts copper and 2 parts tin)
खांडा [*khāṇḍā*] *m* A jag, notch, or indentation (as upon the edge of a tool or weapon). Rebus: *kāṇḍa* 'tools, pots and pans and metal-ware' *ayo ḍhālako* 'alloy metal ingot'

muka 'ladle' (Tamil)(DEDR 4887) Rebus: *mũh* 'ingot' (Santali) *baṭa* = rimless pot (Kannada) Rebus: *baṭa* = a kind of iron (G.)) *bhaṭa* furnace (Gujarati) Thus, iron ingot. *gaṇḍa* 'four' Rebus: *kaṇḍa* 'furnace, fire-altar' (Santali).kolom 'three' Rebus: kolami 'smithy, forge' PLUS *Kur.* xolā tail. *Malt.* qoli id. (DEDR 2135). Rebus: kolhe 'smelter' Thus, copper smelter.

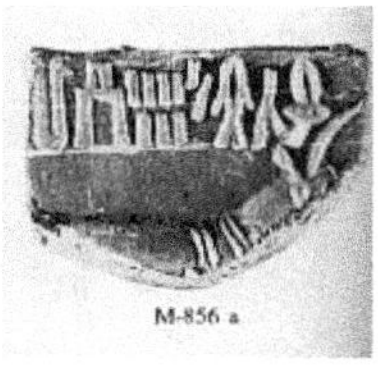

m856a *खोंड [khōṇḍa] m A young bull, a bullcalf. (Marathi) Rebus: kõdār 'turner' (Bengali);* *कोंद kōnda 'engraver, lapidary setting or infixing gems' (Marathi) G. sãghāṛɔ m. 'lathe' ; संघाट joinery; M. sãgaḍ 'double-canoe' Rebus: sangataras 'stone-cutter, mason'*

mogge 'sprout, bud' Rebus: *mũh* 'ingot' (Santali)

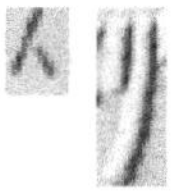

notch+slanted stroke reads rebus: *ḍhālako kāṇḍa* 'ingot, tools, pots and pans and metal-ware'.*dhāḷ* 'a slope'; 'inclination of a plane' (G.); *ḍhāḷiyum* = adj. sloping, inclining (G.) Rebus: *ḍhālako* = a large metal ingot (G.) *ḍhālakī* = a metal heated and poured into a mould; a solid piece of metal; an ingot (Gujarati) PLUS खांडा [*khāṇḍā*] *m* A jag, notch, or indentation (as upon the edge of a tool or weapon). Rebus: *kāṇḍa* 'tools, pots and pans and metal-ware'
ayo 'fish' Rebus: *aya* 'iron' *ayas* 'metal'

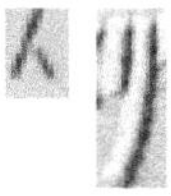

notch+slanted stroke reads rebus: *ḍhālako kāṇḍa* 'ingot, tools, pots and pans and metal-ware'.*dhāḷ* 'a slope'; 'inclination of a plane' (G.); *ḍhāḷiyum* = adj. sloping, inclining (G.) Rebus: *ḍhālako* = a large metal ingot (G.) *ḍhālakī* = a metal heated and poured into a mould; a solid piece of metal; an ingot (Gujarati) PLUS खांडा [*khāṇḍā*] *m* A jag, notch, or indentation (as upon the edge of a tool or weapon). Rebus: *kāṇḍa* 'tools, pots and pans and metal-ware'
|||| Numeral 4: gaṇḍa 'four' Rebus: kaṇḍa 'furnace, fire-altar' (Santali)

||| Numeral 3: *kolom* 'three' Rebus*: kolami* 'smithy, forge'

सांड [sāṇḍa] *f* (षद S) An outlet for superfluous water (as through a dam or mound); a sluice, a floodvent. Rebus: सांडणी [sāṇḍaṇī] *f* (H) An instrument of goldsmiths. It is

hooked or curved at the extremity; and is used to draw things out of the fire.
सांठा [*sāṇṭhā*] *m* (संचय S) A collection, heap, hoard, store, stock.साटें [*sāṭēṃ*] *n* (संचय S) A whole investment; the total quantity of merchandise (brought to market by one merchant).

 kanka 'rim of jar' Rebus: karṇīka 'account (scribe)' karṇī 'supercargo'

m34A *खोंड [khōṇḍa] m A young bull, a bullcalf. (Marathi) Rebus: kōdār 'turner' (Bengali); कोंद kōnda 'engraver, lapidary setting or infixing gems' (Marathi) G. sãghāṛɔ m. 'lathe' ; संघाट joinery; M. sãgaḍ 'double-canoe' Rebus: sangataras 'stone-cutter, mason'*

mogge 'sprout, bud' Rebus: *mũh* 'ingot' (Santali)

 beads: Pa. kandi (pl. -l) necklace, beads. Ga. (Punjabi) kandi (pl. -l) bead, (pl.) necklace; (S.2) kandiṭ bead. (DEDR 1215) Rebus: *கண்டி; kaṇṭi, n. < Mhr. khaṇḍil. [T. Tu. khaṇḍi, M. kaṇḍi.] 1. Candy, a weight, stated to be roughly equivalent to 500 lbs.; பாரமென்னும் நிறையளவு.* खंडीगणती or खंडोगणती [khaṇḍīgaṇatī or khaṇḍōgaṇatī] *ad* By candies; counting or reckoning by candies. खंडीवारी [khaṇḍīvārī] *ad* By scores, heaps, candies. खंडी [khaṇḍī] Applied to a great quantity; as खंडीभर पोरें, खंडीभर मेंढ्या, खंडीभर काम, खंडीभर बोलतो-लिहितो&c

 *kolmo* 'paddy plant' Rebus: *kolami* 'smithy, forge' Vikalpa: *mogge* 'sprout, bud' Rebus: *mũh* 'ingot' (Santali) dolu 'plant of shoot height' Rebus: dul 'cast metal'

 sal 'splinter' Rebus: sal 'workshop'
baraḍo = spine; backbone (Tulu) Rebus: *baran, bharat* 'mixed alloys' (5 copper, 4 zinc and 1 tin) (Punjabi) PLUS gaṇḍa 'four' Rebus: kaṇḍa 'furnace, fire-altar' (Santali)

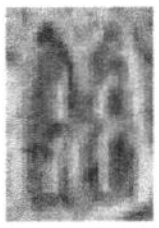 Ligature: two peaks: mēḍu height, rising ground, hillock (Kannada) Rebus: *meḍ* 'iron' (Ho.) dula 'pair' Rebus: dul 'cast metal' PLUS |||| Numeral 4: gaṇḍa 'four' Rebus: kaṇḍa 'furnace, fire-altar' (Santali)

 kanka 'rim of jar' Rebus: karṇīka 'account (scribe)' karṇī 'supercargo'

 'Currycomb' hieroglyph

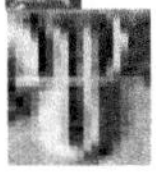

'

|||| Numeral 4: gaṇḍa 'four' Rebus: kaṇḍa 'furnace, fire-altar' (Santali) dula 'pair' Rebus: dul 'cast metal'

H-213 A

h213A h214A First pair of sign turner PLUS turner metalware

H-214 A

hieroglyphs: iron hard alloy (tools, pots and pans)

|||| Numeral 4: Rebus: dul

gaṇḍa 'four' Rebus: kaṇḍa 'furnace, fire-altar' (Santali) dula 'pair' 'cast metal'

 *khareḍo* = a currycomb (Gujarati) खरारा [*kharārā*] *m* (H) A currycomb. 2 Currying a horse. (Marathi) Rebus: करडा [*karaḍā*] Hard from alloy--iron, silver &c. (Marathi) *kharādī* ' turner' (Gujarati)

 कांड *kāṇḍa* 'arrow' Rebus: *kāṇḍa* 'pots and pans, metalware, tools'. Rebus 2: kaṇḍ 'fire-altar' (Santali)

 *khareḍo* = a currycomb (Gujarati) खरारा [*kharārā*] *m* (H) A currycomb. 2 Currying a horse. (Marathi) Rebus: करडा [*karaḍā*] Hard from alloy--iron, silver &c. (Marathi) *kharādī* ' turner' (Gujarati)

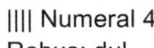

m66a iron hard alloy turner. 'crab' hieroglyph ligatured to 'strands' hieroglyph: *dhatu* 'strands of yarn' rebus: '(Copper) mineral, ore' PLUS *kamaḍha* = crab; *kampaṭṭam* = mint (Tamil) ; *kammaṭa* 'coiner, mint' (Telugu) The first two signs read rebus: iron hard alloy turner PLUS (copper) mineral, ore; mint.

|||| 'pair'

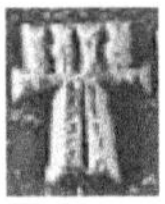

Numeral 4: gaṇḍa 'four' Rebus: kaṇḍa 'furnace, fire-altar' (Santali) dula Rebus: dul 'cast metal'

 *cīmara* 'black ant' Rebus: *cīmara* 'copper'. *cīmara kāra* -- ' coppersmith '

 *mogge* 'sprout, bud' Rebus*: mūh* íngot' sal 'splinter' Rebus: sal 'workshop'

aya kāṇḍa 'alloy metalware'ranku 'liquid measure' Rebus: ranku 'tin'

 *kolmo* 'paddy plant' Rebus: *kolami* 'smithy, forge' Vikalpa: *mogge* 'sprout, bud' Rebus: *mūh* 'ingot' (Santali) dolu 'plant of shoot height' Rebus: dul 'cast metal'

 *kanka* 'rim of jar' Rebus: *karṇīka* 'account (scribe)' *karṇī* 'supercargo'

m242a Pictorial motif: *balad* m. ' ox ', gng. *bald*, (Ku.) *barad*, id. (N. Tarai) Rebus: *bharat* (5 copper, 4 zinc and 1 tin)(Punjabi) pattar 'trough' Rebus: pattar 'guild'. Thus, copper-zinc-tin alloy (worker) guild.

|||| Numeral 4: Rebus: dul  gaṇḍa 'four' Rebus: kaṇḍa 'furnace, fire-altar' (Santali) dula 'pair' 'cast metal'

  Strands of yarn/rope' hieroglyph: Hieroglyph: 'strands of yarn' Rebus reading: *dhā́tu* 'strand of rope' Rebus: *dhatu* 'mineral ore' (Santali) sal 'splinte' Rebus: sal 'workshop'

 dula 'pair' Rebus: dul 'cast (metal)' kolmo 'rice plant' Rebus: kolami 'smithy/forge' metal.

 kanka 'rim of jar' Rebus: karṇīka 'account (scribe)' karṇī 'supercargo'

m251a Pictorial motif: *balad* m. ' ox ', gng. *bald*, (Ku.) *barad*, id. (N. Tarai) Rebus: *bharat* (5 copper, 4 zinc and 1 tin)(Punjabi) pattar 'trough' Rebus: pattar 'guild'. Thus, copper-zinc-tin alloy (worker) guild.

|||| Numeral  4: gaṇḍa 'four' Rebus: kaṇḍa 'furnace, fire-altar' (Santali) dula 'pair' Rebus: dul 'cast metal' *kamaḍha* 'archer, bow' Rebus: *kammaṭa* 'mint, coiner'. sal 'splinter' Rebus: sal 'workshop' kolom 'three' Rebus: kolami 'smithy, forge'

 *kolmo* 'paddy plant' Rebus: *kolami* 'smithy, forge' Vikalpa: *mogge* 'sprout, bud' Rebus: *mūh* 'ingot' (Santali) dolu 'plant of shoot height' Rebus: dul 'cast metal'

m379a

|||| Numeral 4: gaṇḍa 'four' Rebus: kaṇḍa 'furnace, fire-altar' (Santali) dula 'pair' Rebus: dul 'cast metal'

 ḍāg mountain-ridge (H.)(CDIAL 5476). Rebus: dhangar 'blacksmith' (Maithili) *kamaḍha* 'crab' Rebus: *kammaṭa* 'mint, coiner'.*ḍato* = claws of crab (Santali) Rebus: *dhātu* 'mineral ore'

 water-carrier hieroglyph *kuṭi*; Rebus: *kuṭhi* 'smelter furnace'.

 PLUS 'rim of jar': *kanka* (Santali) *karṇika* 'scribe'(Sanskrit)

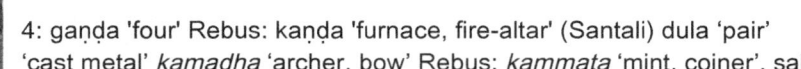

Rebus: *karṇī*, supercargo

'rim-of-jar' hieroglyph *kanka* (Santali) *karṇika* 'scribe'(Sanskrit)

Rebus: *karṇī*, supercargo for a boat shipment. *karṇīka* 'account (scribe)' .कारणी *kāraṇī* 'the supercargo of a ship'

m1972a

 |||| Numeral 4: gaṇḍa 'four' Rebus: kaṇḍa 'furnace, fire-altar' (Santali) dula 'pair' Rebus: dul 'cast metal'

 ḍāg mountain-ridge (H.)(CDIAL 5476). Rebus: dhangar 'blacksmith' (Maithili)

 kanka 'rim of jar' Rebus: karṇīka 'account (scribe)' karṇī 'supercargo' kolom 'three' Rebus: kolami 'smithy, forge' *kamaḍha* 'crab' Rebus: *kammaṭa* 'mint, coiner'.*ḍato* = claws of crab (Santali) Rebus: *dhātu* 'mineral ore' *aya aḍaren (homonym: aduru)*'alloy native metal'

 mēḍu height, rising ground, hillock (Kannada) Rebus: *meḍ* 'iron' (Ho.) kolom 'three' Rebus: kolami 'smithy, forge' Thus, *meḍ kolami* 'iron smithy-forge'

 kanka 'rim of jar' Rebus: karṇīka 'account (scribe)' karṇī 'supercargo'

h1874A,B

 |||| Numeral 4: gaṇḍa 'four' Rebus: kaṇḍa 'furnace, fire-altar' (Santali) dula 'pair' Rebus: dul 'cast metal'

 mēḍu height, rising ground, hillock (Kannada) Rebus: *meḍ* 'iron' (Ho.) kolom 'three' Rebus: kolami 'smithy, forge' Thus, *meḍ kolami* 'iron smithy-forge'

ayo 'fish' Rebus: *aya* 'iron' *ayas* 'metal' sal 'splinter' Rebus: sal 'workshop' gaṇḍa 'four' Rebus: kaṇḍa 'furnace, fire-altar' (Santali) *baṭa* = rimless pot (Kannada) Rebus: *baṭa* = a kind of iron (G.)) *bhaṭa* furnace (Gujarati)

m1679a *खोंड [khōṇḍa] m A young bull, a bullcalf. (Marathi) Rebus: kõdār 'turner' (Bengali); कोंद kōnda 'engraver, lapidary setting or infixing gems' (Marathi) G. sãghārɔ m. 'lathe' ; संघाट joinery; M. sãgaḍ 'double-canoe' Rebus: sangataras 'stone-cutter, mason'*

 |||| Numeral 4: gaṇḍa 'four' Rebus: kaṇḍa 'furnace, fire-altar' (Santali) dula 'pair' Rebus: dul 'cast metal'

 ḍāg mountain-ridge (H.)(CDIAL 5476). Rebus: dhangar 'blacksmith' (Maithili)

 *kanka* (Santali) *karṇika* 'scribe'(Sanskrit) Rebus: *karṇī,* supercargo for a boat shipment. INFIXED खांडा [*khāṇḍā*] *m* A jag, notch, or indentation (as upon the edge of a tool or weapon). Rebus: *kāṇḍa* 'tools, pots and pans and metal-ware'

 *muka* 'ladle' (Tamil)(DEDR 4887) Rebus: *mũh* 'ingot' (Santali) *baṭa* = rimless pot (Kannada) Rebus: *baṭa* = a kind of iron (G.)) *bhaṭa* furnace (Gujarati)

 सांड [sāṇḍa] *f* (षद S) An outlet for superfluous water (as through a dam or mound); a sluice, a floodvent. Rebus: सांडणी [sāṇḍaṇī] *f* (H) An instrument of goldsmiths. It is

hooked or curved at the extremity; and is used to draw things out of the fire.
सांठा [*sāṇṭhā*] *m* (संचय S) A collection, heap, hoard, store, stock.साटें [*sāṭēṃ*] *n* (संचय S) A whole investment; the total quantity of merchandise (brought to market by one merchant).furnace' (Gujarati)

 *baraḍo* = spine; backbone (Tulu) Rebus: *baran, bharat* 'mixed alloys' (5 copper, 4 zinc and 1 tin) (Punjabi) PLUS gaṇḍa 'four' Rebus: kaṇḍa 'furnace, fire-altar' (Santali)

 kanka 'rim of jar' Rebus: karṇīka 'account (scribe)' karṇī 'supercargo'

H-1933 A H-1933 B H-1933 C

h1933A Side C: *karāvu* 'crocodile' Rebus: khara 'blacksmith' (Kashmiri)

 |||| Numeral 4: gaṇḍa 'four' Rebus: kaṇḍa 'furnace, fire-altar' (Santali) dula 'pair' Rebus: dul 'cast metal'

 *khareḍo* = a currycomb (Gujarati) खरारा [*kharārā*] *m* (H) A currycomb. 2 Currying a horse. (Marathi) Rebus: करडा [*karaḍā*] Hard from alloy--iron, silver &c. (Marathi) *kharādī* ' turner' (Gujarati)

 कांड *kāṇḍa* 'arrow' Rebus: *kāṇḍa* 'pots and pans, metalware, tools'. Rebus 2: kaṇḍ 'fire-altar' (Santali)

 *khareḍo* = a currycomb (Gujarati) खरारा [*kharārā*] *m* (H) A currycomb. 2 Currying a horse. (Marathi) Rebus: करडा [*karaḍā*] Hard from alloy--iron, silver &c. (Marathi) *kharādī* ' turner' (Gujarati)
baṭa = rimless pot (Kannada) Rebus: *baṭa* = a kind of iron (G.)) *bhaṭa* furnace (Gujarati) kolom 'three' Rebus: kolami 'smithy, forge'

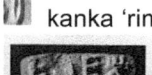

M-1340 A

M-1340 a

m1340a Both sides with same text:

 |||| Numeral 4: gaṇḍa 'four' Rebus: kaṇḍa 'furnace, fire-altar' (Santali) dula 'pair' Rebus: dul 'cast metal'

 kanka 'rim of jar' Rebus: karṇīka 'account (scribe)' karṇī 'supercargo'

 *dāṭu* 'cross'(Telugu) Rebus: *dhatu* 'mineral' (Santali).
dhāḷ 'a slope'; 'inclination of a plane' (Gujarati); *ḍhāḷiyum* = adj. sloping, inclining (Gujarati) Rebus: *ḍhālako* = a large metal ingot (Gujarati) *ḍhālakī* = a metal heated and poured into a mould; a solid piece of metal; an ingot (Gujarati)PLUS*sal* 'splinter' Rebus: *sal* 'workshop'. Thus the composition reads: *ḍhālako sal* 'ingot workshop'.

 *bicha* 'scorpion' (Assamese) Rebus: *bica* 'stone ore' (Santali)

m1129a *खोंड [khōṇḍa] m A young bull, a bullcalf. (Marathi) Rebus: kõdār 'turner' (Bengali); कोंद kōnda 'engraver, lapidary setting or infixing gems' (Marathi) G. sãghārɔ m. 'lathe' ; संघाट joinery; M. sãgaḍ 'double-canoe' Rebus: sangataras 'stone-cutter, mason'*

|||| Numeral 4: gaṇḍa 'four' Rebus: kaṇḍa 'furnace, fire-altar' (Santali) dula 'pair' Rebus: dul 'cast metal'

kanka 'rim of jar' Rebus: karṇīka 'account (scribe)' karṇī 'supercargo'

mēḍu height, rising ground, hillock (Kannada) Rebus: *meḍ* 'iron' (Ho.) kolom 'three' Rebus: kolami 'smithy, forge' Thus, *meḍ kolami* 'iron smithy-forge'

kuṭila 'bent' CDIAL 3230 kuṭi— in cmpd. 'curve', *kuṭika*— 'bent' MBh. Rebus: *kuṭila, katthīl* = bronze (8 parts copper and 2 parts tin)

kanka 'rim of jar' Rebus: karṇīka 'account (scribe)' karṇī 'supercargo' *ḍato* = claws of crab (Santali) Rebus: *dhātu* 'mineral ore' dula 'pair' Rebus: dul 'cast metal'

m800A *खोंड [khōṇḍa] m A young bull, a bullcalf. (Marathi) Rebus: kõdār 'turner' (Bengali); कोंद kōnda 'engraver, lapidary setting or infixing gems' (Marathi) G. sãghārɔ m. 'lathe' ; संघाट joinery; M. sãgaḍ 'double-canoe' Rebus: sangataras 'stone-cutter, mason'*

|||| Numeral 4: gaṇḍa 'four' Rebus: kaṇḍa 'furnace, fire-altar' (Santali) dula 'pair' Rebus: dul 'cast metal'

'Arrow' sign  hieroglyph (variant) This is a ligature of 'lid of pot' hieroglyph superscript on 'a linear stroke' numeral hieroglyph.*aḍaren* 'cover of pot or lid' Rebus: *aduru* 'native, unsmelted metal' PLUS koḍ = one (Santali); koḍ 'workshop' (Gujarati) *ḍhanga* = a crook used for pulling down the branches of trees, for goats, sheep and camels (P.) Rebus:*ḍhangar* blacksmith'. *kanka* (Santali) *karṇika* 'scribe'(Sanskrit)

Rebus: *karṇī,* supercargo for a boat shipment. INFIXED खांडा [*khāṇḍā*] *m* A jag, notch, or indentation (as upon the edge of a tool or weapon). Rebus: *kāṇḍa* 'tools, pots and pans and metal-ware'

dula 'pair' Rebus: *dul* 'cast (metal)' PLUS*kana, kanac* = corner (Santali); Rebus: *kañcu* = bronze (Telugu) PLUS infixed kolmo 'paddy plant' Rebus: kolami 'smithy, forge'. Thus, cast bronze smithy, forge. Or, *mogge* 'sprout, bud' Rebus: *mũh* 'ingot' (Santali)Thus, cast bronze ingot. Read as: *kañcu dul mũh 'bronze cast ingot' aya kāṇḍa* 'alloy metalware'

h2136A

h178A

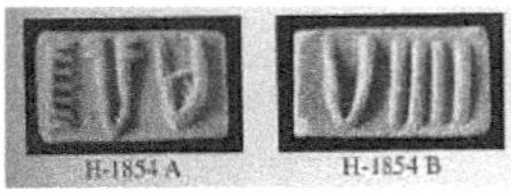

h1854A

 *kharedo* = a currycomb (Gujarati) खरारा [*kharārā*] *m* (H) A currycomb. 2 Currying a horse. (Marathi) Rebus: करडा [*karaḍā*] Hard from alloy--iron, silver &c. (Marathi) *kharādī* ' turner' (Gujarati)

 kanka 'rim of jar' Rebus: karṇīka 'account (scribe)' karṇī 'supercargo'
khuṭo ' leg, foot ', °ṭī ' goat's leg ' Rebus: *khōṭā* 'alloy' (Marathi)

 *baṭa* 'rimless, broad-mouthed pot' Rebus: *bhaṭa* 'furnace' (Gujarati.); *baṭa* 'a kind of iron' (Gujarati)
|||| Numeral 4: gaṇḍa 'four' Rebus: kaṇḍa 'furnace, fire-altar' (Santali

Native metal smith guild: Zebu horns ligatured to a standing person with a tail and bovine legs and upraised hand:

Pict-88 m1224 m1224e Text 1227

Pictorial motif hieroglyph: (man with horns ligatured to a bull's hindpart + tail)

Ligatured zebu horns: *khũṭ* 'zebu' Rebus: '(native metal) guild'

koḍ 'horn' Rebus: koḍ 'workshop'
meḍ 'body' Rebus: meḍ 'iron'
ḍangar 'bull' Rebus: *ḍhangar* 'blacksmith'.
eraka 'upraised arm' Rebus: eraka 'copper'
Thus the pictorial motif denoes: *eraka meḍ ḍhangar koḍ* 'copper-iron-smith workshop, native metal guild'.

Text 1227 hieroglyphs in two lines:

Line 1  Read rebus: From r.: kan- 'copper' + dul 'cast (metal) + kanka 'supercargo scribe' + meḍ 'iron' + kharādī ' turner'. Thus, Line 1 denotes turned supercargo of iron and copper.

Line 2  Read rebus: From r.: kañcu 'bronze' + āra 'brass' +kolami 'smithy, forge' + dul kharādī 'cast metal turner'. Thus, Line 2 denotes smithy/forge of cast metal turner (working) bronze and brass.

Each sign hieroglyph is read rebus:

 meḍ ‘body’ Rebus: meḍ ‘iron’

 *dula* 'pair' Rebus: *dul* 'cast (metal)' PLUS*kana, kanac* = corner (Santali); Rebus: *kañcu* = bronze (Telugu) Thus, cast bronze.

 dula ‘pair’ Rebus: dul ‘cast (metal)’

 kanka ‘rim of jar’ Rebus: *karṇīka* ‘account (scribe)’ *karṇī* ‘supercargo’

 Numeral 6: āra 'six', Rebus: āra 'brass' Vikalpa: dula ‘two’ Rebus: dul ‘cast metal’ PLUS kolom ‘three’ Rebus: kolami ‘smithy, forge’.

 kana, kanac = corner (Santali); Rebus: kañcu = bronze (Telugu) gaṇḍa 'four' Rebus: kaṇḍa 'furnace, fire-altar' (Santali) PLUS sal ‘splinter’ Rebus: sal ‘workshop’

 kharedo = a currycomb (Gujarati) Rebus: kharādī ' turner' ; dula ‘pair’ Rebus: dul ‘cast (metal). Thus, the pair of EE glyphs denote: cast (metal) turner

 kharedo = a currycomb (Gujarati) Rebus: kharādī ' turner'

 kolmo ‘rice plant’ (Munda) Rebus: kolami ‘smithy, forge’ (Telugu)

 Kalibangan 7Ah749A

 *kharedo* = a currycomb (Gujarati) खरारा [*kharārā*] *m* (H) A currycomb. 2 Currying a horse. (Marathi) Rebus: करडा [*karaḍā*] Hard from alloy--iron, silver &c. (Marathi) *kharādī* ' turner' (Gujarati)

 kanka ‘rim of jar’ Rebus: karṇīka ‘account (scribe)’ karṇī ‘supercargo’

m1769a *खोंड [khōṇḍa] m A young bull, a bullcalf. (Marathi) Rebus: kōdār ‘turner’ (Bengali); कोंद kōnda ‘engraver, lapidary setting or infixing gems’ (Marathi) G. sãghāṛɔ m. ‘lathe’ ; संघाट joinery; M. sāgaḍ ‘double-canoe’ Rebus: sangataras ‘stone-cutter, mason’*

| *koḍa* ‘one’ Rebus: *koḍ* ‘workshop’ PLUS |||| Numeral 4: gaṇḍa 'four' Rebus: kaṇḍa 'furnace, fire-altar' (Santali)

 kanka ‘rim of jar’ Rebus: karṇīka ‘account (scribe)’ karṇī ‘supercargo’
dula ‘two’ Rebus: dul ‘cast metal’ *aya kāṇḍa* ‘alloy metalware’

dula ‘two’ Rebus: dul ‘cast metal’

 *kanac* ‘corner’ Rebus: *kañcu* ‘bronze’ sal ‘splinter’ Rebus: sal ‘workshop’

M-317 a

m317a *खोंड [khōṇḍa] m A young bull, a bullcalf. (Marathi) Rebus: kõdār ‘turner’ (Bengali); कोंद kōnda ‘engraver, lapidary setting or infixing gems’ (Marathi) G. sãghāṛɔ m. ‘lathe’ ; संघाट joinery; M. sãgaḍ ‘double-canoe’ Rebus: sangataras ‘stone-cutter, mason’*

dula ‘pair’ Rebus: dul ‘cast metal’ PLUS

 *khareḍo* = a currycomb (Gujarati) खरारा [*kharārā*] *m* (H) A currycomb. 2 Currying a horse. (Marathi) Rebus: करडा [*karaḍā*] Hard from alloy--iron, silver &c. (Marathi) *kharādī* ‘ turner’ (Gujarati)

  *dāṭu* ‘cross’(Telugu) Rebus: *dhatu* ‘mineral’ (Santali).
dhāḷ ‘a slope’; ‘inclination of a plane’ (G.); *ḍhāḷiyum* = adj. sloping, inclining (G.) Rebus: *ḍhālako* = a large metal ingot (G.) *ḍhālakī* = a metal heated and poured into a mould; a solid piece of metal; an ingot (Gujarati) PLUS खांडा [*khāṇḍā*] *m* A jag, notch, or indentation (as upon the edge of a tool or weapon). Rebus: *kāṇḍa* ‘tools, pots and pans and metal-ware’ Thus, the pair of sign hieroglyphs from r. read rebus: copper, bronze ingots, metalware castings.

 kanka ‘rim of jar’ Rebus: karṇīka ‘account (scribe)’ karṇī ‘supercargo’*meḍ* ‘body’ Rebus: *meḍ* ‘iron’ (Ho.) काठी [kāṭhī] *f* (काष्ट S) ‘frame or structure of the body’ (Marathi) Rebus: खंडी [khaṇḍī] measure of weight (Marathi) *கண்டி; kaṇṭi, n. < Mhr. khaṇḍil. [T. Tu. khaṇḍi, M. kaṇḍi.]* Candy, a weight, stated to be roughly equivalent to 500 lbs.

M-1981 a

m1981a

 *khareḍo* = a currycomb (Gujarati) खरारा [*kharārā*] *m* (H) A currycomb. 2 Currying a horse. (Marathi) Rebus: करडा [*karaḍā*] Hard from alloy--iron, silver &c. (Marathi) *kharādī* ‘ turner’ (Gujarati)

 *aḍar* 'harrow'; rebus: *aduru* 'native unsmelted metal'
meḍ ‘body’ Rebus: *meḍ* ‘iron’ (Ho.) काठी [kāṭhī] *f* (काष्ट S) ‘frame or structure of the body’ (Marathi) Rebus: खंडी [khaṇḍī] measure of weight (Marathi) *கண்டி; kaṇṭi, n. < Mhr. khaṇḍil. [T. Tu. khaṇḍi, M. kaṇḍi.]* Candy, a weight, stated to be roughly equivalent to 500 lbs.

 kanka ‘rim of jar’ Rebus: karṇīka ‘account (scribe)’ karṇī ‘supercargo’
kolom ‘three’ Rebus: kolami ‘smithy, forge’

M-1170 a

m1170a Pictorial motif hieroglyph composite:
krammara 'look back' (Telugu) Rebus: kamar 'metalsmith' (Santali)
ṭagara'ram' Rebus: *tagara* 'tin' Thus, tinsmith: *tagara kamar.*

ṭagara'ram' Rebus: *tagara* 'tin' Vikalpa: ranku 'antelope' Rebus: ranku 'tin'

balad m. ' ox ', gng. *bald*, (Ku.) *barad*, id. (N. Tarai) Rebus: *bharat* (5 copper, 4 zinc and 1 tin)(Punjabi) pattar 'trough' Rebus: pattar 'guild'. Thus, copper-zinc-tin alloy (worker) guild.
Text: ligatured hieroglyph sign ligature:
kolmo 'paddy plant' Rebus: kolami 'smithy, forge' Vikalpa: mogge 'sprout, bud' Rebus: *mũh* 'ingot'

 *kharedo* = a currycomb (Gujarati) खरारा [*kharārā*] *m* (H) A currycomb. 2 Currying a horse. (Marathi) Rebus: करडा [*karaḍā*] Hard from alloy--iron, silver &c. (Marathi) *kharādī* ' turner' (Gujarati)
Thus, ingot turner.

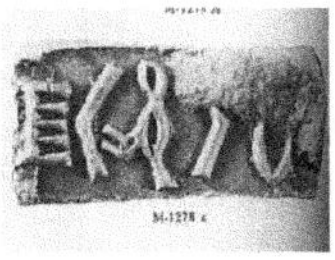

m1278a

 *kharedo* = a currycomb (Gujarati) खरारा [*kharārā*] *m* (H) A currycomb. 2 Currying a horse. (Marathi) Rebus: करडा [*karaḍā*] Hard from alloy--iron, silver &c. (Marathi) *kharādī* ' turner' (Gujarati)

 *kuṭila* 'bent' CDIAL 3230 kuṭi— in cmpd. 'curve', *kuṭika*— 'bent' MBh. Rebus: *kuṭila, katthīl* = bronze (8 parts copper and 2 parts tin) Duplicated: dula 'pair' Rebus: dul 'cast metal' Thus, () circumscript indicates cast bronze or bronze castings. karaṇḍa 'duck' (Sanskrit) karaṛa 'a very large aquatic bird' (Sindhi) Rebus: करडा [*karaḍā*] Hard from alloy--iron, silver &c. (Marathi) *kharādī* ' turner' (Gujarati)

 kanka 'rim of jar' Rebus: karṇīka 'account (scribe)' karṇī 'supercargo'

M-500 a bis

m500a

 *kharedo* = a currycomb (Gujarati) खरारा [*kharārā*] *m* (H) A currycomb. 2 Currying a horse. (Marathi) Rebus: करडा [*karaḍā*] Hard from alloy--iron, silver &c. (Marathi) *kharādī* ' turner' (Gujarati) gaṇḍa 'four' Rebus: kaṇḍa 'furnace, fire-altar' (Santali) PLUS ranku 'liquid measure' Rebus: ranku 'tin'

loa 'ficus religiosa' Rebus: *lo* 'iron' (Sanskrit) PLUS unique ligatures: लोखंड [lōkhaṇḍa] *n* (लोह S) Iron. लोखंडाचे चणे खावविणें or चारणें To oppress grievously.लोखंडकाम [lōkhaṇḍakāma] *n* Iron work; that portion (of a building, machine &c.) which consists of iron. 2 The business of an ironsmith.लोखंडी [lōkhaṇḍī] *a* (लोखंड) Composed of iron; relating to iron. (Marathi) *bhaṭa* 'warrior' (Sanskrit) Rebus: *baṭa* a kind of iron (Gujarati). Rebus: *bhaṭa* 'furnace' (Santali) Thus, together, the ligatured hieroglyph reads rebus: *loa bhaṭa* 'iron furnace'

kolom 'three' Rebus: kolami 'smithy, forge'

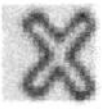 *dāṭu* 'cross'(Telugu) Rebus: *dhatu* 'mineral' (Santali). *baṭa* = rimless pot (Kannada) Rebus:) *baṭa* = a kind of iron (G.)) *bhaṭa* furnace (Gujarati)

Desalpur 3A

 *kolmo* 'paddy plant' Rebus: *kolami* 'smithy, forge' Vikalpa: *mogge* 'sprout, bud' Rebus: *mũh* 'ingot' (Santali) dolu 'plant of shoot height' Rebus: dul 'cast metal'

 *khareḍo* = a currycomb (Gujarati) खरारा [*kharārā*] *m* (H) A currycomb. 2 Currying a horse. (Marathi) Rebus: करडा [*karaḍā*] Hard from alloy--iron, silver &c. (Marathi) *kharādī* ' turner' (Gujarati) dula 'two' Rebus: dul 'cast metal' sal 'splinter' Rebus: sal 'workshop' *kamaḍha* 'archer, bow' Rebus: *kammaṭa* 'mint, coiner'.

 kanka 'rim of jar' Rebus: karṇīka 'account (scribe)' karṇī 'supercargo'

m704a *खोंड [khōṇḍa] m A young bull, a bullcalf. (Marathi) Rebus: kõdār 'turner' (Bengali); कोंद kōnda 'engraver, lapidary setting or infixing gems' (Marathi) G. sãghārɔ m. 'lathe' ; संघाट joinery; M. sãgaḍ 'double-canoe' Rebus: sangataras 'stone-cutter, mason'*

khareḍo =  a currycomb (Gujarati) खरारा [*kharārā*] *m* (H) A currycomb. 2 Currying a horse. (Marathi) Rebus: करडा [*karaḍā*] Hard from alloy--iron, silver &c. (Marathi) *kharādī* ' turner' (Gujarati) dula 'two' Rebus: dul 'cast metal' sal 'splinter' Rebus: sal 'workshop'

 *meḍ* 'body' Rebus: *meḍ* 'iron' (Ho.) काठी [kāṭhī] *f* (काष्ठ S) 'frame or structure of the body' (Marathi) Rebus: खंडी [khaṇḍī] measure of weight (Marathi) *கண்டி; kaṇṭi, n. < Mhr. khaṇḍil. [T. Tu. khaṇḍi, M. kaṇḍi.]* Candy, a weight, stated to be roughly equivalent to 500 lbs.

 *aḍar* 'harrow'; rebus: *aduru* 'native unsmelted metal' खांडा [*khāṇḍā*] *m* A jag, notch, or indentation (as upon the edge of a tool or weapon). Rebus: *kāṇḍa* 'tools, pots and pans and metal-ware'

  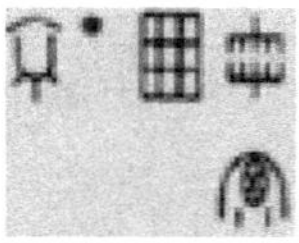

m1101A m1101a Text 2431
khũṭ 'zebu' Rebus: '(native metal) guild'

 The composite, ligature hieroglyph: 'arched wheel-spokes-nave' Rebus reading: *eraka āra* 'copper, bronze' *maṇḍa* 'market'

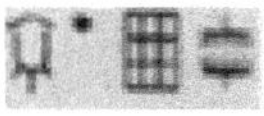 From r.: dula 'two' Rebus: dul 'cast metal'

 *aḍar* 'harrow'; rebus: *aduru* 'native unsmelted metal'

khaṇḍ 'field, division' (Sanskrit) Rebus: *khāṇḍa* 'tools, pots and pans, metal-ware'. Rebus 2: kaṇḍ 'fire-altar' (Santali)

 *aḍaren* 'cover of pot or lid' Rebus: *aduru* 'native, unsmelted metal' Duplicated: dula 'pair' Rebus: dul 'cast metal'

baṭa 'broad-mouthed pot'; *bhaṭa* 'furnace' (Gujarati.); *baṭa* 'a kind of iron' (Gujarati) PLUS *aḍaren* 'lid' Rebus: *aduru* 'native unsmelted metal'.

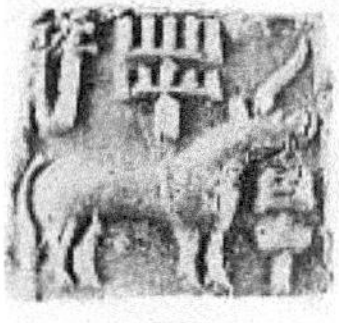
M-938 a
m938A

h475a

m182A

H-2119 A

H-2119 B

h2119A

खोंड [khōṇḍa] m A young bull, a bullcalf. (Marathi) Rebus: kõdār 'turner' (Bengali); कोंद kōnda 'engraver, lapidary setting or infixing gems' (Marathi) G. sãghāṛɔ m. 'lathe' ; संघाट joinery; M. sãgaḍ 'double-canoe' Rebus: sangataras 'stone-cutter, mason'

dula 'two' Rebus: dul 'cast metal'

 *aḍar* 'harrow'; rebus: *aduru* 'native unsmelted metal'

 kanka 'rim of jar' Rebus: karṇīka 'account (scribe)' karṇī 'supercargo'
Side B of h2119: kolom 'three' Rebus: kolami 'smithy, forge'

 *kanac* 'corner' Rebus: *kañcu* 'bronze'

BM 123208 Pictorial motif hieroglyph: *balad* m. ' ox ', gng. *bald*, (Ku.) *barad*, id. (N. Tarai) Rebus: *bharat* (5 copper, 4 zinc and 1 tin)(Punjabi) pattar 'trough' Rebus: pattar 'guild'. Thus, copper-zinc-tin alloy (worker) guild.

 *aḍar* 'harrow'; rebus: *aduru* 'native unsmelted metal'

 *dula* 'pair' Rebus: *dul* 'cast (metal)' PLUS*kana, kanac* = corner (Santali); Rebus: *kañcu* = bronze (Telugu) PLUS infixed kolmo 'paddy plant' Rebus: kolami 'smithy, forge'. Thus, cast bronze smithy, forge. Or, *mogge* 'sprout, bud' Rebus: *mũh* 'ingot' (Santali)Thus, cast bronze ingot. Read as: *kañcu dul mũh 'bronze cast ingot'*

खांडा [*khāṇḍā*] *m* A jag, notch, or indentation (as upon the edge of a tool or weapon). Rebus: *kāṇḍa* 'tools, pots and pans and metal-ware' Thus, mint metalware, ore.

khuṭo ' leg, foot ', °ṭī ' goat's leg ' Rebus: *khōṭā* 'alloy' (Marathi)
kolom 'three' Rebus: kolami 'smithy, forge' sal 'splinter' Rebus: sal 'workshop'

m1222Am741A

M-741 A

M-1222 A

खोंड [khōṇḍa] m A young bull, a bullcalf. (Marathi) Rebus: kõdār 'turner' (Bengali); कोंद kōnda 'engraver, lapidary setting or infixing gems' (Marathi) G. sãghāṛɔ m. 'lathe' ; संघाट joinery; M. sāgaḍ 'double-canoe' Rebus: sangataras 'stone-cutter, mason'

dula 'two' Rebus: dul 'cast metal'

aḍar 'harrow'; rebus: *aduru* 'native unsmelted metal'

water-carrier hieroglyph *kuṭi*; Rebus: *kuṭhi* 'smelter furnace'.
PLUS 'rim of jar': *kanka* (Santali) *karṇika* 'scribe'(Sanskrit)
Rebus: *karṇī,* supercargo
'rim-of-jar' hieroglyph *kanka* (Santali) *karṇika* 'scribe'(Sanskrit)
Rebus: *karṇī,* supercargo for a boat shipment. *karṇīka* 'account (scribe) '.कारणी *kāraṇī* 'the supercargo of a ship' (Marathi)

H-457 a

h457a *खोंड [khōṇḍa] m A young bull, a bullcalf. (Marathi) Rebus: kõdār 'turner' (Bengali); कोंद kōnda 'engraver, lapidary setting or infixing gems' (Marathi) G. sãghāṛɔ m. 'lathe' ; संघाट joinery; M. sāgaḍ 'double-canoe' Rebus: sangataras 'stone-cutter, mason'*
gaṇḍa 'four' Rebus: *kaṇḍa* 'furnace, fire-altar' (Santali).

aḍar 'harrow'; rebus: *aduru* 'native unsmelted metal'
sal 'splinter' Rebus: sal 'workshop' kolom 'three' Rebus: kolami 'smithy, forge' *kamaḍha* 'crab' Rebus: *kammaṭa* 'mint, coiner'.*ḍato* = claws of crab (Santali) Rebus: *dhātu* 'mineral ore'

kanka 'rim of jar' Rebus: karṇīka 'account (scribe)' karṇī 'supercargo'

H-2097 A

H-2097 B

h2097A,B

H-2096 A

H-2096 B

h2096A,B

H-2095 A

H-2095 B

h2095A,B

H-2094 A

H-2094 B

h2094A,B

dula 'two' Rebus: dul 'cast metal'

aḍar 'harrow'; rebus: *aduru* 'native unsmelted metal'

kanac 'corner' Rebus: *kañcu* 'bronze' sal 'splinter' Rebus: sal 'workshop' Side B:

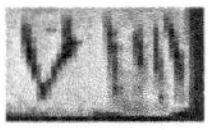

baṭa 'rimless, broad-mouthed pot' Rebus: *bhaṭa* 'furnace' (Gujarati.); *baṭa* 'a kind of iron' (Gujarati)
|||| Numeral 4: gaṇḍa 'four' Rebus: kaṇḍa 'furnace, fire-altar' (Santali)

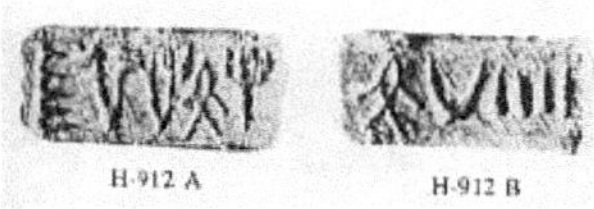

h912A,B

h302A

h1191A,B Side B:

baṭa 'rimless, broad-mouthed pot' Rebus: *bhaṭa* 'furnace' (Gujarati.); *baṭa* 'a kind of iron' (Gujarati)
|||| Numeral 4: gaṇḍa 'four' Rebus: kaṇḍa 'furnace, fire-altar' (Santali) *ayo* 'fish' Rebus: *aya* 'iron' *ayas* 'metal' Side A:

khareḍo = a currycomb (Gujarati) खरारा [*kharārā*] *m* (H) A currycomb. 2 Currying a horse. (Marathi) Rebus: करडा [*karaḍā*] Hard from alloy--iron, silver &c. (Marathi) *kharādī* ' turner' (Gujarati)

dula 'pair' Rebus: dul 'cast (metal)' kolmo 'rice plant' Rebus: kolami 'smithy/forge' metal.

kanka 'rim of jar' Rebus: karṇīka 'account (scribe)' karṇī 'supercargo' *ayo* 'fish' Rebus: *aya* 'iron' *ayas* 'metal'
dula 'two' Rebus: dul 'cast metal'

aḍar 'harrow'; rebus: *aduru* 'native unsmelted metal'

M-1703 a

m1703a खोंड *[khōṇḍa] m A young bull, a bullcalf. (Marathi) Rebus: kõdār 'turner' (Bengali);* कोंद *kõnda 'engraver, lapidary setting or infixing gems' (Marathi) G. sãghāṛɔ m. 'lathe' ;* संघाट *joinery; M. sãgaḍ 'double-canoe' Rebus: sangataras 'stone-cutter, mason'*
dula 'two' Rebus: dul 'cast metal'

aḍar 'harrow';  rebus: *aduru* 'native unsmelted metal' *ayo ḍhālako* 'alloy metal ingot'

meḍ 'body' Rebus: *meḍ* 'iron' (Ho.) PLUS | *koḍa* 'one' Rebus: *koḍ* 'workshop' dula 'pair' Rebus: dul 'cast metal'. Thus, the 'body' flanked by two linear strokes denote: workshop for iron castings.

water-carrier hieroglyph *kuṭi*; Rebus: *kuṭhi* 'smelter furnace'.

m114a खोंड *[khōṇḍa] m A young bull, a bullcalf. (Marathi) Rebus: kõdār 'turner' (Bengali);* कोंद *kōnda 'engraver, lapidary setting or infixing gems' (Marathi) G. sãghāṛɔ m. 'lathe' ;* संघाट *joinery; M. sãgaḍ 'double-canoe' Rebus: sangataras 'stone-cutter, mason'*
dula 'two' Rebus: dul 'cast metal'

 *aḍar* 'harrow'; rebus: *aduru* 'native unsmelted metal' *ayo ḍhālako* 'alloy metal ingot'

  Strands of yarn/rope' hieroglyph: Hieroglyph: 'strands of yarn' Rebus reading: *dhā'tu* 'strand of rope' Rebus: *dhatu* 'mineral ore' (Santali) sal 'splinter' Rebus: sal 'workshop' *ḍhanga* = a crook used for pulling down the branches of trees, for goats, sheep and camels (P.) Rebus:*ḍhangar* blacksmith'.

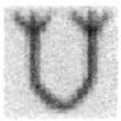 dula 'pair' Rebus: dul 'cast (metal)' kolmo 'rice plant' Rebus: kolami 'smithy/forge' metal.

 kanka 'rim of jar' Rebus: karṇīka 'account (scribe)' karṇī 'supercargo'

m91A खोंड *[khōṇḍa] m A young bull, a bullcalf. (Marathi) Rebus: kõdār 'turner' (Bengali);* कोंद *kōnda 'engraver, lapidary setting or infixing gems' (Marathi) G. sãghāṛɔ m. 'lathe' ;* संघाट *joinery; M. sãgaḍ 'double-canoe' Rebus: sangataras 'stone-cutter, mason'* dula 'two' Rebus: dul 'cast metal'

 *aḍar* 'harrow'; rebus: *aduru* 'native unsmelted metal' *ayo ḍhālako* 'alloy metal ingot'

bicha  'scorpion' (Assamese) Rebus: *bica* 'stone ore' (Santali)

 *kanac* 'corner' Rebus: *kañcu* 'bronze'
sal 'splinter' Rebus: sal 'workshop' dula 'two' Rebus: dul 'cast metal'
ayo 'fish' Rebus: *aya* 'iron' *ayas* 'metal' *kamaḍha* 'crab' Rebus: *kammaṭa* 'mint, coiner'.*ḍato* = claws of crab (Santali) Rebus: *dhātu* 'mineral ore' *bhaṭa* 'warrior' (Sanskrit) Rebus: *baṭa* a kind of iron (Gujarati). Rebus: *bhaṭa* 'furnace' (Santali)

 kanka 'rim of jar' Rebus: karṇīka 'account (scribe)' karṇī 'supercargo'

Lothal 5A खोंड *[khōṇḍa] m A young bull, a bullcalf. (Marathi) Rebus: kõdār 'turner' (Bengali);* कोंद *kōnda 'engraver, lapidary setting or infixing gems' (Marathi) G. sãghāṛɔ m. 'lathe' ;* संघाट *joinery; M. sãgaḍ 'double-canoe' Rebus: sangataras 'stone-cutter, mason'* dula 'two' Rebus: dul 'cast metal'

aḍar  'harrow'; rebus: *aduru* 'native unsmelted metal' *ayo ḍhālako* 'alloy metal ingot'

 *dāṭu* 'cross'(Telugu) Rebus: *dhatu* 'mineral' (Santali).
ḍato = claws of crab (Santali) Rebus: *dhātu* 'mineral ore' PLUS | *koḍa* 'one' Rebus: *koḍ* 'workshop' sal 'splinter' Rebus: sal 'workshop' dula 'two' Rebus: dul 'cast metal' PLUS *ḍato* = claws of crab (Santali) Rebus: *dhātu* 'mineral ore'

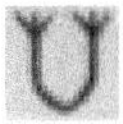 dula 'pair' Rebus: dul 'cast (metal)' kolmo 'rice plant' Rebus: kolami 'smithy/forge' metal.

 kanka 'rim of jar' Rebus: karṇīka 'account (scribe)' karṇī 'supercargo'

m729a *खोंड [khōṇḍa] m A young bull, a bullcalf. (Marathi) Rebus: kõdār 'turner' (Bengali); कोंद kōnda 'engraver, lapidary setting or infixing gems' (Marathi) G. sãghāṛɔ m. 'lathe' ; संघाट joinery; M. sãgaḍ 'double-canoe' Rebus: sangataras 'stone-cutter, mason'*

aḍar 'harrow';  rebus: *aduru* 'native unsmelted metal'

gaṇḍa 'four' Rebus: kaṇḍa 'furnace, fire-altar' (Santali) dula 'pair' Rebus: dul 'cast metal' *aya kāṇḍa* 'alloy metalware'

m1680a *खोंड [khōṇḍa] m A young bull, a bullcalf. (Marathi) Rebus: kõdār 'turner' (Bengali); कोंद kōnda 'engraver, lapidary setting or infixing gems' (Marathi) G. sãghāṛɔ m. 'lathe' ; संघाट joinery; M. sãgaḍ 'double-canoe' Rebus: sangataras 'stone-cutter, mason'*

aḍar  'harrow'; rebus: *aduru* 'native unsmelted metal'
ayo 'fish' Rebus: *aya* 'iron' *ayas* 'metal'

 *khuṭo* ' leg, foot ', °ṭī ' goat's leg ' Rebus: *khōṭā* 'alloy' (Marathi)
kanka 'rim of jar' Rebus: karṇīka 'account (scribe)' karṇī 'supercargo'

m914a *खोंड [khōṇḍa] m A young bull, a bullcalf. (Marathi) Rebus: kõdār 'turner' (Bengali); कोंद kōnda 'engraver, lapidary setting or infixing gems' (Marathi) G. sãghāṛɔ m. 'lathe' ; संघाट joinery; M. sãgaḍ 'double-canoe' Rebus: sangataras 'stone-cutter, mason'*

 *aḍar* 'harrow'; rebus: *aduru* 'native unsmelted metal'

ayo 'fish' Rebus: *aya* 'iron' *ayas* 'metal'
ranku 'antelope' Rebus: ranku 'tin' | *koḍa* 'one' Rebus: *koḍ* 'workshop'

 कांड *kāṇḍa* 'arrow' Rebus: *kāṇḍa* 'pots and pans, metalware, tools'. Rebus 2: kaṇḍ 'fire-altar' (Santali)

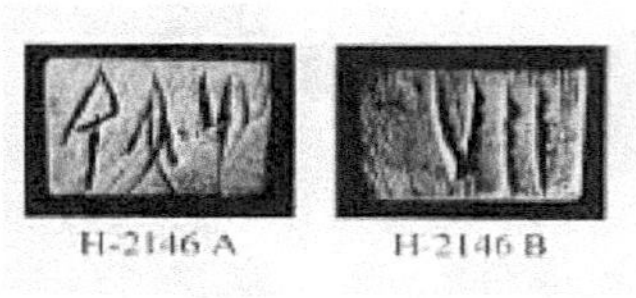

h2146A,B Side A:

aḍar 'harrow'; rebus: *aduru* 'native unsmelted metal'

ayo 'fish' Rebus: *aya* 'iron' *ayas* 'metal'

कांड *kāṇḍa* 'arrow' Rebus:  *kāṇḍa* 'pots and pans, metalware, tools'. Rebus 2: kaṇḍ 'fire-altar' (Santali)

dula 'two' Rebus: dul 'cast metal' *baṭa* = rimless pot (Kannada) Rebus: *baṭa* = a kind of iron (G.)) *bhaṭa* furnace (Gujarati)

m37A *खोंड [khōṇḍa] m A young bull, a bullcalf. (Marathi) Rebus: kõdār 'turner' (Bengali); कोंद kōnda 'engraver, lapidary setting or infixing gems' (Marathi) G. sãghāṛɔ m. 'lathe' ; संघाट joinery; M. sãgaḍ 'double-canoe' Rebus: sangataras 'stone-cutter, mason'*

Read rebus as at Side A of h2146

h786A Side B:

kanac 'corner' Rebus: *kañcu* 'bronze' *kamaḍha* 'archer, bow' Rebus: *kammaṭa* 'mint, coiner'.

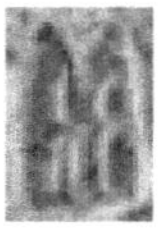

Ligature: two peaks: mēḍu height, rising ground, hillock (Kannada) Rebus: *meḍ* 'iron' (Ho.) dula 'pair' Rebus: dul 'cast metal' PLUS |||| Numeral 4: gaṇḍa 'four' Rebus: kaṇḍa 'furnace, fire-altar' (Santali)

h2240A

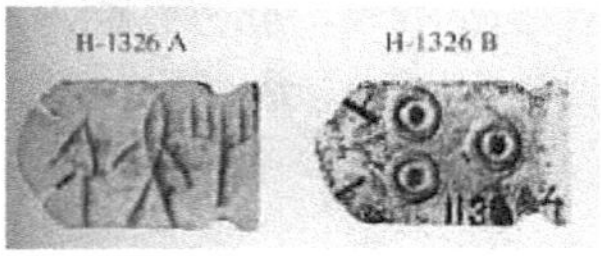

h1326a Read rebus as at Side A of h2146 Side B: dulo 'hole' Rebus: dul 'cast metal' kolom 'three' Rebus: kolami 'smithy, forge'

h940A Read rebus as at 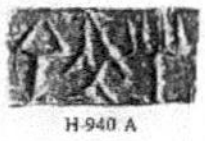 Side A of h2146

h364A Read rebus as at Side A of h2146

H-346 A

h346A Read rebus as at Side A of h2146

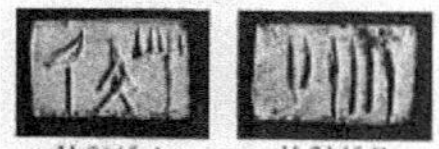
H-2145 A H-2145 B

h2145A,B Read rebus as at Side A of h2146 PLUS Side B: sal 'splinter' Rebus: sal 'workshop' gaṇḍa 'four' Rebus: kaṇḍa 'furnace, fire-altar' (Santali)

h2021A,B

 *aḍar* 'harrow'; unsmelted *aya* 'iron' *ayas*

 mēḍu height, (Kannada) *meḍ* 'iron'

 ḍāg (H.)(CDIAL 'blacksmith' (Maithili)

H-2021 A

H-2021 B

H-2021 C

rebus: *aduru* 'native metal' *ayo* 'fish' Rebus: 'metal'

rising ground, hillock Rebus: *mẽṛhẽt,* (Munda.Ho.)

mountain-ridge 5476). Rebus: dhangar

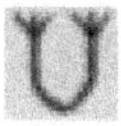 dula 'pair' Rebus: dul 'cast (metal)' kolmo 'rice plant' Rebus: kolami 'smithy/forge' metal.

 kanka 'rim of jar' Rebus: karṇīka 'account (scribe)' karṇī 'supercargo'

Side B:

 *kana, kanac* = corner (Santali); Rebus: *kañcu* = bronze (Telugu) PLUS खांडा [*khāṇḍā*] *m* A jag, notch, or indentation (as upon the edge of a tool or weapon). Rebus: *kāṇḍa* 'tools, pots and pans and metal-ware' Thus, bronze metalware.

 *bicha* 'scorpion' (Assamese) Rebus: *bica* 'stone ore' (Santali)

 'Arrow' sign hieroglyph (variant) This is a ligature of 'lid of pot' hieroglyph superscript on 'a linear stroke' numeral hieroglyph.*aḍaren* 'cover of pot or lid' Rebus: *aduru* 'native, unsmelted metal' PLUS koḍ = one (Santali); koḍ 'workshop' (Gujarati)

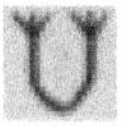 dula 'pair' Rebus: dul 'cast (metal)' kolmo 'rice plant' Rebus: kolami 'smithy/forge' metal.

 kanka 'rim of jar' Rebus: karṇīka 'account (scribe)' karṇī 'supercargo'

Side C:

 *khōṇḍa* A stock or stump (Marathi); 'leafless tree' (Marathi) Rebus: *kõdār* 'turner' (Bengali); *kõdā* 'to turn in a lathe' (Bengali). Allogra

m307A

 *aḍar* 'harrow'; rebus: *aduru* 'native unsmelted metal'

 *ayo* 'fish' Rebus: *aya* 'iron' *ayas* 'metal' Side B: As at Side B h2148 *dula* 'pair' Rebus: *dul* 'cast (metal)' PLUS*kana, kanac* = corner (Santali); Rebus: *kañcu* = bronze (Telugu) Thus, cast bronze. *mogge* 'sprout, bud' Rebus*: mũh* 'ingot'

h2147A

 *aḍar* 'harrow'; rebus: *aduru* 'native unsmelted metal' *ayo* 'fish' Rebus: *aya* 'iron' *ayas* 'metal' Side B: As at Side B h2148

h2148A,B Read rebus as at Side A of h2146 PLUS Side B: *baṭa* 'rimless, broad-mouthed pot' Rebus: *bhaṭa* 'furnace' (Gujarati.); *baṭa* 'a kind of iron' (Gujarati) 'Dance step': meṭṭu step, stair, treading, slipper (Te.)(DEDR 1557). Rebus: *meḍ* 'iron'(Munda); मेढ meḍh'merchant's helper'(Pkt.) *meḍ* iron (Ho.)

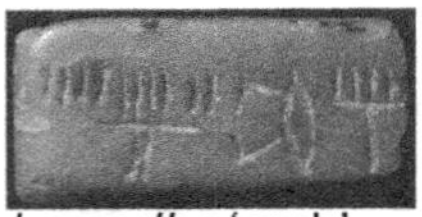

m413A

 *aḍar* 'harrow'; rebus: *aduru* 'native unsmelted metal'

kamaḍha 'crab' Rebus: *kammaṭa* 'mint, coiner'.*ḍato* = claws of crab (Santali) Rebus: *dhātu* 'mineral ore' sal 'splinter' Rebus: sal 'workshop'

 |||| Numeral 4: gaṇḍa 'four' Rebus: kaṇḍa 'furnace, fire-altar' (Santali) dula 'pair' Rebus: dul 'cast metal'

gaṇḍa 'four' Rebus: kaṇḍa 'furnace, fire-altar' (Santali) dula 'pair' Rebus: dul 'cast metal'

 m231a *खोंड [khōṇḍa] m A young bull, a bullcalf. (Marathi) Rebus: kõdār 'turner' (Bengali); कोंद kōnda 'engraver, lapidary setting or infixing gems' (Marathi) G. sãghārɔ m. 'lathe' ; संघाट joinery; M. sãgaḍ 'double-canoe' Rebus: sangataras 'stone-cutter, mason'*

 *aḍar* 'harrow'; rebus: *aduru* 'native unsmelted metal' *bhaṭa* 'warrior' (Sanskrit) Rebus: *baṭa* a kind of iron (Gujarati). Rebus: *bhaṭa* 'furnace' (Santali)

  kanka 'rim of jar' Rebus: karṇīka 'account (scribe)' karṇī 'supercargo' *khareḍo* = a currycomb (Gujarati) खरारा [*kharārā*] *m* (H) A currycomb. 2 Currying a horse. (Marathi) Rebus: करडा [*karaḍā*] Hard from alloy--iron, silver &c. (Marathi) *kharādī* ' turner' (Gujarati)

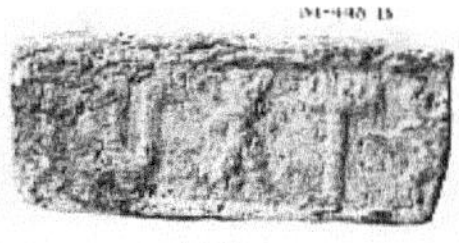

M-450 A

m450A First 3 signs read rebus as at h168

M-1886 a

m1886a Pictorial motif hieroglyph: *balad* m. ' ox ', gng. *bald*, (Ku.) *barad*, id. (N. Tarai) Rebus: *bharat* (5 copper, 4 zinc and 1 tin)(Punjabi) *pattar* 'trough' Rebus: *pattar* 'guild'. Thus, copper-zinc-tin alloy (worker) guild.Read rebus as at first 3 signs h168

H-168 A

h168A

 *aḍar* 'harrow'; rebus: *aduru* 'native unsmelted metal'
bhaṭa 'warrior' (Sanskrit) Rebus: *baṭa* a kind of iron (Gujarati). Rebus: *bhaṭa* 'furnace' (Santali)

 kanka 'rim of jar' Rebus: karṇīka 'account (scribe)' karṇī 'supercargo'

 *meḍ* 'body' Rebus: *meḍ* 'iron' (Ho.) काठी [kāṭhī] *f* (काष्ट S) 'frame or structure of the body' (Marathi) Rebus: खंडी [khaṇḍī] measure of weight (Marathi) கண்டி; *kaṇṭi, n. < Mhr. khaṇḍil. [T. Tu. khaṇḍi, M. kaṇḍi.]* Candy, a weight, stated to be roughly equivalent to 500 lbs.

 *kharedo* = a currycomb (Gujarati) खरारा [*kharārā*] *m* (H) A currycomb. 2 Currying a horse. (Marathi) Rebus: करडा [*karaḍā*] Hard from alloy--iron, silver &c. (Marathi) *kharādī* ' turner' (Gujarati)

M-980 a

m980A *खोंड [khōṇḍa] m A young bull, a bullcalf. (Marathi) Rebus: kōdār 'turner' (Bengali); कोंद kōnda 'engraver, lapidary setting or infixing gems' (Marathi) G. sãghāṛɔ m. 'lathe' ; संघाट joinery; M. sãgaḍ 'double-canoe' Rebus: sangataras 'stone-cutter, mason'*
First 4 signs read rebus as at h168

  *ḍhanga* = a crook used for pulling down the branches of trees, for goats, sheep and camels (P.) Rebus:*ḍhangar* blacksmith' PLUS notch+slanted stroke reads rebus: *ḍhālako kāṇḍa* 'ingot, tools, pots and pans and metal-ware'.*ḍhāḷ* 'a slope'; 'inclination of a plane' (G.); *ḍhāḷiyum* = adj. sloping, inclining (G.) Rebus: *ḍhālako* = a large metal ingot (G.) *ḍhālakī* = a metal heated and poured into a mould; a solid piece of metal; an ingot (Gujarati) PLUS खांडा [*khāṇḍā*] *m* A jag, notch, or indentation (as upon the edge of a tool or weapon). Rebus: *kāṇḍa* 'tools, pots and pans and metal-ware'
kamaḍha 'crab' Rebus: *kammaṭa* 'mint, coiner'.*ḍato* = claws of crab (Santali) Rebus: *dhātu* 'mineral ore'
dula 'pair' Rebus: dul 'cast metal' kolom 'three' Rebus: kolami 'smithy, forge'

 kanka 'rim of jar' Rebus: karṇīka 'account (scribe)' karṇī 'supercargo'

Balakot 5A A variant pictorial hieroglyph of 'young bull' *खोंड [khōṇḍa] m A young bull, a bullcalf. (Marathi) Rebus: kõdār 'turner' (Bengali); कोंद kōnda 'engraver, lapidary setting or infixing gems' (Marathi) G. sãghāṛɔ m. 'lathe' ; संघाट joinery; M. sãgaḍ 'double-canoe' Rebus: sangataras 'stone-cutter, mason'*

If the face of antelope is ligatured to body of 'young bull', the rebus reading is: *ranku* 'antelope' Rebus: *ranku* 'tin'. Thus, tin turner, engraver.

 *aḍar* 'harrow'; rebus: *aduru* 'native unsmelted metal'

 कांड *kāṇḍa* 'arrow' Rebus: *kāṇḍa* 'pots and pans, metalware, tools'. Rebus 2: kaṇḍ 'fire-altar' (Santali)

Rupar 1a

 *khareḍo* = a currycomb (Gujarati) खरारा [*kharārā*] *m* (H) A currycomb. 2 Currying a horse. (Marathi) Rebus: करडा [*karaḍā*] Hard from alloy--iron, silver &c. (Marathi) *kharādī*' turner' (Gujarati) *aya kāṇḍa* 'alloy metalware'

 *aḍar* 'harrow'; rebus: *aduru* 'native unsmelted metal'

h2246B

 *aḍar* 'harrow'; rebus: *aduru* 'native unsmelted metal'

arka) copper (metal); crystal (Kannada) *erako* 'moltencast copper' Duplicated: dula 'pair' Rebus: dul 'cast metal' Thus cast copper, brass casting.

sal 'splinter' Rebus: sal 'workshop' Thus, moltencast copper, brass workshop.

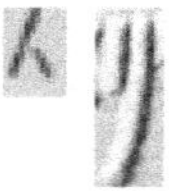 notch+slanted stroke reads rebus: *ḍhālako kāṇḍa* 'ingot, tools, pots and pans and metal-ware'.*dhāḷ* 'a slope'; 'inclination of a plane' (G.); *ḍhāḷiyum* = adj. sloping, inclining (G.) Rebus: *ḍhālako* = a large metal ingot (G.) *ḍhālakī* = a metal heated and poured into a mould; a solid piece of metal; an ingot (Gujarati) PLUS खांडा [*khāṇḍā*] *m* A jag, notch, or indentation (as upon the edge of a tool or weapon). Rebus: *kāṇḍa* 'tools, pots and pans and metal-ware'

dula 'two' Rebus; dul 'cast metal'

 *kanac* 'corner' Rebus: *kañcu* 'bronze'

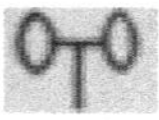 'Cart-frame' sign hieroglyph: Miscellaneous articles

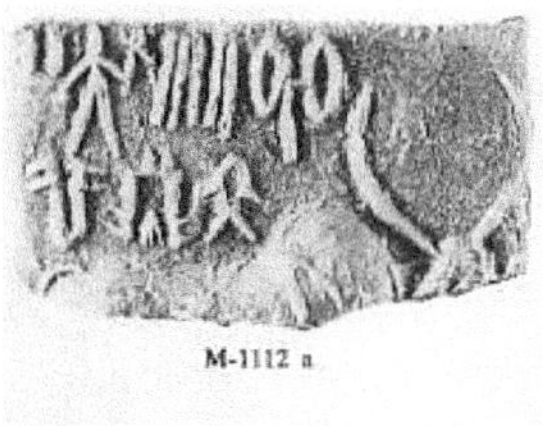

m1112a Text 2366 *khũṭ* 'zebu' Rebus: '(native metal) guild'. The text inscription Line 1: native unsmelted iron workshop, smithy, forge of cast metal; miscellaneous articles:

If frame of a cart is depicted, possible rebus reading: अगडा [agaḍā] *m* The tie connecting the जूं & दांडी of a गाडा or load-cart; the shaft and thill-yoke-tie. Rebus: 'lumber, 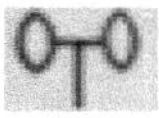 miscellaneous articles': अगडतगड [

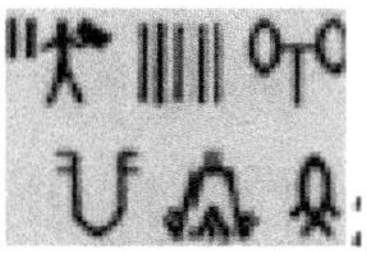

agaḍatagaḍa] *n* अगडबगड *n* (Fanciful formations, or from H) Trash, trumpery, rubbish, lumber, miscellaneous articles.
dula 'pair or two' Rebus: dul 'cast metal'
kolom 'three' Rebus: kolami 'smithy, forge'
meḍ 'body' Rebus: meḍ 'iron' + ligature 'harrow' hieroglyph: *aḍar* 'harrow'; rebus: *aduru* 'native unsmelted metal'
sal 'splinter' Rebus: sal 'workshop'

Line2:
ayo 'fish' Rebus: aya 'iron' (Gujarati) ayas 'metal' (Vedic)
 a  Allograph: सांड [sāṇḍa] *f* (षद S) An outlet for superfluous water (as through dam or mound); a sluice, a floodvent. Rebus: सांडणी [sāṇḍaṇī] *f* (H) An instrument of goldsmiths. It is hooked or curved at the extremity; and is used to draw things out of the fire.
 kanka 'rim of jar' Rebus: *karṇīka* 'account (scribe)' *karṇī* 'supercargo'

h2244A

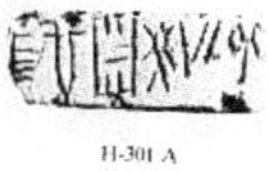

h301A

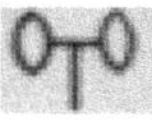

अगडा [agaḍā] *m* The tie connecting the जूं & दांडी of a गाडा or load-cart; the shaft and thill-yoke-tie. Rebus: 'lumber, miscellaneous articles': अगडतगड [*agaḍatagaḍa*] *n* अगडबगड *n* (Fanciful formations, or from H) Trash, trumpery, rubbish, lumber, miscellaneous articles.
dula 'pair' Rebus: dul 'cast metal' PLUS *dhāḷ* 'a slope'; 'inclination of a plane' (G.); *ḍhāḷiyum* = adj. sloping, inclining (G.) Rebus: *ḍhālako* = a large metal ingot (G.) *ḍhālakī* = a metal heated and poured into a mould; a solid piece of metal; an ingot (Gujarati) | *koḍa* 'one' Rebus: *koḍ* 'workshop' *aya kammaṭa.*'coiner, mint alloy'
kəṭhā´r, kc. *kuṭhār* m. ' granary, storeroom '(WPah.)(CDIAL 3550). *koṭhārī m.* ' storekeeper'

(Gujarati)(CDIAL 3551) Thus, storeroom (of) *kolom* 'three' Rebus: *kolami* 'smithy, forge'. Dula 'pair' Rebus: dul 'cast metal' Thus, together *dul kolami kuṭhār* 'metal smithy castings storeroom'

 kanka 'rim of jar' Rebus: karṇīka 'account (scribe)' karṇī 'supercargo'

 *kharedo* = a currycomb (Gujarati) खरारा [*kharārā*] *m* (H) A currycomb. 2 Currying a horse. (Marathi) Rebus: करडा [*karaḍā*] Hard from alloy--iron, silver &c. (Marathi) *kharādī*' turner' (Gujarati)

M-1834 a

m1834a *खोंड [khōṇḍa] m A young bull, a bullcalf. (Marathi) Rebus: kōdār 'turner' (Bengali); कोंद kōnda 'engraver, lapidary setting or infixing gems' (Marathi) G. sãghāṛɔ m. 'lathe' ; संघाट joinery; M. sāgaḍ 'double-canoe' Rebus: sangataras 'stone-cutter, mason'*

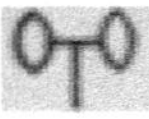

अगडा [agaḍā] *m* The tie connecting the जूं & दांडी of a गाडा or load-cart; the shaft and thill-yoke-tie. Rebus: 'lumber, miscellaneous articles': अगडतगड [*agaḍatagaḍa*] *n* अगडबगड *n* (Fanciful formations, or from H) Trash, trumpery, rubbish, lumber, miscellaneous articles.

kuṭila 'bent' CDIAL 3230 kuṭi— in cmpd. 'curve', *kuṭika—* 'bent' MBh. Rebus: *kuṭila, katthīl* = bronze (8 parts copper and 2 parts tin) *ḍhanga* = a crook used for pulling down the branches of trees, for goats, sheep and camels (P.) Rebus:*ḍhangar* blacksmith'.

kanka (Santali) *karṇika* 'scribe'(Sanskrit) Rebus: *karṇī,* supercargo for a boat shipment. INFIXED खांडा [*khāṇḍā*] *m* A jag, notch, or indentation (as upon the edge of a tool or weapon). Rebus: *kāṇḍa* 'tools, pots and pans and metal-ware'
ranku 'liquid measure' Rebus: ranku 'tin'

ḍāg mountain-ridge (H.)(CDIAL 5476). Rebus: dhangar 'blacksmith' (Maithili)

kanka 'rim of jar' Rebus: karṇīka 'account (scribe)' karṇī 'supercargo' kolom 'three' Rebus: kolami 'smithy, forge'

khaṇḍ 'field, division' (Skt.) Rebus: *khāṇḍa* 'tools, pots and pans, metal-ware'. Rebus 2: kaṇḍ 'fire-altar' (Santali) dula 'pair' Rebus: dul 'cast metal' Thus, duplicated 'division' hieroglyph sign reads: cast metal metal-ware.

karaḍakum 'a streamlet' (Gujarati); [*karaḍamu* 'a wave' (Telugu) Rebus: करडा [*karaḍā*] Hard from alloy--iron, silver &c. (Marathi) *kharādī* ' turner'

m16a *खोंड [khōṇḍa] m A young bull, a bullcalf. (Marathi) Rebus: kōdār 'turner' (Bengali); कोंद kōnda 'engraver, lapidary setting or infixing gems' (Marathi) G. sãghāṛɔ m. 'lathe' ; संघाट joinery; M. sāgaḍ 'double-canoe' Rebus: sangataras 'stone-cutter, mason'*

अगडा [agaḍā] *m* The tie connecting the जूं & दांडी of a गाडा or load-cart; the shaft and thill-yoke-tie. Rebus: 'lumber, miscellaneous articles': अगडतगड [*agaḍatagaḍa*] *n* अगडबगड *n* (Fanciful formations, or from H) Trash, trumpery, rubbish, lumber, miscellaneous articles.
dula 'two' Rebus: dul 'cast metal' kolom 'three' Rebus: kolami 'smithy, forge'

aḍar 'harrow'; rebus: *aduru* 'native unsmelted metal'

meḍ 'body' Rebus: *meḍ* 'iron' (Ho.) काठी [kāṭhī] *f* (काष्ट S) 'frame or structure of the body' (Marathi) Rebus: खंडी [khaṇḍī] measure of weight (Marathi) *கண்டி; kaṇṭi, n. < Mhr. khaṇḍil. [T. Tu. khaṇḍi, M. kaṇḍi.]* Candy, a weight, stated to be roughly equivalent to 500 lbs.

āra 'spokes' Rebus: *āra 'brass'*. cf. erka = ekke (Tbh. of arka) aka (Tbh. of arka) copper (metal); crystal (Kannada) Glyph: *eraka*'nave of wheel' Rebus: eraka 'copper'; cf. erka = ekke (Tbh. of arka) aka (Tbh. of arka) copper (metal); crystal (Kannada) *erako* 'moltencast copper' Duplicated: dula 'pair' Rebus: dul 'cast metal' Thus cast copper, brass casting.

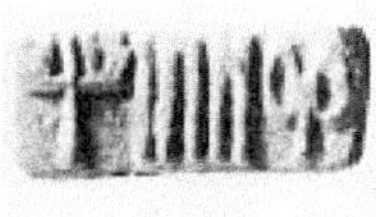

H-219 A

h219A

अगडा [agaḍā] *m* The tie connecting the जूं & दांडी of a गाडा or load-cart; the shaft and thill-yoke-tie. Rebus: 'lumber, miscellaneous articles': अगडतगड [*agaḍatagaḍa*] *n* अगडबगड *n* (Fanciful formations, or from H) Trash, trumpery, rubbish, lumber, miscellaneous articles.

dula 'two' Rebus: dul 'cast metal' kolom 'three' Rebus: kolami 'smithy, forge'

aḍar 'harrow'; rebus: *aduru* 'native unsmelted metal'

M-699 A

m699A *खोंड [khōṇḍa] m A young bull, a bullcalf. (Marathi) Rebus: kōdār 'turner' (Bengali); कोंद kōnda 'engraver, lapidary setting or infixing gems' (Marathi) G. sãghārɔ m. 'lathe' ; संघाट joinery; M. sãgaḍ 'double-canoe' Rebus: sangataras 'stone-cutter, mason'*

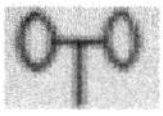

अगडा [agaḍā] *m* The tie connecting the जूं & दांडी of a गाडा or load-cart; the shaft and thill-yoke-tie. Rebus: 'lumber, miscellaneous articles': अगडतगड [*agaḍatagaḍa*] *n* अगडबगड *n* (Fanciful formations, or from H) Trash, trumpery, rubbish, lumber, miscellaneous articles.

dula 'two' Rebus: dul 'cast metal' gaṇḍa 'four' Rebus: kaṇḍa 'furnace, fire-altar' (Santali) sal 'splinter' Rebus: sal 'workshop'

meḍ 'body' Rebus: *meḍ* 'iron' (Ho.) काठी [kāṭhī] *f* (काष्ट S) 'frame or structure of the body' (Marathi) Rebus: खंडी [khaṇḍī] measure of weight (Marathi) *கண்டி; kaṇṭi, n. < Mhr. khaṇḍil. [T. Tu. khaṇḍi, M. kaṇḍi.]* Candy, a weight, stated to be roughly equivalent to 500 lbs.

aḍar 'harrow'; rebus: *aduru* 'native unsmelted metal'

bhaṭa 'warrior' (Sanskrit) Rebus: *baṭa* a kind of iron (Gujarati). Rebus: *bhaṭa* 'furnace' (Santali)

kanka 'rim of jar' Rebus: karṇīka 'account (scribe)' karṇī 'supercargo'

H-2192 A

H-2192 B

h2192Ah2192A,B

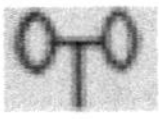 अगडा [agaḍā] *m* The tie connecting the जूं & दांडी of a गाडा or load-cart; the shaft and thill-yoke-tie. Rebus: 'lumber, miscellaneous articles': अगडतगड [*agaḍatagaḍa*] *n* अगडबगड *n* (Fanciful formations, or from H) Trash, trumpery, rubbish, lumber, miscellaneous articles.

kolom 'three' Rebus: kolami 'smithy, forge' *aya kammaṭa.*'coiner, mint alloy' PLUS | *koḍa* 'one' Rebus: *koḍ* 'workshop'

 dula 'two' Rebus: dul 'cast metal' PLUS *kana, kanac* = corner (Santali); Rebus: *kañcu* = bronze (Telugu) PLUS खांडा [*khāṇḍā*] *m* A jag, notch, or indentation (as upon the edge of a tool or weapon). Rebus: *kāṇḍa* 'tools, pots and pans and metal-ware' Thus, bronze metalware.

 kanka 'rim of jar' Rebus: karṇīka 'account (scribe)' karṇī 'supercargo'

Y-shaped sign hieroglyph (Elaborated as 'rimless pot' ligatured with a 'notch': खांडा [*khāṇḍā*] *m* A jag, notch, or indentation (as upon the edge of a tool or weapon). Rebus: *kāṇḍa* 'tools, pots and pans and metal-ware' *PLUS baṭa* = rimless pot (Kannada) Rebus: *baṭa* = a kind of iron (G.)) *bhaṭa* furnace (Gujarati) Thus, furnace tools, *bhaṭa kāṇḍa*

 m810a *खोंड [khōṇḍa] m A young bull, a bullcalf. (Marathi) Rebus: kõdār 'turner' (Bengali); कोंद kōnda 'engraver, lapidary setting or infixing gems' (Marathi) G. sãghāṛɔ m. 'lathe' ; संघाट joinery; M. sãgaḍ 'double-canoe' Rebus: sangataras 'stone-cutter, mason'*

 Furnace tools, *bhaṭa kāṇḍa*
kanka 'rim of jar' Rebus: karṇīka 'account (scribe)' karṇī 'supercargo'

 h449a *खोंड [khōṇḍa] m A young bull, a bullcalf. (Marathi) Rebus: kõdār 'turner' (Bengali); कोंद kōnda 'engraver, lapidary setting or infixing gems' (Marathi) G. sãghāṛɔ m. 'lathe' ; संघाट joinery; M. sãgaḍ 'double-canoe' Rebus: sangataras 'stone-cutter, mason'*
Furnace tools, *bhaṭa kāṇḍa*

 *kolmo* 'paddy plant' Rebus: *kolami* 'smithy, forge' Vikalpa: *mogge* 'sprout, bud' Rebus: *mũh* 'ingot' (Santali) dolu 'plant of shoot height' Rebus: dul 'cast metal'

 dula 'pair' Rebus: dul 'cast (metal)' kolmo 'rice plant' Rebus: kolami 'smithy/forge' metal.

aya kammaṭa.'coiner, mint alloy'
ranku 'liquid measure' Rebus: ranku 'tin'

 *kolmo* 'paddy plant' Rebus: *kolami* 'smithy, forge' Vikalpa: *mogge* 'sprout, bud' Rebus:
 *mũh* 'ingot' (Santali) dolu 'plant of shoot height' Rebus: dul 'cast metal'
kanka 'rim of jar' Rebus: karṇīka 'account (scribe)' karṇī 'supercargo'

M-932 A

m932A *खोंड [khōṇḍa] m A young bull, a bullcalf. (Marathi) Rebus: kõdār 'turner' (Bengali); कोंद kōnda 'engraver, lapidary setting or infixing gems' (Marathi) G. sãghāṛɔ m. 'lathe' ; संघाट joinery; M. sãgaḍ 'double-canoe' Rebus: sangataras 'stone-cutter, mason'*
Furnace tools, *bhaṭa kāṇḍa*

Variant: dula 'pair' Rebus: dul 'cast metal' PLUS | *koḍa* 'one' Rebus: *koḍ* 'workshop' PLUS INFIXED खांडा [*khāṇḍā*] *m* A jag, notch, or indentation (as upon the edge of a tool or weapon). Rebus: *kāṇḍa* 'tools, pots and pans and metal-ware' Thus metware castings workshop.

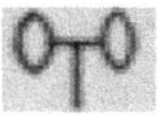

अगडा [agaḍā] *m* The tie connecting the जूं & दांडी of a गाडा or load-cart; the shaft and thill-yoke-tie. Rebus: 'lumber, miscellaneous articles': अगडतगड [*agaḍatagaḍa*] *n* अगडबगड *n* (Fanciful formations, or from H) Trash, trumpery, rubbish, lumber, miscellaneous articles.

muka 'ladle' (Tamil)(DEDR 4887) Rebus: *mũh* 'ingot' (Santali) *baṭa* = rimless pot (Kannada) Rebus: *baṭa* = a kind of iron (G.)) *bhaṭa* furnace (Gujarati) Thus, iron ingot.

kanka 'rim of jar' Rebus: karṇīka 'account (scribe)' karṇī 'supercargo'

H-153 a

h153A Furnace tools, *bhaṭa kāṇḍa*

muka 'ladle' (Tamil)(DEDR 4887) Rebus: *mũh* 'ingot' (Santali) *baṭa* = rimless pot (Kannada) Rebus: *baṭa* = a kind of iron (G.)) *bhaṭa* furnace (Gujarati) Thus, iron ingot.

loa 'ficus religiosa' Rebus: *lo* 'iron' (Sanskrit) PLUS unique ligatures: लोखंड [lōkhaṇḍa] *n* (लोह S) Iron. लोखंडाचे चणे खावविणें or चारणें To oppress grievously.लोखंडकाम [lōkhaṇḍakāma] *n* Iron work; that portion (of a building, machine &c.) which consists of iron. 2 The business of an ironsmith.लोखंडी [lōkhaṇḍī] *a* (लोखंड) Composed of iron; relating to iron. (Marathi)

L-46 A

Lothal 46a Pictorial motif hieroglyph: *balad* m. ' ox ', gng. *bald*, (Ku.) *barad*, id. (N. Tarai) Rebus: *bharat* (5 copper, 4 zinc and 1 tin)(Punjabi) *pattar* 'trough' Rebus*: pattar* 'guild'. Thus, copper-zinc-tin alloy (worker) guild.
Furnace tools, *bhaṭa kāṇḍa*

kanac 'corner' Rebus: *kañcu* 'bronze' sal 'splinter' Rebus: sal 'workshop'

baraḍo = spine; backbone (Tulu) Rebus: *baran, bharat* 'mixed alloys' (5 copper, 4 zinc and 1 tin) (Punjabi) PLUS gaṇḍa 'four' Rebus: kaṇḍa 'furnace, fire-altar' (Santali)

kanka 'rim of jar' Rebus: karṇīka 'account (scribe)' karṇī 'supercargo' *ayo* 'fish' Rebus: *aya* 'iron' *ayas* 'metal'

loa 'ficus religiosa' Rebus: *lo* 'iron' (Sanskrit) PLUS unique ligatures: लोखंड [lōkhaṇḍa] *n* (लोह S) Iron. लोखंडाचे चणे खावविणें or चारणें To oppress grievously.लोखंडकाम [

lōkhaṇḍakāma] *n* Iron work; that portion (of a building, machine &c.) which consists of iron. 2 The business of an ironsmith.लोखंडी [lōkhaṇḍī] *a* (लोखंड) Composed of iron; relating to iron. (Marathi)

dula 'two, pair' Rebus: dul 'cast metal' PLUS *dhāḷ* 'a slope'; 'inclination of a plane' (G.); *ḍhāḷiyum* = adj. sloping, inclining (G.) Rebus: *ḍhālako* = a large metal ingot (G.) *ḍhālakī* = a metal heated and poured into a mould; a solid piece of metal; an ingot (Gujarati) PLUS kolom 'three' Rebus: kolami 'smithy, forge'. Thus cast metal ingot smithy.

'notch infixed ligature of rim-of-jar' hieroglyph

  m1119 Text 2463 *khūṭ* 'zebu' Rebus: '(native metal) guild'

 Ligatured hieroglyph: rim of jar + notch:
kanka 'rim of jar' Rebus: *karṇīka* 'account (scribe)' *karṇī* 'supercargo' PLUS infixed hieroglyph 'notch' Rebus: *kāṇḍa* 'pots and pans, metalware, tools'. Thus, the composite hieroglyph denotes supercargo of metalware.

 *āra* 'spokes' Rebus: *āra 'brass'*. cf. erka = ekke (Tbh. of arka) aka (Tbh. of arka) copper (metal); crystal (Kannada) Glyph: *eraka* 'nave of wheel' Rebus: eraka 'copper'; cf. erka = ekke (Tbh. of arka) aka (Tbh. of arka) copper (metal); crystal (Kannada) *erako* 'moltencast copper' sal 'splinter' Rebus: sal 'workshop'

 *dula* 'pair' Rebus: *dul* 'cast (metal)' PLUS*kana, kanac* = corner (Santali); Rebus: *kañcu* = bronze (Telugu) PLUS infixed kolmo 'paddy plant' Rebus: kolami 'smithy, forge'. Thus, cast bronze smithy, forge. Or, *mogge* 'sprout, bud' Rebus: *mũh* 'ingot' (Santali)Thus, cast bronze ingot. Read as: *kañcu dul mũh 'bronze cast ingot'*

h93a *ibha* 'elephant' Rebus: *ib* 'iron' *ibbo* 'merchant' (Gujarati)

 *baṭa* = rimless pot (Kannada) Rebus: *baṭa* = a kind of iron (G.)) *bhaṭa* furnace (Gujarati) *kamaḍha* 'archer, bow' Rebus: *kammaṭa* 'mint, coiner'.

M-329 a

m329a dula 'two' Rebus: dul 'cast metal' *baṭa* = rimless pot (Kannada) Rebus: *baṭa* = a kind of iron (G.)) *bhaṭa* furnace (Gujarati) Furnace castings.

 *kanac* 'corner' Rebus: *kañcu* 'bronze'
sal 'splinter Rebus: sal 'workshop'

M-1824 a

m1824a *खोंड [khōṇḍa] m A young bull, a bullcalf. (Marathi) Rebus: kõdār 'turner' (Bengali); कोंद kōnda 'engraver, lapidary setting or infixing gems' (Marathi) G. sãghāṛɔ m. 'lathe' ; संघाट joinery; M. sãgaḍ 'double-canoe' Rebus: sangataras 'stone-cutter, mason'*

dula 'two' Rebus: dul 'cast metal' *baṭa* = rimless pot (Kannada) Rebus: *baṭa* = a kind of iron (G.)) *bhaṭa* furnace (Gujarati) Furnace castings. | *koḍa* 'one' Rebus: *koḍ* 'workshop'

kharedo = a currycomb (Gujarati) खरारा [*kharārā*] *m* (H) A currycomb. 2 Currying a horse. (Marathi) Rebus: करडा [*karaḍā*] Hard from alloy--iron, silver &c. (Marathi) *kharādī* ' turner' (Gujarati)

h764B kolom 'three' Rebus: kolami 'smithy, forge' PLUS *baṭa* = rimless pot (Kannada) Rebus: *baṭa* = a kind of iron (G.)) *bhaṭa* furnace (Gujarati) Thus, furnace forge.

m721a *खोंड [khōṇḍa] m A young bull, a bullcalf. (Marathi) Rebus: kōdār 'turner' (Bengali); कोंद kōnda 'engraver, lapidary setting or infixing gems' (Marathi) G. sãghārɔ m. 'lathe' ; संघाट joinery; M. sãgaḍ 'double-canoe' Rebus: sangataras 'stone-cutter, mason'*

dula 'two' Rebus: dul 'cast metal' *baṭa* = rimless pot (Kannada) Rebus: *baṭa* = a kind of iron (G.)) *bhaṭa* furnace (Gujarati) Furnace castings.

meḍ 'body' Rebus: *meḍ* 'iron' (Ho.) काठी [kāṭhī] *f* (काष्ट S) 'frame or structure of the body' (Marathi) Rebus: खंडी [khaṇḍī] measure of weight (Marathi) *கண்டி; kaṇṭi, n. < Mhr. khaṇḍil. [T. Tu. khaṇḍi, M. kaṇḍi.]* Candy, a weight, stated to be roughly equivalent to 500 lbs.

sal 'splinter' Rebus: sal 'workshop' *ayo* 'fish' Rebus: *aya* 'iron' *ayas* 'metal'

m478A

erga = act of clearing jungle (Kui)

Rebus: erako 'moltencast copper'

kuṭi 'tree' Rebus: *kuṭhi* 'smelter'

heraka 'spy' (Sanskrit) Rebus:eraka 'copper' kola 'tiger' Rebus: kolhe 'smelter' kol 'working in iron' krammara 'look back' Rebus: kamar 'smith'

kaṇḍa 'pot' Rebus: 'furnace, fire-altar' (Santali)

Variant:

khōṇḍa A stock or stump (Marathi); 'leafless tree' (Marathi) Rebus: *kõdār* 'turner' (Bengali); *kõdā* 'to turn in a lathe' (Bengali).

aḍaren 'cover of pot or lid' Rebus: *aduru* 'native, unsmelted metal' Duplicated: dula 'pair' Rebus: dul 'cast metal'

Worshipper: *bhaṭā* G. *bhuvɔ* m. ' worshipper in a temple ' rather < bhr̥ta --(CDIAL 9554) Yājñ.com., Rebus: *bhaṭā* ' kiln, furnace'

A variant of 'adorant' hieroglyph sign is shown with a 'rimless, broad-mouthed pot' which is *baṭa* read rebus: *bhaṭa* 'furnace'. If the 'pot' ligature is a phonetic determinant, the gloss for the 'adorant' is *bhaṭa* 'worshipper'. If the 'kneeling' posture is the key hieroglyphic representation, the gloss is *eragu* 'bow' Rebus: *erako* 'moltencast copper'.

Thus, the pair of hieroglyphsl: 'adorant' PLUS 'tiger' connote: *erako kolhe* 'copper smelter'. A pair of 'adorant' PLUS 'pot' connote: *erako bhaṭā* 'copper furnace'.

kuṭi 'tree' Rebus: *kuṭhi* 'smelter'
gaṇḍa 'four' Rebus: *kaṇḍa* 'furnace, fire-altar' (Santali). *baṭa* 'rimless, broad-mouthed pot' Rebus: *bhaṭa* 'furnace' (Gujarati.); *baṭa* 'a kind of iron' (Gujarati)

meḍ 'body' Rebus: *meḍ* 'iron' (Ho.) PLUS | *koḍa* 'one' Rebus: *koḍ* 'workshop' dula 'pair' Rebus: dul 'cast metal'. Thus, the 'body' flanked by two linear strokes denote: workshop for iron castings.

kharedo = a currycomb (Gujarati) खरारा [*kharārā*] *m* (H) A currycomb. 2 Currying a horse. (Marathi) Rebus: करडा [*karaḍā*] Hard from alloy--iron, silver &c. (Marathi) *kharādī* ' turner' (Gujarati)
मेढा [mēḍhā] 'a curl or snarl; twist in thread' (Marathi) Rebus: mẽṛhẽt, meḍ 'iron' (Mu.Ho.)

H-1987 A
H-1987 B

h1987A.B

kuṭila 'bent' CDIAL 3230 kuṭi— in cmpd. 'curve', *kuṭika*— 'bent' MBh. Rebus: *kuṭila, katthīl* = bronze (8 parts copper and 2 parts tin)

kanka 'rim of jar' Rebus: karṇīka 'account (scribe)' karṇī 'supercargo'

beads: Pa. kandi (pl. -l) necklace, beads. Ga. (Punjabi) kandi (pl. -l) bead, (pl.) necklace; (S.2) kandiṭ bead. (DEDR 1215) Rebus: *கண்டி; kaṇṭi, n. < Mhr. khaṇḍil. [T. Tu. khaṇḍi, M. kaṇḍi.] 1. Candy, a weight, stated to be roughly equivalent to 500 lbs.; பாரமென் னும் நிறையளவு.* खंडीगणती or खंडोगणती [khaṇḍīgaṇatī or khaṇḍōgaṇatī] *ad* By candies; counting or reckoning by candies. खंडीवारी [khaṇḍīvārī] *ad* By scores, heaps, candies. खंडी [khaṇḍī] Applied to a great quantity; as खंडीभर पोरें, खंडीभर मेंढ्या, खंडीभर काम, खंडीभर बोलतो-लिहितो&c

mēḍu height, rising ground, hillock (Kannada) Rebus: *meḍ* 'iron' (Ho.) kolom 'three' Rebus: kolami 'smithy, forge' Thus, *meḍ kolami* 'iron smithy-forge'

gaṇḍa 'four' Rebus: kaṇḍa 'furnace, fire-altar' (Santali)

kolmo 'paddy plant' Rebus: *kolami* 'smithy, forge' Vikalpa: *mogge* 'sprout, bud' Rebus: *mũh* 'ingot' (Santali) dolu 'plant of shoot height' Rebus: dul 'cast metal'

Side B: *baṭa* 'rimless, broad-mouthed pot' Rebus: *bhaṭa* 'furnace' (Gujarati.); *baṭa* 'a kind of iron' (Gujarati) gaṇḍa 'four' Rebus: kaṇḍa 'furnace, fire-altar' (Santali) dula

m1985a *bhaṭa* 'warrior' (Sanskrit) Rebus: *baṭa* a kind of iron (Gujarati). Rebus: *bhaṭa* 'furnace' (Santali)

 *kuṭila* 'bent' CDIAL 3230 kuṭi— in cmpd. 'curve', *kuṭika*— 'bent' MBh. Rebus: *kuṭila, katthīl* = bronze (8 parts copper and 2 parts tin) *baṭa* 'rimless, broad-mouthed pot' Rebus: *bhaṭa* 'furnace' (Gujarati.); *baṭa* 'a kind of iron' (Gujarati)

ayo 'fish' Rebus: *aya* 'iron' *ayas* 'metal'

 *aḍar* 'harrow'; rebus: *aduru* 'native unsmelted metal'

 *dula* 'pair' Rebus: *dul* 'cast (metal)' PLUS*kana, kanac* = corner (Santali); Rebus: *kañcu* = bronze (Telugu) PLUS infixed kolmo 'paddy plant' Rebus: kolami 'smithy, forge'. Thus, cast bronze smithy, forge. Or, *mogge* 'sprout, bud' Rebus: *mũh* 'ingot' (Santali)Thus, cast bronze ingot. Read as: *kañcu dul mũh 'bronze cast ingot'*

 *kanka* (Santali) *karṇika* 'scribe'(Sanskrit) Rebus: *karṇī,* supercargo for a boat shipment. INFIXED खांडा [*khāṇḍā*] *m* A jag, notch, or indentation (as upon the edge of a tool or weapon). Rebus: *kāṇḍa* 'tools, pots and pans and metal-ware'

B-8 A

Banawali 8A *ṭagara*'ram' Rebus: *tagara* 'tin' Vikalpa: *miṇḍāl* 'markhor' (Tōrwālī) *meḍho* a ram, a sheep (Gujarati)(CDIAL 10120) Rebus: *mẽṛhẽt, meḍ* 'iron' (Mu.Ho.)

 kanka 'rim of jar' Rebus: karṇīka 'account (scribe)' karṇī 'supercargo'

Read in context, the composite hieroglyph is assumed to be a combination of a slanted stroke ligatured to a notch,which provide possible rebus readings of a smithy/forge: notch+slanted stroke reads rebus: *ḍhālako kāṇḍa* 'ingot, tools, pots and pans and metal-ware'

ḍhāḷ 'a slope'; 'inclination of a plane' (Gujarati); *ḍhāḷiyum* = adj. sloping, inclining (Gujarati) Rebus: *ḍhālako* = a large metal ingot (Gujarati) *ḍhālakī* = a metal heated and poured into a mould; a solid piece of metal; an ingot (Gujarati) PLUS खांडा [*khāṇḍā*] *m* A jag, notch, or indentation (as upon the edge of a tool or weapon). Rebus: *kāṇḍa* 'tools, pots and pans and metal-ware'

H-639 a

h639a

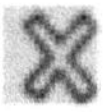 *dāṭu* 'cross'(Telugu) Rebus: *dhatu* 'mineral' (Santali).

muka ‘ladle’ (Tamil)(DEDR 4887) Rebus: *mũh* ‘ingot’ (Santali) *baṭa* = rimless pot (Kannada) Rebus: *baṭa* = a kind of iron (G.)) *bhaṭa* furnace (Gujarati) Thus, iron ingot.

kana, kanac = corner (Santali); Rebus: *kañcu* = bronze (Telugu) PLUS खांडा [*khāṇḍā*] *m* A jag, notch, or indentation (as upon the edge of a tool or weapon). Rebus: *kāṇḍa* ‘tools, pots and pans and metal-ware’ Thus, bronze metalware.

dula ‘pair’ Rebus: *dul* ‘cast (metal)’ PLUS*kana, kanac* = corner (Santali); Rebus: *kañcu* = bronze (Telugu) Thus, cast bronze.

aya aḍaren (homonym: aduru)‘alloy native metal’ sal ‘splinter’ Rebus: sal ‘workshop’ *baṭa* = rimless pot (Kannada) Rebus: *baṭa* = a kind of iron (G.)) *bhaṭa* furnace (Gujarati)

kanka ‘rim of jar’ Rebus: karṇīka ‘account (scribe)’ karṇī ‘supercargo’

m279a *ibha* ‘elephant’ Rebus: *ib* ‘iron’ *ibbo* ‘merchant’ (Gujarati)

baṭa = rimless pot (Kannada) Rebus: *baṭa* = a kind of iron (G.)) *bhaṭa* furnace (Gujarati) sal ‘splinter’ Rebus: sal ‘workshop’

aḍar 'harrow'; rebus: *aduru* 'native unsmelted metal'
ayo ‘fish’ Rebus: *aya* ‘iron’ *ayas* ‘metal’

कांड *kāṇḍa* ‘arrow’ Rebus: *kāṇḍa* ‘pots and pans, metalware, tools’. Rebus 2: kaṇḍ 'fire-altar' (Santali)

m86a *खोंड [khōṇḍa] m A young bull, a bullcalf. (Marathi) Rebus: kõdār ‘turner’ (Bengali); कोंद kōnda ‘engraver, lapidary setting or infixing gems’ (Marathi) G. sãghāṛɔ m. ‘lathe’ ; संघाट joinery; M. sãgaḍ ‘double-canoe’ Rebus: sangataras ‘stone-cutter, mason’*

kanka ‘rim of jar’ Rebus: karṇīka ‘account (scribe)’ karṇī ‘supercargo’

āra 'spokes' Rebus: *āra ‘brass’*. cf. erka = ekke (Tbh. of arka) aka (Tbh. of arka) copper (metal); crystal (Kannada) Glyph: *eraka*‘nave of wheel’ Rebus: eraka ‘copper’; cf. erka = ekke (Tbh. of arka) aka (Tbh. of arka) copper (metal); crystal (Kannada) *erako* ‘moltencast copper’ Duplicated: dula ‘pair’ Rebus: dul ‘cast metal’ Thus cast copper, brass casting.
sal ‘splinter’ Rebus: ‘worrkshop’ *aya kāṇḍa* ‘alloy metalware’

muka ‘ladle’ (Tamil)(DEDR 4887) Rebus: *mũh* ‘ingot’ (Santali) *baṭa* = rimless pot (Kannada) Rebus: *baṭa* = a kind of iron (G.)) *bhaṭa* furnace (Gujarati) Thus, iron ingot.
kolom ‘three’ Rebus: kolami ‘smithy, forge’ *kāṇḍa* ‘arrow’ (Sanskrit) Rebus:*khāṇḍa* ‘tools, pots and pans, metal-ware’. Rebus 2: kaṇḍ 'fire-altar' (Santali) Thus, the three sign sequence reads: iron ingot, furnace smithy, fire-altar metalware.

m196a खोंड [khōṇḍa] m A young bull, a bullcalf. (Marathi) Rebus: kõdār 'turner' (Bengali); कोंद kōnda 'engraver, lapidary setting or infixing gems' (Marathi) G. sãghārɔ m. 'lathe' ; संघाट joinery; M. sãgaḍ 'double-canoe' Rebus: sangataras 'stone-cutter, mason'

kanka 'rim of  jar' Rebus: karṇīka 'account (scribe)' karṇī 'supercargo'

 *kana, kanac* = corner (Santali); Rebus: *kañcu* = bronze (Telugu) PLUS खांडा [*khāṇḍā*] *m* A jag, notch, or indentation (as upon the edge of a tool or weapon). Rebus: *kāṇḍa* 'tools, pots and pans and metal-ware' Thus, bronze metalware.

 *koḍi* 'flag' (Ta.)(DEDR 2049). Rebus 1: *koḍ* 'workshop' (Kuwi) Rebus 2: *khŏḍ* m. 'pit', *khŏḍü* f. 'small pit' (Kashmiri. CDIAL 3947).

 mēḍu height, rising ground, hillock (Kannada) Rebus: *mẽṛhẽt, meḍ* 'iron' (Munda.Ho.)

 *kanac* 'corner' Rebus: *kañcu* 'bronze'

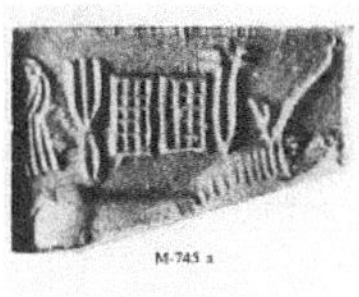

m745a खोंड [khōṇḍa] m A young bull, a bullcalf. (Marathi) Rebus: kõdār 'turner' (Bengali); कोंद kōnda 'engraver, lapidary setting or infixing gems' (Marathi) G. sãghārɔ m. 'lathe' ; संघाट joinery; M. sãgaḍ 'double-canoe' Rebus: sangataras 'stone-cutter, mason'

kanka 'rim of  jar' Rebus: karṇīka 'account (scribe)' karṇī 'supercargo'

 *khaṇḍ* 'field, division' (Skt.) Rebus: *khāṇḍa* 'tools, pots and pans, metal-ware'. Rebus 2: kaṇḍ 'fire-altar' (Santali) dula 'pair' Rebus: dul 'cast metal' Thus, duplicated 'division' hieroglyph sign reads: cast metal metal-ware.

 |||| Numeral 4: gaṇḍa 'four' Rebus: kaṇḍa 'furnace, fire-altar' (Santali) dula 'pair' Rebus: dul 'cast metal'

  Strands of yarn/rope' hieroglyph: Hieroglyph: 'strands of yarn' Rebus reading: *dhā'tu* 'strand of rope' Rebus: *dhatu* 'mineral ore' (Santali)

h599a खोंड [khōṇḍa] m A young bull, a bullcalf. (Marathi) Rebus: kõdār 'turner' (Bengali); कोंद kōnda 'engraver, lapidary setting or infixing gems' (Marathi) G. sãghārɔ m. 'lathe' ; संघाट joinery; M. sãgaḍ 'double-canoe' Rebus: sangataras 'stone-cutter, mason'

kanka (Santali) *karṇika* 'scribe'(Sanskrit) Rebus: *karṇī,* supercargo for a boat shipment. INFIXED खांडा [*khāṇḍā*] *m* A jag, notch, or indentation (as upon the edge of a tool or weapon). Rebus: *kāṇḍa* 'tools, pots and pans and metal-ware'

 ḍãg mountain-ridge (H.)(CDIAL 5476). Rebus: dhangar 'blacksmith' (Maithili)

khaṇḍ 'field, division' (Skt.) Rebus: *khāṇḍa* 'tools, pots and pans, metal-ware'. Rebus 2: kaṇḍ 'fire-altar' (Santali)

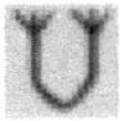
dula 'pair' Rebus: dul 'cast (metal)' kolmo 'rice plant' Rebus: kolami 'smithy/forge' metal.

kanka 'rim of jar' Rebus: karṇīka 'account (scribe)' karṇī 'supercargo'

m1353a *kanka* (Santali) *karṇika* 'scribe'(Sanskrit) Rebus: *karṇī,* supercargo for a boat shipment. INFIXED sal 'splinter' Rebus: sal 'workshop'

mēḍu height, rising ground, hillock (Kannada) Rebus: *mẽṛhẽt, meḍ* 'iron' (Munda.Ho.)

ḍāg mountain-ridge (H.)(CDIAL 5476). Rebus: dhangar 'blacksmith' (Maithili)

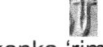

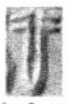
kanka 'rim of jar' Rebus: karṇīka 'account (scribe)' karṇī 'supercargo'

m315A
mogge 'sprout, bud' Rebus: *mũh* 'ingot' (Santali)Thus, cast bronze ingot. Read as: *kañcu dul mũh 'bronze cast ingot'*

kolmo 'paddy plant' Rebus: *kolami* 'smithy, forge' Vikalpa: *mogge* 'sprout, bud' Rebus: *mũh* 'ingot' (Santali) dolu 'plant of shoot height' Rebus: dul 'cast metal' gaṇḍa 'four' Rebus: kaṇḍa 'furnace, fire-altar' (Santali)
sal 'splinter' Rebus: sal 'workshop' *mogge* 'sprout, bud' Rebus*: mũh* 'ingot' *aya kammaṭa.*'coiner, mint alloy'
kanka (Santali) *karṇika* 'scribe'(Sanskrit) Rebus: *karṇī,* supercargo for a boat shipment. INFIXED खांडा [*khāṇḍā*] *m* A jag, notch, or indentation (as upon the edge of a tool or weapon). Rebus: *kāṇḍa* 'tools, pots and pans and metal-ware'

h82a Pictorial motif hieroglyph: *balad* m. ' ox ', gng. *bald*, (Ku.) *barad*, id. (N. Tarai) Rebus: *bharat* (5 copper, 4 zinc and 1 tin)(Punjabi) *pattar* 'trough' Rebus*: pattar* 'guild'. Thus, copper-zinc-tin alloy (worker) guild.
kanka (Santali) *karṇika* 'scribe'(Sanskrit) Rebus: *karṇī,* supercargo for a boat shipment. INFIXED खांडा [*khāṇḍā*] *m* A jag, notch, or indentation (as upon the edge of a tool or weapon). Rebus: *kāṇḍa* 'tools, pots and pans and metal-ware'

mēḍu height, rising ground, hillock (Kannada) Rebus: *meḍ* 'iron' (Ho.) kolom 'three' Rebus: kolami 'smithy, forge' Thus, *meḍ kolami* 'iron smithy-forge'

ayo 'fish' Rebus: *aya* 'iron' *ayas* 'metal' sal 'splinter' Rebus: sal 'workshop'

|||| Numeral 4: gaṇḍa 'four' Rebus: kaṇḍa 'furnace, fire-altar' (Santali)

||| Numeral 3: *kolom* 'three' Rebus*: kolami* 'smithy, forge'

Chanhudaro 5A
खोंड [khōṇḍa] m A young bull, a bullcalf. (Marathi) Rebus: kõdār 'turner' (Bengali); कोंद kōnda 'engraver, lapidary setting or infixing gems' (Marathi) G. sãghārɔ m. 'lathe' ; संघाट joinery; M. sãgaḍ 'double-canoe' Rebus: sangataras 'stone-cutter, mason'

kanka 'rim of jar' Rebus: karṇīka 'account (scribe)' karṇī 'supercargo'

loa 'ficus religiosa' Rebus: *lo* 'iron' (Sanskrit) PLUS unique ligatures: लोखंड [lōkhaṇḍa] *n* (लोह S) Iron. लोखंडाचे चणे खावविणें or चारणें To oppress grievously.लोखंडकाम [lōkhaṇḍakāma] *n* Iron work; that portion (of a building, machine &c.) which consists of iron. 2 The business of an ironsmith.लोखंडी [lōkhaṇḍī] *a* (लोखंड) Composed of iron; relating to iron. (Marathi) *bhaṭa* 'warrior' (Sanskrit) Rebus: *baṭa* a kind of iron (Gujarati). Rebus: *bhaṭa* 'furnace' (Santali) Thus, together, the ligatured hieroglyph reads rebus: *loa bhaṭa* 'iron furnace'

khuṭo ' leg, foot ', °ṭī ' goat's leg ' Rebus: *khōṭā* 'alloy' (Marathi)

Strands of yarn/rope' hieroglyph: Hieroglyph: 'strands of yarn' Rebus reading: *dhā'tu* 'strand of rope' Rebus: *dhatu* 'mineral ore' (Santali)

kanka 'rim of jar' Rebus: karṇīka 'account (scribe)' karṇī 'supercargo'

m1300a kanka 'rim of jar' Rebus: karṇīka 'account (scribe)' karṇī 'supercargo' INFIXED kolom 'three' Rebus: kolami 'smithy, forge' खांडा [*khāṇḍā*] *m* A jag, notch, or indentation (as upon the edge of a tool or weapon). Rebus: *kāṇḍa* 'tools, pots and pans and metal-ware'

meḍ 'body' Rebus: *meḍ* 'iron' (Ho.) काठी [kāṭhī] *f* (काष्ट S) 'frame or structure of the body' (Marathi) Rebus: खंडी [khaṇḍī] measure of weight (Marathi) *கண்டி; kaṇṭi, n. < Mhr. khaṇḍil. [T. Tu. khaṇḍi, M. kaṇḍi.]* Candy, a weight, stated to be roughly equivalent to 500 lbs.

khaṇḍ 'field, division' (Skt.) Rebus: *khāṇḍa* 'tools, pots and pans, metal-ware'. Rebus 2: kaṇḍ 'fire-altar' (Santali) dula 'pair' Rebus: dul 'cast metal' Thus, duplicated 'division' hieroglyph sign reads: cast metal metal-ware.

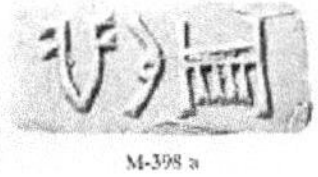

m398a ranku 'antelope' Rebus: ranku 'tin'

kuṭila 'bent' CDIAL 3230 kuṭi— in cmpd. 'curve', *kuṭika—* 'bent' MBh. Rebus:

kuṭila, katthīl = bronze (8 parts copper and 2 parts tin)
kanka 'rim of jar' Rebus: karṇīka 'account (scribe)' karṇī 'supercargo'

m1141a

ibha 'elephant' Rebus: *ib* 'iron' *ibbo* 'merchant' (Gujarati)

kanka 'rim of jar' Rebus: karṇīka 'account (scribe)' karṇī 'supercargo'
baṭa = rimless pot (Kannada) Rebus: *baṭa* = a kind of iron (G.)) *bhaṭa* furnace (Gujaratii)

loa 'ficus  religiosa' Rebus: *lo* 'iron' (Sanskrit) PLUS unique ligatures: लोखंड [lōkhaṇḍa] *n* (लोह S) Iron. लोखंडाचे चणे खावविणें or चारणें To oppress grievously.लोखंडकाम [lōkhaṇḍakāma] *n* Iron work; that portion (of a building, machine &c.) which consists of iron. 2 The business of an ironsmith.लोखंडी [lōkhaṇḍī] *a* (लोखंड) Composed of iron; relating to iron. (Marathi)

 *kuṭila* 'bent' CDIAL 3230 kuṭi— in cmpd. 'curve', *kuṭika—* 'bent' MBh. Rebus: *kuṭila, katthīl* = bronze (8 parts copper and 2 parts tin)

 *cīmara* 'black ant' Rebus: *cīmara* 'copper'. *cīmara kāra* -- ' coppersmith '

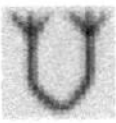 dula 'pair' Rebus: dul 'cast (metal)' kolmo 'rice plant' Rebus: kolami 'smithy/forge' metal.

kanka 'rim of jar' Rebus: karṇīka 'account (scribe)' karṇī 'supercargo'

m1792A *खोंड [khōṇḍa] m A young bull, a bullcalf. (Marathi) Rebus: kõdār 'turner' (Bengali); कोंद kōnda 'engraver, lapidary setting or infixing gems' (Marathi)*
Circumscript: dula 'two' Rebus: dul 'cast metal' PLUS kanka 'rim of jar' Rebus: karṇīka 'account (scribe)' karṇī 'supercargo'
karaṇḍa 'duck' (Sanskrit) karaṛa 'a very large aquatic bird' (Sindhi) Rebus: करडा [*karaḍā*] Hard from alloy--iron, silver &c. (Marathi) *kharādī* ' turner' (Gujarati)
aya kammaṭa.'coiner, mint alloy'

 dula 'pair' Rebus: dul 'cast (metal)' kolmo 'rice plant' Rebus: kolami 'smithy/forge'

kanka 'rim of jar' Rebus: karṇīka 'account (scribe)' karṇī 'supercargo'

h1036a *खोंड [khōṇḍa] m A young bull, a bullcalf. (Marathi) Rebus: kõdār 'turner' (Bengali); कोंद kōnda 'engraver, lapidary setting or infixing gems' (Marathi) G. sãghāṛɔ m. 'lathe' ; संघाट joinery; M. sāgaḍ 'double-canoe' Rebus: sangataras 'stone-cutter, mason' baṭa* = rimless pot (Kannada) Rebus: *baṭa* = a kind of iron (G.)) *bhaṭa* furnace (Gujarati) PLUS | *koḍa* 'one' Rebus: *koḍ* 'workshop'

water-carrier hieroglyph *kuṭi*; Rebus: *kuṭhi* 'smelter furnace'.
PLUS 'rim of jar': *kanka* (Santali) *karṇika* 'scribe'(Sanskrit)
Rebus: *karṇī*, supercargo
'rim-of-jar' hieroglyph *kanka* (Santali) *karṇika* 'scribe'(Sanskrit)
Rebus: *karṇī*, supercargo for a boat shipment. *karṇīka* 'account (scribe)' .कारणी *kāraṇī* 'the supercargo of a ship' (Marathi)

Kalibangan 7A *खोंड [khōṇḍa] m A young bull, a bullcalf. (Marathi) Rebus: kōdār 'turner' (Bengali); कोंद kōnda 'engraver, lapidary setting or infixing gems' (Marathi) G. sãghāṛɔ m. 'lathe' ; संघाट joinery; M. sãgaḍ 'double-canoe' Rebus: sangataras 'stone-cutter, mason'*

baṭa = rimless pot (Kannada) Rebus: *baṭa* = a kind of iron (G.)) *bhaṭa* furnace (Gujarati)

bhaṭa 'warrior' (Sanskrit) Rebus: *baṭa* a kind of iron (Gujarati). Rebus: *bhaṭa* 'furnace' (Santali)
baraḍo = spine; backbone (Tulu) Rebus: *baran, bharat* 'mixed alloys' (5 copper, 4 zinc and 1 tin) (Punjabi) PLUS gaṇḍa 'four' Rebus: kaṇḍa 'furnace, fire-altar' (Santali)

kana, kanac = corner (Santali); Rebus: *kañcu* = bronze (Telugu) PLUS खांडा [*khāṇḍā*] *m* A jag, notch, or indentation (as upon the edge of a tool or weapon). Rebus: *kāṇḍa* 'tools, pots and pans and metal-ware' Thus, bronze metalware.
खांडा [*khāṇḍā*] *m* A jag, notch, or indentation (as upon the edge
ayo 'fish' Rebus: *aya* 'iron' *ayas* 'metal'
dula 'pair' Rebus; dul 'cast metal' PLUS

kamaḍha 'crab' Rebus: *kammaṭa* 'mint, coiner'.*ḍato* = claws of crab (Santali) Rebus: *dhātu* 'mineral ore' PLUS खांडा [*khāṇḍā*] *m* A jag, notch, or indentation (as upon the edge of a tool or weapon). Rebus: *kāṇḍa* 'tools, pots and pans and metal-ware' Thus, mint metalware, ore.
kanka (Santali) *karṇika* 'scribe'(Sanskrit) Rebus: *karṇī*, supercargo for a boat shipment. *karṇīka* 'account (scribe)'.कारणी *kāraṇī* 'the supercargo of a ship' (Marathi)

A Mespotamian seal Pictorial motif hieroglyph: *balad* m. ' ox ', gng. *bald*, (Ku.) *barad*, id. (N. Tarai) Rebus: *bharat* (5 copper, 4 zinc and 1 tin)(Punjabi) *pattar* 'trough' Rebus*: pattar* 'guild'. Thus, copper-zinc-tin alloy (worker) guild.
balad m. ' ox ', gng. *bald*, (Ku.) *barad*, id. (N. Tarai) Rebus: *bharat* (5 copper, 4 zinc and 1 tin)(Punjabi) *pattar* 'trough' Rebus*: pattar* 'guild'. Thus, copper-zinc-tin alloy (worker) guild.

ḍhanga = a crook used for pulling down the branches of trees, for goats, sheep and camels (P.) Rebus:*ḍhangar* blacksmith'.
kamaḍha 'crab' Rebus: *kammaṭa* 'mint, coiner'.*ḍato* = claws of crab (Santali) Rebus: *dhātu* 'mineral ore'
खांडा [*khāṇḍā*] *m* A jag, notch, or indentation (as upon the edge of a tool or weapon). Rebus: *kāṇḍa* 'tools, pots and pans and metal-ware'
kanka 'rim of jar' Rebus: karṇīka 'account (scribe)' karṇī 'supercargo'

h454A *खोंड [khōṇḍa] m A young bull, a bullcalf. (Marathi) Rebus: kõdār 'turner' (Bengali); कोंद kōnda 'engraver, lapidary setting or infixing gems' (Marathi) G. sãghāṛɔ m. 'lathe' ; संघाट joinery; M. sãgaḍ 'double-canoe' Rebus: sangataras 'stone-cutter, mason'*

dula 'pair' Rebus: dul 'cast (metal)' kolmo 'rice plant' Rebus: kolami 'smithy/forge' metal.

kanka 'rim of jar' Rebus: karṇīka 'account (scribe)' karṇī 'supercargo' ranku 'liquid measure' Rebus: ranku 'tin'

kolmo 'paddy plant' Rebus: *kolami* 'smithy, forge' Vikalpa: *mogge* 'sprout, bud' Rebus: *mũh* 'ingot' (Santali) dolu 'plant of shoot height' Rebus: dul 'cast metal'

kanka 'rim of jar' Rebus: karṇīka 'account (scribe)' karṇī 'supercargo'

m802a *खोंड [khōṇḍa] m A young bull, a bullcalf. (Marathi) Rebus: kõdār 'turner' (Bengali); कोंद kōnda 'engraver, lapidary setting or infixing gems' (Marathi) G. sãghāṛɔ m. 'lathe' ; संघाट joinery; M. sãgaḍ 'double-canoe' Rebus: sangataras 'stone-cutter, mason'*

cīmara 'black  ant' Rebus: *cīmara* 'copper'. *cīmara kāra* -- ' coppersmith '

mēḍu height, rising ground, hillock (Kannada) Rebus: *mẽṛhẽt, meḍ* 'iron' (Munda.Ho.)

kanka 'rim of jar' Rebus: karṇīka 'account (scribe)' karṇī 'supercargo' INFIXED खांडा [*khāṇḍā*] *m* A jag, notch, or indentation (as upon the edge of a tool or weapon). Rebus: *kāṇḍa* 'tools, pots and pans and metal-ware'

meḍ 'body' Rebus: *meḍ* 'iron' (Ho.) काठी [kāṭhī] *f* (काष्ट S) 'frame or structure of the body' (Marathi) Rebus: खंडी [khaṇḍī] measure of weight (Marathi) *கண்டி; kaṇṭi, n. < Mhr. khaṇḍil. [T. Tu. khaṇḍi, M. kaṇḍi.]* Candy, a weight, stated to be roughly equivalent to 500 lbs. PLUS

khuṭo ' leg, foot ', °ṭī ' goat's leg ' Rebus: *khōṭā* 'alloy' (Marathi)

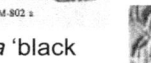

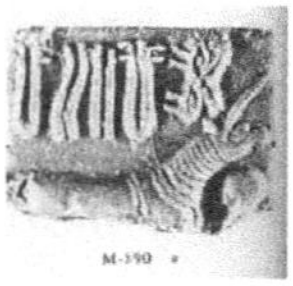

m890a *खोंड [khōṇḍa] m A young bull, a bullcalf. (Marathi) Rebus: kõdār 'turner' (Bengali); कोंद kōnda 'engraver, lapidary setting or infixing gems' (Marathi) G. sãghāṛɔ m. 'lathe' ; संघाट joinery; M. sãgaḍ 'double-canoe' Rebus: sangataras*

'stone-cutter, mason'

 *cīmara* 'black ant' Rebus: *cīmara* 'copper'. *cīmara kāra* -- ' coppersmith '

kanka 'rim of jar' Rebus: karṇīka 'account (scribe)' karṇī 'supercargo'
dula 'two' Rebus: dul 'cast metal'

 *kuṭila* 'bent' CDIAL 3230 kuṭi— in cmpd. 'curve', *kuṭika*— 'bent' MBh. Rebus: *kuṭila, katthīl* = bronze (8 parts copper and 2 parts tin) Duplicated: dula 'pair' Rebus: dul 'cast metal' Thus, cast bronze or bronze castings.
kanka 'rim of jar' Rebus: karṇīka 'account (scribe)' karṇī 'supercargo'

'Bead, beads, chain' sign hieroglyphs

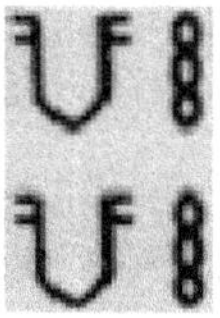

m0324 A,B Text 1252 Zebu horns on composite animal.
ingot (from) iron smelter, tin smelter merchant guild. Focus on 'serpent' tail: *nāga* 'snake' Rebus: *nāga* 'lead' (Sanskrit) anakku 'tin' (Akkadian) *Kur.* xolā tail. *Malt.* qoli id. (DEDR 2135). Focus on human face: mukha, *mũh* 'face' Rebus: *mũh* 'ingot'. Zebu horns: *khũṭ* 'zebu' (Gujarati) Rebus: *khũṭ* '(native metal) community, guild' (Santali) kola 'tiger' Rebus: kolhe 'smelters' kol 'working in iron' ibha 'elephant' Rebus: ib 'iron' body of an ox: balad 'bull' Rebus: *baran, bharat* 'mixed alloys' (5 copper, 4 zinc and 1 tin) (Punjabi) dhatu 'scarf' Rebus: dhatu 'mineral ore'.

Pictorial motif hieroglyphs on m0324B shows a one-horned young bull in front of a standard device.

खोंडी [*khōṇḍī*] *f* An outspread shovelform sack (as formed temporarily out of a कांबळा, to hold or fend off grain, chaff &c.) (Marathi) *koḍiyum* 'rings on neck' (Gujarati)
खोंड [khōṇḍa] m A young bull, a bullcalf. (Marathi) Rebus: kõdār 'turner' (Bengali); कोंद kōnda 'engraver, lapidary setting or infixing gems' (Marathi) G. sãghāṛɔ m. 'lathe' ; संघाट joinery; M. sãgaḍ 'double-canoe' Rebus: sangataras. संगतराश lit. 'to collect stones, stone-cutter, mason.' llcalf. (Marathi) Rebus: kõdār 'turner' (Bengali); *kõdā* 'to turn in a lathe' (Bengali).कोंद kōnda 'engraver, lapidary setting or infixing gems' (Marathi) kōḍu 'horn' Rebus: 'workshop'sãghāṛɔ m. 'lathe' (Gujarati) Rebus: sangataras. संगतराश lit. 'to collect stones, stone-cutter, mason.'*kõdā* 'lathe-turner'. *kũdār* 'turner, brass worker'. कोंद *kōnda* 'engraver, lapidary setting or infixing gems' (Marathi) kũdār, kũdāri (Bengali); kundāru (Oriya) कोंडण [kōṇḍaṇa] f A fold or pen. (Marathi)

sangaḍa 'lathe, portable furnace' Rebus: *sanghāḍo* (Gujarati) cutting stone, gilding (Gujarati); *sangsāru karaṇu* = to stone (Sindhi) *sanghāḍiyo*, a worker on a lathe (Gujarati) sangataras. संगतराश lit. 'to collect stones, stone-cutter, mason.' संगतराश संज्ञा

पुं० [फ़ा०] पत्थर काटने या गढ़नेवाला मजदूर। पत्थरकट। २. एक औजार जो पत्थर काटने के काम में आता है। (Dasa, Syamasundara. Hindi sabdasagara. Navina samskarana. 2nd ed. Kasi : Nagari Pracarini Sabha, 1965-1975.) पत्थर या लकडी पर नकाशी करनेवाला, संगतराश, 'mason'.

Twisted rope: मेढा [mēḍhā] A twist or tangle arising in thread or cord, a curl or snarl.(Marathi)(CDIAL 10312).L. *meṛh* f. 'rope tying oxen to each other and to post on threshing floor'(CDIAL 10317) Rebus: *meḍ* iron'. *mẽṛhet* iron' (Mu.Ho.) Vikalpa: पेंडें [pēṇḍēṃ] n (पेड) A necklace composed of strings of pearls. 2 A loop or ring. Rebus: पेढी (Gujaráthí word.) A shop (Marathi)

kanka 'rim of jar' Rebus: *karṇīka* 'account (scribe)' *karṇī* 'supercargo' Thus, supercargo of iron.

Comparable text messages with 'chain of beads' hieroglyph and variants: Mohenjo-dasro seal m 0046 *खोंड [khōṇḍa] m A young bull, a bullcalf. (Marathi) Rebus: kõdār 'turner' (Bengali); कोंद kōnda 'engraver, lapidary setting or infixing gems' (Marathi) G. sãghāṛɔ m. 'lathe' ; संघाट joinery; M. sãgaḍ 'double-canoe' Rebus: sangataras 'stone-cutter, mason'*
मेढा [mēḍhā] A twist or tangle arising in thread or cord, a curl or snarl.(Marathi) Rebus: *meḍ* iron'. *mẽṛhet* iron' (Mu.Ho.)

notch+slanted stroke reads rebus: *ḍhālako kāṇḍa* 'ingot, tools, pots and pans and metal-ware'.*ḍhāḷ* 'a slope'; 'inclination of a plane' (G.); *ḍhāḷiyum* = adj. sloping, inclining (G.) Rebus: *ḍhālako* = a large metal ingot (G.) *ḍhālakī* = a metal heated and poured into a mould; a solid piece of metal; an ingot (Gujarati) PLUS खांडा [*khāṇḍā*] *m* A jag, notch, or indentation (as upon the edge of a tool or weapon). Rebus: *kāṇḍa* 'tools, pots and pans and metal-ware'
ayo 'fish' Rebus: *aya* 'iron' *ayas* 'metal' sal 'splinter' Rebus: sal 'workshop' *aya aḍaren (homonym: aduru)* 'alloy native metal' *aya kammaṭa.* 'coiner, mint alloy' *kamaḍha* 'crab' Rebus: *kammaṭa* 'mint, coiner'.*ḍato* = claws of crab (Santali) Rebus: *dhātu* 'mineral ore'

kanka 'rim of jar' Rebus: karṇīka 'account (scribe)' karṇī 'supercargo'

H-656 A

Harappa tablet h656A मेढा [mēḍhā] A twist or tangle arising in thread or cord, a curl or snarl.(Marathi) Rebus: *meḍ* iron'. *mẽṛhet* iron' (Mu.Ho.) kanka 'rim of jar' Rebus: karṇīka 'account (scribe)' karṇī 'supercargo'

m324Am324b Side A: composite animal (Zebu horns. Native metal smith guild). Side B: young bull. *खोंड [khōṇḍa] m A young bull, a bullcalf. (Marathi) Rebus: kõdār 'turner' (Bengali); कोंद kōnda 'engraver, lapidary setting or infixing gems' (Marathi)* G. *sãghāṛɔ* m. 'lathe' ; *संघाट joinery; M. sãgaḍ 'double-canoe'* Rebus*: sangataras.* संगतराश lit. 'to collect stones, stone-cutter, mason.'
Read rebus as at h656

Harappa tablet h155a मेढा [mēḍhā] A twist or tangle arising in thread or cord, a curl or snarl.(Marathi) Rebus: *meḍ* iron'. *mẽṛhet* 'iron' (Mu.Ho.)

 *kanac* 'corner' Rebus: *kañcu* 'bronze'

 *koḍi* 'flag' (Ta.)(DEDR 2049). Rebus 1: *koḍ* 'workshop' (Kuwi) Rebus 2: *khŏḍ* m. 'pit', *khŏḍü* f. 'small pit' (Kashmiri. CDIAL 3947). खांडा [*khāṇḍā*] *m* A jag, notch, or indentation (as upon the edge of a tool or weapon). Rebus: *kāṇḍa* 'tools, pots and pans and metal-ware'

 *baraḍo* = spine; backbone (Tulu) Rebus: *baran, bharat* 'mixed alloys' (5 copper, 4 zinc and 1 tin) (Punjabi) PLUS gaṇḍa 'four' Rebus: kaṇḍa 'furnace, fire-altar' (Santali) kanka 'rim of jar' Rebus: karṇīka 'account (scribe)' karṇī 'supercargo'

Harappa seal h446A

खोंड [khōṇḍa] m A young bull, a bullcalf. (Marathi) Rebus: kōdār 'turner' (Bengali); कोंद kōnda 'engraver, lapidary setting or infixing gems' (Marathi) G. sãghāṛɔ m. 'lathe' ; संघाट joinery; M. sãgaḍ 'double-canoe' Rebus: sangataras 'stone-cutter, mason'

मेढा [mēḍhā] A twist or tangle arising in thread or cord, a curl or snarl.(Marathi) Rebus: *meḍ* iron'. *mẽṛhet* 'iron' (Mu.Ho.)

 *kanac* 'corner' Rebus: *kañcu* 'bronze'

sal 'splinter' Rebus: sal 'workshop' kamaḍha 'crab' Rebus: *kammaṭa* 'mint, coiner'.*ḍato* = claws of crab (Santali) Rebus: *dhātu* 'mineral ore'

 सांड [sāṇḍa] *f* (षद S) An outlet for superfluous water (as through a dam or mound); a sluice, a floodvent. Rebus: सांडणी [sāṇḍaṇī] *f* (H) An instrument of goldsmiths. It is hooked or curved at the extremity; and is used to draw things out of the fire.

सांठा [*sāṇṭhā*] *m* (संचय S) A collection, heap, hoard, store, stock.साटें [*sāṭēṃ*] *n* (संचय S) A whole investment; the total quantity of merchandise (brought to market by one merchant). kanka 'rim of jar' Rebus: karṇīka 'account (scribe)' karṇī 'supercargo'

Kalibangan 20A *खोंड [khōṇḍa] m A young bull, a bullcalf. (Marathi) Rebus: kōdār 'turner' (Bengali); कोंद kōnda 'engraver, lapidary setting or infixing gems' (Marathi) G. sãghāṛɔ m. 'lathe' ; संघाट joinery; M. sãgaḍ 'double-canoe' Rebus: sangataras 'stone-cutter, mason'* मेढा [mēḍhā] A twist or tangle arising in thread or cord, a curl or snarl.(Marathi) Rebus: *meḍ* iron'. *mẽṛhet* 'iron' (Mu.Ho.)

 water-carrier hieroglyph *kuṭi*; Rebus: *kuṭhi* 'smelter furnace'.

h94A dulo 'hole' Rebus: dul 'cast metal'

 *kanac* 'corner' Rebus: *kañcu* 'bronze'

meḍ 'body' Rebus: *meḍ* 'iron' (Ho.) काठी [kāṭhī] *f* (काष्ट S) 'frame or structure of the body' (Marathi) Rebus: खंडी [khaṇḍī] measure of weight (Marathi) *கண்டி; kaṇṭi, n. < Mhr. khaṇḍil. [T. Tu. khaṇḍi, M. kaṇḍi.]* Candy, a weight, stated to be roughly equivalent to 500 lbs.

kola 'tiger' Rebus: kolhe 'smelter' kol 'working in iron' pattar 'trough' Rebus: pattar 'guild, goldsmith'

Dholavira *खोंड [khōṇḍa] m A young bull, a bullcalf. (Marathi) Rebus: kõdār 'turner' (Bengali); कोंद kōnda 'engraver, lapidary setting or infixing gems' (Marathi) G. sãghāṛɔ m. 'lathe' ; संघाट joinery; M. sãgaḍ 'double-canoe' Rebus: sangataras 'stone-cutter, mason'*
Read rebus as at h94

m887a *Read rebus as at h94*

m757A *खोंड [khōṇḍa] m A young bull, a bullcalf. (Marathi) Rebus: kõdār 'turner' (Bengali); कोंद kōnda 'engraver, lapidary setting or infixing gems' (Marathi) G. sãghāṛɔ m. 'lathe' ; संघाट joinery; M. sãgaḍ 'double-canoe' Rebus: sangataras 'stone-cutter, mason'*

First sign read rebus as at h94. aya aḍaren (homonym: aduru)'alloy native metal' *ayo ḍhālako* 'alloy metal ingot'

Three sign sequence:

muka 'ladle' (Tamil)(DEDR 4887) Rebus: *mũh* 'ingot' (Santali) Thus, iron ingot.

kolom 'three' Rebus: kolami 'smithy, forge' *kāṇḍa* 'arrow' (Sanskrit) Rebus:*khāṇḍa* 'tools, pots and pans, metal-ware'. Rebus 2: kaṇḍ 'fire-altar' (Santali) Thus, the three sign sequence reads: iron ingot, furnace smithy, fire-altar metalware.

m150a *खोंड [khōṇḍa] m A young bull, a bullcalf. (Marathi) Rebus: kõdār 'turner' (Bengali); कोंद kōnda 'engraver, lapidary setting or infixing gems' (Marathi) G. sãghāṛɔ m. 'lathe' ; संघाट joinery; M. sãgaḍ 'double-canoe' Rebus: sangataras 'stone-cutter, mason'*

kana, kanac = corner (Santali); Rebus: *kañcu* = bronze (Telugu) PLUS खांडा [*khāṇḍā*] *m* A jag, notch, or indentation (as upon the edge of a tool or weapon). Rebus: *kāṇḍa* 'tools, pots and pans and metal-ware' Thus, bronze metalware.

kanka 'rim of jar' Rebus: karṇīka 'account (scribe)' karṇī 'supercargo'

m415A *balad* m. ' ox ', gng. *bald*, (Ku.) *barad*, id. (N. Tarai) Rebus: *bharat* (5 copper, 4 zinc and 1 tin)(Punjabi) *pattar* 'trough' Rebus*: pattar* 'guild'. Thus, copper-zinc-tin alloy (worker) guild.

 *kana, kanac* = corner (Santali); Rebus: *kañcu* = bronze (Telugu) PLUS खांडा [*khāṇḍā*] *m* A jag, notch, or indentation (as upon the edge of a tool or weapon). Rebus: *kāṇḍa* 'tools, pots and pans and metal-ware' Thus, bronze metalware.

 *bicha* 'scorpion' (Assamese) Rebus: *bica* 'stone ore' (Santali)

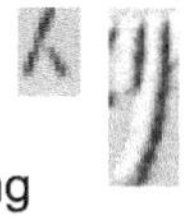 notch+slanted stroke reads rebus: *ḍhālako kāṇḍa* 'ingot, tools, pots and pans and metal-ware'.*ḍhāḷ* 'a slope'; 'inclination of a plane' (G.); *ḍhāḷiyum* = adj. sloping, inclining (G.) Rebus: *ḍhālako* = a large metal ingot (G.) *ḍhālakī* = a metal heated and poured into a mould; a solid piece of metal; an ingot (Gujarati) PLUS खांडा [*khāṇḍā*] *m* A jag, notch, or indentation (as upon the edge of a tool or weapon). Rebus: *kāṇḍa* 'tools, pots and pans and metal-ware'

M-1082 A

m1082A Zebu: native metal smith guild.

 *kana, kanac* = corner (Santali); Rebus: *kañcu* = bronze (Telugu) PLUS खांडा [*khāṇḍā*] *m* A jag, notch, or indentation (as upon the edge of a tool or weapon). Rebus: *kāṇḍa* 'tools, pots and pans and metal-ware' Thus, bronze metalware.

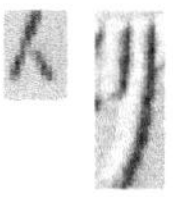 notch+slanted stroke reads rebus: *ḍhālako kāṇḍa* 'ingot, tools, pots and pans and metal-ware'.*ḍhāḷ* 'a slope'; 'inclination of a plane' (G.); *ḍhāḷiyum* = adj. sloping, inclining (G.) Rebus: *ḍhālako* = a large metal ingot (G.) *ḍhālakī* = a metal heated and poured into a mould; a solid piece of metal; an ingot (Gujarati) PLUS खांडा [*khāṇḍā*] *m* A jag, notch, or indentation (as upon the edge of a tool or weapon). Rebus: *kāṇḍa* 'tools, pots and pans and metal-ware'
sal 'splinter' Rebus: sal 'workshop' *aya aḍaren (homonym: aduru)*'alloy native metal'

m456A *खोंड [khōṇḍa] m A young bull, a bullcalf. (Marathi) Rebus: kõdār 'turner' (Bengali); कोंद kōnda 'engraver, lapidary setting or infixing gems' (Marathi) G. sãghāṛɔ m. 'lathe' ; संघाट joinery; M. sãgaḍ 'double-canoe' Rebus: sangataras 'stone-cutter, mason'*

 *kana, kanac* = corner (Santali); Rebus: *kañcu* = bronze (Telugu) PLUS खांडा [*khāṇḍā*] *m* A jag, notch, or indentation (as upon the edge of a tool or weapon). Rebus: *kāṇḍa* 'tools, pots and pans and metal-ware' Thus, bronze metalware.

 *kanac* 'corner' Rebus: *kañcu* 'bronze' sal 'splinter' Rebus: sal 'workshop'

Three sign sequence:

 *muka* 'ladle' (Tamil)(DEDR 4887) Rebus: *mũh* 'ingot' (Santali) Thus, iron ingot. kolom 'three' Rebus: kolami 'smithy, forge' *kāṇḍa* 'arrow' (Sanskrit) Rebus:*khāṇḍa* 'tools, pots and pans, metal-ware'. Rebus 2: kaṇḍ 'fire-altar' (Santali) Thus, the three sign sequence reads: iron ingot, furnace smithy, fire-altar metalware.

m953A खोंड [khōṇḍa] m A young bull, a bullcalf. (Marathi) Rebus: kõdār 'turner' (Bengali); कोंद kōnda 'engraver, lapidary setting or infixing gems' (Marathi) G. sãghāṛɔ m. 'lathe' ; संघाट joinery; M. sãgaḍ 'double-canoe' Rebus: sangataras 'stone-cutter, mason'

dula 'two' Rebus: dul 'cast metal' kana, kanac = corner (Santali); Rebus: *kañcu* = bronze (Telugu) PLUS खांडा [*khāṇḍā*] *m* A jag, notch, or indentation (as upon the edge of a tool or weapon). Rebus: *kāṇḍa* 'tools, pots and pans and metal-ware' Thus, bronze metalware. kanka 'rim of jar' Rebus: karṇīka 'account (scribe)' karṇī 'supercargo'

m1681A खोंड [khōṇḍa] m A young bull, a bullcalf. (Marathi) Rebus: kõdār 'turner' (Bengali); कोंद kōnda 'engraver, lapidary setting or infixing gems' (Marathi) G. sãghāṛɔ m. 'lathe' ; संघाट joinery; M. sãgaḍ 'double-canoe' Rebus: sangataras 'stone-cutter, mason'

kana, kanac = corner (Santali); Rebus: *kañcu* = bronze (Telugu) PLUS खांडा [*khāṇḍā*] *m* A jag, notch, or indentation (as upon the edge of a tool or weapon). Rebus: *kāṇḍa* 'tools, pots and pans and metal-ware' Thus, bronze metalware.

kanac 'corner' Rebus: *kañcu* 'bronze' sal 'splinter' Rebus: sal 'workshop' sal 'splinter' Rebus: sal 'workshop' *kamaḍha* 'crab' Rebus: *kammaṭa* 'mint, coiner'.*ḍato* = claws of crab (Santali) Rebus: *dhātu* 'mineral ore' kanka 'rim of jar' Rebus: karṇīka 'account (scribe)' karṇī 'supercargo' *aya kāṇḍa* 'alloy metalware'

'Arrow' sign hieroglyph (variant) This is a ligature of 'lid of pot' hieroglyph superscript on 'a linear stroke' numeral hieroglyph.*aḍaren* 'cover of pot or lid' Rebus: *aduru* 'native, unsmelted metal' PLUS koḍ = one (Santali); koḍ 'workshop' (Gujarati)

कांड *kāṇḍa* 'arrow' Rebus: *kāṇḍa* 'pots and pans, metalware, tools'. Rebus 2: kaṇḍ 'fire-altar' (Santali)

H-1931 A H-1931 B H-1931 C

m1931A, B, C dula 'two' Rebus: dul 'cast metal' PLUS

kanac 'corner' Rebus: *kañcu* 'bronze'

baraḍo = spine; backbone (Tulu) Rebus: *baran, bharat* 'mixed alloys' (5 copper, 4 zinc and 1 tin) (Punjabi) PLUS gaṇḍa 'four' Rebus: kaṇḍa 'furnace, fire-altar' (Santali) kanka 'rim of jar' Rebus: karṇīka 'account (scribe)' karṇī 'supercargo'

khareḍo = a currycomb (Gujarati) खरारा [*kharārā*] *m* (H) A currycomb. 2 Currying a horse. (Marathi) Rebus: करडा [*karaḍā*] Hard from alloy--iron, silver &c. (Marathi) *kharādī* ' turner' (Gujarati)

Side B: *baṭa* = rimless pot (Kannada) Rebus:) *baṭa* = a kind of iron (G.)) *bhaṭa* furnace (Gujarati) dula 'two' Rebus: dul 'cast metal'

Side C: *karāvu* 'crocodile' Rebus: *khara* 'blacksmith' (Kashmiri)

m833a खोंड [khōṇḍa] m A young bull, a bullcalf. (Marathi) Rebus: kõdār 'turner' (Bengali); कोंद kōnda 'engraver, lapidary setting or infixing gems' (Marathi) G. sãghāṛɔ m. 'lathe' ; संघाट joinery; M. sãgaḍ 'double-canoe' Rebus: sangataras 'stone-cutter, mason'

dulo 'hole' Rebus: dul 'cast metal'

 *kanac* 'corner' Rebus: *kañcu* 'bronze'

kanka 'rim of jar' Rebus: karṇīka 'account (scribe)' karṇī 'supercargo'

Bead hieroglyph: 

M-981 a

m981a *खोंड [khōṇḍa] m A young bull, a bullcalf. (Marathi) Rebus: kõdār 'turner' (Bengali); कोंद kōnda 'engraver, lapidary setting or infixing gems' (Marathi) G. sãghāṛɔ m. 'lathe' ; संघाट joinery; M. sãgaḍ 'double-canoe' Rebus: sangataras 'stone-cutter, mason'*

 beads: Pa. kandi (pl. -l) necklace, beads. Ga. (Punjabi) kandi (pl. -l) bead, (pl.) necklace; (S.2) kandiṭ bead. (DEDR 1215) Rebus: *கண்டி; kaṇṭi, n. < Mhr. khaṇḍil. [T. Tu. khaṇḍi, M. kaṇḍi.] 1. Candy, a weight, stated to be roughly equivalent to 500 lbs.; பாரமென் னும் நிறையளவு.* खंडीगणती or खंडोगणती [khaṇḍīgaṇatī or khaṇḍōgaṇatī] *ad* By candies; counting or reckoning by candies. खंडीवारी [khaṇḍīvārī] *ad* By scores, heaps, candies. खंडी [khaṇḍī] Applied to a great quantity; as खंडीभर पोरें, खंडीभर मेंढ्या, खंडीभर काम, खंडीभर बोलतो-लिहितो&c

 *kolmo* 'paddy plant' Rebus: *kolami* 'smithy, forge' Vikalpa: *mogge* 'sprout, bud' Rebus: *mũh* 'ingot' (Santali) dolu 'plant of shoot height' Rebus: dul 'cast metal' खांडा [*khāṇḍā*] *m* A jag, notch, or indentation (as upon the edge of a tool or weapon). Rebus: *kāṇḍa* 'tools, pots and pans and metal-ware' Thus, cast bronze metalware.

 *meḍ* 'body' Rebus: *meḍ* 'iron' (Ho.) काठी [kāṭhī] *f* (काष्ट S) 'frame or structure of the body' (Marathi) Rebus: खंडी [khaṇḍī] measure of weight (Marathi) *கண்டி; kaṇṭi, n. < Mhr. khaṇḍil. [T. Tu. khaṇḍi, M. kaṇḍi.]* Candy, a weight, stated to be roughly equivalent to 500 lbs.

 *khaṇḍ* 'field, division' (Skt.) Rebus: *khāṇḍa* 'tools, pots and pans, metal-ware'. Rebus 2: kaṇḍ 'fire-altar' (Santali) dula 'pair' Rebus: dul 'cast metal' Thus, duplicated 'division' hieroglyph sign reads: cast metal metal-ware.

m2121a (Inscribed axe) kandiṭ 'bead' Rebus: khaṇḍī 'great quantity'

mogge 'sprout, bud' Rebus: *mũh* 'ingot'

 *kanac* 'corner' Rebus: *kañcu* 'bronze'

āra 'spokes' Rebus: *āra 'brass'.* cf. erka ekke (Tbh. of arka) aka (Tbh. of arka) copper (metal); crystal (Kannada) Glyph: *eraka* 'nave of wheel' Rebus: eraka 'copper'; cf. erka = ekke (Tbh. of arka) aka (Tbh. of arka) copper (metal); crystal (Kannada) *erako* 'moltencast copper' Duplicated: dula 'pair' Rebus: dul 'cast metal' Thus cast copper, brass casting.

m663a *खोंड [khōṇḍa] m A young bull, a bullcalf. (Marathi) Rebus: kõdār 'turner' (Bengali); कोंद kōnda 'engraver, lapidary setting or infixing gems' (Marathi) G. sãghāṛɔ m. 'lathe' ; संघाट joinery; M. sãgaḍ 'double-canoe' Rebus: sangataras 'stone-cutter, mason'*
kandiṭ 'bead' Rebus: khaṇḍī 'great quantity'

 *kanac* 'corner' Rebus: *kañcu* 'bronze'

kanka (Santali) *karṇika* 'scribe'(Sanskrit) Rebus: *karṇī,* supercargo for a boat shipment. INFIXED खांडा [*khāṇḍā*] *m* A jag, notch, or indentation (as upon the edge of a tool or weapon). Rebus: *kāṇḍa* 'tools, pots and pans and metal-ware'
dula 'two' Rebus: dul 'cast metal' *mogge* 'sprout, bud' Rebus: *mũh* 'ingot' (Santali)

m644a *खोंड [khōṇḍa] m A young bull, a bullcalf. (Marathi) Rebus: kõdār 'turner' (Bengali); कोंद kōnda 'engraver, lapidary setting or infixing gems' (Marathi) G. sãghāṛɔ m. 'lathe' ; संघाट joinery; M. sãgaḍ 'double-canoe' Rebus: sangataras 'stone-cutter, mason'*
kandiṭ 'bead' Rebus: *khaṇḍī* 'great quantity'

meḍ 'body' Rebus: *meḍ* 'iron' (Ho.) काठी [kāṭhī] *f* (काष्ट S) 'frame or structure of the body' (Marathi) Rebus: खंडी [khaṇḍī] measure of weight (Marathi) *கண்டி; kaṇṭi, n. < Mhr. khaṇḍil. [T. Tu. khaṇḍi, M. kaṇḍi.]* Candy, a weight, stated to be roughly equivalent to 500 lbs.

 *kanac* 'corner' Rebus: *kañcu* 'bronze' sal 'splinter' Rebus: sal 'workshop' *aya kammaṭa.*'coiner, mint alloy'

 kanka 'rim of jar' Rebus: karṇīka 'account (scribe)' karṇī 'supercargo'
|||| Numeral 4: gaṇḍa 'four' Rebus: kaṇḍa 'furnace, fire-altar' (Santali)
||| Numeral 3: *kolom* 'three' Rebus*: kolami* 'smithy, forge'

 सांड [sāṇḍa] *f* (षद S) An outlet for superfluous water (as through a dam or mound); a sluice, a floodvent. Rebus: सांडणी [sāṇḍaṇī] *f* (H) An instrument of goldsmiths. It is hooked or curved at the extremity; and is used to draw things out of the fire.
सांठा [*sāṇṭhā*] *m* (संचय S) A collection, heap, hoard, store, stock.साटें [*sāṭēṃ*] *n* (संचय S) A whole investment; the total quantity of merchandise (brought to market by one merchant).

 kanka 'rim of jar' Rebus: karṇīka 'account (scribe)' karṇī 'supercargo'

h1711A *kandiṭ* 'bead' Rebus: *khaṇḍī* 'great quantity'
| *koḍa* 'one' Rebus: *koḍ* 'workshop'

 kanka ‘rim of jar’ Rebus: karṇīka ‘account (scribe)’ karṇī ‘supercargo’ INFIXED kolom ‘three’ Rebus: kolami ‘smithy, forge’|
sal ‘splinter’ Rebus: sal ‘workshop’
खांडा [*khāṇḍā*] *m* A jag, notch, or indentation (as upon the edge of a tool or weapon). Rebus: *kāṇḍa* ‘tools, pots and pans and metal-ware’

 *dula* 'pair' Rebus: *dul* 'cast (metal)' PLUS*kana, kanac* = corner (Santali); Rebus: *kañcu* = bronze (Telugu) Thus, cast bronze.

 kanka ‘rim of jar’ Rebus: karṇīka ‘account (scribe)’ karṇī ‘supercargo’

M-1889 A

m1889A *balad* m. ‘ ox ’, gng. *bald*, (Ku.) *barad*, id. (N. Tarai) Rebus: *bharat* (5 copper, 4 zinc and 1 tin)(Punjabi) *pattar* ‘trough’ Rebus*: pattar* ‘guild’. Thus, copper-zinc-tin alloy (worker) guild.
kandiṭ ‘bead’ Rebus: *khaṇḍī* ‘great quantity’ | *koḍa* ‘one’ Rebus: *koḍ* ‘workshop’

 kanka ‘rim of jar’ Rebus: karṇīka ‘account (scribe)’ karṇī ‘supercargo’

 *dula* 'pair' Rebus: *dul* 'cast (metal)' PLUS*kana, kanac* = corner (Santali); Rebus: *kañcu* = bronze (Telugu) Thus, cast bronze.

 *kolmo* ‘paddy plant’ Rebus: *kolami* ‘smithy, forge’ Vikalpa: *mogge* ‘sprout, bud’ Rebus: *mūh* ‘ingot’ (Santali) dolu ‘plant of shoot height’ Rebus: dul ‘cast metal’

m125A *खोंड [khōṇḍa] m A young bull, a bullcalf. (Marathi) Rebus: kõdār ‘turner’ (Bengali); कोंद kōnda ‘engraver, lapidary setting or infixing gems’ (Marathi) G. sãghārɔ m. ‘lathe’ ; संघाट joinery; M. sãgaḍ ‘double-canoe’ Rebus: sangataras ‘stone-cutter, mason’*
kandiṭ ‘bead’ Rebus: *khaṇḍī* ‘great quantity’ | *koḍa* ‘one’ Rebus: *koḍ* ‘workshop’

 *kanka* (Santali) *karṇika* ‘scribe’(Sanskrit) Rebus: *karṇī,* supercargo for a boat shipment. INFIXED खांडा [*khāṇḍā*] *m* A jag, notch, or indentation (as upon the edge of a tool or weapon). Rebus: *kāṇḍa* ‘tools, pots and pans and metal-ware’
kolom ‘three’ Rebus: kolami ‘smithy, forge

M-253 a

m253a *balad* m. ‘ ox ’, gng. *bald*, (Ku.) *barad*, id. (N. Tarai) Rebus: *bharat* (5 copper, 4 zinc and 1 tin)(Punjabi) *pattar* ‘trough’ Rebus*: pattar* ‘guild’. Thus, copper-zinc-tin alloy (worker) guild.
kandiṭ ‘bead’ Rebus: *khaṇḍī* ‘great quantity’

 *koḍi* ‘flag’ (Ta.)(DEDR 2049). Rebus 1: *koḍ* ‘workshop’ (Kuwi) Rebus 2:

khǒḍ m. 'pit', *khǒḍü* f. 'small pit' (Kashmiri. CDIAL 3947). sal 'splinter' Rebus: sal 'workshop'

dula 'pair' Rebus: *dul* 'cast (metal)' PLUS *kana, kanac* = corner (Santali); Rebus: *kañcu* = bronze (Telugu) PLUS infixed kolmo 'paddy plant' Rebus: kolami 'smithy, forge'. Thus, cast bronze smithy, forge. Or, *mogge* 'sprout, bud' Rebus: *mũh* 'ingot' (Santali)Thus, cast bronze ingot. Read as: *kañcu dul mũh 'bronze cast ingot' kamaḍha* = crab; *kampaṭṭam* = mint (Ta.) ; *kammaṭa* 'coiner, mint' (Telugu) Vikalpa: *ḍato* = claws of crab (Santali); *dhātu* = mineral (Sanskrit)

dula 'two, pair' Rebus: dul 'cast metal' PLUS *dhāḷ* 'a slope'; 'inclination of a plane' (G.); *ḍhāḷiyum* = adj. sloping, inclining (G.) Rebus: *ḍhālako* = a large metal ingot (G.) *ḍhālakī* = a metal heated and poured into a mould; a solid piece of metal; an ingot (Gujarati) PLUS kolom 'three' Rebus: kolami 'smithy, forge'. Thus cast metal ingot smithy.

m1a *खोंड [khōṇḍa] m A young bull, a bullcalf. (Marathi) Rebus: kõdār 'turner' (Bengali); कोंद kōnda 'engraver, lapidary setting or infixing gems' (Marathi) G. sãghāṛɔ m. 'lathe' ; sãgāḍā m.*

kandiṭ 'bead' Rebus: *khaṇḍī* 'great quantity'

 *kanac*

 *bicha* 'scorpion' (Assamese) Rebus: *bica* 'stone ore' (Santali) 'corner' Rebus: *kañcu* 'bronze'

koḍi 'flag' (Ta.)(DEDR 2049). Rebus 1: *koḍ* 'workshop' (Kuwi) Rebus 2: *khǒḍ* m. 'pit', *khǒḍü* f. 'small pit' (Kashmiri. CDIAL 3947). खांडा [*khāṇḍā*] *m* A jag, notch, or indentation (as upon the edge of a tool or weapon). Rebus: *kāṇḍa* 'tools, pots and pans and metal-ware'

m12a *खोंड [khōṇḍa] m A young bull, a bullcalf. (Marathi) Rebus: kõdār 'turner' (Bengali); कोंद kōnda 'engraver, lapidary setting or infixing gems' (Marathi) G. sãghāṛɔ m. 'lathe' ; संघाट joinery; M. sãgaḍ 'double-canoe' Rebus: sangataras 'stone-cutter, mason'*

kandiṭ 'bead' Rebus: *khaṇḍī* 'great quantity'

kamaḍha 'archer, bow' Rebus: *kammaṭa* 'mint, coiner'.

Variant: dula 'pair' Rebus: *dul* 'cast (metal)' PLUS *kana, kanac* = corner (Santali); Rebus: *kañcu* = bronze (Telugu) Thus, cast bronze.

koḍi 'flag' (Ta.)(DEDR 2049). Rebus 1: *koḍ* 'workshop' (Kuwi) Rebus 2: *khǒḍ* m. 'pit', *khǒḍü* f. 'small pit' (Kashmiri. CDIAL 3947). sal 'splinter' Rebus: sal 'workshop'

ayo 'fish' Rebus: *aya* 'iron' *ayas* 'metal' ranku 'liquid measure' Rebus: ranku 'tin'

kolmo 'paddy plant' Rebus: *kolami* 'smithy, forge' Vikalpa: *mogge* 'sprout, bud' Rebus: *mũh* 'ingot' (Santali) dolu 'plant of shoot height' Rebus: dul 'cast metal'

kanka 'rim of jar' Rebus: karṇīka 'account (scribe)' karṇī 'supercargo'

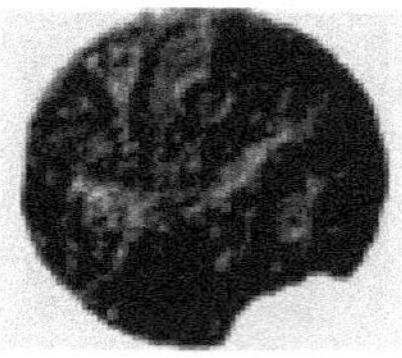

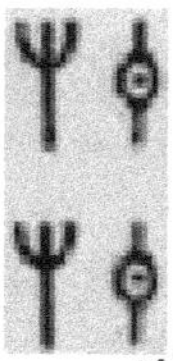

m0436A, B Text 2804

ingot (from) iron smelter, tin smelter merchant guild

The rebus readings are comparable to those provided for m0324 seal with two sides: one side showing a composite animal; the other a young bull and 'chain of beads' hieroglyph. On this seal m0436 the 'rim of jar' hieroglyph is replaced by the hieroglyph: *kolmo* 'paddy plant' Rebus: *kolami* 'smithy, forge'.

खोंड [khōṇḍa] m A young bull, a bullcalf. (Marathi) Rebus: kõdār 'turner' (Bengali); कोंद kōnda 'engraver, lapidary setting or infixing gems' (Marathi) G. sãghāṛɔ m. 'lathe' ; संघाट joinery; M. sāgaḍ 'double-canoe' Rebus: sangataras 'stone-cutter, mason'
kandiṭ 'bead' Rebus: *khaṇḍī* 'great quantity'

kolmo 'paddy plant' Rebus: *kolami* 'smithy, forge' Vikalpa: *mogge* 'sprout, bud' Rebus: *mũh* 'ingot' (Santali) dolu 'plant of shoot height' Rebus: dul 'cast metal'

'Three peaks' sign hieroglyph: *mēḍu* height, rising ground, hillock (Kannada) Rebus: *meḍ* 'iron' (Ho.) kolom 'three' Rebus: kolami 'smithy, forge' Thus *meḍ kolami* 'iron smithy-forge'

h644A Read rebus as at first sign m1150

m1150A *ibha* 'elephant' Rebus: *ib* 'iron' *ibbo* 'merchant' (Gujarati) *kaṇḍo* 'stool, seat' Rebus: *kāṇḍa* 'metalware' *kaṇḍa* 'fire-altar' PLUS mēḍu height, rising ground, hillock (Kannada) Rebus: : *meḍ* 'iron' (Ho.) Thus *meḍ kolami* 'iron smithy-forge' sal 'splinter' Rebus: sal 'workshop' *aya kammaṭa.*'coiner, mint alloy' *ayo ḍhālako* 'alloy metal ingot'

कांड *kāṇḍa* 'arrow' Rebus: *kāṇḍa* 'pots and pans, metalware, tools'. Rebus 2: kaṇḍ 'fire-altar' (Santali) kole.l 'temple' Rebus: kole.l 'smithy'

h874B Side A: Read rebus as at m1150. Side B: First sign read rebus as at m1150 PLUS

kanka 'rim of jar' Rebus: karṇīka 'account (scribe)' karṇī 'supercargo'

kharedo = a currycomb (Gujarati) खरारा [*kharārā*] *m* (H) A currycomb. 2 Currying a horse. (Marathi) Rebus: करडा [*karaḍā*] Hard from alloy--iron, silver &c. (Marathi) *kharādī* ' turner' (Gujarati)

m1909 Rhinoceros/boar: baḍhia = a castrated boar, a hog (Santali) baḍhi 'a caste who work both in iron and wood' (Santali) *baṟea* 'merchant'

aḍaren 'cover of pot or lid' Rebus: *aduru* 'native, unsmelted metal' Duplicated: dula 'pair' Rebus: dul 'cast metal' PLUS *meḍ kolami* 'iron smithy-forge' Thus, smithy-forge iron castings.

 *kanac* 'corner' Rebus: *kañcu* 'bronze' sal 'splinter' Rebus: sal 'workshop' kolom 'three' Rebus: kolami 'smithy, forge' dula 'two' Rebus: dul 'cast metal'

 *koḍi* 'flag' (Ta.)(DEDR 2049). Rebus 1: *koḍ* 'workshop' (Kuwi) Rebus 2: *khŏḍ* m. 'pit', *khōḍü* f. 'small pit' (Kashmiri. CDIAL 3947).

m10a *खोंड [khōṇḍa] m A young bull, a bullcalf. (Marathi) Rebus: kōdār 'turner' (Bengali); कोंद kōnda 'engraver, lapidary setting or infixing gems' (Marathi) G. sãghāṛɔ m. 'lathe' ; संघाट joinery; M. sãgaḍ 'double-canoe' Rebus: sangataras 'stone-cutter, mason'*

 *meḍ kolami* 'iron smithy-forge' Thus, smithy-forge iron castings.

Circumscript: *kuṭila* 'bent' CDIAL 3230 kuṭi— in cmpd. 'curve', *kuṭika—* 'bent' MBh. Rebus: *kuṭila, katthīl* = bronze (8 parts copper and 2 parts tin) Duplicated: dula 'pair' Rebus: dul 'cast metal' Thus, cast bronze or bronze castings. karaṇḍa 'duck' (Sanskrit) karaṛa 'a very large aquatic bird' (Sindhi) Rebus: करडा [*karaḍā*] Hard from alloy--iron, silver &c. (Marathi) *kharādī* ' turner' (Gujarati) sal 'splinter' Rebus: sal 'workshop'

 *dula* 'pair' Rebus: *dul* 'cast (metal)' PLUS*kana, kanac* = corner (Santali); Rebus: *kañcu* = bronze (Telugu) PLUS infixed kolmo 'paddy plant' Rebus: kolami 'smithy, forge'. Thus, cast bronze smithy, forge. Or, *mogge* 'sprout, bud' Rebus: *mũh* 'ingot' (Santali)Thus, cast bronze ingot. Read as: *kañcu dul mũh 'bronze cast ingot' aya aḍaren (homonym: aduru)*'alloy native metal'

 *muka* 'ladle' (Tamil)(DEDR 4887) Rebus: *mũh* 'ingot' (Santali) Thus, iron ingot. kolom 'three' Rebus: kolami 'smithy, forge' dula 'two' Rebus: dul 'cast metal'

 'Arrow' sign hieroglyph (variant) This is a ligature of 'lid of pot' hieroglyph superscript on 'a linear stroke' numeral hieroglyph.*aḍaren* 'cover of pot or lid' Rebus: *aduru* 'native, unsmelted metal' PLUS koḍ = one (Santali); koḍ 'workshop' (Gujarati)

 notch+slanted stroke reads rebus: *ḍhālako kāṇḍa* 'ingot, tools, pots and pans and metal-ware'.*dhāḷ* 'a slope'; 'inclination of a plane' (G.); *ḍhāḷiyum* = adj. sloping, inclining (G.) Rebus: *ḍhālako* = a large metal ingot (G.) *ḍhālakī* = a metal heated and poured into a mould; a solid piece of metal; an ingot (Gujarati) PLUS खांडा [*khāṇḍā*] *m* A jag, notch, or indentation (as upon the edge of a tool or weapon). Rebus: *kāṇḍa* 'tools, pots and pans and metal-ware'

 *kolmo* 'paddy plant' Rebus: *kolami* 'smithy, forge' Vikalpa: *mogge* 'sprout, bud' Rebus: *mũh* 'ingot' (Santali) dolu 'plant of shoot height' Rebus: dul 'cast metal'

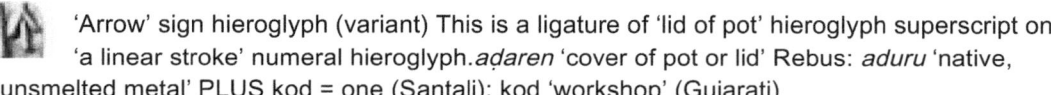

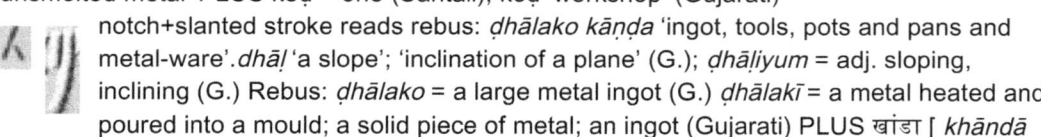

m140A *खोंड [khōṇḍa] m A young bull, a bullcalf. (Marathi) Rebus: kōdār 'turner' (Bengali); कोंद kōnda 'engraver, lapidary setting or infixing gems' (Marathi) G. sãghāṛɔ m. 'lathe' ; संघाट joinery; M. sãgaḍ 'double-canoe' Rebus: sangataras 'stone-cutter, mason'*
meḍ kolami 'iron smithy-forge'
ḍhanga = a crook used for pulling down the branches of trees, for goats, sheep and camels (P.) Rebus:*ḍhangar* blacksmith'.

koḍi 'flag' (Ta.)(DEDR 2049). Rebus 1: *koḍ* 'workshop' (Kuwi) Rebus 2: *khŏḍ* m. 'pit', *khŏḍü* f. 'small pit' (Kashmiri. CDIAL 3947).
ayo 'fish' Rebus: *aya* 'iron' *ayas* 'metal' sal 'splinter' Rebus: sal 'workshop'

Ligature: two peaks: mēḍu height, rising ground, hillock (Kannada) Rebus: *meḍ* 'iron' (Ho.) dula 'pair' Rebus: dul 'cast metal' PLUS |||| Numeral 4: gaṇḍa 'four' Rebus: kaṇḍa 'furnace, fire-altar' (Santali)

kanka  'rim of jar' Rebus: karṇīka 'account (scribe)' karṇī 'supercargo'

m1052a From l.:

kanḍo stool, seat Rebus: *kāṇḍā* 'metalware, tools, pots and pans'(Marathi) PLUS *dhatu* 'mineral ore'.

kanka 'rim of jar' Rebus: *karṇīka* 'account (scribe)' *karṇī* 'supercargo'
ayo 'fish' Rebus: aya 'iron' (Gujarati) ayas 'metal' (Vedic)
dula 'pair' Rebus: dul 'cast metal'

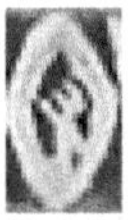
dula 'pair' Rebus: dul 'cast metal'. The circumscribing ligature may be seen as made up of two curved lines back-to-back: ()kuṭila 'bent' CDIAL 3230 kuṭi— in cmpd. 'curve', *kuṭika—* 'bent' MBh. Rebus: kuṭila, katthīl = bronze (8 parts copper and 2 parts tin) [cf. āra-kūṭa, 'brass' (Sanskrit)

ranku 'liquid measue' Rebus: ranku 'tin' PLUS 'notch' hieroglyph Rebus: *kāṇḍā* 'metalware, tools, pots and pans'(Marathi).

Second segment of text inscription

सांड [sāṇḍa] *f* (षद S) An outlet for superfluous water (as through a dam or mound); a sluice, a floodvent. Rebus: सांडणी [sāṇḍaṇī] *f* (H) An instrument of goldsmiths. It is hooked or curved at the extremity; and is used to draw things out of the fire. खांडा [*khāṇḍā*] *m* A jag, notch, or indentation (as upon the edge of a tool or weapon). Rebus: *kāṇḍa* 'tools, pots and pans and metal-ware'
eraka 'raised hand' Rebus: *eraka* 'copper' PLUS 'notch' hieroglyph Rebus: *kāṇḍā* 'metalware, tools, pots and pans'(Marathi).
meḍ 'body' Rebus: *meḍ* 'iron' *koḍa* 'numeral one' Rebus: *koḍ* 'workshop'

Thus, the second segment of the text inscription reads: copper metalware, iron workshop.

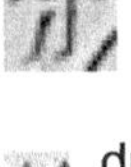
Ligatured sign hieroglyph: 'stool' hieroglyph superscripted on 'ladder' hieroglyph

dula 'pair' Rebus: dul 'cast metal' PLUS | *koḍa* 'one' Rebus: *koḍ* 'workshop' PLUS INFIXED खांडा [*khāṇḍā*] *m* A jag, notch, or indentation (as upon the edge of a tool or weapon). Rebus: *kāṇḍa* 'tools, pots and pans and metal-ware' Thus metalware castings workshop.

maṇḍā 'raised platform, stool' Rebus: maṇḍā 'warehouse' Vikalpa: *kanḍo* stool, seat Rebus: *kāṇḍā* 'metalware, tools, pots and pans'(Marathi).

m648A *खोंड [khōṇḍa] m A young bull, a bullcalf. (Marathi) Rebus: kõdār 'turner' (Bengali); कोंद kōnda 'engraver, lapidary setting or infixing gems' (Marathi) G. sãghārɔ m. 'lathe' ; संघाट joinery; M. sãgaḍ 'double-canoe' Rebus: sangataras 'stone-cutter, mason'*

dula 'pair' Rebus: dul 'cast metal' PLUS | *koḍa* 'one' Rebus: *koḍ* 'workshop' PLUS INFIXED खांडा [*khāṇḍā*] *m* A jag, notch, or indentation (as upon the edge of a tool or weapon). Rebus: *kāṇḍa* 'tools, pots and pans and metal-ware' Thus metalware castings workshop. maṇḍā 'raised platform, stool' Rebus: maṇḍā 'warehouse' Vikalpa: *kanḍo* stool, seat Rebus: *kāṇḍā* 'metalware, tools, pots and pans'(Marathi).

kanka 'rim of jar' Rebus: karṇīka 'account (scribe)' karṇī 'supercargo' dula 'two' Rebus: dul 'cast metal' *ayo* 'fish' Rebus: *aya* 'iron' *ayas* 'metal' *bhaṭa* 'warrior' (Sanskrit) Rebus: *baṭa* a kind of iron (Gujarati). Rebus: *bhaṭa* 'furnace' (Santali) kanka 'rim of jar' Rebus: karṇīka 'account (scribe)' karṇī 'supercargo'

meḍ 'body' Rebus: *meḍ* 'iron' (Ho.) काठी [kāṭhī] *f* (काष्ट S) 'frame or structure of the body' (Marathi) Rebus: खंडी [khaṇḍī] measure of weight (Marathi) கண்டி; *kaṇṭi, n. < Mhr. khaṇḍil. [T. Tu. khaṇḍi, M. kaṇḍi.]* Candy, a weight, stated to be roughly equivalent to 500 lbs.

M-1841 a

m1841a *खोंड [khōṇḍa] m A young bull, a bullcalf. (Marathi) Rebus: kõdār 'turner' (Bengali); कोंद kōnda 'engraver, lapidary setting or infixing gems' (Marathi) G. sãghārɔ m. 'lathe' ; संघाट joinery; M. sãgaḍ 'double-canoe' Rebus: sangataras 'stone-cutter, mason'*

dula 'pair' Rebus: dul 'cast metal' PLUS | *koḍa* 'one' Rebus: *koḍ* 'workshop' PLUS

INFIXED खांडा [*khāṇḍā*] *m* A jag, notch, or indentation (as upon the edge of a tool or weapon). Rebus: *kāṇḍa* 'tools, pots and pans and metal-ware' Thus metalware castings workshop.

notch+slanted stroke reads rebus: *ḍhālako kāṇḍa* 'ingot, tools, pots and pans and metal-ware'.*dhāḷ* 'a slope'; 'inclination of a plane' (G.); *ḍhāḷiyum* = adj. sloping, inclining (G.) Rebus: *ḍhālako* = a large metal ingot (G.) *ḍhālakī* = a metal heated and poured into a mould; a solid piece of metal; an ingot (Gujarati) PLUS खांडा [*khāṇḍā*] *m* A jag, notch, or indentation (as upon the edge of a tool or weapon). Rebus: *kāṇḍa* 'tools, pots and pans and metal-ware' *ayo* 'fish' Rebus: *aya* 'iron' *ayas* 'metal'

bicha 'scorpion' (Assamese) Rebus: *bica* 'stone ore' (Santali) *ayo ḍhālako* 'alloy metal ingot'

dula 'pair' Rebus: dul 'cast (metal)' kolmo 'rice plant' Rebus: kolami 'smithy/forge'

 kanka 'rim of jar' Rebus: karṇīka 'account (scribe)' karṇī 'supercargo'

 m139a खोंड *[khōṇḍa] m A young bull, a bullcalf. (Marathi) Rebus: kõdār 'turner' (Bengali);* कोंद *kōnda 'engraver, lapidary setting or infixing gems' (Marathi) G. sãghāṛɔ m. 'lathe' ;* संघाट *joinery; M. sāgaḍ 'double-canoe' Rebus: sangataras 'stone-cutter, mason'*

 dula 'pair' Rebus: dul 'cast metal' PLUS | *koḍa* 'one' Rebus: *koḍ* 'workshop' PLUS INFIXED खांडा [*khāṇḍā*] *m* A jag, notch, or indentation (as upon the edge of a tool or weapon). Rebus: *kāṇḍa* 'tools, pots and pans and metal-ware' Thus metalware castings workshop. maṇḍā 'raised platform, stool' Rebus: maṇḍā 'warehouse' Vikalpa: *kanḍo* stool, seat Rebus: *kāṇḍā* 'metalware, tools, pots and pans'(Marathi).

kanka 'rim of jar' Rebus: karṇīka 'account (scribe)' karṇī 'supercargo' INFIXED: खांडा [*khāṇḍā*] *m* A jag, notch, or indentation (as upon the edge of a tool or weapon). Rebus: *kāṇḍa* 'tools, pots and pans and metal-ware'
aya kāṇḍa 'alloy metalware'

 *dula* 'pair' Rebus: *dul* 'cast (metal)' PLUS*kana, kanac* = corner (Santali); Rebus: *kañcu* = bronze (Telugu) PLUS infixed kolmo 'paddy plant' Rebus: kolami 'smithy, forge'. Thus, cast bronze smithy, forge. Or, *mogge* 'sprout, bud' Rebus: *mũh* 'ingot' (Santali)Thus, cast bronze ingot. Read as: *kañcu dul mũh 'bronze cast ingot'*
kolom 'three' Rebus: kolami 'smithy, forge'

 m1737a खोंड *[khōṇḍa] m A young bull, a bullcalf. (Marathi) Rebus: kõdār 'turner' (Bengali);* कोंद *kōnda 'engraver, lapidary setting or infixing gems' (Marathi) G. sãghāṛɔ m. 'lathe' ;* संघाट *joinery; M. sāgaḍ 'double-canoe' Rebus: sangataras 'stone-cutter, mason'*

 *āra* 'spokes' Rebus: *āra 'brass'*. cf. erka = ekke (Tbh. of arka) aka (Tbh. of arka) copper (metal); crystal (Kannada) Glyph: *eraka*'nave of wheel' Rebus: eraka 'copper'; cf. erka = ekke (Tbh. of arka) aka (Tbh. of arka) copper (metal); crystal (Kannada) *erako* 'moltencast copper' Duplicated: dula 'pair' Rebus: dul 'cast metal' Thus cast copper, brass casting.

 dula 'pair' Rebus: dul 'cast metal' PLUS | *koḍa* 'one' Rebus: *koḍ* 'workshop' PLUS INFIXED खांडा [*khāṇḍā*] *m* A jag, notch, or indentation (as upon the edge of a tool or weapon). Rebus: *kāṇḍa* 'tools, pots and pans and metal-ware' Thus metalware castings workshop.

 *kuṭila* 'bent' CDIAL 3230 kuṭi— in cmpd. 'curve', *kuṭika—* 'bent' MBh. Rebus: *kuṭila, katthīl* = bronze (8 parts copper and 2 parts tin)

 'Arrow' sign hieroglyph (variant) This is a ligature of 'lid of pot' hieroglyph superscript on 'a linear stroke' numeral hieroglyph.*aḍaren* 'cover of pot or lid' Rebus: *aduru* 'native,

unsmelted metal' PLUS koḍ = one (Santali); koḍ 'workshop' (Gujarati)

 dula 'pair' Rebus: dul 'cast (metal)' kolmo 'rice plant' Rebus: kolami 'smithy/forge'

 kanka 'rim of jar' Rebus: karṇīka 'account (scribe)' karṇī 'supercargo'

h1706A

dula 'pair' Rebus: dul 'cast metal' PLUS | *koḍa* 'one' Rebus: *koḍ* 'workshop' PLUS INFIXED खांडा [*khāṇḍā*] *m* A jag, notch, or indentation (as upon the edge of a tool or weapon). Rebus: *kāṇḍa* 'tools, pots and pans and metal-ware' Thus metalware castings workshop. maṇḍā 'raised platform, stool' Rebus: maṇḍā 'warehouse' Vikalpa: *kanḍo* stool, seat Rebus: *kāṇḍā* 'metalware, tools, pots and pans'(Marathi).

  Strands of yarn/rope' hieroglyph: Hieroglyph: 'strands of yarn' Rebus reading: *dhā'tu* 'strand of rope' Rebus: *dhatu* 'mineral ore' (Santali) sal 'splinter' Rebus: sal 'workshop' *aya aḍaren (homonym: aduru)*'alloy native metal' sal 'splinter' Rebus: sal 'workshop'

Chanhudaro 3A *खोंड [khōṇḍa] m A young bull, a bullcalf. (Marathi) Rebus: kōdār 'turner' (Bengali); कोंद kōnda 'engraver, lapidary setting or infixing gems' (Marathi) G. sãghāṛɔ m. 'lathe' ; संघाट joinery; M. sãgaḍ 'double-canoe' Rebus: sangataras 'stone-cutter, mason'*

dula 'pair' Rebus: dul 'cast metal' PLUS | *koḍa* 'one' Rebus: *koḍ* 'workshop' PLUS INFIXED खांडा [*khāṇḍā*] *m* A jag, notch, or indentation (as upon the edge of a tool or weapon). Rebus: *kāṇḍa* 'tools, pots and pans and metal-ware' Thus metalware castings workshop. maṇḍā 'raised platform, stool' Rebus: maṇḍā 'warehouse' Vikalpa: *kanḍo* stool, seat Rebus: *kāṇḍā* 'metalware, tools, pots and pans'(Marathi).

sal 'splinter' Rebus: sal 'workshop' *āra* 'six' Rebus: *āra* 'brass'

kanka 'rim of jar' Rebus: karṇīka 'account (scribe)' karṇī 'supercargo'

m954a *खोंड [khōṇḍa] m A young bull, a bullcalf. (Marathi) Rebus: kōdār 'turner' (Bengali); कोंद kōnda 'engraver, lapidary setting or infixing gems' (Marathi) G. sãghāṛɔ m. 'lathe' ; संघाट joinery; M. sãgaḍ 'double-canoe' Rebus: sangataras 'stone-cutter, mason'*

dula 'pair' Rebus: dul 'cast metal' PLUS | *koḍa* 'one' Rebus: *koḍ* 'workshop' PLUS INFIXED खांडा [*khāṇḍā*] *m* A jag, notch, or indentation (as upon the edge of a tool or weapon). Rebus: *kāṇḍa* 'tools, pots and pans and metal-ware' Thus metalware castings workshop. maṇḍā 'raised platform, stool' Rebus: maṇḍā 'warehouse' Vikalpa: *kanḍo* stool, seat Rebus: *kāṇḍā* 'metalware, tools, pots and pans'(Marathi).

 *bicha* 'scorpion' (Assamese) Rebus: *bica* 'stone ore' (Santali)

kanka 'rim of jar' Rebus: karṇīka 'account (scribe)' karṇī 'supercargo'मंडप [manḍapa] 'canopy' Rebus: मंडई [manḍī] *f* (H) A green market, the place in a city whither vegetables and fruits

 are brought to be disposed of by wholesale. INFIXED metalware castings workshop.

m44a *खोंड [khōṇḍa] m A young bull, a bullcalf. (Marathi) Rebus: kõdār 'turner' (Bengali); कोंद kōnda 'engraver, lapidary setting or infixing gems' (Marathi) G. sãghāṛɔ m. 'lathe' ; संघाट joinery; M. sãgaḍ 'double-canoe' Rebus: sangataras 'stone-cutter, mason'*

 dula 'pair' Rebus: dul 'cast metal' PLUS | *koḍa* 'one' Rebus: *koḍ* 'workshop' PLUS INFIXED kolom three' Rebus: kolami 'smithy, forge' Thus metalware castings forge.

 *kuṭila* 'bent' CDIAL 3230 kuṭi— in cmpd. 'curve', *kuṭika—* 'bent' MBh. Rebus: *kuṭila, katthīl* = bronze (8 parts copper and 2 parts tin) sal 'splinter' sal 'workshop'

 *dula* 'pair' Rebus: *dul* 'cast (metal)' PLUS*kana, kanac* = corner (Santali); Rebus: *kañcu* = bronze (Telugu) PLUS infixed kolmo 'paddy plant' Rebus: kolami 'smithy, forge'. Thus, cast bronze smithy, forge. Or, *mogge* 'sprout, bud' Rebus: *mũh* 'ingot' (Santali)Thus, cast bronze ingot. Read as: *kañcu dul mũh 'bronze cast ingot'*

 *muka* 'ladle' (Tamil)(DEDR 4887) Rebus: *mũh* 'ingot' (Santali) *baṭa* = rimless pot (Kannada) Rebus:) *baṭa* = a kind of iron (G.)) *bhaṭa* furnace (Gujarati) Thus, iron ingot.

kolom 'three' Rebus: kolami 'smithy, forge'

 dula 'pair' Rebus: dul 'cast (metal)' kolmo 'rice plant' Rebus: kolami 'smithy/forge'

 kanka 'rim of jar' Rebus: karṇīka 'account (scribe)' karṇī 'supercargo'

m129A *खोंड [khōṇḍa] m A young bull, a bullcalf. (Marathi) Rebus: kõdār 'turner' (Bengali); कोंद kōnda 'engraver, lapidary setting or infixing gems' (Marathi) G. sãghāṛɔ m. 'lathe' ; संघाट joinery; M. sãgaḍ 'double-canoe' Rebus: sangataras 'stone-cutter, mason'*

 Variant: dula 'pair' Rebus: dul 'cast metal' PLUS | *koḍa* 'one' Rebus: *koḍ* 'workshop' PLUS INFIXED kolom three' Rebus: kolami 'smithy, forge' Thus metalware castings forge.

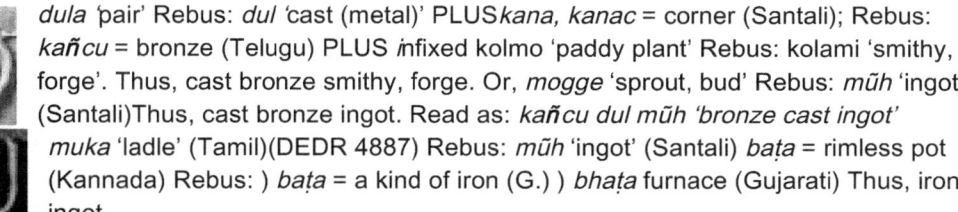

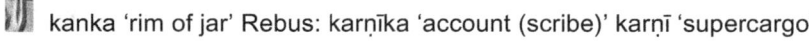

kanka (Santali) *karṇika* 'scribe'(Sanskrit) Rebus: *karṇī,* supercargo for a boat shipment. INFIXED खांडा [*khāṇḍā*] *m* A jag, notch, or indentation (as upon the edge of a tool or weapon). Rebus: *kāṇḍa* 'tools, pots and pans and metal-ware' *aya aḍaren (homonym: aduru)*'alloy native metal' *aya kammaṭa.*'coiner, mint alloy' *ayo ḍhālako* 'alloy metal ingot'

कांड *kāṇḍa* 'arrow' Rebus: *kāṇḍa* 'pots and pans, metalware, tools'. Rebus 2: kaṇḍ 'fire-altar' (Santali)

K-15 A

Kalibangan 15A *खोंड [khōṇḍa] m A young bull, a bullcalf. (Marathi) Rebus: kõdār 'turner' (Bengali); कोंद kōnda 'engraver, lapidary setting or infixing gems' (Marathi) G. sãghāṛɔ m. 'lathe' ; संघाट joinery; M. sāgaḍ 'double-canoe' Rebus: sangataras 'stone-cutter, mason'*

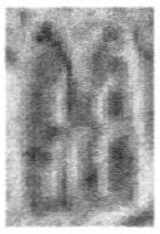

Ligature: two peaks: mēḍu height, rising ground, hillock (Kannada) Rebus: *meḍ* 'iron' (Ho.) dula 'pair' Rebus: dul 'cast metal' PLUS |||| Numeral 4: gaṇḍa 'four' Rebus: kaṇḍa 'furnace, fire-altar' (Santali) *aya aḍaren (homonym: aduru)*'alloy native metal' kolom 'three' Rebus: kolami 'smithy, forge' PLUS *mogge* 'sprout, bud' Rebus: *mũh* 'ingot' (Santali) Circumscript: sal 'splinter' Rebus: sal 'workshop' PLUS gaṇḍa 'four' Rebus: kaṇḍa 'furnace, fire-altar' (Santali) PLUS dulo 'hole' Rebus: dul 'cast metal'

|||| Numeral 4: gaṇḍa 'four' Rebus: kaṇḍa 'furnace, fire-altar' (Santali) dula 'pair' Rebus: dul 'cast metal'
ḍato = claws of crab (Santali) Rebus: *dhātu* 'mineral ore'Duplicated: dula 'two' Rebus: dul 'cast metal'
kanka 'rim of jar' Rebus: karṇīka 'account (scribe)' karṇī 'supercargo'

kharedo = a currycomb (Gujarati) खरारा [*kharārā*] *m* (H) A currycomb. 2 Currying a horse. (Marathi) Rebus: करडा [*karaḍā*] Hard from alloy--iron, silver &c. (Marathi) *kharādī* 'turner' (Gujarati)

kanac 'corner' Rebus: *kañcu* 'bronze'*kuṭila* 'bent' CDIAL 3230 kuṭi— in cmpd. 'curve', *kuṭika—* 'bent' MBh. Rebus: *kuṭila, katthīl* = bronze (8 parts copper and 2 parts tin) Duplicated: dula 'pair' Rebus: dul 'cast metal' Thus, cast bronze or bronze castings. INFIXED dula 'pair' Rebus: dul 'cast metal' PLUS dulo 'hole' Rebus: dul 'cast metal' Thus, bronze castings phonetically-semantically reinforced.

h29A *खोंड [khōṇḍa] m A young bull, a bullcalf. (Marathi) Rebus: kõdār 'turner' (Bengali); कोंद kōnda 'engraver, lapidary setting or infixing gems' (Marathi) G. sãghāṛɔ m. 'lathe' ; संघाट joinery; M. sāgaḍ 'double-canoe' Rebus: sangataras 'stone-cutter, mason'*

kəṭhā´r, kc. *kuṭhār* m. ' granary, storeroom '(Western Pahari)(CDIAL 3550). *koṭhārī m.* ' storekeeper' (Gujarati)(CDIAL 3551) Thus, storeroom (of) *kolom* 'three' Rebus: *kolami* 'smithy, forge'. Dula 'pair' Rebus: dul 'cast metal' Thus, together *dul kolami kuṭhār* 'metal smithy castings storeroom'

loa 'ficus religiosa' Rebus: *lo* 'iron' (Sanskrit) PLUS unique ligatures: लोखंड [lōkhaṇḍa] *n* (लोह S) Iron. लोखंडाचे चणे खावविणें or चारणें To oppress grievously.लोखंडकाम [lōkhaṇḍakāma] *n* Iron work; that portion (of a building, machine &c.) which consists of iron. 2 The business of an ironsmith.लोखंडी [lōkhaṇḍī] *a* (लोखंड) Composed of iron; relating to iron. (Marathi) *bhaṭa* 'warrior' (Sanskrit) Rebus: *baṭa* a kind of iron (Gujarati). Rebus: *bhaṭa* 'furnace' (Santali) Thus, together, th ligatured hieroglyph reads rebus: *loa bhaṭa* 'iron furnace'
ranku 'liquid measure' Rebus: ranku 'tin'.

Chanhudaro 32a *खोंड [khōṇḍa] m A young bull, a bullcalf. (Marathi) Rebus: kōdār 'turner' (Bengali); कोंद kōnda 'engraver, lapidary setting or infixing gems' (Marathi) G. sãghāṛɔ m. 'lathe' ; संघाट joinery; M. sãgaḍ 'double-canoe' Rebus: sangataras 'stone-cutter, mason'*

kəṭhā´r, kc. *kuṭhār* m. ' granary, storeroom '(Western Pahari)(CDIAL 3550). *koṭhārī m.* ' storekeeper' (Gujarati)(CDIAL 3551) Thus, storeroom (of) *kolom* 'three' Rebus: *kolami* 'smithy, forge'. Dula 'pair' Rebus: dul 'cast metal' Thus, together *dul kolami kuṭhār* 'metal smithy castings storeroom'
kolmo 'paddy plant' Rebus: *kolami* 'smithy, forge'

kharedo = a currycomb (Gujarati) खरारा [*kharārā*] *m* (H) A currycomb. 2 Currying a horse. (Marathi) Rebus: करडा [*karaḍā*] Hard from alloy--iron, silver &c. (Marathi) *kharādī* ' turner' (Gujarati)
mogge 'sprout, bud' Rebus: mūh 'ingot' PLUS | *koḍa* 'one' Rebus: *koḍ* 'workshop' dula 'pair' Rebus: dul 'cast metal'. Thus, cast metal ingot.

m1341a From r.:

kəṭhā´r, kc. *kuṭhār* m. ' granary, storeroom '(Western Pahari)(CDIAL 3550). *koṭhārī m.* ' storekeeper' (Gujarati)(CDIAL 3551) Thus, storeroom (of) *kolom* 'three' Rebus: *kolami* 'smithy, forge'. Dula 'pair' Rebus: dul 'cast metal' Thus, together *dul kolami kuṭhār* 'metal smithy castings storeroom'
ranku 'antelope' ranku 'liquid measure' Thus, dula 'pair' Rebus: dul 'cast metal' ranku 'tin'. Thus tin casting.
sal 'splinter' Rebus: sal 'workshop
āra 'six' Rebus: *āra* 'brass'

m845a *खोंड [khōṇḍa] m A young bull, a bullcalf. (Marathi) Rebus: kōdār 'turner' (Bengali); कोंद kōnda 'engraver, lapidary setting or infixing gems' (Marathi) G. sãghāṛɔ m. 'lathe' ; संघाट joinery; M. sãgaḍ 'double-canoe' Rebus: sangataras 'stone-cutter, mason'*

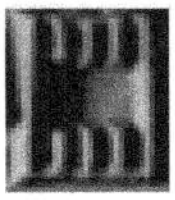

kəṭhā´r, kc. *kuṭhār* m. ' granary, storeroom '(Western Pahari)(CDIAL 3550). *koṭhārī m.* ' storekeeper' (Gujarati)(CDIAL

3551) Thus, storeroom (of) *kolom* 'three' Rebus: *kolami* 'smithy, forge'. Dula 'pair' Rebus: dul 'cast metal' Thus, together *dul kolami kuṭhār* 'metal smithy castings storeroom'

 ḍāg mountain-ridge (Hindi)(CDIAL 5476). Rebus: dhangar 'blacksmith'

sal 'splinter' Rebus: sal 'workshop'

 Read in context, the composite hieroglyph is assumed to be a combination of a slanted stroke ligatured to a notch,which provide possible rebus readings of a smithy/forge: notch+slanted stroke reads rebus: *ḍhālako kāṇḍa* 'ingot, tools, pots and pans and metal-ware' *dhāḷ* 'a slope'; 'inclination of a plane' (Gujarati); *ḍhāḷiyum* = adj. sloping, inclining (Gujarati) Rebus: *ḍhālako* = a large metal ingot (Gujarati) *ḍhālakī* = a metal heated and poured into a mould; a solid piece of metal; an ingot (Gujarati)PLUS खांडा [*khāṇḍā*] *m* A jag, notch, or indentation (as upon the edge of a tool or weapon). Rebus: *kāṇḍa* 'tools, pots and pans and metal-ware'

kanka 'rim of jar' Rebus: karṇīka 'account (scribe)' karṇī 'supercargo'

Balakot 2A *खोंड [khōṇḍa] m A young bull, a bullcalf. (Marathi) Rebus: kõdār 'turner' (Bengali); कोंद kōnda 'engraver, lapidary setting or infixing gems' (Marathi) G. sãghāṛɔ m. 'lathe' ; संघाट joinery; M. sãgaḍ 'double-canoe' Rebus: sangataras 'stone-cutter, mason'*

 *kəṭhā'r*, kc. *kuṭhār* m. ' granary, storeroom '(Western Pahari)(CDIAL 3550). *koṭhārī m.* ' storekeeper' (Gujarati)(CDIAL 3551) Thus, storeroom (of) *kolom* 'three' Rebus: *kolami* 'smithy, forge'. Dula 'pair' Rebus: dul 'cast metal' Thus, together *dul kolami kuṭhār* 'metal smithy castings storeroom'

 *koḍi* 'flag' (Tamil)(DEDR 2049). Rebus 1: *koḍ* 'workshop' (Kuwi) Rebus 2: *khŏḍ* m. 'pit', *khŏḍü* f. 'small pit' (Kashmiri. CDIAL 3947).

sal 'splinter' Rebus: sal 'workshop'

 Read in context, the composite hieroglyph is assumed to be a combination of a slanted stroke ligatured to a notch,which provide possible rebus readings of a smithy/forge: notch+slanted stroke reads rebus: *ḍhālako kāṇḍa* 'ingot, tools, pots and pans and metal-ware' *dhāḷ* 'a slope'; 'inclination of a plane' (Gujarati); *ḍhāḷiyum* = adj. sloping, inclining (Gujarati) Rebus: *ḍhālako* = a large metal ingot (Gujarati) *ḍhālakī* = a metal heated and poured into a mould; a solid piece of metal; an ingot (Gujarati) PLUS खांडा [*khāṇḍā*] *m* A jag, notch, or indentation (as upon the edge of a tool or weapon). Rebus: *kāṇḍa* 'tools, pots and pans and metal-ware'

 *khuṭo* ' leg, foot ', °ṭī ' goat's leg ' Rebus: *khōṭā* 'alloy' (Marathi)

kolmo 'paddy plant' Rebus: *kolami* 'smithy, forge' Thus, together the pair reads: alloy smithy. Vikalpa: *mogge* 'sprout, bud' Rebus: *mũh* 'ingot'

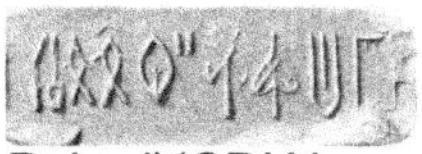 m359a

kəṭhā´r, kc. *kuṭhār* m. ' granary, storeroom '(Western Pahari)(CDIAL 3550). *koṭhārī m.* ' storekeeper' (Gujarati)(CDIAL 3551) Thus, storeroom (of) *kolom* 'three' Rebus: *kolami* 'smithy, forge'. Dula 'pair' Rebus: dul 'cast metal' Thus, together *dul kolami kuṭhār* 'metal smithy castings storeroom'

 *muka* 'ladle' (Tamil)(DEDR 4887) Rebus: *mũh* 'ingot' (Santali) *baṭa* = rimless pot (Kannada) Rebus: *baṭa* = a kind of iron (G.)) *bhaṭa* furnace (Gujarati) Thus, iron ingot. dula 'pair' Rebus: dul 'cast metal' PLUS

 *loa* 'ficus religiosa' Rebus: *lo* 'iron' (Sanskrit) PLUS unique ligatures: लोखंड [lōkhaṇḍa] *n* (लोह S) Iron. लोखंडाचे चणे खावविणें or चारणें To oppress grievously.लोखंडकाम [lōkhaṇḍakāma] *n* Iron work; that portion (of a building, machine &c.) which consists of iron. 2 The business of an ironsmith.लोखंडी [lōkhaṇḍī] *a* (लोखंड) Composed of iron; relating to iron. (Marathi)

sal 'splinter' Rebus: sal 'workshop'

 *dula* 'pair' Rebus: *dul* 'cast (metal)' PLUS*kana, kanac* = corner (Santali); Rebus: *kañcu* = bronze (Telugu) PLUS infixed kolmo 'paddy plant' Rebus: kolami 'smithy, forge'. Thus, cast bronze smithy, forge. Or, *mogge* 'sprout, bud' Rebus: *mũh* 'ingot' (Santali)Thus, cast bronze ingot. Read as: *kañcu dul mũh 'bronze cast ingot' aya aḍaren (homonym: aduru)*'alloy native metal' *ayo* 'fish' Rebus: *aya* 'iron' *ayas* 'metal'

ranku 'liquid measure' Rebus: ranku 'tin'

 *kolmo* 'paddy plant' Rebus: *kolami* 'smithy, forge' Vikalpa: *mogge* 'sprout, bud' Rebus: *mũh* 'ingot' (Santali) dolu 'plant of shoot height' Rebus: dul 'cast metal'

h1035A *खोंड [khōṇḍa] m A young bull, a bullcalf. (Marathi) Rebus: kōdār 'turner' (Bengali); कोंद kōnda 'engraver, lapidary setting or infixing gems' (Marathi) G. sãghāṛɔ m. 'lathe' ; संघाट joinery; M. sāgaḍ 'double-canoe' Rebus: sangataras 'stone-cutter, mason'*

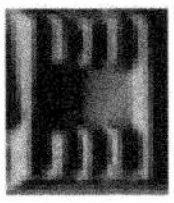 *kəṭhā´r*, kc. *kuṭhār* m. ' granary, storeroom '(Western Pahari)(CDIAL 3550). *koṭhārī m.* ' storekeeper' (Gujarati)(CDIAL 3551) Thus, storeroom (of) *kolom* 'three' Rebus: *kolami* 'smithy, forge'. Dula 'pair' Rebus: dul 'cast metal' Thus, together *dul kolami kuṭhār* 'metal smithy castings storeroom'

 *baraḍo* = spine; backbone (Tulu) Rebus: *baran, bharat* 'mixed alloys' (5 copper, 4 zinc and 1 tin) (Punjabi)

 *dhāḷ* 'a slope'; 'inclination of a plane' (Gujarati); *ḍhāḷiyum* = adj. sloping, inclining (Gujarati) Rebus: *ḍhālako* = a large metal ingot (Gujarati) *ḍhālakī* = a metal heated and poured into a mould; a solid piece of metal; an ingot (Gujarati) PLUS *dula* 'pair'

Rebus: *dul* 'cast *metal' sal* 'splinter' Rebus: *sal* 'workshop'. Thus, *ḍhālako dul sal* 'ingot, cast metal workshop'.

kharedo = a currycomb (Gujarati) खरारा [*kharārā*] *m* (H) A currycomb. 2 Currying a horse. (Marathi) Rebus: करडा [*karaḍā*] Hard from alloy--iron, silver &c. (Marathi) *kharādī*' turner' (Gujarati)

Kalibanga 13A *खोंड [khōṇḍa] m A young bull, a bullcalf. (Marathi) Rebus: kōdār 'turner' (Bengali); कोंद kōnda 'engraver, lapidary setting or infixing gems' (Marathi) G. sãghāṛɔ m. 'lathe' ; संघाट joinery; M. sãgaḍ 'double-canoe' Rebus: sangataras 'stone-cutter, mason'*

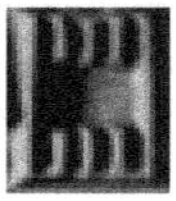
kəṭhā´r, kc. *kuṭhār* m. ' granary, storeroom '(Western Pahari)(CDIAL 3550). *koṭhārī m.* ' storekeeper' (Gujarati)(CDIAL 3551) Thus, storeroom (of) *kolom* 'three' Rebus: *kolami* 'smithy, forge'. Dula 'pair' Rebus: dul 'cast metal' Thus, together *dul kolami kuṭhār* 'metal smithy castings storeroom'

kanka (Santali) *karṇika* 'scribe'(Sanskrit) Rebus: *karṇī,* supercargo for a boat shipment. INFIXED खांडा [*khāṇḍā*] *m* A jag, notch, or indentation (as upon the edge of a tool or weapon). Rebus: *kāṇḍa* 'tools, pots and pans and metal-ware' *gaṇḍa* 'four' Rebus: *kaṇḍa* 'furnace, fire-altar' (Santali).
kolom 'three' Rebus*: kolami* 'smithy, forge'

सांड [sāṇḍa] *f* (षद S) An outlet for superfluous water (as through a dam or mound); a sluice, a floodvent. Rebus: सांडणी [sāṇḍaṇī] *f* (H) An instrument of goldsmiths. It is hooked or curved at the extremity; and is used to draw things out of the fire.
kanka 'rim of jar' Rebus: karṇīka 'account (scribe)' karṇī 'supercargo'

h462A *खोंड [khōṇḍa] m A young bull, a bullcalf. (Marathi) Rebus: kōdār 'turner' (Bengali); कोंद kōnda 'engraver, lapidary setting or infixing gems' (Marathi) G. sãghāṛɔ m. 'lathe' ; संघाट joinery; M. sãgaḍ 'double-canoe' Rebus: sangataras 'stone-cutter, mason'*

kəṭhā´r, kc. *kuṭhār* m. ' granary, storeroom '(Western Pahari)(CDIAL 3550). *koṭhārī m.* ' storekeeper' (Gujarati)(CDIAL 3551) Thus, storeroom (of) *kolom* 'three' Rebus: *kolami* 'smithy, forge'. Dula 'pair' Rebus: dul 'cast metal' Thus, together *dul kolami kuṭhār* 'metal smithy castings storeroom'

kanka (Santali) *karṇika* 'scribe'(Sanskrit) Rebus: *karṇī,* supercargo for a boat shipment. INFIXED खांडा [*khāṇḍā*] *m* A jag, notch, or indentation (as upon the

edge of a tool or weapon). Rebus: *kāṇḍa* 'tools, pots and pans and metal-ware' kolom 'three' Rebus: kolami 'smithy, forge'

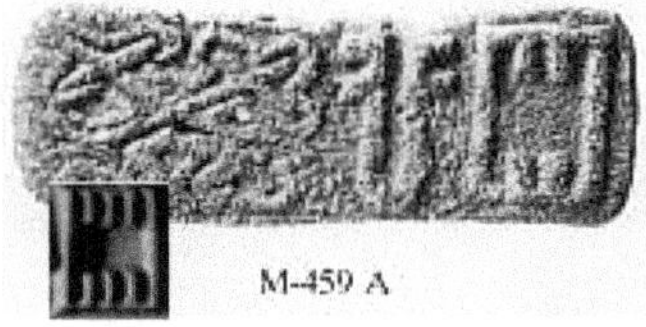

m459APictorial motif hieroglyph: Four altars. *gaṇḍa* 'four' Rebus: *kaṇḍa* 'furnace, fire-altar' (Santali).

kəṭhā´r, kc. *kuṭhār* m. ' granary, storeroom '(Western Pahari)(CDIAL 3550). *koṭhārī m.* ' storekeeper' (Gujarati)(CDIAL 3551) Thus, storeroom (of) *kolom* 'three' Rebus: *kolami* 'smithy, forge'. Dula 'pair' Rebus: dul 'cast metal' Thus, together *dul kolami kuṭhār* 'metal smithy castings storeroom'

kanka 'rim of jar' Rebus: karṇīka 'account (scribe)' karṇī 'supercargo'

gaṇḍa 'four' Rebus: *kaṇḍa* 'furnace, fire-altar' (Santali).

Balakot 3A *खोंड [khōṇḍa] m A young bull, a bullcalf. (Marathi) Rebus: kōdār 'turner' (Bengali); कोंद kōnda 'engraver, lapidary setting or infixing gems' (Marathi) G. sãghāṛɔ m. 'lathe' ; संघाट joinery; M. sãgaḍ 'double-canoe' Rebus: sangataras 'stone-cutter, mason'*

kanka 'rim of jar' Rebus: karṇīka 'account (scribe)' karṇī 'supercargo'

kəṭhā´r, kc. *kuṭhār* m. ' granary, storeroom '(Western Pahari)(CDIAL 3550). *koṭhārī m.* ' storekeeper' (Gujarati)(CDIAL 3551) Thus, storeroom (of) *kolom* 'three' Rebus: *kolami* 'smithy, forge'. Dula 'pair' Rebus: dul 'cast metal' Thus, together *dul kolami kuṭhār* 'metal smithy castings storeroom' *ayo* 'fish' Rebus: *aya* 'iron' *ayas* 'metal'

loa 'ficus religiosa' Rebus: *lo* 'iron' (Sanskrit) PLUS unique ligatures: लोखंड [lōkhaṇḍa] *n* (लोह S) Iron. लोखंडाचे चणे खावविणें or चारणें To oppress grievously.लोखंडकाम [lōkhaṇḍakāma] *n* Iron work; that portion (of a building, machine &c.) which consists of iron. 2 The business of an ironsmith.लोखंडी [lōkhaṇḍī] *a* (लोखंड) Composed of iron; relating to iron. (Marathi)

dula 'pair' Rebus: *dul* 'cast (metal)' PLUS*kana, kanac* = corner (Santali); Rebus: *kañcu* = bronze (Telugu) PLUS infixed kolmo 'paddy plant' Rebus: kolami 'smithy, forge'. Thus, cast bronze smithy, forge. Or, *mogge* 'sprout, bud' Rebus: *mũh* 'ingot' (Santali)Thus, cast bronze ingot. Read as: *kañcu dul mũh 'bronze cast ingot'*

Lothal 45A *balad* m. ' ox ', gng. *bald*, (Ku.) *barad*, id. (N. Tarai) Rebus: *bharat* (5 copper, 4 zinc and 1 tin)(Punjabi) *pattar* 'trough' Rebus*: pattar* 'guild'. Thus, copper-zinc-tin alloy (worker) guild.

kəṭhā´r, kc. *kuṭhār* m. ' granary, storeroom '(Western Pahari)(CDIAL 3550). *koṭhārī m.* ' storekeeper' (Gujarati)(CDIAL 3551) Thus, storeroom (of) *kolom* 'three' Rebus: *kolami* 'smithy, forge'. Dula 'pair' Rebus: dul 'cast metal' Thus, together *dul kolami kuṭhār* 'metal smithy castings storeroom'

kanka (Santali) *karṇika* 'scribe'(Sanskrit) Rebus: *karṇī,* supercargo for a boat shipment. INFIXED खांडा [*khāṇḍā*] *m* A jag, notch, or indentation (as upon the edge of a tool or weapon). Rebus: *kāṇḍa* 'tools, pots and pans and metal-ware' *ayo* 'fish' Rebus: *aya* 'iron' *ayas* 'metal' *aya aḍaren (homonym: aduru)*'alloy native metal' *aya kāṇḍa* 'alloy metalware' *ḍhanga* = a crook used for pulling down the branches of trees, for goats, sheep and camels (P.) Rebus:*ḍhangar* blacksmith'.

khōṇḍa A stock or stump (Marathi); 'leafless tree' (Marathi) Rebus: *kõdār* 'turner' (Bengali); *kõdā* 'to turn in a lathe' (Bengali).

m1221a *खोंड [khōṇḍa] m A young bull, a bullcalf. (Marathi) Rebus: kõdār 'turner' (Bengali); कोंद kōnda 'engraver, lapidary setting or infixing gems' (Marathi) G. sãghāṛɔ m. 'lathe' ; संघाट joinery; M. sãgaḍ 'double-canoe' Rebus: sangataras 'stone-cutter, mason'*

kəṭhā´r, kc. *kuṭhār* m. ' granary, storeroom '(Western Pahari)(CDIAL 3550). *koṭhārī m.* ' storekeeper' (Gujarati)(CDIAL 3551) Thus, storeroom (of) *kolom* 'three' Rebus: *kolami* 'smithy, forge'. Dula 'pair' Rebus: dul 'cast metal' Thus, together *dul kolami kuṭhār* 'metal smithy castings storeroom'

Strands of yarn/rope' hieroglyph: Hieroglyph: 'strands of yarn' Rebus reading: *dhā´tu* 'strand of rope' Rebus: *dhatu* 'mineral ore' (Santali) खांडा [*khāṇḍā*] *m* A jag, notch, or indentation (as upon the edge of a tool or weapon). Rebus: *kāṇḍa* 'tools, pots and pans and metal-ware'
ranku 'antelope' Rebus: ranku 'tin' *bhaṭa* 'warrior' (Sanskrit) Rebus: *baṭa* a kind of iron (Gujarati). Rebus: *bhaṭa* 'furnace' (Santali)
kanka 'rim of jar' Rebus: karṇīka 'account (scribe)' karṇī 'supercargo'

meḍ 'body' Rebus: *meḍ* 'iron' (Ho.) काठी [kāṭhī] *f* (काष्ट S) 'frame or structure of the body' (Marathi) Rebus: खंडी [khaṇḍī] measure of weight (Marathi) *கண்டி; kaṇṭi, n. < Mhr. khaṇḍil. [T. Tu. khaṇḍi, M. kaṇḍi.]* Candy, a weight, stated to be roughly equivalent to 500 lbs.

m921a *खोंड [khōṇḍa] m A young bull, a bullcalf. (Marathi) Rebus: kōdār 'turner' (Bengali); कोंद kōnda 'engraver, lapidary setting or infixing gems' (Marathi) G. sãghāṛɔ m. 'lathe' ; संघाट joinery; M. sãgaḍ 'double-canoe' Rebus: sangataras 'stone-cutter, mason' First 3 signs read rebus as at m1221. PLUS ayo* 'fish' Rebus: *aya* 'iron' *ayas* 'metal'
kanka 'rim of jar' Rebus: karṇīka 'account (scribe)' karṇī 'supercargo'
kamaḍha 'crab' Rebus: *kammaṭa* 'mint, coiner'.*ḍato* = claws of crab (Santali) Rebus: *dhātu* 'mineral ore'

Balakot 4A *खोंड [khōṇḍa] m A young bull, a bullcalf. (Marathi) Rebus: kõdār 'turner' (Bengali); कोंद kōnda 'engraver, lapidary setting or infixing gems' (Marathi) G. sãghāṛɔ m. 'lathe' ; संघाट joinery; M. sãgaḍ 'double-canoe' Rebus: sangataras 'stone-cutter, mason'*

kəṭhā´r, kc. *kuṭhār* m. ' granary, storeroom '(Western Pahari)(CDIAL 3550). *koṭhārī m.* ' storekeeper' (Gujarati)(CDIAL 3551) Thus, storeroom (of) *kolom* 'three' Rebus: *kolami* 'smithy, forge'. Dula 'pair' Rebus: dul 'cast metal' Thus, together *dul kolami kuṭhār* 'metal smithy castings storeroom'

koḍi 'flag' (Ta.)(DEDR 2049). Rebus 1: *koḍ* 'workshop' (Kuwi) Rebus 2: *khŏḍ* m. 'pit', *khŏḍü* f. 'small pit' (Kashmiri. CDIAL 3947).

Strands of yarn/rope' hieroglyph: Hieroglyph: 'strands of yarn' Rebus reading: *dhā´tu* 'strand of rope' Rebus: *dhatu* 'mineral ore' (Santali) *kamaḍha* 'crab' Rebus: *kammaṭa* 'mint, coiner'.*ḍato* = claws of crab (Santali) Rebus: *dhātu* 'mineral ore'

dula two, pair' Rebus: dul 'cast metal' PLUS *dhāḷ* 'a slope'; 'inclination of a plane' (G.); *ḍhāḷiyum* = adj. sloping, inclining (G.) Rebus: *ḍhālako* = a large metal ingot (G.) *ḍhālakī* = a metal heated and poured into a mould; a solid piece of metal; an ingot (Gujarati) PLUS kolom 'three' Rebus: kolami 'smithy, forge'. Thus cast metal ingot smithy.

m8a *खोंड [khōṇḍa] m A young bull, a bullcalf. (Marathi) Rebus: kõdār 'turner' (Bengali); कोंद kōnda 'engraver, lapidary setting or infixing gems' (Marathi) G. sãghārɔ m. 'lathe' ; संघाट joinery; M. sãgaḍ 'double-canoe' Rebus: sangataras 'stone-cutter, mason'*

kəṭhā´r, kc. *kuṭhār* m. ' granary, storeroom '(Western Pahari)(CDIAL 3550). *koṭhārī m.* ' storekeeper' (Gujarati)(CDIAL 3551) Thus, storeroom (of) *kolom* 'three' Rebus: *kolami* 'smithy, forge'. Dula 'pair' Rebus: dul 'cast metal' Thus, together *dul kolami kuṭhār* 'metal smithy castings storeroom'

loa 'ficus religiosa' Rebus: *lo* 'iron' (Sanskrit) PLUS unique ligatures: लोखंड [lōkhaṇḍa

] *n* (लोह S) Iron. लोखंडाचे चणे खावविणें or चारणें To oppress grievously.लोखंडकाम [lōkhaṇḍakāma] *n* Iron work; that portion (of a building, machine &c.) which consists of iron. 2 The business of an ironsmith. लोखंडी [lōkhaṇḍī] *a* (लोखंड) Composed of iron; relating to iron. (Marathi) *bhaṭa* 'warrior' (Sanskrit) Rebus: *baṭa* a kind of iron (Gujarati). Rebus: *bhaṭa* 'furnace' (Santali) Thus, together, th ligatured hieroglyph reads rebus: *loa bhaṭa* 'iron furnace'

muka 'ladle' (Tamil)(DEDR 4887) Rebus: *mũh* 'ingot' (Santali) *baṭa* = a kind of iron (Gujarati) *baṭa* = rimless pot (Kannada) Thus, iron ingot.

m266A *rāngo* 'water buffalo bull' (Ku.N.)(CDIAL 10559) Rebus: rango 'pewter' *pattar* 'trough' Rebus: *pattar* 'guild'.Thus, pewter guild.

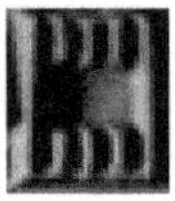

kəṭhā´r, kc. *kuṭhār* m. ' granary, storeroom '(Western Pahari)(CDIAL 3550). *koṭhārī m.* ' storekeeper' (Gujarati)(CDIAL 3551) Thus, storeroom (of) *kolom* 'three' Rebus: *kolami* 'smithy, forge'. Dula 'pair' Rebus: dul 'cast metal' Thus, together *dul kolami kuṭhār* 'metal smithy castings storeroom'

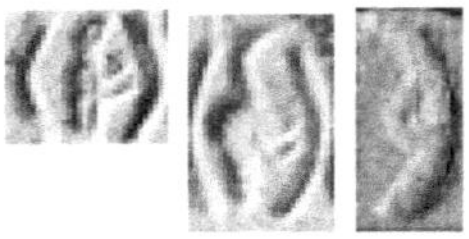 *kuṭila* 'bent' CDIAL 3230 kuṭi— in cmpd. 'curve', *kuṭika—* 'bent' MBh. Rebus: *kuṭila, katthīl* = bronze (8 parts copper and 2 parts tin) dula 'pair' Rebus: dul 'cast metal' Thus, cast bronze PLUS infixed 'bird hieroglyph': *karaṇḍa* 'duck' (Sanskrit) *karaṛa* 'a very large aquatic bird' (Sindhi)
Rebus: करडा [*karaḍā*] Hard from alloy--iron, silver &c. (Marathi) Thus, hard alloy bronze casting.
खांडा [*khāṇḍā*] *m* A jag, notch, or indentation (as upon the edge of a tool or weapon). Rebus: *kāṇḍa* 'tools, pots and pans and metal-ware' *ayo ḍhālako* 'alloy metal ingot' *aya aḍaren (homonym: aduru)*'alloy native metal'
kamaḍha 'crab' Rebus: *kammaṭa* 'mint, coiner'.*ḍato* = claws of crab (Santali) Rebus: *dhātu* 'mineral ore'

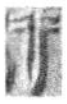 kanka 'rim of jar' Rebus: karṇīka 'account (scribe)' karṇī 'supercargo'
 *kamaḍha* 'crab' Rebus: *kammaṭa* 'mint, coiner'.*ḍato* = claws of crab (Santali) Rebus: *dhātu* 'mineral ore' PLUS kolom 'three' Rebus: kolami 'smithy, forge'

L-39 A

Lothal 39A *खोंड [khōṇḍa] m A young bull, a bullcalf. (Marathi) Rebus: kõdār 'turner' (Bengali); कोंद kōnda 'engraver, lapidary setting or infixing gems' (Marathi) G. sãghāṛɔ m. 'lathe' ; संघाट joinery; M. sãgaḍ 'double-canoe' Rebus: sangataras 'stone-cutter, mason'*

 *kəṭhā´r*, kc. *kuṭhār* m. ' granary, storeroom '(WPah.)(CDIAL 3550). *koṭhārī m.* ' storekeeper' (Gujarati)(CDIAL 3551) Thus, storeroom (of) *kolom* 'three' Rebus: *kolami* 'smithy, forge'. Dula 'pair' Rebus: dul 'cast metal' Thus, together *dul kolami kuṭhār* 'metal smithy castings storeroom'
 *kanac* 'corner' Rebus: *kañcu* 'bronze' sal 'splinter' Rebus: sal 'workshop' dula 'pair' Rebus: dul 'cast metal' PLUS | *koḍa* 'one' Rebus: *koḍ* 'workshop' PLUS INFIXED खांडा [*khāṇḍā*] *m* A jag, notch, or indentation (as upon the edge of a tool or weapon). Rebus: *kāṇḍa* 'tools, pots and pans and metal-ware' Thus metalware castings workshop.

 कांड *kāṇḍa* 'arrow' Rebus: *kāṇḍa* 'pots and pans, metalware, tools'. Rebus 2: kaṇḍ 'fire-altar' (Santali)

L-110 A

Lothal 110A

 *kəṭhā´r*, kc. *kuṭhār* m. ' granary, storeroom '(WPah.)(CDIAL 3550). *koṭhārī m.* ' storekeeper' (Gujarati)(CDIAL 3551) Thus, storeroom (of) *kolom* 'three' Rebus: *kolami* 'smithy, forge'. Dula 'pair' Rebus: dul 'cast metal' Thus, together *dul kolami kuṭhār* 'metal smithy castings storeroom'

  notch+slanted stroke reads rebus: *ḍhālako kāṇḍa* 'ingot, tools, pots and pans and metal-ware'.*dhāḷ* 'a slope'; 'inclination of a plane' (G.); *ḍhāḷiyum* = adj. sloping,

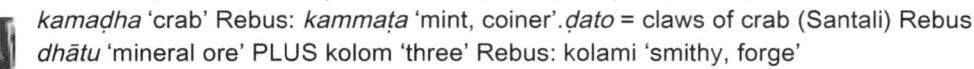

inclining (G.) Rebus: *ḍhālako* = a large metal ingot (G.) *ḍhālakī* = a metal heated and poured into a mould; a solid piece of metal; an ingot (Gujarati) PLUS खांडा [*khāṇḍā*] *m* A jag, notch, or indentation (as upon the edge of a tool or weapon). Rebus: *kāṇḍa* 'tools, pots and pans and metal-ware'

dula 'pair' Rebus: *dul* 'cast (metal)' PLUS*kana, kanac* = corner (Santali); Rebus: *kañcu* = bronze (Telugu) Thus, cast bronze. PLUS खांडा [*khāṇḍā*] *m* A jag, notch, or indentation (as upon the edge of a tool or weapon). Rebus: *kāṇḍa* 'tools, pots and pans and metal-ware' Thus, cast bronze metalware.

kolmo 'paddy plant' Rebus: *kolami* 'smithy, forge' Vikalpa: *mogge* 'sprout, bud' Rebus: *mũh* 'ingot' (Santali) dolu 'plant of shoot height' Rebus: dul 'cast metal'

'Bird' hieroglyphs

m1896a *khũṭ* 'zebu' Rebus: '(native metal) guild': Text message: broze (from) cast metal pit. (of) native metal guild.

kanac 'corner' Rebus: kañcu 'bronze'

Fowl hieroglyphs: கோழி kō̱li, *n.* < கொழு-. [T. *kōḍi*, K. M. *kōli*, Tu. *kōri.*] 1. Gallinaceous fowl; குக்குடம். குப்பை கிளைப்போவாக் கோழிபோல் (நாலடி, 341).Rebus 1: *koḍ* 'workshop' (Kuwi) Rebus 2: *khōḍ* m. 'pit', *khōḍü* f. 'small pit' (Kashmiri. CDIAL 3947). dula 'pair' Rebus: dul 'cast metal' Thus, the pair of hieroglyphs reads: Rebus *dul khōḍ* m. 'cast metal pit'

Seal m107A (with fowl hieroglyphs) *खोंड [khōṇḍa] m A young bull, a bullcalf. (Marathi) Rebus: kõdār 'turner' (Bengali); कोंद kōnda 'engraver, lapidary setting or infixing gems' (Marathi) G. sãghāṛɔ m. 'lathe' ; संघाट joinery; M. sãgaḍ 'double-canoe' Rebus: sangataras 'stone-cutter, mason'* *kōḍi*, 'fowl' Rebus: *koḍ* 'workshop' (Kuwi)

kuṭila 'bent' CDIAL 3230 kuṭi— in cmpd. 'curve', *kuṭika—* 'bent' MBh. Rebus: *kuṭila, katthīl* = bronze (8 parts copper and 2 parts tin) dula 'pair' Rebus: dul 'cast metal' Thus, cast bronze PLUS infixed 'bird hieroglyph': *karaṇḍa* 'duck' (Sanskrit) *karaṛa* 'a very large aquatic bird' (Sindhi)
Rebus: करडा [*karaḍā*] Hard from alloy--iron, silver &c. (Marathi) Thus, hard alloy bronze casting. (with) *ayo* 'fish' Rebus: *aya* 'iron' *ayas* 'metal' sal 'spliner' Rebus: sal 'workshop' *ayo ḍhālako* 'alloy metal ingot'

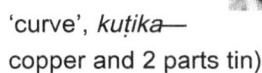

kamaḍha 'crab' Rebus: *kammaṭa* 'mint, coiner'.*ḍato* = claws of crab (Santali) Rebus: *dhātu* 'mineral ore' PLUS
Kur. xolā tail. *Malt.* qoli id. (DEDR 2135). Rebus: kolhe 'smelter' Thus, copper smelter of

kolhe ‘smelters’.

'rim-of-jar' hieroglyph *kanka* (Santali) *karṇika* ‘scribe’(Sanskrit) Rebus: *karṇī,* supercargo for a boat shipment. *karṇīka* ‘account (scribe)’.कारणी *kāraṇī* ‘the supercargo of a ship’ (Marathi)

m451A, B Tablet Text 3235

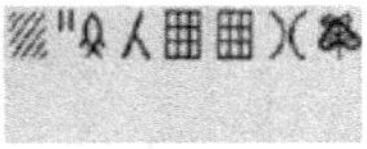

khũṭ ‘zebu’ Rebus: ‘(native metal) guild’ eruvai ‘eagle’ Rebus: eruvai, eraka ‘copper’.

r

loa ‘ficus religiosa’ Rebus: *lo* ‘iron’ (Sanskrit) PLUS unique ligatures: लोखंड [lōkhaṇḍa] *n* (लोह S) Iron. लोखंडाचे चणे खावविणें or चारणें To oppress grievously.लोखंडकाम [lōkhaṇḍakāma] *n* Iron work; that portion (of a building, machine &c.) which consists of iron. 2 The business of an ironsmith.लोखंडी [lōkhaṇḍī] *a* (लोखंड) Composed of iron; relating to iron. (Marathi) Circumscript: *kuṭila* ‘bent’ CDIAL 3230 kuṭi— in cmpd. ‘curve’, *kuṭika—* ‘bent’ MBh. Rebus: *kuṭila, katthīl* = bronze (8 parts copper and 2 parts tin) dula ‘pair’ Rebus: dul ‘cast metal’ Thus, bronze castings.

khaṇḍ ‘field, division’ (Skt.) Rebus: *khāṇḍa* ‘tools, pots and pans, metal-ware’. Rebus 2: kaṇḍ 'fire-altar' (Santali) dula ‘pair’ Rebus: dul ‘cast metal’ Thus, duplicated ‘division’ hieroglyph sign reads: cast metal metal-ware.

notch+slanted stroke reads rebus: *ḍhālako kāṇḍa* ‘ingot, tools, pots and pans and metal-ware’.*dhāḷ* ‘a slope’; ‘inclination of a plane’ (G.); *ḍhāḷiyum* = adj. sloping, inclining (G.) Rebus: *ḍhālako* = a large metal ingot (G.) *ḍhālakī* = a metal heated and poured into a mould; a solid piece of metal; an ingot (Gujarati) PLUS खांडा [*khāṇḍā*] *m* A jag, notch, or indentation (as upon the edge of a tool or weapon). Rebus: *kāṇḍa* ‘tools, pots and pans and metal-ware’

ayo ‘fish’ Rebus: *aya* ‘iron’ *ayas* ‘metal’ sal ‘splinter’ Rebus: sal ‘workshop’

m1183a *खोंड [khōṇḍa] m A young bull, a bullcalf. (Marathi) Rebus: kõdār ‘turner’ (Bengali); कोंद kōnda ‘engraver, lapidary setting or infixing gems’ (Marathi) G. sãghāṛɔ m. ‘lathe’ ; संघाट joinery; M. sãgaḍ ‘double-canoe’ Rebus: sangataras ‘stone-cutter, mason’*

kōḍi, ‘fowl’ Rebus: *koḍ* ‘workshop’ (Kuwi) gaṇḍa 'four' Rebus: kaṇḍa 'furnace, fire-altar' (Santali)

kolmo ‘paddy plant’ Rebus: *kolami* ‘smithy, forge’ Vikalpa: *mogge* ‘sprout, bud’ Rebus: *mũh* ‘ingot’ (Santali) dolu ‘plant of shoot height’ Rebus: dul ‘cast metal’

h452a *खोंड [khōṇḍa] m A young bull, a bullcalf. (Marathi) Rebus: kõdār ‘turner’ (Bengali); कोंद kōnda ‘engraver, lapidary setting or infixing gems’ (Marathi) G. sãghāṛɔ m. ‘lathe’ ; संघाट joinery; M. sãgaḍ ‘double-canoe’ Rebus: sangataras ‘stone-cutter, mason’*

baṭa ‘quail’ Rebus: *baṭha* ‘smelter, furnace’

kanka ‘rim of jar’ Rebus: karṇīka ‘account (scribe)’ karṇī ‘supercargo’

m1673a खोंड *[khōṇḍa] m A young bull, a bullcalf. (Marathi) Rebus: kōdār 'turner' (Bengali);* कोंद *kōnda 'engraver, lapidary setting or infixing gems' (Marathi) G. sãghāṛɔ m. 'lathe' ;* संघाट *joinery; M. sãgaḍ 'double-canoe' Rebus: sangataras 'stone-cutter, mason'*

kōḍi, 'fowl' Rebus: *koḍ* 'workshop' (Kuwi) gaṇḍa 'four' Rebus: kaṇḍa 'furnace, fire-altar' (Santali)

 *koḍi* 'flag' (Ta.)(DEDR 2049). Rebus 1: *koḍ* 'workshop' (Kuwi) Rebus 2: *khŏḍ* m. 'pit', *khōḍü* f. 'small pit' (Kashmiri. CDIAL 3947). *aya kammaṭa.*'coiner, mint alloy' *aya kāṇḍa* 'alloy metalware' *kuṭila* 'bent' CDIAL 3230 kuṭi— in cmpd. 'curve', *kuṭika—* 'bent' MBh. Rebus: *kuṭila, katthīl* = bronze (8 parts copper and 2 parts tin)

 *kanac* 'corner' Rebus: *kañcu* 'bronze'

M-85 a

m85a खोंड *[khōṇḍa] m A young bull, a bullcalf. (Marathi) Rebus: kōdār 'turner' (Bengali);* कोंद *kōnda 'engraver, lapidary setting or infixing gems' (Marathi) G. sãghāṛɔ m. 'lathe' ;* संघाट *joinery; M. sãgaḍ 'double-canoe' Rebus: sangataras 'stone-cutter, mason'*

Bird + wing: *baṭa* 'quail' Rebus: *baṭa* 'iron' (Gujarati) eraka 'wing' Rebus: eraka 'copper'

 'Arrow' sign hieroglyph (variant) This is a ligature of 'lid of pot' hieroglyph superscript on 'a linear stroke' numeral hieroglyph.*aḍaren* 'cover of pot or lid' Rebus: *aduru* 'native, unsmelted metal' Duplicated: dula 'pair' Rebus: dul 'cast metal' LUS koḍ = one (Santali); koḍ 'workshop' (Gujarati) PLUS ligature:

 *kolmo* 'paddy plant' Rebus: *kolami* 'smithy, forge' Vikalpa: *mogge* 'sprout, bud' Rebus: *mūh* 'ingot' (Santali) dolu 'plant of shoot height' Rebus: dul 'cast metal'

 *kanka* (Santali) *karṇika* 'scribe'(Sanskrit) Rebus: *karṇī,* supercargo for a boat shipment. INFIXED खांडा [*khāṇḍā*] *m* A jag, notch, or indentation (as upon the edge of a tool or weapon). Rebus: *kāṇḍa* 'tools, pots and pans and metal-ware' *ayo ḍhālako* 'alloy metal ingot'

 कांड *kāṇḍa* 'arrow' Rebus: *kāṇḍa* 'pots and pans, metalware, tools'. Rebus 2: kaṇḍ 'fire-altar' (Santali)

m411A *baṭa* 'quail' Rebus: *baṭa* 'iron' (Gujarati) *bhaṭa* 'furnace' eraka 'wing' Rebus: eraka 'copper'
kolom 'three' Rebus: kolami 'smithy, forge'

 *kanka* (Santali) *karṇika* 'scribe'(Sanskrit) Rebus: *karṇī,* supercargo for a boat shipment. INFIXED खांडा [*khāṇḍā*] *m* A jag, notch, or indentation (as upon the edge of a tool or weapon). Rebus: *kāṇḍa* 'tools, pots and pans and metal-ware'

 *aya kammaṭa.*'coiner, mint alloy' *ayo ḍhālako* 'alloy metal ingot'*dula* 'pair' Rebus: *dul* 'cast (metal)' PLUS*kana, kanac* = corner (Santali); Rebus: *kañcu* = bronze (Telugu) Thus, cast bronze.

 *kolmo* 'paddy plant' Rebus: *kolami* 'smithy, forge' Vikalpa: *mogge* 'sprout, bud' Rebus: *mũh* 'ingot' (Santali) dolu 'plant of shoot height' Rebus: dul 'cast metal'

m700a *खोंड [khōṇḍa] m A young bull, a bullcalf. (Marathi) Rebus: kõdār 'turner' (Bengali); कोंद kōnda 'engraver, lapidary setting or infixing gems' (Marathi) G. sãghāṛɔ m. 'lathe' ; संघाट joinery; M. sãgaḍ 'double-canoe' Rebus: sangataras 'stone-cutter, mason'*

baṭa 'quail' Rebus: *baṭa* 'iron' (Gujarati) *bhaṭa* 'furnace'

 *koḍi* 'flag' (Ta.)(DEDR 2049). Rebus 1: *koḍ* 'workshop' (Kuwi) Rebus 2: *khŏḍ* m. 'pit', *khŏḍü* f. 'small pit' (Kashmiri. CDIAL 3947).

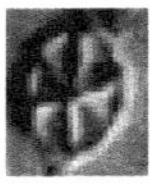 *āra* 'spokes' Rebus: *āra 'brass'*. cf. erka = ekke (Tbh. of arka) aka (Tbh. of arka) copper (metal); crystal (Kannada) Glyph: *eraka*'nave of wheel' Rebus: eraka 'copper'; cf. erka = ekke (Tbh. of arka) aka (Tbh. of arka) copper (metal); crystal (Kannada) *erako* 'moltencast copper'

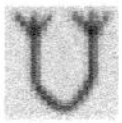 dula 'pair' Rebus: dul 'cast (metal)' kolmo 'rice plant' Rebus: kolami 'smithy/forge'

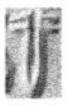 kanka 'rim of jar' Rebus: karṇīka 'account (scribe)' karṇī 'supercargo'

m631A *खोंड [khōṇḍa] m A young bull, a bullcalf. (Marathi) Rebus: kõdār 'turner' (Bengali); कोंद kōnda 'engraver, lapidary setting or infixing gems' (Marathi) G. sãghāṛɔ m. 'lathe' ; संघाट joinery; M. sãgaḍ 'double-canoe' Rebus: sangataras 'stone-cutter, mason' sangataras 'stone-cutter, mason'*

baṭa 'quail' Rebus: *baṭa* 'iron' (Gujarati) *bhaṭa* 'furnace'

 *koḍi* 'flag' (Ta.)(DEDR 2049). Rebus 1: *koḍ* 'workshop' (Kuwi) Rebus 2: *khŏḍ* m. 'pit', *khŏḍü* f. 'small pit' (Kashmiri. CDIAL 3947).

dula 'two' Rebus: dul 'cast metal' ayo ḍhālako 'alloy metal ingot'

aya kammaṭa.'coiner, mint alloy'

 *muka* 'ladle' (Tamil)(DEDR 4887) Rebus: *mũh* 'ingot' (Santali) *baṭa* = rimless pot (Kannada) Rebus:) *baṭa* = a kind of iron (G.)) *bhaṭa* furnace (Gujarati) Thus, iron ingot.kolom 'three' Rebus: kolami 'smithy, forge'

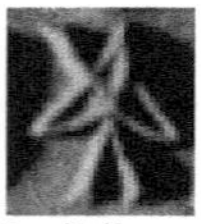 

loa 'ficus religiosa' Rebus: *lo* 'iron' (Sanskrit) PLUS unique ligatures: लोखंड [lōkhaṇḍa] *n* (लोह S) Iron. लोखंडाचे चणे खावविणें or चारणें To oppress grievously.लोखंडकाम [lōkhaṇḍakāma] *n* Iron work; that portion (of a building, machine &c.) which consists of iron. 2 The business of an ironsmith.लोखंडी [lōkhaṇḍī] *a* (लोखंड) Composed of iron; relating to iron. (Marathi) *bhaṭa* 'warrior' (Sanskrit) Rebus: *baṭa* a kind of iron (Gujarati). Rebus: *bhaṭa* 'furnace' (Santali) Thus, together, the ligatured hieroglyph reads rebus: *loa bhaṭa* 'iron furnace'

m1789a *खोंड [khōṇḍa] m A young bull, a bullcalf. (Marathi) Rebus: kõdār 'turner' (Bengali); कोंद kōnda 'engraver, lapidary setting or infixing gems' (Marathi) G. sãghāṛɔ m. 'lathe' ; संघाट joinery; M. sãgaḍ 'double-canoe' Rebus: sangataras 'stone-cutter, mason'*

baṭa 'quail' Rebus: *baṭa* 'iron' (Gujarati) *bhaṭa* 'furnace'

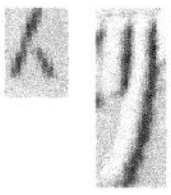

notch+slanted stroke reads rebus: *ḍhālako kāṇḍa* 'ingot, tools, pots and pans and metal-ware'.*dhāḷ* 'a slope'; 'inclination of a plane' (G.); *ḍhāḷiyum* = adj. sloping, inclining (G.) Rebus: *ḍhālako* = a large metal ingot (G.) *ḍhālakī* = a metal heated and poured into a mould; a solid piece of metal; an ingot (Gujarati) PLUS खांडा [*khāṇḍā*] *m* A jag, notch, or indentation (as upon the edge of a tool or weapon). Rebus: *kāṇḍa* 'tools, pots and pans and metal-ware' *sal 'splinter' Rebus: sal 'workshop'*

mēḍu height, rising ground, hillock (Kannada) Rebus: *meḍ* 'iron' (Ho.) kolom 'three' Rebus: kolami 'smithy, forge' Thus, *meḍ kolami* 'iron smithy-forge'

kanka 'rim of jar' Rebus: karṇīka 'account (scribe)' karṇī 'supercargo'

m216a *खोंड [khōṇḍa] m A young bull, a bullcalf. (Marathi) Rebus: kōdār 'turner' (Bengali); कोंद kōnda 'engraver, lapidary setting or infixing gems' (Marathi) G. sãghāṛɔ m. 'lathe' ; संघाट joinery; M. sãgaḍ 'double-canoe' Rebus: sangataras 'stone-cutter, mason'*
sal 'splinter' Rebus: sal 'workshop'

koḍi 'flag' (Ta.)(DEDR 2049). Rebus 1: *koḍ* 'workshop' (Kuwi) Rebus 2: *khōḍ* m. 'pit', *khōḍü* f. 'small pit' (Kashmiri. CDIAL 3947).

water-carrier hieroglyph *kuṭi*; Rebus: *kuṭhi* 'smelter furnace'.

h659a
baṭa 'quail' Rebus: *baṭa* 'iron' (Gujarati) *bhaṭa* 'furnace'

koḍi 'flag' (Ta.)(DEDR 2049). Rebus 1: *koḍ* 'workshop' (Kuwi) Rebus 2: *khōḍ* m. 'pit', *khōḍü* f. 'small pit' (Kashmiri. CDIAL 3947).

kamaḍha 'crab' Rebus: *kammaṭa* 'mint, coiner'.*ḍato* = claws of crab (Santali) Rebus: *dhātu* 'mineral ore' *aya kammaṭa.*'coiner, mint alloy' *ayo* 'fish' Rebus: *aya* 'iron' *ayas* 'metal'

kanka 'rim of jar' Rebus: karṇīka 'account (scribe)' karṇī 'supercargo'

loa 'ficus religiosa' Rebus: *lo* 'iron' (Sanskrit) PLUS unique ligatures: लोखंड [lōkhaṇḍa] *n* (लोह S) Iron. लोखंडाचे चणे खावविणें or चारणें To oppress grievously.लोखंडकाम [lōkhaṇḍakāma] *n* Iron work; that portion (of a building, machine &c.) which consists of iron. 2 The business of an ironsmith.लोखंडी [lōkhaṇḍī] *a* (लोखंड) Composed of iron; relating to iron. (Marathi) *bhaṭa* 'warrior' (Sanskrit) Rebus: *baṭa* a kind of iron (Gujarati). Rebus: *bhaṭa* 'furnace' (Santali) Thus, together, the ligatured hieroglyph reads rebus: *loa bhaṭa* 'iron furnace'

kolmo 'paddy plant' Rebus: *kolami* 'smithy, forge' Vikalpa: *mogge* 'sprout, bud' Rebus: *mũh* 'ingot' (Santali) dolu 'plant of shoot height' Rebus: dul 'cast metal'

dula 'pair' Rebus: *dul* 'cast (metal)' PLUS*kana, kanac* = corner (Santali); Rebus: *kañcu* = bronze (Telugu) Thus, cast bronze.

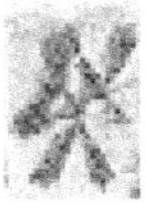

Furnace rebus readings (Pictorial motif/sign hieroglyph 'warrior')

m299a Zeb horns. Native metal smith guild. Sign hieroglyph 'warrior' has been read rebus as 'furnace'.

loa 'ficus religiosa' Rebus: *lo* 'iron' (Sanskrit) PLUS unique ligatures: लोखंड [lōkhaṇḍa] *n* (लोह S) Iron. लोखंडाचे चणे खाववणें or चारणें To oppress grievously.लोखंडकाम [lōkhaṇḍakāma] *n* Iron work; that portion (of a building, machine &c.) which consists of iron. 2 The business of an ironsmith.लोखंडी [lōkhaṇḍī] *a* (लोखंड) Composed of iron; relating to iron. (Marathi) *bhaṭa* 'warrior' (Sanskrit) Rebus: *baṭa* a kind of iron (Gujarati). Rebus: *bhaṭa* 'furnace' (Santali) Thus, together, the ligatured hieroglyph reads rebus: *loa bhaṭa* 'iron furnace'

dula 'pair' Rebus: *dul* 'cast (metal)' PLUS*kana, kanac* = corner (Santali); Rebus: *kañcu* = bronze (Telugu) Thus, cast bronze.

M-1332 a

m1332a

loa 'ficus religiosa' Rebus: *lo* 'iron' (Sanskrit) PLUS unique ligatures: लोखंड [lōkhaṇḍa] *n* (लोह S) Iron. लोखंडाचे चणे खाववणें or चारणें To oppress grievously.लोखंडकाम [lōkhaṇḍakāma] *n* Iron work; that portion (of a building, machine &c.) which consists of iron. 2 The business of an ironsmith.लोखंडी [lōkhaṇḍī] *a* (लोखंड) Composed of iron; relating to iron. (Marathi) *bhaṭa* 'warrior' (Sanskrit) Rebus: *baṭa* a kind of iron (Gujarati). Rebus: *bhaṭa* 'furnace' (Santali) Thus, together, the ligatured hieroglyph reads rebus: *loa bhaṭa* 'iron furnace' *kuṭila* 'bent' CDIAL 3230 kuṭi— in cmpd. 'curve', *kuṭika*— 'bent' MBh. Rebus: *kuṭila, katthīl* = bronze (8 parts copper and 2 parts tin) dula 'two' Rebus: dul 'cast metal'

kharedo = a currycomb (Gujarati) खरारा [*khararā*] *m* (H) A currycomb. 2 Currying a horse. (Marathi) Rebus: करडा [*karaḍā*] Hard from alloy--iron, silver &c. (Marathi) *kharādī* ' turner' (Gujarati)

M-1058 A

m1098A *balad* m. ' ox ', gng. *bald*, (Ku.) *barad*, id. (N. Tarai) Rebus: *bharat* (5 copper, 4 zinc and 1 tin)(Punjabi) *pattar* 'trough' Rebus: *pattar* 'guild'. Thus, copper-zinc-tin alloy (worker) guild.

loa 'ficus religiosa' Rebus: *lo* 'iron' (Sanskrit) PLUS unique ligatures: लोखंड [lōkhaṇḍa

] *n* (लोह S) Iron. लोखंडाचे चणे खावविणें or चारणें To oppress grievously.लोखंडकाम [lōkhaṇḍakāma] *n* Iron work; that portion (of a building, machine &c.) which consists of iron. 2 The business of an ironsmith.लोखंडी [lōkhaṇḍī] *a* (लोखंड) Composed of iron; relating to iron. (Marathi) *bhaṭa* 'warrior' (Sanskrit) Rebus: *baṭa* a kind of iron (Gujarati). Rebus: *bhaṭa* 'furnace' (Santali) Thus, together, the ligatured hieroglyph reads rebus: *loa bhaṭa* 'iron furnace'

dula 'two' Rebus: dul 'cast metal' kolom 'three' Rebus: kolami 'smithy, forge'

kolmo 'paddy plant' Rebus: *kolami* 'smithy, forge' Vikalpa: *mogge* 'sprout, bud' Rebus: *mũh* 'ingot' (Santali) dolu 'plant of shoot height' Rebus: dul 'cast metal'

h1666A *खोंड [khōṇḍa] m A young bull, a bullcalf. (Marathi) Rebus: kõdār 'turner' (Bengali); कोंद kōnda 'engraver, lapidary setting or infixing gems' (Marathi) G. sãghāṛɔ m. 'lathe' ; संघाट joinery; M. sãgaḍ 'double-canoe' Rebus: sangataras 'stone-cutter, mason'*

loa 'ficus religiosa' Rebus: *lo* 'iron' (Sanskrit) PLUS unique ligatures: लोखंड [lōkhaṇḍa

] *n* (लोह S) Iron. लोखंडाचे चणे खावविणें or चारणें To oppress grievously.लोखंडकाम [lōkhaṇḍakāma] *n* Iron work; that portion (of a building, machine &c.) which consists of iron. 2 The business of an ironsmith.लोखंडी [lōkhaṇḍī] *a* (लोखंड) Composed of iron; relating to iron. (Marathi) *bhaṭa* 'warrior' (Sanskrit) Rebus: *baṭa* a kind of iron (Gujarati). Rebus: *bhaṭa* 'furnace' (Santali) Thus, together, the ligatured hieroglyph reads rebus: *loa bhaṭa* 'iron furnace'

kanka (Santali) *karṇika* 'scribe'(Sanskrit) Rebus: *karṇī,* supercargo for a boat shipment. INFIXED खांडा [*khāṇḍā*] *m* A jag, notch, or indentation (as upon the edge of a tool or weapon). Rebus: *kāṇḍa* 'tools, pots and pans and metal-ware'

meḍ 'pair'

'body' Rebus: *meḍ* 'iron' (Ho.) PLUS | *koḍa* 'one' Rebus: *koḍ* 'workshop' dula Rebus: dul 'cast metal'. Thus, the 'body' flanked by two linear strokes denote: workshop for iron castings.

water-carrier hieroglyph *kuṭi*; Rebus: *kuṭhi* 'smelter furnace'.

PLUS

aḍaren 'cover of pot or lid' Rebus: *aduru* 'native, unsmelted metal' Duplicated: dula 'pair' Rebus: dul 'cast metal'

m109a *खोंड [khōṇḍa] m A young bull, a bullcalf. (Marathi) Rebus: kõdār 'turner' (Bengali); कोंद kōnda 'engraver, lapidary setting or infixing gems' (Marathi) G. sãghāṛɔ m. 'lathe' ; संघाट joinery; M. sãgaḍ 'double-canoe' Rebus: sangataras 'stone-cutter, mason'*

loa 'ficus religiosa' Rebus: *lo* 'iron' (Sanskrit) PLUS unique ligatures: लोखंड [lōkhaṇḍa

] *n* (लोह S) Iron. लोखंडाचे चणे खावविणें or चारणें To oppress grievously.लोखंडकाम [lōkhaṇḍakāma] *n* Iron work; that portion (of a building, machine &c.) which consists of iron. 2 The business of an ironsmith.लोखंडी [lōkhaṇḍī] *a* (लोखंड) Composed of iron; relating to iron. (Marathi) *bhaṭa* 'warrior' (Sanskrit) Rebus: *baṭa* a kind of iron (Gujarati). Rebus: *bhaṭa* 'furnace' (Santali) Thus, together, the ligatured hieroglyph reads rebus: *loa bhaṭa* 'iron furnace'

cīmara 'black ant' Rebus: *cīmara* 'copper'. *cīmara kāra* -- ' coppersmith '
PLUS

kolmo 'paddy plant' Rebus: *kolami* 'smithy, forge' Vikalpa: *mogge* 'sprout, bud' Rebus: *mūh* 'ingot' (Santali) dolu 'plant of shoot height' Rebus: dul 'cast metal' Thus, a copper castings smith. sal 'splinter' Rebus: sal 'workshop'

aḍar 'harrow'; rebus: *aduru* 'native unsmelted metal'
ayo 'fish' Rebus: *aya* 'iron' *ayas* 'metal'

kanac 'corner' Rebus: *kañcu* 'bronze' INFIXED S. *akho* m. 'mesh of a net' Rebus: L. P. *akkhā* m. ' one end of a bag or sack thrown over a beast of burden '; Or. *akhā* ' gunny bag '; Bi. *ākhā*, *ākhā* ' grain bag carried by pack animal '; H. *ākhā* m. ' one of a pair of grain bags used as panniers '; M. *ākhā* m. ' netting in which coco -- nuts, &c., are carried ', *ākhẽ* n. ' half a bullock -- load ' (CDIAL 17) అంకెము [aṅkemu] *ankemu.* [Telugu] n. One pack or pannier, being half a bullock load.
kanka 'rim of jar' Rebus: karṇīka 'account (scribe)' karṇī 'supercargo'

m53a *खोंड [khōṇḍa] m A young bull, a bullcalf. (Marathi) Rebus: kõdār 'turner' (Bengali); कोंद kōnda 'engraver, lapidary setting or infixing gems' (Marathi) G. sãghāṛɔ m. 'lathe' ; संघाट joinery; M. sãgaḍ 'double-canoe' Rebus: sangataras 'stone-cutter, mason'*

loa 'ficus religiosa' Rebus: *lo* 'iron' (Sanskrit) PLUS unique ligatures: लोखंड [lōkhaṇḍa] *n* (लोह S) Iron. लोखंडाचे चणे खावविणें or चारणें To oppress grievously.लोखंडकाम [lōkhaṇḍakāma] *n* Iron work; that portion (of a building, machine &c.) which consists of iron. 2 The business of an ironsmith.लोखंडी [lōkhaṇḍī] *a* (लोखंड) Composed of iron; relating to iron. (Marathi) *bhaṭa* 'warrior' (Sanskrit) Rebus: *baṭa* a kind of iron (Gujarati). Rebus: *bhaṭa* 'furnace' (Santali) Thus, together, the ligatured hieroglyph reads rebus: *loa bhaṭa* 'iron furnace'
kuṭila 'bent' CDIAL 3230 kuṭi— in cmpd. 'curve', *kuṭika—* 'bent' MBh. Rebus: *kuṭila, katthīl* = bronze (8 parts copper and 2 parts tin)

cīmara 'black ant' Rebus: *cīmara* 'copper'. *cīmara kāra* -- ' coppersmith '

  Strands of yarn/rope' hieroglyph: Hieroglyph: 'strands of yarn' Rebus reading: *dhā'tu* 'strand of rope' Rebus: *dhatu* 'mineral ore' (Santali)

sal 'splinter' Rebus: sal 'workshop' āra 'six' Rebus: *āra* 'brass' *ayo* 'fish' Rebus: *aya* 'iron' *ayas* 'metal'

 kanka 'rim of jar' Rebus: karṇīka 'account (scribe)' karṇī 'supercargo'

 *meḍ* 'body' Rebus: *meḍ* 'iron' (Ho.) काठी [kāṭhī] *f* (काष्ठ S) 'frame or structure of the body' (Marathi) Rebus: खंडी [khaṇḍī] measure of weight (Marathi) *கண்டி; kaṇṭi, n. < Mhr. khaṇḍil. [T. Tu. khaṇḍi, M. kaṇḍi.]* Candy, a weight, stated to be roughly equivalent to 500 lbs

 m997a *खोंड [khōṇḍa] m A young bull, a bullcalf. (Marathi) Rebus: kõdār 'turner' (Bengali); कोंद kōnda 'engraver, lapidary setting or infixing gems' (Marathi) G. sãghāṛɔ m. 'lathe' ; संघाट joinery; M. sãgaḍ 'double-canoe' Rebus: sangataras 'stone-cutter, mason'*

  *loa* 'ficus religiosa' Rebus: *lo* 'iron' (Sanskrit) PLUS unique ligatures: लोखंड [lōkhaṇḍa] *n* (लोह S) Iron. लोखंडाचे चणे खावविणें or चारणें To oppress grievously.लोखंडकाम [lōkhaṇḍakāma] *n* Iron work; that portion (of a building, machine &c.) which consists of iron. 2 The business of an ironsmith.लोखंडी [lōkhaṇḍī] *a* (लोखंड) Composed of iron; relating to iron. (Marathi) *bhaṭa* 'warrior' (Sanskrit) Rebus: *baṭa* a kind of iron (Gujarati). Rebus: *bhaṭa* 'furnace' (Santali) Thus, together, the ligatured hieroglyph reads rebus: *loa bhaṭa* 'iron furnace'

kuṭila 'bent' CDIAL 3230 kuṭi— in cmpd. 'curve', *kuṭika—* 'bent' MBh. Rebus: *kuṭila, katthīl* = bronze (8 parts copper and 2 parts tin)

 सांड [sāṇḍa] *f* (षद S) An outlet for superfluous water (as through a dam or mound); a sluice, a floodvent. Rebus: सांडणी [sāṇḍaṇī] *f* (H) An instrument of goldsmiths. It is hooked or curved at the extremity; and is used to draw things out of the fire.

सांठा [*sāṇṭhā*] *m* (संचय S) A collection, heap, hoard, store, stock.साटें [*sāṭēṃ*] *n* (संचय S) A whole investment; the total quantity of merchandise (brought to market by one merchant).

 *muka* 'ladle' (Tamil)(DEDR 4887) Rebus: *mũh* 'ingot' (Santali) *baṭa* = rimless pot (Kannada) Rebus: *baṭa* = a kind of iron (G.)) *bhaṭa* furnace (Gujarati) Thus, iron ingot. ranku 'liquid measure' Rebus: ranku 'tin'

 m1016a *balad* m. ' ox ', gng. *bald*, (Ku.) *barad*, id. (N. Tarai) Rebus: *bharat* (5 copper, 4 zinc and 1 tin)(Punjabi) *pattar* 'trough' Rebus*: pattar* 'guild'. Thus, copper-zinc-tin alloy (worker) guild.

First 3 signs read rebus as at m997 PLUS *aya kāṇḍa* 'alloy metalware'

 m280a *ibha* 'elephant' Rebus: *ib* 'iron' *ibbo* 'merchant' (Gujarati) Firsst 2 signs read rebus as at m997. PLUS Circumscript: *gaṇḍa* 'four' Rebus: *kaṇḍa* 'furnace, fire-altar' (Santali).PLUS .साटें [*sāṭēṃ*] *n* (संचय S) A whole investment (of) *ayo* 'fish' Rebus: *aya* 'iron' *ayas* 'metal' sal 'splinter' Rebus: sal 'workshop' *aya kammaṭa.*'coiner, mint alloy'

aḍaren 'cover of pot or lid' Rebus: *aduru* 'native, unsmelted metal' Duplicated: dula 'pair' Rebus: dul 'cast metal'
kanka 'rim of jar' Rebus: karṇīka 'account (scribe)' karṇī 'supercargo'

m1271A

kharedo = a currycomb (Gujarati) खरारा [*kharārā*] *m* (H) A currycomb. 2 Currying a horse. (Marathi) Rebus: करडा [*karaḍā*] Hard from alloy--iron, silver &c. (Marathi) *kharādī* ' turner' (Gujarati) *kaṇḍo* 'stool, seat' Rebus: *kāṇḍa* 'metalware' *kaṇḍa* 'fire-altar'

mēḍu height, rising ground, hillock (Kannada) Rebus: *meḍ* 'iron' (Ho.) kolom 'three' Rebus: kolami 'smithy, forge' Thus, *meḍ kolami* 'iron smithy-forge'

mēḍu height, rising ground, hillock (Kannada) Rebus: *mẽṛhẽt, meḍ* 'iron' (Munda.Ho.)

Ligature: two peaks: mēḍu height, rising ground, hillock (Kannada) Rebus: *meḍ* 'iron' (Ho.) dula 'pair' Rebus: dul 'cast metal' PLUS |||| Numeral 4: gaṇḍa 'four' Rebus: kaṇḍa 'furnace, fire-altar' (Santali)

aḍaren 'cover of pot or lid' Rebus: *aduru* 'native, unsmelted metal' Duplicated: dula 'pair' Rebus: dul 'cast metal' *kuṭila* 'bent' CDIAL 3230 kuṭi— in cmpd. 'curve', *kuṭika*— 'bent' MBh. Rebus: *kuṭila, katthīl* = bronze (8 parts copper and 2 parts tin) *loa* 'ficus religiosa' Rebus: *lo* 'iron' (Sanskrit) PLUS unique ligatures: लोखंड [lōkhaṇḍa] *n* (लोह S) Iron. लोखंडाचे चणे खावविणें or चारणें To oppress grievously.लोखंडकाम [lōkhaṇḍakāma] *n* Iron work; that portion (of a building, machine &c.) which consists of iron. 2 The business of an ironsmith.लोखंडी [lōkhaṇḍī] *a* (लोखंड) Composed of iron; relating to iron. (Marathi) *bhaṭa* 'warrior' (Sanskrit) Rebus: *baṭa* a kind of iron (Gujarati). Rebus: *bhaṭa* 'furnace' (Santali) Thus, together, the ligatured hieroglyph reads rebus: *loa bhaṭa* 'iron furnace'

h1710A

meḍ 'body' Rebus: *meḍ* 'iron' (Ho.) काठी [kāṭhī] *f* (काष्ट S) 'frame or structure of the body' (Marathi) Rebus: खंडी [khaṇḍī] measure of weight (Marathi) *கண்டி; kaṇṭi, n. < Mhr. khaṇḍil. [T. Tu. khaṇḍi, M. kaṇḍi.]* Candy, a weight, stated to be roughly equivalent to 500 lbs.
sāgāḍā m. ' frame of a building ', *°ḍī* f. ' lathe '(CDIAL 12859) Rebus*: sangataras.* संगतराश lit. 'to collect stones, stone-cutter, mason.' *baṭa* 'rimless, broad-mouthed pot' Rebus: *bhaṭa* 'furnace' (Gujarati.); *baṭa* 'a kind of iron' (Gujarati) *kuṭila* 'bent' CDIAL 3230 kuṭi— in cmpd. 'curve', *kuṭika*— 'bent' MBh. Rebus: *kuṭila, katthīl* = bronze (8 parts copper and 2 parts tin) *kamaḍha* 'archer, bow' Rebus: *kammaṭa* 'mint, coiner'. खांडा [*khāṇḍā*] *m* A jag, notch, or indentation (as upon the edge of a tool or weapon). Rebus: *kāṇḍa* 'tools, pots and pans and metal-ware'

baroṭi 'twelve' *bhārata* 'a factitious alloy of copper, pewter, tin' (Marathi) *kuṭila* 'bent' CDIAL 3230 kuṭi— in cmpd. 'curve', *kuṭika*— 'bent' MBh. Rebus: *kuṭila, katthīl* = bronze (8 parts copper and 2 parts tin)

loa 'ficus religiosa' Rebus: *lo* 'iron' (Sanskrit) PLUS unique ligatures: लोखंड [lōkhaṇḍa

] *n* (लोह S) Iron. लोखंडाचे चणे खावविणें or चारणें To oppress grievously.लोखंडकाम [lōkhaṇḍakāma] *n* Iron work; that portion (of a building, machine &c.) which consists of iron. 2 The business of an ironsmith.लोखंडी [lōkhaṇḍī] *a* (लोखंड) Composed of iron; relating to iron. (Marathi) *bhaṭa* 'warrior' (Sanskrit) Rebus: *baṭa* a kind of iron (Gujarati). Rebus: *bhaṭa* 'furnace' (Santali) Thus, together, the ligatured hieroglyph reads rebus: *loa bhaṭa* 'iron furnace'

m1710a *खोंड [khōṇḍa] m A young bull, a bullcalf. (Marathi) Rebus: kōdār 'turner' (Bengali); कोंद kōnda 'engraver, lapidary setting or infixing gems' (Marathi) G. sãghāṛɔ m. 'lathe' ; संघाट joinery; M. sãgaḍ 'double-canoe' Rebus: sangataras 'stone-cutter, mason'*

loa 'ficus religiosa' Rebus: *lo* 'iron' (Sanskrit) PLUS unique ligatures: लोखंड [lōkhaṇḍa] *n* (लोह S) Iron. लोखंडाचे चणे खावविणें or चारणें To oppress grievously.लोखंडकाम [lōkhaṇḍakāma] *n* Iron work; that portion (of a building, machine &c.) which consists of iron. 2 The business of an ironsmith.लोखंडी [lōkhaṇḍī] *a* (लोखंड) Composed of iron; relating to iron. (Marathi) *bhaṭa* 'warrior' (Sanskrit) Rebus: *baṭa* a kind of iron (Gujarati). Rebus: *bhaṭa* 'furnace' (Santali) Thus, together, the ligatured hieroglyph reads rebus: *loa bhaṭa* 'iron furnace'

bicha 'scorpion' (Assamese) Rebus: *bica* 'stone ore' (Santali)

khaṇḍ 'field, division' (Skt.) Rebus: *khāṇḍa* 'tools, pots and pans, metal-ware'. Rebus 2: kaṇḍ 'fire-altar' (Santali) dula 'pair' Rebus: dul 'cast metal' Thus, duplicated 'division' hieroglyph sign reads: cast metal metal-ware.

dāṭu 'cross'(Telugu) Rebus: *dhatu* 'mineral' (Santali).ranku 'antelope' Rebus: ranku 'tin'

m1661a *खोंड [khōṇḍa] m A young bull, a bullcalf. (Marathi) Rebus: kōdār 'turner' (Bengali); कोंद kōnda 'engraver, lapidary setting or infixing gems' (Marathi) G. sãghāṛɔ m. 'lathe' ; संघाट joinery; M. sãgaḍ 'double-canoe' Rebus: sangataras 'stone-cutter, mason'*

loa 'ficus religiosa' Rebus: *lo* 'iron' (Sanskrit) PLUS unique ligatures: लोखंड [lōkhaṇḍa] *n* (लोह S) Iron. लोखंडाचे चणे खावविणें or चारणें To oppress grievously.लोखंडकाम [lōkhaṇḍakāma] *n* Iron work; that portion (of a building, machine &c.) which consists of iron. 2 The business of an ironsmith.लोखंडी [lōkhaṇḍī] *a* (लोखंड) Composed of iron; relating to iron. (Marathi) *bhaṭa* 'warrior' (Sanskrit) Rebus: *baṭa* a kind of iron (Gujarati). Rebus: *bhaṭa* 'furnace' (Santali) Thus, together, the ligatured hieroglyph reads rebus: *loa bhaṭa* 'iron furnace' *kuṭila* 'bent' CDIAL 3230 kuṭi— in cmpd. 'curve', *kuṭika—* 'bent' MBh. Rebus: *kuṭila, katthīl* = bronze (8 parts copper and 2 parts tin) dula 'pair' Rebus: dul 'cast metal' Thus, bronze castings.

कांड *kāṇḍa* 'arrow' Rebus: *kāṇḍa* 'pots and pans, metalware, tools'. Rebus 2: kaṇḍ 'fire-altar' (Santali) dula 'two' Rebus: dul 'cast metal'

kanac 'corner' Rebus: *kañcu* 'bronze' sal 'splinter' Rebus: sal 'workshop' dula 'pair' Rebus: dul 'cast metal':

ayo 'fish' Rebus: *aya* 'iron' *ayas* 'metal'

 *koḍi* 'flag' (Ta.)(DEDR 2049). Rebus 1: *koḍ* 'workshop' (Kuwi) Rebus 2: *khōḍ* m. 'pit', *khōḍü* f. 'small pit' (Kashmiri. CDIAL 3947).

 'Arrow' sign hieroglyph (variant) This is a ligature of 'lid of pot' hieroglyph superscript on 'a linear stroke' numeral hieroglyph.*aḍaren* 'cover of pot or lid' Rebus: *aduru* 'native, unsmelted metal' PLUS koḍ = one (Santali); koḍ 'workshop' (Gujarati)

M-1821 a

m1821a *खोंड [khōṇḍa] m A young bull, a bullcalf. (Marathi) Rebus: kōdār 'turner' (Bengali); कोंद kōnda 'engraver, lapidary setting or infixing gems' (Marathi) G. sãghāṛɔ m. 'lathe' ; संघाट joinery; M. sãgaḍ 'double-canoe' Rebus: sangataras 'stone-cutter, mason'*

loa 'ficus  religiosa' Rebus: *lo* 'iron' (Sanskrit) PLUS unique ligatures: लोखंड [lōkhaṇḍa] *n* (लोह S) Iron. लोखंडाचे चणे खावविणें or चारणें To oppress grievously.लोखंडकाम [lōkhaṇḍakāma] *n* Iron work; that portion (of a building, machine &c.) which consists of iron. 2 The business of an ironsmith.लोखंडी [lōkhaṇḍī] *a* (लोखंड) Composed of iron; relating to iron. (Marathi)

 notch+slanted stroke reads rebus: *ḍhālako kāṇḍa* 'ingot, tools, pots and pans and metal-ware'.*dhāḷ* 'a slope'; 'inclination of a plane' (G.); *ḍhāḷiyum* = adj. sloping, inclining (G.) Rebus: *ḍhālako* = a large metal ingot (G.) *ḍhālakī* = a metal heated and poured into a mould; a solid piece of metal; an ingot (Gujarati) PLUS खांडा [*khāṇḍā*] *m* A jag, notch, or indentation (as upon the edge of a tool or weapon). Rebus: *kāṇḍa* 'tools, pots and pans and metal-ware'

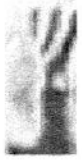 *kolmo* 'paddy plant' Rebus: *kolami* 'smithy, forge' Vikalpa: *mogge* 'sprout, bud' Rebus: *mūh* 'ingot' (Santali) dolu 'plant of shoot height' Rebus: dul 'cast metal'

 *kanka* (Santali) *karṇika* 'scribe'(Sanskrit) Rebus: *karṇī,* supercargo for a boat shipment. INFIXED खांडा [*khāṇḍā*] *m* A jag, notch, or indentation (as upon the edge of a tool or weapon). Rebus: *kāṇḍa* 'tools, pots and pans and metal-ware'

kana,  *kanac* = corner (Santali); Rebus: *kañcu* = bronze (Telugu) PLUS खांडा [*khāṇḍā*] *m* A jag, notch, or indentation (as upon the edge of a tool or weapon). Rebus: *kāṇḍa* 'tools, pots and pans and metal-ware' Thus, bronze metalware.

 kanka 'rim of jar' Rebus: karṇīka 'account (scribe)' karṇī 'supercargo'

h420a *खोंड [khōṇḍa] m A young bull, a bullcalf. (Marathi) Rebus: kōdār 'turner' (Bengali); कोंद kōnda 'engraver, lapidary setting or infixing gems' (Marathi) G. sãghāṛɔ m. 'lathe' ; संघाट joinery; M. sãgaḍ 'double-canoe' Rebus: sangataras 'stone-cutter, mason'*

 *loa* 'ficus religiosa' Rebus: *lo* 'iron' (Sanskrit) PLUS unique ligatures: लोखंड [lōkhaṇḍa] *n* (लोह S) Iron. लोखंडाचे चणे खावविणें or चारणें To oppress grievously.लोखंडकाम [ lōkhaṇḍakāma] *n* Iron work; that portion (of a building, machine &c.) which consists of iron. 2 The business of an ironsmith.लोखंडी [lōkhaṇḍī] *a* (लोखंड) Composed of iron;

relating to iron. (Marathi) *bhaṭa* 'warrior' (Sanskrit) Rebus: *baṭa* a kind of iron (Gujarati). Rebus: *bhaṭa* 'furnace' (Santali) Thus, together, the ligatured hieroglyph reads rebus: *loa bhaṭa* 'iron furnace'

loa 'ficus religiosa' Rebus: *lo* 'iron' (Sanskrit) PLUS unique ligatures: लोखंड [lōkhaṇḍa] *n* (लोह S) Iron. लोखंडाचे चणे खावविणें or चारणें To oppress grievously.लोखंडकाम [lōkhaṇḍakāma] *n* Iron work; that portion (of a building, machine &c.) which consists of iron. 2 The business of an ironsmith.लोखंडी [lōkhaṇḍī] *a* (लोखंड) Composed of iron; relating to iron. (Marathi)
ḍhanga = a crook used for pulling down the branches of trees, for goats, sheep and camels (P.) Rebus:*ḍhangar* blacksmith'

kanka 'rim of jar' Rebus: karṇīka 'account (scribe)' karṇī 'supercargo'खांडा [*khāṇḍā*] *m* A jag, notch, or indentation (as upon the edge of a tool or weapon). Rebus: *kāṇḍa* 'tools, pots and pans and metal-ware' gaṇḍa 'four' Rebus: kaṇḍa 'furnace, fire-altar' (Santali)

mogge 'sprout, bud' Rebus: *mūh* 'ingot' (Santali)

kanka 'rim of jar' Rebus: karṇīka 'account (scribe)' karṇī 'supercargo'

m2098a

khareḍo = a currycomb (Gujarati) खरारा [*kharārā*] *m* (H) A currycomb. 2 Currying a horse. (Marathi) Rebus: करडा [*karaḍā*] Hard from alloy--iron, silver &c. (Marathi) *kharādī*' turner' (Gujarati)
kanka 'rim of jar' Rebus: karṇīka 'account (scribe)' karṇī 'supercargo'

baraḍo = spine; backbone (Tulu) Rebus: *baran, bharat* 'mixed alloys' (5 copper, 4 zinc and 1 tin) (Punjabi) PLUS gaṇḍa 'four' Rebus: kaṇḍa 'furnace, fire-altar' (Santali) *ayo* 'fish' Rebus: *aya* 'iron' *ayas* 'metal'

Lothal 60a

loa 'ficus religiosa' Rebus: *lo* 'iron' (Sanskrit) PLUS unique ligatures:

लोखंड [lōkhaṇḍa] *n* (लोह S) Iron. लोखंडाचे चणे खावविणें or चारणें To oppress grievously.लोखंडकाम [lōkhaṇḍakāma] *n* Iron work; that portion (of a building, machine &c.) which consists of iron. 2 The business of an ironsmith.लोखंडी [lōkhaṇḍī] *a* (लोखंड) Composed of iron; relating to iron. (Marathi) *bhaṭa* 'warrior' (Sanskrit) Rebus: *baṭa* a kind of iron (Gujarati). Rebus: *bhaṭa* 'furnace' (Santali) Thus, together, the ligatured hieroglyph reads rebus: *loa bhaṭa* 'iron furnace'

kanac 'corner' Rebus: *kañcu* 'bronze' kanka 'rim of jar' Rebus: karṇīka 'account (scribe)' karṇī 'supercargo'

m24a खोंड *[khōṇḍa] m A young bull, a bullcalf. (Marathi) Rebus: kõdār 'turner' (Bengali);* कोंद *kōnda 'engraver, lapidary setting or infixing gems' (Marathi) G. sãghāṛɔ m. 'lathe' ;* संघाट *joinery; M. sãgaḍ 'double-canoe' Rebus: sangataras 'stone-cutter, mason'*

loa 'ficus religiosa' Rebus: *lo* 'iron' (Sanskrit) PLUS unique ligatures: लोखंड [lōkhaṇḍa] *n* (लोह S) Iron. लोखंडाचे चणे खावविणें or चारणें To oppress grievously.लोखंडकाम [lōkhaṇḍakāma] *n* Iron work; that portion (of a building, machine &c.) which consists of iron. 2 The business of an ironsmith.लोखंडी [lōkhaṇḍī] *a* (लोखंड) Composed of iron; relating to iron. (Marathi) *bhaṭa* 'warrior' (Sanskrit) Rebus: *baṭa* a kind of iron (Gujarati). Rebus: *bhaṭa* 'furnace' (Santali) Thus, together, the ligatured hieroglyph reads rebus: *loa bhaṭa* 'iron furnace' *kuṭila* 'bent' CDIAL 3230 kuṭi— in cmpd. 'curve', *kuṭika—* 'bent' MBh. Rebus: *kuṭila, katthīl* = bronze (8 parts copper and 2 parts tin) dula 'pair' Rebus: dul 'cast metal' Thus, bronze castings. sal 'splinter' Rebus: sal 'workshop' *aya aḍaren* (homonym: aduru) 'alloy native metal' *aya kammaṭa.*'coiner, mint alloy' kanka 'rim of jar' Rebus: karṇīka 'account (scribe)' karṇī 'supercargo'

meḍ 'body' Rebus: *meḍ* 'iron' (Ho.) काठी [kāṭhī] *f* (काष्ट S) 'frame or structure of the body' (Marathi) Rebus: खंडी [khaṇḍī] measure of weight (Marathi) *கண்டி; kaṇṭi, n. < Mhr. khaṇḍil. [T. Tu. khaṇḍi, M. kaṇḍi.]* Candy, a weight, stated to be roughly equivalent to 500 lbs.

m708a खोंड *[khōṇḍa] m A young bull, a bullcalf. (Marathi) Rebus: kõdār 'turner' (Bengali);* कोंद *kōnda 'engraver, lapidary setting or infixing gems' (Marathi) G. sãghāṛɔ m. 'lathe' ;* संघाट *joinery; M. sãgaḍ 'double-canoe' Rebus: sangataras 'stone-cutter, mason'*

loa 'ficus religiosa' Rebus: *lo* 'iron' (Sanskrit) PLUS unique ligatures: लोखंड [lōkhaṇḍa] *n* (लोह S) Iron. लोखंडाचे चणे खावविणें or चारणें To oppress grievously.लोखंडकाम [lōkhaṇḍakāma] *n* Iron work; that portion (of a building, machine &c.) which consists of iron. 2 The business of an ironsmith.लोखंडी [lōkhaṇḍī] *a* (लोखंड) Composed of iron; relating to iron. (Marathi) *bhaṭa* 'warrior' (Sanskrit) Rebus: *baṭa* a kind of iron (Gujarati). Rebus: *bhaṭa* 'furnace' (Santali) Thus, together, the ligatured hieroglyph reads rebus: *loa bhaṭa* 'iron furnace'

kolmo 'paddy plant' Rebus: *kolami* 'smithy, forge' Vikalpa: *mogge* 'sprout, bud' Rebus: *mũh* 'ingot' (Santali) dolu 'plant of shoot height' Rebus: dul 'cast metal'

sal 'splinter' Rebus: sal 'workshop'

dhāḷ 'a slope'; 'inclination of a plane' (G.); *ḍhāḷiyum* = adj. sloping, inclining (G.) Rebus: *ḍhālako* = a large metal ingot (G.) *ḍhālakī* = a metal heated and poured into a mould; a solid piece of metal; an ingot (Gujarati) PLUS खांडा [*khāṇḍā*] *m* A jag, notch, or indentation (as upon the edge of a tool or weapon). Rebus: *kāṇḍa* 'tools, pots and pans and metal-ware' Thus, the pair of sign hieroglyphs from r. read rebus: copper, bronze ingots, metalware castings.

kanka 'rim of jar' Rebus: karṇīka 'account (scribe)' karṇī 'supercargo'

h505A *खोंड [khōṇḍa] m A young bull, a bullcalf. (Marathi) Rebus: kõdār 'turner' (Bengali); कोंद kōnda 'engraver, lapidary setting or infixing gems' (Marathi) G. sãghāṛɔ m. 'lathe' ; संघाट joinery; M. sãgaḍ 'double-canoe' Rebus: sangataras 'stone-cutter, mason'*

loa 'ficus religiosa' Rebus: *lo* 'iron' (Sanskrit) PLUS unique ligatures: लोखंड [lōkhaṇḍa] *n* (लोह S) Iron. लोखंडाचे चणे खावविणें or चारणें To oppress grievously.लोखंडकाम [lōkhaṇḍakāma] *n* Iron work; that portion (of a building, machine &c.) which consists of iron. 2 The business of an ironsmith.लोखंडी [lōkhaṇḍī] *a* (लोखंड) Composed of iron; relating to iron. (Marathi) *bhaṭa* 'warrior' (Sanskrit) Rebus: *baṭa* a kind of iron (Gujarati). Rebus: *bhaṭa* 'furnace' (Santali) Thus, together, the ligatured hieroglyph reads rebus: *loa bhaṭa* 'iron furnace'

kolom 'three' Rebus: kolami 'smithy, forge' with circumscript dula 'pair' Rebus: dul 'cast metal'. Thus metal smithy castings workshop.

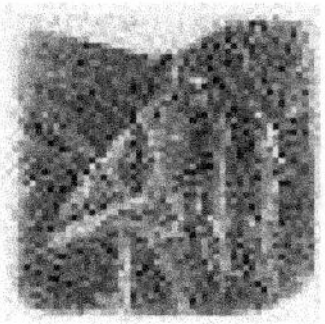

Lothal 118A dula 'two' Rebus: dul 'cast metal'

loa 'ficus religiosa' Rebus: *lo* 'iron' (Sanskrit) PLUS unique ligatures: लोखंड [lōkhaṇḍa] *n* (लोह S) Iron. लोखंडाचे चणे खावविणें or चारणें To oppress grievously.लोखंडकाम [lōkhaṇḍakāma] *n* Iron work; that portion (of a building, machine &c.) which consists of iron. 2 The business of an ironsmith.लोखंडी [lōkhaṇḍī] *a* (लोखंड) Composed of iron; relating to iron. (Marathi) *bhaṭa* 'warrior' (Sanskrit) Rebus: *baṭa* a kind of iron (Gujarati). Rebus: *bhaṭa* 'furnace' (Santali) Thus, together, the ligatured hieroglyph reads rebus: *loa bhaṭa* 'iron furnace'

h1677A *खोंड [khōṇḍa] m A young bull, a bullcalf. (Marathi) Rebus: kõdār 'turner' (Bengali); कोंद kōnda 'engraver, lapidary setting or infixing gems' (Marathi) G. sãghāṛɔ m. 'lathe' ; संघाट joinery; M. sãgaḍ 'double-canoe' Rebus: sangataras 'stone-cutter, mason'*

loa 'ficus religiosa' Rebus: *lo* 'iron' (Sanskrit) PLUS unique ligatures: लोखंड [lōkhaṇḍa] *n* (लोह S) Iron. लोखंडाचे चणे खावविणें or चारणें To oppress grievously.लोखंडकाम [lōkhaṇḍakāma] *n* Iron work; that portion (of a building, machine &c.) which consists of iron. 2 The business of an ironsmith.लोखंडी [lōkhaṇḍī] *a* (लोखंड) Composed of iron; relating to iron. (Marathi) *bhaṭa* 'warrior' (Sanskrit) Rebus: *baṭa* a kind of iron (Gujarati). Rebus: *bhaṭa* 'furnace' (Santali) Thus, together, th ligatured hieroglyph reads rebus: *loa bhaṭa* 'iron furnace'

water-carrier hieroglyph *kuṭi*; Rebus: *kuṭhi* 'smelter furnace'. PLUS 'rim of jar':

kanka 'rim of jar' Rebus: karṇīka 'account (scribe)' karṇī 'supercargo'

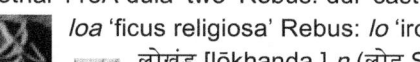

'Set of twelve strokes' hieroglyph

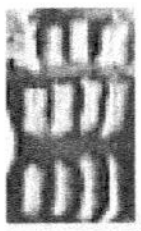 *baroṭi* 'twelve' *bhārata* 'a factitious alloy of copper, pewter, tin' (Marathi)

m988a *खोंड [khōṇḍa] m A young bull, a bullcalf. (Marathi) Rebus: kõdār 'turner' (Bengali); कोंद kōnda 'engraver, lapidary setting or infixing gems' (Marathi) G. sãghāṛɔ m. 'lathe' ; संघाट joinery; M. sãgaḍ 'double-canoe' Rebus: sangataras 'stone-cutter, mason'*

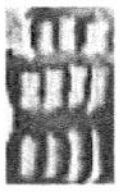 Sign hieroglyph: numeral strokes: three rows of four notches each (with variants). *baroṭi* 'twelve' *bhārata* 'a factitious alloy of copper, pewter, tin' (Marathi)

  water-carrier hieroglyph *kuṭi*; Rebus: *kuṭhi* 'smelter furnace'. PLUS 'rim of jar':

kanka 'rim  of jar' Rebus: karṇīka 'account (scribe)' karṇī 'supercargo'

Thus, supercargo of copper-pewter-tin alloy.

Lothal 47a *खोंड [khōṇḍa] m A young bull, a bullcalf. (Marathi) Rebus: kõdār 'turner' (Bengali); कोंद kōnda 'engraver, lapidary setting or infixing gems' (Marathi) G. sãghāṛɔ m. 'lathe' ; संघाट joinery; M. sãgaḍ 'double-canoe' Rebus: sangataras 'stone-cutter, mason'*

baroṭi 'twelve'  *bhārata* 'a factitious alloy of copper, pewter, tin' (Marathi)
kamaḍha 'crab' Rebus: *kammaṭa* 'mint, coiner'.*ḍato* = claws of crab (Santali) Rebus: *dhātu* 'mineral ore'
sal 'splinter' Rebus: sal 'workshop'

 *aḍaren* 'cover of pot or lid' Rebus: *aduru* 'native, unsmelted metal' Duplicated: dula 'pair' Rebus: dul 'cast metal'

 kanka 'rim of jar' Rebus: karṇīka 'account (scribe)' karṇī 'supercargo'

 *mogge* 'sprout, bud' Rebus: *mũh* 'ingot' (Santali)

m1848a *खोंड [khōṇḍa] m A young bull, a bullcalf. (Marathi) Rebus: kõdār 'turner' (Bengali); कोंद kōnda 'engraver, lapidary setting or infixing gems' (Marathi) G. sãghāṛɔ m. 'lathe' ; संघाट joinery; M. sãgaḍ 'double-canoe' Rebus: sangataras 'stone-cutter, mason'*

On this seal, three rows of numeral strokes are organized alternative slanting positions suggesting that the intent is to present a cluster of 'notches or jags' in three rows. The following epigraphs may be variant presentations totaling twelve numeral strokes again organized in three rows.

 *baroṭi* 'twelve' *bhārata* 'a factitious alloy of copper, pewter, tin' (Marathi)

dula 'pair' Rebus: dul 'cast metal'. Thus, cast alloy of copper-pewter-tin.

MS2645 Pictorial motif hieroglyphs: kamāṭhiyo = archer; kāmaṭhum = a bow; kāmaḍ, kāmaḍum = a chip of bamboo (Gujarati) kāmaṭhiyo a bowman; an archer (Sanskrit) Rebus: kammaṭi a coiner (Kannada); kampaṭṭam coinage, coin, mint (Tamil) kammaṭa = mint, gold furnace (Telugu)
kol 'tiger' Rebus: kolhe 'smelter' *kaṭavai* 'leap, jump' Rebus: *kaḍavu* 'turning lathe' Leaping: *kũdā* Rebus: *kõdār* 'turner' (Bengali); *kõdā* 'to turn in a lathe' (Bengali) Thus the hieroglyph denotes: *kolhe kõdār* 'smelter, turner'
Rhinoceros/boar: baḍhia = a castrated boar, a hog (Santali) baḍhi 'a caste who work both in iron and wood' (Santali) *baṟea* 'merchant'

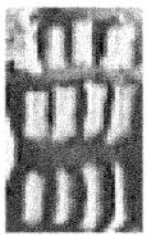

baroṭi 'twelve' *bhārata* 'a factitious alloy of copper, pewter, tin' (Marathi)
kāmaṭhum = a bow Rebus: *kammaṭa* = mint, gold furnace (Telugu) *dula* 'pair' Rebus: *dul* 'cast metal' Thus cast metal mint.
meḍ 'body' Rebus: *meḍ* 'iron' (Ho.)

kāṇḍa 'arrow' (Sanskrit) Rebus:*khāṇḍa* 'tools, pots and pans, metal-ware'. Rebus 2: kaṇḍ 'fire-altar' (Santali)

K-30 A

Kalibangan 30A *balad* m. ' ox ', gng. *bald*, (Ku.) *barad*, id. (N. Tarai) Rebus: *bharat* (5 copper, 4 zinc and 1 tin)(Punjabi) *pattar* 'trough' Rebus: *pattar* 'guild'. Thus, copper-zinc-tin alloy (worker) guild.
dula 'pair' Rebus: *dul* 'cast metal' PLUS kuṭila 'bent' CDIAL 3230 kuṭi— in cmpd. 'curve', *kuṭika*— 'bent' MBh. Rebus: kuṭila, katthīl = bronze (8 parts copper and 2 parts tin) cf. āra-kūṭa, 'brass' (Sanskrit) Thus, cast metal bronze.

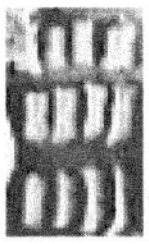

baroṭi 'twelve' *bhārata* 'a factitious alloy of copper, pewter, tin' (Marathi)

h836A *खोंड [khōṇḍa] m A young bull, a bullcalf. (Marathi) Rebus: kõdār 'turner' (Bengali); कोंद kōnda 'engraver, lapidary setting or infixing gems' (Marathi) G. sãghāṛɔ m. 'lathe' ; संघाट joinery; M. sãgaḍ 'double-canoe' Rebus: sangataras 'stone-cutter, mason'*

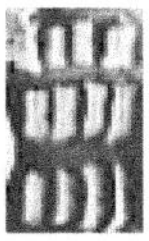

baroṭi 'twelve' *bhārata* 'a factitious alloy of copper, pewter, tin' (Marathi)

koḍi 'flag' (Tamil)(DEDR 2049). Rebus 1: *koḍ* 'workshop' (Kuwi) Rebus 2: *khõḍ* m. 'pit', *khõḍü* f. 'small pit' (Kashmiri. CDIAL 3947). Thus, copper-pewter-tin alloy workshop.

 *kharedo* = a currycomb (Gujarati) खरारा [*kharārā*] *m* (H) A currycomb. 2 Currying a horse. (Marathi) Rebus: करडा [*karaḍā*] Hard from alloy--iron, silver &c. (Marathi) *kharādī* ' turner' (Gujarati)

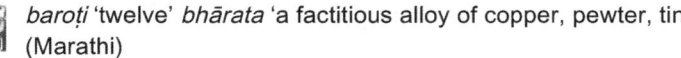

h1797A

 *baroṭi* 'twelve' *bhārata* 'a factitious alloy of copper, pewter, tin' (Marathi)

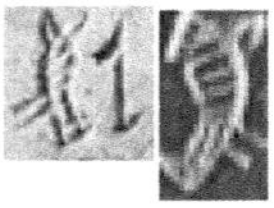 The pair of hieroglyph signs are compositions: 1. *bicha* 'scorpion' (Assamese) Rebus: *bica* 'stone ore' (Santali) The pairing sign is a composition of: sloping stroke PLUS two short strokes of a 'splinter':*dhāḷ* 'a slope'; 'inclination of a plane' (Gujarati); *ḍhāḷiyum* = adj. sloping, inclining (Gujarati) Rebus: *ḍhālako* = a large metal ingot (Gujarati) *ḍhālakī* = a metal heated and poured into a mould; a solid piece of metal; an ingot (Gujarati)PLUS*sal* 'splinter' Rebus: *sal* 'workshop'. Thus the composition reads: *ḍhālako sal* 'ingot workshop'.

 *dāṭu* 'cross'(Telugu) Rebus: *dhatu* 'mineral' (Santali).

kanka 'rim of jar' Rebus: karṇīka 'account (scribe)' karṇī 'supercargo'
dulo 'hole' Rebus: dul 'cast metal' Senatic-phonetic determinant: dula 'two' Rebus: dul 'cast metal' 'ingot' (Santali) *baṭa* = rimless pot (Kannada) Rebus: *baṭa* = a kind of iron (G.)) *bhaṭa* furnace (Gujarati) Thus, furnace metal castings.

m988a *खोंड [khōṇḍa] m A young bull, a bullcalf. (Marathi) Rebus: kōdār 'turner' (Bengali); कोंद kōnda 'engraver, lapidary setting or infixing gems' (Marathi) G. sãghāṛɔ m. 'lathe' ; संघाट joinery; M. sāgaḍ 'double-canoe' Rebus: sangataras 'stone-cutter, mason'*

 *baroṭi* 'twelve' *bhārata* 'a factitious alloy of copper, pewter, tin' (Marathi)

 water-carrier hieroglyph *kuṭi*; Rebus: *kuṭhi* 'smelter furnace'.

m18A *खोंड [khōṇḍa] m A young bull, a bullcalf. (Marathi) Rebus: kōdār 'turner' (Bengali); कोंद kōnda 'engraver, lapidary setting or infixing gems' (Marathi) G. sãghāṛɔ m. 'lathe' ; संघाट joinery; M. sāgaḍ 'double-canoe' Rebus: sangataras 'stone-cutter, mason'*

baroṭi 'twelve' *bhārata* 'a factitious alloy of copper, pewter, tin' (Marathi)
'rim-of-jar' hieroglyph
kanka (Santali) *karṇika* 'scribe'(Sanskrit) Rebus: *karṇī,* supercargo for a boat shipment. *karṇīka* 'account (scribe)'
.कारणी *kāraṇī* 'the supercargo of a ship' (Marathi)

dhā´tu 'strand of rope' Rebus: *dhatu* 'mineral ore' (Santali) PLUS dula 'pair' Rebus: *dul* 'cast metal' PLUS *dhāḷ* 'a slope'; 'inclination of a plane' (Gujarati); *ḍhāḷiyum* = adj. sloping, inclining (Gujarati) Rebus: *ḍhālako* = a large metal ingot (Gujarati) *ḍhālakī* = a metal heated and poured into a mould; a solid piece of metal; an ingot (Gujarati)PLUS *aḍaren* 'cover of pot or lid' Rebus: *aduru* 'native, unsmelted metal'. Thus, the composite hieroglyph reads: native metal cast ingot mineral ore: *aḍaren dul ḍhālako dhatu*

h25a खोंड *[khōṇḍa] m A young bull, a bullcalf. (Marathi) Rebus: kõdār 'turner' (Bengali);* कोंद *kōnda 'engraver, lapidary setting or infixing gems' (Marathi) G. sãghārɔ m. 'lathe' ;* संघाट *joinery; M. sãgaḍ 'double-canoe' Rebus: sangataras 'stone-cutter, mason'*

baroṭi 'twelve' *bhārata* 'a factitious alloy of copper, pewter, tin' (Marathi)
aya aḍaren (homonym: aduru)'alloy native metal'

muka 'ladle' (Tamil)(DEDR 4887) Rebus: *mũh* 'ingot' (Santali) *baṭa* = a kind of iron (Gujarati) *baṭa* = rimless pot (Kannada) Thus, iron ingot.

kolom 'three' Rebus: *kolami* 'smithy, forge'
mogge 'sprout, bud' Rebus*: mũh* 'ingot' PLUS dula 'pair' Rebus: *dul* 'cast metal' kuṭila 'bent' CDIAL 3230 kuṭi— in cmpd. 'curve', *kuṭika*— 'bent' MBh. Rebus: *kuṭila, katthīl* = bronze (8 parts copper and 2 parts tin) cf. āra-kūṭa, 'brass' (Sanskrit) Thus the ligature reads: cast bronze ingot, *dul kuṭila mũh*

kolom 'three' Rebus: kolami 'smithy, forge'
kuṭi— in cmpd. 'curve', *kuṭika*— 'bent' MBh. Rebus: *kuṭila, katthīl* = bronze (8 parts copper and 2 parts tin)

kanka (Santali) *karṇika* 'scribe'(Sanskrit) Rebus: *karṇī,* supercargo for a boat shipment. INFIXED खांडा [*khāṇḍā*] *m* A jag, notch, or indentation (as upon the edge of a tool or weapon). Rebus: *kāṇḍa* 'tools, pots and pans and metal-ware'

 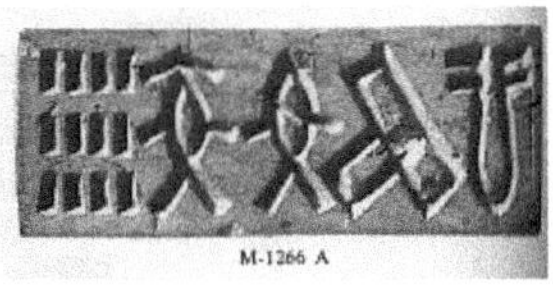

m1266A
baroṭi 'twelve' *bhārata* 'a factitious alloy of copper, pewter, tin' (Marathi)
aya aḍaren (homonym: aduru)'alloy native metal'
ayo ḍhālako 'alloy metal ingot'

Variant

notch+slanted stroke reads rebus: *ḍhālako kāṇḍa* 'ingot, tools, pots and pans and metal-ware'.*dhāḷ* 'a slope'; 'inclination of a plane' (G.); *ḍhāḷiyum* = adj. sloping, inclining (G.) Rebus: *ḍhālako* = a large metal ingot (G.) *ḍhālakī* = a metal heated and poured into a mould; a solid piece of metal; an ingot (Gujarati) PLUS खांडा [*khāṇḍā*] *m* A jag, notch, or indentation (as upon the edge of a tool or weapon). Rebus: *kāṇḍa* 'tools, pots and pans and metal-ware' *kanka* (Santali) *karṇika* 'scribe'(Sanskrit) Rebus: *karṇī,* supercargo for a boat shipment. *karṇīka* 'account (scribe)'.कारणी *kāraṇī* 'the supercargo of a ship' (Marathi)

m368A

baroṭi 'twelve' *bhārata* 'a factitious alloy of copper, pewter, tin' (Marathi)
dula 'pair' Rebus: dul 'cast metal' PLUS
kanac 'corner' Rebus: kañcu 'bronze' PLUS
खांडा [*khāṇḍā*] *m* A jag, notch, or indentation (as upon the edge of a tool or weapon). Rebus: *kāṇḍa* 'tools, pots and pans and metal-ware'
Thus, cast bronze metalware *mogge* 'sprout, bud' Rebus*: mũh* 'ingot'

kamaḍha 'crab' Rebus: *kammaṭa* 'mint, coiner'.*ḍato* = claws of crab (Santali) Rebus: *dhātu* 'mineral ore' PLUS खांडा [*khāṇḍā*] *m* A jag, notch, or indentation (as upon the edge of a tool or weapon). Rebus: *kāṇḍa* 'tools, pots and pans and metal-ware' Thus, mint metalware, ore.

mogge 'sprout, bud' Rebus: *mũh* 'ingot' (Santali)

m1021A

koḍi 'flag' (Ta.)(DEDR 2049). Rebus 1: *koḍ* 'workshop' (Kuwi) Rebus 2: *khŏḍ* m. 'pit', *khōḍü* f. 'small pit' (Kashmiri. CDIAL 3947).

सांड [sāṇḍa] *f* (षद S) An outlet for superfluous water (as through a dam or mound); a sluice, a floodvent. Rebus: सांडणी [sāṇḍaṇī] *f* (H) An instrument of goldsmiths. It is hooked or curved at the extremity; and is used to draw things out of the fire. सांठा [*sāṇṭhā*] *m* (संचय S) A collection, heap, hoard, store, stock.साटें [*sāṭēṃ*] *n* (संचय S) A whole investment; the total quantity of merchandise (brought to market by one merchant).

kanka (Santali) *karṇika* 'scribe'(Sanskrit) Rebus: *karṇī,* supercargo for a boat shipment. INFIXED खांडा [*khāṇḍā*] *m* A jag, notch, or indentation (as upon the edge of a tool or weapon). Rebus: *kāṇḍa* 'tools, pots and pans and metal-ware' *aya aḍaren* (homonym: aduru) 'alloy native metal'
kanka 'rim of jar' Rebus: karṇīka 'account (scribe)' karṇī 'supercargo'

meḍ 'body' Rebus: *meḍ* 'iron' (Ho.) काठी [kāṭhī] *f* (काष्ट S) 'frame or structure of the body' (Marathi) Rebus: खंडी [khaṇḍī] measure of weight (Marathi) *கண்டி; kaṇṭi, n. < Mhr. khaṇḍil. [T. Tu. khaṇḍi, M. kaṇḍi.]* Candy, a weight, stated to be roughly equivalent to 500 lbs.
PLUS ligature: खांडा [*khāṇḍā*] *m* A jag, notch, or indentation (as upon the edge of a tool or weapon). Rebus: *kāṇḍa* 'tools, pots and pans and metal-ware'

Sign ligatured hieroglyph: 'Pillar with ring stones PLUS arch'

h860 and h859: Pictorial hieroglyph: खोंड [khōṇḍa] m A young bull, a bullcalf. (Marathi) Rebus: kōdār 'turner' (Bengali); कोंद kōnda 'engraver, lapidary setting or infixing gems' (Marathi)
G. *sãghāṛɔ* m. 'lathe' ; *संघाट joinery; M. sãgaḍ 'double-canoe'* Rebus*: sangataras.* संगतराश lit. 'to collect stones, stone-cutter, mason.'

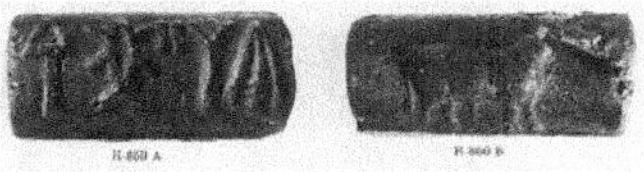

h860A

h859A

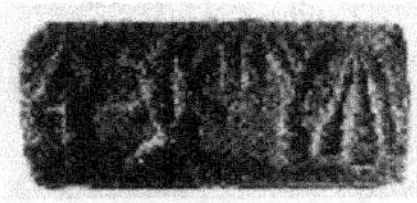

h867A

h265A

h264A

h263A

h262A

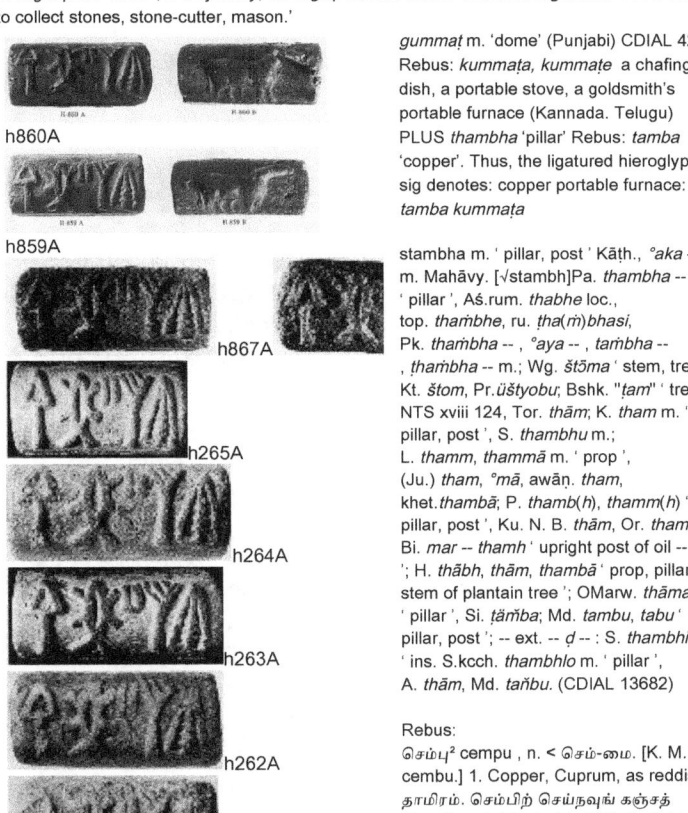

gummaṭ m. 'dome' (Punjabi) CDIAL 4217 Rebus: *kummaṭa, kummaṭe* a chafing dish, a portable stove, a goldsmith's portable furnace (Kannada. Telugu) PLUS *thambha* 'pillar' Rebus: *tamba* 'copper'. Thus, the ligatured hieroglyph sig denotes: copper portable furnace: *tamba kummaṭa*

stambha m. ' pillar, post ' Kāṭh., *°aka* -- m. Mahāvy. [√stambh]Pa. *thambha* -- m. ' pillar ', Aś.rum. *thabhe* loc., top. *thaṁbhe*, ru. *ṭha(ṁ)bhasi*, Pk. *thaṁbha* -- , *°aya* -- , *taṁbha* -- , *ṭhaṁbha* -- m.; Wg. *štōma* ' stem, tree ', Kt. *štom*, Pr.*üštyobu*; Bshk. "*ṭam*" ' tree ' NTS xviii 124, Tor. *thām*; K. *tham* m. ' pillar, post ', S. *thambhu* m.; L. *thamm, thammā* m. ' prop ', (Ju.) *tham, °mā*, awāṇ. *tham*, khet.*thambā*; P. *thamb(h), thamm(h)* ' pillar, post ', Ku. N. B. *thām*, Or. *thamba*; Bi. *mar* -- *thamh* ' upright post of oil -- mill '; H. *thābh, thām, thambā* ' prop, pillar, stem of plantain tree '; OMarw. *thāma* m. ' pillar ', Si. *ṭäm̆ba*; Md. *tambu, tabu* ' pillar, post '; -- ext. -- *ḍ* -- : S. *thambhiṛī* f. ' ins. S.kcch. *thambhlo* m. ' pillar ', A. *thām*, Md. *tam̆bu.* (CDIAL 13682)

Rebus:
செம்பு² cempu , n. < செம்-மை. [K. M. cembu.] 1. Copper, Cuprum, as reddish; தாமிரம். செம்பிற் செய்நவுங் கஞ்சத் தொழிலவும் (சிலப். 14, 174). 2. Gold; பொன். (அக. நி.) 3. [K. Tu. cembu.] Metal vessel; செம்பு முதலியவற்றாற் செய்யப்பட்ட பாத்திரவகை. 4. Liquid measure=3¼ cēr செம்புக்குட்டி cempu-k-kuṭṭi Ta. cempu copper, gold, metal vessel, liquid measure; cempaṉ brown-coloured cow or bull; tampikai a kind of small water-pot. Ma. cempu copper, copper vessel. ? Ko. keby, keb-giṇḍy globular metal drinking-vessel with spout. To. teb copper; ? köb small brass vessel. Ka. cambu, cembu, combu copper, globular copper or glass vessel used

for drinking water; cambige, tambige, tambuge globular copper or glass vessel.Koḍ. cembï copper, small metal pot. Tu. cembu brass, copper, small copper or brass pot; tambigè small, round, metal vessel. Te. cembu goblet, pitcher, ewer; tambuga a sort of drinking-vessel. / Cf. Mar. cābū a metal vessel with a belly and a tapering neck, a goglet. Are the Dr. words influenced by Skt. tāmra-, Pkt. tamba- copper?(DEDR 2775).

tāmrá ' dark red, copper -- coloured ' VS., n. ' copper ' Kauś., *tāmraka* -- n. Yājñ. [Cf. tamrá -- . -- √tam?] Pa. *tamba* -- ' red ', n. ' copper ', Pk. *taṁba* -- adj. and n.; Dm. *trāmba* -- ' red ' (in *trāmba* -- *laçuk* ' raspberry ' NTS xii 192); Bshk. *lām* ' copper, piece of bad pine -- wood (< ' *red wood '?); Phal. *tāmba* ' copper ' (→ Sh.koh. *tāmbā*), K. *trām* m. (→ Sh.gil. gur. *trām* m.), S. *ṭrāmo* m., L. *trāmā*, (Ju.) *tarāmā* m., P. *tāmbā* m., WPah. bhad. *ṭḷām* n., kiūth. *cāmbā*, sod. *cambo*, jaun. *tā̃bō*, Ku. N. *tāmo* (pl. ' young bamboo shoots '), A. *tām*, B. *tā̃bā*, *tāmā*, Or. *tambā*, Bi *tā̃bā*, Mth. *tām*, *tāmā*, Bhoj. *tāmā*, H. *tām* in cmpds., *tā̃bā*, *tāmā* m., G. *trā̃bũ*, *tā̃bũ* n.;M. *tā̃bẽ* n. ' copper ', *tā̃b* f. ' rust, redness of sky '; Ko. *tāmbe* n. ' copper '; Si. *taṁba* adj. ' reddish ', sb. ' copper ', (SigGr) *tam*, *tama*. -- Ext. -- *ira* -- : Pk. *taṁbira* -- ' coppercoloured, red ', L. *tāmrā* ' copper -- coloured (of pigeons) '; -- with -- *ḍa* -- : S. *ṭrāmiṛo* m. ' a kind of cooking pot ', *ṭrāmiṛī* ' sunburnt, red with anger ', f. ' copper pot '; Bhoj. *tāmrā* ' copper vessel '; H. *tā̃bṛā*, *tāmṛā* ' coppercoloured, dark red ', m. ' stone resembling a ruby '; G.*tā̃baṛ* n., *trā̃bṛī*, *tā̃bṛī* f. ' copper pot '; OM. *tāṁbaḍā* ' red '. -- X trápu -- q.v. āmrá -- [< IE. **tomró* -- T. Burrow BSOAS xxxviii 65]S.kcch. *trāmo*, *tām(b)o* m. ' copper ', *trāmbhyo* m. ' an old copper coin '; WPah.kc. *cambo* m. ' copper ', J. *cāmbā* m., kṭg. (kc.) *tambɔ* m. (← P. or H. Him.I 89), Garh.*tāmu*, *tā̃bu*.(CDIAL 5779) tāmrakāra m. ' coppersmith ' [tāmrá -- , kāra -- 1]Or. *tāmbarā* ' id. '.(CDIAL 5780) tāmrakuṭṭa m. ' coppersmith ' R. [tāmrá -- , kuṭṭa --]N. *tamauṭe*, *tamoṭe* ' id. '.(CDIAL 5781) *tāmraghaṭa ' copper pot '. [tāmrá -- , ghaṭa -- 1]Bi. *tamheṛī* ' round copper vessel '; -- *tamheṛā* ' brassfounder ' der. **tamheṛ* ' copper pot ' or < next?(CDIAL 5782) *tāmraghaṭaka ' copper -- worker '. [tāmrá -- , ghaṭa -- 2]Bi. *tamheṛā* ' brass -- founder ' or der. fr. **tamheṛ* see prec. (CDIAL 5783) tāmrapaṭṭa m. ' copper plate (for inscribing) ' Yājñ. [Cf. tāmrapattra -- . -- tāmrá -- , paṭṭa -- 1]M. *tā̃boṭī* f. ' piece of copper of shape and size of a brick '.(CDIAL 5786) tāmrapattra n. ' copper plate (for inscribing) ' [Cf. tāmrapaṭṭa -- . -- tāmrá -- , páttra --]Ku.gng. *tamoti* ' copper plate '. (CDIAL 5787) tāmrapātra n. ' copper vessel ' MBh. [tāmrá -- , pā´tra -- Ku.gng. *tamoi* ' copper vessel for water '.(CDIAL 5788) *tāmrabhāṇḍa ' copper vessel '. [tāmrá -- , bhāṇḍa -- 1]Bhoj. *tāmaṛā*, *tāmṛā* ' copper vessel '; G. *tarbhāṇũ* n. ' copper dish used in religious ceremonies ' (< **taramhā̃ḍũ*).(CDIAL 5789) tāmravarṇa ' copper -- coloured ' TĀr. [tāmrá -- , várṇa -- 1]Si. *taṁbavan* ' copper -- coloured, dark red ' (EGS 61) prob. a Si. cmpd.(CDIAL 5790) tāmrākṣa ' red -- eyed ' MBh. [tāmrá -- , ákṣi --]Pa. *tambakkhin* -- ; P. *tamak* f. ' anger '; Bhoj. *tamakhal* ' to be angry '; H. *tamaknā* ' to become red in the face, be angry '.(CDIAL 5791) tāmrika ' coppery ' Mn. [tāmrá --]Pk. *taṁbiya* -- n. ' an article of an ascetic's equipment (a copper vessel?) '; L. *trāmī* f. ' large open vessel for kneading bread ', poṭh. *trāmbī* f. ' brass plate for kneading on '; Ku.gng. *tāmi* ' copper plate '; A. *tāmi* ' copper vessel used in worship '; B. *tāmī*, *tamiyā* ' large brass vessel for cooking pulses at marriages and other ceremonies '; H.*tambiyā* m. ' copper or brass vessel '. (CDIAL 5792)

Text of inscription read rebus: thamba 'pillar' Rebus: tamba 'copper',

mogge 'sprout, bud' Rebus: *mũh* 'ingot' (Santali)

sal 'splinter Rebus: *sal* 'workshop' *ayas* PLUS *khambhaṛā* m. 'fin' (Lahnda); *khambh* 'wing' (Punjabi) ligatured to ayo 'fish' Hence read rebus as *aya kammaṭa.*'coiner, mint alloy' Rebus: *kammaṭa* 'coiner, mint'. Rebus: *kāṇḍā* 'metalware, tools, pots and pans'(Marathi). Thus, inscription with five hieroglyphs reads: copper axe, metal coiner, mint, metalware.

Harappa. Twisted terra cotta tablet (H2000-4441/2102-464) with a mold-made inscription and narrative motif from the Trench 54 area.

 *kharedo* = a currycomb (Gujarati) खरारा [*kharārā*] *m* (H) A currycomb. 2 Currying a horse. (Marathi) Rebus: करडा [*karaḍā*] Hard from alloy--iron, silver &c. (Marathi) *kharādī* ' turner' (Gujarati)

 kanka 'rim of jar' Rebus: karṇīka 'account (scribe)' karṇī 'supercargo'
kuṭila 'bent' CDIAL 3230 kuṭi— in cmpd. 'curve', *kuṭika*— 'bent' MBh. Rebus: *kuṭila, katthīl* = bronze (8 parts copper and 2 parts tin)

Pictorial motif hieroglyphs:
gummaṭ m. 'dome' (Punjabi) CDIAL 4217 Rebus: *kummaṭa, kummaṭe* a chafing dish, a portable stove, a goldsmith's portable furnace (Kannada. Telugu); *kumpiṭu-caṭṭi* chafing-dish, port- able furnace, potsherd in which fire is kept by goldsmiths (Tamil)(DEDR 1752).

kamaḍha 'penance' Rebus: *kammaṭa* 'coiner, mint'.

 Worshipper: *bhaṭā* G. *bhuvɔ* m. ' worshipper in a temple ' rather < bhṛta --(CDIAL 9554) Yājñ.com., Rebus: *bhaṭā* ' kiln, furnace'

Kur. *kaṇḍō* a stool. Malt. *kanḍo* stool, seat. (DEDR 1179) Rebus: *kaṇḍ* 'stone (ore)' as in: ayaskāṇḍa 'excellent iron' (Panini) *kaṇḍa* 'fire-altar' (Santali) कन्दु [Monier-Williams lexicon, p. 250,1]mf. (√स्कन्द् Un2. i , 15), a boiler , saucepan , or other cooking utensil of iron Sus3r. Ma1lav. Comm. on Ka1tyS3r. *kanḍo* stool, seat Rebus: *kāṇḍā* 'metalware, tools, pots and pans'(Marathi). *kaṇḍ* = a furnace, altar (Santali)

Ta. maṇṭi kneeling, kneeling on one knee as an archer. Ma. maṇṭuka to be seated on the heels. Ka. maṇḍi what is bent, the knee. Tu. maṇḍi knee. Te. maṇḍī kneeling on one knee. Pa. maḍtel knee; maḍi kuḍtel kneeling position. Go. (L.) meṇḍā, (G. Mu. Ma.) minḍa knee (Voc. 2827). Konḍa (BB) meḍa, menḍa id. Pe. menḍa id. Manḍ. menḍe id. Kui menḍa id. Kuwi (F.) menda, (S. Su. P.) menḍa, (Isr.) meṇḍa id. Cf. 4645 Ta. maṭaṅku (maṇi-forms). / ? Cf. Skt. maṇḍūkī- (DEDR 4677)

Allograph: maṇḍa = a branch; a twig; a twig with leaves on it (Telugu)

Rebus: maṇḍhwa, maṇḍua, maṇḍwa 'a temporary shed or booth erected on the occasion of a marriage' (Santali) *maṇḍā* = warehouse, workshop (Kon.) maṇḍā = warehouse, workshop (Konkani) maṇḍī. 'large grain market' (Urdu)

H413A kolom 'three' Rebus: kolami 'smithy, forge' sal 'splinter' Rebus: sal 'workshop'. *gummaṭ* m. 'dome' (Punjabi) CDIAL 4217 Rebus: *kummaṭa, kummaṭe* a chafing dish, a portable stove, a goldsmith's portable furnace (Kannada. Telugu) kolom 'three' Rebus: kolami 'smithy, forge' sal 'splinter' Rebus: sal 'workshop'. Thus, the ligatured hieroglyph reads rebus: *kummaṭa kolami sal* 'portable furnace, smithy/forge workshop'.

m0308 Mohenjodaro seal. Person grappling with two flanking tigers standing and rearing on their hindlegs. Comparable to the Mesopotamian cylinder seal (BM 89538), this Indus seal depicts a person with six hair-knots. *kaṇṇahāra* -- m. 'helmsman, sailor'. (काण *kāṇa* 'one-eyed', *āra* 'six', 'rings of hair' symbolic forms).
kannār 'coppersmiths'; *kan* 'copper'.
arye 'lion' Rebus: *āra* 'brass'. *kol* 'tiger' Rebus: *kol* 'working in iron'; *kolhe* 'smelter'. *dula* 'pair' Rebus: *dul* 'cast metal'.

Text of inscription: *ayaskāṇḍa* 'excellent iron' (Pan) *kāṇḍā* 'metalware, tools, pots and pans'(Marathi). *kaṇḍ* = a furnace, altar (Santali)
sal' splinter' Rebus: sal 'workshop'

śagaḍī = lathe (Gujarati) san:gaḍa, 'lathe, portable furnace'; rebus: battle*; jangaḍiyo* 'military guard who accompanies treasure into the treasury' (Gujarati) Rebus: sanghāḍo (Gujarati) cutting stone, gilding (Gujarati); sangatarāśū = stone cutter (Telugu)

dula 'pair' Rebus: dul 'cast metal' PLUS | *koḍa* 'one' Rebus: *koḍ* 'workshop' PLUS INFIXED kolom
three' Rebus: kolami 'smithy, forge' Thus metalware castings forge.

Nindowari 1A खोंड *[khōṇḍa] m A young bull, a bullcalf. (Marathi) Rebus: kõdār 'turner' (Bengali);* कोंद *kōnda 'engraver, lapidary setting or infixing gems' (Marathi) G. sãghāṛɔ m. 'lathe' ;* संघाट *joinery; M. sãgaḍ 'double-canoe' Rebus: sangataras 'stone-cutter, mason'*

kanka 'rim of jar' Rebus: karṇīka 'account (scribe)' karṇī 'supercargo'

खडी [khaḍī] *f* खटी S) A squirrel (Marathi) Rebus 1:Pa. kandi (pl. -l) necklace, beads. Ga. (Punjabi) kandi (pl. -l) bead, (pl.) necklace; (S.2) kandiṭ bead. (DEDR 1215)

Rebus : खंडी [khaṇḍī] A score (of sheep or goats, and of some certain things). A weight equivalent to 500 lbs. , *n. < Mhr. khaṇḍil. [T. Tu. khaṇḍi, M. kaṇḍi.]*

Allograph 'hare' in front of 'thorny bush': kaṇṭin ' *thorny ' (' name of various plants '). [kaṇṭa -- 1]Pk. *kaṁṭiya* -- ' thorny '; S. *kaṇḍī* f. ' thorn bush '; N. *kāṛe* ' thorny '; A. *kāṭi* ' point of an oxgoad ', *kāiṭīyā* ' thorny '; H. *kāṭī* f. ' thorn bush '; G. *kāṭī* f. ' a kind of fish '; M. *kāṭī, kāṭī* f. ' thorn bush '. -- Ext. with -- *la* -- : S. *kaṇḍiru* ' thorny, bony '; -- with -- *lla* -- : Gy. pal. *ḳāndī́la* ' prickly pear '; H.*kā̃ṭīlā*, *kaṭ°* ' thorny '(CDIAL 2769) Rebus: *khāṇḍa* 'tools, pots and pans, metal-ware'. Rebus 2: kaṇḍ 'fire-altar' (Santali) Pictograph of thorn bush is shown in front of 'hare' hieroglyph on copper plates: kulai, 'hare' (Santali), Meluhha Rebus:kolhe 'smelter'. Thus, together the 'thorn bush' PLUS 'hare' hieroglyphs read: *kolhe khāṇḍa* 'smelter metalware'

Allograph 1: கண்டி[1] kaṇṭi *n.* 1. Buffalo bull; எருமைக் கடா. (தொல். பொ. 623.)

Allograph 2: kāḍi, (*VPK*) kāḍi, kāḍimānu, kāḍimāku, kāṇḍi, kāṇi, kāni, kāvaḍi yoke of plough, etc. (Telugu) *Kol.* (Kin.) kāvaṛi carrying yoke. *Pa.* kāñ- to carry with carrying yoke; kācal carrying yoke. (DEDR 1417).

Allograph 3: కండె [kaṇḍe] *kaṇḍe*. [Telugu] n. A head or ear of millet or maize. జొన్నకంకి.

Allograph 4: 'quadrangular shed': *U. cauk- kaṇḍi. Summer-house; quadrangular shed within a garden; தோப்பில் கட்டப்படுஞ் சவுக்கை. Colloq.*

m1776a *खोंड [khōṇḍa] m A young bull, a bullcalf. (Marathi) Rebus: kõdār 'turner' (Bengali); कोंद kōnda 'engraver, lapidary setting or infixing gems' (Marathi) G. sãghāṛɔ m. 'lathe' ; संघाट joinery; M. sãgaḍ 'double-canoe' Rebus: sangataras 'stone-cutter, mason'*

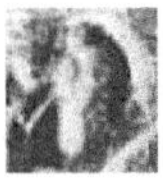

खडी [khaḍī] *f* खटी S) A squirrel (Marathi) Rebus 1:Pa. kandi (pl. -l) necklace, beads. Ga. (Punjabi) kandi (pl. -l) bead, (pl.) necklace; (S.2) kandiṭ bead. (DEDR 1215)

Rebus : खंडी [khaṇḍī] A score (of sheep or goats, and of some certain things). A weight equivalent to 500 lbs. *, n. < Mhr. khaṇḍil. [T. Tu. khaṇḍi, M. kaṇḍi.]*

 kanka 'rim of jar' Rebus: karṇīka 'account (scribe)' karṇī 'supercargo'

There are 15 seals and tablets which include 'black ant' hieroglyph variants:
Signs 54, 55, 57, 58

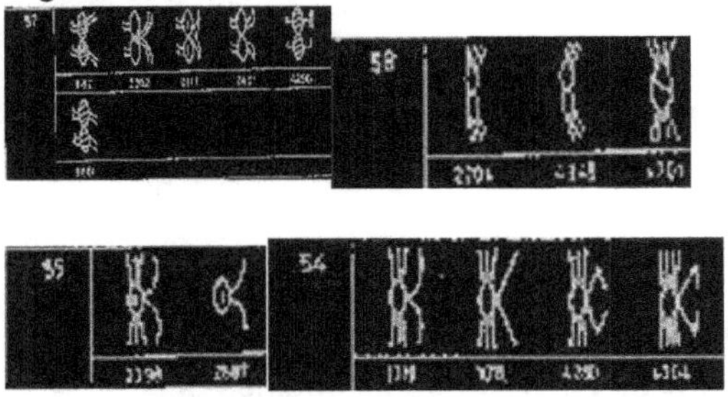

Te. cīma ant. *Kol.* si·ma, (SR.) sime id. *Nk.* śīma id. *Koṇḍa* sīma id. *Kuwi* (F. Su.) sīma, (Punjabi) hīma id. (DEDR 2623)చీమ [cīma] *chīma*. [Telugu] n. An ant. కొండచీమ. The forest ant. రెక్కలచీమ a winged ant. పారేచీమను వింటాడు he can hear an ant crawl, i.e., he is all alive.చీమదూరని అడవి a forest impervious even to an ant. చలిచీమ a black ant ; పై పారేపక్షి క్రిందపారే చీమ (proverb) The bird above, the ant below, i.e., I had no chance with him. చీమంత of the size of an ant. చీమపులి *chīma-puli.* n. The ant lion, an ant-eater.

Cognate etyma in Dravidian related to copper: 2775 *Ta.* cempu copper, gold, metal vessel, liquid measure; cempaṉ brown-coloured cow or bull; tampikai a kind of small water-pot. *Ma.* cempu copper, copper vessel. ? *Ko.* keby, keb-giṇḍy globular metal drinking-vessel with spout. *To.* teb copper; ? köb small brass vessel. *Ka.* cambu, cembu, combu copper, globular copper or glass vessel used for drinking water; cambige, tambige, tambuge globular copper or glass vessel. *Koḍ.* cembï copper, small metal pot. *Tu.* cembu brass, copper, small copper or brass pot; tambigè small, round, metal vessel. *Te.* cembu goblet, pitcher, ewer; tambuga a sort of drinking-vessel. / Cf. Mar. cābū a metal vessel with a belly and a tapering neck, a goglet. Are the Dr. words influenced by Skt. tāmra-, Pkt. tamba- copper? (DEDR 2775).
చీముంత [cīmunta] *chīmunta..* [Telugu] n. A metal vessel. చెంబు.

†cīmara -- 'copper'in *cīmara kāra* -- ' coppersmith ' in Saṁghāṭa -- sūtra Gilgit MS. 37 folio 85 verso, 3 (= *zaṅs -- mkhan* in Tiben Pekin text Vol. 28 Japanese facsimile 285 a 3 which in Mahāvyutpatti 3790 renders *śaulbika* -- BHS ii 533. But the Chinese version (Taishō issaikyō ed. text no. 423 p. 971 col. 3, line 2) has *t'ie* ' iron ': H. W. Bailey 21.2.65). [The Kaf. and Dard. word for ' iron ' appears also in Bur. *čhomār*, *čhumər.*
Turk. *timur* (NTS ii 250) may come from the same unknown source. Semant. cf. lōhá --]
Ash. *ċímä*, *ċimə* ' iron ' (*ċiməkára* ' blacksmith'), Kt. *čimé;*, Wg. *čümā´r*, Pr. *zíme*, Dm. *čimár(r)*, Paš.lauṛ. *čimā´r*, Shum. *čímar*, Woṭ. Gaw. *ċimár*,Kal. *čĩmbar*, Kho. *čúmur*, Bshk. *čimer*, Tor. *čimu*, Mai. *sēwar*, Phal. *čímar*, Sh.gil. *čimĕr* (adj. *čĭmārī*), gur. *čimăr* m., jij. *čimer*, K. *ċamuru* m. (adj.*ċamaruwu*).(CDIAL 14496) cīmara -- Cf. Shgh. *čindōn* ' furnace for smelting iron ' perh. ← Dardic or Kafiri e.g. Kt. *čimə* in cmpds. like *čim -- dur* ' saucepan ']Md. *timara* ' lead, tin '.(CDIAL 4842a)

A cognate in Pali uses the phrase timira akkhin to connote' copper colour': see Pali glosses: Tamba (nt.) [Sk. tāmra, orig. adj.=dark coloured, leaden; cp. Sk. adj. taŋsra id., to tama] copper ("the dark metal"); usually in combinations, signifying colour of or made of (cp. loha bronze), e. g. lākhātamba (adj.) Th 2, 440 (colour of an ox); ˚akkhin Vv 323 (timira˚) Sdhp 286; ˚nakhin J vi.290; ˚nettā (f.)ibid.; ˚bhājana DhA i.395; ˚mattika DhA iv.106;˚vammika DhA iii.208; ˚loha PvA 95 (=loha). Or. *tāmbarā* 'coppersmith' (CDIAL 5780).

h151A

cīmara 'black ant' Rebus: *cīmara* 'copper'. *cīmara kāra* -- ' coppersmith '

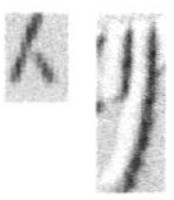

Read in context, the composite hieroglyph is assumed to be a combination of a slanted stroke ligatured to a notch,which provide possible rebus readings of a smithy/forge: notch+slanted stroke reads rebus: *ḍhālako kāṇḍa* 'ingot, tools, pots and pans and metal-ware'

dhāḷ 'a slope'; 'inclination of a plane' (Gujarati); *ḍhāḷiyum* = adj. sloping, inclining (Gujarati) Rebus: *ḍhālako* = a large metal ingot (Gujarati) *ḍhālakī* = a metal heated and poured into a mould; a solid piece of metal; an ingot (Gujarati) PLUS खांडा [*khāṇḍā*] *m* A jag, notch, or indentation (as upon the edge of a tool or weapon). Rebus: *kāṇḍa* 'tools, pots and pans and metal-ware'
|||| Numeral 4: gaṇḍa 'four' Rebus: kaṇḍa 'furnace, fire-altar' (Santali)
||| Numeral 3: kolom 'three' Rebus: kolami 'smithy, forge'
mogge 'sprout, bud' Rebus: *mũh* 'ingot': native cast metal ingot.

h131A

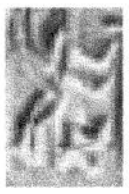

cīmara 'black ant' Rebus: *cīmara* 'copper'. *cīmara kāra* -- ' coppersmith '

ingot. *ḍato* = claws of crab (Santali); *dhātu* = mineral (Sanskrit) Sharp claws ligatured to: *ḍhālako* = a large metal ingot (Gujarati)

सांड [sāṇḍa] *f* (षद S) An outlet for superfluous water (as through a dam or mound); a sluice, a floodvent. Rebus: सांडणी [sāṇḍaṇī] *f* (H) An instrument of goldsmiths. It is hooked or curved at the extremity; and is used to draw things out of the fire.
ranku 'liquid measure' Rebus: ranku 'tin' sal 'splinter' Rebus: sal 'workshop'

baroṭi 'twelve' *bhārata* 'a factitious alloy of copper, pewter, tin' (Marathi)

muka 'ladle' (Tamil)(DEDR 4887) Rebus: *mũh* 'ingot' (Santali) *baṭa* = a kind of iron (Gujarati) *baṭa* = rimless pot (Kannada) Thus, iron ingot.

kolom 'three' Rebus: kolami 'smithy, forge'
aya kammaṭa.'coiner, mint alloy'
ayo ḍhālako 'alloy metal ingot'

kanac 'corner' Rebus: *kañcu* 'bronze' dula 'pair' Rebus: dul 'cast metal' Thus, cast bronze
dula 'pair' Rebus: dul 'cast metal'

kanka 'rim of jar' Rebus: karṇīka 'account (scribe)' karṇī 'supercargo'

h206A h206B

Text 4345
Side A:
kole.l 'temple' Rebus: 'smithy'

muka 'ladle' (Tamil)(DEDR 4887) Rebus: *mũh* 'ingot' (Santali) *baṭa* = a kind of iron (Gujarati) *baṭa* = rimless pot (Kannada) Thus, iron ingot.

cīmara 'black ant' Rebus: *cīmara* 'copper'. *cīmara kāra* -- ' coppersmith '

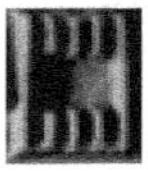

aya kammaṭa.'coiner, mint alloy'
kəṭhā´r, kc. *kuṭhār* m. ' granary, storeroom '(Western Pahari)(CDIAL 3550). *koṭhārī m.* ' storekeeper' (Gujarati)(CDIAL 3551) Thus, storeroom (of) *kolom* 'three' Rebus: *kolami* 'smithy, forge'. Dula 'pair' Rebus: dul 'cast metal' Thus, together *dul kolami kuṭhār* 'metal smithy castings storeroom'

kanka 'rim of jar' Rebus: karṇīka 'account (scribe)' karṇī 'supercargo'

Side B:
kolom 'three' Rebus: kolami 'smithy, forge'
baṭa 'rimless, broad-mouthed pot' Rebus: *bhaṭa* 'furnace' (Gujarati.); *baṭa* 'a kind of iron' (Gujarati)

m1702a *खोंड [khōṇḍa] m A young bull, a bullcalf. (Marathi) Rebus: kõdār 'turner' (Bengali); कोंद kōnda 'engraver, lapidary setting or infixing gems' (Marathi) G. sãghāṛɔ m. 'lathe' ; संघाट joinery; M. sãgaḍ 'double-canoe' Rebus: sangataras 'stone-cutter, mason'*

Variant: *cīmara* 'black ant' Rebus: *cīmara* 'copper'. *cīmara kāra* -- ' coppersmith '
dula 'pair' Rebus: dul 'cast metal'. PLUS *ḍato* = claws of crab (Santali); *dhātu* = mineral (Sanskrit) Thus mineral copper castings.

kanka 'rim of jar' Rebus: karṇīka 'account (scribe)' karṇī 'supercargo'

m730A *खोंड [khōṇḍa] m A young bull, a bullcalf. (Marathi) Rebus: kõdār 'turner' (Bengali); कोंद kōnda 'engraver, lapidary setting or infixing gems' (Marathi) G. sãghāṛɔ m. 'lathe' ; संघाट joinery; M. sãgaḍ 'double-canoe' Rebus: sangataras 'stone-cutter, mason'*

cīmara 'black ant' Rebus: *cīmara* 'copper'. *cīmara kāra* -- ' coppersmith '

kolom 'three' Rebus: kolami 'smithy, forge'

kolmo 'paddy plant' Rebus: *kolami* 'smithy, forge' Vikalpa: *mogge* 'sprout, bud' Rebus: *mũh* 'ingot' (Santali) PLUS 'rim of jar' hieroglyph. Thus, supercargo of smithy, or ingot supercargo.

kuṭila 'bent' CDIAL 3230 kuṭi— in cmpd. 'curve', *kuṭika*— 'bent' MBh. Rebus: *kuṭila, katthīl* = bronze (8 parts copper and 2 parts tin) PLUS *dhāḷ* 'a slope'; 'inclination of a plane' (G.); *ḍhāḷiyum* = adj. sloping, inclining (G.) Rebus: *ḍhālako* = a large metal ingot (G.) *ḍhālakī* = a metal heated and poured into a mould; a solid piece of metal; an

ingot (Gujarati) PLUS खांडा [*khāṇḍā*] *m* A jag, notch, or indentation (as upon the edge of a tool or weapon). Rebus: *kāṇḍa* 'tools, pots and pans and metal-ware' PLUS
meḍ 'body' Rebus: meḍ 'iron' (Ho.) काठी [kāṭhī] f (काष्ट S) 'frame or structure of the body' (Marathi) Rebus: खंडी [khaṇḍī] measure of weight (Marathi) *கண்டி; kaṇṭi, n. < Mhr. khaṇḍil. [T. Tu. khaṇḍi, M. kaṇḍi.]* Candy, a weight, stated to be roughly equivalent to 500 lbs.

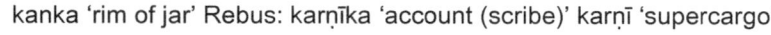

loa 'ficus religiosa' Rebus: *lo* 'iron' (Sanskrit) PLUS unique ligatures: लोखंड [lōkhaṇḍa] *n* (लोह S) Iron. लोखंडाचे चणे खावविणें or चारणें To oppress grievously.लोखंडकाम [lōkhaṇḍakāma] *n* Iron work; that portion (of a building, machine &c.) which consists of iron. 2 The business of an ironsmith.लोखंडी [lōkhaṇḍī] *a* (लोखंड) Composed of iron; relating to iron. (Marathi)

 kanka 'rim of jar' Rebus: karṇīka 'account (scribe)' karṇī 'supercargo'

m735a

खोंड [khōṇḍa] m A young bull, a bullcalf. (Marathi) Rebus: kōdār 'turner' (Bengali); कोंद kōnda 'engraver, lapidary setting or infixing gems' (Marathi) G. sãghārɔ m. 'lathe' ; संघाट joinery; M. sãgaḍ 'double-canoe' Rebus: sangataras 'stone-cutter, mason'

 *cīmara* 'black ant' Rebus: *cīmara* 'copper'. *cīmara kāra* -- ' coppersmith '

kamaḍha 'archer' Rebus: *kammaṭa* 'mint, coiner' PLUS

 *meḍ 'body' Rebus: meḍ 'iron' (Ho.) काठी [kāṭhī] f (काष्ट S) 'frame or structure of the body' (Marathi)* Rebus: खंडी [khaṇḍī] measure of weight (Marathi) *கண்டி; kaṇṭi, n. < Mhr. khaṇḍil. [T. Tu. khaṇḍi, M. kaṇḍi.]* Candy, a weight, stated to be roughly equivalent to 500 lbs.

 *kolmo* 'paddy plant' Rebus: *kolami* 'smithy, forge' Vikalpa: *mogge* 'sprout, bud' Rebus: *mũh* 'ingot' (Santali)
sal 'splinter' Rebus: sal 'workshop'
aya aḍaren (homonym: aduru)'alloy native metal'

 Variant reading: *dula* 'pair' Rebus: dul 'cast metal' *mogge* 'sprout, bud' Rebus: *mũh* 'ingot' (Santali) Thus, cast metal ingot.
dula 'pair' Rebus: dul 'cast (metal)' kolmo 'rice plant' Rebus: kolami 'smithy/forge'

 kanka 'rim of jar' Rebus: karṇīka 'account (scribe)' karṇī 'supercargo'

h170A

 *cīmara* 'black ant' Rebus: *cīmara* 'copper'. *cīmara kāra* -- ' coppersmith '

Ligature:  two peaks: mēḍu height, rising ground, hillock (Kannada) Rebus: *meḍ* 'iron' (Ho.) dula 'pair' Rebus: dul 'cast metal' PLUS |||| Numeral 4: gaṇḍa 'four' Rebus: kaṇḍa 'furnace, fire-altar' (Santali) Thus, iron casting furnace.

kəṭhā´r, kc. *kuṭhār* m. ' granary, storeroom '(WPah.)(CDIAL 3550). *koṭhārī m.* ' storekeeper' (Gujarati)(CDIAL 3551) Thus, storeroom (of) *kolom* 'three' Rebus: *kolami* 'smithy, forge'. Dula 'pair' Rebus: dul 'cast metal' Thus, together *dul kolami kuṭhār* 'metal smithy castings storeroom'

kole.l 'temple' Rebus: kole.l 'smithy' PLUS beads: Pa. kandi (pl. -l) necklace, beads. Ga. (Punjabi) kandi (pl. -l) bead, (pl.) necklace; (S.2) kandiṭ bead. (DEDR 1215) Rebus: *கண்டி; kaṇṭi, n. < Mhr. khaṇḍil. [T. Tu. khaṇḍi, M. kaṇḍi.] 1. Candy, a weight, stated to be roughly equivalent to 500 lbs.; பாரமென் னும் நிறையளவு.* खंडीगणती or खंडोगणती [khaṇḍīgaṇatī or khaṇḍōgaṇatī] *ad* By candies; counting or reckoning by candies. खंडीवारी [khaṇḍīvārī] *ad* By scores, heaps, candies. खंडी [khaṇḍī] Applied to a great quantity; as खंडीभर पोरें, खंडीभर मेंढ्या, खंडीभर काम, खंडीभर बोलतो-लिहितो&c

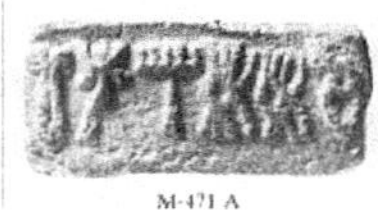

m471A

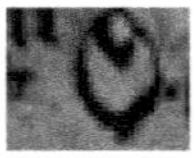

Bronze alloy workshop kañcu sal starting with bronze which is a tin + copper alloy or tin bronze (as distinguished from arsenical bronze, i.e. naturally occurring copper + arsenic).
dula 'pair' Rebus: *dul* 'cast metal' Thus, cast tin bronze.

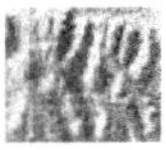

Duplicated black ant hieroglyph:

cīmara 'black ant' Rebus: *cīmara* 'copper'. *cīmara kāra* -- ' coppersmith ' dula 'pair' Rebus: dul 'cast metal'. Thus, cast copper.

aḍar 'harrow'; rebus: *aduru* 'native unsmelted metal'.
bhaṭa 'warrior' (Sanskrit) Rebus: *baṭa* a kind of iron (Gujarati). Rebus: *bhaṭa* 'furnace' (Santali)

kanka 'rim of jar' Rebus: karṇīka 'account (scribe)' karṇī 'supercargo'

m83a *खोंड [khōṇḍa] m A young bull, a bullcalf. (Marathi) Rebus: kõdār 'turner' (Bengali); कोंद kōnda 'engraver, lapidary setting or infixing gems' (Marathi) G. sãghārɔ m. 'lathe' ; संघाट joinery; M. sãgaḍ 'double-canoe' Rebus: sangataras 'stone-cutter, mason'*

m1793a *खोंड [khōṇḍa] m A young bull, a bullcalf. (Marathi) Rebus: kõdār 'turner' (Bengali); कोंद kōnda 'engraver, lapidary setting or infixing gems' (Marathi) G. sãghārɔ m. 'lathe' ; संघाट joinery; M. sãgaḍ 'double-canoe' Rebus: sangataras 'stone-cutter, mason'*
kamaḍha 'crab' Rebus: *kammaṭa* 'mint, coiner'.
ḍato = claws of crab (Santali) Rebus: *dhātu* 'mineral ore'

dhāḷ 'a slope'; 'inclination of a plane' (G.); *ḍhāḷiyum* = adj. sloping, inclining (G.) Rebus: *ḍhālako* = a large metal ingot (G.) *ḍhālakī* = a metal heated and poured into a mould; a

solid piece of metal; an ingot (Gujarati) PLUS खांडा [*khāṇḍā*] *m* A jag, notch, or indentation (as upon the edge of a tool or weapon). Rebus: *kāṇḍa* 'tools, pots and pans and metal-ware' Thus, the pair of sign hieroglyphs from r. read rebus: copper, bronze ingots, metalware
dula 'pair' Rebus: dul 'cast metal'
aya kāṇḍa 'alloy metalware'

h510a *खोंड [khōṇḍa] m A young bull, a bullcalf. (Marathi) Rebus: kõdār 'turner' (Bengali); कोंद kōnda 'engraver, lapidary setting or infixing gems' (Marathi) G. sãghārɔ m. 'lathe' ; संघाट joinery; M. sãgaḍ 'double-canoe' Rebus: sangataras 'stone-cutter, mason'*
kamaḍha 'crab' Rebus: *kammaṭa* 'mint, coiner'.
ḍato = claws of crab (Santali) Rebus: *dhātu* 'mineral ore'

dhāḷ 'a slope'; 'inclination of a plane' (G.); *ḍhāḷiyum* = adj. sloping, inclining (G.) Rebus: *ḍhālako* = a large metal ingot (G.) *ḍhālakī* = a metal heated and poured into a mould; a solid piece of metal; an ingot (Gujarati) PLUS खांडा [*khāṇḍā*] *m* A jag, notch, or indentation (as upon the edge of a tool or weapon). Rebus: *kāṇḍa* 'tools, pots and pans and metal-ware' Thus, the pair of sign hieroglyphs from r. read rebus: copper, bronze ingots, metalware
ranku 'liquid measure' Rebus: *ranku* 'tin'

kolmo 'paddy plant' Rebus: *kolami* 'smithy, forge' Vikalpa: *mogge* 'sprout, bud' Rebus: *mūh* 'ingot' (Santali)

kanka 'rim of jar' Rebus: karṇīka 'account (scribe)' karṇī 'supercargo'

m49a *खोंड [khōṇḍa] m A young bull, a bullcalf. (Marathi) Rebus: kõdār 'turner' (Bengali); कोंद kōnda 'engraver, lapidary setting or infixing gems' (Marathi) G. sãghārɔ m. 'lathe' ; संघाट joinery; M. sãgaḍ 'double-canoe' Rebus: sangataras 'stone-cutter, mason'*

cīmara 'black ant' Rebus: *cīmara* 'copper'. *cīmara kāra* -- ' coppersmith '

dula 'pair' Rebus: *dul* 'cast metal'

|||| Numeral 4: gaṇḍa 'four' Rebus: kaṇḍa 'furnace, fire-altar' (Santali) dula 'pair' Rebus: dul 'cast metal'

Strands of yarn/rope' hieroglyph: Hieroglyph: 'strands of yarn' Rebus reading: *dhā'tu* 'strand of rope' Rebus: *dhatu* 'mineral ore' (Santali)

dula 'pair' Rebus: *dul* 'cast metal'
ayo 'fish' Rebus: *aya* 'iron' *ayas* 'metal'

aya kammaṭa.'coiner, mint alloy'
kamaḍha 'crab' Rebus: *kammaṭa* 'mint, coiner'.
ḍato = claws of crab (Santali) Rebus: *dhātu* 'mineral ore'

m115a
खोंड [khōṇḍa] m A young bull, a bullcalf. (Marathi) Rebus: kõdār 'turner' (Bengali); कोंद kōnda 'engraver, lapidary setting or infixing gems' (Marathi) G. sãghāṛɔ m. 'lathe' ; संघाट joinery; M. sāgaḍ 'double-canoe' Rebus: sangataras 'stone-cutter, mason'

.

cīmara 'black ant' Rebus: *cīmara* 'copper'. *cīmara kāra* -- ' coppersmith '

Strands of yarn/rope' hieroglyph: Hieroglyph: 'strands of yarn' Rebus reading: *dhā´tu* 'strand of rope' Rebus: *dhatu* 'mineral ore' (Santali)

dula 'pair' Rebus: *dul* 'cast (metal)' PLUS*kana, kanac* = corner (Santali); Rebus: *kañcu* = bronze (Telugu) PLUS infixed kolmo 'paddy plant' Rebus: kolami 'smithy, forge'. Thus, cast bronze smithy, forge. Or, mogge 'sprout, bud' Rebus: mũh 'ingot' (Santali)Thus, cast bronze ingot. Read as: kañcu dul mũh 'bronze cast ingot'

baraḍo = spine; backbone (Tulu) Rebus: *baran, bharat* 'mixed alloys' (5 copper, 4 zinc and 1 tin) (Punjabi)

loa 'ficus religiosa' Rebus: *lo* 'iron' (Sanskrit) PLUS unique ligatures: लोखंड [lōkhaṇḍa] *n* (लोह S) Iron. लोखंडाचे चणे खाववणें or चारणें To oppress grievously.लोखंडकाम [lōkhaṇḍakāma] *n* Iron work; that portion (of a building, machine &c.) which consists of iron. 2 The business of an ironsmith.लोखंडी [lōkhaṇḍī] *a* (लोखंड) Composed of iron; relating to iron. (Marathi) *bhaṭa* 'warrior' (Sanskrit) Rebus: *baṭa* a kind of iron (Gujarati). Rebus: *bhaṭa* 'furnace' (Santali) Thus, together, th ligatured hieroglyph reads rebus: *loa bhaṭa* 'iron furnace'

dula 'pair' Rebus: *dul* 'cast (metal)' PLUS*kana, kanac* = corner (Santali); Rebus: *kañcu* = bronze (Telugu) Thus, cast bronze. PLUS खांडा [*khāṇḍā*] *m* A jag, notch, or indentation (as upon the edge of a tool or weapon). Rebus: *kāṇḍa* 'tools, pots and pans and metal-ware' Thus, cast bronze metalware.

kolmo 'paddy plant' Rebus: *kolami* 'smithy, forge' Vikalpa: *mogge* 'sprout, bud' Rebus: *mũh* 'ingot' (Santali)

m1087A Pictorial motif hieroglyph: *balad* m. ' ox ', gng. *bald,* (Ku.) *barad,* id. (N. Tarai) Rebus: *bharat* (5 copper, 4 zinc and 1 tin)(Punjabi) *pattar* 'trough' Rebus*:* *pattar* 'guild'. Thus, copper-zinc-tin alloy (worker) guild.

| *koḍa* 'one' Rebus: *koḍ* 'workshop' dula 'pair' Rebus: dul 'cast metal'. Sal 'splinter' Rebus: sal 'workshop' Thus cast metal workshop.
kamaḍha 'crab' Rebus: *kammaṭa* 'mint, coiner'.
ḍato = claws of crab (Santali) Rebus: *dhātu* 'mineral ore'

dhāḷ 'a slope'; 'inclination of a plane' (G.); *ḍhāḷiyum* = adj. sloping, inclining (G.) Rebus: *ḍhālako* = a large metal ingot (G.) *ḍhālakī* = a metal heated and poured into a mould; a solid piece of metal; an ingot (Gujarati) PLUS खांडा [*khāṇḍā*] *m* A jag, notch, or indentation (as upon the edge of a tool or weapon). Rebus: *kāṇḍa* 'tools, pots and pans and metal-ware' Thus, the pair of sign hieroglyphs from r. read rebus: copper, bronze ingots, metalware

Strands of yarn/rope' hieroglyph: Hieroglyph: 'strands of yarn' Rebus reading: *dhā'tu* 'strand of rope' Rebus: *dhatu* 'mineral ore' (Santali)

h144A

cīmara 'black ant' Rebus: *cīmara* 'copper'. *cīmara kāra* -- ' coppersmith '

kamaḍha 'bow and arrow' Rebus: *kammaṭa* 'mint, coiner'.
kanac 'corner' Rebus: *kañcu* 'bronze' dula 'pair' Rebus: dul 'cast metal' Thus cast bronze.

| *koḍa* 'one' Rebus: *koḍ* 'workshop'

Forging in a smithy using a snarling iron

The basic tool of a smith for forging ingots into metalware is a snarling iron. An example with an inscription is provided from a Chanhudaro artifact.

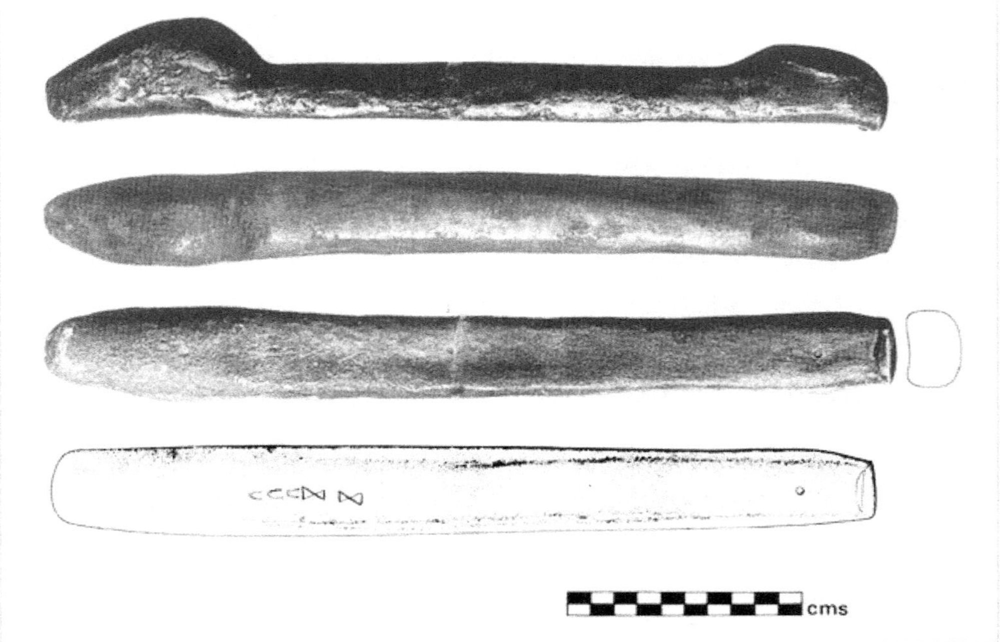

Snarling iron excavated from Chanhudaro, now kept in Purana Qila Fort, Delhi. Dated to ca. mid-third millennium BCE.

Such a snarling iron would hae been held in the center of every working platform, of the type found in Harappa, thus making each circular platform a forge.

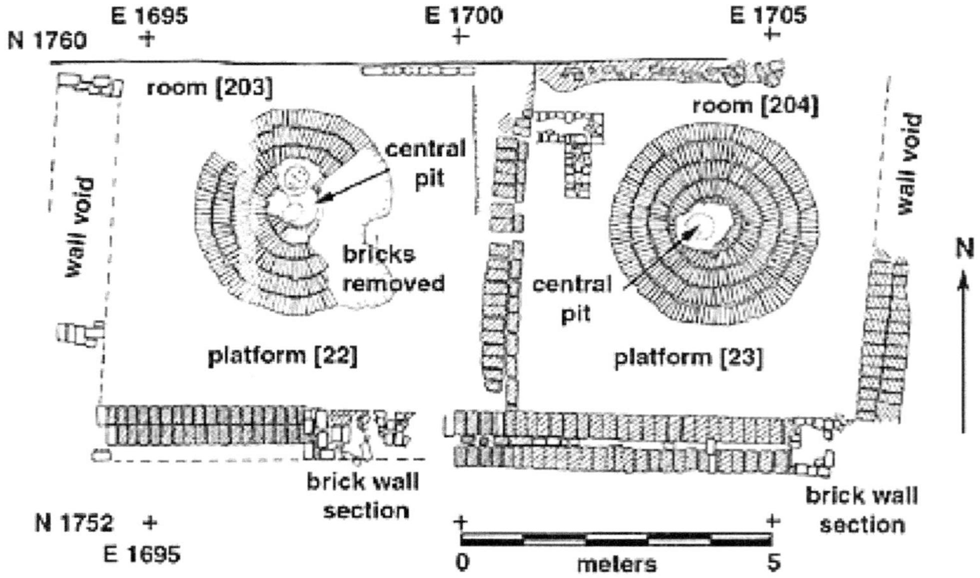

(After Figure 8. Harappa 1998, Mound F, Trench 43: A plan of circular platforms)

Slide 353. harappa.com Circular platforms in the southwestern part of Mound F excavated by M.S. Vats in the 1920s and 1930s, as conserved by the Department of Archaeology and Museums, Government of Pakistan.

Large updraft kiln of the Harappan period (ca. 2400 BCE) found during excavations on Mound E Harappa, 1989 (After Fig. 8.8, Kenoyer, 2000)

Text of inscription on the snarling iron  *dul meḍ* 'iron casting' PLUS *kolami baṭa* 'smithy, kiln'

Read rebus from r.:

meṭ sole of foot, footstep, footprint (Ko.); meṭṭu step, stair, treading, slipper (Te.)(DEDR 1557) Rebus: *meḍ* 'iron' (Ho.) PLUS *dula* 'pair' Rebus: *dul* 'metal casting'. Thus, read as iron metal casting. Thus, *dul meṛed*, cast iron (Mundari) This is distinguished from koṭe meṛed = forged iron.

kolom 'three' Rebus: *kolami* 'smithy, forge' PLUS M. bhaṭṭā m. ' pot of fire ', *baṭi* 'broad-mouthed, rimless metal vessel') *baṭhu* m. 'large pot in which grain is parched.' Rebus: *baṭi* 'smelting furnace'. Rebus: baṭa = a kind of iron (G.) bhaṭa 'furnace' (G.) baṭa = kiln (Santali). bhaṭa = an oven, kiln, furnace (Santali) baṭhi furnace for smelting ore (the same as kuṭhi) (SantaliRebus: *baṭi, bhaṭi* 'furnace' (Hindi) Rebus: mẽṛhẽt baṭi = iron (Ore) furnaces (Santali).A. bhaṭā ' brick -- or lime -- kiln '; B. bhāṭi ' kiln '; Or. bhāṭi ' brick -- kiln, distilling pot '; Mth. bhaṭhī, bhaṭṭī ' brick -- kiln, furnace, still '; Aw.lakh. bhāṭhā ' kiln '; H. bhaṭṭhā m. ' kiln ', bhaṭ f. ' kiln, oven, fireplace '; bhaṭṭī f. 'forge'(CDIAL 9656).

A snarling iron as an anvil could be represented as a hieroglyph:

araṇe 'lizard' Rebus: *airaṇ* 'anvil'. The stylized hieroglyph sig connotes such a snarling iron.

The stylized curved line may denote a lizard's tail. – as seen on many epigraphs such as

Lothal 26 and Harappa 688. The hieroglyph may be a variant of:  *kana, kanac* = corner (Santali); Rebus: *kañcu* = bronze (Telugu) PLUS खांडा [*khāṇḍā*] *m* A jag, notch, or indentation (as upon the edge of a tool or weapon). Rebus: *kāṇḍa* 'tools, pots and pans and metal-ware' Thus, bronze metalware.

Lothal 26a *खोंड [khōṇḍa] m A young bull, a bullcalf. (Marathi) Rebus: kõdār 'turner' (Bengali); कोंद kōnda 'engraver, lapidary setting or infixing gems' (Marathi) G. sãghārɔ m. 'lathe' ; संघाट joinery; M. sãgaḍ 'double-canoe' Rebus: sangataras 'stone-cutter, mason'*

A snarling iron as an anvil could be represented as a hieroglyph:

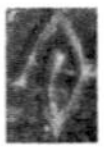

araṇe 'lizard' Rebus: *airaṇ* 'anvil'. The stylized hieroglyph sig connotes such a snarling iron. The hieroglyph may be a variant of:  *kana, kanac* = corner (Santali); Rebus: *kañcu* = bronze (Telugu) PLUS खांडा [*khāṇḍā*] *m* A jag, notch, or indentation (as upon the edge of a tool or weapon). Rebus: *kāṇḍa* 'tools, pots and pans and metal-ware' Thus, bronze metalware.

kanka 'rim of jar' Rebus: karṇīka 'account (scribe)' karṇī 'supercargo'

h688A

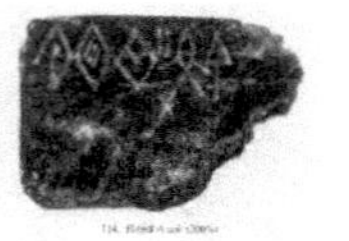

खोंड [khōṇḍa] m A young bull, a bullcalf. (Marathi) Rebus: kõdār 'turner' (Bengali); कोंद kōnda 'engraver, lapidary setting or infixing gems' (Marathi) G. sãghārɔ m. 'lathe' ; संघाट joinery; M. sãgaḍ 'double-canoe' Rebus: sangataras 'stone-cutter, mason'

A snarling iron as an anvil could be represented as a hieroglyph:

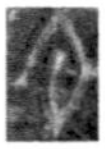

araṇe 'lizard' Rebus: *airaṇ* 'anvil'. The stylized hieroglyph sig connotes such a snarling iron. The hieroglyph may be a variant of:  *kana, kanac* = corner (Santali); Rebus: *kañcu* = bronze (Telugu) PLUS खांडा [*khāṇḍā*] *m* A jag, notch, or indentation (as upon the edge of a tool or weapon). Rebus: *kāṇḍa* 'tools, pots and pans and metal-ware' Thus, bronze metalware.

h40a खोंड *[khōṇḍa] m A young bull, a bullcalf. (Marathi) Rebus: kõdār 'turner' (Bengali);* कोंद *kōnda 'engraver, lapidary setting or infixing gems' (Marathi) G. sãghāṛɔ m. 'lathe' ;* संघाट *joinery; M. sãgaḍ 'double-canoe' Rebus: sangataras 'stone-cutter, mason'*

12859) Rebus*: sangataras.* संगतराश lit. 'to collect stones, stone-cutter, mason.'
A snarling iron as an anvil could be represented as a hieroglyph:

 *araṇe* 'lizard' Rebus: *airaṇ* 'anvil'. The stylized hieroglyph sig connotes such a snarling

iron. The hieroglyph may be a variant of:  *kana, kanac* = corner (Santali); Rebus: *kañcu* = bronze (Telugu) PLUS खांडा [*khāṇḍā*] *m* A jag, notch, or indentation (as upon the edge of a tool or weapon). Rebus: *kāṇḍa* 'tools, pots and pans and metal-ware' Thus, bronze metalware.

 kanka 'rim of jar' Rebus: karṇīka 'account (scribe)' karṇī 'supercargo'

h12a

A snarling iron as an anvil could be represented as a hieroglyph:

araṇe 'lizard' Rebus: *airaṇ* 'anvil'. The stylized hieroglyph sig

connotes such a snarling iron. The hieroglyph may be a variant of:  *kana, kanac* = corner (Santali); Rebus: *kañcu* = bronze (Telugu) PLUS खांडा [*khāṇḍā*] *m* A jag, notch, or indentation (as upon the edge of a tool or weapon). Rebus: *kāṇḍa* 'tools, pots and pans and metal-ware' Thus, bronze metalware.

'Bat' hieroglyph: Pa. *vagguli* -- m.f., *°lī* -- f. ' bat ', Pk. *vagguli* -- m.; G. *vāgoḷ* f. ' flying fox ' Rebus: bagalo = an Arabian merchant vessel (Gujarati) bagala = an Arab boat of a particular description (Kannada); bagalā (Marathi); bagarige, bagarage = a kind of vessel (Kannada)

kanac 'corner' Rebus: *kañcu* 'bronze' *sal* 'splinter' Rebus: *sal* 'workshop'

koḍa 'one' Rebus: *koḍ* 'workshop ayo 'fish' Rebus: aya 'iron' (Gujarati) ayas 'metal' (Vedic)

aya aḍaren (homonym: aduru)'alloy native metal'

 kanka 'rim of jar' Rebus: karṇīka 'account (scribe)' karṇī 'supercargo'

 Read in context, the composite hieroglyph is assumed to be a combination of a slanted stroke ligatured to a notch,which provide possible rebus readings of a smithy/forge: notch+slanted stroke reads rebus: *ḍhālako kāṇḍa* 'ingot, tools, pots and pans and metal-ware'

dhāḷ 'a slope'; 'inclination of a plane' (Gujarati); *ḍhāḷiyum* = adj. sloping, inclining (Gujarati) Rebus: *ḍhālako* = a large metal ingot (Gujarati) *ḍhālakī* = a metal heated and poured into a mould; a solid piece of metal; an ingot (Gujarati) PLUS खांडा [*khāṇḍā*] *m* A jag, notch, or indentation (as upon the edge of a tool or weapon). Rebus: *kāṇḍa* 'tools, pots and pans and metal-ware'

mogge 'sprout, bud' Rebus: *mūh* 'ingot'

m311A Pictorial motif hieroglyph: *khōṇḍa* A stock or stump (Marathi) Rebus: *खोंड [khōṇḍa] m A young bull, a bullcalf. (Marathi) Rebus: kōdār 'turner' (Bengali); कोंद kōnda 'engraver, lapidary setting or infixing gems' (Marathi) G. sãghāṛɔ m. 'lathe' ; संघाट joinery; M. sāgaḍ 'double-canoe' Rebus: sangataras 'stone-cutter, mason'* *ṭagara*'ram' Rebus: *tagara* 'tin' Vikalpa: *miṇḍāl* 'markhor' (Tōrwālī) *meḍho* a ram, a sheep (Gujarati)(CDIAL 10120) Rebus: *mẽṛhẽt, meḍ* 'iron' (Mu.Ho.)

kola 'woman' kol 'tiger' Rebus: kolhe 'smelters'. Thus, the profession is: smelter, tin, turner, engraver.

Text: A snarling iron as an anvil could be represented as a hieroglyph:

araṇe 'lizard' Rebus: *airaṇ* 'anvil'. The stylized hieroglyph sig connotes such a snarling iron. The hieroglyph may be a variant of:  *kana, kanac* = corner (Santali); Rebus: *kañcu* = bronze (Telugu) PLUS खांडा [*khāṇḍā*] *m* A jag, notch, or indentation (as upon the edge of a tool or weapon). Rebus: *kāṇḍa* 'tools, pots and pans and metal-ware' Thus, bronze metalware.

koḍi 'flag' (Tamil)(DEDR 2049). Rebus 1: *koḍ* 'workshop' (Kuwi) Rebus 2: *khōḍ* m. 'pit', *khōḍü* f. 'small pit' (Kashmiri. CDIAL 3947).

khareḍo = a currycomb (Gujarati) खरारा [*kharārā*] *m* (H) A currycomb. 2 Currying a horse. (Marathi) Rebus: करडा [*karaḍā*] Hard from alloy--iron, silver &c. (Marathi) *kharādī* ' turner' (Gujarati) sal 'splinter' Rebus: sal 'workshop' Thus, hard alloys workshop.

m95a *खोंड [khōṇḍa] m A young bull, a bullcalf. (Marathi) Rebus: kōdār 'turner' (Bengali); कोंद kōnda 'engraver, lapidary setting or infixing gems' (Marathi) G. sãghāṛɔ m. 'lathe' ; संघाट joinery; M. sāgaḍ 'double-canoe' Rebus: sangataras 'stone-cutter, mason'*

A snarling iron as an anvil could be represented as a hieroglyph:

araṇe 'lizard' Rebus: *airaṇ* 'anvil'. The stylized hieroglyph sig connotes such a snarling iron.

The hieroglyph may be a variant of:  *kana, kanac* = corner (Santali); Rebus: *kañcu* = bronze (Telugu) PLUS खांडा [*khāṇḍā*] *m* A jag, notch, or indentation (as upon the edge of a tool or weapon). Rebus: *kāṇḍa* 'tools, pots and pans and metal-ware' Thus, bronze metalware.

m211A खोंड [khōṇḍa] m A young bull, a bullcalf. (Marathi) Rebus: kōdār 'turner' (Bengali); कोंद kōnda 'engraver, lapidary setting or infixing gems' (Marathi) G. sãghāṛɔ m. 'lathe' ; संघाट joinery; M. sãgaḍ 'double-canoe' Rebus: sangataras 'stone-cutter, mason'

A snarling iron as an anvil could be represented as a hieroglyph:
araṇe 'lizard' Rebus: *airaṇ* 'anvil'. The stylized hieroglyph sig connotes such a snarling iron.

The hieroglyph may be a variant of:  *kana, kanac* = corner (Santali); Rebus: *kañcu* = bronze (Telugu) PLUS खांडा [*khāṇḍā*] *m* A jag, notch, or indentation (as upon the edge of a tool or weapon). Rebus: *kāṇḍa* 'tools, pots and pans and metal-ware' Thus, bronze metalware. | *koḍa* 'one' Rebus: *koḍ* 'workshop'

ayo 'fish' Rebus: *aya* 'iron' *ayas* 'metal' sal 'splinter' Rebus: sal 'workshop'
bhaṭa 'warrior' (Sanskrit) Rebus: *baṭa* a kind of iron (Gujarati). Rebus: *bhaṭa* 'furnace' (Santali)

kanka 'rim of jar' Rebus: karṇīka 'account (scribe)' karṇī 'supercargo'

meḍ 'body' Rebus: meḍ 'iron' (Ho.) काठी [kāṭhī] f (काष्ट S) 'frame or structure of the body' (Marathi) Rebus: खंडी [khaṇḍī] measure of weight (Marathi) கண்டி; *kaṇṭi, n. < Mhr. khaṇḍil. [T. Tu. khaṇḍi, M. kaṇḍi.]* Candy, a weight, stated to be roughly equivalent to 500 lbs.

Meluhha smithy artisans in Tell Asmar

Glazed steatite . Cylinder seal. 3.4cm high; imported from Indus valley. Rhinoceros, elephant, crocodile (lizard?).Tell Asmar (Eshnunna), Iraq. IM 14674; Frankfort, 1955, No. 642; Collon, 1987, Fig. 610. *Ibha* 'elephant'
Rebus: *ibbo* 'merchant', *ib* 'iron' Rhinoceros*; baḍhia* = a castrated boar, a hog (Santali) *baḍhi* 'a caste who work both in iron and wood' (Santali) *baṟea* 'merchant' Vikalpa: காண்டாமிருகம் kāṇṭā-mirukam , *n.* [M. *kāṇṭāmṛgam.*] கல்யானை. Rebus: *kāṇḍā* 'metalware, tools, pots and pans'.*kāru* 'crocodile' Rebus: *kāru* 'artisan'.
Mohenjo-daro Meluhha artisan guild
Obverse of m1395 and m0441 'Three tigers':
kolom 'three' Rebus: kolami 'smithy, forge'
kol 'tiger' Rebus: kolhe 'smelters'.

sangaḍi = joined animals (Marathi) Rebus: *sãghāṛɔ* m. 'lathe' (Gujarati); *sãgāḍā* m. ' frame of a building ', °*ḍī* f. ' lathe '(CDIAL 12859) *sangataras.* संगतराश lit. 'to collect stones, stone-cutter, mason.'

m1393t

m1394t

m440A

Seal. Mohenjo-
sealing from
depicting a

daro. Terracotta
Mohenjo-daro
collection of animals

m0439t

m1395Bt t

m0441Bt

and some script symbols. In the centre is a lizard (gharial?) surrounded by other animals including a monkey. Source:
http://www.harappa.com/indus/32.html In the center: *araṇe* 'lizard' Rebus: *airaṇ* 'anvil'.(A Tepe Yahya epigraphs clearly indicate a lizard hieroglyph).

meḍ 'body' Rebus: meḍ 'iron' (Ho.) *काठी [kāṭhī] f (काष्ट S) 'frame or structure of the body' (Marathi)* Rebus: खंडी [khaṇḍī] measure of weight (Marathi) *கண்டி; kaṇṭi, n. < Mhr. khaṇḍil. [T. Tu. khaṇḍi, M. kaṇḍi.]* Candy, a weight, stated to be roughly equivalent to 500 lbs.

Ta. kōṭaram monkey. *Ir.* kōḍa (small)monkey; kūḍag monkey. *Ko.* ko·ṛṇ small monkey. *To.* kwṛṇ monkey. *Ka.* kōḍaga monkey, ape. *Koḍ.* ko·ḍë monkey. *Tu.* koḍañji, koḍañja, koḍaṅgů baboon. (DEDR 2196). kuṭhāru = a monkey (Sanskrit) Rebus: kuṭhāru 'armourer or weapons maker'(metal-worker), also an inscriber or writer.

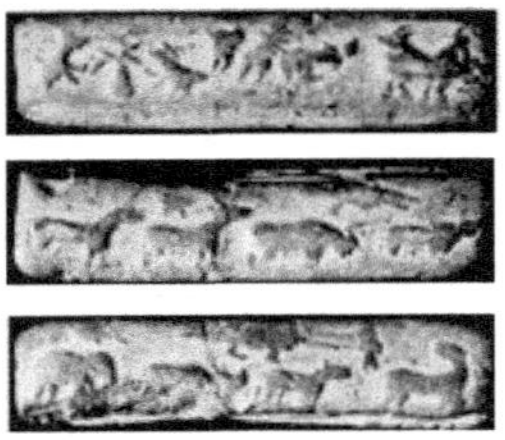

m0489 A, B, C Prism tablet.
Side A:
pasaramu, pasalamu = an animal, a beast, a brute, quadruped (Telugu) Rebus: pasra 'smithy' (Santali)
ranku 'antelope' Rebus: ranku 'tin' dula 'pair' Rebus: dul 'cast metal' Thus cast tin.
ranku 'fornication, adultery' Rebus: ranku 'tin'.
mlekh 'goat' Rebus: milakkha 'copper' PLUS mēḍu height, rising ground, hillock (Kannada) Rebus: *meḍ* 'iron' (Ho.) PLUS dula 'pair' Rebus: dul 'cast metal' Thus iron, copper castings.
Side B: ayakara 'fish + crocodile' Rebus: metalsmith.
meḍho a ram, a sheep (G.)(CDIAL 10120) Rebus: *mẽṛhẽt, meḍ* 'iron' (Mu.Ho.)
balad m. ' ox ', gng. *bald*, (Ku.) *barad*, id. (N. Tarai) Rebus: *bharat* (5 copper, 4 zinc and 1 tin)(Punjabi) *pattar* 'trough' Rebus: *pattar* 'guild'. Thus, copper-zinc-tin alloy (worker) guild.
खोंड [khōṇḍa] m A young bull, a bullcalf. (Marathi) Rebus: kōdār 'turner' (Bengali); कोंद kōnda 'engraver, lapidary setting or infixing gems' (Marathi) G. sãghāṛɔ m. 'lathe' ; संघाट joinery; M. sãgaḍ 'double-canoe' Rebus: sangataras 'stone-cutter, mason'
kul 'tiger' (Santali); *kōlu* id. (Telugu) kōlupuli = Bengal tiger (Te.) कोल्हा [kōlhā] कोल्हें [kōlhēṃ] A jackal (Marathi) Rebus: *kole.l* 'temple, smithy' (Kota.) *kol* = pañcalōha, a metallic alloy containing five metals (Tamil): copper, brass, tin, lead and iron (Sanskrit); an alternative list of five metals: gold, silver, copper, tin (lead), and iron (dhātu; Nānārtharatnākara. 82; Mangarāja's Nighaṇṭu. 498)(Kannada) *kol, kolhe*, 'the *koles*, iron smelters speaking a language akin to that of Santals' (Santali)
krammara 'look back' (Telugu) Rebus: kamar 'metalsmith' (Santali)
baḍhi 'a caste who work both in iron and wood' (Santali) *baṟea* 'merchant'
Ibha 'elephant' Rebus: *ibbo* 'merchant', *ib* 'iron'

Ia. 18

Shahdad seal (Grave 78) *meṭ* sole of foot, footstep, footprint (Ko.); *meṭṭu* step, stair, treading, slipper (Te.)(DEDR 1557) Rebus: *meḍ* 'iron' (Ho.) PLUS *dula* 'pair' Rebus: *dul* 'metal casting'. Thus, read as iron metal casting. Thus, *dul meṛed*, cast iron

(Mundari) This is distinguished from koṭe meṛed = forged iron. Vikalpa: Hieroglyph: *aṭi* foot, footprint (Tamil) Rebus: *aḍe, aḍa, aḍi* the piece of wood on which the five artisans put the article which they happen to operate upon, a support (Kannada) பட்டடை[1] paṭṭaṭai , n. prob. படு[1]- + அடை[1]-. 1. [T. paṭṭika, K. paṭṭaḍe.] Anvil; அடைகல். (பிங்.) *சீரிடங்காணி னெறிதற்குப் பட்ட டை* (குறள், 821). 2. [K. paṭṭaḍi.] Smithy, forge; கொல்லன் களரி.கொல்லன்பட்டடை kollaṉ-paṭṭaṭai , n. < கொல்லன் +. Anvil; அடைகல். (C. G.)அடைகுறடு aṭai-kuṟaṭu , n. < அடை[1]- +. 1. Anvil; கம்மியர் பட்டடை. (பிங்.)

Tepe Yahya. Seal impressions of two sides of a seal. Six-legged lizard and opposing footprints shown on opposing sides of a double-sided steatite stamp seal perforated along the lateral axis. Lamberg- Karlovsky 1971: fig. 2C Shahr-i-Soktha Stamp seal shaped like a foot.

Hieroglyph: araṇe 'lizard' (Tulu) eraṇi f. ' anvil ' (Gujarati); aheraṇ, ahiraṇ, airaṇ, airṇī, haraṇ f. (Marathi)

Hieroglyph: *bhaṭa* 'six' (G.) rebus: *baṭa* = kiln (Santali) *baṭa* = a kind of iron (Gujarati) [Note: six legs shown on the lizard glyph] Vikalpa: *āra 'sx'* Rebus: *āra 'brass'.*

Twisted rope as hieroglyph on a plaque. Hieroglyph: मेढा [mēḍhā] 'a curl or snarl; twist in thread' (Marathi) Rebus: mẽṛhẽt, meḍ 'iron' (Mu.Ho.)
Technical description Votive bas-relief of Dudu, priest of Ningirsu in the time of Entemena, prince of Lagash C. 2400 BCE Tello (ancient Girsu) Bituminous stone H. 25 cm; W. 23 cm; Th. 8 cm De Sarzec excavations, 1881 AO 2354 Plaques perforated in the center and decorated with scenes incised or carved in relief
Twisted rope: मेढा [mēḍhā] A twist or tangle arising in thread or cord, a curl or snarl.(Marathi)(CDIAL 10312).L. *meṛh* f. 'rope tying oxen to each other and to post on threshing floor'(CDIAL 10317) Rebus: *meḍ* 'iron'. *mẽṛhet* 'iron' (Mu.Ho.)
eruvai 'eagle' Rebus: eruvai 'copper' kol 'tiger' Rebus: kolhe 'smelters'
arye 'lion' Rebus: *araa* 'brass'
खोंड [khōṇḍa] m A young bull, a bullcalf. (Marathi) Rebus: kõdār 'turner' (Bengali); कोंद kōnda 'engraver, lapidary setting or infixing gems' (Marathi) G. sãghāṛɔ m. 'lathe' ; संघाट joinery; M. sãgaḍ 'double-canoe' Rebus: sangataras 'stone-cutter, mason'

Section D: Copper, brass

Sign hieroglyph: spokes of wheel, nave of wheel

Starting pair of hieroglyph signs on texts of inscriptions: 'spokes-nave-of-wheel' PLUS 'notch'

āra 'spokes' Rebus: *āra* 'brass'. cf. erka = ekke (Tbh. of arka) aka (Tbh. of arka) copper (metal)

खांडा [*khāṇḍā*] *m* A jag, notch, or indentation (as upon the edge of a tool or weapon). (Marathi) Rebus: *khāṇḍā* 'tools, pots and pans, metal-ware'.

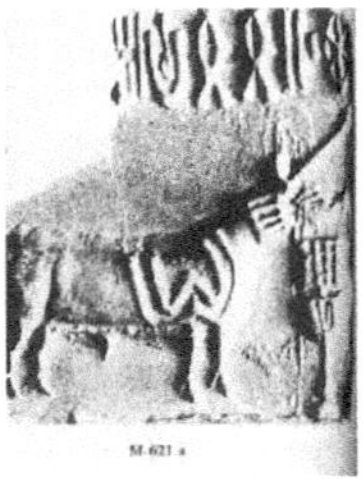

m621a Pictorial motif hieroglyphs;
खोंड [khōṇḍa] m A young bull, a bullcalf. (Marathi) Rebus: kõdār 'turner' (Bengali); कोंद kōnda 'engraver, lapidary setting or infixing gems' (Marathi) G. sãghāṛɔ m. 'lathe' ; संघाट joinery; M. sãgaḍ 'double-canoe' Rebus: sangataras. संगतराश lit. 'to collect stones, stone-cutter, mason.'

Allograph:  'Structural form' hieroglyph

Text hieroglyph signs:

āra 'spokes' Rebus: *āra* 'brass'. cf. erka = ekke (Tbh. of arka) aka (Tbh. of arka) copper (metal)
खांडा [khāṇḍā] *m* A jag, notch, or indentation (as upon the edge of a tool or weapon). (Marathi) Rebus:*khāṇḍā* 'tools, pots and pans, metal-ware'.

dula 'pair' Rebus: dul 'castmetal'
ayo 'fish' Rebus: aya 'iron' (Gujarati) ayas 'metal' (Sanskrit) dula 'pair' Rebus: dul 'cast metal'

m1346a

āra 'spokes' Rebus: *āra* 'brass'. cf. erka = ekke (Tbh. of arka) aka (Tbh. of arka) copper (metal)
खांडा [*khāṇḍā*] *m* A jag, notch, or indentation (as upon the edge of a tool or weapon). (Marathi) Rebus: *khāṇḍā* 'tools, pots and pans, metal-ware'.

dul kuṭila khānḍa 'bronze cast metalware'

ayo 'fish' Rebus*: aya* 'iron' *ayas* 'metal'
dula 'pair' Rebus: *dul* 'cast metal'

m357a
āra 'spokes' Rebus: *āra* 'brass'. cf. erka = ekke (Tbh. of arka) aka (Tbh. of arka) copper (metal)
खांडा [*khāṇḍā*] *m* A jag, notch, or indentation (as upon the edge of a tool or weapon). (Marathi) Rebus: *khāṇḍā* 'tools, pots and pans, metal-ware'.

kaṇḍe 'stalk or stem of metal-ware'. Rebus 2: Rebus: *kuṭila, katthīl* = 'pair' Rebus: dul 'cast metal'. bronze cast metalware *dul kuṭila khānḍa*

straw' Rebus : *khānḍa* 'tools, pots and pans, kaṇḍ 'fire-altar' (Santali) PLUS *kuṭila* 'bent'; bronze (8 parts copper and 2 parts tin) dula Thus the composition hieroglyph sign reads:

aya kammaṭa.'coiner, mint alloy'

கொட்டு² koṭṭu [Tu. *koṭṭu.*] hoe with short handle, weeding-hoe (Tamil) Rebus: खोट [khōṭa] *f* A mass of metal (unwrought or of old metal melted down); an ingot or wedge.(Marathi) PLUS *aḍar* 'harrow'; rebus: *aduru* 'native unsmelted metal' Thus, *aduru khōṭa* 'native alloy metal'.

 bronze cast metalware *dul kuṭila khāṇḍa*

kuṭila 'bent'; Rebus: *kuṭila, katthīl* = bronze (8 parts copper and 2 parts ti*n) dula* 'pair' Rebus: *dul* 'cast metal'

eraka 'upraised arm' Rebus*: erako* 'moltencast copper' PLUS *meḍ 'body' Rebus: meḍ 'iron' (Ho.) काठी [kāṭhī] f (काष्ट S) 'frame or structure of the body' (Marathi) Rebus: खंडी [khaṇḍī] measure of weight (Marathi) கண்டி; kaṇṭi, n. < Mhr. khaṇḍil. [T. Tu. khaṇḍi, M. kaṇḍi.] Candy, a weight, about 500 lbs.*

kana, kanac = corner (Santali); Rebus: *kañcu* = bronze (Telugu)

'rim-of-jar' hieroglyph *kanka* (Santali) karṇika 'scribe'(Sanskrit) Rebus: *karṇī,* supercargo for a boat shipment.

 m157A Epigraph: Pictorial motif hieroglyph composition: turner-stone-cutter. *खोंड [khōṇḍa] m A young bull, a bullcalf. (Marathi) Rebus: kõdār 'turner' (Bengali); कोंद kōnda 'engraver, lapidary setting or infixing gems' (Marathi) G. sãghārɔ m. 'lathe' ; संघाट joinery; M. sãgaḍ 'double-canoe' Rebus: sangataras 'stone-cutter, mason'*

Text: brass metalware +mint + alloyed metal, bronze ingot supercargo

 *āra* 'spokes' Rebus: *āra* 'brass'. cf. erka = ekke (Tbh. of arka) aka (Tbh. of arka) copper (metal)

खांडा [*khāṇḍā*] *m* A jag, notch, or indentation (as upon the edge of a tool or weapon). (Marathi) Rebus: *khāṇḍā* 'tools, pots and pans, metal-ware'.

 *kamaḍha* = crab; *kampaṭṭam* = mint (Tamil) ; *kammaṭa* 'coiner, mint' (Telugu) Vikalpa: *ḍato* = claws of crab (Santali); *dhātu* = mineral (Sanskrit)

ayo 'fish' Rebus: *aya* 'iron' (Gujarati) *ayas* 'metal' (Sanskrit)

खोट [khōṭa] *f* A mass of metal (unwrought or of old metal melted down); an ingot or wedge. Hence 2 A lump or solid bit (as of phlegm, gore, curds, inspissated milk); any concretion or clot. (Marathi)

kuṭila 'bent'; Rebus: *kuṭila, katthīl* = bronze (8 parts copper and 2 parts tin)

'rim-of-jar' hieroglyph *kanka* (Santali) karṇika 'scribe'(Sanskrit) Rebus: *karṇī,* supercargo for a boat shipment.

h26a

खोंड [khōṇḍa] m A young bull, a bullcalf. (Marathi) Rebus: kõdār 'turner' (Bengali); कोंद kōnda 'engraver, lapidary setting or infixing gems' (Marathi) G. sãghārɔ m. 'lathe' ; संघाट joinery; M. sãgaḍ 'double-canoe' Rebus: sangataras 'stone-cutter, mason'

āra 'spokes' Rebus: *āra* 'brass'. cf. erka = ekke (Tbh. of arka) aka (Tbh. of arka) copper (metal)

खांडा [khāṇḍā] *m* A jag, notch, or indentation (as upon the edge of a tool or weapon). (Marathi) Rebus:*khāṇḍā* 'tools, pots and pans, metal-ware'.

kamaḍha = crab; *kampaṭṭam* = mint (Tamil) ; *kammaṭa* 'coiner, mint' (Telugu) Vikalpa: *ḍato* = claws of crab (Santali); *dhātu* = mineral (Sanskrit)

aya kammaṭa.'coiner, mint alloy'

aya aḍaren (homonym: aduru)'alloy native metal'

loa 'ficus religiosa' Rebus: *lo* 'iron' (Sanskrit) PLUS unique ligatures: लोखंड [lōkhaṇḍa] *n* (लोह S) Iron. लोखंडाचे चणे खावविणें or चारणें To oppress grievously.लोखंडकाम [lōkhaṇḍakāma] *n* Iron work; that portion (of a building, machine &c.) which consists of iron. 2 The business of an ironsmith.लोखंडी [lōkhaṇḍī] *a* (लोखंड) Composed of iron; relating to iron. (Marathi)

Another sign hieroglyph which gets almost identical ligatures is: bicha, bichā 'scorpion' (Assamese) Rebus: bica 'stone ore' (Munda) bicha 'scorpion' (Assamese) Rebus: bica 'stone ore' (Munda). meṛed-bica = iron stone ore, in contrast to bali-bica, iron sand ore (Munda) Was there a compound term bicakhaṇḍ 'stone ore metalware'? The assumption is that the ligatures are read: kāṇḍa 'tools, pots and pans and metal-ware'., that is: 'metalware'

खांडा [khāṇḍā] m A jag, notch, or indentation (as upon the edge of a tool or weapon. Rebus: kāṇḍa 'tools, pots and pans and metal-ware'.

'rim-of-jar' hieroglyph *kanka* (Santali) karṇika 'scribe'(Sanskrit) Rebus: *karṇī,* supercargo for a boat shipment.

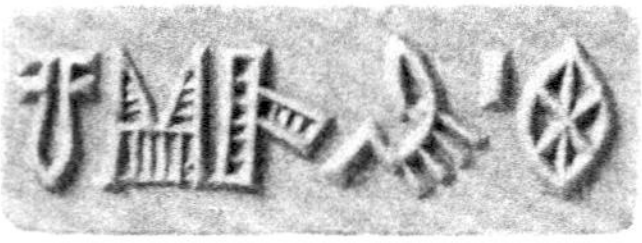

m372a

āra 'spokes'

Rebus: *āra* 'brass'. cf. erka = (Tbh. of arka)

ekke (Tbh. of arka) aka copper (metal)

खांडा [khāṇḍā] *m* A jag, notch, or indentation (as upon the edge of a tool or weapon). (Marathi) Rebus:*khāṇḍā* 'tools, pots and pans, metal-ware'.

baraḍo = spine; backbone (Tulu) Rebus: *baran, bharat* 'mixed alloys' (5 copper, 4 zinc and 1 tin) (Punjabi)

Ladder varian? *sainī, senī* f. ' ladder '(Hindi) Rebus: *sēṇi* -- f. ' guild, division of army' (Pali) workshop' PLUS *ḍhālako* 'metal ingot'

fVariant? *'sãgāḍā* m. ' frame of a building ', k°*ḍī* f. ' lathe '(CDIAL 12859) Rebus*: sangataras.* संगतराश lit. 'to collect stones, stone-cutter, mason' Vikalpa: *ḍānga* 'peak or summit of hill' (Hindi) Rebus: *ḍhangar* 'blacksmith' (Maithili) *dula* 'pair' Rebus: *dul* 'cast metal' PLUS 'four' *gaṇḍā* 'four' Rebus: *kaṇḍā* 'fire-altar'

'rim-of-jar' hieroglyph *kanka* (Santali) karṇika 'scribe'(Sanskrit) Rebus: *karṇī,* supercargo for a boat shipment.

m662a *खोंड [khōṇḍa] m A young bull, a bullcalf. (Marathi) Rebus: kõdār 'turner' (Bengali); कोंद kōnda 'engraver, lapidary setting or infixing gems' (Marathi) G. sãghāṛɔ m. 'lathe' ; संघाट joinery; M. sãgaḍ 'double-canoe' Rebus: sangataras 'stone-cutter, mason'*

āra 'spokes' Rebus: *āra* 'brass'. cf. erka = ekke (Tbh. of arka) aka (Tbh. of arka) copper (metal)

खांडा [khāṇḍā] *m* A jag, notch, or indentation (as upon the edge of a tool or weapon). (Marathi) Rebus:*khāṇḍā* 'tools, pots and pans, metal-ware'.

muka 'ladle' (Tamil)(DEDR 4887) Rebus*: mũh* 'ingot' (Santali) *baṭa* = rimless pot (Kannada) Rebus: *baṭa* = a kind of iron (Gujarati) kolmo 'paddy plant' Rebus: kolami 'smithy, forge'.

h411a

खोंड [khōṇḍa] m A young bull, a bullcalf. (Marathi) Rebus: kõdār 'turner' (Bengali); कोंद kōnda 'engraver, lapidary setting or infixing gems' (Marathi) G. sãghāṛɔ m. 'lathe' ; संघाट joinery; M. sãgaḍ 'double-canoe' Rebus: sangataras 'stone-cutter, mason'

āra 'spokes' Rebus: *āra* 'brass'. cf. erka = ekke (Tbh. of arka) aka (Tbh. of arka) copper (metal)

खांडा [khāṇḍā] *m* A jag, notch, or indentation (as upon the edge of a tool or weapon). (Marathi) Rebus:*khāṇḍā* 'tools, pots and pans, metal-ware'.

aya kammaṭa.'coiner, mint alloy'

ḍhanga = a crook used for pulling down the branches of trees, for goats, sheep and camels (P.) Rebus:*ḍhangar* blacksmith'.

'rim-of-jar' hieroglyph *kanka* (Santali) karṇika 'scribe'(Sanskrit) Rebus: *karṇī,* supercargo for a boat shipment.

m1286A *āra* 'spokes' Rebus: *āra* 'brass'. cf. erka = ekke (Tbh. of arka) aka (Tbh. of arka) copper (metal)

खांडा [khāṇḍā] *m* A jag, notch, or indentation (as upon the edge of a tool or weapon). (Marathi) Rebus:*khāṇḍā* 'tools, pots and pans, metal-ware'.

ayo 'fish' Rebus: aya 'iron' (Gujarati) ayas 'metal' (Vedic) notch (infixed ligature) Rebus: *kāṇḍa* 'pots and pans, metalware', Thus, the composite hieroglyph reads rebus: metalware of alloyed metal. Reading, *aya kāṇḍa*

m1264a

āra 'spokes' Rebus: *āra* 'brass'. cf. erka = ekke (Tbh. of arka) aka (Tbh. of arka) copper (metal)

खांडा [khāṇḍā] *m* A jag, notch, or indentation (as upon the edge of a tool or weapon). (Marathi) Rebus:*khāṇḍā* 'tools, pots and pans, metal-ware'. *kolom* 'three' Rebus: *kolami* 'smithy, forge' PLUS *ḍānga* 'peak or summit of hill' (Hindi) Rebus: *ḍhangar* 'blacksmith' (Maithili) Rebus: *ḍaṅgrɔ* m. ' axe ', poet. *ḍaṅgru* m., °*re* f.; J. *ḍãgrā* m. ' small weapon like axe ', P. *ḍaṅgorī* f. ' small staff or club ' (CDIAL 5520) *Rebus: damgar* 'merchant' (Akkadian) PLUS *kaṇḍō* a stool (Kur.) Malt. *kanḍo* stool, seat. (DEDR 1179) Rebus: *kaṇḍ* 'stone (ore)' The ligatured hieroglyph sign reads: stone ore axe blacksmith forge merchant: *kaṇḍ ḍaṅgrɔ kolami damgar. eraka* 'upraised arm' Rebus: *eraka* 'moltencast copper' PLUS *meḍ 'body' Rebus: meḍ 'iron' (Ho.) काठी [kāṭhī] f (काष्ट S) 'frame or structure of the body' (Marathi) Rebus: खंडी [khaṇḍī] measure of weight (Marathi) கண்டி; kaṇṭi, n. < Mhr. khaṇḍil. [T. Tu. khaṇḍi, M. kaṇḍi.] Candy, a weight, about 500 lbs.*

'rim-of-jar' hieroglyph *kanka* (Santali) karṇika 'scribe'(Sanskrit) Rebus: *karṇī,* supercargo for a boat shipment.

M-205 A

m205A

खोंड [khōṇḍa] m A young bull, a bullcalf. (Marathi) Rebus: kōdār 'turner' (Bengali); कोंद kōnda 'engraver, lapidary setting or infixing gems' (Marathi) G. sãghāṛɔ m. 'lathe' ; संघाट joinery; M. sãgaḍ 'double-canoe' Rebus: sangataras 'stone-cutter, mason'

āra 'spokes' Rebus: *āra* 'brass'. cf. erka = ekke (Tbh. of arka) aka (Tbh. of arka) copper (metal)

खांडा [khāṇḍā] *m* A jag, notch, or indentation (as upon the edge of a tool or weapon). (Marathi) Rebus:*khāṇḍā* 'tools, pots and pans, metal-ware'.

dula 'pair' Rebus: *dul* 'cast metal' *kuṭila* 'bent'; Rebus: *kuṭila, katthīl* = bronze (8 parts copper and 2 parts tin) Thus, cast bronze.

kana, kanac = corner (Santali); Rebus: *kañcu* = bronze (Telugu) PLUS *ḍhālako* 'metal ingot'

Vikalpa: *sal* 'splinter' Rebus: *sal* 'workshop'

m865a

खोंड [khōṇḍa] m A young bull, a bullcalf. (Marathi) Rebus: kõdār 'turner' (Bengali); कोंद kōnda 'engraver, lapidary setting or infixing gems' (Marathi) G. sãghāṛɔ m. 'lathe' ; संघाट joinery; M. sãgaḍ 'double-canoe' Rebus: sangataras 'stone-cutter, mason'

āra 'spokes' Rebus: *āra* 'brass'. cf. erka = ekke (Tbh. of arka) aka (Tbh. of arka) copper (metal)

खांडा [khāṇḍā] *m* A jag, notch, or indentation (as upon the edge of a tool or weapon). (Marathi) Rebus:*khāṇḍā* 'tools, pots and pans, metal-ware'.

aya

aya kammaṭa.'coiner, mint alloy'

rim-of-jar' hieroglyph *kanka* (Santali) karṇika 'scribe'(Sanskrit) Rebus: *karṇī,* supercargo for a boat shipment. *meḍ* 'body' Rebus: *meḍ* 'iron' (Ho.)

m1164a *खोंड [khōṇḍa] m A young bull, a bullcalf. (Marathi) Rebus: kõdār 'turner' (Bengali); कोंद kōnda 'engraver, lapidary setting or infixing gems' (Marathi) G. sãghāṛɔ m. 'lathe' ; संघाट joinery; M. sãgaḍ 'double-canoe' Rebus: sangataras 'stone-cutter, mason'*

āra 'spokes' Rebus: *āra* 'brass'. cf. erka = ekke (Tbh. of arka) aka (Tbh. of arka) copper (metal)

खांडा [khāṇḍā] *m* A jag, notch, or indentation (as upon the edge of a tool or weapon). (Marathi) Rebus:*khāṇḍā* 'tools, pots and pans, metal-ware'.

kana, kanac = corner (Santali); Rebus: *kañcu* = bronze (Telugu) *sainī, senī* f. ' ladder '(Hindi) Rebus: *sēṇi* -- f. ' guild, division of army' (Pali) workshop'

'rim-of-jar' hieroglyph *kanka* (Santali) karṇika 'scribe'(Sanskrit) Rebus: *karṇī,* supercargo for a boat shipment.

m0300 Zebu horns on composite animal. Native metal smith guild. Text 2521

:

ingot (from) iron smelter, tin smelter merchant guild. Focus on 'serpent' tail: *nāga* 'snake' Rebus: *nāga* 'lead' (Sanskrit) anakku 'tin' (Akkadian) *Kur.* xolā tail. *Malt.* qoli id. (DEDR 2135). Focus on human face: mukha, *mũh* 'face' Rebus*: mũh* 'ingot'. Zebu horns: *khũṭ* 'zebu' (Gujarati) Rebus: *khũṭ* '(native metal) community, guild' (Santali) kola 'tiger' Rebus: kolhe 'smelters' kol 'working in iron' ibha 'elephant' Rebus: ib 'iron' body of an ox: balad 'bull' Rebus: *baran, bharat* 'mixed alloys' (5 copper, 4 zinc and 1 tin) (Punjabi) dhatu 'scarf' Rebus: dhatu 'mineral ore'.

āra 'spokes' Rebus: *āra 'brass'*. cf. erka = ekke (Tbh. of arka) aka (Tbh. of arka) copper (metal); crystal (Kannada) Glyph: eraka'nave of wheel' Rebus: eraka 'copper'; cf. erka = ekke (Tbh. of arka) aka (Tbh. of arka) copper (metal); crystal (Kannada)

 Read in context, the composite hieroglyph is assumed to be a combination of a slanted stroke ligatured to a notch,which provide possible rebus readings of a smithy/forge: notch+slanted stroke reads rebus: *ḍhālako kāṇḍa* 'ingot, tools, pots and pans and metal-ware'

dhāḷ 'a slope'; 'inclination of a plane' (Gujarati); *ḍhāḷiyum* = adj. sloping, inclining (Gujarati) Rebus: *ḍhālako* = a large metal ingot (Gujarati) *ḍhālakī* = a metal heated and poured into a mould; a solid piece of metal; an ingot (Gujarati)

PLUS

खांडा [*khāṇḍā*] *m* A jag, notch, or indentation (as upon the edge of a tool or weapon). Rebus: *kāṇḍa* 'tools, pots and pans and metal-ware'

Thus, the first pair of sign hieroglyphs from r. read rebus: copper, bronze ingots, metalware

| खांडा [*khāṇḍā*] *m* A jag, notch, or indentation (as upon the edge of a tool or weapon). Rebus: *kāṇḍa* 'tools, pots and pans and metal-ware'

ranku 'liquid measure' Rebus: ranku 'tin'

 *kanka* 'rim of jar' Rebus: *karṇīka* 'account (scribe)' *karṇī* 'supercargo'
kolmo 'paddy plant' Rebus: kolami 'smithy, forge'

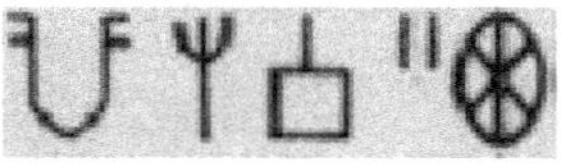

m0437 Tablet Text 2867 *khũṭ* 'zebu' Rebus: '(native metal) guild'

sal 'splinter' Rebus: sal 'workshop'
eraka 'nave of wheel' Rebus: *eraka* 'copper'; *āra* 'spokes' Rebus: āra 'brass'.
ranku 'liquid measure' Rebus: ranku 'tin'
kolmo 'paddy plant' Rebus: kolami 'smithy/forge'

 kanka 'rim of jar' Rebus: *karṇīka* 'account (scribe)' *karṇī* 'supercargo'

Zebu: Native Metal smith guild.

Sign hieroglyphs on m0260

eraka 'nave of wheel' Rebus: *erako* 'moltencast copper'; *āra* 'spokes' Rebus: *āra* 'brass'. PLUS *sal* 'splinter' Rebus*: sal* 'workshop'

Thus, copper, rass workshop.

ayo 'fish' Rebus: *aya* 'iron' (Gujarati) *ayas* 'metal' (Sanskrit)

|||| Numeral 4: gaṇḍa 'four' Rebus: kaṇḍa 'furnace, fire-altar' (Santali) A variant representation of circumscript four short numeral strokes.

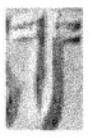

'rim-of-jar' hieroglyph *kanka* (Santali) karṇika 'scribe'(Sanskrit) Rebus: *karṇī,* supercargo for a boat shipment.

*meḍ 'body' Rebus: meḍ 'iron' (Ho.) Rebus: खंडी [khaṇḍī] measure of weight (Marathi) கண்டி; kaṇṭi, n. < Mhr. khaṇḍil. [T. Tu. khaṇḍi, M. kaṇḍi.] Candy, a weight, about 500 lbs.*काठी [kāṭhī] *f* (काष्ट S) 'frame or structure of the body' (Marathi) Rebus: खंडी [khaṇḍī] measure of weight (Marathi) *கண்டி; kaṇṭi, n. < Mhr. khaṇḍil. [T. Tu. khaṇḍi, M. kaṇḍi.]* Candy, a weight, stated to be roughly equivalent to 500 lbs.

m1955a

āra 'spokes' Rebus: *āra 'brass'.* cf. erka = ekke (Tbh. of arka) aka (Tbh. of arka) copper (metal); crystal (Kannada) Glyph: *eraka'*nave of wheel' Rebus: eraka 'copper'; cf. erka = ekke (Tbh. of arka) aka (Tbh. of arka) copper (metal); crystal (Kannada) *erako* 'moltencast copper' PLUS

sal 'splinter' Rebus: sal 'workshop' Thus, moltencast copper, brass workshop.

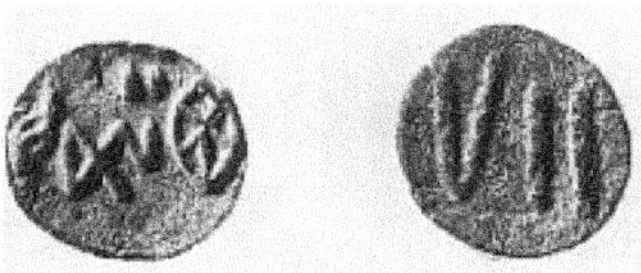

H-833 A bis H-833 B

h833A

āra 'spokes' Rebus: *āra 'brass'.* cf. erka = ekke (Tbh. of arka) aka (Tbh. of arka) copper (metal); crystal (Kannada) Glyph: *eraka'*nave of wheel' Rebus: eraka 'copper'; cf. erka = ekke (Tbh. of arka) aka (Tbh. of arka) copper (metal); crystal (Kannada) *erako* 'moltencast copper'

PLUS

sal 'splinter' Rebus: sal 'workshop' Thus, moltencast copper, brass workshop.

ḍato = claws of crab (Santali) Rebus: *dhātu* 'mineral ore' PLUS *baṭa* = rimless pot (Kannada) Rebus: *baṭa* = a kind of iron (G.)) *bhaṭa* furnace (Gujarati)

dula 'two, pair' Rebus: dul 'cast metal' PLUS *dhāḷ* 'a slope'; 'inclination of a plane' (G.); *ḍhāḷiyum* = adj. sloping, inclining (G.) Rebus: *ḍhālako* = a large metal ingot (G.) *ḍhālakī* = a metal heated and poured into a mould; a solid piece of metal; an ingot (Gujarati) PLUS kolom 'three' Rebus: kolami 'smithy, forge'. Thus cast metal ingot smithy.

Side B: *baṭa* = rimless pot (Kannada) Rebus: *baṭa* = a kind of iron (G.)) *bhaṭa* furnace (Gujarati) dula 'two' Rebus: dul 'cast metal'

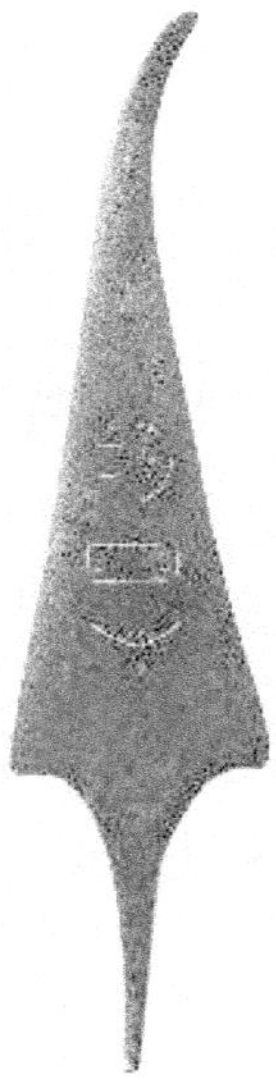

h380Aमंडप [maṇḍapa] 'canopy' Rebus: मंडई [maṇḍī] *f* (H) A green market, the place in a city whither vegetables and fruits are brought to be disposed of by wholesale.
PLUS

eraka 'nave of wheel' Rebus: *erako* 'moltencast copper'; *āra* 'spokes' Rebus: *āra* 'brass'. PLUS *sal* 'splinter' Rebus: *sal* 'workshop' Thus, copper, brass workshop.

kəṭhā´r, kc. *kuṭhār* m. ' granary, storeroom '(WPah.)(CDIAL 3550). *koṭhārī m.* '

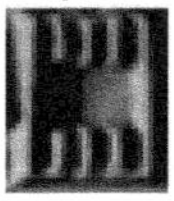

storekeeper' (Gujarati)(CDIAL 3551) Thus, storeroom (of) *kolom* 'three' Rebus: *kolami* 'smithy, forge'. Dula 'pair' Rebus: dul 'cast metal' Thus, together *dul kolami kuṭhār* 'cast metal smithy storeroom'

kuṭila 'bent' Rebus: *kuṭila* 'bronze'.

m651a *खोंड [khōṇḍa] m A young bull, a bullcalf. (Marathi) Rebus: kōdār 'turner' (Bengali);* *कोंद kōnda 'engraver, lapidary setting or infixing gems' (Marathi) G. sãghārɔ m. 'lathe' ; संघाट joinery; M. sãgaḍ 'double-canoe' Rebus: sangataras 'stone-cutter, mason'*

āra 'spokes' Rebus: *āra 'brass'*. cf. erka = ekke (Tbh. of arka) aka (Tbh. of arka) copper (metal); crystal (Kannada) Glyph: *eraka*'nave of wheel' Rebus: eraka 'copper'; cf. erka = ekke (Tbh. of arka) aka (Tbh. of arka) copper (metal); crystal (Kannada) *erako* 'moltencast copper' PLUS

sal 'splinter' Rebus: sal 'workshop' Thus, moltencast copper, brass workshop.
aya kammaṭa.'coiner, mint alloy' *ayo* 'fish' Rebus: *aya* 'iron' *ayas* 'metal'

muka 'ladle' (Tamil)(DEDR 4887) Rebus: *mũh* 'ingot' (Santali) Thus, iron ingot. kolom 'three' Rebus: kolami 'smithy, forge' *kāṇḍa* 'arrow' (Sanskrit)

m117A *खोंड [khōṇḍa] m A young bull, a bullcalf. (Marathi) Rebus: kōdār 'turner' (Bengali); कोंद kōnda 'engraver, lapidary setting or infixing gems' (Marathi) G. sãghārɔ m. 'lathe' ; संघाट joinery; M. sãgaḍ 'double-canoe' Rebus: sangataras 'stone-cutter, mason'*

eraka 'nave of wheel' Rebus: *erako* 'moltencast copper'; *āra* 'spokes' Rebus: *āra* 'brass'. PLUS *sal* 'splinter' Rebus: *sal* 'workshop'

Thus, copper, brass workshop. *baroṭi* 'twelve' *bhārata* 'a factitious alloy of copper, pewter, tin' (Marathi)

smithy/forge (with) fire-altar: *kolami* PLUS *dul kuṭila* 'cast bronze'. Thus, *dul kuṭila kolami* 'cast bronze smithy/forge.
ayo 'fish' Rebus: *aya* 'iron' *ayas* 'metal'

kolom 'three' Rebus: *kolami* 'smithy, forge'
aḍaren 'lid of pot' Rebus: *aduru* 'unsmelted, native metal'. Thus cunsmelted metal (from*) koḍa* 'one' Rebus: *koḍ* 'workshop'

Three sign sequence:

muka 'ladle' (Tamil)(DEDR 4887) Rebus: *mūh* 'ingot' (Santali) Thus, iron ingot.
kolom 'three' Rebus: kolami 'smithy, forge' *kāṇḍa* 'arrow' (Sanskrit) Rebus:*khāṇḍa* 'tools, pots and pans, metal-ware'. Rebus 2: kaṇḍ 'fire-altar' (Santali) Thus, the three sign sequence reads: iron ingot, furnace smithy, fire-altar metalware.

h506a खोंड *[khōṇḍa] m A young bull, a bullcalf. (Marathi) Rebus: kõdār 'turner' (Bengali);* कोंद *kōnda 'engraver, lapidary setting or infixing gems' (Marathi) G. sãghāṛɔ m. 'lathe' ;* संघाट *joinery; M. sāgaḍ 'double-canoe' Rebus: sangataras 'stone-cutter, mason'*

āra 'spokes' Rebus: *āra 'brass'*. cf. erka = ekke (Tbh. of arka) aka (Tbh. of arka) copper (metal); crystal (Kannada) Glyph: *eraka*'nave of wheel' Rebus: eraka 'copper'; cf. erka = ekke (Tbh. of arka) aka (Tbh. of arka) copper (metal); crystal (Kannada) *erako* 'moltencast copper' PLUS

sal 'splinter' Rebus: sal 'workshop' Thus, moltencast copper, brass workshop.

āra 'spokes' Rebus: *āra 'brass'*. cf. erka = ekke (Tbh. of arka) aka (Tbh. of arka) copper (metal); crystal (Kannada) Glyph: *eraka*'nave of wheel' Rebus: eraka 'copper'; cf. erka = ekke (Tbh. of arka) aka (Tbh. of arka) copper (metal); crystal (Kannada) *erako* 'moltencast copper' ranku 'liquid measure' Rebus: ranku 'tin'

|||| Numeral 4: gaṇḍa 'four' Rebus: kaṇḍa 'furnace, fire-altar' (Santali) dula 'pair' Rebus: dul 'cast metal'

Strands of yarn/rope' hieroglyph: Hieroglyph: 'strands of yarn' Rebus reading: *dhā'tu* 'strand of rope' Rebus: *dhatu* 'mineral ore' (Santali)

m1830a खोंड *[khōṇḍa] m A young bull, a bullcalf. (Marathi) Rebus: kõdār 'turner' (Bengali);* कोंद *kōnda 'engraver, lapidary setting or infixing gems' (Marathi) G. sãghāṛɔ m. 'lathe' ;* संघाट *joinery; M. sāgaḍ 'double-canoe' Rebus: sangataras 'stone-cutter, mason'*

āra 'spokes' Rebus: *āra 'brass'*. cf. erka = ekke (Tbh. of arka) aka (Tbh. of arka) copper (metal); crystal (Kannada) Glyph: *eraka*'nave of wheel' Rebus: eraka 'copper'; cf. erka = ekke (Tbh. of arka) aka (Tbh. of arka) copper (metal); crystal (Kannada) *erako* 'moltencast copper' PLUS

sal 'splinter' Rebus: sal 'workshop' Thus, moltencast copper, brass workshop.

loa 'ficus religiosa' Rebus: *lo* 'iron' (Sanskrit) PLUS unique ligatures: लोखंड [lōkhaṇḍa] *n* (लोह S) Iron. लोखंडाचे चणे खावविणें or चारणें To oppress grievously.लोखंडकाम [lōkhaṇḍakāma] *n* Iron work; that portion (of a building, machine &c.) which consists of iron. 2 The business of an ironsmith.लोखंडी [lōkhaṇḍī] *a* (लोखंड) Composed of iron; relating to iron. (Marathi)

kanka 'rim of jar' Rebus: karṇīka 'account (scribe)' karṇī 'supercargo'

h649a

āra 'spokes' Rebus: *āra 'brass'*. cf. erka = ekke (Tbh. of arka) aka (Tbh. of arka) copper (metal); crystal (Kannada) Glyph: *eraka*'nave of wheel' Rebus: eraka 'copper'; cf. erka = ekke (Tbh. of arka) aka (Tbh. of arka) copper (metal); crystal (Kannada) *erako* 'moltencast copper' PLUS

sal 'splinter' Rebus: sal 'workshop' Thus, moltencast copper, brass workshop.

dula 'pair' Rebus: *dul* 'cast (metal)' PLUS*kana, kanac* = corner (Santali); Rebus: *kañcu* = bronze (Telugu) PLUS infixed kolmo 'paddy plant' Rebus: kolami 'smithy, forge'. Thus, cast bronze smithy, forge. Or, *mogge* 'sprout, bud' Rebus: *mũh* 'ingot' (Santali)Thus, cast bronze ingot. Read as: *kañcu dul mũh 'bronze cast ingot'* *aya kammaṭa.*'coiner, mint alloy' *ayo ḍhālako* 'alloy metal ingot'

Three sign sequence:

muka 'ladle' (Tamil)(DEDR 4887) Rebus: *mũh* 'ingot' (Santali) Thus, iron ingot.

kolom 'three' Rebus: kolami 'smithy, forge' *kāṇḍa* 'arrow' (Sanskrit) Rebus:*khāṇḍa* 'tools, pots and pans, metal-ware'. Rebus 2: kaṇḍ 'fire-altar' (Santali) Thus, the three sign sequence reads: iron ingot, furnace smithy, fire-altar metalware.

m38A

āra 'spokes' Rebus: *āra 'brass'*. cf. erka = ekke (Tbh. of arka) aka (Tbh. of arka) copper (metal); crystal (Kannada) Glyph: *eraka*'nave of wheel' Rebus: eraka 'copper'; cf. erka = ekke (Tbh. of arka) aka (Tbh. of arka) copper (metal); crystal (Kannada) *erako* 'moltencast copper' PLUS

sal 'splinter' Rebus: sal 'workshop' Thus, moltencast copper, brass workshop.

dula 'pair' Rebus: *dul* 'cast (metal)' PLUS*kana, kanac* = corner (Santali); Rebus: *kañcu* = bronze (Telugu) PLUS infixed kolmo 'paddy plant' Rebus: kolami 'smithy,

forge'. Thus, cast bronze smithy, forge. Or, *mogge* 'sprout, bud' Rebus: *mũh* 'ingot' (Santali)Thus, cast bronze ingot. Read as: *kañcu dul mũh 'bronze cast ingot'*
kolom 'three' Rebus: kolami 'smithy, forge' kuṭila 'bent' CDIAL 3230 kuṭi— in cmpd. 'curve', *kuṭika—* 'bent' MBh. Rebus: *kuṭila, katthīl* = bronze (8 parts copper and 2 parts tin)
'rim of jar': *kanka* (Santali) *karṇika* 'scribe'(Sanskrit) Rebus: *karṇī,* supercargo

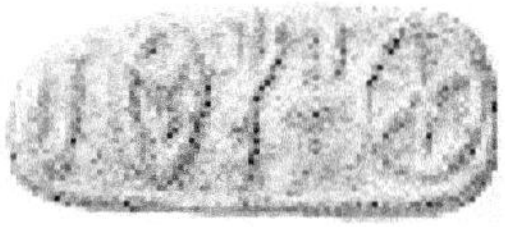

Kalibangan 78A

āra 'spokes' Rebus: *āra 'brass'.* cf. erka = ekke (Tbh. of arka) aka (Tbh. of arka) copper (metal); crystal (Kannada) Glyph: *eraka*'nave of wheel' Rebus: eraka 'copper'; cf. erka = ekke (Tbh. of arka) aka (Tbh. of arka) copper (metal); crystal (Kannada) *erako* 'moltencast copper' PLUS

sal 'splinter' Rebus: sal 'workshop' Thus, moltencast copper, brass workshop.

kolmo 'paddy plant' Rebus: *kolami* 'smithy, forge' Vikalpa: *mogge* 'sprout, bud' Rebus: *mũh* 'ingot' (Santali) dolu 'plant of shoot height' Rebus: dul 'cast metal'

kanac 'corner' Rebus: *kañcu* 'bronze' 'rim of jar': *kanka* (Santali) *karṇika* 'scribe'(Sanskrit) Rebus: *karṇī,* supercargo

M-1306 A

m1306A

āra 'spokes' Rebus: *āra 'brass'.* cf. erka = ekke (Tbh. of arka) aka (Tbh. of arka) copper (metal); crystal (Kannada) Glyph: *eraka*'nave of wheel' Rebus: eraka 'copper'; cf. erka = ekke (Tbh. of arka) aka (Tbh. of arka) copper (metal); crystal (Kannada) *erako* 'moltencast copper' PLUS

sal 'splinter' Rebus: sal 'workshop' Thus, moltencast copper, brass workshop.

dula 'pair' Rebus: *dul* 'cast (metal)' PLUS*kana, kanac* = corner (Santali); Rebus: *kañcu* = bronze (Telugu) PLUS infixed kolmo 'paddy plant' Rebus: kolami 'smithy, forge'. Thus, cast bronze smithy, forge. Or, *mogge* 'sprout, bud' Rebus: *mũh* 'ingot' (Santali)Thus, cast bronze ingot. Read as: *kañcu dul mũh 'bronze cast ingot'*
ranku 'liquid measure' Rebus: ranku 'tin'

mogge 'sprout, bud' Rebus: *mũh* 'ingot' (Santali)
kanka 'rim of jar' Rebus: karṇīka 'account (scribe)' karṇī 'supercargo'

m918A *खोंड [khōṇḍa] m A young bull, a bullcalf. (Marathi) Rebus: kõdār 'turner' (Bengali); कोंद*

M-918 A

kõnda 'engraver, lapidary setting or infixing gems' (Marathi) G. sãghāṛɔ m. 'lathe' ; संघाट joinery; M. sãgaḍ 'double-canoe' Rebus: sangataras 'stone-cutter, mason'

kanac 'corner' Rebus: *kañcu* 'bronze' sal 'splinter' Rebus: sal 'workshop'

 *kanac* 'corner' Rebus: *kañcu* 'bronze' PLUS *mogge* 'sprout, bud' Rebus: *mũh* 'ingot'

 *kolmo* 'paddy plant' Rebus: *kolami* 'smithy, forge' Vikalpa: *mogge* 'sprout, bud' Rebus: *mũh* 'ingot' (Santali) dolu 'plant of shoot height' Rebus: dul 'cast metal' (Santali)

M-726 a

m726a *खोंड [khōṇḍa] m A young bull, a bullcalf. (Marathi) Rebus: kõdār 'turner' (Bengali); कोंद kōnda 'engraver, lapidary setting or infixing gems' (Marathi) G. sãghāṛɔ m. 'lathe' ; संघाट joinery; M. sãgaḍ 'double-canoe' Rebus: sangataras 'stone-cutter, mason'*

 *āra* 'spokes' Rebus: *āra 'brass'*. cf. erka = ekke (Tbh. of arka) aka (Tbh. of arka) copper (metal); crystal (Kannada) Glyph: *eraka*'nave of wheel' Rebus: eraka 'copper'; cf. erka = ekke (Tbh. of arka) aka (Tbh. of arka) copper (metal); crystal (Kannada) *erako* 'moltencast copper' PLUS

sal 'splinter' Rebus: sal 'workshop' Thus, moltencast copper, brass workshop.

 *dula* 'pair' Rebus: *dul* 'cast (metal)' PLUS*kana, kanac* = corner (Santali); Rebus: *kañcu* = bronze (Telugu) PLUS infixed kolmo 'paddy plant' Rebus: kolami 'smithy, forge'. Thus, cast bronze smithy, forge. Or, *mogge* 'sprout, bud' Rebus: *mũh* 'ingot' (Santali)Thus, cast bronze ingot. Read as: *kañcu dul mũh 'bronze cast ingot'* dula 'two' Rebus: dul 'cast metal' *ayo* 'fish' Rebus: *aya* 'iron' *ayas* 'metal' *aya aḍaren* (homonym: aduru) 'alloy native metal' *aya kāṇḍa* 'alloy metalware'

 *loa* 'ficus religiosa' Rebus: *lo* 'iron' (Sanskrit) PLUS unique ligatures: लोखंड [lōkhaṇḍa ] *n* (लोह S) Iron. लोखंडाचे चणे खावविणें or चारणें To oppress grievously.लोखंडकाम [lōkhaṇḍakāma] *n* Iron work; that portion (of a building, machine &c.) which consists of iron. 2 The business of an ironsmith.लोखंडी [lōkhaṇḍī] *a* (लोखंड) Composed of iron; relating to iron. (Marathi) *bhaṭa* 'warrior' (Sanskrit) Rebus: *baṭa* a kind of iron (Gujarati). Rebus: *bhaṭa* 'furnace' (Santali) Thus, together, the ligatured hieroglyph reads rebus: *loa bhaṭa* 'iron furnace'

 *kanac* 'corner' Rebus: *kañcu* 'bronze' | *koḍa* 'one' Rebus: *koḍ* 'workshop'

M-900 a

m900a *खोंड [khōṇḍa] m A young bull, a bullcalf. (Marathi) Rebus: kõdār 'turner' (Bengali); कोंद kōnda 'engraver, lapidary setting or infixing gems' (Marathi) G. sãghāṛɔ m. 'lathe' ; संघाट joinery; M. sãgaḍ 'double-canoe' Rebus: sangataras 'stone-cutter, mason'*

 *āra* 'spokes' Rebus: *āra 'brass'*. cf. erka = ekke (Tbh. of arka) aka (Tbh. of arka) copper (metal); crystal (Kannada) Glyph: *eraka*'nave of wheel' Rebus: eraka 'copper'; cf. erka = ekke (Tbh. of arka) aka (Tbh. of arka) copper (metal); crystal (Kannada) *erako* 'moltencast copper' PLUS

sal ‘splinter’ Rebus: sal ‘workshop’ Thus, moltencast copper, brass workshop.

kana, kanac = corner (Santali); Rebus: *kañcu* = bronze (Telugu) PLUS खांडा [*khāṇḍā*] *m* A jag, notch, or indentation (as upon the edge of a tool or weapon). Rebus: *kāṇḍa* ‘tools, pots and pans and metal-ware’ Thus, bronze metalware.
kamaḍha = crab; *kampaṭṭam* = mint (Ta.) ; *kammaṭa* ‘coiner, mint’ (Telugu) Vikalpa: *ḍato* = claws of crab (Santali); *dhātu* = mineral (Sanskrit)

aḍar 'harrow'; rebus: *aduru* 'native unsmelted metal'
dula ‘pair’ Rebus: dul ‘cast metal’ PLUS *ayo* ‘fish’ Rebus: *aya* ‘iron’ *ayas* ‘metal’
ranku ‘liquid measure’ Rebus: ranku ‘tin’

kolmo ‘paddy plant’ Rebus: *kolami* ‘smithy, forge’ Vikalpa: *mogge* ‘sprout, bud’ Rebus: *mũh* ‘ingot’ (Santali) dolu ‘plant of shoot height’ Rebus: dul ‘cast metal’

kanka ‘rim of jar’ Rebus: karṇīka ‘account (scribe)’ karṇī ‘supercargo’

h514a *खोंड [khōṇḍa] m A young bull, a bullcalf. (Marathi) Rebus: kõdār ‘turner’ (Bengali); कोंद kōnda ‘engraver, lapidary setting or infixing gems’ (Marathi) G. sãghāṛɔ m. ‘lathe’ ; संघाट joinery; M. sãgaḍ ‘double-canoe’ Rebus: sangataras ‘stone-cutter, mason’*

āra 'spokes' Rebus: *āra ‘brass’*. cf. erka = ekke (Tbh. of arka) aka (Tbh. of arka) copper (metal); crystal (Kannada) Glyph: *eraka*’nave of wheel’ Rebus: eraka ‘copper’; cf. erka = ekke (Tbh. of arka) aka (Tbh. of arka) copper (metal); crystal (Kannada) *erako* ‘moltencast copper’ PLUS

sal ‘splinter’ Rebus: sal ‘workshop’ Thus, moltencast copper, brass workshop
āra ‘six’ Rebus: *āra* ‘brass’ *ayo* ‘fish’ Rebus: *aya* ‘iron’ *ayas* ‘metal’

water-carrier hieroglyph *kuṭi*; Rebus: *kuṭhi* ‘smelter furnace’.

m375A

āra 'spokes' Rebus: *āra ‘brass’*. cf. erka = ekke (Tbh. of arka) aka (Tbh. of arka) copper (metal); crystal (Kannada) Glyph: *eraka*’nave of wheel’ Rebus: eraka ‘copper’; cf. erka = ekke (Tbh. of arka) aka (Tbh. of arka) copper (metal); crystal (Kannada) *erako* ‘moltencast copper’ PLUS

sal ‘splinter’ Rebus: sal ‘workshop’ Thus, moltencast copper, brass workshop.
dula ‘two’ Rebus: dul ‘cast metal’
ayo ‘fish’ Rebus: *aya* ‘iron’ *ayas* ‘metal’

ayo ḍhālako 'alloy metal ingot'
bhaṭa 'warrior' (Sanskrit) Rebus: *baṭa* a kind of iron (Gujarati). Rebus: *bhaṭa* 'furnace' (Santali)

 kanka 'rim of jar' Rebus: karṇīka 'account (scribe)' karṇī 'supercargo'

H-1681 A

h1681A *खोंड [khōṇḍa] m A young bull, a bullcalf. (Marathi) Rebus: kõdār 'turner' (Bengali); कोंद kōnda 'engraver, lapidary setting or infixing gems' (Marathi) G. sãghāṛɔ m. 'lathe' ; संघाट joinery; M. sāgaḍ 'double-canoe' Rebus: sangataras 'stone-cutter, mason'*

āra 'spokes' arka) Rebus: eraka

Rebus: *āra 'brass'.* cf. erka = ekke (Tbh. of arka) aka (Tbh. of copper (metal); crystal (Kannada) Glyph: *eraka*'nave of wheel' 'copper'; cf. erka = ekke (Tbh. of arka) aka (Tbh. of arka) copper (metal); crystal (Kannada) *erako* 'moltencast copper' PLUS

sal 'splinter' Rebus: sal 'workshop' Thus, moltencast copper, brass workshop. dula 'two' Rebus: dul 'cast metal'

H-507 a

h507a *खोंड [khōṇḍa] m A young bull, a bullcalf. (Marathi) Rebus: kõdār 'turner' (Bengali); कोंद kōnda 'engraver, lapidary setting or infixing gems' (Marathi) G. sãghāṛɔ m. 'lathe' ; संघाट joinery; M. sāgaḍ 'double-canoe' Rebus: sangataras 'stone-cutter, mason'*

āra 'spokes' Rebus: *āra 'brass'.* cf. erka = ekke (Tbh. of arka) aka (Tbh. of arka) copper (metal); crystal (Kannada) Glyph: *eraka*'nave of wheel' Rebus: eraka 'copper'; cf. erka = ekke (Tbh. of arka) aka (Tbh. of arka) copper (metal); crystal (Kannada) *erako* 'moltencast copper' PLUS

sal 'splinter' Rebus: sal 'workshop' Thus, moltencast copper, brass workshop. dula 'two' Rebus: dul 'cast metal'
ayo 'fish' Rebus: *aya* 'iron' *ayas* 'metal'

m174a *खोंड [khōṇḍa] m A young bull, a bullcalf. (Marathi) Rebus: kõdār 'turner' (Bengali); कोंद kōnda 'engraver, lapidary setting or infixing gems' (Marathi) G. sãghāṛɔ m. 'lathe' ; संघाट joinery; M. sāgaḍ 'double-canoe' Rebus: sangataras 'stone-cutter, mason'*

āra 'spokes' Rebus: *āra 'brass'.* cf. erka = ekke (Tbh. of arka) aka (Tbh. of arka) copper (metal); crystal (Kannada) Glyph: *eraka*'nave of wheel' Rebus: eraka 'copper'; cf. erka = ekke (Tbh. of arka) aka (Tbh. of arka) copper (metal); crystal (Kannada) *erako* 'moltencast copper' PLUS sal ‘splinter’ Rebus: sal ‘workshop’ Thus, moltencast copper, brass workshop. dula ‘two’ Rebus: dul ‘cast metal’

ayo ‘fish’ Rebus: *aya* ‘iron’ *ayas* ‘metal’

kuṭila ‘bent’ CDIAL 3230 kuṭi— in cmpd. ‘curve’, *kuṭika—* ‘bent’ MBh. Rebus: *kuṭila, katthīl* = bronze (8 parts copper and 2 parts tin) dula ‘pair’ Rebus: dul ‘cast metal’ Thus, bronze castings.

'rim-of-jar' hieroglyph *kanka* (Santali) *karṇika* ‘scribe’(Sanskrit) Rebus: *karṇī,* supercargo for a boat shipment. *karṇīka* ‘account (scribe)’.कारणी *kāraṇī* ‘the supercargo of a ship’ (Marathi)

m1960a

āra 'spokes' Rebus: *āra ‘brass’*. cf. erka = ekke (Tbh. of arka) aka (Tbh. of arka) copper (metal); crystal (Kannada) Glyph: *eraka*‘nave of wheel’ Rebus: eraka ‘copper’; cf. erka = ekke (Tbh. of arka) aka (Tbh. of arka) copper (metal); crystal (Kannada) *erako* ‘moltencast copper’ PLUS

sal ‘splinter’ Rebus: sal ‘workshop’ Thus, moltencast copper, brass workshop. *ayo* ‘fish’ Rebus: *aya* ‘iron’ *ayas* ‘metal’ *bhaṭa* ‘warrior’ (Sanskrit) Rebus: *baṭa* a kind of iron (Gujarati). Rebus: *bhaṭa* ‘furnace’ (Santali

'rim-of-jar' hieroglyph *kanka* (Santali) *karṇika* ‘scribe’(Sanskrit) Rebus: *karṇī,* supercargo for a boat shipment. *karṇīka* ‘account (scribe)’.कारणी *kāraṇī* ‘the supercargo of a ship’ (Marathi)

h18A

खोंड [khōṇḍa] m A young bull, a bullcalf. (Marathi) Rebus: kõdār ‘turner’ (Bengali); कोंद kōnda ‘engraver, lapidary setting or infixing gems’ (Marathi) G. sãghāṛɔ m. ‘lathe’ ; संघाट joinery; M. sãgaḍ ‘double-canoe’ Rebus: sangataras ‘stone-cutter, mason’

āra 'spokes' Rebus: *āra ‘brass’*. cf. erka = ekke (Tbh. of arka) aka (Tbh. of arka) copper (metal); crystal (Kannada) Glyph: *eraka*‘nave of wheel’ Rebus: eraka ‘copper’; cf. erka = ekke (Tbh. of arka) aka (Tbh. of arka) copper (metal); crystal (Kannada) *erako* ‘moltencast copper’ PLUS

sal ‘splinter’ Rebus: sal ‘workshop’ Thus, moltencast copper, brass workshop. dula ‘two’ Rebus: dul ‘cast metal’ *ayo* ‘fish’ Rebus: *aya* ‘iron’ *ayas* ‘metal’

m1728a *खोंड [khōṇḍa] m A young bull, a bullcalf. (Marathi) Rebus: kõdār ‘turner’ (Bengali); कोंद kōnda ‘engraver, lapidary setting or infixing gems’ (Marathi) G. sãghāṛɔ m. ‘lathe’ ; संघाट joinery; M. sãgaḍ ‘double-canoe’ Rebus: sangataras ‘stone-cutter, mason’*

āra 'spokes' Rebus: *āra ‘brass’*. cf. erka = ekke (Tbh. of arka) aka (Tbh. of arka) copper (metal); crystal (Kannada) Glyph: *eraka*‘nave of wheel’ Rebus: eraka ‘copper’; cf. erka = ekke (Tbh. of arka) aka (Tbh. of arka) copper (metal); crystal (Kannada) *erako* ‘moltencast copper’ PLUS

sal 'splinter' Rebus: sal 'workshop' Thus, moltencast copper, brass workshop. dula 'two' Rebus: dul 'cast metal' *ayo* 'fish' Rebus: *aya* 'iron' *ayas* 'metal'
aya kammaṭa.'coiner, mint alloy'

 *baroṭi* 'twelve' *bhārata* 'a factitious alloy of copper, pewter, tin' (Marathi)

 water-carrier hieroglyph *kuṭi*; Rebus: *kuṭhi* 'smelter furnace'.
PLUS

कांड  *kāṇḍa* 'arrow' Rebus: *kāṇḍa* 'pots and pans, metalware, tools'. Rebus 2: kaṇḍ 'fire-altar' (Santali)

 m1716a *खोंड [khōṇḍa] m A young bull, a bullcalf. (Marathi) Rebus: kōdār 'turner' (Bengali); कोंद kōnda 'engraver, lapidary setting or infixing gems' (Marathi) G. sãghāṛɔ m. 'lathe' ; संघाट joinery; M. sãgaḍ 'double-canoe' Rebus: sangataras 'stone-cutter, mason'*
āra 'spokes' Rebus: *āra 'brass'*. cf. erka = ekke (Tbh. of arka) aka (Tbh. of arka) copper (metal); crystal (Kannada) Glyph: *eraka*'nave of wheel' Rebus: eraka 'copper'; cf. erka = ekke (Tbh. of arka) aka (Tbh. of arka) copper (metal); crystal (Kannada) *erako* 'moltencast copper' PLUS

sal 'splinter' Rebus: sal 'workshop' Thus, moltencast copper, brass workshop.
 *dula* 'pair' Rebus: *dul* 'cast (metal)' PLUS*kana, kanac* = corner (Santali); Rebus: *kañcu* = bronze (Telugu) PLUS infixed kolmo 'paddy plant' Rebus: kolami 'smithy, forge'. Thus, cast bronze smithy, forge. Or, *mogge* 'sprout, bud' Rebus: *mũh* 'ingot' (Santali)Thus, cast bronze ingot. Read as: *kañcu dul mũh 'bronze cast ingot'*

aya kammaṭa.'coiner, mint alloy' *ayo* 'fish' Rebus: *aya* 'iron' *ayas* 'metal'कांड *kāṇḍa* 'arrow' Rebus: *kāṇḍa* 'pots and pans, metalware, tools'. Rebus 2: kaṇḍ 'fire-altar' (Santali)

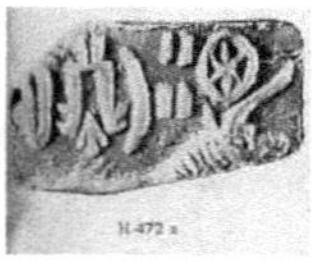 m472a *खोंड [khōṇḍa] m A young bull, a bullcalf. (Marathi) Rebus: kōdār 'turner' (Bengali); कोंद kōnda 'engraver, lapidary setting or infixing gems' (Marathi) G. sãghāṛɔ m. 'lathe' ; संघाट joinery; M. sãgaḍ 'double-canoe' Rebus: sangataras 'stone-cutter, mason'*
 *āra* 'spokes' Rebus: *āra 'brass'*. cf. erka = ekke (Tbh. of arka) aka (Tbh. of arka) copper (metal); crystal (Kannada) Glyph: *eraka*'nave of wheel' Rebus: eraka 'copper'; cf. erka = ekke (Tbh. of arka) aka (Tbh. of arka) copper (metal); crystal (Kannada) *erako* 'moltencast copper' PLUS

sal 'splinter' Rebus: sal 'workshop' Thus, moltencast copper, brass workshop.
kuṭila 'bent' CDIAL 3230 kuṭi— in cmpd. 'curve', *kuṭika*— 'bent' MBh. Rebus: *kuṭila, katthīl* = bronze (8 parts copper and 2 parts tin)
  sal 'splinter' Rebus: sal 'workshop' Thus, bronze workshop.
सांड [sāṇḍa] *f* (षद S) An outlet for superfluous water (as through a dam or mound); a sluice, a floodvent. Rebus: सांडणी [sāṇḍaṇī] *f* (H) An instrument of

goldsmiths. It is hooked or curved at the extremity; and is used to draw things out of the fire. सांठा [*sāṇṭhā*] *m* (संचय S) A collection, heap, hoard, store, stock.साटें [*sāṭēṃ*] *n* (संचय S) A whole investment; the total quantity of merchandise (brought to market by one merchant).

kanka 'rim of jar' Rebus: karṇīka 'account (scribe)' karṇī 'supercargo'
m728a Text read rebus as at m1138 PLUS Pictorial hieroglyphs: *खोंड [khōṇḍa] m A young bull, a bullcalf. (Marathi) Rebus: kõdār 'turner' (Bengali); कोंद kōnda 'engraver, lapidary setting or infixing gems' (Marathi) G. sãghāṛɔ m. 'lathe' ; संघाट joinery; M. sãgaḍ 'double-canoe' Rebus: sangataras 'stone-cutter, mason'*

m1138a Rhinoceros/boar: baḍhia = a castrated boar, a hog (Santali) baḍhi 'a caste who work both in iron and wood' (Santali) *baṟea* 'merchant' pattar 'tough' Rebus: pattar 'guild, goldsmith'

āra 'spokes' Rebus: *āra 'brass'*. cf. erka = ekke (Tbh. of arka) aka (Tbh. of arka) copper (metal); crystal (Kannada) Glyph: *eraka*'nave of wheel' Rebus: eraka 'copper'; cf. erka = ekke (Tbh. of arka) aka (Tbh. of arka) copper (metal); crystal (Kannada) *erako* 'moltencast copper' PLUS

sal 'splinter' Rebus: sal 'workshop' Thus, moltencast copper, brass workshop.
|||| Numeral 4: gaṇḍa 'four' Rebus: kaṇḍa 'furnace, fire-altar' (Santali)

||| Numeral 3: *kolom* 'three' Rebus*: kolami* 'smithy, forge'

सांड [sāṇḍa] *f* (षद S) An outlet for superfluous water (as through a dam or mound); a sluice, a floodvent. Rebus: सांडणी [sāṇḍaṇī] *f* (H) An instrument of goldsmiths. It is hooked or curved at the extremity; and is used to draw things out of the fire.
सांठा [*sāṇṭhā*] *m* (संचय S) A collection, heap, hoard, store, stock.साटें [*sāṭēṃ*] *n* (संचय S) A whole investment; the total quantity of merchandise (brought to market by one merchant).

 kanka 'rim of jar' Rebus: karṇīka 'account (scribe)' karṇī 'supercargo'

m1721a *खोंड [khōṇḍa] m A young bull, a bullcalf. (Marathi) Rebus: kõdār 'turner' (Bengali); कोंद kōnda 'engraver, lapidary setting or infixing gems' (Marathi) G. sãghāṛɔ m. 'lathe' ; संघाट joinery; M. sãgaḍ 'double-canoe' Rebus: sangataras 'stone-cutter, mason'*

āra 'spokes' Rebus: *āra 'brass'*. cf. erka = ekke (Tbh. of arka) aka (Tbh. of arka) copper (metal); crystal (Kannada) Glyph: *eraka*'nave of wheel' Rebus: eraka 'copper'; cf. erka = ekke (Tbh. of arka) aka (Tbh. of arka) copper (metal); crystal (Kannada) *erako* 'moltencast copper' PLUS

sal 'splinter' Rebus: sal 'workshop' Thus, moltencast copper, brass workshop.

kuṭila 'bent' CDIAL 3230 kuṭi— in cmpd. 'curve', *kuṭika*— 'bent' MBh. Rebus: *kuṭila, katthīl* = bronze (8 parts copper and 2 parts tin) PLUS sal 'splinter' Rebus: sal 'workshop' PLUS खांडा [*khāṇḍā*] *m* A jag, notch, or indentation (as upon the edge of a tool or weapon). Rebus: *kāṇḍa* 'tools, pots and pans and metal-ware'

 kanka 'rim of jar' Rebus: karṇīka 'account (scribe)' karṇī 'supercargo'

m1045a *खोंड [khōṇḍa] m A young bull, a bullcalf. (Marathi) Rebus: kõdār 'turner' (Bengali); कोंद kōnda 'engraver, lapidary setting or infixing gems' (Marathi) G. sãghāṛɔ m. 'lathe' ; संघाट joinery; M. sãgaḍ 'double-canoe' Rebus: sangataras 'stone-cutter, mason'*

 *kolmo* 'paddy plant' Rebus: *kolami* 'smithy, forge' Vikalpa: *mogge* 'sprout, bud' Rebus: *mũh* 'ingot' (Santali) dolu 'plant of shoot height' Rebus: dul 'cast metal'

 *āra* 'spokes' Rebus: *āra 'brass'.* cf. erka = ekke (Tbh. of arka) aka (Tbh. of arka) copper (metal); crystal (Kannada) Glyph: *eraka*'nave of wheel' Rebus: eraka 'copper'; cf. erka = ekke (Tbh. of arka) aka (Tbh. of arka) copper (metal); crystal (Kannada) *erako* 'moltencast copper' PLUS

sal 'splinter' Rebus: sal 'workshop' Thus, moltencast copper, brass workshop. dula 'two' Rebus: dul 'cast metal'

 'Arrow' sign hieroglyph (variant) This is a ligature of 'lid of pot' hieroglyph superscript on 'a linear stroke' numeral hieroglyph.*aḍaren* 'cover of pot or lid' Rebus: *aduru* 'native, unsmelted metal' PLUS koḍ = one (Santali); koḍ 'workshop' (Gujarati)

 *aḍar* 'harrow'; rebus: *aduru* 'native unsmelted metal' *bhaṭa* 'warrior' (Sanskrit) Rebus: *baṭa* a kind of iron (Gujarati). Rebus: *bhaṭa* 'furnace' (Santali)

 kanka 'rim of jar' Rebus: karṇīka 'account (scribe)' karṇī 'supercargo'

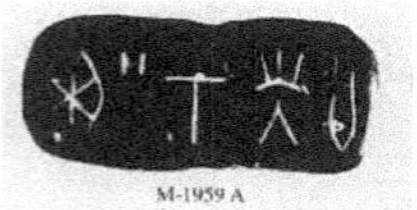

m1959A Text read rebus as at m727

m727a *खोंड [khōṇḍa] m A young bull, a bullcalf. (Marathi) 'turner' (Bengali); कोंद kōnda 'engraver, lapidary setting or (Marathi) G. sãghāṛɔ m. 'lathe' ; संघाट joinery; M. sãgaḍ Rebus: sangataras 'stone-cutter, mason'*

Rebus: kõdār infixing gems' 'double-canoe'

 *āra* 'spokes' Rebus: *āra 'brass'.* cf. erka = ekke (Tbh. of arka) aka (Tbh. of arka) copper (metal); crystal (Kannada) Glyph: *eraka*'nave of wheel' Rebus: eraka 'copper'; cf. erka = ekke (Tbh. of arka) aka (Tbh. of arka) copper (metal); crystal (Kannada) *erako* 'moltencast copper' PLUS

sal 'splinter' Rebus: sal 'workshop' Thus, moltencast copper, brass workshop.

aḍar 'harrow'; rebus: *aduru* 'native unsmelted metal' *bhaṭa* 'warrior' (Sanskrit) Rebus: *baṭa* a kind of iron (Gujarati). Rebus: *bhaṭa* 'furnace' (Santali)

kanka 'rim of jar' Rebus: karṇīka 'account (scribe)' karṇī 'supercargo'

m1878a *balad* m. ' ox ', gng. *bald*, (Ku.) *barad*, id. (N. Tarai) Rebus: *bharat* (5 copper, 4 zinc and 1 tin)(Punjabi) *pattar* 'trough' Rebus*: pattar* 'guild'. Thus, copper-zinc-tin alloy (worker) guild.
Text read rebus as at m727

m595a *खोंड [khōṇḍa] m A young bull, a bullcalf. (Marathi) Rebus: kõdār 'turner' (Bengali); कोंद kōnda 'engraver, lapidary setting or infixing gems' (Marathi) G. sãghāṛɔ m. 'lathe' ; संघाट joinery; M. sāgaḍ 'double-canoe' Rebus: sangataras 'stone-cutter, mason'*

āra 'spokes' Rebus: *āra 'brass'*. cf. erka = ekke (Tbh. of arka) aka (Tbh. of arka) copper (metal); crystal (Kannada) Glyph: *eraka*'nave of wheel' Rebus: eraka 'copper'; cf. erka = ekke (Tbh. of arka) aka (Tbh. of arka) copper (metal); crystal (Kannada) *erako* 'moltencast copper' PLUS

sal 'splinter' Rebus: sal 'workshop' Thus, moltencast copper, brass workshop.

baraḍo = spine; backbone (Tulu) Rebus: *baran, bharat* 'mixed alloys' (5 copper, 4 zinc and 1 tin) (Punjabi) PLUS gaṇḍa 'four' Rebus: kaṇḍa 'furnace, fire-altar' (Santali)

aḍar 'harrow'; rebus: *aduru* 'native unsmelted metal' *bhaṭa* 'warrior' (Sanskrit) Rebus: *baṭa* a kind of iron (Gujarati). Rebus: *bhaṭa* 'furnace' (Santali)

kanka 'rim of jar' Rebus: karṇīka 'account (scribe)' karṇī 'supercargo'

m1088a *balad* m. ' ox ', gng. *bald*, (Ku.) *barad*, id. (N. Tarai) Rebus: *bharat* (5 copper, 4 zinc and 1 tin)(Punjabi) *pattar* 'trough' Rebus*: pattar* 'guild'. Thus, copper-zinc-tin alloy (worker) guild.

āra 'spokes' Rebus: *āra 'brass'*. cf. erka = ekke (Tbh. of arka) aka (Tbh. of arka) copper (metal); crystal (Kannada) Glyph: *eraka*'nave of wheel' Rebus: eraka 'copper'; cf. erka = ekke (Tbh. of arka) aka (Tbh. of arka) copper (metal); crystal (Kannada) *erako* 'moltencast copper' PLUS

sal 'splinter' Rebus: sal 'workshop' Thus, moltencast copper, brass workshop.
dula 'pair' Rebus: dul 'cast metal' PLUS *kamaḍha* 'crab' Rebus: *kammaṭa* 'mint, coiner'.*ḍato* = claws of crab (Santali) Rebus: *dhātu* 'mineral ore' Thus, mint, mineral ore castings.

kanka 'rim of jar' Rebus: karṇīka 'account (scribe)' karṇī 'supercargo'

h1076A

āra 'spokes' Rebus: *āra 'brass'*. cf. erka = ekke (Tbh. of arka) aka (Tbh. of arka) copper (metal); crystal (Kannada) Glyph: *eraka*'nave of wheel' Rebus: eraka 'copper'; cf. erka = ekke (Tbh. of arka) aka (Tbh. of arka) copper (metal); crystal (Kannada) *erako* 'moltencast copper' PLUS

sal 'splinter' Rebus: sal 'workshop' Thus, moltencast copper, brass workshop.

muka 'ladle' (Tamil)(DEDR 4887) Rebus: *mũh* 'ingot' (Santali) *baṭa* = rimless pot (Kannada) Rebus: *baṭa* = a kind of iron (G.)) *bhaṭa* furnace (Gujarati) Thus, iron ingot. *khuṇṭī or khuṭī* a peg or wooden pin (Marathi) *kuṭhi* 'smelting furnace'; *koṭe* 'forged (metal) (Santali)

kanka 'rim of jar' Rebus: karṇīka 'account (scribe)' karṇī 'supercargo'

Unknown 5A

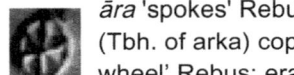

āra 'spokes' Rebus: *āra 'brass'*. cf. erka = ekke (Tbh. of arka) aka (Tbh. of arka) copper (metal); crystal (Kannada) Glyph: *eraka*'nave of wheel' Rebus: eraka 'copper'; cf. erka = ekke (Tbh. of arka) aka (Tbh. of arka) copper (metal); crystal (Kannada) *erako* 'moltencast copper' PLUS

sal 'splinter' Rebus: sal 'workshop' Thus, moltencast copper, brass workshop.

ayo ḍhālako 'alloy metal ingot'

kamaḍha 'crab' Rebus: *kammaṭa* 'mint, coiner'.*ḍato* = claws of crab (Santali) Rebus: *dhātu* 'mineral ore' PLUS खांडा [*khāṇḍā*] *m* A jag, notch, or indentation (as upon the edge of a tool or weapon). Rebus: *kāṇḍa* 'tools, pots and pans and metal-ware' Thus, mint metalware, ore.

m1706a *खोंड [khōṇḍa] m A young bull, a bullcalf. (Marathi) Rebus: kõdār 'turner' (Bengali); कोंद kōnda 'engraver, lapidary setting or infixing gems' (Marathi) G. sãghāṛɔ m. 'lathe' ; संघाट joinery; M. sãgaḍ 'double-canoe' Rebus: sangataras 'stone-cutter, mason'*

āra 'spokes' Rebus: *āra 'brass'*. cf. erka = ekke (Tbh. of arka) aka (Tbh. of arka) copper (metal); crystal (Kannada) Glyph: *eraka*'nave of wheel' Rebus: eraka 'copper'; cf. erka = ekke (Tbh. of arka) aka (Tbh. of arka) copper (metal); crystal (Kannada) *erako* 'moltencast copper' PLUS

sal ‘splinter’ Rebus: sal ‘workshop’ Thus, moltencast copper, brass workshop.
ayo ‘fish’ Rebus: *aya* ‘iron’ *ayas* ‘metal’ dula ‘two’ Rebus: dul ‘cast metal’

dula ‘pair’ Rebus: *dul* ‘cast (metal)’ PLUS*kana, kanac* = corner (Santali); Rebus: *kañcu* = bronze (Telugu) PLUS infixed kolmo ‘paddy plant’ Rebus: kolami ‘smithy, forge’. Thus, cast bronze smithy, forge. Or, *mogge* ‘sprout, bud’ Rebus: *mũh* ‘ingot’ (Santali)Thus, cast bronze ingot. Read as: *kañcu dul mũh ‘bronze cast ingot’*

 kanka ‘rim of jar’ Rebus: karṇīka ‘account (scribe)’ karṇī ‘supercargo’

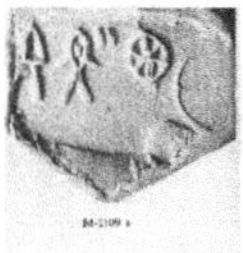

m1109a Zebu. Native metal smith guild.

āra 'spokes' Rebus: *āra ‘brass’.* cf. erka = ekke (Tbh. of arka) aka (Tbh. of arka) copper (metal); crystal (Kannada) Glyph: *eraka*‘nave of wheel’ Rebus: eraka ‘copper’; cf. erka = ekke (Tbh. of arka) aka (Tbh. of arka) copper (metal); crystal (Kannada) *erako* ‘moltencast copper’ PLUS

sal ‘splinter’ Rebus: sal ‘workshop’ Thus, moltencast copper, brass workshop. *aya kāṇḍa* ‘alloy metalware’

कांड *kāṇḍa* ‘arrow’ Rebus: *kāṇḍa* ‘pots and pans, metalware, tools’. Rebus 2: kaṇḍ 'fire-altar' (Santali)

m1136A Rhinoceros/boar: baḍhia = a castrated boar, a hog (Santali) baḍhi ‘a caste who work both in iron and wood’ (Santali) *ba<u>r</u>ea* ‘merchant’ pattar ‘trough’ Rebus: pattar ‘guild, goldsmith’

āra 'spokes' Rebus: *āra ‘brass’.* cf. erka = ekke (Tbh. of arka) aka (Tbh. of arka) copper (metal); crystal (Kannada) Glyph: *eraka*‘nave of wheel’ Rebus: eraka ‘copper’; cf. erka = ekke (Tbh. of arka) aka (Tbh. of arka) copper (metal); crystal (Kannada) *erako* ‘moltencast copper’ PLUS
sal ‘splinter’ Rebus: sal ‘workshop’ Thus, moltencast copper, brass workshop. *aya kammaṭa.*’coiner, mint alloy’
khuṭo ‘ leg, foot ’, °ṭī ‘ goat's leg ’ Rebus: *khōṭā* ‘alloy’ (Marathi)

 kanka ‘rim of jar’ Rebus: karṇīka ‘account (scribe)’ karṇī ‘supercargo’

h273a *खोंड [khōṇḍa] m A young bull, a bullcalf. (Marathi) Rebus: kõdār ‘turner’ (Bengali); कोंद kōnda ‘engraver, lapidary setting or infixing gems’ (Marathi) G. sãghāṛɔ m. ‘lathe’ ; संघाट joinery; M. sãgaḍ ‘double-canoe’ Rebus: sangataras ‘stone-cutter, mason’*

āra 'spokes' Rebus: *āra ‘brass’.* cf. erka = ekke (Tbh. of arka) aka (Tbh. of arka) copper (metal); crystal (Kannada) Glyph: *eraka*‘nave of wheel’ Rebus: eraka ‘copper’; cf. erka = ekke (Tbh. of arka) aka (Tbh. of arka) copper (metal); crystal (Kannada) *erako* ‘moltencast copper’ PLUS

sal ‘splinter’ Rebus: sal ‘workshop’ Thus, moltencast copper, brass workshop. *aya kammaṭa.*’coiner, mint alloy’

m1189a

āra 'spokes' Rebus: *āra 'brass'.* cf. erka = ekke (Tbh. of arka) aka (Tbh. of arka) copper (metal); crystal (Kannada) Glyph: *eraka*'nave of wheel' Rebus: eraka 'copper'; cf. erka = ekke (Tbh. of arka) aka (Tbh. of arka) copper (metal); crystal (Kannada) *erako* 'moltencast copper' PLUS

sal 'splinter' Rebus: sal 'workshop' Thus, moltencast copper, brass workshop. *aya aḍaren* (homonym: aduru) 'alloy native metal'

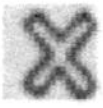 *dāṭu* 'cross'(Telugu) Rebus: *dhatu* 'mineral' (Santali). खांडा [*khāṇḍā*] *m* A jag, notch, or indentation (as upon the edge of a tool or weapon). Rebus: *kāṇḍa* 'tools, pots and pans and metal-ware' dulo 'hole' Rebus: dul 'cast metal' *mogge* 'sprout, bud' Rebus*: mũh* 'ingot'

 *kanac* 'corner' Rebus: *kañcu* 'bronze'

m205A *खोंड [khōṇḍa] m A young bull, a bullcalf. (Marathi) Rebus: kõdār 'turner' (Bengali); कोंद kōnda 'engraver, lapidary setting or infixing gems' (Marathi) G. sãghāṛɔ m. 'lathe' ; संघाट joinery; M. sãgaḍ 'double-canoe' Rebus: sangataras 'stone-cutter, mason'*

āra 'spokes' Rebus: *āra 'brass'.* cf. erka = ekke (Tbh. of arka) aka (Tbh. of arka) copper (metal); crystal (Kannada) Glyph: *eraka*'nave of wheel' Rebus: eraka 'copper'; cf. erka = ekke (Tbh. of arka) aka (Tbh. of arka) copper (metal); crystal (Kannada) *erako* 'moltencast copper' PLUS खांडा [*khāṇḍā*] *m* A jag, notch, or indentation (as upon the edge of a tool or weapon). Rebus: *kāṇḍa* 'tools, pots and pans and metal-ware'
kuṭila 'bent' CDIAL 3230 kuṭi— in cmpd. 'curve', *kuṭika*— 'bent' MBh. Rebus: *kuṭila, katthīl* = bronze (8 parts copper and 2 parts tin) dula 'pair' Rebus: dul 'cast metal' Thus, bronze castings.

 *kana, kanac* = corner (Santali); Rebus: *kañcu* = bronze (Telugu) PLUS खांडा [*khāṇḍā*] *m* A jag, notch, or indentation (as upon the edge of a tool or weapon). Rebus: *kāṇḍa* 'tools, pots and pans and metal-ware' Thus, bronze metalware.

m1137A Rhinoceros/boar: baḍhia = a castrated boar, a hog (Santali) baḍhi 'a caste who work both in iron and wood' (Santali) *baṟea* 'merchant'

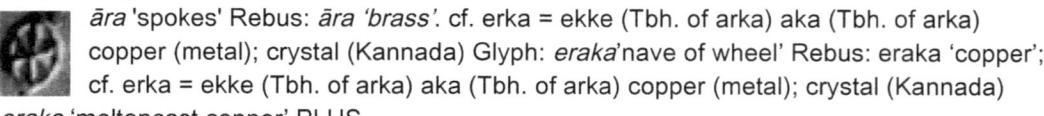

āra 'spokes' Rebus: *āra 'brass'.* cf. erka = ekke (Tbh. of arka) aka (Tbh. of arka) copper (metal); crystal (Kannada) Glyph: *eraka*'nave of wheel' Rebus: eraka 'copper'; cf. erka = ekke (Tbh. of arka) aka (Tbh. of arka) copper (metal); crystal (Kannada) *erako* 'moltencast copper' PLUS

sal 'splinter' Rebus: sal 'workshop' Thus, moltencast copper, brass workshop. *kuṭila* 'bent' CDIAL 3230 kuṭi— in cmpd. 'curve', *kuṭika*— 'bent' MBh. Rebus: *kuṭila, katthīl* = bronze (8 parts copper and 2 parts tin) dula 'pair' Rebus: dul 'cast metal' Thus, bronze castings.

'rim-of-jar' hieroglyph *kanka* (Santali) *karṇika* 'scribe'(Sanskrit) Rebus: *karṇī,* supercargo for a boat shipment. *karṇīka* 'account (scribe)'.कारणी *kāraṇī* 'the supercargo of a ship' (Marathi)

h45a *खोंड [khōṇḍa] m A young bull, a bullcalf. (Marathi) Rebus: kõdār 'turner' (Bengali); कोंद kōnda 'engraver, lapidary setting or infixing gems' (Marathi) G. sãghārɔ m. 'lathe' ; संघाट joinery; M. sāgaḍ 'double-canoe' Rebus: sangataras 'stone-cutter, mason'*

āra 'spokes' Rebus: *āra 'brass'.* cf. erka = ekke (Tbh. of arka) aka (Tbh. of arka) copper (metal); crystal (Kannada) Glyph: *eraka*'nave of wheel' Rebus: eraka 'copper'; cf. erka = ekke (Tbh. of arka) aka (Tbh. of arka) copper (metal); crystal (Kannada) *erako* 'moltencast copper' PLUS

sal 'splinter' Rebus: sal 'workshop' Thus, moltencast copper, brass workshop. *kuṭila* 'bent' CDIAL 3230 kuṭi— in cmpd. 'curve', *kuṭika—* 'bent' MBh. Rebus: *kuṭila, katthīl* = bronze (8 parts copper and 2 parts tin)

Circumscript: *kuṭila* 'bent' CDIAL 3230 kuṭi— in cmpd. 'curve', *kuṭika—* 'bent' MBh. Rebus: *kuṭila, katthīl* = bronze (8 parts copper and 2 parts tin) dula 'pair' Rebus: dul 'cast metal' Thus, bronze castings. *bhaṭa* 'warrior' (Sanskrit) Rebus: *baṭa* a kind of iron (Gujarati). Rebus: *bhaṭa* 'furnace' (Santali)

'rim-of-jar' hieroglyph *kanka* (Santali) *karṇika* 'scribe'(Sanskrit) Rebus: *karṇī,* supercargo for a boat shipment. *karṇīka* 'account (scribe)'.कारणी *kāraṇī* 'the supercargo of a ship' (Marathi)

meḍ 'body' Rebus: *meḍ* 'iron' (Ho.) काठी [kāṭhī] *f* (काष्ट S) 'frame or structure of the body' (Marathi) Rebus: खंडी [khaṇḍī] measure of weight (Marathi) கண்டி; *kaṇṭi, n. < Mhr. khaṇḍil. [T. Tu. khaṇḍi, M. kaṇḍi.]* Candy, a weight, stated to be roughly equivalent to 500 lbs.

M-1139 A

m1139A Rhinoceros/boar: baḍhia = a castrated boar, a hog (Santali) baḍhi 'a caste who work both in iron and wood' (Santali) *baṟea* 'merchant' pattar 'trough' Rebus: pattar 'guild, goldsmith'

āra 'spokes' eraka

Rebus: *āra 'brass'.* cf. erka = ekke (Tbh. of arka) aka (Tbh. of arka) copper (metal); crystal (Kannada) Glyph: *eraka*'nave of wheel' Rebus: 'copper'; cf. erka = ekke (Tbh. of arka) aka (Tbh. of arka) copper (metal); crystal (Kannada) *erako* 'moltencast copper' PLUS

sal 'splinter' Rebus: sal 'workshop' Thus, moltencast copper, brass workshop.
dula 'two' Rebus: dul 'cast metal'

aḍar 'harrow'; rebus: *aduru* 'native unsmelted metal'
kole.l 'temple' Rebus: kole.l 'smithy.

M-1832 a

m1832a *खोंड [khōṇḍa] m A young bull, a bullcalf. (Marathi) Rebus: kõdār 'turner' (Bengali); कोंद kōnda 'engraver, lapidary setting or infixing gems' (Marathi) G. sãghārɔ m. 'lathe' ; संघाट joinery; M. sāgaḍ 'double-canoe' Rebus: sangataras 'stone-cutter, mason'*

āra 'spokes' Rebus: *āra 'brass'.* cf. erka = ekke (Tbh. of arka) aka (Tbh. of arka) copper (metal); crystal (Kannada) Glyph: *eraka*'nave of wheel' Rebus: eraka 'copper'; cf. erka = ekke (Tbh. of arka) aka (Tbh. of arka) copper (metal); crystal (Kannada)

erako 'moltencast copper' PLUS

sal 'splinter' Rebus: sal 'workshop' Thus, moltencast copper, brass workshop.
| *koḍa* 'one' Rebus: *koḍ* 'workshop'
kamaḍha 'crab' Rebus: *kammaṭa* 'mint, coiner'.*ḍato* = claws of crab (Santali) Rebus: *dhātu* 'mineral ore' PLUS Ligature: *baṭa* 'rimless, broad-mouthed pot' Rebus: *bhaṭa* 'furnace' (Gujarati.); *baṭa* 'a kind of iron' (Gujarati)

ḍhanga = a **crook** used for pulling down the branches of trees, for goats, sheep and camels (P.) Rebus:*ḍhangar* blacksmith' PLUS 'notch': खांडा [*khāṇḍā*] *m* A jag, notch, or indentation (as upon the edge of a tool or weapon). Rebus: *kāṇḍa* 'tools, pots and pans and metal-ware'. Thus, blacksmith metalware.

Nausharo 7A *खोंड [khōṇḍa] m A young bull, a bullcalf. (Marathi) Rebus: kõdār 'turner' (Bengali); कोंद kōnda 'engraver, lapidary setting or infixing gems' (Marathi) G. sãghāṛɔ m. 'lathe' ; संघाट joinery; M. sãgaḍ 'double-canoe' Rebus: sangataras 'stone-cutter, mason'*

āra 'spokes' Rebus: *āra 'brass'*. cf. erka = ekke (Tbh. of arka) aka (Tbh. of arka) copper (metal); crystal (Kannada) Glyph: *eraka*'nave of wheel' Rebus: eraka 'copper'; cf. erka = ekke (Tbh. of arka) aka (Tbh. of arka) copper (metal); crystal (Kannada)
erako 'moltencast copper' PLUS
sal 'splinter' Rebus: sal 'workshop' Thus, moltencast copper, brass workshop. kolom 'three' Rebus: kolami 'smithy, forge'

kolmo 'paddy plant' Rebus: *kolami* 'smithy, forge' Vikalpa: *mogge* 'sprout, bud' Rebus: *mũh* 'ingot' (Santali) dolu 'plant of shoot height' Rebus: dul 'cast metal'

M-1806 a

m1806a, m1729a, m1680A *Read rebus as at Nausharo 7.*

M-1729 a

m1729a

H-1680 A

m1680A

Chanhudaro 5A *खोंड [khōṇḍa] m A young bull, a bullcalf. (Marathi) Rebus: kõdār 'turner' (Bengali); कोंद kōnda 'engraver, lapidary setting or infixing gems' (Marathi) G. sãghāṛɔ m. 'lathe' ; संघाट joinery; M. sãgaḍ 'double-canoe' Rebus: sangataras 'stone-cutter, mason'*

āra 'spokes' Rebus: *āra 'brass'*. cf. erka = ekke (Tbh. of arka) aka (Tbh. of arka) copper (metal); crystal (Kannada) Glyph: *eraka*'nave of wheel' Rebus: eraka 'copper'; cf. erka = ekke (Tbh. of arka) aka (Tbh. of arka) copper (metal); crystal (Kannada) *erako* 'moltencast copper' PLUS

sal 'splinter' Rebus: sal 'workshop' Thus, moltencast copper, brass workshop.
āra 'six' Rebus: *āra* 'brass' *ayo* 'fish' Rebus: *aya* 'iron' *ayas* 'metal'

kanka 'rim of jar' Rebus: karṇīka 'account (scribe)' karṇī 'supercargo'

meḍ 'body' Rebus: *meḍ* 'iron' (Ho.) काठी [kāṭhī] *f* (काष्ट S) 'frame or structure of the body' (Marathi) Rebus: खंडी [khanḍī] measure of weight (Marathi) *கண்டி; kaṇṭi, n. < Mhr. khaṇḍil. [T. Tu. khaṇḍi, M. kaṇḍi.]* Candy, a weight, stated to be roughly equivalent to 500 lbs

Kalibangan 12A *खोंड [khōṇḍa] m A young bull, a bullcalf. (Marathi) Rebus: kõdār 'turner' (Bengali); कोंद kōnda 'engraver, lapidary setting or infixing gems' (Marathi) G. sãghārɔ m. 'lathe' ; संघाट joinery; M. sãgaḍ 'double-canoe' Rebus: sangataras 'stone-cutter, mason*

āra 'spokes' Rebus: *āra 'brass'*. cf. erka = ekke (Tbh. of arka) aka (Tbh. of arka) copper (metal); crystal (Kannada) Glyph: *eraka*'nave of wheel' Rebus: eraka 'copper'; cf. erka = ekke (Tbh. of arka) aka (Tbh. of arka) copper (metal); crystal (Kannada) *erako* 'moltencast copper' PLUS
sal 'splinter' Rebus: sal 'workshop' Thus, moltencast copper, brass workshop. kolom 'three' Rebus: kolami 'smithy, forge'
water-carrier hieroglyph *kuṭi*; Rebus: *kuṭhi* 'smelter furnace'.

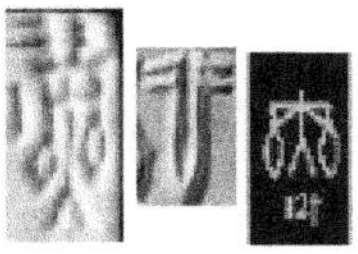
PLUS 'rim of jar': *kanka* (Santali) *karṇika* 'scribe'(Sanskrit)
Rebus: *karṇī,* supercargo
'rim-of-jar' hieroglyph *kanka* (Santali) *karṇika* 'scribe'(Sanskrit)
Rebus: *karṇī,* supercargo for a boat shipment. *karṇīka* 'account (scribe)' .कारणी *kāraṇī* 'the supercargo of a ship' (Marathi)

h149A

āra 'spokes' Rebus: *āra 'brass'*. cf. erka = ekke (Tbh. of arka) aka (Tbh. of arka) copper (metal); crystal (Kannada) Glyph: *eraka*'nave of wheel' Rebus: eraka 'copper'; cf. erka = ekke (Tbh. of arka) aka (Tbh. of arka) copper (metal); crystal (Kannada) *erako* 'moltencast copper' PLUS
sal 'splinter' Rebus: sal 'workshop' Thus, moltencast copper, brass workshop. *aya aḍaren* (homonym: aduru) 'alloy native metal'
kəṭhā´r, kc. *kuṭhār* m. ' granary, storeroom '(WPah.)(CDIAL 3550). *koṭhārī m.* ' storekeeper'

(Gujarati)(CDIAL 3551) Thus, storeroom (of) *kolom* 'three' Rebus: *kolami* 'smithy, forge'. Dula 'pair' Rebus: dul 'cast metal' Thus, together *dul kolami kuṭhār* 'cast metal smithy storeroom'
dulo 'hole' Rebus: dul 'cast metal' *ganḍa* 'four' Rebus: *kanḍa* 'furnace, fire-altar' (Santali).

muka 'ladle' (Tamil)(DEDR 4887) Rebus: *mũh* 'ingot' (Santali) Thus, iron ingot.

kolom ‘three’ Rebus: kolami ‘smithy, forge’

dhāḷ ‘a slope’; ‘inclination of a plane’ (G.); *ḍhāḷiyum* = adj. sloping, inclining (G.) Rebus: *ḍhālako* = a large metal ingot (G.) *ḍhālakī* = a metal heated and poured into a mould; a solid piece of metal; an ingot (Gujarati) PLUS खांडा [*khāṇḍā*] *m* A jag, notch, or indentation (as upon the edge of a tool or weapon). Rebus: *kāṇḍa* ‘tools, pots and pans and metal-ware’ Thus, the pair of sign hieroglyphs from r. read rebus: copper, bronze ingots, metalware castings.

mogge ‘sprout, bud’ Rebus*: mūh* ‘ingot’

h231A

āra 'spokes' Rebus: *āra ‘brass’*. cf. erka = ekke (Tbh. of arka) aka (Tbh. of arka) copper (metal); crystal (Kannada) Glyph: *eraka* ‘nave of wheel’ Rebus: eraka ‘copper’; cf. erka = ekke (Tbh. of arka) aka (Tbh. of arka) copper (metal); crystal (Kannada) *erako* ‘moltencast copper’ PLUS

sal ‘splinter’ Rebus: sal ‘workshop’ Thus, moltencast copper, brass workshop. *aya kammaṭa.* ‘coiner, mint alloy’

aya kāṇḍa ‘alloy metalware’

कांड *kāṇḍa* ‘arrow’ Rebus: *kāṇḍa* ‘pots and pans, metalware, tools’. Rebus 2: kaṇḍ 'fire-altar' (Santali)

m788A *खोंड [khōṇḍa] m A young bull, a bullcalf. (Marathi) Rebus: kõdār ‘turner’ (Bengali); कोंद kōnda ‘engraver, lapidary setting or infixing gems’ (Marathi) G. sãghāṛɔ m. ‘lathe’ ; संघाट joinery; M. sãgaḍ ‘double-canoe’ Rebus: sangataras ‘stone-cutter, mason’*

āra 'spokes' Rebus: *āra ‘brass’*. cf. erka = ekke (Tbh. of arka) aka (Tbh. of arka) copper (metal); crystal (Kannada) Glyph: *eraka* ‘nave of wheel’ Rebus: eraka ‘copper’; cf. erka = ekke (Tbh. of arka) aka (Tbh. of arka) copper (metal); crystal (Kannada) *erako* ‘moltencast copper’ PLUS

sal ‘splinter’ Rebus: sal ‘workshop’ Thus, moltencast copper, brass workshop.

aya aḍaren (homonym: aduru) ‘alloy native metal’

aḍaren ‘cover of pot or lid’ Rebus: *aduru* ‘native, unsmelted metal’ Duplicated: dula ‘pair’ Rebus: dul ‘cast metal’

dulo ‘hole’ Rebus: dul ‘cast metal’

kanka ‘rim of jar’ Rebus: karṇīka ‘account (scribe)’ karṇī ‘supercargo’

m381a

āra 'spokes' Rebus: *āra ‘brass’*. cf. erka = ekke (Tbh. of arka) aka (Tbh. of arka) copper (metal); crystal (Kannada) Glyph: *eraka* ‘nave of wheel’ Rebus: eraka ‘copper’; cf. erka = ekke (Tbh. of arka) aka (Tbh. of arka) copper (metal); crystal (Kannada) *erako* ‘moltencast copper’ PLUS

sal ‘splinter’ Rebus: sal ‘workshop’ Thus, moltencast copper, brass workshop.

kamaḍha 'crab' Rebus: *kammaṭa* 'mint, coiner'.*ḍato* = claws of crab (Santali) Rebus: *dhātu* 'mineral ore'
dula 'two' Rebus: dul 'cast metal'
ayo 'fish' Rebus: *aya* 'iron' *ayas* 'metal'

 *baroṭi* 'twelve' *bhārata* 'a factitious alloy of copper, pewter, tin' (Marathi)

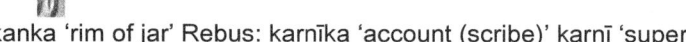

kanka 'rim of jar' Rebus: karṇīka 'account (scribe)' karṇī 'supercargo'

m54a खोंड *[khōṇḍa] m A young bull, a bullcalf. (Marathi) Rebus: kõdār 'turner' (Bengali); कोंद kōnda 'engraver, lapidary setting or infixing gems' (Marathi) G. sãghāṛɔ m. 'lathe' ; संघाट joinery; M. sãgaḍ 'double-canoe' Rebus: sangataras 'stone-cutter, mason'*

āra 'spokes' Rebus: *āra 'brass'.* cf. erka = ekke (Tbh. of arka) aka (Tbh. of arka) copper (metal); crystal (Kannada) Glyph: *eraka*'nave of wheel' Rebus: eraka 'copper'; cf. erka = ekke (Tbh. of arka) aka (Tbh. of arka) copper (metal); crystal (Kannada) *erako* 'moltencast copper' PLUS
sal 'splinter' Rebus: sal 'workshop' Thus, moltencast copper, brass workshop.

 *muka* 'ladle' (Tamil)(DEDR 4887) Rebus: *mũh* 'ingot' (Santali) Thus, iron ingot.
kolom 'three' Rebus: kolami 'smithy, forge'
aya kammaṭa.'coiner, mint alloy' *aya kāṇḍa* 'alloy metalware'

Lothal 18a खोंड *[khōṇḍa] m A young bull, a bullcalf. (Marathi) Rebus: kõdār 'turner' (Bengali); कोंद kōnda 'engraver, lapidary setting or infixing gems' (Marathi) G. sãghāṛɔ m. 'lathe' ; संघाट joinery; M. sãgaḍ 'double-canoe' Rebus: sangataras 'stone-cutter, mason'*

 *āra* 'spokes' Rebus: *āra 'brass'.* cf. erka = ekke (Tbh. of arka) aka (Tbh. of arka) copper (metal); crystal (Kannada) Glyph: *eraka*'nave of wheel' Rebus: eraka 'copper'; cf. erka = ekke (Tbh. of arka) aka (Tbh. of arka) copper (metal); crystal (Kannada) *erako* 'moltencast copper' PLUS
sal 'splinter' Rebus: sal 'workshop' Thus, moltencast copper, brass workshop. | *koḍa* 'one' Rebus: *koḍ* 'workshop'

 *aḍar* 'harrow'; rebus: *aduru* 'native unsmelted metal'

m1667A खोंड *[khōṇḍa] m A young bull, a bullcalf. (Marathi) Rebus: kõdār 'turner' (Bengali); कोंद kōnda 'engraver, lapidary setting or infixing gems' (Marathi) G. sãghāṛɔ m. 'lathe' ; संघाट joinery; M. sãgaḍ 'double-canoe' Rebus: sangataras 'stone-cutter, mason'*

 *āra* 'spokes' Rebus: *āra 'brass'.* cf. erka = ekke (Tbh. of arka) aka (Tbh. of arka) copper (metal); crystal (Kannada) Glyph: *eraka*'nave of wheel' Rebus: eraka 'copper'; cf. erka = ekke (Tbh. of arka) aka (Tbh. of arka) copper (metal); crystal (Kannada) *erako* 'moltencast copper' PLUS cast metal workshop'.

  *khuṭo* ' leg, foot ', °ṭī ' goat's leg ' Rebus: *khōṭā* 'alloy' (Marathi)
P
sal 'splinter' Rebus: sal 'workshop' Thus, moltencast copper, brass, alloy

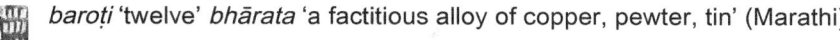

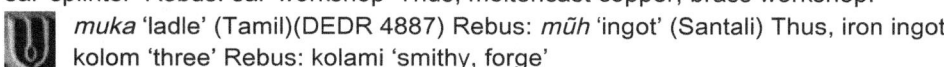

workshop castings
dula 'two' Rebs: dul 'cast metal' *ayo* 'fish' Rebus: *aya* 'iron' *ayas* 'metal'

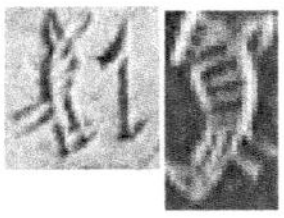

The pair of hieroglyph signs are compositions: 1. *bicha* 'scorpion' (Assamese) Rebus: *bica* 'stone ore' (Santali) The pairing sign is a composition of: sloping stroke PLUS two short strokes of a 'splinter':*dhāḷ* 'a slope'; 'inclination of a plane' (Gujarati); *ḍhāḷiyum* = adj. sloping, inclining (Gujarati) Rebus: *ḍhālako* = a large metal ingot (Gujarati) *ḍhālakī* = a metal heated and poured into a mould; a solid piece of metal; an ingot (Gujarati)PLUS*sal* 'splinter' Rebus: *sal* 'workshop'. Thus the composition reads: *ḍhālako sal* 'ingot workshop'.
mason.'

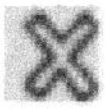 *dāṭu* 'cross'(Telugu) Rebus: *dhatu* 'mineral' (Santali).

kanka 'rim of jar' Rebus: karṇīka 'account (scribe)' karṇī 'supercargo'

m214A *खोंड [khōṇḍa] m A young bull, a bullcalf. (Marathi) Rebus: kōdār 'turner' (Bengali); कोंद kōnda 'engraver, lapidary setting or infixing gems' (Marathi) G. sãghāṛɔ m. 'lathe' ; संघाट joinery; M. sãgaḍ 'double-canoe' Rebus: sangataras 'stone-cutter, mason'*

āra 'spokes' Rebus: *āra 'brass'*. cf. erka = ekke (Tbh. of arka) aka (Tbh. of arka) copper (metal); crystal (Kannada) Glyph: *eraka*'nave of wheel' Rebus: eraka 'copper'; cf. erka = ekke (Tbh. of arka) aka (Tbh. of arka) copper (metal); crystal (Kannada) *erako* 'moltencast copper' PLUSsal 'splinter' Rebus: sal 'workshop' Thus, moltencast copper, brass workshop.

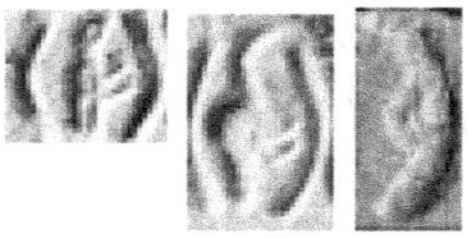

kuṭila 'bent' CDIAL 3230 kuṭi— in cmpd. 'curve', *kuṭika—* 'bent' MBh. Rebus: *kuṭila, katthīl* = bronze (8 parts copper and 2 parts tin) dula 'pair' Rebus: dul 'cast metal' Thus, cast bronze PLUS infixed 'bird hieroglyph': *karaṇḍa* 'duck' (Sanskrit) *karaṛa* 'a very large aquatic bird' (Sindhi)
Rebus: करडा [*karaḍā*] Hard from alloy--iron, silver &c. (Marathi) Thus, hard alloy bronze casting.

 *kharedo* = a currycomb (Gujarati) खरारा [*kharārā*] *m* (H) A currycomb. 2 Currying a horse. (Marathi) Rebus: करडा [*karaḍā*] Hard from alloy--iron, silver &c. (Marathi) *kharādī* ' turner' (Gujarati)

m1979a

āra 'spokes' Rebus: *āra 'brass'*. cf. erka = ekke (Tbh. of arka) aka (Tbh. of arka) copper (metal); crystal (Kannada) Glyph: *eraka*'nave of wheel' Rebus: eraka 'copper'; cf. erka = ekke (Tbh. of arka) aka (Tbh. of arka) copper (metal); crystal (Kannada) *erako* 'moltencast copper' PLUS *aya kammaṭa.*'coiner, mint alloy' *kuṭila* 'bent' CDIAL 3230 kuṭi— in cmpd. 'curve', *kuṭika*— 'bent' MBh. Rebus: *kuṭila, katthīl* = bronze (8 parts copper and 2 parts tin) dula 'pair' Rebus: dul 'cast metal' Thus, cast bronze

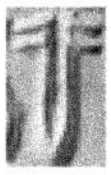
kanka 'rim of jar' Rebus: karṇīka 'account (scribe)' karṇī 'supercargo'

m400A

āra 'spokes' Rebus: *āra 'brass'*. cf. erka = ekke (Tbh. of arka) aka (Tbh. of arka) copper (metal); crystal (Kannada) Glyph: *eraka*'nave of wheel' Rebus: eraka 'copper'; cf. erka = ekke (Tbh. of arka) aka (Tbh. of arka) copper (metal); crystal (Kannada) *erako* 'moltencast copper' PLUS sal 'splinter' Rebus: sal 'workshop' Thus, moltencast copper, brass workshop.PLUS 'notch': खांडा [*khāṇḍā*] *m* A jag, notch, or indentation (as upon the edge of a tool or weapon). Rebus: *kāṇḍa* 'tools, pots and pans and metal-ware'

meḍ 'body' Rebus: *meḍ* 'iron' (Ho.) काठी [kāṭhī] *f* (काष्ट S) 'frame or structure of the body' (Marathi) Rebus: खंडी [khaṇḍī] measure of weight (Marathi) *கண்டி; kaṇṭi, n. < Mhr. khaṇḍil. [T. Tu. khaṇḍi, M. kaṇḍi.]* Candy, a weight, stated to be roughly equivalent to 500 lbs.

khaṇḍ 'field, division' (Sanskrit) Rebus: *khāṇḍa* 'tools, pots and pans, metal-ware'. Rebus 2: kaṇḍ 'fire-altar' (Santali) dula 'pair' Rebus: dul 'cast metal' Thus, duplicated 'division' hieroglyph sign reads: cast metal metal-ware.

m634A *खोंड [khōṇḍa] m A young bull, a bullcalf. (Marathi) Rebus: kõdār 'turner' (Bengali); कोंद kōnda 'engraver, lapidary setting or infixing gems' (Marathi) G. sãghāṛɔ m. 'lathe' ; संघाट joinery; M. sãgaḍ 'double-canoe' Rebus: sangataras 'stone-cutter, mason'*

āra 'spokes' Rebus: *āra 'brass'*. cf. erka = ekke (Tbh. of arka) aka (Tbh. of arka) copper (metal); crystal (Kannada) Glyph: *eraka*'nave of wheel' Rebus: eraka 'copper'; cf. erka = ekke (Tbh. of arka) aka (Tbh. of arka) copper (metal); crystal (Kannada) *erako* 'moltencast copper' PLUS sal 'splinter' Rebus: sal 'workshop' Thus, moltencast copper, brass workshop. *bhaṭa* 'warrior' (Sanskrit) Rebus: *baṭa* a kind of iron (Gujarati). Rebus: *bhaṭa* 'furnace' (Santali)

dula 'pair' Rebus: *dul* 'cast (metal)' PLUS*kana, kanac* = corner (Santali); Rebus: *kañcu* = bronze (Telugu) PLUS infixed kolom 'three' Rebus: kolami 'smithy, forge'. Thus, cast bronze smithy, forge. Or, *mogge* 'sprout, bud' Rebus: *mũh* 'ingot' (Santali)Thus, cast bronze ingot. Read as: *kañcu dul mũh 'bronze cast ingot'*

aḍar 'harrow'; rebus: *aduru* 'native unsmelted metal' *ayo* 'fish' Rebus: *aya* 'iron' *ayas* 'metal'

kanka 'rim of jar' Rebus: karṇīka 'account (scribe)' karṇī 'supercargo'
ayo 'fish' Rebus: *aya* 'iron' *ayas* 'metal' PLUS superscript: 'stool': Kur. *kaṇḍō* a stool.

Malt. *kaṇḍo* stool, seat. (DEDR 1179) Rebus: kaṇḍ 'fire-altar' (Santali) *kāṇḍa* 'tools, pots and pans and metal-ware' (Marathi)

m200a

खोंड [khōṇḍa] m A young bull, a bullcalf. (Marathi) Rebus: kõdār 'turner' (Bengali); कोंद kōnda 'engraver, lapidary setting or infixing gems' (Marathi) G. sãghāṛɔ m. 'lathe' ; संघाट joinery; M. sãgaḍ 'double-canoe' Rebus: sangataras 'stone-cutter, mason'

āra 'spokes' Rebus: *āra 'brass'*. cf. erka = ekke (Tbh. of arka) aka (Tbh. of arka) copper (metal); crystal (Kannada) Glyph: *eraka*'nave of wheel' Rebus: eraka 'copper'; cf. erka = ekke (Tbh. of arka) aka (Tbh. of arka) copper (metal); crystal (Kannada) *erako* 'moltencast copper' PLUS

sal 'splinter' Rebus: sal 'workshop' Thus, moltencast copper, brass workshop.

dula 'pair' Rebus: dul 'cast metal' PLUS

 *kuṭila* 'bent' CDIAL 3230 kuṭi— in cmpd. 'curve', *kuṭika*— 'bent' MBh. Rebus: *kuṭila, katthīl* = bronze (8 parts copper and 2 parts tin) PLUS infixed *ayo* 'fish' Rebus: *aya* 'iron' *ayas* 'metal'. Thus, cast bronze alloy metal.

 kanka 'rim of jar' Rebus: karṇīka 'account (scribe)' karṇī 'supercargo'

m1957a

āra 'spokes' Rebus: *āra 'brass'*. cf. erka = ekke (Tbh. of arka) aka (Tbh. of arka) copper (metal); crystal (Kannada) Glyph: *eraka*'nave of wheel' Rebus: eraka 'copper'; cf. erka = ekke (Tbh. of arka) aka (Tbh. of arka) copper (metal); crystal (Kannada) *erako* 'moltencast copper' PLUS

sal 'splinter' Rebus: sal 'workshop' Thus, moltencast copper, brass workshop.

ḍhanga = a crook used for pulling down the branches of trees, for goats, sheep and camels (P.) Rebus:*ḍhangar* blacksmith'.PLUS

 *kharedo* = a currycomb (Gujarati) खरारा [*kharārā*] *m* (H) A currycomb. 2 Currying a horse. (Marathi) Rebus: करडा [*karaḍā*] Hard from alloy--iron, silver &c. (Marathi) *kharādī* ' turner' (Gujarati)

dula 'pair' Rebus: *dul* 'cast (metal)' PLUS*kana, kanac* = corner (Santali); Rebus: *kañcu* = bronze (Telugu) PLUS infixed kolmo 'paddy plant' Rebus: kolami 'smithy, forge'. Thus,

cast bronze smithy, forge. Or, *mogge* 'sprout, bud' Rebus: *mũh* 'ingot' (Santali)Thus, cast bronze ingot. Read as: *kañcu dul mũh 'bronze cast ingot'* water-carrier hieroglyph *kuṭi*; Rebus: *kuṭhi* 'smelter furnace'. PLUS 'rim of jar': kanka 'rim of jar' Rebus: karṇīka 'account (scribe)' karṇī 'supercargo'

m235a *balad* m. ' ox ', gng. *bald*, (Ku.) *barad*, id. (N. Tarai) Rebus: *bharat* (5 copper, 4 zinc and 1 tin)(Punjabi) *pattar* 'trough' Rebus: *pattar* 'guild'. Thus, copper-zinc-tin alloy (worker) guild.

āra 'spokes' Rebus: *āra 'brass'*. cf. erka = ekke (Tbh. of arka) aka (Tbh. of arka) copper (metal); crystal (Kannada) Glyph: *eraka*'nave of wheel' Rebus: eraka

'copper'; cf. erka = ekke (Tbh. of arka) aka (Tbh. of arka) copper (metal); crystal (Kannada) *erako* 'moltencast copper' PLUS
sal 'splinter' Rebus: sal 'workshop' Thus, moltencast copper, brass workshop.

|||| Numeral 4: gaṇḍa 'four' Rebus: kaṇḍa 'furnace, fire-altar' (Santali) dula 'pair' Rebus: dul 'cast metal'

kamaḍha 'crab' Rebus: *kammaṭa* 'mint, coiner'.
ḍato = claws of crab (Santali) Rebus: *dhātu* 'mineral ore'

kanka 'rim of jar' Rebus: karṇīka 'account (scribe)' karṇī 'supercargo'

m1675a *खोंड [khōṇḍa] m A young bull, a bullcalf. (Marathi) Rebus: kõdār 'turner' (Bengali); कोंद kōnda 'engraver, lapidary setting or infixing gems' (Marathi) G. sãghāṛɔ m. 'lathe' ; संघाट joinery; M. sãgaḍ 'double-canoe' Rebus: sangataras 'stone-cutter, mason'*

āra 'spokes' Rebus: *āra 'brass'*. cf. erka = ekke (Tbh. of arka) aka (Tbh. of arka) copper (metal); crystal (Kannada) Glyph: *eraka*'nave of wheel' Rebus: eraka 'copper'; cf. erka = ekke (Tbh. of arka) aka (Tbh. of arka) copper (metal); crystal (Kannada) *erako* 'moltencast copper' PLUS
sal 'splinter' Rebus: sal 'workshop' Thus, moltencast copper, brass workshop.
dula 'pair' Rebus: *dul* 'cast (metal)' PLUS *kana, kanac* = corner (Santali); Rebus: *kañcu* = bronze (Telugu) Thus, cast bronze. PLUS |||| Numeral 4: gaṇḍa 'four' Rebus: kaṇḍa 'furnace, fire-altar' (Santali)

m103A *खोंड [khōṇḍa] m A young bull, a bullcalf. (Marathi) Rebus: kõdār 'turner' (Bengali); कोंद kōnda 'engraver, lapidary setting or infixing gems' (Marathi) G. sãghāṛɔ m. 'lathe' ; संघाट joinery; M. sãgaḍ 'double-canoe' Rebus: sangataras 'stone-cutter, mason'*

āra 'spokes' Rebus: *āra 'brass'*. cf. erka = ekke (Tbh. of arka) aka (Tbh. of arka) copper (metal); crystal (Kannada) Glyph: *eraka*'nave of wheel' Rebus: eraka 'copper'; cf. erka = ekke (Tbh. of arka) aka (Tbh. of arka) copper (metal); crystal (Kannada) *erako* 'moltencast copper' PLUS
sal 'splinter' Rebus: sal 'workshop' Thus, moltencast copper, brass workshop.
dula 'pair' Rebus: dul 'cast metal' PLUS kolom 'three' Rebus: kolami 'smithy, forge' Thus smithy for casting

kolmo 'paddy plant' Rebus: *kolami* 'smithy, forge' Vikalpa: *mogge* 'sprout, bud' Rebus: *mũh* 'ingot' (Santali) dolu 'plant of shoot height' Rebus: dul 'cast metal'

m385A*āra* 'spokes' Rebus: *āra 'brass'*. cf. erka = ekke (Tbh. of arka) aka (Tbh. of arka) copper (metal); crystal (Kannada) Glyph: *eraka*'nave of wheel' Rebus: eraka 'copper'; cf. erka = ekke (Tbh. of arka) aka (Tbh. of arka) copper (metal); crystal (Kannada) *erako* 'moltencast copper' PLUS

sal 'splinter' Rebus: sal 'workshop' Thus, moltencast copper, brass workshop.

kolmo 'paddy plant' Rebus: *kolami* 'smithy, forge' Vikalpa: *mogge* 'sprout, bud' Rebus: *mũh* 'ingot' (Santali) dolu 'plant of shoot height' Rebus: dul 'cast metal' PLUS |||| Numeral 4: gaṇḍa 'four' Rebus: kaṇḍa 'furnace, fire-altar' (Santali)

m889A *खोंड [khōṇḍa] m A young bull, a bullcalf. (Marathi) Rebus: kõdār 'turner' (Bengali); कोंद kōnda 'engraver, lapidary setting or infixing gems' (Marathi) G. sãghāṛɔ m. 'lathe' ; संघाट joinery; M. sãgaḍ 'double-canoe' Rebus: sangataras 'stone-cutter, mason'*

āra 'spokes' Rebus: *āra 'brass'.* cf. erka = ekke (Tbh. of arka) aka (Tbh. of arka) copper (metal); crystal (Kannada) Glyph: *eraka* 'nave of wheel' Rebus: eraka 'copper'; cf. erka = ekke (Tbh. of arka) aka (Tbh. of arka) copper (metal); crystal (Kannada) *erako* 'moltencast copper' PLUS

sal 'splinter' Rebus: sal 'workshop' Thus, moltencast copper, brass workshop.

dula 'pair' Rebus: *dul* 'cast (metal)' PLUS *kana, kanac* = corner (Santali); Rebus: *kañcu* = bronze (Telugu) PLUS infixed kolmo 'paddy plant' Rebus: kolami 'smithy, forge'. Thus, cast bronze smithy, forge. Or, *mogge* 'sprout, bud' Rebus: *mũh* 'ingot' (Santali)Thus, cast bronze ingot. Read as: *kañcu dul mũh 'bronze cast ingot'*

dula 'pair' Rebus: dul 'cast metal'

loa 'ficus religiosa' Rebus: *lo* 'iron' (Sanskrit)

kanka 'rim of jar' Rebus: karṇīka 'account (scribe)' karṇī 'supercargo'

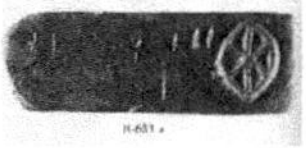

h653a *āra* 'spokes' Rebus: *āra 'brass'.* cf. erka = ekke (Tbh. of arka) aka (Tbh. of arka) copper (metal); crystal (Kannada) Glyph: *eraka* 'nave of wheel' Rebus: eraka 'copper'; cf. erka = ekke (Tbh. of arka) aka (Tbh. of arka)

copper (metal); crystal (Kannada) *erako* 'moltencast copper' PLUS
sal 'splinter' Rebus: sal 'workshop' Thus, moltencast copper, brass workshop.

m623a *खोंड [khōṇḍa] m A young bull, a bullcalf. (Marathi) Rebus: kõdār 'turner' (Bengali); कोंद kōnda 'engraver, lapidary setting or infixing gems' (Marathi) G. sãghāṛɔ m. 'lathe' ; संघाट joinery; M. sãgaḍ 'double-canoe' Rebus: sangataras 'stone-cutter, mason'*

āra 'spokes' Rebus: *āra 'brass'.* cf. erka = ekke (Tbh. of arka) aka (Tbh. of arka) copper (metal); crystal (Kannada) Glyph: *eraka* 'nave of wheel' Rebus: eraka 'copper'; cf. erka = ekke (Tbh. of arka) aka (Tbh. of arka) copper (metal); crystal (Kannada) *erako* 'moltencast copper'

ḍato = claws of crab (Santali) Rebus: *dhātu* 'mineral ore'

Strands of yarn/rope' hieroglyph: Hieroglyph: 'strands of yarn' Rebus reading: *dhā'tu* 'strand of rope' Rebus: *dhatu* 'mineral ore' (Santali)

sal 'splinter' Rebus: sal 'workshop'

kamaḍha = crab; *kampaṭṭam* = mint (Ta.) ; *kammaṭa* 'coiner, mint' (Telugu)

aḍar 'harrow'; rebus: *aduru* 'native unsmelted metal'

baraḍo = spine; backbone (Tulu) Rebus: *baran, bharat* 'mixed alloys' (5 copper, 4 zinc and 1

tin) (Punjabi) dula 'pair' Rebus: dul 'cast metal' Thus cast mixed alloy of opper, zinc and tin.

dula 'pair' Rebus: dul 'cast metal' PLUS kolmo 'paddy plant' Rebus: kolami 'smithy, forge' Thus metal smithy castings.

kanka 'rim of jar' Rebus: karṇīka 'account (scribe)' karṇī 'supercargo'
ayo 'fish' Rebus: aya 'iron' (Gujarati) ayas 'metal' (Vedic)

m558A

āra 'spokes' Rebus: *āra 'brass'*. cf. erka = ekke (Tbh. of arka) aka (Tbh. of arka) copper (metal); crystal (Kannada) Glyph: *eraka* 'nave of wheel' Rebus: eraka 'copper'; cf. erka = ekke (Tbh. of arka) aka (Tbh. of arka) copper (metal); crystal (Kannada) *erako* 'moltencast copper'

dula 'pair' Rebus: dul 'cast metal'

kuṭila 'bent' CDIAL 3230 kuṭi— in cmpd. 'curve', *kuṭika*— 'bent' MBh. Rebus: *kuṭila, katthīl* = bronze (8 parts copper and 2 parts tin) Thus, cast bronze. Infixed with: kolo 'three' Rebus: kolami 'smithy, forge' PLUS *khareḍo* = a currycomb (Gujarati) खरारा [*kharārā*

] *m* (H) A currycomb. 2 Currying a horse. (Marathi) Rebus: करडा [*karaḍā*] Hard from alloy--iron, silver &c. (Marathi) *kharādī* ' turner' (Gujarati) Thus, hard alloys, cast bronze smithy, forge.

ranku 'liquid measure' Rebus: ranku 'tin.'

m108a *खोंड [khōṇḍa] m A young bull, a bullcalf. (Marathi) Rebus: kõdār 'turner' (Bengali); कोंद kōnda 'engraver, lapidary setting or infixing gems' (Marathi) G. sãghāṛɔ m. 'lathe' ; संघाट joinery; M. sãgaḍ 'double-canoe' Rebus: sangataras 'stone-cutter, mason'*

āra 'spokes' Rebus: *āra 'brass'*. cf. erka = ekke (Tbh. of arka) aka (Tbh. of arka) copper (metal); crystal (Kannada) Glyph: *eraka* 'nave of wheel' Rebus: eraka 'copper'; cf. erka = ekke (Tbh. of arka) aka (Tbh. of arka) copper (metal); crystal (Kannada) *erako* 'moltencast copper'

ḍato = claws of crab (Santali) Rebus: *dhātu* 'mineral ore' dula 'pair' Rebus: dul 'cast metal'. Thus, cast mineral ore.

kamaḍha = crab; *kampaṭṭam* = mint (Ta.) ; *kammaṭa* 'coiner, mint' (Telugu)

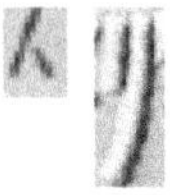

notch+slanted stroke reads rebus: *ḍhālako kāṇḍa* 'ingot, tools, pots and pans and metal-ware'.*ḍhāḷ* 'a slope'; 'inclination of a plane' (G.); *ḍhāḷiyum* = adj. sloping, inclining (G.) Rebus: *ḍhālako* = a large metal ingot (G.) *ḍhālakī* = a metal heated and poured into a mould; a solid piece of metal; an ingot (Gujarati) PLUS खांडा [*khāṇḍā*] *m* A jag, notch, or indentation (as upon the edge of a tool or weapon). Rebus: *kāṇḍa* 'tools, pots and pans and metal-ware' *Thus, together, the pair reads: āra erako khāṇḍā* 'brass, moltencast copper metalware'.

ayo 'fish' Rebus: aya 'iron' (Gujarati) ayas 'metal' (Vedic)

kanac 'corner' Rebus: *kañcu* 'bronze'

khareḍo = a currycomb (Gujarati) खरारा [*kharārā*] *m* (H) A currycomb. 2 Currying a horse. (Marathi) Rebus: करडा [*karaḍā*] Hard from alloy--iron, silver &c. (Marathi) *kharādī* '

turner' (Gujarati)

h19a खोंड *[khōṇḍa] m A young bull, a bullcalf. (Marathi) Rebus: kõdār 'turner' (Bengali);* कोंद *kōnda 'engraver, lapidary setting or infixing gems' (Marathi) G. sãghāṛɔ m. 'lathe' ;* संघाट *joinery; M. sãgaḍ 'double-canoe' Rebus: sangataras 'stone-cutter, mason'*

āra 'spokes' Rebus: *āra 'brass'.* cf. erka = ekke (Tbh. of arka) aka (Tbh. of arka) copper (metal); crystal (Kannada) Glyph: *eraka*'nave of wheel' Rebus: eraka 'copper'; cf. erka = ekke (Tbh. of arka) aka (Tbh. of arka) copper (metal); crystal (Kannada) *erako* 'moltencast copper'

ḍato = claws of crab (Santali) Rebus: *dhātu* 'mineral ore'

kolom 'three' Rebus: kolami 'smithy, forge'

kana, kanac = corner (Santali); Rebus: *kañcu* = bronze (Telugu) Thus, cast bronze. PLUS खांडा [*khāṇḍā*] *m* A jag, notch, or indentation (as upon the edge of a tool or weapon). Rebus: *kāṇḍa* 'tools, pots and pans and metal-ware' Thus, cast bronze metalware.

cīmara 'black ant' Rebus: *cīmara* 'copper'. *cīmara kāra* -- ' coppersmith '

m933A खोंड *[khōṇḍa] m A young bull, a bullcalf. (Marathi) Rebus: kõdār 'turner' (Bengali);* कोंद *kōnda 'engraver, lapidary setting or infixing gems' (Marathi) G. sãghāṛɔ m. 'lathe' ;* संघाट *joinery; M. sãgaḍ 'double-canoe' Rebus: sangataras 'stone-cutter, mason'*

āra 'spokes' Rebus: *āra 'brass'.* cf. erka = ekke (Tbh. of arka) aka (Tbh. of arka) copper (metal); crystal (Kannada) Glyph: *eraka*'nave of wheel' Rebus: eraka 'copper'; cf. erka = ekke (Tbh. of arka) aka (Tbh. of arka) copper (metal); crystal (Kannada) *erako* 'moltencast copper' DUPLICATED dula 'pair' Rebus: dul 'cast metal' Thus, cast copper and brass.

kanka 'rim of jar' Rebus: karṇīka 'account (scribe)' karṇī 'supercargo'
ranku 'liquid measure' Rebus: ranku 'tin' kolmo 'paddy plant' Rebus: kolami 'smithy, forge'

kanka 'rim of jar' Rebus: karṇīka 'account (scribe)' karṇī 'supercargo'

m1811a

m1868a

खोंड *[khōṇḍa] m A young bull, a bullcalf. (Marathi) Rebus: kõdār 'turner' (Bengali);* कोंद *kōnda 'engraver, lapidary setting or infixing gems' (Marathi) G. sãghāṛɔ m. 'lathe' ;* संघाट *joinery; M. sãgaḍ 'double-canoe' Rebus: sangataras 'stone-cutter, mason'*

āra 'spokes' Rebus: *āra 'brass'.* cf. erka = ekke (Tbh. of arka) aka (Tbh. of arka) copper (metal); crystal (Kannada) Glyph: *eraka*'nave of wheel' Rebus: eraka 'copper'; cf. erka = ekke (Tbh. of arka) aka (Tbh. of arka) copper (metal); crystal (Kannada) *erako* 'moltencast copper' DUPLICATED dula 'pair' Rebus: dul 'cast metal' Thus, cast copper and cast brass.

m111a खोंड [khōṇḍa] m A young bull, a bullcalf. (Marathi) Rebus: kõdār 'turner' (Bengali); कोंद kōnda 'engraver, lapidary setting or infixing gems' (Marathi) G. sãghāṛɔ m. 'lathe' ; संघाट joinery; M. sãgaḍ 'double-canoe' Rebus: sangataras 'stone-cutter, mason'

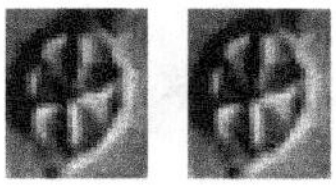

āra 'spokes' Rebus: *āra 'brass'*. cf. erka = ekke (Tbh. of arka) aka (Tbh. of arka) copper (metal); crystal (Kannada) Glyph: *eraka*'nave of wheel' Rebus: eraka 'copper'; cf. erka = ekke (Tbh. of arka) aka (Tbh. of arka) copper (metal); crystal (Kannada) *erako* 'moltencast copper' DUPLICATED dula 'pair' Rebus: dul 'cast metal' Thus, cast copper and brass.

खांडा [*khāṇḍā*] *m* A jag, notch, or indentation (as upon the edge of a tool or weapon). Rebus: *kāṇḍa* 'tools, pots and pans and metal-ware. Thus, the first three hieroglyph signs read: cast copper and brass metalware.

ayo ḍhālako 'alloy metal ingot'

ranku 'antelope' Rebus: ranku 'tin'

kuṭila 'bent' CDIAL 3230 kuṭi— in cmpd. 'curve', *kuṭika*— 'bent' MBh. Rebus: *kuṭila, katthīl* = bronze (8 parts copper and 2 parts tin)

kanka 'rim of jar' Rebus: karṇīka 'account (scribe)' karṇī 'supercargo'

h176A, B Side A:

balad m. ' ox ', gng. *bald*, (Ku.) *barad*, id. (N. Tarai) Rebus: *bharat* (5 copper, 4 zinc and 1 tin)(Punjabi)

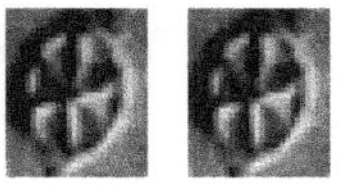

āra 'spokes' Rebus: *āra 'brass'*. cf. erka = ekke (Tbh. of arka) aka (Tbh. of arka) copper (metal); crystal (Kannada) Glyph: *eraka*'nave of wheel' Rebus: eraka 'copper'; cf. erka = ekke (Tbh. of arka) aka (Tbh. of arka) copper (metal); crystal (Kannada) *erako* 'moltencast copper' DUPLICATED dula 'pair' Rebus: dul 'cast metal' Thus, cast copper and brass.

*meḍ 'body' Rebus: meḍ 'iron' (Ho.) Rebus: खंडी [khaṇḍī] measure of weight (Marathi) கண்டி; kaṇṭi, n. < Mhr. khaṇḍil. [T. Tu. khaṇḍi, M. kaṇḍi.] Candy, a weight, about 500 lbs.*काठी [kāṭhī] *f* (काष्ट S) 'frame or structure of the body' (Marathi) Rebus: खंडी [khaṇḍī] measure of weight (Marathi) *கண்டி; kaṇṭi, n. < Mhr. khaṇḍil. [T. Tu. khaṇḍi, M. kaṇḍi.]* Candy, a weight, stated to be roughly equivalent to 500 lbs.

baṭa = rimless pot (Kannada) Rebus: *baṭa* = a kind of iron (Gujarati) : *bhaṭa* 'furnace, kiln' khā́ṭvā- cot; no. 3785, khaṭṭi- bier (*lex.*)(CDIAL 3781) Pa. kaṭeya cot (< Halbi); *Kui* kaṭe id.; *Kur.* khaṭī bedstead, bed; *Malt.* kaṭe, káṭi id. (DEDR 1145) Rebus: काठी [kāṭhī] *f* (काष्ट S) 'frame or structure of the body' (Marathi) Rebus: खंडी [khaṇḍī] measure of weight (Marathi) *கண்டி; kaṇṭi, n. < Mhr. khaṇḍil. [T. Tu. khaṇḍi, M. kaṇḍi.]* Candy, a weight, stated to be roughly equivalent to 500 lbs.

kanka 'rim of jar' Rebus: karṇīka 'account (scribe)' karṇī 'supercargo'

Side B:

kol 'tiger' Rebus: kolhe 'smelters' krammara 'turn back' Rebus: kamar 'blacksmith' *khōṇḍa* A stock or stump (Marathi); 'leafless tree' (Marathi) Rebus: *kõdār* 'turner' (Bengali); Allograph: young bull.

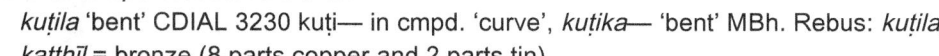

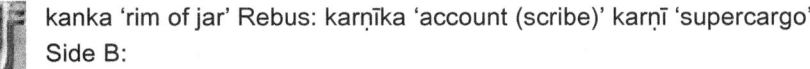

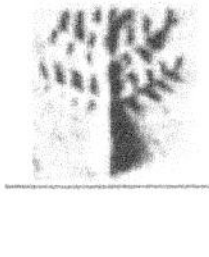

heraka 'spy' Rebus: erako 'moltencast copper'

kamaḍha 'penance' Rebus: *kammaṭa* 'mint, coiner'.
dhatu 'scarf; Rebus: dhatu 'mineral ore'
Kur. *kaṇḍō* a stool. Malt. *kanḍo* stool, seat. (DEDR 1179) Rebus: kaṇḍ 'fire-altar' (Santali)
kāṇḍa 'tools, pots and pans and metal-ware' (Marathi)
Hare + trough+tiger looks back: kulai 'hare' Rebus: kolhe 'smelter' pattar 'trough' Rebus: pattar 'guild' kol kamar 'smelter-artisan' Thus, together, the pictorial composition reads: smelter-artisan guild

m163a *खोंड [khōṇḍa] m A young bull, a bullcalf. (Marathi) Rebus: kõdār 'turner' (Bengali); कोंद kōnda 'engraver, lapidary setting or infixing gems' (Marathi) G. sãghāṛɔ m. 'lathe' ; संघाट joinery; M. sãgaḍ 'double-canoe' Rebus: sangataras 'stone-cutter, mason'*

āra 'spokes' Rebus: *āra 'brass'*. cf. erka = ekke (Tbh. of arka) aka (Tbh. of arka) copper (metal); crystal (Kannada) Glyph: *eraka*'nave of wheel' Rebus: eraka 'copper'; cf. erka = ekke (Tbh. of arka) aka (Tbh. of arka) copper (metal); crystal (Kannada) *erako* 'moltencast copper' PLUS

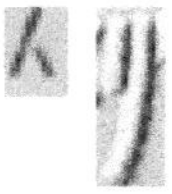
notch+slanted stroke reads rebus: *ḍhālako kāṇḍa* 'ingot, tools, pots and pans and metal-ware'.*ḍhāḷ* 'a slope'; 'inclination of a plane' (G.); *ḍhāḷiyum* = adj. sloping, inclining (G.) Rebus: *ḍhālako* = a large metal ingot (G.) *ḍhālakī* = a metal heated and poured into a mould; a solid piece of metal; an ingot (Gujarati) PLUS खांडा [*khāṇḍā*] *m* A jag, notch, or indentation (as upon the edge of a tool or weapon). Rebus: *kāṇḍa* 'tools, pots and pans and metal-ware' *Thus, together, the pair reads: āra erako khāṇḍā* 'brass, moltencast copper metalware'.

aḍar 'harrow'; rebus: *aduru* 'native unsmelted metal'

ayo 'fish' Rebus: *aya* 'iron' *ayas* 'metal'
kāṇḍa 'arrow' (Sanskrit) Rebus:*khāṇḍa* 'tools, pots and pans, metal-ware'. Rebus 2: kaṇḍ 'fire-altar' (Santali)

M-1369 a

m1369a *āra* 'spokes' Rebus: *āra 'brass'*. cf. erka = ekke (Tbh. of arka) aka (Tbh. of arka) copper (metal); crystal (Kannada) Glyph: *eraka*'nave of wheel' Rebus: eraka 'copper'; cf. erka = ekke (Tbh. of arka) aka (Tbh. of arka) copper (metal); crystal (Kannada) *erako* 'moltencast copper' PLUS

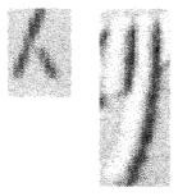
notch+slanted stroke reads rebus: *ḍhālako kāṇḍa* 'ingot, tools, pots and pans and metal-ware'.*ḍhāḷ* 'a slope'; 'inclination of a plane' (G.); *ḍhāḷiyum* = adj. sloping, inclining (G.) Rebus: *ḍhālako* = a large metal ingot (G.) *ḍhālakī* = a metal heated and poured into a mould; a solid piece of metal; an ingot (Gujarati) PLUS खांडा [*khāṇḍā*] *m* A jag, notch, or indentation (as upon the edge of a tool or weapon). Rebus: *kāṇḍa* 'tools, pots and pans and metal-ware' *Thus, together, the pair reads: āra erako khāṇḍā* 'brass, moltencast copper metalware'.

kana, kanac = corner (Santali); Rebus: *kañcu* = bronze (Telugu). PLUS खांडा [*khāṇḍā*] *m* A jag, notch, or indentation (as upon the edge of a tool or weapon). Rebus: *kāṇḍa* 'tools, pots and pans and metal-ware' Thus, bronze metalware.

  *loa* 'ficus religiosa' Rebus: *lo* 'iron' (Sanskrit) PLUS unique ligatures: लोखंड [lōkhaṇḍa] *n* (लोह S) Iron. लोखंडाचे चणे खावविणें or चारणें To oppress grievously.लोखंडकाम [lōkhaṇḍakāma] *n* Iron work; that portion (of a building, machine &c.) which consists of iron. 2 The business of an ironsmith.लोखंडी [lōkhaṇḍī] *a* (लोखंड) Composed of iron; relating to iron. (Marathi) *bhaṭa* 'warrior' (Sanskrit) Rebus: *baṭa* a kind of iron (Gujarati). Rebus: *bhaṭa* 'furnace' (Santali) Thus, together, th ligatured hieroglyph reads rebus: *loa bhaṭa* 'iron furnace'

gaṇḍa 'four' Rebus: *kaṇḍa* 'furnace, fire-altar' (Santali).PLUS ranku 'liquid measure' Rebus:

 ranku 'tin'.

baroṭi 'twelve' *bhārata* 'a factitious alloy of copper, pewter, tin' (Marathi)

m390a

āra 'spokes'  Rebus: *āra 'brass'.* cf. erka = ekke (Tbh. of arka) aka (Tbh. of arka) copper (metal); crystal (Kannada) Glyph: *eraka*'nave of wheel' Rebus: eraka 'copper'; cf. erka = ekke (Tbh. of arka) aka (Tbh. of arka) copper (metal); crystal (Kannada) *erako* 'moltencast copper' PLUS

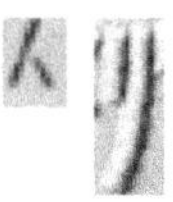 notch+slanted stroke reads rebus: *ḍhālako kāṇḍa* 'ingot, tools, pots and pans and metal-ware'.*ḍhāḷ* 'a slope'; 'inclination of a plane' (G.); *ḍhāḷiyum* = adj. sloping, inclining (G.) Rebus: *ḍhālako* = a large metal ingot (G.) *ḍhālakī* = a metal heated and poured into a mould; a solid piece of metal; an ingot (Gujarati) PLUS खांडा [*khāṇḍā*] *m* A jag, notch, or indentation (as upon the edge of a tool or weapon). Rebus: *kāṇḍa* 'tools, pots and pans and metal-ware' *Thus, together, the pair reads: āra erako khāṇḍā* 'brass, moltencast copper metalware'.

khaṇḍ 'field, division' (Sanskrit) Rebus: *khāṇḍa* 'tools, pots and pans, metal-ware'. खांडा [*khāṇḍā*] *m* A jag, notch, or indentation (as upon the edge of a tool or weapon). Rebus: *kāṇḍa* 'tools, pots and pans and metal-ware'
gaṇḍa 'four' Rebus: kaṇḍa 'furnace, fire-altar' (Santali)

 H. sainī, senī f. ' ladder ' Rebus: Pa. sēṇi -- f. ' guild, division of army '; Pk. sēṇi -- f. ' row, collection '; śrḗṇi (metr. often śrayaṇi --) f. ' line, row, troop ' RV. *śrēṇikā* f. 'house ~ ladder' Rebus:*śreṇi* in meaning "guild" (Sanskrit) Pa. *sēṇi* -- f. ' guild, division of army '(Pali)(CDIAL 10718) *seniya* 'soldier' PLUS खांडा [*khāṇḍā*] *m* A jag, notch, or indentation (as upon the edge of a tool or weapon). Rebus: *kāṇḍa* 'tools, pots and pans and metal-ware' Thus,metalware guild.

 *kuṭila* 'bent' CDIAL 3230 kuṭi— in cmpd. 'curve', *kuṭika—* 'bent' MBh. Rebus: *kuṭila, katthīl* = bronze (8 parts copper and 2 parts tin) PLUS खांडा [*khāṇḍā*] *m* A jag, notch, or indentation (as upon the edge of a tool or weapon). Rebus: *kāṇḍa* 'tools, pots and pans and metal-ware' Thus, bronze metalware.

M-322 a

m322a

खोंड [khōṇḍa] m A young bull, a bullcalf. (Marathi) Rebus: kõdār 'turner' (Bengali); कोंद kōnda 'engraver, lapidary setting or infixing gems' (Marathi) G. sãghāṛɔ m.

'lathe' ; संघाट joinery; M. sãgaḍ 'double-canoe' Rebus: sangataras 'stone-cutter, mason'

āra 'spokes' Rebus: *āra 'brass'.* cf. erka = ekke (Tbh. of arka) aka (Tbh. of arka) copper (metal); crystal (Kannada) Glyph: *eraka*'nave of wheel' Rebus: eraka 'copper'; cf. erka = ekke (Tbh. of arka) aka (Tbh. of arka) copper (metal); crystal (Kannada) *erako* 'moltencast copper' PLUS

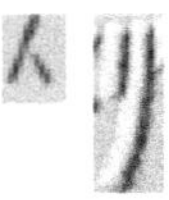

notch+slanted stroke reads rebus: *ḍhālako kāṇḍa* 'ingot, tools, pots and pans and metal-ware'.*dhāḷ* 'a slope'; 'inclination of a plane' (G.); *ḍhāḷiyum* = adj. sloping, inclining (G.) Rebus: *ḍhālako* = a large metal ingot (G.) *ḍhālakī* = a metal heated and poured into a mould; a solid piece of metal; an ingot (Gujarati) PLUS खांडा [*khāṇḍā*] *m* A jag, notch, or indentation (as upon the edge of a tool or weapon). Rebus: *kāṇḍa* 'tools, pots and pans and metal-ware' *Thus, together, the pair reads: āra erako khāṇḍā* 'brass, moltencast copper metalware'.

This pair of signs is duplicated: dula 'pair' Rebus: dul 'cast metal' Thus, cast metal ingot and metalware

kanka 'rim of jar' Rebus: karṇīka 'account (scribe)' karṇī 'supercargo'

m931a

खोंड [khōṇḍa] m A young bull, a bullcalf. (Marathi) Rebus: kõdār 'turner' (Bengali); कोंद kōnda 'engraver, lapidary setting or infixing gems' (Marathi) G. sãghāṛɔ m. 'lathe' ; संघाट joinery; M. sãgaḍ 'double-canoe' Rebus: sangataras 'stone-cutter, mason'

āra 'spokes' Rebus: *āra 'brass'.* cf. erka = ekke (Tbh. of arka) aka (Tbh. of arka) copper (metal); crystal (Kannada) Glyph: *eraka*'nave of wheel' Rebus: eraka 'copper'; cf. erka = ekke (Tbh. of arka) aka (Tbh. of arka) copper (metal); crystal (Kannada) *erako* 'moltencast copper' PLUS

notch+slanted stroke reads rebus: *ḍhālako kāṇḍa* 'ingot, tools, pots and pans and metal-ware'.*dhāḷ* 'a slope'; 'inclination of a plane' (G.); *ḍhāḷiyum* = adj. sloping, inclining (G.) Rebus: *ḍhālako* = a large metal ingot (G.) *ḍhālakī* = a metal heated and poured into a mould; a solid piece of metal; an ingot (Gujarati) PLUS खांडा [*khāṇḍā*] *m* A jag, notch, or indentation (as upon the edge of a tool or weapon). Rebus: *kāṇḍa* 'tools, pots and pans and metal-ware' *Thus, together, the pair reads: āra erako khāṇḍā* 'brass, moltencast copper metalware'.

dula 'pair' Rebus: *dul* 'cast (metal)' PLUS*kana, kanac* = corner (Santali); Rebus: *kañcu* = bronze (Telugu) PLUS infixed kolmo 'paddy plant' Rebus: kolami 'smithy, forge'. Thus, cast bronze smithy, forge. Or, mogge 'sprout, bud' Rebus: mũh 'ingot' (Santali)Thus, cast bronze ingot. Read as: kañcu dul mũh 'bronze cast ingot'

ayo ḍhālako 'alloy metal ingot'

kāṇḍa 'arrow' (Sanskrit) Rebus:*khāṇḍa* 'tools, pots and pans, metal-ware'. Rebus 2: kaṇḍ 'fire-altar' (Santali)

m715A Side B: kol 'tiger' Rebus: kolhe 'smelter' krammara 'look back' Rebus: kamar 'blacksmith' heraka 'spy' Rebus: erako 'moltencast copper'

 *khōṇḍa* A stock or stump (Marathi); 'leafless tree' (Marathi) Rebus: *kõdār* 'turner' (Bengali); Allograph: young bull.

 सांड [sāṇḍa] *f* (षद S) An outlet for superfluous water (as through a dam or mound); a floodvent. Rebus: सांडणी [sāṇḍaṇī] *f* (H) An instrument of goldsmiths. It is hooked or curved at the extremity; and is used to draw things out of the fire.

Side A:

 *āra* 'spokes' Rebus: *āra 'brass'*. cf. erka = ekke (Tbh. of arka) aka (Tbh. of arka) copper (metal); crystal (Kannada) Glyph: *eraka*'nave of wheel' Rebus: eraka 'copper'; cf. erka = ekke (Tbh. of arka) aka (Tbh. of arka) copper (metal); crystal (Kannada) *erako* 'moltencast copper' PLUS

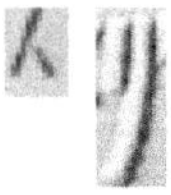 notch+slanted stroke reads rebus: *ḍhālako kāṇḍa* 'ingot, tools, pots and pans and metal-ware'.*dhāḷ* 'a slope'; 'inclination of a plane' (G.); *ḍhāḷiyum* = adj. sloping, inclining (G.) Rebus: *ḍhālako* = a large metal ingot (G.) *ḍhālakī* = a metal heated and poured into a mould; a solid piece of metal; an ingot (Gujarati) PLUS खांडा [*khāṇḍā*] *m* A jag, notch, or indentation (as upon the edge of a tool or weapon). Rebus: *kāṇḍa* 'tools, pots and pans and metal-ware' *Thus, together, the pair reads: āra erako khāṇḍā* 'brass, moltencast copper metalware'.

 *muka* 'ladle' (Tamil)(DEDR 4887) Rebus: *mũh* 'ingot' (Santali) *baṭa* = a kind of iron (G.) *baṭa* = rimless pot (Kannada) Thus, iron ingot.

kolom 'three' Rebus: kolami 'smithy, forge'

kamaḍha 'crab' Rebus: *kammaṭa* 'mint, coiner'.

ḍato = claws of crab (Santali) Rebus: *dhātu* 'mineral ore'

 *dhāḷ* 'a slope'; 'inclination of a plane' (G.); *ḍhāḷiyum* = adj. sloping, inclining (G.) Rebus: *ḍhālako* = a large metal ingot (G.) *ḍhālakī* = a metal heated and poured into a mould; a solid piece of metal; an ingot (Gujarati) dula 'pair' Rebus: dul 'cast metal'. sal splinter' Rebus: sal 'workshop Thu cast metal ingot workshop.

 m1104 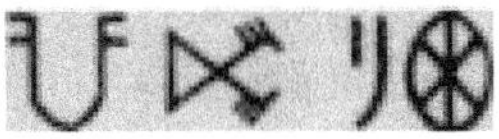 Text 1335 *khũṭ* 'zebu' Rebus: '(native metal) guild'

āra 'spokes' Rebus: *āra 'brass'*. cf. erka = ekke (Tbh. of arka) aka (Tbh. of arka) copper (metal); crystal (Kannada) Glyph: eraka'nave of wheel' Rebus: eraka 'copper'; cf. erka = ekke (Tbh. of arka) aka (Tbh. of arka) copper (metal); crystal (Kannada)

 Read in context, the composite hieroglyph is assumed to be combination of a slanted stroke ligatured to a notch,which provide possible rebus readings of a smithy/forge: notch+slanted stroke reads rebus: *ḍhālako kāṇḍa* 'ingot, tools, pots and pans and metal-ware'

dhāḷ 'a slope'; 'inclination of a plane' (Gujarati); *ḍhāḷiyum* = adj. sloping, inclining (Gujarati) Rebus: *ḍhālako* = a large metal ingot (Gujarati) *ḍhālakī* = a metal heated and poured into a mould; a solid piece of metal; an ingot (Gujarati) PLUS खांडा [*khāṇḍā*] *m* A jag, notch, or indentation (as upon the edge of a tool or weapon). Rebus: *kāṇḍa* 'tools, pots and pans and metal-ware'

Thus, the first pair of sign hieroglyphs from r. read rebus: copper, bronze ingots, metalware

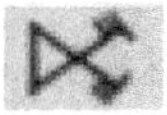

This sign hieroglyph may be a variant of the following rebus readings. This may, therefore, connote the ore smelter for two minerals: *dula dhatu kolhe* 'two minerals, ore smelter'.

Kur. xolā tail. *Malt.* qoli id. (DEDR 2135). Rebus: kolhe 'smelter'

ḍato 'claws or pincers of crab' (Santali) Rebus: *dhatu* 'mineral ore' (Santali) PLUS xola 'tail' Rebus: kolhe 'smelter'. Thus, the ligatured glyph is read rebus as: dhatu kolhe 'mineral, ore smelter'.

kanka 'rim of jar' Rebus: *karṇīka* 'account (scribe)' *karṇī* 'supercargo'

Lothal 122A

āra 'spokes' Rebus: *āra 'brass'.* cf. erka = ekke (Tbh. of arka) aka (Tbh. of arka) copper (metal); crystal (Kannada) Glyph: *eraka* 'nave of wheel' Rebus: eraka 'copper'; cf. erka = ekke (Tbh. of arka) aka (Tbh. of arka) copper (metal); crystal (Kannada) *erako* 'moltencast copper' PLUS

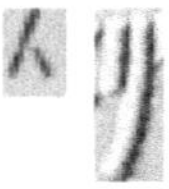

notch+slanted stroke reads rebus: *ḍhālako kāṇḍa* 'ingot, tools, pots and pans and metal-ware'.*ḍhāḷ* 'a slope'; 'inclination of a plane' (G.); *ḍhāḷiyum* = adj. sloping, inclining (G.) Rebus: *ḍhālako* = a large metal ingot (G.) *ḍhālakī* = a metal heated and poured into a mould; a solid piece of metal; an ingot (Gujarati) PLUS खांडा [*khāṇḍā*] *m* A jag, notch, or indentation (as upon the edge of a tool or weapon). Rebus: *kāṇḍa* 'tools, pots and pans and metal-ware' *Thus, together, the pair reads: āra erako khāṇḍā* 'brass, moltencast copper metalware'.

ḍhāḷ 'a slope'; 'inclination of a plane' (G.); *ḍhāḷiyum* = adj. sloping, inclining (G.) Rebus: *ḍhālako* = a large metal ingot (G.) *ḍhālakī* = a metal heated and poured into a mould; a solid piece of metal; an ingot (Gujarati) dula 'pair' Rebus: dul 'cast metal'. sal splinter' Rebus: sal 'workshop Thu cast metal ingot workshop.

kanka 'rim of jar' Rebus: karṇīka 'account (scribe)' karṇī 'supercargo'

kamaḍha 'crab' Rebus: *kammaṭa* 'mint, coiner'.
ḍato = claws of crab (Santali) Rebus: *dhātu* 'mineral ore'
dula 'pair' Rebus: dul 'cast metal; PLUS *ḍhāḷ* 'a slope'; 'inclination of a plane' (G.); *ḍhāḷiyum* = adj. sloping, inclining (G.) Rebus: *ḍhālako* = a large metal ingot (G.) *ḍhālakī* = a metal heated and poured into a mould; a solid piece of metal; an ingot (Gujarati) PLUS खांडा [*khāṇḍā*] *m* A jag, notch, or indentation (as upon the edge of a tool or weapon). Rebus: *kāṇḍa* 'tools, pots and pans and metal-ware' Thus, the pair of sign hieroglyphs ligatured with sal 'splinter' Rebus: sal 'workshop' connote: workshop ingot metalware.

m303a Composite anilmal with zebu horns: Native metal smith guild.

 *āra* 'spokes' Rebus: *āra 'brass'*. cf. erka = ekke (Tbh. of arka) aka (Tbh. of arka) copper (metal); crystal (Kannada) Glyph: *eraka*'nave of wheel' Rebus: eraka 'copper'; cf. erka = ekke (Tbh. of arka) aka (Tbh. of arka) copper (metal); crystal (Kannada) *erako* 'moltencast copper' PLUS

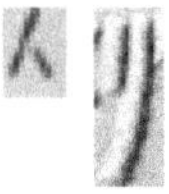 notch+slanted stroke reads rebus: *ḍhālako kāṇḍa* 'ingot, tools, pots and pans and metal-ware'.*dhāḷ* 'a slope'; 'inclination of a plane' (G.); *ḍhāḷiyum* = adj. sloping, inclining (G.) Rebus: *ḍhālako* = a large metal ingot (G.) *ḍhālakī* = a metal heated and poured into a mould; a solid piece of metal; an ingot (Gujarati) PLUS खांडा [*khāṇḍā*

] *m* A jag, notch, or indentation (as upon the edge of a tool or weapon). Rebus: *kāṇḍa* 'tools, pots and pans and metal-ware' *Thus, together, the pair reads: āra erako khāṇḍā* 'brass, moltencast copper metalware'.

muka 'ladle' (Tamil)(DEDR 4887) Rebus: *mũh* 'ingot' (Santali) *baṭa* = a kind of iron (G.) *baṭa* = rimless pot (Kannada) Thus, iron ingot.
kolom 'three' Rebus: kolami 'smithy, forge'
kāṇḍa 'arrow' (Sanskrit) Rebus:*khāṇḍa* 'tools, pots and pans, metal-ware'. Rebus 2: kaṇḍ 'fire-altar' (Santali)

m1804a *खोंड [khōṇḍa] m A young bull, a bullcalf. (Marathi) Rebus: kõdār 'turner' (Bengali); कोंद kōnda 'engraver, lapidary setting or infixing gems' (Marathi) G. sãghāṛɔ m. 'lathe' ; संघाट joinery; M. sãgaḍ 'double-canoe' Rebus: sangataras 'stone-cutter, mason'*

 *āra* 'spokes' Rebus: *āra 'brass'*. cf. erka = ekke (Tbh. of arka) aka (Tbh. of arka) copper (metal); crystal (Kannada) Glyph: *eraka*'nave of wheel' Rebus: eraka 'copper'; cf. erka = ekke (Tbh. of arka) aka (Tbh. of arka) copper (metal); crystal (Kannada) *erako* 'moltencast copper' PLUS

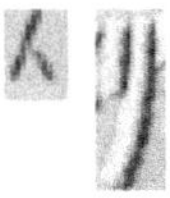 notch+slanted stroke reads rebus: *ḍhālako kāṇḍa* 'ingot, tools, pots and pans and metal-ware'.*dhāḷ* 'a slope'; 'inclination of a plane' (G.); *ḍhāḷiyum* = adj. sloping, inclining (G.) Rebus: *ḍhālako* = a large metal ingot (G.) *ḍhālakī* = a metal heated and poured into a mould; a solid piece of metal; an ingot (Gujarati) PLUS खांडा [*khāṇḍā*] *m* A jag, notch, or indentation (as upon the edge of a tool or weapon). Rebus: *kāṇḍa* 'tools, pots and pans and metal-ware' *Thus, together, the pair reads: āra erako khāṇḍā* 'brass, moltencast copper metalware'.

aya kāṇḍa 'alloy metalware'
kamaḍha 'crab' Rebus: *kammaṭa* 'mint, coiner'.
ḍato = claws of crab (Santali) Rebus: *dhātu* 'mineral ore'

 kanka 'rim of jar' Rebus: karṇīka 'account (scribe)' karṇī 'supercargo'

m1768a

खोंड [khōṇḍa] m A young bull, a bullcalf. (Marathi) Rebus: kõdār 'turner' (Bengali); कोंद kōnda 'engraver, lapidary setting or infixing gems' (Marathi) G. sãghāṛɔ m. 'lathe' ; संघाट joinery; M. sãgaḍ 'double-canoe' Rebus: sangataras 'stone-cutter, mason'

 *āra* 'spokes' Rebus: *āra 'brass'*. cf. erka = ekke (Tbh. of arka) aka (Tbh. of arka) copper (metal); crystal (Kannada) Glyph: *eraka*'nave of wheel' Rebus: eraka 'copper'; cf. erka = ekke (Tbh. of arka) aka (Tbh. of arka) copper (metal); crystal (Kannada) *erako* 'moltencast copper' PLUS

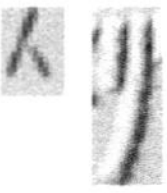 notch+slanted stroke reads rebus: *ḍhālako kāṇḍa* 'ingot, tools, pots and pans and metal-ware'.*dhāḷ* 'a slope'; 'inclination of a plane' (G.); *ḍhāḷiyum* = adj. sloping, inclining (G.) Rebus: *ḍhālako* = a large metal ingot (G.) *ḍhālakī* = a metal heated and poured into a mould; a solid piece of metal; an ingot (Gujarati) PLUS खांडा [*khāṇḍā*] *m* A jag, notch, or indentation (as upon the edge of a tool or weapon). Rebus: *kāṇḍa* 'tools, pots and pans and metal-ware' *Thus, together, the pair reads: āra erako khāṇḍā* 'brass, moltencast copper metalware'.

ayo 'fish' Rebus: *aya* 'iron' *ayas* 'metal'

kamaḍha 'crab' Rebus: *kammaṭa* 'mint, coiner'.

ḍato = claws of crab (Santali) Rebus: *dhātu* 'mineral ore'

 kanka 'rim of jar' Rebus: karṇīka 'account (scribe)' karṇī 'supercargo'

 m31a *खोंड [khōṇḍa] m A young bull, a bullcalf. (Marathi) Rebus: kõdār 'turner' (Bengali); कोंद kōnda 'engraver, lapidary setting or infixing gems' (Marathi) G. sãghāṛɔ m. 'lathe' ; संघाट joinery; M. sãgaḍ 'double-canoe' Rebus: sangataras 'stone-cutter, mason'*

 *āra* 'spokes' Rebus: *āra 'brass'*. cf. erka = ekke (Tbh. of arka) aka (Tbh. of arka) copper (metal); crystal (Kannada) Glyph: *eraka*'nave of wheel' Rebus: eraka 'copper'; cf. erka = ekke (Tbh. of arka) aka (Tbh. of arka) copper (metal); crystal (Kannada) *erako* 'moltencast copper' PLUS

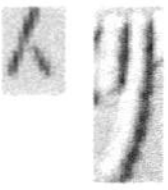 notch+slanted stroke reads rebus: *ḍhālako kāṇḍa* 'ingot, tools, pots and pans and metal-ware'.*dhāḷ* 'a slope'; 'inclination of a plane' (G.); *ḍhāḷiyum* = adj. sloping, inclining (G.) Rebus: *ḍhālako* = a large metal ingot (G.) *ḍhālakī* = a metal heated and poured into a mould; a solid piece of metal; an ingot (Gujarati) PLUS खांडा [*khāṇḍā*] *m* A jag, notch, or indentation (as upon the edge of a tool or weapon). Rebus: *kāṇḍa* 'tools, pots and pans and metal-ware' *Thus, together, the pair reads: āra erako khāṇḍā* 'brass, moltencast copper metalware'.

ayo ḍhālako 'alloy metal ingot'

khaṇḍ 'field, division' (Sanskrit) Rebus: *khāṇḍa* 'tools, pots and pans, metal-ware'. Rebus 2: kaṇḍ 'fire-altar' (Santali) PLUS | *koḍa* 'one' Rebus: *koḍ* 'workshop' . Thus, metalware workshop

  *kuṭila* 'bent' CDIAL 3230 kuṭi— in cmpd. 'curve', *kuṭika*— 'bent' MBh. Rebus: *kuṭila, katthīl* = bronze (8 parts copper and 2 parts tin) dula 'pair' Rebus: dul 'cast metal' Thus, cast bronze PLUS infixed 'bird hieroglyph': *karaṇḍa* 'duck' (Sanskrit) *karaṛa* 'a very large aquatic bird' (Sindhi)

Rebus: करडा [*karaḍā*] Hard from alloy--iron, silver &c. (Marathi) Thus, hard alloy bronze casting.

 kanka 'rim of jar' Rebus: karṇīka 'account (scribe)' karṇī 'supercargo'

m1364C

āra 'spokes' Rebus: *āra 'brass'*. cf. erka = ekke (Tbh. of arka) aka (Tbh. of arka) copper (metal); crystal (Kannada) Glyph: *eraka*'nave of wheel' Rebus: eraka 'copper'; cf. erka = ekke (Tbh. of arka) aka (Tbh. of arka) copper (metal); crystal (Kannada) *erako* 'moltencast copper' PLUS

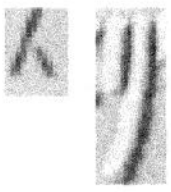

notch+slanted stroke reads rebus: *ḍhālako kāṇḍa* 'ingot, tools, pots and pans and metal-ware'.*dhāḷ* 'a slope'; 'inclination of a plane' (G.); *ḍhāḷiyum* = adj. sloping, inclining (G.) Rebus: *ḍhālako* = a large metal ingot (G.) *ḍhālakī* = a metal heated and poured into a mould; a solid piece of metal; an ingot (Gujarati) PLUS खांडा [*khāṇḍā*] *m* A jag, notch, or indentation (as upon the edge of a tool or weapon). Rebus: *kāṇḍa* 'tools, pots and pans and metal-ware' *Thus, together, the pair reads: āra erako khāṇḍā* 'brass, moltencast copper metalware'.
kolom 'three' Rebus: kolami 'smithy, forge'

mogge 'sprout, bud' Rebus: *mūh* 'ingot' (Santali)

m1906A Rhinoceros/boar: baḍhia = a castrated boar, a hog (Santali) baḍhi 'a caste who work both in iron and wood' (Santali) *baṟea* 'merchant'
pattar 'trough' Rebus: pattar 'guild'

āra 'spokes' Rebus: *āra 'brass'*. cf. erka = ekke (Tbh. of arka) aka (Tbh. of arka) copper (metal); crystal (Kannada) Glyph: *eraka*'nave of wheel' Rebus: eraka 'copper'; cf. erka = ekke (Tbh. of arka) aka (Tbh. of arka) copper (metal); crystal (Kannada) *erako* 'moltencast copper' PLUS

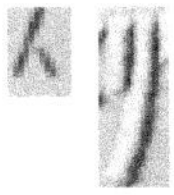

notch+slanted stroke reads rebus: *ḍhālako kāṇḍa* 'ingot, tools, pots and pans and metal-ware'.*dhāḷ* 'a slope'; 'inclination of a plane' (G.); *ḍhāḷiyum* = adj. sloping, inclining (G.) Rebus: *ḍhālako* = a large metal ingot (G.) *ḍhālakī* = a metal heated and poured into a mould; a solid piece of metal; an ingot (Gujarati) PLUS खांडा [*khāṇḍā*] *m* A jag, notch, or indentation (as upon the edge of a tool or weapon). Rebus: *kāṇḍa* 'tools, pots and pans and metal-ware' *Thus, together, the pair reads: āra erako khāṇḍā* 'brass, moltencast copper metalware'.
aya aḍaren (homonym: aduru)'alloy native metal'
ayo ḍhālako 'alloy metal ingot'

 *muka* 'ladle' (Tamil)(DEDR 4887) Rebus: *mūh* 'ingot' (Santali) *baṭa* = a kind of iron (G.) *baṭa* = rimless pot (Kannada) Thus, iron ingot.
kolom 'three' Rebus: kolami 'smithy, forge'
kāṇḍa 'arrow' (Sanskrit) Rebus:*khāṇḍa* 'tools, pots and pans, metal-ware'. Rebus 2: kaṇḍ 'fire-altar' (Santali)

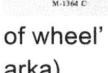

m808A

खोंड *[khōṇḍa] m A young bull, a bullcalf. (Marathi) Rebus: kōdār 'turner' (Bengali);*

कोंद *kōnda 'engraver, lapidary setting or infixing gems' (Marathi) G. sãghāṛɔ m. 'lathe' ; संघाट joinery; M. sãgaḍ 'double-canoe' Rebus: sangataras 'stone-cutter, mason'*

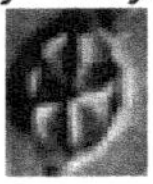
āra 'spokes' Rebus: *āra 'brass'*. cf. erka = ekke (Tbh. of arka) aka (Tbh. of arka) copper (metal); crystal (Kannada) Glyph: *eraka*'nave of wheel' Rebus: eraka 'copper'; cf. erka = ekke (Tbh. of arka) aka (Tbh. of arka) copper (metal); crystal (Kannada) *erako* 'moltencast copper' PLUS

notch+slanted stroke reads rebus: *ḍhālako kāṇḍa* 'ingot, tools, pots and pans and metal-ware'.*dhāḷ* 'a slope'; 'inclination of a plane' (G.); *ḍhāḷiyum* = adj. sloping, inclining (G.) Rebus: *ḍhālako* = a large metal ingot (G.) *ḍhālakī* = a metal heated and poured into a mould; a solid piece of metal; an ingot (Gujarati) PLUS खांडा [*khāṇḍā*] *m* A jag, notch, or indentation (as upon the edge of a tool or weapon). Rebus: *kāṇḍa* 'tools, pots and pans and metal-ware'
Thus, together, the pair reads: āra erako khāṇḍā 'brass, moltencast copper metalware'.
aya aḍaren (homonym: aduru)'alloy native metal'
aya kammaṭa.'coiner, mint alloy'

mēḍu height, rising ground, hillock (Kannada) Rebus: *meḍ* 'iron' (Ho.) kolom 'three' Rebus: kolami 'smithy, forge' Thus, *meḍ kolami* 'iron smithy-forge'

kanka 'rim of jar' Rebus: karṇīka 'account (scribe)' karṇī 'supercargo'

Kalibangan 80A

खोंड [khōṇḍa] m A young bull, a bullcalf. (Marathi) Rebus: kōdār 'turner' (Bengali); कोंद *kōnda 'engraver, lapidary setting or infixing gems' (Marathi) G. sãghāṛɔ m. 'lathe' ; संघाट joinery; M. sãgaḍ 'double-canoe' Rebus: sangataras 'stone-cutter, mason'*

Text inscription:

āra 'spokes' Rebus: *āra 'brass'*. cf. erka = ekke (Tbh. of arka) aka (Tbh. of arka) copper (metal); crystal (Kannada) Glyph: eraka'nave of wheel' Rebus: eraka 'copper'; cf. erka = ekke (Tbh. of arka) aka (Tbh. of arka) copper (metal); crystal (Kannada)

cīmara 'black ant' Rebus: *cīmara* 'copper'. *cīmara kāra* -- ' coppersmith '

koḍi 'flag' (Tamil)(DEDR 2049). Rebus 1: *koḍ* 'workshop' (Kuwi) Rebus 2: *khōḍ* m. 'pit', *khōḍü* f. 'small pit' (Kashmiri. CDIAL 3947).

dhāḷ 'a slope'; 'inclination of a plane' (Gujarati); *ḍhāḷiyum* = adj. sloping, inclining (Gujarati) Rebus: *ḍhālako* = a large metal ingot (Gujarati) *ḍhālakī* = a metal heated and poured into a mould; a solid piece of metal; an ingot (Gujarati) PLUS खांडा [*khāṇḍā*] *m* A jag, notch, or indentation (as upon the edge of a tool or weapon). Rebus: *kāṇḍa* 'tools, pots and pans and metal-ware'

| *koḍa* 'one' Rebus: *koḍ* 'workshop'

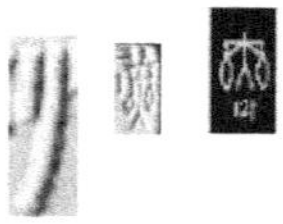
water-carrier hieroglyph *kuṭi*; Rebus: *kuṭhi* 'smelter furnace'. PLUS 'rim of jar':

kanka 'rim of jar' Rebus: karṇīka 'account (scribe)' karṇī 'supercargo'

h88A

Pictorial hieroglyph: pattar 'trough' Rebus: pattar 'guild' *kāṇḍā* 'rhinoceros' (Tamil) Rebus: *khāṇḍā* 'tools, pots and pans, metalware' (Marathi) VIkalpa: c

āra 'spokes' Rebus: *āra 'brass'*. cf. erka = ekke (Tbh. of arka) aka (Tbh. of arka) copper (metal); crystal (Kannada) Glyph: eraka'nave of wheel' Rebus: eraka 'copper'; cf. erka = ekke (Tbh. of arka) aka (Tbh. of arka) copper (metal); crystal (Kannada)

kana, kanac = corner (Santali); Rebus: kañcu = bronze (Telugu) dol 'two' *dula* दुल । युग्मम् m. a pair, a couple, esp. of two similar things (Rām. 966). Rebus: *dul* meṛeḍ cast iron (Mundari. Santali) *dul* 'to cast metal in a mould' (Santali) Rebus: dul 'cast (metal)'

|| dula 'pair' Rebus: dul 'cast metal'. Thus, together, the sign hieroglyphs connote: cast bronze.

'rim-of-jar' hieroglyph *kanka* (Santali) karṇika 'scribe'(Sanskrit)
Rebus: *karṇī,* supercargo for a boat shipment. *karṇīka* 'account (scribe)'.कारणी kāraṇī ' the supercargo of a ship' (Marathi)

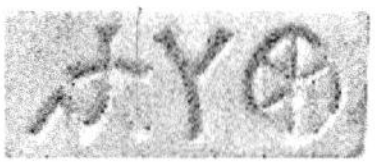

m361A

āra 'spokes' Rebus: *āra 'brass'*. cf. *erka = ekke* (Tbh. of arka) *aka* (Tbh. of arka) copper (metal); crystal (Kannada) Glyph: eraka'nave of wheel' Rebus: *eraka* 'copper'; cf. *erka* = *ekke* (Tbh. of arka) *aka* (Tbh. of arka) copper (metal); crystal (Kannada)

āra 'brass' Variant? muggè, moggè flower-bud, germ; (BRR; Bhattacharya, non-brahmin informant) *mukkè* bud. *Kor.* (O.) *mūke* flower-bud. (Tulu)(DEDR 4893). *mukula-,* () *mudgara-* bud; Pkt. (*DNM*) *moggara* id.; Turner, *CDIAL*, no. 10146 मोख [mōkha] sprout or shoot. (Marathi) *Kuwi* (Su.) *mṛogla* shoot of bamboo; (Punjabi) *moko* sprout (DEDR 4997) *Tu. mugiyuni* to close, contract, shut up; muguru sprout, shoot, bud; tender, delicate; *muguruni, mukuruni* to bud, sprout; *muggè, moggè* flower-bud, germ; (BRR; Bhattacharya, non-brahmin informant) *mukkè* bud. *Kor.* (O.) *mūke* flower-bud. (DEDR 4893) Rebus*: mũh* '(copper) ingot' (Santali) *mũhã* = the quantity of iron produced at one time in a native smelting furnace of the Kolhes; iron produced by the Kolhes and formed like a four-cornered piece a little pointed at each end (Santali) cf. *mlecchamukha* 'copper' (Sanskrit) Allograph: *mũh* 'face' (Hindi) mukha id. (Sanskrit)

*meḍ 'body' Rebus: meḍ 'iron' (Ho.) काठी [kāṭhī] f (काष्ट S) 'frame or structure of the body' (Marathi) Rebus: खंडी [khaṇḍī] measure of weight (Marathi) கண்டி; kaṇṭi, n. < Mhr. khaṇḍil. [T. Tu. khaṇḍi, M. kaṇḍi.] Candy, a weight, about 500 lbs.*PLUS *aḍaren* 'cover of pot or lid' Rebus: *aduru* 'native, unsmelted metal' The ligatured hieroglyph sign reads: unsmelted iron: *aduru meḍ* .

m1761a *खोंड [khōṇḍa] m A young bull, a bullcalf. (Marathi) Rebus: kõdār 'turner' (Bengali); कोंद kōnda 'engraver, lapidary setting or infixing gems' (Marathi) G. sãghāṛɔ m. 'lathe' ; संघाट joinery; M. sãgaḍ 'double-canoe'*

Rebus: sangataras. संगतराश lit. 'to collect stones, stone-cutter, mason.'

 *ranku* 'liquid measure' Rebus: *ranku* 'tin'

 *āra* 'spokes' Rebus: *āra 'brass'*. cf. *erka = ekke* (Tbh. of arka) *aka* (Tbh. of arka) copper (metal); crystal (Kannada) Glyph: *eraka*'nave of wheel' Rebus: eraka 'copper'; cf. *erka* = *ekke* (Tbh. of arka) *aka* (Tbh. of arka) copper (metal); crystal (Kannada)

 *āra* 'spokes'  Rebus: *āra 'brass'*. cf. *erka = ekke* (Tbh. of arka) *aka* (Tbh. of arka) copper (metal); crystal (Kannada) Glyph: eraka'nave of wheel' Rebus: *eraka* 'copper'; cf. *erka* = *ekke* (Tbh. of arka) *aka* (Tbh. of arka) copper (metal); crystal (Kannada)

ranku 'liquid measure' Rebus: *ranku* 'tin'
dula 'pair' Rebus: dul 'cast metal'

*meḍ 'body' Rebus: meḍ 'iron' (Ho.) काठी [kāṭhī] f (काष्ट S) 'frame or structure of the body' (Marathi) Rebus: खंडी [khaṇḍī] measure of weight (Marathi) கண்டி; kaṇṭi, n. < Mhr. khaṇḍil. [T. Tu. khaṇḍi, M. kaṇḍi.] Candy, a weight, about 500 lbs.*PLUS *kana, kanac* = corner (Santali); Rebus: *kañcu* = bronze (Telugu) PLUS *baṭa* = rimless pot (Kannada) Rebus: *baṭa* = a kind of iron (Gujarati) PLUS dulo 'hole' Rebus: dul 'cast metal'

 m1760a *खोंड [khōṇḍa] m A young bull, a bullcalf. (Marathi) Rebus: kõdār 'turner' (Bengali); कोंद kōnda 'engraver, lapidary setting or infixing gems' (Marathi) G. sãghāṛɔ m. 'lathe' ; संघाट joinery; M. sãgaḍ 'double-canoe' Rebus: sangataras 'stone-cutter, mason'*

 *āra* 'spokes' Rebus: *āra 'brass'*. cf. erka = ekke (Tbh. of arka) aka (Tbh. of arka) copper (metal); crystal (Kannada) Glyph: *eraka*'nave of wheel' Rebus: eraka 'copper'; cf. erka = ekke (Tbh. of arka) aka (Tbh. of arka) copper (metal); crystal (Kannada)
erako 'moltencast copper' PLUS

  notch+slanted stroke reads rebus: *ḍhālako kāṇḍa* 'ingot, tools, pots and pans and metal-ware'.*dhāḷ* 'a slope'; 'inclination of a plane' (G.); *ḍhāḷiyum* = adj. sloping, inclining (G.) Rebus: *ḍhālako* = a large metal ingot (G.) *ḍhālakī* = a metal heated and poured into a mould; a solid piece of metal; an ingot (Gujarati) PLUS खांडा [*khāṇḍā*] *m* A jag, notch, or indentation (as upon the edge of a tool or weapon). Rebus: *kāṇḍa* 'tools, pots and pans and metal-ware' *Thus, together, the pair reads: āra erako khāṇḍā* 'brass, moltencast copper metalware'.
aya aḍaren (homonym: aduru)'alloy native metal'
aya kammaṭa.'coiner, mint alloy'

 *kuṭila* 'bent' CDIAL 3230 kuṭi— in cmpd. 'curve', *kuṭika—* 'bent' MBh. Rebus: *kuṭila, katthīl* = bronze (8 parts copper and 2 parts tin)
dula 'pair' Rebus: dul 'cast metal' Thus, cast bronze.

 kanka 'rim of jar' Rebus: karṇīka 'account (scribe)' karṇī 'supercargo'

Lothal 21A

खोंड [khōṇḍa] m A young bull, a bullcalf. (Marathi) Rebus: kōdār 'turner' (Bengali); कोंद kōnda 'engraver, lapidary setting or infixing gems' (Marathi) G. sãghāṛɔ m. 'lathe' ; संघाट joinery; M. sāgaḍ 'double-canoe' Rebus: sangataras 'stone-cutter, mason'

āra 'spokes' Rebus: *āra 'brass'*. cf. erka = ekke (Tbh. of arka) aka (Tbh. of arka) copper (metal); crystal (Kannada) Glyph: *eraka*'nave of wheel' Rebus: eraka 'copper'; cf. erka = ekke (Tbh. of arka) aka (Tbh. of arka) copper (metal); crystal (Kannada) *erako* 'moltencast copper' PLUS

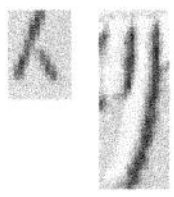

notch+slanted stroke reads rebus: *ḍhālako kāṇḍa* 'ingot, tools, pots and pans and metal-ware'.*dhāḷ* 'a slope'; 'inclination of a plane' (G.); *ḍhāḷiyum* = adj. sloping, inclining (G.) Rebus: *ḍhālako* = a large metal ingot (G.) *ḍhālakī* = a metal heated and poured into a mould; a solid piece of metal; an ingot (Gujarati) PLUS खांडा [*khāṇḍā*] *m* A jag, notch, or indentation (as upon the edge of a tool or weapon). Rebus: *kāṇḍa* 'tools, pots and pans and metal-ware' *Thus, together, the pair reads: āra erako khāṇḍā* 'brass, moltencast copper metalware'.

meḍ 'body' Rebus: meḍ 'iron' (Ho.) काठी [kāṭhī] f (काष्ट S) 'frame or structure of the body' (Marathi) Rebus: खंडी [khaṇḍī] measure of weight (Marathi) *கண்டி; kaṇṭi, n. < Mhr. khaṇḍil. [T. Tu. khaṇḍi, M. kaṇḍi.]* Candy, a weight, stated to be roughly equivalent to 500 lbs.

water-carrier hieroglyph *kuṭi*; Rebus: *kuṭhi* 'smelter furnace'. PLUS 'rim of jar':

kanka 'rim of jar' Rebus: karṇīka 'account (scribe)' karṇī 'supercargo'

M-202 a

m202a *खोंड [khōṇḍa] m A young bull, a bullcalf. (Marathi) Rebus: kōdār 'turner' (Bengali); कोंद kōnda 'engraver, lapidary setting or infixing gems' (Marathi) G. sãghāṛɔ m. 'lathe' ; संघाट joinery; M. sāgaḍ 'double-canoe' Rebus: sangataras 'stone-cutter, mason'*

āra 'spokes' Rebus: *āra 'brass'*. cf. erka = ekke (Tbh. of arka) aka (Tbh. of arka) copper (metal); crystal (Kannada) Glyph: *eraka*'nave of wheel' Rebus: eraka 'copper'; cf. erka = ekke (Tbh. of arka) aka (Tbh. of arka) copper (metal); crystal (Kannada) *erako* 'moltencast copper' PLUS

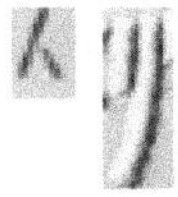

notch+slanted stroke reads rebus: *ḍhālako kāṇḍa* 'ingot, tools, pots and pans and metal-ware'.*dhāḷ* 'a slope'; 'inclination of a plane' (G.); *ḍhāḷiyum* = adj. sloping, inclining (G.) Rebus: *ḍhālako* = a large metal ingot (G.) *ḍhālakī* = a metal heated and poured into a mould; a solid piece of metal; an ingot (Gujarati) PLUS खांडा [*khāṇḍā*] *m* A jag, notch, or indentation (as upon the edge of a tool or weapon). Rebus: *kāṇḍa* 'tools, pots and pans and metal-ware' *Thus, together, the pair reads: āra erako khāṇḍā* 'brass, moltencast copper metalware'.

| *koḍa* 'one' Rebus: *koḍ* 'workshop' dula 'pair'

aya kāṇḍa 'alloy metalware'

 *kharedo* = a currycomb (Gujarati) खरारा [*khararā*] *m* (H) A currycomb. 2 Currying a horse. (Marathi) Rebus: करडा [*karaḍā*] Hard from alloy--iron, silver &c. (Marathi) *kharādī* ' turner' (Gujarati)
khōṇḍa A stock or stump (Marathi); 'leafless tree' (Marathi)

m875a *खोंड [khōṇḍa] m A young bull, a bullcalf. (Marathi) Rebus: kōdār 'turner' (Bengali); कोंद kōnda 'engraver, lapidary setting or infixing gems' (Marathi) G. sãghāṛɔ m. 'lathe' ; संघाट joinery; M. sāgaḍ 'double-canoe' Rebus: sangataras 'stone-cutter, mason'*

āra 'spokes' Rebus: *āra 'brass'.* cf. erka = ekke (Tbh. of arka) aka (Tbh. of arka) copper (metal); crystal (Kannada) Glyph: *eraka*'nave of wheel' Rebus: eraka 'copper'; cf. erka = ekke (Tbh. of arka) aka (Tbh. of arka) copper (metal); crystal (Kannada) *erako* 'moltencast copper' PLUS

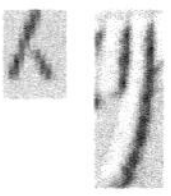

notch+slanted stroke reads rebus: *ḍhālako kāṇḍa* 'ingot, tools, pots and pans and metal-ware'.*dhāḷ* 'a slope'; 'inclination of a plane' (G.); *ḍhāḷiyum* = adj. sloping, inclining (G.) Rebus: *ḍhālako* = a large metal ingot (G.) *ḍhālakī* = a metal heated and poured into a mould; a solid piece of metal; an ingot (Gujarati) PLUS खांडा [*khāṇḍā*] *m* A jag, notch, or indentation (as upon the edge of a tool or weapon). Rebus: *kāṇḍa* 'tools, pots and pans and metal-ware' *Thus, together, the pair reads: āra erako khāṇḍā* 'brass, moltencast copper metalware'.

| *koḍa* 'one' Rebus: *koḍ* 'workshop' dula 'pair'

meḍ 'body' Rebus: meḍ 'iron' (Ho.) काठी [kāṭhī] f (काष्ट S) 'frame or structure of the body' (Marathi) Rebus: खंडी [khaṇḍī] measure of weight (Marathi) கண்டி; *kaṇṭi, n. < Mhr. khaṇḍil. [T. Tu. khaṇḍi, M. kaṇḍi.]* Candy, a weight, stated to be roughly equivalent to 500 lbs.

bhaṭa 'warrior' (Sanskrit) Rebus: *baṭa* a kind of iron (Gujarati). Rebus: *bhaṭa* 'furnace' (Santali)

h992A dula 'pair' Rebus: dul 'cast metal'
kolom 'three' Rebus: kolami 'smithy, forge'

āra 'spokes' Rebus: *āra* 'brass'. cf. erka = ekke (Tbh. of arka) aka (Tbh. of arka) copper (metal); crystal (Kannada) Glyph: *eraka'nave* of wheel' Rebus: *eraka* 'copper'; cf. erka = ekke (Tbh. of arka) aka (Tbh. of arka) copper (metal); crystal (Kannada)

m326b

āra 'spokes' Rebus: *āra* 'brass'. cf. erka = ekke (Tbh. of arka) aka (Tbh. of arka) copper (metal); crystal (Kannada) Glyph: *eraka'nave* of wheel' Rebus: *eraka* 'copper'; cf. erka = ekke (Tbh. of arka) aka (Tbh. of arka) copper (metal); crystal (Kannada)

kolom 'three' Rebus: kolami 'smithy, forge'

X *dāṭu* 'cross'(Telugu) Rebus: *dhatu* 'mineral' (Santali).

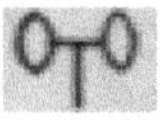

If frame of a cart is depicted, possible rebus reading: अगडा [agaḍā] *m* The tie connecting the जूं & दांडी of a गाडा or load-cart; the shaft and thill-yoke-tie. Rebus: 'lumber, miscellaneous articles': अगडतगड *agaḍatagaḍa*

dula 'pair' Rebus: *dul* 'cast metal'

'slanted stroke': *dhāḷ* 'a slope'; 'inclination of a plane' (Gujarati); *ḍhāḷiyum* = adj. sloping, inclining (Gujarati) Rebus: *ḍhālako* = a large metal ingot (Gujarati) *ḍhālakī* = a metal heated and poured into a mould; a solid piece of metal; an ingot (Gujarati)

m41a *खोंड [khōṇḍa] m A young bull, a bullcalf. (Marathi) Rebus: kõdār 'turner' (Bengali); कोंद kōnda 'engraver, lapidary setting or infixing gems' (Marathi) G. sãghārɔ m. 'lathe' ; संघाट joinery; M. sãgaḍ 'double-canoe' Rebus: sangataras. संगतराश lit. 'to collect stones, stone-cutter, mason.'*

āra 'spokes' Rebus: *āra* 'brass'. cf. erka = ekke (Tbh. of arka) aka (Tbh. of arka) copper (metal); crystal (Kannada) Glyph: *eraka'nave* of wheel' Rebus: *eraka* 'copper'; cf. erka = ekke (Tbh. of arka) aka (Tbh. of arka) copper (metal); crystal (Kannada)

kamaḍha = archer Rebus: *kampaṭṭam* = mint (Tamil) ; *kammaṭa* 'coiner, mint' (Telugu)

kolmo 'paddy plant' Rebus*: kolami* 'smithy, forge'

sal 'splinter' Rebus: *sal* 'workshop'

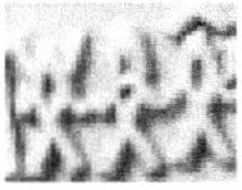

The three fishes read rebus from r.:

aya aduru 'unsmelted native alloy metal'

ayo ḍhālako 'alloy metal ingot'

aya kammaṭa.'coiner, mint alloy

kəṭhā´r, kc. *kuṭhār* m. ' granary, storeroom '(WPah.)(CDIAL 3550). *koṭhārī m.* ' storekeeper'

(Gujarati)(CDIAL 3551) Thus, storeroom (of) *kolom* 'three' Rebus: *kolami* 'smithy, forge'. Dula 'pair' Rebus: dul 'cast metal' Thus, together *dul kolami kuṭhār* 'metal smithy castings storeroom'

'*sãgāḍā* m. ' frame of a building ', k*°ḍī* f. ' lathe '(CDIAL 12859) Rebus*: sangataras.* संगतराश lit. 'to collect stones, stone-cutter, mason.'PLUS infixed 'three': *kolom* 'three' Rebus: *kolami* 'smithy, forge'; infixed 'splinter': *sal* 'splinter' Rebus: *sal* 'workshop'

kəṭhā´r, kc. *kuṭhār* m. ' granary, storeroom '(WPah.)(CDIAL 3550). *koṭhārī m.* ' storekeeper' (Gujarati)(CDIAL 3551) Thus, storeroom (of) *kolom* 'three' Rebus: *kolami* 'smithy, forge'. Dula 'pair' Rebus: dul 'cast metal' Thus, together *dul kolami kuṭhār* 'metal smithy castings storeroom'

'rim-of-jar' hieroglyph *kanka* (Santali) karṇika 'scribe'(Sanskrit)
Rebus: *karṇī,* supercargo for a boat shipment. *karṇīka* 'account (scribe)'.कारणी *kāraṇī* ' the supercargo of a ship' (Marathi)

खोंड [khōṇḍa] m A young bull, a bullcalf. (Marathi) Rebus: kõdār 'turner' (Bengali); कोंद kōnda 'engraver, lapidary setting or infixing gems' (Marathi) G. sãghāṛɔ m. 'lathe' ; संघाट joinery; M. sãgaḍ 'double-canoe' Rebus: sangataras. संगतराश lit. 'to collect stones, stone-cutter, mason.'

Sktd-1 a

Surkotada 1a *खोंड [khōṇḍa] m A young bull, a bullcalf. (Marathi) Rebus: kõdār 'turner' (Bengali); कोंद kōnda 'engraver, lapidary setting or infixing gems' (Marathi) G. sãghāṛɔ m. 'lathe' ; संघाट joinery; M. sãgaḍ 'double-canoe' Rebus: sangataras. संगतराश lit. 'to collect stones, stone-cutter, mason.'*

āra 'spokes' Rebus: *āra* 'brass'. cf. erka = ekke (Tbh. of arka) aka (Tbh. of arka) copper (metal); crystal (Kannada) Glyph: *eraka'nave* of wheel' Rebus: *eraka* 'copper'; cf. erka = ekke (Tbh. of arka) aka (Tbh. of arka) copper (metal); crystal (Kannada)
kamaḍha = archer Rebus: *kampaṭṭam* = mint (Tamil) ; *kammaṭa* 'coiner, mint' (Telugu)
kolmo 'paddy plant' Rebus*: kolami* 'smithy, forge'
sal 'splinter' Rebus: *sal* 'workshop'
|||| Numeral 4: *gaṇḍa* 'four' Rebus: *kaṇḍa* 'furnace, fire-altar' (Santali)
| *koḍa* 'one' Rebus: *koḍ* 'workshop'
m639a
खोंड [khōṇḍa] m A young bull, a bullcalf. (Marathi) Rebus: kõdār 'turner' (Bengali); कोंद kōnda 'engraver, lapidary setting or infixing gems' (Marathi) G. sãghāṛɔ m. 'lathe' ; संघाट joinery; M. sãgaḍ 'double-canoe' Rebus: sangataras. संगतराश lit. 'to collect stones, stone-cutter, mason.'

Supercargo: cast native metal, brass, copper

M-639 a

kanka 'rim of jar' Rebus: karṇīka 'account (scribe)' karṇī 'supercargo'
dula 'pair or two' Rebus: dul 'cast metal' *aḍar* 'harrow'; rebus: *aduru* 'native unsmelted metal' Rebus: *dul aduru* 'cast native unsmelted metal'

āra 'spokes' Rebus: *āra* 'brass'. cf. erka = ekke (Tbh. of arka) aka (Tbh. of arka) copper (metal); crystal (Kannada) Glyph: *eraka'nave* of wheel' Rebus: *eraka* 'copper'; cf. erka = ekke (Tbh. of arka) aka (Tbh. of arka) copper (metal); crystal (Kannada)
aḍar 'harrow'; rebus: *aduru* 'native unsmelted metal' dula 'tw' Rebus: dul 'cast metal'

dhatu 'strands of rope' Rebus: *dhatu* 'mineral ore' (Santali)

cīmara 'black ant' Rebus: *cīmara* 'copper'. *cīmara kāra* -- ' coppersmith '

sal 'splinter' Rebus: *sal* 'workshop' Thus, mineral, coiner, mint workshop: *dhatu kammaṭa*

ayaskāṇḍa 'excellent iron' (Pan) *kāṇḍā* 'metalware, tools, pots and pans'(Marathi). *kaṇḍ* = a furnace, altar (Santali) Thus, alloy metalware.

m268a *rāngo* 'water buffalo bull' (Ku.N.)(CDIAL 10559) Rebus: rango 'pewter' *pattar* 'trough' Rebus: *pattar* 'guild'.Thus, pewter guild.

āra 'spokes' Rebus: *āra 'brass'.* cf. erka = ekke (Tbh. of arka) aka (Tbh. of arka) copper (metal); crystal (Kannada) Glyph: eraka'nave of wheel' Rebus: eraka 'copper
meḍ 'body' Rebus: *meḍ* 'iron' (Ho.)
aḍaren 'lid of pot'; rebus: *aduru* 'native unsmelted metal'
खांडा [khāṇḍā] *m* A jag, notch, or indentation (as upon the edge of a tool or weapon). (Marathi) Rebus:*khāṇḍā* 'tools, pots and pans, metal-ware',
पेंडें [pēṇḍēṃ] n (पेड) A necklace composed of strings of pearls. 2 A loop or ring. Rebus: पेढी (Gujaráthí word.) A shop (Marathi)

Lothal

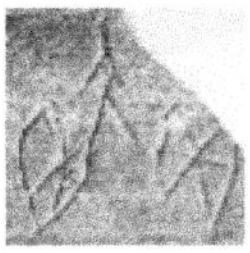

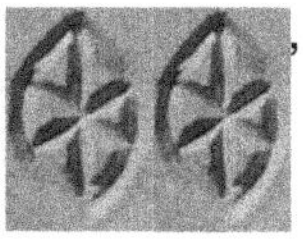

221A
dula 'pair' Rebus: dul 'cast metal' *āra* 'spokes' Rebus: *āra 'brass'.* cf. erka = ekke (Tbh. of arka) aka (Tbh. of arka) copper (metal); crystal (Kannada) Glyph: eraka'nave of wheel' Rebus: eraka 'copper'; cf. *erka = ekke* (Tbh. of arka) *aka* (Tbh. of *arka*) copper (metal); crystal (Kannada)

meḍ 'body' Rebus: *meḍ* 'iron' (Ho.)

Ligatured sign hieroglyph: 'rim-of-jar' PLUS 'water-carrier'

kanka 'rim of jar' Rebus: karṇīka 'account (scribe)' karṇī 'supercargo' कर्णधार [*karṇadhāra*] *m* S (A holder of the ear.) A helmsman or steersman. Thus, together, the ligatured hieroglyph reads: supercargo for a boat.

69: H-1971 A col (200%)

h1971A

āra 'spokes' Rebus: *āra 'brass'.* cf. erka = ekke (Tbh. of arka) aka (Tbh. of arka) copper (metal); crystal (Kannada) Glyph: eraka'nave of wheel' Rebus: eraka 'copper'; cf. *erka = ekke* (Tbh. of arka) *aka* (Tbh. of *arka*) copper (metal); crystal (Kannada)

ibha 'elephant' Rebus: *ib* 'iron' *ibbo* 'merchant' (Gujarati)
kola 'woman' Rebus: *kolhe* 'smelter' (Santali)
kol 'tiger' Rebus: *kolhe* 'smelter' *kol* 'iron, alloy' *dula* 'pair' Rebus: *dul* 'cast metal'
kaṇṇahāra -- m. 'helmsman, sailor' *kannār* 'coppersmiths'; . (काण*kāṇa* 'one-eyed', *āra* 'six', 'rings of hair' symbolic forms). The epigraph reads: Sailor merchant coppersmiths supercargo of cast alloy.

Section E: Bronze, tin

Meluhha glosses: L. awāṇ. *kasērā* ' metal worker ', P. *kaserā* m. ' worker in pewter ' (both ← E with -- *s* --); N. *kasero* ' maker of brass pots '; Bi. H. *kaserā* m. ' worker in pewter '. kāṁsyakāra m. ' worker in bell -- metal or brass ' Yājñ. com., *kaṁsakāra* -- m. BrahmavP. [kā´ṁsya -- , kāra -- 1]N. *kasār* ' maker of brass pots '; A. *kãhār* ' worker in bell -- metal ';

B. *kā̃sāri* ' pewterer, brazier, coppersmith ', Or. *kā̃sārī*, H. *kasārī* m. ' maker of brass pots '; G. *kā̃sārɔ, kas°* m. ' coppersmith '; M. *kā̃sār, kās°* m. ' worker in white metal ', *kāsārḍā* m. ' contemptuous term for the same '.(CDIAL 2988, 2989)

m28a खोंड *[khōṇḍa] m A young bull, a bullcalf. (Marathi) Rebus: kõdār 'turner' (Bengali);* कोंद *kōnda 'engraver, lapidary setting or infixing gems' (Marathi) G. sā̃ghāṛɔ m. 'lathe' ;* संघाट *joinery; M. sā̃gaḍ 'double-canoe' Rebus: sangataras.* संगतराश *lit. 'to collect stones, stone-cutter, mason.'*

Bronze alloy workshop kañcu sal starting with bronze which is a tin + copper alloy or tin bronze (as distinguished from arsenical bronze, i.e. naturally occurring copper + arsenic).'Pair of harrows': *aḍar* 'harrow'; rebus: *aduru* 'native unsmelted metal' *dul aduru* 'cast native unsmelted metal' *kanac* 'corner' Rebus: *kañcu* 'bronze' dula 'pair' Rebus: dul 'cast metal' Thus, cast bronze. *mogge* 'sprout, bud' Rebus*: mũh* 'ingot': native cast metal ingot. dula 'pair' Rebus: dul 'cast metal'. Thus, cast ingot. Or, kolmo 'paddy plant' Rebus: kolami 'smithy, forge'. Thus, metal casting smithy.

kanka 'rim of jar' Rebus: karṇīka 'account (scribe)' karṇī 'supercargo'

mogge 'sprout, bud' Rebus*: mũh* 'ingot'

kamaḍha 'bow and arrow' Rebus: *kammaṭa* 'mint, coiner'.

m1126a *rāngo* 'water buffalo bull' (Ku.N.)(CDIAL 10559) Rebus: rango 'pewter' pattar 'trough' Rebus: pattar 'guild'.

Bronze alloy workshop kañcu sal starting with bronze which is a tin + copper alloy or tin bronze (as distinguished from arsenical bronze, i.e. naturally occurring copper + arsenic). | *koḍa* 'one' Rebus: *koḍ* 'workshop'

āra 'spokes' Rebus: *āra 'brass'*. cf. erka = ekke (Tbh. of arka) aka (Tbh. of arka) copper (metal); crystal (Kannada) Glyph: *eraka* 'nave of wheel' Rebus: eraka 'copper'; cf. erka = ekke (Tbh. of arka) aka (Tbh. of arka) copper (metal); crystal (Kannada) *erako* 'moltencast copper'

h12a खोंड *[khōṇḍa] m A young bull, a bullcalf. (Marathi) Rebus: kõdār 'turner' (Bengali);* कोंद *kōnda 'engraver, lapidary setting or infixing gems' (Marathi) G. sā̃ghāṛɔ m. 'lathe' ;* संघाट *joinery; M. sā̃gaḍ 'double-canoe' Rebus: sangataras.* संगतराश *lit. 'to collect stones, stone-cutter, mason.'*

Bronze alloy workshop kañcu sal starting with bronze which is a tin + copper alloy or tin bronze (as distinguished from arsenical bronze, i.e. naturally occurring copper + arsenic).

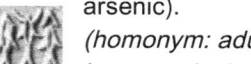

aya aḍaren (homonym: aduru)'alloy native metal'

aya kammaṭa.'coiner, mint alloy'

ayo ḍhālako 'alloy metal ingot'

Circumscript : *kuṭila* 'bent' CDIAL 3230 kuṭi— in cmpd. 'curve', *kuṭika*— 'bent' MBh. Rebus: *kuṭila, katthīl* = bronze (8 parts copper and 2 parts tin) *dula* 'pair' Rebus: *dul* 'cast metal'. Thus two bent lines () together read as circumscript: cast bronze, *dul kuṭila*.

kolmo 'paddy plant' Rebus: *kolami* 'smithy,forge'. Thus the composite hieroglyph with two circumscript ligatures, reads: metalware (from) cast bronze smithy-forge'.

The pair of hieroglyph signs are compositions: bicha 'scorpion' (Assamese) Rebus: *bica* 'stone ore' (Santali) The pairing sign is a composition of: sloping stroke PLUS two short strokes of a 'splinter':*dhāḷ* 'a slope'; 'inclination of a plane' (Gujarati); *ḍhāḷiyum* = adj. sloping, inclining (Gujarati) Rebus: *ḍhālako* = a large metal

ingot (Gujarati) *ḍhālakī* = a metal heated and poured into a mould; a solid piece of metal; an ingot (Gujarati)PLUS*sal* 'splinter' Rebus: *sal* 'workshop'. Thus the composition reads: *ḍhālako sal* 'ingot workshop'.

dāṭu 'cross'(Telugu) Rebus: *dhatu* 'mineral' (Santali).

kanka 'rim of jar' Rebus: *karṇīka* 'account (scribe)' *karṇī* 'supercargo'

m1976a

M-1976 a bis

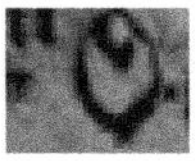

Bronze alloy workshop kañcu sal starting with bronze which is a tin + copper alloy or tin bronze (as distinguished from arsenical bronze, i.e. naturally occurring copper + arsenic). *meḍ* 'body'

Rebus: *meḍ* 'iron' (Ho.) काठी [kāṭhī] *f* (काष्ट S) 'frame or structure of the body' (Marathi) Rebus: खंडी [khaṇḍī] measure of weight (Marathi) *கண்டி; kaṇṭi, n. < Mhr. khaṇḍil. [T. Tu. khaṇḍi, M. kaṇḍi.]* Candy, a weight, stated to be roughly equivalent to 500 lbs.

| *koḍa* 'one' Rebus: *koḍ* 'workshop'

khaṇḍ 'field, division' (Sanskrit) Rebus: *khāṇḍa* 'tools, pots and pans, metal-ware'. Rebus 2: kaṇḍ 'fire-altar' (Santali) dula 'pair' Rebus: dul 'cast metal' Thus, duplicated 'division' hieroglyph sign reads: cast metal metal-ware.

H-1942 A H-1942 B H-1942 C

h1942A Side A:Bronze alloy workshop kañcu sal starting with bronze which is a tin + copper alloy or tin bronze (as distinguished from arsenical bronze, i.e. naturally occurring copper + arsenic). dula 'pair' Rebus: dul 'cast metal' kolom 'three' Rebus: kolami 'smithy, forge' Side C: dulo 'hole' dula 'pair' Rebus: dul 'cast metal' Side B: *baṭa* = rimless pot (Kannada) Rebus:) *baṭa* = a kind of iron (G.)) *bhaṭa* furnace (Gujarati) dula 'pair' Rebus: dul 'cast metal' Thus, iron furnace castings.

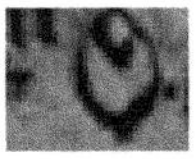

kolmo 'paddy plant' Rebus: *kolami* 'smithy, forge' Vikalpa: *mogge* 'sprout, bud' Rebus: *mũh* 'ingot' (Santali) dolu 'plant of shoot height' Rebus: dul 'cast metal'

M-1762 a

m1762a.

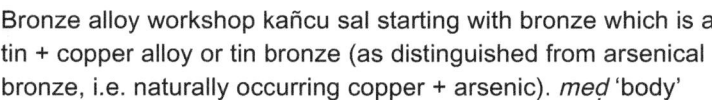

āra 'spokes' Rebus: *āra 'brass'*. cf. erka = ekke (Tbh. of arka) aka (Tbh. of arka) copper (metal); crystal (Kannada) Glyph: eraka'nave of wheel' Rebus: eraka 'copper'; cf. erka = ekke (Tbh. of arka) aka (Tbh. of arka) copper (metal); crystal (Kannada)

खांडा [*khāṇḍā*] *m* A jag, notch, or indentation (as upon the edge of a tool or weapon). Rebus: *kāṇḍa* 'tools, pots and pans and metal-ware'

kañcu 'bronze' hieroglyph is reduplicated (ligatured top-down): *dula* 'pair' Rebus: *dul* 'cast metal' Thus, cast bronze.

dāṭu 'cross'(Telugu) Rebus: *dhatu* 'mineral' (Santali).

m296A Pictorial motifs: nine ficus:
lo, no 'nine' phonetic reinforcement of: *loa* 'ficus' Rebus*: lo* 'copper'
खोंड [khōṇḍa] m A young bull, a bullcalf. (Marathi) Rebus: kõdār 'turner' (Bengali); कोंद kōnda 'engraver, lapidary setting or infixing gems' (Marathi) G. sãghāṛɔ m. 'lathe' ; संघाट joinery; M. sãgaḍ 'double-canoe' Rebus: sangataras 'stone-cutter, mason'

Ligature of copper, brass -- *eraka, āra*; the PLUS bronze -- *kañcu.*

dhāḷ 'a slope'; 'inclination of a plane' (Gujarati); *ḍhāḷiyum* = adj. sloping, inclining (Gujarati) Rebus: *ḍhālako* = a large metal ingot (Gujarati) *ḍhālakī* = a metal heated and poured into a mould; a solid piece of metal; an ingot (Gujarati) PLUS खांडा [*khāṇḍā*] *m* A jag, notch, or indentation (as upon the edge of a tool or weapon). Rebus: *kāṇḍa* 'tools, pots and pans and metal-ware'

ayo 'fish' Rebus: *aya* 'iron' *ayas* 'metal'

kāṇḍa 'arrow' (Sanskrit) Rebus:*khāṇḍa* 'tools, pots and pans, metal-ware'. Rebus 2: kaṇḍ 'fire-altar' (Santali)

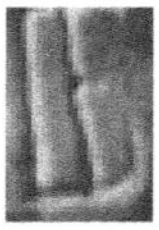
Variant: *kole.l* 'smith, temple' (Kota)

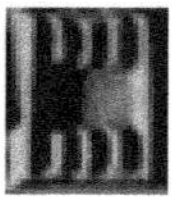
kəṭhā´r, kc. *kuṭhār* m. ' granary, storeroom '(Western Pahari)(CDIAL 3550). *koṭhārī* m. ' storekeeper' (Gujarati)(CDIAL 3551) Thus, storeroom (of) *kolom* 'three' Rebus: *kolami* 'smithy, forge'. Dula 'pair' Rebus: dul 'cast metal' Thus, together *dul kolami kuṭhār* 'metal smithy castings storeroom'

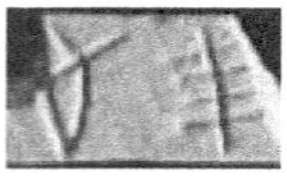
'Pair of hieroglyph signs: bow-and-arrow PLUS | *koḍa* 'one' Rebus: *koḍ* 'workshop' PLUS |||| Numeral 4: gaṇḍa 'four' Rebus: kaṇḍa 'furnace, fire-altar' (Santali) *kamaḍha* 'archer, bow' Rebus: *kammaṭa* 'mint, coiner'.

h2244B

Balakot 1A*खोंड [khōṇḍa] m A young bull, a bullcalf. (Marathi) Rebus: kõdār 'turner' (Bengali); कोंद kōnda 'engraver, lapidary setting or infixing gems'*

(Marathi) G. sãghāṛɔ m. 'lathe' ; संघाट joinery; M. sãgaḍ 'double-canoe' Rebus: sangataras 'stone-cutter, mason'

|||| Numeral 4: gaṇḍa 'four' Rebus: kaṇḍa 'furnace, fire-altar' (Santali) dula 'pair' Rebus: dul 'cast metal'

Strands of yarn/rope' hieroglyph: Hieroglyph: 'strands of yarn' Rebus reading: *dhā'tu* 'strand of rope' Rebus: *dhatu* 'mineral ore' (Santali)

dula 'two' Rebus: dul 'cast metal' kolom 'three' Rebus: kolami 'smithy, forge' *aya kāṇḍa* 'alloy metalware'

m151a *खोंड [khōṇḍa] m A young bull, a bullcalf. (Marathi) Rebus: kõdār 'turner' (Bengali); कोंद kōnda 'engraver, lapidary setting or infixing gems' (Marathi) G. sãghāṛɔ m. 'lathe' ; संघाट joinery; M. sãgaḍ 'double-canoe' Rebus: sangataras 'stone-cutter, mason'*

kana, kanac 'corner' Rebus: *kañcu* 'bronze'. PLUS | *koḍa* 'one' Rebus: *koḍ* 'workshop' PLUS |||| Numeral 4: gaṇḍa 'four' Rebus: kaṇḍa 'furnace, fire-altar' (Santali)*kolom* 'three' Rebus: *kolami* 'smithy, forge'. Thus the composite hieroglyphs reads: bronze smithy granary, *kañcu kolami beṛhi*

slanted stroke ligatured to a notch : *ḍhālako kāṇḍa*, ingot metalware.

ayo 'fish' Rebus: *aya* 'iron' *ayas* 'metal'

Bronze workshops with additional metalwork competence

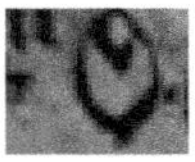
The text sequences starting with the pair of hieroglyph signs indicates bronze workshop: *kanac* 'corner' Rebus: *kañcu* 'bronze' *sal* 'splinter' Rebus: *sal* 'workshop' Thus, *kañcu sal* 'bronze workshop'

This pair is followed by other 'fish' variant signs to indicate specifications of 'ayas' metallurgy:

kañcu sal 'bronze workshop' PLUS ayo 'fish' Rebus: aya 'iron' ayas 'metal' (Vedic) Thus, *kañcu sal ayas* 'bronze workshop, alloy metal'

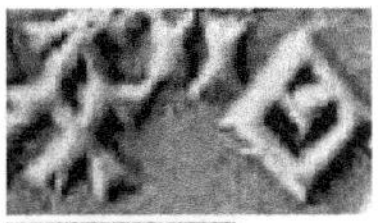
aya aḍaren (homonym: aduru)'alloy native metal'

aya kāṇḍa 'alloy metalware'

aya kammaṭa.'coiner, mint alloy'
ayo 'fish' Rebus: aya 'iron' (Gujarati) ayas 'metal' (Vedic) PLUS ligatured fins: *khambharā* m. 'fin' (Lahnda); khambh 'wing' (Punjabi) Allograph: Garh. *khambu* ' pillar

'.(CDIAL 13640) Rebus: kammaṭa 'coiner, mint'. Thus 'fish' hieroglyph gets ligatured with fins to denote alloyed metal (of) mint to read: *aya kammaṭa.*'coiner, mint alloy'.

Bronze alloy workshop kañcu sal starting with bronze which is a tin + copper alloy or tin bronze (as distinguished from arsenical bronze, i.e. naturally occurring copper + arsenic).

h085 *khũṭ* 'zebu' Rebus: '(native metal) guild'

Bronze alloy workshop kañcu sal starting with bronze which is a tin + copper alloy or tin bronze (as distinguished from arsenical bronze, i.e. naturally occurring copper + arsenic).

ayo 'fish' Rebus: aya 'iron' ayas 'metal'; dula 'pair' Rebus: dul 'cast (metal). Thus, the pair of 'fish' hieroglyphs read rebus: *dul ayas* 'cast alloy metal'.
kaṇḍa 'arrow' Rebus: *kāṇḍa* 'tools, pots and pans and metal-ware.

Thus the message of h085 epigraph is: native metal guild (with) bronze workshop, cast alloy metal tools, pots and pans and metal-ware.

h609a *खोंड [khōṇḍa] m A young bull, a bullcalf. (Marathi) Rebus: kõdār 'turner' (Bengali); कोंद kōnda 'engraver, lapidary setting or infixing gems' (Marathi) G. sãghāṛɔ m. 'lathe' ; संघाट joinery; M. sãgaḍ 'double-canoe' Rebus: sangataras 'stone-cutter, mason'*

Bronze alloy workshop kañcu sal starting with bronze which is a tin + copper alloy or tin bronze (as distinguished from arsenical bronze, i.e. naturally occurring copper + arsenic).

h1042a *खोंड [khōṇḍa] m A young bull, a bullcalf. (Marathi) Rebus: kõdār 'turner' (Bengali); कोंद kōnda 'engraver, lapidary setting or infixing gems' (Marathi) G. sãghāṛɔ m. 'lathe' ; संघाट joinery; M. sãgaḍ 'double-canoe' Rebus: sangataras 'stone-cutter, mason'*

Bronze alloy workshop kañcu sal starting with bronze which is a tin + copper alloy or tin bronze (as distinguished from arsenical bronze, i.e. naturally occurring copper + arsenic).

ayo 'fish' Rebus: *aya* 'iron' *ayas* 'metal'

meḍ 'body' Rebus: *meḍ* 'iron' (Ho.) काठी [kāṭhī] *f* (काष्ट S) 'frame or structure of the body' (Marathi) Rebus: खंडी [khanḍī] measure of weight (Marathi) *கண்டி; kaṇṭi, n. < Mhr. khanḍil. [T. Tu. khanḍi, M. kanḍi.]* Candy, a weight, stated to be roughly equivalent to 500 lbs.

 *kuṭila* 'bent' CDIAL 3230 kuṭi— in cmpd. 'curve', *kuṭika—* 'bent' MBh. Rebus: *kuṭila, katthīl* = bronze (8 parts copper and 2 parts tin)Duplicated: dula 'pair' Rebus: dul 'cast metal' Thus, cast bronze
kanka 'rim of jar' Rebus: karṇīka 'account (scribe)' karṇī 'supercargo'

 h15A *खोंड [khōṇḍa] m A young bull, a bullcalf. (Marathi) Rebus: kōdār 'turner' (Bengali); कोंद kōnda 'engraver, lapidary setting or infixing gems' (Marathi) G. sãghāṛɔ m. 'lathe' ; संघाट joinery; M. sãgaḍ 'double-canoe' Rebus: sangataras 'stone-cutter, mason'*

 Bronze alloy workshop kañcu sal starting with bronze which is a tin + copper alloy or tin bronze (as distinguished from arsenical bronze, i.e. naturally occurring copper + arsenic).
ayo 'fish' Rebus: *aya* 'iron' *ayas* 'metal'

  m453ABronze alloy workshop kañcu sal starting with bronze which is a tin + copper alloy or tin bronze (as distinguished from arsenical bronze, i.e. naturally occurring copper + arsenic).
ayo 'fish' Rebus: *aya* 'iron' *ayas* 'metal'

 m1709a Zebu. Native metal smith guild.
 Bronze alloy workshop kañcu sal starting with bronze which is a tin + copper alloy or tin bronze (as distinguished from arsenical bronze, i.e. naturally occurring copper + arsenic).
ayo 'fish' Rebus: *aya* 'iron' *ayas* 'metal' (Vedic)

kāṇḍa 'arrow' (Sanskrit) Rebus:*khāṇḍa* 'tools, pots and pans, metal-ware'. Rebus 2: kaṇḍ 'fire-altar' (Santali)
kole.l 'temple' Rebus: kole.l 'smithy' (Kota).

 m278A *ibha* 'elephant' Rebus: *ib* 'iron' *ibbo* 'merchant' (Gujarati)

 Bronze alloy workshop kañcu sal starting with bronze which is a tin + copper alloy or tin bronze (as distinguished from arsenical bronze, i.e. naturally occurring copper + arsenic).|||| Numeral 4: *gaṇḍa* 'four' Rebus: *kaṇḍa* 'furnace, fire-altar' (Santali).*mogge* 'sprout, , *mogge* 'sprout, bud' Rebus*: mũh* 'ingot'.
Variant:

  *kəṭhā'r*, kc. *kuṭhār* m. ' granary, storeroom '(Western Pahari)(CDIAL 3550). *koṭhārī m.* ' storekeeper' (Gujarati)(CDIAL 3551) Thus, storeroom (of) *kolom*
 'three' Rebus: *kolami* 'smithy, forge'. Dula 'pair' Rebus: dul 'cast metal' Thus, together *dul kolami kuṭhār* 'metal smithy castings storeroom' Or, variant rebus reading: *kole.l* 'smithy, temple' (Kota)

 m1152A *ibha* 'elephant' Rebus: *ib* 'iron' *ibbo* 'merchant' (Gujarati)

pattar 'trough' (Telugu) Rebus: pattar 'guild' (Tamil)

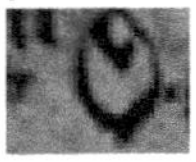 Bronze alloy workshop kañcu sal starting with bronze which is a tin + copper alloy or tin bronze (as distinguished from arsenical bronze, i.e. naturally occurring copper + arsenic).

ayo 'fish' Rebus: *aya* 'iron' *ayas* 'metal' (Vedic)

dula 'pair' Rebus: *dul* 'cast (metal)' PLUS*kana, kanac* = corner (Santali); Rebus: *kañcu* = bronze (Telugu) Thus, cast bronze.
dula 'pair' Rebus: dul 'cast metal'

 kanka 'rim of jar' Rebus: karṇīka 'account (scribe)' karṇī 'supercargo'

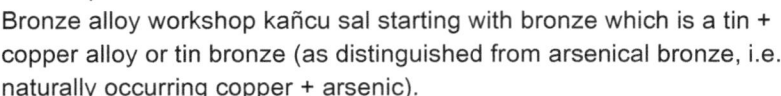

 m1148A *ibha* 'elephant' Rebus: *ib* 'iron' *ibbo* 'merchant'

 Bronze alloy workshop kañcu sal starting with bronze which is a tin + copper alloy or tin bronze (as distinguished from arsenical bronze, i.e. naturally occurring copper + arsenic).

ayo 'fish' Rebus: *aya* 'iron' *ayas* 'metal' *kāṇḍa* 'arrow' (Sanskrit) Rebus:*khāṇḍa* 'tools, pots and pans, metal-ware'. Rebus 2: kaṇḍ 'fire-altar' (Santali) kole.l 'temple' Rebus: kole.l 'smithy' (Kota).

  Lothal 89a Bronze alloy workshop kañcu sal starting with bronze which is a tin + copper alloy or tin bronze (as distinguished from arsenical bronze, i.e. naturally occurring copper + arsenic).

aya aḍaren (homonym: aduru)'alloy native metal' *kamaḍha* 'crab' Rebus: *kammaṭa* 'mint, coiner'.
ḍato = claws of crab (Santali) Rebus: *dhātu* 'mineral ore' PLUS खांडा [*khāṇḍā*] *m* A jag, notch, or indentation (as upon the edge of a tool or weapon). Rebus: *kāṇḍa* 'tools, pots and pans and metal-ware' Thus, cast bronze metalware.

 Variant: *dhāḷ* 'a slope'; 'inclination of a plane' (G.); *ḍhāḷiyum* = adj. sloping, inclining (G.) Rebus: *ḍhālako* = a large metal ingot (G.) *ḍhālakī* = a metal heated and poured into a mould; a solid piece of metal; an ingot (Gujarati) PLUS *dula* 'pair' Rebus: *dul* 'cast *metal'* *sal* 'splinter' Rebus: *sal* 'workshop'. Thus, *ḍhālako dul sal* 'ingot, cast metal workshop'.

 m0259 Text 2132 *khũṭ* 'zebu' Rebus: '(native metal) guild'

kanac 'corner' Rebs: *kañcu* 'bronze'
sal 'splinter' Rebus: *sal* 'workshop'
ayo 'fish' Rebus: aya 'iron' (Gujarati) ayas 'metal' (Vedic) notch (infixed ligature) Rebus: *kāṇḍa* 'pots and pans, metalware', Thus, the composite hieroglyph reads rebus: metalware of alloyed metal.
Thus,

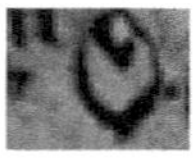 Bronze alloy workshop kañcu sal starting with bronze which is a tin + copper alloy or tin bronze (as distinguished from arsenical bronze, i.e. naturally occurring copper + arsenic). PLUS *aya kāṇḍa* 'alloy metalware'

kāṇḍa 'arrow' Rebus: *kāṇḍa* 'pots and pans, metalware,

 . m1115 Text 1328 *khũṭ* 'zebu' Rebus:

Bronze alloy alloy or tin 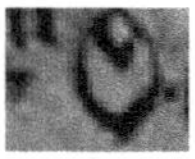 workshop kañcu sal starting with bronze which is a tin + copper bronze (as distinguished from arsenical bronze, i.e. naturally occurring copper + arsenic).

kanac 'corner' Rebus: kañcu 'bronze'
sal 'splinter' Rebus: *sal* 'workshop'
ayo 'fish' Rebus: ayas 'iron' (Gujarati) ayas 'metal' (Vedic) PLUS infixed hieroglyph of slanted stroke: *dhāḷ* 'a slope'; 'inclination of a plane' (Gujarati); *ḍhāḷiyum* = adj. sloping, inclining (Gujarati) Rebus: *ḍhālako* = a large metal ingot (Gujarati) *ḍhālakī* = a metal heated and poured into a mould; a solid piece of metal; an ingot (Gujarati) Thus, the ligatured hieroglyph reads: *ayo ḍhālako* 'native metal ingot'.

sangaḍa 'frame of a building' *sãgaṛh* m. 'line of entrenchments, stone walls for defence (Lahnda)
Rebus: *jangaḍ* 'entrustment articles'. Vikalpa: sangatar Rebus: *jangaḍ* 'entrustment articles'. sangataraas'u 'stone-cutter'.

 kanka 'rim of jar' Rebus: *karṇīka* 'account (scribe)' *karṇī* 'supercargo'

 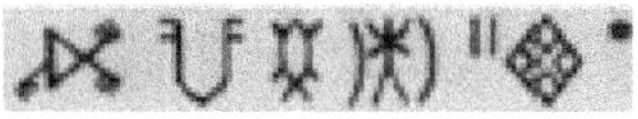 m1107a Text 2306 *khũṭ* 'zebu' Rebus: '(native metal) guild'

kanac 'corner' Rebus: kañcu 'bronze'
sal 'splinter' Rebus: *sal* 'workshop'
kuṭila 'bent' Rebus: kuṭila, katthīl = bronze (8 parts copper and 2 parts tin) dula 'pair' dul 'cast metal' Thus, cast bronze: *dul kuṭila*
meḍ 'body' Rebus: *meḍ* 'iron' *koḍ* 'horn' Rebus: *koḍ* 'workshop'
aya kammaṭa.'coiner, mint alloy'

 kanka 'rim of jar' Rebus: *karṇīka* 'account (scribe)' *karṇī* 'supercargo'

 *Kur.* xolā tail. *Malt.* qoli id. (DEDR 2135). Rebus: kolhe 'smelter'

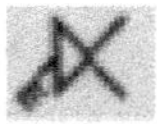 *ḍato* 'claws or pincers of crab' (Santali) Rebus: *dhatu* 'mineral ore' (Santali) PLUS xola 'tail' Rebus: kolhe 'smelter'. Thus, the ligatured glyph is read rebus as: dhatu kolhe 'mineral, ore smelter'.

 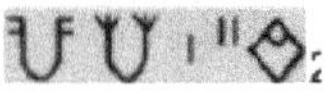 m1177 Composite animal. Zebu horns: Native metal smith guild.Text 2450

ingot (from) iron smelter, tin smelter merchant guild

kanac 'corner' Rebus: kañcu 'bronze'
sal 'splinter' Rebus: sal 'workshop'

खांडा [*khāṇḍā*] *m* A jag, notch, or indentation (as upon the edge of a tool or weapon). Rebus: *kāṇḍa* 'tools, pots and pans and metal-ware'

dula 'pair' Rebus: dul 'cast metal' kolmo 'paddy plant' Rebus: kolami 'smithy, forge'. Thus, the duplicated 'paddyplant' hieroglyph denotes: metal smithy castings.

kanka 'rim of jar' Rebus: karṇīka 'account (scribe)' karṇī 'supercargo'

m21a *खोंड [khōṇḍa] m A young bull, a bullcalf. (Marathi) Rebus: kõdār 'turner' (Bengali); कोंद kōnda 'engraver, lapidary setting or infixing gems' (Marathi) G. sãghāṛɔ m. 'lathe' ; संघाट joinery; M. sãgaḍ 'double-canoe' Rebus: sangataras 'stone-cutter, mason'*

Bronze alloy workshop kañcu sal starting with bronze which is a tin + copper alloy or tin bronze (as distinguished from arsenical bronze, i.e. naturally occurring copper + arsenic).
dula 'two' Rebus: dul 'cast metal'

dāṭu 'cross'(Telugu) Rebus: *dhatu* 'mineral' (Santali).
kaṇḍo 'stool, seat' Rebus: *kāṇḍa* 'metalware' *kaṇḍa* 'fire-altar'
kanka 'rim of jar' Rebus: karṇīka 'account (scribe)' karṇī 'supercargo'

|||| Numeral 4: gaṇḍa 'four' Rebus: kaṇḍa 'furnace, fire-altar' (Santali) dula 'pair' Rebus: dul 'cast metal'

m0258a Native metal smith guild.

Bronze alloy workshop kañcu sal starting with bronze which is a tin + copper alloy or tin bronze (as distinguished from arsenical bronze, i.e. naturally occurring copper + arsenic).

kana, kanac 'corner' Rebus: *kañcu* 'bronze'.
Variant:

khuṭo ' leg, foot ', °ṭī ' goat's leg ' Rebus: *khōṭā* 'alloy' (Marathi)

muka 'ladle' (Tamil)(DEDR 4887) Rebus: *mũh* 'ingot' (Santali) *baṭa* = a kind of iron (Gujarati) *baṭa* = rimless pot (Kannada) Thus, iron ingot.

kamaḍha 'bow and arrow' Rebus: *kammaṭa* 'coiner, mint'.

सांड [sāṇḍa] *f* (षद S) An outlet for superfluous water (as through a dam or mound); a sluice, a floodvent. Rebus: सांडणी [sāṇḍaṇī] *f* (H) An instrument of goldsmiths. It is hooked or curved at the extremity; and is used to draw things out of the fire.

loa 'ficus religiosa' Rebus: *lo* 'iron' (Sanskrit) PLUS unique ligatures: लोखंड [lōkhaṇḍa] *n* (लोह S) Iron. लोखंडाचे चणे खावविणें or चारणें To oppress grievously.लोखंडकाम [lōkhaṇḍakāma] *n* Iron work; that portion (of a building, machine &c.) which consists of iron. 2 The business of an ironsmith.लोखंडी [lōkhaṇḍī] *a* (लोखंड) Composed of iron; relating to iron. (Marathi)

m1961a

Bronze alloy is a tin + copper 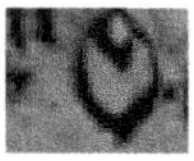 workshop kañcu sal starting with bronze which alloy or tin bronze (as distinguished from arsenical bronze, i.e. naturally occurring copper + arsenic).

 'Arrow' sign hieroglyph (variant) This is a ligature of 'lid of pot' hieroglyph superscript on 'a linear stroke' numeral hieroglyph.*aḍaren* 'cover of pot or lid' Rebus: *aduru* 'native, unsmelted metal' PLUS koḍ = one (Santali); koḍ 'workshop' (G.)

 *kolmo* 'paddy plant' Rebus: *kolami* 'smithy, forge' Vikalpa: *mogge* 'sprout, bud' Rebus: *mũh* 'ingot' (Santali) dolu 'plant of shoot height' Rebus: dul 'cast metal'

m1305A

Variant indicating work with four alloys:

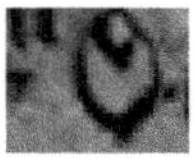 Bronze alloy workshop kañcu sal starting with bronze which is a tin + copper alloy or tin bronze (as distinguished from arsenical bronze, i.e. naturally occurring copper + arsenic).

 water-carrier hieroglyph *kuṭi*; Rebus: *kuṭhi* 'smelter furnace'.

 कांड *kāṇḍa* 'arrow' Rebus: *kāṇḍa* 'pots and pans, metalware, tools'. Rebus 2: kaṇḍ 'fire-altar' (Santali)

 *khareḍo* = a currycomb (Gujarati) खरारा [*kharārā*] *m* (H) A currycomb. 2 Currying a horse. (Marathi) Rebus: करडा [*karaḍā*] Hard from alloy--iron, silver &c. (Marathi) *kharādī* ' turner' (Gujarati)

m874A Bronze, smelting furnace, hard alloys

Read rebus as at m1305

खोंड [khōṇḍa] m A young bull, a bullcalf. (Marathi) Rebus: kōdār 'turner' (Bengali); कोंद kōnda 'engraver, lapidary setting or infixing gems' (Marathi) G. sãghāṛɔ m. 'lathe' ; संघाट joinery; M. sãgaḍ 'double-canoe' Rebus: sangataras 'stone-cutter, mason'

m1696A Turner's workshop *खोंड [khōṇḍa] m A young bull, a bullcalf. (Marathi) Rebus: kōdār 'turner' (Bengali); कोंद kōnda 'engraver, lapidary setting or infixing gems' (Marathi) G. sãghāṛɔ m. 'lathe' ;*

संघाट joinery; M. sāgaḍ 'double-canoe' Rebus: sangataras 'stone-cutter, mason'

kanac 'corner' Rebus: *kañcu* 'bronze' (Telugu) sal 'splinter' Rebus: sal 'workshop' Bronze-workshop.

aḍar 'harrow'; rebus: *aduru* 'native unsmelted metal'
ayo 'fish' Rebus: *aya* 'iron' *ayas* 'metal'

muka 'ladle' (Tamil)(DEDR 4887) Rebus*: mũh* 'ingot' (Santali) *baṭa* = rimless pot (Kannada) Rebus: *baṭa* = a kind of iron (Gujarati)
kolom 'three' Rebus: *kolami* 'smithy, forge. *kaṇḍa* 'arrow' Rebus: *kāṇḍa* 'tools, pots and pans and metal-ware.

m388A *खोंड [khōṇḍa] m A young bull, a bullcalf. (Marathi) Rebus: kõdār 'turner' (Bengali); कोंद kōnda 'engraver, lapidary setting or infixing gems' (Marathi) G. sãghāṛɔ m. 'lathe' ; संघाट joinery; M. sāgaḍ 'double-canoe' Rebus: sangataras 'stone-cutter, mason'*

Bronze alloy workshop kañcu sal starting with bronze which is a tin + copper alloy or tin bronze (as distinguished from arsenical bronze, i.e. naturally occurring copper + arsenic).

dula 'pair' Rebus: *dul* 'cast (metal)' PLUS*kana, kanac* = corner (Santali); Rebus: *kañcu* = bronze (Telugu) PLUS infixed kolmo 'paddy plant' Rebus: kolami 'smithy, forge'. Thus, cast bronze smithy, forge. Or, *mogge* 'sprout, bud' Rebus: *mũh* 'ingot' (Santali)Thus, cast bronze ingot. Read as: *kañcu dul mũh 'bronze cast ingot'*
aya kāṇḍa 'alloy metalware' Variant:

mogge 'sprout, bud' Rebus*: mũh* 'ingot' PLUS *dul kuṭila* 'cast bronze'. Thus, *dul kuṭila mũh* 'cast bronze ingot'
kolmo 'paddy plant' Rebus: *kolami* 'smithy, forge'
Last sign: *kanac* 'corner' Rebus: *kañcu* 'bronze' (Telugu) PLUS 'notch' Rebus: *kāṇḍa* 'tools, pots and pans and metal-ware. Thus, bronze metalware

Three sign sequence:

muka 'ladle' (Tamil)(DEDR 4887) Rebus: *mũh* 'ingot' (Santali) Thus, iron ingot.
kolom 'three' Rebus: kolami 'smithy, forge' *kāṇḍa* 'arrow' (Sanskrit) Rebus:*khāṇḍa* 'tools, pots and pans, metal-ware'. Rebus 2: kaṇḍ 'fire-altar' (Santali) Thus, the three sign sequence reads: iron ingot, furnace smithy, fire-altar metalware.

M-77 a

m77a
First 3 signs read rebus as at m388. *खोंड [khōṇḍa] m A young bull, a bullcalf. (Marathi) Rebus: kõdār 'turner' (Bengali); कोंद kōnda 'engraver, lapidary setting or infixing gems' (Marathi) G. sãghāṛɔ m. 'lathe' ; संघाट joinery; M. sāgaḍ 'double-canoe' Rebus: sangataras 'stone-cutter, mason'*

Variant:

mogge 'sprout, bud' Rebus*: mũh* 'ingot' PLUS *dul kuṭila* 'cast bronze'. Thus, *dul kuṭila mũh* 'cast bronze ingot'
kolmo 'paddy plant' Rebus: *kolami* 'smithy, forge'
Last sign: *kanac* 'corner' Rebus: *kañcu* 'bronze' (Telugu) PLUS 'notch' Rebus: *kāṇḍa* 'tools, pots and pans and metal-ware. Thus, bronze metalware

kolmo 'paddy plant' Rebus: *kolami* 'smithy, forge' Vikalpa: *mogge* 'sprout, bud' Rebus: *mũh* 'ingot' (Santali) dolu 'plant of shoot height' Rebus: dul 'cast metal'

kana, kanac = corner (Santali); Rebus: *kañcu* = bronze (Telugu) PLUS खांडा [*khāṇḍā*] *m* A jag, notch, or indentation (as upon the edge of a tool or weapon). Rebus: *kāṇḍa* 'tools, pots and pans and metal-ware' Thus, bronze metalware.

m166a *खोंड [khōṇḍa] m A young bull, a bullcalf. (Marathi) Rebus: kõdār 'turner' (Bengali); कोंद kōnda 'engraver, lapidary setting or infixing gems' (Marathi) G. sãghāṛɔ m. 'lathe' ; संघाट joinery; M. sãgaḍ 'double-canoe' Rebus: sangataras 'stone-cutter, mason'*

Bronze alloy workshop kañcu sal starting with bronze which is a tin + copper alloy or tin bronze (as distinguished from arsenical bronze, i.e. naturally occurring copper + arsenic).

dula 'pair' Rebus: *dul* 'cast (metal)' PLUS*kana, kanac* = corner (Santali); Rebus: *kañcu* = bronze (Telugu) PLUS infixed kolmo 'paddy plant' Rebus: kolami 'smithy, forge'. Thus, cast bronze smithy, forge. Or, *mogge* 'sprout, bud' Rebus: *mũh* 'ingot' (Santali)Thus, cast bronze ingot. Read as: *kañcu dul mũh 'bronze cast ingot'*
aya kammaṭa.'coiner, mint alloy'

dula 'pair' Rebus: *dul* 'cast (metal)' PLUS *kana, kanac* = corner (Santali); Rebus: *kañcu* = bronze (Telugu) Thus, cast bronze.

kolmo 'paddy plant' Rebus: *kolami* 'smithy, forge' Vikalpa: *mogge* 'sprout, bud' Rebus: *mũh* 'ingot' (Santali) dolu 'plant of shoot height' Rebus: dul 'cast metal'

m118A *खोंड [khōṇḍa] m A young bull, a bullcalf. (Marathi) Rebus: kõdār 'turner' (Bengali); कोंद kōnda 'engraver, lapidary setting or infixing gems' (Marathi) G. sãghāṛɔ m. 'lathe' ; संघाट joinery; M. sãgaḍ 'double-canoe' Rebus: sangataras 'stone-cutter, mason'*

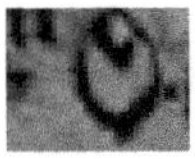

Bronze alloy workshop kañcu sal starting with bronze which is a tin + copper alloy or tin bronze (as distinguished from arsenical bronze, i.e. naturally occurring copper + arsenic).

dula 'pair' Rebus: *dul* 'cast (metal)' PLUS*kana, kanac* = corner (Santali); Rebus: *kañcu* = bronze (Telugu) PLUS infixed kolmo 'paddy plant' Rebus: kolami 'smithy, forge'. Thus, cast bronze smithy, forge. Or, *mogge* 'sprout, bud' Rebus: *mũh* 'ingot'

(Santali)Thus, cast bronze ingot. Read as: *kañcu dul mũh 'bronze cast ingot'*

ayo ḍhālako 'alloy metal ingot' *muka* 'ladle' (Tamil)(DEDR 4887) Rebus: *mũh* 'ingot' (Santali) *baṭa* = rimless pot (Kannada) Rebus:) *baṭa* = a kind of iron (G.)) *bhaṭa* furnace (G.) Thus, iron ingot. kolom 'three' Rebus: kolami 'smithy, forge'

| *koḍa* 'one' Rebus: *koḍ* 'workshop' PLUS gaṇḍa 'four' Rebus: kaṇḍa 'furnace, fire-altar' (Santali) sal 'splinter' Rebus: sal 'workshop' *mogge* 'sprout, bud' Rebus*: mũh* 'ingot': native cast metal ingot

kanka 'rim of jar' Rebus: karṇīka 'account (scribe)' karṇī 'supercargo'

m501a

m819a *खोंड [khōṇḍa] m A young bull, a bullcalf. (Marathi) Rebus: kõdār 'turner' (Bengali); कोंद kōnda 'engraver, lapidary setting or infixing gems' (Marathi) G. sãghāṛɔ m. 'lathe' ; संघाट joinery; M. sãgaḍ 'double-canoe' Rebus: sangataras 'stone-cutter, mason'*

dula 'pair' Rebus: *dul* 'cast (metal)' PLUS*kana, kanac* = corner (Santali); Rebus: *kañcu* = bronze (Telugu) PLUS infixed kolmo 'paddy plant' Rebus: kolami 'smithy, forge'. Thus, cast bronze smithy, forge. Or, *mogge* 'sprout, bud' Rebus: *mũh* 'ingot' (Santali)Thus, cast bronze ingot. Read as: *kañcu dul mũh 'bronze cast ingot'*

aya kammaṭa.'coiner, mint alloy'

ayo ḍhālako 'alloy metal ingot'

kāṇḍa 'arrow' (Sanskrit) Rebus:*khāṇḍa* 'tools, pots and pans, metal-ware'. Rebus 2: kaṇḍ 'fire-altar' (Santali)

m410a*खोंड [khōṇḍa] m A young bull, a bullcalf. (Marathi) Rebus: kõdār 'turner' (Bengali); कोंद kōnda 'engraver, lapidary setting or infixing gems' (Marathi) G. sãghāṛɔ m. 'lathe' ; संघाट joinery; M. sãgaḍ 'double-canoe' Rebus: sangataras. संगतराश lit. 'to collect stones, stone-cutter, mason.'*

Bronze alloy workshop kañcu sal starting with bronze which is a tin + copper alloy or tin bronze (as distinguished from arsenical bronze, i.e. naturally occurring copper + arsenic).

kana, kanac = corner (Santali); Rebus: *kañcu* = bronze (Telugu) PLUS खांडा [*khāṇḍā*] *m* A jag, notch, or indentation (as upon the edge of a tool or weapon). Rebus: *kāṇḍa* 'tools, pots and pans and metal-ware'

dula 'pair' Rebus: *dul* 'cast (metal)' PLUS*kana, kanac* = corner (Santali) Rebus: *kañcu* = bronze (Telugu Thus, cast bronze.

koḍi 'flag' (Ta.)(DEDR 2049). Rebus 1: *koḍ* 'workshop' (Kuwi) Rebus 2: *khõḍ* m. 'pit', *khõḍü* f. 'small pit' (Kashmiri. CDIAL 3947).

Chanhudaro 4A

खोंड [khōṇḍa] m A young bull, a bullcalf. (Marathi) Rebus: kõdār 'turner' (Bengali); कोंद kōnda 'engraver, lapidary setting or infixing gems' (Marathi) G.

sãghāṛɔ m. 'lathe' ; संघाट joinery; M. sãgaḍ 'double-canoe' Rebus: sangataras 'stone-cutter, mason'

Bronze alloy workshop kañcu sal starting with bronze which is a tin + copper alloy or tin bronze (as distinguished from arsenical bronze, i.e. naturally occurring copper + arsenic).

dula 'pair' Rebus: *dul* 'cast (metal)' PLUS*kana, kanac* = corner (Santali); Rebus: *kañcu* = bronze (Telugu) PLUS infixed kolmo 'paddy plant' Rebus: kolami 'smithy, forge'. Thus, cast bronze smithy, forge. Or, *mogge* 'sprout, bud' Rebus: *mũh* 'ingot' (Santali)Thus, cast bronze ingot. Read as: *kañcu dul mũh 'bronze cast ingot'*

aya aḍaren (homonym: aduru)'alloy native metal'

'Arrow' sign hieroglyph (variant) This is a ligature of 'lid of pot' hieroglyph superscript on 'a linear stroke' numeral hieroglyph.*aḍaren* 'cover of pot or lid' Rebus: *aduru* 'native, unsmelted metal' PLUS koḍ = one (Santali); koḍ 'workshop' (G.)

m405a

खोंड [khōṇḍa] m A young bull, a bullcalf. (Marathi) Rebus: kõdār 'turner' (Bengali); कोंद kōnda 'engraver, lapidary setting or infixing gems' (Marathi) G. sãghāṛɔ m. 'lathe' ; संघाट joinery; M. sãgaḍ 'double-canoe' Rebus: sangataras 'stone-cutter, mason'

Bronze alloy workshop kañcu sal starting with bronze which is a tin + copper alloy or tin bronze (as distinguished from arsenical bronze, i.e. naturally occurring copper + arsenic) PLUS

kolmo 'paddy plant' Rebus: *kolami* 'smithy, forge' Vikalpa: *mogge* 'sprout, bud' Rebus: *mũh* 'ingot' (Santali) dolu 'plant of shoot height' Rebus: dul 'cast metal' Thus, bronze casting.

.

aya aḍaren (homonym: aduru)'alloy native metal' PLUS *aya kāṇḍa* 'alloy metalware'

Dholavira

खोंड [khōṇḍa] m A young bull, a bullcalf. (Marathi) Rebus: kõdār 'turner' (Bengali); कोंद kōnda 'engraver, lapidary setting or infixing gems' (Marathi) G. sãghāṛɔ m. 'lathe' ; संघाट joinery; M. sãgaḍ 'double-canoe' Rebus: sangataras 'stone-cutter, mason'

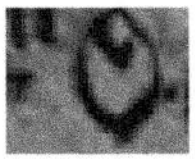

Bronze alloy workshop kañcu sal starting with bronze which is a tin + copper alloy or tin bronze (as distinguished from arsenical bronze, i.e. naturally occurring copper + arsenic). *dula* 'pair' Rebus: *dul* 'cast (metal)' PLUS*kana, kanac* = corner (Santali);

Rebus: *kañcu* = bronze (Telugu) PLUS infixed kolmo 'paddy plant' Rebus: kolami 'smithy, forge'. Thus, cast bronze smithy, forge. Or, *mogge* 'sprout, bud' Rebus: *mũh* 'ingot' (Santali)Thus, cast bronze ingot. Read as: *kañcu dul mũh 'bronze cast ingot'*

aḍar  'harrow'; rebus: *aduru* 'native unsmelted metal' DUPLICATED: dula 'pair' Rebus: dul 'cast metal' Thus cast native metal.

ayo ḍhālako 'alloy metal ingot' PLUS*kana, kanac* = corner (Santali); Rebus: *kañcu* = bronze (Telugu)

kanka 'rim of jar' Rebus: karṇīka 'account (scribe)' karṇī 'supercargo'PLUS infixed notch: खांडा [*khāṇḍā*] *m* A jag, notch, or indentation (as upon the edge of a tool or weapon). Rebus: *kāṇḍa* 'tools, pots and pans and metal-ware'

araṇe 'lizard' Rebus: *airaṇ* 'anvil'. The stylized hieroglyph sig connotes such a snarling iron.The stylized curved line may denote a lizard's tail. – as seen on many epigraphs such as Lothal 26 and Harappa 688. The hieroglyph may be a variant of:  *kana, kanac* = corner (Santali); Rebus: *kañcu* = bronze (Telugu) PLUS खांडा [*khāṇḍā*] *m* A jag, notch, or indentation (as upon the edge of a tool or weapon). Rebus: *kāṇḍa* 'tools, pots and pans and metal-ware' Thus, bronze metalware.

Pk. *vagguli* -- m. 'bat'; G. *vāgoḷ* f. ' flying fox ', M. *vāgūḷ, °gaḷ, vāghūḷ, °ghaḷ* f.n., Rebus: bagalo = an Arabian merchant vessel (Gujarati) bagala = an Arab boat of a particular description (Kannada)

h21A *खोंड [khōṇḍa] m A young bull, a bullcalf. (Marathi) Rebus: kōdār 'turner' (Bengali); कोंद kōnda 'engraver, lapidary setting or infixing gems' (Marathi) G. sãghāṛɔ m. 'lathe' ; संघाट joinery; M. sãgaḍ 'double-canoe' Rebus: sangataras 'stone-cutter, mason'*

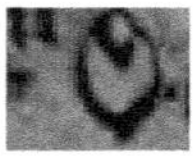

Bronze alloy workshop kañcu sal starting with bronze which is a tin + copper alloy or tin bronze (as distinguished from arsenical bronze, i.e. naturally occurring copper + arsenic). *dula* 'pair' Rebus: *dul* 'cast (metal)' PLUS*kana, kanac* = corner (Santali);

Rebus: *kañcu* = bronze (Telugu) PLUS infixed kolmo 'paddy plant' Rebus: kolami 'smithy, forge'. Thus, cast bronze smithy, forge. Or, *mogge* 'sprout, bud' Rebus: *mũh* 'ingot' (Santali)Thus, cast bronze ingot. Read as: *kañcu dul mũh 'bronze cast ingot'* *aya aḍaren (homonym: aduru)*'alloy native metal' *ayo ḍhālako* 'alloy metal ingot'

kamaḍha 'crab' Rebus: *kammaṭa* 'mint, coiner'.

ḍato = claws of crab (Santali) Rebus: *dhātu* 'mineral ore'

dhāḷ 'a slope'; 'inclination of a plane' (G.); *ḍhāḷiyum* = adj. sloping, inclining (G.) Rebus: *ḍhālako* = a large metal ingot (G.) *ḍhālakī* = a metal heated and poured into a mould; a solid piece of metal; an ingot (Gujarati) DUPLICATED: dula 'pair' Rebus: dul 'cast metal' Thus, cast ingot. PLUS sal 'splinter' Rebus: sal 'workshop' Thus, cast ingot workshop.

Slanted line: *ḍhālako* = a large metal ingot (Gujarati)

kanka 'rim of jar' Rebus: *karṇīka* 'account (scribe)' *karṇī* 'supercargo'

m656A

खोंड [khōṇḍa] m A young bull, a bullcalf. (Marathi) Rebus: kōdār 'turner' (Bengali); कोंद kōnda 'engraver, lapidary setting or infixing gems' (Marathi) G. sãghāṛɔ m. 'lathe' ; संघाट joinery; M. sãgaḍ 'double-canoe' Rebus: sangataras 'stone-cutter, mason'

Bronze alloy workshop kañcu sal starting with bronze which is a tin + copper alloy or tin bronze (as distinguished from arsenical bronze, i.e. naturally occurring copper + arsenic).

dula 'pair' Rebus: *dul* 'cast (metal)' PLUS*kana, kanac* = corner (Santali); Rebus: *kañcu* = bronze (Telugu) PLUS infixed kolmo 'paddy plant' Rebus: kolami 'smithy, forge'. Thus, cast bronze smithy, forge. Or, *mogge* 'sprout, bud' Rebus: *mũh* 'ingot' (Santali)Thus, cast bronze ingot. Read as: *kañcu dul mũh 'bronze cast ingot'*

muka 'ladle' (Tamil)(DEDR 4887) Rebus: *mũh* 'ingot' (Santali) *baṭa* = a kind of iron (G.) *baṭa* = rimless pot (Kannada) Thus, iron ingot.

kuṭila 'bent' CDIAL 3230 kuṭi— in cmpd. 'curve', *kuṭika*— 'bent' MBh. Rebus: *kuṭila, katthīl* = bronze (8 parts copper and 2 parts tin)

m1297A

Bronze alloy workshop kañcu sal starting with bronze which is a tin + copper alloy or tin bronze (as distinguished from arsenical bronze, i.e. naturally occurring copper + arsenic).

dula 'pair' Rebus: *dul* 'cast (metal)' PLUS*kana, kanac* = corner (Santali); Rebus: *kañcu* = bronze (Telugu) PLUS infixed kolmo 'paddy plant' Rebus: kolami 'smithy, forge'. Thus, cast bronze smithy, forge. Or, *mogge* 'sprout, bud' Rebus: *mũh* 'ingot' (Santali)Thus, cast bronze ingot. Read as: *kañcu dul mũh 'bronze cast ingot'*

Lothal 92A

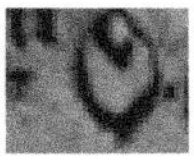
Bronze alloy workshop kañcu sal starting with bronze which is a tin + copper alloy or tin bronze (as distinguished from arsenical bronze, i.e. naturally occurring copper + arsenic).

kanac 'corner' Rebus: *kañcu* 'bronze'

baraḍo = spine; backbone (Tulu) Rebus: *baran, bharat* 'mixed alloys' (5 copper, 4 zinc and 1 tin) (Punjabi) *kāṇḍa* 'arrow' (Sanskrit) Rebus:*khāṇḍa* 'tools, pots and pans, metal-ware'. Rebus 2: kaṇḍ 'fire-altar' (Santali)

m869A *खोंड [khōṇḍa] m A young bull, a bullcalf. (Marathi) Rebus: kõdār 'turner' (Bengali); कोंद kōnda 'engraver, lapidary setting or infixing gems' (Marathi) G. sãghāṛɔ m. 'lathe' ; संघाट joinery; M. sãgaḍ 'double-canoe' Rebus: sangataras 'stone-cutter, mason'*

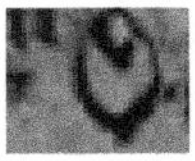
Bronze alloy workshop kañcu sal starting with bronze which is a tin + copper alloy or tin bronze (as distinguished from arsenical bronze, i.e. naturally occurring copper + arsenic).

aḍar 'harrow'; rebus: *aduru* 'native unsmelted metal' *bhaṭa* 'warrior' (Sanskrit) Rebus:

baṭa a kind of iron (Gujarati). Rebus: *bhaṭa* 'furnace' (Santali)

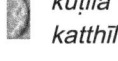

meḍ 'body' Rebus: *meḍ* 'iron' (Ho.) काठी [kāṭhī] *f* (काष्ट S) 'frame or structure of the body' (Marathi) Rebus: खंडी [khaṇḍī] measure of weight (Marathi) *கண்டி; kaṇṭi, n. < Mhr. khaṇḍil. [T. Tu. khaṇḍi, M. kaṇḍi.]* Candy, a weight, stated to be roughly equivalent to 500 lbs.

m839A Read rebus as at the epigraph on m869A PLUS

m850A Read rebus as at the epigraph on m869A PLUS

kanka 'rim of jar' Rebus: karṇīka 'account (scribe)' karṇī 'supercargo'

m658a *खोंड [khōṇḍa] m A young bull, a bullcalf. (Marathi) Rebus: kõdār 'turner' (Bengali); कोंद kõnda 'engraver, lapidary setting or infixing gems' (Marathi) G. sãghāɽɔ m. 'lathe' ; संघाट joinery; M. sãgaḍ 'double-canoe' Rebus: sangataras 'stone-cutter, mason'*

Bronze alloy or tin 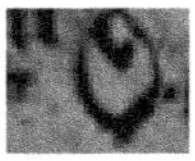 alloy workshop kañcu sal starting with bronze which is a tin + copper bronze (as distinguished from arsenical bronze, i.e. naturally occurring copper + arsenic).

'Arrow' sign hieroglyph (variant) This is a ligature of 'lid of pot' hieroglyph superscript on 'a linear stroke' numeral hieroglyph.*aḍaren* 'cover of pot or lid' Rebus: *aduru* 'native, unsmelted metal' PLUS koḍ = one (Santali); koḍ 'workshop' (G.)
sal 'splinter' Rebus: sal 'workshop'.

m116a

खोंड [khōṇḍa] m A young bull, a bullcalf. (Marathi) Rebus: kõdār 'turner' (Bengali); कोंद kõnda 'engraver, lapidary setting or infixing gems' (Marathi) G. sãghāɽɔ m. 'lathe' ; संघाट joinery; M. sãgaḍ 'double-canoe' Rebus: sangataras 'stone-cutter, mason'

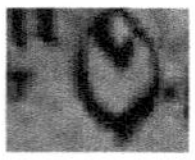

Bronze alloy workshop kañcu sal starting with bronze which is a tin + copper alloy or tin bronze (as distinguished from arsenical bronze, i.e. naturally occurring copper + arsenic).

'rim-of-jar' hieroglyph *kanka* (Santali) *karṇika* 'scribe'(Sanskrit)
sal 'splinter' Rebus: sal 'workshop' PLUS 'notch': खांडा [*khāṇḍā*] *m* A jag, notch, or indentation (as upon the edge of a tool or weapon). Rebus: *kāṇḍa* 'tools, pots and pans and metal-ware' *dula* 'pair' Rebus: *dul* 'cast (metal)' PLUS*kana, kanac* = corner (Santali); Rebus: *kañcu* = bronze (Telugu) Thus, cast bronze.

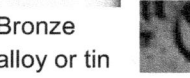

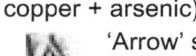

baraḍo = spine; backbone (Tulu) Rebus: *baran, bharat* 'mixed alloys' (5 copper, 4 zinc and 1 tin) (Punjabi) *bhaṭa* 'warrior' (Sanskrit) Rebus: *baṭa* a kind of iron (Gujarati).
Rebus: *bhaṭa* 'furnace' (Santali)

Rebus: *karṇī,* supercargo for a boat shipment. *karṇīka* 'account (scribe)'.कारणी *kāraṇī*' the supercargo of a ship' (Marathi)

h783a *खोंड [khōṇḍa] m A young bull, a bullcalf. (Marathi) Rebus: kōdār 'turner' (Bengali); कोंद kōnda 'engraver, lapidary setting or infixing gems' (Marathi) G. sãghāṛɔ m. 'lathe' ; संघाट joinery; M. sãgaḍ 'double-canoe' Rebus: sangataras 'stone-cutter, mason'*

Bronze alloy workshop kañcu sal starting with bronze which is a tin + copper alloy or tin bronze (as distinguished from arsenical bronze, i.e. naturally occurring copper + arsenic).

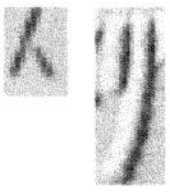

notch+slanted stroke reads rebus: *ḍhālako kāṇḍa* 'ingot, tools, pots and pans and metal-ware'.*dhāḷ* 'a slope'; 'inclination of a plane' (G.); *ḍhāḷiyum* = adj. sloping, inclining (G.) Rebus: *ḍhālako* = a large metal ingot (G.) *ḍhālakī* = a metal heated and poured into a mould; a solid piece of metal; an ingot (Gujarati) PLUS खांडा [*khāṇḍā*] *m* A jag, notch, or indentation (as upon the edge of a tool or weapon). Rebus: *kāṇḍa* 'tools, pots and pans and metal-ware'

water-carrier hieroglyph *kuṭi*; Rebus: *kuṭhi* 'smelter furnace'.

H-1864 A H-1864 B

h1864A,B

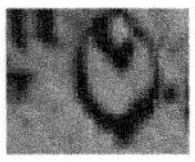

Bronze alloy workshop kañcu sal starting with bronze which is a tin + copper alloy or tin bronze (as distinguished from arsenical bronze, i.e. naturally occurring copper + arsenic).

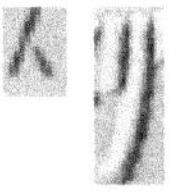

notch+slanted stroke reads rebus: *ḍhālako kāṇḍa* 'ingot, tools, pots and pans and metal-ware'.*dhāḷ* 'a slope'; 'inclination of a plane' (G.); *ḍhāḷiyum* = adj. sloping, inclining (G.) Rebus: *ḍhālako* = a large metal ingot (G.) *ḍhālakī* = a metal heated and poured into a mould; a solid piece of metal; an ingot (Gujarati) PLUS खांडा [*khāṇḍā*] *m* A jag, notch, or indentation (as upon the edge of a tool or weapon). Rebus: *kāṇḍa* 'tools, pots and pans and metal-ware'

meḍ 'body' Rebus: *meḍ* 'iron' (Ho.) काठी [kāṭhī] *f* (काष्ट S) 'frame or structure of the body' (Marathi) Rebus: खंडी [khaṇḍī] measure of weight (Marathi) *கண்டி; kaṇṭi, n. < Mhr. khaṇḍil. [T. Tu. khaṇḍi, M. kaṇḍi.]* Candy, a weight, stated to be roughly equivalent to 500 lbs.

kanka 'rim of jar' Rebus: karṇīka 'account (scribe)' karṇī 'supercargo' Side B: dula 'pair' Rebus: dul 'cast metal' *baṭa* = rimless pot (Kannada) Rebus: *baṭa* = a kind of iron (G.) *bhaṭa* 'furnace'. Thus iron casting furnace.

m408A

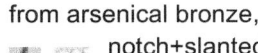

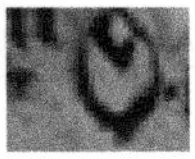

Bronze alloy workshop kañcu sal starting with bronze which is a tin + copper alloy or tin bronze (as distinguished from arsenical

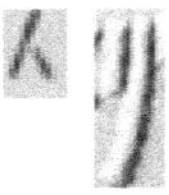 notch+slanted stroke reads rebus: *ḍhālako kāṇḍa* 'ingot, tools, pots and pans and metal-ware'.*dhāḷ* 'a slope'; 'inclination of a plane' (G.); *ḍhāḷiyum* = adj. sloping, inclining (G.) Rebus: *ḍhālako* = a large metal ingot (G.) *ḍhālakī* = a metal heated and poured into a mould; a solid piece of metal; an ingot (Gujarati)

 *kolmo* 'paddy plant' Rebus: *kolami* 'smithy, forge' Vikalpa: *mogge* 'sprout, bud' Rebus: *mũh* 'ingot' (Santali) dolu 'plant of shoot height' Rebus: dul 'cast metal'

m309A

kuṭi 'tree' Rebus: *kuṭhi* 'smelter'

 *khōṇḍa* A stock or stump (Marathi); 'leafless tree' (Marathi) Rebus: *kõdār* 'turner' (Bengali); Allograph: young bull.

kol 'tiger' Rebus: kolhe 'smelter' krammara 'look back' Rebus: kamar 'smith' heraka 'spy' Rebus: erako 'moltencast copper'

 Bronze alloy workshop kañcu sal starting with bronze which is a tin + copper alloy or tin bronze (as distinguished from arsenical bronze, i.e. naturally occurring copper + arsenic).

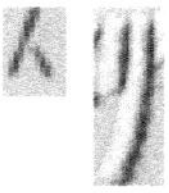 notch+slanted stroke reads rebus: *ḍhālako kāṇḍa* 'ingot, tools, pots and pans and metal-ware'.*dhāḷ* 'a slope'; 'inclination of a plane' (G.); *ḍhāḷiyum* = adj. sloping, inclining (G.) Rebus: *ḍhālako* = a large metal ingot (G.) *ḍhālakī* = a metal heated and poured into a mould; a solid piece of metal; an ingot (Gujarati)

 kanka 'rim of jar' Rebus: karṇīka 'account (scribe)' karṇī 'supercargo'

 *koḍi* 'flag' (Ta.)(DEDR 2049). Rebus 1: *koḍ* 'workshop' (Kuwi) Rebus 2: *khōḍ* m. 'pit', *khōḍü* f. 'small pit' (Kashmiri. CDIAL 3947).

ayo 'fish' Rebus: *aya* 'iron' *ayas* 'metal'
PLUS | *koḍa* 'one' Rebus: *koḍ* 'workshop'

m717a

m823A

m164A

खोंड [khōṇḍa] m A young bull, a bullcalf. (Marathi) Rebus: kõdār 'turner' (Bengali); कोंद kōnda 'engraver, lapidary setting or infixing gems' (Marathi) G. sãghārɔ m. 'lathe' ; संघाट joinery; M. sãgaḍ 'double-canoe' Rebus: sangataras 'stone-cutter, mason'

 Bronze alloy workshop kañcu sal starting with bronze which is a tin + copper alloy or tin bronze (as distinguished from arsenical bronze, i.e. naturally occurring copper + arsenic).

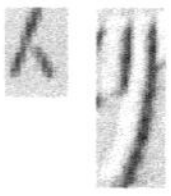 notch+slanted stroke reads rebus: *ḍhālako kāṇḍa* 'ingot, tools, pots and pans and metal-ware'.*dhāḷ* 'a slope'; 'inclination of a plane' (G.); *ḍhāḷiyum* = adj. sloping, inclining (G.) Rebus: *ḍhālako* = a large metal ingot (G.) *ḍhālakī* = a metal heated and poured into a mould; a solid piece of metal; an ingot (Gujarati)

 *meḍ* 'body' Rebus: *meḍ* 'iron' (Ho.) काठी [kāṭhī] *f* (काष्ट S) 'frame or structure of the body' (Marathi) Rebus: खंडी [khaṇḍī] measure of weight (Marathi) *கண்டி; kaṇṭi, n.* <

Mhr. khaṇḍil. [T. Tu. khaṇḍi, M. kaṇḍi.] Candy, a weight, stated to be roughly equivalent to 500 lbs.
kanka 'rim of jar' Rebus: karṇīka 'account (scribe)' karṇī 'supercargo'

m204A *खोंड [khōṇḍa] m A young bull, a bullcalf. (Marathi) Rebus: kōdār 'turner' (Bengali); कोंद kōnda 'engraver, lapidary setting or infixing gems' (Marathi) G. sãghāṛɔ m. 'lathe' ; संघाट joinery; M. sãgaḍ 'double-canoe' Rebus: sangataras 'stone-cutter, mason'*

Bronze alloy workshop kañcu sal starting with bronze which is a tin + copper alloy or tin bronze (as distinguished from arsenical bronze, i.e. naturally occurring copper + arsenic).

Variant:

dula 'pair' Rebus: dul 'cast metal' PLUS | *koḍa* 'one' Rebus: *koḍ* 'workshop' PLUS INFIXED खांडा [*khāṇḍā*] *m* A jag, notch, or indentation (as upon the edge of a tool or weapon). Rebus: *kāṇḍa* 'tools, pots and pans and metal-ware' Thus metware castings workshop.

खांडा [*khāṇḍā*] *m* A jag, notch, or indentation (as upon the edge of a tool or weapon). Rebus: *kāṇḍa* 'tools, pots and pans and metal-ware'

koḍi 'flag' (Ta.)(DEDR 2049). Rebus 1: *koḍ* 'workshop' (Kuwi) Rebus 2: *khŏḍ* m. 'pit', *khŏḍü* f. 'small pit' (Kashmiri. CDIAL 3947).

kanka 'rim of jar' Rebus: karṇīka 'account (scribe)' karṇī 'supercargo'

m1788A

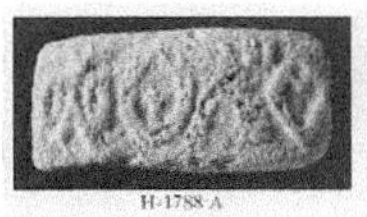

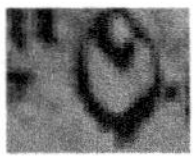

Bronze alloy workshop kañcu sal starting with bronze which is a tin + copper alloy or tin bronze (as distinguished from arsenical bronze, i.e. naturally occurring copper + arsenic).

notch+slanted metal-sloping, inclining

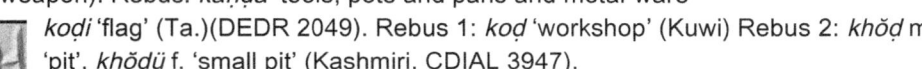

stroke reads rebus: *ḍhālako kāṇḍa* 'ingot, tools, pots and pans and ware'.*dhāḷ* 'a slope'; 'inclination of a plane' (G.); *ḍhāḷiyum* = adj. (G.) Rebus: *ḍhālako* = a large metal ingot (G.) *ḍhālakī* = a metal heated and poured into a mould; a solid piece of metal; an ingot (Gujarati)

dula 'pair' Rebus: *dul* 'cast (metal)' PLUS*kana, kanac* = corner (Santali); Rebus: *kañcu* = bronze (Telugu) PLUS infixed kolmo 'paddy plant' Rebus: kolami 'smithy, forge'. Thus, cast bronze smithy, forge. Or, *mogge* 'sprout, bud' Rebus: *mũh* 'ingot' (Santali)Thus, cast bronze ingot. Read as: *kañcu dul mũh 'bronze cast ingot'*

water-carrier hieroglyph *kuṭi*; Rebus: *kuṭhi* 'smelter furnace'. PLUS 'rim of jar':

kanka 'rim of jar' Rebus: karṇīka 'account (scribe)' karṇī 'supercargo'

Unknown 6A,B

Bronze alloy workshop kañcu sal starting with bronze which is a tin + copper alloy or tin bronze (as distinguished from arsenical bronze, i.e. naturally occurring copper + arsenic).

notch+slanted stroke reads rebus: *ḍhālako kāṇḍa* 'ingot, tools, pots and pans and metal-ware'.*dhāḷ* 'a slope'; 'inclination of a plane' (G.); *ḍhāḷiyum* = adj. sloping, inclining (G.) Rebus: *ḍhālako* = a large metal ingot (G.) *ḍhālakī* = a metal heated and poured into a mould; a solid piece of metal; an ingot (Gujarati)
baṭa = rimless pot (Kannada) Rebus:) *baṭa* = a kind of iron (G.)) *bhaṭa* furnace (G.) sal 'splinter' Rebus: sal 'workshop' Thus iron ingot furnace

kanka 'rim of jar' Rebus: karṇīka 'account (scribe)' karṇī 'supercargo'

Side B: dula 'pair' Rebus: dul 'cast metal' *baṭa* = rimless pot (Kannada) Rebus: *baṭa* = a kind of iron (G.) *bhaṭa* 'furnace'. Thus iron casting furnace.

m803a खोंड *[khōṇḍa] m A young bull, a bullcalf. (Marathi) Rebus: kõdār 'turner' (Bengali);* कोंद *kōnda 'engraver, lapidary setting or infixing gems' (Marathi) G. sãghāṛɔ m. 'lathe' ;* संघाट *joinery; M. sãgaḍ 'double-canoe' Rebus: sangataras 'stone-cutter, mason'*

Bronze alloy workshop kañcu sal starting with bronze which is a tin + copper alloy or tin bronze (as distinguished from arsenical bronze, i.e. naturally occurring copper + arsenic). PLUS 'notch': खांडा [*khāṇḍā*] *m* A jag, notch, or indentation (as upon the edge of a tool or weapon). Rebus: *kāṇḍa* 'tools, pots and pans and metal-war
ranku 'liquid measure' Rebus: ranku 'tin'.
'notch': खांडा [*khāṇḍā*] *m* A jag, notch, or indentation (as upon the edge of a tool or weapon). Rebus: *kāṇḍa* 'tools, pots and pans and metal-ware' PLUS

kolmo 'paddy plant' Rebus: *kolami* 'smithy, forge' Vikalpa: *mogge* 'sprout, bud' Rebus: *mũh* 'ingot' (Santali) dolu 'plant of shoot height' Rebus: dul 'cast metal'

m1708a खोंड *[khōṇḍa] m A young bull, a bullcalf. (Marathi) Rebus: kõdār 'turner' (Bengali);* कोंद *kōnda 'engraver, lapidary setting or infixing gems' (Marathi) G. sãghāṛɔ m. 'lathe' ;* संघाट *joinery; M. sãgaḍ 'double-canoe' Rebus: sangataras 'stone-cutter, mason'*

Bronze alloy workshop kañcu sal starting with bronze which is a tin + copper alloy or tin bronze (as distinguished from arsenical bronze, i.e. naturally occurring copper + arsenic).
|||| Numeral 4: gaṇḍa 'four' Rebus: kaṇḍa 'furnace, fire-altar' (Santali)
kolom 'three' Rebus: kolami 'smithy, forge'

सांड [sāṇḍa] *f* (षद S) An outlet for superfluous water (as through a dam or mound); a sluice, a floodvent. Rebus: सांडणी [sāṇḍaṇī] *f* (H) An instrument of goldsmiths. It is hooked or curved at the extremity; and is used to draw things out of the fire.

kanka 'rim of jar' Rebus: karṇīka 'account (scribe)' karṇī 'supercargo'

dāṭu 'cross'(Telugu) Rebus: *dhatu* 'mineral' (Santali). Ligatured with: *kanḍo* stool, seat Rebus: *kāṇḍā* 'metalware, tools, pots and pans'(Marathi). *kanḍ* = a furnace, altar (Santali) Thus 'metalware mineral'. This mineral could be either tin or zinc to create bronze or brass tools and metalware. That it is related to tin is seen in the variant of this X hieroglyph on Haifa tin ingots together with a 'notch' ligature.

Lothal 84a

m776a Read rebus as at m1708a PLUS *dula* 'pair' Rebus: *dul* 'cast (metal)' PLUS*kana, kanac* = corner (Santali); Rebus: *kañcu* = bronze (Telugu) Thus, cast bronze. dula 'two' Rebus: dul 'cast metal'

m1711a

As at m895a

m895a *खोंड [khōṇḍa] m A young bull, a bullcalf. (Marathi) Rebus: kõdār 'turner' (Bengali); कोंद kōnda 'engraver, lapidary setting or infixing gems' (Marathi) G. sãghāṛɔ m. 'lathe' ; संघाट joinery; M. sãgaḍ 'double-canoe' Rebus: sangataras 'stone-cutter, mason'*

Bronze alloy workshop kañcu sal starting with bronze which is a tin + copper alloy or tin bronze (as distinguished from arsenical bronze, i.e. naturally occurring copper + arsenic).

|||| Numeral 4: gaṇḍa 'four' Rebus: kaṇḍa 'furnace, fire-altar' (Santali)

kolom 'three' Rebus: kolami 'smithy, forge'

kuṭila 'bent' CDIAL 3230 kuṭi— in cmpd. 'curve', *kuṭika*— 'bent' MBh. Rebus: *kuṭila, katthīl* = bronze (8 parts copper and 2 parts tin)

dula 'pair' Rebus: dul 'caat metal' Thus, cast bronze.

kanka 'rim of jar' Rebus: karṇīka 'account (scribe)' karṇī 'supercargo'

Lothal 166A As at m895a PLUS

Lothal 161A *ibha* 'elephant' Rebus: *ib* 'iron' *ibbo* 'merchant' (Gujarati)

m792A *खोंड [khōṇḍa] m A young bull, a bullcalf. (Marathi) Rebus: kõdār 'turner' (Bengali); कोंद kōnda 'engraver, lapidary setting or infixing gems' (Marathi) G. sãghāṛɔ m. 'lathe' ; संघाट joinery; M. sãgaḍ 'double-canoe' Rebus: sangataras 'stone-cutter, mason'*

 Bronze alloy workshop kañcu sal starting with bronze which is a tin + copper alloy or tin bronze (as distinguished from arsenical bronze, i.e. naturally occurring copper + arsenic).

|||| Numeral 4: gaṇḍa 'four' Rebus: kaṇḍa 'furnace, fire-altar' (Santali)

kolom 'three' Rebus: kolami 'smithy, forge'

 सांड [sāṇḍa] *f* (षद S) An outlet for superfluous water (as through a dam or mound); a sluice, a floodvent. Rebus: सांडणी [sāṇḍaṇī] *f* (H) An instrument of goldsmiths. It is hooked or curved at the extremity; and is used to draw things out of the fire.

 kanka 'rim of jar' Rebus: karṇīka 'account (scribe)' karṇī 'supercargo'

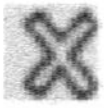 *dāṭu* 'cross'(Telugu) Rebus: *dhatu* 'mineral' (Santali).

h597c

 Bronze alloy workshop kañcu sal starting with bronze which is a tin + copper alloy or tin bronze (as distinguished from arsenical bronze, i.e. naturally occurring copper + arsenic).

PLUS as at h597a

 h597a *खोंड [khōṇḍa] m A young bull, a bullcalf. (Marathi) Rebus: kõdār 'turner' (Bengali); कोंद kōnda 'engraver, lapidary setting or infixing gems' (Marathi) G. sãghāṛɔ m. 'lathe' ; संघाट joinery; M. sãgaḍ 'double-canoe' Rebus: sangataras 'stone-cutter, mason'*

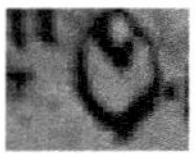 Bronze alloy workshop kañcu sal starting with bronze which is a tin + copper alloy or tin bronze (as distinguished from arsenical bronze, i.e. naturally occurring copper + arsenic).

dula 'two' Rebus: dul 'cast metal'.

 'Arrow' sign hieroglyph (variant) This is a ligature of 'lid of pot' hieroglyph superscript on 'a linear stroke' numeral hieroglyph.*aḍaren* 'cover of pot or lid' Rebus: *aduru* 'native, unsmelted metal' PLUS koḍ = one (Santali); koḍ 'workshop' (G.)

ranku 'liquid measure' Rebus: dul 'cast metal'

 *kolmo* 'paddy plant' Rebus: *kolami* 'smithy, forge' Vikalpa: *mogge* 'sprout, bud' Rebus: *mũh* 'ingot' (Santali) dolu 'plant of shoot height' Rebus: dul 'cast metal'

kanka 'rim of jar' Rebus: karṇīka 'account (scribe)' karṇī 'supercargo'

 m1763a *खोंड [khōṇḍa] m A young bull, a bullcalf. (Marathi) Rebus: kõdār 'turner' (Bengali); कोंद kōnda 'engraver, lapidary setting or infixing gems' (Marathi) G. sãghāṛɔ m. 'lathe' ; संघाट joinery; M. sãgaḍ 'double-canoe' Rebus: sangataras 'stone-cutter, mason'*

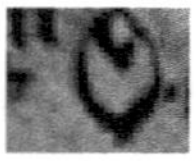 Bronze alloy workshop kañcu sal starting with bronze which is a tin + copper alloy or tin bronze (as distinguished from arsenical bronze, i.e. naturally occurring copper + arsenic).

dula 'two' Rebus: dul 'cast metal'. *ayo* 'fish' Rebus: *aya* 'iron' *ayas* 'metal'

 kanka ‘rim of jar’ Rebus: karṇīka ‘account (scribe)’ karṇī ‘supercargo’

kamaḍha ‘crab’ Rebus: *kammaṭa* ‘mint, coiner’.
ḍato = claws of crab (Santali) Rebus: *dhātu* ‘mineral ore’
‘notch’: खांडा [*khāṇḍā*] *m* A jag, notch, or indentation (as upon the edge of a tool or weapon). Rebus: *kāṇḍa* ‘tools, pots and pans and metal-ware
Circumscript: gaṇḍa 'four' Rebus: kaṇḍa 'furnace, fire-altar' (Santali) PLUS

 *aḍar* 'harrow'; rebus: *aduru* 'native unsmelted metal' PLUS dula ‘pair’ Rebus: dul ‘cast metal. Thus, cast native metal.

 m1044aखोंड *[khōṇḍa] m A young bull, a bullcalf. (Marathi) Rebus: kõdār ‘turner’ (Bengali);* कोंद *kōnda ‘engraver, lapidary setting or infixing gems’ (Marathi) G. sãghāṛɔ m. ‘lathe’ ;* संघाट *joinery; M. sãgaḍ ‘double-canoe’ Rebus: sangataras ‘stone-cutter, mason’*

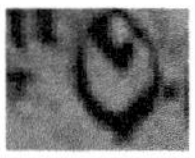 Bronze alloy workshop kañcu sal starting with bronze which is a tin + copper alloy or tin bronze (as distinguished from arsenical bronze, i.e. naturally occurring copper + arsenic).
dula ‘two’ Rebus: dul ‘cast metal’ *ayo* ‘fish’ Rebus: *aya* ‘iron’ *ayas* ‘metal’ *kāṇḍa* ‘arrow’ (Sanskrit) Rebus:*khāṇḍa* ‘tools, pots and pans, metal-ware’. Rebus 2: kaṇḍ 'fire-altar' (Santali)
kanka ‘rim of jar’ Rebus: karṇīka ‘account (scribe)’ karṇī ‘supercargo’

 m1704a खोंड *[khōṇḍa] m A young bull, a bullcalf. (Marathi) Rebus: kõdār ‘turner’ (Bengali);* कोंद *kōnda ‘engraver, lapidary setting or infixing gems’ (Marathi) G. sãghāṛɔ m. ‘lathe’ ;* संघाट *joinery; M. sãgaḍ ‘double-canoe’ Rebus: sangataras ‘stone-cutter, mason’*

 Bronze alloy workshop kañcu sal starting with bronze which is a tin + copper alloy or tin bronze (as distinguished from arsenical bronze, i.e. naturally occurring copper + arsenic).
dula ‘two’ Rebus: dul ‘cast metal’

 *kolmo* ‘paddy plant’ Rebus: *kolami* ‘smithy, forge’ Vikalpa: *mogge* ‘sprout, bud’ Rebus: *mūh* ‘ingot’ (Santali) dolu ‘plant of shoot height’ Rebus: dul ‘cast metal’ DUPLICATED: dula ‘pair’ Rebus: dul ‘cast metal’ Thus, smithy castings.

 kanka ‘rim of jar’ Rebus: karṇīka ‘account (scribe)’ karṇī ‘supercargo’

 h140A

 Bronze alloy workshop kañcu sal starting with bronze which is a tin + copper alloy or tin bronze (as distinguished from arsenical bronze, i.e. naturally occurring copper + arsenic).

 dula ‘two’ Rebus: dul ‘cast metal’ *loa* ‘ficus religiosa’ Rebus: *lo* ‘iron’ (Sanskrit)

kanka 'rim of jar' Rebus: karṇīka 'account (scribe)' karṇī 'supercargo'

m444a *खोंड [khōṇḍa] m A young bull, a bullcalf. (Marathi) Rebus: kõdār 'turner' (Bengali); कोंद kōnda 'engraver, lapidary setting or infixing gems' (Marathi) G. sãghāṛɔ m. 'lathe' ; संघाट joinery; M. sãgaḍ 'double-canoe' Rebus: sangataras 'stone-cutter, mason'*

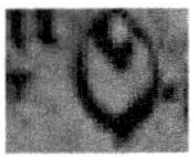

Bronze alloy workshop kañcu sal starting with bronze which is a tin + copper alloy or tin bronze (as distinguished from arsenical bronze, i.e. naturally occurring copper + arsenic). dula 'two' Rebus: dul 'cast metal' *ayo* 'fish' Rebus: *aya* 'iron' *ayas* 'metal' *aya kāṇḍa* 'alloy metalware' circumscript: *aya kammaṭa.*'coiner, mint alloy' Thus, alloys used in mint.

m221a *खोंड [khōṇḍa] m A young bull, a bullcalf. (Marathi) Rebus: kõdār 'turner' (Bengali); कोंद kōnda 'engraver, lapidary setting or infixing gems' (Marathi) G. sãghāṛɔ m. 'lathe' ; संघाट joinery; M. sãgaḍ 'double-canoe' Rebus: sangataras 'stone-cutter, mason'*

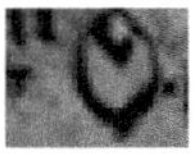

Bronze alloy workshop kañcu sal starting with bronze which is a tin + copper alloy or tin bronze (as distinguished from arsenical bronze, i.e. naturally occurring copper + arsenic). dula 'two' Rebus: dul 'cast metal' *ayo* 'fish' Rebus: *aya* 'iron' *ayas* 'metal'

Ligature: two peaks: mēḍu height, rising ground, hillock (Kannada) Rebus: *meḍ* 'iron' (Ho.) dula 'pair' Rebus: dul 'cast metal' PLUS |||| Numeral 4: gaṇḍa 'four' Rebus: kaṇḍa 'furnace, fire-altar' (Santali)

kolmo 'paddy plant' Rebus: *kolami* 'smithy, forge' Vikalpa: *mogge* 'sprout, bud' Rebus: *mũh* 'ingot' (Santali) dolu 'plant of shoot height' Rebus: dul 'cast metal' DUPLICATED: dula 'pair' Rebus: dul 'cast metal' Thus, smithy castings.

kanka 'rim of jar' Rebus: karṇīka 'account (scribe)' karṇī 'supercargo'

m720a *खोंड [khōṇḍa] m A young bull, a bullcalf. (Marathi) Rebus: kõdār 'turner' (Bengali); कोंद kōnda 'engraver, lapidary setting or infixing gems' (Marathi) G. sãghāṛɔ m. 'lathe' ; संघाट joinery; M. sãgaḍ 'double-canoe' Rebus: sangataras 'stone-cutter, mason'*

Bronze alloy workshop kañcu sal starting with bronze which is a tin + copper alloy or tin bronze (as distinguished from arsenical bronze, i.e. naturally occurring copper + arsenic). dula 'two' Rebus: dul 'cast metal' *ayo* 'fish' Rebus: *aya* 'iron' *ayas* 'metal'

 *kuṭila* 'bent' CDIAL 3230 kuṭi— in cmpd. 'curve', *kuṭika—* 'bent' MBh. Rebus: *kuṭila, katthīl* = bronze (8 parts copper and 2 parts tin)
Duplicated: dula 'pair' Rebus: dul 'cast metal' Thus, cast bronze
kanka 'rim of jar' Rebus: karṇīka 'account (scribe)' karṇī 'supercargo'

m722a *खोंड [khōṇḍa] m A young bull, a bullcalf. (Marathi) Rebus: kōdār 'turner' (Bengali); कोंद kōnda 'engraver, lapidary setting or infixing gems' (Marathi) G. sãghāṛɔ m. 'lathe' ; संघाट joinery; M. sãgaḍ 'double-canoe' Rebus: sangataras 'stone-cutter, mason'*

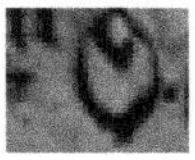 Bronze alloy workshop kañcu sal starting with bronze which is a tin + copper alloy or tin bronze (as distinguished from arsenical bronze, i.e. naturally occurring copper + arsenic).dula 'two' Rebus: dul 'cast metal' *ayo* 'fish' Rebus: *aya* 'iron' *ayas* 'metal' *aya kammaṭa.*'coiner, mint alloy'

 सांड [sāṇḍa] *f* (षद S) An outlet for superfluous water (as through a dam or mound); a sluice, a floodvent. Rebus: सांडणी [sāṇḍaṇī] *f* (H) An instrument of goldsmiths. It is hooked or curved at the extremity; and is used to draw things out of the fire.
kanka 'rim of jar' Rebus: karṇīka 'account (scribe)' karṇī 'supercargo'

m723a*खोंड [khōṇḍa] m A young bull, a bullcalf. (Marathi) Rebus: kōdār 'turner' (Bengali); कोंद kōnda 'engraver, lapidary setting or infixing gems' (Marathi) G. sãghāṛɔ m. 'lathe' ; संघाट joinery; M. sãgaḍ 'double-canoe' Rebus: sangataras 'stone-cutter, mason'*

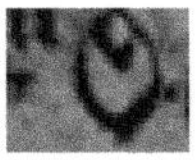 Bronze alloy workshop kañcu sal starting with bronze which is a tin + copper alloy or tin bronze (as distinguished from arsenical bronze, i.e. naturally occurring copper + arsenic).
dula 'two' Rebus: dul 'cast metal' *ayo* 'fish' Rebus: *aya* 'iron' *ayas* 'metal' *aya aḍaren (homonym: aduru)*'alloy native metal'

 सांड [sāṇḍa] *f* (षद S) An outlet for superfluous water (as through a dam or mound); a sluice, a floodvent. Rebus: सांडणी [sāṇḍaṇī] *f* (H) An instrument of goldsmiths. It is hooked or curved at the extremity; and is used to draw things out of the fire.

 ḍãg mountain-ridge (H.)(CDIAL 5476). Rebus: dhangar 'blacksmith' damgar 'merchant' (Akkadian)

 kanka 'rim of jar' Rebus: karṇīka 'account (scribe)' karṇī 'supercargo'

Chanhudaro 10a *खोंड [khōṇḍa] m A young bull, a bullcalf. (Marathi) Rebus: kōdār 'turner' (Bengali); कोंद kōnda 'engraver, lapidary setting or infixing gems' (Marathi) G. sãghāṛɔ m. 'lathe' ; संघाट joinery; M. sãgaḍ 'double-canoe' Rebus: sangataras 'stone-cutter, mason'*

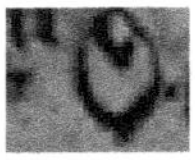

Bronze alloy workshop kañcu sal starting with bronze which is a tin + copper alloy or tin bronze (as distinguished from arsenical bronze, i.e. naturally occurring copper + arsenic). dula 'two' Rebus: dul 'cast metal' *aya* 'iron' *ayas* 'metal' *aya kāṇḍa* 'alloy metalware'

kanka 'rim of jar' Rebus: karṇīka 'account (scribe)' karṇī 'supercargo'

\m1788a *खोंड [khōṇḍa] m A young bull, a bullcalf. (Marathi) Rebus: kõdār 'turner' (Bengali); कोंद kōnda 'engraver, lapidary setting or infixing gems' (Marathi) G. sãghāṛɔ m. 'lathe' ; संघाट joinery; M. sãgaḍ 'double-canoe' Rebus: sangataras 'stone-cutter, mason'*

Bronze alloy workshop kañcu sal starting with bronze which is a tin + copper alloy or tin bronze (as distinguished from arsenical bronze, i.e. naturally occurring copper + arsenic). dula 'two' Rebus: dul 'cast metal' *aya* 'iron' *ayas* 'metal'

h640A

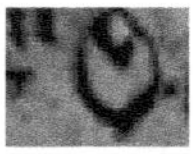

Bronze alloy workshop kañcu sal starting with bronze which is a tin + copper alloy or tin bronze (as distinguished from arsenical bronze, i.e. naturally occurring copper + arsenic). dula 'two' Rebus: dul 'cast metal' *aya* 'iron' *ayas* 'metal'

m853a*खोंड [khōṇḍa] m A young bull, a bullcalf. (Marathi) Rebus: kõdār 'turner' (Bengali); कोंद kōnda 'engraver, lapidary setting or infixing gems' (Marathi) G. sãghāṛɔ m. 'lathe' ; संघाट joinery; M. sãgaḍ 'double-canoe' Rebus: sangataras 'stone-cutter, mason'*

Bronze alloy workshop kañcu sal starting with bronze which is a tin + copper alloy or tin bronze (as distinguished from arsenical bronze, i.e. naturally occurring copper + arsenic). dula 'two' Rebus: dul 'cast metal' PLUS*kana, kanac* = corner (Santali); Rebus: *kañcu* = bronze (Telugu) PLUS 'notch': खांडा [*khāṇḍā*] *m* A jag, notch, or indentation (as upon the edge of a tool or weapon). Rebus: *kāṇḍa* 'tools, pots and pans and metal-ware'

kanka 'rim of jar' Rebus: karṇīka 'account (scribe)' karṇī 'supercargo'

meḍ 'body' Rebus: *meḍ* 'iron' (Ho.) काठी [kāṭhī] *f* (काष्ट S) 'frame or structure of the body' (Marathi) Rebus: खंडी [khaṇḍī] measure of weight (Marathi) கண்டி; *kaṇṭi, n. < Mhr. khaṇḍil. [T. Tu. khaṇḍi, M. kaṇḍi.]* Candy, a weight, stated to be roughly equivalent to 500 lbs.

Lothal 57A

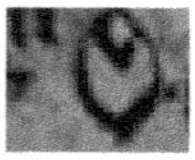

Bronze alloy workshop kañcu sal starting with bronze which is a tin + copper alloy or tin bronze (as distinguished from arsenical bronze, i.e. naturally occurring copper + arsenic).

kana, kanac = corner (Santali); Rebus: *kañcu* = bronze (Telugu) PLUS खांडा [*khāṇḍā*] *m* A jag, notch, or indentation (as upon the edge of a tool or weapon). Rebus: *kāṇḍa* 'tools, pots and pans and metal-ware'. Thus, bronze metalware workshop.

m142A *खोंड [khōṇḍa] m A young bull, a bullcalf. (Marathi) Rebus: kõdār 'turner' (Bengali); कोंद kōnda 'engraver, lapidary setting or infixing gems' (Marathi) G. sãghāṛɔ m. 'lathe' ; संघाट joinery; M. sãgaḍ 'double-canoe' Rebus: sangataras 'stone-cutter, mason'*

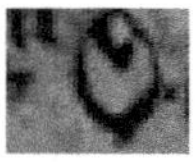

Bronze alloy workshop kañcu sal starting with bronze which is a tin + copper alloy or tin bronze (as distinguished from arsenical bronze, i.e. naturally occurring copper + arsenic).

bhaṭa 'warrior' (Sanskrit) Rebus: *baṭa* a kind of iron (Gujarati). Rebus: *bhaṭa* 'furnace' (Santali)

meḍ 'body' Rebus: *meḍ* 'iron' (Ho.) काठी [kāṭhī] *f* (काष्ट S) 'frame or structure of the body' (Marathi) Rebus: खंडी [khaṇḍī] measure of weight (Marathi) *கண்டி; kaṇṭi, n. < Mhr. khaṇḍil. [T. Tu. khaṇḍi, M. kaṇḍi.]* Candy, a weight, stated to be roughly equivalent to 500 lbs.

Lothal 11a

खोंड [khōṇḍa] m A young bull, a bullcalf. (Marathi) Rebus: kõdār 'turner' (Bengali); कोंद kōnda 'engraver, lapidary setting or infixing gems' (Marathi) G. sãghāṛɔ m. 'lathe' ; संघाट joinery; M. sãgaḍ 'double-canoe' Rebus: sangataras. संगतराश lit. 'to collect stones, stone-cutter, mason.'

Bronze alloy workshop kañcu sal starting with bronze which is a tin + copper alloy or tin bronze (as distinguished from arsenical bronze, i.e. naturally occurring copper + arsenic).

dula 'pair' Rebus: dul 'cast metal' PLUS *kāṇḍa* 'arrow' (Sanskrit) Rebus:*khāṇḍa* 'tools, pots and pans, metal-ware'. Rebus 2: kaṇḍ 'fire-altar' (Santali) Thus, cast metal metalware PLUS *kamaḍha* 'crab' Rebus: *kammaṭa* 'mint, coiner'.

ḍato = claws of crab (Santali) Rebus: *dhātu* 'mineral ore' Thus, cast metal metalware and mint mineral ore.

The pair of hieroglyph signs are compositions: *bicha* 'scorpion' (Assamese) Rebus: *bica* 'stone ore' (Santali) The pairing sign is a composition of: sloping stroke PLUS two short strokes of a 'splinter' sal 'splinter Rebus: sal 'workshop':

dhāḷ 'a slope'; 'inclination of a plane' (G.); *ḍhāḷiyum* = adj. sloping, inclining (G.) Rebus: *ḍhālako* = a large metal ingot (G.) *ḍhālakī* = a metal heated and poured into a mould; a solid piece of metal; an ingot (Gujarati) PLUS *sal* 'splinter' Rebus: *sal* 'workshop'. Thus the composition reads: *ḍhālako sal* 'ingot workshop'. Together, the pair of hieroglyph signs read: *bica ḍhālako sal* 'stone ore ingot workshop'.

ranku 'liquid measure' Rebus: ranku 'tin'.

muka 'ladle' (Tamil)(DEDR 4887) Rebus: *mũh* 'ingot' (Santali) *baṭa* = rimless pot

(Kannada) Rebus:) *baṭa* = a kind of iron (G.)) *bhaṭa* furnace (G.) Thus, iron ingot.

m316a

Bronze alloy workshop kañcu sal starting with bronze which is a tin + copper alloy or tin bronze (as distinguished from arsenical bronze, i.e. naturally occurring copper + arsenic).

baṭa = rimless pot (Kannada) Rebus:) *baṭa* = a kind of iron (G.)) *bhaṭa* furnace (G.) Thus, iron furnace PLUS

Vikalpa: *mogge* 'sprout, bud' Rebus: *mũh* 'ingot' (Santali) dolu 'plant of shoot height' Rebus: dul 'cast metal' Thus, together, iron cast metal ingot furnace

kolmo 'paddy plant' Rebus: *kolami* 'smithy, forge'

koḍi 'flag' (Ta.)(DEDR 2049). Rebus 1: *koḍ* 'workshop' (Kuwi) Rebus 2: *khŏḍ* m. 'pit', *khŏḍü* f. 'small pit' (Kashmiri. CDIAL 3947).

m362a

Bronze alloy workshop kañcu sal starting with bronze which is a tin + copper alloy or tin bronze (as distinguished from arsenical bronze, i.e. naturally occurring copper + arsenic).

mēḍu height, rising ground, hillock (Kannada) Rebus: *mẽṛhẽt, meḍ* 'iron' (Munda.Ho.)

|||| Numeral 4: gaṇḍa 'four' Rebus: kaṇḍa 'furnace, fire-altar' (Santali)

||| Numeral three: kolom 'three' Rebus: kolami 'smithy, forge'

kanka 'rim of jar' Rebus: karṇīka 'account (scribe)' karṇī 'supercargo'

m245A *balad* m. ' ox ', gng. *bald*, (Ku.) *barad*, id. (N. Tarai) Rebus: *bharat* (5 copper, 4 zinc and 1 tin)(Punjabi) *pattar* 'trough' Rebus*: pattar* 'guild'. Thus, copper-zinc-tin alloy (worker) guild.

Bronze alloy workshop kañcu sal starting with bronze which is a tin + copper alloy or tin bronze (as distinguished from arsenical bronze, i.e. naturally occurring copper + arsenic).

mēḍu height, rising ground, hillock (Kannada) Rebus: *mẽṛhẽt, meḍ* 'iron' (Munda.Ho.)

ḍãg mountain-ridge (H.)(CDIAL 5476). Rebus: dhangar 'blacksmith' (Maithili)

kanka 'rim of jar' Rebus: karṇīka 'account (scribe)' karṇī 'supercargo'

m58a *खोंड [khōṇḍa] m A young bull, a bullcalf. (Marathi) Rebus: kõdār 'turner' (Bengali); कोंद kōnda 'engraver, lapidary setting or infixing gems' (Marathi) G. sãghāṛɔ m. 'lathe' ; संघाट joinery; M. sãgaḍ 'double-canoe' Rebus: sangataras. संगतराश lit. 'to collect stones, stone-cutter, mason.'*

Bronze alloy workshop kañcu sal starting with bronze which is a tin + copper alloy or tin bronze (as distinguished from arsenical bronze, i.e. naturally occurring copper +

arsenic).

mēḍu height, rising ground, hillock (Kannada) Rebus: *mẽṛhẽt, meḍ* 'iron' (Munda.Ho.)

ḍāg mountain-ridge (H.)(CDIAL 5476). Rebus: dhangar 'blacksmith' damgar 'merchant' (Akkadian)
(Maithili)

kanka 'rim of jar' Rebus: karṇīka 'account (scribe)' karṇī 'supercargo'

m14a *खोंड [khōṇḍa] m A young bull, a bullcalf. (Marathi) Rebus: kõdār 'turner' (Bengali); कोंद kōnda 'engraver, lapidary setting or infixing gems' (Marathi) G. sãghārɔ m. 'lathe' ; संघाट joinery; M. sãgaḍ 'double-canoe' Rebus: sangataras 'stone-cutter, mason'*

Bronze alloy workshop kañcu sal starting with bronze which is a tin + copper alloy or tin bronze (as distinguished from arsenical bronze, i.e. naturally occurring copper + arsenic).

mēḍu height, rising ground, hillock (Kannada) Rebus: *mẽṛhẽt, meḍ* 'iron' (Munda.Ho.)

mogge 'sprout, bud' Rebus*: mũh* 'ingot'. kolom 'three' Rebus: kolami 'smithy, forge'. Thus ingot smithy.
kanka 'rim of jar' Rebus: karṇīka 'account (scribe)' karṇī 'supercargo'

h13a *खोंड [khōṇḍa] m A young bull, a bullcalf. (Marathi) Rebus: kõdār 'turner' (Bengali); कोंद kōnda 'engraver, lapidary setting or infixing gems' (Marathi) G. sãghārɔ m. 'lathe' ; संघाट joinery; M. sãgaḍ 'double-canoe' Rebus: sangataras 'stone-cutter, mason'*

Bronze alloy workshop kañcu sal starting with bronze which is a tin + copper alloy or tin bronze (as distinguished from arsenical bronze, i.e. naturally occurring copper + arsenic).

mēḍu height, rising ground, hillock (Kannada) Rebus: *mẽṛhẽt, meḍ* 'iron' (Munda.Ho.)

khaṇḍ 'field, division' (Sanskrit) Rebus: *khānḍa* 'tools, pots and pans, metal-ware'. Rebus 2: kaṇḍ 'fire-altar' (Santali) dula 'pair' Rebus: dul 'cast metal' Thus, duplicated 'division' hieroglyph sign reads: cast metal metal-ware.

dula 'pair' Rebus: dul 'cast metal' *mogge* 'sprout, bud' Rebus: *mũh* 'ingot' (Santali) Thus, cast metal ingot.

kanka 'rim of jar' Rebus: karṇīka 'account (scribe)' karṇī 'supercargo'

h612f

Bronze alloy workshop kañcu sal starting with bronze which is a tin + copper alloy or tin bronze (as distinguished from arsenical bronze, i.e. naturally occurring copper + arsenic).

mēḍu height, rising ground, hillock (Kannada) Rebus: *mẽṛhẽt, meḍ* 'iron' (Munda.Ho.) *khaṇḍ* 'field, division' (Sanskrit) Rebus: *khāṇḍa* 'tools, pots and pans, metal-ware'.

kanka 'rim of jar' Rebus: karṇīka 'account (scribe)' karṇī 'supercargo'
h1850a

M-1850 a bis

खोंड [khōṇḍa] m A young bull, a bullcalf. (Marathi) Rebus: kõdār 'turner' (Bengali); कोंद kōnda 'engraver, lapidary setting or infixing gems' (Marathi) G. *sãghārɔ m. 'lathe' ; संघाट joinery; M. sãgaḍ 'double-canoe' Rebus: sangataras 'stone-cutter, mason'*

Bronze alloy workshop kañcu sal starting with bronze which is a tin + copper alloy or tin bronze (as distinguished from arsenical bronze, i.e. naturally occurring copper + arsenic).

mēḍu height, rising ground, hillock (Kannada) Rebus: *mẽṛhẽt, meḍ* 'iron' (Munda.Ho.) PLUS *kanḍo* stool, seat Rebus: *kāṇḍā* 'metalware, tools, pots and pans'(Marathi). *kaṇḍ* = a furnace, altar (Santali) Circumscript: Four strokes: gaṇḍa 'four' Rebus: kaṇḍa 'furnace, fire-altar' (Santali) Thus, furnace for iron metalware.

h1667A*खोंड [khōṇḍa] m A young bull, a bullcalf. (Marathi) Rebus: kõdār 'turner' (Bengali); कोंद kōnda 'engraver, lapidary setting or infixing gems' (Marathi) G. sãghārɔ m. 'lathe' ; संघाट joinery; M. sãgaḍ 'double-canoe' Rebus: sangataras 'stone-cutter, mason'*

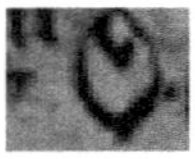
Bronze alloy workshop kañcu sal starting with bronze which is a tin + copper alloy or tin bronze (as distinguished from arsenical bronze, i.e. naturally occurring copper + arsenic).

kamaḍha 'crab' Rebus: *kammaṭa* 'mint, coiner'.Duplicated: dula 'pair' Rebus: dul 'cast metal' Thus, mint metal castings.

ḍato = claws of crab (Santali) Rebus: *dhātu* 'mineral ore'
kanka 'rim of jar' Rebus: karṇīka 'account (scribe)' karṇī 'supercargo'

m100a *खोंड [khōṇḍa] m A young bull, a bullcalf. (Marathi) Rebus: kõdār 'turner' (Bengali); कोंद kōnda 'engraver, lapidary setting or infixing gems' (Marathi) G. sãghārɔ m. 'lathe' ; संघाट joinery; M. sãgaḍ 'double-canoe' Rebus: sangataras 'stone-cutter, mason'*

Bronze alloy workshop kañcu sal starting with bronze which is a tin + copper alloy or tin bronze (as distinguished from arsenical bronze, i.e. naturally occurring copper + arsenic).

muka 'ladle' (Tamil)(DEDR 4887) Rebus: *mũh* 'ingot' (Santali) *baṭa* = rimless pot (Kannada) Rebus:) *baṭa* = a kind of iron (G.)) *bhaṭa* furnace (G.) Thus, iron ingot.

bicha 'scorpion' (Assamese) Rebus: *bica* 'stone ore' (Santali) The pairing sign is a composition of: sloping stroke PLUS two short strokes of a 'splinter': *bica sal* 'stone ore workshop.'

 kanka 'rim of jar' Rebus: karṇīka 'account (scribe)' karṇī 'supercargo'

 *meḍ* 'body' Rebus: *meḍ* 'iron' (Ho.) काठी [kāṭhī] *f* (काष्ट S) 'frame or structure of the body' (Marathi) Rebus: खंडी [khaṇḍī] measure of weight (Marathi) *கண்டி; kaṇṭi, n. < Mhr. khaṇḍil. [T. Tu. khaṇḍi, M. kaṇḍi.]* Candy, a weight, stated to be roughly equivalent to 500 lbs.

 h781A *खोंड [khōṇḍa] m A young bull, a bullcalf. (Marathi) Rebus: kõdār 'turner' (Bengali); कोंद kōnda 'engraver, lapidary setting or infixing gems' (Marathi) G. sãghāṛɔ m. 'lathe' ; संघाट joinery; M. sãgaḍ 'double-canoe' Rebus: sangataras. संगतराश lit. 'to collect stones, stone-cutter, mason.'*

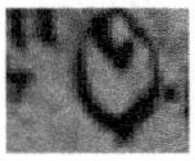 Bronze alloy workshop kañcu sal starting with bronze which is a tin + copper alloy or tin bronze (as distinguished from arsenical bronze, i.e. naturally occurring copper + arsenic).

 *muka* 'ladle' (Tamil)(DEDR 4887) Rebus: *mũh* 'ingot' (Santali) *baṭa* = rimless pot (Kannada) Rebus:) *baṭa* = a kind of iron (G.)) *bhaṭa* furnace (G.) Thus, iron ingot. kolom 'three' Rebus: kolami 'smithy, forge'. *kāṇḍa* 'arrow' (Sanskrit) Rebus:*khāṇḍa* 'tools, pots and pans, metal-ware'. Rebus 2: kaṇḍ 'fire-altar' (Santali)

 m787A*खोंड [khōṇḍa] m A young bull, a bullcalf. (Marathi) Rebus: kõdār 'turner' (Bengali); कोंद kōnda 'engraver, lapidary setting or infixing gems' (Marathi) G. sãghāṛɔ m. 'lathe' ; संघाट joinery; M. sãgaḍ 'double-canoe' Rebus: sangataras 'stone-cutter, mason'*

 Bronze alloy workshop kañcu sal starting with bronze which is a tin + copper alloy or tin bronze (as distinguished from arsenical bronze, i.e. naturally occurring copper + arsenic).

 *muka* 'ladle' (Tamil)(DEDR 4887) Rebus: *mũh* 'ingot' (Santali) *baṭa* = rimless pot (Kannada) Rebus:) *baṭa* = a kind of iron (G.)) *bhaṭa* furnace (G.) Thus, iron ingot.
bicha 'scorpion' (Assamese) Rebus: *bica* 'stone ore' (Santali) The pairing sign is a composition of: sloping stroke PLUS two short strokes of a 'splinter': *bica sal* 'stone ore workshop.'
kanka 'rim of jar' Rebus: karṇīka 'account (scribe)' karṇī 'supercargo'

 h383a*खोंड [khōṇḍa] m A young bull, a bullcalf. (Marathi) Rebus: kõdār 'turner' (Bengali); कोंद kōnda 'engraver, lapidary setting or infixing gems' (Marathi) G. sãghāṛɔ m. 'lathe' ; संघाट joinery; M. sãgaḍ 'double-canoe' Rebus: sangataras 'stone-cutter, mason'*

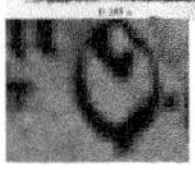 Bronze alloy workshop kañcu sal starting with bronze which is a tin + copper alloy or tin bronze (as distinguished from arsenical bronze, i.e. naturally occurring copper + arsenic).

arsenic).

 *muka* 'ladle' (Tamil)(DEDR 4887) Rebus: *mũh* 'ingot' (Santali) *baṭa* = rimless pot (Kannada) Rebus:) *baṭa* = a kind of iron (G.)) *bhaṭa* furnace (G.) Thus, iron ingot.
kolom 'three' Rebus: kolami 'smithy, forge'
|||| Numeral 4: gaṇḍa 'four' Rebus: kaṇḍa 'furnace, fire-altar' (Santali) PLUS
||| Numeral three: kolom 'three' Rebus: kolami 'smithy, forge' Thus, fire-altar smithy.

 सांड [sāṇḍa] *f* (षद S) An outlet for superfluous water (as through a dam or mound); a sluice, a floodvent. Rebus: सांडणी [sāṇḍaṇī] *f* (H) An instrument of goldsmiths. It is hooked or curved at the extremity; and is used to draw things out of the fire.

 kanka 'rim of jar' Rebus: karṇīka 'account (scribe)' karṇī 'supercargo'

m1880a *balad* m. ' ox ', gng. *bald*, (Ku.) *barad*, id. (N. Tarai) Rebus: *bharat* (5 copper, 4 zinc and 1 tin)(Punjabi) *pattar* 'trough' Rebus*: pattar* 'guild'. Thus, copper-zinc-tin alloy (worker) guild.

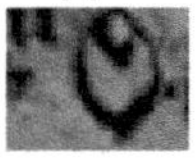 Bronze alloy workshop kañcu sal starting with bronze which is a tin + copper alloy or tin bronze (as distinguished from arsenical bronze, i.e. naturally occurring copper + arsenic).

 *baraḍo* = spine; backbone (Tulu) Rebus: *baran, bharat* 'mixed alloys' (5 copper, 4 zinc and 1 tin) (Punjabi)

 water-carrier hieroglyph *kuṭi*; Rebus: *kuṭhi* 'smelter furnace'.

m15a

खोंड [khōṇḍa] m A young bull, a bullcalf. (Marathi) Rebus: kõdār 'turner' (Bengali); कोंद kōnda 'engraver, lapidary setting or infixing gems' (Marathi) G. sãghāṛɔ m. 'lathe' ; संघाट joinery; M. sãgaḍ 'double-canoe' Rebus: sangataras 'stone-cutter, mason'

 Bronze alloy workshop kañcu sal starting with bronze which is a tin + copper alloy or tin bronze (as distinguished from arsenical bronze, i.e. naturally occurring copper + arsenic).

 *baraḍo* = spine; backbone (Tulu) Rebus: *baran, bharat* 'mixed alloys' (5 copper, 4 zinc and 1 tin) (Punjabi)

 kanka 'rim of jar' Rebus: karṇīka 'account (scribe)' karṇī 'supercargo'

 *meḍ* 'body' Rebus: *meḍ* 'iron' (Ho.) काठी [kāṭhī] *f* (काष्ट S) 'frame or structure of the body' (Marathi) Rebus: खंडी [khaṇḍī] measure of weight (Marathi) *கண்டி; kaṇṭi, n. < Mhr. khaṇḍil. [T. Tu. khaṇḍi, M. kaṇḍi.]* Candy, a weight, stated to be roughly equivalent to 500 lbs.

m1268a

 Bronze alloy workshop kañcu sal starting with bronze which is a tin + copper alloy or tin bronze (as distinguished from arsenical bronze, i.e. naturally occurring copper + arsenic).

 *baraḍo* = spine; backbone (Tulu) Rebus: *baran, bharat* 'mixed alloys' (5 copper, 4 zinc and 1 tin) (Punjabi)

 mēḍu height, rising ground, hillock (Kannada) Rebus: *meḍ* 'iron' (Ho.) kolom 'three' Rebus: kolami 'smithy, forge' Thus, *meḍ kolami* 'iron smithy-forge'

 kanka 'rim of jar' Rebus: karṇīka 'account (scribe)' karṇī 'supercargo'

  m963a

m1755a *खोंड [khōṇḍa] m A young bull, a bullcalf. (Marathi) Rebus: kōdār 'turner' (Bengali); कोंद kōnda 'engraver, lapidary setting or infixing gems' (Marathi) G. sãghāṛɔ m. 'lathe' ; संघाट joinery; M. sãgaḍ 'double-canoe' Rebus: sangataras 'stone-cutter, mason'*

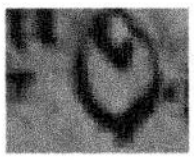 Bronze alloy workshop kañcu sal starting with bronze which is a tin + copper alloy or tin bronze (as distinguished from arsenical bronze, i.e. naturally occurring copper + arsenic).

 *baraḍo* = spine; backbone (Tulu) Rebus: *baran, bharat* 'mixed alloys' (5 copper, 4 zinc and 1 tin) (Punjabi)

 kanka 'rim of jar' Rebus: karṇīka 'account (scribe)' karṇī 'supercargo'

 m1267a

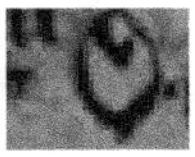 Bronze alloy workshop kañcu sal starting with bronze which is a tin + copper alloy or tin bronze (as distinguished from arsenical bronze, i.e. naturally occurring copper + arsenic).

 *baraḍo* = spine; backbone (Tulu) Rebus: *baran, bharat* 'mixed alloys' (5 copper, 4 zinc and 1 tin) (Punjabi)

 *dula* 'pair' Rebus: dul 'cast metal' *mogge* 'sprout, bud' Rebus: *mũh* 'ingot' (Santali) Thus, cast metal ingot.

 kanka 'rim of jar' Rebus: karṇīka 'account (scribe)' karṇī 'supercargo'

 *aḍar* 'harrow'; rebus: *aduru* 'native unsmelted metal' Duplicated: dula 'pair' Rebus: dul 'cast metal' PLUS 'notch': खांडा [*khāṇḍā*] *m* A jag, notch, or indentation (as upon the edge of a tool or weapon). Rebus: *kāṇḍa* 'tools, pots and pans and metal-war' Thus, native metal castings.

 Lothal 95A

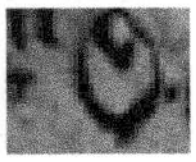 Bronze alloy workshop kañcu sal starting with bronze which is a tin + copper alloy or tin bronze (as distinguished from arsenical bronze, i.e. naturally occurring copper + arsenic).

 *baraḍo* = spine; backbone (Tulu) Rebus: *baran, bharat* 'mixed alloys' (5 copper, 4 zinc and 1 tin) (Punjabi)

'svastika' hieroglyph: Rebus: jasta 'zinc'

 kanka 'rim of jar' Rebus: karṇīka 'account (scribe)' karṇī 'supercargo'

m650a

खोंड [khōṇḍa] m A young bull, a bullcalf. (Marathi) Rebus: kõdār 'turner' (Bengali); कोंद kōnda 'engraver, lapidary setting or infixing gems' (Marathi) G. sãghāṛɔ m. 'lathe' ; संघाट joinery; M. sãgaḍ 'double-canoe' Rebus: sangataras 'stone-cutter, mason'

Bronze alloy workshop kañcu sal starting with bronze which is a tin + copper alloy or tin bronze (as distinguished from arsenical bronze, i.e. naturally occurring copper + arsenic).

'Arrow' sign hieroglyph (variant) This is a ligature of 'lid of pot' hieroglyph superscript on 'a linear stroke' numeral hieroglyph.*aḍaren* 'cover of pot or lid' Rebus: *aduru* 'native, unsmelted metal' PLUS koḍ = one (Santali); koḍ 'workshop' (G.)
Duplicated: dula 'pair' Rebus: dul 'cast metal' Thus, native metal casting workshop.

aḍar 'harrow'; rebus: *aduru* 'native unsmelted metal'
ayo 'fish' Rebus: *aya* 'iron' *ayas* 'metal'
kāṇḍa 'arrow' (Sanskrit) Rebus:*khāṇḍa* 'tools, pots and pans, metal-ware'. Rebus 2: kaṇḍ 'fire-altar' (Santali)

m327a *खोंड [khōṇḍa] m A young bull, a bullcalf. (Marathi) Rebus: kõdār 'turner' (Bengali); कोंद kōnda 'engraver, lapidary setting or infixing gems' (Marathi) G. sãghāṛɔ m. 'lathe' ; संघाट joinery; M. sãgaḍ 'double-canoe' Rebus: sangataras. संगतराश lit. 'to collect stones, stone-cutter, mason.'*

Bronze alloy workshop kañcu sal starting with bronze which is a tin + copper alloy or tin bronze (as distinguished from arsenical bronze, i.e. naturally occurring copper + arsenic).

'Arrow' sign hieroglyph (variant) This is a ligature of 'lid of pot' hieroglyph superscript on 'a linear stroke' numeral hieroglyph.*aḍaren* 'cover of pot or lid' Rebus: *aduru* 'native, unsmelted metal' PLUS koḍ = one (Santali); koḍ 'workshop' (G.)
Duplicated: dula 'pair' Rebus: dul 'cast metal' Thus, native metal casting workshop.
kanka 'rim of jar' Rebus: karṇīka 'account (scribe)' karṇī 'supercargo'

m225A *खोंड [khōṇḍa] m A young bull, a bullcalf. (Marathi) Rebus: kõdār 'turner' (Bengali); कोंद kōnda 'engraver, lapidary setting or infixing gems' (Marathi) G. sãghāṛɔ m. 'lathe' ; संघाट joinery; M. sãgaḍ 'double-canoe' Rebus: sangataras 'stone-cutter, mason'*

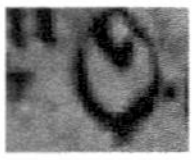

Bronze alloy workshop kañcu sal starting with bronze which is a tin + copper alloy or tin bronze (as distinguished from arsenical bronze, i.e. naturally occurring copper + arsenic).

aya kāṇḍa 'alloy metalware'

m110A

खोंड [khōṇḍa] m A young bull, a bullcalf. (Marathi) Rebus: kõdār 'turner' (Bengali); कोंद kōnda 'engraver, lapidary setting or infixing gems'

(Marathi) G. sãghāṛɔ m. 'lathe' ; संघाट joinery; M. sãgaḍ 'double-canoe' Rebus: sangataras 'stone-cutter, mason'

Bronze alloy workshop kañcu sal starting with bronze which is a tin + copper alloy or tin bronze (as distinguished from arsenical bronze, i.e. naturally occurring copper + arsenic). *aya kāṇḍa* 'alloy metalware'

Kalibangan 33a : *rāngo* 'water buffalo bull' (Ku.N.)(CDIAL 10559) Rebus: rango 'pewter' pattar 'trough' Rebus: pattar 'guild, goldsmith'

Bronze alloy workshop kañcu sal starting with bronze which is a tin +
copper alloy or tin bronze (as distinguished from arsenical bronze, i.e. naturally
occurring copper + arsenic).*aya kāṇḍa* 'alloy metalware'

m144A *खोंड [khōṇḍa] m A young bull, a bullcalf. (Marathi) Rebus: kõdār 'turner' (Bengali); कोंद kōnda 'engraver, lapidary setting or infixing gems' (Marathi) G. sãghāṛɔ m. 'lathe' ; संघाट joinery; M. sãgaḍ 'double-canoe' Rebus: sangataras 'stone-cutter, mason'*

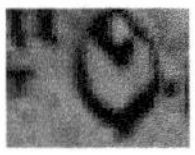

Bronze alloy workshop kañcu sal starting with bronze which is a tin + copper alloy or tin bronze (as distinguished from arsenical bronze, i.e. naturally occurring copper + arsenic).

aya kammaṭa.'coiner, mint alloy'

aḍar 'harrow'; rebus: *aduru* 'native unsmelted metal'

bhaṭa 'warrior' (Sanskrit) Rebus: *baṭa* a kind of iron (Gujarati). Rebus: *bhaṭa* 'furnace' (Santali)

kanka 'rim of jar' Rebus: karṇīka 'account (scribe)' karṇī 'supercargo'

m199A Read rebus as at m144A PLUS

meḍ 'body' Rebus: *meḍ* 'iron' (Ho.) काठी [kāṭhī] *f* (काष्ट S) 'frame or structure of the body' (Marathi) Rebus: खंडी [khaṇḍī] measure of weight (Marathi) *கண்டி; kaṇṭi, n. < Mhr. khaṇḍil. [T. Tu. khaṇḍi, M. kaṇḍi.]* Candy, a weight, stated to be roughly equivalent to 500 lbs.

m285a *ibha* 'elephant' Rebus: *ib* 'iron' *ibbo* 'merchant' (Gujarati)

Bronze alloy workshop kañcu sal starting with bronze which is a tin + copper alloy or tin bronze (as distinguished from arsenical bronze, i.e. naturally occurring copper + arsenic).

aya kammaṭa.'coiner, mint alloy'

 |||| Numeral 4: gaṇḍa 'four' Rebus: kaṇḍa 'furnace, fire-altar' (Santali) dula 'pair' Rebus: dul 'cast metal'

 mēḍu height, rising ground, hillock (Kannada) Rebus: *mẽṛhẽt, meḍ* 'iron' (Munda.Ho.) PLUS *kanḍo* stool, seat Rebus: *kāṇḍā* 'metalware, tools, pots and pans'(Marathi). *kaṇḍ* = a furnace, altar (Santali) Thus, furnace for iron metalware.

m1746a *खोंड [khōṇḍa] m A young bull, a bullcalf. (Marathi) Rebus: kõdār 'turner' (Bengali); कोंद*

 *kōnda 'engraver, lapidary setting or infixing gems' (Marathi) G. sãghāṛɔ m. 'lathe' ; संघाट joinery; M. sãgaḍ 'double-canoe' Rebus: sangataras 'stone-cutter, mason'*

Bronze 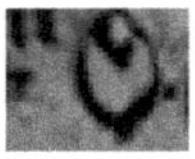 alloy workshop kañcu sal starting with bronze which is a tin + copper alloy or tin bronze (as distinguished from arsenical bronze, i.e. naturally occurring copper + arsenic).

aya kammaṭa.'coiner, mint alloy' sal 'splinter' Rebus: sal 'workshop. Thus, mint workshop
| *koḍa* 'one' Rebus: *koḍ* 'workshop' (with a pit furnace) sal 'splinter' Rebus: sal 'workshop'
bhaṭa 'warrior' (Sanskrit) Rebus: *baṭa* a kind of iron (Gujarati). Rebus: *bhaṭa* 'furnace' (Santali)

 kanka 'rim of jar' Rebus: karṇīka 'account (scribe)' karṇī 'supercargo'

 *meḍ* 'body' Rebus: *meḍ* 'iron' (Ho.) काठी [kāṭhī] *f* (काष्ट S) 'frame or structure of the body' (Marathi) Rebus: खंडी [khaṇḍī] measure of weight (Marathi) *கண்டி; kaṇṭi, n. < Mhr. khaṇḍil. [T. Tu. khaṇḍi, M. kaṇḍi.]* Candy, a weight, stated to be roughly equivalent to 500 lbs.

 m246A *balad* m. ' ox ', gng. *bald*, (Ku.) *barad*, id. (N. Tarai) Rebus: *bharat* (5 copper, 4 zinc and 1 tin)(Punjabi) *pattar* 'trough' Rebus*: pattar* 'guild'. Thus, copper-zinc-tin alloy (worker) guild.

Bronze 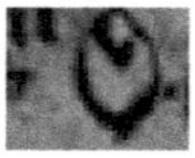 alloy workshop kañcu sal starting with bronze which is a tin + copper alloy or tin bronze (as distinguished from arsenical bronze, i.e. naturally occurring copper + arsenic).

ayo ḍhālako 'alloy metal ingot'

aya aḍaren (homonym: aduru)'alloy native metal'

 mēḍu height, rising ground, hillock (Kannada) Rebus: *mẽṛhẽt, meḍ* 'iron' (Munda.Ho.)

(Illegible hieroglyph)

खोंड [khōṇḍa] m A young bull, a bullcalf. (Marathi) Rebus: kõdār 'turner' (Bengali); कोंद kōnda 'engraver, lapidary setting or infixing gems' (Marathi) G. sãghāṛɔ m. 'lathe' ; संघाट joinery; M. sãgaḍ 'double-canoe' Rebus: sangataras 'stone-cutter, mason'

 Bronze alloy workshop kañcu sal starting with bronze which is a tin + copper alloy or tin bronze (as distinguished from arsenical bronze, i.e. naturally occurring copper + arsenic).

aya kammaṭa.'coiner, mint alloy'

dula 'two' Rebus: dul 'cast metal' kolom 'three' Rebus: kolami 'smithy, forge' Thus, smithy for castings.

dula 'pair' Rebus: dul 'cast metal' *mogge* 'sprout, bud' Rebus: *mũh* 'ingot' (Santali) Thus, cast metal ingot.

 kanka 'rim of jar' Rebus: karṇīka 'account (scribe)' karṇī 'supercargo'

 m42a *खोंड [khōṇḍa] m A young bull, a bullcalf. (Marathi) Rebus: kõdār 'turner' (Bengali); कोंद kōnda 'engraver, lapidary setting or infixing gems' (Marathi) G. sãghārɔ m. 'lathe' ; संघाट joinery; M. sãgaḍ 'double-canoe' Rebus: sangataras 'stone-cutter, mason'*

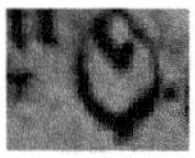 Bronze alloy workshop kañcu sal starting with bronze which is a tin + copper alloy or tin bronze (as distinguished from arsenical bronze, i.e. naturally occurring copper + arsenic).

aya kammaṭa.'coiner, mint alloy'

kamaḍha = crab; *kampaṭṭam* = mint (Ta.) ; *kammaṭa* 'coiner, mint' (Telugu) Vikalpa: *ḍato* = claws of crab (Santali); *dhātu* = mineral (Sanskrit)

 *dhāḷ* 'a slope'; 'inclination of a plane' (G.); *ḍhāḷiyum* = adj. sloping, inclining (G.) Rebus: *ḍhālako* = a large metal ingot (G.) *ḍhālakī* = a metal heated and poured into a mould; a solid piece of metal; an ingot (Gujarati) dula 'pair' Rebus: dul 'cast metal'. sal splinter' Rebus: sal 'workshop Thu cast metal ingot workshop.

 Lothal 83A

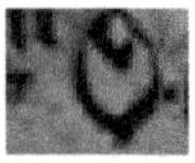 Bronze alloy workshop kañcu sal starting with bronze which is a tin + copper alloy or tin bronze (as distinguished from arsenical bronze, i.e. naturally occurring copper + arsenic). *aya kammaṭa.*'coiner, mint alloy'

  *dula* 'pair' Rebus: *dul* 'cast (metal)' PLUS*kana, kanac* = corner (Santali); Rebus: *kañcu* = bronze (Telugu) PLUS infixed kolmo 'paddy plant' Rebus: kolami 'smithy, forge'. Thus, cast bronze smithy, forge. Or, *mogge* 'sprout, bud' Rebus: *mũh* 'ingot' (Santali)Thus, cast bronze ingot. Read as: *kañcu dul mũh 'bronze cast ingot'*

dula 'pair' Rebus: dul 'cast metal' *mogge* 'sprout, bud' Rebus: *mũh* 'ingot' (Santali) Thus, cast metal ingot.

 m289A kol 'tiger' Rebus: kolhe 'smelters'. pattar 'trough' Rebus: pattar 'guild'

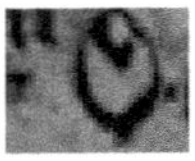

Bronze alloy workshop kañcu sal starting with bronze which is a tin + copper alloy or tin bronze (as distinguished from arsenical bronze, i.e. naturally occurring copper + arsenic).*aya kammaṭa.*'coiner, mint alloy' *aya kammaṭa.*'coiner, mint alloy'

baraḍo = spine; backbone (Tulu) Rebus: *baran, bharat* 'mixed alloys' (5 copper, 4 zinc and 1 tin) (Punjabi)

kanka 'rim of jar' Rebus: karṇīka 'account (scribe)' karṇī 'supercargo'

m1753a *खोंड [khōṇḍa] m A young bull, a bullcalf. (Marathi) Rebus: kõdār 'turner' (Bengali); कोंद kōnda 'engraver, lapidary setting or infixing gems' (Marathi) G. sãghārɔ m. 'lathe' ; संघाट joinery; M. sãgaḍ 'double-canoe' Rebus: sangataras. संगतराश lit. 'to collect stones, stone-cutter, mason.'*

Bronze alloy workshop kañcu sal starting with bronze which is a tin + copper alloy or tin bronze (as distinguished from arsenical bronze, i.e. naturally occurring copper + arsenic). *aya kammaṭa.*'coiner, mint alloy'

'Arrow' sign hieroglyph (variant) This is a ligature of 'lid of pot' hieroglyph superscript on 'a linear stroke' numeral hieroglyph.*aḍaren* 'cover of pot or lid' Rebus: *aduru* 'native, unsmelted metal' PLUS koḍ = one (Santali); koḍ 'workshop' (G.)

dula 'pair' Rebus: dul 'cast metal' *mogge* 'sprout, bud' Rebus: *mũh* 'ingot' (Santali) Thus, cast metal ingot.

kanka 'rim of jar' Rebus: karṇīka 'account (scribe)' karṇī 'supercargo'
h1130B

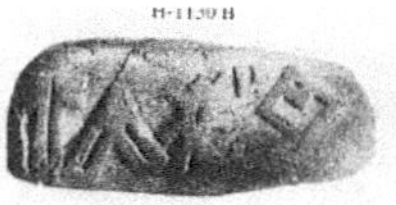

Bronze alloy workshop kañcu sal starting with bronze which is a tin + copper alloy or tin bronze (as distinguished from arsenical bronze, i.e. naturally occurring copper + arsenic). *aya kammaṭa.*'coiner, mint alloy'

dhāḷ 'a slope'; 'inclination of a plane' (G.); *ḍhāḷiyum* = adj. sloping, inclining (G.) Rebus: *ḍhālako* = a large metal ingot (G.) *ḍhālakī* = a metal heated and poured into a mould; a solid piece of metal; an ingot (Gujarati) PLUS खांडा [*khāṇḍā*] *m* A jag, notch, or indentation (as upon the edge of a tool or weapon). Rebus: *kāṇḍa* 'tools, pots and pans and metal-ware'

Thus, the pair of sign hieroglyphs from r. read rebus: copper, bronze ingots, metalware
kanka 'rim of jar' Rebus: *karṇīka* 'account (scribe)' *karṇī* 'supercargo'

h1048A

खोंड [khōṇḍa] m A young bull, a bullcalf. (Marathi) Rebus: kõdār 'turner' (Bengali); कोंद kōnda 'engraver, lapidary setting or infixing gems' (Marathi) G. sãghārɔ m. 'lathe' ; संघाट joinery; M. sãgaḍ 'double-canoe' Rebus: sangataras. संगतराश lit. 'to collect stones, stone-cutter, mason.'

Bronze alloy workshop kañcu sal starting with bronze which is a tin + copper alloy or tin bronze (as distinguished from arsenical bronze, i.e. naturally occurring copper + arsenic). *ayo ḍhālako* 'alloy metal ingot'. *dula* 'pair' Rebus: *dul* 'cast (metal)' PLUS*kana, kanac* = corner (Santali); Rebus: *kañcu* = bronze (Telugu) Thus, cast bronze.

dula ‘two’ Rebus: dul ‘cast metal’

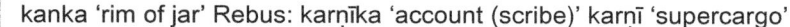

 kanka ‘rim of jar’ Rebus: karṇīka ‘account (scribe)’ karṇī ‘supercargo’

m1670a *खोंड [khōṇḍa] m A young bull, a bullcalf. (Marathi) Rebus: kõdār ‘turner’ (Bengali); कोंद kōnda ‘engraver, lapidary setting or infixing gems’ (Marathi) G. sãghāṛɔ m. ‘lathe’ ; संघाट joinery; M. sãgaḍ ‘double-canoe’ Rebus: sangataras. संगतराश lit. ‘to collect stones, stone-cutter, mason.’*

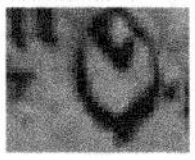 Bronze alloy workshop kañcu sal starting with bronze which is a tin + copper alloy or tin bronze (as distinguished from arsenical bronze, i.e. naturally occurring copper + arsenic). *ayo ḍhālako* ‘alloy metal ingot’. PLUS | *koḍa* ‘one’ Rebus: *koḍ* ‘workshop’

 *dula* ‘pair’ Rebus: dul ‘cast metal’ *mogge* ‘sprout, bud’ Rebus: *mũh* ‘ingot’ (Santali) Thus, cast metal ingot.

 'rim-of-jar' hieroglyph *kanka* (Santali) *karṇika* ‘scribe’(Sanskrit) Rebus: *karṇī,* supercargo for a boat shipment. *karṇīka* ‘account (scribe)’.कारणी *kāraṇī* ‘the supercargo of a ship’

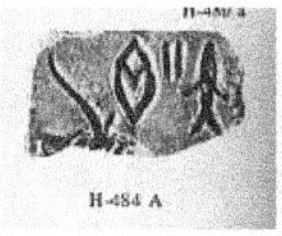 Jukar 2a   m794a h459A  h484A

खोंड [khōṇḍa] m A young bull, a bullcalf. (Marathi) Rebus: kõdār ‘turner’ (Bengali); कोंद kōnda ‘engraver, lapidary setting or infixing gems’ (Marathi) G. sãghāṛɔ m. ‘lathe’ ; संघाट joinery; M. sãgaḍ ‘double-canoe’ Rebus: sangataras. संगतराश lit. ‘to collect stones, stone-cutter, mason.’

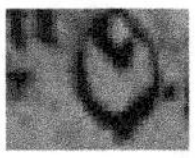 Bronze alloy workshop kañcu sal starting with bronze which is a tin + copper alloy or tin bronze (as distinguished from arsenical bronze, i.e. naturally occurring copper + arsenic). *ayo ḍhālako* ‘alloy metal ingot’

Marathi)

 h484A

 m1860a

खोंड [khōṇḍa] m A young bull, a bullcalf. (Marathi) Rebus: kõdār ‘turner’ (Bengali); कोंद kōnda ‘engraver, lapidary setting or infixing gems’ (Marathi) G. sãghāṛɔ m. ‘lathe’ ; संघाट joinery; M. sãgaḍ ‘double-canoe’ Rebus: sangataras. संगतराश lit. ‘to collect stones, stone-cutter, mason.’

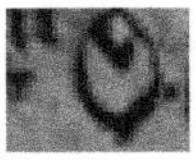 Bronze alloy workshop kañcu sal starting with bronze which is a tin + copper alloy or tin bronze (as distinguished from arsenical bronze, i.e. naturally occurring copper + arsenic). *aya aḍaren (homonym: aduru)*‘alloy native metal’

 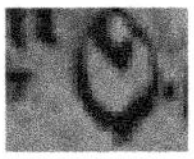 m1299a Bronze alloy workshop kañcu sal starting with bronze which is a tin + copper alloy or tin bronze (as distinguished from arsenical bronze, i.e. naturally occurring copper + arsenic). *ayo ḍhālako* ‘alloy metal ingot’

 *muka* ‘ladle’ (Tamil)(DEDR 4887) Rebus: *mũh* ‘ingot’ (Santali) *baṭa* = rimless pot (Kannada) Rebus:) *baṭa* = a kind of iron (G.)) *bhaṭa* furnace (G.) Thus, iron ingot.

kolom ‘three’ Rebus: kolami ‘smithy, forge’ *kamaḍha* ‘crab’ Rebus: *kammaṭa* ‘mint, coiner’.

ḍato = claws of crab (Santali) Rebus: *dhātu* 'mineral ore'

dhāḷ 'a slope'; 'inclination of a plane' (G.); *ḍhāḷiyum* = adj. sloping, inclining (G.) Rebus: *ḍhālako* = a large metal ingot (G.) *ḍhālakī* = a metal heated and poured into a mould; a solid piece of metal; an ingot (Gujarati) dula 'pair' Rebus: dul 'cast metal'. sal splinter' Rebus: sal 'workshop Thu cast metal ingot workshop.

h137a First five sign hieroglyphs read rebus as at m1299a PLUS

loa 'ficus religiosa' Rebus: *lo* 'iron' (Sanskrit) *ḍhanga* = a crook used for pulling down the branches of trees, for goats, sheep and camels (P.)
Rebus:*ḍhangar* blacksmith'.PLUS 'notch': खांडा [*khāṇḍā*] *m* A jag, notch, or indentation (as upon the edge of a tool or weapon). Rebus: *kāṇḍa* 'tools, pots and pans and metal-ware'. Thus, blacksmith tools.

kanka 'rim of jar' Rebus: karṇīka 'account (scribe)' karṇī 'supercargo'

m1110 Text 1334 *khũṭ* 'zebu' Rebus: '(native metal) guild'
kanac 'corner' Rebus: *kañcu* 'bronze' (Telugu)
sal 'splinter' Rebus: *sal* 'workshop'
meḍ 'body' Rebus: *meḍ* 'iron' *aḍaren* 'cover of pot or lid' Rebus: *aduru* 'native metal'
khaṇḍ 'field, division' (Sanskrit) Rebus: *khāṇḍa* 'tools, pots and pans, metal-ware'. Rebus 2: kaṇḍ 'fire-altar' (Santali) *aḍaren* 'cover of pot or lid' Rebus: *aduru* 'native, unsmelted metal' PLUS

meḍ 'body' Rebus: *meḍ* 'iron' (Ho.) काठी [kāṭhī] *f* (काष्ट S) 'frame or structure of the body' (Marathi) Rebus: खंडी [khaṇḍī] measure of weight (Marathi) கண்டி; *kaṇṭi, n.* < *Mhr. khaṇḍil. [T. Tu. khaṇḍi, M. kaṇḍi.]* Candy, a weight, stated to be roughly

kanka 'rim of jar' Rebus: *karṇīka* 'account (scribe)' *karṇī* 'supercargo'

m1899a *khũṭ* 'zebu' Rebus: '(native metal) guild': Text message: bronze workshop, iron, moltencast copper, brass
kanac 'corner' Rebus: *kañcu* 'bronze'
sal 'splinter' Rebus: *sal* 'workshop'
meḍ 'body' Rebus: *meḍ* 'iron' PLUS ligature: eraka 'upraised arm' Rebus; erako 'moltencast copper'
kuṭila 'bent' CDIAL 3230 *kuṭi*— in cmpd. 'curve', *kuṭika*— 'bent' MBh. Rebus: kuṭila, *katthīl* = bronze (8 parts copper and 2 parts tin) cf. *āra-kūṭa*, 'brass' (Sanskrit)

kanka 'rim of jar' Rebus: karṇīka 'account (scribe)' karṇī 'supercargo'

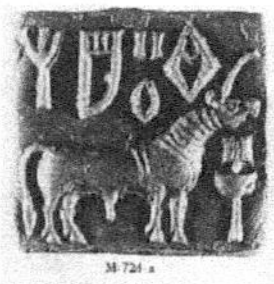

m724A*खोंड [khōṇḍa] m A young bull, a bullcalf. (Marathi) Rebus: kõdār 'turner' (Bengali); कोंद kōnda 'engraver, lapidary setting or infixing gems' (Marathi) G. sãghāṛɔ m. 'lathe' ; संघाट joinery; M. sãgaḍ 'double-canoe' Rebus: sangataras. संगतराश lit. 'to collect stones, stone-cutter, mason.'*

Bronze alloy workshop kañcu sal starting with bronze which is a tin + copper alloy or tin bronze (as distinguished from arsenical bronze, i.e. naturally occurring copper + arsenic). dola 'hole' Rebus: dol 'cast metal'

baṭa = rimless pot (Kannada) Rebus:) *baṭa* = a kind of iron (G.)) *bhaṭa* furnace (G.) Thus, iron ingot.
kolmo 'paddy plant' Rebus: kolami 'smithy, forge'. Vikalpa: *mogge* 'sprout, bud' Rebus*: mũh* 'ingot'

h1851A Side B: *baṭa* = rimless pot (Kannada) Rebus:) *baṭa* = a kind of iron (G.)) *bhaṭa* furnace
||| Numeral three: kolom 'three' Rebus: kolami 'smithy, forge Side A:
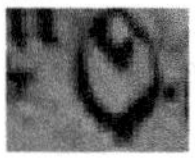
Bronze alloy workshop kañcu sal starting with bronze which is a tin + copper alloy or tin bronze (as distinguished from arsenical bronze, i.e. naturally occurring copper + arsenic).
| *koḍa* 'one' Rebus: *koḍ* 'workshop'
kamaḍha 'bow and arrow' Rebus: *kammaṭa* 'mint, coiner'.

dula 'pair' Rebus: *dul* 'cast (metal)' PLUS*kana, kanac* = corner (Santali); Rebus: *kañcu* = bronze (Telugu) PLUS infixed kolmo 'paddy plant' Rebus: kolami 'smithy, forge'. Thus, cast bronze smithy, forge. Or, *mogge* 'sprout, bud' Rebus: *mũh* 'ingot' (Santali)Thus, cast bronze ingot. Read as: *kañcu dul mũh 'bronze cast ingot'*

kanka 'rim of jar' Rebus: karṇīka 'account (scribe)' karṇī 'supercargo'

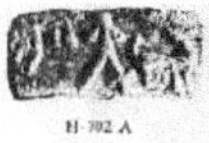

h702A Side B: ranku 'antelope' Rebus: ranku 'tin' krammara 'look back' Rebus: kamar 'blacksmith' *baṭa* = rimless pot (Kannada) Rebus:) *baṭa* = a kind of iron (G.)) *bhaṭa* furnace
||| Numeral three: kolom 'three' Rebus: kolami 'smithy, forge

Bronze alloy workshop kañcu sal starting with bronze which is a tin + copper alloy or tin bronze (as distinguished from arsenical bronze, i.e. naturally occurring copper + arsenic).

meḍ 'body' Rebus: *meḍ* 'iron' (Ho.) काठी [kāṭhī] *f* (काष्ट S) 'frame or structure of the body' (Marathi) Rebus: खंडी [khaṇḍī] measure of weight (Marathi) *கண்டி; kaṇṭi, n. < Mhr. khaṇḍil. [T. Tu. khaṇḍi, M. kaṇḍi.]* Candy, a weight, stated to be roughly equivalent to 500 lbs.

m825a

h651a

h292A

m646A 'Young bull' hieroglyph: कोंद *kōnda 'engraver,*
Bronze alloy workshop kañcu sal starting with bronze which is a tin + copper alloy or tin bronze (as distinguished from arsenical bronze, i.e. naturally occurring copper + arsenic).

m1913A *ibha* 'elephant' Rebus: *ib* 'iron' *ibbo* 'merchant' (Gujarati) kanac 'corner'

Rebus: *kañcu sal* 'splinter' Rebus: 'workshop'

aḍar 'harrow'; rebus: *aduru* 'native unsmelted metal'

m835a

खोंड [khōṇḍa] m A young bull, a bullcalf. (Marathi) Rebus: kõdār 'turner' (Bengali); कोंद kōnda 'engraver, lapidary setting or infixing gems' (Marathi) G. sãghāṛɔ m. 'lathe' ; संघाट joinery; M. sãgaḍ 'double-canoe' Rebus: sangataras 'stone-cutter, mason'

 Bronze alloy workshop kañcu sal starting with bronze which is a tin + copper alloy or tin bronze (as distinguished from arsenical bronze, i.e. naturally occurring copper + arsenic).

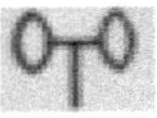

If frame of a cart is depicted, possible rebus reading: अगडा [agaḍā] *m* The tie connecting the जूं & दांडी of a गाडा or load-cart; the shaft and thill-yoke-tie. Rebus: 'lumber, miscellaneous articles': अगडतगड [*agaḍatagaḍa*] *n* अगडबगड *n* (Fanciful formations, or from H) Trash, trumpery, rubbish, lumber, miscellaneous articles.

dula 'two' Rebus: dul 'cast metal' kolom 'three' Rebus: kolami 'smithy, forge'

 *kanka* 'rim of jar' Rebus: *karṇika* 'account (scribe)' *karṇī* 'supercargo'

h164a

  Bronze alloy workshop kañcu sal starting with bronze which is a tin + copper alloy or tin bronze (as distinguished from arsenical bronze, i.e. naturally occurring copper + arsenic).

 *meḍ* 'body' Rebus: *meḍ* 'iron' (Ho.) काठी [kāṭhī] *f* (काष्ट S) 'frame or structure of the body' (Marathi) Rebus: खंडी [khaṇḍī] measure of weight (Marathi) *கண்டி; kaṇṭi, n. < Mhr. khaṇḍil. [T. Tu. khaṇḍi, M. kaṇḍi.]* Candy, a weight, stated to be roughly equivalent to 500 lbs.

| *koḍa* 'one' Rebus: *koḍ* 'workshop'

 water-carrier hieroglyph *kuṭi*; Rebus: *kuṭhi* 'smelter furnace'. PLUS *kāṇḍa* 'arrow' (Sanskrit) Rebus: *khāṇḍa* 'tools, pots and pans, metal-ware'. Rebus 2: kaṇḍ 'fire-altar' (Santali)

 Chanhudaro 18a *खोंड [khōṇḍa] m A young bull, a bullcalf. (Marathi) Rebus: kõdār 'turner' (Bengali); कोंद kōnda 'engraver, lapidary setting or infixing gems' (Marathi) G. sãghāṛɔ m. 'lathe' ; संघाट joinery; M. sãgaḍ 'double-canoe' Rebus: sangataras 'stone-cutter, mason'*

 Bronze alloy workshop kañcu sal starting with bronze which is a tin + copper alloy or tin bronze (as distinguished from arsenical bronze, i.e. naturally occurring copper + arsenic). *koḍa* 'one' Rebus: *koḍ* 'workshop' *kamaḍha* 'crab' Rebus: *kammaṭa* 'mint, coiner'. *ḍato* = claws of crab (Santali) Rebus: *dhātu* 'mineral ore'

 h1042

खोंड [khōṇḍa] m A young bull, a bullcalf. (Marathi) Rebus: kõdār 'turner' (Bengali); कोंद kōnda 'engraver, lapidary setting or infixing gems' (Marathi) G. sãghāṛɔ m. 'lathe' ; संघाट joinery; M. sãgaḍ 'double-canoe' Rebus: sangataras 'stone-cutter, mason'

 Bronze alloy workshop kañcu sal starting with bronze which is a tin + copper alloy or tin bronze (as distinguished from arsenical bronze, i.e. naturally occurring copper + arsenic).
ayo 'fish' Rebus: aya 'iron' (Gujarati) ayas 'metal' (Vedic) dula 'pair' Rebus: dul 'cast metal' Thus, cast metal alloy. Vikalpa: *ayo ḍhālako* 'alloy metal ingot'

 *kuṭila* 'bent' CDIAL 3230 kuṭi— in cmpd. 'curve', *kuṭika—* 'bent' MBh. Rebus: *kuṭila,*

 *katthīl* = bronze (8 parts copper and 2 parts tin)
kanka 'rim of jar' Rebus: karṇīka 'account (scribe)' karṇī 'supercargo'

 m79a *खोंड [khōṇḍa] m A young bull, a bullcalf. (Marathi) Rebus: kõdār 'turner' (Bengali); कोंद kōnda 'engraver, lapidary setting or infixing gems' (Marathi) G. sãghāṛɔ m. 'lathe' ; संघाट joinery; M. sãgaḍ 'double-canoe' Rebus: sangataras 'stone-cutter, mason'*

 Bronze alloy workshop kañcu sal starting with bronze which is a tin + copper alloy or tin bronze (as distinguished from arsenical bronze, i.e. naturally occurring copper + arsenic).
ayo ḍhālako 'alloy metal ingot'
aya kammaṭa.'coiner, mint alloy'
meḍ 'body' Rebus: meḍ 'iron' (Ho.) काठी [kāṭhī] f (काष्ट S) 'frame or structure of the body' (Marathi) Rebus: खंडी [khaṇḍī] measure of weight (Marathi) கண்டி; kaṇṭi, n. < Mhr. khaṇḍil. [T. Tu. khaṇḍi, M. kaṇḍi.] Candy, a weight, about 500 lbs.bhaṭa 'warrior' (Sanskrit) Rebus: *baṭa* a kind of iron (Gujarati). Rebus: *bhaṭa* 'furnace' (Santali)

 kanka 'rim of jar' Rebus: karṇīka 'account (scribe)' karṇī 'supercargo'
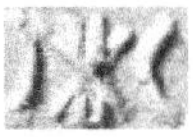 kuṭila 'bent' CDIAL 3230 kuṭi— in cmpd. 'curve', *kuṭika—* 'bent' MBh. Rebus: kuṭila, katthīl = bronze (8 parts copper and 2 parts tin) Variant:
 *dāṭu* 'cross'(Telugu) Rebus: *dhatu* 'mineral' (Santali). Sal 'splinter' Rebus: sal 'workshop' dula 'pair' Rebus: dul 'cast metal'. Thus metalworkshop for casting bronze and iron.

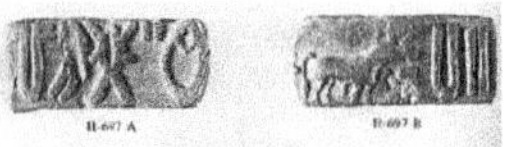 h697A

h1100A Side B:  *baṭa* = rimless pot (Kannada) Rebus:) *baṭa* = a kind of iron (G.)) *bhaṭa* furnace (Gujarati) PLUS dula 'two; Rebus: dul 'cast metal' Thus iron furnace castings. 'Young bull' hieroglyph ligatured with two horns of zebu. Native metal smith guild. PLUS *baṭa* = a kind of iron (Gujarati) *baṭa* = rimless pot (Kannada) dula 'two' Rebus: dul 'cast metal' Thus, cast iron.*खोंड [khōṇḍa] m A young bull, a bullcalf. (Marathi) Rebus: kõdār 'turner' (Bengali); कोंद kōnda 'engraver, lapidary setting or infixing gems' (Marathi) G. sãghāṛɔ m. 'lathe' ; संघाट joinery; M. sãgaḍ 'double-canoe' Rebus: sangataras. संगतराश lit. 'to collect stones, stone-cutter, mason.'* Side A:

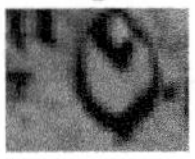 Bronze alloy workshop kañcu sal starting with bronze which is a tin + copper alloy or tin bronze (as distinguished from arsenical bronze, i.e. naturally occurring copper + arsenic).
aya kammaṭa.'coiner, mint alloy'
kuṭila 'bent' CDIAL 3230 kuṭi— in cmpd. 'curve', *kuṭika—* 'bent' MBh. Rebus: kuṭila, katthīl = bronze (8 parts copper and 2 parts tin) dula 'pair' Rebus: dul 'cast metal'. Thus cast bronze.

kanka 'rim of jar' Rebus: karṇīka 'account (scribe)' karṇī 'supercargo'

Lothal 41a खोंड *[khōṇḍa] m A young bull, a bullcalf. (Marathi) Rebus: kõdār 'turner' (Bengali);* कोंद *kōnda 'engraver, lapidary setting or infixing gems' (Marathi) G. sãghāṛɔ m. 'lathe' ;* संघाट *joinery; M. sãgaḍ 'double-canoe' Rebus: sangataras.* संगतराश *lit. 'to collect stones, stone-cutter, mason.'*

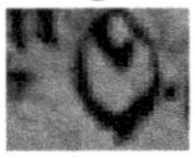

Bronze alloy workshop kañcu sal starting with bronze which is a tin + copper alloy or tin bronze (as distinguished from arsenical bronze, i.e. naturally occurring copper + arsenic).

ayo ḍhālako 'alloy metal ingot'

kanka 'rim of jar' Rebus: karṇīka 'account (scribe)' karṇī 'supercargo'

meḍ 'body' Rebus: *meḍ* 'iron' (Ho.) काठी [kāṭhī] *f* (काष्ट S) 'frame or structure of the body' (Marathi) Rebus: खंडी [khaṇḍī] measure of weight (Marathi) *கண்டி; kaṇṭi, n. < Mhr. khaṇḍil. [T. Tu. khaṇḍi, M. kaṇḍi.]* Candy, a weight, stated to be roughly equivalent to 500 lbs.

h51A खोंड *[khōṇḍa] m A young bull, a bullcalf. (Marathi) Rebus: kõdār 'turner' (Bengali);* कोंद *kōnda 'engraver, lapidary setting or infixing gems' (Marathi) G. sãghāṛɔ m. 'lathe' ;* संघाट *joinery; M. sãgaḍ 'double-canoe' Rebus: sangataras.* संगतराश *lit. 'to collect stones, stone-cutter, mason.'*

aya kammaṭa.'coiner, mint alloy'

kəṭhā'r, kc. *kuṭhār* m. ' granary, storeroom '(Western Pahari)(CDIAL 3550). *koṭhārī m.* ' storekeeper' (Gujarati)(CDIAL 3551) Thus, storeroom (of) *kolom* 'three' Rebus: *kolami* 'smithy, forge'. Dula 'pair' Rebus: dul 'cast metal' Thus, together *dul kolami kuṭhār* 'metal smithy castings storeroom'

kanka 'rim of jar' Rebus: karṇīka 'account (scribe)' karṇī 'supercargo'

m868A

खोंड *[khōṇḍa] m A young bull, a bullcalf. (Marathi) Rebus: kõdār 'turner' (Bengali);* कोंद *kōnda 'engraver, lapidary setting or infixing gems' (Marathi) G. sãghāṛɔ m. 'lathe' ;* संघाट *joinery; M. sãgaḍ 'double-canoe' Rebus: sangataras 'stone-cutter, mason'*

Bronze alloy workshop kañcu sal starting with bronze which is a tin + copper alloy or tin bronze (as distinguished from arsenical bronze, i.e. naturally occurring copper + arsenic).

ayo 'fish' Rebus: aya 'iron' (Gujarati) ayas 'metal' dula 'pair' Rebus: dul 'cast metal' Thus, cast alloy metal *aya aḍaren (homonym: aduru)*'alloy native metal'

muka 'ladle' (Tamil)(DEDR 4887) Rebus: *mũh* 'ingot' (Santali) *baṭa* = a kind of iron (Gujarati) *baṭa* = rimless pot (Kannada) Thus, iron ingot.

kolom 'three' Rebus: kolami 'smithy, forge'

kāṇḍa ‘arrow’ (Sanskrit) Rebus:*khāṇḍa* ‘tools, pots and pans, metal-ware’. Rebus 2: kaṇḍ 'fire-altar' (Santali)

m677a Rebus as at m868A PLUS
aya kammaṭa.’coiner, mint alloy’
aya kāṇḍa ‘alloy metalware’

muka  ‘ladle’ (Tamil)(DEDR 4887) Rebus: *mũh* ‘ingot’ (Santali) *baṭa* = a kind of iron (Gujarati) *baṭa* = rimless pot (Kannada) Thus, iron ingot. kolom ‘three’ Rebus: kolami ‘smithy, forge’
(Ilegible hieroglyph)

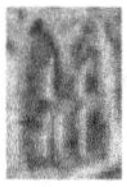

Ligature: two peaks: mēḍu height, rising ground, hillock (Kannada) Rebus: *meḍ* ‘iron’ (Ho.) dula ‘pair’ Rebus: dul ‘cast metal’ PLUS |||| Numeral 4: gaṇḍa 'four' Rebus: kaṇḍa 'furnace, fire-altar' (Santali)
aḍaren ‘cover of pot or lid’ Rebus: *aduru* ‘native, unsmelted metal’ PLUS koḍ = one (Santali); koḍ ‘workshop’ (Gujarati)
kuṭila ‘bent’ CDIAL 3230 kuṭi— in cmpd. ‘curve’, *kuṭika*— ‘bent’ MBh. Rebus: kuṭila, katthīl =

bronze (8 parts copper and 2 parts tin dula ‘pair’ Rebus: dul ‘cast metal’ Thus cast bronze
kanka ‘rim of jar’ Rebus: karṇīka ‘account (scribe)’ karṇī ‘supercargo’

m1726a Rebus as at m677a PLUS

mēḍu height, rising ground, hillock (Kannada) Rebus: *mẽṛhẽt, meḍ* ‘iron’ (Munda.Ho.) *khaṇḍ* ‘field, division’ (Sanskrit) Rebus: *khāṇḍa* ‘tools, pots and pans, metal-ware’.

m1166a kol

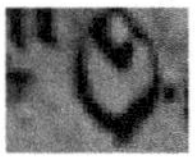

tin

‘tiger’ Rebus: kolhe ’smelter’ pattar ‘trough’ Rebus: pattar ‘guild. Bronze alloy workshop kañcu sal starting with bronze which is a + copper alloy or tin bronze (as distinguished from arsenical bronze, i.e. naturally occurring copper + arsenic).
aya *kammaṭa.*’coiner, mint alloy’
kuṭila ‘bent’ CDIAL 3230 kuṭi— in cmpd. ‘curve’, *kuṭika*— ‘bent’ MBh. Rebus: kuṭila, katthīl =

bronze (8 parts copper and 2 parts tin dula ‘pair’ Rebus: dul ‘cast metal’ Thus cast bronze
kanka ‘rim of jar’ Rebus: karṇīka ‘account (scribe)’ karṇī ‘supercargo’

m827A*खोंड [khōṇḍa] m A young bull, a bullcalf. (Marathi) Rebus: kōdār ‘turner’ (Bengali); कोंद kōnda ‘engraver, lapidary setting or infixing gems’ (Marathi) G. sãghāṛɔ m. ‘lathe’ ; संघाट joinery; M. sãgaḍ ‘double-canoe’ Rebus: sangataras. संगतराश lit. ‘to collect stones, stone-cutter, mason.’*

Bronze alloy workshop kañcu sal starting with bronze which is a tin + copper alloy or tin bronze (as distinguished from arsenical bronze, i.e. naturally occurring copper + arsenic).*aya kammaṭa.*’coiner, mint alloy’ *aya kāṇḍa* ‘alloy metalware’

6112

6112

Bronze alloy workshop kañcu sal starting with bronze which is a tin + copper alloy or tin bronze (as distinguished from arsenical bronze, i.e. naturally occurring copper + arsenic).

aya kammaṭa.'coiner, mint alloy'

kəṭhā´r, kc. *kuṭhār* m. ' granary, storeroom '(Western Pahari)(CDIAL 3550). *koṭhārī m.* ' storekeeper' (Gujarati)(CDIAL 3551) Thus, storeroom (of) *kolom* 'three' Rebus: *kolami* 'smithy, forge'. Dula 'pair' Rebus: dul 'cast metal' Thus, together *dul kolami kuṭhār* 'metal smithy castings storeroom' sal 'splinter' Rebus: sal 'workshop' thus, storeroom of the workshop.

kanka 'rim of jar' Rebus: *karṇīka* 'account (scribe)' *karṇī* 'supercargo'

m834a*खोंड [khōṇḍa] m A young bull, a bullcalf. (Marathi) Rebus: kõdār 'turner' (Bengali); कोंद kōnda 'engraver, lapidary setting or infixing gems' (Marathi) G. sãghāṛɔ m. 'lathe' ; संघाट joinery; M. sãgaḍ 'double-canoe' Rebus: sangataras. संगतराश lit. 'to collect stones, stone-cutter, mason.'*

Bronze alloy workshop kañcu sal starting with bronze which is a tin + copper alloy or tin bronze (as distinguished from arsenical bronze, i.e. naturally occurring copper + arsenic).kuṭila 'bent' CDIAL 3230 kuṭi— in cmpd. 'curve', *kuṭika*— 'bent' MBh. Rebus: kuṭila, katthīl = bronze (8 parts copper and 2 parts tin)

ranku 'liquid measure' Rebus; ranku 'tin.

kolmo 'paddy plant' Rebus: kolami 'smithy, forge

water-carrier hieroglyph *kuṭi*; Rebus: *kuṭhi* 'smelter furnace'.

m701a*खोंड [khōṇḍa] m A young bull, a bullcalf. (Marathi) Rebus: kõdār 'turner' (Bengali); कोंद kōnda 'engraver, lapidary setting or infixing gems' (Marathi) G. sãghāṛɔ m. 'lathe' ; संघाट joinery; M. sãgaḍ 'double-canoe' Rebus: sangataras 'stone-cutter, mason'*

Bronze 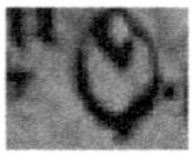 alloy workshop kañcu sal starting with bronze which is a tin + copper alloy or tin bronze (as distinguished from arsenical bronze, i.e. naturally occurring copper + arsenic).

kuṭila 'bent' CDIAL 3230 kuṭi— in cmpd. 'curve', *kuṭika*— 'bent' MBh. Rebus: kuṭila, katthīl = bronze (8 parts copper and 2 parts tin)

meḍ 'body' Rebus: *meḍ* 'iron' (Ho.) काठी [kāṭhī] *f* (काष्ट S) 'frame or structure of the body' (Marathi) Rebus: खंडी [khaṇḍī] measure of weight (Marathi) *கண்டி; kaṇṭi, n. < Mhr. khaṇḍil. [T. Tu. khaṇḍi, M. kaṇḍi.]* Candy, a weight, stated to be roughly equivalent to 500 lbs.

h658A

Bronze alloy workshop kañcu sal starting with bronze which is a tin + copper 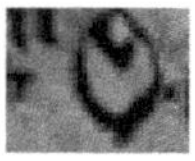 alloy or tin bronze (as distinguished from arsenical bronze, i.e. naturally occurring copper + arsenic).

kuṭila 'bent' CDIAL 3230 kuṭi— in cmpd. 'curve', *kuṭika*— 'bent' MBh. Rebus: kuṭila, katthīl = bronze (8 parts copper and 2 parts tin)

m816Aखोंड [khōṇḍa] m A young bull, a bullcalf. (Marathi) Rebus: kōdār 'turner' (Bengali); कोंद kōnda 'engraver, lapidary setting or infixing gems' (Marathi) G. sãghāṛɔ m. 'lathe' ; संघाट joinery; M. sāgaḍ 'double-canoe' Rebus: sangataras. संगतराश lit. 'to collect stones, stone-cutter, mason.'

Bronze alloy workshop kañcu sal starting with bronze which is a tin + copper alloy or tin bronze (as distinguished from arsenical bronze, i.e. naturally occurring copper + arsenic).

The pair of hieroglyph signs are compositions: bicha 'scorpion' (Assamese) Rebus: *bica* 'stone ore' (Santali) The pairing sign is a composition of: sloping stroke PLUS two short strokes of a 'splinter':

dhāḷ 'a slope'; 'inclination of a plane' (Gujarati); *ḍhāḷiyum* = adj. sloping, inclining (Gujarati) Rebus: *ḍhālako* = a large metal ingot (Gujarati) *ḍhālakī* = a metal heated and poured into a mould; a solid piece of metal; an ingot (Gujarati) PLUS *sal* 'splinter' Rebus: *sal* 'workshop'. Thus the composition reads: *ḍhālako sal* 'ingot workshop'.

 *dāṭu* 'cross'(Telugu) Rebus: *dhatu* 'mineral' (Santali).

 kanka 'rim of jar' Rebus: karṇīka 'account (scribe)' karṇī 'supercargo'

m1206eBronze alloy workshop kañcu sal starting with bronze which is a tin + copper alloy or tin bronze (as distinguished from arsenical bronze, i.e. naturally occurring copper + arsenic).
kuṭila 'bent' CDIAL 3230 kuṭi— in cmpd. 'curve', *kuṭika—* 'bent' MBh. Rebus: kuṭila, katthīl = bronze (8 parts copper and 2 parts tin)

The pair of hieroglyph signs are compositions: bicha 'scorpion' (Assamese) Rebus: *bica* 'stone ore' (Santali) The pairing sign is a composition of: sloping stroke PLUS two short strokes of a 'splinter':*dhāḷ* 'a slope'; 'inclination of a plane' (Gujarati); *ḍhāḷiyum* = adj. sloping, inclining (Gujarati) Rebus: *ḍhālako* = a large metal ingot (Gujarati) *ḍhālakī* = a metal heated and poured into a mould; a solid piece of metal; an ingot (Gujarati)PLUS*sal* 'splinter' Rebus: *sal* 'workshop'. Thus the composition reads: *ḍhālako sal* 'ingot workshop'.

 *dāṭu* 'cross'(Telugu) Rebus: *dhatu* 'mineral' (Santali).

 kanka 'rim of jar' Rebus: karṇīka 'account (scribe)' karṇī 'supercargo'

m1833aखोंड [khōṇḍa] m A young bull, a bullcalf. (Marathi) Rebus: kōdār 'turner' (Bengali); कोंद kōnda 'engraver, lapidary setting or infixing gems' (Marathi) G. sãghāṛɔ m. 'lathe' ; संघाट joinery; M. sāgaḍ 'double-canoe' Rebus: sangataras. संगतराश lit. 'to collect stones, stone-cutter, mason.'

Bronze alloy workshop kañcu sal starting with bronze which is a tin + copper alloy or tin bronze (as distinguished from arsenical bronze, i.e. naturally occurring copper + arsenic).kolom 'three' Rebus: kolami 'smithy, forge' dula 'two' Rebus: dul 'cast metal'

mogge 'sprout, bud' Rebus*: mũh* 'ingot'

h1045a Rebus as at m1833a PLUS
kuṭila 'bent' CDIAL 3230 kuṭi— in cmpd. 'curve', *kuṭika*— 'bent' MBh. Rebus: kuṭila, katthīl = bronze (8 parts copper and 2 parts tin)
kanka 'rim of jar' Rebus: karṇīka 'account (scribe)' karṇī 'supercargo'

m72a *खोंड [khōṇḍa] m A young bull, a bullcalf. (Marathi) Rebus: kõdār 'turner' (Bengali); कोंद kōnda 'engraver, lapidary setting or infixing gems' (Marathi) G. sãghārɔ m. 'lathe' ; संघाट joinery; M. sãgaḍ 'double-canoe' Rebus: sangataras. संगतराश lit. 'to collect stones, stone-cutter, mason.'*

Bronze alloy workshop kañcu sal starting with bronze which is a tin + copper alloy or tin bronze (as distinguished from arsenical bronze, i.e. naturally occurring copper + arsenic).

kolom 'three' Rebus: kolami 'smithy, forge' kanka 'rim of jar' Rebus: karṇīka 'account (scribe)' karṇī 'supercargo'
loa 'ficus religiosa' Rebus: *lo* 'iron' (Sanskrit) PLUS unique ligatures: लोखंड [lōkhaṇḍa

] *n* (लोह S) Iron. लोखंडाचे चणे खावविणें or चारणें To oppress

grievously.लोखंडकाम [lōkhaṇḍakāma] *n* Iron work; that portion (of a building, machine &c.) which consists of iron. 2 The business of an ironsmith.लोखंडी [lōkhaṇḍī] *a* (लोखंड) Composed of iron; relating to iron. (Marathi) *bhaṭa* 'warrior' (Sanskrit) Rebus: *baṭa* a kind of iron (Gujarati). Rebus: *bhaṭa* 'furnace' (Santali) Thus, together, th ligatured hieroglyph reads rebus: *loa bhaṭa* 'iron furnace'
muka 'ladle' (Tamil)(DEDR 4887) Rebus: *mũh* 'ingot' (Santali) *baṭa* = a kind of iron (Gujarati) *baṭa* = rimless pot (Kannada) Thus, iron ingot.

The pair of hieroglyph signs are compositions: *bicha* 'scorpion' (Assamese) Rebus: *bica* 'stone ore' (Santali)

kanka 'rim of jar' Rebus: karṇīka 'account (scribe)' karṇī 'supercargo'

m1697A m712A m32a m407Am177A

खोंड [khōṇḍa] m A young bull, a bullcalf. (Marathi) Rebus: kõdār 'turner' (Bengali); कोंद kōnda 'engraver, lapidary setting or infixing gems' (Marathi) G. sãghārɔ m. 'lathe' ; संघाट joinery; M. sãgaḍ 'double-canoe' Rebus: sangataras. संगतराश lit. 'to collect stones, stone-cutter, mason.'
Bronze alloy workshop kañcu sal starting with bronze which is a tin + copper alloy or tin bronze (as distinguished from arsenical bronze, i.e. naturally occurring copper + arsenic). kolom 'three' Rebus: kolami 'smithy, forge' *mogge* 'sprout, bud' Rebus*: mũh* 'ingot'

Kalibangan 82A*खोंड [khōṇḍa] m A young bull, a bullcalf. (Marathi) Rebus: kõdār 'turner' (Bengali); कोंद kōnda 'engraver, lapidary setting or infixing gems' (Marathi) G. sãghārɔ m. 'lathe' ; संघाट joinery; M. sãgaḍ 'double-canoe' Rebus: sangataras.*

संगतराश *lit. 'to collect stones, stone-cutter, mason.'*

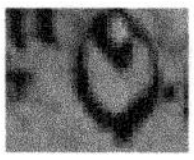
Bronze alloy workshop kañcu sal starting with bronze which is a tin + copper alloy or tin bronze (as distinguished from arsenical bronze, i.e. naturally occurring copper + arsenic).kolom 'three' Rebus: kolami 'smithy, forge' *mogge* 'sprout, bud' Rebus*: mũh* ingot'

h1043a*खोंड [khōṇḍa] m A young bull, a bullcalf. (Marathi) Rebus: kõdār 'turner' (Bengali); कोंद kōnda 'engraver, lapidary setting or infixing gems' (Marathi) G. sãghāṛɔ m. 'lathe' ; संघाट joinery; M. sãgaḍ 'double-canoe' Rebus: sangataras. संगतराश lit. 'to collect stones, stone-cutter, mason.'*

Bronze alloy workshop kañcu sal starting with bronze which is a tin + copper alloy or tin bronze (as distinguished from arsenical bronze, i.e. naturally occurring copper + arsenic).kolom 'three' Rebus: kolami 'smithy, forge' *ayo* 'fish' Rebus: *aya* 'iron' *ayas* 'metal'*kolmo* 'paddy plant' Rebus: *kolami* 'smithy, forge' dula 'pair' Rebus: dul 'cast metal' Thus, metal smithy castings.

water-carrier hieroglyph *kuṭi*; Rebus: *kuṭhi* 'smelter furnace'. PLUS 'rim of jar':

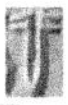
kanka 'rim of jar' Rebus: karṇīka 'account (scribe)' karṇī 'supercargo'

h134ABronze alloy workshop kañcu sal starting with bronze which is a tin + copper alloy or tin bronze (as distinguished from arsenical bronze, i.e. naturally

occurring copper + arsenic).kolom 'three' Rebus: kolami 'smithy, forge'*ayo* 'fish' Rebus: *aya* 'iron' *ayas* 'metal'ranku 'liquid measure' Rebus: ranku 'tin'*mogge* 'sprout, bud' Rebus*: mũh* ingot'

kanka 'rim of jar' Rebus: karṇīka 'account (scribe)' karṇī 'supercargo'

m872A*खोंड [khōṇḍa] m A young bull, a bullcalf. (Marathi) Rebus: kõdār 'turner' (Bengali); कोंद kōnda 'engraver, lapidary setting or infixing gems' (Marathi) G. sãghāṛɔ m. 'lathe' ; संघाट joinery; M. sãgaḍ 'double-canoe' Rebus: sangataras. संगतराश lit. 'to collect stones, stone-cutter, mason.'*

Bronze alloy workshop kañcu sal starting with bronze which is a tin + copper alloy or tin bronze (as distinguished from arsenical bronze, i.e. naturally occurring copper + arsenic).kolom 'three' Rebus: kolami 'smithy, forge' dula 'pair' Rebus: dul 'cast metal' Thus metal smithy castings.*mogge* 'sprout, bud' Rebus*: mũh* ingot'

m1658a

Bronze alloy workshop kañcu sal starting with bronze which is a tin + copper alloy or tin bronze (as distinguished from arsenical bronze, i.e. naturally occurring copper + arsenic).
kolom 'three' Rebus: kolami 'smithy, forge' dula 'pair' Rebus: dul 'cast metal' Thus metal smithy castings.

Read in context, the composite hieroglyph is assumed to be a combination of a slanted stroke ligatured to a notch,which provide possible rebus readings of a smithy/forge: notch+slanted stroke reads rebus: *ḍhālako kāṇḍa* 'ingot, tools, pots and pans and metal-ware' *ḍhāḷ* 'a slope'; 'inclination of a plane' (Gujarati); *ḍhāḷiyum* = adj. sloping, inclining (Gujarati) Rebus: *ḍhālako* = a large metal ingot (Gujarati) *ḍhālakī* = a metal heated and poured into a mould; a solid piece of metal; an ingot (Gujarati) PLUS खांडा [

khāṇḍā] *m* A jag, notch, or indentation (as upon the edge of a tool or weapon). Rebus: *kāṇḍa* 'tools, pots and pans and metal-ware'

h42A खोंड [khōṇḍa] m A young bull, a bullcalf. (Marathi) Rebus: kõdār 'turner' (Bengali); कोंद kōnda 'engraver, lapidary setting or infixing gems' (Marathi) G. sãghāṛɔ m. 'lathe' ; संघाट joinery; M. sãgaḍ 'double-canoe' Rebus: sangataras. संगतराश lit. 'to collect stones, stone-cutter, mason.'

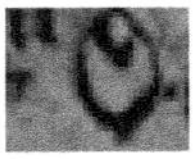

Bronze alloy workshop kañcu sal starting with bronze which is a tin + copper alloy or tin bronze (as distinguished from arsenical bronze, i.e. naturally occurring copper + arsenic). *aya aḍaren (homonym: aduru)*'alloy native metal' *aḍaren* 'cover of pot or lid' Rebus: *aduru* 'native, unsmelted metal'

kanka 'rim of jar' Rebus: *karṇīka* 'account (scribe)' *karṇī* 'supercargo'

m47a*खोंड [khōṇḍa] m A young bull, a bullcalf. (Marathi) Rebus: kõdār 'turner' (Bengali); कोंद kōnda 'engraver, lapidary setting or infixing gems' (Marathi) G. sãghāṛɔ m. 'lathe' ; संघाट joinery; M. sãgaḍ 'double-canoe' Rebus: sangataras. संगतराश lit. 'to collect stones, stone-cutter, mason.'*

Bronze alloy workshop kañcu sal starting with bronze which is a tin + copper alloy or tin bronze (as distinguished from arsenical bronze, i.e. naturally occurring copper + arsenic).*aya aḍaren (homonym: aduru)*'alloy native metal'

kolmo 'paddy plant' Rebus: kolami 'smithy, forge' PLUS *mogge* 'sprout, bud' Rebus*: mũh* ingot' Thus, ingot smithy.

kanka 'rim of jar' Rebus: karṇīka 'account (scribe)' karṇī 'supercargo'

m1842a*खोंड [khōṇḍa] m A young bull, a bullcalf. (Marathi) Rebus: kõdār 'turner' (Bengali); कोंद kōnda 'engraver, lapidary setting or infixing gems' (Marathi) G. sãghāṛɔ m. 'lathe' ; संघाट joinery; M. sãgaḍ 'double-canoe' Rebus: sangataras 'stone-cutter, mason'*

Bronze alloy workshop kañcu sal starting with bronze which is a tin + copper alloy or tin bronze (as distinguished from arsenical bronze, i.e. naturally occurring copper + arsenic).*aya aḍaren (homonym: aduru)*'alloy native metal' *ayo ḍhālako* 'alloy metal ingot'*kāṇḍa* 'arrow' (Sanskrit) Rebus:*khāṇḍa* 'tools, pots and pans, metal-ware'. Rebus 2: kaṇḍ 'fire-altar' (Santali)

m703a*खोंड [khōṇḍa] m A young bull, a bullcalf. (Marathi) Rebus: kõdār 'turner' (Bengali); कोंद kōnda 'engraver, lapidary setting or infixing gems' (Marathi) G. sãghāṛɔ m. 'lathe' ; संघाट joinery; M. sãgaḍ 'double-canoe' Rebus: sangataras 'stone-cutter, mason'*

Bronze alloy workshop kañcu sal starting with bronze which is a tin + copper alloy or tin bronze (as distinguished from arsenical bronze, i.e. naturally occurring copper + arsenic).*aya aḍaren (homonym: aduru)*'alloy native metal'*ayo ḍhālako* 'alloy metal ingot'

(Last hieroglyph sign/s illegible, due to a broken corner of the seal)

m1343A

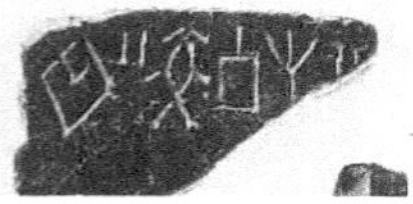

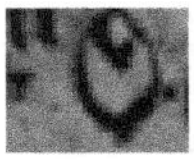

Bronze alloy workshop kañcu sal starting with bronze which is a tin + copper alloy or tin bronze (as distinguished from arsenical bronze, i.e. naturally occurring copper + arsenic).

aya aḍaren (homonym: aduru)'alloy native metal' ranku 'liquid measure' Rebus: ranku 'tin' kolmo 'paddy plant' Rebus: kolami 'smithy, forge'

Rebus: *karṇī,* supercargo for a boat shipment. *karṇīka* 'account (scribe)'.कारणी *kāraṇī*' the supercargo of a ship' (Marathi)

m897ARebus as at m 934a

m934aखोंड *[khōṇḍa] m A young bull, a bullcalf. (Marathi) Rebus: kõdār 'turner' (Bengali);* कोंद *kōnda 'engraver, lapidary setting or infixing gems' (Marathi) G. sãghārɔ m. 'lathe' ;* संघाट *joinery; M. sãgaḍ 'double-canoe' Rebus: sangataras.* संगतराश *lit. 'to collect stones, stone-cutter, mason.'*

Bronze alloy workshop kañcu sal starting with bronze which is a tin + copper alloy or tin bronze (as distinguished from arsenical bronze, i.e. naturally occurring copper + arsenic).

aya aḍaren (homonym: aduru)'alloy native metal'

kamaḍha 'crab' Rebus: *kammaṭa* 'mint, coiner'.
ḍato = claws of crab (Santali) Rebus: *dhātu* 'mineral ore' PLUS 'notch' hieroglyph sign ligature: खांडा [*khāṇḍā*] *m* A jag, notch, or indentation (as upon the edge of a tool or weapon). Rebus: *kāṇḍa* 'tools, pots and pans and metal-ware'

Two slanted strokes ligatured (joined) with 'splinter' hieroglyph: *dhāḷ* 'a slope'; 'inclination of a plane' (Gujarati); *ḍhāḷiyum* = adj. sloping, inclining (Gujarati) Rebus: *ḍhālako* = a large metal ingot (Gujarati) *ḍhālakī* = a metal heated and poured into a mould; a solid piece of metal; an ingot (Gujarati) Two strokes: dula 'pair' Rebus: dul 'cast metal'. Thus *dul ḍhālako* 'cast metal ingot'. *sal* 'splinter' Rebus: *sal* 'workshop'. Thus the ligatured hieroglyph sign reads: cast metal ingot workshop, *dul ḍhālako sal*

m1778aखोंड *[khōṇḍa] m A young bull, a bullcalf. (Marathi) Rebus: kõdār 'turner' (Bengali);* कोंद *kōnda 'engraver, lapidary setting or infixing gems' (Marathi) G. sãghārɔ m. 'lathe' ;* संघाट *joinery; M. sãgaḍ 'double-canoe' Rebus: sangataras 'stone-cutter, mason'*

Bronze alloy workshop kañcu sal starting with bronze which is a tin + copper alloy or tin bronze (as distinguished from arsenical bronze, i.e. naturally occurring copper + arsenic).

aya aḍaren (homonym: aduru)'alloy native metal'

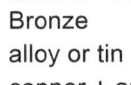

kanka 'rim of jar' Rebus: karṇīka 'account (scribe)' karṇī 'supercargo'

m653a Rebus as at 1778a PLUS

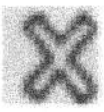

dāṭu 'cross'(Telugu) Rebus: *dhatu* 'mineral' (Santali)
kaṇḍo 'stool, seat' Rebus: *kāṇḍa* 'metalware' *kaṇḍa* 'fire-altar'

m732a*खोंड [khōṇḍa] m A young bull, a bullcalf. (Marathi) Rebus: kõdār 'turner' (Bengali); कोंद kōnda 'engraver, lapidary setting or infixing gems' (Marathi) G. sãghāṛɔ m. 'lathe' ; संघाट joinery; M. sãgaḍ 'double-canoe' Rebus: sangataras. संगतराश lit. 'to collect stones, stone-cutter, mason.'*

Bronze alloy workshop kañcu sal starting with bronze which is a tin + copper alloy or tin bronze (as distinguished from arsenical bronze, i.e. naturally occurring copper + arsenic).

Variant:

|||| Numeral 4: gaṇḍa 'four' Rebus: kaṇḍa 'furnace, fire-altar' (Santali) dula 'pair' Rebus: dul 'cast metal'

kharedo = a currycomb (Gujarati) खरारा [*kharārā*] *m* (H) A currycomb. 2 Currying a horse. (Marathi) Rebus: करडा [*karaḍā*] Hard from alloy--iron, silver &c. (Marathi) *kharādī*' turner' (Gujarati) *aḍaren* 'cover of pot or lid' Rebus: *aduru* 'native, unsmelted metal' PLUS koḍ = one (Santali); koḍ 'workshop' (Gujarati)

Dholavira

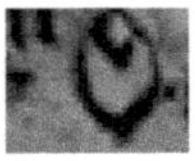

Bronze alloy workshop kañcu sal starting with bronze which is a tin + copper alloy or tin bronze (as distinguished from arsenical bronze, i.e. naturally occurring copper + arsenic). 'Pair of harrows': *aḍar* 'harrow'; rebus: *aduru* 'native unsmelted metal' *dul aduru* 'cast native unsmelted metal'

'rim-of-jar' hieroglyph

kanka (Santali) *karṇika* 'scribe'(Sanskrit) Rebus: *karṇī,* supercargo for a boat shipment. *karṇīka* 'account (scribe)'.कारणी *kāraṇī* 'the supercargo of a ship' (Marathi)

m1085A *balad* m. ' ox ', gng. *bald,* (Ku.) *barad,* id. (N. Tarai) Rebus: *bharat* (5 copper, 4 zinc and 1 tin)(Punjabi) *pattar* 'trough' Rebus*: pattar* 'guild'. Thus, copper-zinc-tin alloy (worker) guild.

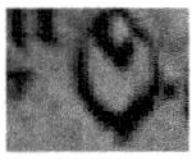

Bronze alloy workshop kañcu sal starting with bronze which is a tin + copper alloy or tin bronze (as distinguished from arsenical bronze, i.e. naturally occurring copper + arsenic).

Variant:

|||| Numeral 4: gaṇḍa 'four' Rebus: kaṇḍa 'furnace, fire-altar' (Santali) dula 'pair'

ḍãg mountain-ridge (Hindi)(CDIAL 5476). Rebus: dhangar 'blacksmith' (Maithili)

kamaḍha 'crab' Rebus: *kammaṭa* 'mint, coiner'.*ḍato* = claws of crab (Santali) Rebus: *dhātu* 'mineral ore'*aḍar* 'harrow'; rebus: *aduru* 'native unsmelted metal
bhaṭa 'warrior' (Sanskrit) Rebus: *baṭa* a kind of iron (Gujarati). Rebus: *bhaṭa* 'furnace' (Santali) PLUS *kharedo* = a currycomb (Gujarati) खरारा [*kharārā*] *m* (H) A currycomb. 2 Currying a

horse. (Marathi) Rebus: करडा [*karaḍā*] Hard from alloy--iron, silver &c. (Marathi) *kharādī*' turner' (Gujarati)

kanka 'rim of jar' Rebus: karṇīka 'account (scribe)' karṇī 'supercargo'

m364A

Bronze alloy workshop kañcu sal starting with bronze which is a tin + copper alloy or tin bronze (as distinguished from arsenical bronze, i.e. naturally occurring copper + arsenic).

Variant:

|||| Numeral 4: gaṇḍa 'four' Rebus: kaṇḍa 'furnace, fire-altar' (Santali) dula 'pair' Rebus: dul 'cast metal' Thus, cast metal furnace.

'rim-of-jar' hieroglyph *kanka* (Santali) *karṇika* 'scribe'(Sanskrit)

Rebus: *karṇī,* supercargo for a boat shipment. *karṇīka* 'account (scribe)'.कारणी *kāraṇī* 'the supercargo of a ship' (Marathi)

m1063a

m2003A

m984a

m1785A

m719A

m1750A

m1844A *खोंड [khōṇḍa] m A young bull, a bullcalf. (Marathi) Rebus: kõdār 'turner' (Bengali); कोंद kōnda 'engraver, lapidary setting or infixing gems' (Marathi) G. sãghāṛɔ m. 'lathe' ; संघाट joinery; M. sãgaḍ 'double-canoe' Rebus: sangataras 'stone-cutter, mason'*
Bronze alloy workshop kañcu sal starting with bronze which is a tin + copper alloy or tin bronze (as distinguished from arsenical bronze, i.e. naturally occurring copper + arsenic).
|||| Numeral 4: *gaṇḍa* 'four' Rebus: *kaṇḍa* 'furnace, fire-altar' (Santali).

mogge 'sprout, , *mogge* 'sprout, bud' Rebus*: mũh* 'ingot'.
खांडा [*khāṇḍā*] *m* A jag, notch, or indentation (as upon the edge of a tool or weapon). Rebus: *kāṇḍa* 'tools, pots and pans and metal-ware'

m75A*खोंड [khōṇḍa] m A young bull, a bullcalf. (Marathi) Rebus: kõdār 'turner' (Bengali); कोंद kōnda 'engraver, lapidary setting or infixing gems' (Marathi) G. sãghāṛɔ m. 'lathe' ; संघाट joinery; M. sãgaḍ 'double-canoe' Rebus: sangataras. संगतराश lit. 'to collect stones, stone-cutter, mason.'*

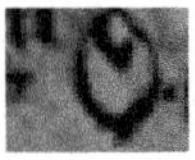
Bronze alloy workshop kañcu sal starting with bronze which is a tin + copper alloy or tin bronze (as distinguished from arsenical bronze, i.e. naturally occurring copper + arsenic).
|||| Numeral 4: *gaṇḍa* 'four' Rebus: *kaṇḍa* 'furnace, fire-altar' (Santali).
ayo 'fish' Rebus: aya 'iron' (Gujarati) ayas 'metal' (Vedic)

 *kānḍa* 'arrow' (Sanskrit) Rebus:*khānḍa* 'tools, pots and pans, metal-ware'. Rebus 2: kaṇḍ 'fire-altar' (Santali)

Sequence of four hieroglyph signs

h1692A

  Bronze alloy workshop kañcu sal starting with bronze which is a tin + copper alloy or tin bronze (as distinguished from arsenical bronze, i.e. naturally occurring copper + arsenic).

| *koḍa* 'one' Rebus: *koḍ* 'workshop' ranku 'liquid measure' Rebus: ranku 'tin' kolmo 'paddy plant' Rebus: kolami 'smithy, forge'. Thus smithy, forge workshop for bronze alloy and tin workshop

m851Aखोंड *[khōṇḍa] m A young bull, a bullcalf. (Marathi) Rebus: kōdār 'turner' (Bengali);* कोंद *kōnda 'engraver, lapidary setting or infixing gems' (Marathi) G. sãghāṛɔ m. 'lathe' ;* संघाट *joinery; M. sãgaḍ 'double-canoe' Rebus: sangataras 'stone-cutter, mason'*

  Bronze alloy workshop kañcu sal starting with bronze which is a tin + copper alloy or tin bronze (as distinguished from arsenical bronze, i.e. naturally occurring copper + arsenic).

| *koḍa* 'one' Rebus: *koḍ* 'workshop' ranku 'liquid measure' Rebus: ranku 'tin' kolmo 'paddy plant' Rebus: kolami 'smithy, forge'. Thus smithy, forge workshop for bronze alloy and tin

 kanka 'rim of jar' Rebus: karṇīka 'account (scribe)' karṇī 'supercargo'

kəṭhā´r, kc. *kuṭhār* m. ' granary, storeroom '(WPah.)(CDIAL 3550). *koṭhārī m.* ' storekeeper'

 (Gujarati)(CDIAL 3551) Thus, storeroom (of) *kolom* 'three' Rebus: *kolami* 'smithy, forge'. Dula 'pair' Rebus: dul 'cast metal' Thus, together *dul kolami kuṭhār* 'metal smithy castings storeroom'

m813A

खोंड [khōṇḍa] m A young bull, a bullcalf. (Marathi) Rebus: kōdār 'turner' (Bengali); कोंद *kōnda 'engraver, lapidary setting or infixing gems' (Marathi) G. sãghāṛɔ m. 'lathe' ;* संघाट *joinery; M. sãgaḍ 'double-canoe' Rebus: sangataras 'stone-cutter, mason'*

 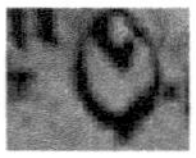 Bronze alloy workshop kañcu sal starting with bronze which is a tin + copper alloy or tin bronze (as distinguished from arsenical bronze, i.e. naturally occurring copper + arsenic).

| *koḍa* 'one' Rebus: *koḍ* 'workshop' ranku 'liquid measure' Rebus: ranku 'tin' kolmo 'paddy plant' Rebus: kolami 'smithy, forge'. Thus smithy, forge workshop for bronze alloy and tin

water-carrier hieroglyph *kuṭi*; Rebus: *kuṭhi* 'smelter furnace'.

PLUS

kānḍa 'arrow' (Sanskrit) Rebus:*khānḍa* 'tools, pots and pans, metal-ware'. Rebus 2: kaṇḍ 'fire-altar' (Santali)

m90A

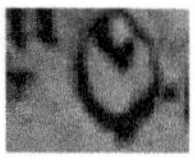

Bronze alloy workshop kañcu sal starting with bronze which is a tin + copper alloy or tin bronze (as distinguished from arsenical bronze, i.e. naturally occurring copper + arsenic).

| *koḍa* 'one' Rebus: *koḍ* 'workshop'
sal 'splinter' Rebus: sal 'workshop' PLUS 'notch': खांडा [*khāṇḍā*] *m* A jag, notch, or indentation (as upon the edge of a tool or weapon). Rebus: *kāṇḍa* 'tools, pots and pans and metal-ware' Thus, metalware workshop.

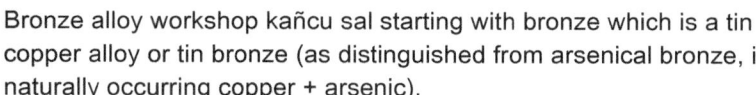

kanac 'corner' Rebus: *kañcu* 'bronze' dula 'pair' Rebus: dul 'cast metal' Thus, cast bronze.
kanka 'rim of jar' Rebus: karṇīka 'account (scribe)' karṇī 'supercargo'

Sequence of five hieroglyph signs:

tin +

Bronze alloy workshop kañcu sal starting with bronze which is a copper alloy or tin bronze (as distinguished from arsenical bronze, i.e. naturally occurring copper + arsenic).

kamaḍha 'crab' Rebus: *kammaṭa* 'mint, coiner'.
ḍato = claws of crab (Santali) Rebus: *dhātu* 'mineral ore'
aḍar 'harrow'; rebus: *aduru* 'native unsmelted metal'
ayo 'fish' Rebus: *aya* 'iron' *ayas* 'metal'
Together, the rebus reading: bronze workshop, mint (with) mineral ore, native metal, alloyed metal.

m1954a

Bronze alloy workshop kañcu sal starting with bronze which is a tin + copper alloy or tin bronze (as distinguished from arsenical bronze, i.e. naturally occurring copper + arsenic).

kamaḍha 'crab' Rebus: *kammaṭa* 'mint, coiner'.
ḍato = claws of crab (Santali) Rebus: *dhātu* 'mineral ore'
aḍar 'harrow'; rebus: *aduru* 'native unsmelted metal'
ayo 'fish' Rebus: *aya* 'iron' *ayas* 'metal'
Together, the rebus reading: bronze workshop, mint (with) mineral ore, native metal, alloyed metal.

muka 'ladle' (Tamil)(DEDR 4887) Rebus: *mũh* 'ingot' (Santali) *baṭa* = a kind of iron (Gujarati) *baṭa* = rimless pot (Kannada) Thus, iron ingot.

kolom 'three' Rebus: kolami 'smithy, forge' Thus iron ingot smithy.

'Rimless pot ligatured with unique ligatures to denote a gloss comparable to *lokhaṇḍa* on 'ficus' and 'scorpion' hieroglyphs, thus offering a cipher of *khaṇḍa* for the unique ligatures] *m* A jag, notch, or indentation (as upon the edge of a tool or weapon). Rebus: *kāṇḍa* 'tools, pots and pans and metal-ware'
baṭa = a kind of iron (Gujarati) *baṭa* = rimless pot (Kannada) PLUS खांडा [*khāṇḍā*] *m* A jag, notch, or indentation (as upon the edge of a tool or weapon). Rebus: *kāṇḍa* 'tools, pots and pans and metal-ware' Thus, iron furnace metalware, *baṭa khāṇḍā.*
| *koḍa* 'one' Rebus: *koḍ* 'workshop Thus, the pair reads: *baṭa khāṇḍā koḍ* 'iron furnace metalware workshop' (or, a forge).

m1426A

Bronze alloy workshop kañcu sal starting with bronze which is a tin + copper alloy or tin bronze (as distinguished from arsenical bronze, i.e. naturally occurring copper + arsenic).

kamaḍha 'crab' Rebus: *kammaṭa* 'mint, coiner'.
ḍato = claws of crab (Santali) Rebus: *dhātu* 'mineral ore'
aḍar 'harrow'; rebus: *aduru* 'native unsmelted metal'
ayo 'fish' Rebus: *aya* 'iron' *ayas* 'metal'
Together, the rebus reading: bronze workshop, mint (with) mineral ore, native metal, alloyed metal.

kolmo 'three' Rebus: kolami 'smithy, forge' dula 'pair' Rebus: dul 'cast metal' Thus, metal smithy castings.

'Rimless pot ligatured with unique ligatures to denote a gloss comparable to *lokhaṇḍa* superscript ligatures on 'ficus' and 'scorpion' hieroglyphs, thus offering a cipher of *khaṇḍa* for the unique ligatures] *m* A jag, notch, or indentation (as upon the edge of a tool or weapon). Rebus: *kāṇḍa* 'tools, pots and pans and metal-ware'
baṭa = a kind of iron (Gujarati) *baṭa* = rimless pot (Kannada) PLUS खांडा [*khāṇḍā*] *m* A jag, notch, or indentation (as upon the edge of a tool or weapon). Rebus: *kāṇḍa* 'tools, pots and pans and metal-ware' Thus, iron furnace metalware, *baṭa khāṇḍā.*
| *koḍa* 'one' Rebus: *koḍ* 'workshop Thus, the pair reads: *baṭa khāṇḍā koḍ* 'iron furnace metalware workshop' (or, a forge).

kanka 'rim of jar' Rebus: karṇīka 'account (scribe)' karṇī 'supercargo'

m22a *खोंड [khōṇḍa] m A young bull, a bullcalf. (Marathi) Rebus: kõdār 'turner' (Bengali); कोंद kōnda 'engraver, lapidary setting or infixing gems' (Marathi) G. sãghāṛɔ m. 'lathe' ; संघाट joinery; M. sãgaḍ 'double-canoe' Rebus: sangataras. संगतराश lit. 'to collect stones, stone-cutter, mason.'*

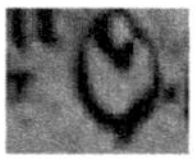

Bronze alloy workshop kañcu sal starting with bronze which is a tin + copper alloy or tin bronze (as distinguished from arsenical bronze, i.e. naturally occurring copper + arsenic).

kamaḍha 'crab' Rebus: *kammaṭa* 'mint, coiner'.
ḍato = claws of crab (Santali) Rebus: *dhātu* 'mineral ore'. Thus, together, rebus reading is: mineral ore, mint, bronze workshop.

dula 'pair' Rebus: dul 'cast metal'
ayo 'fish' Rebus: *aya* 'iron' *ayas* 'metal'. Thus, together, the pair read: cast alloy metal.

baraḍo = spine; backbone (Tulu) Rebus: *baran, bharat* 'mixed alloys' (5 copper, 4 zinc and 1 tin) (Punjabi)

kuṭila 'bent' CDIAL 3230 kuṭi— in cmpd. 'curve', *kuṭika—* 'bent' MBh. Rebus: *kuṭila, katthīl* = bronze (8 parts copper and 2 parts tin)
dula 'pair' Rebus: dul 'cast metal'. Thus, cast bronze, *dul kuṭila*

kanka 'rim of jar' Rebus: karṇīka 'account (scribe)' karṇī 'supercargo'

Sequence of three hieroglyph signs

Bronze alloy workshop kañcu sal starting with bronze which is a tin + copper alloy or tin bronze (as distinguished from arsenical bronze, i.e. naturally occurring copper + arsenic).
kamaḍha 'crab' Rebus: *kammaṭa* 'mint, coiner'.
ḍato = claws of crab (Santali) Rebus: *dhātu* 'mineral ore'. Thus, together, rebus reading is: mineral ore, mint, bronze workshop.

m1051A *खोंड [khōṇḍa] m A young bull, a bullcalf. (Marathi) Rebus: kōdār 'turner' (Bengali); कोंद kōnda 'engraver, lapidary setting or infixing gems' (Marathi) G. sãghārɔ m. 'lathe' ; संघाट joinery; M. sãgaḍ 'double-canoe' Rebus: sangataras. संगतराश lit. 'to collect stones, stone-cutter, mason.'*

 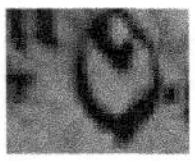
Bronze alloy workshop kañcu sal starting with bronze which is a tin + copper alloy or tin bronze (as distinguished from arsenical bronze, i.e. naturally occurring copper + arsenic).
kamaḍha 'crab' Rebus: *kammaṭa* 'mint, coiner'.
ḍato = claws of crab (Santali) Rebus: *dhātu* 'mineral ore'. Thus, together, rebus reading is: mineral ore, mint, bronze workshop.
ranku 'antelope' Rebus: ranku 'tin'

kuṭila 'bent' CDIAL 3230 kuṭi— in cmpd. 'curve', *kuṭika—* 'bent' MBh. Rebus: *kuṭila, katthīl* = bronze (8 parts copper and 2 parts tin)

|||| Numeral 4: *gaṇḍa* 'four' Rebus: *kaṇḍa* 'furnace, fire-altar' (Santali).
||| Numeral 3: *kolom* 'three' Rebus: *kolami* 'smithy, forge'.

सांड [sāṇḍa] *f* (षद S) An outlet for superfluous water (as through a dam or mound); a sluice, a floodvent. Rebus: सांडणी [sāṇḍaṇī] *f* (H) An instrument of goldsmiths. It is hooked or curved at the extremity; and is used to draw things out of the fire.

kanka 'rim of jar' Rebus: karṇīka 'account (scribe)' karṇī 'supercargo'

 *kharedo* = a currycomb (Gujarati) खरारा [*kharārā*] *m* (H) A currycomb. 2 Currying a horse. (Marathi) Rebus: करडा [*karaḍā*] Hard from alloy--iron, silver &c. (Marathi) *kharādī* ' turner' (Gujarati)

m1973a

Bronze alloy
tin + copper alloy

 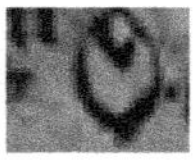

workshop kañcu sal starting with bronze which is a or tin bronze (as distinguished from arsenical bronze, i.e. naturally occurring copper + arsenic).

kamaḍha 'crab' Rebus: *kammaṭa* 'mint, coiner'.
ḍato = claws of crab (Santali) Rebus: *dhātu* 'mineral ore'. Thus, together, rebus reading is: mineral ore, mint, bronze workshop.

ayo ḍhālako 'alloy metal ingot'

|||| Numeral 4: *ganḍa* 'four' Rebus: *kanḍa* 'furnace, fire-altar' (Santali).
||| Numeral 3: *kolom* 'three' Rebus: *kolami* 'smithy, forge'.

 सांड [sāṇḍa] *f* (षद S) An outlet for superfluous water (as through a dam or mound); a sluice, a floodvent. Rebus: सांडणी [sāṇḍaṇī] *f* (H) An instrument of goldsmiths. It is hooked or curved at the extremity; and is used to draw things out of the fire.

 kanka 'rim of jar' Rebus: karṇīka 'account (scribe)' karṇī 'supercargo'

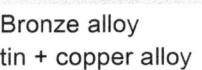

m815A *खोंड [khōṇḍa] m A young bull, a bullcalf. (Marathi) Rebus: kōdār 'turner' (Bengali); कोंद kōnda 'engraver, lapidary setting or infixing gems' (Marathi) G. sãghāṛɔ m. 'lathe' ; संघाट joinery; M. sãgaḍ 'double-canoe' Rebus: sangataras. संगतराश lit. 'to collect stones, stone-cutter, mason.'*

 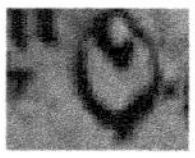

Bronze alloy workshop kañcu sal starting with bronze which is a tin + copper alloy or tin bronze (as distinguished from arsenical bronze,i.e. naturally occurring copper + arsenic).

kamaḍha 'crab' Rebus: *kammaṭa* 'mint, coiner'.
ḍato = claws of crab (Santali) Rebus: *dhātu* 'mineral ore'. Thus, together, rebus reading is: mineral ore, mint, bronze workshop.

ayo ḍhālako 'alloy metal ingot'

 'Arrow' sign hieroglyph (variant) This is a ligature of 'lid of pot' hieroglyph superscript on 'a linear stroke' numeral hieroglyph.*aḍaren* 'cover of pot or lid' Rebus: *aduru* 'native, unsmelted metal' PLUS koḍ = one (Santali); koḍ 'workshop' (Gujarati)
kānḍa 'arrow' (Sanskrit) Rebus:*khānḍa* 'tools, pots and pans, metal-ware'. Rebus 2: kaṇḍ 'fire-altar' (Santali)

m629A

खोंड [khōṇḍa] m A young bull, a bullcalf. (Marathi) Rebus: kōdār 'turner' (Bengali); कोंद kōnda 'engraver, lapidary setting or infixing gems' (Marathi) G.

 *sãghārɔ m. 'lathe' ; संघाट joinery; M. sãgaḍ 'double-canoe' Rebus: sangataras 'stone-cutter, mason'*

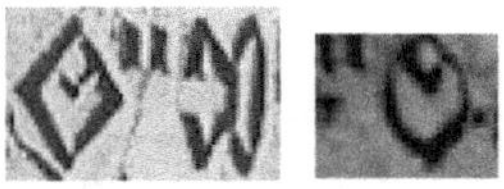

Bronze alloy workshop kañcu sal starting with bronze which is a tin + copper alloy or tin bronze (as distinguished from arsenical bronze,i.e. naturally occurring copper + arsenic).

kamaḍha 'crab' Rebus: *kammaṭa* 'mint, coiner'.

ḍato = claws of crab (Santali) Rebus: *dhātu* 'mineral ore'. Thus, together, rebus reading is: mineral ore, mint, bronze workshop.

aya kammaṭa.'coiner, mint alloy'

 *baraḍo* = spine; backbone (Tulu) Rebus: *baran, bharat* 'mixed alloys' (5 copper, 4 zinc and 1 tin) (Punjabi)

kanka 'rim of jar' Rebus: karṇīka 'account (scribe)' karṇī 'supercargo'

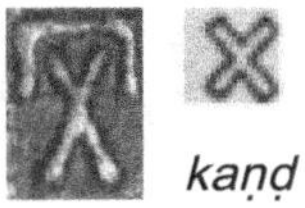 *dāṭu* 'cross'(Telugu) Rebus: *dhatu* 'mineral' (Santali). Ligatured with: *kanḍo* stool, seat Rebus: *kāṇḍā* 'metalware, tools, pots and pans'(Marathi). *kaṇḍ* = a furnace, altar (Santali) Thus 'metalware mineral'. This mineral could be either tin or zinc to create bronze or brass tools and metalware. That it is related to tin is seen in the variant of this X hieroglyph on Haifa tin ingots together with a 'notch' ligature.

 m50a *खोंड [khōṇḍa] m A young bull, a bullcalf. (Marathi) Rebus: kōdār 'turner' (Bengali); कोंद kōnda 'engraver, lapidary setting or infixing gems' (Marathi) G. sãghārɔ m. 'lathe' ; संघाट joinery; M. sãgaḍ 'double-canoe' Rebus: sangataras. संगतराश lit. 'to collect stones, stone-cutter, mason.'*

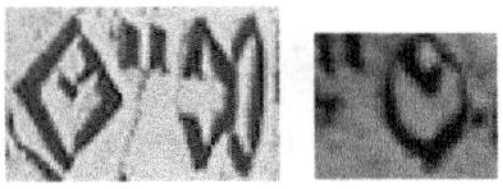

Bronze alloy workshop kañcu sal starting with bronze which is a tin + copper alloy or tin bronze (as distinguished from arsenical bronze,i.e. naturally occurring copper + arsenic).

kamaḍha 'crab' Rebus: *kammaṭa* 'mint, coiner'.

ḍato = claws of crab (Santali) Rebus: *dhātu* 'mineral ore'. Thus, together, rebus reading is: mineral ore, mint, bronze workshop.

aya kammaṭa.'coiner, mint alloy'

 *muka* 'ladle' (Tamil)(DEDR 4887) Rebus: *mũh* 'ingot' (Santali) *baṭa* = a kind of iron (Gujarati) *baṭa* = rimless pot (Kannada) Thus, iron ingot.

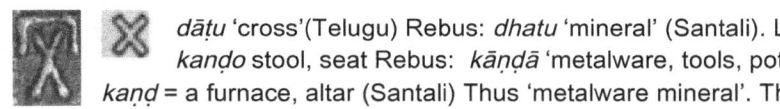

kolom 'three' Rebus: kolami 'smithy, forge'

|||| Numeral 4: *gaṇḍa* 'four' Rebus: *kaṇḍa* 'furnace, fire-altar' (Santali).
||| Numeral 3: *kolom* 'three' Rebus: *kolami* 'smithy, forge'.

 सांड [sāṇḍa] *f* (षद S) An outlet for superfluous water (as through a dam or mound); a sluice, a floodvent. Rebus: सांडणी [sāṇḍaṇī] *f* (H) An instrument of goldsmiths. It is hooked or curved at the extremity; and is used to draw things out of the fire.

 kanka 'rim of jar' Rebus: karṇīka 'account (scribe)' karṇī 'supercargo'

Chanhdaro 7a *खोंड [khōṇḍa] m A young bull, a bullcalf. (Marathi) Rebus: kõdār 'turner' (Bengali); कोंद kōnda 'engraver, lapidary setting or infixing gems' (Marathi) G. sãghāṛɔ m. 'lathe' ; संघाट joinery; M. sãgaḍ 'double-canoe' Rebus: sangataras 'stone-cutter, mason'*

 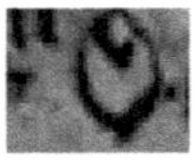

Bronze alloy workshop kañcu sal starting with bronze which is a tin + copper alloy or tin bronze (as distinguished from arsenical bronze,i.e. naturally occurring copper + arsenic).
kamaḍha 'crab' Rebus: *kammaṭa* 'mint, coiner'.
ḍato = claws of crab (Santali) Rebus: *dhātu* 'mineral ore'. Thus, together, rebus reading is: mineral ore, mint, bronze workshop.

aya kammaṭa.'coiner, mint alloy'

 *muka* 'ladle' (Tamil)(DEDR 4887) Rebus: *mũh* 'ingot' (Santali) *baṭa* = a kind of iron (Gujarati) *baṭa* = rimless pot (Kannada) Thus, iron ingot.

kolom 'three' Rebus: kolami 'smithy, forge'

kāṇḍa 'arrow' (Sanskrit) Rebus:*khāṇḍa* 'tools, pots and pans, metal-ware'. Rebus 2: kaṇḍ 'fire-altar' (Santali)

M-793 A

m793A

खोंड [khōṇḍa] m A young bull, a bullcalf. (Marathi) Rebus: kõdār 'turner' (Bengali); कोंद kōnda 'engraver, lapidary setting or infixing gems' (Marathi) G. sãghāṛɔ m. 'lathe' ; संघाट joinery; M. sãgaḍ 'double-canoe' Rebus: sangataras 'stone-cutter, mason'

Bronze alloy workshop kañcu sal starting with bronze which is a tin + copper alloy or tin bronze (as distinguished from arsenical bronze,i.e. naturally occurring copper + arsenic).
kamaḍha 'crab' Rebus: *kammaṭa* 'mint, coiner'.
ḍato = claws of crab (Santali) Rebus: *dhātu* 'mineral ore'. Thus, together, rebus reading is: mineral ore, mint, bronze workshop.

aya kammaṭa.'coiner, mint alloy'
aya aḍaren (homonym: aduru)'alloy native metal'

 *loa* 'ficus religiosa' Rebus: *lo* 'iron' (Sanskrit) PLUS unique ligatures: लोखंड [lōkhaṇḍa

] *n* (लोह् S) Iron. लोखंडाचे चणे खावविणें or चारणें To oppress grievously.लोखंडकाम [lōkhaṇḍakāma] *n* Iron work; that portion (of a building, machine &c.) which consists of iron. 2 The business of an ironsmith.लोखंडी [lōkhaṇḍī] *a* (लोखंड) Composed of iron; relating to iron. (Marathi)
kanka 'rim of jar' Rebus: karṇīka 'account (scribe)' karṇī 'supercargo'

m198A*खोंड [khōṇḍa] m A young bull, a bullcalf. (Marathi) Rebus: kõdār 'turner' (Bengali); कोंद kōnda 'engraver, lapidary setting or infixing gems' (Marathi) G. sãghārɔ m. 'lathe' ; संघाट joinery; M. sãgaḍ 'double-canoe' Rebus: sangataras. संगतराश lit. 'to collect stones, stone-cutter, mason.'*

Bronze alloy  workshop kañcu sal starting with bronze which is a tin + copper alloy or tin bronze (as distinguished from arsenical bronze, i.e. naturally occurring copper + arsenic).

dula 'pair' Rebus: dul 'cast metal' PLUS *kamaḍha* 'crab' Rebus: *kammaṭa* 'mint, coiner'. *ḍato* = claws of crab (Santali) Rebus: *dhātu* 'mineral ore' Thus, mint + mineral castings.

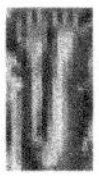

dula 'pair' Rebus: dul 'cast metal' *mogge* 'sprout, bud' Rebus: *mũh* 'ingot' (Santali) Thus, cast metal ingot. *dula* 'pair' Rebus: *dul* 'cast (metal)' PLUS*kana, kanac* = corner (Santali); Rebus: *kañcu* = bronze (Telugu) Thus, cast bronze.

kanka 'rim of jar' Rebus: *karṇīka* 'account (scribe)' *karṇī* 'supercargo'

m1752a*खोंड [khōṇḍa] m A young bull, a bullcalf. (Marathi) Rebus: kõdār 'turner' (Bengali); कोंद kōnda 'engraver, lapidary setting or infixing gems' (Marathi) G. sãghārɔ m. 'lathe' ; संघाट joinery; M. sãgaḍ 'double-canoe' Rebus: sangataras. संगतराश lit. 'to collect stones, stone-cutter, mason.'*

Bronze alloy workshop kañcu sal starting with bronze which is a tin + copper alloy or tin bronze (as distinguished from arsenical bronze, i.e. naturally occurring copper + arsenic).
baṭa = rimless pot (Kannada) Rebus:) *baṭa* = a kind of iron (G.)) *bhaṭa* furnace (Gujarati) Thus, iron ingot. PLUS 'notch': खांडा [*khāṇḍā*] *m* A jag, notch, or indentation (as upon the edge of a tool or weapon). Rebus: *kāṇḍa* 'tools, pots and pans and metal-ware'

dula 'pair' Rebus: dul 'cast metal' *mogge* 'sprout, bud' Rebus: *mũh* 'ingot' (Santali)

kanka 'rim of jar' Rebus: *karṇīka* 'account (scribe)' *karṇī* 'supercargo'

M-1851 A bis

m1851A*खोंड [khōṇḍa] m A young bull, a bullcalf. (Marathi) Rebus: kõdār 'turner' (Bengali); कोंद kōnda 'engraver, lapidary setting or infixing gems' (Marathi) G. sãghārɔ m. 'lathe' ; संघाट joinery; M. sãgaḍ 'double-canoe' Rebus: sangataras. संगतराश lit. 'to collect stones, stone-cutter, mason.'*

Bronze  alloy workshop kañcu sal starting with bronze which is a tin + copper alloy or tin bronze (as distinguished from arsenical bronze, i.e. naturally occurring copper + arsenic).

kanka 'rim of jar' Rebus: karṇīka 'account (scribe)' karṇī 'supercargo'

kəṭhā´r, kc. *kuṭhār* m. ' granary, storeroom '(WPah.)(CDIAL 3550). *koṭhārī m.* ' storekeeper'
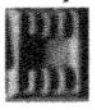
(Gujarati)(CDIAL 3551) Thus, storeroom (of) *kolom* 'three' Rebus: *kolami* 'smithy, forge'. Dula 'pair' Rebus: dul 'cast metal' Thus, together *dul kolami kuṭhār* 'metal smithy castings storeroom'

dula 'pair' Rebus: dul 'cast metal'

'Duck' hieroglyph: *karaṇḍa* 'duck' (Sanskrit) *karaṛa* 'a very large aquatic bird' (Sindhi)

Rebus: करडा [*karaḍā*] Hard from alloy--iron, silver &c. (Marathi) () dula 'pair' Rebus: dul 'cast metal' PLUS *kuṭila* 'bent' CDIAL 3230 kuṭi— in cmpd. 'curve', *kuṭika*— 'bent' MBh. Rebus: *kuṭila, katthīl* = bronze (8 parts copper and 2 parts tin) Thus, cast bronze.

kolmo 'paddy plant' Rebus: *kolami* 'smithy, forge' Vikalpa: *mogge* 'sprout, bud' Rebus: *mũh* 'ingot' (Santali) dolu 'plant of shoot height' Rebus: dul 'cast metal'

kana, kanac = corner (Santali); Rebus: *kañcu* = bronze (Telugu) infixed: खांडा [*khāṇḍā*] *m* A jag, notch, or indentation (as upon the edge of a tool or weapon). Rebus: *kāṇḍa* 'tools, pots and pans and metal-ware' Thus, bronze metalware.

h301B

h787B
h786B

Bronze alloy workshop kañcu sal starting with bronze which is a tin + copper alloy or tin bronze (as distinguished from arsenical bronze, i.e. naturally occurring copper + arsenic). *kamaḍha* 'bow and arrow' Rebus: *kammaṭa* 'mint, coiner'.

| *koḍa* 'one' Rebus: *koḍ* 'workshop' PLUS |||| Numeral 4: gaṇḍa 'four' Rebus: kaṇḍa 'furnace, fire-altar' (Santali)

Unnumbered *खोंड [khōṇḍa] m A young bull, a bullcalf. (Marathi) Rebus: kōdār 'turner' (Bengali); कोंद kōnda 'engraver, lapidary setting or infixing gems' (Marathi) G. sãghāṛɔ m. 'lathe' ; संघाट joinery; M. sãgaḍ 'double-canoe' Rebus: sangataras. संगतराश lit. 'to collect stones, stone-cutter, mason.'*

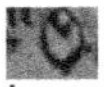
Bronze alloy workshop kañcu sal starting with bronze which is a tin + copper alloy or tin bronze (as distinguished from arsenical bronze, i.e. naturally occurring copper + arsenic). *kamaḍha* 'bow and arrow' Rebus: *kammaṭa* 'mint, coiner'. Duplicated: dula 'pair' Rebus: dul 'cast metal' Thus, cast metal mint *aya kammaṭa.*'coiner, mint alloy' *aya aḍaren (homonym: aduru)*'alloy native metal' PLUS circumscript |||| Numeral 4: gaṇḍa 'four' Rebus: kaṇḍa 'furnace, fire-altar' (Santali)

m295A kol 'tiger' Rebus: kolhe 'smelter' kolom 'three' Rebus: kolami 'smithy, forge'. Thus, the message is: smelter's forge.

kole.l 'temple' Rebus: kole.l 'smithy'

Bronze  alloy workshop kañcu sal starting with bronze which is a tin + copper alloy or tin bronze (as distinguished from arsenical bronze, i.e. naturally occurring copper + arsenic).

kanka 'rim of jar' Rebus: karṇīka 'account (scribe)' karṇī 'supercargo'

meḍ 'body' Rebus: *meḍ* 'iron' (Ho.) काठी [kāṭhī] *f* (काष्ट S) 'frame or structure of the body' (Marathi) Rebus: खंडी [khanḍī] measure of weight (Marathi) *கண்டி; kaṇṭi, n.*
< *Mhr. khanḍil. [T. Tu. khanḍi, M. kanḍi.]* Candy, a weight, stated to be roughly

equivalent to 500 lbs.

h177A

 Bronze alloy workshop kañcu sal starting with bronze which is a tin + copper alloy or tin bronze (as distinguished from arsenical bronze, i.e. naturally occurring copper + arsenic). | *koḍa* 'one' Rebus: *koḍ* 'workshop'

 *muka* 'ladle' (Tamil)(DEDR 4887) Rebus: *mũh* 'ingot' (Santali) *baṭa* = rimless pot (Kannada) Rebus:) *baṭa* = a kind of iron (G.)) *bhaṭa* furnace (Gujarati) Thus, iron ingot.

 water-carrier hieroglyph *kuṭi*; Rebus: *kuṭhi* 'smelter furnace'.
kolom 'three' Rebus: kolami 'smithy, forge'.

 *kanka* 'rim of jar' Rebus: *karṇika* 'account (scribe)' *karṇī* 'supercargo'

m941a *खोंड [khōṇḍa] m A young bull, a bullcalf. (Marathi) Rebus: kõdār 'turner' (Bengali); कोंद kōnda 'engraver, lapidary setting or infixing gems' (Marathi) G. sãghāṛɔ m. 'lathe' ; संघाट joinery; M. sãgaḍ 'double-canoe' Rebus: sangataras. संगतराश lit. 'to collect stones, stone-cutter, mason.'*

 Bronze alloy workshop kañcu sal starting with bronze which is a tin + copper alloy or tin bronze (as distinguished from arsenical bronze, i.e. naturally occurring copper + arsenic). | *koḍa* 'one' Rebus: *koḍ* 'workshop'*aya kammaṭa*.'coiner, mint alloy'

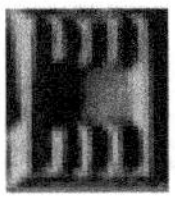 *kəṭhā´r*, kc. *kuṭhār* m. ' granary, storeroom '(WPah.)(CDIAL 3550). *koṭhārī m.* ' storekeeper' (Gujarati)(CDIAL 3551) Thus, storeroom (of) *kolom* 'three' Rebus: *kolami* 'smithy, forge'. Dula 'pair' Rebus: dul 'cast metal' Thus, together *dul kolami kuṭhār* 'metal smithy castings storeroom'

 *kanka* 'rim of jar' Rebus: *karṇika* 'account (scribe)' *karṇī* 'supercargo'

m1161a *ibha* 'elephant' Rebus: *ib* 'iron' *ibbo* 'merchant' (Gujarati) | *koḍa* 'one' Rebus: *koḍ* 'workshop' *ayo* 'fish' Rebus: *aya* 'iron' *ayas* 'metal' *kāṇḍa* 'arrow' (Sanskrit) Rebus:*khāṇḍa* 'tools, pots and pans, metal-ware'. Rebus 2: kaṇḍ 'fire-altar' (Santali)

m1914A *ibha* 'elephant' Rebus: *ib* 'iron' *ibbo* 'merchant' (Gujarati)

 Bronze alloy workshop kañcu sal starting with bronze which is a tin + copper alloy or tin bronze (as distinguished from arsenical bronze, i.e. naturally occurring copper + arsenic).

kana, kanac = corner (Santali); Rebus: *kañcu* = bronze (Telugu) PLUS खांडा [*khāṇḍā*] *m* A jag, notch, or indentation (as upon the edge of a tool or weapon). Rebus: *kāṇḍa* 'tools, pots and pans and metal-ware' Thus, bronze metalware.

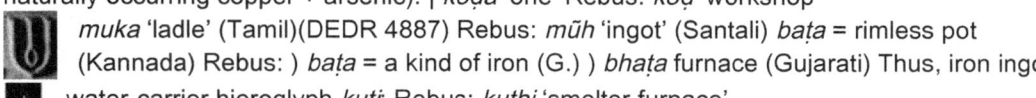

m19A

h266Aखोंड *[khōṇḍa] m A young bull, a bullcalf. (Marathi) Rebus: kõdār 'turner' (Bengali);* कोंद *kōnda 'engraver, lapidary setting or infixing gems' (Marathi) G. sãghāṛɔ m. 'lathe' ;* संघाट *joinery; M. sãgaḍ 'double-canoe' Rebus: sangataras.* संगतराश *lit. 'to collect stones, stone-cutter, mason.'*

 Bronze alloy workshop kañcu sal starting with bronze which is a tin + copper alloy or tin bronze (as distinguished from arsenical bronze, i.e. naturally occurring copper + arsenic).

H-154 a

h154A

 Bronze alloy workshop kañcu sal starting with bronze which is a tin + copper alloy or tin bronze (as distinguished from arsenical bronze, i.e. naturally occurring copper + arsenic). *ḍhanga* = a crook used for pulling down the branches of trees, for goats, sheep and camels (P.) Rebus:*ḍhangar* blacksmith'

 PLUS

kharedo = a currycomb (Gujarati) खरारा [*kharārā*] *m* (H) A currycomb. 2 Currying a horse. (Marathi) Rebus: करडा [*karaḍā*] Hard from alloy--iron, silver &c. (Marathi) *kharādī*' turner' (Gujarati)

 *dula* 'pair' Rebus: *dul* 'cast (metal)' PLUS*kana, kanac* = corner (Santali); Rebus: *kañcu* = bronze (Telugu) PLUS infixed kolmo 'paddy plant' Rebus: kolami 'smithy, forge'. Thus, cast bronze smithy, forge. Or, *mogge* 'sprout, bud' Rebus: *mũh* 'ingot' (Santali)Thus, cast bronze ingot. Read as: *kañcu dul mũh 'bronze cast ingot'*

  water-carrier hieroglyph *kuṭi*; Rebus: *kuṭhi* 'smelter furnace'. PLUS 'rim of jar':

 kanka 'rim of jar' Rebus: karṇīka 'account (scribe)' karṇī 'supercargo'

Dlp-1 a

Dlv-1 A

Dholavira 1a*खोंड [khōṇḍa] m A young bull, a bullcalf. (Marathi) Rebus: kõdār 'turner' (Bengali);* कोंद *kōnda 'engraver, lapidary setting or infixing gems' (Marathi) G. sãghāṛɔ m. 'lathe' ;* संघाट *joinery; M. sãgaḍ 'double-canoe' Rebus: sangataras.* संगतराश *lit. 'to collect stones, stone-cutter, mason.'*

Bronze alloy workshop kañcu sal starting with bronze which is a tin + copper alloy or tin bronze (as distinguished from arsenical bronze, i.e. naturally occurring copper + arsenic).

PLUS 'notch': खांडा [*khāṇḍā*] *m* A jag, notch, or indentation (as upon the edge of a tool or weapon). Rebus: *kāṇḍa* 'tools, pots and pans and metal-ware'

loa 'ficus religiosa' Rebus: *lo* 'iron' (Sanskrit)

water-carrier hieroglyph *kuṭi*; Rebus: *kuṭhi* 'smelter furnace'. PLUS 'rim of jar':

kanka 'rim of jar' Rebus: karṇīka 'account (scribe)' karṇī 'supercargo'

Desalpur 1a

 Bronze alloy workshop kañcu sal starting with bronze which is a tin + copper alloy or tin bronze (as distinguished from arsenical bronze, i.e. naturally occurring copper + arsenic).

PLUS 'notch': खांडा [*khāṇḍā*] *m* A jag, notch, or indentation (as upon the edge of a tool or weapon). Rebus: *kāṇḍa* 'tools, pots and pans and metal-ware' *aya kammaṭa.*'coiner, mint alloy' *ayo ḍhālako* 'alloy metal ingot'
ranku 'antelope' Rebus: ranku 'tin'

 *kuṭila* 'bent' CDIAL 3230 kuṭi— in cmpd. 'curve', *kuṭika—* 'bent' MBh. Rebus: *kuṭila, katthīl* = bronze (8 parts copper and 2 parts tin)

 *kanka* 'rim of jar' Rebus: *karṇīka* 'account (scribe)' *karṇī* 'supercargo'

h1713A

 Bronze alloy workshop kañcu sal starting with bronze which is a tin + copper alloy or tin bronze (as distinguished from arsenical bronze, i.e. naturally occurring copper + arsenic).

kolom 'three' Rebus: kolami 'smithy, forge'

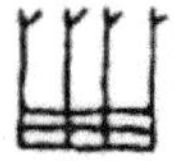 Vikalpa 1: ढांक [ḍhāṅka] *n* ढांकळ *f* C An old and decaying tree: also the stump or naked stalks and stem remaining (of a little plant).(Marathi)
WPah.ktg. *ḍāṅg* f. (obl. -- *a*) ' stick ', *ḍaṅgrɔ* m. ' stalk (of a plant) ' Allograph: डांग [ḍāṅga] *m n* (H Peak or summit of a hill.) A name for the wild, hilly, and ascending tract along

the range (esp. of the upper or eastern side) of the Sayhádri gháṭs in the North Desh. डांग is, in the northern division of the Sayhádri range (about Náshik &c.), what मावळ is in the southern (about Satárá &c.)(Marathi)

Rebus:*ḍhangar* blacksmith' *ḍaṅgrɔ* m. ' axe ', poet. *ḍaṅgru* m., °*ref*.; J. *ḍãgrā* m. ' small weapon like axe ', P. *ḍaṅgorī* f. ' small staff or club ' (Him.I 84).(CDIAL 5520).

gaṇḍā 'four' Rebus: kaṇḍā 'fire-altar'
Vikalpa 2: కండె [kaṇḍe] *kaṇḍe*. [Telugu] n. A head or ear of millet or maize. జొన్నకంకి (Telugu) *kāṛ* 'stack of stalks of large millet' (Maithili) kãḍ 2 काँड् m. a section, part in general; a cluster, bundle, multitude (Śiv. 32). kãḍ 1 काँड् । काण्डः m. the stalk or stem of a reed, grass, or the like, straw. In the compound with dan 5 (p. 221*a*, l. 13) the word is spelt kãḍ.

kaṇḍe 'stalk or stem of straw' Rebus : *khāṇḍa* 'tools, pots and pans, metal-ware'. Rebus 2: kaṇḍ 'fire-altar' (Santali)

m1818a खोंड *[khōṇḍa] m A young bull, a bullcalf. (Marathi) Rebus: kõdār 'turner' (Bengali);* कोंद *kōnda 'engraver, lapidary setting or infixing gems' (Marathi) G. sãghāṛɔ m. 'lathe' ;* संघाट *joinery; M. sãgaḍ 'double-canoe' Rebus: sangataras.* संगतराश *lit. 'to collect stones, stone-cutter, mason.'*

 *kanac* 'corner' Rebus: *kañcu* 'bronze'

 notch+slanted stroke reads rebus: *ḍhālako kāṇḍa* 'ingot, tools, pots and pans and metal-ware'.*ḍhāḷ* 'a slope'; 'inclination of a plane' (G.); *ḍhāḷiyum* = adj. sloping, inclining (G.) Rebus: *ḍhālako* = a large metal ingot (G.) *ḍhālakī* = a metal heated and poured into a mould; a solid piece of metal; an ingot (Gujarati) PLUS खांडा [*khāṇḍā*] *m* A jag, notch, or indentation

(as upon the edge of a tool or weapon). Rebus: *kāṇḍa* 'tools, pots and pans and metal-ware'

Thus, together, the pair reads: āra erako khāṇḍā 'brass, moltencast copper metalware'.

kanka 'rim of jar' Rebus: *karṇīka* 'account (scribe)' *karṇī* 'supercargo'

m1869Aखोंड *[khōṇḍa] m A young bull, a bullcalf. (Marathi) Rebus: kõdār 'turner' (Bengali); कोंद kōnda 'engraver, lapidary setting or infixing gems' (Marathi) G. sãghārɔ m. 'lathe' ; संघाट joinery; M. sãgaḍ 'double-canoe' Rebus: sangataras. संगतराश lit. 'to collect stones, stone-cutter, mason.'*

kanac 'corner' Rebus: *kañcu* 'bronze'

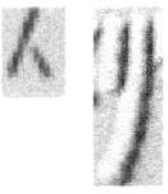

notch+slanted stroke reads rebus: *ḍhālako kāṇḍa* 'ingot, tools, pots and pans and metal-ware'.*dhāḷ* 'a slope'; 'inclination of a plane' (G.); *ḍhāḷiyum* = adj. sloping, inclining (G.) Rebus: *ḍhālako* = a large metal ingot (G.) *ḍhālakī* = a metal heated and poured into a mould; a solid piece of metal; an ingot (Gujarati) PLUS खांडा [*khāṇḍā*] *m* A jag, notch, or indentation (as upon the edge of a tool or weapon). Rebus: *kāṇḍa* 'tools, pots and pans and metal-ware' *Thus, together, the pair reads: āra erako khāṇḍā* 'brass, moltencast copper metalware'.

kanka 'rim of jar' Rebus: *karṇīka* 'account (scribe)' *karṇī* 'supercargo'

h511Aखोंड *[khōṇḍa] m A young bull, a bullcalf. (Marathi) Rebus: kõdār 'turner' (Bengali); कोंद kōnda 'engraver, lapidary setting or infixing gems' (Marathi) G. sãghārɔ m. 'lathe' ; संघाट joinery; M. sãgaḍ 'double-canoe' Rebus: sangataras. संगतराश lit. 'to collect stones, stone-cutter, mason.'*

kanac 'corner' Rebus: *kañcu* 'bronze'

kolmo 'paddy plant' Rebus: *kolami* 'smithy, forge' Vikalpa: *mogge* 'sprout, bud' Rebus: *mūh* 'ingot' (Santali) dolu 'plant of shoot height' Rebus: dul 'cast metal'

m492B *balad* m. ' ox ', gng. *bald*, (Ku.) *barad*, id. (N. Tarai) Rebus: *bharat* (5 copper, 4 zinc and 1 tin)(Punjabi). Duplicated: dula 'pair' Rebus: dul 'cast metal'. Thus cast bharat (alloy of copper, zinc and tin).

kanac 'corner' Rebus: *kañcu* 'bronze'

kəṭhā´r, kc. *kuṭhār* m. ' granary, storeroom '(WPah.)(CDIAL 3550). *koṭhārī m.* ' storekeeper' (Gujarati)(CDIAL 3551) Thus, storeroom (of) *kolom* 'three' Rebus: *kolami* 'smithy, forge'. Dula 'pair' Rebus: dul 'cast metal' Thus, together *dul kolami kuṭhār* 'metal smithy castings storeroom' Or, kole.l 'temple' Rebus: kole.l 'smithy'.

m170Aखोंड *[khōṇḍa] m A young bull, a bullcalf. (Marathi) Rebus: kõdār 'turner' (Bengali); कोंद kōnda 'engraver, lapidary setting or infixing gems' (Marathi) G.*

sãghāṛɔ m. 'lathe' ; संघाट joinery; M. sāgaḍ 'double-canoe' Rebus: sangataras. संगतराश lit. 'to collect stones, stone-cutter, mason.'
kanac 'corner' Rebus: *kañcu* 'bronze'

muka 'ladle' (Tamil)(DEDR 4887) Rebus: *mũh* 'ingot' (Santali) *baṭa* = rimless pot (Kannada) Rebus:) *baṭa* = a kind of iron (G.)) *bhaṭa* furnace (Gujarati) Thus, iron ingot.
dula 'two' Rebus: dul 'cast metal'

'Arrow' sign hieroglyph (variant) This is a ligature of 'lid of pot' hieroglyph superscript on 'a linear stroke' numeral hieroglyph.*aḍaren* 'cover of pot or lid' Rebus: *aduru* 'native, unsmelted metal' PLUS koḍ = one (Santali); koḍ 'workshop' (G.)

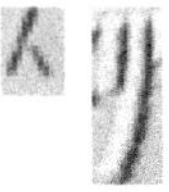
notch+slanted stroke reads rebus: *ḍhālako kāṇḍa* 'ingot, tools, pots and pans and metal-ware'.*dhāḷ* 'a slope'; 'inclination of a plane' (G.); *ḍhāḷiyum* = adj. sloping, inclining (G.) Rebus: *ḍhālako* = a large metal ingot (G.) *ḍhālakī* = a metal heated and poured into a mould; a solid piece of metal; an ingot (Gujarati) PLUS खांडा [*khāṇḍā*] *m* A jag, notch, or indentation (as upon the edge of a tool or weapon). Rebus: *kāṇḍa* 'tools, pots and pans and metal-ware' *Thus, together, the pair reads: āra erako khāṇḍā* 'brass, moltencast copper metalware'.

kolmo 'paddy plant' Rebus: *kolami* 'smithy, forge' Vikalpa: *mogge* 'sprout, bud' Rebus: *mũh* 'ingot' (Santali) dolu 'plant of shoot height' Rebus: dul 'cast metal'
mogge 'sprout, bud' Rebus*: mũh* 'ingot'

kanka 'rim of jar' Rebus: *karṇīka* 'account (scribe)' *karṇī* 'supercargo'

Chanhudaro 13A

dula 'pair' Rebus: dul 'cast metal' *mogge* 'sprout, bud' Rebus: *mũh* 'ingot' (Santali) Thus, cast metal ingot.
PLUS

kanka 'rim of jar' Rebus: *karṇīka* 'account (scribe)' *karṇī* 'supercargo'
Thus, cast metal ingot supercargo

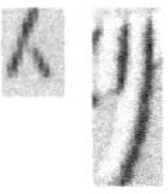
notch+slanted stroke reads rebus: *ḍhālako kāṇḍa* 'ingot, tools, pots and pans and metal-ware'.*dhāḷ* 'a slope'; 'inclination of a plane' (G.); *ḍhāḷiyum* = adj. sloping, inclining (G.) Rebus: *ḍhālako* = a large metal ingot (G.) *ḍhālakī* = a metal heated and poured into a mould; a solid piece of metal; an ingot (Gujarati) PLUS खांडा [*khāṇḍā*] *m* A jag, notch, or indentation (as upon the edge of a tool or weapon). Rebus: *kāṇḍa* 'tools, pots and pans and metal-ware' *Thus, together, the pair reads: āra erako khāṇḍā* 'brass, moltencast copper metalware'.
dula 'two' Rebus: dul 'cast metal'

ayo 'fish' Rebus: *aya* 'iron' *ayas* 'metal'

meḍ 'body' Rebus: *meḍ* 'iron' (Ho.) काठी [kāṭhī] *f* (काष्ट S) 'frame or structure of the body' (Marathi) Rebus: खंडी [khaṇḍī] measure of weight (Marathi) *கண்டி; kaṇṭi, n. < Mhr. khaṇḍil. [T. Tu. khaṇḍi, M. kaṇḍi.]* Candy, a weight, stated to be roughly equivalent

to 500 lbs.

h102a खोंड *[khōṇḍa] m A young bull, a bullcalf. (Marathi) Rebus: kõdār 'turner' (Bengali);* कोंद *kōnda 'engraver, lapidary setting or infixing gems' (Marathi) G. sãghāṛɔ m. 'lathe' ;* संघाट *joinery; M. sãgaḍ 'double-canoe' Rebus: sangataras.* संगतराश *lit. 'to collect stones, stone-cutter, mason.'*

 *kanac* 'corner' Rebus: *kañcu* 'bronze'

dula 'pair' Rebus:  dul 'cast metal' *mogge* 'sprout, bud' Rebus: *mũh* 'ingot' (Santali) Thus, cast metal ingot.

aya kammaṭa.'coiner, mint alloy'

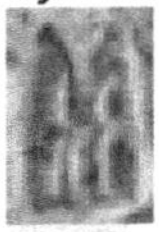 Ligature: two peaks: mēḍu height, rising ground, hillock (Kannada) Rebus: *meḍ* 'iron' (Ho.) dula 'pair' Rebus: dul 'cast metal' PLUS |||| Numeral 4: gaṇḍa 'four' Rebus: kaṇḍa 'furnace, fire-altar' (Santali)

 *kanka* 'rim of jar' Rebus: *karṇīka* 'account (scribe)' *karṇī* 'supercargo'

m282a *ibha* 'elephant' Rebus: *ib* 'iron' *ibbo* 'merchant' (Gujarati)

 Bronze alloy workshop kañcu sal starting with bronze which is a tin + copper alloy or tin bronze (as distinguished from arsenical bronze, i.e. naturally occurring copper + arsenic).

 *koḍi* 'flag' (Ta.)(DEDR 2049). Rebus 1: *koḍ* 'workshop' (Kuwi) Rebus 2: *khõḍ* m. 'pit', *khõḍü* f. 'small pit' (Kashmiri. CDIAL 3947).

 *meḍ* 'body' Rebus: *meḍ* 'iron' (Ho.) काठी [kāṭhī] *f* (काष्ट S) 'frame or structure of the body' (Marathi) Rebus: खंडी [khaṇḍī] measure of weight (Marathi) *கண்டி; kaṇṭi, n. < Mhr. khaṇḍil. [T. Tu. khaṇḍi, M. kaṇḍi.]* Candy, a weight, stated to be roughly equivalent to 500 lbs.

  water-carrier hieroglyph *kuṭi*; Rebus: *kuṭhi* 'smelter furnace'. PLUS 'rim of jar':

 kanka 'rim of jar' Rebus: karṇīka 'account (scribe)' karṇī 'supercargo'

m849A खोंड *[khōṇḍa] m A young bull, a bullcalf. (Marathi) Rebus: kõdār 'turner' (Bengali);* कोंद *kōnda 'engraver, lapidary setting or infixing gems' (Marathi) G. sãghāṛɔ m. 'lathe' ;* संघाट *joinery; M. sãgaḍ 'double-canoe' Rebus: sangataras 'stone-cutter, mason'*

kanac 'corner' Rebus: *kañcu* 'bronze'

kanac 'corner' Rebus: *kañcu* 'bronze'

 *koḍi* 'flag' (Ta.)(DEDR 2049). Rebus 1: *koḍ* 'workshop' (Kuwi) Rebus 2: *khõḍ* m. 'pit', *khõḍü* f. 'small pit' (Kashmiri. CDIAL 3947).

aya kāṇḍa 'alloy metalware'

kāṇḍa 'arrow' (Sanskrit) Rebus:*khāṇḍa* 'tools, pots and pans, metal-ware'. Rebus 2: kaṇḍ 'fire-altar' (Santali)
mēḍu height, rising ground, hillock (Kannada) Rebus: : *meḍ* 'iron' (Ho.)
ranku 'liquid measure' Rebus: ranku 'tin'

 *dhāḷ* 'a slope'; 'inclination of a plane' (G.); *ḍhāḷiyum* = adj. sloping, inclining (G.) Rebus: *ḍhālako* = a large metal ingot (G.) *ḍhālakī* = a metal heated and poured into a mould; a solid piece of metal; an ingot (Gujarati) PLUS खांडा [*khāṇḍā*] *m* A jag, notch, or indentation (as upon the edge of a tool or weapon). Rebus: *kāṇḍa* 'tools, pots and pans and metal-ware' dola 'hole' Rebus: dul 'cast metal'.

m1687a खोंड [khōṇḍa] m A young bull, a bullcalf. (Marathi) Rebus: kõdār 'turner' (Bengali); कोंद kōnda 'engraver, lapidary setting or infixing gems' (Marathi) G. sãghāṛɔ m. 'lathe' ; संघाट joinery; M. sāgaḍ 'double-canoe' Rebus: sangataras 'stone-cutter, mason'

kanac 'corner' Rebus: *kañcu* 'bronze'
ayo 'fish' Rebus: *aya* 'iron' *ayas* 'metal'

kāṇḍa 'arrow' (Sanskrit) Rebus:*khāṇḍa* 'tools, pots and pans, metal-ware'. Rebus 2: kaṇḍ 'fire-altar' (Santali)

m1714a खोंड [khōṇḍa] m A young bull, a bullcalf. (Marathi) Rebus: kõdār 'turner' (Bengali); कोंद kōnda 'engraver, lapidary setting or infixing gems' (Marathi) G. sãghāṛɔ m. 'lathe' ; संघाट joinery; M. sāgaḍ 'double-canoe' Rebus: sangataras 'stone-cutter, mason'

kanac 'corner' Rebus: *kañcu* 'bronze'

 kanka 'rim of jar' Rebus: karṇīka 'account (scribe)' karṇī 'supercargo'
| *koḍa* 'one' Rebus: *koḍ* 'workshop' *ayo* 'fish' Rebus: *aya* 'iron' *ayas* 'metal'
|||| Numeral 4: gaṇḍa 'four' Rebus: kaṇḍa 'furnace, fire-altar' (Santali)
||| Numeral 3: kolom 'three' Rebus: kolami 'smithy, forge'

m1717a

खोंड [khōṇḍa] m A young bull, a bullcalf. (Marathi) Rebus: kõdār 'turner' (Bengali); कोंद kōnda 'engraver, lapidary setting or infixing gems' (Marathi) G. sãghāṛɔ m. 'lathe' ; संघाट joinery; M. sāgaḍ 'double-canoe' Rebus: sangataras 'stone-cutter, mason'

kanac 'corner' Rebus: *kañcu* 'bronze'

 *koḍi* 'flag' (Ta.)(DEDR 2049). Rebus 1: *koḍ* 'workshop' (Kuwi) Rebus 2: *khõḍ* m. 'pit', *khõḍü* f. 'small pit' (Kashmiri. CDIAL 3947).
mēḍu height, rising ground, hillock (Kannada) Rebus: *mẽṛhẽt, meḍ* 'iron' (Munda.Ho.)
|||| Numeral 4: gaṇḍa 'four' Rebus: kaṇḍa 'furnace, fire-altar' (Santali)
||| Numeral 3: kolom 'three' Rebus: kolami 'smithy, forge'

 kanka 'rim of jar' Rebus: karṇīka 'account (scribe)' karṇī 'supercargo'
dola 'hole' Rebus: dul 'cast metal'.

H-300 B

h300B *kanac* 'corner' Rebus: *kañcu* 'bronze'

 *koḍi* 'flag' (Ta.)(DEDR 2049). Rebus 1: *koḍ* 'workshop' (Kuwi) Rebus 2: *khŏḍ* m. 'pit', *khŏḍü* f. 'small pit' (Kashmiri. CDIAL 3947).

dāṭu

 'cross'(Telugu) Rebus: *dhatu* 'mineral' (Santali).

Lothal 29a Repeated as epigraph on h54 Seal

PLUS *aḍaren* 'lid of pot' Rebus: aduru 'native metal'

h54a

खोंड [khōṇḍa] m A young bull, a bullcalf. (Marathi) Rebus: kõdār 'turner' (Bengali); कोंद kōnda 'engraver, lapidary setting or infixing gems' (Marathi) G. sãghāṛɔ m. 'lathe' ; संघाट joinery; M. sãgaḍ 'double-canoe' Rebus: sangataras 'stone-cutter, mason'

kanac 'corner' Rebus: *kañcu* 'bronze'

koḍi 'flag' (Ta.)(DEDR 2049). Rebus 1: *koḍ* 'workshop' (Kuwi) Rebus 2: *khŏḍ* m. 'pit', *khŏḍü* f. 'small pit' (Kashmiri. CDIAL 3947).

kolom 'three' Rebus: kolami 'smithy, forge

kolmo 'paddy plant' Rebus: *kolami* 'smithy, forge' Vikalpa: *mogge* 'sprout, bud' Rebus: *mũh* 'ingot' (Santali) dolu 'plant of shoot height' Rebus: dul 'cast metal'

Thus, together, ||| plus paddy plant read: cast smithy, *dul kolami.*

h694a

खोंड [khōṇḍa] m A young bull, a bullcalf. (Marathi) Rebus: kõdār 'turner' (Bengali); कोंद kōnda 'engraver, lapidary setting or infixing gems' (Marathi) G. sãghāṛɔ m. 'lathe' ; संघाट joinery; M. sãgaḍ 'double-canoe' Rebus: sangataras 'stone-cutter, mason'

kanac 'corner' Rebus: *kañcu* 'bronze'

 *koḍi* 'flag' (Ta.)(DEDR 2049). Rebus 1: *koḍ* 'workshop' (Kuwi) Rebus 2: *khŏḍ* m. 'pit', *khŏḍü* f. 'small pit' (Kashmiri. CDIAL 3947).

aya aḍaren (homonym: aduru)'alloy native metal'
ranku 'liquid measure' Rebus: ranku 'tin'
kolmo 'paddy plant' Rebus: kolami 'smithy, forge'

kanka ‘rim of jar’ Rebus: karṇīka ‘account (scribe)’ karṇī ‘supercargo’

m944a

खोंड [khōṇḍa] m A young bull, a bullcalf. (Marathi) Rebus: kõdār ‘turner’ (Bengali); कोंद kōnda ‘engraver, lapidary setting or infixing gems’ (Marathi) G. sãghāṛɔ m. ‘lathe’ ; संघाट joinery; M. sãgaḍ ‘double-canoe’ Rebus: sangataras ‘stone-cutter, mason’

kanac ‘corner’ Rebus: *kañcu* ‘bronze’

koḍi ‘flag’ (Ta.)(DEDR 2049). Rebus 1: *koḍ* ‘workshop’ (Kuwi) Rebus 2: *khōḍ* m. ‘pit’, *khōḍü* f. ‘small pit’ (Kashmiri. CDIAL 3947).

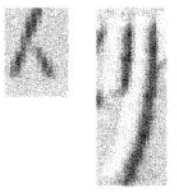

notch+slanted stroke reads rebus: *ḍhālako kāṇḍa* ‘ingot, tools, pots and pans and metal-ware’.*dhāḷ* ‘a slope’; ‘inclination of a plane’ (G.); *ḍhāḷiyum* = adj. sloping, inclining (G.) Rebus: *ḍhālako* = a large metal ingot (G.) *ḍhālakī* = a metal heated and poured into a mould; a solid piece of metal; an ingot (Gujarati) PLUS खांडा [*khāṇḍā*] *m* A jag, notch, or indentation (as upon the edge of a tool or weapon). Rebus: *kāṇḍa* ‘tools, pots and pans and metal-ware’ Thus, together, the three hieroglyph signs read: workshop metalware.

ayo ‘fish’ Rebus: *aya* ‘iron’ *ayas* ‘metal’

kanka ‘rim of jar’ Rebus: *karṇīka* ‘account (scribe)’ *karṇī* ‘supercargo’

meḍ ‘body’ Rebus: *meḍ* ‘iron’ (Ho.) काठी [kāṭhī] *f* (काष्ट S) ‘frame or structure of the body’ (Marathi) Rebus: खंडी [khaṇḍī] measure of weight (Marathi) *கண்டி; kaṇṭi, n. < Mhr. khaṇḍil. [T. Tu. khaṇḍi, M. kaṇḍi.]* Candy, a weight, stated to be roughly equivalent to 500 lbs.

m80a

खोंड [khōṇḍa] m A young bull, a bullcalf. (Marathi) Rebus: kõdār ‘turner’ (Bengali); कोंद kōnda ‘engraver, lapidary setting or infixing gems’ (Marathi) G. sãghāṛɔ m. ‘lathe’ ; संघाट joinery; M. sãgaḍ ‘double-canoe’ Rebus: sangataras ‘stone-cutter, mason’

kanac ‘corner’ Rebus: *kañcu* ‘bronze’

koḍi ‘flag’ (Ta.)(DEDR 2049). Rebus 1: *koḍ* ‘workshop’ (Kuwi) Rebus 2: *khōḍ* m. ‘pit’, *khōḍü* f. ‘small pit’ (Kashmiri. CDIAL 3947).

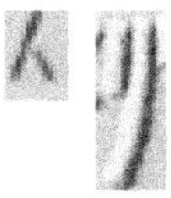

notch+slanted stroke reads rebus: *ḍhālako kāṇḍa* ‘ingot, tools, pots and pans and metal-ware’.*dhāḷ* ‘a slope’; ‘inclination of a plane’ (G.); *ḍhāḷiyum* = adj. sloping, inclining (G.) Rebus: *ḍhālako* = a large metal ingot (G.) *ḍhālakī* = a metal heated and poured into a mould; a solid piece of metal; an ingot (Gujarati) PLUS खांडा [*khāṇḍā*

] *m* A jag, notch, or indentation (as upon the edge of a tool or weapon). Rebus: *kāṇḍa* 'tools, pots and pans and metal-ware' Thus, together, the three hieroglyph signs read: workshop metalware.
kolom 'three' Rebus: kolami 'smithy, forge'

  water-carrier hieroglyph *kuṭi*; Rebus: *kuṭhi* 'smelter furnace'. PLUS 'rim of jar':

 kanka 'rim of jar' Rebus: karṇīka 'account (scribe)' karṇī 'supercargo'

H-102 b

h102b *kanac* 'corner' Rebus: *kañcu* 'bronze'

 kanka 'rim of jar' Rebus: karṇīka 'account (scribe)' karṇī 'supercargo'

M-1796 A

m1796A *खोंड [khōṇḍa] m A young bull, a bullcalf. (Marathi) Rebus: kõdār 'turner' (Bengali); कोंद kōnda 'engraver, lapidary setting or infixing gems' (Marathi) G. sãghārɔ m. 'lathe' ; संघाट joinery; M. sãgaḍ 'double-canoe' Rebus: sangataras 'stone-cutter, mason'*

kanac 'corner' Rebus: *kañcu* 'bronze'
mēḍu height, rising ground, hillock (Kannada) Rebus: *meḍ* 'iron' (Ho.) kolom 'three' Rebus: kolami 'smithy, forge' Thus, *meḍ kolami* 'iron smithy-forge'

 kanka 'rim of jar' Rebus: karṇīka 'account (scribe)' karṇī 'supercargo'
dula 'pair' Rebus: *dul* 'cast (metal)' PLUS*kana, kanac* = corner (Santali); Rebus: *kañcu* = bronze (Telugu) Thus, cast bronze.
dula 'pair' Rebus: 'cast metal'
 kanka 'rim of jar' Rebus: karṇīka 'account (scribe)' karṇī 'supercargo'

M-1888 a

m1888a *balad* m. ' ox ', gng. *bald*, (Ku.) *barad*, id. (N. Tarai) Rebus: *bharat* (5 copper, 4 zinc and 1 tin)(Punjabi) *pattar* 'trough' Rebus*: pattar* 'guild'. Thus, copper-zinc-tin alloy (worker) guild.

PLUS*kana, kanac* = corner (Santali); Rebus: *kañcu* = bronze (Telugu)
kolom 'three' Rebus: kolami 'smithy, forge'

  water-carrier hieroglyph *kuṭi*; Rebus: *kuṭhi* 'smelter furnace'. PLUS 'rim of

 jar':
kanka 'rim of jar' Rebus: karṇīka 'account (scribe)' karṇī 'supercargo'

m306A dula ‘pair’ Rebus: dul ‘cast metal’ kol ‘tiger’ Rebus: kolhe ‘smelters’ kol ‘working in iron’
kola ‘woman’ Rebus: kol ‘working in iron’
kole.l ‘temple’ Rebus: kole.l ‘smithy’

 kanka ‘rim of jar’ Rebus: karṇīka ‘account (scribe)’ karṇī ‘supercargo’
kamaḍha ‘crab’ Rebus: *kammaṭa* ‘mint, coiner’.
ḍato = claws of crab (Santali) Rebus: *dhātu* ‘mineral ore’

dula ‘pair’ Rebus: *dul* ‘cast (metal)’ PLUS*kana, kanac* = corner (Santali); Rebus: *kañcu* = bronze (Telugu) PLUS infixed kolmo ‘paddy plant’ Rebus: kolami ‘smithy, forge’. Thus, cast bronze smithy, forge. Or, mogge ‘sprout, bud’ Rebus: mũh ‘ingot’ (Santali)Thus, cast bronze ingot. Read as: kañcu dul mũh ‘bronze cast ingot’

‘Notch’ infixed: खांडा [*khāṇḍā*] *m* A jag, notch, or indentation (as upon the edge of a tool or weapon). Rebus: *kāṇḍa* ‘tools, pots and pans and metal-ware’ Thus, cast bronze metalware.

 kanka ‘rim of jar’ Rebus: karṇīka ‘account (scribe)’ karṇī ‘supercargo’
sangada 'lathe', 'portable furnace'
G. *sãghāṛɔ* m. ‘lathe’ ; *sãgāḍā* m. ‘ frame of a building ’, *°ḍī* f. ‘ lathe

kanac ‘corner’ Rebus: *kañcu* ‘bronze’

h778A *kanac* ‘corner’ Rebus: *kañcu* ‘bronze’
|||| Numeral 4: gaṇḍa 'four' Rebus: kaṇḍa 'furnace, fire-altar' (Santali)
kolmo ‘paddy plant’ Rebus: kolami ‘smithy, forge’

m1424B *balad* m. ‘ ox ’, gng. *bald*, (Ku.) *barad*, id. (N. Tarai) Rebus: *bharat* (5 copper, 4 zinc and 1 tin)(Punjabi) *pattar* ‘trough’ Rebus: *pattar* ‘guild’. Thus, copper-zinc-tin alloy (worker) guild.

Text of inscription:
kanac ‘corner’ Rebus: *kañcu* ‘bronze’

 kanka ‘rim of jar’ Rebus: karṇīka ‘account (scribe)’ karṇī ‘supercargo’

 *loa* ‘ficus religiosa’ Rebus: *lo* ‘iron’ (Sanskrit)
kamaḍha ‘archer Rebus: *kammaṭa* ‘mint, coiner’.

 m1874a *kanac* ‘corner’ Rebus: *kañcu* ‘bronze’

m0143AText 2002

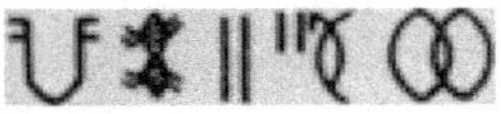

2002

kuṭila 'bent' CDIAL 3230 kuṭi— in cmpd. 'curve', *kuṭika—* 'bent' MBh. Rebus: *kuṭila, katthīl* = bronze (8 parts copper and 2 parts tin)

This is a ligature of two hieroglyphs: 'bent line' denoting bronze PLUS 'slanted stroke + numeral linear stroke': | *koḍa* 'one' Rebus: *koḍ* 'workshop' dula PLUS *dhāḷ* 'a slope'; 'inclination of a plane' (Gujarati); *ḍhāḷiyum* = adj. sloping, inclining (Gujarati) Rebus: *ḍhālako* = a large metal ingot (Gujarati) *ḍhālakī* = a metal heated and poured into a mould; a solid piece of metal; an ingot (Gujarati) Thus, together: bronze ingot workshop *kuṭila ḍhālako koḍ*

An ancient gloss of Indian *sprachbund* is attested to denote a metalworker: *ċiməkára* ' blacksmith')(Ash.), In Sumerian, *bad tibira* meant 'metalworking fort' attesting to cimara, tibira, timira as related to tamb(r)a 'copper'. *tibira* in Sumerian also meant 'merchant'.

Thus Text 2002 renders rebus:
kanac 'corner' Rebus: *kañcu* 'bronze' dula 'pair' Rebus: dul 'cast metal' Thus, cast bronze

kuṭila 'bent' CDIAL 3230 kuṭi— in cmpd. 'curve', *kuṭika—* 'bent' MBh. Rebus: *kuṭila, katthīl* = bronze (8 parts copper and 2 parts tin)
dula 'pair' Rebus: dul 'cast metal' Thus, cast bronze

cīmara 'black ant' Rebus: *cīmara* 'copper'. *cīmara kāra* -- ' coppersmith '

sal 'splinter' Rebus: sal 'workshop'. Thus, coppersmith workshop

'rim-of-jar' hieroglyph *kanka* (Santali) *karṇika* 'scribe'(Sanskrit) Rebus: *karṇī,* supercargo for a boat shipment. *karṇīka* 'account (scribe)'
.कारणी *kāraṇī* 'the supercargo of a ship' (Marathi)
'Pair of corners hieroglyph' ligatured sign hieroglyph
Rebus reading: *kanac* 'corner' Rebus: *kañcu* 'bronze' dula 'pair' Rebus: dul 'cast metal' Thus, the ligatured hieroglyph connotes *dul kañcu* 'cast bronze'.
The ligatures on 'rhombus' connote *sal* 'splinter' Rebus: *sal* 'workshop' PLUS *gaṇḍa* 'four' Rebus: *kaṇḍa* 'furnace, fire-altar' (Santali). Thus, *kañcu sal kaṇḍa* 'bronze workshop fire-altar'.

m275A Rhinoceros/boar: baḍhia = a castrated boar, a hog (Santali) baḍhi 'a caste who work both in iron and wood' (Santali) *baṟea* 'merchant' pattar 'trough' Rebus: pattar 'guild, goldsmith'

kañcu sal kaṇḍa 'bronze workshop fire-altar'.
khuṭo ' leg, foot ', °ṭī ' goat's leg ' Rebus: *khōṭā* 'alloy' (Marathi)

dula 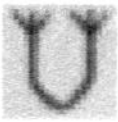 'pair' Rebus: dul 'cast (metal)' kolmo 'rice plant' Rebus: kolami 'smithy/forge' metal.

kanka 'rim of jar' Rebus: karṇīka 'account (scribe)' karṇī 'supercargo'

meḍ 'body' Rebus: *meḍ* 'iron' (Ho.) काठी [kāṭhī] *f* (काष्ट S) 'frame or structure of the body' (Marathi) Rebus: खंडी [khaṇḍī] measure of weight (Marathi) கண்டி; *kaṇṭi, n. < Mhr. khaṇḍil. [T. Tu. khaṇḍi, M. kaṇḍi.]* Candy, a weight, stated to be roughly equivalent to 500 lbs.

m1077a 'Two horns' on a 'young bull' emphasise the semantics of *kōḍu* 'horn' Rebus: *kōḍ* 'turner-engraver's workshop' So does the first sign fom r. of ligatured rhombus hieroglyph connote a workshop: *kañcu sal kaṇḍa* 'bronze workshop fire-altar'.

खोंड [khōṇḍa] m A young bull, a bullcalf. (Marathi) Rebus: kõdār 'turner' (Bengali); कोंद kōnda 'engraver, lapidary setting or infixing gems' (Marathi) G. sãghāṛɔ m. 'lathe' ; संघाट joinery; M. sãgaḍ 'double-canoe' Rebus: sangataras 'stone-cutter, mason' kañcu sal kaṇḍa 'bronze workshop fire-altar'.

bhaṭa 'warrior' (Sanskrit) Rebus: *baṭa* a kind of iron (Gujarati). Rebus: *bhaṭa* 'furnace' (Santal

aḍar 'harrow'; rebus: *aduru* 'native unsmelted metal'

loa 'ficus religiosa' Rebus: *lo* 'iron' (Sanskrit) PLUS unique ligatures: लोखंड [lōkhaṇḍa] *n* (लोह S) Iron. लोखंडाचे चणे खावविणें or चारणें To oppress grievously.लोखंडकाम [lōkhaṇḍakāma] *n* Iron work; that portion (of a building, machine &c.) which consists of iron. 2 The business of an ironsmith.लोखंडी [lōkhaṇḍī] *a* (लोखंड) Composed of iron; relating to iron. (Marathi) *bhaṭa* 'warrior' (Sanskrit) Rebus: *baṭa* a kind of iron (Gujarati). Rebus: *bhaṭa* 'furnace' (Santali) Thus, together, the ligatured hieroglyph reads rebus: *loa bhaṭa* 'iron furnace'.

baṭa 'rimless, broad-mouthed pot' Rebus: *bhaṭa* 'furnace' (Gujarati.); *baṭa* 'a kind of iron' (Gujarati)

m281A *ibha* 'elephant' Rebus: *ib* 'iron' *ibbo* 'merchant' (Gujarati) *kañcu sal kaṇḍa* 'bronze workshop fire-altar'.

kuṭila  'bent' CDIAL 3230 kuṭi— in cmpd. 'curve', *kuṭika—* 'bent' MBh. Rebus: *kuṭila, katthīl* = bronze (8 parts copper and 2 parts tin)

ranku 'liquid measure' Rebus: ranku 'tin' | *koḍa* 'one' Rebus: *koḍ* 'workshop'

ḍāg mountain-ridge (H.)(CDIAL 5476). Rebus: dhangar 'blacksmith' (Maithili) खांडा [*khāṇḍā*] *m* A jag, notch, or indentation (as upon the edge of a tool or weapon). Rebus: *kāṇḍa* 'tools, pots and pans and metal-ware'

 kanka 'rim of jar' Rebus: karṇīka 'account (scribe)' karṇī 'supercargo'

m1876a Pictorial motif hieroglyph: *balad* m. ' ox ', gng. *bald,* (Ku.) *barad,* id. (N. Tarai) Rebus: *bharat* (5 copper, 4 zinc and 1 tin)(Punjabi) *pattar* 'trough' Rebus: *pattar* 'guild'. Thus, copper-zinc-tin alloy (worker) guild. *kañcu sal kaṇḍa* 'bronze workshop fire-altar'.

ayo ḍhālako 'alloy metal ingot'

 *aḍar* 'harrow'; rebus: *aduru* 'native unsmelted metal'

 m195A *खोंड [khōṇḍa] m A young bull, a bullcalf. (Marathi) Rebus: kõdār 'turner' (Bengali); कोंद kōnda 'engraver, lapidary setting or infixing gems' (Marathi) G. sãghāṛɔ m. 'lathe' ; संघाट joinery; M. sãgaḍ 'double-canoe' Rebus: sangataras 'stone-cutter, mason' kañcu sal kaṇḍa* 'bronze workshop fire-altar'.

 *kuṭila* 'bent' CDIAL 3230 kuṭi— in cmpd. 'curve', *kuṭika—* 'bent' MBh. Rebus: *kuṭila, katthīl* = bronze (8 parts copper and 2 parts tin)

 dula 'pair' Rebus: dul 'cast metal' PLUS | *koḍa* 'one' Rebus: *koḍ* 'workshop' PLUS INFIXED kolom
'three' Rebus: kolami 'smithy, forge' Thus metware castings forge.
ranku 'liquid measure' Rebus: ranku 'tin'

 |||| Numeral 4: gaṇḍa 'four' Rebus: kaṇḍa 'furnace, fire-altar' (Santali) dula 'pair' Rebus: dul 'cast metal'

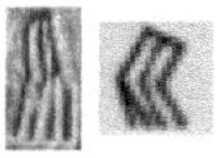 Strands of yarn/rope' hieroglyph: Hieroglyph: 'strands of yarn' Rebus reading: *dhāˊtu* 'strand of rope' Rebus: *dhatu* 'mineral ore' (Santali)

 m184a *खोंड [khōṇḍa] m A young bull, a bullcalf. (Marathi) Rebus: kõdār 'turner' (Bengali); कोंद kōnda 'engraver, lapidary setting or infixing gems' (Marathi) G. sãghāṛɔ m. 'lathe' ; संघाट joinery; M. sãgaḍ 'double-canoe' Rebus: sangataras 'stone-cutter, mason' kañcu sal kaṇḍa* 'bronze workshop fire-altar'.
kañcu sal kaṇḍa 'bronze workshop fire-altar'.

 *kuṭila* 'bent' CDIAL 3230 kuṭi— in cmpd. 'curve', *kuṭika—* 'bent' MBh. Rebus: *kuṭila, katthīl* = bronze (8 parts copper and 2 parts tin)
bhaṭa 'warrior' (Sanskrit) Rebus: *baṭa* a kind of iron (Gujarati). Rebus: *bhaṭa* 'furnace' (Santali)
Circumscript:

 *kuṭila* 'bent' CDIAL 3230 kuṭi— in cmpd. 'curve', *kuṭika—* 'bent' MBh. Rebus: *kuṭila, katthīl* = bronze (8 parts copper and 2 parts tin) Duplicated: dula 'pair' Rebus: dul 'cast metal' Thus, cast bronze or bronze castings.

 kanka 'rim of jar' Rebus: karṇīka 'account (scribe)' karṇī 'supercargo'

 *meḍ* 'body' Rebus: *meḍ* 'iron' (Ho.) काठी [kāṭhī] *f* (काष्ट S) 'frame or structure of the body' (Marathi) Rebus: खंडी [khanḍī] measure of weight (Marathi) *கண்டி; kaṇṭi, n. < Mhr. khanḍil. [T. Tu. khanḍi, M. kanḍi.]* Candy, a weight, stated to be roughly equivalent to 500 lbs.

m1224 B,E *खोंड [khōṇḍa] m A young bull, a bullcalf. (Marathi) Rebus: kõdār 'turner' (Bengali); कोंद kōnda 'engraver, lapidary setting or infixing gems' (Marathi) G. sãghāṛɔ m. 'lathe' ; संघाट joinery; M. sãgaḍ 'double-canoe' Rebus: sangataras 'stone-cutter, mason'*

Side E has a bull ligatured with zebu's horns and with the person shown with upraised arm denoting rebus a coppersmith, a native metalsmith guild: *eraka* 'upraised arm' Rebus: *erako* 'moltencast copper'. Zebu horns: native metalsmith guild: *khũṭ* 'zebu' Rebus: '(native metal) guild'. *khũṭ,* 'zebu' 'guild', A synonym is *aḍar ḍangra* Rebus: *aduru ḍhangar* 'native-metal- or black-smith' (Kannada.Santali). dangra 'bull' (Punjabi) Rebus: *ḍhangar* 'blacksmith' (Maithili) *adar dangra* 'zebu' *bos indicus* (Santali) Rebus: ಗಣಿಯಿಂದ ತೆಗದು ಕರಗದೆ ಇರುವ ಅದುರು (Kannada) aduru *gan.iyinda tegadu karagade iruva aduru* = ore taken from the mine and not subjected to melting in a furnace (Ka. Siddhānti Subrahmaṇya' Śastri's new interpretation of the AmarakoŚa, Bangalore, Vicaradarpana Press, 1872, p.330). *adar* = fine sand (Tamil) *aduru* native metal (Kannada); *ayil* iron (Tamil) *ayir, ayiram* any ore (Malayalam); *ajirda karba* very hard iron (Tulu)(DEDR 192).

kañcu sal kaṇḍa 'bronze workshop fire-altar'.

dula 'pair' Rebus: dul 'cast metal' kolom 'three' Rebus: kolami 'smithy, forge'

 *kolmo* 'paddy plant' Rebus: *kolami* 'smithy, forge' Vikalpa: *mogge* 'sprout, bud' Rebus: *mũh* 'ingot' (Santali) dolu 'plant of shoot height' Rebus: dul 'cast metal'

dula 'pair' Rebus: dul 'cast metal' PLUS

 *kharedo* = a currycomb (Gujarati) खरारा [*kharārā*] *m* (H) A currycomb. 2 Currying a horse. (Marathi) Rebus: करडा [*karaḍā*] Hard from alloy--iron, silver &c. (Marathi) *kharādī* ' turner' (Gujarati)

m104a *खोंड [khōṇḍa] m A young bull, a bullcalf. (Marathi) Rebus: kōdār 'turner' (Bengali);* कोंद *kōnda 'engraver, lapidary setting or infixing gems' (Marathi) G. sãghāṛɔ m. 'lathe' ;* संघाट *joinery; M. sãgaḍ 'double-canoe' Rebus: sangataras 'stone-cutter, mason'*

kañcu sal kaṇḍa 'bronze workshop fire-altar'.

aya aḍaren (homonym: aduru)'alloy native metal'

aya kāṇḍa 'alloy metalware'

 kanka 'rim of jar' Rebus: karṇīka 'account (scribe)' karṇī 'supercargo'

 *meḍ* 'body' Rebus: *meḍ* 'iron' (Ho.) काठी [kāṭhī] *f* (काष्ट S) 'frame or structure of the body' (Marathi) Rebus: खंडी [khaṇḍī] measure of weight (Marathi) *கண்டி; kaṇṭi, n. < Mhr. khaṇḍil. [T. Tu. khaṇḍi, M. kaṇḍi.]* Candy, a weight, stated to be roughly equivalent to 500 lbs.

h80a Pictorial motif hieroglyph: *balad* m. ' ox ', gng. *bald,* (Ku.) *barad,* id. (N. Tarai) Rebus: *bharat* (5 copper, 4 zinc and 1 tin)(Punjabi) *pattar* 'trough' Rebus: *pattar* 'guild'. Thus, copper-zinc-tin alloy (worker) guild.

kanac  'corner' Rebus: *kañcu* 'bronze'

 dula 'pair' Rebus: dul 'cast metal' PLUS | *koḍa* 'one' Rebus: *koḍ* 'workshop' PLUS INFIXED खांडा [*khāṇḍā*] *m* A jag, notch, or indentation (as upon the edge of a tool or weapon). Rebus: *kāṇḍa* 'tools, pots and pans and metal-ware' Thus metware castings workshop.

kanka (Santali) *karṇika* 'scribe'(Sanskrit) Rebus: *karṇī,* supercargo for a boat shipment. INFIXED खांडा [*khāṇḍā*] *m* A jag, notch, or indentation (as upon the edge of a tool or weapon). Rebus: *kāṇḍa* 'tools, pots and pans and metal-ware'

aḍar 'harrow'; rebus: *aduru* 'native unsmelted metal' *bhaṭa* 'warrior' (Sanskrit) Rebus: *baṭa* a kind of iron (Gujarati). Rebus: *bhaṭa* 'furnace' (Santali)

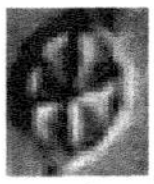

āra 'spokes' Rebus: *āra 'brass'.* cf. erka = ekke (Tbh. of arka) aka (Tbh. of arka) copper (metal); crystal (Kannada) Glyph: *eraka'*nave of wheel' Rebus: eraka 'copper'; cf. erka = ekke (Tbh. of arka) aka (Tbh. of arka) copper (metal); crystal (Kannada) *erako* 'moltencast copper' Duplicated: dula 'pair' Rebus: dul 'cast metal' Thus cast copper, brass casting.

ranku 'liquid measure' Rebus: ranku 'tin'

h764A dulo 'hole' Rebus; dul 'cast metal'

khuṭo ' leg, foot ', °ṭī ' goat's leg ' Rebus: *khōṭā* 'alloy' (Marathi)

kanka 'rim of jar' Rebus: karṇīka 'account (scribe)' karṇī 'supercargo'

m131a *खोंड [khōṇḍa] m A young bull, a bullcalf. (Marathi) Rebus: kõdār 'turner' (Bengali); कोंद kōnda 'engraver, lapidary setting or infixing gems' (Marathi) G. sãghārɔ m. 'lathe' ; संघाट joinery; M. sãgaḍ 'double-canoe' Rebus: sangataras 'stone-cutter, mason'*

dulo 'hole' Rebus: dul 'cast metal'

kolmo 'paddy plant' Rebus: *kolami* 'smithy, forge' Vikalpa: *mogge* 'sprout, bud' Rebus: *mũh* 'ingot' (Santali) dolu 'plant of shoot height' Rebus: dul 'cast metal'

kanka (Santali) *karṇika* 'scribe'(Sanskrit) Rebus: *karṇī,* supercargo for a boat shipment. INFIXED खांडा [*khāṇḍā*] *m* A jag, notch, or indentation (as upon the edge of a tool or weapon). Rebus: *kāṇḍa* 'tools, pots and pans and metal-ware'

ranku 'liquid measure' Rebus: ranku 'tin'

kolmo 'paddy plant' Rebus: *kolami* 'smithy, forge' Vikalpa: *mogge* 'sprout, bud' Rebus: *mũh* 'ingot' (Santali) dolu 'plant of shoot height' Rebus: dul 'cast metal'

kanka 'rim of jar' Rebus: karṇīka 'account (scribe)' karṇī 'supercargo'

Chanhudaro 22a Pictorial motif hieroglyph: *balad* m. ' ox ', gng. *bald,* (Ku.) *barad,* id. (N. Tarai) Rebus: *bharat* (5 copper, 4 zinc and 1 tin)(Punjabi) *pattar* 'trough' Rebus*: pattar* 'guild'. Thus, copper-zinc-tin alloy (worker) guild.

dulo 'hole' Rebus: dul 'cast metal'

kolmo 'paddy plant' Rebus: *kolami* 'smithy, forge' Vikalpa: *mogge* 'sprout, bud' Rebus: *mũh* 'ingot' (Santali) dolu 'plant of shoot height' Rebus: dul 'cast metal'

 *koḍi* ‘flag’ (Ta.)(DEDR 2049). Rebus 1: *koḍ* ‘workshop’ (Kuwi) Rebus 2: *khŏḍ* m. ‘pit’, *khŏḍü* f. ‘small pit’ (Kashmiri. CDIAL 3947). sal ‘splinter’ Rebus: sal ‘workshop’

 *kolmo* ‘paddy plant’ Rebus: *kolami* ‘smithy, forge’ Vikalpa: *mogge* ‘sprout, bud’ Rebus: *mũh* ‘ingot’ (Santali) dolu ‘plant of shoot height’ Rebus: dul ‘cast metal’

 m1002a *खोंड [khōṇḍa] m A young bull, a bullcalf. (Marathi) Rebus: kõdār ‘turner’ (Bengali); कोंद kōnda ‘engraver, lapidary setting or infixing gems’ (Marathi) G. sãghāṛɔ m. ‘lathe’ ; संघाट joinery; M. sãgaḍ ‘double-canoe’ Rebus: sangataras ‘stone-cutter, mason’*

 *kanac* ‘corner’ Rebus: *kañcu* ‘bronze’

 dula ‘pair’ Rebus: dul ‘cast metal’ PLUS | *koḍa* ‘one’ Rebus: *koḍ* ‘workshop’ PLUS INFIXED खांडा [*khāṇḍā*] *m* A jag, notch, or indentation (as upon the edge of a tool or weapon). Rebus: *kāṇḍa* ‘tools, pots and pans and metal-ware’ Thus metware castings workshop.

sal ‘splinter’ Rebus: sal ‘workshop’

| *koḍa* ‘one’ Rebus: *koḍ* ‘workshop’ dulo ‘hole’ Rebus: dul ‘cast metal’ sal ‘splinter’ Rebus: sal ‘workshop’

 kanka ‘rim of jar’ Rebus: karṇīka ‘account (scribe)’ karṇī ‘supercargo’

 Allahdino 8a *ibha* ‘elephant’ Rebus: *ib* ‘iron’ *ibbo* ‘merchant’ (Gujarati) PLUS G. *sãghāṛɔ* m. ‘lathe’ ; *संघाट joinery; M. sãgaḍ ‘double-canoe’* Rebus: *sangataras.* संगतराश lit. ‘to collect stones, stone-cutter, mason dula ‘pair’ Rebus: dul ‘cast metal’ PLUS

 *kanac* ‘corner’ Rebus: *kañcu* ‘bronze’ sal ‘splinter’ Rebus: sal ‘workshop’

 mēḍu height, rising ground, hillock (Kannada) Rebus: *mẽṛhẽt, meḍ* ‘iron’ (Munda.Ho.) *ḍhanga* = a crook used for pulling down the branches of trees, for goats, sheep and camels (P.) Rebus:*ḍhangar* blacksmith’.

 kanka ‘rim of jar’ Rebus: karṇīka ‘account (scribe)’ karṇī ‘supercargo’

 m172A *खोंड [khōṇḍa] m A young bull, a bullcalf. (Marathi) Rebus: kõdār ‘turner’ (Bengali); कोंद kōnda ‘engraver, lapidary setting or infixing gems’ (Marathi) G. sãghāṛɔ m. ‘lathe’ ; संघाट joinery; M. sãgaḍ ‘double-canoe’ Rebus: sangataras ‘stone-cutter, mason’*

 *kanac* ‘corner’ Rebus: *kañcu* ‘bronze’

 kanka 'rim of jar' Rebus: karṇīka 'account (scribe)' karṇī 'supercargo' PLUS | *koḍa* 'one' Rebus: *koḍ* 'workshop' sal 'splinter' Rebus: sal 'workshop' *ayo* 'fish' Rebus: *aya* 'iron' *ayas* 'metal'

dula 'pair' Rebus: dul 'cast metal' PLUS
|||| Numeral 4: gaṇḍa 'four' Rebus: kaṇḍa 'furnace, fire-altar' (Santali) *mogge* 'sprout, bud' Rebus*: mũh* 'ingot'

m99A

खोंड [khōṇḍa] m A young bull, a bullcalf. (Marathi) Rebus: kõdār 'turner' (Bengali); कोंद kōnda 'engraver, lapidary setting or infixing gems' (Marathi) G. sãghārɔ m. 'lathe' ; संघाट joinery; M. sãgaḍ 'double-canoe' Rebus: sangataras 'stone-cutter, mason'

 *kanac* 'corner' Rebus: *kañcu* 'bronze'

 *meḍ* 'body' Rebus: *meḍ* 'iron' (Ho.) काठी [kāṭhī] *f* (काष्ट S) 'frame or structure of the body' (Marathi) Rebus: खंडी [khaṇḍī] measure of weight (Marathi) *கண்டி; kaṇṭi, n. < Mhr. khaṇḍil. [T. Tu. khaṇḍi, M. kaṇḍi.]* Candy, a weight, stated to be roughly equivalent to 500 lbs.

 *koḍi* 'flag' (Ta.)(DEDR 2049). Rebus 1: *koḍ* 'workshop' (Kuwi) Rebus 2: *khŏḍ* m. 'pit', *khŏḍü* f. 'small pit' (Kashmiri. CDIAL 3947).

Twisted rope: मेढा [*mēḍhā*] A twist or tangle arising in thread or cord, a curl or snarl.(Marathi)(CDIAL 10312).L. *meṛh* f. 'rope tying oxen to each other and to post on threshing floor'(CDIAL 10317) Rebus: *meḍ* 'iron'. *mẽṛhet* 'iron' (Mu.Ho.)

 kanka 'rim of jar' Rebus: karṇīka 'account (scribe)' karṇī 'supercargo'

Chanhudaro 24A

 *kanac* 'corner' Rebus: *kañcu* 'bronze'

aḍaren 'cover  of pot or lid' Rebus: *aduru* 'native, unsmelted metal' Duplicated: dula 'pair' Rebus: dul 'cast metal'खांडा [*khāṇḍā*] *m* A jag, notch, or indentation (as upon the edge of a tool or weapon). Rebus: *kāṇḍa* 'tools, pots and pans and metal-ware' sal 'splinter' Rebus: sal 'workshop' dula 'two' Rebus: dul 'cast metal' *aya kāṇḍa* 'alloy metalware'

 *kolmo* 'paddy plant' Rebus: *kolami* 'smithy, forge' Vikalpa: *mogge* 'sprout, bud' Rebus: *mũh* 'ingot' (Santali) dolu 'plant of shoot height' Rebus: dul 'cast metal'
baṭa 'rimless, broad-mouthed pot' Rebus: *bhaṭa* 'furnace' (Gujarati.); *baṭa* 'a kind of iron' (Gujarati) sal 'splimnter' Rebus: sal 'workshop'.

h1951 dulo 'hole' Rebus: dul 'cast metal' kolom 'three' Rebus: kolami 'smithy, forge'
kamaḍha 'crab' Rebus: *kammaṭa* 'mint, coiner'.*ḍato* = claws of crab (Santali) Rebus: *dhātu* 'mineral ore'

khaṇḍ 'field, division' (Skt.) Rebus: *khāṇḍa* 'tools, pots and pans, metal-ware'. Rebus 2: kaṇḍ 'fire-altar' (Santali) dula 'pair' Rebus: dul 'cast metal' Thus, duplicated 'division' hieroglyph sign reads: cast metal metal-ware.

dula 'pair' Rebus: dul 'cast metal' *mogge* 'sprout, bud' Rebus: *mũh* 'ingot' (Santali) Thus, cast metal ingot.

मंडप [maṇḍapa] 'canopy' Rebus: मंडई [maṇḍī] *f* (H) A green market, the place in a city whither vegetables and fruits are brought to be disposed of by wholesale.

loa 'ficus religiosa' Rebus: *lo* 'iron' (Sanskrit) PLUS unique ligatures: लोखंड [lōkhaṇḍa] *n* (लोह S) Iron. लोखंडाचे चणे खावविणें or चारणें To oppress grievously.लोखंडकाम [lōkhaṇḍakāma] *n* Iron work; that portion (of a building, machine &c.) which consists of iron. 2 The business of an ironsmith.लोखंडी [lōkhaṇḍī] *a* (लोखंड) Composed of iron; relating to iron. (Marathi)
meḍ 'body' Rebus: *meḍ* 'iron' (Ho.) काठी [kāṭhī] *f* (काष्ट S) 'frame or structure of the body' (Marathi) Rebus: खंडी [khaṇḍī] measure of weight (Marathi) *கண்டி; kaṇṭi, n. < Mhr. khaṇḍil. [T. Tu. khaṇḍi, M. kaṇḍi.]* Candy, a weight, stated to be roughly equivalent to 500 lbs. Ligature: *Kur.* xolā tail. *Malt.* qoli id. (DEDR 2135). Rebus: kolhe 'smelter' Thus, copper smelter. dhatu 'scarf' Rebus: dhatu 'mineral ore'.

h1951A *खोंड [khōṇḍa] m A young bull, a bullcalf. (Marathi) Rebus: kõdār 'turner' (Bengali); कोंद kōnda 'engraver, lapidary setting or infixing gems' (Marathi) G. sãghārɔ m. 'lathe' ; संघाट joinery; M. sãgaḍ 'double-canoe' Rebus: sangataras 'stone-cutter, mason'*
dulo 'hole' Rebus: dul 'cast metal' kolom 'three' Rebus: kolami 'smithy, forge' kamaḍha 'crab' Rebus: *kammaṭa* 'mint, coiner'.*ḍato* = claws of crab (Santali) Rebus: *dhātu* 'mineral ore'

khaṇḍ 'field, division' (Skt.) Rebus: *khāṇḍa* 'tools, pots and pans, metal-ware'. Rebus 2: kaṇḍ 'fire-altar' (Santali) dula 'pair' Rebus: dul 'cast metal' Thus, duplicated 'division' hieroglyph sign reads: cast metal metal-ware.

h385a *खोंड [khōṇḍa] m A young bull, a bullcalf. (Marathi) Rebus: kõdār 'turner' (Bengali); कोंद kōnda 'engraver, lapidary setting or infixing gems' (Marathi) G. sãghārɔ m. 'lathe' ; संघाट joinery; M. sãgaḍ 'double-canoe' Rebus: sangataras 'stone-cutter, mason'*
dulo 'hole' Rebus: dul 'cast metal'

|||| Numeral 4: gaṇḍa 'four' Rebus: kaṇḍa 'furnace, fire-altar' (Santali) dula 'pair' Rebus: dul 'cast metal'

kəṭhā´r, kc. *kuṭhār* m. ' granary, storeroom '(WPah.)(CDIAL 3550). *koṭhārī m.* ' storekeeper'

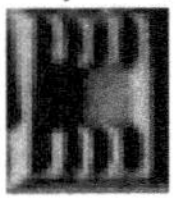

(Gujarati)(CDIAL 3551) Thus, storeroom (of) *kolom* 'three' Rebus: *kolami* 'smithy, forge'. Dula 'pair' Rebus: dul 'cast metal' Thus, together *dul kolami kuṭhār* 'metal smithy castings storeroom'

ranku 'liquid measure' Rebus; ranku 'tin' sal 'splinter' Rebus: sal 'workshop'

ayo 'fish' Rebus: *aya* 'iron' *ayas* 'metal'

h479A *खोंड [khōṇḍa] m A young bull, a bullcalf. (Marathi) Rebus: kõdār 'turner' (Bengali); कोंद kōnda 'engraver, lapidary setting or infixing gems' (Marathi) G. sãghāṛɔ m. 'lathe' ; संघाट joinery; M. sāgaḍ 'double-canoe' Rebus: sangataras 'stone-cutter, mason'*

dulo 'hole' Rebus; dul 'cast metal' ranku 'liquid measure' Rebus: ranku 'tin' mogge 'sprout, bud' Rebus: *mūh* 'ingot' (Santali)

 kanka 'rim of jar' Rebus: karṇīka 'account (scribe)' karṇī 'supercargo'

h1149A dulo 'hole' Rebus: dul 'cast metal'

 kanka 'rim of jar' Rebus: karṇīka 'account (scribe)' karṇī 'supercargo'

 *kharedo* = a currycomb (Gujarati) खरारा [*kharārā*] *m* (H) A currycomb. 2 Currying a horse. (Marathi) Rebus: करडा [*karaḍā*] Hard from alloy--iron, silver &c. (Marathi) *kharādī* ' turner' (Gujarati)

h841A Read rebus as at h1149

h1810A

 *kanac* 'corner' Rebus: *kañcu* 'bronze'

 kanka 'rim of jar' Rebus: karṇīka 'account (scribe)' karṇī 'supercargo'

Circumscript:

 *kuṭila* 'bent' CDIAL 3230 kuṭi— in cmpd. 'curve', *kuṭika*— 'bent' MBh. Rebus: *kuṭila, katthīl* = bronze (8 parts copper and 2 parts tin) Duplicated: dula 'pair' Rebus: dul 'cast metal' Thus, cast bronze or bronze castings.

|||| Numeral 4: gaṇḍa 'four' Rebus: kaṇḍa 'furnace, fire-altar' (Santali)

||| Numeral 3: *kolom* 'three' Rebus*: kolami* 'smithy, forge'

Side B: | *koḍa* 'one' Rebus: *koḍ* 'workshop' sal 'splinter' Rebus: sal 'workshop' gaṇḍa 'four' Rebus: kaṇḍa 'furnace, fire-altar' (Santali)

 सांड [sāṇḍa] *f* (षद S) An outlet for superfluous water (as through a dam or mound); a sluice, a floodvent. Rebus: सांडणी [sāṇḍaṇī] *f* (H) An instrument of goldsmiths. It is hooked or curved at the extremity; and is used to draw things out of the fire.

सांठा [*sāṇṭhā*] *m* (संचय S) A collection, heap, hoard, store, stock.साटें [*sāṭēṃ*] *n* (संचय S) A whole investment; the total quantity of merchandise (brought to market by one merchant).

 Ligature: two peaks: mēḍu height, rising ground, hillock (Kannada) Rebus: *meḍ* 'iron' (Ho.) dula 'pair' Rebus: dul 'cast metal' PLUS |||| Numeral 4: gaṇḍa 'four' Rebus: kaṇḍa 'furnace, fire-altar' (Santali)

baṭa 'rimless, broad-mouthed pot' Rebus: *bhaṭa* 'furnace' (Gujarati.); *baṭa* 'a kind of iron' (Gujarati) kolom 'three' Rebus: kolami 'smithy, forge'

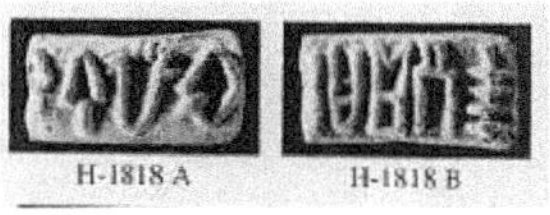

h1818B

 *kanac* 'corner' Rebus: *kañcu* 'bronze'

kanka 'rim of jar' Rebus: karṇīka 'account (scribe)' karṇī 'supercargo'
sal 'splinter' Rebus: sal 'workshop'

 कांड *kāṇḍa* 'arrow' Rebus: *kāṇḍa* 'pots and pans, metalware, tools'. Rebus 2: kaṇḍ 'fire-altar' (Santali)
Side B: Read rebus as at Side B h1810

m1771a *खोंड [khōṇḍa] m A young bull, a bullcalf. (Marathi) Rebus: kõdār 'turner' (Bengali); कोंद kōnda 'engraver, lapidary setting or infixing gems' (Marathi) G. sãghāṛɔ m. 'lathe' ; संघाट joinery; M. sãgaḍ 'double-canoe' Rebus: sangataras 'stone-cutter, mason'*

 *kanac* 'corner' Rebus: *kañcu* 'bronze'

 *kanka* (Santali) *karṇika* 'scribe'(Sanskrit) Rebus: *karṇī,* supercargo for a boat shipment. INFIXED खांडा [*khāṇḍā*] *m* A jag, notch, or indentation (as upon the edge of a tool or weapon). Rebus: *kāṇḍa* 'tools, pots and pans and metal-ware'

 *loa* 'ficus religiosa' Rebus: *lo* 'iron' (Sanskrit) PLUS unique ligatures: लोखंड [lōkhaṇḍa] *n* (लोह S) Iron. लोखंडाचे चणे खावविणें or चारणें To oppress grievously.लोखंडकाम [lōkhaṇḍakāma] *n* Iron work; that portion (of a building, machine &c.) which consists of iron. 2 The business of an ironsmith.लोखंडी [lōkhaṇḍī] *a* (लोखंड) Composed of iron; relating to iron. (Marathi)

 kanka 'rim of jar' Rebus: karṇīka 'account (scribe)' karṇī 'supercargo'

m293a *karāvu* 'crocodile' Rebus: khara 'blacksmith' (Kashmiri)

kanka (Santali) *karṇika* 'scribe'(Sanskrit) Rebus: *karṇī,* supercargo for a boat shipment. INFIXED खांडा [*khāṇḍā*] *m* A jag, notch, or indentation (as upon the edge of a tool or weapon). Rebus: *kāṇḍa* 'tools, pots and pans and metal-ware' dula 'two' Rebus; dul 'cast metal' PLUS

 *aḍar* 'harrow'; rebus: *aduru* 'native unsmelted metal'

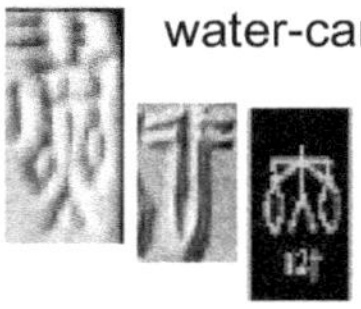

water-carrier hieroglyph *kuṭi*; Rebus: *kuṭhi* 'smelter furnace'.
PLUS 'rim of jar': *kanka* (Santali) *karṇika* 'scribe'(Sanskrit)
Rebus: *karṇī,* supercargo
'rim-of-jar' hieroglyph *kanka* (Santali) *karṇika* 'scribe'(Sanskrit)
Rebus: *karṇī,* supercargo for a boat shipment. *karṇīka* 'account (scribe) '.कारणी *kāraṇī* 'the supercargo of a ship' (Marathi)

h1989, h1990, h1998:
Side B: | *koḍa* 'one' Rebus: *koḍ* 'workshop' sal 'splinter' Rebus: sal 'workshop' gaṇḍa 'four' Rebus: kaṇḍa 'furnace, fire-altar' (Santali)

 सांड [sāṇḍa] *f* (षद S) An outlet for superfluous water (as through a dam or mound); a sluice, a floodvent. Rebus: सांडणी [sāṇḍaṇī] *f* (H) An instrument of goldsmiths. It is hooked or curved at the extremity; and is used to draw things out of the fire.
सांठा [*sāṇthā*] *m* (संचय S) A collection, heap, hoard, store, stock.साटें [*sāṭēṃ*] *n* (संचय S) A whole investment; the total quantity of merchandise (brought to market by one merchant).

 Ligature: two peaks: mēḍu height, rising ground, hillock (Kannada) Rebus: *meḍ* 'iron' (Ho.) dula 'pair' Rebus: dul 'cast metal' PLUS |||| Numeral 4: gaṇḍa 'four' Rebus: kaṇḍa 'furnace, fire-altar' (Santali)

baṭa 'rimless, broad-mouthed pot' Rebus: *bhaṭa* 'furnace' (Gujarati.); *baṭa* 'a kind of iron' (Gujarati) *gaṇḍa* 'four' Rebus: *kaṇḍa* 'furnace, fire-altar' (Santali).

Side A:

 *aḍaren* 'cover of pot or lid' Rebus: *aduru* 'native, unsmelted metal' Duplicated: dula 'pair' Rebus: dul 'cast metal'

 kanka 'rim of jar' Rebus: karṇīka 'account (scribe)' karṇī 'supercargo'

 *muka* 'ladle' (Tamil)(DEDR 4887) Rebus: *mũh* 'ingot' (Santali) *baṭa* = rimless pot (Kannada) Rebus: *baṭa* = a kind of iron (G.)) *bhaṭa* furnace (Gujarati) Thus, iron ingot.

 ḍãg mountain-ridge (H.)(CDIAL 5476). Rebus: dhangar 'blacksmith' (Maithili)

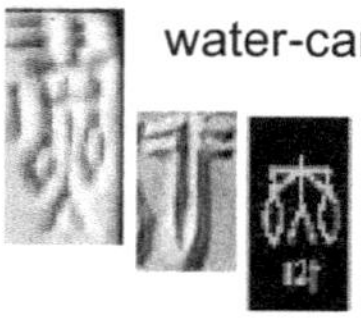

water-carrier hieroglyph *kuṭi*; Rebus: *kuṭhi* 'smelter furnace'.
PLUS 'rim of jar': *kanka* (Santali) *karṇika* 'scribe'(Sanskrit)
Rebus: *karṇī,* supercargo
'rim-of-jar' hieroglyph *kanka* (Santali) *karṇika* 'scribe'(Sanskrit)
Rebus: *karṇī,* supercargo for a boat shipment. *karṇīka* 'account (scribe)'.कारणी *kāraṇī* 'the supercargo of a ship' (Marathi)

Chanhudaro 17a *खोंड [khōṇḍa] m A young bull, a bullcalf. (Marathi) Rebus: kõdār 'turner' (Bengali); कोंद kōnda 'engraver, lapidary setting or infixing gems' (Marathi) G. sãghāṛɔ m. 'lathe' ; संघाट joinery; M. sāgaḍ 'double-canoe' Rebus: sangataras 'stone-cutter, mason'*
dulo 'hole' Rebus: dul 'cast metal

 kanka 'rim of jar' Rebus: karṇīka 'account (scribe)' karṇī 'supercargo'
bhaṭa 'warrior' (Sanskrit) Rebus: *baṭa* a kind of iron (Gujarati). Rebus: *bhaṭa* 'furnace' (Santali)

 *meḍ* 'body' Rebus: *meḍ* 'iron' (Ho.) काठी [kāṭhī] *f* (काष्ट S) 'frame or structure of the body' (Marathi) Rebus: खंडी [khaṇḍī] measure of weight (Marathi) *கண்டி; kaṇṭi, n. < Mhr. khaṇḍil. [T. Tu. khaṇḍi, M. kaṇḍi.]* Candy, a weight, stated to be roughly equivalent to 500 lbs.

h668A dulo 'hole' Rebus: dul 'cast metal'

 kanka 'rim of jar' Rebus: karṇīka 'account (scribe)' karṇī 'supercargo'

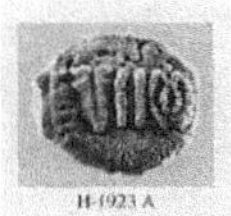

H-1923 A

h1923A,B
dula 'pair' Rebus: *dul* 'cast (metal)' PLUS*kana, kanac* = corner (Santali); Rebus: *kañcu* = bronze (Telugu) Thus, cast bronze.
dula 'two' Rebus: dul 'cast metal'

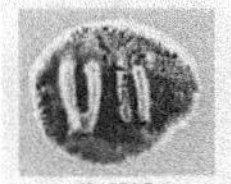

H-1923 B

kanka 'rim of  jar' Rebus: karṇīka 'account (scribe)' karṇī 'supercargo' *kharedo* = a currycomb (Gujarati) खरारा [*kharārā*] *m* (H) A currycomb. 2 Currying a horse. (Marathi) Rebus: करडा [*karaḍā*] Hard from alloy--iron, silver &c. (Marathi) *kharādī*' turner' (Gujarati) *baṭa* 'rimless, broad-mouthed pot' Rebus: *bhaṭa* 'furnace' (Gujarati.); *baṭa* 'a kind of iron' (Gujarati) dula 'two' Rebus: dul 'cast metal'

M-1224 A

m1224A, *खोंड [khōṇḍa] m A young bull, a bullcalf. (Marathi) Rebus: kõdār 'turner' (Bengali); कोंद kōnda 'engraver, lapidary setting or infixing gems' (Marathi) G. sãghāṛɔ m. 'lathe' ; संघाट joinery; M. sāgaḍ 'double-canoe' Rebus: sangataras 'stone-cutter, mason'*

dula 'pair' Rebus: *dul* 'cast (metal)' PLUS*kana, kanac* = corner (Santali); Rebus: *kañcu* = bronze (Telugu) Thus, cast bronze. dula 'two' Rebus: dul 'cast metal'

H-668 A

kanka 'rim of jar' Rebus: karṇīka 'account (scribe)' karṇī 'supercargo'

 *meḍ* 'body' Rebus: *meḍ* 'iron' (Ho.) काठी [kāṭhī] *f* (काष्ट S) 'frame or structure of the body' (Marathi) Rebus: खंडी [khaṇḍī] measure of weight (Marathi)

கண்டி; *kaṇṭi, n. < Mhr. khaṇḍil. [T. Tu. khaṇḍi, M. kaṇḍi.]* Candy, a weight, stated to be roughly equivalent to 500 lbs.

 *kharedo* = a currycomb (Gujarati) खरारा [*kharārā*] *m* (H) A currycomb. 2 Currying a horse. (Marathi) Rebus: करडा [*karaḍā*] Hard from alloy--iron, silver &c. (Marathi) *kharādī* ' turner' (Gujarati)

Lothal 59a Read rebus as first 3 signs at m1224

h723A

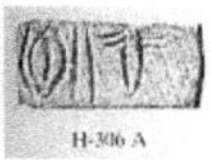

h306A

h182A 3 signs read rebus as at m1224. *kul* 'tiger' (Santali); *kōlu* id. (Telugu) kōlupuli = Bengal tiger (Te.) कोल्हा [kōlhā] कोल्हें [kōlhēṃ] A jackal (Marathi) Rebus: *kole.l* 'temple, smithy' (Kota.) *kol* = pañcalōha, a metallic alloy containing five metals (Tamil): copper, brass, tin, lead and iron (Sanskrit); an alternative list of five metals: gold, silver, copper, tin (lead), and iron (dhātu; Nānārtharatnākara. 82; Mangarāja's Nighaṇṭu. 498)(Kannada) *kol, kolhe*, 'the *koles*, iron smelters speaking a language akin to that of Santals' (Santali) dhol 'drum' Rebus: dul 'cast metal' 2+3 svastika: dula 'two' Rebus: dul 'cast metal' PLUS kolom 'three' Rebus: kolami 'smithy, forge' Rebu: sattva, jasta 'zinc' Or, five parts of zinc added to copper to create alloy brass.

dula 'pair' Rebus: *dul* 'cast (metal)' PLUS*kana, kanac* = corner (Santali); Rebus: *kañcu* = bronze (Telugu) Thus, cast bronze

m828A *खोंड [khōṇḍa] m A young bull, a bullcalf. (Marathi) Rebus: kōdār 'turner' (Bengali); कोंद kōnda 'engraver, lapidary setting or infixing gems' (Marathi) G. sãghāṛɔ m. 'lathe' ; संघाट joinery; M. sāgaḍ 'double-canoe' Rebus: sangataras 'stone-cutter, mason'*

dula 'pair' Rebus: *dul* 'cast (metal)' PLUS*kana, kanac* = corner (Santali); Rebus: *kañcu* = bronze (Telugu) Thus, cast bronze

dula 'two' Rebus: dul 'cast metal'

The hieroglyph may be a variant of:  *kana, kanac* = corner (Santali); Rebus: *kañcu* = bronze (Telugu) PLUS kolom 'three' Rebus: kolami 'smithy, forge.

ranku 'liquid measure' Rebus: ranku 'tin'

m619A

dula 'pair' Rebus: *dul* 'cast (metal)' PLUS*kana, kanac* = corner (Santali); Rebus: *kañcu* = bronze (Telugu) Thus, cast bronze. dula 'two' Rebus: dul 'cast metal'

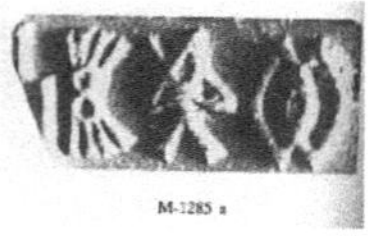

m1285a

 *dula* 'pair' Rebus: *dul* 'cast (metal)' PLUS*kana, kanac* = corner (Santali); Rebus: *kañcu* = bronze (Telugu) Thus, cast bronze

loa   'ficus religiosa' Rebus: *lo* 'iron' (Sanskrit) PLUS unique ligatures: लोखंड [lōkhaṇḍa] *n* (लोह S) Iron. लोखंडाचे चणे खावविणें or चारणें To oppress grievously.लोखंडकाम [lōkhaṇḍakāma] *n* Iron work; that portion (of a building, machine &c.) which consists of iron. 2 The business of an ironsmith.लोखंडी [lōkhaṇḍī] *a* (लोखंड) Composed of iron; relating to iron. (Marathi) *bhaṭa* 'warrior' (Sanskrit) Rebus: *baṭa* a kind of iron (Gujarati). Rebus: *bhaṭa* 'furnace' (Santali) Thus, together, the ligatured hieroglyph reads rebus: *loa bhaṭa* 'iron furnace'

 *cīmara* 'black ant' Rebus: *cīmara* 'copper'. *cīmara kāra* -- ' coppersmith '
ranku 'liquid measure' Rebus:ranku 'tin'

m1807a

  m1795a *खोंड [khōṇḍa] m A young bull, a bullcalf. (Marathi) Rebus: kōdār 'turner' (Bengali); कोंद kōnda 'engraver, lapidary setting or infixing gems' (Marathi) G. sãghāṛɔ m. 'lathe' ; संघाट joinery; M. sãgaḍ 'double-canoe' Rebus: sangataras 'stone-cutter, mason'*

 *dula* 'pair' Rebus: *dul* 'cast (metal)' PLUS*kana, kanac* = corner (Santali); Rebus: *kañcu* = bronze (Telugu) Thus, cast bronze

 *kolmo* 'paddy plant' Rebus: *kolami* 'smithy, forge' Vikalpa: *mogge* 'sprout, bud' Rebus: *mũh* 'ingot' (Santali) dolu 'plant of shoot height' Rebus: dul 'cast metal'

 *khareḍo* = a currycomb (Gujarati) खरारा [*kharārā*] *m* (H) A currycomb. 2 Currying a horse. (Marathi) Rebus: करडा [*karaḍā*] Hard from alloy--iron, silver &c. (Marathi) *kharādī* ' turner' (Gujarati)

 m56A *खोंड [khōṇḍa] m A young bull, a bullcalf. (Marathi) Rebus: kōdār 'turner' (Bengali); कोंद kōnda 'engraver, lapidary setting or infixing gems' (Marathi) G. sãghāṛɔ m. 'lathe' ; संघाट joinery; M. sãgaḍ 'double-canoe' Rebus: sangataras 'stone-cutter, mason'*

 *dula* 'pair' Rebus: *dul* 'cast (metal)' PLUS*kana, kanac* = corner (Santali); Rebus: *kañcu* = bronze (Telugu) Thus, cast bronze

kaṇḍo 'stool, seat' Rebus: *kāṇḍa* 'metalware' *kaṇḍa* 'fire-altar' PLUS | *koḍa* 'one' Rebus: *koḍ* 'workshop' *kamaḍha* 'crab' Rebus: *kammaṭa* 'mint, coiner'.*ḍato* = claws of crab (Santali) Rebus: *dhātu* 'mineral ore'

 *dhāḷ* 'a slope'; 'inclination of a plane' (G.); *ḍhāḷiyum* = adj. sloping, inclining (G.) Rebus: *ḍhālako* = a large metal ingot (G.) *ḍhālakī* = a metal heated and poured into a mould; a solid piece of metal; an ingot (Gujarati) PLUS खांडा [*khāṇḍā*] *m* A jag, notch, or indentation (as upon the edge of a tool or weapon). Rebus: *kāṇḍa* 'tools, pots and pans and metal-ware' Thus, the pair of sign hieroglyphs from r. read rebus: copper, bronze ingots, metalware castings. *aya aḍaren (homonym: aduru)*'alloy native metal'
dula 'two' Rebus: dul 'cast metal'

 *kanac* 'corner' Rebus: *kañcu* 'bronze'

kanka 'rim of jar' Rebus: karṇīka 'account (scribe)' karṇī 'supercargo'

m143A *खोंड [khōṇḍa] m A young bull, a bullcalf. (Marathi) Rebus: kōdār 'turner' (Bengali); कोंद kōnda 'engraver, lapidary setting or infixing gems' (Marathi) G. sãghāṛɔ m. 'lathe' ; संघाट joinery; M. sãgaḍ 'double-canoe' Rebus: sangataras 'stone-cutter, mason'*

 *dula* 'pair' Rebus: *dul* 'cast (metal)' PLUS*kana, kanac* = corner (Santali); Rebus: *kañcu* = bronze (Telugu) Thus, cast bronze

 *kuṭila* 'bent' CDIAL 3230 kuṭi— in cmpd. 'curve', *kuṭika—* 'bent' MBh. Rebus: *kuṭila, katthīl* = bronze (8 parts copper and 2 parts tin) *ḍhanga* = a crook used for pulling down the branches of trees, for goats, sheep and camels (P.) Rebus:*ḍhangar* blacksmith'.

sal 'splinter' Rebus: sal 'workshop' dula 'two' dul 'cast metal'

 *cīmara* 'black ant' Rebus: *cīmara* 'copper'. *cīmara kāra* -- ' coppersmith '

 kanka 'rim of jar' Rebus: karṇīka 'account (scribe)' karṇī 'supercargo'

m1089A Pictorial motif hieroglyph: *balad* m. ' ox ', gng. *bald*, (Ku.) *barad*, id. (N. Tarai) Rebus: *bharat* (5 copper, 4 zinc and 1 tin)(Punjabi) *pattar* 'trough' Rebus: *pattar* 'guild'. Thus, copper-zinc-tin alloy (worker) guild.

 *dula* 'pair' Rebus: *dul* 'cast (metal)' PLUS*kana, kanac* = corner (Santali); Rebus: *kañcu* = bronze (Telugu) Thus, cast bronze

mogge 'sprout, bud' Rebus: *mũh* 'ingot' (Santali) sal 'splinter' Rebus: sal 'workshop' ranku 'liquid measure' Rebus: ranku 'tin'

 *kolmo* 'paddy plant' Rebus: *kolami* 'smithy, forge' Vikalpa: *mogge* 'sprout, bud' Rebus: *mũh* 'ingot' (Santali) dolu 'plant of shoot height' Rebus: dul 'cast metal'

 water-carrier hieroglyph *kuṭi*; Rebus: *kuṭhi* 'smelter furnace'.

m1202A Pictorial motif hieroglyph: *balad* m. ' ox ', gng. *bald*, (Ku.) *barad*, id. (N. Tarai) Rebus: *bharat* (5 copper, 4 zinc and 1 tin)(Punjabi) *pattar* 'trough' Rebus: *pattar* 'guild'. Thus, copper-zinc-tin alloy (worker) guild.

dula 'pair' Rebus: *dul* 'cast (metal)' PLUS*kana, kanac* = corner (Santali); Rebus: *kañcu* = bronze (Telugu) Thus, cast bronze

खडी [khaḍī] *f* खटी S) A squirrel (Marathi) Rebus 1:Pa. kandi (pl. -l) necklace,

beads. Ga. (Punjabi) kandi (pl. -l) bead, (pl.) necklace; (S.2) kandiṭ bead. (DEDR 1215)

Rebus : खंडी [khaṇḍī] A score (of sheep or goats, and of some certain things). A weight equivalent to 500 lbs. , *n. < Mhr. khaṇḍil. [T. Tu. khaṇḍi, M. kaṇḍi.]*

 kanka 'rim of jar' Rebus: karṇīka 'account (scribe)' karṇī 'supercargo'

 *aḍar* 'harrow'; rebus: *aduru* 'native unsmelted metal') *bhaṭa* 'warrior' (Sanskrit) Rebus: *baṭa* a kind of iron (Gujarati). Rebus: *bhaṭa* 'furnace' (Santali)

 kanka 'rim of jar' Rebus: karṇīka 'account (scribe)' karṇī 'supercargo'

dulo 'hole' Rebus: dul 'cast metal'

'Liquid measue' sign glyph: ranku 'liquid measure'' Rebus: ranku 'tin' (Santali)

Kalibangan 39A
Rhinoceros/boar: baḍhia = a castrated boar, a hog (Santali) baḍhi 'a caste who work both in iron and wood' (Santali) *baṟea* 'merchant'
ranku 'liquid measure'' Rebus: ranku 'tin' (Santali)

 *koḍi* 'flag' (Ta.)(DEDR 2049). Rebus 1: *koḍ* 'workshop' (Kuwi) Rebus 2: *khŏḍ* m. 'pit', *khŏḍü* f. 'small pit' (Kashmiri. CDIAL 3947).

 *kolmo* 'paddy plant' Rebus: *kolami* 'smithy, forge' Vikalpa: *mogge* 'sprout, bud' Rebus: *mūh* 'ingot' (Santali) dolu 'plant of shoot height' Rebus: dul 'cast metal'

m638a *kondh 'heifer'. kōḍu horn (Kannada. Tulu. Tamil) खोंड [khōṇḍa] m A young bull, a bullcalf. (Marathi) Rebus: kõdār 'turner' (Bengali); kõdā 'to turn in a lathe' (Bengali). कोंद kōnda 'engraver, lapidary setting or infixing gems' (Marathi)* G. *sãghāṛɔ* m. 'lathe' ; *sãgāḍā* m. ' frame of a building ', *°ḍī* f. ' lathe '(CDIAL 12859) Rebus*: sangataras.* संगतराश lit. 'to collect stones, stone-cutter, mason.' ranku 'liquid measure'' Rebus: ranku 'tin' (Santali)

 *kanka* 'rim of jar' Rebus: *karṇīka* 'account (scribe)' *karṇī* 'supercargo'

 *kanka* 'rim of jar' Rebus: *karṇīka* 'account (scribe)' *karṇī* 'supercargo' INFIXED kolom 'three' Rebus: kolami 'smithy, forge' *aya aḍaren (homonym: aduru)*'alloy native metal' *aya kammaṭa.*'coiner, mint alloy'

  *baroṭi* 'twelve' *bhārata* 'a factitious alloy of copper, pewter, tin' (Marathi) *aḍaren* 'cover of pot or lid' Rebus: *aduru* 'native, unsmelted metal' Duplicated: dula 'pair' Rebus: dul 'cast metal

Hulas 1A ranku 'liquid measure" Rebus: ranku 'tin' (Santali)

kuṭila 'bent'  CDIAL 3230 kuṭi— in cmpd. 'curve', *kuṭika—* 'bent' MBh. Rebus: *kuṭila, katthīl* = bronze (8 parts copper and 2 parts tin) Duplicated: dula 'pair' Rebus: dul 'cast metal' Thus, cast bronze or bronze castings.

 *kanka* 'rim of jar' Rebus: *karṇīka* 'account (scribe)' *karṇī* 'supercargo'

Lothal 112a ranku 'liquid measure" Rebus: ranku 'tin' (Santali)
ḍato = claws of crab (Santali) Rebus: *dhātu* 'mineral ore'PLUS dula 'pair' Rebus: dul 'cast metal' sal 'splinter' Rebus: sal 'workshop' Variant:

dula 'pair' Rebus: dul 'cast metal' PLUS | *koḍa* 'one' Rebus: *koḍ* 'workshop' PLUS INFIXED kolom
three' Rebus: kolami 'smithy, forge' Thus metalware castings forge. PLUS dula 'two' Rebus: dul 'cast metal'

 *dula* 'pair' Rebus: dul 'cast metal' *mogge* 'sprout, bud' Rebus: *mũh* 'ingot' (Santali) Thus, cast metal ingot.

 *kanka* 'rim of jar' Rebus: *karṇīka* 'account (scribe)' *karṇī* 'supercargo'

m378A ranku 'liquid measure" Rebus: ranku 'tin' (Santali)
 *kanka* 'rim of jar' Rebus: *karṇīka* 'account (scribe)' *karṇī* 'supercargo'

 *kanka* 'rim of jar' Rebus: *karṇīka* 'account (scribe)' *karṇī* 'supercargo' INFIXED kolom 'three' Rebus: kolami 'smithy, forge' खांडा [*khāṇḍā*] *m* A jag, notch, or indentation (as upon the edge of a tool or weapon). Rebus: *kāṇḍa* 'tools, pots and pans and metal-ware' *PLUS* dula 'two' Rebus: dul 'cast metal' PLUS kolom 'three' Rebus: kolami 'smithy, forge'

 *kolmo* 'paddy plant' Rebus: *kolami* 'smithy, forge' Vikalpa: *mogge* 'sprout, bud' Rebus: *mũh* 'ingot' (Santali) dolu 'plant of shoot height' Rebus: dul 'cast metal'

m1203A खोंड *[khōṇḍa] m A young bull, a bullcalf. (Marathi) Rebus: kõdār 'turner' (Bengali);* कोंद *kōnda 'engraver, lapidary setting or infixing gems' (Marathi) G. sãghāṛɔ m. 'lathe' ;* संघाट *joinery; M. sāgaḍ 'double-canoe' Rebus: sangataras 'stone-cutter, mason'*

G. *sãghāṛɔ* m. 'lathe' ; *sãgāḍā* m. ' frame of a building ', °*ḍī* f. ' lathe '(CDIAL 12859) Rebus*:* *sangataras.* संगतराश lit. 'to collect stones, stone-cutter, mason.'
ranku 'liquid measure" Rebus: ranku 'tin' (Santali) gaṇḍa 'four' Rebus: kaṇḍa 'furnace, fire-altar' (Santali)

 *muka* 'ladle' (Tamil)(DEDR 4887) Rebus: *mũh* 'ingot' (Santali) *baṭa* = rimless pot (Kannada) Rebus: *baṭa* = a kind of iron (G.)) *bhaṭa* furnace (Gujarati) Thus, iron ingot.

  *loa* 'ficus religiosa' Rebus: *lo* 'iron' (Sanskrit) PLUS unique ligatures: लोखंड [lōkhaṇḍa] *n* (लोह S) Iron. लोखंडाचे चणे खावविणें or चारणें To oppress grievously.लोखंडकाम [lōkhaṇḍakāma] *n* Iron work; that portion (of a building, machine &c.) which consists of iron. 2 The business of an ironsmith.लोखंडी [lōkhaṇḍī] *a* (लोखंड) Composed of iron; relating to iron. (Marathi) *bhaṭa* 'warrior' (Sanskrit) Rebus: *baṭa* a kind of iron (Gujarati). Rebus: *bhaṭa* 'furnace' (Santali) Thus, together, the ligatured hieroglyph reads rebus: *loa bhaṭa* 'iron furnace'

 m25A *खोंड [khōṇḍa] m A young bull, a bullcalf. (Marathi) Rebus: kōdār 'turner' (Bengali); कोंद kōnda 'engraver, lapidary setting or infixing gems' (Marathi) G. sãghārɔ m. 'lathe' ; संघाट joinery; M. sãgaḍ 'double-canoe' Rebus: sangataras 'stone-cutter, mason'* G. *sãghārɔ* m. 'lathe' ; *sãgāḍā* m. ' frame of a building ', *°ḍī* f. ' lathe '(CDIAL 12859) Rebus*: sangataras.*संगतराश lit. 'to collect stones, stone-cutter, mason.'
ranku 'liquid measure" Rebus: ranku 'tin' (Santali)

 *muka* 'ladle' (Tamil)(DEDR 4887) Rebus: *mũh* 'ingot' (Santali) *baṭa* = rimless pot (Kannada) Rebus: *baṭa* = a kind of iron (G.)) *bhaṭa* furnace (Gujarati) Thus, iron ingot.

 *aya aḍaren (homonym: aduru)*'alloy native metal'*khanḍ* 'field, division' (Skt.) Rebus: *khānḍa* 'tools, pots and pans, metal-ware'. Rebus 2: kanḍ 'fire-altar' (Santali) dula 'pair' Rebus: dul 'cast metal' Thus, duplicated 'division' hieroglyph sign reads: cast metal metal-ware.

 m74a *खोंड [khōṇḍa] m A young bull, a bullcalf. (Marathi) Rebus: kōdār 'turner' (Bengali); कोंद kōnda 'engraver, lapidary setting or infixing gems' (Marathi) G. sãghārɔ m. 'lathe' ; संघाट joinery; M. sãgaḍ 'double-canoe' Rebus: sangataras 'stone-cutter, mason'* G. *sãghārɔ* m. 'lathe' ; *sãgāḍā* m. ' frame of a building ', *°ḍī* f. ' lathe '(CDIAL 12859) Rebus*: sangataras.* संगतराश lit. 'to collect stones, stone-cutter, mason.'
ranku 'liquid measure" Rebus: ranku 'tin' (Santali)

 सांड [sāṇḍa] *f* (षद S) An outlet for superfluous water (as through a dam or mound); a sluice, a floodvent. Rebus: सांडणी [sāṇḍaṇī] *f* (H) An instrument of goldsmiths. It is hooked or curved at the extremity; and is used to draw things out of the fire.
सांठा [*sāṇṭhā*] *m* (संचय S) A collection, heap, hoard, store, stock.साटें [*sāṭēṃ*] *n* (संचय S) A whole investment; the total quantity of merchandise (brought to market by one merchant).
muka 'ladle' (Tamil)(DEDR 4887) Rebus: *mũh* 'ingot' (Santali) *baṭa* = rimless pot (Kannada)
 Rebus: *baṭa* = a kind of iron (G.)) *bhaṭa* furnace (Gujarati) Thus, iron ingot.
loa 'ficus religiosa' Rebus: *lo* 'iron' (Sanskrit) PLUS unique ligatures: लोखंड [lōkhaṇḍa
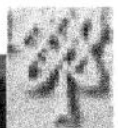 ] *n* (लोह S) Iron. लोखंडाचे चणे खावविणें or चारणें To oppress grievously.लोखंडकाम [lōkhaṇḍakāma] *n* Iron work; that portion (of a building, machine &c.) which consists of iron. 2 The business of an ironsmith.लोखंडी [lōkhaṇḍī] *a* (लोखंड) Composed of iron; relating to iron. (Marathi) *bhaṭa* 'warrior' (Sanskrit) Rebus: *baṭa* a kind of iron (Gujarati). Rebus: *bhaṭa* 'furnace' (Santali) Thus, together, the ligatured hieroglyph reads rebus: *loa bhaṭa* 'iron furnace'

m958a *खोंड [khōṇḍa] m A young bull, a bullcalf. (Marathi) Rebus: kõdār 'turner' (Bengali); कोंद kōnda 'engraver, lapidary setting or infixing gems' (Marathi) G. sãghāṛɔ m. 'lathe' ; संघाट joinery; M. sãgaḍ 'double-canoe' Rebus: sangataras 'stone-cutter, mason'* G. *sãghāṛɔ* m. 'lathe' ; *sãgāḍā* m. ' frame of a building ', °*ḍī* f. ' lathe '(CDIAL 12859) Rebus*: sangataras.* संगतराश lit. 'to collect stones, stone-cutter, mason.'

ranku 'liquid measure'' Rebus: ranku 'tin' (Santali) kolom 'three' Rebus: kolami 'smithy, forge'

kuṭila 'bent' CDIAL 3230 kuṭi— in cmpd. 'curve', *kuṭika—* 'bent' MBh. Rebus: *kuṭila, katthīl* = bronze (8 parts copper and 2 parts tin)

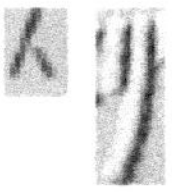

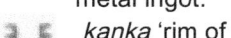

notch+slanted stroke reads rebus: *ḍhālako kāṇḍa* 'ingot, tools, pots and pans and metal-ware'.*dhāḷ* 'a slope'; 'inclination of a plane' (G.); *ḍhāḷiyum* = adj. sloping, inclining (G.) Rebus: *ḍhālako* = a large metal ingot (G.) *ḍhālakī* = a metal heated and poured into a mould; a solid piece of metal; an ingot (Gujarati) PLUS खांडा [*khāṇḍā*] *m* A jag, notch, or indentation (as upon the edge of a tool or weapon). Rebus: *kāṇḍa* 'tools, pots and pans and metal-ware' *aya kammaṭa.*'coiner, mint alloy'

Ligatured sign hieroglyph: 'Pair of harrows': *dul aduru* 'cast native unsmelted metal' PLUS kolmo 'paddy plant' Rebus: kolami 'smithy, forge'. Thus the composite hieroglyph denotes native metal smithy castings. Or, *mogge* 'sprout, bud' Rebus*: mũh* 'ingot': native cast metal ingot.

kanka 'rim of jar' Rebus: *karṇīka* 'account (scribe)' *karṇī* 'supercargo'

m979a *खोंड [khōṇḍa] m A young bull, a bullcalf. (Marathi) Rebus: kõdār 'turner' (Bengali); कोंद kōnda 'engraver, lapidary setting or infixing gems' (Marathi) G. sãghāṛɔ m. 'lathe' ; संघाट joinery; M. sãgaḍ 'double-canoe' Rebus: sangataras 'stone-cutter, mason'* G. *sãghāṛɔ* m. 'lathe' ; *sãgāḍā* m. ' frame of a building ', °*ḍī* f. ' lathe '(CDIAL 12859) Rebus*: sangataras.* संगतराश lit. 'to collect stones, stone-cutter, mason.'

ranku 'liquid measure'' Rebus: ranku 'tin' (Santali) kolom 'three' Rebus: kolami 'smithy, forge'

kuṭila 'bent' CDIAL 3230 kuṭi— in cmpd. 'curve', *kuṭika—* 'bent' MBh. Rebus: *kuṭila, katthīl* = bronze (8 parts copper and 2 parts tin) sal 'splinter' Rebus: sal 'workshop' *aya kammaṭa.*'coiner, mint alloy'

kolmo 'paddy plant' Rebus: *kolami* 'smithy, forge' Vikalpa: *mogge* 'sprout, bud' Rebus: *mũh* 'ingot' (Santali) dolu 'plant of shoot height' Rebus: dul 'cast metal'
Ligaure:

aḍar 'harrow'; rebus: *aduru* 'native unsmelted metal'

kanka 'rim of jar' Rebus: *karṇīka* 'account (scribe)' *karṇī* 'supercargo'

m1854a *खोंड [khōṇḍa] m A young bull, a bullcalf. (Marathi) Rebus: kõdār 'turner' (Bengali); कोंद kōnda 'engraver, lapidary setting or infixing gems'*

(Marathi) G. sãghāṛɔ m. 'lathe' ; संघाट joinery; M. sãgaḍ 'double-canoe' Rebus: sangataras 'stone-cutter, mason' G. *sãghāṛɔ* m. 'lathe' ; *sãgāḍā* m. ' frame of a building ', *°ḍī* f. ' lathe '(CDIAL 12859) Rebus*: sangataras.* संगतराश lit. 'to collect stones, stone-cutter, mason.' ranku 'liquid measure'' Rebus: ranku 'tin' (Santali) *kamaḍha* 'archer, bow' Rebus: *kammaṭa* 'mint, coiner'.

h611a ranku 'liquid measure'' Rebus: ranku 'tin' (Santali) *kamaḍha* 'archer, bow' Rebus: *kammaṭa* 'mint, coiner'. sal 'splinter' Rebus: sal 'workshop' *kamaḍha* 'crab' Rebus: *kammaṭa* 'mint, coiner'.

dula 'two, pair' Rebus: dul 'cast metal' PLUS *dhāḷ* 'a slope'; 'inclination of a plane' (G.); *ḍhāḷiyum* = adj. sloping, inclining (G.) Rebus: *ḍhālako* = a large metal ingot (G.) *ḍhālakī* = a metal heated and poured into a mould; a solid piece of metal; an ingot (Gujarati) PLUS kolom 'three' Rebus: kolami 'smithy, forge'. Thus cast metal ingot smithy.

m522A Copper plate.
ranku 'liquid measure'' Rebus: ranku 'tin' (Santali)
ranku 'antelope' Rebus: ranku 'tin' PLUS *Kur.* xolā tail. *Malt.* qoli id. (DEDR 2135). Rebus: kolhe 'smelter' Thus, copper smelter. dulo 'hole' Rebus: dul 'cast metal' *khaṇḍ* 'field, division' (Skt.) Rebus: *khāṇḍa* 'tools, pots and pans, metal-ware'. Rebus 2: kaṇḍ 'fire-altar' (Santali) dula 'pair' Rebus: dul 'cast metal' Thus cast metalware or metalware castings.

m248A *balad* m. ' ox ', gng. *bald*, (Ku.) *barad*, id. (N. Tarai) Rebus: *bharat* (5 copper, 4 zinc and 1 tin)(Punjabi) *pattar* 'trough' Rebus*: pattar* 'guild'. Thus, copper-zinc-tin alloy (worker) guild.

ranku 'liquid measure'' Rebus: ranku 'tin' (Santali)

muka 'ladle' (Tamil)(DEDR 4887) Rebus: *mũh* 'ingot' (Santali) *baṭa* = rimless pot (Kannada) Rebus: *baṭa* = a kind of iron (G.)) *bhaṭa* furnace (Gujarati) Thus, iron ingot. sal 'splinter' Rebus: sal 'workshop'

aḍar 'harrow'; rebus: *aduru* 'native unsmelted metal' *bhaṭa* 'warrior' (Sanskrit) Rebus: *baṭa* a kind of iron (Gujarati). Rebus: *bhaṭa* 'furnace' (Santali)

kanka 'rim of jar' Rebus: *karṇīka* 'account (scribe)' *karṇī* 'supercargo'

m1290A ranku 'liquid measure'' Rebus: ranku 'tin' (Santali)

āra 'spokes' Rebus: *āra 'brass'.* cf. erka = ekke (Tbh. of arka) aka (Tbh. of arka) copper (metal); crystal (Kannada) Glyph: *eraka*'nave of wheel' Rebus: eraka 'copper'; cf. erka = ekke (Tbh. of arka) aka (Tbh. of arka) copper (metal); crystal (Kannada) *erako* 'moltencast copper' Duplicated: dula 'pair' Rebus: dul 'cast metal' Thus cast copper, brass casting.

 *muka* 'ladle' (Tamil)(DEDR 4887) Rebus: *mūh* 'ingot' (Santali) *baṭa* = rimless pot

H-299 B

(Kannada) Rebus: *baṭa* = a kind of iron (G.)) *bhaṭa* furnace (Gujarati) Thus, iron ingot.
h299B ranku 'liquid measure" Rebus: ranku 'tin' (Santali)

 *muka* 'ladle' (Tamil)(DEDR 4887) Rebus: *mūh* 'ingot' (Santali) *baṭa* = rimless pot (Kannada) Rebus: *baṭa* = a kind of iron (G.)) *bhaṭa* furnace (Gujarati) Thus, iron ingot.

 *kanac* 'corner' Rebus: *kañcu* 'bronze'

h1708A ranku 'liquid measure" Rebus: ranku 'tin' (Santali)
kəṭhā'r, kc. *kuṭhār* m. ' granary, storeroom '(WPah.)(CDIAL 3550). *koṭhārī m.* ' storekeeper' (Gujarati)(CDIAL 3551) Thus, storeroom (of) *kolom* 'three' Rebus: *kolami* 'smithy, forge'. Dula 'pair' Rebus: dul 'cast metal' Thus, together *dul* *kolami kuṭhār* 'metal smithy castings storeroom'

INFIXED dulo 'hole' Rebus: dul 'cast metal' PLUS *kamaḍha* 'crab' Rebus: *kammaṭa* 'mint, coiner'.
ḍato = claws of crab (Santali) Rebus: *dhātu* 'mineral ore

h558a ranku 'liquid measure" Rebus: ranku 'tin' (Santali)

 *kana, kanac* = corner (Santali); Rebus: *kañcu* = bronze (Telugu) PLUS खांडा [*khāṇḍā*] *m* A jag, notch, or indentation (as upon the edge of a tool or weapon). Rebus: *kāṇḍa* 'tools, pots and pans and metal-ware' Thus, bronze metalware. INFIXED kolom 'three' Rebus: kolami 'smithy, forge' PLUS *khareḍo* = a currycomb (Gujarati) खरारा [*kharārā*] *m* (H) A currycomb. 2 Currying a horse. (Marathi) Rebus: करडा [*karaḍā*] Hard from alloy--iron, silver &c. (Marathi) *kharādī* ' turner' (Gujarati)

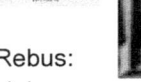

 *āra* 'spokes' Rebus: *āra 'brass'*. cf. erka = ekke (Tbh. of arka) aka (Tbh. of arka) copper (metal); crystal (Kannada) Glyph: *eraka*'nave of wheel' Rebus: eraka 'copper'; cf. erka = ekke (Tbh. of arka) aka (Tbh. of arka) copper (metal); crystal (Kannada) *erako* 'moltencast copper' Duplicated: dula 'pair' Rebus: dul 'cast metal' Thus cast copper, brass casting.

h645A ranku 'liquid measure" Rebus: ranku 'tin' (Santali)
kəṭhā'r, kc. *kuṭhār* m. ' granary, storeroom '(WPah.)(CDIAL 3550). *koṭhārī m.* ' storekeeper' (Gujarati)(CDIAL 3551) Thus, storeroom (of) *kolom* 'three' Rebus: *kolami* 'smithy, forge'. Dula 'pair' Rebus: dul 'cast metal' Thus, together *dul* *kolami kuṭhār* 'metal smithy castings storeroom'

 *kanka* 'rim of jar' Rebus: *karṇīka* 'account (scribe)' *karṇī* 'supercargo' *kamaḍha* 'crab' Rebus: *kammaṭa* 'mint, coiner'.
ḍato = claws of crab (Santali) Rebus: *dhātu* 'mineral ore'

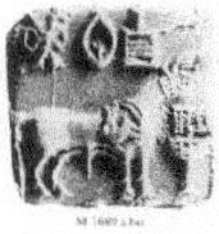

m1689a *खोंड [khōṇḍa] m A young bull, a bullcalf. (Marathi) Rebus: kõdār 'turner' (Bengali); कोंद kōnda 'engraver, lapidary setting or infixing gems' (Marathi) G. sãghāṛɔ m. 'lathe' ; संघाट joinery; M. sãgaḍ 'double-canoe' Rebus: sangataras 'stone-cutter, mason')* G. *sãghāṛɔ* m. 'lathe' ; *sãgāḍā* m. ' frame of a building ', *°ḍī* f. ' lathe '(CDIAL 12859) Rebus*: sangataras.* संगतराश lit. 'to collect stones, stone-cutter, mason.

ranku 'liquid measure" Rebus: ranku 'tin' (Santali)

dula 'pair' Rebus: *dul* 'cast (metal)' PLUS*kana, kanac* = corner (Santali); Rebus: *kañcu* = bronze (Telugu) PLUS infixed kolmo 'paddy plant' Rebus: kolami 'smithy, forge'. Thus, cast bronze smithy, forge. Or, *mogge* 'sprout, bud' Rebus: *mũh* 'ingot' (Santali)Thus, cast bronze ingot. Read as: *kañcu dul mũh 'bronze cast ingot'*

water-carrier hieroglyph *kuṭi*; Rebus: *kuṭhi* 'smelter furnace'.

PLUS 'rim of jar': *kanka* (Santali) *karṇika* 'scribe'(Sanskrit) Rebus: *karṇī,* supercargo 'rim-of-jar' hieroglyph *kanka* (Santali) *karṇika* 'scribe'(Sanskrit)

Rebus: *karṇī,* supercargo for a boat shipment. *karṇīka* 'account (scribe)'.कारणी *kāraṇī* 'the supercargo of a ship.

h1046a *खोंड [khōṇḍa] m A young bull, a bullcalf. (Marathi) Rebus: kõdār 'turner' (Bengali); कोंद kōnda 'engraver, lapidary setting or infixing gems' (Marathi) G. sãghāṛɔ m. 'lathe' ; संघाट joinery; M. sãgaḍ 'double-canoe' Rebus: sangataras 'stone-cutter, mason'*

ranku 'liquid measure" Rebus: ranku 'tin' (Santali)

khōṇḍa A stock or stump (Marathi); 'leafless tree' (Marathi) Rebus: *kõdār* 'turner' (Bengali); *kõdā* 'to turn in a lathe' (Bengali).

water-carrier hieroglyph *kuṭi*; Rebus: *kuṭhi* 'smelter furnace'.

PLUS 'rim of jar': *kanka* (Santali) *karṇika* 'scribe'(Sanskrit) Rebus: *karṇī,* supercargo 'rim-of-jar' hieroglyph *kanka* (Santali) *karṇika* 'scribe'(Sanskrit) Rebus: *karṇī,* supercargo for a

boat shipment. *karṇīka* 'account (scribe)'.कारणी *kāraṇī* 'the supercargo of a ship'

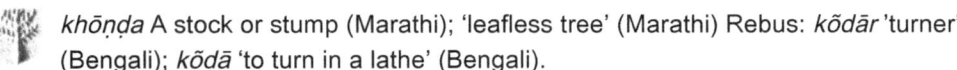

m998a *खोंड [khōṇḍa] m A young bull, a bullcalf. (Marathi) Rebus: kõdār 'turner' (Bengali); कोंद kōnda 'engraver, lapidary setting or infixing gems' (Marathi) G. sãghāṛɔ m. 'lathe' ; संघाट joinery; M. sãgaḍ 'double-canoe' Rebus: sangataras 'stone-cutter, mason'* G. *sãghāṛɔ* m. 'lathe' ; *sãgāḍā* m. ' frame of a building ', *°ḍī* f. ' lathe '(CDIAL 12859) Rebus*: sangataras.* संगतराश lit. 'to collect stones, stone-cutter, mason.'

ranku 'liquid measure" Rebus: ranku 'tin' (Santali)

kolmo 'paddy plant' Rebus: *kolami* 'smithy, forge' Vikalpa: *mogge* 'sprout, bud' Rebus: *mũh* 'ingot' (Santali) dolu 'plant of shoot height' Rebus: dul 'cast metal'

āra 'spokes' Rebus: *āra 'brass'.* cf. erka = ekke (Tbh. of arka) aka (Tbh. of arka) copper (metal); crystal (Kannada) Glyph: *eraka*'nave of wheel' Rebus: eraka 'copper'; cf. erka = ekke (Tbh. of arka) aka (Tbh. of arka) copper (metal); crystal (Kannada) *erako* 'moltencast copper' Duplicated: dula 'pair' Rebus: dul 'cast metal' Thus cast copper, brass casting.

h816A Read rebus as at h75a

h75a *खोंड [khōṇḍa] m A young bull, a bullcalf. (Marathi) Rebus: kõdār 'turner' (Bengali); कोंद kōnda 'engraver, lapidary setting or infixing gems' (Marathi) G. sãghāṛɔ m. 'lathe' ; संघाट joinery; M. sãgaḍ 'double-canoe' Rebus: sangataras 'stone-cutter, mason'* G. *sãghāṛɔ* m. 'lathe' ; *sãgāḍā* m. ' frame of a building ', *°ḍī* f. ' lathe '(CDIAL 12859) Rebus*: sangataras.* संगतराश lit. 'to collect stones, stone-cutter, mason.'

ranku 'liquid measure" Rebus: ranku 'tin' (Santali)

kolmo 'paddy plant' Rebus: *kolami* 'smithy, forge' Vikalpa: *mogge* 'sprout, bud' Rebus: *mũh* 'ingot' (Santali) dolu 'plant of shoot height' Rebus: dul 'cast metal'

kanka 'rim of jar' Rebus: *karṇīka* 'account (scribe)' *karṇī* 'supercargo'

kharedo = a currycomb (Gujarati) खरारा [*kharārā*] *m* (H) A currycomb. 2 Currying a horse. (Marathi) Rebus: करडा [*karaḍā*] Hard from alloy--iron, silver &c. (Marathi) *kharādī* ' turner' (Gujarati)

h158A First three signs read rebus as at h75a

खांडा [*khāṇḍā*] *m* A jag, notch, or indentation (as upon the edge of a tool or weapon). Rebus: *kāṇḍa* 'tools, pots and pans and metal-ware' *ḍhanga* = a crook used for pulling down the branches of trees, for goats, sheep and camels (P.) Rebus:*ḍhangar* blacksmith'. PLUS

kharedo = a currycomb (Gujarati) खरारा [*kharārā*] *m* (H) A currycomb. 2 Currying a horse. (Marathi) Rebus: करडा [*karaḍā*] Hard from alloy--iron, silver &c. (Marathi) *kharādī* ' turner' (Gujarati)

dula 'pair' Rebus: *dul* 'cast (metal)' PLUS*kana, kanac* = corner (Santali); Rebus: *kañcu* = bronze (Telugu) PLUS infixed kolmo 'paddy plant' Rebus: kolami 'smithy, forge'. Thus, cast bronze smithy, forge. Or, *mogge* 'sprout, bud' Rebus: *mũh* 'ingot' (Santali)Thus, cast bronze ingot. Read as: *kañcu dul mũh 'bronze cast ingot'*

water-carrier hieroglyph *kuṭi*; Rebus: *kuṭhi* 'smelter furnace'. PLUS 'rim of jar': *kanka* (Santali) *karṇika* 'scribe'(Sanskrit) Rebus: *karṇī,* supercargo

'rim-of-  jar' hieroglyph *kanka* (Santali) *karṇika* 'scribe'(Sanskrit) Rebus: *karṇī,* supercargo for a boat shipment. *karṇīka* 'account (scribe)'.कारणी *kāraṇī* 'the supercargo of a ship'

m968A *खोंड [khōṇḍa] m A young bull, a bullcalf. (Marathi) Rebus: kõdār 'turner' (Bengali); कोंद kōnda 'engraver, lapidary setting or infixing gems' (Marathi) G. sãghāṛɔ m. 'lathe' ; संघाट joinery; M. sãgaḍ 'double-canoe' Rebus: sangataras 'stone-*

cutter, mason' G. *sãghāṛɔ* m. 'lathe' ; *sãgāḍā* m. ' frame of a building ', *°ḍī* f. ' lathe '(CDIAL 12859) Rebus*: sangataras.* संगतराश lit. 'to collect stones, stone-cutter, mason.'
ranku 'liquid measure'' Rebus: ranku 'tin' (Santali)

kolmo 'paddy plant' Rebus: *kolami* 'smithy, forge' Vikalpa: *mogge* 'sprout, bud' Rebus: *mũh* 'ingot' (Santali) dolu 'plant of shoot height' Rebus: dul 'cast metal'

kanka (Santali) *karṇika* 'scribe'(Sanskrit) Rebus: *karṇī,* supercargo for a boat shipment. INFIXED खांडा [*khāṇḍā*] *m* A jag, notch, or indentation (as upon the edge of a tool or weapon). Rebus: *kāṇḍa* 'tools, pots and pans and metal-ware'

kuṭila 'bent' CDIAL 3230 kuṭi— in cmpd. 'curve', *kuṭika—* 'bent' MBh. Rebus: *kuṭila, katthīl* = bronze (8 parts copper and 2 parts tin) Duplicated: dula 'pair' Rebus: dul 'cast metal' Thus, cast bronze or bronze castings.

kanka 'rim of jar' Rebus: karṇīka 'account (scribe)' karṇī 'supercargo'

m734A *खोंड [khōṇḍa] m A young bull, a bullcalf. (Marathi) Rebus: kõdār 'turner' (Bengali);* कोंद *kōnda 'engraver, lapidary setting or infixing gems' (Marathi) G. sãghāṛɔ m. 'lathe' ;* संघाट *joinery; M. sãgaḍ 'double-canoe' Rebus: sangataras 'stone-cutter, mason'* G. *sãghāṛɔ* m. 'lathe' ; *sãgāḍā* m. ' frame of a building ', *°ḍī* f. ' lathe '(CDIAL 12859) Rebus*: sangataras.* संगतराश lit. 'to collect stones, stone-cutter, mason.'

ranku 'liquid measure'' Rebus: ranku 'tin' (Santali)

kolmo 'paddy plant' Rebus: *kolami* 'smithy, forge' Vikalpa: *mogge* 'sprout, bud' Rebus: *mũh* 'ingot' (Santali) dolu 'plant of shoot height' Rebus: dul 'cast metal'

koḍi 'flag' (Ta.)(DEDR 2049). Rebus 1: *koḍ* 'workshop' (Kuwi) Rebus 2: *khõḍ* m. 'pit', *khõḍü* f. 'small pit' (Kashmiri. CDIAL 3947).
kolom 'three' Rebus: kolami 'smithy, forge' Duplicated: dula 'pair' Rebus: dul 'cast metal' Thus smithy for castings.

m1592A Read rebus as at Allahdino 1A.

m1301A Read rebus as at Allahdino 1A

h533A 
First 2 signs read rebus as at Allahdino 1A

Allahdino 1A *खोंड [khōṇḍa] m A young bull, a bullcalf. (Marathi) Rebus: kõdār 'turner' (Bengali);* कोंद *kōnda 'engraver, lapidary setting or infixing gems' (Marathi) G. sãghāṛɔ m. 'lathe' ;* संघाट *joinery; M. sãgaḍ 'double-canoe'*

Rebus: sangataras 'stone-cutter, mason' G. *sãghāṛɔ* m. 'lathe' ; *sãgāḍā* m. ' frame of a building ', *°ḍī* f. ' lathe '(CDIAL 12859) Rebus*: sangataras.* संगतराश lit. 'to collect stones, stone-cutter, mason.

ranku 'liquid measure" Rebus: ranku 'tin' (Santali)

kolmo 'paddy plant' Rebus: *kolami* 'smithy, forge' Vikalpa: *mogge* 'sprout, bud' Rebus: *mūh* 'ingot' (Santali) dolu 'plant of shoot height' Rebus: dul 'cast metal'

kanka 'rim of jar' Rebus: *karṇīka* 'account (scribe)' *karṇī* 'supercargo'

Chanhudaro 2a खोंड *[khōṇḍa] m A young bull, a bullcalf. (Marathi) Rebus: kōdār 'turner' (Bengali);* कोंद *kōnda 'engraver, lapidary setting or infixing gems' (Marathi) G. sãghāṛɔ m. 'lathe' ;* संघाट *joinery; M. sãgaḍ 'double-canoe' Rebus: sangataras 'stone-cutter, mason'* G. *sãghāṛɔ* m. 'lathe' ; *sãgāḍā* m. ' frame of a building ', *°ḍī* f. ' lathe '(CDIAL 12859) Rebus*: sangataras.* संगतराश lit. 'to collect stones, stone-cutter, mason.'

ranku 'liquid measure" Rebus: ranku 'tin' (Santali)

khōṇḍa A stock or stump (Marathi); 'leafless tree' (Marathi) Rebus: *kõdār* 'turner' (Bengali); *kõdā* 'to turn in a lathe' (Bengali). Allograph

kanka 'rim of jar' Rebus: karṇīka 'account (scribe)' karṇī 'supercargo'

m1452B *krammara* 'head turned back' Rebus: *kamar* 'artisan, blacksmith' खोंड *[khōṇḍa] m A young bull, a bullcalf. (Marathi) Rebus: kōdār 'turner' (Bengali);* कोंद *kōnda 'engraver, lapidary setting or infixing gems' (Marathi) G. sãghāṛɔ m. 'lathe' ;* संघाट *joinery; M. sãgaḍ 'double-canoe' Rebus: sangataras 'stone-cutter, mason'* G. *sãghāṛɔ* m. 'lathe' ; *sãgāḍā* m. ' frame of a building ', *°ḍī* f. ' lathe '(CDIAL 12859) Rebus*: sangataras.* संगतराश lit. 'to collect stones, stone-cutter, mason.'
Kur. xolā tail. *Malt.* qoli id. (DEDR 2135). Rebus: kolhe 'smelter' Thus, copper smelter.

ranku 'liquid measure" Rebus: ranku 'tin' (Santali) *kolmo* 'paddy plant' Rebus: *kolami* 'smithy, forge' Vikalpa: *mogge* 'sprout, bud' Rebus: *mūh* 'ingot' (Santali) dolu 'plant of shoot height' Rebus: dul 'cast metal'

kanka 'rim of jar' Rebus: *karṇīka* 'account (scribe)' *karṇī* 'supercargo'

h682a

muka 'ladle' (Kannada)

(Tamil)(DEDR 4887) Rebus: *mūh* 'ingot' (Santali) *baṭa* = rimless pot Rebus: *baṭa* = a kind of iron (G.)) *bhaṭa* furnace (Gujarati) Thus, iron ingot.

ranku 'liquid measure" Rebus: ranku 'tin' (Santali) *kamaḍha* 'archer, bow' Rebus: *kammaṭa* 'mint, coiner'.

dula 'pair' Rebus: dul 'cast metal' PLUS | *koḍa* 'one' Rebus: *koḍ* 'workshop' PLUS INFIXED kolom

three' Rebus: kolami 'smithy, forge' Thus metalware castings forge.

 *kanac* 'corner' Rebus: *kañcu* 'bronze'

h389A *खोंड [khōṇḍa] m A young bull, a bullcalf. (Marathi) Rebus: kõdār 'turner' (Bengali); कोंद kōnda 'engraver, lapidary setting or infixing gems' (Marathi) G. sãghāṛɔ m. 'lathe' ; संघाट joinery; M. sãgaḍ 'double-canoe' Rebus: sangataras 'stone-cutter, mason'* G. *sãghāṛɔ* m. 'lathe' ; *sãgāḍā* m. ' frame of a building ', *°ḍī* f. ' lathe '(CDIAL 12859) Rebus*: sangataras.* संगतराश lit. 'to collect stones, stone-cutter, mason.'

 *kanac* 'corner' Rebus: *kañcu* 'bronze'

aḍaren 'cover of pot or lid' Rebus: *aduru* 'native, unsmelted metal' Duplicated: dula 'pair' Rebus: dul 'cast metal'

koḍ = one (Santali); koḍ 'workshop' (Gujarati)

sal 'splinter' Rebus: sal 'workshop' PLUS *aya aḍaren (homonym: aduru)*'alloy native metal'

ranku 'liquid measure" Rebus: ranku 'tin' (Santali) *kolmo* 'paddy plant' Rebus: *kolami* 'smithy, forge' Vikalpa: *mogge* 'sprout, bud' Rebus: *mũh* 'ingot' (Santali) dolu 'plant of shoot height' Rebus: dul 'cast metal'

 *kanka* 'rim of jar' Rebus: *karṇīka* 'account (scribe)' *karṇī* 'supercargo'

m331a

 *kanac* 'corner' Rebus: *kañcu* 'bronze'

 *kuṭila* 'bent' CDIAL 3230 kuṭi— in cmpd. 'curve', *kuṭika*— 'bent' MBh. Rebus: *kuṭila, katthīl* = bronze (8 parts copper and 2 parts tin) Ligature: खांडा [*khāṇḍā*] *m* A jag, notch, or indentation (as upon the edge of a tool or weapon). Rebus: *kāṇḍa* 'tools, pots and pans and metal-ware'

 Circumscript: *kuṭila* 'bent' CDIAL 3230 kuṭi— in cmpd. 'curve', *kuṭika*— 'bent' MBh. Rebus: *kuṭila, katthīl* = bronze (8 parts copper and 2 parts tin) Duplicated: dula 'pair' Rebus: dul 'cast metal' Thus, cast bronze or bronze castings.

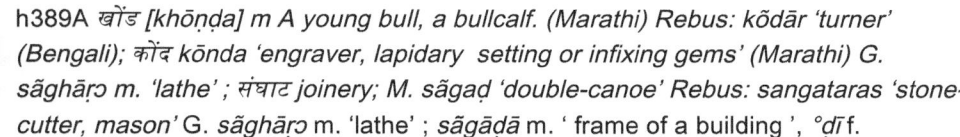

'Arrow' sign hieroglyph (variant) This is a ligature of 'lid of pot' hieroglyph superscript on 'a linear stroke' numeral hieroglyph.*aḍaren* 'cover of pot or lid' Rebus: *aduru* 'native, unsmelted metal' PLUS koḍ = one (Santali); koḍ 'workshop' (Gujarati)

gaṇḍa 'four' Rebus: kaṇḍa 'furnace, fire-altar' (Santali)

 mēḍu height, rising ground, hillock (Kannada) Rebus: *mẽṛhẽt, meḍ* 'iron' (Munda.Ho.) kolom 'three' Rebus: kolami 'smithy, forge' sal 'splinter' Rebus: sal 'workshop'.

h6A *खोंड [khōṇḍa] m A young bull, a bullcalf. (Marathi) Rebus: kõdār 'turner' (Bengali); कोंद kōnda 'engraver, lapidary setting or infixing gems' (Marathi) G. sãghāṛɔ m. 'lathe' ; संघाट joinery; M. sãgaḍ 'double-canoe' Rebus: sangataras 'stone-cutter, mason'* G. *sãghāṛɔ* m. 'lathe' ; *sãgāḍā* m. ' frame of a building ', *°ḍī* f. ' lathe '(CDIAL 12859) Rebus*: sangataras.* संगतराश lit. 'to collect stones, stone-cutter, mason.'

 *kanac* 'corner' Rebus: *kañcu* 'bronze'

kolom 'three' Rebus: kolami 'smithy, forge' INFIXED *mogge* 'sprout, bud' Rebus: *mũh* 'ingot' (Santali) dula 'two' Rebus: dul 'cast metal' PLUS खांडा [*khāṇḍā*] *m* A jag, notch, or indentation (as upon the edge of a tool or weapon). Rebus: *kāṇḍa* 'tools, pots and pans and metal-ware' Thus, mint metalware, ore.

kamaḍha 'archer, bow' Rebus: *kammaṭa* 'mint, coiner'.

 dula 'pair' Rebus: dul 'cast metal' PLUS | *koḍa* 'one' Rebus: *koḍ* 'workshop' PLUS INFIXED kolom three' Rebus: kolami 'smithy, forge' Thus metalware castings forge.

Section F: *Cire perdue* (lost wax) castings, forge

Note on *cīmara* and *dhokra*

Both the words *cīmara* and *dhokra* are attested in Meluhha hieroglyphs.

cīmara -- ' copper ' *cīmara -- kāra* -- ' coppersmith ' (Pali) Shgh. *čindōn* ' furnace for smelting iron ' perh. ← Dardic or Kafiri e.g. Kt. *čimə* in cmpds. like *čim -- dur* ' saucepan ' Md. *timara* ' lead, tin '(CDIAL 4842) [The Kaf. and Dard. word for ' iron ' appears also in Bur. *čhomār*, *čhumər*. Turk. *timur* (NTS ii 250) may come from the same unknown source. Semant. cf. lōhá --]Ash. *ċímä*, *ċimə* ' iron ' (*ċiməkára* ' blacksmith '), Kt. *čimédotdot;*, Wg. *čümā´r*, Pr. *zíme*, Dm. *čimár(r)*, Paš.lauṛ. *čimā´r*, Shum. *čímar*, Woṭ. Gaw. *ċimár*, Kal. *čĩmbar*, Kho. *čúmur*, Bshk. *čimer*, Tor. *čimu*, Mai. *sēwar*, Phal. *čímar*, Sh.gil. *čimĕr* (adj. *čĭmārī*), gur. *čimăr* m., jij. *čimer*, K. *ċamuru* m. (adj. *ċamaruwu*).(CDIAL 14496).

The lexical entry notes that the phrase *cīmara -- kāra* occurs in Buddhist Hybrid Sanskrit text called *Saṁghāṭa sūtra* Gilgit MS. 37 folio 85 verso, 3 (= *zaṅs-- mkhan* in Tibetan Pekin text Vol. 28 Japanese facsimile 285 a 3 which in Mahāvyutpatti 3790 renders *śaulbika*-- BHS ii 533. But the Chinese version (Taishō issaikyō ed. text no. 423 p. 971 col. 3, line 2) has *t'ie* 'iron': H. W. Bailey 21.2.65). Āryasamghāṭa sūtram is an unpublished Digital Sanskrit Buddhist Canon. http://www.dsbcproject.org/node/7683 cf. Editor: Oskar von Hinüber

The term '*dhokra kamar*' refers in Hindu tradition, to artisans working with lost wax casting techniques for alloy metal castings.

A note on the 27 manuscripts available in Khotanese and the Sogdian SghS appears in an article by Ilya Yakubovich and Yutaka Yoshida, '2005, The Sogdian fragments of *Saṁghāṭa* sutra in the German Turfan Collection' in: Weber, Dieter, ed., *Languages of Iran: past and present – Iranian studies in memoriam David Neil MacKenzie*, Harrassowitz Verlag, Wiesbaden.
https://www.academia.edu/582862/The_Sogdian_fragments_of_Samghata_Sutra_the_German_Turfan_Collection

The word *saṁghāṭa* means: 'fitting and joining of timber, joinery , carpentry'. The text involves artisans in the inquiry mentioned in the fragments of the Bauddham text. The semantics of *saṁghāṭa* provide a rebus interpretation for the 'standard device' or 'lahe-cum-portable furnace' hieroglyph shown in front of the young bull on hundreds of epigraphs. The Meluhha ciphertext reading of this hieroglyph is: . *sãghāṛɔ* m. 'lathe' (Gujarati) The plain text rendering as *saṁghāṭa* 'joinery' is consistent with the work of the 'turner' artisan: *kōdār* 'turner'.

The specialist working with metals using the specialized technique of *cire perdue* (lost-wax casting) during the early bronze age was called in Meluhha language: *dhokra kamar*.

This professional title, *dhokra kamar*, is evidenced by Meluhha hieroglyphs on a seal from Mohenjo-daro and on a tablet from Dholavira of Sarasvati Civilization. In ancient Indian texts, the *cire perdue* technique is referred to as *madhucchiṣṭa vidhānam*. मधु madhu -उच्छिष्टम्,-उत्थभ्,-उत्थितभ् 1 bees'-wax; शस्त्रासवमधूच्छिष्टं मधु लाक्षा च बर्हिषः Y.3.37; मधूच्छिष्टेन केचिच्च जध्रुरन्योन्यमुत्कटाः Rām.5.62.11.-2 the casting of an image in wax; Mānasāra; the name of 68th chapter. This technique was clearly attested in the Epic *Rāmāyaṇa*.मधुशिष्ट madhuśiṣṭa 'wax' (Monier-Williams, p. 780).

Muhly speculates on the possible reason for using of hard alloy for lost-wax castings:

"...perhaps arsenical copper was used at Nahal Mishmar not because it was harder, more durable metal but because it would have facilitated the production of intricate lost-wax castings." (Muhly, J., 1986, The beginnings of metallurgy in the old world. In Maddin R, ed., The beginning of the use of metals and alloys, pp. 2-20. Zhengzhou: Second International conference on the beginning of the use of metals and alloys.)

Lost-wax casting. Bronze statue, Mohenjo-daro. Bronze statue of a woman holding a small bowl, Mohenjo-daro; copper alloy made using cire perdue method (DK 12728; Mackay 1938: 274, Pl. LXXIII, 9-11)

'Dancing girl' 10.8 cm. from Mohenjo-daro of Sarasvati civilization dates to the early 2nd millennium BCE. (Marshall, 1931, *Mohenjo-daro and the Indus civilization*, Vol. I, London, Arthus Probsthain, p. 345; pl. 94)."Metallurgists smelted silver, lead, and copper and worked gold too. Coppersmiths employed tin bronze as in Sumer, but also an alloy of copper with from 3.4 to 4.4 per cent of arsenic, an alloy used also at Anau in Transcaspia. They could cast *cire perdue* (lost wax) and rivet, but never seem to have resorted to brazing or soldering." (Childe, Gordon, 1952, New light on the most ancien East, New York, Frederick A. Praeger)

Dance step Meluhha hieroglyph: meṭ sole of foot, footstep, footprint (Ko.); meṭṭu step, stair, treading, slipper (Te.)(DEDR 1557). Rebus: *meḍ* 'iron'(Munda); मेढ meḍh'merchant's helper'(Pkt.) *meḍ* iron (Ho.) *meṛed-bica* = iron stone ore, in contrast to bali-bica, iron sand ore (Munda)

Meluhha hieroglyph: young girl: *kṝtā* -- 'girl' (RV); *kuṛä´* 'girl' (Ash.); *kola* 'woman' (Nahali); 'wife'(Assamese). *kuḍa1 ' boy, son ', *°ḍī* ' girl, daughter '. [Prob. ← Mu. (Sant. Muṇḍari *koṛa* ' boy ', *kuṛi* ' girl ', Ho *koa, kui*, Kūrkū *kōn, kōnjē*); or ← Drav. (Tam. *kuṟa* ' young ', Kan.*koḍa* ' youth ') T. Burrow BSOAS xii 373. Prob. separate from RV. *kṝtā* -- ' girl ' H. W. Bailey TPS 1955, 65. -- Cf. *kuḍáti* ' acts like a child ' Dhātup.] NiDoc. *kuḍ'aǵa* ' boy ', *kuḍ'i* ' girl '; Ash. *kū´ṛə* ' child, foetus ', *istrimalī -- kuṛä´* ' girl '; Kt. *kŕū, kuŕuk* ' young of animals '; Pr. *kyútru* ' young of animals, child ', *kyurú* ' boy ',*kurī´* ' colt, calf '; Dm. *kúŕa* ' child ', Shum. *kuṛ*, Kal. *kūr*lk* ' young of animals '; Phal. *kuṝī* ' woman, wife '; K. *kūrü* f. ' young girl ', kash. *kōṛī*, ram. *kuṛhī*; L. *kuṛā* m. ' bridegroom ',*kuṛī* f. ' girl, virgin, bride ', awāṇ. *kuṛī* f. ' woman '; P. *kuṛī* f. ' girl, daughter ', P. bhaṭ. WPah. khaś. *kuṛi*, cur. *kuḷī*, cam. *kŏḷā* ' boy ', *kuṛī* ' girl '; -- B. *ā̃ṭ -- kuṛā* ' childless ' (*ā̃ṭa* ' tight ')? -- X pṓta -- 1: WPah. bhad. *kō* ' son ', *kūī* ' daughter ', bhal. *ko* m., *koi* f., pāḍ.*kuā, kōī*, paṅ. *koā, kūī.* (CDIAL 3245)

Rebus: kōla1 m. ' name of a degraded tribe ' Hariv. Pk. *kōla* -- m.; B. *kol* ' name of a Muṇḍā tribe'(CDIAL 3532). kolhe 'smelters.*Ta.* kol working in iron, blacksmith kollaṉ blacksmith. *Ma.* kollan blacksmith,artificer.*Ko.* kole·l smithy, temple in Kota village. *To.* kwala·l Kota smithy. *Ka.* kolime, kolume, kulame, kulime, kulume, kulme fire-pit, furnace ; (Bell.; U.P.U.) konimi blacksmith (Gowda kolla id. *Koḍ.* kollë blacksmith. *Te.* kolimi furnace. *Go.* kollusānā to mend implements; (Ph.) kolstānā, kulsānā to forge ; (Tr.)kōlstānā to repair (of ploughshares); (SR.) kolmi smithy (*Voc.* 948). *Kuwi* (F.) kolhali to forge. (DEDR 2133).

Nahal Mishmar. Crown with building facade decoration and birds.

Hieroglyphs on Nahal Mishkar crown artifact::

'Duck' hieroglyph: *karaṇḍa* 'duck' (Sanskrit) *karaṛa* 'a very large aquatic bird' (Sindhi)
Rebus: करडा [*karaḍā*] Hard from alloy--iron, silver &c. (Marathi) *dula* 'pair' Rebus: *dul* 'cast metal'.

'Six' knobs on the frame of the structure: *āra* 'six' Rebus: *āra* 'brass'. *sãgāḍā* m. ' frame of a building ' (M.)(CDIAL 12859) Rebus: *jaṅgaḍ* 'entrustment articles' *sãgaṛh* m. ' line of entrenchments, stone walls for defence ' (Lahnda).(CDIAL 12845) Allograph: *saṅgaḍa* 'lathe'. 'potable furnace'. *sang* 'stone', *gaḍa* 'large stone'. *dula* 'pair' Rebus: *dul* 'cast metal'. *koḍ* 'horns' Rebus: *koḍ* 'artisan's workshop'.

'Ibex' hieroglyph: Dm. mraṅ m. 'markhor' Wkh. merg f. 'ibex' (CDIAL 9885) Tor. miṇḍ 'ram', miṇḍāl 'markhor' (CDIAL 10310) Rebus: meḍ (Ho.); mẽṛhet 'iron' (Munda.Ho.) dula 'pair' Rebus: dul 'cast metal'.

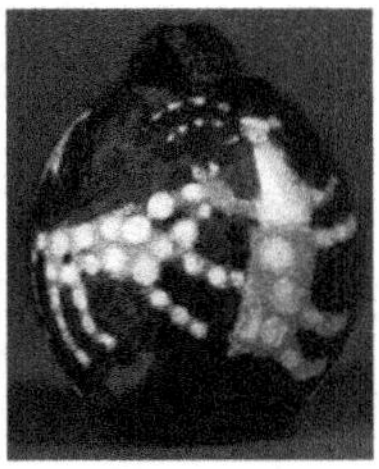

The Leopards weight from Shahi Tump - Photography and 30 MeV accelerator tomodensimetry showing the copper shell and the lead filling.(Science for Cultural Heritage: Technological Innovation and Case Studies in Marine and Land Archaeology in the Adriatic Region and Inland : VII International Conference on Science, Arts and Culture : August 28-31, 2007, Veli Lošinj, Croatia, World Scientific, 2010. The aim of the conference was to discuss the contribution of physics and other sciences in archaeological research and in the preservation of cultural heritage.)

Pictorial hieroglyphs on Shahi Tump weight: *karaḍa* 'panther' Rebus: *karaḍa* 'hard alloy'. mlekh 'goat' Rebus: milakkhu 'copper' (Pali)

Cireperdue method was used in Uruk, ca. 3500 BCE. to make a recumbent ram in silver which is mounted on pins and dowelled into the center of a cylinder seal. This was a hieroglyph, tagged to cylinder seal method of writing by impressing an agreement to a transaction or to indicate ownership. This cylinder seal is carved with figures of cattle. Ashmolean Museum, Univ. of Oxford. "The Ashmolean Museum describes this item as a cylinder seal showing a herd of cattle and reed huts containing calves and vessels. The seal itself is made of magnesite ($MgCO_3$) with small (a few centimeters) cast silver ram-shaped finial. No claim is made by the museum that it was produced by the Lost Wax process and it is dated by the museum to the Late Uruk period or "around 3200 BCE". The item has been purchased by the museum but its provenance is unknown and therefore cannot be precisely dated." (Shlomo Guil)

'Young bull' hieroglyph on Uruk cylinder seal:
खोंड [khōṇḍa] m A young bull, a bullcalf. (Marathi) Rebus: kõdār 'turner' (Bengali); कोंद kōnda 'engraver, lapidary setting or infixing gems' (Marathi) G. sãghāṛɔ m. 'lathe' ; संघाट joinery; M. sãgaḍ 'double-canoe' Rebus: sangataras 'stone-cutter, mason'
'Mudhif' hieroglyph: *mūdh* ' ridge of roof ' (Assamese)(CDIAL 10247) Rebus: *mund* 'Toda *mund* hut, house, temple' (Toda)

'Six' rings atop the reed of the Mudhif depicted on Uruk cylinder seal: *āra* 'six' Rebus: *āra* 'brass' Thus, signifying, brass (making) hut, *āra 'mund.*

Allolgraph: ||| Numeral three strokes: mūnḍ, (L.) munḍ, (Pat.) muḍu three (Go.); mūnd three things.(Kur.)(DEDR 5052). Vikalpa: *kolom* 'three' (Santali) Rebus: kolami 'smithy, forge'.

Bronze bull. 5 in. h. X 7 in. l. Empty eye-sockets possibly held semiprecious stones. The small hump on its back, amove the forelegs, identifies this as a "Zebu bull" (*Bos indicus*), a species that originated in India , but which was present in the Near East as early as the fourth millennium B.C.E. Prof. Amihai Mazar, 1983, Bronze Bull Found in Israelite "High Place" from the Time of the Judges, *BAR* 9:05, Sep/Oct 1983 notes that the discovery was made on the summit of a hill in northern Samaria.

Copper bull's head from the Dilmun era, found at. Barbar Temple, along with early Dilmun seals.

Meluhha rebus readings:

khũṭ 'zebu'. Rebus: *khũṭ* 'guild, community'; *adar ḍaṅgra* 'zebu or humped bull'; rebus: *aduru* 'native metal' (Kannada); *ḍhangar* 'blacksmith' (Hindi) *balad* m. ' ox ', gng. *bald*, (Ku.) *barad*, id. (N. Tarai) Rebus: *bharat* (5 copper, 4 zinc and 1 tin)(Punjabi)

A brief account of the remarkable find is provided: Bronze Bull, c. 1200 BCE

Rebus: *koḍ* 'workshop' (Gujarati)
kāruvu 'crocodile' Rebus: *khar* 'blacksmith' (Kashmiri)

m1919 Pict-103 (Female with breasts hanging down?) with a tail and bovine legs standing near a tree, fisting a hornd tiger rearing on its hindlegs and looking back. Text 1357

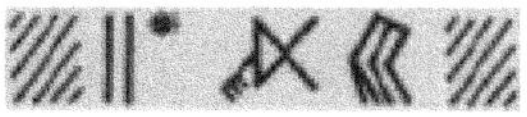

Pictorial motif hieroglyphs: Tiger is ligatured with zebu horns and hence the ligature denotes 'native metal smith guild'. Leaping: *kūdā* Rebus: *kõdār* 'turner' (Bengali); *kõdā* 'to turn in a lathe' (Bengali) Thus the hieroglyph denotes: *kolhe kõdār* 'smelter, turner'

kola 'tiger' Rebus: *kol* 'working in iron', 'pañcaloha, alloy of five metals'.

Hieroglyph: dhokra 'decrepit woman with breasts hanging down'. Rebus: *dhokra kamar* 'artisan caster using lost-wax technique'.

The ligature to a bull's hindlegs + tail denotes: dangra 'bull' Rebus: ḍhangar 'blacksmith'.

Hieroglyph ligatured to the woman: koḍ 'horn' Rebus: koḍ 'workshop'

Hieroglyph: Ku. ḍokro, ḍokhro ' old man '; B. ḍokrā ' old, decrepit ', Or. ḍokarā; H. ḍokrā ' decrepit '; G. ḍokɔ m. ' penis ', ḍokrɔ m. ' old man ', M. ḍokrā m. -- Kho. (Lor.) duk ' hunched up, hump of camel '; K. ḍŏku ' humpbacked ' perh. < *ḍōkka -- 2. Or. dhokaṛa ' decrepit, hanging down (of breasts) '(CDIAL 5567).

Hieroglyph: upraised arm: *eraka* 'upraised arm' Rebus; *eraka* 'copper'.

Rebus: *dhokra* 'cire perdue' or 'lost-wax metal casting technique'. Thus, together the composite hieroglyph denotes: dhokra ḍhangar 'metalsmith, coppersmith *cire perdue* artisan'; synonym: *dhokra kamar.*

khōṇḍa A stock or stump (Marathi); 'leafless tree' (Marathi). Rebus: *kõdār* 'turner' (Bengali); *kõdā* 'to turn in a lathe' (Bengali).

kul 'tiger' (Santali); *kōlu* id. (Telugu) kōlupuli = Bengal tiger (Telugu)कोल्हा [kōlhā] कोल्हें [kōlhēṃ] A jackal (Marathi) Rebus: *kole.l* 'temple, smithy' (Kota.) *kol* = pañcalōha, a metallic alloy containing five metals (Tamil): copper, brass, tin, lead and iron (Sanskrit); an alternative list of five metals: gold, silver, copper, tin (lead), and iron (dhātu; Nānārtharatnākara. 82; Mangarāja's Nighaṇṭu. 498)(Kannada) *kol, kolhe,* 'the *koles*, iron smelters speaking a language akin to that of Santals' (Santali) krammara 'look back' (Telugu) Rebus: kamar 'metalsmith' (Santali)

Text 1357 Text hieroglyphs:

The three hieroglyph 'signs' are read rebus in sequence from r. to l.: dhatu 'strands' rebus: 'mineral, ore'; dhatu kolhe 'mineral, ore smelter'; dul 'cast (metal)'. Thus the text denotes the competence of the dhokra kamar 'cire perdue artisan' to work with smelter for casting mineral ore (copper). Copper ore is indicated by the use of the gloss dhatu which denotes 'reddish, copper ore'.

Each sign hieroglyph is read rebus:

 dula 'pair' Rebus: dul 'cast (metal)

Ligaturing glyph:

 *Kur.* xolā tail. *Malt.* qoli id. (DEDR 2135). Rebus: kolhe 'smelter'

ḍato 'claws or pincers of crab' (Santali) Rebus: *dhatu* 'mineral ore' (Santali) PLUS xola 'tail' Rebus: kolhe 'smelter'. Thus, the ligatured glyph is read rebus as: dhatu kolhe 'mineral, ore smelter'.

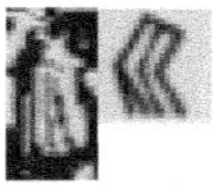 Hieroglyph: 'strands of yarn' Rebus reading: *dhā́tu* 'strand of rope' Rebus: dhatu 'mineral ore' (Santali)

dhā́tu *strand of rope ' (cf. tridhā́tu -- ' threefold ' RV., ayugdhātu -- ' having an uneven number of strands ' KātyŚr.) S. dhāī f. ' wisp of fibres added from time to time to a rope that is being twisted ', L. dhāī̃ f.(CDIAL 6773) Rebus: dhā́tu n. ' substance ' RV., m. ' element ' MBh., ' metal, mineral, ore (esp. of a red colour) ' Mn.Pk. dhāu -- m. ' metal, red chalk '; N. dhāu ' ore (esp. of copper) '; Or. ḍhāu ' red chalk, red ochre ' (whence ḍhāuā ' reddish '; M. dhāū, dhāv m.f. ' a partic. soft red stone ' (whence dhāvaḍ m. ' a caste of iron -- smelters ', dhāvḍī ' composed of or relating to iron ')(CDIAL 6773)

Dholavira (Obverse: *dhokra kamar*)

After Fig. 16 Two-faced tablet from Dholavira, Kutch, Gujarat, suggesting child sacrifice (lower picture) connected with crocodile cult (upper picture). After Parpola 2011: 41 fig. 48 (sketch AP). 'Crocodile in the Indus civilization and later south Asian traditions'. In Linguistics, archaeology and the human past: occasional paper 12, ed. Toshiki Osada & Hitoshi Endo. Pp. 1-58. Kyoto: Indus Project, Research Institute for Humanity and Nature.

'Crocodile' hieroglyphs *karā* 'crocodile' Rebus: *khara* 'blacksmith' (Kashmiri) dula 'pair' Rebus; dul 'cast metal' Thus, blacksmith casting

Hieroglyph: Ku. ḍokro, ḍokhro ' old man '; B. ḍokrā ' old, decrepit ', Or. ḍokarā; H. ḍokrā ' decrepit '; G. ḍokɔ m. ' penis ', ḍokrɔ m. ' old man ', M. ḍokrā m. -- Kho. (Lor.) duk ' hunched up, hump of camel '; K. ḍŏ̄ku ' humpbacked ' perh. < *ḍŏkka -- 2. Or. dhokaṛa ' decrepit, hanging down (of breasts) '.(CDIAL 5567). M. ḍhẽg n. ' groin ', ḍhẽgā m. ' buttock '. M. dhõgā m. ' buttock '. (CDIAL 5585). Glyph: Br. kōnḍō on all fours, bent double. (DEDR 204a) Rebus: kunda 'turner' kundār turner (A.); kũdār, kũdāri (B.); kundāru (Or.); kundau to turn on a lathe, to carve, to chase; kundau dhiri = a hewn stone; kundau murhut = a graven image (Santali) kunda a turner's lathe (Sanskrit)(CDIAL 3295) Tiger has head turned backwards. క౯రమ౯మర krammara. adv. క౯రమ౯మర౯ల౯లు or క౯రమరబడు Same as క౯రమ౯మరు (Telugu). Rebus: krəm back'(Kho.)(CDIAL 3145) karmāra 'smith, artisan' (Sanskrit) kamar 'smith' (Santali) Hieroglyph: krəm back'(Khotanese)(CDIAL 3145) Rebus: karmāra 'smith, artisan' (Sanskrit) kamar 'smith' (Santali)

Hieroglyphs to children held aloft on a seated person's hands: *dula* 'pair' Rebus: *dul 'cast metal' kuṛī* 'girl, child' Rebus: *kuṭhi* 'smelter furnace' (Santali) *kuṛī* f. 'fireplace' (H.); *krvṛī* f. 'granary (WPah.); kuṛī, kuṛohouse, building'(Ku.)(CDIAL 3232) *kuṭi* 'hut made of boughs' (Sanskrit) *guḍi* temple (Telugu)

'Horned woman' hieroglyph: Pa. kōḍ (pl. kōḍul) horn; Ka. kōḍu horn, tusk, branch of a tree; kōr horn Tu. kōḍů, kōḍu horn Ko. kṛ (obl. kṭ-)((DEDR 2200) Paš. kōṇḍā 'bald', Kal. rumb. kōṇḍa 'hornless'.(CDIAL 3508). Kal. rumb. khōṇḍ a 'half' (CDIAL 3792).

kuṭila 'bent' CDIAL 3230 kuṭi— in cmpd. 'curve', *kuṭika*— 'bent' MBh. Rebus: *kuṭila, katthīl* = bronze (8 parts copper and 2 parts tin)

sal 'splinter' Rebus: sal 'workshop'

'Arrow' sign hieroglyph (variant) This is a ligature of 'lid of pot' hieroglyph superscript on 'a linear stroke' numeral hieroglyph.*aḍaren* 'cover of pot or lid' Rebus: *aduru* 'native, unsmelted metal' PLUS koḍ = one (Santali); koḍ 'workshop' (G.)

Duplicated 'arrow': dula 'pair' Rebus: dul 'cast metal'. Thus, native metal casting workshop.

kanka 'rim of jar' Rebus: karṇīka 'account (scribe)' karṇī 'supercargo'

Note on dula gloss:

" 'Splinter' hieroglyph sign: Pk. *dula, duijja 'second' (CDIAL 6402)* K. *dula* m. ' pair, couple (of anything) *'(CDIAL 10489)*

Allograph 1: *dula 'hole'(Ku.N.);* M. *ḍuḷũ* n. ' little hole ', *ḍolā* m. (CDIAL 6452)

dula 'pair' Rebus: *dul* 'cast (metal)' PLUS*kana, kanac* = corner (Santali); Rebus: *kañcu* = bronze (Telugu) Thus, cast bronze. PLUS खांडा [*khāṇḍā*] *m* A jag, notch, or indentation (as upon the edge of a tool or weapon). Rebus: *kāṇḍa* 'tools, pots and pans and metal-ware' Thus, cast bronze metalware.

Allograph 2: Pk. *ḍulaï* ' shakes '; -- altern. < 2: K. *ḍulun* ' to roll '; Ku. *ḍulṇo* ' to wander '; N. *ḍulnu* ' to walk about '; B. *dulā* ' to swing '; H.*dulnā, ḍu°* ' to move '.dul 'swing, wander' dōlayati'swings' (Sanskrit)(CDIAL 6453, 6585). (CDIAL 6582) Note the person holding aloft two children and swining them – a narrative on Dholavira tablet.]

Allograph 3: K. *ḍula* m. ' rolling stone ',(CDIAL 6582)

Allograph 4: Pk. *ḍōla* -- m. ' eye ' M. *ḍoḷā* m. ' eye ' Or. *doḷā*, *ḍoḷā* ' pupil of eye '

kuṭila 'bent' CDIAL 3230 kuṭi— in cmpd. 'curve', *kuṭika*— 'bent' MBh. Rebus: *kuṭila, katthīl* = bronze (8 parts copper and 2 parts tin) Thus, the hieroglyph sign may denote: bronze casting.

Allograph 5: *Konḍa* dolu a creeper plant, shrub, plant of shoot height. *Pe.* dol plant; stem, trunk. *Manḍ.* dul plant; sapling. *Kui.*(Mah. p. 96) kūḍi-ḍoḍu rice plant; (p. 102) ḍoḍu tree. *Kuwi* (Mah.) kūli-dolu rice plant; (Isr.) dulomi plant.(DEDR 3517)

kolmo 'paddy plant' Rebus: *kolami* 'smithy, forge' Vikalpa: *mogge* 'sprout, bud' Rebus: *mũh* 'ingot' (Santali) dolu 'plant of shoot height' Rebus: dul 'cast metal'

Rebus 1: *dul* 'cast metal' (Santali. Munda) May refer to *cire perdue* method of metal casting.

Rebus 2: Bshk. *ḍōl* ' brass pot '; K. *ḍol* m. ' bucket ', S. *ḍolu* m., P. *ḍol* m., WPah.bhal. *ḍol* n., Ku. N. B. Mth. *ḍol*, Aw. lakh. *ḍōlu*, H. *dol,ḍol* m., G. *ḍol* f., M. *ḍol* m.Bshk. *ḍōl* ' brass pot '; WPah.poet. *ḍōr* m. ' small pot ', kṭg. *ḍōl* m. ' bucket ', J. *ḍōl* m. ← H. or < **dōlla* --). (CDIAL 6583)

The frequent use of doubling (*dula* 'pair') a Meluhha hieroglyph on hundreds of epigraphs is significant. It indicates the possible use of cire perdue metallurgical technique to create alloy and metal castings for trade in Bronze Age products. The rebus gloss *dul* 'cast metal' is signified by the cognate *dullu* 'work' in Ancient Near East (3rd millennium BCE Akkadian gloss) –a signifier of artisanal workmanship, a possible derivative from Meluhhan speech of earlier millennia. Cognate Meluhha etyma: *Ta.* toṟil act, action, deed, work, office, calling, profession; toṟuvar servants, agriculturalists, ploughmen; *Ma.* toṟil business, occupation; *Tu.* toḷilů trade, business
(DEDR3524).

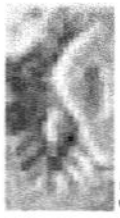

Sign hieroglyph Read rebus as *kolhe cīmara* 'smelter-coppersmith' Ligatured hieroglyph:

cīmara 'black ant' Rebus: *cīmara* 'copper'. *cīmara kāra* -- ' coppersmith ' Ligatured to: *Kur.* xolā tail. *Malt.* qoli id. (DEDR 2135). Rebus: kolhe 'smelter' Thus, copper smelter.

m1895a *khũṭ* 'zebu' Rebus: '(native metal) guild'

Text: 

Ligaturing glyph to the first sign hieroglyph from r.:
Kur. xolā tail. *Malt.* qoli id. (DEDR 2135). Rebus: kolhe 'smelter'

Read rebus as *kolhe cīmara* 'smelter-coppersmith'

ayo 'fish' Rebus: aya 'iron' (Gujarati) ayas 'metal' (Vedic)

kuṭila 'bent' CDIAL 3230 kuṭi— in cmpd. 'curve', *kuṭika—* 'bent' MBh. Rebus: kuṭila, katthīl = bronze (8 parts copper and 2 parts tin) cf. āra-kūṭa, 'brass' (Sanskrit)

kanka 'rim of jar' Rebus: *karṇīka* 'account (scribe)' *karṇī* 'supercargo'

ibha 'elephant' Rebus: *ib* 'iron' *ibbo* 'merchant' (Gujarati)

Read rebus as *kolhe cīmara* 'smelter-coppersmith' sal 'splinter' Rebus: sal 'workshop' *aya aḍaren (homonym: aduru)* 'alloy native metal'
ayo 'fish' Rebus: *aya* 'iron' *ayas* 'metal'
kamaḍha 'archer, bow' Rebus: *kammaṭa* 'mint, coiner'.
ranku 'liquid measure' Rebus: ranku 'tin'

kolmo 'paddy plant' Rebus: *kolami* 'smithy, forge' Vikalpa: *mogge* 'sprout, bud' Rebus: *mũh* 'ingot' (Santali) dolu 'plant of shoot height' Rebus: dul 'cast metal'

kanka 'rim of jar' Rebus: *karṇīka* 'account (scribe)' *karṇī* 'supercargo'

m43a *खोंड [khōṇḍa] m A young bull, a bullcalf. (Marathi) Rebus: kõdār 'turner' (Bengali); कोंद kōnda 'engraver, lapidary setting or infixing gems' (Marathi) G. sãghāṛɔ m. 'lathe' ; संघाट joinery; M. sãgaḍ 'double-canoe' Rebus: sangataras 'stone-cutter, mason'*

Read rebus as *kolhe cīmara* 'smelter-coppersmith'

baroṭi 'twelve' *bhārata* 'a factitious alloy of copper, pewter, tin' (Marathi) sal 'splinter' Rebus: sal 'workshop' *aya kāṇḍa* 'alloy metalware' *kamaḍha* 'crab' Rebus: *kammaṭa* 'mint, coiner'.*ḍato* = claws of crab (Santali) Rebus: *dhātu* 'mineral ore'

kanka 'rim of jar' Rebus: karṇīka 'account (scribe)' karṇī 'supercargo'

'Ladder ligatured to double ingots'

Lothal 218A

dula 'pair' Rebus: dul 'cast metal' PLUS | *koḍa* 'one' Rebus: *koḍ* 'workshop' PLUS INFIXED kolom 'three' Rebus: kolami 'smithy, forge' Thus metware castings forge.

ranku 'liquid measure' Rebus: ranku 'tin'

meḍ 'body' Rebus: *meḍ* 'iron' (Ho.) काठी [kāṭhī] *f* (काष्ट S) 'frame or structure of the body' (Marathi) Rebus: खंडी [khaṇḍī] measure of weight (Marathi) *கண்டி; kaṇṭi, n. < Mhr. khaṇḍil. [T. Tu. khaṇḍi, M. kaṇḍi.]* Candy, a weight, stated to be roughly equivalent to 500 lbs. PLUS *baṭa* = rimless pot (Kannada) Rebus: *baṭa* = a kind of iron (G.)) *bhaṭa* furnace (Gujarati)

Lothal 52a

dula 'two, pair' Rebus: dul 'cast metal' PLUS *dhāḷ* 'a slope'; 'inclination of a plane' (G.); *ḍhāḷiyum* = adj. sloping, inclining (G.) Rebus: *ḍhālako* = a large metal ingot (G.) *ḍhālakī* = a metal heated and poured into a mould; a solid piece of metal; an ingot (Gujarati) PLUS kolom 'three' Rebus: kolami 'smithy, forge'. Thus cast metal ingot smithy. *kamaḍha* 'crab' Rebus: *kammaṭa* 'mint, coiner'.*ḍato* = claws of crab (Santali) Rebus: *dhātu* 'mineral ore'

m965a *खोंड [khōṇḍa] m A young bull, a bullcalf. (Marathi) Rebus: kõdār 'turner' (Bengali); कोंद kōnda 'engraver, lapidary setting or infixing gems' (Marathi) G. sãghāṛɔ m. 'lathe' ; संघाट joinery; M. sãgaḍ 'double-canoe' Rebus: sangataras 'stone-cutter, mason'*

dula 'two, pair' Rebus: dul 'cast metal' PLUS *dhāḷ* 'a slope'; 'inclination of a plane' (G.); *ḍhāḷiyum* = adj. sloping, inclining (G.) Rebus: *ḍhālako* = a large metal ingot (G.) *ḍhālakī* = a metal heated and poured into a mould; a solid piece of metal; an ingot (Gujarati) PLUS kolom 'three' Rebus: kolami 'smithy, forge'. Thus cast metal ingot smithy.

'rim-of-jar' hieroglyph *kanka* (Santali) *karṇika* 'scribe'(Sanskrit) Rebus: *karṇī,* supercargo for a boat shipment. *karṇīka* 'account (scribe)'.कारणी *kāraṇī* 'the supercargo of a ship'

(Marathi) PLUS infixed notch: खांडा [*khāṇḍā*] *m* A jag, notch, or indentation (as upon the edge of a tool or weapon). Rebus: *kāṇḍa* 'tools, pots and pans and metal-ware'. Thus, metalware supercarg

dula 'two' Rebus: dul 'cast metal' ranku 'liquid measure' Rebus: ranku 'tin' PLUS infixed kolmo 'paddy plant' Rebus: kolami 'smithy, forge'. Thus, cast bronze smithy, forge. Or, *mogge* 'sprout, bud' Rebus: *mũh* 'ingot' (Santali)Thus, cast bronze ingot. Read as: *kañcu dul mũh 'bronze cast ingot'*

kolmo 'paddy plant' Rebus: *kolami* 'smithy, forge' Vikalpa: *mogge* 'sprout, bud' Rebus: *mũh* 'ingot' (Santali) dolu 'plant of shoot height' Rebus: dul 'cast metal'

kanka 'rim of jar' Rebus: karṇīka 'account (scribe)' karṇī 'supercargo'

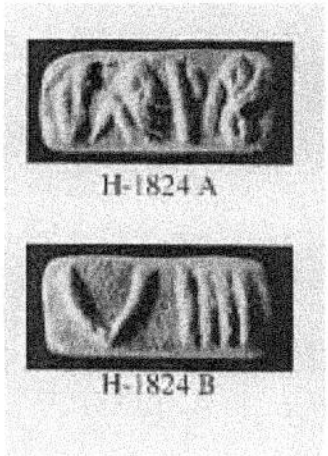

h1824A

 *kana, kanac* = corner (Santali); Rebus: *kañcu* = bronze (Telugu) PLUS खांडा [*khāṇḍā*] *m* A jag, notch, or indentation (as upon the edge of a tool or weapon). Rebus: *kāṇḍa* 'tools, pots and pans and metal-ware' Thus, bronze metalware.

dula 'pair' Rebus: dul 'cast metal' PLUS ligature:

dula 'pair' Rebus: dul 'cast metal' PLUS | *koḍa* 'one' Rebus: *koḍ* 'workshop' PLUS INFIXED kolom

'three' Rebus: kolami 'smithy, forge' Thus metware castings forge.

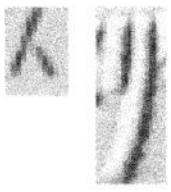 notch+slanted stroke reads rebus: *ḍhālako kāṇḍa* 'ingot, tools, pots and pans and metal-ware'.*dhāḷ* 'a slope'; 'inclination of a plane' (G.); *ḍhāḷiyum* = adj. sloping, inclining (G.) Rebus: *ḍhālako* = a large metal ingot (G.) *ḍhālakī* = a metal heated and poured into a mould; a solid piece of metal; an ingot (Gujarati) PLUS खांडा [*khāṇḍā*] *m* A jag, notch, or indentation (as upon the edge of a tool or weapon). Rebus: *kāṇḍa* 'tools, pots and pans and metal-ware' | *koḍa* 'one' Rebus: *koḍ* 'workshop'

 *baraḍo* = spine; backbone (Tulu) Rebus: *baran, bharat* 'mixed alloys' (5 copper, 4 zinc and 1 tin) (Punjabi) PLUS gaṇḍa 'four' Rebus: kaṇḍa 'furnace, fire-altar' (Santali)

 kanka 'rim of jar' Rebus: karṇīka 'account (scribe)' karṇī 'supercargo'

 *baṭa* 'rimless, broad-mouthed pot' Rebus: *bhaṭa* 'furnace' (Gujarati.); *baṭa* 'a kind of iron' (Gujarati)

|||| Numeral 4: gaṇḍa 'four' Rebus: kaṇḍa 'furnace, fire-altar' (Santali)

h17A *खोंड [khōṇḍa] m A young bull, a bullcalf. (Marathi) Rebus: kõdār 'turner' (Bengali); कोंद kōnda 'engraver, lapidary setting or infixing gems' (Marathi) G. sãghāṛɔ m. 'lathe' ; संघाट joinery; M. sāgaḍ 'double-canoe' Rebus: sangataras 'stone-cutter, mason'*

First sign read rebus as at h1824A 'metalware castings forge'

 *dhāḷ* 'a slope'; 'inclination of a plane' (G.); *ḍhāḷiyum* = adj. sloping, inclining (G.) Rebus: *ḍhālako* = a large metal ingot (G.) *ḍhālakī* = a metal heated and poured into a mould; a solid piece of metal; an ingot (Gujarati) PLUS खांडा [*khāṇḍā*] *m* A jag, notch, or indentation (as upon the edge of a tool or weapon). Rebus: *kāṇḍa* 'tools, pots and pans and metal-ware' Thus, the pair of sign hieroglyphs from r. read rebus: copper, bronze ingots, metalware castings.

aya kammaṭa.'coiner, mint alloy' *ayo ḍhālako* 'alloy metal ingot'

 कांड *kāṇḍa* 'arrow' Rebus: *kāṇḍa* 'pots and pans, metalware, tools'. Rebus 2: kaṇḍ 'fire-altar' (Santali)

M-1739 a bis

m1739a खोंड *[khōṇḍa] m A young bull, a bullcalf. (Marathi) Rebus: kõdār 'turner' (Bengali);* कोंद *kōnda 'engraver, lapidary setting or infixing gems' (Marathi) G. sãghāṛɔ m. 'lathe' ;* संघाट *joinery; M. sãgaḍ 'double-canoe' Rebus: sangataras 'stone-cutter, mason'*

First sign read rebus as at h1824A 'metalware castings forge'

 *dhāḷ* 'a slope'; 'inclination of a plane' (G.); *ḍhāḷiyum* = adj. sloping, inclining (G.) Rebus: *ḍhālako* = a large metal ingot (G.) *ḍhālakī* = a metal heated and poured into a mould; a solid piece of metal; an ingot (Gujarati) PLUS खांडा [*khāṇḍā*] *m* A jag, notch, or indentation (as upon the edge of a tool or weapon). Rebus: *kāṇḍa* 'tools, pots and pans and metal-ware' Thus, the pair of sign hieroglyphs from r. read rebus: copper, bronze ingots, metalware castings.

dula 'two' Rebus: dul 'cast metal'

ranku 'liquid measure' Rebus: ranku 'tin'

 *kolmo* 'paddy plant' Rebus: *kolami* 'smithy, forge' Vikalpa: *mogge* 'sprout, bud' Rebus: *mūh* 'ingot' (Santali) dolu 'plant of shoot height' Rebus: dul 'cast metal'

kanka 'rim of jar' Rebus: karṇīka 'account (scribe)' karṇī 'supercargo'

h61a खोंड *[khōṇḍa] m A young bull, a bullcalf. (Marathi) Rebus: kõdār 'turner' (Bengali);* कोंद *kōnda 'engraver, lapidary setting or infixing gems' (Marathi) G. sãghāṛɔ m. 'lathe' ;* संघाट *joinery; M. sãgaḍ 'double-canoe' Rebus: sangataras 'stone-cutter, mason'*

First sign read rebus as at h1824A 'metalware castings forge'

 *dhāḷ* 'a slope'; 'inclination of a plane' (G.); *ḍhāḷiyum* = adj. sloping, inclining (G.) Rebus: *ḍhālako* = a large metal ingot (G.) *ḍhālakī* = a metal heated and poured into a mould; a solid piece of metal; an ingot (Gujarati) PLUS खांडा [*khāṇḍā*] *m* A jag, notch, or indentation (as upon the edge of a tool or weapon). Rebus: *kāṇḍa* 'tools, pots and pans and metal-ware' Thus, the pair of sign hieroglyphs from r. read rebus: copper, bronze ingots, metalware castings.

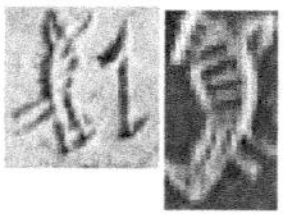 The pair of hieroglyph signs are compositions: 1. *bicha* 'scorpion' (Assamese) Rebus: *bica* 'stone ore' (Santali) The pairing sign is a composition of: sloping stroke PLUS two short strokes of a 'splinter':*dhāḷ* 'a slope'; 'inclination of a plane' (Gujarati); *ḍhāḷiyum* = adj. sloping, inclining (Gujarati) Rebus: *ḍhālako* = a large metal ingot (Gujarati) *ḍhālakī* = a metal heated and poured into a mould; a solid piece of metal; an ingot (Gujarati)PLUS*sal* 'splinter' Rebus: *sal* 'workshop'. Thus the composition reads: *ḍhālako sal* 'ingot workshop'.

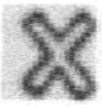 *dāṭu* 'cross'(Telugu) Rebus: *dhatu* 'mineral' (Santali).

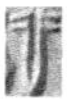 kanka 'rim of jar' Rebus: karṇīka 'account (scribe)' karṇī 'supercargo'

h386a खोंड [khōṇḍa] m A young bull, a bullcalf. (Marathi) Rebus: kõdār 'turner' (Bengali); कोंद kōnda 'engraver, lapidary setting or infixing gems' (Marathi) G. sãghāṛɔ m. 'lathe' ; संघाट joinery; M. sãgaḍ 'double-canoe' Rebus: sangataras 'stone-cutter, mason'

First sign read rebus as at h1824A 'metalware castings forge'

 *dhāḷ* 'a slope'; 'inclination of a plane' (G.); *ḍhāḷiyum* = adj. sloping, inclining (G.) Rebus: *ḍhālako* = a large metal ingot (G.) *ḍhālakī* = a metal heated and poured into a mould; a solid piece of metal; an ingot (Gujarati) PLUS खांडा [*khāṇḍā*] *m* A jag, notch, or indentation (as upon the edge of a tool or weapon). Rebus: *kāṇḍa*

'tools, pots and pans and metal-ware' Thus, the pair of sign hieroglyphs from r. read rebus: copper, bronze ingots, metalware castings.

kamaḍha 'crab' Rebus: *kammaṭa* 'mint, coiner'.*ḍato* = claws of crab (Santali) Rebus: *dhātu* 'mineral ore'

sal 'splinter' Rebus: sal 'workshop' PLUS | *koḍa* 'one' Rebus: *koḍ* 'workshop'

sal 'splinter' Rebus: sal 'workshop'

 *baroṭi* 'twelve' *bhārata* 'a factitious alloy of copper, pewter, tin' (Marathi)

 kanka 'rim of jar' Rebus: karṇīka 'account (scribe)' karṇī 'supercargo'

 *kamaḍha* 'crab' Rebus: *kammaṭa* 'mint, coiner'.*ḍato* = claws of crab (Santali) Rebus: *dhātu* 'mineral ore' PLUS खांडा [*khāṇḍā*] *m* A jag, notch, or indentation (as upon the edge of a tool or weapon). Rebus: *kāṇḍa* 'tools, pots and pans and metal-ware' Thus, mint metalware, ore.

Splinter sign hieroglyph; 'Two linear strokes' hieroglyph;  'splinter PLUS notch' ligature

h469a खोंड [khōṇḍa] m A young bull, a bullcalf. (Marathi) Rebus: kõdār 'turner' (Bengali); कोंद kōnda 'engraver, lapidary setting or infixing gems' (Marathi) G. sãghāṛɔ m. 'lathe' ; संघाट joinery; M. sãgaḍ 'double-canoe' Rebus: sangataras 'stone-cutter, mason'

sal 'splinter' Rebus: sal 'workshop'

खांडा [*khāṇḍā*] *m* A jag, notch, or indentation (as upon the edge of a tool or weapon). Rebus: *kāṇḍa* 'tools, pots and pans and metal-ware'

 *dula* 'pair' Rebus: *dul* 'cast (metal)' PLUS*kana, kanac* = corner (Santali); Rebus: *kañcu* = bronze (Telugu) Thus, cast bronze.

dula  'pair' Rebus: dul 'cast (metal)' kolmo 'rice plant' Rebus: kolami 'smithy/forge' metal.

 kanka 'rim of jar' Rebus: karṇīka 'account (scribe)' karṇī 'supercargo'

Allahdino 6A Rhinoceros/boar: baḍhia = a castrated boar, a hog (Santali) baḍhi 'a caste who work both in iron and wood' (Santali) *baṟea* 'merchant'

sal 'splinter' Rebus: sal 'workshop'

खांडा [*khāṇḍā*] *m* A jag, notch, or indentation (as upon the edge of a tool or weapon). Rebus: *kāṇḍa* 'tools, pots and pans and metal-ware'

dula 'pair' Rebus: *dul* 'cast (metal)' PLUS*kana, kanac* = corner (Santali); Rebus: *kañcu* = bronze (Telugu) Thus, cast bronze.

kanka 'rim of jar' Rebus: karṇīka 'account (scribe)' karṇī 'supercargo'

Circumscript: | *koḍa* 'one' Rebus: *koḍ* 'workshop'

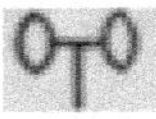

अगडा [agaḍā] *m* The tie connecting the जूं & दांडी of a गाडा or load-cart; the shaft and thill-yoke-tie. Rebus: 'lumber, miscellaneous articles': अगडतगड [*agaḍatagaḍa*] *n* अगडबगड *n* (Fanciful formations, or from H) Trash, trumpery, rubbish, lumber, miscellaneous articles.

dulo 'hole' Rebus: dul 'cast metal'

'Arrow' sign hieroglyph (variant) This is a ligature of 'lid of pot' hieroglyph superscript on 'a linear stroke' numeral hieroglyph.*aḍaren* 'cover of pot or lid' Rebus: *aduru* 'native, unsmelted metal' PLUS koḍ = one (Santali); koḍ 'workshop' (Gujarati)

m1915a *ibha* 'elephant' Rebus: *ib* 'iron' *ibbo* 'merchant' (Gujarati)

h924A

h147a

sal 'splinter' Rebus: sal 'workshop'

खांडा [*khāṇḍā*] *m* A jag, notch, or indentation (as upon the edge of a tool or weapon). Rebus: *kāṇḍa* 'tools, pots and pans and metal-ware'

dula 'pair' Rebus: *dul* 'cast (metal)' PLUS*kana, kanac* = corner (Santali); Rebus: *kañcu* = bronze (Telugu) Thus, cast bronze. kanka 'rim of jar' Rebus: karṇīka 'account (scribe)' karṇī 'supercargo'

h1774a

Lothal 22a

खोंड [khōṇḍa] m A young bull, a bullcalf. (Marathi) Rebus: kōdār 'turner' (Bengali); कोंद kōnda 'engraver, lapidary setting or infixing

gems'

(Marathi) G. sãghāṛɔ m. 'lathe' ; संघाट joinery; M. sāgaḍ 'double-

canoe'

Rebus: sangataras 'stone-cutter, mason' Read rebus as at h147.

m1872A

 *kuṭila* 'bent' CDIAL 3230 kuṭi— in cmpd. 'curve', *kuṭika*— 'bent' MBh. Rebus: *kuṭila, katthīl* = bronze (8 parts copper and 2 parts tin) Duplicated: dula 'pair' Rebus: dul 'cast metal' Thus, cast bronze or bronze castings.

ayo 'fish' Rebus: *aya* 'iron' *ayas* 'metal'
dula 'two' Rebus: dul 'cast metal' sal 'splinter' Rebus: sal 'workshop'

M-1127 a

m1127a: *rāngo* 'water buffalo bull' (Ku.N.)(CDIAL 10559) Rebus: rango 'pewter' *pattar* 'trough' Rebus: *pattar* 'guild'.Thus, pewter guild.
sal 'splinter' Rebus: sal 'workshop'

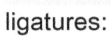

ligatures:   *loa* 'ficus religiosa' Rebus: *lo* 'iron' (Sanskrit) PLUS unique लोखंड [lōkhaṇḍa] *n* (लोह S) Iron. लोखंडाचे चणे खावविणें or चारणें To oppress grievously.लोखंडकाम [lōkhaṇḍakāma] *n* Iron work; that portion (of a building, machine &c.) which consists of iron. 2 The business of an ironsmith.लोखंडी [lōkhaṇḍī] *a* (लोखंड) Composed of iron; relating to iron. (Marathi) *bhaṭa* 'warrior' (Sanskrit) Rebus: *baṭa* a kind of iron (Gujarati). Rebus: *bhaṭa* 'furnace' (Santali) Thus, together, the ligatured hieroglyph reads rebus: *loa bhaṭa* 'iron furnace'
Circumscript:

 *kuṭila* 'bent' CDIAL 3230 kuṭi— in cmpd. 'curve', *kuṭika*— 'bent' MBh. Rebus: *kuṭila, katthīl* = bronze (8 parts copper and 2 parts tin) Duplicated: dula 'pair' Rebus: dul 'cast metal' Thus, cast bronze or bronze castings. PLUS *baṭa* 'quail' Rebus: *baṭha* 'smelter, furnace' kanka 'rim of jar' Rebus: karṇīka 'account (scribe)' karṇī 'supercargo'
 *dāṭu* 'cross'(Telugu) Rebus: *dhatu* 'mineral' (Santali).

 *dhāḷ* 'a slope'; 'inclination of a plane' (G.); *ḍhāḷiyum* = adj. sloping, inclining (G.) Rebus: *ḍhālako* = a large metal ingot (G.) *ḍhālakī* = a metal heated and poured into a mould; a solid piece of metal; an ingot (Gujarati) PLUS खांडा [*khāṇḍā*] *m* A jag, notch, or indentation (as upon the edge of a tool or weapon). Rebus: *kāṇḍa* 'tools, pots and pans and metal-ware' Thus, the pair of sign hieroglyphs from r. read rebus: copper, bronze ingots, metalware castings.

M-762 a

m762a *खोंड [khōṇḍa] m A young bull, a bullcalf. (Marathi) Rebus: kōdār 'turner' (Bengali); कोंद kōnda 'engraver, lapidary setting or infixing gems' (Marathi) G. sãghāṛɔ m. 'lathe' ; संघाट joinery; M. sāgaḍ 'double-canoe' Rebus: sangataras 'stone-cutter, mason'*
sal 'splinter' Rebus: sal 'workshop'

  *loa* 'ficus religiosa' Rebus: *lo* 'iron' (Sanskrit) PLUS unique ligatures: लोखंड [lōkhaṇḍa] *n* (लोह S) Iron. लोखंडाचे चणे खावविणें or चारणें To oppress grievously.लोखंडकाम [lōkhaṇḍakāma] *n* Iron work; that portion (of a building, machine &c.) which consists of iron. 2 The business of an ironsmith.लोखंडी [lōkhaṇḍī] *a* (लोखंड) Composed of iron; relating to iron. (Marathi) *bhaṭa* 'warrior' (Sanskrit) Rebus: *baṭa* a

kind of iron (Gujarati). Rebus: *bhaṭa* 'furnace' (Santali) Thus, together, the ligatured hieroglyph reads rebus: *loa bhaṭa* 'iron furnace'
aya kāṇḍa 'alloy metalware'

Lothal 87A dula 'two' Rebus: dul 'cast metal' PLUS *mogge* 'sprout, bud' Rebus: *mũh* 'ingot' (Santali)

dula 'pair' Rebus: *dul* 'cast (metal)' PLUS*kana, kanac* = corner (Santali); Rebus: *kañcu* = bronze (Telugu) Thus, cast bronze. dula 'pair' Rebus: dul 'cast metal' *aya kāṇḍa* 'alloy metalware'

ayo 'fish' Rebus: *aya* 'iron' *ayas* 'metal'
dula 'two' Rebus: dul 'cast metal'

ḍhāḷ 'a slope'; 'inclination of a plane' (G.); *ḍhāḷiyum* = adj. sloping, inclining (G.) Rebus: *ḍhālako* = a large metal ingot (G.) *ḍhālakī* = a metal heated and poured into a mould; a solid piece of metal; an ingot (Gujarati) PLUS खांडा [*khāṇḍā*] *m* A jag, notch, or indentation (as upon the edge of a tool or weapon). Rebus: *kāṇḍa* 'tools, pots and pans and metal-ware' Thus, the pair of sign hieroglyphs from r. read rebus: copper, bronze ingots, metalware castings.

kana, kanac = corner (Santali); Rebus: *kañcu* = bronze (Telugu) PLUS खांडा [*khāṇḍā*] *m* A jag, notch, or indentation (as upon the edge of a tool or weapon). Rebus: *kāṇḍa* 'tools, pots and pans and metal-ware' Thus, bronze metalware. INFIXED S. *akho* m. 'mesh of a net' Rebus: L. P. *akkhā* m. ' one end of a bag or sack thrown over a beast of burden '; Or. *akhā* ' gunny bag '; Bi. *ākhā, ãkhā* ' grain bag carried by pack animal '; H. *ākhā* m. ' one of a pair of grain bags used as panniers '; M. *ākhā* m. ' netting in which coco -- nuts, &c., are carried ', *ākhẽ* n. ' half a bullock -- load ' (CDIAL 17) అంకెము [aṅkemu] *ankemu.* [Telugu] n. One pack or pannier, being half a bullock load.

m1718a
खोंड [khōṇḍa] m A young bull, a bullcalf. (Marathi) Rebus: kõdār 'turner' (Bengali); कोंद kōnda 'engraver, lapidary setting or infixing gems' (Marathi)

beads: Pa. kandi (pl. -l) necklace, beads. Ga. (Punjabi) kandi (pl. -l) bead, (pl.) necklace; (S.2) kandiṭ bead. (DEDR 1215) Rebus: *கண்டி; kanṭi, n. < Mhr. khaṇḍil. [T. Tu. khaṇḍi, M. kaṇḍi.] 1. Candy, a weight, stated to be roughly equivalent to 500 lbs.; பாரமென் னும் நிறையளவு.* खंडीगणती or खंडोगणती [khaṇḍīgaṇatī or khaṇḍōgaṇatī] *ad* By candies; counting or reckoning by candies. खंडीवारी [khaṇḍīvārī] *ad* By scores, heaps, candies. खंडी [khaṇḍī] Applied to a great quantity; as खंडीभर पोरें, खंडीभर मेंढ्या, खंडीभर काम, खंडीभर बोलतो-लिहितो&c

sal 'splinter' Rebus sal 'workshop'
āra 'spokes' Rebus: *āra 'brass'.* cf. erka = ekke (Tbh. of arka) aka (Tbh. of arka) copper (metal); crystal (Kannada) Glyph: *eraka*'nave of wheel' Rebus: eraka 'copper'; cf. erka = ekke (Tbh. of arka) aka (Tbh. of arka) copper (metal); crystal (Kannada) *erako* 'moltencast copper'

kanka 'rim of jar' Rebus: karṇīka 'account (scribe)' karṇī 'supercargo'

 *baroṭi* 'twelve' *bhārata* 'a factitious alloy of copper, pewter, tin' (Marathi)

M-982 a

m982a खोंड *[khōṇḍa] m A young bull, a bullcalf. (Marathi) Rebus: kõdār 'turner' (Bengali);* कोंद *kōnda 'engraver, lapidary setting or infixing gems' (Marathi) G. sãghāṛɔ m. 'lathe' ;* संघाट *joinery; M. sãgaḍ 'double-canoe' Rebus: sangataras 'stone-cutter, mason'*

sal 'splinter' Rebus: sal 'workshop'

 *kana, kanac* = corner (Santali); Rebus: *kañcu* = bronze (Telugu) PLUS खांडा [*khāṇḍā*] *m* A jag, notch, or indentation (as upon the edge of a tool or weapon). Rebus: *kāṇḍa* 'tools, pots and pans and metal-ware' Thus, bronze metalware. INFIXED S. *akho* m. 'mesh of a net' Rebus: L. P. *akkhā* m. ' one end of a bag or sack thrown over a beast of burden '; Or. *akhā* ' gunny bag '; Bi. *ākhā, ãkhā* ' grain bag carried by pack animal '; H. *ākhā* m. ' one of a pair of grain bags used as panniers '; M. *ãkhā* m. ' netting in which coco -- nuts, &c., are carried ', *ãkhẽ* n. ' half a bullock -- load ' (CDIAL 17) అంకెము [aṅkemu] *ankemu.* [Telugu] n. One pack or pannier, being half a bullock load.

kanka 'rim of jar' Rebus: karṇīka 'account (scribe)' karṇī 'supercargo'

Banawali 5A Variant with two horns:

खोंड *[khōṇḍa] m A young bull, a bullcalf. (Marathi) Rebus: kõdār 'turner' (Bengali);* कोंद *kōnda 'engraver, lapidary setting or infixing gems' (Marathi) G. sãghāṛɔ m. 'lathe' ;* संघाट *joinery; M. sãgaḍ 'double-canoe' Rebus: sangataras 'stone-cutter, mason'*

sal 'splinter' Rebus: sal 'workshop'

 *kanac* 'corner' Rebus: *kañcu* 'bronze'

miṇḍāl 'markhor' (Tōrwālī) *meḍho* a ram, a sheep (Gujarati)(CDIAL 10120) Rebus: *mẽṛhẽt, meḍ* 'iron' (Mu.Ho.)

Banawali 15A Read rebus as at Banawali 5: Bronze workshop. PLUS

Rhinoceros/boar: baḍhia = a castrated boar, a hog (Santali) baḍhi 'a caste who work both in iron and wood' (Santali) *baṟea* 'merchant'

m272A *miṇḍāl* 'markhor' (Tōrwālī) *meḍho* a ram, a sheep (Gujarati)(CDIAL 10120) Rebus: *mẽṛhẽt, meḍ* 'iron' (Mu.Ho.) krammara 'look back' Rebus: kamar 'blacksmith' Read rebus as at Banawali 5: Bronze workshop.

K-27 a

Kalibangab 27a With the horns of zebu signifying 'native metal smith guild': खोंड *[khōṇḍa] m A young bull, a bullcalf. (Marathi) Rebus: kõdār 'turner' (Bengali);* कोंद *kōnda 'engraver, lapidary setting or infixing gems' (Marathi) G. sãghāṛɔ m. 'lathe' ;* संघाट *joinery; M. sãgaḍ 'double-canoe' Rebus: sangataras 'stone-cutter, mason' Read rebus as at Banawali 5: Bronze Workshop.*

Banawali 7A *rāngo* 'water buffalo bull' (Ku.N.)(CDIAL 10559) Rebus: rango 'pewter'

Read rebus as at Banawali 5: Bronze Workshop.

m1400A  sal 'splinter' Rebus: sal 'workshop'

 *koḍi* 'flag' (Ta.)(DEDR 2049). Rebus 1: *koḍ* 'workshop' (Kuwi) Rebus 2: *khŏḍ* m. 'pit', *khŏḍü* f. 'small pit' (Kashmiri. CDIAL 3947). kanka 'rim of jar' Rebus: karṇīka 'account (scribe)' karṇī 'supercargo'

Circumscript:

 *kuṭila* 'bent' CDIAL 3230 kuṭi— in cmpd. 'curve', *kuṭika*— 'bent' MBh. Rebus: *kuṭila, katthīl* = bronze (8 parts copper and 2 parts tin) Duplicated: dula 'pair' Rebus: dul 'cast metal' Thus, cast bronze or bronze castings.

 *bicha* 'scorpion' (Assamese) Rebus: *bica* 'stone ore' (Santali)

 *kanac* 'corner' Rebus: *kañcu* 'bronze'

H-2209 A

H-2209 B

H-2209 C

h2209 Side B: *baṭa* 'rimless, broad-mouthed pot' Rebus: *bhaṭa* 'furnace' (Gujarati.); *baṭa* 'a kind of iron' (Gujarati) PLUS kolom 'three' Rebus: kolami 'smithy, forge'

SideA:sal 'splinter' Rebus: sal 'workshop' kolom 'three' Rebus: kolami 'smithy, forge' dula 'two' Rebus: dul 'cast metal' kanka 'rim of jar' Rebus: karṇīka 'account (scribe)' karṇī 'supercargo' lathe' (Bengali). Allograph: young bull.

 *kharedo* = a currycomb (Gujarati) खरारा [*kharārā*] *m* (H) A currycomb. 2 Currying a horse. (Marathi) Rebus: करडा [*karaḍā*] Hard from alloy--iron, silver &c. (Marathi) *kharādī* ' turner' (Gujarati)

Side C: *ayo* 'fish' Rebus: *aya* 'iron' *ayas* 'metal'

H-2204 A

H-2204 B

H-2204 C

h2204A

Side B:

 *baṭa* 'rimless, broad-mouthed pot' Rebus: *bhaṭa* 'furnace' (Gujarati.); *baṭa* 'a kind of iron' (Gujarati)

|||| Numeral 4: gaṇḍa 'four' Rebus: kaṇḍa 'furnace, fire-altar' (Santali)

Side A: Read rebus as at h2209A

m40a *खोंड [khōṇḍa] m A young bull, a bullcalf. (Marathi) Rebus: kōdār 'turner' (Bengali); कोंद kōnda 'engraver, lapidary setting or infixing gems' (Marathi) G. sãghāṛɔ m. 'lathe' ; संघाट joinery; M. sāgaḍ 'double-canoe' Rebus: sangataras 'stone-cutter, mason'*

dula 'two' Rebus: dul 'cast metal' kolom 'three' Rebus: kolami 'smithy, forge'

 *ḍhanga* = a crook used for pulling down the branches of trees, for goats, sheep and camels (P.) Rebus:*ḍhangar* blacksmith'. PLUS
 *kharedo* = a currycomb (Gujarati) खरारा [*kharārā*] *m* (H) A currycomb. 2 Currying a horse. (Marathi) Rebus: करडा [*karaḍā*] Hard from alloy--iron, silver &c. (Marathi) *kharādī* ' turner' (Gujarati)

 *dula* 'two, pair' Rebus: dul 'cast metal' PLUS *dhāḷ* 'a slope'; 'inclination of a plane' (G.); *ḍhāḷiyum* = adj. sloping, inclining (G.) Rebus: *ḍhālako* = a large metal ingot (G.) *ḍhālakī* = a metal heated and poured into a mould; a solid piece of metal; an ingot (Gujarati) PLUS kolom 'three' Rebus: kolami 'smithy, forge'. Thus cast metal ingot smithy.
sal 'splinter' Rebus: sal 'workshop'
 *kolmo* 'paddy plant' Rebus: *kolami* 'smithy, forge' Vikalpa: *mogge* 'sprout, bud' Rebus: *mũh* 'ingot' (Santali) dolu 'plant of shoot height' Rebus: dul 'cast metal'

m1316A dula 'two' Rebus: dul 'cast metal' *kamaḍha* 'archer, bow' Rebus: *kammaṭa* 'mint, coiner'. mint metal castings.
dula 'two' Rebus: dul 'cast metal'
 *loa* 'ficus religiosa' Rebus: *lo* 'iron' (Sanskrit) PLUS unique ligatures: लोखंड [lōkhaṇḍa] *n* (लोह S) Iron. लोखंडाचे चणे खावविणें or चारणें To oppress grievously.लोखंडकाम [lōkhaṇḍakāma] *n* Iron work; that portion (of a building, machine &c.) which consists of iron. 2 The business of an ironsmith.लोखंडी [lōkhaṇḍī] *a* (लोखंड) Composed of iron; relating to iron. (Marathi)
  Strands of yarn/rope' hieroglyph: Hieroglyph: 'strands of yarn' Rebus reading: *dhā'tu* 'strand of rope' Rebus: *dhatu* 'mineral ore' (Santali)

ranku 'liquid measure' Rebus: ranku 'tin'
dula 'two' Rebus: dul 'cast metal' kolom 'three' Rebus: kolami 'smithy, forge'

Nausharo 9A markhor horn: *miṇḍāl* 'markhor' (Tōrwālī) *meḍho* a ram, a sheep (G.)(CDIAL 10120) Rebus: *mẽṛhẽt, meḍ* 'iron' (Mu.Ho.)
kūdī 'bunch of twigs' (Sanskrit) Rebus: *kuṭhi* 'smelter furnace' (Santali)
dhatu 'scarf' Rebus; dhatu 'mineral ore' kola 'tiger' Rebus: kolhe 'smelter' kol 'working in iron'
sal 'splinter' Rebus: sal 'workshop' *mogge* 'sprout, bud' Rebus*: mũh* 'ingot'

  Strands of yarn/rope' hieroglyph: Hieroglyph: 'strands of yarn' Rebus reading: *dhā'tu* 'strand of rope' Rebus: *dhatu* 'mineral ore' (Santali)

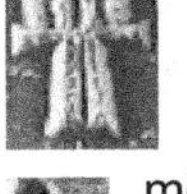 |||| Numeral 4: gaṇḍa 'four' Rebus: kaṇḍa 'furnace, fire-altar' (Santali) dula 'pair' Rebus: dul 'cast metal'

 mēḍu height, rising ground, hillock (Kannada) Rebus: *mẽṛhẽt, meḍ* 'iron' (Munda.Ho.)
 *kana, kanac* = corner (Santali); Rebus: *kañcu* = bronze (Telugu) PLUS खांडा [*khāṇḍā*] *m* A jag, notch, or indentation (as upon the edge of a tool or weapon). Rebus: *kāṇḍa* 'tools, pots and pans and metal-ware' Thus, bronze metalware.

 *dhāḷ* 'a slope'; 'inclination of a plane' (G.); *ḍhāḷiyum* = adj. sloping, inclining (G.) Rebus: *ḍhālako* = a large metal ingot (G.) *ḍhālakī* = a metal heated and poured into a mould; a solid piece of metal; an ingot (Gujarati) PLUS खांडा [*khāṇḍā*] *m* A jag, notch, or indentation (as upon the edge of a tool or weapon). Rebus: *kāṇḍa* 'tools, pots and pans and metal-ware' Thus, the pair of sign hieroglyphs from r. read rebus: copper, bronze ingots, metalware castings.

 *meḍ* 'body' Rebus: *meḍ* 'iron' (Ho.) काठी [kāṭhī] *f* (काष्ट S) 'frame or structure of the body' (Marathi) Rebus: खंडी [khaṇḍī] measure of weight (Marathi) கண்டி; *kaṇṭi, n. < Mhr. khaṇḍil. [T. Tu. khaṇḍi, M. kaṇḍi.]* Candy, a weight, stated to be roughly equivalent to 500 lbs.

dulo 'hole' Rebus: dul 'cast metal'

 kanka 'rim of jar' Rebus: karṇīka 'account (scribe)' karṇī 'supercargo'.

H-844 A

h844A sal 'splinter' Rebus; sal 'workshop'

 *dula* 'pair' Rebus: *dul* 'cast (metal)' PLUS*kana, kanac* = corner (Santali); Rebus: *kañcu* = bronze (Telugu) Thus, cast bronze.

kanka  'rim of jar' Rebus: karṇīka 'account (scribe)' karṇī 'supercargo'.

M-942 a

m942a खोंड [khōṇḍa] m A young bull, a bullcalf. (Marathi) Rebus: kōdār 'turner' (Bengali); कोंद kōnda 'engraver, lapidary setting or infixing gems' (Marathi) G. sãghāṛɔ m. 'lathe' ; संघाट joinery; M. sãgaḍ 'double-canoe' Rebus: sangataras 'stone-cutter, mason' sal 'splinter' Rebus: sal 'workshop'

 *kuṭila* 'bent' CDIAL 3230 kuṭi— in cmpd. 'curve', *kuṭika*— 'bent' MBh. Rebus: *kuṭila, katthīl* = bronze (8 parts copper and 2 parts tin) sal 'splinter' Rebus: sal 'workshop' खांडा [*khāṇḍā*] *m* A jag, notch, or indentation (as upon the edge of a tool or weapon). Rebus: *kāṇḍa* 'tools, pots and pans and metal-ware

kanka 'rim of jar' Rebus: karṇīka 'account (scribe)' karṇī 'supercargo'

Chanhudaro 29A

dula 'two' Rebus; dul 'cast metal'

kəṭhā´r, kc. *kuṭhār* m. ' granary, storeroom '(WPah.)(CDIAL 3550). *koṭhārī m.* '  storekeeper' (Gujarati)(CDIAL 3551) Thus, storeroom (of) *kolom* 'three' Rebus: *kolami* 'smithy, forge'. Dula 'pair' Rebus: dul 'cast metal' Thus, together *dul kolami kuṭhār* 'metal smithy castings storeroom'

 *dula* 'pair' Rebus: *dul* 'cast (metal)' PLUS*kana, kanac* = corner (Santali); Rebus: *kañcu* = bronze (Telugu) Thus, cast bronze.

  Strands of yarn/rope' hieroglyph: Hieroglyph: 'strands of yarn' Rebus reading: *dhā´tu* 'strand of rope' Rebus: *dhatu* 'mineral ore' (Santali)

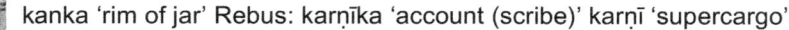

dula 'two' Rebus: dul 'cast metal'

loa 'ficus religiosa' Rebus: *lo* 'iron' (Sanskrit) PLUS unique ligatures: लोखंड [lōkhaṇḍa] *n* (लोह S) Iron. लोखंडाचे चणे खावविणें or चारणें To oppress grievously.लोखंडकाम [lōkhaṇḍakāma] *n* Iron work; that portion (of a building, machine &c.) which consists of iron. 2 The business of an ironsmith.लोखंडी [lōkhaṇḍī] *a* (लोखंड) Composed of iron; relating to iron. (Marathi) kanka 'rim of jar' Rebus: karṇīka 'account (scribe)' karṇī 'supercargo'
ḍhālako kāṇḍa 'ingot, tools, pots and pans and metal-ware'.*dhāḷ* 'a slope'; 'inclination of a plane' (G.); *ḍhāḷiyum* = adj. sloping, inclining (G.) Rebus: *ḍhālako* = a large metal ingot (G.) *ḍhālakī* = a metal heated and poured into a mould; a solid piece of metal; an ingot (Gujarati)

dula 'two' Rebus: dul 'cast metal'

m1692a *खोंड [khōṇḍa] m A young bull, a bullcalf. (Marathi) Rebus: kõdār 'turner' (Bengali); कोंद kōnda 'engraver, lapidary setting or infixing gems' (Marathi) G. sãghāṛɔ m. 'lathe' ; संघाट joinery; M. sãgaḍ 'double-canoe' Rebus: sangataras 'stone-cutter, mason'*

dula 'two' Rebus: dul 'cast metal'

kəṭhā´r, kc. *kuṭhār* m. ' granary, storeroom '(WPah.)(CDIAL 3550). *koṭhārī m.* ' storekeeper'

(Gujarati)(CDIAL 3551) Thus, storeroom (of) *kolom* 'three' Rebus: *kolami* 'smithy, forge'. Dula 'pair' Rebus: dul 'cast metal' Thus, together *dul kolami kuṭhār* 'metal smithy castings storeroom'

kamaḍha 'archer, bow' Rebus: *kammaṭa* 'mint, coiner'.

cīmara 'black ant' Rebus: *cīmara* 'copper'. *cīmara kāra* -- ' coppersmith '
sal 'splinter' Rebus: sal 'workshop'

khaṇḍ 'field, division' (Skt.) Rebus: *khāṇḍa* 'tools, pots and pans, metal-ware'. Rebus 2: kaṇḍ 'fire-altar' (Santali) dula 'pair' Rebus: dul 'cast metal' Thus, duplicated 'division' hieroglyph sign reads: cast metal metal-ware.

| *koḍa* 'one' Rebus: *koḍ* 'workshop'

kolmo 'paddy plant' Rebus: *kolami* 'smithy, forge' Vikalpa: *mogge* 'sprout, bud' Rebus: *mũh* 'ingot' (Santali) dolu 'plant of shoot height' Rebus: dul 'cast metal'

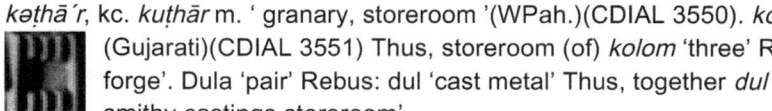

m1169A *खोंड [khōṇḍa] m A young bull, a bullcalf. (Marathi) Rebus: kõdār 'turner' (Bengali); कोंद kōnda 'engraver, lapidary setting or infixing gems' (Marathi) G. sãghāṛɔ m. 'lathe' ; संघाट joinery; M. sãgaḍ 'double-canoe' Rebus: sangataras 'stone-cutter, mason'*

ṭagara 'ram' Rebus: *tagara* 'tin' Vikalpa: *miṇḍāl* 'markhor' (Tōrwālī) *meḍho* a ram, a sheep (Gujarati)(CDIAL 10120) Rebus: *mẽṛhẽt, meḍ* 'iron' (Mu.Ho.)

balad m. ' ox ', gng. *bald*, (Ku.) *barad*, id. (N. Tarai) Rebus: *bharat* (5 copper, 4 zinc and 1 tin)(Punjabi) Thus, copper-zinc-tin alloy (worker).

The three animal hieroglyphs ligatured connote: copper-zinc-tin alloy (worker), iron worker, turner, engraver – that is, lapidary-smith artisan (guild indicated by the ligatured togetherness.)
dula 'two' Rebus: dul 'cast metal'

kəṭhā´r, kc. *kuṭhār* m. ' granary, storeroom '(WPah.)(CDIAL 3550). *koṭhārī m.* ' storekeeper'
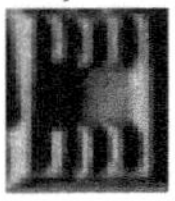
(Gujarati)(CDIAL 3551) Thus, storeroom (of) *kolom* 'three' Rebus: *kolami* 'smithy, forge'. Dula 'pair' Rebus: dul 'cast metal' Thus, together *dul kolami kuṭhār* 'metal smithy castings storeroom'

Circumscript:

kuṭila 'bent' CDIAL 3230 kuṭi— in cmpd. 'curve', *kuṭika*— 'bent' MBh. Rebus: *kuṭila, katthīl* = bronze (8 parts copper and 2 parts tin) Duplicated: dula 'pair' Rebus: dul 'cast metal' Thus, cast bronze or bronze castings. karaṇḍa 'duck' (Sanskrit) karaṛa 'a very large aquatic bird' (Sindhi) Rebus: करडा [*karaḍā*] Hard from alloy--iron, silver &c. (Marathi) *kharādī* ' turner' (Gujarati)sal 'splinter' Rebus: sal 'workshop'dulo 'hole' Rebus: dul 'cast metal' dula 'two' Rebus: dul 'cast metal' *ayo* 'fish' Rebus: *aya* 'iron' *ayas* 'metal'

muka 'ladle' (Tamil)(DEDR 4887) Rebus: *mũh* 'ingot' (Santali) *baṭa* = rimless pot (Kannada) Rebus:) *baṭa* = a kind of iron (G.)) *bhaṭa* furnace (Gujarati) Thus, iron ingot.

kolom 'three' Rebus: kolami 'smithy, forge'

'Arrow' sign hieroglyph (variant) This is a ligature of 'lid of pot' hieroglyph superscript on 'a linear stroke' numeral hieroglyph.*aḍaren* 'cover of pot or lid' Rebus: *aduru* 'native, unsmelted metal' PLUS koḍ = one (Santali); koḍ 'workshop' (Gujarati) *aya kāṇḍa* 'alloy metalware'

Kalibangan 1A *खोंड [khōṇḍa] m A young bull, a bullcalf. (Marathi) Rebus: kōdār 'turner' (Bengali); कोंद kōnda 'engraver, lapidary setting or infixing gems' (Marathi) G. sãghāṛɔ m. 'lathe' ; संघाट joinery; M. sãgaḍ 'double-canoe' Rebus: sangataras 'stone-cutter, mason' dula 'two' Rebus; dul 'cast metal'*

kəṭhā´r, kc. *kuṭhār* m. ' granary, storeroom '(WPah.)(CDIAL 3550). *koṭhārī m.* ' storekeeper'

(Gujarati)(CDIAL 3551) Thus, storeroom (of) *kolom* 'three' Rebus: *kolami* 'smithy, forge'. Dula 'pair' Rebus: dul 'cast metal' Thus, together *dul kolami kuṭhār* 'metal smithy castings storeroom'

mēḍu height, rising ground, hillock (Kannada) Rebus: *mẽṛhẽt, meḍ* 'iron' (Munda.Ho.)

kaṇḍo 'stool, seat' Rebus: *kāṇḍa* 'metalware' *kaṇḍa* 'fire-altar' PLUS | *koḍa* 'one' Rebus: *koḍ* 'workshop'

खोंड [khōṇḍa] m A young bull, a bullcalf. (Marathi) Rebus: kōdār 'turner' (Bengali); कोंद kōnda 'engraver, lapidary setting or infixing gems' (Marathi) G. sãghāṛɔ m. 'lathe' ; संघाट joinery; M. sãgaḍ 'double-canoe' Rebus: sangataras 'stone-cutter, mason'

dula 'two' Rebus: dul 'cast metal'

kəṭhā´r, kc. *kuṭhār* m. ' granary, storeroom '(WPah.)(CDIAL 3550). *koṭhārī m.* ' storekeeper'

(Gujarati)(CDIAL 3551) Thus, storeroom (of) *kolom* 'three' Rebus: *kolami* 'smithy, forge'. Dula 'pair' Rebus: dul 'cast metal' Thus, together *dul kolami kuṭhār* 'metal smithy castings storeroom' boat shipment. *karṇīka* 'account (scribe)'.कारणी *kāraṇī* 'the

supercargo of a ship' (Marathi)

koḍi 'flag' (Ta.)(DEDR 2049). Rebus 1: *koḍ* 'workshop' (Kuwi) Rebus 2: *khōḍ* m. 'pit', *khōḍü* f. 'small pit' (Kashmiri. CDIAL 3947).

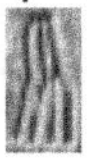 
Strands of yarn/rope' hieroglyph: Hieroglyph: 'strands of yarn' Rebus reading: *dhā´tu* 'strand of rope' Rebus: *dhatu* 'mineral ore' (Santali)

pots and pans and metal-ware'

dhāḷ 'a slope'; 'inclination of a plane' (G.); *ḍhāḷiyum* = adj. sloping, inclining (G.) Rebus: *ḍhālako* = a large metal ingot (G.) *ḍhālakī* = a metal heated and poured into a mould; a solid piece of metal; an ingot (Gujarati) PLUS खांडा [*khāṇḍā*] *m* A jag, notch, or indentation (as upon the edge of a tool or weapon). Rebus: *kāṇḍa* 'tools, pots and pans and metal-ware' Thus, the pair of sign hieroglyphs from r. read rebus: copper, bronze ingots, metalware castings.

aya kammaṭa.'coiner, mint alloy'

ḍāg mountain-ridge (H.)(CDIAL 5476). Rebus: dhangar 'blacksmith' (Maithili)

'Arrow' sign hieroglyph (variant) This is a ligature of 'lid of pot' hieroglyph superscript on 'a linear stroke' numeral hieroglyph.*aḍaren* 'cover of pot or lid' Rebus: *aduru* 'native, unsmelted metal' PLUS koḍ = one (Santali); koḍ 'workshop' (Gujarati)

कांड *kāṇḍa* 'arrow' Rebus: *kāṇḍa* 'pots and pans, metalware, tools'. Rebus 2: kaṇḍ 'fire-altar' (Santali)

m38a खोंड *[khōṇḍa] m A young bull, a bullcalf. (Marathi) Rebus: kōdār 'turner' (Bengali); कोंद kōnda 'engraver, lapidary setting or infixing gems' (Marathi) G. sãghāṛɔ m. 'lathe' ; संघाट joinery; M. sāgaḍ 'double-canoe' Rebus: sangataras 'stone-cutter, mason'*

dula 'two' Rebus: dul 'cast metal'

kəṭhā´r, kc. *kuṭhār* m. ' granary, storeroom '(WPah.)(CDIAL 3550). *koṭhārī m.* ' storekeeper'

(Gujarati)(CDIAL 3551) Thus, storeroom (of) *kolom* 'three' Rebus: *kolami* 'smithy, forge'. Dula 'pair' Rebus: dul 'cast metal' Thus, together *dul kolami kuṭhār* 'metal smithy castings storeroom'

kamaḍha 'archer, bow' Rebus: *kammaṭa* 'mint, coiner'.

kolmo 'paddy plant' Rebus: *kolami* 'smithy, forge' Vikalpa: *mogge* 'sprout, bud' Rebus: *mũh* 'ingot' (Santali) dolu 'plant of shoot height' Rebus: dul 'cast metal'

sal 'splinter' Rebus: sal 'workshop' *aya aḍaren (homonym: aduru)*'alloy native metal' *aya kammaṭa.*'coiner, mint alloy'

dula 'two' Rebus: dul 'cast metal' *ayo* 'fish' Rebus: *aya* 'iron' *ayas* 'metal'

The pair of hieroglyph signs are compositions: 1. *bicha* 'scorpion' (Assamese) Rebus: *bica* 'stone ore' (Santali) The pairing sign is a composition of: sloping stroke PLUS two short strokes of a 'splinter':*dhāḷ* 'a slope'; 'inclination of a plane' (Gujarati); *ḍhāḷiyum* = adj. sloping, inclining (Gujarati) Rebus: *ḍhālako* = a large

metal ingot (Gujarati) *ḍhālakī* = a metal heated and poured into a mould; a solid piece of metal; an ingot (Gujarati)PLUS*sal* 'splinter' Rebus: *sal* 'workshop'. Thus the composition reads: *ḍhālako sal* 'ingot workshop'.

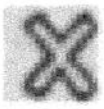
dāṭu 'cross'(Telugu) Rebus: *dhatu* 'mineral' (Santali).
kanka 'rim of jar' Rebus: karṇīka 'account (scribe)' karṇī 'supercargo'

M-1767 a

m1767a *खोंड [khōṇḍa] m A young bull, a bullcalf. (Marathi) Rebus: kōdār 'turner' (Bengali); कोंद kōnda 'engraver, lapidary setting or infixing gems' (Marathi) G. sãghāṛɔ m. 'lathe' ; संघाट joinery; M. sãgaḍ 'double-canoe' Rebus: sangataras 'stone-cutter, mason' First 3 signs as at m38.*

'rim-of-jar' hieroglyph *kanka* (Santali) *karṇika* 'scribe'(Sanskrit) Rebus: *karṇī,* supercargo for a boat shipment. *karṇīka* 'account (scribe)'.कारणी *kāraṇī* 'the supercargo of a ship' (Marathi)

|||| Numeral 4: gaṇḍa 'four' Rebus: kaṇḍa 'furnace, fire-altar' (Santali) dula 'pair' Rebus: dul 'cast metal'

Strands of yarn/rope' hieroglyph: Hieroglyph: 'strands of yarn' Rebus reading: *dhā'tu* 'strand of rope' Rebus: *dhatu* 'mineral ore' (Santali)

khareḍo = a currycomb (Gujarati) खरारा [*kharārā*] *m* (H) A currycomb. 2 Currying a horse. (Marathi) Rebus: करडा [*karaḍā*] Hard from alloy--iron, silver &c. (Marathi) *kharādī* ' turner' (Gujarati)

h92a
ibha 'elephant' Rebus: *ib* 'iron' *ibbo* 'merchant' (Gujarati) dula 'two' Rebus: dul 'cast metal' PLUS *ḍhālako kāṇḍa* 'ingot, tools, pots and pans and metal-ware'.*dhāḷ* 'a slope'; 'inclination of a plane' (G.); *ḍhāḷiyum* = adj. sloping, inclining (G.) Rebus: *ḍhālako* = a large metal ingot (G.) *ḍhālakī* = a metal heated and poured into a mould; a solid piece of metal; an ingot (Gujarati) Thus, metal ingot castings
sal 'splinter' Rebus: sal 'workshop' dula 'two' Rebus: dul 'cast metal'

aḍar 'harrow'; rebus: *aduru* 'native unsmelted metal' *ayo* 'fish' Rebus: *aya* 'iron' *ayas* 'metal'

beads: Pa. kandi (pl. -l) necklace, beads. Ga. (Punjabi) kandi (pl. -l) bead, (pl.) necklace; (S.2) kandiṭ bead. (DEDR 1215) Rebus: *கண்டி; kaṇṭi, n. < Mhr. khaṇḍil. [T. Tu. khaṇḍi, M. kaṇḍi.] 1. Candy, a weight, stated to be roughly equivalent to 500 lbs.; பாரமென் னும் நிறையளவு.* खंडीगणती or खंडोगणती [khaṇḍīgaṇatī or khaṇḍōgaṇatī] *ad* By candies; counting or reckoning by candies. खंडीवारी [khaṇḍīvārī] *ad* By scores, heaps, candies. खंडी [khaṇḍī] Applied to a great quantity; as खंडीभर पोरें, खंडीभर मेंढ्या, खंडीभर काम, खंडीभर बोलतो-लिहितो&c

baraḍo = spine; backbone (Tulu) Rebus: *baran, bharat* 'mixed alloys' (5 copper, 4 zinc and 1 tin) (Punjabi) PLUS gaṇḍa 'four' Rebus: kaṇḍa 'furnace, fire-altar' (Santali)
water-carrier hieroglyph *kuṭi*; Rebus: *kuṭhi* 'smelter furnace'.

PLUS 'rim of jar': *kanka* (Santali) *karṇika* 'scribe'(Sanskrit) Rebus: *karṇī,* supercargo
'rim-of-jar' hieroglyph *kanka* (Santali) *karṇika* 'scribe'(Sanskrit) Rebus: *karṇī,* supercargo

for a boat shipment. *karṇīka* 'account (scribe)'.कारणी *kāraṇī* 'the supercargo of a ship' (Marathi)

m1766a खोंड *[khōṇḍa] m A young bull, a bullcalf. (Marathi) Rebus: kõdār 'turner' (Bengali); कोंद kōnda 'engraver, lapidary setting or infixing gems' (Marathi) G. sãghāṛɔ m. 'lathe' ; संघाट joinery; M. sãgaḍ 'double-canoe' Rebus: sangataras 'stone-cutter, mason'*

dula 'two' Rebus: dul 'cast metal'

kana, kanac = corner (Santali); Rebus: *kañcu* = bronze (Telugu) PLUS खांडा [*khāṇḍā*] *m* A jag, notch, or indentation (as upon the edge of a tool or weapon). Rebus: *kāṇḍa* 'tools, pots and pans and metal-ware' Thus, bronze metalware.

beads: Pa. kandi (pl. -l) necklace, beads. Ga. (Punjabi) kandi (pl. -l) bead, (pl.) necklace; (S.2) kandiṭ bead. (DEDR 1215) Rebus: *கண்டி; kaṇṭi, n. < Mhr. khaṇḍil. [T. Tu. khaṇḍi, M. kaṇḍi.] 1. Candy, a weight, stated to be roughly equivalent to 500 lbs.; பாரமென் னும் நிறையளவு.* खंडीगणती or खंडोगणती [khaṇḍīgaṇatī or khaṇḍōgaṇatī] *ad* By candies; counting or reckoning by candies. खंडीवारी [khaṇḍīvārī] *ad* By scores, heaps, candies. खंडी [khaṇḍī] Applied to a great quantity; as खंडीभर पोरें, खंडीभर मेंढ्या, खंडीभर काम, खंडीभर बोलतो-लिहितो&c खांडा [*khāṇḍā*] *m* A jag, notch, or indentation (as upon the edge of a tool or weapon). Rebus: *kāṇḍa* 'tools, pots and pans and metal-ware'

Circumscript:

kuṭila 'bent' CDIAL 3230 kuṭi— in cmpd. 'curve', *kuṭika—* 'bent' MBh. Rebus: *kuṭila, katthīl* = bronze (8 parts copper and 2 parts tin) Duplicated: dula 'pair' Rebus: dul 'cast metal' Thus, cast bronze or bronze castings.

karaṇḍa 'duck' (Sanskrit) karaṛa 'a very large aquatic bird' (Sindhi) Rebus: करडा [*karaḍā*] Hard from alloy--iron, silver &c. (Marathi) *kharādī* ' turner' (Gujarati)

sal 'splinter' Rebus: sal 'workshop' *ayo* 'fish' Rebus: *aya* 'iron' *ayas* 'metal'

dula 'pair' Rebus: *dul* 'cast (metal)' PLUS*kana, kanac* = corner (Santali); Rebus: *kañcu* = bronze (Telugu) Thus, cast bronze.

dula 'two' Rebus: dul 'cast metal'kanka 'rim of jar' Rebus: karṇīka 'account (scribe)' karṇī 'supercargo'

m165a खोंड *[khōṇḍa] m A young bull, a bullcalf. (Marathi) Rebus: kõdār 'turner' (Bengali); कोंद kōnda 'engraver, lapidary setting or infixing gems' (Marathi) G. sãghāṛɔ m. 'lathe' ; संघाट joinery; M. sãgaḍ 'double-canoe' Rebus: sangataras 'stone-cutter, mason'*

dula 'two' Rebus: dul 'cast metal

kolmo 'paddy plant' Rebus: *kolami* 'smithy, forge' Vikalpa: *mogge* 'sprout, bud' Rebus: *mũh* 'ingot' (Santali) dolu 'plant of shoot height' Rebus: dul 'cast metal'

kanka (Santali) *karṇika* 'scribe'(Sanskrit) Rebus: *karṇī,* supercargo for a boat shipment. INFIXED खांडा [*khāṇḍā*] *m* A jag, notch, or indentation (as upon the edge of a tool or weapon). Rebus: *kāṇḍa* 'tools, pots and pans and metal-ware'

खांडा [*khāṇḍā*] *m* A jag, notch, or indentation (as upon the edge of a tool or weapon). Rebus: *kāṇḍa* 'tools, pots and pans and metal-ware'

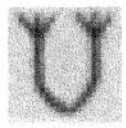

dula 'pair' Rebus: dul 'cast (metal)' kolmo 'rice plant' Rebus: kolami 'smithy/forge'

kanka 'rim of jar' Rebus: karṇīka 'account (scribe)' karṇī 'supercargo'

ḍato = claws of crab (Santali) Rebus: *dhātu* 'mineral ore' kanka 'rim of jar' Rebus: karṇīka 'account (scribe)' karṇī 'supercargo'

kanac 'corner' Rebus: *kañcu* 'bronze'

M-1835 a

m1835a *खोंड [khōṇḍa] m A young bull, a bullcalf. (Marathi) Rebus: kõdār 'turner' (Bengali); कोंद kōnda 'engraver, lapidary setting or infixing gems' (Marathi) G. sãghārɔ m. 'lathe' ; संघाट joinery; M. sãgaḍ 'double-canoe' Rebus: sangataras 'stone-cutter, mason'*

dula 'two' Rebus: dul 'cast metal'
kolmo 'paddy plant' Rebus: *kolami* 'smithy, forge' Vikalpa: *mogge* 'sprout, bud' Rebus: *mũh* 'ingot' (Santali) dolu 'plant of shoot height' Rebus: dul 'cast metal'
खांडा [*khāṇḍā*] *m* A jag, notch, or indentation (as upon the edge of a tool or weapon). Rebus: *kāṇḍa* 'tools, pots and pans and metal-ware' Thus, mint metalware, ore.

gaṇḍa 'four' Rebus: kaṇḍa 'furnace, fire-altar' (Santali)
kuṭila 'bent' CDIAL 3230 kuṭi— in cmpd. 'curve', *kuṭika—* 'bent' MBh. Rebus: *kuṭila, katthīl* = bronze (8 parts copper and 2 parts tin)

water-carrier hieroglyph *kuṭi*; Rebus: *kuṭhi* 'smelter furnace'.
PLUS 'rim of jar': *kanka* (Santali) *karṇika* 'scribe'(Sanskrit)
Rebus: *karṇī,* supercargo
'rim-of-jar' hieroglyph *kanka* (Santali) *karṇika* 'scribe'(Sanskrit)
Rebus: *karṇī,* supercargo for a boat shipment. *karṇīka* 'account (scribe)'.कारणी *kāraṇī* 'the supercargo of a ship' (Marath

m274A
Rhinoceros/boar: baḍhia = a castrated boar, a hog (Santali) baḍhi 'a caste who work both in iron and wood' (Santali) *baṟea* 'merchant' pattar 'trough' Rebus: pattar 'guild, goldsmith'
dula 'two' Rebus: dul 'cast metal'
dula 'pair' Rebus: dul 'cast metal' PLUS | *koḍa* 'one' Rebus: *koḍ* 'workshop' PLUS INFIXED खांडा [*khāṇḍā*] *m* A jag, notch, or indentation (as upon the edge of a tool or weapon). Rebus: *kāṇḍa* 'tools, pots and pans and metal-ware' Thus metware castings workshop.
kanka (Santali) *karṇika* 'scribe'(Sanskrit) Rebus: *karṇī,* supercargo for a boat shipment. INFIXED खांडा [*khāṇḍā*] *m* A jag, notch, or indentation (as upon the edge of a tool or weapon). Rebus: *kāṇḍa* 'tools, pots and pans and metal-ware' *aya kāṇḍa* 'alloy metalware' karaṇḍa 'duck' (Sanskrit) karaṛa 'a very large aquatic bird' (Sindhi) Rebus: करडा [*karaḍā*] Hard from alloy--iron, silver &c. (Marathi) *kharādī* ' turner' (Gujaratij)

dula 'pair' Rebus: dul 'cast (metal)' kolmo 'rice plant' Rebus: kolami 'smithy/forge' kanka 'rim of jar' Rebus: karṇīka 'account (scribe)' karṇī 'supercargo'

m169a *खोंड [khōṇḍa] m A young bull, a bullcalf. (Marathi) Rebus: kōdār 'turner' (Bengali); कोंद kōnda 'engraver, lapidary setting or infixing gems' (Marathi) G. sãghāṛɔ m. 'lathe' ; संघाट joinery; M. sãgaḍ 'double-canoe' Rebus: sangataras 'stone-cutter, mason'*

dula 'two' Rebus: dul 'cast metal'

notch+slanted stroke reads rebus: *ḍhālako kāṇḍa* 'ingot, tools, pots and pans and metal-ware'.*ḍhāḷ* 'a slope'; 'inclination of a plane' (G.); *ḍhāḷiyum* = adj. sloping, inclining (G.) Rebus: *ḍhālako* = a large metal ingot (G.) *ḍhālakī* = a metal heated and poured into a mould; a solid piece of metal; an ingot (Gujarati) PLUS खांडा [*khāṇḍā*] *m* A jag, notch, or indentation (as upon the edge of a tool or weapon). Rebus: *kāṇḍa* 'tools, pots and pans and metal-ware'

sal 'splinter' Rebus: sal 'workshop' kolom 'three' Rebus: kolami 'smithy, forge'

सांड [sāṇḍa] *f* (षंद S) An outlet for superfluous water (as through a dam or mound); a sluice, a floodvent. Rebus: सांडणी [sāṇḍaṇī] *f* (H) An instrument of goldsmiths. It is hooked or curved at the extremity; and is used to draw things out of the fire.

सांठा [*sāṇṭhā*] *m* (संचय S) A collection, heap, hoard, store, stock.साटें [*sāṭēṃ*] *n* (संचय S) A whole investment; the total quantity of merchandise (brought to market by one merchant).

kanka 'rim of jar' Rebus: karṇīka 'account (scribe)' karṇī 'supercargo'

m1033a *खोंड [khōṇḍa] m A young bull, a bullcalf. (Marathi) Rebus: kōdār 'turner' (Bengali); कोंद kōnda 'engraver, lapidary setting or infixing gems' (Marathi) G. sãghāṛɔ m. 'lathe' ; संघाट joinery; M. sãgaḍ 'double-canoe' Rebus: sangataras 'stone-cutter, mason'*

dula 'two' Rebus: dul 'cast metal'

kanac 'corner' Rebus: *kañcu* 'bronze'

Kur. xolā tail. *Malt.* qoli id. (DEDR 2135). Rebus: kolhe 'smelter' Thus, copper smelter.

sal 'splinter' Rebus: sal 'workshop'

कांड *kāṇḍa* 'arrow' Rebus: *kāṇḍa* 'pots and pans, metalware, tools'. Rebus 2: kaṇḍ 'fire-altar' (Santali)

mēḍu height, rising ground, hillock (Kannada) Rebus: *mẽṛhẽt, meḍ* 'iron' (Munda.Ho.)

ayo 'fish' Rebus: *aya* 'iron' *ayas* 'metal'

h598c Circumscript: dula 'two' Rebus: dul 'cast metal'

āra 'spokes' Rebus: *āra 'brass'*. cf. erka = ekke (Tbh. of arka) aka (Tbh. of arka) copper (metal); crystal (Kannada) Glyph: *eraka*'nave of wheel' Rebus: eraka 'copper'; cf. erka = ekke (Tbh. of arka) aka (Tbh. of arka) copper (metal); crystal (Kannada) *erako* 'moltencast copper' Duplicated: dula 'pair' Rebus: dul 'cast metal' Thus cast copper, brass casting.

m1309A dula 'two' Rebus; dul 'cast metal'*āra* 'spokes' Rebus: *āra 'brass'*. cf. erka = ekke (Tbh. of arka) aka

(Tbh. of arka) copper (metal); crystal (Kannada) Glyph: *eraka*'nave of wheel' Rebus: eraka 'copper'; cf. erka = ekke (Tbh.

of arka) aka (Tbh. of arka) copper (metal); crystal (Kannada) *erako* 'moltencast copper' Duplicated: dula 'pair' Rebus: dul 'cast metal' Thus cast copper, brass casting.

 *kanac* 'corner' Rebus: *kañcu* 'bronze'

 h27A *खोंड [khōṇḍa] m A young bull, a bullcalf. (Marathi) Rebus: kõdār 'turner' (Bengali); कोंद kōnda 'engraver, lapidary setting or infixing gems' (Marathi) G. sãghāṛɔ m. 'lathe' ; संघाट joinery; M. sãgaḍ 'double-canoe' Rebus: sangataras 'stone-cutter, mason'*

dula 'two' Rebus: dul 'cast metal'

 *kanac* 'corner' Rebus: *kañcu* 'bronze'

 kanka 'rim of jar' Rebus: karṇīka 'account (scribe)' karṇī 'supercargo' PLUS खांडा [*khāṇḍā*] *m* A jag, notch, or indentation (as upon the edge of a tool or weapon). Rebus: *kāṇḍa* 'tools, pots and pans and metal-ware'

 *ḍhanga* = a crook used for pulling down the branches of trees, for goats, sheep and camels (P.) Rebus:*ḍhangar* blacksmith'. PLUS

 *kharedo* = a currycomb (Gujarati) खरारा [*kharārā*] *m* (H) A currycomb. 2 Currying a horse. (Marathi) Rebus: करडा [*karaḍā*] Hard from alloy--iron, silver &c. (Marathi) *kharādī* ' turner' (Gujarati)

 *dula* 'pair' Rebus: *dul* 'cast (metal)' PLUS*kana, kanac* = corner (Santali); Rebus: *kañcu* = bronze (Telugu) PLUS infixed kolmo 'paddy plant' Rebus: kolami 'smithy, forge'. Thus, cast bronze smithy, forge. Or, *mogge* 'sprout, bud' Rebus: *mũh* 'ingot' (Santali)Thus, cast bronze ingot. Read as: *kañcu dul mũh 'bronze cast ingot'*

water-carrier hieroglyph *kuṭi*; Rebus: *kuṭhi* 'smelter furnace'.

   PLUS 'rim of jar': *kanka* (Santali) *karṇika* 'scribe'(Sanskrit)

Rebus: *karṇī,* supercargo

'rim-of-jar' hieroglyph *kanka* (Santali) *karṇika* 'scribe'(Sanskrit)

Rebus: *karṇī,* supercargo for a boat shipment. *karṇīka* 'account (scribe)' .कारणी *kāraṇī* 'the supercargo of a ship' (Marathi)

 h143a dula 'two' Rebus: dul 'cast metal'

kanac 'corner'  Rebus: *kañcu* 'bronze' *kanka* (Santali) *karṇika* 'scribe'(Sanskrit) Rebus: *karṇī,* supercargo

खांडा [*khāṇḍā*] *m* A jag, notch, or indentation (as upon the edge of a tool or weapon). Rebus: *kāṇḍa* 'tools, pots and pans and metal-ware'

 *ḍhanga* = a crook used for pulling down the branches of trees, for goats, sheep and camels (P.) Rebus:*ḍhangar* blacksmith'. PLUS

 *kharedo* = a currycomb (Gujarati) खरारा [*kharārā*] *m* (H) A currycomb. 2 Currying a horse. (Marathi) Rebus: करडा [*karaḍā*] Hard from alloy--iron, silver &c.

(Marathi) *kharādī* ' turner' (Gujarati)

dula 'pair' Rebus: *dul* 'cast (metal)' PLUS*kana, kanac* = corner (Santali); Rebus: *kañcu* = bronze (Telugu) PLUS infixed kolmo 'paddy plant' Rebus: kolami 'smithy, forge'. Thus, cast bronze smithy, forge. Or, *mogge* 'sprout, bud' Rebus: *mũh* 'ingot'

 water-carrier hieroglyph *kuṭi*; Rebus: *kuṭhi* 'smelter furnace'.

  PLUS 'rim of jar': *kanka* (Santali) *karṇika* 'scribe'(Sanskrit) Rebus: *karṇī,* supercargo

'rim- of-jar' hieroglyph *kanka* (Santali) *karṇika* 'scribe'(Sanskrit) Rebus: *karṇī,* supercargo for a boat shipment. *karṇīka* 'account (scribe)'.कारणी *kāraṇī* 'the supercargo of a ship' (Marathi)

h586A Native metal smith guild. dula 'two' Rebus: dul 'cast metal

 *kanac* 'corner' Rebus: *kañcu* 'bronze'

kanka 'rim  of jar' Rebus: karṇīka 'account (scribe)' karṇī 'supercargo'

m683a *खोंड [khōṇḍa] m A young bull, a bullcalf. (Marathi) Rebus: kōdār 'turner' (Bengali); कोंद kōnda 'engraver, lapidary setting or infixing gems' (Marathi) G. sãghāṛɔ m. 'lathe' ; संघाट joinery; M. sãgaḍ 'double-canoe' Rebus: sangataras 'stone-cutter, mason' dula 'two' Rebus: dul 'cast metal'*

ḍãg mountain-ridge (H.)(CDIAL 5476). Rebus: dhangar 'blacksmith' (Maithili)

Strands of yarn/rope' hieroglyph: Hieroglyph: 'strands of yarn' Rebus reading: *dhā'tu* 'strand of rope' Rebus: *dhatu* 'mineral ore' (Santali)

sal 'splinter' Rebus: sal 'workshop' *aya kāṇḍa* 'alloy metalware' *kamaḍha* 'crab' Rebus: *kammaṭa* 'mint, coiner'.*ḍato* = claws of crab (Santali) Rebus: *dhātu* 'mineral or

 kanka 'rim of jar' Rebus: karṇīka 'account (scribe)' karṇī 'supercargo'

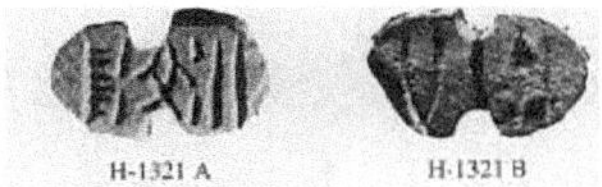

H-1321 A H-1321 B

h1321A Side A: dula 'two' Rebus: dul 'cast metal'
aya aḍaren (homonym: aduru)'alloy native metal'
aya kāṇḍa 'alloy metalware'

khareḍo = a currycomb (Gujarati) खरारा [*kharārā*] *m* (H) A currycomb. 2 Currying a horse. (Marathi) Rebus: करडा [*karaḍā*] Hard from alloy--iron, silver &c. (Marathi) *kharādī* ' turner' (Gujarati)

dulo 'hole' Rebus: dul 'cast metal' kolom 'three' Rebus: kolami 'smithy, forge' *baṭa* = rimless pot (Kannada) Rebus:) *baṭa* = a kind of iron (G.)) *bhaṭa* furnace (Gujarati

m892A खोंड *[khōṇḍa] m A young bull, a bullcalf. (Marathi) Rebus: kõdār 'turner' (Bengali);* कोंद *kōnda 'engraver, lapidary setting or infixing gems' (Marathi) G. sãghāṛɔ m. 'lathe' ;* संघाट *joinery; M. sãgaḍ 'double-canoe' Rebus: sangataras 'stone-cutter, mason' dula 'two' Rebus: dul 'cast metal'*

muka 'ladle' (Tamil)(DEDR 4887) Rebus: *mũh* 'ingot' (Santali) *baṭa* = rimless pot (Kannada) Rebus:) *baṭa* = a kind of iron (G.)) *bhaṭa* furnace (Gujarati) Thus, iron ingot.

kanka 'rim of jar' Rebus: karṇīka 'account (scribe)' karṇī 'supercargo'

INFIXED sal 'splinte' Rebus: sal 'workshop'

|||| Numeral 4: gaṇḍa 'four' Rebus: kaṇḍa 'furnace, fire-altar' (Santali) dula 'pair' Rebus: dul 'cast metal'

ḍãg mountain-ridge (H.)(CDIAL 5476). Rebus: dhangar 'blacksmith' (Maithili)

kamaḍha 'crab' Rebus: *kammaṭa* 'mint, coiner'.*ḍato* = claws of crab (Santali)
Rebus: *dhātu* 'mineral ore'
kanka 'rim of jar' Rebus: karṇīka 'account (scribe)' karṇī 'supercargo'

m957a खोंड *[khōṇḍa] m A young bull, a bullcalf. (Marathi) Rebus: kõdār 'turner' (Bengali);* कोंद *kōnda 'engraver, lapidary setting or infixing gems' (Marathi) G. sãghāṛɔ m. 'lathe' ;* संघाट *joinery; M. sãgaḍ 'double-canoe' Rebus: sangataras 'stone-cutter, mason'*
dula 'two' Rebus: dul 'cast metal'

सांड [sāṇḍa] *f* (षद S) An outlet for superfluous water (as through a dam or mound); a sluice, a floodvent. Rebus: सांडणी [sāṇḍaṇī] *f* (H) An instrument of goldsmiths. It is hooked or curved at the extremity; and is used to draw things out of the fire.
सांठा [*sāṇṭhā*] *m* (संचय S) A collection, heap, hoard, store, stock.साटें [*sāṭēṃ*] *n* (संचय S) A whole investment; the total quantity of merchandise (brought to market by one merchant).
dula 'two' Rebus: dul 'cast metal' sal 'splinter' Rebus: sal 'workshop'

muka 'ladle' (Tamil)(DEDR 4887) Rebus: *mũh* 'ingot' (Santali) *baṭa* = rimless pot (Kannada) Rebus: *baṭa* = a kind of iron (G.)) *bhaṭa* furnace (Gujarati) Thus, iron ingot.

dula 'pair' Rebus: dul 'cast (metal)' kolmo 'rice plant' Rebus: kolami 'smithy/forge'

kanka 'rim of jar' Rebus: karṇīka 'account (scribe)' karṇī 'supercargo'

h442A खोंड *[khōṇḍa] m A young bull, a bullcalf. (Marathi) Rebus: kõdār 'turner' (Bengali);* कोंद *kōnda 'engraver, lapidary setting or infixing gems' (Marathi) G. sãghāṛɔ m. 'lathe' ;* संघाट *joinery; M. sãgaḍ 'double-canoe' Rebus: sangataras 'stone-cutter, mason' Circumscript: dula 'two' Rebus: dul 'cast metal' ayo* 'fish'

Rebus: *aya* 'iron' *ayas* 'metal'

 *kanac* 'corner' Rebus: *kañcu* 'bronze'

m1362A dula 'two' Rebus: dul 'cast metal' *ayo* 'fish' Rebus: *aya* 'iron' *ayas* 'metal'

'Arrow' sign hieroglyph (variant) This is a ligature of 'lid of pot' hieroglyph superscript on 'a linear stroke' numeral hieroglyph.*aḍaren* 'cover of pot or lid' Rebus: *aduru* 'native, unsmelted metal' PLUS koḍ= one (Santali); koḍ 'workshop' (Gujarati)

 *kolmo* 'paddy plant' Rebus: *kolami* 'smithy, forge' Vikalpa: *mogge* 'sprout, bud' Rebus: *mūh* 'ingot' (Santali) dolu 'plant of shoot height' Rebus: dul 'cast metal'

m512A

m511A Copper plate. dula 'two' Rebus: dul 'cast metal' *ayo* 'fish' Rebus: *aya* 'iron' *ayas* 'metal'

baraḍo = spine; backbone (Tulu) Rebus: *baran, bharat* ' mixed alloys' (5 copper, 4 zinc and 1 tin) (Punjabi) PLUS gaṇḍa 'four' Rebus: kaṇḍa 'furnace, fire-altar' (Santali)

 kanka 'rim of jar' Rebus: karṇīka 'account (scribe)' karṇī 'supercargo'

m999A *खोंड [khōṇḍa] m A young bull, a bullcalf. (Marathi) Rebus: kōdār 'turner' (Bengali); कोंद kōnda 'engraver, lapidary setting or infixing gems' (Marathi) G. sãghārɔ m. 'lathe' ; संघाट joinery; M. sãgaḍ 'double-canoe' Rebus: sangataras 'stone-cutter, mason'*

dula 'two' Rebus: dul 'cast metal'

ayo 'fish' Rebus: *aya* 'iron' *ayas* 'metal' *aya kāṇḍa* 'alloy metalware'

h502a *खोंड [khōṇḍa] m A young bull, a bullcalf. (Marathi) Rebus: kōdār 'turner' (Bengali); कोंद kōnda 'engraver, lapidary setting or infixing gems' (Marathi) G. sãghārɔ m. 'lathe' ; संघाट joinery; M. sãgaḍ 'double-canoe' Rebus: sangataras 'stone-cutter, mason' dula 'two' Rebus: dul 'cast metal' ayo* 'fish' Rebus: *aya* 'iron' *ayas* 'metal'

 kanka 'rim of jar' Rebus: karṇīka 'account (scribe)' karṇī 'supercargo'

 *meḍ* 'body' Rebus: *meḍ* 'iron' (Ho.) काठी [kāṭhī] *f* (काष्ट S) 'frame or structure of the body' (Marathi) Rebus: खंडी [khaṇḍī] measure of weight (Marathi) *கண்டி; kaṇṭi, n. < Mhr. khaṇḍil. [T. Tu. khaṇḍi, M. kaṇḍi.]* Candy, a weight, stated to be roughly equivalent to 500 lbs.

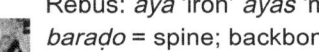

h669A dula 'two' Rebus: dul 'cast metal' *ayo* 'fish' Rebus: *aya* 'iron' *ayas* 'metal' kanka 'rim of jar' Rebus: karṇīka 'account (scribe)' karṇī 'supercargo'

h601A खोंड [khōṇḍa] m A young bull, a bullcalf. (Marathi) Rebus: kõdār 'turner' (Bengali); कोंद kōnda 'engraver, lapidary setting or infixing gems' (Marathi) G. sãghāṛɔ m. 'lathe' ; संघाट joinery; M. sãgaḍ 'double-canoe' Rebus: sangataras 'stone-cutter, mason' dula 'two' Rebus: dul 'cast metal' *ayo* 'fish' Rebus: *aya* 'iron' *ayas* 'metal'

khuṭo ' leg, foot ', °ṭī ' goat's leg ' Rebus: *khōṭā* 'alloy' (Marathi)

kanka 'rim of jar' Rebus: karṇīka 'account (scribe)' karṇī 'supercargo'

h1678A खोंड [khōṇḍa] m A young bull, a bullcalf. (Marathi) Rebus: kõdār 'turner' (Bengali); कोंद kōnda 'engraver, lapidary setting or infixing gems' (Marathi) G. sãghāṛɔ m. 'lathe' ; संघाट joinery; M. sãgaḍ 'double-canoe' Rebus: sangataras 'stone-cutter, mason'
dula 'two' Rebus: dul 'cast metal' *ayo* 'fish' Rebus: *aya* 'iron' *ayas* 'metal' *aya kammaṭa.*'coiner, mint alloy' *ayo ḍhālako* 'alloy metal ingot'

कांड *kāṇḍa* 'arrow' Rebus: *kāṇḍa* 'pots and pans, metalware, tools'. Rebus 2: kaṇḍ 'fire-altar' (Santali)

m319a pattar 'trough' Rebus: pattar 'guild, goldsmith' *kul* 'tiger' (Santali); *kōlu* id. (Telugu) kōlupuli = Bengal tiger (Te.) कोल्हा [kōlhā] कोल्हें [kōlhēṃ] A jackal (Marathi) Rebus: *kole.l* 'temple, smithy' (Kota.) *kol* = pañcalōha, a metallic alloy containing five metals (Tamil): copper, brass, tin, lead and iron (Sanskrit); an alternative list of five metals: gold, silver, copper, tin (lead), and iron (dhātu; Nānārtharatnākara. 82; Mangarāja's Nighaṇṭu. 498)(Kannada) *kol, kolhe*, 'the *koles*, iron smelters speaking a language akin to that of Santals' (Santali) dula 'two' Rebus: dul 'cast metal'
aya kammaṭa.'coiner, mint alloy'
ayo 'fish' Rebus: *aya* 'iron' *ayas* 'metal' kolom 'three' Rebus: kolami 'smithy, forge'

kana, kanac = corner (Santali); Rebus: *kañcu* = bronze (Telugu) PLUS खांडा [*khāṇḍā*] *m* A jag, notch, or indentation (as upon the edge of a tool or weapon). Rebus: *kāṇḍa* 'tools, pots and pans and metal-ware' Thus, bronze metalware.

INFIXED kolom 'three' Rebus: kolami 'smithy, forge'
kanka 'rim of jar' Rebus: karṇīka 'account (scribe)' karṇī 'supercargo

m124a खोंड [khōṇḍa] m A young bull, a bullcalf. (Marathi) Rebus: kõdār 'turner' (Bengali); कोंद kōnda 'engraver, lapidary setting or infixing gems' (Marathi) G. sãghāṛɔ m. 'lathe' ; संघाट joinery; M. sãgaḍ 'double-canoe' Rebus: sangataras 'stone-cutter, mason' dula 'two' Rebus: dul 'cast metal'
ayo 'fish' Rebus: *aya* 'iron' *ayas* 'metal'

kuṭila 'bent' CDIAL 3230 kuṭi— in cmpd. 'curve', *kuṭika—* 'bent' MBh. Rebus: *kuṭila, katthīl* = bronze (8 parts copper and 2 parts tin) Duplicated: dula 'pair' Rebus: dul 'cast

metal' Thus, cast bronze or bronze castings. kanka 'rim of jar' Rebus: karṇīka 'account (scribe)' karṇī 'supercargo'

m523A dulo 'two' Rebus: dul 'cast metal'
ayo 'fish' Rebus: *aya* 'iron' *ayas* 'metal'

kolmo 'paddy plant' Rebus: *kolami* 'smithy, forge' Vikalpa: *mogge* 'sprout, bud' Rebus: *mũh* 'ingot' (Santali) dolu 'plant of shoot height' Rebus: dul 'cast metal'

h43A *खोंड [khōṇḍa] m A young bull, a bullcalf. (Marathi) Rebus: kõdār 'turner' (Bengali); कोंद kōnda 'engraver, lapidary setting or infixing gems' (Marathi) G. sãghāṛɔ m. 'lathe' ; संघाट joinery; M. sãgaḍ 'double-canoe' Rebus: sangataras 'stone-cutter, mason' dula 'two' Rebus: dul 'cast metal'*
Variant:

dāṭu 'cross'(Telugu) Rebus: *dhatu* 'mineral'

kolmo 'paddy plant' Rebus: *kolami* 'smithy, forge' Vikalpa: *mogge* 'sprout, bud' Rebus: *mũh* 'ingot' (Santali) dolu 'plant of shoot height' Rebus: dul 'cast metal' (Santali).

m1159A *ibha* 'elephant' Rebus: *ib* 'iron' *ibbo* 'merchant' (Gujarati)
dula 'two' Rebus: dul 'cast metal'

water-  carrier hieroglyph *kuṭi*; Rebus: *kuṭhi* 'smelter furnace'.

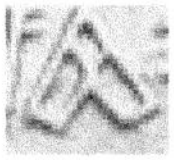

PLUS
aḍaren 'cover of pot or lid' Rebus: *aduru* 'native, unsmelted metal' Duplicated: dula 'pair' Rebus: dul 'cast metal'
sal 'splinter' Rebus: sal 'workshop' dula 'two' Rebus; dul 'cast metal' *ayo* 'fish' Rebus: *aya* 'iron' *ayas* 'metal'

aya kāṇḍa 'alloy metalware' *aya aḍaren (homonym: aduru)*'alloy native metal.

h455A *खोंड [khōṇḍa] m A young bull, a bullcalf. (Marathi) Rebus: kõdār 'turner' (Bengali); कोंद kōnda 'engraver, lapidary setting or infixing gems' (Marathi) G. sãghāṛɔ m. 'lathe' ; संघाट joinery; M. sãgaḍ 'double-canoe' Rebus: sangataras 'stone-cutter, mason' dula 'two' Rebus: dul 'cast metal'*

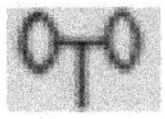

अगडा [agaḍā] *m* The tie connecting the जूं & दांडी of a गाडा or load-cart; the shaft and thill-yoke-tie. Rebus: 'lumber, miscellaneous articles': अगडतगड [*agaḍatagaḍa*] *n* अगडबगड *n* (Fanciful formations, or from H) Trash, trumpery, rubbish, lumber, miscellaneous articles.
sal 'splinter' Rebus: sal 'workshop'

Three sign sequence:

muka 'ladle' (Tamil)(DEDR 4887) Rebus: *mũh* 'ingot' (Santali) Thus, iron ingot.

kolom 'three' Rebus: kolami 'smithy, forge' *kāṇḍa* 'arrow' (Sanskrit) Rebus:*khāṇḍa* 'tools, pots and pans, metal-ware'. Rebus 2: kaṇḍ 'fire-altar' (Santali) Thus, the three sign sequence reads: iron ingot, furnace smithy, fire-altar metalware.

m675A *खोंड [khōṇḍa] m A young bull, a bullcalf. (Marathi) Rebus: kõdār 'turner' (Bengali); कोंद kōnda 'engraver, lapidary setting or infixing gems' (Marathi) G. sãghāṛɔ m. 'lathe' ; संघाट joinery; M. sãgaḍ 'double-canoe' Rebus: sangataras 'stone-cutter, mason'*
dula 'two' Rebus: dul 'cast metal'

kuṭila 'bent' CDIAL 3230 kuṭi— in cmpd. 'curve', *kuṭika*— 'bent' MBh. Rebus: *kuṭila, katthīl* = bronze (8 parts copper and 2 parts tin) *ḍhanga* = a crook used for pulling down the branches of trees, for goats, sheep and camels (P.) Rebus:*ḍhangar* blacksmith'.
aya aḍaren (homonym: aduru)'alloy native metal' *ayo ḍhālako* 'alloy metal ingot'

muka 'ladle' (Tamil)(DEDR 4887) Rebus: *mũh* 'ingot' (Santali) *baṭa* = rimless pot (Kannada) Rebus:) *baṭa* = a kind of iron (G.)) *bhaṭa* furnace (Gujarati) Thus, iron ingot.
kolom 'three' Rebus: kolami 'smithy, forge' Circumscript: gaṇḍa 'four' Rebus: kaṇḍa 'furnace, fire-altar' (Santali)

dula 'pair' Rebus: *dul* 'cast (metal)' PLUS*kana, kanac* = corner (Santali); Rebus: *kañcu* = bronze (Telugu) PLUS infixed kolmo 'paddy plant' Rebus: kolami 'smithy, forge'. Thus, cast bronze smithy, forge. Or, *mogge* 'sprout, bud' Rebus: *mũh* 'ingot' (Santali)Thus, cast bronze ingot. Read as: *kañcu dul mũh 'bronze cast ingot'*

loa 'ficus religiosa' Rebus: *lo* 'iron' (Sanskrit) PLUS unique ligatures: लोखंड [lōkhaṇḍa] *n* (लोह S) Iron. लोखंडाचे चणे खावविणें or चारणें To oppress grievously.लोखंडकाम [lōkhaṇḍakāma] *n* Iron work; that portion (of a building, machine &c.) which consists of iron. 2 The business of an ironsmith.लोखंडी [lōkhaṇḍī] *a* (लोखंड) Composed of iron; relating to iron. (Marathi)
dulo 'hole' Rebs: dul 'cast metal'

Dholavira *खोंड [khōṇḍa] m A young bull, a bullcalf. (Marathi) Rebus: kõdār 'turner' (Bengali); कोंद kōnda 'engraver, lapidary setting or infixing gems' (Marathi) G. sãghāṛɔ m. 'lathe' ; संघाट joinery; M. sãgaḍ 'double-canoe' Rebus: sangataras 'stone-cutter, mason' dula 'two' Rebus: dul 'cast metal' kamaḍha* 'archer, bow' Rebus: *kammaṭa* 'mint, coiner'.

water-carrier hieroglyph *kuṭi*; Rebus: *kuṭhi* 'smelter furnace'.

m1665a *खोंड [khōṇḍa] m A young bull, a bullcalf. (Marathi) Rebus: kõdār 'turner' (Bengali); कोंद kōnda 'engraver, lapidary setting or infixing gems' (Marathi) G. sãghāṛɔ m. 'lathe' ; संघाट joinery; M. sãgaḍ 'double-canoe' Rebus: sangataras 'stone-cutter, mason' dula 'two' Rebus: dul 'cast metal' kamaḍha* 'archer, bow' Rebus: *kammaṭa* 'mint, coiner'. Variant: *khuṇṭī or khuṭī* a peg or wooden pin (Marathi) *kuṭhi* 'smelting furnace'; *koṭe* 'forged (metal) (Santali) sal 'splinter' Rebus: sal 'workshop' *aya kammaṭa.*'coiner, mint alloy' *ayo ḍhālako* 'alloy metal ingot'

Three sign sequence:

muka 'ladle' (Tamil)(DEDR 4887) Rebus: *mũh* 'ingot' (Santali) Thus, iron ingot.

kolom 'three' Rebus: kolami 'smithy, forge' *kāṇḍa* 'arrow' (Sanskrit) Rebus:*khāṇḍa* 'tools, pots and pans, metal-ware'. Rebus 2: kaṇḍ 'fire-altar' (Santali) Thus, the three sign sequence reads: iron ingot, furnace smithy, fire-altar metalware.

h74a *खोंड [khōṇḍa] m A young bull, a bullcalf. (Marathi) Rebus: kõdār 'turner' (Bengali); कोंद kōnda 'engraver, lapidary setting or infixing gems' (Marathi) G. sãghāṛɔ m. 'lathe' ; संघाट joinery; M. sãgaḍ 'double-canoe' Rebus: sangataras 'stone-cutter, mason' dula 'two' Rebus: dul 'cast metal' kamaḍha* 'archer, bow' Rebus: *kammaṭa* 'mint, coiner' *khuṇṭī or khuṭī* a peg or wooden pin (Marathi) *kuṭhi* 'smelting furnace'; *koṭe* 'forged (metal) (Santali) sal 'splinter' Rebus; sal 'workshop'

m1791a *खोंड [khōṇḍa] m A young bull, a bullcalf. (Marathi) Rebus: kõdār 'turner' (Bengali); कोंद kōnda 'engraver, lapidary setting or infixing gems' (Marathi) G. sãghāṛɔ m. 'lathe' ; संघाट joinery; M. sãgaḍ 'double-canoe' Rebus: sangataras 'stone-cutter, mason' dula 'two' Rebus: dul 'cast metal'*

dula 'pair' Rebus: *dul* 'cast (metal)' PLUS*kana, kanac* = corner (Santali); Rebus: *kañcu* = bronze (Telugu) Thus, cast bronze.

sal 'splinter' Rebus: sal 'workshop' karaṇḍa 'duck' (Sanskrit) karaṛa 'a very large aquatic bird' (Sindhi) Rebus: करडा [*karaḍā*] Hard from alloy--iron, silver &c. (Marathi) *kharādī* ' turner' (Gujarati)

dula 'pair' Rebus: dul 'cast (metal)' kolmo 'rice plant' Rebus: kolami 'smithy/forge'

kanka 'rim of jar' Rebus: karṇīka 'account (scribe)' karṇī 'supercargo'

m190a *खोंड [khōṇḍa] m A young bull, a bullcalf. (Marathi) Rebus: kõdār 'turner' (Bengali); कोंद kōnda 'engraver, lapidary setting or infixing gems' (Marathi) G. sãghāṛɔ m. 'lathe' ; संघाट joinery; M. sãgaḍ 'double-canoe' Rebus: sangataras 'stone-cutter, mason' Circumscript: dula 'two' Rebus: dul 'cast metal'*

dula 'pair' Rebus: *dul* 'cast (metal)' PLUS*kana, kanac* = corner (Santali); Rebus: *kañcu* = bronze (Telugu) Thus, cast bronze.

water-carrier hieroglyph *kuṭi*; Rebus: *kuṭhi* 'smelter furnace'.

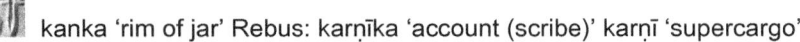

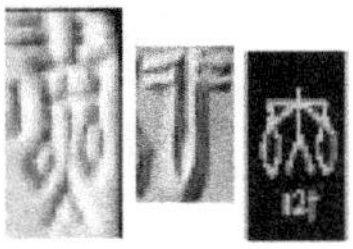

PLUS 'rim of jar': *kanka* (Santali) *karṇika* 'scribe'(Sanskrit)

Rebus: *karṇī,* supercargo

'rim-of-jar' hieroglyph *kanka* (Santali) *karṇika* 'scribe'(Sanskrit)

Rebus: *karṇī,* supercargo for a boat shipment. *karṇīka* 'account (scribe)' .कारणी *kāraṇī* 'the supercargo of a ship' (Marathi)

m45A *खोंड [khōṇḍa] m A young bull, a bullcalf. (Marathi) Rebus: kõdār 'turner' (Bengali); कोंद kōnda 'engraver, lapidary setting or infixing gems' (Marathi) G. sãghārɔ m. 'lathe' ; संघाट joinery; M. sãgaḍ 'double-canoe' Rebus: sangataras 'stone-cutter, mason' dula 'two' Rebus: dul 'cast metal'*

dula 'pair' Rebus: *dul* 'cast (metal)' PLUS*kana, kanac* = corner (Santali); Rebus: *kañcu* = bronze (Telugu) Thus, cast bronze.

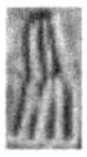 

Strands of yarn/rope' hieroglyph: Hieroglyph: 'strands of yarn' Rebus reading: *dhā´tu* 'strand of rope' Rebus: *dhatu* 'mineral ore' (Santali) sal 'splinter' Rebus: sal 'workshop'खांडा [*khāṇḍā*] *m* A jag, notch, or indentation (as upon the edge of a tool or weapon). Rebus: *kāṇḍa* 'tools, pots and pans and metal-ware'

kana, kanac = corner (Santali); Rebus: *kañcu* = bronze (Telugu) PLUS खांडा [*khāṇḍā*] *m* A jag, notch, or indentation (as upon the edge of a tool or weapon). Rebus: *kāṇḍa* 'tools, pots and pans and metal-ware' Thus, bronze metalware. INFIXED kolom 'three' Rebus: kolami 'smithy, forge'

khaṇḍ 'field, division' (Skt.) Rebus: *khāṇḍa* 'tools, pots and pans, metal-ware'. Rebus 2: kaṇḍ 'fire-altar' (Santali) dula 'pair' Rebus: dul 'cast metal' Thus, duplicated 'division' hieroglyph sign reads: cast metal metal-ware.

H-285 a

h285a sal 'splinter' Rebus: sal 'workshop'

loa 'ficus religiosa' Rebus: *lo* 'iron' (Sanskrit) PLUS unique ligatures: लोखंड [lōkhaṇḍa] *n* (लोह S) Iron. लोखंडाचे चणे खाववणें or चारणें To oppress grievously.लोखंडकाम [lōkhaṇḍakāma] *n* Iron work; that portion (of a building, machine &c.) which consists of iron. 2 The business of an ironsmith.लोखंडी [lōkhaṇḍī] *a* (लोखंड) Composed of iron; relating to iron. (Marathi)

kanka 'rim of jar' Rebus: karṇīka 'account (scribe)' karṇī 'supercargo

m746a *खोंड [khōṇḍa] m A young bull, a bullcalf. (Marathi) Rebus: kõdār 'turner' (Bengali); कोंद kōnda 'engraver, lapidary setting or infixing gems' (Marathi) G. sãghārɔ m. 'lathe' ; संघाट joinery; M. sãgaḍ 'double-canoe' Rebus: sangataras 'stone-cutter, mason' dula 'two' Rebus: dul 'cast metal' ranku 'liquid measure' Rebus: ranku 'tin'*

kolmo 'paddy plant' Rebus: *kolami* 'smithy, forge' Vikalpa: *mogge* 'sprout, bud' Rebus: *mūh* 'ingot' (Santali) dolu 'plant of shoot height' Rebus: dul 'cast metal'

kanka (Santali) *karṇika* 'scribe'(Sanskrit) Rebus: *karṇī,* supercargo for a boat shipment. INFIXED खांडा [*khāṇḍā*] *m* A jag, notch, or indentation (as upon the edge of a tool or weapon). Rebus: *kāṇḍa* 'tools, pots and pans and metal-ware'

dula 'two' Rebus: dul 'cast metal' *ayo ḍhālako* 'alloy metal ingot' *ḍhanga* = a crook used for pulling down the branches of trees, for goats, sheep and camels (P.)

Rebus:*ḍhangar* blacksmith'.

kanka 'rim of jar' Rebus: karṇīka 'account (scribe)' karṇī 'supercargo

h464a *खोंड [khōṇḍa] m A young bull, a bullcalf. (Marathi) Rebus: kõdār 'turner' (Bengali); कोंद kōnda 'engraver, lapidary setting or infixing gems' (Marathi) G. sãghāṛɔ m. 'lathe' ; संघाट joinery; M. sãgaḍ 'double-canoe' Rebus: sangataras 'stone-cutter, mason'*

dula 'two' Rebus: dul 'cast metal' ranku 'liquid measure' Rebus: ranku 'tin'

kamaḍha 'crab' Rebus: *kammaṭa* 'mint, coiner'.*ḍato* = claws of crab (Santali) Rebus: *dhātu* 'mineral ore'

sal 'splinter' Rebus: sal 'workshop'

 *kanac* 'corner' Rebus: *kañcu* 'bronze'

 *muka* 'ladle' (Tamil)(DEDR 4887) Rebus: *mũh* 'ingot' (Santali) *baṭa* = rimless pot (Kannada) Rebus: *baṭa* = a kind of iron (G.)) *bhaṭa* furnace (Gujarati) Thus, iron ingot.

h515a *खोंड [khōṇḍa] m A young bull, a bullcalf. (Marathi) Rebus: kõdār 'turner' (Bengali); कोंद kōnda 'engraver, lapidary setting or infixing gems' (Marathi) G. sãghāṛɔ m. 'lathe' ; संघाट joinery; M. sãgaḍ 'double-canoe' Rebus: sangataras 'stone-cutter, mason' dula 'two' Rebus: dul 'cast metal' ranku 'liquid measure' Rebus: ranku 'tin'*

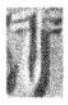 kanka 'rim of jar' Rebus: karṇīka 'account (scribe)' karṇī 'supercargo'

 *muka* 'ladle' (Tamil)(DEDR 4887) Rebus: *mũh* 'ingot' (Santali) *baṭa* = rimless pot (Kannada) Rebus: *baṭa* = a kind of iron (G.)) *bhaṭa* furnace (Gujarati) Thus, iron ingot.

 mēḍu height, rising ground, hillock (Kannada) Rebus: *mẽṛhẽt, meḍ* 'iron' (Munda.Ho.) *kamaḍha* 'crab' Rebus: *kammaṭa* 'mint, coiner'.*ḍato* = claws of crab (Santali) Rebus: *dhātu* 'mineral ore' PLUS | *koḍa* 'one' Rebus: *koḍ* 'workshop'

m915a *खोंड [khōṇḍa] m A young bull, a bullcalf. (Marathi) Rebus: kõdār 'turner' (Bengali); कोंद kōnda 'engraver, lapidary setting or infixing gems' (Marathi) G. sãghāṛɔ m. 'lathe' ; संघाट joinery; M. sãgaḍ 'double-canoe' Rebus: sangataras 'stone-cutter, mason'*

| *koḍa* 'one' Rebus: *koḍ* 'workshop'

 *meḍ* 'body' Rebus: *meḍ* 'iron' (Ho.) PLUS | *koḍa* 'one' Rebus: *koḍ* 'workshop' dula 'pair' Rebus: dul 'cast metal'. Thus, the 'body' flanked by two linear strokes denote: workshop for iron castings.

 water-carrier hieroglyph *kuṭi*; Rebus: *kuṭhi* 'smelter furnace'.

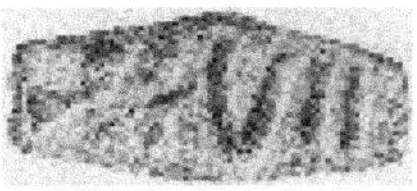

h230B Read rebus as at Kalibangan 68.

h697B *Read*

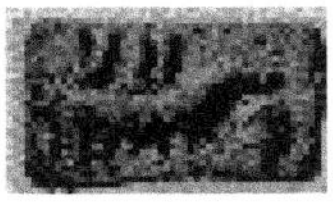

rebus as at Kalibangan 68B

Kalibangan 68B *खोंड [khōṇḍa] m A young bull, a bullcalf. (Marathi) Rebus: kõdār 'turner' (Bengali); कोंद kōnda 'engraver, lapidary setting or infixing gems' (Marathi) G. sãghārɔ m. 'lathe' ; संघाट joinery; M. sãgaḍ 'double-canoe' Rebus: sangataras 'stone-cutter, mason' dula 'two' Rebus: dul 'cast metal baṭa* = rimless pot (Kannada) Rebus:) *baṭa* = a kind of iron (G.)) *bhaṭa* furnace (Gujarati

h1774B Read rebus as at Kalibangan 68. *खोंड [khōṇḍa] m A young bull, a bullcalf. (Marathi) Rebus: kõdār 'turner' (Bengali); कोंद kōnda 'engraver, lapidary setting or infixing gems' (Marathi) G. sãghārɔ m. 'lathe' ; संघाट joinery; M. sãgaḍ 'double-canoe' Rebus: sangataras 'stone-cutter, mason'*

A variant of 'adorant' hieroglyph sign is shown with a 'rimless, broad-mouthed pot' which is *baṭa* read rebus: *bhaṭa* 'furnace'. If the 'pot' ligature is a phonetic determinant, the gloss for the 'adorant' is *bhaṭa* 'worshipper'. If the 'kneeling' posture is the key hieroglyphic representation, the gloss is *eragu* 'bow' Rebus: *erako* 'moltencast copper'. Thus, the pair of hieroglyphsl: 'adorant' PLUS 'tiger' connote: *erako kolhe* 'copper smelter'. A pair of 'adorant' PLUS 'pot' connote: *erako bhaṭā* 'copper furnace'.

h849B 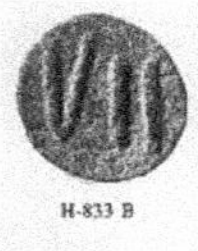 h833B  h813B 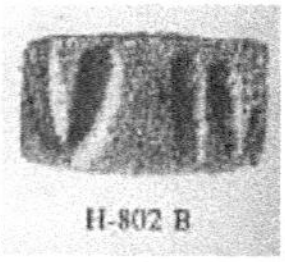 h802B

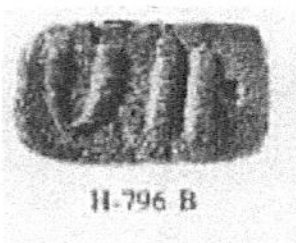 h796B  h768B 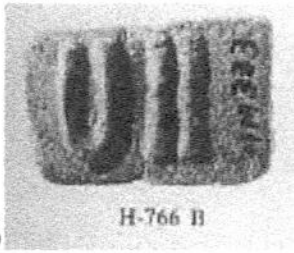 h766B 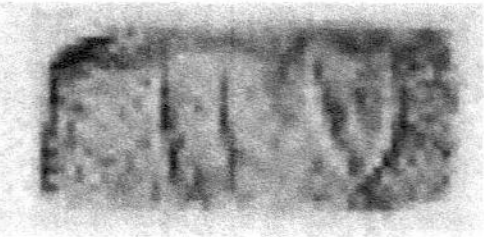

h359B 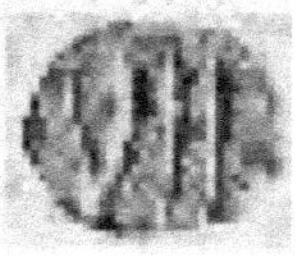 h315B 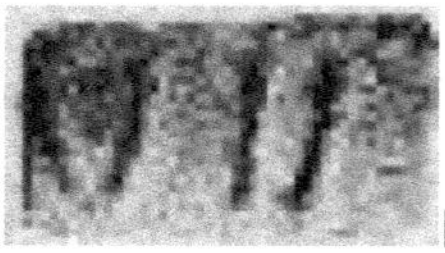 h217B 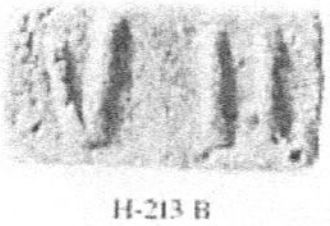 h213B

Read rebus as at Kalibangan 68. dula 'two' Rebus: dul 'cast metal'
baṭa 'rimless, broad-mouthed pot' Rebus: *bhaṭa* 'furnace' (Gujarati.); *baṭa* 'a kind of iron' (Gujarati) dula 'two' Rebus:dul 'cast metal'. Thus, cast metal furnace.

Lothal 109a *dula 'two' Rebus: dul 'cast metal' bhaṭa* 'warrior' (Sanskrit) Rebus: *baṭa* a kind of iron (Gujarati). Rebus: *bhaṭa* 'furnace' (Santali) sal 'splinter' Rebus: sal 'workshop; Semantic-Phonetic determinant: *baṭa* 'rimless, broad-mouthed pot' Rebus: *bhaṭa* 'furnace' (Gujarati.); *baṭa* 'a kind of iron' (Gujarati) dula 'two' Rebus:dul 'cast metal'. Thus, cast metal furnace. Y-shaped hieroglyph: *baṭa* 'rimless, broad-mouthed pot' Rebus: *bhaṭa* 'furnace' (Gujarati.) PLUS | *koḍa* 'one' Rebus: *koḍ* 'workshop'खांडा [*khāṇḍā*] *m* A jag, notch, or indentation (as upon the edge of a tool or weapon). Rebus: *kāṇḍa* 'tools, pots and pans and metal-ware' Thus metware castings workshop.

H-1714 A

h1714A dula ‘two’ Rebus: dul ‘cast metal’

 *kanac* ‘corner’ Rebus: *kañcu* ‘bronze’

 *kolmo* ‘paddy plant’ Rebus: *kolami* ‘smithy, forge’ Vikalpa: *mogge* ‘sprout, bud’ Rebus: *mũh* ‘ingot’ (Santali) dolu ‘plant of shoot height’ Rebus: dul ‘cast metal’

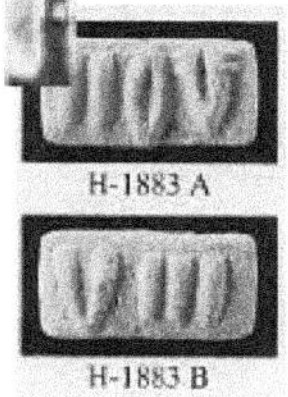
H-1883 A
H-1883 B

h1883A,B *baṭa* ‘rimless, broad-mouthed pot’ Rebus: *bhaṭa* ‘furnace’ (Gujarati.); *baṭa* ‘a kind of iron’ (Gujarati)

 *kanac* ‘corner’ Rebus: *kañcu* ‘bronze’ Vikalpa: dulo ‘hole’ Rebus: dul ‘cast metal’

dula ‘two’ Rebus: dul ‘cast metal’

Side H: *baṭa* ‘rimless, broad-mouthed pot’ Rebus: *bhaṭa* ‘furnace’ (Gujarati.); *baṭa* ‘a kind of iron’ (Gujarati) kolom ‘three’ Rebus: kolami ‘smithy, forge’

M-733 a

m733a *खोंड [khōṇḍa] m A young bull, a bullcalf. (Marathi) Rebus: kõdār ‘turner’ (Bengali); कोंद kōnda ‘engraver, lapidary setting or infixing gems’ (Marathi) G. sãghāṛɔ m. ‘lathe’ ; संघाट joinery; M. sãgaḍ ‘double-canoe’ Rebus: sangataras ‘stone-cutter, mason’ dula ‘two’ Rebus: dul ‘cast metal’*

 *kanac* ‘corner’ Rebus: *kañcu* ‘bronze’

ranku ‘liquid measure’ Rebus: ranku ‘tin’

kamaḍha ‘archer, bow’ Rebus: *kammaṭa* ‘mint, coiner’.

ayo ‘fish’ Rebus: *aya* ‘iron’ *ayas* ‘metal’

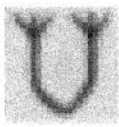 dula ‘pair’ Rebus: dul ‘cast (metal)’ kolmo ‘rice plant’ Rebus: kolami ‘smithy/forge’

kanka ‘rim of jar’ Rebus: karṇīka ‘account (scribe)’ karṇī ‘supercargo’

water-carrier hieroglyph *kuṭi*; Rebus: *kuṭhi* ‘smelter furnace’.

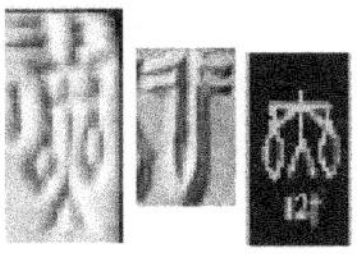

PLUS ‘rim of jar’: *kanka* (Santali) *karṇika* ‘scribe’(Sanskrit)

Rebus: *karṇī,* supercargo

'rim-of-jar' hieroglyph *kanka* (Santali) *karṇika* ‘scribe’(Sanskrit)

Rebus: *karṇī,* supercargo for a boat shipment. *karṇīka* ‘account (scribe)’ .कारणी *kāraṇī* ‘the supercargo of a ship’ (Marathi)

H-664 A bis

h664A

dula ‘two’ Rebus: dul ‘cast metal’

 *kanac* ‘corner’ Rebus: *kañcu* ‘bronze’. Thus, bronze castings.

m571A,B Zebu horns on elephant hieroglyph: Native metal smith guild. *ibha* 'elephant' Rebus: *ib* 'iron' *ibbo* 'merchant' (Gujarati)
dula 'two' Rebus: dul 'cast metal' *ayo* 'fish' Rebus: *aya* 'iron' *ayas* 'metal'
dula 'pair' Rebus: dul 'cast metal' PLUS

aḍar  'harrow'; rebus: *aduru* 'native unsmelted metal'
PLUS
Kur. xolā tail. *Malt.* qoli id. (DEDR 2135). Rebus: kolhe 'smelter' Thus, copper smelter.

 'rim-of-jar' hieroglyph *kanka* (Santali) *karṇika* 'scribe'(Sanskrit) Rebus: *karṇī,* supercargo for a boat shipment. *karṇīka* 'account (scribe)'.कारणी *kāraṇī* 'the supercargo of a ship' (Marathi)

A Meluhha narrative in hieroglyphic precision on furnace metal work – an executive summary on an ancient tablet of Meluhha metal hieroglyphs

87: M-488 A col (300%)

88: M-488 B col (300%)

89: M-488 C col (300%)

m488A, B, C Side A: krammara 'look back' Rebus: kamar 'blacksmith' kola 'tiger' Rebus: kolhe 'smelter' kol 'working in iron' heraka 'spy' Rebus: erako 'moltencast copper' *kuṭi* 'tree' Rebus: *kuṭhi* 'smelter'

 *khōṇḍa* A stock or stump (Marathi); 'leafless tree' (Marathi) Rebus: *kõdār* 'turner' (Bengali); *kõdā* 'to turn in a lathe' (Bengali).
Svastika Rebus: sattva, jasta 'zinc'

ibha 'elephant' Rebus: *ib* 'iron' *ibbo* 'merchant' (Gujarati)

Side B: *खोंड [khōṇḍa] m A young bull, a bullcalf. (Marathi) Rebus: kõdār 'turner' (Bengali); कोंद kōnda 'engraver, lapidary setting or infixing gems' (Marathi) G. sãghāṛɔ m. 'lathe' ; संघाट joinery; M. sãgaḍ 'double-canoe' Rebus: sangataras 'stone-cutter, mason'*

  *loa* 'ficus religiosa' Rebus: *lo* 'iron' (Sanskrit) PLUS unique ligatures: लोखंड [lōkhaṇḍa] *n* (लोह S) Iron. लोखंडाचे चणे खावविणें or चारणें To oppress grievously.लोखंडकाम [lōkhaṇḍakāma] *n* Iron work; that portion (of a building, machine &c.) which consists of iron. 2 The business of an ironsmith.लोखंडी [lōkhaṇḍī] *a* (लोखंड) Composed of iron; relating to iron. (Marathi) *bhaṭa* 'warrior' (Sanskrit) Rebus: *baṭa* a kind of iron (Gujarati). Rebus: *bhaṭa* 'furnace' (Santali) Thus, together, the ligatured hieroglyph reads rebus: *loa bhaṭa* 'iron furnace'

 *loa* 'ficus religiosa' Rebus: *lo* 'iron' (Sanskrit) PLUS unique ligatures: लोखंड [lōkhaṇḍa] *n* (लोह S) Iron. लोखंडाचे चणे खावविणें or चारणें To oppress grievously.लोखंडकाम [

lōkhaṇḍakāma] *n* Iron work; that portion (of a building, machine &c.) which consists of iron. 2 The business of an ironsmith.लोखंडी [lōkhaṇḍī] *a* (लोखंड) Composed of iron; relating to iron. (Marathi)

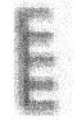
khareḍo = a currycomb (Gujarati) खरारा [*kharārā*] *m* (H) A currycomb. 2 Currying a horse. (Marathi) Rebus: करडा [*karaḍā*] Hard from alloy--iron, silver &c. (Marathi) *kharādī* ' turner' (Gujarati)

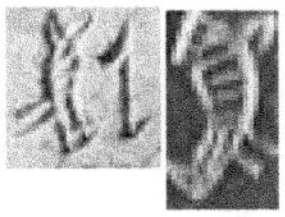
The pair of hieroglyph signs are compositions: 1. *bicha* 'scorpion' (Assamese) Rebus: *bica* 'stone ore' (Santali) The pairing sign is a composition of: sloping stroke PLUS two short strokes of a 'splinter':*dhāḷ* 'a slope'; 'inclination of a plane' (Gujarati); *ḍhāḷiyum* = adj. sloping, inclining (Gujarati) Rebus: *ḍhālako* = a large metal ingot (Gujarati) *ḍhālakī* = a metal heated and poured into a mould; a solid piece of metal; an ingot (Gujarati)PLUS*sal* 'splinter' Rebus: *sal* 'workshop'. Thus the composition reads: *ḍhālako sal* 'ingot workshop'.

khaṇḍ 'field, division' (Skt.) Rebus: *khāṇḍa* 'tools, pots and pans, metal-ware'. Rebus 2: kaṇḍ 'fire-altar' (Santali) dula 'pair' Rebus: dul 'cast metal' Thus, duplicated 'division' hieroglyph sign reads: cast metal metal-ware.

Side C: *kōḍu horn Rebus: 'workshop' meḍ* 'body' Rebus: *meḍ* 'iron' (Ho.) मंडप [maṇḍapa] 'canopy' Rebus: मंडई [maṇḍī] *f* (H) A green market, the place in a city whither vegetables and fruits are brought to be disposed of by wholesale.

lo, no 'nine' (Assamese) Rebus: lo 'iron, copper'

loa 'ficus religiosa' Rebus: *lo* 'iron' (Sanskrit) PLUS unique ligatures: लोखंड [lōkhaṇḍa] *n* (लोह S) Iron. लोखंडाचे चणे खावविणें or चारणें To oppress grievously.लोखंडकाम [lōkhaṇḍakāma] *n* Iron work; that portion (of a building, machine &c.) which consists of iron. 2 The business of an ironsmith.लोखंडी [lōkhaṇḍī] *a* (लोखंड) Composed of iron; relating to iron. (Marathi)

Composite animal: Markhor horns: *miṇḍāl* 'markhor' (Tōrwālī) *meḍho* a ram, a sheep (G.)(CDIAL 10120) Rebus: *mẽṛhẽt, meḍ* 'iron' (Mu.Ho.) scarf: dhatu 'scarf' Rebus: dhatu 'mineral ore' Ligature: *Kur.* xolā tail. *Malt.* qoli id. (DEDR 2135). Rebus: kolhe 'smelter' Thus, copper smelter.

Worshipper: *bhaṭā* G. *bhuvɔ* m. ' worshipper in a temple ' rather < bhr̥ta --(CDIAL 9554) Yājñ.com., Rebus: *bhaṭā* ' kiln, furnace' *kōḍu horn Rebus: 'workshop' kūdī* 'bunch of twigs' (Sanskrit) Rebus: *kuṭhi* 'smelter furnace' (Santali)

Scarf: dhatu 'scarf' Rebus: dhatu 'mineral ore' As a phonetic-semantic reinforcement, the worshipper holds a 'pot': 'rimless, broad-mouthed pot' which is *baṭa* read rebus: *bhaṭa* 'furnace'.

kaṇḍo 'stool, seat' Rebus: *kāṇḍa* 'metalware' *kaṇḍa* 'fire-altar' erugu = to bow, to salute or make obeisance (Te.) er-agu = obeisance (Ka.), ir_ai (Ta.) [Note image of an offering adorant]eraka, erka = copper (Ka.) erako 'moltencast copper' (Gujarati)

మండి [*maṇḍi]* or మండీ *maṇḍi*. [Tel.] n. Kneeling down with one leg, an attitude in archery, ఒక కాలితో నేలమీద మోకరించుట, ఆలీఢపాదము. Rebus: *maṇḍi* 'market'.

About book...

Meluhha hieroglyphs document Bronze Age trade on Tin Road from Malhar, India to Haifa, Israel. Meluhha hieroglyphs constitute Indus Script. The readings of Meluhha hieroglyphs are presented as a decipherment of Indus script. The script transcribes Proto-Indian speech -- Meluhha (mleccha) language glosses. Rebus cipher -- homonymous glosses of Meluhha -- provide plaintext readings of hieroglyphs and ciphertext rebus renderings of traded resources and products of Bronze Age , mostly stone, mineral, metal and alloyed artifacts. A remarkable semantic unity among present-day Indian languages is established traceable to the days of Sarasvati Hindu civilization ca 4th millennium BCE. Many glosses identified by the deciphered Meluhha Indus Script hieroglyphs are demonstrated in ciphertexts of the lexical repertoire of all Indian languages validating a hypothesis that Meluhha-Mleccha was the fountain-spring of Indian *sprachbund* and a veritable *lingua franca* of the nation founded by the organized brilliance of the Bronze Age experts like smelters, artisans , metal- and stone-workers, stone-cutters, inventors of new metal alloys, *cire perdue* casting experts, in particular and traders. This semantic unity of Indian *sprachbund* from Bronze Age days, explains why anyone of the present-day glosses from any one of the Indian languages adequately explains and validates Meluhha rebus cipher. Metallurgical repertoire of Meluhhans in Bronze Age is well articulated in Meluhha language.)

About Author...

S. Kalyanaraman a former executive of Asian Development Bank, has a Ph.D in Public Administration and is the author of *Philosophy of symbolic forms in Meluhha Cipher, Meluhha a visible language, Indus Script Cipher* and 17 other books on Sarasvati Civilization. Other books include *Ramasetu, Indian lexicon, a comparative dictionary of 25+ Indian languages, Indian Alchemy – Soma in the Veda*. He is a recipient of the Vakankar Award (2000); Shivananda Eminent Citizens' Award (2008) and Dr. Hedgewar Prajna Samman (2008); Mythic Society Centenary Award (2009). He is on the Board of Directors of the World Association of Vedic Studies, and is associated with many research and non-governmental voluntary organizations including Rashtrotthana Research and Communications Center in Bengaluru, India.

aḍar, 17, 30, 33, 41, 45, 51, 53, 59, 63, 64, 68, 162, 175, 176, 179, 198, 199, 200, 207, 216, 225, 236, 239, 240, 241, 258, 269, 281, 301, 302, 307, 312, 356, 362, 371, 384, 386, 387, 390, 422, 423, 427, 428, 436, 438, 477, 487, 489, 504, 506, 507, 508, 509, 510, 511, 512, 513, 514, 515, 516, 517, 518, 519, 525, 526, 566, 588, 601, 629, 632, 636, 650, 652, 662, 665, 667, 675, 685, 686, 687, 693, 704, 707, 708, 727, 728, 729, 730, 736, 741, 744, 745, 776, 792
aḍaren, 8, 9, 10, 39, 40, 41, 49, 51, 52, 53, 54, 56, 57, 101, 158, 163, 164, 175, 178, 187, 191, 192, 193, 194, 196, 199, 202, 205, 206, 210, 213, 214, 215, 222, 226, 230, 234, 236, 243, 248, 253, 259, 261, 269, 270, 271, 272, 273, 274, 275, 276, 277, 278, 279, 280, 281, 282, 283, 284, 287, 288, 289, 290, 291, 293, 294, 295, 296, 301, 307, 308, 309, 310, 311, 312, 315, 317, 324, 329, 332, 333, 338, 339, 346, 356, 365, 369, 370, 373, 376, 380, 381, 382, 385, 386, 388, 390, 391, 393, 396, 397, 399, 404, 405, 407, 414, 415, 420, 424, 427, 430, 434, 437, 439, 445, 453, 458, 459, 462, 486, 488, 489, 490, 499, 501, 507, 513, 523, 526, 534, 536, 537, 538, 543, 544, 547, 548, 550, 553, 556, 558, 561, 565, 568, 570, 572, 574, 577, 578, 587, 595, 602, 609, 643, 644, 645, 646, 651, 652, 655, 658, 661, 665, 666, 668, 674, 677, 686, 688, 690, 691, 692, 696, 697, 702, 703, 704, 710, 712, 714, 719, 722, 729, 732, 736, 739, 741, 743, 751, 759, 761, 766, 774, 775, 781, 783, 785, 786
agaḍā, 172, 310, 316, 417, 425, 480, 493, 517, 518, 519, 520, 521, 649, 694, 766, 785
agate, 59
Akkadian, 5, 20, 23, 24, 28, 30, 37, 61, 62, 96, 108, 109, 110, 115, 117, 119, 121, 152, 161, 171, 184, 276, 284, 285, 328, 410, 424, 427, 494, 533, 604, 606, 677, 681, 760
alligator, 71
allograph, 14, 169, 199, 344
antelope, 72, 100, 108, 109, 111, 115, 121, 157, 184, 189, 214, 228, 234, 253, 254, 256, 257, 258, 259, 274, 280, 285, 289, 295, 402, 415, 431, 456, 491, 505, 511, 516, 529, 551, 556, 569, 598, 635, 693, 709, 717, 745
antimony, 13, 14, 30, 50, 129
āra, 22, 23, 27, 33, 40, 51, 62, 63, 100, 132, 162, 163, 165, 167, 172, 173, 174, 179, 180, 202, 224, 225, 226, 229, 235, 241, 260, 261, 264, 269, 275, 279, 280, 306, 308, 310, 321, 322, 341, 348, 359, 364, 377, 386, 387, 394, 398, 399, 406, 411, 433, 453, 466, 469, 470, 483, 487, 502, 503, 506, 519, 522, 526, 540, 547, 548, 551, 562, 567, 582, 599, 600, 601, 602, 603, 604, 605, 606, 607, 608, 609, 610, 611, 612, 613, 614, 615, 616, 617, 618, 619, 620, 621, 622, 623, 624, 625, 626, 627, 628, 629, 630, 631, 632, 633, 634, 635, 636, 637, 638, 639, 640, 641, 642, 643, 644, 645, 646, 647, 648, 649, 650, 651, 652, 653, 718, 719, 730, 745, 746, 748, 755, 756, 768, 779
archer, 37, 38, 41, 55, 169, 219, 247, 256, 260, 261, 269, 271, 281, 313, 314, 315, 344, 346, 353, 378, 395, 401, 416, 434, 453, 459, 469, 479, 486, 487, 488, 489, 490, 491, 492, 498, 506, 512, 522, 542, 568, 575, 581, 587, 649, 650, 654, 725, 745, 751, 752, 761, 771, 773, 775, 786, 787, 791
arrow, 8, 9, 40, 42, 46, 48, 49, 52, 54, 55, 94, 101, 112, 174, 193, 196, 199, 205, 206, 208, 209, 210, 215, 218, 219, 228, 230, 238, 240, 241, 246, 252, 253, 267, 269, 277, 278, 279, 281, 287, 289, 290, 291, 292, 297, 299, 301, 307, 308, 309, 310, 313, 314, 315, 322, 323, 331, 338, 341, 342, 344, 345, 350, 353, 354, 357, 374, 381, 382, 385, 386, 388, 391, 401, 415, 421, 423, 424, 427, 430, 438, 446, 457, 458, 461, 484, 486, 487, 488, 491, 497, 500, 511, 512, 516, 526, 536, 537, 538, 543, 550, 558, 561, 569, 575, 591, 636, 638, 641, 643, 652, 654, 656, 657, 658, 659, 660, 662, 664, 667, 675, 679, 683, 686, 693, 694, 697, 702, 706, 710, 712, 714, 715, 721, 735, 759, 763, 775, 779, 784, 786, 787
arsenic, 9, 14, 42, 46, 54, 55, 56, 57, 69, 124, 126, 129, 178, 180, 183, 261, 588, 652, 653, 656, 657, 658, 659, 660, 661, 662,

663, 664, 665, 666, 667, 668, 669, 670, 671, 672, 673, 674, 675, 676, 677, 678, 679, 680, 681, 682, 683, 684, 685, 686, 687, 688, 689, 690, 691, 692, 693, 694, 695, 696, 697, 698, 699, 700, 701, 702, 703, 704, 705, 706, 707, 708, 709, 710, 711, 712, 713, 714, 715, 716, 717, 720, 754
asūrta, 19
axe, 32, 33, 37, 146, 539, 581, 604, 717
backbone, 10, 18, 41, 48, 158, 159, 182, 187, 204, 205, 207, 208, 210, 217, 218, 219, 220, 221, 222, 223, 240, 254, 260, 269, 276, 286, 296, 299, 300, 302, 309, 315, 318, 336, 356, 364, 387, 402, 412, 430, 431, 441, 442, 448, 449, 473, 490, 496, 500, 521, 531, 535, 538, 553, 571, 590, 603, 633, 667, 668, 684, 685, 690, 709, 711, 763, 776, 783
Bactria, 107
bagalo, 44, 51, 232, 403, 595, 666
Bagchi, 156
Bahrain, 115, 116, 119, 123, 124
baraḍo, 10, 18, 41, 48, 158, 159, 182, 187, 204, 205, 207, 208, 210, 217, 218, 219, 220, 221, 222, 223, 240, 254, 260, 269, 276, 286, 296, 299, 300, 302, 309, 315, 318, 336, 356, 364, 387, 402, 412, 430, 431, 441, 442, 448, 449, 473, 490, 496, 500, 521, 531, 535, 538, 553, 571, 590, 603, 633, 667, 668, 684, 685, 690, 709, 711, 763, 776, 783
baran, 10, 18, 41, 48, 157, 158, 159, 182, 184, 187, 204, 205, 207, 208, 210, 217, 218, 219, 220, 221, 222, 223, 240, 254, 260, 269, 276, 284, 286, 296, 299, 300, 302, 309, 315, 318, 329, 336, 356, 364, 387, 412, 430, 431, 441, 442, 448, 449, 473, 490, 496, 500, 521, 531, 533, 535, 538, 553, 571, 590, 603, 606, 633, 667, 668, 684, 685, 690, 709, 711, 763, 776, 783
baroṭi, 41, 158, 159, 161, 179, 212, 237, 238, 255, 270, 273, 275, 283, 297, 300, 305, 349, 393, 395, 401, 487, 489, 568, 574, 575, 576, 577, 578, 585, 609, 637, 741, 761, 765, 769
baṭa, 9, 11, 18, 28, 34, 40, 41, 42, 44, 46, 47, 48, 49, 53, 55, 57, 60, 61, 101, 161, 171, 173, 182, 183, 184, 185, 193, 195, 197, 199, 202, 205, 206, 207, 208, 209, 210, 214, 215, 216, 217, 218, 219, 220, 222, 223, 225, 228, 230, 231, 232, 234, 236, 238, 241, 245, 246, 247, 250, 252, 255, 258, 259, 265, 266, 267, 270, 273, 274, 277, 280, 283, 286, 287, 288, 291, 298, 300, 302, 310, 312, 313, 315, 322, 330, 331, 332, 334, 338, 339, 343, 346, 347, 348, 349, 350, 357, 361, 367, 368, 373, 377, 379, 381, 382, 384, 385, 387, 388, 393, 394, 395, 397, 398, 400, 401, 403, 404, 408, 413, 418, 419, 422, 423, 426, 428, 429, 430, 434, 436, 437, 438, 439, 441, 444, 445, 448, 449, 452, 453, 457, 459, 460, 462, 463, 464, 465, 466, 467, 469, 470, 474, 475, 476, 477, 478, 480, 481, 482, 483, 485, 490, 491, 494, 495, 499, 500, 502, 505, 506, 507, 509, 510, 512, 514, 515, 519, 520, 521, 522, 523, 524, 525, 526, 529, 530, 531, 538, 546, 549, 551, 553, 556, 557, 560, 561, 562, 563, 564, 565, 566, 567, 568, 569, 571, 572, 573, 576, 577, 585, 586, 588, 590, 593, 597, 599, 603, 629, 635, 637, 639, 641, 643, 646, 648, 653, 660, 662, 664, 667, 668, 669, 672, 679, 680, 682, 683, 684, 687, 688, 691, 693, 695, 696, 697, 700, 704, 707, 708, 711, 712, 713, 715, 719, 727, 728, 730, 732, 735, 736, 737, 739, 741, 742, 743, 745, 746, 750, 762, 763, 767, 770, 774, 781, 782, 786, 789, 790, 791, 792, 793
BB Lal, 80
beads, 15, 81, 82, 87, 100, 103, 104, 161, 197, 258, 281, 283, 304, 329, 364, 442, 496, 524, 533, 534, 539, 543, 582, 583, 588, 741, 768, 776, 777
bharata, 6, 61, 62, 157, 182, 183, 305, 402
bhaṭa, 9, 11, 18, 34, 41, 42, 43, 46, 48, 49, 53, 55, 60, 61, 101, 161, 171, 182, 183, 193, 195, 197, 199, 202, 205, 206, 207, 208, 209, 210, 214, 215, 216, 217, 218, 219, 220, 222, 223, 225, 228, 230, 231, 232, 234, 236, 238, 241, 245, 246, 247, 250, 252, 255, 258, 259, 265, 266, 267, 270, 273, 274, 277, 280, 283, 286, 287, 288, 291, 300, 302, 310, 312, 313, 315, 322, 330, 331, 332, 334, 338, 339, 343, 346, 348, 349, 350, 357, 361, 367, 368, 373, 377, 379, 381, 382, 384, 385, 387, 388, 393, 394, 395, 397, 398, 400, 401, 403, 404, 408, 410, 413, 418, 419, 422, 423, 426, 428, 429, 430, 434, 436, 437, 438,

439, 441, 444, 445, 448, 449, 452, 453, 457, 459, 460, 462, 463, 464, 465, 466, 467, 469, 470, 474, 475, 476, 477, 478, 480, 481, 482, 483, 485, 490, 491, 494, 495, 499, 500, 502, 505, 506, 507, 509, 510, 512, 514, 515, 519, 520, 521, 522, 523, 524, 525, 526, 529, 530, 531, 538, 546, 549, 551, 553, 556, 557, 561, 562, 563, 564, 565, 566, 567, 568, 569, 571, 572, 573, 576, 586, 588, 590, 593, 597, 599, 629, 635, 637, 648, 653, 664, 667, 668, 669, 672, 679, 680, 682, 683, 684, 687, 688, 691, 693, 695, 700, 704, 713, 715, 719, 727, 728, 730, 732, 735, 736, 737, 739, 741, 742, 743, 745, 746, 750, 762, 763, 767, 770, 774, 781, 782, 786, 789, 790, 791, 792, 793
bhaṭā, 42, 43, 407, 423, 523, 524, 581, 593, 790, 793
Bisht, 96, 163
Bison, 402
boar, 218, 235, 262, 279, 285, 298, 320, 390, 393, 398, 432, 475, 543, 575, 597, 643, 726, 741, 766, 769, 778
boat, 10, 18, 44, 45, 46, 48, 51, 56, 68, 69, 70, 72, 104, 168, 178, 185, 232, 349, 351, 353, 359, 378, 396, 397, 403, 407, 416, 419, 421, 424, 426, 430, 440, 451, 455, 461, 476, 481, 488, 490, 491, 498, 499, 501, 508, 518, 525, 527, 528, 531, 540, 541, 550, 554, 555, 560, 561, 565, 570, 576, 577, 578, 595, 601, 602, 603, 604, 605, 607, 645, 649, 651, 666, 669, 691, 703, 704, 705, 726, 730, 735, 736, 747, 748, 749, 762, 774, 776, 777, 778, 780, 781, 787, 788, 791, 792
bos indicus, 17, 23, 30, 34, 63, 65, 66, 67, 729
buffalo, 137, 145, 184, 186, 266, 285, 298, 327, 389, 421, 431, 432, 439, 451, 456, 478, 489, 557, 652, 687, 767, 770
bush, 13, 14, 582
canopy, 173, 317, 549, 608, 733, 793
carnelian, 15, 81, 84, 85, 108, 124
cīmara, 54, 230, 239, 256, 259, 308, 323, 353, 361, 382, 384, 395, 399, 404, 497, 530, 532, 533, 566, 584, 585, 586, 587, 588, 589, 590, 591, 634, 644, 726, 739, 740, 760, 761, 773
composite animal, 7, 68, 177, 181, 184, 284, 402, 475, 493, 533, 534, 543, 605
coppersmith, 54, 70, 230, 239, 256, 259, 308, 323, 353, 361, 382, 384, 395, 399, 404, 497, 530, 532, 533, 566, 580, 584, 585, 586, 587, 588, 589, 590, 591, 634, 644, 652, 726, 729, 739, 740, 757, 760, 773
copulation, 71
crocodile, 45, 71, 145, 153, 156, 157, 204, 326, 376, 379, 395, 500, 538, 597, 598, 735, 757, 758
cylinder seal, 13, 24, 30, 59, 60, 62, 64, 65, 92, 109, 115, 120, 127, 128, 138, 140, 141, 145, 285, 582, 756
ḍāg, 37, 63, 161, 181, 194, 195, 262, 263, 267, 320, 321, 322, 352, 357, 366, 377, 411, 417, 427, 498, 499, 513, 518, 527, 528, 552, 604, 677, 680, 681, 704, 717, 727, 736, 775, 781, 782
dance, 79
dhā´tu, 38, 41, 180, 233, 269, 279, 324, 340, 355, 356, 357, 392, 450, 464, 469, 479, 486, 492, 498, 510, 527, 529, 548, 556, 557, 567, 577, 589, 590, 591, 632, 655, 728, 758, 771, 772, 775, 776, 781, 788
ḍhālako, 8, 9, 10, 38, 40, 42, 43, 47, 49, 51, 52, 53, 57, 102, 130, 159, 172, 173, 174, 176, 179, 186, 188, 193, 195, 196, 197, 200, 203, 204, 205, 208, 209, 211, 213, 214, 218, 221, 224, 225, 226, 227, 228, 230, 231, 237, 241, 242, 245, 246, 247, 251, 256, 260, 268, 273, 274, 275, 276, 277, 278, 279, 280, 286, 287, 289, 290, 291, 292, 293, 295, 296, 297, 298, 299, 300, 302, 303, 304, 305, 308, 309, 310, 314, 315, 316, 317, 318, 319, 320, 332, 336, 337, 340, 342, 348, 350, 353, 354, 355, 357, 358, 359, 360, 361, 362, 363, 364, 365, 366, 367, 368, 369, 370, 371, 372, 374, 375, 376, 377, 381, 382, 383, 386, 389, 395, 396, 397, 403, 405, 406, 407, 408, 410, 411, 412, 413, 414, 416, 420, 424, 428, 429, 430, 431, 433, 436, 439, 440, 446, 447, 449, 450, 451, 452, 454, 455, 456, 458, 465, 468, 469, 471, 472, 475, 476, 477, 480, 482, 486, 491, 492, 495, 500, 504, 509, 510, 515, 516, 517, 522, 525, 534, 536, 537, 542, 543, 544, 546, 550, 552, 553, 557, 558, 559, 560, 561, 562, 563, 570, 572, 576, 577, 584, 585, 586, 588, 589, 591, 595, 603, 605, 606, 633, 635, 636, 637, 638, 639, 640, 641, 642, 643, 644, 646, 647, 648,

649, 652, 653, 654, 655, 658, 659, 664, 666, 669, 670, 671, 672, 679, 688, 689, 690, 691, 692, 695, 696, 699, 701, 702, 703, 710, 717, 718, 719, 721, 723, 726, 727, 739, 744, 745, 762, 763, 764, 765, 767, 768, 771, 772, 773, 775, 776, 779, 784, 786, 787, 788, 793
ḍhangar, 17, 22, 30, 33, 38, 40, 59, 62, 63, 64, 65, 66, 67, 68, 140, 162, 171, 176, 187, 226, 227, 230, 235, 236, 237, 239, 243, 251, 252, 255, 259, 277, 294, 298, 300, 303, 308, 323, 329, 330, 342, 343, 352, 365, 366, 367, 391, 410, 411, 415, 424, 429, 437, 439, 440, 458, 460, 466, 485, 501, 502, 510, 515, 518, 531, 544, 556, 571, 603, 604, 630, 692, 716, 717, 729, 731, 740, 748, 756, 757, 771, 780, 786, 788
dhokra, 13, 17, 19, 63, 67, 74, 148, 753, 754, 757, 758
Dilmun, 61, 62, 100, 108, 115, 118, 119, 756
dotted circle, 33, 56, 100, 102
elephant, 7, 53, 68, 149, 150, 153, 156, 157, 176, 177, 184, 186, 189, 236, 276, 284, 303, 308, 328, 336, 373, 393, 415, 432, 446, 461, 475, 522, 526, 530, 533, 543, 567, 597, 598, 606, 651, 657, 658, 673, 687, 693, 715, 720, 727, 731, 761, 766, 776, 785, 792
Emeneau, 7
Failaka, 61, 62, 100
ficus religiosa, 9, 34, 37, 39, 48, 53, 62, 159, 168, 169, 172, 184, 190, 205, 211, 214, 232, 244, 245, 246, 255, 264, 265, 266, 267, 268, 280, 285, 302, 303, 304, 312, 313, 341, 342, 346, 357, 359, 360, 374, 377, 379, 382, 383, 384, 385, 387, 391, 393, 394, 405, 419, 435, 452, 453, 459, 460, 465, 466, 468, 469, 470, 474, 505, 521, 529, 530, 551, 553, 555, 557, 560, 562, 563, 564, 565, 566, 567, 568, 569, 570, 571, 572, 573, 587, 590, 602, 632, 637, 675, 692, 700, 712, 716, 725, 727, 733, 735, 739, 743, 767, 771, 773, 786, 788, 792, 793
flag, 54, 68, 70, 72, 189, 197, 202, 216, 219, 226, 243, 265, 308, 310, 319, 326, 329, 343, 347, 374, 377, 378, 382, 390, 433, 435, 441, 449, 459, 460, 465, 487, 492, 527, 535, 541, 542, 544, 545, 552, 557, 561, 562, 563, 570, 575, 578, 596, 644, 664, 670, 671, 680, 720, 721, 722, 723, 731, 732, 741, 749, 770, 775
gimlet, 100, 102
Haifa, 5, 17, 107, 108, 109, 110, 113, 114, 118, 119, 146, 673, 711
hare, 13, 14, 582, 636
Hunter, 46
iron ore, 45, 71, 160, 234
jackal, 22, 43, 146, 330, 407, 408, 442, 598, 738, 757, 784
Kalyanaraman, 106, 114, 132, 146
kamar, 13, 17, 19, 39, 43, 67, 74, 137, 138, 148, 169, 196, 204, 233, 347, 432, 443, 505, 523, 598, 635, 636, 638, 670, 693, 750, 753, 754, 757, 758, 759, 769, 792
kammaṭa, 37, 38, 41, 47, 52, 53, 55, 57, 158, 163, 164, 168, 169, 171, 175, 186, 193, 197, 199, 206, 207, 208, 215, 219, 221, 222, 223, 224, 225, 226, 227, 230, 231, 233, 234, 235, 236, 237, 238, 239, 240, 241, 246, 247, 254, 256, 260, 261, 263, 265, 269, 271, 272, 275, 276, 281, 283, 287, 288, 289, 293, 298, 302, 304, 306, 307, 309, 313, 314, 315, 332, 336, 337, 343, 344, 346, 352, 353, 355, 375, 378, 379, 383, 388, 389, 395, 396, 398, 400, 401, 403, 413, 416, 422, 423, 424, 430, 431, 432, 433, 434, 436, 453, 459, 462, 463, 467, 469, 473, 474, 479, 481, 486, 487, 488, 489, 490, 491, 492, 497, 498, 499, 506, 508, 510, 512, 514, 515, 522, 531, 534, 535, 538, 542, 556, 557, 558, 559, 563, 568, 574, 575, 578, 581, 587, 588, 589, 590, 591, 601, 602, 631, 632, 633, 636, 639, 640, 641, 642, 649, 650, 652, 654, 656, 658, 660, 666, 675, 679, 682, 689, 691, 693, 694, 703, 704, 707, 708, 709, 710, 711, 712, 713, 714, 725, 733, 739, 745, 746, 751, 752, 761, 762, 765, 771, 773, 775, 781, 782, 786, 787, 789, 791
kañcu, 5, 8, 9, 10, 11, 13, 14, 37, 38, 40, 41, 42, 45, 46, 47, 48, 49, 51, 53, 54, 55, 56, 57, 60, 68, 69, 70, 102, 163, 164, 167, 168, 171, 174, 178, 180, 181, 186, 187, 188, 189, 194, 196, 197, 198, 199, 200, 201, 202, 203, 204, 205, 206, 207, 208, 209, 210, 211, 212, 213, 214, 215, 216, 219, 220, 221, 224, 226, 227, 228, 229, 230, 231, 235, 236, 238, 241, 242, 244, 247, 248, 249, 251, 252, 253, 254, 256, 257, 258, 259, 261, 264, 272, 274, 277, 279,

282, 283, 286, 289, 290, 293, 294, 295, 297, 298, 300, 304, 305, 307, 312, 313, 314, 315, 317, 318, 319, 321, 322, 323, 324, 326, 329, 330, 332, 334, 335, 341, 346, 347, 348, 349, 351, 352, 355, 356, 362, 367, 372, 378, 379, 380, 382, 383, 388, 390, 398, 400, 401, 405, 406, 412, 414, 415, 416, 418, 419, 420, 422, 428, 429, 435, 437, 439, 440, 441, 442, 449, 450, 453, 458, 462, 464, 466, 467, 469, 476, 484, 486, 488, 489, 490, 491, 501, 502, 503, 504, 507, 508, 510, 512, 513, 514, 516, 520, 521, 522, 525, 526, 527, 528, 531, 535, 536, 537, 538, 539, 540, 541, 542, 544, 547, 549, 550, 553, 555, 558, 559, 561, 564, 566, 569, 570, 571, 578, 585, 588, 590, 591, 594, 595, 596, 597, 601, 605, 629, 630, 631, 632, 633, 634, 636, 638, 645, 646, 652, 653, 654, 655, 656, 657, 658, 659, 660, 661, 662, 663, 664, 665, 666, 667, 668, 669, 670, 671, 672, 673, 674, 675, 676, 677, 678, 679, 680, 681, 682, 683, 684, 685, 686, 687, 688, 689, 690, 691, 692, 693, 694, 695, 696, 697, 698, 699, 700, 701, 702, 703, 704, 705, 706, 707, 708, 709, 710, 711, 712, 713, 714, 715, 716, 717, 718, 719, 720, 721, 722, 723, 724, 725, 726, 727, 728, 729, 731, 732, 734, 735, 737, 738, 739, 740, 746, 747, 748, 751, 752, 759, 762, 763, 765, 766, 768, 769, 770, 771, 772, 777, 778, 779, 780, 781, 783, 784, 786, 787, 788, 789, 791

kandiṭ, 100, 197, 258, 281, 283, 304, 329, 364, 442, 496, 524, 539, 540, 541, 542, 543, 582, 583, 588, 741, 768, 776, 777

karaṇḍa, 132, 137, 146, 196, 239, 254, 263, 264, 347, 387, 403, 418, 420, 505, 530, 544, 558, 559, 628, 642, 714, 755, 774, 777, 778, 787

Kazanas, 19

Kenoyer, 14, 32, 34, 98, 593

khāṇḍa, 9, 27, 40, 41, 42, 46, 48, 54, 55, 94, 101, 171, 174, 185, 186, 192, 193, 196, 199, 205, 208, 209, 210, 215, 218, 219, 228, 230, 238, 240, 241, 243, 244, 252, 253, 259, 260, 261, 262, 263, 267, 268, 269, 270, 278, 279, 281, 287, 289, 290, 291, 292, 294, 297, 299, 301, 308, 309, 326, 327, 328, 339, 345, 377, 395, 407, 410, 425, 427, 430, 433, 446, 447, 449, 455, 457, 458, 461, 463, 467, 477, 478, 482, 488, 507, 518, 526, 527, 528, 529, 536, 537, 539, 560, 569, 575, 583, 600, 629, 636, 637, 638, 641, 642, 643, 653, 654, 657, 658, 664, 667, 675, 679, 681, 682, 683, 686, 692, 694, 697, 702, 706, 710, 712, 715, 717, 721, 733, 743, 745, 773, 786, 787, 788, 793

khareḍo, 8, 40, 49, 55, 94, 101, 158, 159, 181, 185, 191, 197, 217, 219, 222, 223, 236, 238, 240, 242, 243, 244, 252, 260, 261, 263, 265, 266, 267, 271, 272, 273, 277, 281, 282, 287, 288, 289, 290, 292, 293, 294, 295, 296, 298, 300, 301, 306, 309, 310, 315, 317, 320, 325, 328, 332, 378, 383, 393, 395, 396, 397, 415, 417, 422, 424, 426, 428, 434, 435, 438, 440, 443, 449, 453, 455, 457, 460, 461, 462, 468, 474, 476, 479, 484, 497, 500, 502, 503, 504, 505, 506, 509, 514, 515, 516, 517, 523, 524, 538, 543, 550, 551, 554, 564, 568, 571, 576, 581, 596, 628, 630, 633, 648, 661, 704, 710, 716, 729, 734, 737, 738, 739, 746, 748, 770, 771, 776, 780, 781, 793

khōṇḍa, 22, 36, 43, 60, 61, 100, 146, 157, 234, 285, 323, 407, 441, 442, 513, 523, 556, 596, 635, 639, 648, 747, 750, 757, 792

khōṭā, 10, 14, 49, 171, 173, 187, 194, 195, 226, 299, 304, 308, 311, 312, 313, 314, 315, 319, 343, 390, 396, 406, 427, 429, 451, 502, 508, 511, 529, 532, 552, 660, 726, 730, 784

kolhe, 14, 22, 26, 27, 33, 36, 42, 43, 54, 60, 61, 65, 71, 146, 175, 176, 177, 184, 186, 191, 194, 204, 225, 231, 232, 233, 238, 246, 254, 275, 276, 281, 284, 294, 318, 328, 330, 333, 348, 379, 407, 408, 419, 430, 431, 432, 436, 442, 444, 462, 464, 465, 466, 493, 494, 495, 523, 524, 533, 536, 559, 575, 582, 583, 596, 597, 598, 599, 606, 635, 636, 638, 640, 651, 659, 670, 689, 697, 714, 725, 733, 738, 745, 750, 755, 757, 758, 760, 761, 771, 779, 784, 790, 792, 793

kuṭhār, 46, 47, 200, 201, 229, 230, 235, 247, 286, 293, 294, 305, 319, 343, 352, 359, 399, 413, 421, 439, 452, 459, 517, 550, 551, 552, 553, 554, 555, 556, 557, 558, 586, 588, 649, 654, 657, 696, 698, 706,

714, 715, 718, 734, 746, 772, 773, 774, 775
kuṭhi, 11, 12, 13, 43, 44, 54, 61, 65, 71, 100, 163, 164, 185, 199, 201, 203, 204, 207, 208, 217, 229, 232, 244, 248, 249, 253, 263, 266, 267, 270, 275, 277, 281, 285, 286, 288, 300, 301, 320, 326, 332, 334, 356, 358, 373, 385, 389, 393, 395, 397, 403, 404, 407, 408, 409, 411, 413, 415, 419, 421, 424, 425, 426, 429, 431, 435, 439, 440, 443, 444, 445, 454, 461, 463, 472, 477, 485, 489, 493, 498, 508, 509, 523, 524, 531, 535, 563, 565, 573, 574, 576, 593, 620, 630, 644, 647, 669, 671, 684, 694, 698, 701, 706, 715, 716, 720, 724, 736, 740, 747, 748, 759, 771, 776, 778, 780, 781, 785, 786, 787, 789, 791, 792, 793
lapidary, 8, 9, 10, 11, 12, 13, 18, 24, 41, 45, 47, 48, 50, 51, 54, 55, 56, 57, 59, 69, 94, 105, 130, 177, 178, 179, 180, 181, 185, 186, 187, 188, 189, 190, 191, 192, 193, 194, 195, 198, 201, 203, 204, 205, 206, 207, 208, 209, 210, 212, 213, 214, 215, 216, 218, 219, 220, 221, 222, 223, 225, 226, 227, 228, 229, 230, 233, 234, 235, 236, 237, 238, 239, 242, 245, 246, 247, 248, 249, 250, 251, 252, 253, 255, 256, 257, 258, 259, 260, 261, 262, 263, 264, 265, 267, 268, 269, 271, 272, 274, 277, 278, 279, 280, 281, 282, 283, 284, 286, 287, 288, 289, 291, 292, 293, 294, 298, 299, 300, 301, 302, 303, 304, 305, 306, 307, 309, 311, 312, 316, 317, 318, 320, 321, 322, 323, 324, 325, 327, 330, 331, 334, 335, 336, 337, 338, 340, 341, 342, 343, 344, 347, 348, 349, 350, 351, 352, 353, 354, 355, 356, 357, 358, 359, 361, 364, 365, 366, 367, 368, 369, 370, 371, 372, 374, 375, 376, 377, 378, 379, 380, 381, 383, 384, 385, 386, 387, 388, 389, 390, 391, 392, 393, 394, 395, 396, 397, 398, 399, 400, 401, 403, 404, 405, 406, 407, 408, 410, 411, 412, 414, 415, 416, 417, 418, 419, 420, 421, 422, 423, 425, 426, 427, 428, 429, 433, 434, 435, 436, 437, 438, 439, 440, 441, 442, 443, 446, 448, 449, 450, 451, 452, 454, 455, 456, 457, 458, 459, 460, 461, 462, 463, 465, 466, 467, 468, 469, 470, 472, 473, 474, 475, 477, 478, 479, 480, 482, 486, 487, 488, 489, 490, 491, 492, 493, 495, 496, 499, 501, 503, 504, 506, 507, 508, 509, 510, 511, 512, 514, 515, 516, 518, 519, 520, 521, 522, 523, 526, 527, 529, 530, 531, 532, 533, 534, 535, 536, 537, 538, 539, 540, 541, 542, 543, 544, 546, 547, 548, 549, 550, 551, 552, 553, 554, 555, 556, 557, 558, 559, 560, 561, 562, 563, 565, 566, 567, 569, 570, 572, 573, 574, 575, 576, 577, 579, 582, 583, 586, 587, 588, 589, 590, 594, 595, 596, 597, 598, 599, 600, 601, 602, 603, 604, 605, 608, 609, 611, 612, 613, 614, 615, 616, 617, 618, 619, 620, 621, 622, 623, 624, 625, 626, 627, 628, 629, 630, 631, 632, 633, 634, 635, 636, 637, 638, 641, 642, 644, 645, 646, 647, 648, 649, 650, 652, 654, 655, 656, 657, 660, 661, 662, 663, 664, 665, 666, 667, 668, 669, 670, 671, 672, 673, 674, 675, 676, 677, 678, 679, 680, 681, 682, 683, 684, 685, 686, 687, 688, 689, 690, 691, 692, 694, 695, 696, 697, 698, 699, 700, 701, 702, 703, 704, 705, 706, 708, 709, 710, 711, 712, 713, 714, 715, 716, 717, 718, 720, 721, 722, 723, 724, 727, 728, 729, 730, 731, 732, 733, 734, 735, 737, 738, 739, 740, 741, 742, 743, 744, 747, 748, 749, 750, 751, 752, 756, 761, 762, 763, 764, 765, 766, 767, 768, 769, 770, 772, 773, 774, 775, 776, 777, 778, 779, 780, 781, 782, 783, 784, 785, 786, 787, 788, 789, 790, 791, 792
lizard, 205, 395, 594, 595, 596, 597, 598, 599, 666
Mackay, 17, 103, 754
Markhor, 168, 444, 793
meḍho, 37, 60, 100, 187, 216, 232, 268, 284, 285, 326, 329, 402, 444, 448, 480, 494, 525, 596, 598, 769, 771, 773, 793
mēṭu, 432
miner, 121
mountain-ridge, 63, 161, 181, 194, 195, 262, 263, 267, 320, 321, 322, 352, 357, 366, 377, 410, 411, 417, 424, 427, 498, 499, 513, 518, 527, 528, 552, 677, 680, 681, 704, 727, 736, 775, 781, 782
mũh, 9, 38, 40, 41, 45, 46, 47, 48, 49, 50, 54, 57, 60, 69, 171, 173, 177, 178, 180, 184, 189, 192, 193, 194, 196, 197, 198, 199, 200, 201, 202, 203, 204, 205, 206, 207, 208, 209, 210, 211, 212, 213, 214, 215, 216, 218, 219, 221, 224, 225, 227, 228, 229, 230, 231, 232, 235, 238, 239, 241,

242, 244, 247, 249, 252, 255, 256, 257, 258, 259, 261, 262, 266, 270, 272, 273, 274, 275, 276, 277, 281, 282, 284, 285, 286, 287, 288, 289, 290, 292, 293, 295, 296, 297, 298, 300, 303, 304, 305, 306, 307, 311, 312, 313, 314, 315, 319, 321, 322, 323, 324, 325, 327, 328, 330, 332, 333, 335, 337, 340, 345, 346, 349, 350, 351, 352, 353, 355, 356, 357, 358, 361, 362, 363, 367, 368, 369, 372, 373, 376, 378, 379, 380, 381, 384, 388, 392, 394, 398, 400, 401, 402, 403, 404, 406, 412, 414, 415, 416, 417, 418, 419, 420, 421, 422, 423, 427, 428, 429, 430, 432, 434, 435, 438, 439, 440, 441, 442, 446, 448, 449, 450, 451, 452, 453, 454, 455, 456, 457, 459, 460, 462, 464, 466, 470, 473, 476, 479, 481, 483, 485, 488, 490, 491, 492, 493, 495, 496, 497, 498, 499, 501, 505, 506, 507, 514, 520, 521, 522, 524, 525, 526, 528, 532, 533, 536, 537, 539, 540, 541, 542, 543, 544, 547, 549, 550, 551, 552, 553, 555, 557, 559, 560, 561, 562, 564, 565, 566, 567, 570, 571, 572, 574, 577, 578, 580, 585, 586, 587, 589, 590, 596, 603, 606, 629, 630, 631, 632, 638, 639, 641, 643, 645, 652, 653, 657, 660, 661, 662, 663, 664, 665, 666, 667, 670, 671, 672, 674, 675, 676, 679, 680, 681, 682, 683, 684, 685, 689, 690, 691, 693, 696, 697, 700, 701, 702, 705, 707, 711, 712, 713, 714, 715, 716, 718, 719, 720, 722, 725, 729, 730, 731, 732, 733, 734, 736, 739, 740, 741, 742, 743, 744, 745, 746, 747, 748, 749, 750, 751, 752, 760, 761, 762, 764, 768, 771, 773, 774, 775, 777, 778, 780, 781, 782, 783, 785, 786, 787, 788, 789, 791

muka, 9, 40, 46, 48, 49, 57, 171, 173, 184, 193, 199, 202, 208, 209, 210, 214, 215, 218, 219, 225, 228, 230, 232, 238, 241, 255, 259, 273, 274, 277, 286, 287, 288, 313, 330, 332, 349, 350, 368, 373, 379, 381, 384, 388, 398, 400, 401, 403, 404, 418, 422, 438, 439, 441, 446, 452, 460, 464, 483, 485, 488, 491, 495, 499, 521, 526, 536, 537, 544, 549, 553, 557, 562, 567, 577, 585, 586, 603, 639, 641, 643, 660, 662, 664, 667, 679, 682, 683, 684, 691, 696, 697, 700, 707, 711, 712, 715, 719, 736, 742, 743, 745, 746, 750, 774, 782, 786, 787, 789

nāga, 30, 137, 184, 186, 276, 284, 285, 328, 389, 432, 494, 533, 606

offering, 43, 84, 182, 708, 793

peak, 60, 439, 603, 604

pewter, 5, 6, 13, 30, 41, 50, 61, 62, 70, 137, 157, 158, 159, 161, 179, 181, 182, 183, 184, 186, 204, 212, 237, 238, 255, 266, 270, 273, 275, 283, 285, 297, 298, 300, 305, 327, 349, 389, 393, 395, 401, 403, 421, 432, 439, 451, 456, 478, 487, 489, 557, 568, 574, 575, 576, 577, 578, 585, 609, 637, 650, 651, 652, 741, 761, 765, 767, 769, 770

Pleiades, 232

Possehl, 24, 34

Rakhigarhi, 375

rhinoceros, 125, 393, 432, 645

sāṇḍa, 172, 189, 190, 200, 237, 242, 248, 251, 255, 258, 287, 288, 292, 295, 297, 320, 334, 339, 344, 345, 346, 347, 348, 349, 350, 351, 352, 353, 354, 355, 380, 385, 391, 392, 400, 411, 437, 475, 477, 495, 499, 517, 535, 540, 545, 554, 567, 578, 585, 639, 661, 672, 674, 677, 684, 709, 710, 712, 734, 736, 743, 779, 782

scorpion, 30, 47, 64, 69, 104, 112, 158, 159, 195, 200, 213, 218, 265, 268, 278, 304, 336, 359, 362, 393, 394, 395, 404, 414, 416, 439, 441, 456, 470, 484, 500, 510, 513, 537, 542, 546, 549, 569, 576, 602, 653, 679, 683, 699, 700, 708, 764, 770, 775, 793

seat, 22, 53, 65, 130, 213, 228, 229, 232, 238, 242, 254, 285, 289, 304, 308, 312, 330, 345, 348, 374, 376, 379, 404, 405, 407, 409, 411, 413, 421, 424, 432, 481, 543, 545, 546, 547, 548, 549, 568, 581, 604, 629, 636, 673, 682, 688, 703, 711, 739, 774, 793

spinner, 21, 22

storeroom, 46, 47, 117, 200, 201, 229, 230, 235, 247, 286, 293, 294, 305, 319, 343, 352, 359, 399, 413, 421, 439, 452, 459, 517, 550, 551, 552, 553, 554, 555, 556, 557, 558, 586, 588, 649, 654, 657, 696, 698, 706, 714, 715, 718, 734, 746, 772, 773, 774, 775

substrate, 121, 141

Susa, 20, 21, 88, 96, 117, 119, 122, 135, 143, 169, 170

tabernae Montana, 59

Tepe Yahya, 117, 125, 598, 599

tiger, 7, 14, 22, 26, 27, 33, 34, 36, 42, 43, 59, 60, 64, 65, 68, 71, 108, 113, 137, 145, 146, 175, 176, 177, 184, 191, 194, 225, 231, 233, 275, 276, 281, 284, 285, 294, 328, 330, 333, 379, 402, 407, 408, 419, 431, 432, 442, 444, 494, 523, 524, 533, 536, 575, 582, 596, 597, 598, 599, 606, 635, 636, 638, 651, 670, 689, 697, 714, 725, 738, 757, 771, 784, 790, 792
Tiwari, 73, 74
Tocharian, 19, 105, 107
Turner, 7, 493, 645, 661
Twig, 444
vagguli, 51, 595, 666
Vats, 99, 103, 593
Vidale, 145, 148
weight, 9, 10, 14, 50, 53, 55, 56, 69, 92, 100, 101, 117, 181, 191, 197, 223, 232, 233, 239, 244, 245, 250, 254, 257, 258, 263, 264, 265, 270, 272, 278, 279, 281, 282, 283, 285, 286, 290, 292, 297, 299, 304, 308, 311, 312, 316, 320, 329, 330, 334, 338, 339, 343, 348, 352, 354, 355, 364, 373, 379, 384, 389, 391, 392, 393, 394, 405, 410, 420, 421, 422, 424, 431, 432, 433, 434, 435, 436, 440, 442, 444, 445, 447, 454, 455, 460, 461, 464, 468, 470, 473, 482, 483, 485, 489, 492, 496, 504, 506, 515, 519, 523, 524, 529, 532, 536, 539, 540, 546, 556, 567, 568, 572, 578, 582, 583, 587, 588, 597, 598, 601, 604, 607, 629, 635, 645, 646, 647, 648, 653, 656, 668, 669, 670, 678, 679, 683, 684, 687, 688, 692, 693, 694, 695, 696, 698, 714, 719, 720, 723, 727, 728, 729, 732, 733, 737, 741, 755, 762, 768, 772, 776, 777, 783
worshipper, 18, 42, 122, 232, 407, 423, 523, 581, 790, 793
zinc, 4, 8, 10, 12, 18, 26, 41, 42, 48, 61, 62, 141, 156, 157, 158, 159, 182, 183, 184, 187, 189, 197, 199, 204, 205, 207, 208, 209, 210, 217, 218, 219, 220, 221, 222, 223, 235, 240, 241, 246, 254, 260, 269, 270, 272, 273, 276, 277, 278, 283, 284, 285, 286, 290, 292, 295, 296, 298, 299, 300, 301, 302, 309, 310, 315, 318, 323, 324, 327, 329, 332, 336, 337, 339, 340, 346, 356, 363, 364, 382, 387, 393, 401, 402, 404, 409, 412, 418, 428, 430, 431, 441, 442, 445, 446, 448, 449, 456, 470, 473, 480, 483, 490, 494, 496, 498, 500, 505, 507, 515, 521, 528, 531, 533, 535, 536, 538, 541, 553, 555, 565, 567, 571, 575, 590, 591, 598, 603, 606, 633, 635, 667, 668, 673, 680, 684, 685, 688, 690, 704, 709, 711, 718, 724, 725, 727, 729, 730, 738, 740, 745, 756, 763, 773, 776, 783, 792

www.ingramcontent.com/pod-product-compliance
Lightning Source LLC
Chambersburg PA
CBHW080611230426
43664CB00019B/2855
* 9 7 8 0 9 9 1 1 0 4 8 3 3 *